The United Nations and Human Rights

D0168978

The United Nations and Human Rights

A CRITICAL APPRAISAL

Edited by

Philip Alston

CLARENDON PRESS · OXFORD

Oxford University Press, Walton Street, Oxford OX2 6DP
Oxford New York Toronto
Delhi Bombay Calcutta Madras Karachi
Kuala Lumpur Singapore Hong Kong Tokyo
Nairobi Dar es Salaam Cape Town
Melbourne Auckland Madrid
and associated companies in
Berlin Ibadan

Oxford is a trade mark of Oxford University Press

Published in the United States
by Oxford University Press Inc., New York

© Oxford University Press 1992, except where otherwise stated

First published 1992

All rights reserved. No part of this publication may be reproduced, stored in a retrieval system, or transmitted, in any form or by any means, without the prior permission in writing of Oxford University Press. Within the UK, exceptions are allowed in respect of any fair dealing for the purpose of research or private study, or criticism or review, as permitted under the Copyright, Designs and Patents Act, 1988, or in the case of reprographic reproduction in accordance with the terms of the licences issued by the Copyright Licensing Agency. Enquiries concerning reproduction outside these terms and in other countries should be sent to the Rights Department, Oxford University Press, at the address above

British Library Cataloguing in Publication Data
Data available.

Library of Congress Cataloging in Publication Data
The United Nations and Human Rights: a critical appraisal /
edited by Philip Alston.
Includes bibliographical references and index.
1. Human rights. 2. United Nations—Commissions. I. Alston, Philip.
K3240.4.H844 1992 341,4'81—dc20 91-43943
ISBN 0-19-825450-4

3 5 7 9 10 8 6 4 2

Printed in Great Britain
on acid-free paper by
Antony Rowe Ltd., Chippenham

RICHARD J. WILSON

Property of:
DISABILITY RIGHTS
INTERNATIONAL
202-296-0800 | info@driadvocacy.org

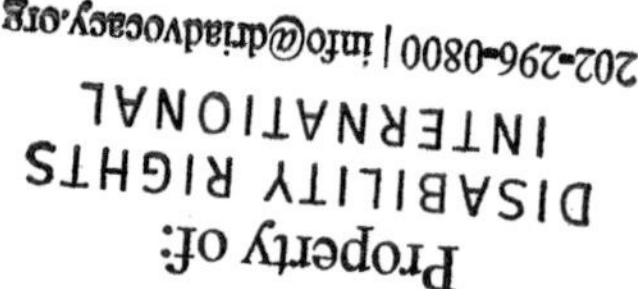

PREFACE

In his annual Report on the Work of the Organization, for 1990, the United Nations Secretary-General observed that '[t]he past year has seen the conversion of human rights from a subsidiary theme of the international discourse to a dominant concern'. He went on to add that the UN had, 'from its very inception . . . engaged itself in elaborating human rights instruments and establishing bench-marks against which standards of behaviour can be measured'.[1] He did not, however, venture an evaluation of how far the world organization has succeeded in those endeavours.

In the 1990s the pre-eminent human rights concern of the international community will be the establishment and development of effective procedures and mechanisms for sustained monitoring and for rapid and constructive responses to violations. The end of the Cold War should facilitate more open and critical scrutiny of existing arrangements and should enable major improvements to be effected. These expectations are clearly reflected in the agenda for the 1993 World Conference on Human Rights which calls for an evaluation of the 'effectiveness of the methods and mechanisms used by the United Nations in the field of human rights' and the formulation of 'concrete recommendations for improving' that effectiveness.[2]

It is precisely to these issues that the essays in the present volume address themselves. The functions, procedures, and performance of each of the major United Nations organs dealing with human rights matters are reviewed. The essays do not purport to provide a detailed account of all of the issues dealt with by each body, let alone of the innumerable resolutions, decisions, and other measures they have adopted. Rather the focus is on their functioning as institutional mechanisms—in the past, present, and future.

The coverage is comprehensive, although two organs that might have been covered are not included. Thus the International Court of Justice has been omitted because of its tangential relevance to a study of institutional arrangements for the promotion and protection of human rights (despite the importance of its jurisprudential contribution in this field). Similarly, the experience of the Committee on the Rights of the Child, which met for the first time in September 1991, is much too recent to permit any meaningful evaluation at this point.

The volume has taken a long time to come to fruition. This is due in part to

[1] A/45/1, p. 10 [2] GA Res. 45/155 (1990), para. 1.

the difficulty of focusing on a variety of moving targets, for each of which the speed and direction of movement has been inconstant and unpredictable. It has also been due to the difficulty of co-ordinating inputs by such a large number of heavily committed contributors. But despite the delays, for which the editor must bear the lion's share of the responsibility, the volume is up to date as of July 1991. The only exceptions in that regard are the chapters on the Security Council (current as of mid-1989) and that on the Human Rights Committee (current as of January 1991).

In the preparation of the volume the Editor has incurred an inordinate number of debts to various individuals and institutions. The project would never have got off the ground but for the support and enthusiasm of Torkel Opsahl and the financial support of what is now the Norwegian Human Rights Institute. Crucial encouragement and advice were also received from Georges Abi-Saab, Theo van Boven, and Klaus Samson. Financial or administrative support was also received from the Ford Foundation, the European Human Rights Foundation, The Harvard Law School Human Rights Program, and the Centre for International and Public Law at the Australian National University. Mara Bustelo's advice and assistance were, as always, invaluable.

Among many other individuals who have also been generous with their support in the preparation of this volume are: Hilary Charlesworth, Emilija Beswick, Maryam Elahi, Shepard Forman, Connie Monaco, Margo Picken, Cecelia Tancred, and Katie Zoglin. Rachel Tan and Bernard Fung provided invaluable assistance in editing and preparing the index and Richard Hart and Peter Momtchiloff of Oxford University Press were ever helpful and patient. Finally, the volume is dedicated to Helen, Sylvie, and Theresa, without whose constant encouragement it would not have been completed.

P.A.

Centre for International and Public Law
Australian National University
1991

CONTENTS

NOTES ON CONTRIBUTORS

PHILIP ALSTON (Australia) is Professor of Law and Director of the Centre for International and Public Law at the Australian National University. He was previously on the faculty of Harvard Law School (1984–9) and the Fletcher School of Law and Diplomacy at Tufts University (1985–9) and was an official of the UN Centre for Human Rights in Geneva from 1978 to 1984. Since 1987 he has been Rapporteur and then Chairman of the UN Committee on Economic, Social and Cultural Rights. He is the author or editor of various works, including *The International Dimensions of Human Rights* (2 vols., 1982), *The Right to Food* (1984), *A Commentary on the Convention on the Rights of the Child* (forthcoming), and *Children, Rights and the Law* (forthcoming).

SYDNEY D. BAILEY (United Kingdom) has served as representative of the Friends World Committee (Quakers) at the United Nations in New York, and as United Nations correspondent for *The Economist*, and has been involved in the activities of a wide range of non-governmental organizations. He is the author of numerous books, including *The Procedure of the UN Security Council* (2nd edn., 1988), *How Wars End* (1982), and the editor of *Human Rights and Responsibilities in Britain and Ireland* (1988).

THEO C. VAN BOVEN (Netherlands) is Professor of Law at the University of Limburg in Maastricht. He has been the Netherlands representative on the UN Commission on Human Rights, from 1970 to 1975, and a member of the Sub-Commission on Prevention of Discrimination and Protection of Minorities, from 1975 to 1977 and from 1987 to the present. He was Director of the UN Division of Human Rights from 1977 to 1982 and is currently a member of the ILO group of independent experts to follow up and monitor the implementation of sanctions and other forms of action against apartheid.

ANDREW BYRNES (Australia) is a Lecturer in the Faculty of Law at the University of Hong Kong. He has previously worked for the Australian Attorney-General's Department and the Australian Human Rights Commission, and has taught at the University of Sydney. He has also worked with a number of non-governmental organizations active in the field of international human rights. He has written various articles dealing in particular with anti-discrimination law and women's human rights under international law.

Each of the contributions in this volume reflects the personal views of the author.

ANTONIO CASSESE (Italy) is Professor of International Law and Relations at the European University Institute in Florence. He was a Member, and Rapporteur, of the Sub-Commission on Prevention of Discrimination and Protection of Minorities in 1977. As Special Rapporteur he prepared a study on the impact of foreign economic aid and assistance in respect of human rights in Chile. He has been a member of the Italian delegation to the General Assembly on several occasions, Chairman of the Council of Europe's Steering Committee for Human Rights (1987–8), and is currently Chairman of the European Committee for the Prevention of Torture. He is also the author or editor of a wide range of books in the field of international law, including *International Law in a Divided World* (1986) and *Human Rights in a Changing World* (1990).

ASBJØRN EIDE (Norway) is Director of the Norwegian Human Rights Institute. He is a former Executive Director of the International Peace Research Institute, Oslo, and former Secretary-General of the International Peace Research Association. He has been a member of the Sub-Commission on Prevention of Discrimination and Protection of Minorities from 1981 to 1983 and again since 1988. He was a member of the Norwegian Delegation to the Diplomatic Conference on the Reaffirmation and Development of International Humanitarian Law and is the author of several books and many articles on human rights, humanitarian law, militarism, disarmament, and development.

ROBERTA JACOBSON (United States) is a graduate of the Fletcher School of Law and Diplomacy in Boston and, since 1986, an official of the US Department of State. She worked from 1982 to 1984 with the UN Centre for Social Development and Humanitarian Affairs where her responsibilities included assisting in the work of the Committee on the Elimination of Discrimination against Women.

VIRGINIA A. LEARY (United States) is Professor of International Law at the State University of New York in Buffalo. She is a former official of the International Labour Office in Geneva, is on the board of directors of several non-governmental organizations concerned with human rights, and has published extensively on the ILO, human rights, and specific country situations.

DECLAN O'DONOVAN (Ireland) is an official of the Irish Ministry of Foreign Affairs. He represented Ireland at the Third Committee of the General Assembly, the Economic and Social Council, and the Commission on Human Rights from 1977 to 1983. He was acting Chairman of the Second Committee of the Economic and Social Council (which dealt with human rights) in 1979 and Vice-Chairman of the Third Committee of the Council (which dealt with programme and co-ordination matters) in 1980. He was Chairman of the Third Committee of the General Assembly in 1981.

TORKEL OPSAHL (Norway) is Professor of Constitutional Law at the University of Oslo and, since 1987, Chairman of the Board of the Norwegian Institute of Human Rights. He was a member of the United Nations Human Rights Committee from 1977 to 1986 (as well as Vice-Chairman, 1977–8, and Rapporteur, 1983–4). He was also a member of the European Human Rights Commission from 1970 to 1984 and, in both 1985 and 1988, undertook missions on behalf of the UN Secretary-General to investigate the situation of prisoners of war involved in the Iran–Iraq war. He has published extensively on human rights issues and is the founding editor of a Scandinavian journal devoted to human rights.

KARL JOSEF PARTSCH (Germany) (Dr Jur Freiburg, 1937) was in the diplomatic service of the Federal Republic of Germany from 1950 to 1957. Since 1957 he has been Professor of Public Law at the Universities of Kiel, Mainz, and Bonn (Rector 1968/9). From 1970 until 1989 he was a Member of the Committee on the Elimination of Racial Discrimination and was its Rapporteur from 1979 to 1985. His principal publications are in the fields of human rights and humanitarian law in armed conflicts.

JOHN QUINN (Australia) is Director of the Services Trade Section of the Australian Department of Foreign Affairs and Trade. From 1985 to 1988 he represented Australia in the Third Committee of the General Assembly.

LAURA REANDA (Italy) holds an M.Phil. degree in comparative politics and African studies from Columbia University in New York. She joined the United Nations Secretariat in 1973 as a Political Officer and has occupied a number of positions, dealing primarily with national self-determination issues. From 1978 to 1984, she was a Human Rights Officer dealing with contemporary forms of slavery.

KLAUS T. SAMSON (United Kingdom) was an official of the International Labour Office in Geneva from 1964 to 1987. He was Chief of the ILO's Application of Standards Section and subsequently Co-ordinator for Human Rights Questions. He has also been an Adjunct Professor at the Graduate Institute of International Studies in Geneva.

ABBREVIATIONS

ABAJ	*American Bar Association Journal*
ABA Sec. Int'l & Comp. L.	*American Bar Association Section of International and Comparative Law*
Am. J. Int'l L.	*American Journal of International Law*
Am. Soc. Int'l L. Proc.	*American Society of International Law, Proceedings*
An. de derecho int'l	*Anuario de derecho internacional*
Ann. de droit de Louvain	*Annuaire de droit de Louvain*
Ann. français de droit int'l	*Annuaire français de droit international*
Ann. of the Am. Acad. of Pol. and Soc. Science	*Annual of the American Academy of Political and Social Sciences*
BC Int'l & Comp. L. Rev.	*British Columbia International and Comparative Law Review*
Bull. of Peace Proposals	*Bulletin of Peace Proposals*
Calif. L. Rev.	*California Law Review*
Canadian Hum. Rts. YB	*Canadian Human Rights Year Book*
Colum. J. Transnat'l L.	*Columbia Journal of Transnational Law*
Conn. Bus. J.	*Connecticut Business Journal*
Cornell Int'l LJ	*Cornell International Law Journal*
Den. J. Int'l L. & Pol.	*Denver Journal of International Law and Policy*
De Paul L. Rev.	*De Paul Law Review*
Dep. St. Bull.	*Department of State Bulletin*
Duke LJ	*Duke University Law Journal*
ECOSOC	Economic and Social Council
Foreign Aff.	*Foreign Affairs*
Ga. J. Int'l & Comp. L.	*Georgia Journal of International and Comparative Law*
Harv. Hum. Rts. Yb.	*Harvard Human Rights Yearbook*
Hum. Rts. LJ	*Human Rights Law Journal*
Hum. Rts. Monitor	*Human Rights Monitor*
Hum. Rts. Q.	*Human Rights Quarterly*
Hum. Rts. Rev.	*Human Rights Review*
ICJ Review	*International Commission of Jurists Review*
Int'l Aff.	*International Affairs*

Int'l & Comp. LQ	*International and Comparative Law Quarterly*
Int'l J. Legal Info.	*International Journal of Legal Information*
Int'l LQ	*International Law Quarterly*
Int'l Org.	*International Organization*
Int'l Stud. Q.	*International Studies Quarterly*
Law & Contemp. Prob.	*Law and Contemporary Problems*
Law QJ of the Indian L. Inst.	*Law Quarterly Journal of the Indian Law Institute*
Neths Q. of Hum. Rts	*Netherlands Quarterly of Human Rights*
Nordic J. Int'l L.	*Nordic Journal of International Law*
Nw. UL Rev.	*Northwestern University Law Review*
NY St. BJ	*New York State Bar Journal*
NYUJ Int'l L. & Pol.	*New York University Journal of International Law and Politics*
Pol. Sci. Q.	*Political Science Quarterly*
Rec. des cours	*Recueil des cours de l'Académie de Droit International*
Rev. égypt. de droit int'l	*Revue égyptien de droit international*
Rev. gén. de droit int'l pub.	*Revue général de droit international public*
Rev. inst. interam. de derechos hum.	*Revista instituto interamericano de derechos humanitarios*
Rev. of Contemp. L.	*Review of Contemporary Law*
Rev. of Int'l Aff.	*Review of International Affairs*
Rev. roum. d'ét. int'l	*Revue roumaine d'études internationales*
U. Pa. L. Rev.	*University of Pennsylvania Law Review*
Va. J. Int'l L.	*Virginia Journal of International Law*
Yale J. Int'l L.	*Yale Journal of International Law*

1
Appraising the United Nations Human Rights Regime

PHILIP ALSTON

For present purposes, the international human rights regime consists of those international norms, processes, and institutional arrangements, as well as the activities of domestic and international pressure groups, that are directly related to promoting respect for human rights.[1] The United Nations[2] is only one part of the broader international regime which, by any definition, must also embrace at least: the authentically human rights-conscious UN agencies such as the International Labour Organisation (ILO) and the United Nations Educational, Scientific and Cultural Organization (UNESCO); mechanisms such as the Conference on Security and Co-operation in Europe; and various regional organizations such as the Council of Europe, the Organization of American States, and the Organization of African Unity.

But while the United Nations has a central and direct role with respect to only one part of the broader regime as thus defined, its activities have, nevertheless, contributed in very large measure to the task of creating, shaping, and implementing that regime as a whole. As a result, it would be difficult, if not impossible, to understand, let alone evaluate, the overall regime without an understanding of the functions performed by the relevant United Nations 'organs'. This is confirmed by the fact that most observers have treated the totality of UN human rights activities as constituting, at least for the purpose of analysis, a regime in themselves.[3]

The present chapter seeks to do two things. The first is to sketch the evolution of the institutional component of the UN regime by providing a brief overview of the individual human rights organs and of their relationship to one another. The second is to consider what is, or should be, involved in

[1] This definition does not purport to satisfy the nuances identified by different 'regime theorists'. See for example Krasner, 'Structural Causes and Regime Consequences: Regimes as Intervening Variables', 36 *Int'l Org.* 185 (1982); and Donnelly, 'International Human Rights: A Regime Analysis', 40 *Int'l Org.* 599 (1986).

[2] The term United Nations is used in this sense to refer to the UN itself, as distinct from the far wider UN family of agencies.

[3] Donnelly, 'International Human Rights'; and Forsythe, 'The United Nations and Human Rights, 1945–1985', 100 *Pol. Sci. Q.* 249 (1985), reprinted in a slightly revised form in id., *The Internationalization of Human Rights* (1991), Chap. 3.

the process of evaluating or appraising the effectiveness of the UN human rights regime as a whole and of individual organs.

A. *A Sketch of the UN Human Rights System and its Evolution*

1. THE REALITY OF UNPLANNED GROWTH

The years since 1946, and particularly since 1966, have seen a dramatic increase in the number of UN 'organs' devoted primarily to dealing with human rights matters, as well as a major increase in the time devoted by some of the existing organs to the human rights part of their mandates. Any depiction of this growth as being systematic, gradual, or even rational is largely unwarranted. The system has grown 'like Topsy' and the boundaries between the different organs are often only poorly delineated. For the most part, this pattern has hardly been accidental. Rather, it is the inevitable result of a variety of actors seeking to achieve diverse, and perhaps sometimes even irreconcilable, objectives within the same overall institutional framework. If an existing body could not do a particular job, whether because of some intrinsic defects, sheer incompetence, or, more likely, political intransigence, the preferred response was to set up yet another. In a very short space of time States and individual actors would develop a vested interest in the maintenance of the new body in the same form. This pattern simply repeated itself when a new policy agenda, to which none of the existing bodies was sufficiently responsive, emerged.

In general then, the evolution of the regime has reflected specific political developments. Its expansion has depended upon the effective exploitation of the opportunities which have arisen in any given situation from the prevailing mix of public pressures, the cohesiveness or disarray of the key geopolitical blocks, the power and number of the offending state(s) and the international standing of their current governments, and a variety of other, often rather specific and ephemeral, factors. For that reason, efforts to identify and describe steady and principled patterns in the evolution of the various procedures are generally misplaced. Pragmatism, rather than principal, has been the touchstone of the UN's evolution. This is especially apparent in almost any aspect of the activities of the Charter-based organs. Examples include: the reticence of those organs to spell out the normative basis on which they are acting in specific cases in condemning violations, especially in relation to states which are not parties to relevant treaty regimes; their failure to adopt any particular framework designed to enhance the integrity and perceived objectivity of fact-finding activities; and their reluctance to identify principles which would assist in determining the circumstances under which technical assistance (advisory services) should be offered to states as well as the kind of assistance that might appropriately be provided when violations are involved. In each case, the main organs have tended to adopt *ad hoc* approaches from which lessons might or might not be drawn for application in subsequent cases.

It is tempting to speak in terms which are unstintingly critical of this evolution and to rue the lack of co-ordination, of a rational division of labour, or of any clear institutional blueprint. But while there is indeed much to criticize, it must also be borne in mind that this unstated preference for 'letting a hundred flowers blossom' was largely responsible for the limited capacity that the system exhibited for responding to new circumstances and taking advantage of new opportunities. But, whatever the causes, the fact remains that the UN human rights system consists of a wide range of disparate, and often only formally related, bodies with overlapping mandates and different, perhaps sometimes even inconsistent, approaches.

2. CLASSIFYING THE ORGANS

In order to obtain an overview, the identification of a limited number of categories into which each of the organs might be fitted, at least for purposes of analysis, is a highly desirable goal in this context. Descriptions of the UN's activities, as opposed to its institutional arrangements, have traditionally seized upon three or more 'phases' of activity since 1947. They are standard-setting (1947–54), promotion (1955–66), and protection (since 1967) and each phase is said to have been dominated by the activity in question.[4] Leaving aside the accuracy or utility of such neat phases, that approach is not very helpful in relation to efforts to describe or understand the process of institutional evolution within the system, or its consequences.

For that reason, other analytical classifications have been proposed. Most of them reflect the UN's own distinction between organs composed of experts—perhaps elected, perhaps appointed, but virtually always nominated by governments—and those composed of governmental representatives. From that starting-point, analysts have suggested several dichotomies—expert/governmental, expert/political, legal/political, and so on—to describe variously the composition, the *modus operandi*, or the basis of decision-making.[5] To those categories may be added judicial/non-judicial (with quasi-judicial as a commonly used intermediate classification). But, it is submitted that, at least for the purpose at hand, these categories are for the most part unhelpful and often serve only to mask the reality. They are, of course, convenient labels both for those governmental representatives who would wish to emphasize

[4] For a detailed description of this approach see Marie, *La Commission des droits de l'homme de l'O.N.U.* (1975).

[5] e.g. van Boven, '"Political" and "Legal" Control Mechanisms: Their Competition and Co-Existence', unpub. manuscript (1988).

their representativeness and thus their dominance in the decision-making hierarchy as well as for those 'experts' who would wish to disclaim any political, or non-technical, influences upon their analyses. Moreover, in UN institutional terms, such distinctions (for example, 'X' is an expert committee, whereas 'Y' is a political body) are very useful since they convey an indication as to the type of membership profiles to be expected, the procedures to be used, and the types of outcome envisaged.

But for analytical purposes, such distinctions are much less helpful. The different connotations that attach to terms such as 'expert' or 'political' derive less from any natural or inherent meaning than from the usage that has grown up around the terms in UN practice. It is thus unsurprising that insights from theory as well as practice confirm their very limited utility for other purposes. A major recent study by March and Olsen concluded that, despite certain characteristics that are usually associated with each approach, 'a sharp division of labor between specialists and policy-makers is impossible to sustain, either conceptually or behaviorally'.[6] Similarly, on the basis of an examination of the very early work of the Sub-Commission on Prevention of Discrimination and Protection of Minorities, Inis Claude rejected 'the notion that every participant in the work of international organization can be stuffed into one of two categories—"governmental representative" or "uninstructed expert"—without doing Procrustean violence to the facts'.[7] In some respects the same comment applies to the bodies themselves.

A more useful distinction for analytical purposes, although still with its own shortcomings, is between those organs whose establishment may be justified by reference to the provisions of the UN Charter (Charter-based organs) and those whose creation is justified by reference to the provisions of specific treaties (treaty-based organs). This distinction was, of course, unavailable—or at least meaningless—until 1970 when the first of the UN's human rights treaty bodies met for its inaugural session. Since that time a clearly discernible two-track approach to institutional arrangements has emerged.

Put succinctly, the essential role of each of the treaty bodies is to monitor and encourage compliance with a specific treaty regime, while the political organs have a much broader mandate to promote awareness, to foster respect, and to respond to violations of human rights standards. Each treaty-based organ has been established either pursuant to the terms of a specific treaty or for the specific purpose of monitoring compliance with such a treaty. The Charter-based organs on the other hand derive their legitimacy and their mandate, in the broadest sense, from the human rights-related provisions of the Charter.

Within that overall framework the treaty-based organs are distinguished by:

[6] March and Olsen, *Rediscovering Institutions: The Organizational Basis of Politics* (1989), p. 30.

[7] Claude, 'The Nature and Status of the Subcommission on Prevention of Discrimation and Protection of Minorities', 5 *Int'l Org.* 300 (1951).

a limited clientele, consisting only of States Parties to the treaty in question; a clearly delineated set of concerns reflecting the terms of the treaty; a particular concern with developing the normative understanding of the relevant rights; a limited range of procedural options for dealing with matters of concern; caution in terms of setting precedents; consensus-based decision-making to the greatest extent possible; and a non-adversarial relationship with States Parties based on the concept of a 'constructive dialogue'.

By contrast, the political organs generally: focus on a diverse range of issues; insist that every state is an actual or potential client (or respondent), regardless of its specific treaty obligations; work on the basis of a constantly expanding mandate, which should be capable of responding to crises as they emerge; engage, as a last resort, in adversarial actions *vis-à-vis* states; rely more heavily upon NGO inputs and public opinion generally to ensure the effectiveness of their work; take decisions by often strongly contested majority voting; pay comparatively little attention to normative issues; and are very wary about establishing specific procedural frameworks within which to work, preferring a more *ad hoc* approach in most situations.

It is, of course, easy to overstate the differences between the two types of organ and to underestimate the ability of one type to emulate certain characteristics of the other. Thus a Charter-based organ might choose to play down its political character and devote some of its efforts to a systematic clarification of the normative content of a specific right while a treaty-based organ might play down its constructive dialogue approach in order to indicate its strong disapproval of a state's behaviour. Nevertheless, the differences of mandate, content, and style between the two types of organs are sufficiently clear and consistent as to justify using this as the principal distinction for purposes of the present analysis.

3. EVOLUTION OF THE CHARTER-BASED ORGANS

The diagram contained in Figure 1 shows, in the form of an inner circle, those bodies specifically designated by the UN Charter as 'principal organs'. While the International Court of Justice, the Trusteeship Council, the General Assembly, the Economic and Social Council (ECOSOC), the Security Council, and the Secretariat were all defined as organs of equal importance, this institutional formalism did little to conceal the deeper assumptions of the framers of the UN Charter as to the existence of an implicit organizational hierarchy. Thus the Security Council, with the veto power vested in each of the five Permanent Members, was clearly at the head of the pecking order, with the General Assembly next in line. While the other organs were each allocated significant spheres of institutional competence, they were, in any general political sense, inferior to the other two. The

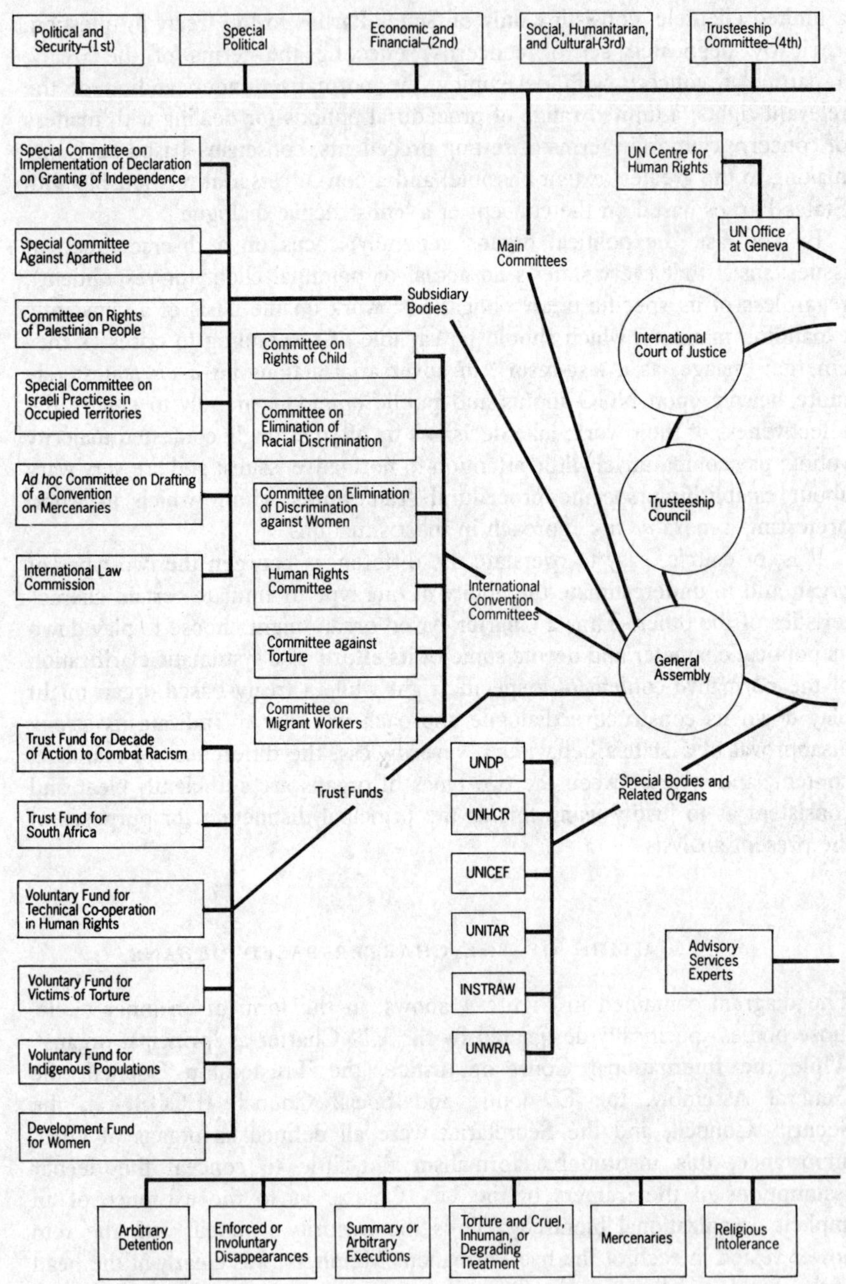

FIG. 1. UN Organs with Responsibilities in the Human Rights Area

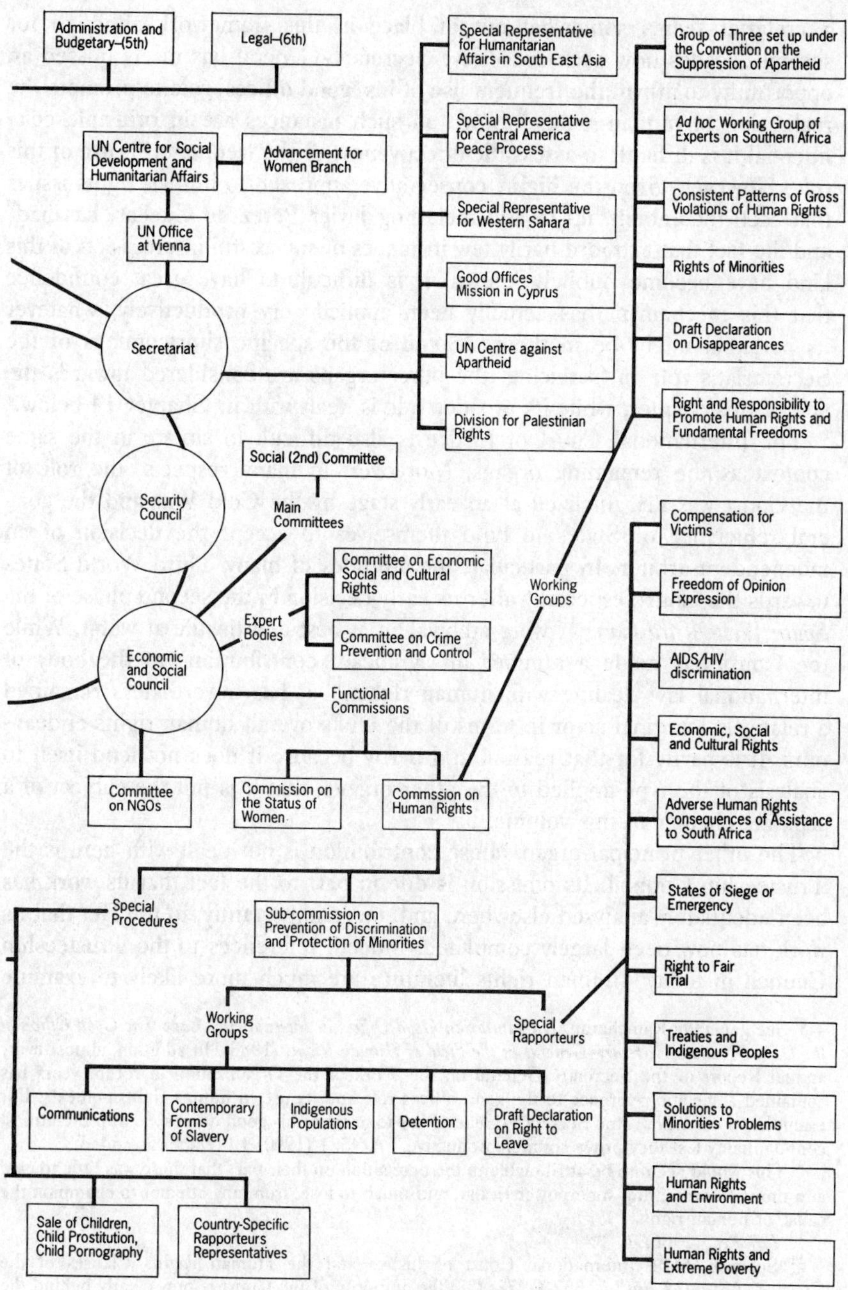
Administration and Budgetary–(5th)
Legal–(6th)
UN Centre for Social Development and Humanitarian Affairs
Advancement for Women Branch
UN Office at Vienna
Secretariat
Security Council
Economic and Social Council
Social (2nd) Committee
Main Committees
Committee on Economic Social and Cultural Rights
Committee on Crime Prevention and Control
Expert Bodies
Functional Commissions
Committee on NGOs
Commission on the Status of Women
Commssion on Human Rights
Special Representative for Humanitarian Affairs in South East Asia
Special Representative for Central America Peace Process
Special Representative for Western Sahara
Good Offices Mission in Cyprus
UN Centre against Apartheid
Division for Palestinian Rights
Working Groups
Group of Three set up under the Convention on the Suppression of Apartheid
Ad hoc Working Group of Experts on Southern Africa
Consistent Patterns of Gross Violations of Human Rights
Rights of Minorities
Draft Declaration on Disappearances
Right and Responsibility to Promote Human Rights and Fundamental Freedoms
Compensation for Victims
Freedom of Opinion Expression
AIDS/HIV discrimination
Economic, Social and Cultural Rights
Adverse Human Rights Consequences of Assistance to South Africa
States of Siege or Emergency
Right to Fair Trial
Treaties and Indigenous Peoples
Solutions to Minorities' Problems
Human Rights and Environment
Human Rights and Extreme Poverty
Special Procedures
Sub-commission on Prevention of Discrimination and Protection of Minorities
Working Groups
Special Rapporteurs
Communications
Contemporary Forms of Slavery
Indigenous Populations
Detention
Draft Declaration on Right to Leave
Sale of Children, Child Prostitution, Child Pornography
Country-Specific Rapporteurs Representatives

Source: Adapted from a diagram prepared by Human Rights Internet (Ottawa) in A. Roberts and B. Kingsbury (eds.), *United Nations: Divided World* (Clarendon Press, Oxford, 1988).

Secretariat seems somewhat out of place in this framework although for several decades now each successive Secretary-General has rarely missed an opportunity to affirm the frequent use of his 'good offices' role to promote the realization of human rights.[8] Since all such instances are in principle confidential it is difficult to assess the effectiveness or the frequency of use of this role. However, given the highly conservative approach to human rights issues that each incumbent, up to and including Javier Pérez de Cuellar, has had[9] and the fact that extraordinarily few instances of successful intercession of this kind have become publicly known, it is difficult to have great confidence that this mechanism has actually been applied very productively, whatever its potential might be in theory. Some of the specific shortcomings of the Secretariat's role in 'servicing' the other organs are considered towards the end of this chapter, while its broader role is dealt with in Chapter 14 below.

The International Court of Justice is also difficult to situate in the same context as the remaining organs. Moreover, in many respects, the role of the Court was marginalized at an early stage by the Cold War and the general reluctance of States to bind themselves to accept the decision of an independent arbiter. In particular, the attitudes of many Third World States towards the Court, especially after its early decision in the second phase of the *South West Africa Cases*,[10] were ambivalent at best and hostile at worst. While the Court has made a number of significant contributions to the body of international law dealing with human rights,[11] it has nevertheless remained a relatively marginal actor in terms of the UN's overall human rights endeavours. It is partly for that reason, and partly because it does not lend itself to analysis of the type applied to the other organs, that it is not the subject of a separate chapter in this volume.

The other principal organ whose contribution is not dealt with here is the Trusteeship Council. Its omission is due in part to the fact that its work has been adequately analysed elsewhere and, more importantly, to the fact that its work has now been largely completed. Indeed, references to the Trusteeship Council in today's human rights literature are much more likely to examine

[8] See generally Ramcharan, *Humanitarian Good Offices in International Law: The Good Offices of the United Nations Secretary-General in the Field of Human Rights* (1983). In addition, almost every annual Report of the Secretary-General on the Work of the Organization in recent years has contained a specific reference to the good offices role and its use in human rights contexts. For example: "*Very often* . . . the Secretary-General has to exercise his good offices . . . with the utmost confidentiality lest they prove counter-productive." A/45/1 (1990) 10 (emphasis added).

[9] This would seem to be attributable to the perception on their part that there was little to gain at a time of unremitting superpower rivalry, and much to lose, from any attempt to champion the cause of human rights.

[10] *ICJ Rep*. (1966), 6.

[11] Schwelb, 'The International Court of Justice and the Human Rights Clauses of the Charter', 66 *Am. J. Int'l L*. 337 (1972) ("[T]he authority of the Court is now clearly behind the [expansive] interpretation of the human rights clauses of the Charter as presented almost a generation ago by Lauterpacht and others." Ibid. 350); and Rodley, 'Human Rights and Humanitarian Intervention: The Case Law of the World Court', 38 *Int'l & Comp. LQ* 321 (1989).

how the Council can be transformed into a super-Human Rights Commission than to consider the tiny and ever-dwindling agenda that it still retains.

The remaining principal organs form part of a definite hierarchy with the Security Council at the apex. The problem, however, is that the Council has a long history of refusing to consider itself as an organ for the promotion of respect for human rights, except in so far as a given situation constitutes a threat to international peace and security.[12] Although there are many examples of the Council taking up human rights issues (they are systematically reviewed in Chapter 8 below) its reluctance to alter its stance still persists, despite hopes that its response to the crisis involving the Kurdish and Shiah populations in northern Iraq in the aftermath of the 1990–1 Gulf War signalled a fundamental change in attitude. While future developments might well impel the Council to adopt a less restrictive approach, the great majority of its members made it abundantly clear during the Iraq/Kuwait War aftermath that they did not consider themselves to be creating any precedents in this regard.[13] The Security Council's position thus remains (artificially) detached from that of the remaining principal organs.

We thus come to the formal hierarchy with which any analysis of human rights within the Charter-based organs must be primarily concerned. It consists of the General Assembly and ECOSOC as principal organs and, underneath them as 'functional commissions',[14] the Commission on Human Rights and the Commission on the Status of Women. This is as far as the system goes in terms of specific Charter authorization. However, each of these organs is entitled to create whatever subsidiary mechanisms it considers necessary to enable it to carry out its own responsibilities and functions under the Charter. It is at this point that the proliferation begins, as Figure 1 well illustrates. The only such body to which specific attention need be drawn in this context is the Sub-Commission on Prevention of Discrimination and Protection of Minorities. It has long stood out because of its relative independence, its flexible agenda and working methods, its preparedness to act as a pressure group *vis-à-vis* its parent body (the Commission), and its ambiguous and often antagonistic relationship with that parent.

While in principle, the lines of authority are reasonably clear-cut and obvious, in practice they are much less so. The ECOSOC, which once played a major role as an intermediary between the Assembly and the Commission, is now little more than a rubber stamp. The Assembly, on the other hand, has come to play an important initiating role in a number of areas while at the same time deferring (in substance, although not in form) to the Commission

[12] White, *The UN and the Maintenance of International Peace and Security* (1990), 36.

[13] S/PV.2982 (1991), 1–72 *passim*.

[14] This terminology is taken from Article 68 of the UN Charter which provides that 'The Economic and Social Council shall set up commissions in economic and social fields and for the promotion of human rights, and such other commissions as may be required for the performance of its functions.'

in many respects. Similarly, any analysis that portrayed the Sub-Commission as little more than a subsidiary organ to advise the Commission and do its bidding (and no more) might be an accurate reflection of the initial design as seen by some of its creators, but would otherwise be singularly out of touch with today's reality. The result of these various evolutionary trends is a much more complex interrelationship among the group of bodies than any diagram or flow-chart could ever convey.

4. EVOLUTION OF THE TREATY-BASED ORGANS

Since the Committee on the Elimination of Racial Discrimination (CERD) first met in January 1970, the treaty-based system has expanded at a rate which is without precedent in the field of international organization. By September 1991, when the Committee on the Rights of the Child (CRC) began its first session, there were eight treaty bodies already operating and another one foreshadowed once the International Convention on the Protection of the Rights of All Migrant Workers and Members of Their Families[15] enters into force. Of these eight, five are almost identical in form and basic mandate. They are, in addition to the two already mentioned, the Human Rights Committee (HRC) (which first met in 1976), the Committee on the Elimination of Discrimination against Women (CEDAW) (1982), and the Committee against Torture (CAT) (1988).

Of the other three, two relate to apartheid issues. They both tend to have somewhat different functions and procedures by comparison with the other treaty supervisory mandates. In addition, of course, their mandates are far narrower and more clearly centred around developments in one country. They are the Group of Three, composed of governmental representatives, established under the Convention on the Suppression and Punishment of the Crime of Apartheid[16] and the Commission against Apartheid in Sports, established pursuant to Article 11 of the International Convention against Apartheid in Sports.[17] The latter is composed of fifteen elected members, 'of high moral character and committed to the struggle against apartheid, particular attention being paid to participation of persons having experience in sports administration'. Unlike members of the other committees, they are not said to be serving in their 'personal capacities'. For various reasons, neither has succeeded in generating the type of precedents or practice that would warrant separate consideration in this volume.

The final treaty body, the Committee on Economic, Social and Cultural Rights (CESCR), is a curious hybrid in that it has been established by a Charter-based organ (the ECOSOC), ostensibly to advise it on the im-

[15] GA Res.45/158 (1990).
[16] GA Res.3068 (XXVIII) (1973), Annex.
[17] GA Res.40/64 G, (1985) Annex.

plementation of the relevant treaty (the Covenant on Economic, Social and Cultural Rights), but in reality to perform virtually all of the Council's relevant treaty-based functions on its behalf. While the Committee can thus be abolished at any moment by the Council, it has been given a quasi-independent existence by being authorized by the latter to imitate in every significant way the role and working methods of the five other bodies that operate pursuant to specific treaty provisions.

In brief, each of the treaty bodies performs the task of monitoring States Parties' compliance with their obligations under the relevant treaty. Each of the five analysed in this volume (HRC, CERD, CEDAW, CAT, and CESCR) does so through a dialogue with the representatives of each of the States Parties on the basis of a detailed report (an 'initial' report, followed by 'periodic' reports at approximately four- to five-year intervals). The principal outcome of this process is the record of the resulting dialogue and the Committee's own summary of the key points, which provide an opportunity for individual members, or the Committee as a whole, to indicate the extent to which the State Party appears to be in compliance, or otherwise. Each of the Committees also adopts carefully drafted statements in the form of General Comments (or some comparable terminology), which purport to be based directly on the Committees' work in examining reports, and which seek to elaborate upon the normative content of specific rights or to address specific issues that have arisen. Four of the five Committees also deal with complaints from individuals alleging violations of their rights under the treaty concerned. The exception is the CESCR, but it will be joined by the new committee (CRC) in having no procedure to enable it to respond to individual petitions. Finally, there is an interstate complaints mechanism which can be invoked before three of the treaty bodies (HRC, CERD, and CAT). The latter mechanism has attracted no attention from States and seems unlikely to generate any 'business' in the foreseeable future, although the rekindling of long-dormant ethnic disputes among the States of Central and Eastern Europe might well provide an occasion for rewriting this record.

There is no formal hierarchy among the treaty bodies, although the Human Rights Committee tends to have the potentially most comprehensive mandate and to have been endowed with the greatest resources in terms of meeting time and Secretariat assistance. The relationship among the treaty bodies and the need for measures to promote better co-ordination, to reduce overlapping, and to rationalize the burden imposed on States that are parties to many of the treaties, have only recently begun to be addressed by UN organs.[18] The main opportunity to do so is in the Meeting of the Chairpersons of the Human Rights Treaty Bodies which has so far been convened in 1984, 1988, and 1990, but which is likely to be held on a biennial basis henceforth.[19] This

[18] See e.g. A/44/668 (1989). [19] GA Res.45/85 (1990).

forum has to date, however, made only a very limited amount of progress in this direction.

B. *Appraising Effectiveness*

Evaluation of the UN human rights regime has, in effect, been placed at the top of the international community's human rights agenda by virtue of the objectives adopted by the UN General Assembly for the World Conference on Human Rights to be held in Berlin in June 1993. The stated aims of the Conference include: a review and assessment of progress made in the field of human rights since 1948 and the identification of obstacles in this regard and ways of overcoming them; an examination of ways and means 'to improved implementation of existing human rights standards and instruments'; an evaluation of the 'effectiveness of the methods and mechanisms used by the United Nations in the field of human rights'; and the formulation of 'concrete recommendations for improving' that effectiveness.[20]

The essays that follow seek to appraise the achievements and shortcomings of each of the various UN organs which play a major role in human rights terms. That is not to say that they all share a common framework for evaluation, and indeed they do not. For that reason, and in light of the objectives of the World Conference, it is important to explore what is involved in any such evaluation and to identify a possible framework within which further work might be undertaken. It should be noted, however, that the present chapter does not purport to present an evaluation of effectiveness to date. By the same token, the essays that follow do provide the essential raw material that is required in order to undertake any such evaluations.

In attempting to evaluate the effectiveness of the UN's human rights regime two preliminary issues must first be addressed. The first is to identify the benchmarks that are appropriate as a basis on which to undertake an evaluation. The second is to determine a methodology that can be used in measuring performance in relation to specific benchmarks or objectives once they have been identified.

1. IDENTIFYING APPROPRIATE CRITERIA

The UN's effectiveness in this domain has been the subject of much casual comment but remarkably little systematic evaluation. But since evaluation is, as the word itself connotes, a value-based undertaking, the starting-point for any such exercise must be the identification of the criteria against which an informed and balanced assessment can be attempted. While this is hardly a

[20] GA Res.45/155 (1990), para. 1.

great insight, it stands in stark contrast to the approach adopted in practice by most of those who have in the past purported to offer an assessment of the UN's human rights programme. The same criticism also applies in the international organization field more generally. Thus, for example, the UN system as a whole has recently been the focus of a series of evaluation exercises, both internal and external in nature,[21] but few if any of them have gone beyond vague references to efficiency and effectiveness in describing their criteria for assessment.[22]

In the human rights field the explanation for this failure to specify the criteria being used lies, to a significant extent, in the unquestioning acceptance of the assumption that the Organization's central function is to respond effectively to violations of human rights wherever they occur. What constitutes an 'effective' response is usually not spelled out. Thus some critics might be satisfied with a focused discussion in an international forum of any relevant situation, others might insist upon a formal condemnation or at least the establishment of a fact-finding and reporting mechanism wherever appropriate, while still others might be unsatisfied with anything less than the imposition of sanctions or even the mounting of a military exercise designed to restore respect for human rights.

In other words, some evaluators might start with a very strong 'world order' set of assumptions while others might be firmly convinced of the need to protect 'state sovereignty' and the principle of non-intervention (as narrowly defined). Many will see the mobilization and pursuit of international pressures, primarily by or through the UN, as the key component in any global endeavour to protect human rights while others will relegate UN action to a secondary role, perhaps, at best. All of these factors will have a major and direct influence on the outcome of an evaluation exercise. In other words, the assumptions (usually unstated and often even unexplored) that are taken into an evaluation process, will have a determining influence on the outcome. Thus for example if we accept the criticism that the UN has applied double standards in its approach to human rights violations, the policy prescription that follows will be determined not by that diagnosis itself but by the critic's unstated preference either to reduce all action to a lowest common denominator or to move in the opposite direction so that the highest rather

[21] See e.g. *Report of the Group of High-Level Intergovernmental Experts to Review the Efficiency of the Administrative and Financial Functioning of the UN*, A/42/49 (1986); and *Report of the Special Commission of the Economic and Social Council on the In-Depth Study of the UN Intergovernmental Structure and Functions in the Economic and Social Fields*, E/CSN.1/L.1 (1988).

[22] The difficulties in this regard are well illustrated by the following statement contained in a major Nordic evaluation study: 'Effectiveness and organization can only be judged against what the UN is supposed, mandated or expected to do. If that remains unclear or subject to widely divergent interpretations, then no amount of reforms is going to make it into an effective institution. Efficiency on the other hand, can be improved through institutional arrangements or rearrangements.' *The UN in Development: Reform Issues in the Economic and Social Fields*, Final Report by the Nordic UN Project (1991), 33.

than the lowest standards are applied uniformly. The latter approach will, of course, rarely be favoured by States which rely upon the double standards criticism since their aim is usually to make the case that a particular situation ought not to be the subject of scrutiny or other measures.

What then are the key questions that need to be asked in evaluating the effectiveness of the UN regime. It is generally accepted in the academic literature that there are five such questions: When? Where?, For Whom?, What?, and Why?[23] *When?* raises the issue of an appropriate time-frame. The 1993 World Conference, for example, has been asked 'to review and assess progress . . . since the adoption of the Universal Declaration' in 1948.[24] It is indisputable that by almost any measure immense progress has been achieved since that time. But other time-frames could equally well have been chosen. Since the first World Conference in 1968, for example, or over the last decade, the results might look significantly different, although much would still depend on how the other questions were framed. The importance of the time-frame chosen is well illustrated by the extent to which analyses of the UN's human rights performance that are unrelentingly negative are very often rooted in the details of the period during the 1960s and 1970s when the UN's response to violations was essentially limited to criticizing the unholy trinity of South Africa, Israel in respect of the Occupied Territories, and Chile. It is easy to cite a string of situations during the 1970s in particular which involved egregious violations but which failed to attract any specific UN sanction. On the other hand a review of the 1980s in isolation will yield an infinitely more favourable balance sheet of action and inaction.

Where? refers to the scope and focus of the evaluation. Donnelly, for example, in his analysis of the human rights regime looks specifically only at the Human Rights Committee and the Commission on Human Rights.[25] From a feminist perspective this immediately biases the outcome by excluding the Commission on the Status of Women and CEDAW. Excluding the other treaty bodies as well as the Assembly and the Sub-Commission also ensures the presentation of only a partial picture. On the other hand, as this volume confirms, attempting to cover the entire regime provides a potentially unmanageable focus.

The question *for whom?* poses an immediate problem in terms of the human rights regime. The outcome of the evaluation will be radically different depending on whether the standpoint adopted is primarily that of the victims of violations, human rights activists, governments, UN officials, or the press. The answer is by no means self-evident when the UN is asked to undertake

[23] See generally Nakamura and Smallwood, *The Politics of Policy Implementation* (1980); Williams, *et al.* (eds.), *Studying Implementation; Methodological and Administrative Issues* (1982); and Pressman and Wildavsky, *Implementation* (3rd. edn., 1984).

[24] GA Res.54/155 (1990), para. 1(*a*).

[25] Donnelly, 'International Human Rights'.

the evaluation, since its approach in general seeks to balance the concerns of its different constituencies, while at the same time playing down any suggestion that trade-offs are being made. For this reason, another question is appropriately added in the present context: *by whom?* On occasion, the UN uses independent experts, but more often than not such people will be 'insiders' of one kind or another with strong vested interests in maintenance of the status quo. Should members of the expert committees, for example, be asked to evaluate their own activities, as has been requested?[26] How objective, or outspoken, can the Secretariat be in such a context? What weight should be placed on NGO evaluations? Presumably, evaluators from a range of backgrounds are required but then the frame of reference of each can still differ radically from those of others, thereby diminishing the comparability of the results.

What? adds another level of questions after *where?* Having determined, for example, that the focus will be on the Human Rights Committee it must still be decided whether its interstate complaints jurisdiction is best ignored as being certainly unproductive or is carefully examined in the hope of breathing life into a potentially important procedure. Similarly, should the task of developing a sophisticated jurisprudence based on the Covenant be treated as being of primary or only secondary importance? A focus on the Commission raises an even more complex array of issues, particularly the question of the importance attached to its function of responding to violations.

Finally, the question *why?* will be answered rather differently by an academic, an activist, a government minister, and an international official. The answers might range from a general quest to gain a better understanding of modes of international co-operation, or a desire to increase efficiency defined in managerial terms, or a mandate 'to formulate concrete recommendations for improving [overall] effectiveness' (as in the case of the World Conference),[27] through to a desire to ensure an immediate and productive response to all future reports of alleged violations.

A more formal or legalistic approach to evaluation, and one more consonant with the past practice of the UN, is to ignore most of these questions (implicitly dismissing them as practically or politically unanswerable) and to seek to compare existing practice with the stated objectives of the system. The problem, of course, is that the 'system' *per se* does not exist in such terms. Thus, the evaluator might turn either to the mandate provided in the UN Charter or to the more specific terms of reference outlined in the constituent instruments relating to each of the organs in question.[28] But in the case of the

[26] A/45/636 (1990), para. 67.

[27] GA Res.54/155 (1990), para. 1(*e*).

[28] In other words, the UN Charter in the case of the Security Council, the Assembly, and ECOSOC, the UN resolution(s) establishing the organ in the case of each of the other Charter-based bodies, and the text of the relevant treaties in the case of the various supervisory committees.

principal Charter-based organs, the terms of the Charter provisions give little practical guidance for evaluation purposes and the constituent instruments may not be a great deal more helpful. In the case of the Commission, for example, its standard-setting mandate refers only to three specific issues, with respect to one of which (freedom of information) it has been able to achieve virtually nothing. Yet that is unlikely to be a major item on the World Conference's evaluation agenda. Similarly, the word 'protection' is only mentioned in relation to 'minorities', but it is unthinkable that the Commission's success in providing 'protection' could be evaluated solely in that regard. In reality, most of the Commission's activities are justified by reference to the catch-all provision in its mandate referring to 'any other matter concerning human rights'.[29] That hardly constitutes a meaningful yardstick for evaluation purposes, however.

The easy solution to this dilemma is to turn to the resolutions adopted by the body in question, say the Commission, as an authoritative description of its objectives. But, even leaving aside the virtual impossibility of gathering together all such mandates, questions arise as to what interpretation can properly be given to a directive such as that given by the Assembly to the Commission in 1966 'to put a stop to violations of human rights wherever they may occur'.[30] Should this be taken literally; should it be subject to all sorts of unstated caveats; or should violations be defined as having occurred only when the Commission recognizes them? Just as statements of goals contained in constituent instruments can change radically over time, so can more narrowly defined and more recent mandates. As March and Olsen note: 'Institutions develop and redefine goals while making decisions and adapting to institutional pressures, and initial intent can be lost. . . . [A]ctions taken (for whatever reasons) become the source of a new definition of objectives.'[31]

But the UN does actually prepare a document which purports to state the objectives of the 'Human Rights Programme' as a whole and even to offer some indication as to the activities which are expected to be carried out in relation to each objective. The Medium-Term Plan is drawn up by the Secretariat and reflects the principal 'mandates' adopted by the various bodies.[32] Its principal purpose, however, is to justify proposed allocations of human and financial resources, rather than to record the type of benchmarks against which the overall programme might be evaluated. While the Plan is formally submitted to, and approved by, the Commission it is subjected to little real scrutiny, presumably because it is assumed that very little hinges upon it. Nevertheless, when the Secretariat did actually undertake an evaluation of the human rights programme, in 1989, it was based largely on the

[29] ESC Res.5(I) (1946), para. (*e*).
[30] GA Res.2144 A (XXI) (1966).
[31] March and Olsen, *Rediscovering Institutions*, 66.
[32] A/39/38 (1984).

framework used in the Medium-Term Plan.[33] While it is entirely understandable that an internal/institutional evaluation would opt for such an approach, its shortcomings from an external, policy-oriented, perspective should also be acknowledged. The Medium-Term Plan focuses on what is being done rather than on what might have been done given the existing mandate, let alone what could be or should have been done given minor modifications to the mandate. It is, in essence, an evaluation of efficiency which takes the appropriateness of established approaches largely for granted.

How then have academic observers sought to overcome these problems? The principal answer has to be that they have not. For the most part, as noted earlier, evaluations have been produced without any detailed attempt to specify the criteria, benchmarks, or assumptions on which they are based. For example, one book identifies 'enforcement' as the goal of the international human rights regime but then defines enforcement as 'comprising all measures intended and proper to induce respect for human rights'.[34] Perhaps not surprisingly, the attempts at evaluation that follow are not especially informative.[35]

There are, however, several more sophisticated analyses from which some useful insights might be gained. Jack Donnelly, in particular, in his 1986 study of the international human rights regime, has sought to provide an appropriate evaluative framework. He identifies four different types of activities that the regime can be expected to perform:

> *enforcement* activities involve international decision making and the stronger forms of international monitoring. International *implementation* activities include weaker monitoring procedures, policy coordination and some form of information exchange. *Promotional* activities may involve international information exchange, promotion or assistance, and perhaps even weak monitoring of international guidelines. . . . Finally, *declaratory* regimes involve international norms but no international decision making (except in the creation of norms).[36]

Donnelly concludes by classifying the UN regime, as of 1985, as being a 'strong promotional' one, having only 'weak monitoring' procedures.[37]

Forsythe, by contrast, arrives at a generally favourable evaluation of the

[33] 'In-Depth Evaluation of the Human Rights Programme', E/AC.51/1989/2. See also 'Situation and Developments Regarding the Logistical and Human Rights [sic] Resources Support for the Activities of the Centre for Human Rights in the Field of Human Rights', E/1990/50.

[34] Bernhardt, 'General Report' in Bernhardt and Jolowicz (eds.), *International Enforcement of Human Rights* (1985), 143 at 145.

[35] e.g.: 'An over-all judgement on the effectiveness of the different reporting systems is hardly possible. . . . It is to be hoped that reporting systems will improve respect for human rights' (ibid. 147); and 'An evaluation of international human rights courts is dependent upon the personal views and experiences of the observer' (ibid. 152).

[36] Donnelly, 'International Human Rights', 604–5 (emphasis in original).

[37] Ibid. 634.

UN in 1991 largely as a consequence of his starting assumption that 'the organization does not normally utilize its authority and power for short-term protection'.[38] In his view '[t]he sum total of UN activity is supposed to socialize or educate actors into changing their views and policies over time towards a cosmopolitan (universal) human rights standard as defined by UN instruments'.[39] A comparable approach is also adopted by Henkin whose 'optimistic, almost triumphant'[40] conclusions are facilitated by an emphasis upon the role of individual states and their legal and political systems rather than on that of the international community. Similarly, while noting that 'the influence of United Nations bodies . . . to induce compliance by states generally with international human rights standards is difficult to appraise',[41] he seems prepared to countenance a singularly undemanding benchmark for evaluation by suggesting that '[i]t may be that the international community could not abandon or desist from pursuing an international human rights program even if doubts as to its efficacy were overwhelming.'[42]

Perhaps the most challenging academic evaluation of the UN programme has come from Allott. He argues that after 1945 the 'idea of human rights quickly became perverted by the self-misconceiving of international society. Human rights were quickly appropriated by governments, embodied in treaties, made part of the stuff of primitive international relations, swept up into the maw of an international bureaucracy.'[43] In sum, he concludes that 'the deterrent effect of bureaucratized human rights is negligible'.[44] While a detailed review of Allott's thesis is well beyond the scope of the present analysis, one of its implications is particularly worthy of note in this context. That is that a non-bureaucratic and truly probing evaluation would take as its starting-point some vision of the arrangements required in order to prevent human rights violations to the greatest extent possible and to respond to them in as comprehensive a manner as possible when they do occur. The existing UN and other arrangements would then be compared with that benchmark rather than on their own 'bureaucratic' and thus inevitably very limited terms.

C. *Problems of Methodology*

It is one thing to determine the objectives with respect to which an evaluation might be undertaken, but quite another to identify a feasible and effective methodology for doing so. In particular, the question of causality presents

[38] Forsythe, *The Internationalization of Human Rights* (1991), 77.

[39] Ibid.

[40] Steiner, 'The Youth of Rights' (Review of Henkin, *The Age of Rights*), 104 *Harv. L. Rev.* 917 (1991).

[41] Henkin, *The Age of Rights* 24 (1990).

[42] Ibid 29.

[43] Allott, *Eunomia: New Order for a New World* (1990), 288.

[44] Ibid, 336.

major difficulties in evaluation in general,[45] and in this domain in particular.[46] It is difficult enough to measure significant long-term impacts (even an immediate change in government or a direct reversal of offending policies may have little to do with UN measures) on issues such as the treatment of detainees, police harassment, freedom of the press, the fairness of the political system, freedom of association, etc. But it is even more difficult to attribute such impacts, even in part, to the actions taken by the UN or other international organizations.[47] The representative of a newly democratic Chile illustrated the problem of causality very effectively when, in seeking to laud the UN's efforts to respond to violations in Chile between 1973 and 1989, he told the Economic and Social Council in May 1990 that: 'There can be no doubt that the noble attitude maintained by the [UN] contributed decisively to bringing about the international conditions needed to lend support to the main task within the country, which made Chile's return to democracy possible.'[48] He was not seeking to damn with faint praise, but it may have been his concern not to make any rash assertions as to causality that led him close to doing so. Academic commentators have proven hardly more successful in seeking to evaluated the effectiveness of international pressures in specific cases.[49] Indeed, rather than undertake an evaluation *per se*, most have opted to compare the performance of two or more organizations.[50] The question of whether either has actually been effective can thus be overlooked in favour of concluding that one did more than the other.

Within the UN itself there has tended to be an emphasis upon what might be termed bureaucratic indicators such as the number of pages of documents 'processed' by the Centre for Human Rights,[51] the number of meetings serviced,[52] the number of trips undertaken,[53] or the number of observers and NGOs at meetings. An academic variation on this theme was an empirical

[45] Ripley and Franklin, *Bureaucracy and Policy Implementation* (1982), Chap. 8.

[46] For a domestic analogy in the US context see Bullock and Lamb, *Implementation of Civil Rights Policy* (1984).

[47] 'Viewing the human rights movement as a determining or important influence on these changes [in Eastern Europe and in countries such as Argentina and South Africa] may constitute as much an act of faith as a finding of positive social science'. Steiner, 'The Youth of Rights', 926.

[48] Full text of statement by Ambassador Juan Somavia, Social Committee of the ECOSOC, agenda item 3, New York, 15 May 1990, 4.

[49] For an unusually detailed, and highly instructive, effort in this regard see Guest, *Behind the Disappearances: Argentina's Dirty War Against Human Rights and the United Nations* (1990).

[50] e.g. Shelton, 'Utilization of Fact-Finding Missions to Promote and Protect Human Rights: The Chile Case, 2 *Hum. Rts LJ* 1 (1981); and Weissbrodt and Bartolomei, 'The Effectiveness of International Human Rights Pressures: The Case of Argentina, 1976–1983', 75 *Minnesota L. Rev.* 1009 (1991).

[51] The figure has gone from 45,497 pages in 1985 to 64,307 in 1989, an increase of 41%. E/1990/50, para. 55.

[52] The figure has gone from 405 meetings in 1985 to 648 in 1989, a 60% increase. Ibid. para. 56.

[53] The figure has gone from 498 'official travel authorizations issued' in 1985 to 789 in 1989, a 58.4% increase. Ibid. para. 57.

investigation of the validity of alleged bias on the part of the UN in its human rights work by taking the amount of meeting time devoted to a given issue as an indicator of the importance attached to it. Although there would seem to be strong arguments in favour of preferring the number of resolutions adopted on each issue,[54] or combining that indicator with meeting time, this attempt clearly has the great merit of being better empirically grounded than the vast majority of evaluations proffered.

Another rather novel approach, reflected in a 1989 UN evaluation, was to survey the accessible academic literature and to draw conclusions from it as to the perceived effectiveness of specific UN bodies and programmes.[55] But given the paucity of such evaluations, as well as the relative superficiality of many of them, such an approach could hardly have been expected to yield results that were any more scientific or revealing than its source material would permit.

It is clear from this brief survey that no particular methodology will be suitable for all evaluation-related purposes. But it is equally clear that the identification of at least some methodology is an indispensable prerequisite to any sustained attempt at evaluation that aspires to be taken seriously. There is therefore a dire need for more creative and empirical research to be undertaken with a view to exploring the advantages and disadvantages of different approaches.

D. *A Possible Framework for Evaluation*

Much of the foregoing analysis has aimed at identifying the shortcomings of some of the evaluative frameworks that have been used in different contexts to appraise the UN's human rights programme. The message sought to be conveyed is not, however, that they are all fatally flawed. Nor is it that there is any particularly scientific means of arriving at an appropriate set of criteria. Rather, it is that some serious consideration needs to be given to such criteria as a prelude to any evaluation and that the criteria being applied should be spelled out.

In that context, it seems appropriate to offer a framework which the present writer believes would be a useful starting-point for attempts to evaluate the UN programme as a whole. It is one that could easily be used within the framework of the 1993 World Conference. Although it must be conceded that it seems unlikely in view of past performances that the international community of States would be prepared to structure its deliberations in such a

[54] An approach which the author explicitly rejects, although hardly in convincing fashion. Donnelly, 'Human Rights at the United Nations 1955–85: The Question of Bias', 32 *Int'l Studs Q.* 275 at 278 (1988).

[55] E/AC.51/1989/2.

methodical fashion, despite the comparatively systematic approach called for in the Assembly's resolution defining the Conference's objectives.

The framework is divided into three parts, as follows:

I. Standards

(*a*) Setting standards.

(*b*) Deepening normative understanding.

(*c*) Issue analysis (studies, etc.).

II. Promotion

(*a*) Promoting rights-consciousness.

(*b*) Encouraging and facilitating the adoption of international norms in domestic legal systems.

(*c*) Encouraging and facilitating institution building at the national level.

(*d*) Developing an international institutional network with arrangements for information exchange, co-ordination, and joint activities, as appropriate with: regional human rights bodies; United Nations development and other agencies; and other international bodies.

III. Establishing accountability

(*a*) Development of an accepted international legal framework.

(*b*) Monitoring respect for obligations by means of authoritative, regular reviews.

(*c*) Anticipating and seeking to prevent violations through early-warning systems, mediation, conciliation, publicity, pressure, etc. as appropriate.

(*d*) Responding to violations through, *inter alia*: effective fact-finding; mobilization of shame; and, as a last resort, enforcement through sanctions, etc.

(*e*) Securing relief and redress for victims of violations.

This framework has several significant features: (1) it treats both the Charter-based and treaty-based organs as though they are both parts of a single integrated programme; (2) the 'protection' mandate, which often tends to become an exclusive feature of the criteria applied (often only implicitly) by many observers, is but one part of the overall set of criteria; and (3) the work of the UN is seen in its wider context in terms of the need to reach out beyond the UN's own programme to take full account of the opportunities offered for collaboration and co-ordination with other extant regimes.

I
UN Charter-Based Organs

2
The General Assembly: Historical Perspective 1945–1989

ANTONIO CASSESE

A. *The Drafting of the Charter*

It is well known that in 1944–5, while the USSR thought that the world organization soon to be set up should concentrate on security problems and therefore hinge on one main body, the Security Council, the United States suggested that the UN should also deal with other questions, in particular economic, social, and humanitarian issues. To this effect it proposed that another body, the General Assembly, should be vested with recommendatory powers covering an extensive range of issues. Among the questions to be entrusted to the jurisdiction of the Assembly were those concerning human rights. In the spring of 1944, after throwing out suggestions that soon proved unrealistic (such as the drafting, at San Francisco, along with the Charter, of an International Bill of Rights, to be ratified together with the statute of the new organization,[1] the US confined itself to suggesting in its 'Tentative Proposals for a General International Organisation'[2] that the General Assembly should, among other things, be empowered to 'initiate studies and make recommendations' for 'the promotion of the observance of basic human rights in accordance with principles or undertakings agreed upon by States members of the international organisation'.[3]

It is apparent from the above that even the very State that championed the inclusion of human rights among the matters under the jurisdiction of the UN, proceeded with utmost caution and took pains to spell out that the Organisation should have limited powers only, and that in addition the standards on human rights by which member States should be guided were to be first accepted by them through the traditional process of treaty-making, or, at any rate, by agreement.

At the Dumbarton Oaks Conference, the initial opposition of the UK and the USSR[4] led the US somewhat to water down its proposals on human

[1] Russell and Muther, *A History of the United Nations Charter* (1958), 327.
[2] 18 July 1944, ibid. 329.
[3] Provision B(c) (3).
[4] Russell and Muther, *History*, 423.

rights and in fact the provision on the matter produced by the Four Powers (US, USSR, UK, and China) was rather weak.[5] However, when the San Francisco Conference began, the four Sponsoring Powers were confronted with a spate of bold amendments on human rights, mostly emanating from Latin American countries. This, as well as the conversion of the USSR to the cause of human rights (this State put forward specific proposals on the matter, particularly on non-discrimination and self-determination of peoples), led the Four Powers to consider it advisable to strengthen their proposals on human rights. Accordingly they suggested a few provisions that included explicit references to this matter;[6] in particular, these rights were mentioned in the general statement of purposes and in the clause concerning the powers of the General Assembly.

At the San Francisco Conference three alignments emerged. On the one hand, there was a group of vocal Latin American countries (chiefly Brazil, Colombia, Chile, Cuba, the Dominican Republic, Ecuador, Mexico, Panama, and Uruguay) plus a few Western countries (Australia, New Zealand, and Norway) and such Third World countries as India. These States put forward amendments substantially calculated to lay down an obligation to respect human rights. Mention should be made in particular of the steps taken by Australia with a view to establishing, in Article 56, that member States should not only co-operate with the Organisation in the promotion of human rights, but also pledge themselves to take *separate* and joint action to *achieve respect* for human rights.[7] Then there was a group of States including some major powers, which—though favourable to the promotion of human rights—opposed the attempt to expand the sphere of action of the UN, as well as the laying down of any definite obligation to respect human rights. The US took the lead on this score, by strongly objecting to the broadening of Article 56 and also by insisting on the need to lay down a safeguard clause protecting State sovereignty (the proviso that later became Article 2(7). One can finally discern a third group of States, consisting of the socialist countries led by the USSR (Byelorussia, Czechoslovakia, and Ukraine), which, although substantially upholding the restrictive attitude of the second group just mentioned, distinguished itself by the fact that they stressed the importance of the right of peoples to self-determination (a right that major Western countries, plus such colonial powers as Belgium, strongly opposed). The upshot of the lengthy discussions was that the first group did not obtain any substantial gain, while the other two groups reached a compromise that accommodated their mutual demands to some extent. The compromise consisted of the following

[5] Ibid. 1019–21.

[6] On the Soviet proposals, see ibid. 779; see also *United Nations Conference on International Organization*, Doc. 909, II/11, 8 *UNCIO* 56 (1945). Arts. I(3) and V(B)(6) were Four Power suggestions.

[7] *United Nations Conference on International Organization*, 3 *UNCIO* (1945).

elements: (*a*) no specific obligation to take separate action for the promotion, let alone the protection, of human rights was upheld (Article 56); (*b*) the right of self-determination of people was proclaimed (Articles 1 and 55), but only as a guiding principle for the Organisation and in the emasculated version of 'self-government'; and (*c*) the powers of the General Assembly in the field of human rights, which were already very weak (they were limited to the making of recommendations and studies) were further limited by the proviso of Article 2(7).[8]

B. *The Charter System*

The scheme for the protection of human rights resulting from the San Francisco deliberations might appear to be rather disappointing indeed. As stated above, the powers of the General Assembly were limited. It could act in the following ways:

(i) 'discuss' any question or matter concerning human rights, subject, however, to the proviso laid down in Article 2(7);[9]
(ii) 'initiate studies' for the purpose of 'assisting in the realization of human rights and fundamental freedoms for all without distinction as to race, sex, language, or religion;[10]
(iii) 'make recommendations' for the same purpose;[11]
(iv) draft international conventions;[12]
(v) establish 'such subsidiary organs as it deems necessary for the performance of its functions';[13] and
(vi) co-ordinate and stimulate the action of the other UN organs as well as of the Specialized Agencies.[14]

Plainly, the tasks entrusted to the General Assembly boiled down to discussion, exhortation, and the drafting of treaties. On top of it all, these powers (except for the elaboration of conventions) were put under that sword of Damocles constituted by Article 2(7). This provision had been worded so loosely as to give no idea whatsoever of the standards by which to appraise human rights questions. The only things that emerged clearly from the text and the preparatory work were that: (*a*) the provision was intended to bar the Organisation from *even discussing* any question falling within the domestic jurisdiction of member States; and (*b*) the dropping of the reference to

[8] See generally Russell and Muther, *History*, 422–9, 614–16, and 777–891.
[9] See below, 32–5 and 43–4.
[10] Art. 13(1)(b).
[11] Ibid.
[12] e.g. Art. 62(3).
[13] Art. 22.
[14] See e.g. Arts. 58 and 66.

international law contained in Article 15 of the League of Nations Covenant[15] and the use of the word 'essentially' in lieu of 'exclusively' entailed a broadening of the States' domestic jurisdiction and a correlative restriction of the Organisation's field of action (plainly, the expansion of the field of activity of international institutions prompted States to shield from this activity matters that, albeit covered by international treaties, normally did not constitute the subject of international legal obligations). However, no measuring rods were provided to determine precisely at what point the world organization was to stop, lest it should trespass on State sovereignty. In addition, certain other indications emerged from the preparatory work. The authority of the Organisation to 'intervene' on specific issues was confined to cases where violations of human rights endangered peace or 'obstructed the application' of the Charter. This was spelled out in the following terms:

> assuring or protecting such fundamental rights is primarily the concern of each State. If, however, such rights and freedoms are grievously outraged so as to create conditions which threaten peace or to obstruct the application of provisions of the Charter, then they cease to be the sole concern of each State.[16]

However, even this pronouncement did not furnish any clear-cut guidelines, and eventually left the Assembly free to decide when and how to 'intervene'.

Faced with this normative framework, member States of the UN were called upon to decide how to make use of the broad and vague formulas of the Charter. It was of course they who had to choose, not the Assembly itself, for, as Nicholas has noted, the Assembly is 'the exact reverse of Blackstone's parliament... [and] can only do what sovereign member States will let it'.[17] Broadly speaking, two possible courses of action were available to members of the UN. First, they might confine themselves to using the Assembly as a mere 'talking shop',[18] as 'a regular diplomatic conference',[19] and accordingly draft conventions or stimulate States to pursue certain objectives by addressing general recommendations to them, in keeping with a strict construction of Article 2(7). Arguably, this would by no means have been a poor performance, for the mere fact of detailing and spelling out in international instruments the human rights and fundamental freedoms for the promotion of which States should strive, constituted a major accomplishment.

[15] Art. 15(8) of the League of Nations Covenant provided as follows: 'If the dispute between the parties is claimed by one of them, and is found by the Council, to arise out of a matter which by international law is solely within the domestic jurisdiction of that party, the Council shall so report, and shall make no recommendation as to its settlement.'

[16] *United Nations Conference on International Organization*, Doc. 723, I/1/A/19, 6 *UNCIO* 705 (1945).

[17] Nicholas, *The United Nations as a Political Institution* (1975), 109.

[18] Ibid. 108.

[19] Xidis, 'The General Assembly', in J. Barros (ed.), *The United Nations: Past, Present and Future* (1972), 64.

A less moderate course of action was also open to States. By placing a liberal interpretation on Article 2(7) they might go beyond the mere preparation of international standards on human rights and call States to account, at least in cases of massive infringements of human rights. To this effect, they might emphasize that after all the Assembly was to be 'regarded as the highest organ of the United Nations', and indeed possessed 'the highest moral authority in so far as it could discuss (and thus criticize) the competence and functions of any other organ', because 'the competence of the Assembly comprises every subject coming within the scope of the Charter'.[20] The Assembly might therefore act as the 'conscience of the world': in addition to its 'quasi-legislative' functions it might be given the task of watch-dog for the purpose of forestalling or castigating egregious deviations from basic standards on human rights.

We shall see below that member States of the UN eventually chose the second course of action, albeit gradually and amidst much hesitation.

C. *Main Questions to be Examined*

Before dealing with the evolution of UN practice in the years following the adoption of the Charter, it should be emphasized that the Assembly, being composed of States, cannot but directly reflect the views and tendencies prevailing among the members of the Organisation. It would be erroneous to speak of an 'Assembly philosophy' or 'strategy' of human rights. In actual fact, 'the views of the Assembly' are those injected into its resolutions by the various groups of States prevailing at any specific time within that body (and consequently within the Organisation as a whole). In examining the policy lines on human rights elaborated by the Assembly we shall therefore have to concentrate on the concept of human rights propounded by the majority prevailing within it. Since, as we shall see, that majority has changed over time, one can discern three different phases or stages in the Assembly's evolution. The first stage, which goes from the adoption of the Charter to the late 1950s, was characterized by the domination of the West and its doctrine. The second stage starts around 1955 with the strengthening of the Socialist group which stimulated and supported developing countries. It has as its main feature the need for the West to come to terms with the other two groups, and the striking of a number of compromises necessary to take account of Socialist and Third World demands. The third stage, which starts around the middle 1970s, sees the prevalence of the Third World and their launching of a new doctrine of human rights that eventually gains the upper hand and aims at supplanting the views previously upheld by the General Assembly.

[20] Ross, *Constitution of the United Nations* (1950), 57.

For each of these three stages, I shall try to outline the prevailing doctrine, the achievements made on the plane of standard-setting and supervision, as well as the extent to which the Assembly (i.e., the majority of States within it) has 'interfered' with the domestic jurisdiction of member States.

Another general remark may prove apposite. In the pages below we shall have to ask ourselves the following questions: can one say that the Assembly, being the highest UN body in the sense pointed out above, has been able to 'instruct' the other UN organs about the way they should deal with human rights, or have those other bodies developed their own outlook autonomously? In other words, can we conclude from an examination of UN practice that the directives given by the General Assembly in the field of human rights have been merely taken up and implemented by the minor bodies concerned with the same issues? Or have these bodies gone beyond those higher guidelines and propounded an original view of human rights, or raised problems that the Assembly had not seen, or focused on issues neglected by the higher body? By way of hypothesis, we can postulate the existence in the UN system of another 'pole', constituted by a body that, although much lower in the hierarchical order, is totally different from the Assembly, namely the Sub-Commission on the Prevention of Discrimination and the Protection of Minorities. This organ is different from the Assembly in two very important respects: (*a*) it consists of individuals acting in their personal capacity (hence in a much freer position than delegates, who have to comply with the instructions of their government); (*b*) its membership is relatively small (26 persons), and it can therefore work more expeditiously and fruitfully than the Assembly, which is rather cumbersome and unwieldy. As the Sub-Commission's action is dealt with in Chapter 6 of this book I shall not examine its role and output. However, after examining the performance of the General Assembly we shall have to ask ourselves whether the two organs have merely had a one-way relationship of dominance by the higher one, or whether instead there has been mutual stimulation and feeding.

D. *The Practice of the General Assembly*

I. THE FIRST STAGE: FROM THE ADOPTION OF THE CHARTER TO THE LATE 1950S

(*a*) *Policy-Making and First Steps towards International 'Legislation'*

The first phase was characterized by efforts on the part of the General Assembly to draw up an international document on human rights which would be acceptable to all the members of the UN—to States so dissimilar ideologically and politically as the US and the USSR, to States with such different economic and political structures as the Western countries on the one hand and Ethiopia, Saudi Arabia, and Afghanistan on the other, to

Christian countries (like those of the West and Latin America), Muslim countries (like Saudi Arabia, Afghanistan, Turkey, and Pakistan, etc.), Hindu countries (like India), and Buddhist countries (like China).

It was therefore necessary to find a lowest common denominator, both as regards the conception of the relationship between the State and the individual and that of freedom and the rights of the individual. The attempt to forge a single, collective view, a general 'philosophy' of human dignity, was successful, although agreement was only reached after lengthy discussions. The political document which was the result, the Universal Declaration, and which was to be observed from 10 December 1948,[21] has two basic characteristics: one to do with its formal structure and the other with its content. In formal terms it is not legally binding, so possesses only moral and political force. In other words, it is simply a recommendation to States.

About the content of the Declaration a bit more needs to be said. On the whole, the view of human rights expressed in it is *Western*. More space and importance are allotted to civil and political rights than to economic, social, and cultural rights and no mention at all is made of the rights of peoples (the right of self-determination is completely absent). The position taken with regard to colonized peoples, partially or completely denied their right to freedom, is purely formal. The existence of dependent peoples is not ignored: the preamble states that the Universal Declaration is to be observed 'both among the peoples of member States and among the peoples of territories under their jurisdiction'. Moreover, Article 2(2) lays down that 'no distinction shall be made on the basis of the political, jurisdictional or international status of the country or territory to which a person belongs, whether it be independent, trust or non-self-governing or under any other limitation of sovereignty.'

However, these remain entirely formal and abstract pronouncements because the particular economic, political, and social circumstances of dependent countries were not taken into account by giving specific instructions to the States holding power over these countries. Nor does the Declaration say anything about economic inequalities between States, or consider the fact that some of them, being economically underdeveloped, will find it hard to grant full freedom to their citizens and in any case will not be in a position to guarantee certain basic economic and social rights, such as the right to work, to education, to suitable housing, etc.

How did the West succeed in imposing its 'philosophy' of human rights? The Socialist countries were in a minority (although they put up a strong resistance to the fact that so little importance was being attributed to economic, social, and cultural rights, and eventually abstained).[22] Also they had

[21] Universal Declaration of Human Rights, adopted by GA Res.217 A (III) (1948), in *Human Rights: A Compilation of International Instruments* (1988), 1.

[22] The Declaration was adopted by a vote of 48 to 0, with 8 abstentions, those of the Eastern European countries (Byelorussia, Czechoslovakia, Poland, Soviet Union, Ukraine, and Yugoslavia) plus Saudi Arabia and South Africa; GA Res.217 A (III) (1948).

not yet fully worked out a clear strategy of their own on the subject. As for the Third World, it was at this stage to a large extent made up of Latin American countries with a Western outlook; the remaining countries simply did not have the strength or authority to stand up to the Western powers, which incidentally numbered among their delegates influential figures such as Eleanor Roosevelt and René Cassin.

Even though the Declaration was not a true reflection of the various different approaches to human rights, nevertheless it was of great importance as a spur to international promotion of human rights and as a guiding star to direct this action.

(b) The Gradual Restriction by the Assembly of States' Domestic Jurisdiction

I have pointed out above that in the aftermath of the adoption of the Charter the General Assembly was faced with a difficult and important choice as regards the application of Article 2(7): it had to decide whether to adopt a restrictive view of human rights and consequently limit its 'interventions' in the matter as much as possible, or, by contrast, expand its field of action by overruling possible objections based on the notion of domestic jurisdiction. It did so, however, by adding a qualification based on the concept of these rights upheld in the Charter, namely that human rights must be respected as a means of safeguarding international peace. Starting from this assumption, the Assembly took the view that whenever an issue concerning human rights amounted to a situation likely to impair friendly relations among States, it was authorized to 'intervene'. A second justification for the Assembly's authority to pass judgement on matters relating to human rights was found in the possible existence of an international treaty (be it bilateral or multilateral) or at any rate an international legal obligation on the matter. The new doctrine was aptly summarized in 1948 by the French delegate to the Sixth Committee who pointed out that:

> If... the General Assembly were to have competence [in matters concerning human rights] either there must be an international agreement, or the situation must be such as to be likely to impair friendly relations among nations. Even if the first of those alternatives were not established, the recognition of the second would make it possible for the General Assembly to have competence in the matter.[23]

This doctrine, which constituted an imaginative and forward-looking way of expanding the jurisdiction of the Organisation (and, at least as far as the existence of international treaties was concerned, clearly departed from the spirit of Article 2(7) as it emerged from the preparatory work), was upheld by the Assembly on various occasions, among which the following stand out: the case of the treatment of Indians in the Union of South Africa;[24] the case of

[23] In the 'case of the Russian wives', A/C.6/SR.137, 3 (Part 1) GAOR C.6 (1948), 750.

[24] See GA Res.44 (I) (1946), and the subsequent resolutions on the matter adopted up to 1962.

the Russian wives in 1948;[25] the question concerning the observance of human rights in Bulgaria, Hungary, and Romania in 1949;[26] and the question of racial conflict in South Africa resulting from the policies of apartheid.[27]

Two interesting points should be stressed. First, in dismissing the plea of domestic jurisdiction, the Assembly gradually evolved the notion that the various provisions of the Charter enshrining human rights actually lay down obligations for member States. This was first done in 1949, in the resolution adopted on the question of the Russian wives. There, the Assembly stated that 'Article 1(3) of the Charter *binds* all Members to encourage "respect for human rights..."'; and that in Article 55(c) of the Charter the Members undertook to 'promote universal respect...' for human rights. The Assembly then 'declared' that 'the measures which prevent or coerce the wives of citizens of other nationalities from leaving their country of origin with their husbands or in order to join them abroad, are not in conformity with the Charter'.[28]

In the same vein, it stated in 1952 with respect to apartheid that 'governmental policies of Member States which are not directed towards these goals [i.e., racial harmony and respect for human rights] but which are designed to perpetuate or increase discrimination, are inconsistent with the pledges of Members under Article 56 of the Charter', and called upon 'all Member States to bring their policies into conformity with their obligation under the Charter to promote the observance of human rights and fundamental freedoms.'[29]

The second point to be emphasized regards the gradual emergence of a concept of domestic jurisdiction unrelated to the two elements stressed by the Assembly (namely the existence of an international treaty binding the State concerned, or the likelihood of the situation to impair friendly relations among States). The new concept tended to differentiate between two sets of situations, that of individual or isolated violations of human rights (to be left under the domestic jurisdiction of the State concerned), and that of large-scale infringements of human rights (to be regarded instead as coming within the province of the Assembly). In the first stage under consideration this distinction was merely hinted at on a few occasions, by single members of the UN or by minor UN bodies; later on, as we shall see, it became the official Assembly doctrine of domestic jurisdiction. It is worth briefly mentioning that the first to propound this view was a Polish delegate to the Assembly, Mr Katz-Suchy, who on the occasion of the discussion in 1949 on the question of observance of human rights in Bulgaria, Hungary, and Romania, said the following:

25 See GA Res.285 (III) (1949).

26 See GA Res.272 (III) (1949) and 385 (V) (1950).

27 See GA Res.616 A-B (VII) (1952), 721 (VIII) (1953), and the subsequent resolutions on apartheid adopted since then by the General Assembly (see n. 41, below).

28 GA Res.285 (III) (1949).

29 GA Res.616 (B) (VII) (1952), paras. 2–3.

The matter [concerning Article 2(7)] could be settled as follows: whenever, in law or in fact, a Member State denied the exercise of human rights to its whole population, the United Nations was entitled to intervene as a body. That point of view had been adopted when the General Assembly had studied the question of the treatment of Indians in South Africa. On the other hand, there was no legal clause authorizing any intervention whatsoever in the case of individual violations of human rights particularly when such violations were imaginary and when it was possible to prove that the allegations to that effect were totally without foundation.[30]

A similar line of thought was taken by the UN Commission on the Racial Situation in the Union of South Africa, in its 1953 report. Dismissing the argument that in upholding its jurisdiction on matters concerning human rights the Assembly would not be acting cautiously and showing a clear sense of responsibility, the Commission said the following:

Thus, for example, if an isolated instance of violation of fundamental human rights should arise in a country where the citizens enjoy legal facilities for seeking and obtaining redress, there would be no case for making it an international question. The United Nations organs would be failing to perform their duties under the Charter in a responsible and cautious manner were they to interfere in a domestic situation which, though incompatible with the principles of the Charter, is due to certain well-defined historical conditions and circumstances which cannot be changed overnight but which the State concerned is endeavouring gradually to eliminate. On the other hand, to go to the opposite extreme, the United Nations is unquestionably justified in deciding that a matter is outside the essentially domestic jurisdiction of a State when it involves systematic violation of the Charter's principles concerning human rights, and more especially that of non-discrimination, above all when such actions affect millions of human beings, and have provoked grave international alarm, and when the State concerned clearly displays an intention to aggravate the position.[31]

(*c*) *Supervision*

In this first period, the Assembly did not engage—on a large scale—in international scrutiny of States' misbehaviour. First, in the early years of UN concern with human rights, the main issue was still the elaboration of international standards by which to appraise the conduct of member States. Secondly, States were still very insistent on their right to reject possible interference by the UN in their domestic jurisdiction; the majority in the Assembly therefore felt that it was too early to submit the action of members to regular and continuous supervision. As a consequence, the Assembly confined itself to setting up special bodies entrusted with supervisory tasks in those few exceptional instances in which it decided to 'intervene'.

In 1951 the Assembly set up a commission of enquiry to investigate the

[30] A/BUR/SR.58, 3 (Part 2) GAOR General C. (1949), 14.

[31] *Report of the United Nations Commission on the Racial Situation in the Union of South Africa*, A/2505 (1953), para. 159.

conditions for holding free elections in Germany.[32] Even more significant was the setting up, in 1952, of a body responsible for keeping a grave situation of violations of human rights under review: the Assembly established a three-member 'Commission on the Racial Situation in the Union of South Africa', 'to study the racial situation' in that State 'in the light of the Purposes and Principles of the Charter, with due regard to the provisions of Article 2(7)'.[33] The Commission submitted a report to the Assembly, which then prolonged its mandate.[34] It is common knowledge that South Africa never heeded the recommendations of the Commission nor, for that matter, of the General Assembly.

II. THE SECOND STAGE: FROM THE LATE 1950S TO 1974

(*a*) *General: The New Doctrines of Human Rights*

Two important international political events heralded the beginning of the second phase: the socialist group was strengthened in 1955 owing to the admission of four socialist countries to the UN, and the Cold War gradually drew to an end. Eastern European countries thus became more and more vocal and assertive and their presence was even more strongly felt on account of the support of a growing number of developing nations, which joined the Organisation in the late 1950s and early 1960s. Above all, the socialist group perfected its doctrine and strategy of human rights and the West began to find itself on the defensive. This whole stage is consequently marked by the confrontation and the occasional convergence in the General Assembly of *two schools of thought*: that of the West and that of socialist countries supported by the Third World. The whole output of the Assembly cannot be appraised without taking account of this all-important phenomenon.

(*b*) *The Elaboration of International Standards: Their Reflection of the Emerging Doctrines of Human Rights*

Several very important treaties were the product of the contrast and compromise between these two different schools of thought: first and foremost the two International Covenants of 1966, the 1965 Convention on the Elimination of all Forms of Racial Discrimination, the 1968 Convention on the Non-Applicability of Statutory Limitations to War Crimes and Crimes against Humanity, and the 1973 Convention on the Suppression and Punishment of the Crime of Apartheid.[35] Some important resolutions were also passed on

[32] GA Res.510 (VI) (1951).
[33] GA Res.616 A (VII) (1952), para. 1.
[34] GA Res.721 (VIII) (1953).
[35] International Covenant on Economic, Social and Cultural Rights, adopted by GA Res.2200 A (XXI) (1966), *International Instruments*, 7; International Covenant on Civil and Political Rights,

the subject of self-determination: the 1960 Declaration on the Granting of Independence to Colonial Countries and Peoples and the Resolution of 1962 on Permanent Sovereignty over Natural Resources.[36] The three main groups of States (Western, Socialist, and Third World) basically agreed on the need to translate the general principles of the Universal Declaration into legally binding instruments; there was also considerable agreement—though some Western countries dragged their feet—that the principle of self-determination, which the Declaration had ignored, should be given international recognition on a 'legislative' level. For the West this only meant proclaiming a general principle to serve as a guideline for individual States to follow gradually. The socialists and the Third World countries, on the other hand, wanted a clear legal obligation to be laid down, which would be binding and immediately applicable. Compromise was finally reached and embodied first in the two resolutions passed at the beginning of the 1960s and then in the two Covenants.

We should now go back to the treaties on human rights drawn up in this period. A brief glance at the choice of rights favoured and the formulation of the respective measures is enough to see that the Socialist countries and the Third World countries which sided with them had by this time won the upper hand—even if they had, of course, to compromise with the West on more than one point.

First, the two majority groups succeeded in attributing great importance to the principle of self-determination in both Covenants; it is proclaimed in both, in identical terms. Secondly, the right to property does not figure in either Covenant. That is, it was no longer considered a value worthy of international protection on a universal level (this omission went along with the trend to erode and revise the international customary law which in the past had protected the private property of foreigners, requiring 'prompt, adequate and effective' compensation in the case of expropriation or nationalization).

Thirdly, for the first time in an international legal document we find the concept that formal or legal equality makes little sense if deep practical inequalities exist. This being the case, it appears right to give legal sanction to certain types of distinction when they are designed to make account of marked factual inequalities. Thus, Article 2(3) of the Covenant on Economic, Social and Cultural Rights lays down that developing countries can establish to what extent they mean to allow foreigners the economic rights specified by

adopted by GA Res.2200 A (XXI) (1966), ibid. 18; International Convention on the Elimination of all Forms of Racial Discrimination, adopted by GA Res.2106 A (XX) (1965), ibid. 56; Convention on the Non-Applicability of Statutory Limitations to War Crimes and Crimes against Humanity, adopted by GA Res.2391 (XXIII) (1968), ibid. 147; International Convention on the Suppression and Punishment of the Crime of Apartheid, adopted by GA Res.3068 (XXVIII) (1973), ibid. 69.

[36] Adopted by GA Res.1514 (XV) (1960) and 1803 (XVII) (1962), ibid. 47 and 49 respectively.

the Covenant. In other words, they are authorized to discriminate between nationals and foreigners (so long as this is justified by the country's economic circumstances and is not tantamount to discrimination against citizens of a particular State, and so long as this refusal to award the same status to foreigners and nationals does not lead to serious violations of other human rights).

In the fourth place, Socialist States, as well as a number of Third World countries, succeeded in weakening the system of international control over the application of the two Covenants proposed by the West, and also in making at least the most incisive part of it voluntary (supervision of observance of the Covenant on Civil and Political Rights, exercisable on individual request, is foreseen in an Optional Protocol[37] and not in the Covenant itself).

It should be added that the Socialist and developing countries also played a decisive part in deciding which rights were to be given special protection in the form of separate international treaties. It is certainly no accident that a draft convention on religious freedom—a subject dear above all to certain Western democracies—was brought before the organs of the UN time and again without success,[38] whereas the Convention on Racial Discrimination and the conventions mentioned above on apartheid and on war crimes and crimes against humanity—subjects towards which the Western attitude was distinctly lukewarm, if not downright hostile—were passed by the Assembly in no time at all.[39]

(c) *The Gradual Consolidation of the General Assembly's Position*

In this second stage the Assembly first took up the trend that had previously emerged as regards domestic jurisdiction, then gradually dropped the two conditions on which it had rested its authority to 'intervene' (existence of an international treaty or some legally binding rule; or the likelihood of the situation to impair the friendly relations of States), and turned to the view whereby large-scale and massive violations of human rights justified its dealing with them, whereas isolated instances of infringements of such rights did not warrant its 'intervention'. This gradual evolution appears clearly in the question of apartheid in South Africa. For some years the Assembly continued to affirm that its authority to discuss and pass resolutions condemning South

[37] Optional Protocol to the International Covenant on Civil and Political rights, adopted by GA Res.2200 A (XXI) (1966), ibid. 38.

[38] The drafting of a Declaration and a Convention began in 1962. In 1981 the Assembly adopted the Declaration on the Elimination of all Forms of Intolerance and Discrimination Based on Religion or Belief. GA Res.36/55 (1981), ibid. 125. The debate over whether to proceed with the drafting of a Convention has continued in the years since the Declaration was completed but no final decision had been taken by the end of 1989. See the report by T. van Boven on, *inter alia*, 'the issues and factors which should be considered before any drafting of a further binding international instrument'. E/CN.4/Sub.2/1989/32.

[39] See n. 35, above.

Africa derived from the fact that the situation constituted a serious danger to international peace and security.[40] Then the Assembly began to label apartheid 'a crime against humanity' and no longer rested its authority on the 'dangerous' character of apartheid for international peace, but rather on its being an international crime, i.e. a most egregious violation of the basic tenets of humanity.[41] To be sure, it continued to emphasize that the policy of apartheid amounted to a threat to the peace but it stated this only for the purpose of urging the Security Council to adopt adequate measures under Chapter VII of the Charter.[42]

(*d*) *Supervision*

In the early 1960s many member States of the UN became more and more aware of the urgent need to devise some form of international machinery for monitoring the way domestic authorities complied with the international standards elaborated, or in the process of being hammered out, by the Assembly. For a number of reasons, the need for such supervisory mechanisms was felt more acutely by Western countries, while Socialist and Third World States soon appeared to be rather reluctant to accept international control. The opposition of these two groups accounts for the meagre results achieved by the Assembly in this field.

The Assembly dealt with supervision on *three different levels*: (i) the institution of monitoring devices within the framework of the two Covenants and other international instruments that it was in the process of drafting; (ii) the direct setting up of fact-finding bodies for the purpose of scrutinizing gross violations perpetrated by certain countries; and (iii) endorsement of the creation of control machinery in 1967 and 1970 by the Sub-Commission, the Commission and the Council. I shall briefly examine each of these three areas in turn.

As for the Covenants and the other international conventions elaborated by the Assembly, it is common knowledge that Socialist and numerous Third World countries advanced the claim that international supervision would easily lend itself to possible forms of undue encroachment of international organs on State sovereignty and that in particular such organs would be used by Western countries to interfere with domestic matters within the Socialist and developing countries. This claim—no doubt substantially unfounded—led the majority in the Assembly to water down the control mechanisms

[40] See e.g. GA Res.1761 (XVII) (1962) and 2054 (XX) (1965), as well as 2307 (XXII)(1967).

[41] The relevant resolutions are contained in *Compilation of United Nations Resolutions and Decisions Relevant to the Struggle against Racism, Racial Discrimination and Apartheid: General Assembly Resolutions*, A/CONF.119/15 (Part II (1946–78)) and (Part III (1979–82)) (1983).

[42] The new trend can be discerned in various resolutions, among which mention should be made, by way of example, of GA Res.2396 (XXIII) (1968), 2506 A (XXIV) (1969), 3671 F (XXV) (1970), 2764 (XXVI) (1971), 2775 E (XXVI) (1971), and so on.

proposed by some Western countries, for the two Covenants and also for the Convention on Racial Discrimination, to such an extent that—as pointed out above—they were essentially deprived of their 'teeth' (although of course what remains is better than nothing).

The Assembly made more headway in some specific areas where it set up fact-finding bodies directly. The first attempt was made in 1963, when it sent a mission to South Vietnam to investigate alleged persecutions of Buddhists by the government.[43] It should be stressed, however, that this case was at the time unique because the proposal to send a mission was made by the very government under attack. In addition, the report submitted to the Assembly by the fact-finding mission was not discussed and no action was taken, because in the mean time the government had been toppled. More illustrative of the evolution of General Assembly action in the field of human rights is the setting up of two investigatory bodies: (1) the Special Committee on apartheid, with the tasks of (*a*) keeping 'the racial policies of the Government of South Africa under review when the Assembly is not in session', and (*b*) 'reporting either to the Assembly or to the Security Council or to both, as may be appropriate, from time to time';[44] and (2) the Special Committee on Israeli practices in territories occupied after the 1967 war, with the task of reporting on the violations of human rights committed by the occupying Power.[45] Unfortunately, in neither case has the State complained of co-operated with the UN fact-finding body, and this in many respects has resulted in limiting the effectiveness of the action taken.

Although it is not possible in the present context to go into any detail, mention should also be made of two other UN bodies: the Committee of 24[46] (which has dealt with human rights issues of dependent countries on many occasions) and the Committee on the Exercise of the Inalienable Rights of the Palestinian People.[47]

As stated before, the Assembly also dealt with control in a third way which, unlike the two previous ones, was only *indirect*. Indeed, it took account of the control procedures set up by its subordinate bodies, without opposing or trying to thwart them when it considered the reports of those organs. A few words about these procedures may be fitting. In 1967 the Commission established an Ad Hoc Group of Experts to investigate the plight of prisoners, detainees, and others in police custody in South Africa.[48] In 1967 and then in

[43] See the report contained in E/5630 (1973).
[44] The Committee was established by GA Res.1761 (XVII) (1962).
[45] Set up by GA Res.2443 (XXIII) (1968).
[46] The complete title of the Committee of 24 is the Special Committee on the Situation with Regard to the Implementation of the Declaration on the Granting of Independence to Colonial Countries and Peoples, established by GA Res.1654 (XVI) (1961). For details of its work, see *United Nations Action in the Field of Human Rights*, ST/HR/2/Rev.3 (1988), 56–7.
[47] See generally ibid. 59–62.
[48] CHR Res.2 (XXIII) (1967).

1970 the Council set up two special procedures for dealing with gross violations of human rights; the 1235 and 1503 procedures respectively.[49] Despite all their shortcomings,[50] these two procedures marked a great step forward in international action for effective respect for human rights. The Assembly must be given credit for not having opposed or stifled them, although they clearly emanated from UN bodies more sensitive than the Assembly to the need to deal with large-scale violations of human rights.

To sum up, the contention can be made that in this second stage, the Assembly, although sensitized by some Western countries to the urgent need to cater to international supervision, did not go a long way in this area. In fact, it was extremely cautious with regard to control mechanisms relating to the international conventions it drafted, while the progress it made by directly establishing some fact-finding and reporting bodies was to some extent motivated by the exceptional gravity of the situations to be monitored and also by the political considerations underlying UN concern for those situations (this holds true in particular for the Special Committee on Israeli practices). It should therefore not be surprising that possibly the Assembly's major achievements lay in not undoing the attempts made in this area by the subordinate bodies referred to above.

III. THE THIRD STAGE: FROM THE MIDDLE 1970S TO 1989

(*a*) *General*

As pointed out above, the third stage was, to a large extent, dominated by the Third World. In the early 1970s developing countries managed to elaborate their own philosophy and strategy of human rights, which to some extent did not coincide with that of Socialist countries. Thanks to their numerical superiority and their vociferousness, they managed to propound their own views without necessarily needing the support of Eastern European countries. In actual fact, however, the latter tended to endorse and corroborate their views, with the result that the West increasingly stood on the defensive.

As we shall see, the general Third World dominance was also apparent in the work of the Assembly on human rights. The fears expressed by some Western authors that this would gradually entail a complete suppression of Western ideals was, as we shall see, groundless, for in some important respects the Assembly's majority never went so far as to disregard some of the basic Western demands, particularly as regards implementation and responses to very grave violations such as torture, forced 'disappearances', etc.

[49] Provided for in ESC Res.1235 (XLII) (1967) and 1503 (XLVIII) (1970). For a discussion on these procedures, see Chap. 6, below.

[50] See Cassese, 'The Admissibility of Communications to the UN on Human Rights Violations', 5 *Rev. des droits de l'homme* 375 (1972).

(*b*) *The New General Assembly Strategy, Elaborated at the Instigation of the Developing Countries: Virtues and Defects*

The turning-point was 1974 when a series of important documents concerning the New International Economic Order were approved.[51] They not only made the reform of the international economic and social order a precondition for greater respect for human rights in developing countries; they also made very little mention of human rights at all. This approach was applied specifically to human rights issues in resolution 32/130 approved by the General Assembly in 1977. It was proposed by Argentina, Cuba, Yugoslavia, the Philippines, and Iran. It was significant, above all, because it made it clear, once and for all, that when considering important and delicate matters such as human rights, one could not take an abstract and metahistorical view of the international situation. On the contrary, in the opinion of its sponsors, one had constantly to bear in mind the fact that States could be divided into two main groups (developed and developing) and that different expectations held true for the two groups even in the field of human rights. The resolution also marked a definite step forward by stating the need to deal with the fundamental cause of so many violations of human rights: that is, 'structural violence' or, in other words, the grave injustices which derive from inequality between countries and the unfair distribution of wealth in the world. It rightly stressed this imbalance and also other phenomena connected with it (colonialism, foreign occupation or domination, racial discrimination, etc.). The corollary to this postulate also seems correct: it is not sufficient to condemn individual States for grave violations of human rights. The historical and social causes for these violations need to be understood so as to be able to work towards their removal, thus promoting respect for human rights, not of a temporary and ephemeral kind, but radical and permanent.

These important merits should not, however, blind us to the undeniable limitations and ambiguities of this resolution. First, one should at once be put on one's guard by the fact that among the countries which took an important part in its framing were Third World States which had (and in some cases, still have) authoritarian governments. It cannot be ruled out that these countries were motivated *in part* by the desire to squash the Western proposal to create a UN High Commissioner for Human Rights with the job of making sure that human rights are respected.[52] The 'neutralization' of the High Commissioner proposal and the simultaneous evolution of the stragegy expressed in resolution 32/130, which places the stress above all on social and economic rights, could have been thought up by these authoritarian governments as a means of distracting international attention from the grave violations committed in their own countries.

[51] See GA Res.3201 (S-VI) (1974), 3202 (S-VI) (1974), and 3281 (XXIX) (1974).
[52] See generally Clark, *A United Nations High Commissioner for Human Rights* (1972).

In the second place, it is undisputedly important to stress structural conditions (such as colonialism, attempts to deny the right of ownership of natural resources, etc.), both because this can serve to highlight the sins of some developed countries and because it is true that many violations of human rights in some developing countries result from appalling material conditions. Nevertheless, this approach can result in paying too little attention to grave violations (by some Third World countries) which are not among those listed in the resolution: for example, torture, genocide, denial of the most elementary civil and political liberties, etc. These appear to be the fruit of unjustified and arbitrary forms of authoritarian rule; they are not dictated by conditions of economic underdevelopment, but are the consequences of abuses perpetrated by individuals or groups.

Thirdly, the resolution does not throw enough light on a phenomenon which is by no means uncommon in developing countries and which is often the cause of grave violations of human rights. It may happen that the ruling minority has the backing of large-scale foreign interests and pursues ends which are not in the interests of the whole population; this minority often uses the support of foreign governments or powerful foreign economic interests to oppress the population. The despotic methods of these governments are to some extent the result of underdevelopment, but cannot be eliminated by economic aid alone (which will often be used by the ruling class to strengthen the repressive structures.) International pressure must also be exerted to denounce the authoritarian nature of the government.

(*c*) *Legislation and Control*

What have been the results of this new strategy? Briefly, it can be said that its chief result has been to stimulate the formulation of new rights: the right to development (which according to some is a right of the individual, and according to others, of peoples), the right to peace, the right to a just and fair international order (already adumbrated in the 1948 Universal Declaration), the right to a healthy environment free from pollution, and the right of peoples to use their own natural resources.[53]

Not a great deal was done during this time in the way of drawing up international conventions: the principal exception was the 1979 Convention on the Elimination of all Forms of Discrimination against Women.[54] Until 1984, the preparation of a Convention against Torture[55] proceeded very slowly, partly because of the inherent difficulty of the subject, and partly because a few countries, mainly from the Third World, were reluctant to be bound by detailed rules on this subject.

[53] See generally Crawford (ed.), *The Rights of Peoples* (1988).
[54] Adopted by GA Res.34/180 (1979), *International Instruments*, 112
[55] Adopted by GA Res.39/46 (1984), ibid. 212.

It has also been difficult to draw up new international standards in some fields with respect to which widespread violations currently occur. These include: (1) the rights of detainees (especially political prisoners);[56] (2) politically motivated 'kidnappings' and 'disappearances';[57] (3) abuses of declarations in the form of 'states of emergency' as a means of seriously limiting the enjoyment of human rights for prolonged periods.[58]

It was certainly no accident that during the late 1970s and early 1980s there was considerable progress in the formulation of new rights and relatively little towards the approval of new standards in other areas. Those areas concerned civil and political rights which were apparently of little interest to many Third World and Eastern European countries, whereas the new rights were of the kind which most concerned the majority.

(*d*) *Domestic Jurisdiction*

After 1974 the doctrine that had previously emerged, whereby the plea of domestic jurisdiction could be overruled whenever gross violations of human rights were at stake, definitively consolidated itself. Two things contributed to this result. First, the functioning of the two procedures for dealing with gross violations of human rights, referred to above, led States increasingly to accept the idea that large-scale infringements could not be regarded as coming within the purview of their domestic jurisdiction. Secondly, in 1974 the General Assembly began to deal with a new situation of massive disregard of human rights: that of Chile. Interestingly, all resolutions that the Assembly adopted after 1974 on Chile stressed that the situation obtaining there revealed massive violations, but made no mention of the likelihood of that situation impairing friendly relations (nor, for that matter, did they place special emphasis on violations of its treaty obligations by Chile).[59] Thus, the Assembly's 'intervention' on Chile both exemplified and reinforced the new trends in the field of domestic jurisdiction.

It should be added, however, that the majority prevailing in the Assembly during the 1970s and 1980s also made itself felt with negative results. In 1981 the Assembly strongly 'deplored' the fact that the US had extradited to Israel Mr Ziad Abu Eain, 'a Palestinian national from occupied Palestinian territory

[56] A draft instrument on this issue was completed by the Sub-Commission in 1978 but it took an entire decade for the General Assembly to finalize its review and adopt the Body of Principles for the Protection of all Persons under any Form of Detention or Imprisonment, GA Res.43/173 (1988), Annex.

[57] The Sub-Commission's Working Group on Detention has continued to work on this issue during the early 1990s. See e.g. the draft declaration contained in E/CN.4/Sub.2/1990/32 and also E/CN.4/1992/19.

[58] See Questiaux, 'Study of the Implications for Human Rights of Recent Developments Concerning Situations Known as States of Siege or Emergency', E/CN.4/Sub.2/1982/15.

[59] See e.g. GA Res.3219 (XXIX) (1974), 3348 (XXX) (1975), 31/124 (1976), and 32/118 (1977).

and a Jordanian citizen . . . illegally detained in prison in the United States of America for two years'.[60] It also demanded that Mr Ziad Abu Eain be immediately released by Israel and that the US government, 'being responsible for his safety, should facilitate his safe transfer to the country of his choice'. This resolution was adopted by a vote of 75 in favour, to 21 against (all Western countries), with 43 abstentions. Both Israel and the US declared that the passing of the resolution was in clear violation of Article 2 para. 7. In the view of the former:

> The bringing to justice of an individual accused of the criminal offences mentioned above [murder, attempted murder and causing bodily harm with aggravating intent] is clearly within the domestic jurisdiction of the prosecuting State. In accordance with Article 2 para. 7 of the Charter, it is thus *ultra vires* for the United Nations to intervene in such matters.[61]

It is suggested that these objections were well founded. Indeed, the resolution markedly departed from the previous consolidated practice of the Assembly without any convincing justification being given for such a radical step. And there seemed in fact to be no solid ground on which the Assembly could rest its 'intervention' on the issue. The resolution was an unfortunate move that did not contribute either to the cause of human rights or to the settlement of the tricky and numerous problems of the Middle East situation. It is to be hoped that in the future the Assembly will avoid passing resolutions that can only contribute to dividing and estranging the various parties and also perhaps to exacerbating the conflicts.

(*e*) *Supervision*

Some authors, very critical of the new course of action begun in the 1970s by the Assembly, suggested that the new strategy championed by the Third World with the support of Socialist countries had, among other things, a negative impact on the actual implementation of human rights. This critical assessment cannot be shared. In the period after 1974 the Assembly not only continued to refrain from hampering in any way the working of the two procedures for dealing with gross violations of human rights, referred to above, but also proved capable of extending its concern to gross violations other than the 'traditional' ones (i.e., South Africa and Israel). Before considering this interesting development, it should be pointed out that the critics of the Assembly's performance were right in asserting that its then majority wrongly thwarted what the West considered a most significant device for monitoring large-scale disregard of human rights, namely the High Commissioner for Human Rights. The derailment of the (mainly Western) move to set up the High Commissioner must no doubt be regretted, for it is not

[60] GA Res.36/171 (1981).

[61] 21 *Int'l Legal Materials* 444 (1982).

true that it would only have looked into violations of civil and political rights, nor would it have interfered in the domestic affairs of developing and socialist countries. There is no gainsaying that the High Commissioner might have had a tremendous role in casting light on so many situations of 'structural violence', i.e., social and economic injustice, and might also have suggested the most appropriate ways of contributing towards solving those problems. Be that as it may, the failure to establish the High Commissioner did not mean that the new majority was blind to situations revealing a consistent pattern of gross violations of human rights. After 1974 the Assembly adopted a two-pronged course of action in this regard. First, it emphasized, in general terms, the need to come to grips with massive violations and in addition called attention to some particularly serious categories of such infringements. Secondly, it drew the attention of Member States to the human rights situation obtaining in some specific countries. The details of these developments are provided in Chapter 3 of this book and will not be repeated in the present chapter.

It could be argued that in adopting various resolutions of a general kind the Assembly merely drew the attention of members to some particularly glaring instances of gross violations, without, however, pointing to infringements occurring in specific countries, nor setting up special machinery for investigating such violations wherever they occurred. Nevertheless, the Assembly often requested the Commission to enquire into such matters. Furthermore, it is significant that the highest UN body should have indicated to all States its concern about some classes of grave violations of human rights.

Undoubtedly, the second line of action, consisting in passing resolutions on specific countries and keeping them under scrutiny appears to have been more satisfactory in some respects.

Arguably, the method chosen by the Assembly for dealing with countries such as Chile, Bolivia, El Salvador, Guatemala, Poland, Afghanistan, Iran, Romania, and others of (*a*) urging the government concerned to discontinue its gross violations, (*b*) requesting the Commission to investigate the matter, possibly by appointing a special rapporteur, and (*c*) deciding to keep the matter under consideration as long as the massive violations continue,[62] is flexible and fairly adequate. It seems that the setting up of a single supervisory body, urged by a few countries, would be opposed by the majority of States, which prefer solutions based on a case-by-case approach. The major shortcoming of the Assembly action in this field lies somewhere else, namely in the fact that many other situations of gross and systematic violations have never been the subject of adequate supervisory measures by either the Assembly or the Commission. The political alignments that take shape in the Assembly

[62] For details of these different country studies, see *United Nations Action in the Field of Human Rights*, 266–79.

should be blamed for this unsatisfactory state of affairs. Given the very recent changes in the political constellation, it seems probable that things will improve in the medium run.

E. *Achievements and Defects of the Assembly Action: A Tentative Appraisal*

I. CONFRONTATION AND CONVERGENCE OF THE VARIOUS DOCTRINES OF HUMAN RIGHTS

What conclusions can be drawn about the work of the General Assembly which we briefly examined? We should distinguish between two different levels: that of the 'doctrines' on human rights, put forward by the various groups of States between 1945 and the late 1980s in the Assembly, and that of the actual legislative and institutional action taken. The two levels are closely connected and influence each other; nevertheless, it is useful to distinguish between them, if only for the sake of clarity.

As regards 'doctrine', we have seen how the Western view lost its dominant position in the face of the conceptions favoured by the Third World and Socialist countries. The fact should not be ignored that although the three principal 'doctrines' influenced each other to some extent, they remained distinct and also, in a way, opposed to each other. Despite all its efforts and the successes it had even in this field, the Assembly did not succeed in merging these conflicting views. There remained a fundamental rift between two different doctrines: on the one hand, the Western philosophy; on the other, that of the Third World and Socialist countries. The latter doctrine—which sometimes led to unduly neglecting civil and political rights—must be given credit for having prompted the Assembly to spread a deep sense of social justice and indignation against 'structural violence', in particular with respect to those historical situations (such as colonial or neo-colonial exploitation and apartheid) which deprived whole human groups of basic rights and freedoms. As Bert Röling rightly pointed out, the Assembly:

> has been instrumental in bringing about a new concept of world justice based on the universal recognition of human rights. The implementation of this new concept of justice has contributed to conflict and violence in many parts of the world in that it calls for a fundamental change in international relations, the abolition of traditional privileges of the rich part of the world and the granting of rights whose exercise clashes with substantial interests of States that formerly ruled the world.[63]

[63] Röling, 'Peace Research and Peace-Keeping', in A. Cassese (ed.), *United Nations Peace-Keeping: Legal Essays* (1978), 251.

In other words, the Assembly (together with other UN bodies) succeeded in moving from a static concept of human rights (conceived as a means of realizing international peace) to a dynamic concept that went as far as to promote physical violence and the disruption of the status quo for the sake of introducing social justice and respect for the dignity of man (this, as Röling has correctly underscored, is what happened in the case of apartheid in Southern Africa and Rhodesia, where the UN willingly promoted rebellion against structural violence in the form of white rule).

Let us now go back to the contrast between the two main approaches to human rights, that of the West and that of the other two groups of States. This conflict did not lead to a deadlock. In fact, in spite of the many differences, a limited consensus which came to be shared by all three groups of States emerged from the Assembly's debates. At the same time, certain States changed their views under the influence of those views of other States. Let us consider these phenomena.

As had regards the first, it can, I think, be said that the main groups of States had agreed on the following essential points by the late 1980s:

(i) '*Freedom and dignity for each human being*' constituted an essential value which every State should try to protect, regardless of considerations of nationality, sex, etc. There were, without a doubt, differences of opinion concerning the practical steps to be taken both domestically and internationally to achieve this end; there was, however, full agreement that every State—whatever its internal structure or ideological and political standpoint—should do its utmost to safeguard those rights which are essential to the integrity of the person.

(ii) It was also necessary to aim at the achievement of some fundamental rights of groups and peoples. Between 1919 and 1945 concern was mostly for minorities (linguistic, ethnic, and religious), whereas in the years immediately after the Second World War, protection of the rights of individuals appeared of paramount importance. Later, however, there seemed to be general agreement that other groups as well needed protection; it is now accepted that peoples have a right to their own integrity (and hence to protection against genocide) and to self-determination.

(iii) There was full agreement in condemning *racial discrimination*, and, in particular apartheid, which was universally considered (and rightly so) to be one of the most repulsive and inhuman features of the present age. It is significant that the 1965 Convention on the Elimination of all Forms of Racial discrimination has been ratified by more countries than any other international instrument on human rights: 130 countries had ratified it as of 1 January 1991.[64] In particular, as regards apartheid, even Western countries

[64] 'Human Rights: Status of the International Instruments as at 1 January 1991', ST/HR/5 (1991).

—which rely heavily on South African exports of four key minerals (chromium, manganese, vanadium, and platinum) essential to their industry and defence —came to realize how loathsome the policy of discrimination pursued by the authorities in that country was, and increasingly called for radical changes. Indicative of the mood emerging in the West, and also of the motivations behind it, was a statement made in 1982 by Robert S. McNamara:

> Unless South Africa's racial policies are fundamentally redesigned, they will eventually lead to a catastrophic racial conflict that will have serious ramifications throughout the Western world, and most especially in the United States . . . If what is left of the 1980s does not witness real movement toward sharing of political power . . . then South Africa may, and I believe will, become as great a threat to the peace of the world in the 1990s as the Middle East is today.[65]

(iv) Even though some States might find it hard, both for economic and social reasons and for organizational and political reasons, to grant full respect for human rights, no State must perpetrate grave, repeated, and large-scale violations of whole categories of human rights. When this did occur, the international community was justified in 'intervening', by addressing recommendations and solicitations to the country concerned or helping it to put an end to the practices criticized. The concept of 'state sovereignty' then, no longer protected countries from UN intervention in the case of exceptionally serious and flagrant deviations from the most elementary rules concerning the protection of the rights of individuals or groups. It was thanks to the United Nations and to the possibility it offered for States to come together and exchange their different views and ideas and try to reduce the area of conflict, that it was possible to form a common approach, at least on the basic points just listed.

We should now look at the other positive result of the coming together of conflicting views inside the UN: changes of opinion brought about, *inter alia*, by the persuasive influence of one school of thought on another.

One example has been the increasing preparedness of the Western countries to take economic, social, and cultural rights seriously, a tendency which was partly responsible for the Council's 1985 decision to establish a fully-fledged expert committee to monitor States parties compliance with their obligations under the Covenant on Economic, Social and Cultural Rights.[66] It seems clear that this greater willingness to promote economic rights—which is certainly more in tune with modern needs and closer to the reality of the international situation—also resulted from the demands of developing countries and their campaign to draw the attention of industrialized nations to

[65] McNamara, 'South Africa Threatens to be the Middle East of the 1990's', *International Herald Tribune* (25 Oct. 1982), 5.
[66] ESC Res.1985/17.

the pressing problems of the 'have-nots'. It is of course a matter of regret that the United States has, since 1981, refused to recognize these rights as rights.

By the same token, the Western approach to human rights influenced, at least to some extent, the doctrines of the other two groups of States. I have suggested above that resolution 32/130, setting forth the new UN strategy in the field of human rights, was marred by some ambiguity. In particular, it lent itself to over-emphasizing the importance of implementing economic, social, and cultural rights to the detriment of civil and political rights. It has been asserted that the resolution actually threw the latter category of human rights into the waste-paper basket;[67] this is no doubt excessive. A better view seems to be that the resolution was tainted with some ambiguity that might have led to overrating the importance of the former category of rights. And in fact a number of developing countries, together with the Socialist States, set out to enhance the role of such rights and, by the same token, to pass over the other category in silence. The West must be given credit for insisting on the crucial role of both categories, and it seems to have soundly influenced the other groups. This, to my mind, was evidenced by a number of Assembly resolutions where emphasis was placed on the need 'to promote and protect civil and political rights as well as economic, social and cultural rights'. Thus, for example, in 1982 the Assembly stated that:

> the international community should accord, or continue to accord, priority to the search for solutions to mass and flagrant violations of human rights of the peoples and individuals affected by situations such as those mentioned in para. 1(e) of Res. 32/130 [i.e., situations resulting from apartheid, from all forms of racial discrimination, from colonialism, from foreign domination and occupation, from aggression and threats against national sovereignty, national unity and territorial integrity, as well as from the refusal to recognize the fundamental rights of peoples to self-determination and of every nation to the exercise of full sovereignty over its wealth and natural resources] *paying due attention also to other situations of violations of human rights*' (italics added).[68]

This provision implied that the resolution under consideration, authored by developing and Socialist countries, upheld one of the basic tenets of the West. This, however, should not lead us to over-emphasize the extent to which Western ideas had been injected into the dominant doctrine of human rights.

(*a*) *Legislative Achievements*

In terms of practical achievements, the results of the co-operation and compromise among the different groups of states since 1945 should not be underestimated. First, numerous international conventions were adopted. In other

[67] e.g. Donnelly, 'Recent Trends in UN Human Rights Activity: Description and Polemic', 35 *Int'l Org.* 633 (1981); but cf. Alston, 'The Alleged Demise of Political Rights at the UN: A Reply to Donnelly', 37 *Int'l Org.* 537 (1983).

[68] GA Res.36/133 (1981), para. 3.

words, an international legislative framework was created which is binding on a large number of States, and which now regulates the most important aspects of human rights and fundamental freedoms. In general these conventions had the widespread support of the three main groups of States. Only a few were drawn up by one or other of the groups, without the support of the other group. One such was the 1968 Convention on the Non-Applicability of Statutory Limitations to War Crimes and Crimes against Humanity, and another the 1973 Convention on the Crime of Apartheid.[69] In both cases the initiative of the Afro-Asian and Socialist countries did not meet with the approval of the West, which tried to hinder the passage of the Conventions in several ways. As a result, although the Conventions were adopted by the Assembly they have only been ratified by a relatively low number of States (respectively 31 and 89 as of 1 January 1991);[70] no Western country has ratified either.

A second positive aspect of this legislative activity was that it also led to the gradual emergence of certain important customary rules: for example, the rule forbidding grave, repeated, and systematic violations of human rights, and those banning genocide, racial discrimination, or denial of the right to self-determination of peoples. It should be noted that these rules are not only binding on all States which belong to the international community, whether they have ratified conventions on the subject or not, but also impose obligations *erga omnes*, as has been stressed by the International Court of Justice.[71] Moreover, some of these norms have also acquired the status of *jus cogens*.

(*b*) *Institutional Achievements*

Among the most important accomplishments of the Assembly since 1945, mention should be made first of all of the expansion of the UN's authority in the field of human rights and the correlative restriction of States' domestic jurisdiction. As we have seen above, no member State any longer questions the authority of the Assembly (as well as the other competent organs) to discuss, investigate, and pass resolutions upon situations revealing a consistent pattern of gross violations of human rights. For such situations to be considered by the Assembly no requirement is made that they should be likely to impair friendly relations among States. Indeed, as I have pointed out above, on a number of occasions the Assembly has passed resolutions and recommended action that ran counter to the requirement of safeguarding peaceful relations.

A second major achievement was the setting up, on a case-by-case

[69] See n. 35, above.

[70] 'Human Rights: Status of the International Instruments as at 1 January 1991', ST/HR/5 (1991).

[71] See generally Rodley, 'Human Rights and Humanitarian Intervention: The Case Law of the World Court', 38 *Int'l & Comp. LQ* 321 (1989).

basis, of special bodies entrusted with enquiring into specific situations. An important 1980s trend was to request the Commission on Human Rights to institute such fact-finding bodies, and this can be regarded as a positive development—except, however, for the cases where urgent investigation was needed and consequently the delegation to the Commission of the task of appointing a person or a team proved time-consuming.

Finally, one may well number among the Assembly's achievements the fact that it neither opposed nor endeavoured to stifle the two procedures for dealing with human rights violations set up by ECOSOC in 1967 and 1970 respectively. Although they have not yet yielded conspicuous results, they might have aroused strong opposition among those numerous States which object to any international scrutiny of the way they behave in their domestic sphere, the more so because the initiative to bring cases of gross violations to the attention of international bodies is left to individuals or groups of individuals. The fact that the Assembly tacitly endorsed the creation of the two procedures was, in itself, a positive result.

(*c*) *Major Deficiencies of General Assembly Action up until the Late 1980s*

First of all, in the human rights field, the Assembly increasingly indulged in a practice that could also be noticed in other fields of its activity: the passing of a great number of resolutions each year, in the awareness that most of them constituted mere paper solutions to serious problems and that no domestic authority would ever heed them. The staggering increase in Assembly resolutions became a serious phenomenon that should have given rise to the utmost concern on the part of all those who believed in the Assembly's crucial importance. It seemed that the more impotent the Assembly felt in the face of difficult problems, the more often it resorted to paper solutions. One is reminded of the Queen of Hearts in *Alice in Wonderland*, who had only one way of settling all difficulties, great or small, namely to order 'off with his head', but nobody paid any attention to her commands and no beheading was ever carried out.

A second major shortcoming was the ambiguity of the doctrine of human rights expounded in resolution 32/130 and subsequently taken up in various other resolutions. Admittedly, as I have stressed above, the new approach set forth in that landmark resolution had a lot of merit. Nevertheless, it was ambiguous as regards the nexus between civil and political rights on the one hand and economic, social, and cultural rights on the other. In particular, it failed to state that the existence of serious social injustice due to economic backwardness could not by any means warrant the suppression of some important human rights such as the right to life and security, nor could it justify such appalling practices as torture or forced 'disappearances'. Although, as I have shown above, the Assembly tried to tackle this question in later resolutions, it seems to me that it was still a long way from satisfactorily clarifying the complex connections between the two sets of rights. It is to be hoped that the new era in the 1990s will see it engage in this important exercise.

A third drawback lay in the scant attention given by the Assembly to the suggestions emanating from the Sub-Commission—which, as I have stressed above, represents the other pole of action in the UN in that, being composed of persons acting in their individual capacity, it is in a better position to give voice to the demands of individuals and non-governmental groups for a more effective and extensive protection of human rights. The Assembly often neglected the Sub-Commission's demands for more imaginative and concrete action. Linked in part to this neglect was a failure to pursue the policy implications of its new approach which involved looking at the structural causes underlying specific human rights violations. An illustration of what might be done—with respect to which the present writer finds himself in a rather awkward position, since he was personally involved in the business—can be found in decisions by the Sub-Commission and the Commission in 1977 to supplement UN action on Chile by undertaking an examination of the impact that foreign economic assistance to Chile had on respect for human rights in that country. The idea of thus expanding the UN's action constituted a forward-looking and momentous decision and was intended to provide a means of coming to grips with the root causes of continuing disregard of human rights in that particular country.

Another major shortcoming of the Assembly—or rather of the majority of States therein—was inadequate attention to the demands and suggestions of non-governmental organizations (NGOs). This was a very serious defect indeed, for NGOs offer a wealth of first-hand information, raise new points often neglected by governmental agencies, and expose situations that would otherwise be neglected by States.

Furthermore, the Assembly proved unable to deal swiftly and efficaciously with situations that needed urgent intervention. This by no means reflected an inherent incapacity to cope with emergency situations. If the political will to take action expeditiously had existed, the Assembly could have devised appropriate means of intervention (one such means was precisely to be the High Commissioner) or could have entrusted one of its subordinate bodies with this task. Political interests accounted for the Assembly's failure to meet this demand. It follows that—to use the metaphor of a famous Austrian thinker—Assembly resolutions often conjured up the 'ugly picture of mills which grind so slowly that, before the flour is ready, men are dead of hunger'.

Finally, it is a matter of regret that many studies and reports prepared by the UN—either by the Secretariat or by the special rapporteurs or working groups appointed by various UN bodies—were of little value except for the information they gathered from various official sources. This was probably due to the idea that they should tend to be compilations of material rather than original contributions to the study of specific questions. Unfortunately, with very few exceptions, the reports produced by the UN continue to be of scant cognitive value, offer very few imaginative solutions, and very seldom break new ground. Consequently, they are known and cited only by other UN bodies. There are probably many reasons for this state of affairs: rapporteurs are required to be 'neutral' at all costs; appointments are often not made on the basis of the intellectual qualities of the rapporteurs, but on the basis of political considerations; and the bulk of the research and drafting is carried out by the UN Secretariat which strives to be 'neutral' and is reluctant to venture into new fields.

F. *Desirable Improvements: A Few Modest Proposals*

After the shortcomings of the 1980s, there are several steps that warrant consideration by the Assembly in the 1990s. A first improvement would be radically to diminish the number of resolutions it passes. The Assembly should become selective, and take action only on a few issues deserving special emphasis. By the same token, it should seek to make its resolutions better known to national authorities and, even more importantly, relevant within the domestic legal systems of member States. In this way resolutions could have a far greater (moral, psychological, and political) impact on national authorities. It is suggested that the fewer the resolutions, the greater their possible bearing on domestic authorities. Of course, this would mean that States ought to give up some of their demands. It is common knowledge that, at present, the multiplication of resolutions on certain items such as apartheid is due to the need for the sponsors to command the support of certain groups of States. This is obtained by devoting specific resolutions to some issues which can be supported by States which would not vote for them if those issues were inserted in other resolutions they feel unable to endorse for political reasons. Admittedly, the drastic reduction in Assembly resolutions would result in some of the 'amalgamated' resolutions gaining little support, or even in the abandonment of certain issues which would be unlikely to draw the support of some groups of States. Would this be a great loss? Would it not contribute to more clarity in international relations, i.e., in a better appreciation of where States really stand and what they really support or reject?

A second change might be to try to do away with the ambiguity that currently mars too many Assembly resolutions. The Assembly should try to engage in an in-depth discussion of the basic approach to be taken to human rights, and then consistently adhere to the decisions taken. If the majority feels that it cannot accommodate the demands of the minority, it had better say so in so many words. The minority would then have to decide whether to go along or, more probably, to dissociate itself from the proposed decisions. False unanimity, or paper consensuses, do not serve much purpose.

A further improvement would be to pay greater attention to both the Sub-Commission and to NGOs. They should be given a greater role to play; the Assembly should listen more carefully to their proposals and seek to take greater account of them.

Finally, a drastic change should be introduced in the quality of the reports and studies prepared under the aegis of the UN. One should not fear to entrust them to persons having the requisite intellectual capabilities and ask them to express their viewpoint and make suggestions in full independence. In this way, a great wealth of ideas, suggestions, and viewpoints would eventually enrich the work of UN bodies and offer the intellectual basis and stimulation for more effective action.

3
The General Assembly into the 1990s

JOHN QUINN

Introduction

In this chapter a modest attempt is made to address the ambitious question of how well placed the General Assembly is to deal with some of the pressing human rights issues now on the international agenda, as well as those new challenges which are likely to emerge as this decade unfolds. The focus is squarely on the practical dimension: how does the Assembly go about its human rights business, and what could be done to improve its performance? Strangely perhaps, the proceedings of the Assembly's recent sessions have not been the subject of the close scrutiny accorded to other parts of the UN's labyrinthine human rights machinery. This chapter tries to fill this gap in the belief that the history of the Assembly over the last decade offers a number of useful pointers to productive reforms of this body. Indeed, it will be argued that major reform of the Assembly is necessary to realize its undoubtedly significant and largely untapped potential, and that a clearer definition of the Assembly's human rights responsibilities will have beneficial spin-off effects for other UN human rights bodies. In the 1990s, as human rights are increasingly intertwined with other major issues on the rapidly evolving international agenda, the unique potential of the Assembly to explore these interlinkages will become even more important. The chapter concludes with some speculative thoughts about how the international human rights agenda might change over this decade.

A critical examination of the General Assembly's recent contribution to protection and promotion of human rights reveals some paradoxes. On the one hand, the Assembly's proceedings attest to the fact that human rights issues have now assumed an important place on the international political agenda. Human rights issues permeate beyond the Third Committee, as the traditional focus of this debate, to most of the organs of the Assembly including the Plenary,[1] and are the subject of many resolutions and lengthy debates. Within the UN system itself, the Assembly's place at the top of the

The views expressed in this chapter are the author's own, and do not represent the views of the Australian government.

[1] During the General Debate, and under specific items, notably apartheid.

UN's legislative hierarchy[2] gives it special authority and a unique oversight role in relation to the UN's human rights activities. In a context of tight resource constraints facing the UN (as well as most of its member States), the Assembly's budgetary and administrative powers give it a special importance as far as the UN's human rights programme is concerned. On the other hand, the Assembly's effectiveness and relevance are being increasingly questioned. Much of the formal multilateral machinery sought by proponents of an active UN human rights programme in the 1970s is now well established around the core body, the Commission on Human Rights (the 'CHR' or the 'Commission'). Looking at this framework, it is reasonable to ask: what *distinctive* contribution is the Assembly really making to the advancement of human rights, especially when so much of its output seems to replicate what is being done by the Commission and other subsidiary bodies? Others complain with justification that the Assembly has failed to act against egregious human rights violations in a number of countries, and, that when it has dealt with specific situations, the results have been mixed. Another criticism is that the Assembly's human rights activities are marginal to the most important international action to address violations, which takes place through bilateral contacts between governments, or as a result of the endeavours of NGOs working outside the UN framework. Attention is also drawn to the Assembly's overcrowded agenda, the limited time which it allocates for human rights (about half of its seven- to eight-week annual sessions) and the relative paucity of human rights specialists and NGOs in attendance,[3] all of which have not been conducive to effective in-depth debate, or innovation. Belying its overview/supervisory status, the Assembly has, moreover, devoted only limited attention to priority setting, improving co-ordination of human rights activities throughout the UN system, or mobilizing the resources of this system as a whole to achieve human rights objectives. In short, the Assembly has failed to give the sort of political and administrative/budgetary leadership which might be expected from a body with its mandate and functions.

Before embarking on an analysis of the way in which the Assembly has handled its human rights agenda over recent years, and how its performance could be improved, some discussion seems warranted as to why so little critical attention has been devoted to this body, either by delegations themselves or by outside observers. There are a number of possible explanations for this neglect of the Assembly. In the first place, the focus of academic

[2] The Security Council could be regarded as 'superior' because it adopts binding resolutions, but is not of course of universal membership, and has a narrower agenda related to international peace and security. The Security Council has nevertheless addressed human rights issues, notably in the context of apartheid and recently the Iraq/Kuwait crisis.

[3] A small number of countries such as Canada, France, Australia, Denmark, the United States, and The Netherlands have followed the practice of including parliamentarians or other special advisers in their delegations.

interest seems to have shifted to the Commission since the Assembly concluded its major work on standard-setting. This has led some to the conclusion that the Assembly is really only of marginal relevance as a 'rubber stamp' for the important decisions of the subsidiary bodies. Another explanation may be that access to the General Assembly is much more restricted than to the Commission or the Commission Sub-Commission, where both NGOs and academics have been prominent and active participants. Furthermore, the Assembly is often characterized as intrinsically 'political', and therefore, in some eyes, beyond rigorous analysis.

A more compelling rationale for the dearth of critical commentary on the Assembly may have been the understandable reluctance on the part of supporters of an active UN human rights programme to open the 'reform gate' in relation to politically sensitive activities and structures in the human rights field which have evolved over years of difficult negotiation. While these activities and structures are now reasonably well established, it must be acknowledged that opponents of UN involvement in human rights issues could still take advantage of calls for 'rationalization' to hobble worthwhile procedures, activities, and structures. Nevertheless, resource constraints facing the UN now require difficult choices to be made such as between conference services, reports, and other documents on the one hand, and substantive programmes such as support for the work of special rapporteurs on the other.[4]

It is perhaps even more surprising that so little attention has been paid to the relationship between the General Assembly, ECOSOC, and the Commission on Human Rights. Perhaps this is because supporters of UN human rights activities have generally taken the 'empirical' view that 'more is better'. Repetition of debate and of resolutions about violations in various bodies, especially in the 'superior' universal membership Assembly, is seen by many as reinforcing international pressure. While there may have been clear justification for this view when the Assembly offered one of the few mechanisms through which to air human rights concerns internationally, times have changed, and a more sophisticated analysis of its role is now required, especially given the scramble for resources which accompanied the UN's budget crisis in the 1980s.

When the Special Commission of ECOSOC was established to tackle reform of ECOSOC and its subsidiary bodies as a flow-on of the Report of the 'Group of 18' on UN reform presented to the Assembly in 1987,[5] the role of

[4] In concluding his analysis of the thematic procedures established by the Commission on Human Rights, Rodley highlights the challenges posed by budget cuts to these important UN activities. See 'UN Action Procedures against Disappearances, Summary or Arbitrary Executions, and Torture', 8. *Hum. Rts. Q.* 700 (1986).

[5] This Special Commission was set up pursuant to GA Res.41/213 (1986), which dealt with the report of the so-called 'Group of 18' on UN reform, A/41/48 (1986).

the General Assembly in economic and social matters was also put directly under the microscope. This occurred primarily as a result of a proposal by the developing countries ('the Group of 77') that ECOSOC become a universal rather than limited membership body,[6] a suggestion which naturally provoked a series of fundamental questions. If ECOSOC membership were to be universalized, what would the Second and Third Committees do? Should they be abolished, shortened, or otherwise recast? How should the General Assembly deal with the report of ECOSOC? In particular, what kind of human rights debate should take place at the Assembly?

A variety of options emerged from the Special Commission's deliberations. Some European Community delegations and the United States suggested that the Commission on Human Rights, as the only subsidiary body of ECOSOC with a pedigree directly from the UN Charter, should report directly to the General Assembly, bypassing the intermediate step of ECOSOC. The EC proposed that the ACABQ could handle any necessary financial authorizations for the Commission's activities. It was argued that such an organizational structure would reflect more accurately the institutional strength and stature of the Commission. The alternative view was that ECOSOC could not be circumvented because the Council provided an important (albeit under-utilized) opportunity for co-ordination between human rights and other programmes, especially those in the development sphere. Moreover, it was argued that ECOSOC, having a central role under the terms of the International Covenant on Economic, Social and Cultural Rights, could not be bypassed without producing distortions in the human rights programme. There was also resistance in some quarters to the Commission on Human Rights being given elevated status *vis à vis* other subsidiary bodies of ECOSOC.

In trying to analyse the Assembly's role in the human rights field, the Special Commission was confronted with a significant threshold obstacle which still remains to be overcome—the vagueness and overlapping character of the mandates of the respective UN bodies. Article 10 of the UN Charter provides some pointers to the Assembly's role—'essentially a deliberative, supervisory and reviewing organ'. The report of the Special Commission to ECOSOC in May 1988 elaborated upon this definition: 'The General Assembly should function as the principal forum for policy making and the establishment of overall priorities for the United Nations system as a whole . . .'. ECOSOC's task is differentiated as 'monitoring and evaluation of implementation of these overall strategies, overall co-ordination of economic

[6] Unfortunately, no summary records, and very few other official records were prepared in relation to the Special Commission. These comments are based on the author's recollections, and a series of informal conference room papers which were produced during the proceedings.

and social activities of the UN system, and assistance in preparation of the work of the Assembly'.[7] Unfortunately these formulations do not take us very far. As the Chairman of the Special Commission, Ambassador Badawi of Egypt conceded in his closing statement to the Special Commission on 11 May 1988 one of the key stumbling-blocks to successful agreement on a reform package was the Special Commission's 'inability to make a clear cut logical and implementable division of labour between the General Assembly and a universalized Economic and Social Council'.[8]

Given the chequered history of reform efforts in the UN economic and social fields, it came as no real surprise that the Special Commission was unable to produce an agreed package of reforms. Nevertheless, at its 1990 session the Assembly called for further negotiations on proposals to restructure and revitalize the UN in the economic and social fields. This led to a resumed session of the Assembly in May 1991 which proceeded to adopt a package of significant ECOSOC reforms, including the consolidation of the annual Council meetings from two to one sessions (alternating between Geneva and New York), the introduction of a high level segment, with Ministerial participation on major policy themes, and another segment on co-ordination covering the specialized agencies. In addition, the Assembly endorsed a forward work programme which provided, *inter alia*, for reviews of the subsidiary bodies of ECOSOC, and of the complementarity of activities undertaken by the GA and ECOSOC. The Assembly is scheduled to consider progress achieved in these reform efforts at its regular session in 1993 at which time the membership of ECOSOC itself will be reviewed. Such developments raise hopes that the Assembly may finally be coming to grips with the need for comprehensive reform of ECOSOC.[9]

At the outset, several broad areas of Assembly human rights activity can be identified: standard-setting, development and application of procedures to deal with violations, both in country-specific and non-specific ('thematic') ways, provision of practical assistance to build infrastructure in states experiencing human rights problems, and philosophical/ideological developments. These areas are dealt with in turn in this chapter. While the focus is on the role of the Third Committee, some comments are offered on the role of the Plenary and the other Committees of the Assembly in the field of human rights.

[7] E/SCN.1/L.1 (1988), 10.

[8] The Chairman's statement was circulated as an informal conference room paper.

[9] GA Res.45/264 (1991). Annex. While the easing of the UN's financial crisis slowed some of the momentum behind UN reform, the central role of the UN in the Gulf crisis and the increasing level of co-operation among the permanent five have improved prospects for substantial and lasting progress in reforming the UN's economic and social activities and machinery.

A. *The Third Committee 'Culture'*

Before embarking on an examination of specific areas, it is important to draw attention to some distinctive institutional aspects of the Third Committee which are often overlooked. It is necessary to bear in mind that the procedural framework for consideration of human rights issues in multilateral forums such as the Assembly and CHR is the result of gradual evolution over a period of years rather than 'quantum leaps'. Because UN machinery and approaches usually reflect compromises on deeper political and other differences, progress is often measured in relatively minor procedural adjustments which open the way for new forms of multilateral action.

As has already been noted, the Third Committee is encumbered with a very heavy agenda covering a broad range of issues in the social sphere. Over the last decade, increasing attention by delegations from all regional groups has been paid to the advancement of women, international efforts to curb illicit drug trafficking and abuse, the problems of the disabled, of youth and, of the ageing, and other social development questions such as crime prevention and control. Some have interpreted this increased attention to these 'other' social issues as the result of a conscious strategy initiated by the Eastern Europeans and some developing countries in the 1970s to downgrade the human rights (specifically civil and political rights) agenda of the Third Committee. While certain delegations have undoubtedly approached human rights and social issues in zero sum game terms, it is worth recalling that a number of the most active supporters of the UN human rights programme have also been at the forefront of efforts to revitalize the General Assembly's consideration of other 'social' questions. Moreover, distinctions between 'social' and 'human rights' questions can of course be artificial.

Indeed, the 'cohabitation' of these two sets of issues on the Third Committee's agenda should not be seen exclusively through the optic of mutually exclusive competition for resources and attention. The development of a more sophisticated social agenda at the UN, in which the Third Committee has played a central role, has put human rights issues into an appropriately broad context and initiated a degree of helpful cross-referencing and model-sharing between various programmes. For example, attempts to 'mainstream' the UN Charter-mandated objective of advancing the status of women across a range of UN programmes, especially economic and development-related, have direct relevance to the UN human rights programme if it is to avoid being marginalized, both as regards policy prominence and resource endowment. The debate about women in development has reinforced the arguments of proponents of more sensitivity to human rights concerns on the part of the UN's development agencies. It is encouraging that other more direct linkages are being made between human rights programmes and the advancement of women. The Committee on the Elimination of Discrimination against Women ('CEDAW'), which has its own agenda item in the Third Committee, has also been dealt with in the Assembly's resolutions on reporting obligations under various human rights treaties, now an annual feature.[10] CEDAW has, with encouragement from the Assembly, begun to draw on the procedural precedents established by other human rights treaty bodies in considering reports of States Parties to the Convention on the Elimination of all Forms of Discrimination Against Women.

The sharp compartmentalization between human rights and 'social' items is breaking down in other ways. Recent Assembly resolutions on crime and the administration of justice have brought human rights questions together with crime prevention and criminal justice issues. Thus, for example, the Seventh and Eighth UN Congresses on the Prevention of Crime and Treatment of Offenders, in 1985 and 1990, proposed a number of international instruments to the Assembly for endorsement which deal squarely with human rights. Notable among these were the Declaration on Victims of Crime and Abuse of Power, and the Beijing Rules on the Treatment of Juvenile Offenders and the UN Standard Minimum Rules for Non-Custodial Measures (the Tokyo Rules).[11] In 1987, under the 'social' item on disability, the Assembly held a vigorous debate about whether to accept a recommendation that work should begin on drafting an international convention on the rights of disabled persons.[12]

The Third Committee's heavy agenda has brought with it intense time pressures which have limited in-depth consideration of complex human rights issues. Smaller delegations in particular face formidable difficulties in following agenda items effectively. For this reason, Morocco circulated a proposal in 1986 to 'biennialize' a number of items.[13] While most delegations supported this idea *in principle*, the modalities for selecting which items should only be considered every second year were less easily resolved, with the result that the Moroccan proposal was shelved. The following year, a Belgian 'non-paper' developing biennialization proposals was circulated informally among delegations in New York and referred to in the Third Committee's debate. Once again, developing countries declined to enter into negotiations on this kind of reform, on the ground that they did not wish to prejudge the outcome of the deliberations of the Special Commission of ECOSOC. By 1990, however, a consensus had emerged and the Assembly agreed to an important package of reforms affecting the work of the Third Committee. A number of matters will

[10] e.g. GA Res.42/105 (1987).

[11] The standard-setting output of the 1985 Congress is contained in A/40/881 (1985); and that of the 1990 Congress in A/CONF. 144/28 (1990).

[12] This recommendation was made by the Global Meeting of Experts to Review the Implementation of the World Programme of Action Concerning Disabled Persons at the Mid-point of the UN Decade of Disabled Persons, held in Stockholm in August 1987, the report of which is contained in CSOM/DDP/OML.7 (1987).

[13] Contained in A/C.3/41/L.80 (1986).

be dealt with only biennially and the overall debate will be structured within three sub-items of the agenda.[14]

In general, the Third Committee has taken a less technical approach to human rights issues than the Commission. Many Assembly resolutions have simply repeated or paraphrased language adopted by the Commission. An informal tradition appears to have developed that major innovations or reopening of work done by the subsidiary organs should generally be avoided by the Assembly. This conservative approach may be sound in many cases, but, as a result, out of the 80 or more resolutions and decisions on all subjects adopted each session by the Third Committee over recent years, only a small proportion involve new issues, or even significant recasting of old ones. Symbolic reaffirmations of principle have their place, but, in the more sophisticated international human rights debate of the 1990s, more should perhaps be expected of the Assembly.

One recent factor militating against innovation and creativity in the Assembly (and other human rights bodies) has been the severe financial constraints under which the UN has been operating. As a result, any proposal which cannot be funded from within the existing regular budget can usually be expected to encounter strong resistance when put forward in the Third Committee. In its deliberations, final consideration of the financial implications (which takes place in the Fifth Committee) is closer at hand than in the subsidiary bodies such as the Commission which do not have authority to approve expenditure.

The location of the substantive UN Secretariat servicing the UN human rights programme in Geneva is another complication affecting the work of the Assembly in New York. Only a handful of staff from the Geneva-based UN Centre for Human Rights are usually able to attend the Assembly because of the travel costs involved. The Centre has a miniscule liaison office in New York which must also deal, *inter alia*, with the business generated by the significant number of missions in New York of member States which are not represented in Geneva at all. The capacity of the Secretariat to provide technical support on human rights issues dealt with in New York has thus been very limited. This poses particular problems for standard-setting exercises undertaken by the Assembly where technical advice is so important.

Several other distinctive aspects of the Third Committee 'culture' are worthy of mention. The absence of substantial NGO input has had an impact on the atmosphere and proceedings in the Third Committee. Relatively few 'outsiders' participate in or even observe the Third Committee. Surprisingly,

[14] GA Res.45/175 (1990), Annex. The three sub-items are: (*a*) Implementation of human rights instruments; (*b*) Human rights questions, including alternative approaches for improving the effective enjoyment of human rights and fundamental freedoms; and (*c*) Human rights situations and reports of special rapporteurs and representatives.

despite the presence of many human rights NGOs in New York, relatively few follow the activities of the Assembly closely. Delegates to the Third Committee have generally been New York-based working-level diplomatic officers rather than experts from capitals or Ambassadors who comprise a significant component of representatives at the Commission.[15] This tends to generate a more pragmatic, result-oriented atmosphere, with greater emphasis on procedure and often more superficial treatment of substance.

At the Assembly, as at all multilateral conferences, individual delegates wield considerable influence, especially those with extensive experience and expertise, coupled with a strong interest in human rights issues.[16] Commentators have generally tended to be dismissive about the capacity of diplomats to play a proactive and constructive role in relation to human rights because such a role is seen as inimical to diplomacy's main task of encouraging good relations among states.[17] This assessment seems not only at odds with the way in which multilateral human rights activities have evolved, but also overlooks the development of human rights diplomacy as an increasingly important element in bilateral relations between states.

By UN standards, the Third Committee's proceedings are characterized by relative informality. Multiple negotiations take place concurrently 'in the corridors' of the Committee, often in the margins of the conference room itself, to the chagrin of delegates trying to deliver speeches during the debates.[18] These factors have led to descriptions of the Committee as an 'oriental bazaar', and have no doubt contributed to its reputation among UN

[15] Bertrand identifies adverse implications flowing from lower-level representation at UN social and economic meetings. He concludes that 'ministerial councils would produce better results than conferences attended by diplomats'. See Bertrand, *The Role of the United Nations in the Economic and Social Fields* (1987), 16–17. The increasing specialization of human rights diplomacy, the expanding agenda, and case load, as well as the impracticality of regular ministerial meetings, cast some doubt on this conclusion.

[16] Perhaps the most famous Third Committee delegate still active in its proceedings is Mr Halima Warzazi (Morocco), who chaired the Committee at the time of the adoption of the Covenants, and has attended sessions since 1966.

[17] Vincent's reflections are indicative: 'To summarise the view of the foreign policy professionals, they are not excited by [human rights]. They are uncomfortable, even if they favour human rights in principle, about dealing with individual cases of human rights violation. They prefer the setting of international standards. They are happier that this be done in multilateral rather than bilateral diplomacy, public debate tending "towards issues of principle" while private negotiation "inclines towards compromise, and understanding of the other man's point of view" ... they place great stress on the efficacy of "quiet diplomacy" ... taken up reluctantly by diplomats in response to small but articulate domestic lobbies, human rights are perceived as a problem not a solution. They get in the way of ordinary diplomacy ... There are no diplomatic triumphs to be pulled off in this area ... Let human rights remain on the periphery, or on the periphery of the periphery.' Vincent, *Human Rights, and International Relations* (1986), 136–7.

[18] In contrast, the Second (Economic) Committee of the Assembly conducts a series of structured 'informal consultations'. Usually, only a limited number of delegations intervene (e.g. those chairing the G77, EC, etc.) in these meetings which are generally presided over by a member of the Committee's bureau.

delegates as unruly.[19] Nevertheless, this method of work, while tending to downgrade the importance of the formal debate, has provided a relatively cost-efficient and flexible way of handling a large volume of diverse business.

Moreover, proceedings in the Third Committee have reflected the relative looseness of bloc caucusing. It is not uncommon for alliances between delegations to shift according to the issue under consideration. For some purposes, the Group of 77 has caucused relatively effectively. But on other issues, even the right to development, sharp divergences of view between developing countries are evident. On the whole, therefore, the Group of 77 is a relatively flexible grouping in the Third Committee, especially when compared to the situation pertaining elsewhere in the Assembly and in many other UN bodies. Nor do regional groupings play a decisive role on most issues. Delegations which profess a strong commitment to human rights have worked constructively together across regional group 'lines', while other members of the same regional groups have been passive or actively opposed initiatives. Some of the liveliest arguments have erupted within regional groups in the Third Committee. By way of illustration, the diversity of Asian or Latin American and Caribbean countries' attitudes to human rights needs no elaboration here. Indeed, the complexity of attitudes of developing countries to human rights issues is rarely done justice.[20] The extent to which specific delegations tend to be associated with certain issues (either as prime sponsors, co-sponsors, supporters, or opponents of resolutions—and sometimes over many years) is another complicating factor, and often gives rise to 'proprietorial' instincts, further blurring divisions along regional or group lines.

Over recent sessions of the Assembly, there is evidence that new informal alliances are developing in the Third Committee. For example, the emergence of an Islamic caucus, partly as a response to developments concerning the status of women and capital punishment, has important longer-term implications for the UN's social and human rights programmes.

While perhaps rather obvious, it is often forgotten that the Third Committee's organization of work also affects the substantive consideration of particular issues. The human rights items have been dealt with in four main clusters over recent years:

(*a*) self-determination and racial discrimination;
(*b*) 'alternative approaches' to protect and promote human rights;

[19] In 1987, the Third Committee Chairman, Ambassador Ritter (Panama), suggested in his concluding remarks that more time should be devoted to organized informal consultations after complaining that important statements had been lost 'in a sea of confusion' in the Committee. (Statement not reflected in UN official summary records.)

[20] The analysis of policy attitudes developed by D. P. Forsythe does not, for example, adequately reflect the spectrum of developing country positions on many human rights issues ranging from the abolition of capital punishment to religious freedom. See Forsythe, *Human Rights and World Politics* (1983), 81–4.

(*c*) a cluster of 'thematic' items including the International Covenants, religious intolerance, and torture; and

(*d*) a mixed cluster of thematic and country-specific issues under the rubric of the report of ECOSOC (traditionally dealt with under item 12 of the Assembly's agenda).

This structure offers advantages—notably streamlining debate and grouping together related items. But it also brings disadvantages—including artificiality and a degree of illogicality. For example, delegations could legitimately deliver similar statements under each of the four different clusters if they so wished.

B. *Standard-setting*

The most tangible output of the United Nations in the human rights field is the series of international instruments built on the foundation of the Universal Declaration of Human Rights and the International Covenants. Much of the work of negotiating these instruments has taken place in working groups of the Commission on Human Rights, but the General Assembly has almost always played the role of final arbiter, giving its *imprimatur*, with adjustments as considered nccessary, to texts which have emerged from the subsidiary bodies. In a few instances, the Assembly itself has undertaken substantial drafting, either in one of its Committees, or at sessional and inter-sessional working groups. The variety of approaches taken by the UN in relation to standard-setting in recent years and the variable quality of the resulting instruments point to the need for a more rational and consistent set of procedures.

In the case of the Declaration on the Right to Development,[21] adopted by the Assembly in 1986, a Working Group of the Commission on Human Rights had earlier reached an impasse. A controversial decision was taken by the Commission to transmit the report of the Working Group directly to the General Assembly in a bid to break what was essentially a political log-jam. Behind the scenes work by a number of experts produced a text on which consensus appeared possible. In the end, the Declaration was adopted with only the United States voting against and Japan, the Federal Republic of Germany, the United Kingdom, the Nordics (minus Norway), and Israel abstaining. The Assembly thus played a role in forcing the pace on an issue of pressing concern to a substantial majority of UN members, even though consensus eluded the negotiations at the end of the day. In similar vein, the adoption by the Assembly in 1989 of the Second Protocol to the ICCPR on the abolition of the death penalty marked an important breakthrough

[21] GA Res.41/128 (1986), A/41/925 (1986).

in relation to an issue which had been formally on its agenda for almost a decade.[22]

With regard to the Convention against Torture and Other Cruel, Inhuman, or Degrading Forms of Treatment or Punishment, the Assembly's job was, by and large, to give its *imprimatur* to technical work done by a Commission on Human Right's Working Group, and to resolve several outstanding issues with political repercussions, including the shape of implementation machinery and the nature of recommendations which could be made by the supervisory body. In 1984, the Third Committee was able to resolve outstanding questions and to adopt the Convention without a vote.[23]

The Assembly's work in drafting an International Convention on the Rights of Migrant Workers and their Families threw into relief the problem identified by Alston of 'quality control' in developing new standards.[24] Work on this Convention, undertaken since 1980 by a sessional Working Group of open-ended membership meeting in the first two weeks of the Third Committee's session and at one inter-sessional meeting mid-year, was finally completed when the instrument was adopted by the Assembly in 1990.[25] The initial draft had contained many provisions which were inconsistent with existing international standards and revealed inadequate attention to myriad technical issues. Partly as a result of work by members of the so-called 'MESCA Group' (a loose group of delegations including Mexico, which chaired the negotiations, Mediterranean, and Scandinavian countries), considerable improvement of the text was achieved. Nevertheless, only a limited number of delegates involved in the negotiations had specialist expertise, which was unfortunate given the complexity of much of the subject-matter. Even more regrettably, many developing countries, including those which are significant receivers and senders of migrant workers, did not participate in the negotiations. Nor did the UN Secretariat provide adequate technical support for the drafting process as it unfolded, although Secretariat input increased as the negotiations entered their final phase.

The Assembly's adoption of a Declaration on the Human Rights of Individuals who are not Nationals of the Country in which they Live in 1985, after five years' deliberations in a Working Group of the Assembly, involved similar difficulties. Such were the doubts about the scope of the instrument which

[22] GA Res.44/128 (1989). The vote was 59–26–48.

[23] Convention against Torture, and other Cruel, Inhuman or Degrading Treatment of Punishment, adopted by GA Res.39/46 (1984), in United Nations, *Human Rights: A Compilation of International Instruments* (1988), 212.

[24] Alston, 'Conjuring Up New Human Rights: A Proposal for Quality Control', 78 *Am. J. Int'l L.* 607 (1984).

[25] The decision to undertake drafting of this instrument in the General Assembly probably reflected the overtly political North/South origins of this initiative, as well as a concern by its proponents to assert the competence of the UN itself rather than the ILO in this field. See GA Res.34/172 (1979).

had been agreed by the Working Group that the chairperson made a statement before adoption of the Declaration underlining that it was not to be read as prejudicing the rights of non-citizens under other international instruments.[26]

There has been growing sentiment that the major phase of United Nations activity in standard-setting is drawing to a close and that, while drafting on a few instruments will continue, more attention should now be devoted to *implementation* of existing standards. The adoption of GA Resolution 41/120 of 4 December 1986 reflected some of these concerns. The Assembly, as the highest legislative authority with overall responsibility for the human rights programme, is uniquely placed to provide guidelines to be applied throughout the UN system in relation to standard-setting. The provisions of GA Resolution 41/120 cover, *inter alia*, the importance of effective preparation before drafting is commenced, the need for realistic and effective implementation machinery pursuant to conventions, and the value of establishing certain criteria which should be satisfied before drafting an international instrument is contemplated.

This Resolution was invoked to useful effect by the Commission to launch a 'technical review' by the UN Secretariat of the draft Convention on the Rights of the Child in 1988. In 1989 the Assembly requested a similar review of the draft Migrant Workers Convention.[27] The Resolution also influenced the Commission and the Assembly to restrain precipitate commencement of work on a draft convention against religious intolerance until adequate preparation, including an examination of the modalities for drafting, had been undertaken, and until more had been done to implement the existing Declaration on this subject. Outside the UN, the Council of Europe has devoted attention to human rights standard-setting processes in the wake of Resolution 41/120, conducting expert seminars on the subject.

A number of academic commentators have examined the standard-setting procedures of the UN, including the role of the General Assembly. Alston has suggested a seven-stage procedure for dealing with 'new rights'.[28] Meron has proposed what seems a rather impractical suggestion: a new body in the style of the International Law Commission to devote itself exclusively to the preparation of new human rights instruments.[29] Ramcharan also broaches this subject. After citing a study undertaken by the UN's Administrative Co-ordination Committee, he suggests a series of conclusions about how standard-setting should be conducted.[30] A detailed review of these analyses is

[26] See A/C.3/40/12.

[27] See GA Res.44/155, operative para. 2.

[28] Alston, 'Conjuring Up New Human Rights', 620.

[29] Meron, 'Reform of Lawmaking in the United Nations: The Human Rights Instance' 79 *Am. J. Int'l L.* 664 (1985).

[30] Ramcharan, 'Standard-setting: Future Perspectives', in id. (ed.), *Human Rights: Thirty Years after the Universal Declaration* (1979), 107.

beyond the scope of this chapter, but they demonstrate the need to look much more carefully at the methods of work of the Assembly as a complement to the activities of the Commission and other UN bodies, including the specialized agencies (notably UNESCO and the ILO), which are involved in treaty-making in the human rights field.

C. *Implementation of International Standards*

In the related area of treaty implementation and supervision, the Assembly receives reports from the Human Rights Committee, the Committee on Economic, Social and Cultural Rights,[31] the Committee on the Elimination of Racial Discrimination, the Committee on the Elimination of Discrimination against Women, and the Committee against Torture. It is thus uniquely placed to suggest reforms aimed at bringing about a more effective and better integrated system of accountability for human rights performance within the different parameters laid down by the relevant treaties. But, until recently, little had been achieved in this regard. Some delegations have been and remain resistant to the idea that the Assembly should exercise a supervisory role over the activities of the independent treaty bodies, particularly as not all UN members are of course parties to these treaties. Others have expressed reluctance to endorse any proposals which could be seen as taking the pressure off States Parties to meet their treaty obligations. This argument was also raised in opposition to proposals floated at the Assembly to adjust the reporting arrangements under the Racial Discrimination Convention which require States Parties to submit reports every two years, a challenging timetable even for well-organized governments with adequate resources. Despite these misgivings, the dependence (to varying degrees) of the treaty bodies on the UN regular budget approved by the Assembly, and the general mood of reform and interest in greater efficiency have provided more fertile ground for active Assembly scrutiny of the activities of the treaty bodies.

The Assembly, through the item on reporting obligations under human rights treaties, has begun to engage in efforts to enhance co-ordination of these reporting procedures. A wide variety of delegations have complained about the onerous burden of reporting which falls upon conscientious States Parties to the human rights treaties, and have drawn attention to the need for reform of both reporting guidelines and procedures, as well as for practical assistance, especially for developing countries, struggling to meet reporting obligations. Because individual treaties contain specific provisions on reporting requirements, there are, however, limits to the amount of harmonization which is possible.

[31] Pursuant to ESC Res.1987/5.

In 1987 the Assembly's consensus resolution under the reporting obligations item provided a detailed draft agenda for a meeting of chairpersons of the treaty bodies to be held in Geneva in October 1988. This meeting was the sequel to a similar event held in 1984 which yielded disappointing results. The Assembly also sought, through the resolution, to register its approval of innovations which could be emulated by other treaty bodies, and to give encouragement to those committees which had made progress in rationalizing and streamlining procedures.[32] This approach seems to have been effective since the report of the 1988 meeting yielded considerably more constructive suggestions than had its predecessor. In 1989 and 1990, the Assembly took its consideration of these issues further, receiving a study from an independent expert on reform of the UN human rights treaty bodies and then considering the recommendations of the third meeting of chairpersons of the treaty bodies.[33]

Over recent years the General Assembly has thus begun to play a distinctive and valuable role in relation to the operation of the human rights treaties, a role which could be further developed in the future. Better use could, for example, be made of the wealth of material submitted by States Parties as well as the comments made in the Committees by the independent experts and governments in relation to particular reports. In addition, where applicable, this information should be related to the work done by special rapporteurs on specific country situations and on themes such as torture and summary executions. The Assembly could strengthen these linkages and generate a much wider awareness of the treaty procedures. Moreover, it could facilitate input from the Specialized Agencies into the treaty reporting processes, an important step in mobilizing the information and other resources of the UN system to achieve human rights objectives. At a more modest level, the Assembly could do more to reinforce the efforts of the treaty bodies to press States Parties to come forward with overdue periodic reports.

An important corollary of the Assembly's examination of all five existing treaty bodies on a comparable basis has been to draw the Committee on the Elimination of all Forms of Discrimination against Women more closely into the UN human rights system. This Committee, serviced by the UN Centre for Social Development and Humanitarian Affairs ('CSDHA') in Vienna, has benefited from the application of procedural precedents established by other treaty bodies, notably the Human Rights Committee, as well as providing some lessons of its own.

The Assembly has also dealt with the reports of treaty bodies on an individual basis under respective agenda items. At recent sessions of the

[32] GA Res.42/105 (1987).

[33] See A/44/668, Annex: 'Study on possible long term approaches to enhancing the effective operation of existing, and prospective bodies established under UN instruments on human rights.' See also GA Res.45/85 (1990).

Assembly, the preoccupation in relation to the Racial Discrimination Convention has been the failure of States Parties to pay their modest assessed contributions to fund CERD.[34] The Assembly has been addressing the financial crisis afflicting CERD since 1986, and, while little concrete progress has been made in this regard, the discussions have facilitated the work of States Parties at their own meetings where the crisis has been discussed in more detail.[35]

The General Assembly's consideration of the two Covenants has been primarily of a symbolic, rather than substantive, character. By and large, the Assembly has simply endorsed the activities of the Human Rights Committee and repeated language already used in resolutions adopted by the Commission. With the presentation of the report of the new Committee on Economic, Social and Cultural Rights for the first time to the Assembly in 1987, the traditional resolution on the Covenants was adjusted to give more adequate coverage to economic, social, and cultural rights.[36]

In addition, there has been some debate in the Assembly about the performance of the Committees monitoring compliance with the Covenants, especially their procedures. The Human Rights Committee has fared reasonably well in these assessments, although some criticisms have emerged.[37] The Committee on Economic, Social and Cultural Rights, which first met in 1987, has attracted positive comment from a wide range of delegations at the Assembly, although, perhaps surprisingly, several Eastern European delegations initially took a more critical approach to the Committee's innovative procedures. Poland even suggested that the Committee should be a little less zealous in examining periodic reports in order not to discourage countries from presenting them.[38]

For many years the Assembly has witnessed disputes of an ideological character about the relationship between the two sets of rights in the Covenants.[39]

[34] The States Parties only bear the costs of travel, and subsistence of the members of CERD, while the conference servicing costs of CERD's meetings are met by the UN Regular Budget.

[35] In 1986, for example, the General Assembly gave approval for a special meeting of the States Parties to discuss the financial crisis facing the Committee on the Elimination of Racial Discrimination (CERD), which was duly held in January 1987; GA Res.41/105 (1986), para. 5(d). The role of meetings of States Parties to various instruments—a subject beyond the scope of this chapter—has received scant attention but is worthy of examination in the context of the General Assembly's human rights agenda. The States Parties to the Racial Discrimination Convention, and the Women's Discrimination Convention have requested the Secretary-General to bring decisions adopted at their meetings to the attention of the General Assembly.

[36] GA Res.42/103 (1987).

[37] The German Democratic Republic, for example, took issue with the Committee's procedures in handling second periodic reports (see A/C.3/42/SR.40 (1987), para. 2). Some of the Committee's 'general comments', notably on the right to life and disarmament, have also been controversial.

[38] A/C.3/42/SR.40 (1987), para. 17.

[39] It will be interesting to observe how Eastern Europe countries and the former USSR deal with these issues at future sessions of the Assembly in the wake of the revolutionary events since 1989.

In 1985, the German Democratic Republic launched a resolution on the inter-dependence and indivisibility of the rights in the Covenants[40] which provoked disquiet among many Western delegations who saw it as an attempt to downgrade civil and political rights by making respect for them dependent on certain levels of economic development. Such ideological arguments have not had any material effect on the operation of the treaty bodies. Nor indeed have they taken the focus off civil and political rights which continue to dominate the Third Committee's deliberations.

The Assembly has seen the emergence of resolutions on specific rights plucked by delegations from the Covenant on Economic, Social and Cultural Rights, notably literacy and adequate housing.[41] But these resolutions have been general in character, and have added little to existing UN legislative mandates. Unless a more rational, systematic, and co-ordinated approach is developed in addressing various specific rights at the Assembly (and other UN bodies), there is a real risk of a flood of uncoordinated and unproductive resolutions. One option would be for the Assembly, in co-ordination with ECOSOC and the Commission, to adopt a future programme of work giving prominence to particular rights or sets of related rights at each session. ECOSOC must also remain integrally involved in consideration of economic, social, and cultural rights, given the Council's specific responsibilities under the Covenant embodying these rights.

A more serious challenge to the Covenants was launched by the Islamic Republic of Iran, with indirect support from some other delegations in the late 1980s. Iran took issue with the universality of the principles in the Covenants because they were not, in its view, fully consistent with the tenets of Islam. As another ramification of this conflict, some Islamic delegations have also displayed sensitivity to criticism of reservations lodged by their countries upon ratifying human rights treaties, asserting the sovereign right to make whatever reservations they regard as appropriate. This sensitivity has been particularly acute in relation to the Convention on the Elimination of Discrimination against Women which expressly prohibits sweeping reservations, but it has also arisen in relation to the Covenants.[42]

D. *The Thematic Approach to Violations*

The role of the General Assembly in non-country-specific activities to deal with human rights violations, has generally been limited to endorsing initiatives

[40] GA Res.40/114 (1985).

[41] GA Res.41/146 (1986) and 42/104 (1987).

[42] See Art. 28(2) of the Convention on the Elimination of all Forms of Discrimination against Women, adopted by GA Res.34/180 (1979), International Instruments, 112. In 1987, Egypt and Tunisia expressed disquiet about operative para. 11 of GA Resolution 42/103 which contained a general exhortation to States Parties to lift reservations to the International Covenants. See A/42/PV.93 (1987), 35 and 36.

taken at the Commission on Human Rights. Resolutions on subjects like summary and arbitrary executions, disappearances, and torture have passed through the Assembly without much controversy or even much attention at recent sessions. While the Third Committee is not, like some other parts of the UN, tied to the consensus principle, this has been an important objective in most of its negotiations, especially on 'thematic' issues where it is seen as enhancing the universal applicability of the concepts and procedures under consideration.

Nevertheless, there are often difficult trade-offs to be made between sending unequivocal messages which provoke sharp responses, and seeking to draw as many delegations as possible into support for resolutions. What use, it is often argued, are texts to which relevant countries remain implacably opposed and from which they can distance themselves, especially if such texts relate to matters of fundamental principle? Overall, it seems fair to conclude that, while some of these resolutions constitute valuable endorsements by the universal membership of the UN of important activities and principles, some 'diminishing of the currency' has occurred through a proliferation of lowest common denominator paper. There has also been a degree of arbitrariness about what 'thematic issues' are brought to the attention of the Assembly. Why, for example, has substantive discussion of the rights of minorities been generally confined to the Commission and the Sub-Commission?[43]

As a universal membership body, the Assembly has provided a unique forum for discussion of a few complex issues in relation to which pluralism, dialogue, and a global perspective are particularly important. While not breaking much new ground, discussion of religious intolerance at sessions of the Assembly since the mid-1980s has been notable for the broad participation of delegations with different social and political systems. Despite occasional polemics, a wide range of delegations, including developing countries and the Eastern Europeans, have made thoughtful and comprehensive interventions on their national policies relating to religion. It is unfortunate that this debate, like most of the Third Committee's deliberations, has received minimal publicity. Similarly, on the rights of the child, the Assembly's debate has provided an opportunity for a range of delegations to contribute to discussion on an issue of universal concern where overt political considerations usually take a back seat.

For the most part, the Assembly's 'thematic' activities have generally not been very innovative. The human rights and science and technology item has, for example, been dominated by unproductive attention to disarmament,

[43] Minority rights issues have of course been prominent in a number of international trouble spots. The rapid changes sweeping Eastern Europe and the USSR in recent years have focused even more attention on nationalism based on ethnic and cultural factors, and on the assertion of minority rights.

while the ethical implications of new medical technology, computers and privacy, and other pressing contemporary issues have not been given adequate coverage.[44]

Nevertheless, the door to innovation at the Assembly has not been closed. In 1986 the United States proposed a major new 'thematic' initiative—a resolution on the right to private property. This right, embodied in the Universal Declaration of Human Rights, is not developed in the Covenants. The US initiative predictably generated considerable ideological conflict, but was, in the end, adopted convincingly.[45]

The following year, the United States circulated a novel proposal on democracy and free and fair elections under the self-determination item. This linkage had been made before, including at the Commission, but the US decision to launch a major initiative at the Assembly seemed to reflect a concern to give the Assembly's human rights debate a new, specific orientation in support of democratic processes. The draft resolution invoked provisions concerning elections contained in 'general principles on freedom and non-discrimination in the matter of political rights' prepared by the Sub-Commission in 1962.[46] The US Delegation's introduction of the draft resolution included the following pertinent comments: 'one of the rights necessary to uphold the principle of self-determination is the right of everyone to take part in the government of his country . . . [This is] an important, but not the only component of self-determination'.[47] The draft was withdrawn later that session after exhaustive negotiations in the face of hostile amendments relating to the Palestinians and Namibia put forward by a group of developing countries. It was, however, adopted without vote, in modified form, at the Assembly's forty-forth session in 1989.[48]

One interesing objection raised to these initiatives was that they should have been introduced at the Commission rather than at the Assembly. This argument did not, however, cut much ice as there are no guidelines as to whether it is appropriate to launch such proposals in either body. Indeed it is

[44] Useful modest resolutions have, however, been adopted under this item which deal with the abuse of psychiatry. See GA Res.42/98 (1987).

[45] GA Res.41/132 (1986). At the same Assembly session, the German Democratic Republic attempted unsuccessfully to neutralize this text by proposing extensive amendments. At the subsequent session, a competing text was put forward by the German Democratic Republic, and also adopted by vote, as GA Res.41/115 (1987). This text provided an 'alternative' philosophy of property addressing, *inter alia*, social justice and the activities of transnational corporations in South Africa.

[46] UN Document A/C.3/42/L.15, and Rev.1–3 (1987).

[47] US Mission Press Release USUN 71–(87) of 26 Oct. 1987, 1–2.

[48] See GA Res.44/146 (1989) on 'Enhancing the Effectiveness of the Principle of Periodic and Genuine Elections', adopted without vote. Some delegations registered their reservations by pressing for the adoption (by vote) of a counterpoint resolution at the same session entitled: 'Respect for Principles of National Sovereignty, and Non-interference in the Internal Affairs of States in their Electoral Processes', GA Res.44/147 (1989).

difficult to see how such guidelines could ever be agreed. The bottom line must remain that sovereign states have the right to make any proposals they deem fit in any bodies of the UN system, provided that the proposals lie within relevant mandates.

Occasionally, the timing of the Assembly's discussion of thematic issues has given its role more immediate importance, particularly when connected with standard-setting. In the case of the Torture Convention, the Assembly adopted a useful resolution in 1987, just after the establishment of the new Committee against Torture, which set out some pertinent considerations, including the need for an adequate financial and administrative basis for the long-term viability of the Committee.[49] The Assembly also acted to step up the momentum of negotiations on the Convention on the Rights of the Child, encouraging the Commission to have a final text ready for adoption by the Assembly in 1989. In taking this line and meeting its 1989 target for adoption of the Convention, the Assembly seemed to recognize that successful negotiations on this instrument would be a fillip both to the whole UN human rights programme and to the UN as an institution.[50]

In addition, it should be borne in mind that the Assembly's thematic work on human rights has helped to reinforce some important connections between various parts of the UN system. Austria has piloted resolutions on human rights and the administration of justice through the Assembly (and the Commission) for a number of years. These resolutions have, *inter alia*, encouraged improved co-ordination between the Centre for Human Rights in Geneva and the Centre for Social Development and Humanitarian Affairs in Vienna.[51] While this message may seem self-evident, the 'atomization' of the UN system into discrete programmes directed independently from New York, Geneva, and Vienna has had adverse implications for co-ordination and consolidation of social, humanitarian, and other activities which should be mutually reinforcing.

The Assembly's modest resolutions on human rights and mass exoduses have highlighted an important and axiomatic relationship. The Third Committee's joint refugee and human rights responsibilities, as well as its universal membership, give it a unique opportunity to explore this relationship further. However, some countries have resisted such efforts, especially any suggestion that the Secretary-General could play a preventive role in relation to mass exoduses.[52]

There has been debate about whether thematic rapporteurs and other

[49] GA Res.42/123 (1987).

[50] GA Res.42/101 (1987) and GA Res.44/25 (1989).

[51] See GA Res.42/143 (1987).

[52] A further procedural complication has affected the handling of this issue – related work of the Special Political Committee which received the report of a group of intergovernmental experts on massive outflows of refugees in 1986. See A/41/324 (1986).

analogous mechanisms, such as the Working Group on disappearances set up by the Commission, should present interim reports to the General Assembly, in the manner of the special rapporteurs and representatives on specific country situations. As some of these mechanisms have developed a more specific approach to violations in their public reports, it has been argued that the higher public profile of the Assembly could lend important new momentum to the thematic debate at the Assembly.[53] Moreover, delegations have demonstrated increasing willingness to raise specific cases and countries under the 'thematic' cluster of human rights items at the Assembly (and the Commission). This has raised the political temperature of this debate, and some argue that important humanitarian activities requiring the co-operation of governments are prejudiced as a result. Despite the risks, there seems on balance to be a good case for such interim thematic reports to the Assembly.

The Assembly's 'thematic' contribution has not been limited to the penultimate cluster of items and item 12 (the report of ECOSOC). As has been demonstrated, the first cluster of Third Committee items—self-determination and racial discrimination—is also relevant to this discussion. Since the early 1980s, these items have been relatively lack-lustre, partly because the real 'action' takes place elsewhere at the Assembly—such as in Plenary (apartheid) and in the Fourth Committee (de-colonization). Given the importance of these issues to the human rights debate, greater effort could be made by the Third Committee to identify what distinctive *human rights* contribution it could make in these fields, rather than simply repeating what is said and done in Plenary and the other Committees.

On apartheid, the Plenary of the Assembly has the primary role, adopting a series of related resolutions each year. The Third Committee has made a modest complementary contribution over recent years, primarily by following up efforts at the Commission to focus more attention on the individual victims of apartheid. In 1987, for example, the Third Committee adopted a resolution on torture against children in detention in South Africa.[54] The Committee has also addressed the controversial International Convention on the Suppression and Punishment of the Crime of Apartheid in resolutions which have not attracted the support of Western countries.

Not surprisingly, the racism debate has been one of the more overtly political aspects of the Third Committee's agenda. Unfortunately its deliberations have not yielded much new thinking about this complex subject. Indeed, it can be argued that the global character and seriousness of racism and racial discrimination demand a more effective response from the Assembly. Apart from attention to apartheid, this debate has been characterized by unproductive verbal skirmishing between Arab delegations and Israel, and between

[53] See Denmark's statement on behalf of the European Community in 1987, A/C.3/42/SR.52 (1987), para. 5.

[54] GA Res.42/124 (1987).

other countries with serious bilateral problems in the Third Committee. GA Resolution 3379 adopted in 1975 which equated racism and Zionism (destroying the first World Racism Conference by precipitating a Western walkout and prompting the United States to maintain a position of non-participation in the Second World Racism Decade) has surfaced from time to time in debates but should now have less impact after its rescission by the Assembly in 1991. Divisions over the Western Sahara and the Falklands–Malvinas surfaced in relation to the resolution on the report of CERD in the early to mid-1980s, disrupting consensus adoption of the resolution on this important body. Since then, however, the emphasis has been more concrete, focusing largely on the financial crisis of CERD.

It is encouraging that practical strategies to tackle racial discrimination as a global phenomenon—such as human rights teaching, and development of national institutions and legislation—have been endorsed by a wide range of delegations at the Assembly. The Secretary-General's 1987 report on the Second Racism Decade[55] contained a useful list of suggested activities for the second half of the Second Racism Decade, many of which have application to the societies of virtually all UN member states. While this report generated some discussion in the Committee, it seems unlikely that it got into the hands of many relevant national authorities which are actually responsible for programmes to combat racial discrimination among their citizens.

The self-determination item has usually offered a vehicle for Third Committee delegations to rehearse well-established positions on major international political issues such as Cambodia, Afghanistan, and Namibia which have been recorded fully during other UN debates. While little new light has been shed on the human rights aspects of self-determination, statements by delegations and the recent US initiative on free elections (discussed above) reflect a greater interest in theoretical aspects, notably the post-colonial application of self-determination. Given its political and de-colonization responsibilities, the Assembly should be well placed to carry forward discussion of these issues.[56]

The risk of duplication with other activities of the Assembly emerged starkly in relation to Nigerian-led initiatives to focus more attention on the activities of mercenaries (in the context of subversion of the right to self-determination) through the appointment of a special rapporteur on the

[55] A/42/493 (1987), paras. 35–57.

[56] The suggestion has been made that the UN Trusteeship Council, which is nearing the end of its work, should be wound up or converted into a forum for other purposes (such as handling environmental issues). It has also been argued that the Fourth Committee should be merged with the Special Political Committee of the General Assembly. Implementation of these suggestions would add weight to the case for the Third Committee becoming more involved in post-decolonization issues and problems. Another dimension of self-determination which has assumed renewed prominence in the wake of events in Eastern Europe is its relationship to the rights of minorities.

subject.[57] There was resistance from some delegations to these proposals because of perceived overlap with the work of the Sixth Committee which has established a Working Group to draft an international convention against mercenaries. Not unexpectedly, the political imperatives prevailed, leading eventually to the appointment by the Commission of a Special Rapporteur on the activities of mercenaries.

Looking at the balance sheet, the Assembly's contribution on 'thematic' issues has been mixed. This forum's global membership offers certain advantages in relation to consideration of human rights issues, especially those where dialogue is so important—such as religious intolerance, or where broader political aspects loom large—such as self-determination. On the other hand, the Assembly is generally less well suited than the Commission to conduct technical, in-depth studies.

E. *Specific Country Situations*

The area which has probably received the most critical attention in the Assembly's basket of human rights activities is its consideration of specific country situations. Since the mid-1980s, the Assembly has received interim reports from the special rapporteurs and representatives appointed by the Commission to examine a limited range of human rights situations—Chile, El Salvador, Guatemala, Iran, and Afghanistan. Its usual role has thus been to complement and follow-up the work of the Commission which initiates formal action. This secondary role for the Assembly is illustrated in several ways. For example, its resolutions on country situations sometimes contain 'invitations' to the Commission to perform certain tasks, but the language conveys a strong implication that the latter has primary responsibility rather than subordinate status in these matters.

It is difficult to assess the impact of the Assembly's deliberations on actual respect for human rights in countries targeted for critical attention, either by resolution or in the course of the debate. The Third Committee's major debate under item 12 provides an opportunity for all member States of the UN to comment on human rights violations in specific countries in all parts of the world. While many delegations do not avail themselves of this opportunity, a surprisingly broad cross-section does address human rights issues in statements to the Third Committee. Western delegations have predictably covered a broader range of specific country situations, but it is more significant that delegations from all other regional groups, including the Eastern Europeans, have raised situations not covered by special rapporteurs. Over the last decade, debate has addressed situations as diverse as those in, *inter alia*,

[57] GA Res.41/102 (1986).

Bulgaria, Cuba, Cyprus, Iraq, Nicaragua, Peru, the Philippines, Romania, Sri Lanka, Surinam, Turkey, the USSR, and Zaire. Some delegations have taken a theme such as torture, or human rights violations against children as the basis for a global review, including comment on specific country situations. EC members make a lengthy joint statement on human rights to the Third Committee each year which has become an important means by which to co-ordinate, develop, and enunciate EC policy. It is striking that, despite criticism by some delegations about inadequate attention to economic, social, and cultural rights, interventions from all regional groups have continued to give primary attention to civil and political rights issues at the Assembly.

The impact of public exposure of violations of human rights in the Assembly's debate has undoubtedly been uneven. Nevertheless, it is incontestable that governments, whatever their ideological persuasion, recognize that such exposure carries costs for them. Most governments make strenuous efforts to avoid being cited in this way, and respond with vigour to criticism. It is of course difficult to isolate the effect of Assembly consideration from that by the Commission or other forms of international pressure, but several recent cases, notably Cuba, seem to reflect some improvements as a result of UN pressure.

It should also be acknowledged that the non-binding character of GA Resolutions inhibits the capacity of this body to influence events in many fields, not just human rights. The Assembly must be judged on the basis of realistic criteria. As Cassese has rightly observed: 'criticism levelled at UN action in the field of implementation of human rights has been particularly harsh. In my opinion, it is largely unfounded for these critics would like to see the UN doing things that it is not capable of doing'.[58]

The very fact that public debate and dialogue about certain specific human rights situations takes place at all can sometimes be judged as a significant breakthrough. A number of countries have delivered detailed responses to allegations made against them in the Assembly. Their responses are thereby placed on the international record, and can be scrutinized by governments, NGOs, and others. All too often, however, rights of reply have been polemical cross-claims, having little relation to the allegations tendered. The proliferation of such empty rights of reply has, despite the imposition of tight time-limits, consumed increasing amounts of expensive UN meeting time, generally shedding limited new light on the issues, while generating considerable political heat. Firmer chairmanship of the Committee might help to confine speakers exercising their right of reply to answering allegations made against them.

While criticism of a country in debate can have some impact, making it the

[58] Cassese, 'Progressive Transnational Promotion of Human Rights', *Human Rights: Thirty Years After*, 249.

subject of a specific GA Resolution raises the stakes much higher. The Assembly has generally taken its cue from the Commission in determining which countries should be the subject of resolutions. Moreover, in terms of content, the Assembly's resolutions have usually followed the paths laid down by the Commission, with appropriate adjustment to reflect the more up-to-date information contained in the interim reports provided to the Assembly by the Commission's rapporteurs.

The responses of countries which have been the subject of GA Resolutions repay careful attention. All of these countries have now agreed to allow special rapporteurs and representatives to visit their territories to inspect conditions, although the extent to which some of these visits have been unfettered is a moot point.[59] All have made lengthy statements in defence of their reputations. None has challenged the fundamental legitimacy of the procedures, although all have complained about politicization.

Undoubtedly, consideration by the Assembly and the Commission has focused international attention on human rights violations in these countries, and brought some pressure to bear on the governments responsible. One indication of the impact of such scrutiny is perhaps the difficulty now associated with launching new resolutions in the Assembly on any country situation not previously covered by the Commission. Nevertheless, the initial impact of being cited in such resolutions appears to fade as the texts become part of the multilateral landscape over successive sessions.

One way of putting the Assembly's role in this field into sharper focus is to ask an important threshold question: what is distinctive about Assembly, as opposed to the Commission, attention to specific country situations? The main argument, made with some justification, is that the higher profile of the General Assembly, and its universal membership, warrant the reaffirmation of key elements of resolutions adopted by the Commission. But what else could the Assembly offer on specific country situations? Let us consider some possibilities.

With a broader mandate than the Commission's, the Assembly could examine human rights in their wider political and economic context. A more thorough examination of the causes of human rights violations should, for example, be within its competence. In the same vein, the nexus between human rights violations and armed conflict could be explored further. If the UN's peacekeeping efforts gather further momentum, as now seems inevitable, the Assembly could witness a more thoughtful debate about longer-term strategies to keep the peace, and remove sources of conflict. This debate would logically involve human rights considerations. Moreover, the Assembly,

[59] Iran finally agreed in 1989 to allow the Special Representative appointed by CHR to visit the country, thus facilitating adoption without vote for the first time of a UN resolution on human rights in that country. See GA Res.44/163 (1989).

as a 'higher authority', could focus more attention on countries which refuse to co-operate with the Commission, and other UN human rights procedures, thus enhancing the capacity of the UN system to provide more clearly graduated responses to human rights violations.

Some have suggested that the Third Committee's broad debate should be replaced by a more focused discussion of the rapporteurs' reports. It is argued that these reports should be given more serious and thorough attention by the Assembly, and that the presence of the rapporteurs during the proceedings offers opportunities for useful dialogue which have not been explored sufficiently. On the other hand, restricting the Assembly's attention to the limited number of countries covered by specific rapporteurs' reports would undercut one of the most useful aspects of its human rights work—its wide-ranging debate about violations throughout the world. Plainly, the effectiveness of such a strategy would in the end depend heavily on the quality of the reports of the rapporteurs, which have been criticized from time to time by delegations, NGOs, and other commentators.

Attention has been drawn by a variety of commentators to the conflicts between the fact-finding, and good offices/diplomatic conciliation roles of rapporteurs on specific countries. In 1985, for example, Denmark observed in the Third Committee that the rapporteurs' reports

> revealed considerable differences as to methodology, substance, and commentary. The reports on Afghanistan and El Salvador seemed thoroughly researched and the authors' comments were useful. The other three did not quite meet expectations; it was hoped that they could be improved considerably before submission in final form to the CHR.

Denmark went on to suggest that the reports should include at least a broad description of the general situation, and a systematic review of the situation in relation to various rights set out in the Covenants. The reporting should be 'more even-handed, and balanced'. Two sessions later, Finland made the suggestion that these reports should contain 'information of a condensed, and substantial character which was not available elsewhere'. NGOs have also weighed in heavily on this subject.[60]

There has also been widespread concern that the Assembly has not done enough to broaden the political and geographical scope of resolutions on specific situations. Indeed the Assembly continues to be criticized, justifiably, for what US Assistant Secretary of State for Human Rights, and Humanitarian Affairs Richard Schifter has called 'selective indignation'.[61] The political numbers game in the Assembly has only permitted nine countries

[60] See respectively A/C.3/40/SR.65 (1985), paras. 31–2; A/C.3/42/SR.57 para. 86; and Watch Committees, *Four Failures: A Report on the United Nations Special Rapporteurs on Human Rights in Chile, Guatemala, Iran, and Poland* (1986).

[61] A/C.3/39/SR.65 (1984), para. 34.

to be the subject of specific resolutions over recent years. Initially, the focus was exclusively on right-wing Latin American regimes—Chile, El Salvador, and Guatemala. In 1985, Iran and Afghanistan were added to this list when the Commission decided that the relevant rapporteurs should present interim reports to the Assembly. Since then, despite egregious violations of human rights in a number of other countries, this list has only been expanded to include the situation in 'occupied Kuwait' in 1990, with Iraq, Burma and Haiti being addressed in Assembly resolutions in 1991. Moreover, the geographical spread of the Assembly's enquiries has been more limited than that of the Commission, partly because there is no parallel at the Assembly to the confidential procedures established pursuant to the ESC Resolution 1503. The absence of NGO participation (discussed above) has also affected the content and tone of the Third Committee's debate.

Delegations have, nevertheless, tried to launch resolutions in the Assembly on other countries. Not surprisingly given the protagonists, the result of these efforts has been to increase the political temperature of the Assembly's proceedings considerably. The United States attempted in vain to launch a resolution on human rights in Cuba late in the Assembly's session in 1986. Cuba retaliated by tabling draft resolutions on human rights violations in the United States against blacks, American Indians, and Puerto Ricans. In the end, a motion to take no action on all these texts was adopted without vote.[62] The following year, Chile launched a retaliatory text on human rights in Mexico (a traditional co-sponsor of UN resolutions on Chile), a manœuvre which prompted heavy criticism.[63] These sharp confrontations between Cuba and the United States, and Chile and Mexico, did not reflect well on the Assembly's capacity to deal objectively and effectively with human rights issues.

An unfortunate trend in UN human rights bodies over recent years has been the increasingly common resort to procedural means to avoid substantive action on country situations, and other controversial proposals. This form of procedural manœuvring was exemplified when Syria moved unsuccessfully at the Assembly in 1985 to adjourn the debate (i.e., to take no action) on both draft resolutions on human rights in Afghanistan and Iran taken together.[64]

[62] A/C.3/41 L.97/Rev.1 (1986) and A/C.3/41/1.98/Rev.1 (1986) respectively. One argument adduced to attack the United States initiative was that only situations previously considered at the Commission on Human Rights should be the subject of resolutions at the General Assembly. See Panama's statement, A/C.3/42/SR.60 (1987), para. 61. The United States subsequently relaunched its Cuba initiative at the Commission on Human Rights in 1987 and 1988, in the latter case achieving adoption of a resolution.

[63] A/C.3/42/L.71 (1987).

[64] The Hungarian Chairman of the Committee, Ambassador Zador, ruled that this motion was in order, on the basis of advice from the UN Legal Counsel. This ruling was subsequently overturned decisively by vote in the Committee. Separate Syrian motions to take no action on each of the texts were then defeated.

Resort to such procedures has serious implications for UN human rights activities. There will often be a majority of states in favour of avoiding taking positions on difficult issues by procedural means, whereas, on the issues of substance, resolutions will carry, albeit with a significant number of abstentions.

Other critics of the Assembly argue with justification that it has not managed very successfully to deal with situations where, although serious human rights violations continue, some progress has been made. Because of the 'quantum leap' involved in securing adoption of resolutions on specific country situations, and the eagerness of countries to 'get off the hook', it is difficult to maintain the political spotlight on such countries, especially in the Assembly. The UN's handling of Guatemala illustrates these difficulties.

Nor has the Assembly (or the Commission for that matter) developed a capacity to deal with urgent cases of human rights violations, or to play much of a preventive role. Canada observed in 1986 that the UN lacked the 'ability to act rapidly in urgent cases, a capacity to establish fact-finding, and conciliation missions, and a longer term strategic approach'.[65] One remedial measure could be to give the Bureau of the Third Committee, or at least its Chairperson, an inter-sessional role to act in urgent humanitarian cases, an approach which has been followed to a modest extent at the Commission. The potential role of the Secretary-General in urgent cases is also particularly important in this regard, and should be encouraged by the Assembly which is in a better position to work with the Secretary-General than the Geneva-based human rights bodies.

One disturbing trend which has marked sessions of the Assembly (and the Commission) since the mid-1980s is the perceptible strengthening of regional caucusing on human rights country situations, especially those in Central America. Latin American delegations have asserted that they are the best qualified to negotiate satisfactory texts on countries such as El Salvador and Guatemala. In 1987, this sentiment almost derailed the adoption of a GA Resolution on the former country. Although it is apparent that many Latin American countries have important political and other interests in Central America, this trend is nevertheless subversive of the universality of the UN's human rights endeavours because it excludes input from other regions from negotiations, especially once a regional consensus has been forged.

This brief account illustrates the need to consider more carefully the Assembly's role in addressing violations in particular countries. The international debate has moved on from the days when the UN offered one of the very few effective channels to pursue human rights issues. A number of countries have active bilateral human rights policies, making representations on particular cases, and raising broad 'thematic' issues at ministerial and

[65] A/C.3/41/SR.56 (1986), para. 44.

official levels with bilateral interlocutors.[66] Australia, Canada, the Nordic countries, and the United States have especially active policies in this regard. Similarly, the European Community often makes joint *démarches* and public statements on human rights issues. The Helsinki (or CSCE) process provides another forum for human rights deliberations, while regional activities, despite their variable effectiveness, also have an important role to play.

In addition, a network of international human rights professionals, concentrated in non-governmental bodies such as Amnesty International, the International Commission of Jurists, and other lawyers' groups, the Watch Committees, and religious organizations, provides a wealth of information about violations. Much of this material is published. The Commission on Human Rights offers NGOs a unique international forum for promoting their concerns, and, as already noted, has become the multilateral focal point for consideration of specific human rights issues.

Against this background, the Assembly's role must be to build on all these diverse activities to protect and promote human rights. In this section, some modest suggestions have been offered on ways in which the General Assembly's distinctive characteristics could be exploited to enhance its effectiveness and impact, and to complement, and reinforce other endeavours, notably the work of the Commission. At the same time, an assessment of some of the more ambitious tasks suggested for the Assembly might be in order. One proposal which has emerged is that the Assembly could strive to adopt an omnibus resolution on the global human rights situation, based on an incisive survey of international trends. Several member States have pressed for such a global report to be prepared by the Secretary-General as a means of overcoming the selectivity and politicization of UN procedures for dealing with specific countries.[67]

But it is not difficult to foresee that such a project would confront formidable obstacles. For a start, it would be unrealistic to expect the Secretariat to produce a global human rights survey involving such political sensitivity and complexity. Would member States report fully, and frankly? If an independent rapporteur were to be assigned by the Assembly to perform this task, this would undoubtedly be seen as establishing a High Commissioner for Human Rights 'by the back door', and thus generate opposition. Moreover, finding language for inclusion in a global resolution to satisfy the universal membership of the Assembly would be a daunting challenge which, if achieved, would probably represent a lowest common denominator result of limited value.

[66] The International Commission of Jurists has produced useful reports on a series of *colloquia* involving officials responsible for management of human rights issues which reflect the increasing complexity and importance of this aspect of foreign relations.

[67] In 1987 Ecuador explained its vision of a global report by the Secretary General prepared on the basis of information from member States. This approach would convert the item 12 debate into a mechanism by which all countries account to the international community for their human rights performance. A/C.3/42/SR.57 (1987), para. 12.

A more encouraging untapped potential role for the Assembly which has already been mentioned is in relation to the exercise of the Secretary-General's 'good offices' in human rights cases.[68] While much of this activity should be confidential, and 'behind the scenes', there should be scope for the Secretary-General to report to the Assembly on overall trends, even if specific details of cases examined are not published. Such a report would at least alert the international community to a little-known procedure which has important application in urgent humanitarian cases. The presence of so many Heads of Government and Foreign Ministers for the Assembly's General Debate each year in New York would provide convenient opportunities for the Secretary-General to exercise his or her good offices for human rights purposes.

F. *The Philosophical/Ideological Debate about Human Rights*

The Third Committee, like the rest of the General Assembly, became a major forum for North-South issues in the 1970s and early 1980s. General GA Resolution 32/130, the landmark invitation to the international community to pursue 'alternative approaches' to human rights, set in train several major strands of discussion about the nature of human rights. These strands are still evident in the proceedings of more recent sessions of the Assembly, but with significant changes of direction, and emphasis.[69]

The most concrete follow-up of the economic/North–South aspects of Resolution 32/130 has probably been the adoption of the Declaration on the Right to Development in 1986. While some Group of 77 countries continue to press for an early start to negotiations on a binding international convention on this subject, consideration of the right to development at the Assembly since the adoption of the Declaration has been notable for its moderate tone. This situation partly reflects a wider trend over the last five years at the UN—towards greater moderation on North-South issues.[70] It may also indicate a recognition of the formidable difficulties inherent in drafting a binding international treaty on the right to development.

A key motivation behind Resolution 32/130 was to broaden the focus of UN inquiries beyond classical civil liberties issues, and to tackle economic and social aspects of human rights in an integrated fashion.[71] With the establish-

[68] UN Under-Secretary-General Buffum drew attention to the mechanism in introducing the 'Alternative Approaches' debate in 1986. A/C.3/41/SR.36 (1986), para. 4.

[69] For a critique of GA Res.32/130, see van Boven, 'United Nations Policies, and Strategies: Global Perspectives?', *Human Rights: Thirty Years After*, 88–9.

[70] This may be a temporary phenomenon. It is argued below that improved East–West relations could lead to greater North–South conflict at the UN.

[71] In 1984 the Philippines delegation argued, for example, that the General Assembly 'should not concentrate on social issues in isolation from the economic questions covered by the report of ECOSOC. Instead, it should encourage a clear direct link between human rights, poverty, hunger,

ment of the new Committee on Economic, Social and Cultural Rights, both the Assembly and the Commission have devoted more attention to economic, social, and cultural rights. But, as the foregoing analysis has revealed, despite both this advance and the continuing emphasis of developing country delegations on those rights, the 'cutting edge' of Assembly action undoubtedly remains civil and political rights.

Concerns voiced in the late seventies and early eighties about a flood of demands for 'third generation' rights have not so far been realized at the General Assembly. While new instruments have been adopted or are under negotiation, their focus is generally on the application or refinement of existing rights to special categories of persons, rather than the wholesale creation of new rights as such. This process has occasionally raised new rights including those which are distinctive to groups (such as in the case of minorities or indigenous populations), but delegations have generally approached new rights with circumspection.[72]

The emphasis of Resolution 32/130 on 'massive, and flagrant violations' of human rights such as apartheid (rather than abuses of the rights of individuals) was sustained by the Soviets and their allies working with a number of developing countries, but this theme has been more muted over recent sessions. Relatively predictable resolutions, adopted at the instigation of Cuba under the 'alternative approaches' item of the agenda, continue to emphasize 'massive, and flagrant' violations. These texts have only limited impact on the main orientation of the Assembly's debate, and no delegation has seriously challenged the legitimacy of efforts to raise violations of the human rights of individuals at recent sessions of the General Assembly. The international prominence given to individual victims (Nelson Mandela, for example) would make it difficult for proponents of this line of reasoning to sustain their objections. Indeed, a perusal of the summary records of recent sessions of the Assembly confirms that, while some developing countries would undoubtedly prefer the UN to discontinue its scrutiny of human rights violations against individuals, many hold the opposite view, and are quite prepared to raise concerns about human rights in other countries, risking in the process criticism of their own human rights performance.[73]

The controversial subject of the rights of peoples and other collective rights

disease, and illiteracy on the one hand, and the questions of survival and development and the inter-dependence of states on the other'. A/C.3/39/SR.54, para. 43.

[72] Looking ahead, it seems likely that pressures from some developing countries will grow for renewed attention to 'third generation rights', especially as East–West tensions diminish. In this context, the Colombian initiative to inscribe 'Human rights based on solidarity' with emphasis on extreme poverty, as a new item on the Assembly's agenda, is noteworthy. GA Res.44/148 (1989).

[73] The invocation of human rights by such a range of delegations has done much to entrench this subject on the UN's agenda. It is paradoxical that, in many instances, human rights have been invoked in order to legitimate, and add weight to, a wide variety of political, and other demands and concerns.

is still raised from time to time in the Assembly, but with less passion than in the days when these issues took centre stage at UNESCO.[74] Discussion of the 'rights of peoples' is not confined to the Eastern Europeans, and their developing country allies. In 1987, New Zealand made an interesting intervention encouraging more open-minded examination of collective rights.[75]

As already noted, a recent theme at the Assembly has been the growing chorus of concern expressed by delegations about the politicization and selectivity of the UN's human rights programme. A wide variety of delegations, including Western countries, have argued that the credibility of the UN's procedures is at risk if its procedures are manipulated for political ends. There are various suggestions as to what should be done to address this problem. Some delegations have been pragmatic: it is a political world where human rights will inevitably be caught up in wider issues, but 'best endeavours' to resist politicization should be sustained. Others are less flexible: UN human rights procedures are made untenable if compromised by political pressures, and objective criteria must be developed to minimize scope for political manipulation.

'Political manipulation' is of course a rather subjective, and sometimes elusive concept. The Ukrainian SSR sought to pursue the question of 'illegitimate use of the human rights issues for political purposes' in a draft resolution first circulated in 1985. This text foundered after several developing countries, including Zimbabwe, made the axiomatic point that human rights and politics could not, of course, be separated. Zimbabwe cited South Africa, and the Middle East to illustrate this proposition.[76]

A variation on this theme emerged in a further draft resolution, again circulated by the Ukrainian SSR, in 1986. This text extolled the virtues of 'international co-operation' in the field of human rights. The 'co-operation' theme wove together several interrelated strands—the avoidance of confrontation and polemic in discussion of human rights problems, the implicit rejection of the use of UN human rights forums to 'name names', and to make accusations against other countries, the desirability of generating dialogue about complex issues, with the focus on constructive solutions rather than condemnation, and the primordial importance of maintaining friendly relations among states.[77]

[74] Ironically, the Ukrainian SSR circulated draft resolutions on people's rights in 1985 and 1986 (see A/C.3/41/L.91 (1986)), but did not press to take action on this text, perhaps because of its troubling implications for national minorities in the Soviet Union.

[75] A/C.3/42/SR.57 (1987), paras. 89–92.

[76] The Ukrainian SSR invoked the Declaration on the Inadmissibility of Intervention and Interference in the Internal Affairs of States as the legal foundation of their resolution. See A/C.3/40/L.83/Rev.1 (1985).

[77] This Ukrainian resolution complemented Soviet initiatives in other Committees of the Assembly, notably the First (Disarmament and Arms Control) Committee, to promote Gorbachev's concept of 'international co-operation' across the UN agenda—the interlinkage of political security, economic, and humanitarian issues. It was launched in the Third Committee

This 'co-operation' theme reappeared in more elaborate form the following year, and the response of a variety of delegations was sceptical. 'Western, and other' countries in particular took issue with the fundamental premiss of the new Ukrainian text that the maintenance of friendly relations among States should be the paramount consideration governing the human rights work of the UN. Ireland and others defended the unique focus of the human rights programme on the fundamental human rights, and freedoms *of the individual*, even if this focus meant friction in bilateral relations. Suggestions were made to amend the Ukrainian text, including the insertion, at Costa Rica's initiative, of language on the importance of 'co-operation' with UN procedures, including the First Optional Protocol to the ICCPR. Eventually, after accepting some changes, the Ukrainians decided not to insist on their text, ostensibly because more time was required for consultations.[78]

Such efforts to define the 'legitimate' human rights activities of the UN could be interpreted as representing a reappearance, in more sophisticated guise, of the traditional objection to these activities—interference in the domestic affairs of member States. The obstacles to be overcome in assessing objectively the motivation behind various human rights proposals, and of developing generalized 'guidelines' to prevent abuse seem insurmountable. Inevitably, attempts to separate human rights from politics seem destined to fail, for obvious reasons.

The emergence of the 'co-operation' theme was also significant as a reflection of evolving Soviet attitudes to human rights. The approach of Russia and the other Republics to the Third Committee at future sessions of the Assembly should provide interesting insights into progress in reform. Under President Gorbachev, the USSR took a number of steps to underline its support for multilateralism, and for the UN system, including payment of peacekeeping arrears, as part of its attachment to a broader central theme of global interdependence.[79] The Third Committee now offers challenges and opportunities for new leaders in the former USSR. The UN's focus on individual human rights traditionally discomforted the Soviet bloc for ideological and practical reasons. Gorbachev, however, publicly embraced the importance of respect for individual rights, and of their international verification. No doubt, some powerful sections of society will resist efforts to expose events in the former USSR to full outside scrutiny and influence, including by the UN. Reform commitments could thus be squarely put to the test by UN human rights procedures.

with a parallel text (from the USSR delegation) on 'co-operation in international humanitarian issues', and, after negotiation to near consensus adoption as GA Res.41/155 (1986), it was finally adopted without vote at UNGA 43.

[78] See A/C.3/42/SR.60 (1987), paras. 132–6; A/C.3/42/SR.62 (1987), paras. 33–49; and A/C.3/42/SR.63 (1987), paras. 1–6.

[79] See Gorbachev's interview in *International Herald Tribune* (23 May 1988), 4.

Whatever the ultimate fate of *glasnost*, and *perestroika*, the constructive approach adopted by Soviet delegations at recent UN human rights meetings (including the Assembly) on some significant issues has offered new opportunities to advance the multilateral human rights agenda. If professed commitments to multilateral processes extend fully to human rights issues, a number of significant procedural and other logjams inhibiting the effective development of UN human rights activities may now be capable of resolution. Some of the opportunities (and problems) which could arise from 'new thinking in Eastern Europe', and improved East–West relations are discussed briefly in the last section of this chapter.

An increasingly important theme in the human rights debate in the Third Committee relates to cultural relativities. The Islamic Republic of Iran, for example, has taken a robust approach in arguing that the UN's human rights activities reflect a western liberal democratic bias, and that existing structures need to be replaced. In 1984, Iran proposed that 'certain concepts in the Universal Declaration of Human Rights should be revised', and concluded that 'any conventions, declarations, and resolutions of international organizations which were contrary to Islam had no validity for Iran'.[80] Three years later, Iran argued in the Third Committee that the Group of 77 no longer represented the views of many developing countries, and that an Islamic grouping would be more appropriate. Other delegations have taken a more muted position on the relativism issue, suggesting that the UN should take fuller account of social and cultural differences, as well as stages of development, when addressing human rights issues.[81]

Some have viewed the philosophical debate in the Assembly, especially the 'alternative approaches' item, as subversive of respect for human rights by introducing extraneous political issues, and challenging the status of established international norms. While such problems and challenges have emerged from time to time, the overall record of the Assembly does not bear out this negative assessment. Nor is it difficult, moreover, to see why the UN human rights programme should not be allowed to become static and insensitive in the face of the evolving views of the broad international community. If it falls into these traps, it will simply become increasingly irrelevant. Therefore, if the Assembly is to retain the mantle of providing overall policy guidance in relation to the UN's human rights activities, the debate about the philosophical underpinnings of this system should continue in a universal

[80] A/C.3/39/SR.65 (1984), para. 92.

[81] In 1984, Singapore's delegation commented, for example, that: 'it was patently unfair to expect developing countries to conform immediately to standards [of] Western developed countries which had had several centuries to evolve relatively stable social and political systems. Democratic institutions appeared to function most effectively when there was a broad consensus on basic values, but many new countries like Singapore were forced to forge such a consensus very rapidly while attempting to prevent the centrifugal forces of racial, linguistic, and religious diversity from tearing the fragile state apart.' A/C.3/39/SR.62 (1984), para. 37.

membership body such as the Third Committee, and should be allowed to evolve.

At the same time, it must be conceded that the Assembly's all-inclusive approach to human rights, as reflected in the wide variety of resolutions which it has adopted, has produced a rather fragmented overall picture. The traditional Cuban resolution on alternative approaches seeks to provide an 'overview', but, as a selective, biased, and unenlightening litany of well-worn UN formulas, seems decreasingly relevant to efforts to answer the hard questions about human rights and development.[82] Moreover, while the UN Secretary-General has regularly presented reports on the 'international conditions affecting the global human rights situation' under the alternative approaches item, these documents have been non-specific, descriptive rather than analytical, and generally devoid of useful content.[83] To be fair, as has already been observed, it is probably unrealistic at this stage to expect the Assembly to produce a credible overall assessment of the state of human rights in the world or a coherent strategy to improve it. Despite its limitations, the Assembly could, however, devote much more attention to exploiting more effectively its unique global perspectives.

The pressures associated with the Assembly's hectic agenda have no doubt affected the capacity of many delegations to contribute fruitfully to this wider debate. Nevertheless, the range of pertinent issues already raised attests to the relevance of its role as a global forum. It is also encouraging that such a wide range of views can be accommodated within the existing framework, and that delegations, by participating in the human rights debate, are implicitly recognizing its universal relevance and applicability, as well as its evolutionary character.

G. *Advisory Services and other Measures of Constructive Assistance*

In his valedictory speech to the Commission on Human Rights in 1986, the retiring Director of the Centre of Human Rights, Dr Kurt Herndl, identified the provision of constructive assistance to member States to rebuild infrastructure, to train officials, and to take other remedial steps to curb or prevent human rights abuses, as the most important challenge then facing the UN human rights programme. These comments struck a responsive chord among many delegations. Strangely, the Assembly, despite having established the consolidated Advisory Services Programme of expert assistance, fellowships, and seminars in 1955,[84] has only played a modest role in the field. There is

[82] GA Res.42/119 (1987).

[83] In 1987, Canada described this report as 'seriously incomplete', and 'badly distorted'. A/C.3/42/SR.37 (1987), para. 1.

[84] By GA Res.926 (X) (1955).

for example no parallel at the Assembly to the advisory services debate which takes place at the Commission.

The advisory services strategy has, however, begun to figure more prominently in the Assembly over recent sessions, partly as a result of pressures from some delegations to substitute this procedure for public scrutiny of countries through resolutions under agenda item 12. The United States, for example, has argued for several years that the situations in El Salvador and Guatemala should be dealt with in this way. The constructive orientation of advisory services is argued to be a more appropriate response than the spotlight of international criticism to the bona fide efforts of the governments concerned to deal with legacies of violence and oppression. At the Commission in 1987, the situation in Guatemala was shifted into the advisory services procedural framework, despite the objections of some delegations. This change effectively ended formal consideration of Guatemala by the Assembly, notwithstanding the fact that serious violations were continuing in that country. It would be unfortunate indeed if public scrutiny and the provision of advisory services came to be viewed as mutually exclusive UN responses to human rights violations in particular countries. In the political environment of the Assembly, where there are growing pressures to change the way in which individual country situations are addressed, the temptation to substitute the 'softer' option of advisory services could be difficult to resist.

The establishment of a Voluntary Fund for Advisory Services has also focused greater attention on practical strategies to assist countries to protect and promote human rights. Given the Assembly's crowded agenda, and the need for a thorough re-examination of the advisory services programme, it would seem desirable to give prime carriage of this issue to the Commission, with support as necessary from ECOSOC. Nevertheless, the Assembly may be able to add momentum to the development of effective advisory services by bringing its existence to the attention of all member States, and highlighting its relevance to other activities conducted by the UN such as peacekeeping, election monitoring, and de-colonization.

The 'alternative approaches' discussion, and the item on the report of ECOSOC, provide some opportunities for the Assembly to consider other constructive strategies, notably the development of public information, national institutions, and regional arrangements in the field of human rights. Despite this, the role of the Assembly in these fields has generally been limited to consolidating initiatives launched at the Commission.

The Assembly's contribution has probably been most significant in relation to public information strategies, and activities which have been addressed in a series of GA Resolutions over recent sessions.[85] The Assembly has a long history of involvement in this field dating back to Resolution 217D (III) of 10

[85] See GA Res.42/118 (1987).

December 1948 which adopted the Universal Declaration of Human Rights, and urged that it be widely disseminated. As far back as 1968, the Assembly drew attention to the importance of teaching human rights.[86] Once again this legislative effort has sought to reinforce the activities of the Commission, resulting in a series of similar parallel resolutions on public information emanating from both of these bodies over recent years.

The Assembly should be ideally placed in institutional terms to advance the UN's efforts to promote human rights through public information. In theory, the Assembly has some oversight role in relation to the Specialised Agencies (of which UNESCO is particularly relevant in this context). It also supervises the UN Department of Public Information, through the Special Political Committee which receives the report of the Committee on Information, and through the Fifth Committee's broader budgetary and administrative review. In principle, therefore, the Assembly should be able to legislate with authority, and to mobilize the resources of the UN system as a whole to achieve public information objectives. However, in practice, despite clear legislative direction from the Assembly, the response of the Secretariat and of the Specialized Agencies has been disappointing, and very little has been accomplished. This partly reflects institutional realities such as the autonomy of the Specialized Agencies, the absence of any coherent information strategy in DPI, and the paralysis of the UN Committee on Information over ideological issues. Regrettably, this failure also reflects a lack of political will at the UN to look seriously and professionally at information issues which are of crucial importance to human rights programmes, and to accord them sufficient resources. Both the Assembly and the Commission have sensibly drawn attention to the need for information activities in this field to be targeted, to make use of modern technology, especially audio and visual media, to tap the UN's extensive network of Information Centres, and to give priority to developing human rights teaching materials. Recently, however, the Secretariat appears to be giving public information higher priority, and it is hoped that this signals the end of a period of neglect of a central element in any human rights activity.

As a final note on publicity, it should also be remembered that decisions on 'international years', anniversaries, and other such symbolic events have traditionally been taken by the Assembly on the basis of guidelines developed by ECOSOC. Some delegations have more enthusiasm for such events than others, key concerns of the sceptics being 'devaluing the currency', and diverting scarce resources to public relations, and away from other critical substantive UN programmes. Nevertheless, the fortieth anniversary of the adoption of the Universal Declaration of Human Rights, celebrated in 1988, provided a useful occasion to generate greater public awareness of human rights issues. That event was also followed by the launching of a major UN

[86] GA Res.2445 (XXIII) (1968).

public information campaign on human rights, which was approved by the Assembly in 1988 and a 1990 decision to hold a World Conference on Human Rights in 1993.[87]

The Assembly has played a more modest role in encouraging the development of national institutions to protect and promote human rights by adopting a series of non-controversial resolutions during the 1980s. These initiatives date back to 1963, and took their most concrete form in guidelines for national institutions endorsed by the Assembly in 1978.[88] More recently, it has encouraged revision of these guidelines to enhance their practical relevance to member States.[89] This debate has continued concurrently in the Commission, and, while this subject should be drawn to the attention of the global membership of the Assembly from time to time, it could perhaps be more productively pursued at the Commission where more in-depth attention is possible.

Another recondite part of the Assembly's agenda has been its consideration of regional human rights arrangements. Proposals for such regional arrangements for Africa which emerged from a UN seminar in Monrovia, Liberia, in 1979 precipitated the Assembly's interest in a subject which had been broached by the Commission since 1967. The Assembly duly noted the Monrovia seminar's report, and encouraged the development of regional machinery in parts of the world where it had not already been established. More recently, with the advent of the African Charter of Human and Peoples Rights, biennial resolutions of the Assembly have repeated this broad exhortation. In addition, encouragment of Asian–Pacific regional arrangements has been the subject of biennial resolutions following up a UN seminar in Colombo in 1982.[90]

While subject to criticism for challenging the universality of the UN's activities and instruments, regional structures have taken root, and their relationship to UN activities would benefit from more careful global oversight. Indeed, the General Assembly, with its broad membership, and a key role in relation to the human rights treaty system, should be well placed to be more active in efforts to co-ordinate and harmonize regional activities, both between themselves, and with the UN system. In Plenary, the Assembly already considers items on co-operation between the UN and regional political organizations such as the Organization of African Unity. The Third Committee could build on these foundations.

[87] See GA Res.42/118 (1987), para. 3, and also GA Res.42/131 (1987) and 41/150 (1986), which listed proposed UN activities for this Anniversary. The 'World Public Information Campaign for Human Rights' was launched by GA Res.43/128 (1988), para. 7. In relation to the World Conference see GA Res.45/155 (1990).

[88] See GA Res.33/46 (1978).

[89] GA Res.42/116 (1987), esp. para. 6.

[90] See GA Res.41/153 (1986).

H. *Budgets, Resources, and Co-ordination*

Over recent sessions, as concerns about UN finances and administration have intensified, the Assembly has provided an increasingly important forum for consideration of budget, personnel, and planning issues affecting all UN programmes. Human rights is no exception. In 1986, many delegations spoke out at the Assembly against the Secretary-General's decision to impose a 30 per cent across-the-board cut to the human rights programme. Delegations used statements under all human rights items to register their views, and followed up in the Fifth Committee which considered the specific aspects of the Secretary-General's budget cuts package. Of particular concern was the effect of these cuts on the Centre for Human Rights, and particularly in relation to special procedures where temporary staff whose contacts were not to be renewed had played a prominent role. The Assembly's 1986 resolution on reporting obligations under the treaty bodies also put down an unequivocal marker for the Secretary-General—that the summary records for these bodies should be preserved.[91]

Given the likelihood that budget shortfalls will continue to afflict the UN, the Third Committee provides an important 'window' through which to keep track of resource allocations to the human rights programme, and to ensure that the Secretariat remains accountable to member States for decisions with significant ramifications for priority programmes. It is equally important that budget, personnel, and planning processes in other UN organs are watched carefully because of the direct impact of their decisions on the human rights programme. The Fifth Committee, the Committee for Programme and Co-ordination ('CPC'), and the Advisory Committee on Administrative and Budgetary Questions ('ACABQ') are the most significant bodies in this regard.

Another noteworthy development over recent sessions of the Assembly has been its endorsement of the establishment of voluntary funds for specific human rights activities—for the rehabilitation of victims of torture, indigenous populations, and advisory services. While this method of funding is likely to be given increasing emphasis as UN regular budget resources are squeezed, it carries some disadvantages. Apart from the challenge of co-ordinating a proliferation of funds, and ensuring that these resources are used effectively, voluntary funding undercuts the principle that UN Charter-mandated activities should receive adequate regular budget funding. The universality of the UN's human rights programme could be compromised by excessive reliance on voluntary contributions from a limited number and range of delegations such as the developed countries.

Despite all the rhetoric of the UN reform debate over the last few years, the

[91] GA Res.41/121 (1986).

Assembly's ultimate responsibility for co-ordination in the human rights field has received scant detailed attention. Effective co-ordination is of course increasingly important as UN procedures proliferate, and become more complex, and as pressures on UN resources intensify. Farer has drawn attention to a useful organizational diagram which 'unfocusses the eye with its complex mix of boxes, circles, and lines representing, and commenting on various human rights bodies of the UN system'.[92] The Assembly's co-ordination role is no doubt complicated by uncertainty about ECOSOC's responsibilities in this regard, as well as by the strength of the Commission. Whatever the respective mandates of these bodies, ECOSOC has not done its job, placing greater responsibilities on the Assembly, and the Commission remains constrained by its status as a subsidiary of ECOSOC in dealing with other parts of the UN.

Two separate aspects of co-ordination should also be distinguished—co-ordination within the human rights programme itself, and between human rights and other parts of the UN system. While some progress has been made in the former respect, little has been accomplished in the latter. To date, system-wide co-ordination mechanisms, at both intergovernmental, and secretariat levels, have not proved very effective, despite or perhaps because of their elaborate nature.[93] The Assembly could do more to fill this institutional gap, especially given its role as final arbiter on resources. However, the fate of co-ordination as it affects the human rights programme will ultimately depend on the wider question of co-ordination in the UN systems as a whole. Given both resource constraints facing the human rights programme and its relevance to UN development activities, an early priority should be to enhance links between these areas. In theory, ECOSOC's cross-organizational mandate should give it a central role in drawing together the UN's economic and social agendas, but, in practice, the Council has failed to discharge this crucial function. It is hoped that further reform efforts will give this deficiency priority attention.

I. *Human Rights and other Organs of the General Assembly*

As will already be apparent from this analysis, other parts of the Assembly play an often overlooked but none the less important role in human rights. The General Debate in the Assembly's Plenary which allows heads of government and foreign ministers to expound their views on the international political agenda has served as a vehicle to air human rights concerns. Moreover,

[92] Farer, 'The UN and Human Rights: More than a Wimper, Less than a Roar', 9 *Hum. Rts. Q.*, 550 and 561 (1987).

[93] See Bertrand, *Some Reflections on Reform of the United Nations: Joint Inspection Unit Report*, A/40/1988 (1985), and the review by the Committee on Programme and Co-ordination, E/AC.51/1987/2.

Afghanistan, apartheid, Cambodia, the Middle East (Occupied Territories), and Namibia are inscribed as separate Plenary items, and constitute crucial human rights-related components of the Assembly's agenda. Discussion in the Fourth (De-colonization) Committee frequently picks up human rights issues. As Farer has observed, the UN's de-colonization procedures developed two important precedents now applied by the human rights programme—'vigorous investigation, and exposure in detail of official acts violating international norms, and action based on communications from petitioners'.[94]

In addition to its budgetary, and other administrative responsibilities, the Fifth Committee addresses human rights violations against individual UN staff members under an item dealing with their privileges and immunities. This item spilled over into the First Committee in 1986, when efforts were begun to secure adoption of a resolution relating to the detention of a Romanian national who had headed the UN Disarmament Research Institute. He was subsequently released, and became a Special Adviser in the Centre for Human Rights in Geneva.

It is an institutional peculiarity of the UN system that legal and human rights issues have been kept separate, both in intergovernmental, and Secretariat structures. Surprisingly, therefore, the Sixth (Legal) Committee has played only a limited role in human rights discussions over the last few years. The Sixth Committee's most significant recent contribution flowed from the decision taken by the Third Committee to transmit to the Sixth Committee draft principles on the rights of persons under detention (the 'Nettel principles'). A sessional Working Group of the Sixth Committee struggled with this instrument for several years before adopting a final text in 1988. Unfortunately the text does not represent a major advance over existing international standards, notably the Standard Minimum Rules for the treatment of prisoners adopted in 1955. The only other major human rights input from the Sixth Committee during the mid- to late 1980s was the adoption of a Declaration on the Social and Legal Principles Relating to the Protection and Welfare of Children, with Special Reference to Foster Placement and Adoption Nationally and Internationally in 1986.[95]

In most cases, the allocation of human rights items to Assembly organs other than the Third Committee has a clear logic. The uniquely grave and abhorrent character of apartheid justifies direct handling by the Plenary without reference to a main committee. Similarly, the Fifth Committee is probably best equipped to deal with personnel matters. In addition, it can be argued that these 'cross-over' issues demonstrate the validity of the important proposition that human rights items cannot be separated from other central

[94] Farer, 'The UN and Human Rights', 566.

[95] See GA Res.43/173 (1988) and 41/85 (1986) respectively. Russel Barsh has provided a useful analysis of budgetary aspects of the UN human rights programme in 'Making the United Nations Human Rights Machinery Cost-Effective', 56 *Nordic J. Int'l L.* 187.

functions of the UN organization. By contrast, in other cases, the justification for the current allocation of various items is less readily apparent, and tends to dissipate the focus of the Assembly's inquiries. Proposals to give the Assembly's General Committee more scope to rationalize the Assembly's agenda could help to consolidate human rights issues in the Third Committee. Other creative options such as joint meetings of two or more relevant committees could also be explored in order to counteract the tendency at the Assembly for the work of each Committee to be considered discretely. Moreover, consideration could be given to using the Plenary more effectively to raise the profile of priority human rights issues. If, as the meeting of former Presidents of the Assembly in 1985 suggested, the General Debate in Plenary could be devoted to one or two main topics each year, could not human rights issues be given this special treatment from time to time?[96]

J. *Overview*

A critical evaluation of the work of the General Assembly would not be complete without some comment on the overall impact of its debate and resolutions. As already noted, governments make vigorous efforts to avoid being cited for violations of human rights during the Assembly's proceedings, and, if such action cannot be avoided, all will attempt to contain adverse repercussions for them. In addition, the Assembly's activities which are not country specific have also influenced international thinking on human rights issues. In particular, the Assembly's role in standard-setting and implementation has left an enduring legacy. In these and other ways, the political authority and visibility of the Assembly have helped to make it an important mechanism for the protection and promotion of human rights.

It must, however, be acknowledged that the Assembly has lapsed into predictable patterns of activity over the years, casting doubts on the value of some of its resolutions, and other work. This criticism is particularly pertinent to 'thematic' and other non-specific resolutions which are now numerous, and generally only procedural and declaratory in character. Despite its supervisory and priority setting mandate, the Assembly has no effective method of follow-up or evaluation of implementation of its resolutions. The Secretary-General's reports, all too often requested by delegations semi-automatically, without regard to purpose or resource implications, are by and large bureaucratic set-pieces which do little to advance understanding of the issues.

[96] A/40/377 (1985), para. 16.

Such problems are of course not unique to the Assembly nor even to the UN's human rights work. Reform efforts so far, including those initiated in the Assembly's General Committee, have made little headway. It has also been pointed out earlier in this chapter that, while, in theory, ECOSOC has a vital role in co-ordinating UN human rights activities, and linking them to the UN's economic programmes, in practice, its contribution has been very limited indeed. Its failures have placed more pressure on the Assembly, and this pressure seems set to increase. The resource constraints upon the UN, the growing complexity of the UN system, and the increasing focus on economic social, and cultural rights demand that efforts to give ECOSOC a more meaningful role be intensified. The Assembly thus has good reason not to allow the ECOSOC reform to be returned to the back burner.

The foregoing analysis has sought to highlight another important remedial step: giving more effective publicity to the work of the Assembly. Media interest is very low, and the UN's own information programmes are generally modest, unsophisticated, unimaginative, and oriented towards written materials rather than more cost-effective and influential media such as radio. These seems little doubt that if the Assembly had a higher public profile internationally, its work would be more relevant, and responsive to current human rights preoccupations.

While continuing reform and rationalization of the Assembly's procedures will have an important effect on the future viability of the UN's human rights programme, the value of the Assembly's work in human rights will, at the risk of stating the obvious, depend to a significant extent on the standing of the Assembly, and the UN as a whole. It is unfortunate therefore that the phase of major development of UN human rights procedures, and the entrenchment of human rights on the international political agenda since the early 1980s has coincided with a period of weaker international commitment to multilateral processes. However, after positive movement on long-standing regional conflicts, and in the wake of the Gulf crisis, the UN's stocks appear to be rising.[97] This changed mood should have positive implications for the human rights programme which must be pursued more vigorously if progress is to be consolidated. Throughout this chapter, it has been argued that the Assembly provides a range of potentially very significant mechanisms to advance the cause of human rights which have not been exploited to best effect. The challenge now rests with member States, NGOs, academics, and others in the international community to demonstrate their commitment, and to do more to explore and tap the potential of the Assembly to make a more effective and distinctive contribution.

[97] See Wilenski, 'Reforming the United Nations for the Post-Cold War Era', in Bustelo and Alston, *Whose New World Order: What Role for the United Nations?* (1991), 122.

K. *The Future*

A survey of the Third Committee's human rights role would not be complete without a few speculative thoughts about the future. Recent changes in the international political and economic environment should have significant repercussions for multilateral human rights activities, including those of the General Assembly. The most striking geopolitical changes over the last few years have of course included the end of the Cold War, the wave of democratization which has swept Eastern Europe, the reunification of Germany, and the dissolution of the USSR. Sharp ideological differences between East and West have been a feature of the human rights debate since its inception, marring both thoughtful discussion and practical results. It therefore seems obvious that a priority task should now be to identify which areas of multilateral human rights activity can now be advanced in the light of Russia's more forthcoming and co-operative approach, and the commitments made by new leaderships in Eastern Europe to give high priority to human rights. One such field is the development of procedures to deal with human rights violations, where the former USSR and East Europeans have in the past adopted a restrictive and cautious approach.

Looking ahead over the next five years, the broad question of verification of compliance with international agreements on arms control as well as on human rights seems set to assume an increasingly crucial place in East–West relations. It is possible to imagine the emergence of some important 'cross-overs' of verification precedents and models between these and other different fields. In the same vein, the UN could also act as an important database for information about bilateral human-rights-related agreements such as those covering human contacts between East and West, if all such agreements were registered with the UN. Another beneficiary of reduced East–West tensions could be UN consideration of economic, social, and cultural rights which has for too long been seriously impeded by ideological polarization.

Recent developments suggest that the CSCE will play an increasingly important role in relations between East and West Europe. A central element in the CSCE process has been, and is likely to remain, its human rights basket. CSCE's evolution provides challenges and opportunities for the UN. On the one hand there is some risk that UN human rights procedures will be marginalized from the events unfolding in Eastern Europe which could increasingly be seen as 'European' business. On the other hand, the UN's activities could receive a significant boost as a result of new procedures and concepts developed through the CSCE, and other European processes.

An important spin-off of improved relations between the superpowers has been the easing of serious regional conflicts such as those in Afghanistan, Cambodia, and Namibia. The political temperature of the Assembly's human rights debate was raised significantly during the 1970s and 1980s by sharp differences among delegations over these issues. Settlements of regional conflicts should thus improve the general negotiating atmosphere at the UN, offering the Third Committee an opportunity to devote more attention to practical problem solving. The co-operation among the permanent five members of the Security Council during the Gulf crisis, and the central role of the UN in providing the political framework to deal with Iraq's aggression against Kuwait, should also have valuable spin-offs in the human rights field.

By the same token, these changes in the international political environment will also present the Assembly with new challenges. For example, the Assembly will have to address squarely the problem of strengthening human rights infrastructures after the withdrawal of foreign military forces, the cessation of violent internal conflicts, or the transition from military to civilian rule. The link between respect for human rights and the achievement of durable political settlements should become more apparent as the international community is faced with the challenge of making various regional settlement accords stick. The UN has already become involved in election monitoring projects such as in Namibia, and may come under increasing pressure to do more to help countries reconstruct their political and legal institutions. At the same time, there will be strong *realpolitik* pressures for the Assembly to discontinue its close focus on human rights violations against individuals once the major geo-political dimensions of regional conflicts are resolved.[98]

Settlements in Namibia, Afghanistan, and Cambodia could also allow the Third Committee to look more closely at the issue of self-determination beyond the traditional contexts of de-colonization, or foreign military occupation or intervention. A closer focus on self-determination could have important repercussions across the broad human rights agenda, including its economic, social, and cultural dimensions. For example, a more sophisticated conception of self-determination is, arguably, central to the processes of political and economic liberalization, as well as to the resolution of minorities problems, including those now confronting the former USSR and other Eastern European countries.[99]

In addition, the UN could do more to lend momentum to positive developments, rather than being seen primarily as a focus for international criticism of human rights failures. Fundamental political changes in the USSR and Eastern Europe became a major international preoccupation in the late 1980s. Countries in Latin America and Asia have also made significant progress in relation to human rights and democracy over recent years. A key question which now arises is how the UN, and the Assembly in particular, can

[98] The muted international reaction to serious human rights violations in Afghanistan which continue after the withdrawal of Soviet troops suggests that this concern might be well-founded.

[99] Zbigniew Brzezinski addresses some of the complexities confronting western policy-makers in dealing with the rising tide of nationalism in Eastern Europe and the USSR in 'Post-Communist Nationalism', *Foreign Affairs* (Winter 1989/90), 1–25.

reinforce these positive trends, without playing into the hands of those wishing to gloss over continuing serious human rights problems?

One way might be to provide governments with a showcase for their human rights achievements, thus aiming to reward them as well as locking them more fully into their international human rights obligations. President Gorbachev used the UN very effectively to present his 'new thinking' to the international community. The *quid pro quo* should be that the UN keeps a close watch on the performance of countries making such undertakings, especially where instruments of repression remain substantially in place. The Assembly could also give greater support and encouragement to a variety of countries which have moved away from authoritarianism, both in public declarations, and through practical assistance.

The UN's Advisory Services Programme is beginning to attract significant voluntary contributions, and could expand considerably if member States give higher priority to practical assistance to countries to protect and promote human rights. There is also growing recognition that multilateral aid agencies should factor human rights considerations more fully into their programmes, both to improve the effectiveness of their development assistance, and to maintain the political and financial support of donors.

Despite these positive developments, there are sound reasons why supporters of an effective UN human rights programme should not be complacent about the international political environment of the 1990s. In the former USSR and Eastern Europe, for example, important forces in these societies remain decidedly circumspect about human rights, democratization and other daring experiments in reform which have overturned the ideological, strategic, and economic foundations of the order prevailing in Europe since the late 1940s. At the same time, the prospect of a significant rise in ethnic and nationalities tensions leading to serious violence (as has occurred in Yugoslavia) or other upheavals in the former USSR and Eastern Europe poses difficult challenges for the international community and the UN's human rights programme. In the former USSR, in particular, leaders might feel compelled to use more forceful measures to deal with nationalities, thus sorely testing their public commitments to international accountability in the field of human rights.

The UN's human rights deliberations are likely to be complicated by other factors. Some developing countries, always suspicious of superpower 'collusion', could choose to place increasing importance on group solidarity in response to greater co-operation between East and West at the UN. One possible consequence could be to reinforce the tendency for countries to close ranks around other members of their region in order to protect them from UN scrutiny, well illustrated by the fate of efforts to put cases of African countries on the UN agenda. Moreover, some developing countries which object to UN procedures and principles, but which kept a low profile when the USSR took the running in this regard, are already becoming more forthright in their criticism.

The increasing multi-polarity of the international scene as a result of the declining dominance of the superpowers seems likely to complicate the UN's human rights deliberations in other ways as well. Countries such as India, Brazil, and Egypt which have traditionally been influential at the UN, could become even more important. How will China, as the world's most populous nation, approach the UN human rights programme in view of its forceful crackdown against dissent in 1989, and its unequivocal rejection of international criticism of its human rights record?

Other emerging players could become more vocal and influential in the UN's human rights debate. The positive economic prognosis for a number of states in the Asian region over the next five to ten years suggests that these countries will develop greater global political influence and confidence. Asian countries have generally maintained a low profile in the human rights deliberations of the UN. However, economic dynamism and achievement are already encouraging a number of Asian countries to be more active and assertive internationally. Japan stands out among such countries, and has already made plain its intention to develop an international political profile which is more in keeping with its status as an economic superpower. Among Japan's strategies to achieve this result is greater involvement in multilateral activities. Japan has close links with the United States and other Western countries, and has given emphasis to the importance it places on its international responsibilities. Significantly also, Japan has signalled its concern to give more emphasis in its foreign policy to its Asian credentials and links. Japan's role in the UN human rights debate will, in particular, be influenced by the evolution of Japanese society over the next decade.

Against this broad background, it is possible to foresee the emergence of more forceful and effective advocacy of alternative perspectives in the human rights debate at the General Assembly. Many non-Western countries emphasize, for example, the importance of consensus, and the avoidance of confrontation, as well as the predominance of collective considerations over the rights of the individual and the responsibility of the individual to society.

As has been emphasized, however, attempts to generalize about non-Western countries' interests and perspectives in relation to the UN's human rights debate can be misleading. It is therefore difficult to foresee a clear pattern of concerns emerging from these countries. Indeed, we can expect sharp divisions and differences to persist, especially over regional issues which often have nationalistic, ethnic, or religious overtones, and as the pace of social change accelerates. By way of example, experience over the last few years, in the Assembly, and outside it, suggests that fundamentalist Islamic concerns might figure more prominently in the international human rights debate in the 1990s, including at the UN. More serious and effective multilateral consideration of social and cultural rights might help to address the concerns of countries which take issue with perceived imbalance and cultural bias in the international human rights debate.

The increasing multi-polarity of international relations will also bring important changes in relation to Western countries. To begin with the United States, its decreased capacity, *acting on its own*, to determine international developments could have mixed results for multilateral human rights activities over the next decade. On the one hand, the United States might, in response, attach greater significance to multilateral processes, seeing its interests advanced through compromise and coalition with other like-minded countries, rather than through unilateral action. It is noteworthy in this regard that the Bush Administration has accorded the UN new priority, exemplified by its strategy in response to the Iraq–Kuwait crisis in 1990–1. We could see the US pushing harder in UN human rights deliberations, also given the new era in East–West relations and closer co-operation among the permanent five. On the other hand, a more isolationist US could in the future retreat from multilateral processes, thus reducing some of the momentum behind the UN's human rights work. The United States might also consider that the significant democratic advances made in Eastern Europe and elsewhere lessen the importance of UN human rights activities, especially if the Eastern Europe 'case-load' is taken up by CSCE or other European processes. It would be ironic if the commitment of the United States to the UN's work on human rights were to falter at a time when major international trends point towards democracy and political liberalization.

The movement towards economic and political integration in Europe, highlighted by the launching of the European Community's Single Market scheduled for 1992, and the moves being made by reformist leaderships in Eastern Europe to become an integral part of a new Europe, could have significant implications for the UN's human rights programme. There is a risk that EC members will become increasingly preoccupied with European developments including the rapid change in East Europe, at the expense of their global interests and responsibilities. It will be interesting in this regard to observe how EC countries handle immigration, refugee, and asylum issues over the next decade. European alienation from other regions of the world would be reinforced if the Single Market ushered in protectionist trade policies. Such developments would be a particular set-back in the human rights field where Western Europeans have been so prominent, and where the maintenance of the universal, non-culture-specific character of UN codes of behaviour has been so important. To mention another potential problem of a different order, greater pressure for collective EC action could impede rapid responses to emerging human rights problems, and produce cautious, lowest common denominator results in EC decision-making.

Despite these risks, the EC seems likely to continue to give prominence to human rights issues, and to maintain its global perspective on them. The European Human Rights Commission and European Court are important elements in the system of European institutions. Progress on human rights issues will of course remain central to better relations between Western and Eastern Europe. In addition, the close collaboration between EC countries in relation to international human rights issues has become an important element in the European Political Co-operation process, partly because there is such a broad measure of agreement between EC members in this field. It is interesting to note in this context that the General Assembly has become a major forum for the public exposition of EC views on human rights issues as European Political Co-operation has intensified. The EC, as a collective force, has thus become increasingly important in sustaining the momentum behind the UN's human rights proramme, especially during the recent period of tight resource constraints. On balance, therefore, the increasing global leverage of the EC countries should result in a stronger UN human rights programme.

Another major change in the international environment over recent years has been an increasing preoccupation with economic issues. Debate at the Assembly was of course dominated by the North-South dialogue from the mid-1970s to the early 1980s. The focus then was on social justice, and redistribution of wealth from developed to developing countries. Now, however, much of the emphasis has shifted to structural adjustment, free trade, reform, and deregulation as paths to economic prosperity for developing countries. The Assembly figures much less prominently as a forum for these discussions, having been displaced by GATT, the International Financial Institutions, and other mechanisms, including those outside the multilateral framework such as the 'Group of Seven' industrialized nations. At the same time, greater attention is being paid to the social consequences of these economic policies, notably the pressure which they place on the sustainability of democracy. Harsh economic austerity programmes also tend to affect the poorest disproportionately. Latin American countries have used the General Assembly, and other forums to highlight the adverse social and political repercussions of their crushing external debt burdens. It is likely that the tone of this international debate about the social and political costs of structural adjustment will sharpen over the next few years as the stresses on many developing countries intensify.

For Africa, as economic stocks fall further, the multilateral system could become an increasingly important mechanism by which to amplify the continent's international voice. Apartheid has given this voice its primary focus in the human rights debate over the last twenty-five years, and it is conceivable that pressures within South Africa could increase to such an extent that the apartheid issue assumes even greater urgency in the General Assembly's deliberations. Nevertheless, as their economic plight becomes increasingly serious, African states might be expected to given higher billing to the nexus between human rights and development, especially if positive political developments in South Africa such as current moves towards multiracial democracy sustained.

We can therefore expect the North–South dimension of the UN's human rights debate to loom large again, but under different guises, reflecting new political and economic realities such as the increasingly divergent interests of different developing countries. To illustrate, few countries would now be prepared to argue baldly that their low level of economic development precludes them from respecting the human rights of their citizens. Nevertheless, as a variation on this old theme, more countries are making the point that growing economic pressures are making it increasingly difficult to hold the line against social and political upheaval which erodes the institutions and practices which serve to protect and promote human rights.

Greater international emphasis on economics has implications for UN human rights activities in another way: it coincides with a growing interest in the relationship between economic and political liberalization. This relationship has been highlighted by the stresses experienced in the centrally planned economies as they attempt economic reform. It is also relevant to some of the successful newly industrialized economies which have attributed their remarkable growth to 'developmental authoritarianism'—tight political control and social cohesion to ensure that ambitious economic objectives are met. Some of these countries such as the South Korea have publicly committed themselves to significant political reform, implicitly recognizing its close connection with deregulation, and decentralization of economic decision-making.[100] There seems little doubt that in the years ahead, these linkages, which have come into particularly sharp focus in the wake of events in Eastern Europe and China since 1989, will attract even greater international attention. The Assembly could provide an appropriate forum for consideration of these complex themes, perhaps within a framework of discussion in the Third Committee about economic rights and their relationship with civil and political rights, or perhaps in a debate conducted jointly by the Second and Third Committees of the Assembly.

Against a background of a greater international attention to economic issues, the UN human rights debate could be used more creatively to reflect the pressing concerns of member States. It could conceivably be argued, for example, that increasing global protectionism is inimical to the exercise of the individual's economic rights. Innovation along these lines would offer some attractions to the large number of developing countries dependent primarily

[100] Ross Garnaut examines the relationship between economic and political liberalization in his report to the Australian government: *Australia and the Northeast Asian Ascendency*, Chap. 6 (1989). See also John Girling, 'Development and Democracy in Southeast Asia', 4 *Pac. Rev.* (1988).

on commodity exports, the volatile returns for which are often linked to access to markets in industrialized countries, and to the general health of the global economy.

Another striking aspect of the world political scene as we move into the 1990s is the rapid rise of environmental concerns, as both international and domestic issues. In the multilateral domain, the Brundtland report on the environment, presented to the General Assembly in 1987, placed 'sustainable development' firmly on the international agenda. A moment's reflection reveals a variety of linkages between the international human rights framework and efforts to deal with the environment. At one level, respect for civil and political rights is central to the involvement of individuals in crucial political processes affecting the environment.[101] Plainly, the enjoyment or denial of economic, social, and cultural rights is also directly relevant to the handling of environmental issues. To be more specific, the UN's discussion of the right to development could benefit from more carefully considered input on environmental dimensions. In the case of indigenous populations, the environment–human rights nexus is already firmly established, and well illustrates the human dimensions of problems relating to the balance between economic development and environmental protection.

But perhaps the most fundamental positive spin-off for human rights of greater international attention to environmental issues could be a greater sense of global community, interdependence, shared interests, and values. Such a sense of community seems destined to be strengthened, albeit unevenly, as the 'information revolution' gathers momentum, and economic processes including the division of labour and the deployment of capital become more internationalized. Traditional concepts of national sovereignty and territorial integrity will come under increasing challenge over the next decade.[102] Non-State actors, including international NGOs, will play a major role in shaping international agendas in fields such as the environment. All these trends have important implications for multilateral human rights activities.

Looking into the 1990s, there is clearly a need for more concerted and creative thinking about the General Assembly's human rights agenda as it might look at the end of the century. Much of the pioneering work of

[101] In a speech given to the National Governors Association on 26 February 1990, United States Secretary of State James Baker highlighted the role of environmental issues in raising political consciousness and encouraging grass-roots political activity and organization in Eastern European countries, which have since been swept by a wave of reform and democratization. 'Baker Says Environment Key Part of United States Policy', United States Information Service Press Release (1 Mar. 1990), 2–3.

[102] George Shultz contributed a thought-provoking article in the *Washington Post* suggesting that evolving less absolute concepts of sovereignty and security could facilitate a peaceful resolution of Arab–Israeli conflict. 'Middle East: Diplomacy for the New Facts of Life', reprinted in *International Herald Tribute* (1 Mar. 1990).

establishing machinery to protect and promote civil and political rights has been done, and a wide range of procedures are in place. But the necessary political will has not been displayed to make the multilateral system really effective, and the full potential of the UN's elaborate human rights machinery has not been realized. The challenge for the Assembly is to take the lead in the UN system in forward thinking about desirable objectives, and the most realistic strategies by which to achieve them.

4

The Economic and Social Council

DECLAN O'DONOVAN

Introduction

Human institutions do not always develop as expected. Use confers power and power unused diminishes. Almost half a century ago, the victorious nations of the Second World War established the United Nations and provided it with an elaborate structure. The Economic and Social Council (ECOSOC) was a principal feature of that structure but it has become the major casualty of the Organisation's life in the interim. Other chapters in this book are about the growth of human rights bodies. This chapter is about decline.

A. *The Mandate of the Council*

The founders of the UN foresaw an important role for the Council and gave it considerable powers in the UN Charter, *inter alia*: to make or initiate studies and reports and to make recommendations to the General Assembly, Member States, and the Specialized Agencies; to prepare draft conventions for submission to the General Assembly and call international conferences; subject to the General Assembly's approval, to enter into agreement with any of the specialized agencies defining the terms in which the agency concerned should be brought into relationship with the United Nations; to co-ordinate the activities of the specialized agencies through consultation with and recommendations to such agencies and through recommendations to the General Assembly and to the members of the United Nations; to furnish information to, and, upon request, assist, the Security Council.

These powers and functions are detailed in Chapter X of the Charter. Chapter IX (Articles 55–60) confers further responsibilities which are directly relevant to human rights. By Article 60, responsibility for the discharge of these functions is vested in the General Assembly and, under its authority, in the Council.

The Council's origins lie in rather ambitious proposals drawn up in 1939 within the framework of the League of Nations. In response to the success of the League's technical activities in the economic and social fields, in contrast to the relative failure of its political endeavours, a League Committee, known as the Bruce Committee after its Chairman, proposed the establishment of a 'Central Committee for Economic and Social Questions', one-fourth of the composition of which would consist of independent experts.[1] Although the proposal was shelved for the duration of the War it is clear from the Charter, and confirmed by reports of the proceedings of the founding conferences at Dumbarton Oaks in 1944 and San Francisco in 1945, that there was a determination to make the ECOSOC the decisive body in its field. This is clearly confirmed by the extent of the explicit powers given to it under the Charter.

B. *Characteristics of the Council*

I. SIZE

There was a division of opinion at Dumbarton Oaks and at San Francisco about the number of seats on the Council. The United States suggested a Council of 24, more than twice the number envisaged for the Security Council. The United Kingdom and others argued, however, for a small Council on the grounds that such a body would be more effective. At San Francisco a compromise was reached on the figure of 18 and this was inserted in Article 61 of the Charter.[2] In 1963, the Council was increased from 18 to 27[3] and it was enlarged further in 1971 to 54.[4] In each case the Charter required to be amended in respect of Article 61. Although there has been a further increase in membership of the United Nations since 1971, there has been no increase in the size of the Council. There has been, however, a major increase in the size of a number of subsidiary bodies, notably the Commission on Human Rights, which now has fifty-three seats. Recently, there have been proposals, not yet generally acceptable, to increase the size of the Council and even make it a body of universal membership. While the resolution adopted by the General Assembly in May 1991 seemed to imply that the Council's size would not be enlarged, it left open the possibility of a changed geographical allocation of seats.[5]

II. ELECTIONS

Unlike the Security Council, there was no provision made for permanent membership of the Council. In effect, however, the United States, the Soviet

[1] One commentator has noted that there is a striking resemblance between the suggestions contained in the Bruce Report and the proposals for the creation of ECOSOC. See Ranshofen-Wertheimer, *The International Secretariat* (1945), 166.

[2] See generally Russell and Muther, *A History of the United Nations Charter* (1958).

[3] GA Res.1991B (XVIII) (1963).

[4] GA Res.2847 (XXVI) (1971).

[5] GA Res.45/264 (1991). Annex, para. 6(2).

Union, the United Kingdom, France, and China are permanent members by repeated election. Other economic powers such as Japan and Germany are frequent members. This pattern reflects the importance of these countries and a general recognition that they should be represented on the Council. To an extent, however, their ease of election is due to a lack of interest in the Council as compared to other bodies, such as the Governing Body of the United Nations Development Programme (UNDP), and even a lack of interest compared to certain of the Commission's subsidiary bodies. The competition of States for election to bodies such as the Commission on Human Rights, the Commission on the Status of Women, and the Commission on Narcotic Drugs is much more intense than that for election to the Council itself. A measure of the intensity is that in recent years permanent members of the Security Council have all lost such elections (e.g. the United States for the Statistical Commission, France and the United Kingdom for the Commission on Human Rights).

An important reason, therefore, for seeking election to the Council itself is the opportunity to influence election to the subsidiary bodies and to the major associated bodies such as UNDP and the United Nations Children Fund (UNICEF) by use of the vote conferred by membership. Council members tend to trade votes in order to help each other, although not in all circumstances.

Members of the Council are elected by the General Assembly for a term of three years. Disputed elections are the exception rather than the rule, the candidates being endorsed by their regional groups, sometimes in accordance with a pre-arranged pattern. For example, the Western European and Others Group, is divided into sub-groups for the purpose of taking turns on the Council, an agreement which is rare in that group and which has proved impossible to obtain for elections to the subsidiary bodies of the Council.

III. REPRESENTATION

It was envisaged by many that representatives on the Council would be high-calibre political figures, preferably of cabinet rank. As the substantive areas of the Council's work have dwindled, however, and as the Council has turned more and more to minor questions of co-ordination and oversight, governments have seen no particular need to send high-ranking political figures as their representatives. At present, the representative of a State at sessions of the Council is usually its Permanent Representative in New York or in Geneva, depending on the site of the session. The Permanent Representatives are assisted at the Spring and Summer sessions by the officers dealing with economic and social ministries or legal offices. The officers dealing with human rights matters are usually spokesmen for their Countries in the Second Committee (human rights) and in the Plenary of the Council when human rights questions arise there. They are most often of middle rank. In contrast, representatives in the Commission tend to be of high political or diplomatic rank or are persons of prestige from the judicial and academic worlds.

Unlike the International Labour Organisation, the Council is a body composed of the representatives of States only. Provision for participation by non-members of the Council is liberal.[6] For practical purposes, non-members have all the rights of members except the right to vote. There is also provision for observation and participation in the Council's work by Specialized Agencies, but without the right to vote.

IV. NON-GOVERNMENTAL ORGANIZATIONS

It was originally envisaged at Dumbarton Oaks that the subsidiary functional commissions of the Council should be composed of experts, following the experience of the League of Nations. It was finally left to the Council to decide on this question and, to the dismay of both NGOs and old hands from the League of Nations, the Council decided by vote that its Commissions should be composed of Government representatives only. Had private experts been permitted membership, the way would have been open to direct influence of the commissions by NGOs. Instead, the rights of NGOs remained limited. There is no question of their participation; rather, the Charter speaks of consultation and permits the Council in vague terms to make 'suitable arrangements' (Article 71).

The Council has established three categories of consultation for NGO applicants.[7] Category I organizations are the major ones and those which have an interest in a number of areas.[8] Category II includes those which have an interest in specific aspects of the Council's work and are (or were) reasonably well known.[9] The third group is called the Roster and includes NGOs with very limited interests or no proven record.[10] All categories may send representatives to public meetings of the Council and its subsidiary bodies. Categories I and II may submit written statements for circulation to Members of the Council and Category I may make oral presentations as of right. NGOs on the Roster are not excluded from being read or heard, but they must receive a Council invitation for each debate. Promotion and demotion is possible within the system of categories.

There are many hundreds of NGOs in consultative status with the Council which maintains a Committee to keep track of them, monitor their activities

[6] Rule 72 of the Council's Rules of Procedure, E/5715/Rev.1 (1983).

[7] The Council's original arrangements were set out in its Resolution 288B (X) (1950) which has now been superseded by ESC Res.1296 (XLIV) (1968).

[8] Ibid. para. 16(a).

[9] Ibid. paras. 16(b), 17, and 18.

[10] Ibid. para. 19.

and recommend acceptance into one or other of the three categories of status.[11] The Committee on NGOs' work is informed by considerable political prejudice depending on the activities of the NGO and which State(s) it annoys. The Committee meets every second year and is currently composed of representatives of nineteen States. A well-known NGO will not normally be rejected, however, and once in consultative status it has been fairly rare for a NGO to lose status or to suffer demotion.[12] In 1991, for example, the Committee agreed after an eight-year wait to recommend the granting of consultative status to the Lawyers Committee for Human Rights. Status was also given to International Alert, Article 19, the Refugee Policy Group, and International Service for Human Rights, among others. At the same time, however, it effectively rejected (by means of deferring consideration) applications by Human Rights Watch and the International Movement Against All Forms of Discrimination and Racism.[13] There have been attempts in recent years to cut back on the few rights and privileges which NGOs have, including the right of access to buildings and conference rooms (which implies access to government representatives). Many States still tend towards paranoia in their view of certain NGOs from East and West, and the grounds for restrictions must be suspect.

For example at its 1991 session the Committee on NGOs heard criticism of Human Rights Watch and the International League for Human Rights by Cuba. The Cuban representative even submitted a written attack denouncing the activities of the former group.[14] Rather than taking any specific action in response to such criticisms the Committee contented itself with a general appeal to all NGOs to observe the relevant rules.[15] To some extent the objections have been brought on by security considerations and by over-zealous lobbying of delegates by some NGOs, some of which have permitted themselves to be used as flags of convenience by opposition groups in various countries which would not otherwise gain easy access to those voting on resolutions. Any curtailment of NGOs would be unfortunate. NGOs have been an important aid and influence in the elaboration of human rights standards (very notably on the Convention against Torture and the Convention on the Rights of the Child) and have been successful in directing attention to human rights abuses. Not all NGOs are useful but the body of NGOs continues to represent, even if weakly and erratically, major strands of public

[11] The work of the Committee is reviewed exhaustively in Chiang, *Non-Governmental Organizations at the United Nations* (1981).

[12] In 1950 the International Association of Democratic Lawyers and the International Organization of Journalists were expelled from consultative status while the World Federation of Democratic Youth was demoted to the Register. ESC Res.334A (XI) (1950). Four years later the Women's International Democratic Federation was also expelled. ESC Res.529B (XVII) (1954).

[13] E/1991/20, paras. 5–15.

[14] E/1991/43.

[15] E/1987/22, paras. 26–45.

opinion that are in the nature of things not represented by Govenment delegates; and they are some corrective to the inevitably bureaucratic approach of the latter. The Council itself set an important precedent in 1987 when it agreed to arrangements by which NGOs can make written submissions to the Committee on Economic, Social and Cultural Rights in connection with its consideration of reports by States Parties to the Covenant.[16] The NGO Committee took a potentially important step in 1991 when it agreed to establish an inter-sessional working group to develop technical guidelines for future admission and review decisions. The group will also seek to identify means by which to improve the Committee's effectiveness in carrying out its mandate.

V. SESSIONS OF THE COUNCIL

In recent years the Council has pruned its meeting time. Up until the end of 1991 it held two regular sessions of four weeks each. The first was held in New York in May and the second in Geneva in July. An organizational session of two days or so was held in New York in February. There were three regular sessional committees of the Council, the second of which deals with human rights. The work of the Second Committee dominated the first regular session in May. Most of the human rights work of the Council was done in this committee, but some questions arose directly in the plenary of the Council also and some others indirectly in the First (Economic) and Third (Programme and Co-ordination) Committees which met in Geneva in July.

In 1986 the Group of High-Level Intergovernmental Experts to Review the Efficiency of the Administrative and Financial Functioning of the UN (hereafter, 'the Group of 18') recommended the Council in future hold a single annual session.[17]

Accordingly, the General Assembly decided in May 1991 that, as from 1992, the Council will hold an organizational session of up to four days in New York in early February each year and one substantive annual session of four to five weeks to take place in alternate years in New York and Geneva between May and July. The latter session will consist of: 'a high-level segment' of four days 'with ministerial participation, devoted to the consideration of one or more major economic and/or social policy themes'; a segment of four to five days devoted to UN-system co-ordination issues; a two to three-day segment devoted to 'operational activities' of the UN system; and a segment during which two separate committees meet simultaneously 'to consider and take decisions on the reports' of the Council's subsidiary bodies.

[16] ESC Res.1987/5, para. 6.
[17] A/41/49, 6, Recommendation 2(a).

Committee discussions are supposed to be decision-oriented, to focus on specific recommendations and issues, and not to involve a general debate.[18]

From 1979 to 1986 there was a Sessional Working Group of the Council dealing with the implementation of the International Covenant on Economic, Social and Cultural Rights. As of 1987, the Council delegated this responsibility to an expert Committee on Economic, Social and Cultural Rights, which reports annually to the Council. The work of both the Committee and its predecessor is discussed in Chapter 12, below.

C. *How has the Council Responded to its Mandate?*

1. GENERAL ISSUES, STUDIES, CONVENTIONS, CONFERENCES

The Council played an active role in human rights issues in the early years. Its role as the parent body of a number of subsidiary organs was initially pursued with such vigour that it actually sought to abolish the Sub-Commission on Prevention of Discrimination and Protection of Minorities. It failed in this endeavour, although only as a result of intervention by the General Assembly, but it nevertheless succeeded in effectively dictating a different policy-line to the Sub-Commission. It also succeeded in bringing about the demise, in 1952, of the Sub-Commission on Freedom of Information.[19] In 1963 the Commission itself became a target when the Council cancelled its 1964 session. The ostensible reason was a shortage of conference facilities but the real aim was to force all of the Council's functional commissions to meet only biennially. The Assembly, however, effectively reversed the Council's decision in so far as it applied to the Human Rights Commission.

On a more constructive note it was the Council itself, rather than the Commission, which was responsible for most of the work done to draft the Genocide Convention of 1948. Its role in the drafting of the Covenants was minimal although in 1954 it did ask the Commission to reconsider its proposed article on self-determination, a tactic which yielded nothing more than a reaffirmation by the Commission.

In the late 1940s and early 1950s, when the Commission was preoccupied with the drafting of the Covenants, the Council was, in effect, the principal arena for the study of several major human rights problems. Its decision in 1947 to affirm the Commission's own view that it (the Commission) had no power to act in response to alleged violations helped to reinforce its role in

[18] GA Res.45/264 (1991), Annex, para. 5.

[19] These activities are recounted in Green, *The United Nations and Human Rights* (1956), 76–95.

this regard. Thus while a wide range of specific violations was being debated by the General Assembly (e.g., the plight of prisoners in Spain and Greece, the problem of the wives of Russian foreign nationals, the treatment of Indians in South Africa) it was the Council which took action to deal with several problems of general, rather than specific, significance.

Thus for example it resumed the efforts begun by the League of Nations by appointing an *Ad Hoc* Committee on Slavery in 1949 and five years later appointed a Rapporteur on the same issue. Also, in 1949 it began a long series of debates on the issue of forced labor which culminated in the establishment of a joint UN/ILO committee which prepared an exhaustive report on that subject. Similarly, in 1950, after extensive inter-agency negotiations the Council and the ILO agreed to a procedure for the investigation of infringements of trade union rights in any member State of either organization. According to Green, the resulting Fact-Finding and Conciliation Commission on Freedom of Association constituted 'the first standing international agency (outside the special fields of minorities, mandates and the trustee system) ever empowered to examine allegations concerning violations of human rights.'[20]

In 1948, the Council formed a special Human Rights Committee of the Whole to consider a number of questions, although it never got around to discussing those raised in the report of the Commission on Human Rights. This experiment was not repeated, but there has been renewed interest recently in establishing occasional sessional committees of the whole on particular topics. This interest has arisen in the economic area but it could be usefully applied to human rights questions.

By the mid-1950s the Council's role in human rights issues began to fade as a result of more external factors rather than its own lack of interest. The Commission and the Assembly were heavily involved at that time in the drafting of the Covenants, an activity in which the Council played an insignificant part. Moreover, the diminished enthusiasm of the United States for human rights endeavours and the rapid expansion of the Council's economic and social activities both contributed to a shift in focus.

The Council's power to make studies and reports, which it had exercised with respect to slavery and forced labour, was to be used only rarely thereafter. In 1953 it adopted a formal policy decision[21] to farm out such projects to the Specialized Agencies or to its subsidiary bodies.

One area in which the Council *has* exercised its powers is that of convening international conferences several of which have been called and prepared by the Council rather than the General Assembly, although the latter has taken care to approve the Council's action. The original initiative has not been in the Council. Certain conferences have been called by the General Assembly

[20] Ibid. 137.
[21] ESC Res.502H (XVI) (1953).

without reference to the Council. Perhaps most notable in this regard was the International Conference on Human Rights held in Teheran in 1968. The decision to convene the Conference was taken by the Assembly in 1965[22] and the subsequent arrangements were made by the Preparatory Committee of the Assembly without any formal involvement on the part of the Council.

If subsidiary bodies possessed the power to call and prepare Conferences as well as propose them, it is likely they would have done so. None the less, much of the work that goes into holding a World Conference can be done in the Council and was done in the case of the Conferences against Racism held in 1978 and 1983.

II. OBSERVANCE OF HUMAN RIGHTS

The Council has been reluctant to exercise its major power to promote respect for the observance of human rights and fundamental freedoms under Articles 60 and 62 of the Charter. This applies especially to the initiation of measures and recommendations to deal with specific situations of human rights violations. The Council has been pushed along in this area by the General Assembly, the Commission, and the Sub-Commission. As late as 1969, the authors of the *Charter of the United Nations: Commentary and Documents* were able to say with confidence that 'the Council has recognized from the beginning that studies or reports involving field surveys or investigations within the territories of individual states can only be undertaken with the concurrence of the Governments concerned or upon their request.'[23]

The Council was asked in a number of instances to investigate allegations or reports concerning violations of human rights in specific states or territories and to recommend remedial action. The authors of the work mentioned above note that in 1949 the Council considered allegations of violations of trade union rights by a number of member and non-member States, but rejected a draft proposal making recommendations to those states. According to the authors, 'the Council has in such cases limited itself to stating its evaluations and making its recommendations in general terms without naming individual states.'[24] The early unwillingness of the Council to deal with complaints received from individuals or to consider specific situations of human rights abuses was again quite deliberate.

The first action of the Council to ensure against such a development was its decision that the members of its subsidiary bodies should be representatives of the states rather than individuals. The nuclear commissions established by the Council in 1946 to advise on the number of commissions of the Council

[22] GA Res.2081 (XX) (1965).

[23] Goodrich, Hambro, and Simons, *Charter of the United Nations, Commentary and Documents* (1969), 416.

[24] Ibid.

to be established, and to advise also on their composition and mandate, recommended with one exception (the nuclear social commission) that the Commission should be composed of members serving in a personal capacity. The nuclear commission concerned with human rights[25] stipulated explicitly that the commission should be composed of 'non-governmental representatives' or 'experts not bound by instructions of their respective governments'. It was agreed, however, that representatives could not be appointed by governments. The Council rejected this advice and provided instead for State representation. It made one concession. It agreed that representatives should not be appointed by governments. Rather, they were to be designated by governments 'after consultation with the Secretary-General' who would then notify the designated person to the Council 'for confirmation'.[26] The way was open in this procedure for the Secretary-General to protest at the choice of person or to indicate his views to the Council and it was certainly open to the Council to refuse to confirm a nominee. Neither the Secretary-General nor the Council seems to have taken action and, in effect, the designations of governments are now treated as appointments. This decision by the Council caused much unhappiness to outside supporters of the United States who saw in the decision a bad omen for the future.[27]

The nuclear Commission of Human Rights had put forward the view that the promotion and observance of human rights required by the Charter could be fulfilled only if provisions were made for the implementation as well as the promulgation of standards. The nuclear Commission suggested that pending the eventual establishment of an agency of implementation, the Commission on Human Rights should be recognized as qualified to aid the appropriate organs of the United Nations. The Council's response to this recommendation was to request the Commission 'to submit at an early date suggestions regarding the ways and means for the effective implementation of human rights and fundamental freedoms with a view to assisting the Economic and Social Council in working out arrangements for such implementations with other appropriate organs of the United Nations'.[28] Thus, it was immediately clear that the Council would not hand over responsibility for implementation to the Commission but would retain it in its own hands.

In the earlier years, the Council at times took a poor view of the Commission's wandering into fields not explicitly authorized by its terms of reference, and until the mid-1960s at least sought to keep its grip on the reins of the Commission.

[25] A body of 9 members acting in their personal capacity which met at Hunter College, New York, in Apr.–May 1946.

[26] Rule 12 of the *Rules of Procedure of the Functional Commissions of the Economic and Social Council*, E/5975/Rev.1 (1983).

[27] See e.g. Loveday, 'An Unfortunate Decision', 1 *Int'l Org.* 247 (1947).

[28] *UN Yearbook 1946/47*, 523–4.

III. REPORTS OF HUMAN RIGHTS ABUSES

At the first Session of the Commission in January/February 1947, the Commission considered what should be done about communications from the public alleging abuses of human rights. It was decided to propose to the Council that the Secretary General be asked to compile a confidential list of the communications received concerning human rights abuses before each session of the Commission, and to furnish this to the members of the Commission on request, enabling them to consult the originals; and that the Secretary-General be asked to inform writers that their communications would be brought to the Commission's attention. Such communications were to be reviewed by the Chairman and Vice-Chairman and the one or two co-opted members before each session of the Commission with the intention that they would bring the Commission's attention to selected communications. The Council received this proposal coolly, deferring consideration.[29] At the Council's Fifth Session in July/August 1947, the Commission's decision was taken up again. There was considerable discussion and several proposals and amendments were submitted. Although the greatest criticism came from Eastern European states, it is clear that other states also had certain doubts on the subject. Finally, the Council adopted Resolution 75(V) by 14 votes to 2 with 2 abstentions on 5 August 1947. In this, the first resolution on the question of how the UN should deal with communications it received on violations of human rights, the Council went out of its way to approve a statement contained in the report of the Commission recognizing that it (the commission) 'has no power to take any action in regard to any complaints regarding human rights'.

IV. DEVELOPMENT OF PROCEDURES FOR HANDLING COMMUNICATIONS CONCERNING HUMAN RIGHTS ABUSES

This first resolution of the Council dealing with a procedure for communications seems almost bureaucratic, a matter of simply deciding what to do with embarrassing pieces of paper. Not only was it established that the Commission itself would take no action on these pieces of paper, but it was also established that the pieces of paper themselves should be strictly confidential, so confidential that the Secretary-General was asked to compile a list of communications without divulging the identity of the authors. The Secretary-General was also instructed to reply to the authors 'where necessary' that the Commission had no power to take any action in regard to any complaint concerning human rights. It was this resolution which also estab-

[29] Ibid. 528.

lished an *ad hoc* committee to meet shortly before the Commission's session for the purpose of reviewing the confidential list of communications prepared by the Secretary-General and of recommending which of these communications should be made available to members of the Commission on request. A somewhat similar resolution (76(V)) was adopted by the Council in respect to the Commission on the Status of Women.[30]

The Council resolutions on procedures were drafted by the Commission itself, taking its cue from the Council's consideration of the recommendation of the United Nations Preparatory Commission and the Nuclear Commission on Human Rights. Council delegates discussing the draft procedures emphasized extreme caution, a view which was shared by all Western as well as Eastern European countries. The United States, New Zealand, and the Soviet Union were all in favour of *not* modifying the original procedure in Resolution 75(V). The United States representative in the Council thought, for example, 'that the impression should not be created that the Commission dealt with individual complaints as such or that it could be used as publicity for worthless facts or documents'.[31] The Council only slightly amended Resolution 75(V), in its Resolution 116A(VI) which allowed authors to be identified where they had already stated that they had divulged or intended to divulge their names or that they had no objection to their names being divulged. The same resolution gave the members of the Sub-Commission a role in dealing with communications.

The Council, prompted by the Commission, continued to review the procedures for communications in the 1940s and 1950s making only minor revisions. In 1955, the procedures were consolidated in a new resolution. Council Resolution 728F(XXVIII) reaffirmed that the Commission had 'no power to take any action in regard to any complaints concerning human rights'. It then went on to provide, unlike Resolution 116A(VI), that the Secretary-General should draw up confidential statistics of human rights by individual petitioners. The resolution did not envisage any action by the Commission; indeed, the Council contemplated that the Commission would take no action at all and went out of its way to rewrite a part of 75(V) in order to make it clearer to petitioners that the Commission could take no action on their complaints.

V. A CHANGE OF ATTITUDE IN THE COUNCIL

It was twenty years before the Commission was given authority to take any action on complaints received concerning human violations. In 1967, the Council, on the recommendation of the Commission, adopted Resolution 1235(XLII) which decided that the Commission could 'make a thorough

[30] See Chap. 7, below.
[31] *UN Yearbook 1947/48*, 579.

study of situations which reveal a consistent pattern of violations of human rights, as exemplified by the policy of apartheid'.

The reasons for this new attitude in the Economic and Social Council were, briefly, the changing composition of the United Nations, the process of de-colonization, and the development of a human rights conscience among Western nations. By 1967, the composition of the United Nations had changed considerably;[32] in particular, a large number of African countries had come to independence and, within the United Nations, had begun to campaign against apartheid. Apartheid was not an issue which had figured very prominently in the proceedings of the Commission, in part because the Africans themselves did not want it treated as a human rights question but as an internal matter for the South African government, a position also taken by those who opposed the placing of apartheid on the UN agenda. Indeed, the 1946 complaint by India to the General Assembly was handled as an interstate problem between India and South Africa and was not taken up in the Third Committee (Human Rights), but in the First (Political) and Sixth (Legal) Committees and later in the *Ad Hoc* (now Special) Political Committee. Today, the human rights rubric can make many things possible in the United Nations, but until the late 1960s, the possibility of action by the international community on specific human rights violations was so negligible as to discourage the Africans from seeking to have apartheid discussed in any substantial way as a human rights issue.

A large part of the reason for the failure of the conferees at Dumbarton Oaks and San Francisco to approve implementation powers in the human rights field stemmed from the nervousness of the Western Powers on the issue of race. By the mid-1960s Western members of the United Nations had divested themselves of many of their colonies and were less sensitive to the raising of racial discrimination. Western societies had become increasingly preoccupied by human rights issues and Western public opinion increasingly assertive (most strikingly in the United States). That interest extended to foreign issues, the discussion of which began to assume the language of human rights. The relative indifference of Western opinion to the civil war in the Congo at the beginning of the decade gave way to major debate on the rights and wrongs of the Biafran revolt in Nigeria at the decade's end. The same could be said in the case of South-East Asia. But the classic issue which marked out the new Western preoccupation with civil rights was apartheid.

It was, in fact, in 1967—the same year that the new procedure of Council Resolution 1235 was established—that for the first time the Commission on Human Rights proposed to establish an *Ad Hoc* Working Group of the Commission to consider violations of human rights in southern Africa. The Council accepted the proposal.

[32] There were 82 members of the UN in 1957. Ten years later there were 123.

It is important to note that Resolution 1235 did not involve action by the Commission on just any kind of human rights violations. It specified 'situations which reveal a consistent pattern of violations of human rights, *as exemplified by the policy of apartheid*'. The anti-apartheid campaign was, therefore, a spur to a more general development of the human rights role of the United Nations. Other spurs were the de-colonization movement, the Arab–Israeli conflict, and the Third World's efforts to concentrate the attention of the UN on its development problems. Through the influence of the Afro-Asians, the right to self-determination was at last not only acknowledged by Western countries but given priority in the two human rights Covenants adopted by the General Assembly in 1966. Two years later, there occurred the International Conference on Human Rights at Teheran which prompted a major effort by radical developing countries to reshape the human rights agenda, emphasizing anti-colonialism and economic development.

Arab interest in the possibility of action by the United Nations on human rights grounds did not develop significantly until the 1973 war in the Middle East. The Committee on the Inalienable Rights of the Palestinian People was established in 1975 to monitor the implementation of the major General Assembly Resolution 3236 (XXIX) adopted the previous year.[33] These resolutions were taken in Plenary by the Assembly rather than in the Third (Human Rights) Committee but they were couched mainly in human rights terms. The Arabs attempted, also in 1975, to equate Zionism with Racism. Indeed, General Assembly Resolution 3379 (XXX) does precisely that, but it has been abandoned at least for the present and the Arabs have pursued the racism angle more obliquely, though none the less persistently, since 1975.

Although these developments by no means covered all that was wrong with the world, or even all issues that were worthy of being addressed, and although their motivation was often ideological or political, they had wider consequences. In summary, the fact that by the 1970s many UN legislative organs were in the control of the developing countries may have allowed the Organization to develop a more active concern for human rights than was possible in the 1950s or even for part of the 1960s when action by the United Nations on human rights issues might have been interpreted as action in the political interest of the Western Powers, especially the United States. The argument on the issue of domestic jurisdiction, on whether action could be taken, receded. In its place came the argument on whether and how UN action could be strengthened or made more general and less political. The attention paid to apartheid and de-colonization, and later the Middle East, helped to make it possible for other cases to be raised, first Chile in 1974 and a large number of other situations more recently.

The Afro-Asian efforts were focused on the General Assembly and to some

[33] GA Res.3376 (XXX) (1975).

extent the Commission, rather than the Council. The reason for the focus on the Assembly is clear. It was the supreme body in the UN system, it had power in the system, it got the attention of the Western media, and the Afro-Asians, when they agreed, could control it by simple majority. By contrast, the power of the Council was restricted, the developed countries were over-represented in numerical terms, and it attracted little publicity. The Assembly consciously offered a focus within the system and made policy, often controversially, every autumn. The Afro-Asians established prestigious committees on Apartheid, De-colonization, and Palestinian Rights each of which reported direct to the Assembly, undercutting the Council's role and influencing its conduct of business by their own publicity-wise practices of sending telegrams, organizing visits, and calling for reports by special rapporteurs. The Council, on the other hand, delegated its powers, transferred its functions, and got lost in its own sprawl of activities. The beneficiary of the Council's policy or lack of one was the Commission. It was active. It was the main forum for the elaboration of the first human rights standards. And it had glamour, having included among its members over the years a significant number of internationally known personalities (Eleanor Roosevelt chaired its early sessions) and many other first-class minds.

VI. RECENT PROGRESS

The developments of the last twenty years require detailed examination of the Commission's work and are dealt with in chapter 5 below. While the Commission's actions have been the subject of heated debate in the Council, almost none of its decisions has been overturned. The only decision to have been vitiated, because the Council refused endorsement, was a decision by the Commission to make public the documentation relating to Albania under the 1503 resolution.[34]

Conclusion: Decline of the Council's Importance

There has been greatly increased interest in the human rights topic in recent years and in the bodies inside and outside the United Nations in which human rights are discussed. Academic research has also intensified, reflecting the coming into force of the two human rights covenants and other international instruments and the adoption of more determined methods within the United Nations to deal with abuses of human rights. There has been a certain amount of literature over the years on the proceedings of the General Assembly and the Commission; however, little attention has been paid to

[34] See CHR draft decision 2, proposed by CHR Res.1988/17.

the role of the Council. Whatever interest was once shown has diminished steadily over the years. No recent work has been published exclusively on the powers and functions of the ECOSOC in the human rights field.

There has been a double failure here: first, the failure of the Council to deal substantively with human rights issues; and secondly, its failure to relate human rights issues to the wider economic and social field. Conceptually, the debate on an integrated approach to human rights and on their importance in assessing development problems has passed the Council by. Operationally, the Council has made little effort to co-ordinate the work of the Commission on Human Rights with other bodies and agencies. Even within its own immediate domain, the Council has allowed itself to follow separate and independent tracks where human rights are concerned. Neither the Specialized Agencies nor the UN Secretariat have had much guidance from the Council in their attempts to place their human rights work in context, whereas the Assembly, the Commission, and the Sub-Commission have been vigorously urging particular views, although not always consistently. Some of the reasons for this bashfulness, or indifference, is that human rights questions are considered to be more immediately political than economic or social and have always fitted uneasily in the Council's ambit. Up until 1992 the economic specialists in the Council, who also occupy themselves with issues of co-ordination, worked for the most part in the Summer in Geneva; the human rights specialists worked entirely in the Spring in New York. There has been regrettably little contact between the two even when the former were constructing schemes for the regeneration of the Council. The problem is compounded by the separation, physical and philosophical, between the human rights secretariat in Geneva and the Council and economic secretariats in New York. Secretariat studies of the Council's problems and its recipes for better co-ordination of the economic and social fields are capable of omitting any useful reference to the Council's human rights role.[35]

The other part of the problem is that, because of the range of the economic and social programme of the UN, the Council has difficulty in even monitoring what its various subsidiary bodies and associated bodies and agencies are doing. This point is strongly emphasized in the 1986 report of the Group of 18 which contains many explicit and implicit criticisms of the Council's role to date. Whereas the General Assembly has three months and seven committees to exercise its monitoring functions, the Council has had three committees of partial membership each of them meeting for four weeks. The recent tendency of the Council to 'rationalize' its work by cutting down on its meeting time, by dispensing with reports, and by ignoring others altogether has saved time for everyone involved but has reduced the potential significance of the Council still further.

[35] See e.g. Hill, *The United Nations System: Coordinating its Economic and Social Work* (1978), and Bertrand, *Reporting to the Economic and Social Council*, J1U/REP/84/7 (1984).

In the recent past the only moment of glory for the Council has been the annual debate on the world economic situation which took place in July in Geneva. This debate was an echo of the economic responsibilities entrusted to the Council, which, over the years, have devolved upon two bodies in particular, the United Nations Conference on Trade and Development (UNCTAD) and, so far as the Charter responsibility of assistance to member States is concerned, the United Nations Development Programme (UNDP).

In addition, many other important bodies have been established subsequent to the creation of the Council. They include: the Office of the UN High Commissioner for Refugees, the UN Childrens Fund, the UN Fund for Population Activities, the World Food Programme, the World Food Council, the UN Environment Programme, and the UN Industrial Development Organization.

Thus the substantive work of the Council in the economic sphere has been parcelled out over the years to bodies which report to the General Assembly directly. Those bodies also report to the Council but it rarely offers serious comments in response, partly because of time restrictions. The decline of the Council has been emphasized again in very recent years by the holding of General Assembly Special Sessions and by the establishment of a Committee of the Whole of the General Assembly to discuss economic problems. There have been efforts to devise means of 'restructuring' or 'revitalizing' the Council so as to give it greater significance. The major resolution in this field during the 1970s, General Assembly Resolution 32/197 of 1977, attempted to reaffirm the role of the Council as a central forum for the discussion of international economic and social issues of a global or interdisciplinary nature, for the monitoring and evaluation of the implementation of overall strategies, policies, and priorities established by the General Assembly, for ensuring the overall co-ordination of the activities of the organizations of the UN system in the economic, social, and related fields, and for carrying out comprehensive policy reviews of operational activities in the system. These efforts resulted mainly in organizational changes in the Secretariat, changes in the presentation and distribution of documents, and changes in the calendar of UN conferences. Some of the changes effectively recognized the Council's diminished role by dispensing with debates on reports by associated bodies of the Council or by the Secretariat.

These changes have essentially been confirmed and strengthened by the reforms adopted in 1991 as a result of the lengthy and tedious discussions throughout the second half of the 1980s, on restructuring and revitalization.[36]

This brief indication of general developments in the Council's work shows the deterioration of its importance in the overall system. The Council has, however, not only lost out to bodies created to deal with specific problems which the Council felt it could not handle itself: it has suffered almost as

[36] GA Res.45/264 (1991), Annex. See generally E/1990/75.

much *vis-à-vis* bodies which are clearly subordinate to it and which report to it and *not* directly to the General Assembly. These are the bodies which were established by the Council in 1946 upon the recommendation of the nuclear commissions. They include the Statistical Commission, the Commission for Social Development, the Population Commission, the Commission on the Status of Women, the Commission on Narcotic Drugs, and, most notably, the Commission on Human Rights which, unlike the other Commissions, has regular annual meetings. The Commissions generally meet for two weeks, except for the Commission on Human Rights which meets for six weeks in full session. Working Groups of the Commission now meet for a further week prior to the full session. The Commission on Human Rights in particular has come to overshadow the Council in importance, especially in the last decade. The membership of the Commission is now 53, which compares with 54 for the Council. The present attendance at the Commission includes some 60 Observer States bringing the total number of States formally indicating attendance (not all actually attend) to well over 100, about two-thirds of the total United Nations membership. On any given day, the number of States represented as participants or observers at the Commission is likely to be greater, or even far greater, than the number attending the Session of the Council. Far more NGOs attend the Commission on Human Rights than attend the Council.

The Council has proved superfluous to the UN system for substantive purposes and has been unable to perform the co-ordinating role *vis-à-vis* other bodies and Specialized Agencies, envisaged in the Charter. The Council does have power of life and death over its own subsidiary bodies and also has disciplinary powers *vis-à-vis* various Agencies by the terms of their Agreements with the UN, but perhaps wisely the Council has chosen not to exercise these powers. For their part, the Specialized Agencies have shown little willingness to be co-ordinated by the General Assembly, let alone the Council, and the Council's efforts to promote any greater coherence in the system than exists at present have had little effect.

The Council was created without the small composition or the weighted voting of the Security Council: nor was it immediately given a large membership. It, therefore, fell between two stools. It did not engage the full responsibility of the major powers which, conceivably, might have been accomplished by giving them a stronger say in the Council's affairs. In economic discussions, States which were not members of the Council saw no reason to entrust their trade or other important interests to those that were. The result has been that, over the years, the new members of the United Nations, comprised mostly of developing countries, have viewed the Council as of little practical use for their purposes. The Council contained a relatively high proportion of Western members and it was soon clear to the developing countries that the General Assembly and other universal bodies, which could be influenced by the bloc voting of the Non-aligned Movement and the Group of 77 countries, offered much better prospects than the Council for steering the economic and social debate in a desired direction. These basic problems are not new. The Secretariat was already reviewing and reappraising the Council thirty years ago and the first alarms go back at least to 1951.[37]

It is doubtful if the Council will ever achieve the prompting, guiding, and co-ordinating role which has been mapped out for it in countless plans by delegates and secretariat officials over the years. It has all the characteristics of a holding operation. It has already been joined or superseded in status by bodies which are its offshoots, and the same may happen with others such as the Commission on Human Rights.

[37] See Loveday, 'Suggestions for the Reform of the United Nations Economic and Social Machinery', 7 *Int'l Org.* 325–41 (1953), and *Secretary-General's Report on the Council*, A/3109 (1965).

5

The Commission on Human Rights

PHILIP ALSTON

Introduction

Between its first session in 1947 and its forty-seventh in 1991, the Commission on Human Rights has undergone a profound transformation in terms of its role and functions within the international community. In the process, it has firmly established itself as the single most important United Nations organ in the human rights field, despite its subordinate status as one of several specialized ('functional') commissions answerable to the Economic and Social Council and, through it, to the General Assembly.

In the analysis that follows, consideration is given to the functioning of the Commission as well as to its evolving roles, including its activities in terms of standard-setting, monitoring, promotion, and conceptual development. The strongest emphasis, however, is on the protection role and the extent to which the Commission has succeeded in developing effective procedures for responding to violations. Moreover, since the evolution of the Commission's role cannot properly be understood unless its contemporary activities are situated clearly within their broader historical context, considerable attention is given to the historical record.

A. *The Commission's Mandate*

I. TERMS OF REFERENCE

While the details of the deeper historical antecedents of UN concern with human rights are beyond the scope of this chapter, a brief résumé is indispensable to an understanding of why strongly divergent expectations attended the birth of the Commission. The key issue with respect to the Commission's terms of reference was whether its mandate was to be *limited* and thus restricted to specified objectives or *general* and therefore open-ended.

Partly due to the determined lobbying efforts of non-governmental organizations, the San Francisco Conference in 1945 included a series of human rights provisions in the UN Charter. One concern of a number of delegations at the Conference was to secure the adoption of a declaration of rights. The main proponents were Chile, Cuba, and Panama and the last even went so far as to provide a draft 'Declaration of Essential Human Rights' which it wanted appended to the Charter.[1] These efforts were unsuccessful but there emerged from the Conference a clear expectation, as noted by President Truman in his closing speech, that the major task of the Commission on Human Rights, the establishment of which was provided for in the Charter, would be the drafting of an international Bill of Rights.[2] Similarly in his official report on the Conference, the Chairman of the US delegation expressed the view that the discussions at the Conference had been 'highly suggestive of the scope of its [the Commission's] possible activities'.[3] These included the drafting of an International Bill of Human Rights and of conventions on various specific subjects. The tenor of the report indicated a strong preference for a limited promotional role concentrating primarily on standard-setting rather than an open-ended protection role.

Subsequently, the Preparatory Commission which met in London in late 1945 to make provisional arrangements for the different UN organs, suggested that the work of the Commission should be directed towards:

(*a*) formulation of an international bill of rights;

(*b*) formulation of recommendations for an international declaration or convention on such matters as civil liberties, status of women, freedom of information;

(*c*) protection of minorities;

(*d*) prevention of discrimination on grounds of race, sex, language, or religion; and

(*e*) any matters within the field of human rights considered likely to impair the general welfare or friendly relations among nations.[4]

Through the inclusion of (*e*) in the proposed terms of reference the Preparatory Commission clearly envisaged a relatively open-ended, and thus politically active, mandate for the Commission. This was in accordance with the expectations not only of a number of States but of the large majority of contemporary academic commentators.[5] It should be noted, however, that this version of paragraph (*e*) could easily have been interpreted as reflecting a strong sense of deference to the assumption that the UN's human rights activities would be limited to matters which did not involve interference in the

[1] *Documents of the United Nations Conference on International Organization* (1945), vi. 545–9. This draft was subsequently referred by the General Assembly to the Commission for consideration: GA Res.43 (I) (1946).

[2] US Dept. of State, *Bulletin* (1946), xiii. 5.

[3] Quoted in Nolde, 'Possible Functions of the Commission on Human Rights', 243 *Ann. of the Am. Acad. of Pol. and Soc. Science* 150 (1946).

[4] *Report of the Preparatory Commission of the United Nations*, PC/20, chap. 3, sect. 4, paras. 14–16 (1945).

[5] Nolde, 'Possible Functions of the Commission on Human Rights'.

domestic affairs of states. But even with this implicit limitation the paragraph was deleted by the Council at its first session, thus providing the preparatory session of the Commission (the so-called 'nuclear' session) with only a limited mandate.

However, when the Nuclear Commission of nine members met at Hunter College, New York, in April–May 1946, with Eleanor Roosevelt as Chairman, it expressed a definite preference for an expansive approach. In its report to ECOSOC it advocated that the Commission be composed of independent experts and that it be given an open-ended mandate including a general brief not only to assist ECOSOC and the Assembly in their work but also to 'aid the Security Council in the task entrusted to it by Article 39 of the Charter, by pointing to cases where a violation of human rights committed in one country may, by its gravity, its frequency, or its systematic nature, constitute a threat to the peace'.[6] In some respects, this would have amounted to a restoration of the approach reflected in paragraph (*e*). The Nuclear Commission clearly expected the Commission to do much more than drafting; its vision was of a Commission endowed with a wide-ranging political mandate which would enable it to be truly effective in promoting 'universal respect for, and observance of, human rights'.[7] But this conception proved to be anathema to the governments represented in ECOSOC which, at its second session, in June 1946, promptly scrapped the proposals for an independent membership and for a role in dealing with violations constituting a threat to peace. However, perhaps by way of compensation, it agreed not to limit the mandate to the specific issues already listed, but to add a new version of paragraph (*e*), giving the Commission a role with respect to 'any other matter concerning human rights not covered by items (*a*) (*b*) (*c*) and (*d*)'.[8] Thus, after a lengthy battle, the Commission was endowed with a *general* mandate. In fact, the new provision was even more open-ended and susceptible to a broad and flexible interpretation than was the original proposal.

In reality, however, the first twenty years of the Commission's existence were to demonstrate that the *limited* conception of its mandate remained, for all intents and purposes, the dominant one. Before examining the Commission's interpretation in practice of its mandate it is relevant to note that several proposals have since been made to expand further the Commission's terms of reference but only one of these has been formally adopted. Thus in 1979 ECOSOC agreed that the Commission's mandate would henceforth include assisting it 'in the co-ordination of activities concerning human rights in the United Nations system'.[9] In 1967 the Commission failed to persuade ECOSOC to include in its terms of reference 'the

[6] E/38/Rev.1 (1946), 7.
[7] UN Charter, Art. 55(c).
[8] E/38/Rev.1 (1946), 7.
[9] ESC Res.1979/36.

power to recommend and adopt general and specific measures to deal with violations of human rights' without prejudice to the functions and powers of other organs.[10] But despite this refusal to take formal action, the same result was achieved anyway through the Council's adoption of resolutions 1235 (XLII) in 1967 and 1503 (XLVIII) in 1970 which had the effect of widening the Commission's effective terms of reference to enable it to deal with gross violations of human rights. In 1979 proposals to incorporate the concepts contained in General Assembly resolution 32/130 into the Commission's terms of reference failed even to reach the stage of a draft resolution in the Commission.[11]

II. THE COMMISSION'S INTERPRETATION OF ITS MANDATE

For the first twenty years of its existence the Commission struggled valiantly and successfully to avoid becoming an overtly political organ. Despite the significant human rights dimensions of the Cold War, the decolonization debate and many other matters being brought before the Assembly and the Security Council, the Commission managed to confine its efforts to standard-setting with a variety of other technical pursuits thrown in for good measure. In 1947 the Commission adopted its oft-criticized statement that it had 'no power to take any action in regard to any complaints concerning human rights',[12] thereby effectively removing itself from the front line of the vast majority of human rights-related political battles. The following year Eleanor Roosevelt, Chairman of the Commission at its first seven sessions, opined 'that the work of the Human Rights Commission should be directed for years to come' to the drafting of 'many conventions on special subjects'.[13] On this basis she saw the main purpose of the Commission's work as educational. Both of these trends were consistently upheld until 1967 when the Commission first began to tackle specific violations issues. As we shall see later in this chapter, the Assembly, ECOSOC, and the Trusteeship Council never felt constrained about debating specific alleged violations, provided only that a political majority was in favour of such action. Yet at no time were any of these issues formally debated in the Commission, nor did the Assembly or ECOSOC contemplate that they should be.

In fact the Commission played a role akin to that of the International Law Commission, albeit with a restricted mandate. Writing in 1969 John Humphrey (Director of the Human Rights Division from 1946 to 1965) conceded that there is 'some truth in the proposition' that 'the Commission

[10] CHR Res.9 (XXIII) (1967).

[11] See generally Quinn, 'The General Assembly into the 1990s', chap. 3, above, text accompanying nn. 69–73.

[12] E/259 (1947), paras. 21–2.

[13] Roosevelt, 'The Promise of Human Rights', 26 *Foreign Aff.* 475 (1948).

has been little more than a drafting committee for the General Assembly'.[14] Even in that role many of the most difficult political issues were resolved not by the Commission but by the Assembly. Indeed the Commission was so preoccupied with drafting the Covenants that: in 1948 it had no time to consider the draft Genocide Convention; in 1951 it was unable to take up the question of self-determination as the Assembly had requested it to do; and it was not until 1953 that the 1951 and 1952 reports of the Sub-Commission were considered by the Commission (despite, or perhaps also partly because of, the political battle which was then raging in the Assembly and ECOSOC over whether or not the Sub-Commission should be disbanded). Similarly, it is symptomatic that it was ECOSOC and not the Commission which absorbed the functions of two human rights bodies which were carried over from the days of the League of Nations: (1) the *Ad Hoc* Committee on Slavery; and (2) the International Penal and Penitentiary Commission which dealt with the treatment and conditions of prisoners. While it would seem natural for the functions of these bodies to have been given to the Commission, such an allocation of responsibility would not readily have been reconciled with efforts to keep it divorced from politics.

This historical review is revealing in so far as many commentators have failed to recognize that the Commission's non-involvement in concrete issues came about more by overall design than as a result of political manœuvring on the part of individual states or blocs. Its failure to take any action on communications and the ineffectiveness of its so-called 'promotional' activities are more readily understood in the light of the Commission's own perception that it could, and even should, be a technical rather than a political body. The foregoing review also serves to underline the significance of the Commission's gradual abandonment of its purportedly apolitical posture after 1967. Seen in this light, current criticism that the Commission's activities are too politicized represents either an attempt to take it back to the pre-1967 days of drafting (and avoiding or skirting around concrete issues) or a failure to see that a politically composed commission dealing with human rights must, if it is to be effective, work in an inherently political milieu.

This is not to argue that the Commission's twenty years of apolitical functionalism[15] were not justified at the time. As Humphrey has written:

> In adopting the conservative course which it did during the first two decades of its history the Commission probably followed the path of wisdom having regard to its terms of reference, the overriding constitutional authority of the Council and, above all, the great importance of the legislative work on which it was engaged.[16]

[14] Humphrey, 'The United Nations Commission on Human Rights and its Parent Body', in *René Cassin: Amicorum Discipulorumque Liber* (1969), i. 111.

[15] See generally Fatouros, 'On the Hegemonic Role of International Functional Organization', 23 *German YB Int'l L.* 9 (1980).

[16] Humphrey, 'The United Nations Commission', 111.

Indeed it is clear with hindsight that the basic drafting of the Universal Declaration of Human Rights, for which the Commission must take most of the credit and which took less than 18 months, would probably not be accomplished in as many years if the process were begun today.

B. *The Commission's Functions and their Evolution*

I. THE STANDARD-SETTING ROLE OF THE COMMISSION[17]

The drafting of international instruments in the field of human rights has been a continuous occupation of the Commission and its achievements in this regard are by no means confined to the first decade of its existence. Indeed, until the early 1970s standard-setting continued to be by far its most productive and enduring activity. Even in the early 1990s, it is apparent that the development of new standards in a range of specialized fields will continue to occupy much of the Commission's agenda for the foreseeable future, albeit through the work of subsidiary groups created for the purpose rather than in plenary session, as was the case with much of the drafting work carried out in the 1950s and 1960s.

In the space of only two sessions, in 1947–8, the Commission completed a comprehensive draft of the Universal Declaration, which was proclaimed by the Assembly less than six months later. By 1954, after a remarkably sustained and intensive drafting effort, the Commission had completed its drafts of the two Covenants and forwarded them on to the Assembly. Nevertheless, several of the most controversial political issues which arose during the Commission's deliberations on the Covenants during this period were left unresolved by the Commission and turned over to the Assembly to grapple with; thus beginning a practice which was to be repeated fairly frequently in the years ahead. These issues included decisions as to: (1) whether there would be two Covenants rather than one; (2) whether the right of self-determination would be included in the Covenants; and (3) whether a territorial or colonial clause would be included.[18]

But the Commission's effectiveness in preparing the first draft of the Covenants also came at the cost of its non-involvement in the drafting of an

[17] Two official sources are particularly informative as to the history of the Commission, and indeed the United Nations in general, in the field of standard-setting. They are: *Review of the Multilateral Treaty-Making Process* (1985), 177–216, and *United Nations Action in the Field of Human Rights* (1988), *passim*. In the analysis that follows, citations are not provided for individual instruments. They are contained in *Human Rights: A Compilation of International Instruments* (1988).

[18] See generally Bossuyt, *Guide to the 'Travaux Préparatoires' of the International Covenant on Civil and Political Rights* (1987).

important range of other human rights instruments during the same period. Thus, for example, the Convention on the Prevention and Punishment of the Crime of Genocide was adopted without a single comment having been made on the draft by the Commission. Several conventions relating to the rights of women were drafted by the Commission on the Status of Women, and subsequently adopted by the General Assembly, without any input even being sought from the Commission. Similarly, the Convention for the Suppression of the Traffic in Persons and of the Exploitation of the Prostitution of Others, adopted in 1949, was drafted solely by the UN Social Commission while the Supplementary Convention on the Abolition of Slavery was adopted in 1956 having been drafted by an International Conference set up by ECOSOC. In addition, the Commission was assiduously excluded from any role in the drafting of various instruments relating to freedom of information and freedom of the press. Between 1947 and 1954 these issues demanded considerable attention from the Council, from a UN Conference on Freedom of Information held in Geneva in 1948, and from the Commission's own Sub-Commission on Freedom of Information and of the Press. While a Convention on the International Right of Correction was adopted in 1952, these activities otherwise generated more controversy than positive results.[19] The Commission, however, was by-passed entirely on these issues, despite the fact that the Covenants that it was drafting dealt with some of the same issues. In sum, during most of its first decade, the Commission had neither the time, nor the political will, nor the responsibility for co-ordination, to be involved in many standard-setting activities of direct relevance to its mandate.

But if this exclusion had served to fuel any aspirations on the part of the Commission to be more actively involved in future standard-setting, they received a major rebuff in the early 1950s when it became apparent that powerful forces in the United States were becoming increasingly opposed to the principle of making human rights a matter of enforceable treaty obligations. In 1951 a 'sense of the Senate' resolution was proposed by Senator Bricker and others that condemned the draft covenant as being prejudicial to the rights already protected in the US Bill of Rights and urged the US government 'to withdraw from further negotiations with respect to the Covenant on Human Rights, and all other covenants, treaties, and conventions which seek to prescribe restrictions on individual liberty . . .'.[20] The proposed resolution was not acted upon, but the advent of the Eisenhower Administration in 1953 set the scene for a fundamental reversal of US human rights policy at the United Nations. In April 1953 Secretary of State Dulles, prompted at least in part by a desire to lay the proposed Constitutional

[19] In fact, the issue of a draft convention on freedom of information remained on the General Assembly's agenda from 1950 to 1980, without result. *See United Nations Action in the Field of Human Rights*, paras. 310–53, and Green, *The United Nations and Human Rights* (1958), 716–28.

[20] S. Res.177, 82 Cong. I Sess. (17 July 1951)

amendment known as 'the Bricker amendment' to rest, announced that the United States intended 'to encourage the promotion everywhere of human rights and individual freedoms, but to favor methods of persuasion, education and example rather than formal undertakings'.[21] He added that the US did not intend to become a party to the Covenants or to even submit them to the Senate for its consideration. The Covenants thus joined the 1948 Havana Charter for the establishment of an International Trade Organization[22] as another victim of US reluctance to adhere to an international agreement which it had strongly supported initially but which, in the process of negotiations, had assumed not only a different profile from that envisaged by its initiators, but also one which they found unattractive.

This repudiation of the entire concept of international human rights standard-setting on the part of the single most influential member of the United Nations did not deter the Commission from completing its work on the Covenants by 1954 but it did put a damper on other standard-setting activities during the remainder of the 1950s. There were two principal exceptions, however. In 1956 the French launched a strong, and ultimately successful, push to address the issue of asylum which had not been satisfactorily dealt with in the draft Covenants. By 1960 the Commission had completed a comprehensive draft Declaration on the Right of Asylum which it then sent on to the Assembly.[23] The latter took another seven years before finally adopting the draft. The Commission's only other major involvement in the 1950s concerned the draft Declaration on the Rights of the Child. It had received a completed draft from the UN Social Commission in 1951 but had done nothing at all until 1957 when it held a brief general debate on the draft and decided to seek further comments from governments.[24] It then devoted almost half of its session in 1959 to the revision of the draft[25] which was adopted later in the same year by the General Assembly. Of course both of these exceptions to the US policy according to which the Commission ought not to engage in further standard-setting took the form of non-binding declarations rather than treaties.

Two other standard-setting exercises which could easily have been undertaken by the Commission in the 1950s concerned discrimination in employment and in education. The need for new standards was identified in studies prepared for the Sub-Commission but the decision was wisely taken, espec-

[21] US Dept. of State, *Bulletin*, (1953), xxviii. 592. See also Kaufman and Whiteman, 'Opposition to Human Rights Treaties in the United States Senate: The Legacy of the Bricker Amendment', 10 *Hum. Rts Q.* 309 (1988).

[22] See generally Gardner, *Sterling-Dollar Diplomacy in Current Perspective* (1956), chap. 17.

[23] For the original decision of the Commission see CHR Res.V (XII) (1956). The principal work on the draft declaration is reflected in Report on the Sixteenth Session, E/3335 (1960), paras. 63–147.

[24] Report on the Thirteenth Session, E/2970/Rev.1 (1957), paras. 108–16.

[25] Report on the Fifteenth Session, E/3229 (1959), paras. 104–97.

ially since binding rather than hortatory standards were sought, to let the ILO and UNESCO respectively take the necessary steps. The results were ILO Convention (No. 111) Concerning Discrimination in Respect of Employment and Occupation, of 1958 and the Convention against Discrimination in Education adopted by UNESCO in 1960.

The period between 1961 and 1976 represented a decade and a half during which the Commission, in terms of standard-setting, initiated very little and in which its principal contribution was to act as a technical advisory body to the Assembly on a limited range of issues. Thus, at a time when the United Nations as a whole was making major progress in standard-setting, the role of the Commission was not particularly distinguished. Its first major exercise in the 1960s was to draft a declaration and a convention on the elimination of religious intolerance. It received a detailed draft from the Sub-Commission in 1960, held preliminary discussions in 1962, engaged in intensive drafting between 1964 and 1967, and then turned a radically incomplete draft over to the Assembly. There it languished until the Commission took it up again in 1974 at the Assembly's instigation.[26] It then took the Commission another eight years to complete the job, thus enabling the Assembly to adopt the Declaration on the Elimination of all Forms of Intolerance and of Discrimination Based on Religion or Belief.[27] The role of the Commission in the other major achievements of this period was limited although none the less important. And it spent a single session in 1963[28] revising a Sub-Commission draft that the General Assembly adopted later the same year as the Declaration on the Elimination of all Forms of Racial Discrimination. It spent most of its next session turning the Declaration into a Convention on the same subject[29] which the Assembly adopted in 1965 (having been unable to do so in 1964 because of a financial crisis). In these cases the Commission was drawing heavily upon work done by the Sub-Commission and was acting under explicit instructions from the Assembly. The emergent Third World majority in the Assembly ensured that there would be no political delays involved and the Commission was able to act with considerable speed.

When the General Assembly adopted the Covenants in 1966 it also added an Optional Protocol to the Covenant on Civil and Political Rights. The Protocol was proposed, debated, and adopted exclusively in the Assembly. Consultation with the Commission on the issue was apparently considered to

[26] See generally Claydon, 'The Treaty Protection of Religious Rights: UN Draft Convention on the Elimination of all Forms of Intolerance and of Discrimination Based on Religion or Belief', *12 Santa Clara Law* 403 (1972); and Clark, 'The United Nations and Religious Freedom', 11 *NYU J Int'l L. & Pol.* 197 (1978).

[27] See generally Sullivan, 'Advancing the Freedom of Religion or Belief through the UN Declaration on the Elimination of Religious Intolerance and Discrimination', 82 *Am. J. Int'l L.* 487 (1988).

[28] Report on the Nineteenth Session, E/3743 (1963), paras. 89–145.

[29] Report on the Twentieth Session, E/3873 (1964), paras. 16–288.

be unnecessary. In the case of the Convention on the Non-Applicability of Statutory Limitations to War Crimes and Crimes against Humanity, adopted by the Assembly in 1968, the Commission had worked on the initial draft between 1965 and 1967 but, having found itself deadlocked, had sent an incomplete draft to the Assembly.[30] The latter was left with considerable work to do on it in 1967 and 1968. In 1971, at the Assembly's request, the Commission began drafting a convention for the protection of journalists. The draft articles that it sent to the Assembly the following year[31] drew considerable fire in the Third Committee and, after several years of delay, there was relief all around when the matter was conveniently deemed to have been taken care of by the inclusion of the provisions of Article 79 of the 1977 Additional Protocol I to the 1949 Geneva Conventions.

The International Convention on the Suppression and Punishment of the Crime of Apartheid was adopted by the Assembly in 1973. Although a draft of the convention had been sent to the Commission by the Assembly for review, the former devoted only a very general discussion to it and made no real contribution to its final form.[32] Similarly, the Assembly adopted the Declaration on the Protection of all Persons from being Subjected to Torture and Other Cruel, Inhuman or Degrading Treatment or Punishment in 1975 without ever having referred the draft to the Commission. In the same year the Assembly did, however, request the Commission to take up work on the rights of detainees which it had begun in a different context as long ago as 1962.[33] The Commission immediately passed the task on to the Sub-Commission and approved its work without comment three years later.[34]

Thus, during this fifteen-year period the Commission proved its technical competence as a drafting body but was unable to resolve many of the difficult political issues that arose in the course of drafting the various instruments. As a result it was the Assembly, and not the Commission that: took the initiative in the great majority of cases; had to iron out the major problems; and, in several important instances, acted unilaterally. Moreover, the Commission came to rely quite heavily on the Sub-Commission either to prepare initial drafts or to do the entire job.

Starting in 1977 the Commission's standard-setting role entered a new, and ultimately very productive, phase. In that year the Assembly, which had chosen to ignore it in drafting the Declaration against Torture, chose the Commission as the preferred forum in which to draft a Convention on the same subject. Also, in 1978, the Polish government selected the Commission

[30] Report on the Twenty-Third Session, E/4322 (1967), paras. 135–85.
[31] Report on the Twenty-Eighth Session, E/5113 (1972), paras. 87–103.
[32] Ibid. paras. 37–48.
[33] See the Draft Principles annexed to the *Study of the Right of Everyone to be Free from Arbitrary Arrest, Detention and Exile*, E/CN.4/826/Rev.1 (1964).
[34] Report on the Thirty-Fifth Session, E/1979/36, paras. 184–6.

as the place to launch an initiative designed to produce a convention on childrens' rights. These initiatives resulted in the adoption of Conventions of major importance in 1984 and 1989 respectively. In each case virtually all of the drafting work was done by the Commission. Another major achievement during this period was the 1986 Declaration on the Right to Development. Although the Commission was nominally responsible for the preparation of the draft, all of the work was done by a Working Group of Governmental Experts set up in 1981, which in practice had rather little to do with the Commission. The Commission also set up Working Groups to draft declarations on minorities, the rights of human rights defenders and the rights of mental patients. While the latter two exercises are expected to result in declarations adopted by the Assembly by the end of 1993,[35] the first has moved at a notably unhurried pace with little enthusiasm being shown by governments for its completion.[36] In 1992 a working group to draft a declaration on disappearances will meet to continue the previous work done by the Sub-Commission.[37] In addition, efforts have been revived to persuade the Commission to consider the adoption of an optional protocol to the Torture Convention.[38]

Thus the Commission worked effectively in generating new standards throughout the 1980s, although it was still far from enjoying a monopoly in that regard. For example, the Assembly insisted on doing all of the work to draft the 1990 Migrant Workers Convention on its own, despite the background work that the Sub-Commission and Commission had done on the subject. The Assembly also played a major role in the drafting of the Second Optional Protocol (aimed at the elimination of the death penalty and adopted in 1989) and the Body of Principles for the Protection of All Persons under Any Form of Detention or Imprisonment (adopted in 1988). In addition, as demonstrated in the chapter on the Sub-Commission in this volume, that body continued to play an important role both as an initiator and as a drafter of standards.

In sum then the Commission has played a consistently important role in standard-setting although in this domain its relationship *vis-à-vis* the Assembly and the Sub-Commission has never been particularly clear. Moreover, the Assembly has, on occasion, retained an exclusive standard-setting role for itself or has permitted other bodies to perform the drafting of human

35 The Commission adopted the draft 'Body of Guidelines, Principles and Guarantees for the Protection of Mentally-Ill Persons' at its 1991 session, CHR Res.1991/46. For the text, see E/CN.4/1991/39.

36 For the situation as of Feb. 1991, see E/CN.4/1991/52 and Add.1. and E/CN.4/1991/53.

37 A draft declaration adopted by the Sub-Commission is contained in E/CN.4/Sub.2/1990/32.

38 It would, *inter alia*, provide for a system of visits to places of detention, based on a 'preventive and non-judicial system'. A sophisticated draft, prepared by various NGOs, was sent to the Commission in 1991 by Costa Rica. E/CN.4/1991/66.

rights instruments without any concern over the resulting exclusion of the Commission. If this were simply a matter of jurisdiction or institutional 'turf' it would be of little relevance. However, at a time when there is growing concern over the proliferation of new standards and well-justified fears that existing co-ordination mechanisms are inadequate in this regard,[39] the Commission's position is less than ideal. But the Assembly's reluctance to reduce its own room for manœuvre by giving co-ordinating authority to the Commission was underscored in a significant 1986 resolution in which it reaffirmed 'the important role of the Commission ... in the development of international instruments in the field of human rights' but could not resist inserting, after the word 'Commission', 'among other appropriate United Nations bodies'.[40] In the longer term, it is clear that the Council will never exert a co-ordinating influence in this domain and it seems equally unlikely that the Assembly will do so. Thus the Commission itself should be encouraged to assume that responsibility, at least in practice.[41] In the absence of such a development, the practice of forum-shopping, which states have so far pursued with considerable skill and determination in order to ensure that the desired standards are set by the forum which is most favourably disposed towards them, will continue to thrive.

In terms of quality it is difficult to assess the Commission's drafting work, especially in view of the diverse range of instruments involved and the peculiarities of each individual exercise. Some commentators (usually former participants in the process) have expressed great satisfaction with its work. A former British delegate, for example, praised the Commission's work as having 'been carried out with thoroughness and skill'.[42] Others have been far more critical.[43] One for example has focused particularly on what he considers to be the problems flowing from the Commission's preference for consensus decision-making.[44] But although the quest for consensus has indeed foiled many of the more radical and innovative initiatives, the Commision has not always been deterred by strong disagreements registered by influential States. It adopted the draft Universal Declaration over Soviet objections that it was

[39] See generally A/44/668 (1989), paras. 137–74.

[40] GA Res.41/120 (1986), para. 4.

[41] The Commission took a step in this direction in 1991 by asking that an inventory of all ongoing standard-setting exercises be drawn up. CHR Res.1991/20, para. 17.

[42] Hoare, 'The UN Commission on Human Rights', in Luard (ed.), *The International Protection of Human Rights* (1967), 92.

[43] Thus, for example, speaking on behalf of the members of the European Community when the Convention on the Rights of the Child was adopted, the French delegate observed that 'some members of the ... Community had noted some inadequacies in the process of negotiating the draft'. A/C.3/44/SR.36 (1989), para. 24. By contrast, the Secretary-General subsequently opined that 'the process of its drafting was a model of how our Organization can and should strive to achieve common goals'. A/44/PV.61 (1989), 8.

[44] Tolley, *The UN Commission on Human Rights* (1987), 136.

'weak, and in many ways, absolutely unsatisfactory'.[45] Similarly the draft Convention against Apartheid was approved despite implacable opposition by many Western States. More importantly, it should be noted that the quest to achieve a consensus has not always served only to promote a lowest common denominator approach. On many occasions it has been used as a means of pressuring recalcitrant states to agree to higher standards or at least to drop their previously implacable opposition to certain proposals, as is particularly well illustrated by the case of the Convention against Torture.[46]

Nevertheless, there are criticisms which can justly be directed at the Commission's performance. In brief, they concern: its failure to indicate some sense of priorities in terms of standard-setting; its complete neglect of human rights standards drafted by organs other than by itself or its Sub-Commission; the lack of any procedures, no matter how flexible, designed to promote efficiency and the availability of the necessary expertise during the drafting process; and the lack of any substantive role, at least since the 1960s, for the Secretariat,[47] thus leaving research etc. to the vagaries of the interests of individual delegations or interest groups. The Commission should therefore look carefully at its standard-setting procedures in future with a view to ensuring: a more careful choice of topics; a more thorough preparatory phase; a more realistic allocation of meeting time for the designated drafting groups; a more substantive role for the Secretariat; the preparation of far better *travaux préparatoires*; and a better system for keeping track of human rights drafting exercises being undertaken by other bodies.[48]

II. RESPONDING TO VIOLATIONS

All too frequently the sole criterion which is used for judging the performance and achievements of the Commission is the extent to which it has succeeded in responding to specific violations of human rights and providing a degree of protection to actual and potential victims. While there are strong grounds for insisting that the Commission's performance be judged on the basis of a much broader range of considerations, the reality is that its effectiveness in responding to violations remains the benchmark which the great majority of governments and other observers continue to use. Its record in this regard thus warrants very detailed scrutiny.

[45] A/PV.183 (1948), 923 (Mr Vyshynsky).

[46] e.g. Baehr, 'The General Assembly: Negotiating the Convention on Torture', in Forsythe (ed.), *The United Nations in the World Political Economy* (1989), 36.

[47] For a generous description of the role of the Secretariat during the drafting of the Universal Declaration, see Humphrey, *Human Rights and the United Nations: A Great Adventure* (1984); cf. Alston, 'Book Review', 6 *Hum. Rts Q.* 224 (1984).

[48] For an elaboration of these proposals, see A/44/668 (1989).

(a) *The Historical Evolution: An Overview*

Although it is tempting to evaluate the Commission's performance solely on the basis of recent developments, any such assessment is likely to be grossly distorted if it is not placed carefully in historical perspective. In brief, there have been three very distinct phases: (1) 1946–66, during which time the Commission was not prepared to address the issue of specific violations at all; (2) 1967–78, when the Commission struggled to evolve procedures which were initially designed to respond only to problems associated with racism and colonialism; and (3) 1979 to the present, when the procedures developed earlier have been applied in an increasingly creative and tailored fashion to an ever-widening range of countries and types of violations. Thus any meaningful evaluation must at least recognize these distinct phases and acknowledge that it is only in the present (third) phase that the member States of the United Nations have made any serious effort to respond to violations in a manner that at all purports to be objective and even-handed. Thus any evaluation of recent actions by comparing them with those of a decade or more ago is the equivalent of seeking to compare apples and oranges.

Before moving towards any form of evaluation it is necessary first of all to review each of the three historical phases, at least in broad outline.

(i) *1946–1966: Abdication of Responsibility* For twenty years, until 1967, the official and oft-repeated position of the Commission was that it had 'no power to take any action in regard to any complaints concerning human rights'.[49] The genesis of this 'doctrine' was a statement to that effect in the February 1947 report of the Commission's Sub-Committee on the Handling of Communications which was subsequently endorsed by both the Commission itself and by ECOSOC. Although the first draft of the Universal Declaration of Human Rights, compiled by the Secretariat earlier in 1947, had included the right of petition, that provision was deleted by the Commission's Drafting Committee[50] and did not appear in the Declaration as adopted by the General Assembly in December 1948.

The appropriateness of the 1947 doctrine was effectively called into question by the Secretariat itself in 1949 in a report which, *inter alia*, warned that the doctrine 'is bound to lower the prestige and the authority not only of the Commission' but of the United Nations as a whole.[51] The decision was

[49] ESC Res.75 (V) (1947).

[50] For an analysis of the debate, see Lauterpacht, *International Law and Human Rights* (1950), 244–51.

[51] *Report on the Present Situation with Regard to Communications Concerning Human Rights*, E/CN.4/165 (1949), 5. In that report the Secretary-General recommended that, in cases affecting very great numbers of persons or having international repercussions, the Commission after consultation with the government concerned should bring appropriate cases to the attention of the Council. The Commission effectively ignored the recommendation.

also roundly condemned by a number of prominent academics. The most uncompromising position was taken by the distinguished British jurist Hersch Lauterpacht who condemned the doctrine as constituting an 'extraordinary degree of... abdication' of the UN's proper functions.[52] In his view, UN organs, and the Commission in particular, 'are under a duty to receive petitions alleging violations of human rights, to examine them, and, on the basis of such examination, to take all requisite action short of intervention'.[53] Otherwise, he warned, the United Nations would fail in 'perhaps *the* crucial' aspect of its purpose. Although in one thirteen-month period in 1951–2, for which statistics are available, the Commission received more than 25,000 communications,[54] the token procedure embodied in resolution 75(V) was not further developed until 1967 despite recognition from time to time by all relevant UN organs that the situation was unsatisfactory.[55] Under the procedure, the Commission was simply informed, on a confidential basis and in the most telegraphic fashion, of the complaints that were being received, without any information as to the identity of the authors involved. No action of any description was taken as a result and the sole justification for the ensuing charade was that Commission members could gain a better idea of the sort of concrete problems existing in the world at any given time.

In 1959 the Council adopted resolution 728 F (XXVIII) consolidating a number of minor amendments which had been made to the procedure laid down in resolution 75 (V). Under the 728 F procedure the Secretary-General was required to compile a non-confidential list of all communications dealing with general human rights principles and a separate confidential list giving brief indication of the substance of other relevant communications. The latter list was furnished to all members of the Commission in private meeting and a copy of any communication referring to a particular state was sent to the government concerned which could, if it wished, submit a reply to the Commission. Although both resolutions 75 (V) and 728 F (XXVIII) suggested the establishment by the Commission of an *ad hoc* committee to review the confidential list, the Commission followed that practice only at two sessions prior to 1967.[56] It was clear even at the time when these arrangements were being made that the submission of a communication under these procedures was an exercise in futility, except in so far as the information contained in the communication had an educative effect on the members of the Commission. In any event, there is no question that this highly restrictive

[52] Lauterpacht, *International Law and Human Rights*, 236.

[53] Ibid. 230.

[54] Report of the Ninth Session, E/2447 (1953), para. 293.

[55] See Schwelb and Alston, 'The Principal Institutions and other Bodies Founded under the Charter', in Vasak and Alston (eds.), *International Dimensions of Human Rights* (1982), i. 271–2.

[56] The Ad Hoc Committee met only at the Commission's Second and Third Sessions. For a detailed history, see Zuijdwijk, *Petitioning the United Nations: A Study in Human Rights* (1982), 58–61 n. 81.

and unproductive procedure failed to do justice to the concerns and hopes of the tens of thousands who petitioned the United Nations annually. In the telling words of the official responsible for all of the Secretariat's assistance to the Commission at the time, the system became 'the world's most elaborate waste-paper basket'.[57] It also contributed significantly to a loss of credibility by the United Nations in human rights matters.

It must thus be asked why the Commission failed to concern itself with problems of human rights violations for the first twenty years of its existence? According to the author of the most exhaustive study of this issue '[i]t is not easy to explain' this inaction at a time 'when the Western bloc had a comfortable majority in the United Nations'.[58] But such a comment contains within itself the seeds of a compelling and accurate explanation. The Western bloc was anxious to ensure that the United Nations would not begin examining alleged violations, given the certainty that Western states would, and probably sooner rather than later, become the focus of such procedures. The United States, for example, was worried about the certainty of complaints alleging racial discrimination (already in 1947 the Commission had been sent a petition, said to be on behalf of 13 million American 'negroes', alleging such discrimination) while the United Kingdom, France, Belgium, Portugal and the other colonial powers feared complaints about conditions and practices in their colonies. The Western states were joined in an unacknowledged alliance by their Eastern European adversaries who opposed such a procedure, ostensibly on the grounds that it would involve a breach of Article 2(7) of the Charter. But underlying their opposition was a clear sense that some of the more brutal dimensions of Stalinism and even the very ideology of Marxism–Leninism would probably be priority targets for any adversarial international complaints procedures. As a result, initiatives taken at various times in different organs by states such as Egypt, India, and the Philippines to establish some form of general human rights petition procedure, were to no avail.

In addition to this unholy alliance, there were other arguments which could be used to justify the Commission's inaction. The first, which was not articulated at the time but tends to make some sense in retrospect, is that specific violations could be, and actually were being, dealt with by other UN organs during this period. Indeed, at the same time that the major specialist human rights organ was repeatedly proclaiming that it had no power to act on violations, its superior organs, the General Assembly and ECOSOC, were deeply immersed in a wide range of highly controversial human rights issues. Thus for example in 1949 ECOSOC set up its own *Ad Hoc* Committee on Slavery and two years later it appointed a joint UN/ILO *Ad Hoc* Committee on Forced Labour. Similarly the General Assembly dealt with issues such

[57] Humphrey, 'The United Nations Commission', 110.
[58] Zuijdwijk, *Petitioning the United Nations*, 14.

as racial discrimination in South Africa (taken up in 1946), violations of human rights in Bulgaria, Hungary, and Romania and the continued holding of prisoners of war, especially in Eastern Europe. In 1963 the Assembly appointed a fact-finding team (composed of seven governmental representatives) to investigate alleged violations in South Vietnam. In the event, its detailed report was not acted upon in the wake of the overthrow of the government concerned.[59] Even individual cases were taken up on matters such as: the Soviet wives of foreign nationals (1947–9); death sentences passed by a Greek military tribunal on the leaders of a seamen's union (1948–9); and the Spanish strikers sentenced to death by a military tribunal (1951–2).

Another reason sometimes cited to justify the Commission's inaction, and one which was strongly supported by René Cassin, the French delegate who was among the Commission's staunchest defenders of human rights, was that the Covenants, when adopted, would provide the desired avenue for redress.[60] In the mean time, it was argued, nothing should be done to jeopardize or inhibit progress with respect to their drafting. The validity of this argument is difficult to accept, however, given the avowed determination of the United States at that time never to ratify the Covenants and the unlikelihood of any significant proportion of the UN's membership agreeing to any treaty-based complaints procedures for many years to come. Indeed, with hindsight, we now know that almost forty years after this argument was first put forward less than one-third of the UN's member states have ratified the Optional Protocol.

But while it is tempting to criticize the Commission, even perhaps unreservedly, for its abdication of concern with violations during this period, it must be conceded that, at least up until 1954, the Commission's drafting work had a strong, if not absolute, claim to priority. It can be convincingly argued that simultaneous efforts to draft pioneering, norm-entrenching instruments and to respond to country-specific violations would only have produced a counter-productive and even destructive result. Nevertheless, after 1954 this argument loses much, if not all, of its force. Thereafter, the real barrier, as noted above, was the existence of a political consensus on the part of a majority in the Commission and ECOSOC not to open the floodgates. By the mid-1950s this policy amounted to a simple abdication of responsibility, since it had no foundation in either the Charter or the Commission's terms of reference. Rather it was the product of a rare agreement on the part of the major powers at a time when their combined voting strength was almost beyond challenge.

(ii) *1967–1978: A Gradual Assumption of Responsibility* By the mid-1960s several developments coincided to produce a climate in which a breakthrough

[59] A/5630 (1963).
[60] Zuijdwijk, *Petitioning the United Nations*, 4.

was achieved and the 1947 doctrine was abandoned. First and foremost was the dramatic change in the composition of the major UN organs as a reflection of the influx of new members, mainly newly independent Asian and African States. In 1961 ECOSOC had enlarged the membership of the Commission from its original 18 to 21 but this made little difference in policy terms. However, in 1966 ECOSOC decided that, as of the following year, membership would be increased to 32 (20 of which would come from the Third World).

Another important development was the adoption of the Convention on the Elimination of All Forms of Racial Discrimination (CERD) in 1965 which included provision, in Article 14, for the submission of complaints by individuals or groups against States which accepted the procedure. This development was intimately linked with the emergence of the new Third World majority and the preparedness, indeed determination, of that majority to make racism a major concern and to develop whatever procedures might be necessary in order to combat it. In any such endeavours they were virtually assured the support of the Eastern Europeans who were happy to encourage attention to what were assumed to be quintessentially Western sins. By the mid-1960s they also had a significant (but by no means unqualified) degree of support from an American government which had committed itself to the implementation of civil rights domestically and had nominated black Americans to both ECOSOC (Clyde Ferguson) and the Sub-Commission (Beverly Carter). The willingness of the Third World majority to develop new procedures applied even though there was a significant 'risk' that the scope or reach of the procedure might eventually be extended to address problems other than racism.

The adoption of the CERD complaints procedure cleared the way for an Optional Protocol to the Covernant on Civil and Political Rights to be adopted the following year. It too enabled complaints to be brought against States Parties. These two procedures, even though they were not to bear much fruit for another couple of decades and would in any event apply only to the small number of ratifying states, constituted very important breakthroughs in terms of the principles involved, particularly that of accountability.

The most significant development, however, was a decision by the Third World countries, strongly supported by the Eastern Europeans, that a general, non-treaty-based communications-type procedure would be useful as an additional means by which to pursue the struggle against racist and colonialist policies, particularly in southern Africa. The Trusteeship Council had long made effective use of a petitions procedure (based on 87 (b) of the Charter). The acceptance of communications from organizations and individuals and the conduct of hearings had also become accepted as appropriate practice in the work of the UN Commission on the Racial Situation in South Africa, and its successor, the Special Committee on the Policies of Apartheid of the

Government of the Republic of South Africa.[61] It was on the initiative of the Special Committee on Decolonization, in 1965, that the attention of the Commission was drawn to petitions alleging human rights violations in southern Africa. The following year ECOSOC accordingly invited the Commission to consider urgently the question of the violation of human rights, including policies of racial discrimination and segregation and of apartheid in all countries, with particular reference to colonial and other dependent countries and territories, and to submit its recommendations on measures to halt those violations.[62] In the Commission the view prevailed that an artificial restriction of such a mandate to only a single category of countries was not justified. As a result, the ambiguity of the Commission's original mandate was resolved by a General Assembly request that it give urgent consideration to ways and means of improving the capacity of the United Nations to put a stop to violations of human rights *wherever they may occur*.[63] This latter phrase was to prove to be of vital importance, despite the clear desire of most of the resolution's key proponents to confine the focus to racist and colonialist situations.[64]

These developments resulted in the adoption of what eventually turned out to be two separate procedures. The procedure established under ECOSOC Resolution 1235 (XLII) established the principle that violations could be examined and responded to, and provided the necessary authorization for the Commission to engage in public debate on the issue each year. The procedure under ECOSOC Resolution 1503 (XLVIII) provided a carefully and deliberately constrained procedure by which situations which appear to reveal 'a consistent pattern of gross and reliably attested violations of human rights' could be pursued with the governments concerned, but in private.

The details of these procedures, as well as information on how they have functioned in practice, are provided below.[65] For present purposes it is sufficient to note that both procedures generated considerable controversy and engendered high hopes while actually accomplishing relatively little during their first decade in operation. The inevitable teething problems involved in taking procedures which had been established on the basis of a hotchpotch of competing aspirations and transforming them into flexible and effective tools for inquiry and assessment, backed by at least a minimum of political will, were to take up almost all of the 1970s.

[61] See generally Ozgür, *Apartheid: The United Nations and Peaceful Change in South Africa* (1984).
[62] ESC Res.1102 (XL) (1966).
[63] GA Res.2144 A (XXI) (1966).
[64] e.g., the Tanzanian iniatives during this period, described in Zuijdwijk, *Petitioning the United Nations*, 22–4.
[65] See text accompanying nn. 67 and 68, below.

(iii) *1979 to the Present: Evolution Towards an Effective Response* It was not until more than a decade had elapsed after the adoption of the 1235 procedure that a convergence of factors facilitated the next quantum leap in United Nations practice in response to violations. This took the form of: a more active and (albeit minimally) more public approach to the 1503 confidential procedures; increasing acceptance that confidential consideration did not preclude public consideration with respect to any given State; and a substantially expanded range of fact-finding activities. Unlike 1967 when the impetus had come primarily from a change in the composition of the Commission and ECOSOC, the developments in the late 1970s were environmental. The Commission had excelled itself in 1976–7 by a failure to act publicly with regard to horrendous violations in Pol Pot's Democratic Kampuchea, Amin's Uganda, Bokassa's Central African Empire, Macias' Equatorial Guinea, the military's Argentina and Uruguay, and several other situations. Thus a 1976 investigation by the (London) *Sunday Times* concluded that the Commission worked 'in almost total secrecy' and had deliberately constructed 'a bureaucratic and procedural maze' as a result of which 'delay has been institutionalized and the aim has not been to protect the victims but the oppressors'.[66]

But the developing consciousness of public opinion (almost by definition among the élites in the West and a limited number of Third World countries), combined with the higher profile given to human rights issues by the Carter Administration and several of its allies contributed to a climate in which task expansion was almost an imperative. That the West was prepared to take the initiative, despite the fact that many of its 'allies' were among the worst offenders, facilitated the mobilization of majorities in favour of action. Inevitably, it also resulted in an imbalance in the range of states against which action was taken. The demise of *détente*, especially after the Soviet invasion of Afghanistan, will probably facilitate a correction of that imbalance. A final but somewhat intangible factor in the Commission's expansion of focus was the more assertive advocacy role played by the new executive head of the Secretariat responsible for servicing the Commission between its 1978 and 1982 sessions.

In order to put post-1979 developments in perspective it is necessary to trace the evolution of the principal procedures through which these achievements have been accomplished. We therefore turn to an in-depth review of the 1503, 1235, and 'thematic' procedures.

(*b*) *The 1503 Procedure*

Although the 1503 procedure had its origins in the efforts begun in the late 1940s to give substance to the right to submit a petition to the United Nations

[66] Shawcross, Terry, and Pringle, 'Human Rights, A Conspiracy to Oppress', *Sunday Times* (14 Mar. 1976), 24.

in order to seek redress of human rights violations, it is not properly called a 'petition-redress' procedure since it offers no solace, or redress, to individual victims. It is better characterized as a 'petition-information' system[67] because its objective is to use complaints as a means by which to assist the Commission in identifying situations involving 'a consistent pattern of gross and reliably attested violations'. In that sense, an individual victim is but a piece of evidence whose case might, if accompanied by a sufficient number of related cases, spur the United Nations into action of some kind.

In numerical terms the United Nations has never had problems attracting complaints about the behaviour of governments. This has remained true despite various efforts to discourage their submission.[68] Even in the late 1940s and early 1950s, when the complaints were virtually ignored, annual figures of 20,000 or so appear not to have been uncommon. From the time when the 1503 procedure began functioning (in 1972) until the mid-1980s an average of 25,000 complaints were received annually. In 1988 and 1989 the numbers rose to 200,000 and 300,000 respectively.[69] Although much of the increase is due to well orchestrated letter-writing campaigns involving a handful of situations, the numbers still attest to a significant awareness of the procedures combined with an apparent faith, on the part of at least a few groups, in their potential effectiveness.

In the first seven years of its existence the procedure evolved significantly beyond the terms of the authorizing resolution. Those innovations were formally reflected by the Commission in the arrangements adopted in 1978.[70] In broad terms therefore the procedure currently consists of the following four steps. Firstly, the Communications Working Group of the Sub-Commission begins the procedure by sorting through the various complaints that have been received in the preceding year. The group consists of five Sub-Commission members and each takes primary responsibility for complaints dealing with a specific cluster of rights. Thus, for example, the politics of the situation apparently required that the Eastern European group (invariably represented by the Soviet expert) take the lead on all complaints relating to the right to leave and return. The Group required an affirmative majority vote before any 'situation' could be forwarded on to the Sub-Commission in plenary. The resolution itself provides any number of potential justifications

[67] See generally Tardu, 'United Nations Response to Gross Violations of Human Rights: The 1503 Procedure', 20 *Santa Clara L. Rev.* 561 (1980).

[68] The most public instance of such discouragement was the decision taken by the then Secretary-General in 1969 to direct UN Information Offices around the world to discontinue the long-standing practice of receiving such complaints and forwarding them to the UN Secretariat. The decision resulted from Soviet pressure but was no doubt welcomed by many other governments as well. See Lillich, 'The UN and Human Rights Complaints: U Thant as Strict Constructionist', 64 *Am. J. Int'l L.* 610 (1970).

[69] E/1990/50, para. 49.

[70] Möller, 'Petitioning the United Nations', 1 *Univ. Hum. Rts.* 69–70 (1979).

for not taking action on a given situation. Thus, for example, rejection of a complaint is justifiable in any of the following cases: it is anonymous; 'clear evidence' is lacking; it is deemed to be 'essentially abusive' in its entirety; it is prompted by 'manifestly political motivations'; it is 'based exclusively on reports disseminated by mass media'; if potentially viable domestic remedies have not been exhausted or if it is submitted too long after they have been; if a 'consistent pattern' is not established; or if the violations are not 'gross'.

In recent years the Sub-Commission's Working Group has sent its parent a list of about eight to ten countries a year on average. It might also identify a few situations for specific consideration the following year, thus implicitly serving notice on the governments concerned. At the second stage, when the full Sub-Commission considers each of its Working Group's 'nominees', it opts by a simple majority vote to send the country on to the Commission, to drop it, or to reconsider it the following year. While the complainant is not informed at this stage, the government concerned is invited to submit written observations and to defend itself before the Commission, thus creating a clear inequality of opportunities to participate in the proceedings. As the third stage of the procedure the Commission also establishes a Communications Working Group.[71] Its task is to draft recommendations as to the action which the Commission might wish to take on each country situation that is put before it. At the fourth stage the Commission itself devotes several days at each of its annual sessions to a consideration of all the relevant material. At the end of its deliberations its Chairman announces the names of the countries that have been considered and the names of those that have been let off the hook. He or she does not, however, provide any details as to the nature of the allegations or the specific action taken by the Commission. As to the latter, several options are available—in addition to dropping the case altogether. The first is to keep it 'under review' which means that more evidence will be admitted next year and the government concerned will be called to account again. It also provides an incentive for at least cosmetic measures to be adopted and for strong lobbying to be undertaken in the meantime. The second option is to send an envoy to seek further information on the spot and report back to the Commission. The third is to appoint an *ad hoc* committee which, with the approval of the state concerned, can conduct a confidential investigation aimed at finding a 'friendly solution'. The Committee then reports to the Commission 'with such observations and suggestions as it may deem appropriate'.[72] This procedure has, as of the end of the 1991 session, never been invoked. The fourth and final option is for the Commission to transfer the case to the 1235 procedure, thereby going public and permitting 'a

[71] Its composition is regionally balanced. In 1991, for example, members were from the Federal Republic of Germany, Bulgaria, Peru, China, and Morocco.

[72] ESC Res.1503 (1970), paras. 6(b) and 7.

thorough study by the Commission and a report and recommendations thereon to the Council'.[73] The role of the Council in this respect has so far proved to be absolutely minimal.[74]

Thus, in the absence of a decision to go public, the entire procedure is shrouded in secrecy, with each of its stages being accomplished in confidential sessions by the bodies concerned. Nevertheless, the details have invariably been leaked to the media for one reason or another and the complete documentation on several country situations has been made available as a result of Commission decisions to release all the relevant documentation in cases concerning Equatorial Guinea, Uruguay, Argentina, and the Philippines.

In statistical terms, the 1503 procedure has 'touched' an impressive number of countries. On the basis of unofficial sources it seems that at least forty-five countries have been reported to the Commission under the procedure since 1972. More authoritatively, however, it can be said that since the Commission began to officially identify the situations before it, in 1978, thirty-nine States have been subject to scrutiny as of the end of the 1991 session.[75] Of these, twelve were in Africa, twelve in Asia, twelve in Latin America, two in Eastern Europe, and one in Western Europe.

Before seeking to evaluate the procedure, it is essential to review the often skimpy concrete evidence that is in the public domain. It can be said at the outset, however, that most of the available snapshots provide few grounds for optimism as to the procedure's effectiveness. Thus, for example, the first attempt to put specific situations on the Commission's 1503 agenda, in 1972, rapidly became bogged down at the level of the Sub-Commission which was loathe to act on its own Working Group's recommendation that the focus be on Greece, Iran, and Portugal. The choice of such a list served to put those who had championed the 1503 procedure, in the hope that it would become a potent tool in the struggle against racism and colonialism, quickly on notice that the procedure could equally well be applied to other offenders. While one of three was a colonial power and another was from the Western group, the latter case involved the sort of violations of which many of the Third World regimes might equally stand accused, if not today perhaps tomorrow. Establishing such a precedent, especially right from the outset, would not augur well. In addition, the other accused State was actually from the Third World, thus indicating that the racists and imperialists might not be able to monopolize the spotlight as had been hoped by many of the procedure's

[73] Ibid. para. 6(a).

[74] Although in 1988 the Council refused to act on the Commission's recommendation that the 1503 material concerning Albania should be made public in view of the government's non co-operation. CHR Res.1988/17.

[75] These are listed by Tolley, *The UN Commission on Human Rights*, for the period 1973–9 (p. 77) and the period 1978–86 (p. 128). Between 1987 and 1991 the following additional countries were examined: Brunei, Chad, Grenada, Honduras, Iraq, Myanmar, Somalia, Sudan, and Syria.

original sponsors. The Sub-Commission decided to do nothing for a year so that the governments concerned might be given more time to respond to the allegations if they so wished. The International Commission of Jurists deplored this decision and, in the diplomatic language of the day, accused the Sub-Commission of being 'affected by undue regard for the susceptibilities of governments'.[76] The subsequent fate of at least one of these cases, that of Greece, is particularly well documented.[77] In brief the Sub-Commission managed to defer any action until 1974, by which time the military government had been overthrown.

Another notorious case in the early years was that of Uganda under President Idi Amin. In 1974, confronted by allegations that Amin had killed 75,000 people since coming to power in 1970, the Sub-Commission placed the case on the Commission's agenda. But because Amin was then chairman of the Organization of African Unity, he had little difficulty in mobilizing the support needed to have the case struck off the Commission's agenda. Although Uganda was again placed on the list, it was not until 1978 that the Commission finally sought to send an envoy to Amin, still on a confidential basis. But before this could have any effect Amin had been overthrown after an invasion by Tanzanian troops.[78] Among the many troubling aspects of this case was the fact that a brutal regime had managed, by virtue of playing the 1503 game, to keep its case off the Commission's public agenda over a four-year period. Another case in respect of which the relevant documentation is now available is that of Uruguay which was on the Commission's 1503 list from 1978 to 1985.[79] Human rights NGOs had reported thousands of cases of arbitrary arrest and torture, a significant number of disappearances and deaths and the 'destruction of the rule of law'.[80] The first violation to be found by the Human Rights Committee under the Optional Protocol had concerned the treatment of a detainee in Uruguay.[81] The Committee began consideration of the case in August 1977.

Faced with an imposing dossier of allegations, the Commission requested the then Secretary-General (Waldheim) to undertake a direct contacts mission to investigate prison conditions. He appointed Javier Pérez de Cuellar (later to become UN Secretary-General) as his envoy. Pérez de Cuellar's report was soon leaked to the press and provides a dismal insight into the type of fact-finding reports that can be produced when the glare of publicity is eliminated

[76] 'Disappointing Start to New UN Procedure on Human Rights', 9 *Int'l Commission of Jurists Rev.* 5 (1972).
[77] Lillich and Newman, *International Human Rights* (1979), 318–87.
[78] For details, see Guest, *Behind the Disappearances: Argentina's Dirty War against Human Rights and the United Nations* (1990), 440–1.
[79] Consideration was terminated by CHR Dec. 1985/107 and ESC Dec. 1985/139.
[80] E/CN.4/R.27 (1977), para. 3(f).
[81] *Report of the Human Rights Committee*, A/34/40 (1979), Annex VII, Communication No. R.1/5.

in the context of human rights procedures. It is: aridly descriptive; openly predicated on the assumption that respect for, and co-operation with, the government is the principal ground rule for the mission; determinedly unprobing; apologist in its emphasis on the 'justifications' cited by the government; and entirely at odds with authoritative reports by the International Committee of the Red Cross and other groups in concluding blandly that prisoners were being held 'under normal detention conditions'.[82] In the view of one commentator this episode showed that the 1503 procedure had turned 'dialogue' into an end in itself. '"Dialogue", to the United Nations, meant "cooperating", and cooperation brought its reward: the case stayed confidential. If it felt under any pressure, an astute government could always introduce minor changes and present them as "improvements". There was endless room to maneuver for clever diplomats . . .'.[83] In the event the Commission, instead of appointing a Special Rapporteur as had been proposed, accepted an Argentinian amendment to maintain direct contacts with the government. But in doing so it also gave the thumbs down to Pérez de Cuellar's report by noting that it had 'been helpful to the Commission in elucidating the views of the Government'[84]—a function which it had hardly been intended to achieve.

Another major failure of the 1503 procedure which has recently been documented in great detail is that of the disappearances in Argentina during the 1970s and early 1980s. At the first try, in 1977, the case failed to get past the Sub-Commission's Working Group. The following year it reached the Sub-Commission but went no further. By 1979 the situation was so grave that the Commission began to seek a public response under the 1235 procedure even though the case had still not reached it under 1503. The latter event occurred in 1980 and it remained on the 1503 agenda until 1985.[85] Following an exhaustive assessment of the procedure in the case of Argentina, Iain Guest concluded that it had, if anything, been positively harmful to the cause of those wishing to put an end to the continuing violations under the military government.[86] This resulted primarily from the ready availability of opportunities to manipulate the procedure at each stage.

In concluding this review of some specific country studies, it must be conceded that the range of 1503 cases in respect of which public documentation is available is not only limited but now also somewhat dated. In recent years, however, the record would not appear to be much better. In the late

[82] E/CN.4/R.50/Add.2, 11. See extracts from the report in Guest, *Behind the Disappearances*, 420–3.

[83] Ibid. 492 n. 21.

[84] 'Confidential Decision Relating to Uruguay', E/CN.4/R.64 (1980), 14, 2nd pream. para.

[85] Subsequent to the election of the Alfonsin government in 1983 the case was terminated under 1503 in 1985 'in view of the full restoration of human rights' in Argentina. ESC Dec. 1985/156.

[86] Guest, *Behind the Disappearances*, 117–19 and 440–1.

1980s and in 1990 NGO observers have tended to be highly critical of the results obtained (or, rather, not obtained) by the procedure, both in general, and in specific cases such as China, Iraq, Somalia, Syria, Zaire, etc.[87]

The experience gained with the 1503 procedure over almost twenty years is sufficient to enable some general observations to be made about it. With respect to the range of situations taken up it appears that: (*a*) alleged violations of economic, social, and cultural rights have never been examined seriously, despite a resolution by the Commission urging that they should be;[88] (*b*) the Commission has responded to violations of only a limited range of civil and political rights, which in turn has ensured that while Third World countries are disproportionately represented on the 1503 blacklist, developed countries (both West and East) have only very rarely been called to account;[89] (*c*) there is probably a *de facto* limit of 6 to 8 on the number of countries that the Commission is prepared to take on at any one time, but since a similar principle applies to the public country-specific procedures 1503 effectively doubles the number of countries that can be 'named'; (*d*) despite the focus on 'situations' some individuals have been directly assisted under the procedure; and (*e*) many of the situations dealt with under the Commission's public procedures have been raised earlier in the 1503 context.[90]

With respect to the actual functioning of the procedure it is clear that some of the early wrinkles were effectively ironed out in the course of the first decade. In particular, the relationship between the public and private procedures, which was often invoked in an effort to confine discussions to the latter domain in the 1970s,[91] was resolved in such a way as to make it clear that only the proceedings themselves and the details of decisions taken were confidential. There is thus no bar to focusing on the same country in both procedures at the same time. Nevertheless, the procedure is designed to move extremely slowly and deliberations are, as a result, too often based on outdated information. As one Filipina activist put it, use of the 1503 procedure to put pressure on the Marcos regime 'was not done with any illusion that immediate specific relief would be forthcoming'. Rather, it 'was used simply as another device to generate adverse propaganda against' the regime.[92] Another criticism of the functioning of the procedure concerns the

[87] e.g. Int'l Service for Hum. Rts, 4 *Hum. Rts. Monitor*, 38 (1989): '[T]his year, the procedure was more than abused—it was quite deformed'; and International Commission of Jurists, 44 *The Review* 25 (1990): 'The Commission once again failed even to consider action regarding some of the worst situations.'

[88] CHR Res.5 (XXXIII) (1977), para. 2.

[89] The rare exceptions are Albania, the German Democratic Republic, and Turkey.

[90] Nevertheless, the nature of the relationship between these two developments is often murky at best. Thus, public debate has sometimes only begun after no effective action has been taken in private. Cf. Bossuyt, 'The Development of Special Procedures of the United Nations Commission on Human Rights', 6 *Hum. Rts L. J.* 184 and 202–3.

[91] See Zuijdwijk, *Petitioning the United Nations*, 43–54.

[92] Yorac, 'Case Study: The Philippines' (mimeo., 1988).

Commission's apparent failure to structure its working methods under 1503. Consequently, the response in one situation will often bear little relationship to that adopted in another generally comparable one. While no two situations are identical and attempts to draw comparisons are often flawed, there is still room to seek some consistency in responses, to seek a more uniform structure for reports prepared, and to question States representatives in a more systematic fashion. From the records that are available, the 'dialogue' that takes place is usually unadulterated political horse-trading rather than a probing inquiry into the facts and a quest for the most effective potential response. Thus, those who have observed the procedure in practice have noted that the level of debate in the closed sessions is sometimes abysmally low and reveals that delegations have done little, if any, serious preparation.[93]

Providing a general evaluation of the 1503 procedure is difficult but necessary. The question is whether the procedure provides adequate returns in terms of the investments of faith, time, energy, and media attention that have been made in it; whether, on balance, it succeeds in putting enough pressure on enough countries in ways that could not more effectively be achieved by other means. Some of those means might already be in existence, others might more easily be created if the 1503 procedure were to be eliminated.

The first point to be made is that the historical value of the 1503 procedure cannot be doubted. In many ways it laid the groundwork for the development of the potentially effective public (i.e., resolution 1235-based) response to violations which began to come into its own after 1979. It put paid once and for all to the domestic jurisdiction *canard*; it accustomed States to the need to defend themselves and gave them practice in examining (and prosecuting) the performance of others; it galvanized some of the NGOs at a time when some of the other procedures offered even lower rates of return; and it exposed the Commission and Sub-Commission to the real world of violations more effectively than any earlier exercise had. But a valuable historical role does not of itself justify the procedure's retention in the 1990s. Among commentators, the procedure has had both its defenders and its critics. Among the latter was Amnesty International which, in the mid-1970s, characterized the confidentiality of 1503 as 'an undisguised stratagem for using the United Nations, not as an instrument for promoting and protecting and exposing large-scale violations of human rights, but rather for concealing their occurrence'.[94] In a similar vein the then Director of the UN's human rights Secretariat, Theo van Boven, asked in a thinly veiled allusion to the procedure in his opening statement to the Commission in 1980:

[93] Alston and Rodriguez-Bustelo, *Taking Stock of United Nations Human Rights Procedures: Workshop Report* (1988), 13.

[94] Quoted in Shawcross, *The Quality of Mercy: Cambodia, Holocaust and Modern Conscience* (1984), 66–7.

Is it satisfactory to place so much emphasis on the consideration of situations in confidential procedures thereby shutting out the international community and oppressed peoples? Are certain procedures in danger of becoming, in effect, screens of confidentiality to prevent cases discussed thereunder from being aired in public? While there is probably no alternative to trying to co-operate with the Governments concerned, should we allow this to result in the passage of several years while the victims continue to suffer and nothing meaningful is really done?[95]

Writing a decade later, in 1990, Iain Guest concluded that 'confidentiality has not persuaded governments to cooperate with the United Nations' and that '1503 has become truly dangerous to human rights—and that it offers a useful refuge to repressive regimes'.[96]

While some of the procedure's proponents would disagree strongly with such assessments, their enthusiasm is nevertheless usually rather restrained. Writing in 1980, Tardu was optimistic about the procedure's future while conceding that its past performance had left much to be desired.[97] In 1982 Zuijdwijk, after an exhaustive study of the procedure, damned it with faint praise by concluding that it is 'worth sending a petition to the United Nations under resolution 1503 (XLVIII) but petitioners should limit their expectations'.[98] Tolley is equally sparing in his praise for 1503 although he attaches importance to the fact that most target governments feel threatened by it and that 'only four states have failed to have observers at two consecutive [Commission] sessions when their government was under Resolution 1503 review'.[99] An experienced Sub-Commission member, Marc Bossuyt, has strongly defended the procedure on the grounds that: (1) 1503 review facilitates subsequent consideration of a country under the public procedures—a hypothesis that would appear to be at least questionable; and (2) that it enables attention to be paid to situations that would otherwise be ignored. His views are predicated on the assumptions that a government's reputation suffers from remaining under 1503 review and that a continuing dialogue is the key to success in dealing with human rights violations.[100] While in some instances these may be valid, they would seem to be applicable only with great difficulty to many of the cases in which 1503 has clearly failed during the 1980s.

Probably the best-informed NGO observer, David Weissbrodt, concedes that 'the 1503 process is painfully slow, complex, secret, and vulnerable to political influence at many junctures' but none the less supports it as 'an

[95] Statement of 4 Feb. 1980, reprinted in van Boven, *People Matter: Views on International Human Rights Policy* (1982), 65.

[96] Guest, *Behind the Disappearances*, 441.

[97] Tardu, 'United Nations Response to Grass Violations', 598–9.

[98] Zuijdwijk, *Petitioning the United Nations*, 377.

[99] Tolley, *The UN Commission on Human Rights*, 211.

[100] Bossuyt, 'The Development of Special Procedures', 183–4.

incremental technique for placing gradually increasing pressure on offending governments'.[101] He suggests that in many individual cases the procedure has been effective, although this proposition is supported only by reference to East Germany's tendency to permit emigration by individuals who petitioned under 1503 (concessions which he notes might better be explained by the money paid in each case by the West German government) and the assertion that '[m]any governments, including the US, regularly respond to 1503 communications'. While the latter proposition is undoubtedly correct, there is little if any evidence that these responses have led to significant reversals of existing policy or practice in such states.

In general, it would seem to the present author that the shortcomings of the procedure are so considerable, its tangible achievements so scarce, the justifications offered in its favour so modest, and the need for an effective and universally applicable petition procedure so great, that it is time to re-evaluate its future. The principal options are major reform or abolition. If the procedure were to be reformed the following issues could profitably be addressed: (1) the administrative delays which call for communications to be submitted long before they might be considered by the Commission should be reduced;[102] it is surely unacceptable for a procedure which self-consciously restricts itself to dealing with the worst violations to produce virtually no results for at least a year; (2) in practice, a government's failure to respond to the allegations in question should give rise to the presumption that the allegations are well-founded; (3) a secret ballot should be introduced at the level of the Sub-Commission and its Working Group in order to reduce the political pressures involved (Commission resolution 1991/81 goes some way in this direction); (4) the list of countries could be revealed at the completion of the Sub-Commission's discussion of the matter; i.e., six months sooner than at present; (5) the author of a complaint should be allowed to furnish additional information to the Commission and its Working Group so as to ensure the currency of the complaint and to respond to government denials; (6) governments should be prevailed upon to take the procedure more seriously at the Commission level and to make a concerted effort to develop more systematic procedures for examining situations; (7) a higher standard of fact-finding and reporting should be insisted upon; (8) use should be made of the techniques already built into the procedure which provide for in-depth studies to be undertaken and Working Groups to be established; (9) a time-limit of 2–3 years (allowing for some, limited, flexibility) should be established after which a specific situation should be terminated or referred to the public procedures; (10) some details as to the nature of the Commission's

[101] Newman and Weissbrodt, *International Human Rights* (1990), 123, where Weissbrodt's final assessment is that '[i]f the objective is to obtain prompt publicity or public action for serious human rights violations, the 1503 procedure is inappropriate'.

[102] Cf. Sub-Commission Dec. 1990/112 and 1989/102.

decision should be given at the same time as the list of countries under consideration is announced to the Commission; (11) the transparency of the procedure should be increased by, for example, publishing statistics about cases treated and giving details (without country names, if necessary) of any results achieved; (12) after a specific period a report should be made public on the action taken in each situation, as is the case under the ILO's Freedom of Association procedure which is initially confidential; and (13) a period should be specified (perhaps ten years) after which all of the confidential records would automatically be released, thus providing some minimal incentives to governments to behave decently, even in private.[103]

To date, however, proposals for reform have fared badly. It has also been widely assumed that any attempt to reopen the procedural arrangements would provide a perfect opportunity for those who wish to abolish the procedure or at least neutralize it further. It is to be hoped that under the changed circumstances of the 1990s these fears may be less compelling. But whether they are or not two propositions would seem valid. The first is that many of the needed reforms could be introduced without formal authorization. The second is that an unreformed 1503 procedure would seem to have outlived whatever usefulness it might have had in the 1960s and 1970s.

(*c*) *The 1235 Procedure*

(i) *Origins* ECOSOC resolution 1235 (XLII) of 6 June 1967 established the procedure on the basis of which the Commission holds an annual public debate focusing on gross violations of human rights. It is in this context that it has developed an array of methods by which to investigate and apply pressure to individual states. The 1235 procedure illustrates, perhaps better than any other single example, the gradual evolutionary manner in which the Commission's mandate has been expanded over the years. The ways in which violations are dealt with by the Commission in the 1990s, always under the rubric of 'the 1235 procedure', bears only a passing resemblance to the actual procedure formally authorized by that resolution.

The tortuous path leading to the adoption of resolution 1235 is an unusually good example of the complementarity of the roles played by the different UN organs involved: the Assembly, the Council, the Commission and the Sub-Commission. Each was to play an indispensable part in the construction of a procedure which would enable the Commission's 'no-power to act' doctrine to be definitively repudiated. The immediate origins of 1235 lay in the struggle against racism in general and apartheid in particular. The ball was

[103] For suggested reforms, see Alston and Rodriguez-Bustelo, *Taking Stock of United Nations*, 10–15; intervention by Niall MacDermot of the International Commission of Jurists, E/CN.4/1984/SR.61, paras. 44–50; and Newman, 'The New UN Procedures for Human Rights Complaints: Reform, Status Quo, or Chamber of Horrors', in Lillich and Newman, *International Human Rights*, 371–2.

set rolling in 1965 by the Committee of 24 (the Special Committee on Decolonization) when it requested the Commission to do something in response to the petitions that the Committee had been receiving about the situation in southern Africa.[104] The Council responded by inviting the Commission to consider the question of violations 'in all countries'.[105] The latter phrase was to constitute the crucial turning-point because it was agreed to in place of a proposal which would have restricted the focus to situations involving racism or colonialism.[106] Over the next two years that debate was to be replayed in each of the UN organs concerned, with the United States and its allies insisting upon the broader mandate and the USSR and its friends vigorously promoting a more limited focus upon situations involving colonialism or foreign occupation.[107] In the end a compromise was reached which enabled the Commission to inscribe on its agenda an item entitled: 'Question of the violation of human rights and fundamental freedoms, including policies of racial discrimination and segregation and of apartheid, in all countries, with particular reference to colonial and other dependent countries and territories.'[108] The same wording continues to be on the Commission's agenda almost a quarter of a century later.

It was thus established that while *any* violations were fair game, those involving racism and colonialism were (for the time being) a priority concern. While it was ECOSOC resolution 1235 that authorized this development, it was two Commission resolutions of 1967 that heralded the dawning of the new era. In resolution 2 (XXIII) the Commission established the *Ad Hoc* Working Group of Experts on Human Rights in Southern Africa, thus establishing a vital precedent in terms of a formal investigation by the Commission of the situation in specific countries. In the second resolution, 8 (XXIII), the terms of which were subsequently endorsed by Council resolution 1235, a procedure for the consideration of situations involving violations was created. It envisaged three phases. First, the Sub-Commission would examine all communications with a view to identifying consistent patterns of violations. Secondly, the Commission would then investigate any such situations referred to it and, in the third phase, could report its findings and recommendations to the Council. With the passage of time the separation of these phases has become thoroughly blurred and the key parts of the resulting mandate on which the Commission continues to draw are the authority: (1) to hold an annual public debate; and (2) to study and investigate situations, by whatever means the Commission may deem appropriate. The role of the Sub-Commission in this area, particularly as a catalyst, is still important, but since

[104] A/6000/Rev.1 (1965), para. 463.
[105] ESC Res.1102 (XL) (1966).
[106] E/L.1111 (1966).
[107] For a blow-by-blow account, see Zuijdwijk, *Petitioning the United Nations*, 14–30.
[108] CHR Res.8 (XXIII) (1967).

1969 its input has not been seen as a necessary prelude to Commission action.[109] Similarly, the role of the Council is now marginal at best.

Before seeking to understand the functioning of 1235 in practice it is necessary to understand the political motivations of the principal actors involved in establishing and designing it. In a nutshell, the Third World wanted action against violations in southern Africa and other colonial situations. The Eastern Europeans were happy with that focus since they had no colonies and were equally happy for racism in the West to be targeted. The West, well aware that it did not have the numbers to block action and in any event wary about appearing to condone racism, calculated that the resulting procedures would be applied in a far more balanced fashion if all states, as opposed to just those which might potentially be labelled racists and colonialists, were liable to be 'indicted'.

(ii) *The Early Years* The new 1235 procedure got off to a predictably stormy start. This was ensured in part by the Sub-Commission's 1967 decision to add Haiti and Greece to a list of otherwise exclusively colonial situations to be brought to the Commission's attention.[110] When these recommendations came before the Commission in 1968 'an assortment of currents swirled and surged over a period of several days, buffeting but finally leaving intact the flimsy structures' (i.e., the 1235 procedure).[111] The actual result was a stalemate which resulted in no action under 1235[112] except in response to the six-day war in the Middle East. In the latter context a resolution calling for human rights to be respected in the occupied territories and for displaced persons to be able to return to their homes[113] was to lay the groundwork for the creation of a new 1235 mandate. The *Ad Hoc* Working Group created to deal with the situation in southern Africa was transformed into a Special Working Group of Experts to investigate alleged violations in the Occupied Territories.[114] Israel did not co-operate with the Group although various of its neighbours did. The group was disbanded in 1970 because the General Assembly had, in the mean time, been able to appoint its own Special Committee to Investigate Israeli Practices Affecting the Human

[109] 1968 was the only year in which a general report under CHR Res.8 (XXIII) was prepared for the Commission by the Sub-Commission. However, in recent years, proposals have been made to revive the practice. Its proponents have noted that in the preceding years most of the cases brought to the Commission's attention by the Sub-Commission 'were already under close public scrutiny by the Commission'. E/CN.4/Sub.2/1988/43, para. 4. The proposal continues to be considered by the Sub-Commission which established a Working Group for that purpose in 1990. See E/CN.4/Sub.2/1990/14.

[110] Sub-Commission Res.3 (XX) (1967).

[111] Carey, *UN Protection of Civil and Political Rights* (1970), 87.

[112] Report on the Twenty-Fourth Session, E/4475 (1968), paras. 140–210.

[113] CHR Res.6 (XXIV) (1968).

[114] Ibid. (XXV) (1969).

Rights of the Population of the Occupied Territories.[115] Although the latter has been reporting directly to the Assembly since that time, its reports are also sent to, and debated by, the Commission each year. In the present context, however, the important point is that a second precedent had been set in the use of the 1235 procedure to undertake a country-specific investigation.

In the early 1970s the Commission heard many allegations under the 1235 procedure but it remained unmoved by incidents such as the mass killings that accompanied efforts to suppress the secession of East Pakistan (subsequently Bangladesh)[116] and the mass expulsion of Asians from Uganda. The case that finally drew a response was that of Chile. In setting up an *Ad Hoc* Working Group of five of its members to investigate the human rights situation arising out of the military *coup d'état* against President Allende, the Commission was setting another vital precedent. Chile was the first situation, which involved neither colonialism nor racism, to be investigated by the Commission. In principle at least, the door had finally been opened, albeit only a fraction, to permit the effective use of 1235 in virtually any situation, provided only that the political will could be mustered. There are several reasons why Chile was able to play this vital role: it had a long history of democracy; the circumstances of the coup were particularly bloody; the government that had been overthrown was a member of the Non-Aligned Movement and of the Socialist International; the involvement of the United States in the coup was documented; the ILO had already appointed a Commission of Inquiry; and the resulting international campaign was intensive.

It is important to note at this point that each of the three precedent-setting investigations (the 'unholy trinity' as South Africa liked to term the trio) had been authorized on the 'understanding' that it would not in fact create a precedent. Rather, each situation was presented as though it were *sui generis*. The investigation into southern Africa involved institutionalized racism at every level of society and it could thus not be cited as a precedent which would justify examining the situation in, for example, Australia, the United States, or elsewhere. Similarly, the situation in the Occupied Territories was presented as being unique and the sponsors of the inquiry confidently believed that no precedent of potentially wider application was being set. By the time Chile was added to the list the assumption that no precedent was being set was not an especially credible one, despite the protestations of those who sponsored the proposal. Nevertheless, the remainder of the 1970s was to demonstrate that the *sui generis* myth would, because of the immunity to investigation that it seemed to offer to most governments, take time to be destroyed. Between 1975 and 1979 an impressive succession of horror

115 See Bender, '*Ad Hoc* Committees and Human Rights Investigations: A Comparative Case Study in the Middle East', 38 *Soc. Res.*241 (1971).

116 Salzberg, 'UN Prevention of Human Rights Violations: The Bangladesh Case' 27 *Int'l Org.* 115 (1973).

stories was presented to the Commission but none was deemed worthy of an inquiry under the 1235 provisions. Idi Amin's atrocities in Uganda, Emperor Bokassa's barbarisms in the Central African Empire, Pol Pot's genocidal regime in Democratic Kampuchea, the annexation of East Timor and the abuse of its people by Indonesia, the systematic disappearances and the widespread terror that accompanied them in Argentina and Uruguay, the brutality of the military regime in Brazil, and many other comparable situations were all ignored in the 1235 context.

(iii) *The Opening-up of the Procedure* By 1979, however, the situation had changed. NGOs such as Amnesty International and others had created a far better informed public opinion and governments were beginning to be subjected to domestic pressure to do something about human rights. The United Nations forum provided a convenient setting in which to take a stand. The Carter Administration's heavy-handed but none the less pioneering efforts, building upon continuing Congressional efforts, had dramatically elevated the international profile of human rights issues.

The Commission's first tentative move to open up its procedures came in 1978. It asked the government of Democratic Kampuchea to respond to allegations brought against it and requested the Sub-Commission to consider that response and any other material and report to the Commission.[117] Shawcross termed the resulting report 'superb and unequivocal'[118] but when the Commission considered it in 1979 it was paralysed by political manœuvring and postponed its discussion.[119] It was justifiably accused of acting 'with its customary tortoise-like caution'.[120] In the same year the Commission did, however, condemn the Somoza regime in Nicaragua for violations and requested the Secretary-General to report back to it at its next session.[121] It also sent a telegram to the Guatemalan government expressing concern over the 'assassination' of a former Minister for Foreign Affairs. It also took action under resolution 1235 against Equatorial Guinea. The situation in that country was chronic and attempts to deal with it since 1977 under the 1503 procedure had simply been ignored by the government. The case was transferred to the public procedure thereby making it the first country to be 'graduated' from 1503 in this way and the first outside of 'the unholy trinity' to be subjected to an investigation by the Commission. Taken together these developments opened the door much wider than before and set the scene for

117 CHR Dec. 9 (XXXIV) (1978).

118 Shawcross, *The Quality of Mercy*, 330.

119 E/CN.4/SR.1510 (1979). The Vietnamese invasion of Kampuchea later in 1979 enabled the Commission to take up the issue the following year, but under its self-determination rather than its 1235 agenda item. It also requested a Sub-Commission report on current developments in Kampuchea each year until 1983.

120 *Time* magazine, cited in Shawcross, *The Quatity of Mercy*, 67.

121 CHR Res.14 (XXXV) (1979).

a comparatively rapid development of the means by which the United Nations could use the 1235 procedure to respond to violations.

At the same time, a struggle was going on within the various human rights organs to ensure an effective, although belated, response to the disappearances in Argentina. This culminated in the establishment of the Disappearances Working Group in 1980. Although this development is considered below under the rubric of 'thematic procedures' it should be borne in mind that these procedures are an integral part of the 1235 response to violations.

In 1980, the Assembly requested the Commission to take action in cases concerning Bolivia and El Salvador, which it did the following year. From then on, the 1980s witnessed a steady stream of resolutions under the 1235 procedure calling for a variety of 'special procedures' to be undertaken. As of the end of its 1991 session the Commission had, since 1979, taken the following country-specific actions under the 1235 procedure:[122]

(*a*) *Appointment of a special rapporteur*: Afghanistan 1984–present;[123] Chile 1979–90;[124] Equatorial Guinea 1979;[125] Guatemala 1982–5;[126] Romania 1989–present;[127] 'Occupied Kuwait' 1991–present;[128] Iraq 1991–present.[129]

(*b*) *Appointment of a special representative*: El Salvador 1981–present;[130] Guatemala 1986–7;[131] Iran 1984–present;[132] Cuba 1991–present.[133]

(*c*) *Appointment of an expert*: Equatorial Guinea 1980,[134] 1984.[135]

(*d*) *Appointment of an independent expert*: Haiti 1990–present;[136] Guatemala 1990–present.[137]

[122] Not all of these situations have continued to be considered by the Commission under the 1235 agenda item. Some such as Chile, Southern Africa, and the Occupied Territories have subsequently been accorded separate agenda items.

[123] Reports: E/CN.4/1986/24; E/CN.4/1987/22; E/CN.4/1988/25; E/CN.4/1989/24; E/CN.4/1990/25; E/CN.4/1991/31.

[124] A/34/583 (1980); E/CN.4/1362 (1981); E/CN.4/1484 (1982); E/CN.4/1983/9; E/CN.4/1984/7; A/39/631 (1985); E/CN.4/1986/2; E/CN.4/1987/7; E/CN.4/1988/7; E/CN.4/1989/7; E/CN.4/1990/5.

[125] E/CN.4/1371 (1980).

[126] E/CN.4/1984/30; E/CN.4/1985/19; E/CN.4/1986/23.

[127] E/CN.4/1990/28 and Add.1; E/CN.4/1991/30.

[128] CHR Res.1991/67.

[129] CHR Res.1991/74.

[130] E/CN.4/1502 (1982); E/CN.4/1983/20; E/CN.4/1984/25; E/CN.4/1985/18; E/CN.4/1986/22; E/CN.4/1987/21; E/CN.4/1988/23; E/CN.4/1989/23; E/CN.4/1990/26; E/CN.4/1991/34.

[131] E/CN.4/1987/24; E/CN.4/1988/42.

[132] E/CN.4/1985/20; A/40/847 (1986); E/CN.4/1987/23; E/CN.4/1988/24; E/CN.4/1989/26; E/CN.4/1990/24; E/CN.4/1991/35.

[133] CHR Res.1991/68.

[134] E/CN.4/1439 (1980).

[135] E/CN.4/1985/9 and Add.1.

[136] E/CN.4/1991/33.

[137] E/CN.4/1991/5 and Add.1. This appointment was made not under resolution 1235 but under the advisory services item. In 1990 the Commission left open the question as to the agenda

(*e*) *Appointment of a working group*: Southern Africa 1967–present;[138] Israeli Occupied Territories 1968–present;[139] Chile 1975–9.[140]

(*f*) *Appointment of a Commission delegation (6 members)*: Cuba 1988.[141]

(*g*) *Secretary-General to maintain direct contacts*: Iran–1982;[142] Cuba 1989–91.[143]

(*h*) *Review of available information by Sub-Commission member*: Democratic Kampuchea 1979–83.[144]

(*i*) *Report to the Commission by the Secretary-General*: Nicaragua 1979;[145] Albania 1990–present.[146]

(*j*) *Report to the Commission by the Secretary-General or his designated representative*: Poland 1982–4.[147]

(iv) *The Selection of Countries Targeted* Although since 1979, country-specific special procedures have been set up in respect of only seventeen States, this figure reflects only a small part of the overall number of situations debated by the Commission under the 1235 and related procedures. An enormous range of situations has been specifically discussed under the 1235 item, and in some of those cases, the mere expression of serious concern or the threat of a resolution has been sufficient to provoke a constructive response from the government concerned. In addition, the Commission has adopted a number of country-specific resolutions and decisions which stop short of initiating a special procedure.[148] A new technique, pioneered in 1991, is for the Chairman to make a formal (pre-agreed) 'statement' on a specific situation.[149] Moreover, the agenda items on self-determination, advisory

item under which the independent expert's report would be considered in 1991 (CHR Res.1990/80). In the event, it opted for the advisory services item but the resulting resolution still called for continued monitoring (CHR Res.1991/51).

[138] E/CN.4/950 (1968); E/CN.4/984 and Add.1–19 (1969); E/CN.4/1020 and Add.1–3 (1970); E/CN.4/1050 (1971); E/CN.4/1075 and 1076 (1972); E/CN.4/1111 (1973); E/CN.4/1135 (1974); E/CN.4/1159 (1975); E/CN.4/1187 (1976); E/CN.4/1222 (1977); E/CN.4/1270 (1978); E/CN.4/1311 (1979); E/CN.4/1365 (1980); E/CN.4/1429 and 1430 (1981); E/CN.4/1485 (1982); E/CN.4/1983/10, 37 and 38; E/CN.4/1984/8; E/CN.4/1985/8; E/CN.4/1986/9; E/CN.4/1987/8; E/CN.4/1988/8; E/CN.4/1989/8; E/CN.4/1990/7 and Add.1; E/CN.4/1991/10.

[139] Technically, this Working Group is established under a mandate from the General Assembly but, in light of the extensive Commission debate over its reports, it warrants a mention in this context.

[140] E/CN.4/1188 (1976); E/CN.4/1221 (1977); E/CN.4/1266 (1978); For its most recent reports see: A/45/84 (1990); A/45/306 (1990); A/45/576 (1990) and A/46/6 (1991). E/CN.4/1310 (1979).

[141] E/CN.4/1989/46.

[142] E/CN.4/1983/53.

[143] E/CN.4/1991/28.

[144] E/CN.4/1335 (1979); E/CN.4/1437 (1981); E/CN.4/1491 (1982); E/CN.4/1983/12.

[145] E/CN.4/Sub.2/426 (1979); E/CN.4/1372 (1980).

[146] E/CN.4/1990/27; E/CN.4/1991/29.

[147] E/CN.4/1983/18; E/CN.4/1984/26.

[148] e.g. CHR Res.1987/61 concerning Sri Lanka.

[149] This occurred in 1991 in relation to the situation in the Baltic States.

TABLE 5.1 *Special Procedures Launched under the 1235 Procedure, by Region*

Africa	Asia	Latin America	Eastern Europe	Western Europe
Equatorial Guinea	Afghanistan	Bolivia	Poland	—
South Africa	Democratic Kampuchea	Chile	Romania	
	Iran	Cuba		
	Iraq	El Salvador		
	Occupied Kuwait	Guatemala		
	Occupied Territories	Haiti		
		Nicaragua		

services, slavery, and other matters have provided important opportunities for discussing specific violations.[150] The thematic procedures, discussed below, have also provided the occasion for a large and diverse range of countries to be named in connection with possible violations. While the potential impact of these procedures in terms of putting pressure upon governments should not be underestimated, it is nevertheless inevitable that the Commission's overall effectiveness is judged, at least in part, on the basis of the range of special procedures it has initiated.

In this regard, the record since 1979 is impressive when compared with that which preceded it. Four of the five principal UN geopolitical regional groupings have been the subject of investigations, Communist governments have not been free of scrutiny, and countries with very close links to one or more of the major powers have nevertheless been called to account. Most important of all is the fact that, unlike the situation which prevailed until the late 1970s, no country is necessarily immune from scrutiny in the future. But, in addition to these credits, the 1235 balance sheet also has its debit side. Thus, for example, Table 5.1, which shows countries targeted, according to region, demonstrates a continuing imbalance.

The table reveals several shortcomings. Apart from South Africa the only African State to have been targeted is Equatorial Guinea. No Arab State had been targeted until Iraq and Occupied Kuwait were taken up in 1991, although one Islamic State (Iran) has been. Only two Eastern European States have been targeted despite the widespread abuses of human rights that have been acknowledged by the governments concerned since the fall of the Berlin Wall. Not a single Western European State has been targeted. Even Turkey which, throughout the 1980s, was subjected to strong and continuing criticism

[150] e.g. the Commission has adopted resolutions on self-determination relating to, *inter alia*, Panama, Afghanistan, East Timor, Western Sahara, and Grenada.

in the Council of Europe context for its human rights violations escaped any investigation.

Without seeking to justify these apparent imbalances, a number of factors help to explain them. In the first place, the great powers (such as the United States, the USSR, China, the United Kingdom, and France) and the major regional powers (such as India and Brazil) have all enjoyed a degree of immunity resulting from their political and economic clout. The case of China in 1990, when no State was prepared to introduce a much discussed and very watered-down draft resolution,[151] best illustrates this regrettable phenomenon. The close allies of the great powers (e.g., El Salvador, Guatemala, Cuba, Poland, and Afghanistan) have not, however, avoided the spotlight. Secondly, regional solidarity has been an important means of preventing African and Arab nations from being scrutinized. It has been less effective in Asia and Latin America. Thirdly, it is clear that the Commission was only moved to action in cases involving widespread, documented repression of a serious kind. The 'mere' suppression of democracy, the violation of economic and social rights, the denial of the cultural and other rights of minorities and indigenees, and comparable violations were not deemed sufficient to warrant the creation of a special procedure. As a general rule it seems that blood needed to be spilled, and in large quantities. The main exceptions (such as Cuba and Poland) resulted from the investment of massive political capital (especially by the United States).

Finally, the disproportionately strong focus on Latin America may be explained by: the strength of (the myth surrounding) the democratic/rights tradition in that region,[152] the brutality of the violations, the close involvement of the United States and thus the special concern of activist American NGOs, the detailed and powerful reporting of the Inter-American Commission on Human Rights in the late 1970s and early 1980s, and the very active role of NGOs and the churches in the countries concerned. But, notwithstanding the plausibility of such explanatory factors, the focus on Latin America during the 1980s provoked persistent accusations that the Commission applied double standards. American support for many of the governments that the Commission had singled out as 'gross violators' led the US Representative to the United Nations, Jeanne Kirkpatrick, to tell the General Assembly in 1981 that: '[H]uman rights has become a bludgeon to be wielded by the strong against the weak, by the majority against the isolated, by the blocs against the unorganized . . . The activities of the United Nations with respect to Latin

[151] The Commission decided, by a vote of 17 in favour, 15 against, and 11 abstentions, 'to take no decision on draft resolution E/CN.4/1990/L.47'. CHR Dec. 190/106.

[152] This was not confined only to domestic traditions. Thus in the early UN debates Latin American countries 'not only valiantly supported the cause of human rights, but were sometimes bolder than the industrialized countries of the West in suggesting solutions . . .'. Cassese, *Human Rights in a Changing World* (1990), 33.

America offer a particularly egregious example of moral hypocrisy.'[153] Even a decade later US officials were condemning the Commission for 'a shameful history of double standards'.[154] It must be said, however, that the credibility of criticisms emanating from such sources is at least open to question when it is accompanied, not by a preparedness to bring about a significant across-the-board expansion of the Commission's focus, but rather by suggestions that the United States' principal ideological adversaries alone should be added to the target group. Nevertheless, while allegations of egregious hypocrisy can no longer he sustained, it remains true that double standards have prevailed and that many countries which have been thoroughly deserving of scrutiny have been intentionally overlooked. Only time and a political preparedness on the part of states that are members of the Commission to be critical of their allies (when such criticism is warranted) can cure this defect. By the same token, the Commission's achievements in relation to the countries that have been targeted should not be under estimated simply on the grounds that other States should also have been selected.[155]

(v) *The Complementary Role of Different Organs* The protracted negotiations that led to the establishment of the 1235 and 1503 procedures were an excellent example of the Assembly, the Council, the Commission, and the Sub-Commission playing complementary roles in such a way that the obstacles in the way of action by one body were able to be overcome by the different political forces prevailing in another. Since that time the role of the Council has been marginal at best, but the Commission has continued to interact very effectively with the Assembly and the Sub-Commission. In some instances, the latter has taken the initiative of bringing situations to the Commission's attention, thus virtually compelling debate on them. This strategy was directly effective in the cases of Iran and Afghanistan, but was unproductive in other cases including those of Sri Lanka, East Timor, Albania, Pakistan, and China.[156] In each of those cases Sub-Commission proposals that the Commission take action provoked a debate but failed to culminate in the adoption of a resolution by the Commission. In other cases in which the Sub-Commission itself has been unable to agree to target a specific situation, such as with Turkey and Iraq,[157] the Commission has been content

[153] 'Human Rights and Wrongs in the United Nations', reprinted in Kirkpatrick, *The Reagan Phenomenon—And other Speeches on Foreign Policy* (1983), 49.

[154] Williamson, 'Rethinking the U.N.: Agencies of Change', *American Enterprise*, 73 (Nov./Dec. 1990).

[155] For useful analyses addressing the question of bias, see Donnelly, 'Human Rights at the United Nations 1955–85: The Question of Bias', 32 *Int'l Stud. Q.* 275 (1988) ('Systemic bias . . . is declining in the case of the Commission, and has never bveen entirely consistent or completely debilitating', ibid. 296); and Forsythe, 'The Politics of Efficacy: The United Nations and Human Rights', in Finkelstein (ed.), *Politics in the United Nations System* (1988), 246.

[156] See respectively Sub-Commission resolutions 1984/24, 1985/20, 1985/21, and 1989/5.

[157] E/CN.4/1988/37, Chap. 7.

also to ignore the situation. The implications in this regard of the proposal (pending as of April 1991) to provide the Commission with a comprehensive annual report detailing situations appearing to involve gross violations are unclear.[158] Such a report would ensure that a wider range of situations is brought before the Commission but the pressure to respond might be relaxed accordingly. If that happened the actions of the Sub-Commission itself might simply assume greater significance, even at the Commission's expense.

There have also been instances, notably those involving Chile, Bolivia, and El Salvador, in which the initial impetus for action by the Commission has come from the General Assembly. The latter has also played an important role in supporting efforts to establish the various thematic mechanisms.

(vi) *Designation and Selection of Rapporteurs* The implementation of special procedures has been entrusted to a wide range of entities. While 'working groups' and 'special rapporteurs' were initially the favoured means of fact-finding, various other designations have been added over the years. They include: 'rapporteurs', 'envoys', 'special representatives', 'experts', 'independent experts', 'delegations', etc. The different terminology was originally intended to reflect an unstated hierarchy according to the gravity of the response. But the Commission's creativity, combined with its inconsistency in this regard, has served to blur the significance of these distinctions, at least in the minds of all but those diplomats who continue to fight with such vigour and enthusiasm to secure one designation rather than another. Of much greater importance today is the agenda item under which the appointment is made. If made under the advisory services item it has been presumed to have a far less negative connotation than if made under the violations item. But the significance of this distinction may also disappear in time if the Commission continues to blur the lines between the two items, as has clearly been the case in respect of Haiti and Guatemala.

The selection of rapporteurs (using the term generically) has been a quintessentially political process, the mechanics of which do little to ensure that expertise and competence will be the principal qualities sought. The composition of the UN groups investigating violations in southern Africa and the Occupied Territories has been subject to widespread criticism. Writing in 1973 a former UN official complained that '[t]he members . . . have been, generally, neither independent of their governments nor impartial to the governments whose policies they investigated.'[159] The principal objection was that most of the members were representatives of States which had already expressed unmistakably hostility to the governments under review. Nevertheless, the members of the 1988 mission to Cuba were also governmental

[158] See n. 109, above.

[159] Miller, 'United Nations Fact-Finding Missions in the Field of Human Rights', 5 *Australian YB Int'l L.* 48 (1970–3). See also Bender, '*Ad Hoc* Committees', *passim*.

representatives and the reaction to their report was generally very favourable.[160] In more recent country-specific endeavours an effort has generally been made to avoid the appointment of individuals from the same region as the country being investigated (e.g., a Spaniard was appointed for El Salvador, an Austrian for Afghanistan, a Guatemalan for Iran, a Senegalese and a Mauritian for Chile, and a Costa Rican for Equatorial Guinea). But there have also been cases where this principle has not been followed (e.g., a Uruguayan for Bolivia). The task of identifying individuals to undertake the special procedures has generally been left to the Chairman of the Commission who is expected to 'consult' with the regional groups before making an appointment. The target country has sometimes been closely involved in the selection process, an approach which has not always been welcomed by human rights activists.[161]

When the task of reporting on the situation in Poland was entrusted to a representative of the Secretary-General the resulting reports were brief, superficial, and unduly solicitous of the government's viewpoint.[162] In light of a similarly unsatisfactory experience under the confidential procedures there would appear to be very good grounds for concluding that the task of objective fact-finding is inherently incompatible with the 'neutrality' which Secretaries-General seem to assume they must demonstrate, even in human rights matters.[163] The Secretary-General's 1991 report on his direct contacts with Cuba would seem only to confirm this conclusion.[164]

There is no doubt that there has been great uneveness in the quality of the reports produced by different rapporteurs. Some have been accused of being 'in the pockets' of the government being investigated[165] while the efforts of others have been deemed 'spineless' and 'needlessly apologetic'.[166] One proposed solution is that they be 'appointed by a body that is insulated from political pressure and whose members serve for sufficient time so that they can be called to account for their choices over a period of years'.[167] But the feasibility of such a system in the United Nations' inevitably polticized milieu is at best questionable. The present system at least enables some pressure to be brought to bear on the Chairman not to appoint an individual who is patently unqualified. A better approach would seem to be that proposed in a

[160] e.g. Neier, 'Cuba: The Human Rights Show', *The NY Rev. of Books*, 33 (1989): 'The report's studied neutrality reflects an effort to maintain a consensus within the politically diverse delegation . . . But if the report is read closely, a telling picture emerges from it . . .'.

[161] On the appointment of Lord Colville as Special Rapporteur on Guatemala, see Guest, *Behind the Disappearances*, 369.

[162] E/CN.4/1983/18 and E/CN.4/1984/26.

[163] See generally van Boven, 'The Role of the United Nations Secretariat', Chap. 14, below.

[164] E/CN.4/1991/28.

[165] Anti-Slavery Society, *Guatemala: UN Whitewash?* (1984).

[166] *New York Times* (25 Nov. 1985), A18 (concerning a report on Iran).

[167] Americas Watch, *et al.*, *Four Failures: A Report on the U.N. Special Rapporteurs on Human Rights in Chile, Guatemala, Iran and Poland* (1986), 38.

UN report in 1970 according to which violations would be investigated by a standing body which would be 'scrupulously non-political' and 'should strive to offer all guarantees of impartiality, efficiency and rectitude'.[168] Such a system would also have its potential defects but it is difficult to accept that they would outweigh those inherent in the existing approach.

Another valid criticism is that the range of people from which the Commission generally draws its rapporteurs is unduly narrow. No woman has ever been appointed under the public procedures. The nominees are usually diplomats, and expertise in human rights law or in the politics and culture of the region concerned is often not prominent among their attributes. In future a greater effort on the part of the Secretariat to build up a list of qualified and capable potential rapporteurs could assist in improving the calibre of nominees. There is no intrinsic reason why the Commission could not move away from its present practice of opting for semi-political or diplomatic appointees and instead follow the approach of the ILO which attaches far greater importance to expertise and independence.[169] Ultimately, however, an equally significant problem with the present system may well lie in the uncertain and often intentionally ambivalent mandates that are given to the rapporteurs—a matter of major importance to which we now turn.

(vii) *The Mandate: Prosecutors, Solution Seekers or Fact-finders?* The terms used to describe the formal mandates given to country rapporteurs have varied considerably. But whether they have been asked to 'study', 'inquire into', 'investigate', or 'examine', most rapporteurs have tended to assume considerable flexibility and to approach each situation as they see fit. The Commission, for its part, has generally not sought to impose any procedural straitjackets and has been reluctant to criticize the approach adopted by individual rapporteurs. Not surprisingly, this lack of structure has resulted in enormous disparities of style, methodology, content, and focus from one report to another. It has also enabled individual rapporteurs to assume that they have a *carte blanche* in determining the nature of their reports.

For analytical purposes, three principal approaches to country-reporting may be discerned. The first emphasizes the *fact-finding and documentation function*. In this view the function of reporting is to record the facts, to provide a reliable historical record, and to provide the necessary raw material against the background of which the political organs can determine the best strategy under the circumstances. In this approach, facts and their substantiation are the key. The report prepared by the Special Commission appointed in

[168] A/8052 (1970), para. 77.
[169] See Valticos, 'Foreword' and von Potobsky, 'The Experience of the ILO', in Ramcharan (ed.), *International Law and Fact-Finding in the Field of Human Rights* (1982), pp. vii and 160 respectively.

Argentina in 1984 is an excellent example in this regard.[170] The second approach assumes that the *prosecutorial/publicity function* is paramount. Thus the rapporteur's role is not to establish whether violations have occurred but to marshal as much evidence as possible to support a condemnation that, in many instances, will already have been made. Thus Bailey has described the Special Committee on southern Africa as a fact-finding body 'only in the sense that it collects and collates facts in pursuit of a predetermined political aim'.[171] The goal in such cases is to mobilize world public opinion and to provide the basis on which the earlier conviction can be justified. The third approach is to emphasize the *conciliation function*. The rapporteur's role is not to confront the violators but to seek solutions which will improve, even if not necessarily resolve, the situation. The perceived challenge is to steer a middle course between the positions of the accused and their accusers and the emphasis is on dialogue and co-operation between the Commission and the government. The high (or some would say low) point of this approach was the report on Guatemala in 1984 in which the Rapporteur stated his 'belief that the Commission . . . wishes to encourage as well as condemn'. He concluded by urging the Commission to adopt 'a constructive approach'.[172] In a subsequent report, the same person, albeit redesignated as a Special Representative, concluded (again to the dismay of most observers) that the relevant government's efforts to guarantee human rights, 'even if not yet perfect or complete, should receive the support of the international community'.[173]

Although each of these models has had its adherents among the various rapporteurs the Commission itself has never acknowledged that different situations appear to call for different approaches. It would seem wholly inappropriate, and even unfair, for such an important decision to be left to the predisposition of the rapporteur. It is inevitably unseemly and most probably unproductive for a rapporteur to engage in haggling with a government over whether his report will be 'constructive' and mild, or 'condemnatory' and uncompromising. An exercise which purports to be engaged in 'fact-finding', but then denies or plays down the seriousness of the violations in order to maintain a conciliatory stance, insults the victims, misleads the public and the Commission, and discredits the United Nations. It is the Commission itself which should determine what type of report is called for and it would be possible to draw up some general (perhaps informal) guidelines for that purpose. For example: if the facts are genuinely unclear or the issue is a

170 CONADEP (The Argentine National Commission on the Disappeared), *Nunca Mas* (1986; English edn.)

171 Bailey, 'U.N. Fact-Finding and Human Rights Complaints', 48 *Int'l Aff.* 256 (1972).

172 E/CN.4/1984/30, paras. 8.2 and 8.10. He also expressed the hope that, in future, 'the security forces [would be able to] distinguish small babies and elderly people from villagers who may perhaps be realistically suspected of involvement in subversion . . .'. Ibid.

173 E/CN.4/1987/24, para. 8.

highly controversial one the first model might be followed and the Commission be left to draw its own conclusions based on a thorough, factual report submitted do it. If the government concerned refuses all co-operation, or if the report is a prelude to further action, then the second model might be warranted. If the situation is genuinely open to conciliation the rapporteur's task ought to be defined accordingly, and a clear indication given of the point at which such efforts would be abandoned if they are unproductive. The potential policy variations are clearly too numerous to enable a thorough review in this context. Nevertheless, those States Members of the Commission which are serious about improving the 1235-related procedures must acknowledge that the same mandate cannot effectively serve a diversity of undefined purposes, unless the Commission is simply to abdicate its political and legal functions to the whims of an individual rapporteur.[174]

(viii) *Procedures and Fact-finding Methodology* It has been persuasively argued that 'if fact-finding is to become more than another chimera, the sponsoring institutions must develop universally applicable minimal standards of due process to control both the way the facts are established and what is done with them afterwards'.[175] But in these respects the Commission's procedures got off to a bad start and have yet to recover fully. The first two situations dealt with (apartheid and Israeli occupation) were hardly conducive to dispassionate and objective reporting and the resulting precedents were strongly criticized.[176] As a result, the 1968 International Conference on Human Rights, held in Teheran, recognized 'the importance of well defined rules of procedure for the orderly and efficient discharge of their functions' by UN human rights bodies and called for 'model rules' to be prepared.[177] A Working Group of the Commission subsequently took five years to come up with an incomplete draft[178] which was never adopted but which ECOSOC requested be brought to the attention of all relevant bodies.[179] In principle,

[174] This is underscored by comments by one of the Commission's most effective fact-finders, who has been a member of the Working Group on Disappearances since 1984. Otherwise, however, his viewpoint contrasts with that expressed here: 'A nimble person with a narrow mandate will, in fact, have greater room for manoeuvre than someone of more moderate talents whose mandate is more broadly defined. Dexterity is much more important than definition. You [i.e., the rapporteur] basically do what you think is best, *and* what you think you can get away with.' Van Dongen, 'Finding Fact, Finding Fault: The United Nations Experience', (mimeo., Geneva, 1990), 6.

[175] Franck and Fairley, 'Procedural Due Process in Human Rights Fact-Finding by International Agencies', 74 *Am. J. Int'l L.* 309 (1980).

[176] See e.g. Ermacora, 'International Enquiry Commissions in the Field of Human Rights' 1 *Hum. Rts J.* 180 (1968). The role of the fact-finding groups seems to be 'to support the preconceived assumptions of the UN as regards the facts'. Ibid. 205.

[177] *Final Act of the International Conference on Human Rights*, A/CONF.32/41 (1968) Res.X, 12.

[178] E/CN.4/1021/Rev.1; E/CN.4/1086; and E/CN.4/1134 (1974). For governmental comments, see E/CN.4/1071 and Add.1–6. The Model Rules and proposals by the Secretary-General are reprinted in Ramcharan, *International Law and Fact-Finding*, 231–48.

[179] ESC Res.1870 (LVI) (1974).

therefore, the model rules are still relevant but, in practice, they have long since been forgotten. The only other comparable attempts to devise procedures designed to ensure both fairness and effectiveness were the rules drawn up by a fact-finding mission to South Vietnam in 1963[180] and the arrangements contained in a memorandum between the Working Group on Chile and the Chilean government in connection with the Group's on-site visit in 1978.[181]

Despite the lack of any formal guidelines it has been suggested that the various rapporteurs do in fact generally follow certain 'basic rules and procedures'.[182] But insofar as this may be the case, the rules in question are so rudimentary that they do not go anywhere near ensuring the degree of integrity of process that most commentators would agree to be essential if consistency, credibility, effectiveness, and fairness are to be achieved.[183] Thus, for example, one rapporteur could happily observe that he was 'much indebted to the Army . . . for their safe-keeping and their transport, with many other kindnesses and facilities',[184] without thereby running foul of any procedural rules for independent fact-finding. In brief, the existing methodology for fact-finding by UN rapporteurs is *ad hoc*, inconsistent, and often unsatisfactory. Perhaps the clearest demonstration of their inferiority is to compare the reports produced by UN fact-finders with those produced by their Inter-American counterparts. In the case of Guatemala and, albeit to a slightly lesser extent, Chile, the difference in quality and thoroughness is enormous.[185] Similarly invidious comparisons may be made with respect to the ILO, with the case of Poland being especially telling.[186] Yet in spite of these patent shortcomings, the Commission has tended to operate on the assumption that any attempt to move towards a more carefully structured and credible process would only be hijacked by those opposed to effective fact-finding. But it is now time to challenge that assumption and to move towards a methodology which would ensure that UN reports consistently pass muster in terms of their procedural probity. A small step in this direction was the Commission's call in 1990 for efforts to ensure that individuals and groups

[180] The group was appointed by the General Assembly rather than the Commission. The rules are contained in A/5630 (1963), Annex II. See also the subsequent report of the Secretary-General on methods of fact-finding in A/5694 (1964).

[181] A/33/331 (1978), Annexes VI and VII.

[182] Herndl, 'Recent Developments Concerning United Nations Fact-Finding in the Field of Human Rights', in Nowak, *et al.* (eds.), *Festschrift für Felix Ermacora: Progress in the Spirit of Human Rights* (1988), 28.

[183] See e.g. the International Law Association's 'Belgrade Minimal Rules of Procedure for International Human Rights Fact-Finding Missions', reproduced in 75 *Am. J. Int'l L.* 163–5 (1981).

[184] E/CN.4/1987/24, para. 7.

[185] Norris, 'Observations In Loco: Practice and Procedure of the Inter-American Commission on Human Rights', 15 *Texas Int'l L. J.* 46 (1980); and 19 *Texas Int'l L. J.* 285 (1984).

[186] See ILO, *Official Bulletin*, Special Supplement, 67 (1984), para. 1.

were accorded free access to UN human rights procedures, including fact-finding exercises.[187] The resulting report indicates that significant problems have been experienced in terms of reprisals against witnesses and relatives and other acts of harassment.[188]

(ix) *The Preparedness of Governments to Co-operate* The picture in this regard is a very mixed one. Neither South Africa nor Israel have ever formally co-operated with the Commission's investigative organs. Chile permitted the Working Group to visit on only one occasion and almost certainly considered that to have been a grave mistake given the Group's uncompromising report on its findings. At a later stage, the Chilean government relented after a new rapporteur released what a leading NGO termed an 'informal, summary and highly selective' report in 1985.[189] As a result the rapporteur was able to conduct on-site investigations each year from 1986 to 1989.[190] Poland was singularly uncooperative although a visit by the Secretary-General's representative was eventually tolerated. Afghanistan was entirely negative at first and then changed its tune dramatically to permit a visit by the rapporteur in 1987. Iran took a similar approach while Guatemala, Bolivia, and El Salvador have all permitted relatively unrestricted access to the respective rapporteurs. Cuba and Romania (after the fall of President Ceaucescu) have also been prepared to admit the Commission's representatives.

Overall, the factors that induce governmental co-operation seem to be rather diverse and to depend very much on a calculation, taking account of all of the relevant circumstances, as to the relative costs of co-operation versus non co-operation. The costs of the latter are being steadily increased but they are still far from being consistently prohibitive. But whether or not an on-site visit is permitted, the great majority of governments have sought to defend themselves systematically and vigorously within the Commission. Thus detailed rebuttals of country-specific reports are now very much the norm rather than the exception.

(x) *The Commission's Response to Reports* The Commission's response to a rapporteur's report is dictated in part by the approach adopted in the report itself. If extensive conclusions and recommendations are offered by the rapporteur, as is usually the case whether or not the Commission has specifically requested them, the latter's room for manœuvre is very limited. It cannot readily reach a conclusion which is at odds with that of its fact-finder without putting the government concerned in a strong position to denounce the fairness of the process. Thus, for example, in the case of Guatemala the

[187] CHR Res.1990/76.
[188] E/CN.4/1991/24.
[189] See above, n. 167, 14.
[190] See E/CN.4/1986/2; E/CN.4/1987/7; E/CN.4/1988/7; and E/CN.4/1989/7.

rapporteur's conclusions (including his resignation) left the Commission with little choice but to terminate its investigation despite the strong feeling on the part of some members and most NGO observers that the situation clearly warranted continuing scrutiny. The principal example of the opposite approach, by which the rapporteur gathers and analyses all the facts but leaves the Commission to draw its own conclusions, was the report on Cuba. In that instance the approach of the delegation was close to that followed by ILO fact-finding missions.

The Commission's debates are rarely the occasion for any serious and sustained analysis of the content of the reports it has commissioned. Delegate's speeches are usually taken up by general justifications of the position which that State proposes to take in response to the report. The real action is in the corridors where the content of the draft resolution is determined. Determined lobbying can also take place in the capitals and the content of the report is at best a minor element in such negotiations. Thus, for example, in the case of Cuba the 'United States lobbied vigorously in national capitals prior to the 1988 [Commission] meeting. President Reagan, Vice-President Bush, and Secretary of State Shultz were personally involved in writing, phoning, and meeting with [Commission] members.'[191] The following year President Bush sent a personal message to the Commission criticizing its past record and calling upon 'all countries that value freedom' to vote to continue Commission monitoring of the situation in Cuba.[192] Similar lobbying had taken place in the case of Poland earlier in the decade. At the Commission level, however, political decision-making is not only inevitable, it is also desirable. What is neither inevitable nor desirable is the politicization of the fact-finding process itself.

(xi) *The Effectiveness of the 1235 Procedure* Evaluating effectiveness of any procedure in the human rights field is a vexing issue. The principal question concerns the criteria to be applied. Objectives range from general consciousness-raising to the actual saving of lives. It would seem difficult to sustain many strong claims on behalf of the 1235 procedure at the latter end of the spectrum. The response time is too great, the potential sanction too distant (or un-immediate), and the range of other relevant pressures in most situations too vast to be able to say with confidence in any given situation that 1235 made the crucial difference. This is borne out by the few studies which have sought to evaluate the United Nations' impact within the context of specific situations.[193]

[191] Williamson, 'Rethinking the U.N.', 73.

[192] E/CN.4/1989/74, Annex, 2.

[193] e.g. Shelton, 'Utilization of Fact-Finding Missions to Promote and Protect Human Rights: The Chile Case', 2 *Hum. Rts LJ.* 1 (1981). In the Chile case, 'the perception of bias . . . delayed the work' of the United Nations. Ibid. 35.

As a measure for dealing with issues on an emergency basis the 1235 procedure is deeply flawed, especially because of the fact that the Commission meets but once a year. This criticism is mitigated by the agreement in 1990 that the Commission may, in exceptional circumstances, meet between sesssions.[194] It remains to be seen if that procedure can be invoked effectively but it seems unlikely to be used in any but the most egregious (and headline-grabbing) situations. The problem of a single annual Commission meeting is further mitigated by the UN's annual calendar of meetings which ensures that one or other of the main human rights organs is meeting, or is about to meet, at any given time of the year. Nevertheless the Commission's response is not usually of an urgent nature and the time taken for ECOSOC to approve new special procedures, for a rapporteur to be appointed; and for the resulting report to be reviewed, is considerable. In these respects, 1235 is slow, cumbersome, and indirect, in addition to being methodologically weak. Seen from the perspective of Commission members who have struggled valiantly to improve the procedure, such criticisms will seem unfair. They will note, with ample justification, that an enormous amount has been achieved in a short period of time and that further improvements will come gradually. Account must also be taken of the great tribute paid to the 1235 procedure by those states, such as Argentina,[195] China, Cuba, Poland, and others which have all lobbied furiously at one time or other to avoid or terminate scrutiny. Similarly, equally determined lobbying efforts on the part of countries such as the United States and others, including the topping-up or withholding of development aid funds, aimed at gaining or sustaining condemnatory resolutions have been widely reported.

While an overall assessment cannot be made without taking account of the panoply of other UN techniques and procedures and their complex interaction with 1235, it is difficult to escape the conclusion that the glass is at best half full. Although that is an achievement that should not be underestimated it is nevertheless difficult to accept that, after almost half a century of concerted efforts, the principal UN procedures for responding to violations are quite as embryonic, marginally effective and unevenly applied as they are.

(*d*) *The Thematic Procedures*

Just as the reinvigoration of the 1235 procedure resulted in part from the horrors of the 1970s and the accompanying unresponsiveness of the UN's human rights organs, so too did the evolution of various 'thematic' procedures. The first of these procedures, the Working Group on Enforced or

[194] ESC Res.1990/48, para. 3.

[195] For a very detailed treatment of measures taken by the Argentinian government during the 1970s and early 1980s, see Guest, *Behind the Disappearances, passim*; and Cassese, *Human Rights in a Changing World*, 127–9.

Involuntary Disappearances,[196] was established in 1980 in response to developments in Argentina and Chile. In the latter case the Commission's rapporteur had devoted considerable attention not only to the phenomenon of disappearances but also to establishing the responsibility of the government for actions of which it denied all knowledge.[197] In the case of Argentina, both the scale and the ramifications of the widespread disappearances had been known since 1976 but nothing had been done, largely because of the determined and highly professional lobbying efforts of that country's diplomatic representatives in Geneva and New York. By 1980 a major NGO campaign launched by Amnesty International was in full swing and UN action was virtually inevitable. At this point the Argentinians took a calculated gamble that an initiative which focused on a particular 'theme' (i.e., disappearances) rather than on the general situation in one particular country (Argentina) would diffuse some of the heat that the resulting investigations might generate. Moreover, because a range of countries would be threatened by such a mechanism they could calculate that the Group's prospects of survival beyond a year or two were not great.

Once again, as with the opening up of the 1235 procedure after 1979, the establishment of the Disappearances Group served as a vital precedent that enabled other comparable initiatives to be taken in later years. Thus in 1982 a Special Rapporteur on Summary or Arbitrary Executions was appointed,[198] in response to various factors such as another Amnesty campaign, some well-publicized mass executions in Liberia and Suriname, and an important resolution of the Sixth UN Crime Congress.[199] In 1985, after the Convention against Torture had been adopted but well before the Committee was established, a Special Rapporteur on Torture was appointed.[200] The following year the United States, at least partly motivated by a desire to focus the spotlight on Eastern Europe, was instrumental in the appointment of a Special Rapporteur on Religious Intolerance.[201] A year later, another initiative which was aimed in part at the activities of US supported groups in Nicaragua, Angola, and elsewhere, led to the appointment of a Special Rapporteur on

[196] Its reports are contained in: E/CN.4/1435 and Add.1 (1981); E/CN.4/1492 and Add.1 (1982); E/CN.4/1983/14; E/CN.4/1984/21 and Add.1–2; E/CN.4/1985/15 and Add.1; E/CN.4/1986/18 and Add.1; E/CN.4/1987/15 and Add.1; E/CN.4/1988/19 and Add.1; E/CN.4/1989/18 and Add.1; E/CN.4/1990/13; E/CN.4/1991/20 and Add.1.

[197] A/34/583/Add.1 (1979), 87–92.

[198] Reports: E/CN.4/1983/16; E/CN.4/1984/29; E/CN.4/1985/17; E/CN.4/1986/21; E/CN.4/1987/20; E/CN.4/1988/22 and Add.1–2; E/CN.4/1989/25; E/CN.4/1990/22; E/CN.4/1991/36.

[199] A/CONF.87/14/Rev.1, Res.5; GA Res.35/172.

[200] Reports: E/CN.4/1986/15; E/CN.4/1987/13; E/CN.4/1988/17 and Add.1; E/CN.4/1989/10; E/CN.4/1990/17 and Add.1; E/CN.4/1991/17.

[201] Reports: E/CN.4/1987/35; E/CN.4/1988/45 and Add.1; E/CN.4/1989/44; E/CN.4/1990/46; E/CN.4/1991/56.

Mercenaries.[202] In many respects the wheel had turned full circle with each of the regional groups being prepared to endorse new thematic procedures aimed at their adversaries, while being unable to get the votes needed to disband those which seemed to affect themselves. Finally, attempts begun in 1988 to establish a procedure dealing with political imprisonment in 1988 and 1989 eventually bore fruit in 1991 when a Working Group on Arbitrary Detention was created.[203] The creation of such a group was largely inspired by the work of the Sub-Commission's working group on detention and was very actively promoted by France and the UK, in addition to several of the most influential NGOs.

Initially, the thematic procedures might have been seen as being located in-between the 1503 and 1235 procedures. Their work was not to be confidential but nor was it to be country-specific in the full sense. The procedure was more co-operative than adversarial in design and condemnations were neither the goal nor the likely result of the exercise. Indeed the term 'fact-finding' was of dubious application to the procedures that were envisaged. But, despite the procedures' initially very modest aspirations, they have over the course of their first decade proven to be far more flexible, innovative, and persistent than either their original detractors or proponents would have dared to think. We turn now to a brief review of the ways in vhich they have functioned.[204] In this context, special emphasis is placed on the most effective, innovative, and longstanding of the procedures, the Disappearances Working Group.

(i) *Mandates and Procedures* Each of the procedures has been endowed with slightly different terms of reference, although the resulting differences have gradually been diminished, if not eliminated, over time. The Disappearances Group was empowered to 'examine questions' relating to the problem, to 'bear in mind the need to be able to respond effectively' and to 'work with discretion'.[205] The latter element was reiterated in 1981 when the Commission specified that such discretion was needed to 'protect persons providing information' as well as 'to limit the dissemination of information provided by Governments'. The Commission also characterized the Group's objectives as 'strictly humanitarian'.[206] By 1990, however, the Group's practice had evolved to the point where its mandate 'to examine questions' was the

[202] Reports: E/CN.4/1988/14; E/CN.4/1989/14; E/CN.4/1990/11; E/CN.4/1991/14.

[203] CHR Res.1991/42.

[204] At the time of writing the Working Group on Arbitrary Detention had not yet begun to function. For the best comparative analysis, see Kamminga, 'The Thematic Procedures of the UN Commission on Human Rights', 34 *Netherlands Int'l. L. Rev.* 299 (1987). See also Rodley, *The Treatment of Prisoners under International Law* (1986).

[205] CHR Res.20 (XXXVI) (1980).

[206] CHR Res.10 (XXXVII) (1981).

one to which it gave the greatest emphasis, thus playing down many of the constraints implicit in some of the other language used at one time or other by the Commission to describe its mandate. In this context it has worked at three different levels, examining: (1) individual cases; (2) overall country situations; and (3) the 'dynamics' of the phenomenon of disappearances. In the latter context it has focused on systemic factors such as the role of paramilitary groups, harassment of witnesses and relatives, impunity for perpetrators, and the role of military courts and of amnesties. It has also consistently advocated the adoption of a new international instrument dealing with disappearances.

The injunctions to examine or study the relevant phenomenon and to seek to 'respond effectively' is common to the mandates of most of the thematic rapporteurs. The principal exception is the Rapporteur on Mercenaries whose mandate is somewhat different as a result of the nature of the phenomenon with which he is dealing and of its status in international law. Thus his mandate is closely linked to the right to self-determination and he is specifically directed to 'develop further the position that mercenary acts are means of violating human rights and thwarting the self-determination of peoples'.[207]

The vagueness of the definition of the themes being inquired into has also provided important opportunities for the relevant rapporteurs to define their own mandates. While a certain core content is readily discernible in each case, the Commission has left other matters open for determination over time. This has clearly favoured the evolution of an expansive approach, usually after an initially cautious period devoted to the establishment of procedures and the consolidation of political support.[208]

The Disappearances Working Group and the Rapporteurs were all initially appointed for a single year. Putting them on such a short leash was intended to restrain their enthusiasm. It also succeeded in causing problems for the procedures in terms of the available staff, the continuity of the work and the political clout which it carried.[209] In 1988 it was agreed that all the thematic mandates should be extended for two years at a time and in 1990 ECOSOC agreed to three-year extensions.[210]

(ii) *Sources of Information* Unlike other United Nations efforts to monitor human rights violations, the thematic procedures have never been hobbled in terms of the sources of information on which they are authorized to rely. The Disappearances Group was empowered to make use of information from any 'reliable sources', a term which placed only a minimal limitation upon it. It has

[207] CHR Res.1990/7, para. 16.

[208] The Rapporteur on Summary Executions was an exception in this regard. See Weissbrodt, 'The Three "Theme" Special Rapporteurs of the UN Commission on Human Rights', 80 *Am. J. Int'l L.* 688–93 (1986).

[209] Guest, *Behind the Disappearances*, 306–9.

[210] ESC Res.1990/48, para. 4.

sought to develop working relationships with as wide a variety of NGOs and others as possible and in its 1990 report lists ninety-eight different groups with which it has been in contact since its inception.[211] The other thematic rapporteurs have been restricted to seeking or obtaining information from NGOs or even from NGOs in consultative status with ECOSOC. But these restrictions have not been permitted to hinder their activities. Thus, for example, as noted below, a significant number of on-site visits has been undertaken under each of the thematic procedures. Such visits should, and usually do, provide unrivalled opportunities for the collection of information. In the words of one commentator, 'all procedures appear to have had a healthy disregard for formality and to have employed a wider range of sources than officially permitted'.[212]

Given the artificiality of the different provisions and the indispensable need for access to all available sources, such an approach is surely appropriate. Indeed, this assumption was explicitly endorsed by the Commission in an important 1990 resolution aimed at publicizing the extent to which intimidation, threats, and various forms of reprisals have been used to inhibit or punish co-operation with both the thematic and country rapporteurs. In a significant statement of generally applicable principles, the Commission called upon 'all Governments receiving representatives of United Nations human rights bodies to provide effective advance information to them, to allow unhampered contacts between private individuals and such representatives and to remove all legal and practical obstacles which would unduly prevent or discourage such contacts from taking place'.[213]

(iii) *Means of Pressure* While each of the thematic procedures has experimented with different priorities in terms of the various means by which pressure can be exerted upon governments, the type of approaches used by the Disappearances Working Group have been broadly representative. For analytical purposes, five different techniques may be identified: routine requests for information; urgent action requests; country visits; prompt interventions; and reporting to the Commission.

The first, and most widely used, consists of requests for information. The Group transmits the essence of any plausible allegations that it receives to the government concerned with a request for information. The Group's overriding concern is to clarify the circumstances surrounding each individual case. Its enquiry is thus designed to pressure the government to ensure that no further harm comes to individuals who are still alive and that a full investigation is undertaken in all other cases. The Group styles its approach as

211 E/CN.4/1990/13, Annex I.
212 Kamminga, 'The Thematic Procedures', 309.
213 CHR Res.1990/76, para. 1. See also n. 188, above.

'non-accusatory' and notes that it 'does not engage in the attribution of responsibility' to individual perpetrators, a task which remains the responsibility of the State.[214] Between its creation in 1980 and its 1991 report to the Commission the Group had examined well over 50,000 cases, of which almost 20,000 had been transmitted to the forty-five governments concerned. The Group notes that most governments respond to it, at least orally, but concedes that many of the responses are entirely unproductive. Of the total, the Group estimates that there is a 7 per cent 'clarification' rate. In assessing its own performance in this regard the Group has been almost disarmingly frank. It believes that its approach to individual cases has been 'strong' in the sense that affected individuals have been allowed 'to address the pertinent human rights body swiftly and directly'. But its approach has also been 'weak' 'in the sense that the Group seeks to clarify cases of disppearances through co-operation with governments which probably were responsible for them in the first place and who have little, if anything, to gain by strenuous investigations'. It defends its approach as 'the only real option available to it' and notes that disappearances can only be eliminated 'through co-operation and dialogue with States'.[215] In reality, however, this candour is somewhat misleading since the Group's real strategy is far less 'co-operative' and considerably more confrontational than it would wish to acknowledge. This is best seen through the other techniques that it uses.

The second is the urgent action procedure by which the Chairman of the Group is authorized to make immediate representations to a government in cases where a disappearance is alleged to have occurred within the past three months. This innovation, which bears an uncanny resemblance to a procedure widely used by Amnesty International, was introduced at the Group's very first meeting in 1980 (after its first Chairman, an Iraqi, himself disappeared[216]). The Group claims that this procedure has achieved a clarification rate of 25 per cent[217] and it seems clear that, depending upon the country and the circumstances, it can provide an individual victim with a significant degree of protection from further harm. The technique has since been emulated by each of the thematic rapporteurs.

The third technique consists of on-site country visits. In the words of the Working Group: 'Not only does a visit provide an opportunity to obtain first-hand information [on] the matter, it also puts the Group in direct contact with family members, witnesses and non-governmental groups, as well as with the competent authorities at different levels. Working relationships established in

[214] E/CN.4/1990/13, para. 347.
[215] Ibid. para. 349.
[216] This sad episode is recounted in Guest, *Behind the Disappearances*, 204–5.
[217] E/CN.4/1990/13, para. 351.

the course of a visit usually continue afterwards.'[218] Between 1985 and February 1991 visits were undertaken to Peru (twice), Guatemala, Colombia, and the Philippines. The resulting reports have been detailed, well structured, balanced, and far from reticent. They have given rise to very precise, and often rather far-reaching recommendations. The Group has, however, expressed its dismay at the neglect of its recommendations by the first three governments concerned.[219] Each of the other thematic rapporteurs has also undertaken a number of country visits although the thoroughness of the resulting reports varies considerably from one to another.

The fourth technique has been termed a 'prompt intervention' procedure. Under this procedure the Group's Chairman, acting on an urgent basis, sends a cable to the Minister of Foreign Affairs of the country concerned requesting that immediate steps be taken to protect all the rights of, *inter alia*, 'relatives of missing persons, witnesses to disappearances and their families, members of relatives' organizations, as well as other non-governmental organizations and its [*sic*] members persecuted or threatened as a reprisal for their activities on behalf of victims of disappearances or for their efforts to eliminate such practice [*sic*]'.[220] Since this procedure was only adopted by the Group in the course of 1990 it is still too early to evaluate its effectiveness.

The fifth and final means by which the Group and each of the thematic Rapporteurs can apply pressure on governments is through their annual reports to the Commission. UN organs have always placed great faith in the power of annual reports, but it may be that this is less a reflection of the demonstrated effectiveness of such reports than of the perceived lack of any feasible alternative. The Disappearances Group has made an enormous effort to report in a balanced and carefully structured fashion on each of the countries reviewed and its reports contain very detailed analyses which, at least by UN standards, are frank and incisive. As a result, an enormous amount of authoritative primary material is placed on the public record. But while effective use has been made of such information by NGOs and in US State Department reports, the Commission itself has been much less assiduous in using the Group's material.[221] In its consideration of such items the Commission continues to rely upon 'debates' which, for the most part, are unfocused and rhetorical, often consist of interventions drafted well in advance, and all too rarely reflect a careful reading of the relevant reports. Indeed, it is particularly striking to compare the manner in which debates

[218] Ibid. para. 352.

[219] E/CN.4/1991/20, para. 413.

[220] Ibid. paras. 26 and 411.

[221] Thus, for example, FEDEFAM, one of the most important of the NGOs monitoring the work of the Disappearances Working Group, told the Group in 1984 that 'the debate in the Commission was very poor and very few ideas were incorporated in the Group's mandate, resulting in very little progress'. E/CN.4/15, Annex II, 1.

unfold in bodies such as the Governing Body of the ILO or the ILO Conference Committees and the undisciplined and unstructured proceedings of the Commission. As a result it comes as no surprise that the rapporteurs sometimes complain that their reports have been treated as superfluous in important debates and that their specific recommendations are either ignored altogether or endorsed and then ignored. The Commission has yet to adopt procedures which would ensure automatic follow-up to its recommendations and the rapporteurs have been slow to recognize that they must unilaterally take that task upon themselves.

(iv) *Evaluating Effectiveness* The thematic rapporteurs have generally been less activist than the Disappearances Group and have tended to play a more reactive role. It must be said, however, that the differences among them are sufficiently great as to limit severely the utility of most generalizations. Nevertheless, it would seem that the thematic procedures have, in a number of important respects, been more effective than either the 1235 or 1503 procedures. In terms of the fact-finding function, as narrowly defined, the country visits being undertaken with increasing frequency under the auspices of the thematic procedures may well turn out to be more effective than the country-specific procedures under resolution 1235. Their working methods, while far from uniform across the different mandates, are generally better developed and more sophisticated than those of their 1235 counterparts. Their missions have been generally better prepared, their co-operation with NGOs and other sources more comprehensive and they have demonstrated a greater willingness to tackle some of the structural dimensions of the problems with which they are dealing. Perhaps none of this should be surprising in view of the ability of the thematic rapporteurs to pick and choose their priorities, their greater insulation from political pressures generated by individual governments, and, in most cases, the stronger Secretariat support that they have received.

In terms of the public relations function, the thematic rapporteurs have also been very effective, especially in comparative terms. They have developed and maintained contacts with a wide range of NGOs, they have reached out systematically to the victims and their supporters,[222] and they have succeeded in generating a better informed public debate around the relevant issues. In particular, most of the procedures have played an important role as catalysts to the develpment of new international instruments. Finally, in terms of the conciliation function, the thematic procedures have often succeeded in pro-

222 There have, of course, been many exceptions in this regard. For an account of the 1984 boycott of the Disappearances Group by one of the major NGOs see ibid. (the boycott was designed to show 'the depth of the families' [of the disappeared] disillusionment with the United Nations . . .'). See also Guest, *Behind the Disappearances*, 376–9.

ducing highly critical analyses while at the same time reassuring the governments concerned that co-operation was all that they sought.

Several criticisms may, however, be levelled at the thematic procedures. In the first place, the range of issues that they cover is clearly skewed. While disappearances, summary executions, torture, religious intolerance, and the use of mercenaries are all issues of the utmost importance, there remain many other important issues that are not being accorded comparable attention, and efforts to reduce and limit the overall number of thematic procedures have already been foreshadowed.[223] Such imbalance risks creating a *de facto* hierarchy of rights within the UN context, despite the inconsistency of such an outcome with the theoretical foundations of international endeavours.

A more telling criticism of the thematic procedures is that they do not succeed in putting much pressure upon individual countries. This is best illustrated by several very serious cases of States that have simultaneously been the subject of major attention by several of the thematic procedures (e.g., Colombia and Iraq) but have still not been given any particular attention by the Commission itself. In this regard, it is clear that the thematic procedures should be given particular weight in the process of identifying countries that deserve to be targeted under the 1235 procedure. Yet no country has so far been graduated in this way. As a result it is feared that the thematic procedures might only make the development of the 1235 procedure even more difficult, thus enabling States to shield behind the less targeted and inevitably much more narrowly focused thematic procedures.

III. MONITORING AND PROMOTIONAL ACTIVITIES

Analyses of UN human rights activities have traditionally distinguished between 'protection' activities on the one hand and 'promotional' activities on the other.[224] The distinction is by no means watertight but it is useful for analytical purposes. In essence, any activity designed to protect the rights of specific individuals or to respond to violations that have already occurred (i.e., any activity targeted to a particular group) may be classified under the heading of protection. Any activity of a more general, less-targeted, nature is considered to be promotional. In reality, this latter category is a grab-bag which accomodates a multitude of activities that do not otherwise have a lot in common. The United Nations' involvement in promotional activities was begun largely in response to US antipathy in the early Cold War years to the drafting of the Covenants.

[223] Brody, *et al.*, 'Major Developments in 1990 at the UN Commission on Human Rights', 12 *Hum. Rts Q.* 581 (1990).

[224] On the use of this distinction, see Marie, 'La Pratique de la Commission des droits de l'homme de l'ONU en matière de violation des droits de l'homme', 15 *Revue belge de droit int'l* 355 (1980); and id., 'Article 55(c)', in Cot and Pellet (eds.), *La Charte des Nations Unies* (1986), 863.

The response of the Eisenhower Administration to the Bricker amendment went considerably beyond the repudiation of international standard-setting activities described above.[225] In 1953, in an effort to put a positive face on its rejection of the main component of the UN's human rights programme the United States launched what it euphemistically called an 'action plan'. Its principal components were a system of periodic reports by States, a series of studies, and a seminar programme (characterized as the provision of 'advisory services'). This initiative was, in essence, little more than an effort to steer the UN programme in directions that the West (the United States and the United Kingdom in particular) felt confident it could control. Thus while action in response to violations was never contemplated as part of the 'action plan', no opportunities would be lost to study or discuss issues with respect to which the West's political adversaries were perceived to be in a weak position.[226] In time, of course, that strategy would begin to backfire on the West, particularly as the Third World influx began to influence the priorities. The early years of the new promotional regime have been described in detail elsewhere.[227] Thus the focus of this section is mostly on the current legacy of the 'action plan' launched by the United States at the Commission in 1953.

The Commission's current programme of promotional activities was very significantly expanded following its decision in 1987 to establish a Voluntary Fund for Advisory Services and Technical Assistance in the Field of Human Rights (UNFASTA).[228] By October 1990 that fund had received contributions of US $2,114,682, over 95 per cent of which had come from fourteen Western States (excluding the United States, which had not contributed).[229] While some regular budget funds are also available for the same purposes, the voluntary fund provides far greater resources and considerably more flexibility. In addition, it provides an opportunity for the priorities of the funders, rather than of the Commission as a whole, to influence heavily the types of activity to be funded.[230] While this is consistent with trends throughout the UN system, those trends have been said to raise 'serious questions with regard to accountability and governance . . .'.[231] While the Commission

225 See text accompanying n. 20–1, above.

226 See generally Eide, 'The Sub-Commission on Prevention of Discrimination and Protection of Minorities', Chap. 6, below.

227 e.g. Humphrey, *Human Rights and the United Nations*; Tolley, *The UN Commission on Human Rights*; and Marie, *La Commission des droits de l'homme de l'ONU* (1975), 177–232.

228 CHR Res.1987/38.

229 E/CN.4/1991/55, Annex II.

230 The official statement of the position is more guarded: 'The Centre [for Human Rights] will continue . . . to hold regular, informal meetings with donors and other interested countries on various aspects of the utilization of the Voluntary Fund . . .'. E/CN.4/1991/55, para. 17. There is also an internal 'advisory group' of senior UN officials which 'meets regularly to review requests and to identify projects'. Ibid. para. 15.

231 Edgren and Möller, *The Agencies at a Crossroads* (1990), 3. (The study notes that 58% of FAO activities are funded by extra-budgetary resources. It is 54% for WHO, 41% for ILO, and 32% for UNESCO.)

has an opportunity to influence the direction of the programme by virtue of resolutions adopted on the basis of an annual report by the Secretary-General,[232] neither the debate nor the ensuing resolutions have been especially well focused in this regard.

We turn now to review the principal component parts of the Commission's promotional activities.

(*a*) *Periodic Reports*

A 1950 proposal by the Commission, which was turned down by ECOSOC, would have required States to submit an annual report 'on the manner in which they have promoted respect for, and the progress of human rights'.[233] The US proposals in 1953 revived that idea and, after some delay, ECOSOC acted on the suggestion in 1956 by establishing a system of triennial reporting under which States were requested to describe 'developments and the progress achieved during the preceding three years in the field of human rights, and measures taken to safeguard human liberty'.[234] The Council emphasized that the objective was 'not to criticize individual governments' but simply to 'ascertain the results obtained and difficulties encountered'. Initially, the Commission's task was to study not the reports but summaries of them prepared by the Secretariat. This was revised in 1964 so that the Commission received the reports in full thereafter. In 1961 the Commission established a Committee on Periodic Reports which, in the space of one week, was expected to review all the reports (in 1962, for example, there were sixty-seven for the period 1957–9) and make recommendations on the basis of them.[235] In fact, no critical examination of the reports was ever undertaken by the Committee. In 1965 an attempt was made to improve reporting standards[236] and to delegate the review function to the Sub-Commission. Controversy erupted, however, at the Sub-Commission's first attempt to deal with the reports in 1967.[237] The difficulties were caused by NGO submissions in connection with the reporting system, which, in disregard of the traditional niceties, alleged specific violations. This was completely unacceptable to many States and the Commission subsequently used the rescheduling of the Sub-Commission's session as a convenient justification for relieving the Sub-Commission of its responsibility for reviewing the reports.[238] After a number of singularly unproductive years of reviewing, or purporting to review, the

[232] See e.g. the Medium-Term Plan of Activities outlined in E/CN.4/1988/40. For a detailed critique of that plan see Rädda Barnen and Int'l Comm. of Jurists, Swedish Section, *UN Assistance for Human Rights* (1988).

[233] E/CN.4/517 (1951), 2.

[234] CHR Res.1 (XII) (1956), para. 1.

[235] E/3456 (1961).

[236] ESC Res.1074 C (1965).

[237] See Eide, 'The Sub-Commission on Prevention of Discrimination'.

[238] CHR Res.16 (XXIII) (1967).

reports, the Commission began to defer the relevant agenda item on a regular basis. By 1975 the number of reports being received was down to forty-seven despite the increase in UN membership in the preceding years. It was not until 1981 that it finally voted to abolish a system which, in the mean time, had not only wasted a great number of trees but had established precedents (with respect to the submission of reports which were largely devoid of substance) which the treaty bodies would find very hard to overturn.[239]

(*b*) *Studies and Seminars*

Throughout the late 1950s and 1960s the Commission sponsored a series of seminars on specific human rights topics. The topics were determined not by the Commission itself but by the governments that hosted the meetings and were expected to foot much of the bill. It is hardly surprising, therefore, that the issues chosen were often very broadly defined and the approach adopted was usually rather abstract and 'safe'. Between 1957 and 1987 the United Nations organized some 35 world-wide seminars and over 40 regional seminars.[240] This program was vigorously defended by its principal Secretariat sponsor on the grounds that it was no mean feat merely to keep the human rights flag flying at a time when the Cold War was otherwise poisoning the atmosphere.[241] But even allowing for such obstacles, it is difficult in retrospect to be impressed by what was achieved, other than to marvel at the regularity of the events and at the impressive distances travelled by some of the more persistent participants. Among the more recent of the seminars, two in particular stand out as having made important contributions. They are the 1978 Geneva world-wide Seminar on National and Local Institutions for the Promotion and Protection of Human Rights, which gave a major push to initiatives to establish human rights comnmissions and the like at the country level, and the 1979 Monrovia regional Seminar on The Establishment of Regional Commissions with Special Reference to Africa,[242] which eventually led to the adoption of the African Charter on Human and People's Rights.

Since 1987 the emphasis of the seminar programme has changed significantly. This was inspired to some extent by a successful Ford Foundation-funded, UNITAR-run series of regional training programmes in the mid-1980s focusing on reporting procedures under UN human rights instruments. The changes were also facilitated by the availability of far more resources flowing from the creation of the voluntary fund. In 1990, for example, training courses and workshops were held in Asunción, Manila, Moscow, Montevideo, and New Delhi; and an international seminar was held in Geneva.[243] While it

[239] CHR Dec. 10 (XXXVII) (1981).

[240] For the period to 1982 they are listed in *United Nations Action in the Field of Human Rights*, ST/HR/2/Rev.3 (1988), 343–5.

[241] Humphrey, *Human Rights and the United Nations*, 278.

[242] For reports, see ST/HR/SER.A/2 (1978) and ST/HR/SER.A/4 (1979).

[243] E/CN.4/1991/55, paras. 39–40.

is perhaps too soon to evaluate this new programme, it would still seem to suffer from many of the shortcomings that afflicted its predecessor.

(c) Fellowships

The awarding of fellowships to candidates nominated by their governments was an important part of the original package of proposals approved in the mid-1950s. About 30 fellowships are awarded each year[244] but the programme appears to have achieved rather little over the years. In some respects, it might be viewed as a way of providing some reward at UN expense to a small number of government officials involved in human rights matters.[245]

(d) Advisory Services

In terms of its origins, this part of the original 1953 US 'action plan' was strongly influenced by the technical assistance programs that the United Nations was increasingly undertaking in the context of de-colonization and related activities. According to Tolley, the United States and its allies 'hoped that predemocratic societies would solicit legal advice on fashioning a constitution, criminal code or election procedures'.[246] But despite the controversy that surrounded this part of the original package, limited enthusiasm and even more limited funding ensured that only a few token activities were undertaken between 1955 and 1980.[247] Requests relating to Bolivia, Equatorial Guinea, Guatemala, Guinea, Haiti, and Uganda were all dealt with favourably during the 1980s[248] and, although those experiences were not especially happy ones, the technical assistance dimension of the programme was substantially developed towards the end of the decade. Thus the active solicitation of requests from governments for assistance had yielded a very lengthy list of possible programme activities by 1991.[249]

While questions have been posed as to whether UN funding for such activities is the most appropriate and cost-effective means of spending money avaliable for human rights purposes, both the design and the execution of the programme as a whole have also given rise to more troubling questions. In the case of assistance provided to successive regimes in Haiti, the Commission's own expert queried whether the monitoring of violations might not be more

[244] 29 were awarded in 1990. E/CN.4/1991/55, para. 53.

[245] For a detailed critique, see Alston, 'Towards an Effective Advisory Services Program', in Rädda Barnen, *et al.*, *UN Assistance for Human Rights*, 78–83. Changes made to the programme since 1988 have done little to affect these criticisms.

[246] Tolley, *The UN Commission on Human Rights*, 35.

[247] See n. 240, above, 342.

[248] The best reviews of the entire advisory services programme are Picken, 'A Review of the UN Advisory and Technical Assistance Programs for Human Rights' and 'Country Cases: Advisory Services in Practice', in Rädda Barnen, *et al.*, *UN Assistance for Human Rights*, 18–52 and 110–50 respectively.

[249] E/CN.4/1991/55, paras. 91–135.

appropriate under the circumstances than the provision of technical assistance.[250] Similarly, the Commission's advisory services activities in Guatemala have been strongly criticized. In one very detailed report the Lawyers Committee for Human Rights concluded that the Guatemala programme itself had been deficient and that the reports to the Commission were 'often misleading and in some cases inaccurate'. The Lawyers Committee also argued that monitoring and assistance are incompatible activities and could not be carried out effectively by the Commission in one country at the same time.[251] In 1990 and 1991, however, the Commission explicitly rejected this contention by appointing an 'independent expert' in the case of Guatemala to both monitor violations and supervise the provision of advisory services.[252]

The need for the establishment of criteria in order to ensure that technical assistance is not provided to governments engaged in serious human rights violations and that assistance is, at least potentially, constructive in its impact has also been called for by various commentators.[253] The Commission has responded by requesting the Secretary-General 'to elaborate guidelines . . . with special emphasis on defining priorities and developing criteria for project appraisal and follow-up'.[254] Although such guidelines were subsequently drawn up, the Commission was told in 1990 that they remained part of an 'internal document . . . based on standard procedures developed by UNDP'. Given the difficulties confronting any non-governmental group seeking to scrutinize UNDP's own country programme procedures, it is at least questionable whether such an approach guarantees the 'transparency' specifically sought by the Commission.[255]

An equally important issue is whether governments that have had, or are still having, serious human rights problems are capable of making effective use of external assistance, except for the most technical of purposes. In this regard the experience of the first country to receive major advisory services assistance is far from encouraging. Equatorial Guinea has been given advice and assistance under this programme for more than a decade. In his 1991 report, the Commission's Expert was rather despondent about the results: 'The Expert is deeply concerned that since his first visit to Equatorial Guinea in 1979,

[250] E/CN.4/1989/40.

[251] Lawyers Committee for Human Rights, *Abandoning the Victims: The UN Advisory Services Program in Guatemala* (1990), 92–7.

[252] CHR Res.1990/80. Cf. a statement to the Commission by Amnesty International condemning continuing violations in Guatemala and calling upon the Commission to respond to them. E/CN.4/1991/NGO/14.

[253] Ireland, speaking on behalf of the European Community, told ECOSOC in 1990 that the advisory services programme 'will be of benefit only where governments are genuinely committed to human rights reforms and have themselves taken the necessary measures to provide a basic level of human rights protection . . .'. Verbatim text of remarks delivered to the Second Committee of ECOSOC, 15 May 1990, 10. See also Lawyers Committee, *Abandoning the Victims*, 3–4; and Alston, n. 242, above, 87–100.

[254] CHR Res.1990/59, para. 11.

[255] Ibid. para. 12.

representative democracy has still not been established in the country and that consequently there is no adequate institutional framework for the protection of human rights'.[256] Amnesty International was even less impressed by what had been achieved. It told the Commission in 1991 that '[e]fforts by the United Nations... to encourage respect for human rights in Equatorial Guinea appear to have had little positive effect.'[257] The Commission has been remarkably reluctant to draw the conclusions which would seem to follow from this experience. Given the similarity between such conclusions and the negative lessons derived from earlier United States-led efforts to transpose norms and institutions from developed countries, there would seem to be strong reasons for reassessing both the feasibility of, and the appropriate modalities for delivering, such assistance in the future. Until such an appraisal is undertaken it will be difficult to accept that money spent on this form of advisory services is being spent as well as it could be.

(*e*) *Public Information*

One of the major promotional activities overseen by the Commission is the public information programme. Initially, the focus was on the Human Rights Yearbook which was initially true to its name but is now biennial. It has been a rather formalistic affair for many years now but States have been reluctant either to upgrade it or to perform euthanasia on it. In the 1980s the Commission itself began to attach much greater emphasis to general public information activities and sought to prompt a reluctant and under-resourced Secretariat into action through a series of resolutions. Towards the end of the decade a new Under-Secretary-General for Human Rights included among his priorities the preparation and production of brochures and booklets and the translation of the basic international instruments.[258] Nevertheless, despite the resulting flurry of activity, the role played by the Commission in this field has been a minor one.[259] This situation was also confirmed by the fact that a World Public Information Campaign on Human Rights was launched not on the initiative of the Commission but of the Assembly.[260]

IV. DEEPENING THE CONCEPTUAL FOUNDATIONS OF HUMAN RIGHTS

For almost two decades, academic commentators and many others have seized upon the terminology of 'generations' in an attempt to encapsulate con-

[256] E/CN.4/1991/54, para. 13. (Poverty 'is no excuse for failing to establish the basic and indispensible [*sic*] machinery for the operation of representative democracy'. Ibid.)

[257] E/CN.4/1991/NGO/27, para. 1.

[258] See the list of activities described in E/CN.4/1991/22.

[259] See generally Alston and Rodriguez-Bustelo, *Taking Stock of United Nations Human Rights Procedures*, 45–54.

[260] GA Res.43/128 (1988); GA Res.44/61 (1989); and GA Res.45/99 (1990).

veniently the evolution of international thinking about human rights. But, in so far as such analyses purport to be applicable to the United Nations' approach, they are misleading at best and a distortion of the historical record at worst. The record of the Commission is the best illustration in this regard. The Universal Declaration, for which the Commission was principally responsible, gave near-equal weight to the two sets of rights (as they only later came to be known, once the Commission had been directed by the Council to adopt two separate Covenants). Thus the first two generations arrived in the United Nations at the same time. The third generation, so-called, consists of peoples' rights and solidarity rights. But solidarity rights have their foundations in various articles of the UN Charter and in Article 28 of the Universal Declaration. Peoples rights have their origins in the Minority Treaty regime of the League of Nations and soon found expression in the right to self-determination which the United Nations recognized, as a human right, in the early 1950s.

Nevertheless, while generational terminology is unproductive in this context, it must equally be noted that the Commission has, over almost five decades, been in the frontline of a struggle to deepen the conceptual foundations of the package of rights contained in the Universal Declaration and subsequently the Covenants. This struggle has, however, been played out within a largely theoretical context and its practical ramifications have so far been somewhat limited. In the 1990s it is now possible to discern a number of changes that have gradually begun to take root, but their gestation period has been long. In particular, the concept of peoples' rights is beginning to assume new meaning and a greater effort has been made to give content to political participation rights, an effort which, by general geopolitical consensus (i.e., East, South, and West), has been conscientiously and systematically fudged by the Commission. But cultural and economic rights both remain late starters with virtually nothing having been done on the former and the latter being consigned to the Sub-Commission and the relevant treaty body for action. We turn now to a brief examination of each of these key areas in which the Commission has sought to deepen the conceptual foundations of human rights.

(*a*) *Peoples' Rights and Cultural Rights*

Although the Organization of African Unity has adopted a comprehensive regional Charter proclaiming the integral relationship between human rights and peoples' rights, the UN Commission has made only very limited progress in that direction. Indeed, one way to trace the history of its conceptual endeavours would be through a review of the rearguard actions that have consistently been fought, with considerable success, to block efforts to move towards the recognition of peoples' rights. The rights of minorities were consigned from the outset to the Sub-Commission and the Commission's principal contribution was to make sure that the former's debates were never conclusive. It was then not until the late 1970s that the Commission began drafting a declaration on the rights of minorities and, some thirteen years later (1991), it had still not succeeded in resolving some rather elementary questions such as whether some of the rights are vested in the minority as a collectivity rather than in each member of the group in his and her individual capacities.[261]

The right of peoples to self-determination is another issue on which considerable time has been spent but with relatively little to show for it. That is not to say that the practical consequences of the Commission's work on self-determination in the 1950s and 1960s was not very substantial. It would, however, be virtually impossible to demonstrate a convincing causal link between that work and the many practical manifestations of peoples asserting and achieving their right to self-determination. In an effort to resolve the principal definitional controversies (how is a people to be defined for these purposes and is the right of continuing validity beyond situations of colonialism and foreign occupation?) the Commission took the highly unusual step of appointing two Rapporteurs to study marginally different aspects of the same topics. The reports, by a Romanian[262] and an Uruguayan,[263] inevitably reached conflicting conclusions and the resulting recommendation that a new instrument be drafted on self-determination[264] got nowhere. As was the case in the 1950s, the conceptual foundations have been clarified far more in practice than through such conceptual excursions. Thus, for example, in the context of the rights of indigenous peoples the Commission has provided active encouragement to Sub-Commission efforts which could substantially extend the notion of self-determination.[265]

As the world heads into a post-Cold War era in which demands for realization of the right to self-determination will become ever more frequent, in the context not only of Eastern Europe but of Africa and Asia as well, the Commission's failure to have developed any more sophisticated notions of self-determination will inevitably return to haunt it. Of course, in a forum composed exclusively of governments, the ramifications of that deficiency will take some time to be appreciated. Nevertheless, it is clear that the concepts with which the Commission is working will require considerable deepening in the years ahead if they are to be responsive to the most pressing needs of peoples and societies throughout the world.

261 See n. 36, above.

262 Cristescu, *The Right to Self-Determination: Historical and Current Developments on the Basis of United Nations Instruments*, UN Sales No. E.80.XIV.3 (1981).

263 Gros Espiell, *The Right to Self-Determination: Implementation of United Nations Resolutions*, UN Sales No. E.79.XIV.5 (1980).

264 Ibid. 69, para. 288.

265 The best comprehensive survey of these developments is Hannum, *Autonomy, Sovereignty, and Self-Determination: The Accomodation of Conflicting Rights* (1990).

In the area of cultural rights, the Commission has done very little except in the context of other concerns such as minority and indigenous rights. Cultural rights *per se*, however, have been very largely neglected and they remain unexplored terrain as far as the Commission is concerned. One excuse for this situation is that UNESCO is, or should be, the lead agency in this domain, but this is not a policy position that has been invoked in any other area. Moreover, given the rather limited progress made by UNESCO to date in this regard, the need for further study and debate remains.

Finally, the concept of solidarity rights, which some believe capable of providing an overarching conceptual umbrella in this area, is being explored by the Assembly, with virtually no inputs from the Commission.[266]

(*b*) *Economic Rights and the Economics of Rights*

The Commission has played an inconsistent and rather ineffectual role in seeking to develop the concept of economic and social rights. Initially, it steered well clear of such issues, except in so far as they arose within the context of studies commissioned in the 1950s and 1960s on different dimensions of discrimination.[267] The Teheran Conference in 1968 provided the necessary impetus to force the Commission to begin to explore some of the more fundamental issues.[268] These had been touched upon by some of the seminars organized during the 1960s but the Commission's agenda and its priorities were entirely unmoved by such exercises. Immediately after the Teheran Conference the Secretary-Gerneral produced an excellent survey of the major issues that demanded attention.[269] This laid the groundwork for an Iranian rapporteur to be appointed by the Commission to produce a major study seeking to answer some of the key questions. The report, produced on an extraordinarily lavish budget and with the help of a host of consultants, was a most impressive compilation of poverty-related statistics and analysis.[270] But it actually shed remarkably little light on the major issues. The Commission made few comments on the progress reports that it received and the 1973 final report led to little more than a tame annual debate. Proposals to update the report were made for the rest of the decade but (mercifully) never quite succeeded.

In the mean time, the focus was shifted as a result of a Commission resolution in 1977 proclaiming the existence of a right to development and asking that its 'international dimensions' be explored in a Secretariat study.[271]

[266] GA Res.44/148 (1989). Cf. CHR Res.1990/15, para. 2.
[267] e.g. Ammoun, *Study of Discrimination in Education*, E/CN.4/Sub.2/181/Rev.1 (1957).
[268] See n. 177, above, Res.XXI, 16.
[269] E/CN.4/988 and Add.1 (1969).
[270] Ganji, *The Realization of Economic, Social and Cultural Rights: Problems, Policies, Progress*, UN Sales No. E.75.XIV.2 (1975).
[271] CHR Res.4 (XXXIII) (1977).

The resulting document[272] presented the Commission with a wide range of topics on which further progress might have been made but the latter opted instead to pursue a standard-setting exercise. The Commission delegated that task to a group of governmental experts who laboured for some five years before a Declaration on the Right to Development was adopted by the Assembly in 1986. The significance of the Declaration remains a matter of some dispute but it cannot be said that the Commission's efforts to examine the economic and other structures underlying and supporting many human rights violations were a success. Its most recent approach seems to recognize this fact by focusing on 'the need for a continuing evaluation mechanism so as to ensure the promotion, encouragement and reinforcement of the principles contained in the Declaration'.[273] In other words, the Commission would like the task to be performed by a body other than itself.

Overall, therefore, the Commission's lengthy debates have done very little to promote understanding of the core normative content of economic rights let alone the human rights dimensions of debt, world trade, and development co-operation.[274] Similarly, a major effort in the late 1980s to study the content and significance of the right to private property, which was recognized in the Universal Declaration but omitted from the Covenants, was initiated by the General Assembly[275] rather than the Commission and the latter has done little to enrich the ensuing debates.[276] While the Commission has taken up the issue of 'extreme poverty', the approach it has adopted provides a perfect demonstration of its inability to deal with such issues effectively. Thus, it has drawn the attention 'of the General Assembly and all United Nations bodies' to the issue, urged the Committee on Economic, Social and Cultural Rights to give the issue 'the necessary attention' and requested the Sub-Commission to study it.[277]

Indeed in recent years the Commission has almost conceded its inadequacy in this general field by calling for a major study on economic, social, and cultural rights to be undertaken by the Sub-Commission[278] and by following closely the work of the Committee on Economic, Social and Cultural Rights.[279]

[272] E/CN.4/1334 (1978). See also E/CN.4/1421 (1980) and E/CN.4/1488 (1981).

[273] CHR Res.1990/18, para. 4.

[274] Cf. 'Report on the Global Consultation on the Realization of the Right to Development as a Human Right', E/CN.4/1990/9.

[275] GA Res.41/132 (1986); GA Res.43/123 (1988); and GA Res.45/98 (1990).

[276] Although the Assembly has requested it, in the context of its agenda item on economic and social rights, to 'consider the means whereby and the degree to which respect for the right to own property alone as well as in association with others contributes to the development of individual liberty and initiative, which serve to foster, strengthen and enhance the exercise of other human rights'. GA Res.45/98 (1990).

[277] CHR Res.1990/15.

[278] Preliminary reports are contained in E/CN.4/Sub.2/1989/19 and E/CN.4/Sub.2/1990/19.

[279] e.g. CHR Res.1990/17.

It may be that the results of these separate endeavours will, in the course of time, equip the Commission with the conceptual tools that it has so clearly been unable to develop for itself in this area.

A closely related issue, into which some occasional but none the less important forays have been made, is that of the economic dimensions of human rights violations. The Commission has acknowledged the significance of the issue in the context of racism and has held several seminars focusing on different aspects of the topic. Its most significant work, however, has been on the role of multinational corporations and other commercial enterprises in sustaining apartheid in southern Africa.[280] As important as these efforts have been, their conceptual foundations remain underdeveloped. By contrast, an earlier attempt by a member of the Sub-Commission to examine comparable concerns in the context of Chile produced a first-rate report which the Commission largely ignored.[281] It did, however, pay enough attention to it to ensure that the author, Antonio Cassese, was not re-elected to the Sub-Commission.

(*c*) *Participation Rights*

This is another area in which the Commission has done relatively little to develop the conceptual foundations. Despite the purported centrality of participation rights to the very concept of human rights, the various formulations used in the major international instruments are notoriously vague, flexible, and open-ended.[282] The need for the Commission to seek to bring greater clarity to the relevant debates would seem both obvious and urgent. Yet it has done very little in this regard. In the early 1980s it undertook a study of the right to popular participation as a human right. While the study yielded some interesting observations by governments,[283] it failed to produce any particular insights that were to make their way into Commission resolutions. In the late 1980s as democracy and free elections became central issues in Eastern Europe, Central America, and elsewhere it was the General Assembly[284] rather than the Commission[285] which took the initiative to relate those values to human rights and to promote concrete measures in that regard.

[280] Khalifa, *Adverse Consequences for the Enjoyment of Human Rights of Political, Military, Economic and other Forms of Assistance Given to the Racist and Colonialist Régime of South Africa*, E/CN.4/Sub.2/1987/Rev.1. See also CHR Res.1990/22.

[281] E/CN.4/Sub.2/412 (1978).

[282] See Steiner, 'Political Participation as a Human Right', 1 *Harv. Hum. Rts. Yb.* 77 (1988) ('For a right regarded as foundational, political participation suffers from serious infirmities. The norms defining it are either vague or, when explicit, bear sharply disputed meanings.' Ibid.

[283] E.g. E/CN.4/1985/10 and E/CN.4/1990/8.

[284] GA Res.43/157 (1988); GA Res.44/146 (1989); and GA Res.45/150 (1990). Cf. GA Res.45/151 (1990) (an 'alternative' resolution emphasizing the principle of non-interference in the internal affairs of States with particular reference to the holding of elections).

[285] Cf. CHR Res.1989/51.

C. *The Functioning of the Commission*

I. COMPOSITION

The composition of the Commission has changed radically in slightly under half a century. At least part of the story is best told through the statistics. At its first session, in 1947, it had eighteen members. Two UN agencies sent observers and three NGOs were present. The resulting report, in both English and French combined, was six pages long. It contained a handful of unnumbered resolutions. By 1992 the Commission will consist of fifty-three members. In 1990 there were 116 member States actively participating either as members or observers. There were also four non-member States of the United Nations represented by observers, ten international agencies, and three national liberation movements. Some 111 NGOs in consultative status were in attendance as were many others without such status. The Commission's final report was contained in two volumes comprising 424 pages. It adopted 81 resolutions and 16 decisions in its own right and forwarded 9 draft resolutions and 29 draft decisions to the Council for adoption. In all, these instruments took up 175 pages of single-spaced text. The sheer magnitude of the exercise attests to the importance that many governments and other actors attach to it, although this does not preclude there being an inverse relationship between size on the one hand and effectiveness and efficiency on the other.

Perhaps the Commission's single most important characteristic is that it is composed of governmental representatives. Proposals made in 1946 to the effect that it should consist of independent experts were decisively rejected by the Council.[286] As a 'compromise' it was agreed that the Secretary-General should consult with the governments elected to the Commission before the representatives are 'finally nominated . . . and confirmed by the Council'. This was designed to ensure that representatives were of a high calibre and reflected a 'balanced representation in the various fields covered by the Commission'.[287] However, the procedure immediately degenerated into a formality devoid of all practical significance. Since that time, the Commission has never purported to be other than a political body in which decisions are taken on political lines, albeit in the light of appropriate international legal standards and the desirability of consistency and fairness in decision-making. The concerted lobbying and the accompanying horse-trading which virtually all of the key actors have engaged in at one time or other is a testament not only to the importance attached to the Commission but also to its inherently

[286] See n. 6, above.
[287] ESC Res.9 (II) (1946).

political nature. But despite this reality, demands that the Commission should de-politicize its deliberations continue to come from all sides.[288] While there is much to be said in favour of the elimination of double standards and of the quest for procedural fairness and substantive consistency, such discussions cannot ultimately ignore the quintessentially governmental and political nature of the Commission.

Hersch Lauterpacht observed in 1950 that 'the Commission will not attain the full stature of moral authority and practical effectiveness until it includes, in addition to persons appointed by governments, private individuals of distinction, full independence and experience, chosen irrespective of nationality by a selective process . . .'.[289] This, of course, it has not done. Nevertheless, it would be wrong to assume that the Commission has not managed to build up considerable expertise and even distinction within its ranks. Over the years a number of individuals have succeeded in exercising leadership roles by virtue of their personal qualities rather than their diplomatic clout. Several Western European States have also developed a general policy of appointing individual experts (often academics) to head their delegations, thus seeking to emphasise expertise over diplomacy. In addition, several NGO representatives have achieved the status of widely respected advisers to the Commission.

The level of diplomatic representation in the Commission is unusually high by United Nations standards. Many delegations are large and are headed by very senior diplomats, sometimes sent especially from capitals or from New York. Representation of women as heads of delegation has been strikingly poor, despite the Commission's own rhetoric of equality.

The role played by the Secretariat has been more difficult to gauge, if only because it is expected to be subtle and usually indirect. While the various executive directors have each played important roles, the Secretariat as a whole has probably exerted less influence upon the Commission than is the case in many comparable international bodies. This is a result, in part, of many years of objections being lodged by various States at the slightest sign of any initiative having been shown by the Secretariat.

The membership of the Commission has been expanded gradually from 18 in 1946 to 21 in 1962, 32 in 1967, 43 in 1980, and 53 in 1992. On each occasion the rationale has been to ensure a more equitable geographical balance (i.e., to diminish the role of Western and Eastern Europe and enhance that of the Third World). Each time the expectation has been that the political equilibrium would be altered significantly. To some extent it has, but the frequent predictions of radical change have rarely come to pass. On each occasion, adjustments have had to be made to take account of ever-

[288] For a useful discussion of the concept of 'politicization' and of the contexts in which it is most often used, see Wells, *The UN, UNESCO and the Politics of Knowledge* (1987), 1–22.

[289] Lauterpacht, *International Law and Human Rights*, 257.

growing lists of speakers, expanding agendas, and more time-consuming negotiations and voting. But on the issues of greatest import the role of the various geopolitical blocs is not always so straightforward and their ability to prevent the emergence of ephemeral or shifting coalitions is by no means as great as is sometimes suggested.

Some historical analysis of the Commission has sought to demonstrate that the different blocs have, at different stages, wielded a consistently determining influence. Tolley, for example, depicts the West as being 'dominant' from 1946 to 1967. Nevertheless, the right to self-determination was definitively recognized early in this period, the Covenants were adopted despite a lack of enthusiasm on the part of the United States and the seeds were sown for many of the initiatives that blossomed later on. Tolley also portrays the Non-Aligned Movement (NAM) as having 'control [of the Commission] for a decade after 1967' but this belies the effectiveness of the blocking tactics used by the West on issues such as economic rights and the very limited effectiveness of the Commission on the NAM's pet issues of South Africa and Israel. In the first half of the 1980s Tolley saw a 'tenuous balance . . . between the blocs'.[290] More recently, a deep North–South divide has been discerned by various commentators.[291] But while each observer would probably attach different weight to the relative strengths of the various blocs at any given time it would seem that the Commission is, for the most part, no longer susceptible to being 'captured' definitively by any given bloc. This is due to the increasing range of issues being dealt with, the impact of public opinion and inter-governmental pressures, the increased salience of human rights attitudes to domestic politics in many countries, and the growing sophistication of some of the procedures that have been created. Whilst the fragility of many such procedures is striking, the extent of their evolution and the attention they command in diverse situations is equally remarkable. This is not to say that individual country initiatives will not be prevented by obstinate bloc voting: for they assuredly will be.[292] But, in the longer term, the latest enlargement notwithstanding, the Commission will continue to break down the barriers to effective action and to develop, albeit sometimes with a deeply frustrating gradualism, the precedents that it requires in order to be able to respond to the hard cases. In the mean time, commentators will continue to conjure up the bogyman of bloc voting, especially by the NAM. The irony, however, is that the Western group is better organized and more cohesive than any of the others on probably the majority of issues.

290 Tolley, *The UN Commission on Human Rights*, 219.

291 Brody, *et al.*, 'Major Developments in 1990', 587; and Zoller, 'North–South Tension and Human Rights', 8 *Human Rights Monitor*, 3.

292 Zoller, 'North–South Tension', 6, suggests that a strategy of 'regionalization' developed by the Latin Americans 'has since been emulated by the Asian and African countries to the point where no decision affecting any one country can be taken without the agreement of its regional group'.

II. METHODS OF WORK

Since 1949 the Commission has met every year for a single session. In both 1947 and 1948 it met twice. Efforts have been made, particularly under United States sponsorship in the late 1950s and early 1960s, to reduce the frequency to a biennial basis.[293] But although they came close in 1964 when the Council voted not to hold a Commission session, these efforts were unsuccessful. Since the early 1980s each session has been of six weeks duration with an extra week for pre-sessional working groups. Sessional working groups have been widely used despite the enormous pressure thus put on small delegations.

The Commission's agenda is lengthy and the formal listing provides no indication of the real, as opposed to the nominal, importance attached to different issues. Some items have consistently generated mainly token resolutions that change little from one year to the next while others have proven to be genuinely open-ended and thus somewhat unpredictable in terms of their 'yield'. The inscription or maintenance of an item on the agenda can thus sometimes prove to be a pyrrhic victory. Similarly, the length of time devoted to debating a given agenda item will often be in inverse proportion to the likelihood of anything tangible or useful being achieved thereby.[294] But even in such cases, when the politics of symbolism reign supreme, the parties involved may well feel the exercise to have been well worth while. Debates can thus fulfil many functions. These include: reaffirming the principle of sovereign equality of states by permitting Fiji to speak for as long as the United States on an item; enabling ideas to be floated; signalling changes in previous positions; placing positions on the public record; serving notice of discontent to allies as much as to antagonists; satisfying domestic constituencies; stimulating media interest; and appealing to public opinion.[295] Statements made in debate one year can also return to haunt governments at a later stage and to limit their perceived policy options.

By the same token, many debates in the Commission are singularly sterile affairs. This may be because they are dominated (or plagued) by bilateral antipathies and give rise to a ping-pong game of abusive statements, rights of reply, written documents, etc. Or it may be because an issue is so current and complex that representatives are left no room for manœuvre and must instead confine themselves to the delivery of speeches drafted and approved in their capitals by officials with little or no 'feel' for the Commission and its debates.

The Commission's principal tangible output consists of resolutions and

293 e.g. Report of the Fourteenth Session, E/3088 (1958), paras. 198–208.

294 'The weakest members shout the loudest, the most radical seek the most attention, and the most paranoid are the most critical.' Puchala (ed), *Issues before the Thirty–Eighth General Assembly* (1983), 344.

295 See generally Peterson, *The General Assembly in World Politics* (1986), 103–11.

decisions. The methods by which these are negotiated have changed significantly over the years as a result of the expanded membership, the vastly more active role of observer States, and the increasing resort to consensus decision-making. In the early years, there were procedural incentives to lodge draft resolutions as soon as possible and then to negotiate amendments in public debate. This procedure was time-consuming and eventually proved impossible given the growing number of participants and the increase in resolutions.

In 1990, 77 per cent of the 97 resolutions and decisions adopted by the Commission were adopted by consensus. In 1991, six of the ten resolutions under the violations item were also adopted by consensus. Inter-bloc negotiations have thus become a key ingredient of the drafting process and for that purpose one member of each bloc is usually designated as the principal negotiator on a given item. This system has generally worked well, although it has given rise to situations in which a country being scrutinized for human rights violations can play a very active role in determining the content of the relevant Commission resolution. The greater emphasis on consensus has reduced the time taken for the adoption of resolutions and has greatly diminished the spectacle of procedural wrangling over competing drafts in public sessions.

III. REFORM AND INNOVATION

The Commission has succeeded in transforming itself over the decades from an almost exclusively standard-setting body into one which is capable of responding more or less effectively to violations, while at the same time pursuing a wide range of other initiatives designed to strengthen the rule of law and respect for human rights. But the reform process has been spasmodic rather than gradual and has been fuelled more by confrontation than by rational debate. There have been at least four major efforts at task-expansion (i.e., the addition of extra functions to the Commission's *de facto* mandate). The first came in the 1950s when the United States was anxious to stop, or at least to play down, the standard-setting function. As we have seen, it produced the Advisory Services Programme, the periodic reporting system, and the seminar programme. Those reforms were feasible because they were determinedly non-threatening in nature, at least as far as the great majority of Commission members was concerned. The next push came in the wake of successful decolonization efforts and led to the adoption of the 1235 and 1503 procedures and a much more effective focus on racism and colonialism. Then, between 1977 and 1986 a major effort was made by Third World States in particular to make the Commission more attuned to structural and economic factors underlying human rights violations and to identify an unjust international economic order as one of the principal culprits in that regard. These efforts, which included a proposal to reflect the principles recognized in General Assembly resolution 32/130 within the Commission's formal terms of reference, made remarkably little impact on the priorities of the Commission despite the successful launching (in 1977) of the right to development[296] and the subsequent adoption of a Declaration on the subject by the Assembly in 1986. At the same time the West countered with a set of proposals, including a revived High Commissioner plan,[297] provision for emergency sessions, an inter-sessional role for the bureau (office-holders), and such like. They were equally unsuccessful although the relevant agenda item ('alternative ways and means' etc.) generated large numbers of meetings and a considerable volume of paper.[298] The 1979 expansion of the Commission's membership from 32 to 43, the extension of the Commission's annual session to six weeks, and formal recognition of the Commission's role in assisting the Council to co-ordinate all UN human rights activities were the principal outcome of this reform phase.[299] In addition, the Commission succeeded in redesignating the Division of Human Rights as a Centre[300] and in upgrading its head from a Director to an Assistant- and subsequently an Under-Secretary-General. Having discussed a package of reforms at each session from 1978 onwards the Commission finally agreed to terminate this phase of its efforts to achieve reforms in 1984.

The fourth phase came in 1989 when the Non-Aligned States made it clear that they wanted additional representation on the Commission as well as on other bodies. The proposal to expand the Commission was clearly signalled in a 1989 General Assembly resolution.[301] The Western counter-move was to link the proposed enlargement with proposals for 'enhancement' of the Commission's effectiveness and to insist that both elements had to be part of a package deal. When the matter was taken up by the Commission, the Western group identified a number of specific reforms to be seen as a *quid pro quo* for enlargement. The Non-Aligned group, which clearly had the numbers to guarantee enlargement, responded with its own definition of enhancement. Its radical package of reforms (drafted by India and Pakistan) included proposals that: the Commission's approach should be 'constructive and remedial' and

[296] CHR Res.4 (XXXIII) (1977), para. 4.

[297] Among the key reports on this issue, see: A/5963 (1965); A/10235 (1975); A/32/178 (1977); E/CN.4/Sub.2/1982/26; and E/CN.4/Sub.2/1982/36. See also CHR Res.14 (XXIII) (1967); CHR Res.22 (XXXIV) (1978); and CHR Res.1982/22.

[298] The reports of the Commission's Working Group on Further Promotion and Encouragement of Human Rights are contained in: E/CN.4/L.1413 (1978); E/CN.4/L.1482 (1979); E/CN.4/L.1577 (1981); E/CN.4/L.1577 (1982); E/CN.4/1983/65; E/CN.4/1983/64; E/CN.4/1984/73. The last document contains a brief review of the various proposals that remained outstanding when the process was abandoned.

[299] ESC Res.1979/36.

[300] CHR Res.22 (XXXVI) (1980).

[301] GA Res.44/167, paras. 1 and 3.

that 'judgemental, selective or inquisitorial approaches' should be eschewed; any reforms should involve no additional financial or personnel costs; the time for debate allocated to each item should reflect the importance accorded to it by the international community; all thematic procedures should be undertaken by five-member Working Groups, consisting in part of Geneva-based diplomats, rather than by individual Special Rapporteurs; country rapporteurs be chosen 'from amongst individuals commanding a thorough knowledge and familiarity of [*sic*] the specificities and complexities of the country in question'; the Sub-Commission should no longer adopt any resolutions and should not concern itself with violations; all communications should be dealt with solely under the 1503 procedure and not by the thematic rapporteurs; and the role of NGOs should be restricted. This package was subsequently described as being 'aimed at eviscerating serious Commission scrutiny of violations'.[302]

After the Commission proved unable to resolve the competing proposals it referred the matter to ECOSOC. The latter adopted a package which approved enlargement while at the same time accepting many of the Western proposals including authorization for emergency special sessions (provided a majority of Commission members agrees), three-year mandates for all thematic rapporteurs, and a week-long meeting of the Commission's Bureau to explore organizational reforms.[303]

Despite the relative success achieved by each of these efforts, the great majority of proposals for specific reforms have been unsuccessful. One result is the emergence of a rather defeatist mentality whenever proposals for major changes are made. Thus, for example, proposals to achieve a major overhaul of the 1503 procedure, significant improvement of fact-finding procedures, or a substantial reorganization of the Commission's agenda and of its working methods, would all be actively discouraged by most observers on the grounds of futility. In essence, the arguments most often confronted are that: what has been achieved should not be tampered with; opening up the procedures to debate will only provide opportunities for those wishing to reduce their effectiveness; overlapping and duplication is desirable in order to ensure that if one procedure is neutralized another might nevertheless be able to function effectively; the ethos of the Commission would never tolerate efficient and effective procedures comparable to those already functioning in the ILO, Council of Europe, and (at least with respect to fact-finding) the Organization of American States.

The result is that major innovations have usually been achieved as a result of equally major political confrontations. Sometimes the reforms have simply been pushed through by a determined majority, while in other cases the reforms have been the price that the majority has been prepared to pay in

[302] Brody, *et al.*, 'Major Developments in 1990', 563.
[303] ESC Res.1990/48.

order to achieve some other objective. Thus orderly change and rational step-by-step reforms have been the exception rather than the rule in the functioning of the Commission on Human Rights. This is especially well illustrated by the fate of persistent attempts to rationalize the agenda.

Complaints about the Commission's failure to consider all items on its agenda at any given session are frequently heard. The deferral of certain items year after year, and the unseemly haste with which other items are sometimes dispatched for want of time, provide ample justification for such complaints. In response, the Commission has sought, on several occasions,[304] to streamline its agenda and to devise a long-term programme of work. For the most part, however, these approaches have not produced significant results. In fact, it would be surprising had it been otherwise. The reality is that the Commission invariably finds or makes time to consider those items which the majority considers to be pressing or even relevant; it often fails to do so where the proponents of an item are in a small minority and are unable to bring sufficient pressure to bear, or where there is an unspoken (even unacknowledged) consensus that a matter would best be deferred (which occurs as often for political reasons as for want of time).

Thus for example the Commission deferred its consideration of the items on human rights and scientific and technological developments in 1979 and 1980 and on advisory services in 1976, 1977, and 1979 at least in part because there was little to be said or done under the relevant items. Similarly the abolition of the periodic reports system in 1981 was preceded by the postponement of the relevant item several years in a row because the exercise was known to be futile to all concerned. Thus the quest for technical solutions in the form of a revamped agenda or long-term work programme is often a misplaced response to an essentially political problem.

This was implicitly recognized in the report by the Bureau of the Commission's 1976 session which was convened for three days in advance of the 1977 session to make proposals for rationalizing and planning the Commission's future work. The Bureau rejected a proposal to split the agenda into two groups, each dealing with a particular set of rights; rejected the notion of long-term planning—on the grounds that circumstances are constantly changing; concluded that the grouping together of different agenda items should be decided on an *ad hoc* basis; and, with respect to priorities, proposed that items, other than violations, 'would be dealt with in accordance with their importance and urgency at a given session'.[305]

IV. RELATIONSHIPS WITH OTHER BODIES

The Commission has long sought a key co-ordinating role in terms of human rights activities throughout the UN system. This has involved it in seeking to

[304] e.g. CHR Res.2 (XXV) (1969); CHR Res.7 (XXXII) (1976); and CHR Res.1982/40.
[305] E/CN.4/1243 (1977), para. 8.

develop and consolidate both its *vertical* and *horizontal* relationships within the system. In *vertical* terms, the Commission is part of a formal hierarchy consisting of the Assembly, ECOSOC, itself and the Sub-Commission (originally, there were two Sub-Commissions[306]). In *horizontal* terms, the Commission must relate to other UN bodies and agencies and to the regionhal human rights bodies.

The Commission's vertical relationship has evolved very significantly over the years. In the early years, ECOSOC was an important force and so was the Assembly. Over time, the role of the former waned so that by the 1980s it had become a virtual rubber stamp for the Commission. By contrast, the relationship between the Assembly and the Commission has remained fairly constant over recent years. The Commission enjoys a far greater degree of autonomy from the Assembly than any hierarchical depiction of the arrangements would imply. On the one hand, the level of seniority of Commission representatives is far higher than that of Assembly Third Committee delegates. This helps to ensure that issues will not readily be reopened once the Commission has pronounced itself. One the other hand, the Commission has continued to play an important role as a forum in which human rights activities can be initiated. In some instances the mandate might then be passed on to the Commission for implementation or the locus of activity might remain the Assembly itself. Thus in recent years matters such as studies on private property and on solidarity rights, the free elections initiative, the World Campaign for Human Rights, and the second World Conference on Human Rights (scheduled for 1993) have all originated in the Assembly rather than the Commission.

The Commission's relationship with the Sub-Commission has been rather more convoluted and is described elsewhere in this volume.[307] Suffice it to say in the present context that the two bodies have been effective partners,

[306] In 1947, on the advice of the Commission, the Council had established two sub-commissions. But although one of them—the Sub-Commission on the Freedom of Information and of the Press—dealt with issues of clear human rights significance, the Council requested it to report to it directly. As a result, the Commission did little more than take note of its reports, e.g., Report of the Second Session, E/600 (1947), paras. 31–3, and Report of the Third Session, E/800 (1948), para. 19. The Commission nevertheless recommended the extension of the Sub-Commission's mandate at its Second Session and elected a new set of members to the Sub-Commission in 1949. Report of the Fourth Session, E/1315 (1949), para. 5. As it transpired, this detachment was a blessing given the controversial nature of that Sub-Commission's work and its inability, in the face of dramatic East–West policy disagreements, to achieve anything substantial. According to one observer: 'It was asserted that the sub-commission was attempting too many different projects at the same time, that its recommendations were often unrealistic and its work unfruitful, and that it neglected political barriers to freedom of information while concentrating on technical problems.' Green, *The United Nations and Human Rights*, 724. The Sub-Commission was wound up in 1952 after five sessions and replaced by a Rapporteur who proved to be so blunt and outspoken that his mandate was also terminated after a year. Ibid. 724–8. '[T]he very frankness of the report, which contained detailed statements about governmental controls and censorship, subjected the rapporteur to considerable abuse in the Council'. Ibid. 725. The report was: López, *Freedom of Information*, E/2426 and Add.1–5 (1953–4).

[307] See Chap. 6, below.

and have complemented one another, much more than one might expect from reading the Commission's own debates on the subject.

The Commission has been far less successful in its horizontal relationships. Many of its shortcomings in this regard are documented in Chapter 16 of the present volume. In addition to those difficulties, the Commission has had only a very formalistic relationship with each of the three regional human rights commissions despite the similarity of their tasks. In the case of the African Commission a greater effort has been made in recent years but, in general, the Commission still gives the impression of a body that operates without regard to its peers.

V. THE ROLE OF NON-GOVERNMENTAL ORGANIZATIONS (NGOS)

From the outset, NGOs have played a vital role in the work of the Commission. Nevertheless, the relationship has been sometimes stormy and never easy. Old habits die hard and even the new-found enthusiasm of the Eastern Europeans and various other former antagonists has not led to any significant easing of the formal restrictions that were designed to keep NGOs at arm's length in all of the Commission's endeavours.

The initial rules drawn up by ECOSOC for the granting of consultative status to NGOs were not especially restrictive. Only groups 'discredited by past collaboration in fascist activities' were excluded.[308] But the Cold War and the growing importance of human rights issues led to a change in the early 1950s which made it clear that naming specific governments as violators was unacceptable.[309] It was not to be until 1980 that NGOs were to enjoy relative freedom to name names in their comments to the Commission.[310] In the intervening period major attacks were launched upon many of the leading NGOs in both the Commission and other forums. The rules that were formulated in 1968 and are still applicable are permissive in some respects and highly restrictive in others. Their operation in practice depends on the interpretation applied to them by various actors (the Secretariat, the Chairman of the Commission, etc.) and on the ethos which develops in the relevant body.

In the Commission there has always been a major disparity between the formal (*de jure*) role permitted to NGOs and the real (*de facto*) role that they actually play. While one significantly affects the other, it is the latter

308 ESC Res.2/3 (1946) Part I.

309 ESC Res.288 B (X) (1950). See generally Chiang, *Non-Governmental Organizations at the United Nations: Identity, Role and Function* (1981).

310 For a good overview of this struggle, see Kamminga and Rodley, 'Direct Intervention at the UN: NGO Participation in the Commission on Human Rights and its Sub-Commission', in Hannum (ed.), *Guide to International Human Rights Practice* (1984), 186.

that ultimately counts. In the context of the Commission's standard-setting activities the real role has evolved considerably over the years. Thus, in some recent exercises such as the drafting of the Convention on the Rights of the Child and of a draft declaration on human rights monitors[311] NGOs have been treated as full participants (i.e., on a par with States) for most purposes other than voting. Their resulting influence has been very considerable, although it is usually seen to be in their best interests to refrain from blowing their own trumpets in this regard. In terms of protection activities it has always been the NGOs that have applied the real pressure for reform of the Commission's procedures and the great majority of the 'evidence' of violations continues to be generated directly by NGOs. Indeed many of the country-specific reports prepared for the Commission have been very heavily dependent upon NGOs for their content. Similarly, the relationships between the thematic rapporteurs and NGOs have generally been very close. NGOs have also come to play a key role in briefing delegates on various issues and in securing support for resolutions, some of which may have been drafted by the NGOs themselves.

Over the past decade or so NGOs have become increasingly sophisticated in their approach to the Commission. Amnesty International now has a permanent Geneva office, and other influential NGOs such as the International Commission of Jurists and Defence for Children International have long played important co-ordinating roles within the NGO community. Since the late 1980s a major effort has been made by NGOs to present shared positions and to submit documents which have widespread support. Thus, for example, a 1990 document on reform of the Commission's procedures was submitted on behalf of 35 different NGOs.[312] Even Amnesty, which for many years sought to remain aloof from such co-operative lobbying exercises, is now an active partner in many of them.

The observation has frequently been made that the NGOs represented at the Commission are predominantly from the North.[313] This is undoubtedly true, although on issues such as disappearances, development, and indigenous peoples the involvement of groups from the South has been significant. Nevertheless, initiatives such as the greater use of trust funds to facilitate the participation of NGOs from the South in the Commission's meetings deserve greater consideration than they have received to date.

Despite the fact that NGOs are indispensable to the effective functioning of the Commission, their position will never be accepted more than grudgingly by the States that make up the Commission. If it were otherwise it would be

[311] E/CN.4/1990/47 and CHR Res.1990/47.
[312] E/CN.4/1990/WG.3/WP.5.
[313] E/CN.4/1990/WG.3/WP.4, and Blaser, 'Human Rights in the Third World and Development of International Nongovernmental Organizations', in Shepherd and Nanda (eds.), *Human Rights and Third World Development* (1985), Chap. 11.

safe to say that NGOs were not behaving as they should: in an informed, independent, critical, and uncompromising manner. Thus, no geopolitical group has a monopoly on anti-NGO sentiments. Even in the United States, critics have suggested that the 'primary "hidden agenda" of most activist [human rights] organizations' is to cast 'into doubt the moral status of American foreign policy'.[314] It therefore comes as no surprise that the concessions won by NGOs in terms of their standing *vis-à-vis* the Commission have been piecemeal, hard-fought, fragile, and incomplete. Similarly, the prospects for positive, formal changes in the future are regrettably slim.

D. *The Commission's Place in the World*

Policy-oriented recommendations relating to the different functions performed by the Commission have been made in the context of each of the major preceding sections of this chapter. They will not be repeated here. Suffice it to say that most governments have tended to underestimate not only the need for major procedural reforms in the way the Commission works but also the political feasibility of achieving such reforms. The reality is that very little governmental time or effort has been devoted to reviewing the Commission's functioning. This is not surprising given the heavy political and administrative burdens that membership of the Commission entails. Nevertheless, there is a strong case to be made in favour of the propositions that major reforms are possible and that they could, if undertaken, yield significant savings in terms of time and energy, as well as enhancing effectiveness.

What remains to be done in this final section is to assess the significance of the Commission's work. We need to try to answer the question: does it make any real difference that the UN Commission on Human Rights has adopted a particular stance on a given issue? If it does, in what contexts and in what ways? These questions assume even greater importance for those who have witnessed only one, or at most two, sessions of the Commission and are very likely to have concluded that it is a frustratingly slow-moving and inherently ineffectual talking shop. The Commission's culture is a rarefied and alien one and cannot readily be grasped by those who do not take the time to understand how it really functions.

For analytical purposes the Commission can be seen to function in two main ways. It provides a forum in which various activities can be undertaken and it is itself an actor playing the roles of a catalyst, a manager, a generator of norms, and a protector of rights. We turn now to examine the effectiveness of each of these functions.

314 Kristol, '"Human Rights": The Hidden Agenda', *The National Interest* (Winter 1986/7), 6.

I. THE COMMISSION AS A FORUM

The Commission provides a forum for at least four different types of activities. The first and most general is for consultation within and among the different geopolitical and other groupings. Each of the major groups has a reasonably well known, although often only vaguely articulated, stance on the major human rights issues facing the international community. On a fairly regular basis, some individual Western States issue detailed policy statements, the Non-Aligned Movement regularly adopts group positions, the European Community and the Nordic nations prepare joint statements from time to time and so on. But in the context of the Commission, each of the groups, and indeed each individual member State, is forced to address an enormous range of specific topics of current import and to adopt a policy stance thereon. The Commission thus provides a forum for consultation on human rights issues that is of unequalled importance. The consequences of such consultation go well beyond particular votes in the Commission framework. It involves also an important socialization process by which competing conceptions are not just communicated but explained and justified. It provides a degree of personal interaction which can greatly enhance the effectiveness of subsequent bilateral and multilateral discussions on related issues.

The second type of activity for which the Commission provides a forum is seeking co-operative solutions to problems. The word 'co-operative' does not necessarily imply that such quests are always amiable or that they are free of political pressures. They might indeed be rather confrontational affairs in which one State learns the real depth of concern at its human rights policies on the part of some of its peers while the latter are forced to temper their demands in the hope of promoting a genuine improvement in the situation. Such issues will be discussed differently in a multilateral forum than they usually can be in a bilateral setting. Evidence of the Commission's effectiveness in performing this function is, almost by definition, difficult to gather. Nevertheless, in a number of country situations, and certainly in terms of promotional and other activities, the Commission has succeeded in prompting considerably greater co-operation than might otherwise have been the case.

The Commission also provides a useful forum for the canvassing of new issues. When the human rights dimensions of matters such as the AIDS disease, environmental degradation, or child labour (to mention but a few) are raised for the first time, the Commission, usually in conjunction with the Sub-Commission, can provide a forum for analysis, discussion, and consciousness-raising which is not readily available elsewhere. Similarly, the inscription of such issues on the Commission's agenda can, over time, provide an important degree of legitimacy to those issues in terms of domestic human rights and public policy agendas.

Finally, the Commission also provides a forum for the pursuit of conflict, especially between neighbouring States. Debates over various conflicts (such as those involving Arabs and Israelis, Greece and Turkey, Kampuchea and Vietnam, Iran and Iraq, South Africa and others) have succeeded in generating large quantities of often poisonous invective, leading some observers to question the value of the whole exercise and to suggest that matters might only be made worse as a result. It is true that significant chunks of discussion time have been taken up by seemingly futile 'to and fro' debates and that a large amount of documentation has been generated in the process. It may be questioned, however, whether these battles are, in fact, entirely futile or whether the debates do serve useful educative, symbolic, or frustration-release functions for the aggrieved sides and in relation to the public at large. Positions might be more carefully honed in the Commission context than elsewhere and the human rights legal dimensions given closer attention than would otherwise be the case. These justifications might not always be applicable, but they would seem to be valid in a considerable number of cases.

Moreover, the Commission's most important contribution is not in the context of these highly polarized and deeply entrenched 'hard' cases, but in relation to the more typical cases such as El Salvador, Romania, or Iran. In the latter case, for example, the Commission was able to generate a significant amount of information about a situation that was not otherwise well documented by 'impartial' sources. The responses by the government and by the relevant NGOs to the Commission's reports may have been heated and highly critical but they nevertheless serve the purpose of making the debate more precise, more sophisticated and more clearly focused on international norms.

II. THE COMMISSION AS AN ACTOR

The very suggestion that the Commission is an actor in its own right immediately provokes the response that its performance is solely a reflection of the aggregated strengths and shortcomings of the governments that compose it. Several decades ago Lauterpacht warned of 'the danger of attributing to a collective body, called "the Commission on Human Rights" the responsibility which rests upon the Governments concerned'.[315] There is much to be said for such an approach. If, by way of example, the Commission fails to take action against China in the wake of the crushing of the democracy movement, it is not because the Commission as a collective entity is pusillanimous or has different priorities, but because a majority of the member States does not wish to act. But by the same token, the Commission is in many other respects, considerably more than the sum of its formal constituent parts. The Commission as an entity includes, in addition to the member States: the

[315] Lauterpacht, *International Law and Human Rights*, 257.

governmental observers, who can have a major impact upon the voting behaviour of members; the Secretariat which has many an opportunity to influence outcomes if it so wishes; and the NGOs whose representatives can significantly influence governmental understanding of issues and especially their assessments of the political import of those issues. The Commission also has its own 'corporate culture' built up over many years of experience. That culture is often negative, in that it errs on the side of protecting the status quo and encourages undue deference to repressive governments. But it also has its positive side which can result in a stronger collective sensitivity to human rights issues being shown by a group than would be the case if the members were acting alone. There is thus good reason, in addition to convenience of expression, to treat the Commission as an entity for analytical purposes, even in situations in which the sum of the views of the member States is all that really matters.

As an actor in its own right the Commission has acted as an important catalyst to the preparation and dissemination of information on human rights issues by individuals and groups all over the world. Those aggrieved by governmental behaviour can turn to the Commission (and its Sub-Commission) to an extent that is unequalled by any other international body. The Assembly and the Council are effectively closed to NGOs and lobbyists, and most of the treaty bodies remain determinedly aloof from activist groups. The Commission provides not only a rallying-point for concerned groups but also a forum in which many of them can speak and issue statements. Even though these 'privileges' are qualified in very many respects, their symbolic importance cannot be overestimated. The Commission often confers an important aura of legitimacy upon activities that might otherwise be too readily denigrated as merely subversive or whatever.

As an actor, the Commission also plays the role of a manager. In principle, it is to the Commission that the Secretariat should be accountable for its activities in a wide range of areas. Yet in practice the Commission has proven to be a poor manager. In areas such as public information, advisory services, seminars, and the like, the Commission's real influence has been less than it should have. Similarly, it has only recently begun to tackle, and then rather timidly, the problem of the enormous number of requests for information directed to governments by the various human rights bodies.[316] In budgetary matters, the division of responsibilities between the Commission on the one hand, and the Third and Fifth Committees of the General Assembly on the other hand, is so unclear that appropriate lines of responsibility have never really been established. While the Assembly must ultimately control the purse strings, the Commission itself should have some means of determining budgetary and staffing priorities. Its existing role in this regard (which is

[316] CHR Res.1990/70.

largely confined to noting the financial implications of its proposals) is far from statisfactory.

Another aspect of its management role is to co-ordinate the UN's human rights programme in general. But here too the Commission's effectiveness has been limited. The co-ordination mandate bestowed upon it in 1979 has been rarely used,[317] although in recent years it has begun to play a much more active and constructive role *vis-à-vis* the treaty bodies. Many of the suggestions generated by the Meetings of the Chairpersons of the Human Rights Treaty Bodies,[318] which the Assembly has noted but done little about, have been taken up by the Commission, especially at its 1991 session.[319]

Another of the Commission's roles has been as a generator of norms. In terms of formal standard-setting activities it has been the principal locus for some (e.g., conventions on torture and children's rights and a declaration on development), a player but not the dominant influence in others (e.g., a protocol on the death penalty and a declaration on the rights of the mentally ill) and has been largely irrelevant in others (e.g., the migrant workers convention). But its major contribution in this area has been as a legitimator of norms once they have been adopted. The example *par excellence* is the Universal Declaration of Human Rights. While its formal standing in international law remains a matter of some controversy,[320] the Commission has treated it as a universally applicable set of norms and its approach is responsible, to a significant extent, for the extremely high standing that it now enjoys.

The Commission's final role as an actor is as a protector of individuals and groups. Because of its size and nature as well as its rigid meeting schedule, the Commission can generally only aspire to react rapidly to alleged or anticipated violations through the agency of its Chairman or one of its rapporteurs. The role of the former has varied considerably from one incumbent to another and there would seem to be significant scope for seeking to expand the role in the future. To date, however, most of the occupants of the position have used their influence sparingly. The thematic rapporteurs have, by using the model developed by the Disappearances Working Group (and pioneered by Amnesty International), begun to evolve a significant capacity for prompt responses. They are, however, confined to the use of telegrams and the like and have not yet moved very far towards seeking the immediate mobilization of public or governmental opinion (an option that many observers would, in any event, counsel them not to use). The Commission's other rapporteurs have been more timid in this regard, perhaps assuming that such interventions

[317] Some efforts were initiated in 1991 to remedy this deficiency, but they have yet to bear fruit. See CHR Res.1991/22.

[318] A/39/484 (1984); A/44/98 (1989); A/45/636 (1990).

[319] CHR Res.1991/[L.13].

[320] Meron, *Human Rights and Humanitarian Norms as Customary Law* (1990).

would jeopardize their fact-finding and conciliation functions. The result of these activities is that the Commission is far more responsive to violations and more interventionist *vis-à-vis* governments than most observers would have dared to hope as recently as ten years ago. But, if we apply a different measure, the Commission remains depressingly detached from most of the atrocities that occur in the world today and its role remains less that of a protector than a recorder of the facts and a much needed forum for post-mortem examinations. Even in the case of UN staff members whose rights have been violated, the Commission has been a reluctant and less than forceful source of protection.[321]

It may be that, as a protector, the Commission's most effective role is an indirect one. Its very existence as a forum in which most gross violations are likely to be raised, perhaps sooner, perhaps later, generates significant pressure upon governments. Similarly, the greater weight that the Commission's activities are capable of imparting to the efforts of NGOs and to bilateral governmental initiatives should not be underestimated.

III. CONCLUDING OBSERVATION

In concluding, it would do an injustice to the Commission if mention were not made of the tangible, external signs of its place in the world. In the first place, competition among States for membership of the Commission is unusually intense. While the cynic will respond that all foxes are anxious to guard their local chicken coops, it is rarely very productive in the human rights area to evaluate governmental action on the basis of the underlying motivation involved. Secondly, as noted above, the level of general participation by the international community as broadly defined is greater than in virtually any other UN arena. Thirdly, NGOs and others have seen fit to devote enormous amounts of time, energy, and resources to attending its sessions, lobbying its members, and preparing very detailed submissions.[322] Finally, governmental lobbying has at times been extremely intense, a practice which must signify that some importance is attached to the Commission's position on at least some issues.

Although the Commission rarely provides enough drama or transparency to attract the sustained attention of the media, there have been exceptions. One such story provides a good illustration of the ability of the Commission to 'get up the nose' even of a superpower. In 1983 when the Reagan Administration's activities in Central America and its policies on Eastern Europe and elsewhere were bringing it into conflict with the Commission on certain issues, *Newsweek* ran a major story which concluded:

[321] CHR Res.1990/31.

[322] e.g. the 353-page hard-cover book produced by the Secretariat of the National Council of Resistance of Iran entitled *Human Rights Betrayed: Galindo Pohl's Report Under Scrutiny* (1990).

The Human Rights Commission has *nothing* to say for itself. It costs $10 million a year. At very best, its resolutions have no effect at all. And the annual spectacle of its partial, partisan debates must be repugnant to any serious advocate of human rights and dignity. If the West is serious in its moralizing about reviving the United Nations, it could start by starving this preposterous commission out of existence.[323]

But it would seem odd for such passion to be excited by a body whose ineffectiveness is anywhere near as great as the authors purport to believe.

[323] *Newsweek* (28 Feb. 1983), 22.

6
The Sub-Commission on Prevention of Discrimination and Protection of Minorities

ASBJØRN EIDE

Introduction

It is significant that a major outcry from the human rights community was heard in 1986, when the annual session of the Sub-Commission on Prevention of Discrimination and Protection of Minorities was cancelled, ostensibly because of the UN's financial crisis. NGOs convened a protest meeting in Geneva, attended by numerous experts and government observers, in an effort to make sure that such cancellations would not happen again.[1] The outcry occurred because the Sub-Commission has come to play a unique role in the international dynamics of human rights, due mainly to the independence of its members and its exceptional openness to participation by NGOs, as well as to its mandate which has continuously been stretched, without formal amendments, to accommodate new tasks.

The Sub-Commission is an expert body subordinate to the Commission and ECOSOC established to provide analysis and advice to the former. But it has also become a link between the official, intergovernmental institutions and the general public, as represented by the NGOs. As a consequence, it has repeatedly shown more independence than expected by its parent bodies. Controversy over its role has been endemic since its creation in 1947. Although the Commission recognizes the obvious usefulness of the Sub-Commission, relations between the two bodies are never likely to be entirely harmonious.

The task initially given the Sub-Commission was to recommend standards to be adopted in the fields of prevention of discrimination and protection of minorities, though it was recognized that it might also be entrusted with other functions.[2] In 1948, the year of the adoption of the Universal Declaration, the

[1] The report and recommendations from the seminar were submitted by the delegation of the United Kingdom to the General Assembly. See A/41/926 (1986).

[2] When the Commission decided to establish a Sub-Commission on Prevention of Discrimination and Protection of Minorities, it 'decided that the functions of the Sub-Commission should be: (a) In the first instance, to examine what provisions should be adopted in

emphasis on standard-setting was diminished and the Sub-Commission was henceforth to undertake studies, particularly in the light of the Universal Declaration, and to make recommendations to the Commission.[3] Since 1949, no formal revision of the mandate has been made, but since the existing mandate is open-ended its functions have been considerably expanded at the request of the Commission and ECOSOC;[4] the Sub-Commission has also repeatedly expanded its mandate on its own initiative, most, but not all, instances of which have been accepted by the Commission, however, grudgingly.

The Sub-Commission now has twenty-six members, elected by the Commission, based on regional distribution from among individuals nominated by their governments; there is a requirement that members shall be 'independent experts' but no formal criteria for evaluating the qualifications of nominees have been established. It has one annual session, lasting four weeks and preceded by pre-sessional working groups of one or two weeks' duration. A large number of observers attends the sessions, including NGO representatives, a sprinkling of representatives of intergovernmental organizations, and a growing number of governmental observers. The often confrontational nature of the interaction between NGOs and government observers, over human rights violations, has contributed to an increasing politicization of the Sub-Commission. While the role of the NGOs has been essential to the evolution of the United Nations' protection role, a stage appears to have been reached during the last years of the 1980s where the confrontation between NGOs and government observers was becoming dysfunctional unless more sophisticated methods to deal with violations were found. Taking into account, however, the resistance both by Socialist and many Third World countries to any improvement in the mechanisms of handling violations, it appeared to be almost impossible to resolve this dilemma.

At the beginning of the 1990s the situation has changed as a consequence of the political evolution in Central and Eastern Europe. From these countries, much more support is now forthcoming for international human

defining the principles to be applied in the field of the prevention of discrimination on grounds of race, sex, language or religion, and in the field of the protection of minorities, and to make recommendations to the Commission on urgent problems in these fields. (b) To perform any other functions which may be entrusted to it by the Economic and Social Council or the Commission on Human Rights' (*Report of the Commission on Human Rights in 1947* [First Session], E/259 (1947), para. 19).

[3] In 1949, the Commission amended section (a) of the previous mandate (ibid.) to read: '(a) to undertake studies, particularly in the light of the Universal Declaration of Human Rights concerning the prevention of discrimination of any kind relating to human rights and fundamental freedoms and the protection of racial, national, religious and linguistic minorities'. Section (b) was maintained as before: 'Terms of Reference of the Sub-Commission', CHR Res. on the Prevention of Discrimination and the Protection of Minorities, in *Report of the Commission on Human Rights in 1949* [Fifth Session], E/1371 (1949), para. 13, sect. A.

[4] ESC Res.1334 (XLIV) (1968); ESC Dec. 1978/21; and ESC Res.1986/35.

rights mechanisms. This also includes greater acceptance of the role of NGOs. At the time of writing, it remains to be seen how the various Third World countries will react to the new situation. Most probably they will not react as a monolithic bloc. While some will remain negative to international human rights monitoring, a wide scope of new possibilities seems to have opened up.

A. *Evolution of the Mandate*

Initially the Sub-Commission seemed to have a limited field to cover: prevention of discrimination and protection of minorities. There were other Sub-Commissions established to deal with other tasks: one to focus on the rights of women, another to deal with freedom of information and the press. The former was subsequently transformed into the Commission on the Status of Women;[5] the latter was cancelled in 1952.[6] Consequently, there remained only one Sub-Commission, to which the Commission has come to turn for tasks far beyond its original terms of reference. At the outset, however, prevention of discrimination and protection of minorities were the main goals to be pursued.

Not that these goals were straightforward: they turned out to contain innumerable problems with which the Sub-Commission has had to struggle throughout its existence. In the early years, the Western powers (which then dominated the United Nations) were lukewarm at best to the prevention of discrimination,[7] and overtly hostile to the protection of minorities.[8]

During its first session, in 1947, the Sub-Commission innocently assumed that its tasks were to be taken seriously. It sought as a first step to clarify the meaning of its mandate. It defined 'prevention of discrimination' as the prevention of any action which denied individuals or groups equality of treatment which they might wish,[9] and interpreted the 'protection of minorities' as

[5] See Chap. 7, below.

[6] ESC Res.1986/35.

[7] In the United States, the civil rights struggle for racial equality was a dominant and deeply divisive factor. The American Bar Association, which came to have considerable influence on US human rights policies, for many years took a conservative position on civil rights, an attitude which it also pursued in its international policies. Racial discrimination was also a significant reality in the colonial empires still held by several Western European States.

[8] Both the United States and Latin American governments, dominated by descendants of settlers which had come from many different European countries, strongly supported assimilationist policies towards minorities. European states had mixed feelings: colonial powers feared that the minority issue would be used in the anti-colonial struggle; others had bad memories of the way in which Nazi Germany had exploited the minority issue in Central and Eastern Europe as part of its policy of destabilization and conquest. On the other hand, it was recognized that some real minority issues had to be faced in Europe.

[9] *Report of the Sub-Commission in 1947*, E/CN.4/52 (1947), sect. V, 13.

the protection of non-dominant groups which generally wanted equality of treatment, while acknowledging or permitting a measure of differential treatment in order for the minorities to preserve their traditional characteristics, if they so desired.[10] According to the mandate the relevant characteristics were race, nationality, religion, and language.

Limitations on the protection to be accorded to minorities were envisaged, however. For example, they were to be accorded differential treatment only so long as it did not conflict with the welfare of the community as a whole. The minorities were to owe their individual allegiance to the government of the State in which they lived, in addition to being nationals of that State. Furthermore, if individuals belonging to such minorities wanted to become assimilated with the majority, but were prevented from doing so, it would constitute discrimination.

The Secretariat later issued a memorandum,[11] which was largely endorsed by the Sub-Commission in 1949,[12] elaborating on the relationship between prevention of discrimination and protection of minorities. The memorandum emphasized the fundamental differences between the two objectives, and concluded that the two had to be handled very differently.

Discrimination implied any act or conduct which denied equality of treatment to certain individuals because they belonged to particular groups. In order to prevent discrimination, some method had to be found to suppress or eliminate any conduct which denied or restricted a person's right to equality. The protection of minorities, by contrast, consisted of enforcing distinctions, voluntarily maintained by the group concerned, which to a large extent required positive action. The memorandum referred to the rendering of services, such as the establishment of schools in which teaching would be in the child's mother tongue. This was required, according to the memorandum, in order to achieve real equality. If the child was not taught in his or her own language, he or she would be discriminated against when compared to the majority who were taught in their mother tongue.

In theoretical terms, the memorandum was logical, but in practice not very helpful. Applied to concrete situations, the principles espoused were bound to create political controversy and practical problems. Numerous dilemmas have arisen. One problem, albeit minor, is caused by the conflicting aspirations of many individual members of minorities groups; they may want differential treatment and equality at the same time. Alternately, programmes to protect minorities can become shields behind which racial discrimination is perpetuated under the pretext of differential treatment. For example, in the

[10] Ibid.

[11] 'Definition and Classification of Minorities. Memorandum Submitted by the Secretary-General', E/CN.4/Sub.2/85 (1950).

[12] Sub-Commission Res. D, *Report of the Sub-Commission in 1950*, E/CN.4/358 (1950), paras. 29–38.

United States, debate on the 'separate but equal' doctrine was finally laid to rest by the Supreme Court only in 1954.[13] In South Africa, the doctrine of apartheid, officially proclaimed in 1948, also purported to provide special 'protection' to racial groups. In response to such claims, the Sub-Commission emphasized that only those who desired to preserve their separate characteristics should be granted protection.

Most governments are generally reluctant to accept the existence of minorities on their territory. In an effort to allay governmental fears of separatist or secessionist claims the Sub-Commission stated that members of minorities should owe undivided allegiance to the State in which they lived. Nevertheless, the fact remained that international recognition of minority rights might encourage separatist ambitions endangering territorial integrity and could provoke conflicts among different national groups over access to land and public resources. Thus, the Sub-Commission's mandate contained the seeds of significant conflict with governments and between different ethnic groups.

I. PREVENTION OF DISCRIMINATION

The initial task of the Sub-Commission in 1947 was to comment on the Commission's draft of the non-discrimination clause (Article 2) to be included in the Universal Declaration. The Sub-Commission suggested the addition of 'political or other opinion' and 'material condition, national or social origin'.[14] With minor modifications, the Sub-Commission's recommendations were accepted by the Commission and, with some elaboration, by the Third Committee of the General Assembly as well.[15]

The main activity of the Sub-Commission in this field has taken the form of studies, exploring different aspects of discrimination in some depth. The revised 1969 mandate[16] called on the Sub-Commission to undertake 'studies, particularly in the light of the Universal Declaration'. While the prevention of discrimination had been incorporated in the Universal Declaration, the protection of minorities had not; the Sub-Commission therefore had a further standard-setting task to be performed in the latter field. As it turned out, that effort brought the Sub-Commission to the brink of extinction.[17] By 1952, it was a chastened Sub-Commission which finally turned to an elaboration of its study programme, in the knowledge that Western members, led by the United States, were antipathetic to its continued existence. It sought, therefore, to develop a study programme, which was acceptable to the West. The result came to colour its subsequent priorities significantly.

[13] *Brown et al.* v. *Board of Education of Topeka et al.*, 347 US 483 (1954).
[14] *Report of the Sub-Commission in 1947*, E/CN.4/52 (1947), 4.
[15] *See Report of the Third Committee in 1948*, A/777 (1948).
[16] 'Terms of Reference of the Sub-Commission', n. 3, above.
[17] See text accompanying n. 194, below.

The programme was launched in 1952 with the aim of presenting recommendations or concrete measures 'for hastening the eradication of discrimination'.[18] It remains probably the greatest achievement of the Sub-Commission, if for no other reason than because it was the only field in which it was allowed to develop its own profile. It represented, however, a marked retreat from the Sub-Commission's early involvement in the drafting of standards.

In seeking less controversial methods than standard-setting, the Sub-Commission also responded to a change in United States policy following the election of the new Republican administration in 1952. In 1953, the United States declared that the international protection of human rights should not proceed through the adoption and implementation of international instruments. Instead, 'methods of persuasion, education and example' should be employed.[19] Thus the studies programme was initially adopted to allay fears, harboured primarily by Western States, of an overtly activist approach by the Sub-Commission with respect to issues which were not perceived to be in the interest of these States.

Discussion of the focus of the programme in the Sub-Commission was initially based upon a report of the Secretary-General to ECOSOC on possible UN activities in the fields of discrimination and minorities, on the assumption that the mandate of the Sub-Commission would be discontinued.[20] The report had proposed 'objective studies of actual conditions in various parts of the world'.[21] It immediately ran into difficulties on political grounds when the Sub-Commission sought to implement it. The proposal to study 'actual conditions' gave rise to fears on the part of the United Kingdom and other colonial powers that the situation in their colonies would be investigated. Accordingly, the United Kingdom and its Western allies sought in the Commission, in 1953 and 1954, to amend the study programme in order to prevent the Sub-Commission from considering specific cases of discrimination, to limit the studies to the purpose of drawing only general, rather than country-specific, conclusions, and to restrict the use of information from non-governmental sources.[22]

The UK representative at the 1953 session of the Commission invoked

[18] CHR Res. E, in *Report of the Commission in 1953*, E/2447 (1953), Annex IV.

[19] 'The present administration intends to encourage the promotion everywhere of human rights, but to favour methods of persuasion, education, and example rather than formal undertakings which commit one part of the world to impose its particular standards upon another part of the world community, which has different standards'. *US Dep. St. Bull.* 592 (1953).

[20] 'Report by the Secretary-General under Council Resolution 414 B II (XIII) on the Future Work of the United Nations in the Fields of Prevention of Discrimination and Protection of Minorities', E/2229 (1952). ECOSOC decided, however, not to discuss the substance of the report, since the General Assembly had, in the mean time, ordered it to authorize the continuation of the Sub-Commission. GA Res.532 B (VI) (1952).

[21] E/2229 (1952), para. 71.

[22] See *Report of the Commission on Human Rights in 1953*, E/2447 (1953), Annex IV, paras. 63–82; and *Report of the Commission on Human Rights in 1954*, E/2573 (1954), paras. 373–418.

Article 2(7) of the Charter[23] and also argued that the Sub-Commission's plan seemed to be a 'purely expert approach', evidently meaning that political realities were not properly taken into account. Initially, the Soviet expert was also reluctant to accept the study programme. He preferred the Sub-Commission to work directly on standard-setting rather than to carry out what he called 'academic work'.[24]

The initial plan for the study programme was adopted in the Commission by 10 votes to 1 (France) with 5 abstentions, most of them Western.[25] The terms of reference for Sub-Commission studies, drafted by the Sub-Commission in 1953, were approved by the Commission in 1954 by 11 votes to 4, with 2 abstentions, with most Western States either voting against or abstaining.[26] The United States, however, voted in favour.

Once adopted, the programme was sought to be used in the East–West confrontation which was intensifying at that time. This was done by seeking to select for study such aspects of discrimination as might be particularly relevant to the situation in the Soviet Union and Eastern Europe. In general, three sets of issues emerged: (*a*) discrimination on what *grounds*; (*b*) discrimination in regard to what *rights*; and (*c*) discrimination by *whom*?

In choosing among the *grounds* of discrimination to be investigated, Article 2 of the Universal Declaration refers us to 'race, colour, sex, language, religion, political or other opinion, national or social origin, property, birth or other status'. Discrimination on the ground of sex has largely been dealt with in the Commission on the Status of Women. The other grounds, however, would form proper subjects for the Sub-Commission. Not surprisingly, the preferences of the geopolitical groups differ. Western countries are less interested in investigating discrimination on the grounds of race or colour, since white people have rarely been the victims of such discrimination, while Europeans and their descendants elsewhere have often been on the offending side. Quite the reverse is the position of African and Asian countries. Emotional memories of discrimination due to race and colour have led to a strong sense of solidarity wherever such discrimination takes place. Socialist countries have until recently tended to line up with African and Asian countries on such matters.

Discrimination on the grounds of religion, or based on political or other opinion, is a different matter. This is an area in which the Western countries have fewer problems but where the Socialist countries in the past and some Islamic countries at present are vulnerable to criticism.

[23] 'Nothing contained in the present Charter shall authorize the United Nations to intervene in matters which are essentially within the domestic jurisdiction of any state . . .'. Art. 2(7), Charter of the United Nations.

[24] See E/CN.4/SR.402 (1953), 17.

[25] *Report of the Commission on Human Rights in 1953*, E/2447 (1953), Annex IV, paras. 63–82.

[26] E/CN.4/SR.459 (1954), 4–13.

The choice of the rights or benefits in regard to which discrimination occurs, when determining the focus of a study, has been another area of controversy. This is well illustrated by one study, the focus of which was completely changed from the time of the initial decision by the Sub-Commission until its authorization by ECOSOC in which the Western countries held a clear majority at the time. The original proposal concerned discrimination in immigration and travel.[27] ECOSOC transformed the focus so that the study ended up dealing with the right to leave any country and to return to one's own country, as provided for in Article 13(2) of the Universal Declaration.[28] This caused considerable resentment by many Third World, and particularly Socialist experts, against whose States' practices the study was now primarily directed.[29]

Although all but one of the Special Rapporteurs selected in the decade or so after 1952 came from the Third World (Lebanon, India, Chile, the Philippines, and Sudan) the studies principally dealt with issues which were of most immediate concern to the developed States.[30] From the mid-1960s, East–West rivalry in the context of the study programme became less marked, as Third World concerns came rapidly to the fore. With the sudden increase of UN Afro-Asian membership, voting power in the General Assembly shifted in favour of a Third World majority. While not immediately reflecting itself in the Sub-Commission's composition, the concerns of this new majority were injected more and more into its deliberations. Thus, for example, a British effort to exclude the consideration of the issue of self-determination from the study of discrimination in the matter of political rights was unsuccessful,[31] and the final report condemned all forms of colonialism.[32] Similarly, the Sub-Commission became increasingly concerned with racial rather than political discrimination. The issue of apartheid emerged in the mid-1960s, in a number of different contexts, and came to occupy an increasing part of the Sub-Commission's time thereafter.

A special report on the 'adverse consequences for the enjoyment of human rights of political, military, economic, and other forms of assistance given to the colonial and racist regimes of Southern Africa'[33] was prepared, and was subsequently followed by a listing of banks, transnational corporations, and

[27] See *Report of the Sub-Commission in 1952*, E/CN.4/670 (1952), paras. 253–9 and Annex I, draft Res. F, Part A, para. 1.

[28] ESC Res.545 D (XVIII) (1954).

[29] See the discussion in the relevant Committee of the ESC, E/AC.7/SR.289 (1954), 14–18.

[30] For a complete list of studies undertaken by Sub-Commission Rapporteurs, see Section 5 of the Bibliography, below.

[31] See E/CN.4/SR.471 (1954), 13–14.

[32] Santa Cruz, *Study of Discrimination in the Matter of Political Rights*, E/CN.4/Sub.2/213/Rev.1 (1962), 42.

[33] Khalifa, *Adverse Consequences for the Enjoyment of Human Rights of Political, Military, Economic and other Forms of Assistance Given to the Colonial and Racist Regimes in Southern Africa*, E/CN.4/Sub.2/469 and Add.1.

other organizations assisting the colonial and racist regimes in Southern Africa. This list is presently updated annually.[34]

The Sub-Commission's activities in this area have been of great importance, not only for their own sake but also because they have set precedents which have been used in relation to other situations. Like other UN bodies, the Sub-Commission has, however, notably failed to co-ordinate its anti-apartheid studies with those being undertaken elsewhere in the UN system.

II. PROTECTION OF MINORITIES

One of the two dimensions of the Sub-Commission's original mandate concerned the protection of minorities. It has turned out to be a near-impossible task. For reasons noted earlier, many countries of the 'new world' favoured policies of assimilation, while the 'old world', and in particular Arab, Asian, and Socialist European countries supported efforts to develop some system for the protection of minorities.

The original Secretariat draft of the Universal Declaration contained a provision based on the pre-war experiences with minorities, recognizing the rights of persons belonging to certain minorities to maintain their own schools and religious and cultural institutions and to have resources made available for that purpose, and to use their own language in the press, public meetings, and the courts and tribunals of the State.[35] The Commission's Drafting Committee toned it down by omitting the right to obtain resources for the above purposes,[36] and transferred the draft to the Sub-Commission in 1947. After a long debate, the Sub-Commission proposed the following text:

> In States inhabited by well-defined ethnic, linguistic or other groups which are clearly distinguished from the rest of the population, and which want to be accorded differential treatment, persons belonging to such groups shall have the right, as far as is compatible with public order and security, to establish and maintain their own schools and cultural or religious institutions, and to use their own language and script in the Press, in public assembly and before the courts and other authorities of the State, if they so choose.[37]

The most important addition made by the Sub-Commission was that only those groups which wanted differential treatment should have the right to it. This was to prevent abuses such as the imposition of segregation *against* the will of those concerned. The debate in the Sub-Commission also acknowledged the rights of non-citizens under the minority protection system. Despite

[34] See E/CN.4/Sub.2/1990/13 and Add.1 for an updated version.

[35] Art. 46 of the Secretariat draft, in E/CN.4/21 (1947), Annex A, 23.

[36] *Report of the Commission on Human Rights in 1947* [Second Session], E/600, Annex A, Art. 31 ('Text Proposed by the Drafting Committee').

[37] Ibid. ('Text Proposed by the Sub-Commission on Prevention of Discrimination and Protection of Minorities').

strong protests, the majority proposed a formulation which did *not* limit the protection to nationals of the State involved.[38]

In the Commission, however, the majority was opposed to the inclusion of any reference to the protection of minorities in the Universal Declaration and the draft forwarded to the General Assembly contained no such provision.[39] Positions were also sharply divided in the Assembly's Third Committee[40] and no such provision was ultimately included. However, as a compromise, and simultaneously with the adoption of the Universal Declaration, the Assembly adopted a resolution calling on the Sub-Commission 'to make a thorough study of the problem of minorities, in order that the United Nations may be able to take effective measures for the protection of racial, national, religious or linguistic minorities'.[41]

It was thus increasingly evident that the United Nations was deeply split over the desirability of a system of protection of minorities. Nevertheless, the Assembly resolution was essentially a reaffirmation of the Sub-Commission's responsibility to pursue its mandate in this field. In response, the Sub-Commission, in 1949, identified three steps required in order to carry out the 'thorough study' requested: (*a*) definition of minorities; (*b*) classification, according to categories of protection required; and (*c*) collection of information about the situation of minorities. The Sub-Commission also proposed that a special provision be inserted in the Covenant on Civil and Political Rights, which was then being drafted.[42] Its debate on the proposed provision revealed the existence of two broad schools of thought. For the first, the minority group itself was the beneficiary of the protection to be afforded, while for the second, the beneficiary was the individual member of the group. The draft proposed by the Sub-Commission and subsequently adopted by the General Assembly (as Article 27 of the Covenant), despite continuing reluctance on the part of the Council and the Commission, read: 'Persons belonging to ethnic, religious or linguistic minorities shall not be denied the right, in community with other members of their group, to enjoy their own culture, to profess and practice their own religion or to use their own language.'[43]

This was a substantially weaker approach than the one taken by the Sub-Commission at its first session, in two regards. First, the right was vested in individuals, not groups, and second, it imposed a purely passive obligation on States.

Other proposals made by the Sub-Commission were either ignored or

38 *Report of the Sub-Commission in 1947*, E/CN.4/52 (1947), 9–10.
39 E/CN.4/SR.74 (1948), 5.
40 See A/C.3/SR.161–2 (1948).
41 GA Res.217 C (III) (1948), para. 5.
42 *Report of the Sub-Commission in 1950*, E/CN.4/358 (1950), paras. 39–41.
43 Ibid. paras. 42–7.

rejected. The Commission and ECOSOC turned down proposals for the collection of information and for interim measures of protection.[44] They evaded those issues by asking for further work on the definition of minorities, to which the Sub-Commission responded in 1954 by pointing out that it had repeatedly presented proposals for definitions on which neither the Commission nor ECOSOC had commented.[45] There thus seemed little point in continuing work on minorities and the Sub-Commission let it lapse, having achieved nothing more than the insertion of Article 27 in the Covenant on Civil and Political Rights.

It did not resume its efforts until several years after the adoption of the Covenant in 1966. In 1971, it appointed Francesco Capotorti as Special Rapporteur to undertake a study on the implications of Article 27 of the Covenant.[46] The resulting study, which was completed in 1977, remains the most thorough UN report on the subject. In a manner which is unusually forthright by UN standards, the rapporteur notes in his preface some of the obstacles to genuine acceptance by States of the idea of special protection for minorities: (*a*) any international system may be viewed as a pretext for interference in States' internal affairs; (*b*) the usefulness of a uniform approach in such profoundly different situations is questionable; (*c*) preservation of the identity of minorities is seen as a threat to State unity and stability; and (*d*) the need for special protection could be used to justify reverse discrimination. 'In short', he concluded, 'governments would prefer to have a free hand in their treatment of minorities.'[47] His principal suggestions for future action focused on: (*a*) the formulation of standards to supplement Article 27; (*b*) the development of new international methods for implementation; and (*c*) the adoption of bilateral or regional arrangements.[48]

Given the political realities surrounding the issue, it is hardly surprising that the only real follow-up to the report has been an effort by the Commission to draft a declaration on the rights of minorities[49]—an effort which, from 1979 to 1990, was characterized by a singular lack of enthusiasm and progress. In 1984 the Commission requested the Sub-Commission to define for it the term 'minority',[50] a task curiously reminiscent of that which it had been given more than 30 years earlier. For that purpose Jules Deschênes

[44] *Report of the Commission on Human Rights in 1950* [Sixth Session], E/1681 (1950), paras. 58–69; *Report of the Commission on Human Rights in 1953*, E/2447 (1953), paras. 236–45.

[45] Sub-Commission Res. F (1954), pream. para. 4; see also *Report of the Commission on Human Rights in 1954*, E/2573 (1954), paras. 422–3.

[46] Capotorti, *The Rights of Persons belonging to Ethnic, Religious and Linguistic Minorities*, E/CN.4/Sub.2/384 and Add.1–6 (1977).

[47] Ibid. p. iv.

[48] Ibid.

[49] See E/CN.4/1988/36 and the Final Report of the Commission's Working Group contained in E/CN.4/1992/48.

[50] CHR Res.1984/62, para. 2.

presented a comprehensive analysis in 1985, in which he suggested that a definition should exclude (*a*) indigenous populations, (*b*) non-citizens, and (*c*) oppressed majorities. He proposed the following definition of a minority:

A group of citizens of a State constituting a numerical minority and in a non-dominant position in that State, endowed with ethnic, religious or religious characteristics which differ from those of the majority of the population, having a sense of solidarity with one another, motivated, if only implicitly, by a collective will to survive and whose aim is to achieve equality with the majority in fact and in law.[51]

In the debate that followed[52] points of disagreement and doubt were expressed on almost every aspect of the definition. Some felt that the definition could not be limited to citizens. With one exception, all members agreed that indigenous peoples should be treated separately from minorities. The requirement that the group was to be a 'numerical minority', combined with the requirement of being 'non-dominant', created some problems, since some groups could be in a majority in a region of a country and/or be dominant there, though it might have neither status in the State as a whole. Some members also felt that other characteristics than 'ethnic, religious or linguistic' should be taken into account, such as cultural or nationalist links of cohesion within the group. The study was passed on to the Commission by a resolution making it clear that there were different opinions in the Sub-Commission and that the definition proposed by Mr Deschênes 'did not command general approval by the Sub-Commission'.[53]

It is now apparent that no general, authoritative definition of minorities will be adopted by the United Nations in the foreseeable future. The best path is probably to separate out for special treatment particular aspects of the underlying problems, or particular groups. This is what the Sub-Commission has done with regard to indigenous peoples, which are now the subject of a separate standard-setting exercise. Similarly, the Declaration on the Elimination of All Forms of Religious Intolerance has some implicit consequences for the protection of religious minorities.[54] It would thus seem appropriate to heed the warning made by Capotorti and to proceed in a pragmatic way, dealing with those parts of the issues which are manageable.

III. 'ANY OTHER FUNCTION': THE GENERALIZED MANDATE

The mandate of the Sub-Commission encompasses any functions entrusted to it by the Commission or the Council. Initiatives to add extra functions can

[51] Deschênes, *Proposal Concerning a Definition of the Term 'Minority'*, E/CN.4/Sub.2/1985/31, para. 181.

[52] See *Report of the Sub-Commission in 1985*, E/CN.4/1986/5, paras. 403–20.

[53] Sub-Commission Res.1985/6, pream. para. 5.

[54] GA Res.36/55 (1981). See in particular Art. 6 of the Declaration.

come from either of those bodies or from the Sub-Commission itself. In practice, the range of functions has expanded very considerably over the years. In a number of instances, tasks have been given to the Sub-Commission in an effort to circumvent or conceal deep conflicts within the Commission. While that tactic has sometimes succeeded, it has also failed on a number of occasions because the problems are intrinsic and must be confronted when the issue is referred back again to the Commission. The problem is well illustrated by a case study from the mid-1960s.

In 1965 the Sub-Commission was asked to undertake an 'initial study' of periodic reports on the implementation of human rights which the Council had previously requested from governments under a voluntary reporting system, initiated in 1956.[55] Until 1965, however, the reports had not been given serious attention by any UN body.[56] The reasons were primarily political. Any reviewing system was bound to give rise to dispute over the degree of government compliance—or otherwise—with the provisions of the Universal Declaration. In the Commission, profound political divergences had already surfaced with regard to the assessment of human rights performance. The most controversial question was the utilization of information and comments from NGOs.

When the Commission had first begun to receive periodic reports, some members had complained that most of them focused mainly on legislative measures, while giving no information about violations or practical difficulties. Blatant discrepancies had been claimed to exist between the theory and the reality. In 1962, at the Commission's suggestion, the Council invited NGOs 'to submit comments and observations of an objective character . . . to assist the Commission in its considerations of the summarized periodic reports.'[57] However, ECOSOC did not make it clear how the comments should be utilized and distributed. In 1967 the Sub-Commission's Rapporteur drafted a report which contained a summary of the periodic reports and appended to it a summary of the comments made by the NGOs and replies by governments to those comments.[58] Sub-Commission members from Eastern European countries strongly attacked the annex and were supported by most of the Third World members, whereas Western States wanted to retain it. The latter lost, however, and the annex was deleted from the report.[59] The Sub-Commission asked for further clarification on what it should do with the

[55] ESC Res.624 B (XXII) (1956).

[56] See Questiaux, 'La Procédure des rapports trienniaux devant la Commission des droits de l'homme', 1 *Rev. des droits de l'homme* 544 (1968).

[57] ESC Res.888 B (XXXIV) (1962), para. 10.

[58] 'Periodic Reports on Human Rights and Reports on Freedom of Information', E/CN.4/Sub.2/L.458 (1967), paras. 5–7.

[59] E/CN.4/Sub.2/SR.504–6 (1967). The vote was 8 for deletion, 6 for the maintenance of the NGO comments, with 4 abstentions.

replies.[60] The Commission, being unable to settle this question, called on ECOSOC to withdraw the request to the Sub-Commission to study the reports.[61] Some lessons can be drawn from this experience. One is that the Sub-Commission cannot, in spite of its 'expert' status, escape the deeper political controversies which split the Commission. The other is that comments and information from NGOs can be dynamite in the context of deliberations of intergovernmental bodies.

Perhaps the most significant overall expansion of the Sub-Commission's mandate is the role which it has come to play in dealing with alleged violations of human rights. While the way in which it has functioned in this role will be analysed below,[62] it is instructive to trace briefly the way in which the relevant mandate evolved. Under Commission Resolution 8 (XXIII) and Council Resolution 1235 (XLII), the Sub-Commission was required to prepare a report containing information 'from all available sources' on violations on human rights. The intention was to have a general report on the occurrence of human rights violations in the world. The Sub-Commission was also requested, by the first of these resolutions, to bring to the attention of the Commission any situation which it had reasonable cause to believe revealed a consistent pattern of gross violations of human rights. These resolutions represented a major policy turn-around on the part of the UN's human rights organs which had previously refused to consider even reliably attested communications alleging violations. Resolution 1235 (XLII), which authorized the Sub-Commission and the Commission to do what was intended in Commission Resolution 8 (XXII), referred to cases of 'gross violations of human rights and fundamental freedoms, including policies of racial discrimination and segregation and apartheid, as exemplified by the policy of apartheid'. The majority of the Sub-Commission members understood this to mean *any* gross violation, not only those which involved racial discrimination or violation of minority rights, and that the contribution of the Sub-Commission should be correspondingly wide.

In its first—and only—report[63] under the new procedure, in 1967, the Sub-Commission referred to gross violations in Southern Africa (South Africa, Namibia, Southern Rhodesia, and the territories still under Portugese colonial rule). All of these could be seen as cases involving racial discrimination. But it also referred to Greece, where a military junta had seized power, and to Haiti.[64] These cases represented gross violations which had nothing to

[60] Sub-Commission Res.4 (XIX) (1967), para. 3.

[61] *Report of the Commission on Human Rights in 1967*, E/4322 (1967), draft Res.V; adopted by ESC Res.1230 (XLII) (1967).

[62] See text accompanying nn. 166–79, below.

[63] Annexed to Sub-Commission Res.3 (XX) (1967), *Report of the Sub-Commission in 1967*, E/CN.4/947 (1967), para. 95.

[64] Ibid.; para. 1 of the resolution focused on the African cases, para. 2 on the situation in Greece and Haiti.

do with racial discrimination and marked the first time that specified countries were named by the United Nations beyond those involved in the Southern African problems of apartheid and colonialism. At the Commission's session in 1968, this report created a stir. The representative of Tanzania attacked the Sub-Commission[65] and presented a draft resolution intended to criticize it for going beyond its mandate by including cases not related to racial discrimination. Counter-proposals were presented, and the outcome was that no decision was taken by the Commission.[66] Thus, the Sub-Commission continued to interpret its mandate to include gross violations wherever they might occur, but it has not subsequently done so in the context of a single report. Rather, it has opted to bring to the attention of the Commission various situations with respect to which it has adopted separate resolutions or decisions. As noted below, it has also come to play a significant role in the handling of communications on human rights violations.

The case studies described above illustrate some of the functions which the Sub-Commission has been asked to fill over the past forty odd years. In addition, the Sub-Commission has undertaken studies on a diverse range of topics, some of which touch only tangentially, if at all, on the problems of minorities or discrimination. It has also provided the Commission with policy analyses of contentious issues such as the terms of reference for a possible UN High Commissioner for Human Rights,[67] methods by which to monitor the declaration of states of emergency[68] and the uses and limitations of laws providing amnesty.[69] It has established Working Groups to examine in detail issues such as contemporary forms of slavery, the rights of detainees, the rights of indigenous peoples, and the possibility of encouraging States to ratify human rights instruments.[70] Its agenda has also explored issues such as the relevance of the programme for a New International Economic Order to human rights,[71] the rights of disabled persons[72] and of mental patients,[73] and

[65] E/CN.4/SR.968 (1968), 292–3.

[66] For a report of the discussion, see *Report of the Commission on Human Rights in 1968*, E/4475 (1968), paras. 140–99. One outcome of this discussion, however, was the recommendation by the Commission (draft resolution III in the Report) to expand the number of Sub-Commission members in order to have more seats for African and Asian States. ECOSOC endorsed this resolution in the same year as ESC Res.1334 (XLIV) (1968).

[67] See Sub-Commission Res.1982/26 and the report of the Sub-Commission's informal Working Group on the issue. E/CN.4/Sub.2/1982/36.

[68] Questiaux, *Study of the Implications for Human Rights of Recent Developments Concerning Situations known as States of Siege or Emergency*, E/CN.4/Sub.2/1982/15. For subsequent work, see the annual reports on the same issue prepared by L. Despouy, including E/CN.4/Sub.2/1987/19 and E/CN.4/Sub.2/1988/18; and E/CN.4/Sub.2/1990/33 and Add.1 and Add.2.

[69] *Joint Study on Amnesty Laws and their Role in the Safeguard and Promotion of Human Rights*, E/CN.4/Sub.2/1985/16.

[70] For a discussion of the role of the working groups, see text accompanying nn. 93–125.

[71] Ferrero, *The New International Economic Order and the Promotion of Human Rights*, E/CN.4/Sub.2/1983/24/Rev.1 (1986).

[72] Despouy, *Human Rights and Disability*, E/CN.4/Sub.2/1991/31.

[73] Daes, *Principles, Guidelines and Guarantees for the Protection of Persons Detained on Grounds of Mental Ill Health or Suffering from Mental Disorder*, E/CN.4/Sub.2/1983/17/Rev.1 (1986).

selected human rights issues covering women[74] and children.[75] This diversity underscores the extent to which its open-ended mandate can be used to justify a focus on almost any issue which the Sub-Commission deems worthy of its consideration. Equally importantly the relevant decisions reflect a belief that bodies such as the Commission on Social Development, the Commission on the Status of Women, and the UN Development Programme, each of which has long been active in dealing with relevant issues, are unlikely to adopt a 'human rights approach' to them.

B. *Methods of Work*

In 1947, the twelve original members of the Sub-Commission met for two weeks annually to deal with an agenda which consisted of only three or four substantive points.[76] In 1991, its twenty-six members met for four weeks to discuss an agenda of nearly twenty substantive issues and, prior to the plenary session, members also met in several working groups for either one or two weeks. In the early years, the activities were all carried out by means of debates in plenary. With the launching of the studies programme in 1952, a new pattern emerged, whereby considerable preparatory work was undertaken prior to each session. In the 1970s, a further dimension was added when the use of working groups became institutionalized.

I. METHODS IN PREPARING STUDIES

The basic guidelines which still govern the method of preparing studies were laid down by the Sub-Commission in 1954 in connection with the study of discrimination in education.[77] They provide that the sources of information for studies are: governments, the Secretary-General, the specialized agencies, NGOs, and 'recognized scholars and scientists'. The Sub-Commission decided that its studies would be global, dealing with all grounds of discrimination mentioned in the Universal Declaration. Because of the anxiety of many States that the studies would be used to criticize a particular State, it was agreed that emphasis was to be given to occurrences of discrimination which were 'typical of general tendencies' and also to instances of successful

[74] In 1987 the Sub-Commission implicitly criticized its own past performance by resolving in future to 'devote greater attention to the prevention of discrimination against women, particularly in relation to development . . .'. Sub-Commission Res.1987/26, 6th pream. para.

[75] Bouhdiba, *Exploitation of Child Labour*, E/CN.4/Sub.2/479/Rev.1 (1982); report by the Sec. Gen. on *The Role of Children*, E/CN.4/Sub.2/1988/30; van Boven, *Prevention of the Disappearance of Children*, E/CN.4/Sub.2/1988/19.

[76] *Report of the Sub-Commission in 1947*, E/CN.4/52 (1947).

[77] The guidelines are detailed in the *Report of the Commission on Human Rights in 1954*, E/2573 (1954), chap. 7, sect. C, paras. 376–418.

eradication of discrimination. Studies were to be factual and objective and deal with both *de facto* and *de jure* situations with respect to discrimination. They were to indicate general trends in legislation and practice and deal with the causes of discrimination in particular contexts. Studies were to be designed not only to lead to recommendations by the Sub-Commission, but also to educate public opinion.

The original intention was that each study would be based upon country reports, each of which would give a detailed description of conditions in an individual State. The UN Secretariat, under the supervision of the Special Rapporteur responsible for the study, was to prepare 'country monographs' which would be sent to the governments concerned for their comments.[78] Since information from NGOs was to be taken fully into account in the preparation of the country reports, it was considered important that States be given the chance to correct any inaccuracies or errors. This system was also supposed to have the advantage of indirectly making States aware of how their legislation and practice measured up to international standards. The system of preparing country monographs was used in the preparation of quite a number of Sub-Commission studies. Thus, for example, the study on rights of persons belonging to ethnic, religious, and linguistic minorities was based in part on monographs examining the situation in seventy-six countries.[79] However, the preparation of the monographs placed very considerable demands upon the limited resources of the Secretariat and only fragmentary information was available in some cases. By 1974, the Secretariat finally succeeded in convincing the Sub-Commission that Special Rapporteurs should dispense with country monographs, at least where the requisite information is already available from official and UN sources.[80] The study on discrimination against indigenous populations, which was initiated in 1972 and completed in 1984,[81] was the last study to make use of country monographs. In any event, a 1957 decision not to publicize the monographs had already substantially reduced their value. Some States, in particular the United States, were opposed to the original decision not to issue the monographs as public documents, because the reports were seen as a means of obtaining publicity critical of the practices of other States.[82] The Soviet Union, on the other hand, supported the decision on the basis that the reports were inherently unreliable documents in so far as they were based on other than government-supplied information.[83]

The system of appointing a Special Rapporteur to take the responsibility for

[78] See *Report of the Sub-Commission in 1954*, E/CN.4/703 (1954), paras. 29–33; and Sub-Commission Res.B (VI) (1954), sect. I.

[79] See Capotorti, *The Rights of Persons*, Annex I, paras. 11–13.

[80] See *Report of the Sub-Commission in 1974*, E/CN.4/1160 (1974), paras. 18–27.

[81] See Martinez-Cobo, *The Problem of Discrimination against Indigenous Populations*, E/CN.4/Sub.2/1986/7 and Add.1–3.

[82] *Report of the Sub-Commission in 1958*, E/CN.4/764 (1958), paras. 168–73.

[83] Ibid.

each study was created because in the words of the Secretariat, the studies involve matters 'too difficult or delicate to entrust... to the Secretary-General'.[84] While the Sub-Commission's original decision does not require that each Special Rapporteur be chosen solely from among its own ranks, such has been the consistent practice. It was always assumed that the Secretariat would provide substantive assistance to the Special Rapporteur, although it was hoped at one stage that the latter would receive an honorarium to enable him or her to do most of the work personally. However, the General Assembly decided in 1952 that the rapporteurs of all UN bodies, with the sole exception of the International Law Commission, would be ineligible to receive honoraria for their work.[85] Both the Sub-Commission and the Secretary-General were critical of this decision on the grounds that the Secretariat should not thereby be forced into a position of having to prepare studies of a controversial or creative character.[86] Nevertheless, in 1954, the General Assembly, on the advice of the Advisory Committee on Administrative and Budgetary Questions (ACABQ) reaffirmed its refusal.[87] Similarly, requests that travel and per diem allowances be provided for Sub-Commission Special Rapporteurs have been refused by the ACABQ and the Fifth Committee of the Assembly, except for consultations to be held between the Special Rapporteur and the Secretariat. However, by the early 1990s it seemed that the latter practice was gradually being abandoned.

Thus until the late 1970s, all studies were prepared essentially by the Secretariat, with the Special Rapporteur supplying his or her imprimatur following a more or less thorough revision of the draft. In some instances, the preparation of a study has involved very substantial inputs of Secretariat manpower over a period of several years. However, in 1979 an administrative reform implemented by the Secretariat changed the situation dramatically, without publicity and (initially at least) without controversy. It was decided that henceforth Special Rapporteurs would be provided only with 'technical assistance' which would not involve the drafting of any substantive part of the report. In effect, the Secretariat now provides secretarial and translation services and acts as a 'post box' for Rapporteurs.

The resulting situation can only be characterized as unsatisfactory on every score. Sub-Commission members who already work for up to six weeks a year for no more than a per diem, and who, almost without exception, are performing full-time jobs, are also expected to take additional time off from their jobs to prepare studies of critical importance. In return they receive no substantive drafting assistance from the Secretariat, no honorarium from the

[84] E/CN.4/Sub.2/SR.113 (1954), 8.

[85] GA Res.677 (VII) (1952).

[86] See *Report of the Sub-Commission in 1954*, E/CN.4/703 (1954), para. 33; and 'Report of the Secretary-General to the Ninth Session of the General Assembly on the System of Allowances...', A/2687 (1954), paras. 19–20 and para. 24 (proposal B(a)).

[87] GA Res.875 B (IX) (1954); and *Report of the Advisory Committee on Administrative and Budgetary Questions in 1954*, A/2688 (1954), paras. 264–9.

UN or from the governments from whom they are in any event supposed to be independent, and very rarely are funds made available for travel or per diem to enable on-the-spot inquiries in connection with their studies.

Since the original rationale for refusing to pay an honorarium (that the real work was to be done by the Secretariat) has been invalidated, the entire matter should now be reconsidered. Consideration should be given to providing funds which would enable an expert consultant to be employed by the Special Rapporteur, and enable the convening of a small private meeting of experts to contribute to the preparation of the reports. The appointment of non-Sub-Commission members as Special Rapporteurs (perhaps in conjunction with a member) might also warrant consideration.

While country monographs are no longer prepared, information is normally requested from governments, specialized agencies, and other intergovernmental organizations, and from NGOs. The information from these sources is usually reproduced in a summary form in the report or by way of surveys and tables appended to the studies. NGOs can, and in some cases do, play an important role in the preparation of studies. In preparing their responses to requests for information, they may enlist the help of qualified experts in the field whose views and insights might be of great value for the academic or professional content of the study. The overall impression, however, is that they do not utilize this possibility as fully as they could. This may be because they are not fully aware of the possibilities open to them. Alternatively, it may be because they attach low priority to Sub-Commission studies or because they now receive so many formal requests for their views that they are unable to determine which of them are worth a thoughtful response.

When a report is completed, it is submitted to the Sub-Commission for discussion. At times, the members take a keen interest in the studies and make valuable comments; at other times they limit themselves to rather formal and non-committal statements. It is thus not always clear how far a completed study reflects the views of the Sub-Commission as a whole. Each report is normally sent on to the Commission, with or without the Sub-Commission's express endorsement of the recommendations it contains.

The Commission tends to treat the reports in a rather summary manner. On the face of it, the final outcome in some cases is simply a recommendation to the Council that the report be printed and distributed. In practice, however, the subject covered in the study is, more often than not, pursued further in a number of different ways. The follow-up can take the form of a subsequent updating of the study, in order to take into account subsequent events and new insights, as was the case with updates of reports on genocide and slavery.[88] Certain aspects of the problems discussed are also often singled out

[88] Whitaker, *Updating of the Report on Slavery*, E/CN.4/Sub.2/1982/20 and Add.1; and Whitaker, *Updated Report on the Question of the Prevention and Punishment of the Crime of Genocide*, E/CN.4/Sub.2/1985/16.

for more detailed study, or for action in other ways. An illustration is the process which started in 1968 with the commissioning of a study on minorities.[89] On, the one hand, it gave rise to a more specialized study on indigenous populations,[90] which in turn gave rise to the creation of a working group on the rights of indigenous populations, which has now begun drafting international standards in this area.[91] On the other hand it led to a decision by the Commission to prepare a Declaration on the Rights of Persons belonging to Minorities, a task pursued by a Working Group of the Commission and completed in 1991.[92]

The Sub-Commission's studies cover a wide range of subjects and serve different functions. Some are preparatory to standard-setting, others seek to clarify the more precise interpretation of standards adopted, and still others are aimed at the promotion or implementation of certain specified rights. In many cases, broad general studies have been carried out first, later followed by more specific studies exploring limited dimensions of the wider issue. Taken together, they constitute an enormously rich source of information which has so far been fully tapped neither in research nor in action.

II. WORKING GROUPS

One major innovation during the last decade has been the use of semi-permanent working groups, meeting before or during the sessions. They relieve the pressure of time during the session and facilitate more flexible participation. They are composed of at least one resentative from each of the five regions into which Sub-Commission members are grouped. The information provided to each working group is therefore available to at least one expert from each of the regions. Two of the pre-sessional working groups, and both of those which are in operation during the sessions, are open to participation by observers and have become important forums on the issue under examination. It makes it possible for specialist institutions and organizations to participate for the sole purpose of discussing a particular subject. The working groups have also made it possible, in a relatively subtle manner to hear allegations of violations and give governments concerned an opportunity to respond to them. By contrast, the Working Group on Communications operates under strict confidentiality.

(a) *The Working Group on Communications*

As noted earlier, Council Resolution 1503 (XLVIII) of 1970, authorized the Sub-Commission to appoint a pre-sessional working group to consider com-

89 CHR Res.11 (XXIV) (1968).

90 See n. 81, above.

91 See *Report of the Working Group on Indigenous Populations*, E/CN.4/Sub.2/1990/42.

92 See n. 49, above.

munications (i.e. complaints) received by the Secretary General under Council Resolution 728 (XXVIII) of 1959, together with any government replies, and on that basis, to inform the Commission about situations appearing to reveal a consistent pattern of gross and reliably attested violations of human rights. The Working Group is the first stage in determining the admissibility of a communication, and in assessing whether or not it appears to reveal a consistent pattern of gross violations. Nobody attends its meetings other than its five members and the necessary Secretariat officals. Thus neither government, nor NGO, nor specialized agency officials can be present. The examination is made solely on the basis of the written submissions. The number of communications fluctuates somewhat, but is always very high; on occasion there have been as many as 250,000 to examine.

In 1971 the Sub-Commission adopted detailed rules of admissibility for these communications.[93] They may originate from a person or group of persons who can be presumed to be the victims of violations, or from persons who have direct and reliable knowledge of those violations. Very often, however, communications originate from NGOs; these are considered admissible if the organization acts 'in good faith'. This vague requirement can be used by members of the Working Group, or at a later stage by members of the Sub-Commission, to oppose communications from organizations they do not like. The NGOs concerned are also required not to 'resort to politically motivated stands contrary to the provisions of the Charter', an even more general requirement which is often invoked when determining admissibility. But it bears emphasizing that only politically motivated stands *contrary to the provisions of the Charter* shall be deemed to make the communication non-admissible. While many NGOs have only 'second-hand' knowledge of alleged violations, this does not make the communication inadmissible, provided that it is accompanied by persuasive evidence. Some NGOs are more skilful than others at framing their communications so as to fulfil the requirements for admissibility. This, however, does not guarantee success since even highly professional NGOs are accused by some Sub-Commission experts of being politically motivated. However, these claims often fail to prove that the alleged political motivation is contrary to the United Nations Charter.

The quality of communications varies greatly. While they should contain a clear description of the facts, and indicate the purpose of the communication, as well as the rights that have been violated, some only contain criticism of governments with insufficient attention to the facts, and without specifying what human rights provisions have been violated.

The first action by the Working Group is to divide up the communications so that each member is given responsibility for the initial examination of all communications dealing with a certain group of human rights. That individual

[93] Sub-Commission Res.1 (XXIV) (1971).

alone goes through all of the relevant communications; other members have to depend on the assessment made by him. If he recommends the forwarding of a given communication, the others have the opportunity to examine it and agree or disagree; if, on the other hand, he decides not to make such a recommendation, the other members have little opportunity to disagree. The Working Group makes its decisions by majority vote. Proposals have been made to require consensus, the effect of which would be to give each member a veto; but this has not been accepted either by the Sub-Commission or by its parent bodies.

The Working Group reports to the Sub-Commission, giving a list of those situations which appear to it to reveal a consistent pattern of gross violations. Appended to the report is the full text of the relevant communications. They form only a very small percentage of the total number of communications originally received, estimated at about 1 per cent.

The Sub-Commission examines the communications brought to it by the Working Group in closed meetings. Those withheld are never seen by the Sub-Commission members who are not on the Working Group. Either by vote or consensus, the Sub-Commission as a whole then decides which ones to forward to the Commission. The number of situations transmitted to the Commission can therefore be further reduced, but not increased, by the Sub-Commission acting in plenary. The report to the Commission, also confidential, thus lists only those situations which appear to the Sub-Commission to warrant further consideration. But the final decision is left for the Commission.

(*b*) *The Working Group on Contemporary Forms of Slavery*[94]

The Working Group on Slavery began its work in 1975.[95] Its establishment represented the continuation of a long-standing concern in international organizations for the complete abolition of all forms of slavery.[96] The Universal Declaration as well as the International Covenant on Civil and Political Rights both prohibit slavery, servitude, and the slave trade. No derogation can be made from these provisions. In 1956 the General Assembly adopted the Supplementary Convention on the Abolition of Slavery, Slave Trade, and Institutions and Practices Similar to Slavery. It covers a wider list of slavery-like institutions and practices than the 1926 Convention, including

[94] Until 1988, the name was Working Group on Slavery. The Sub-Commission recommended in 1987, and the the Commission in its Res.1988/42 endorsed, a change in the name to emphasize that traditional slavery is not the main concern of the group.

[95] Its establishment was authorized by ESC Res.16 (LVI) (1974).

[96] The League of Nations established its Temporary Slavery Commission in 1924 and was instrumental in the drafting of the International Slavery Convention of 1926. Several years later, an Advisory Committee of Experts on Slavery was set up by the Assembly of the League and met for its first session in 1935.

a section on 'Institutions and Practices Similar to Slavery'.[97] One of the practices mentioned is 'debt bondage', which exists when an individual's services are pledged as collateral for a debt, but the services are undervalued so that the debt can never be paid off. The effect is that the individual is enslaved, even though the phenomenon does not fit within the traditional definition of slavery. A second slavery-like condition is 'serfdom', where an individual is bound to live and to work on another's land and is unable to leave. In addition, the Supplementary Convention condemns a number of abusive forms of treatment of women and children.[98] In spite of its name, therefore, it covers a number of current phenomena involving extreme exploitation.

No implementation machinery was established for implementation of the Supplementary Convention. For many years, an NGO, the Anti-Slavery Society for the Protection of Human Rights, endeavoured to obtain the establishment of some machinery to supervise these conventions. Success came only in 1973 when the Sub-Commission proposed the creation of a body which would review developments in the field of slavery based on all available information and would recommend appropriate action. Following authorization by the Council the Working Group on Slavery has met annually since 1975.[99]

NGOs have been particularly central to its work. The Anti-Slavery Society has played the major role. In 1982, nineteen NGOs attended, including the International Abolitionist Federation, whose main concern is the elimination of prostitution, the Minority Rights Group, and the International Federation of Women Lawyers. In subsequent years, the number of NGOs declined, particularly because of a lack of sufficient focus in its work. This is now being remedied.

While the ILO has actively participated in the work of the Group, other UN agencies have largely neglected it. Initially, member States did not pay much attention to the group, but since 1981 their representatives have taken part in increasing numbers, which indicates the growing significance of the Working Group. Its mandate is to 'review developments in the field of slavery and the slave trade in all their practices and manifestations . . .' based on the two slavery conventions (1926 and 1956) and the Convention for the Suppression of the Traffic in Persons and of the Exploitation of the Prostitution of Others of 1949. Six general topics have been dealt with: (*a*) slavery and the slave trade, (*b*) the sale of children, (*c*) the exploitation of child labour, (*d*) debt bondage, (*e*) the traffic in persons and exploitation of the prostitution of others, and (*f*) the slavery-like practices of apartheid and colonialism.

[97] In *Human Rights: A Compilation of International Instruments* (1988), 160–1 (Arts. 1 and 2).
[98] Ibid. Art. 1, paras. (a), (b), (c), (d).
[99] See generally Zoglin, 'United Nations Action against Slavery. *A Critical Evaluation*', 8 *Hum. Rts. Q.* 306 (1986).

A detailed report on many of these issues was presented by Ben Whitaker[100] in 1982 in the form of an updated version of an earlier study of slavery by Mohammed Awad, which had been published in 1966.[101] The Whitaker Report presented a variety of recommendations for action by governments, all of which were subsequently endorsed by the Working Group. The group also sought authorization to provide special studies on serious situations, but did not receive it until 1981 when the situation in Mauritania became a hot issue. The Anti-Slavery Society had reported that in Mauritania, where slavery had recently become outlawed, the practice was still flourishing. The government denied the allegation in a cable sent to the Working Group, but subsequently invited the Sub-Commission to send a delegation to examine the situation. A fact-finding mission was undertaken in 1984 by Marc Bossuyt (the Belgian Sub-Commission expert). He was accompanied by Peter Davies, Director of the Anti-Slavery Society. A series of reports was presented, the last of which was issued in 1987.[102] The Rapporteur concluded that although the government was taking measures to enforce the prohibition against slavery, only economic development would enable the government to eliminate the traditional economy which was the principal vehicle for maintaining slavery-like practices. For that reason, a group of UN agencies were requested to see what relevant assistance might be provided.[103] This case illustrates that the non-realization of human rights may sometimes be due not to bad will on the part of the government but to a lack of resources, to which the international community should respond.

With respect to children, the Group has been presented with disturbing information on the sale of children, sometimes for the purpose of commercially-motivated transnational adoption, and sometimes for other forms of exploitation, including child prostitution.[104] In 1989 the Group adopted a detailed 'draft programme of action for prevention of sale of children, child prostitution and child pornography'. Suggestions for improvements made by governments and other groups were subsequently referred back to the Sub-Commission in 1991 to enable the Group to present a revised programme.[105] Another major concern has been child labour. Following a comprehensive 1981 study by Mr A. Bouhdiba, the Working Group proposed a '35-point Programme of Action for the Elimination of the Exploitation of Child Labour' which the Commission adopted in 1991.[106]

[100] Whitaker, *Updating of the Report on Slavery*, n. 88, above.

[101] Awad, *Report on Slavery*, E/4168 and Add.1–5 (1966).

[102] Bossuyt, *Final Follow-up Report on the Mission to Mauritania*, E/CN.4/Sub.2/1987/27. See also the initial report (E/CN.4/Sub.2/1984/23) and interim follow-up report (E/CN.4/Sub.2/1985/26).

[103] *Final Follow-up Report on the Mission to Mauritania*, E/CN.4/Sub.2/1987/27, para. 22.

[104] Whitaker, *Updating of the Report on Slavery*, paras. 68–9.

[105] See E/CN.4/1990/50, Annex and CHR Res.1991/54, Pt.I, para.4.

[106] See Bouhdiba, *Exploitation of Child Labour*, E/CN.4/Sub.2/479/Rev.1 (1981). For the Programme of Action see Sub-Commission Res.1990/31 and CHR Res.1991/54, Pt.II, para. 10.

Reports and statements by NGOs on forced labour and slavery-like practices, particularly in specific African and Latin American countries, have caused the Group to call for a response by the governments concerned. These and other activities have caused the Working Group to be criticized on occasion by some members of the Sub-Commission and the Commission for overstepping its mandate. As a result, since 1982, somewhat greater caution has been shown in directly requesting governments to respond to allegations.

In 1983 the UN Committee for Program and Coordination, in reviewing the overall budget for the 1984–5 UN human rights programme, proposed to cut off the funding needed to enable the Working Group on Slavery to meet. This proposal was not based on discussion in the Working Group, the Sub-Commission or the Commission. It required a concerted effort by certain governments, with strong urging by NGOs, to persuade the General Assembly's Fifth Committee to overrule this somewhat underhand attempt to eliminate the Group.[107]

The Working Group has served an important function as a forum for concerned NGOs and aggrieved groups. One of its weaknesses, however, has been the absence of a clear focus, and of effective procedures to follow up the conclusions reached and the recommendations made. This was remedied in 1988 by the adoption of a programme of action providing for a major theme each year.[108] In 1989 the main theme was sale of children and sexual exploitation of children; in 1990 it was bonded labour and child labour; and in 1991 it was traffic in persons and the exploitation of the prostitution of others as well as 'child soldiers'.

(*c*) *The Working Group on the Rights of Indigenous Populations*

In recent years, American Indians, Inuits of the Arctic regions, Australian Aborigines, and Samis of Northern Scandinavia, among others, have discovered the Sub-Commission and its possible uses. When the Working Group on the Rights of Indigenous Populations[109] was set up in 1982, it provided the first international forum allowing for continuing participation by representatives of indigenous peoples. Its establishment represents the most practical effort made pursuant to the mandate to protect minorities. Proposals during the early years to develop a general system had failed altogether. The 1978 study on minorities by Francesco Capotorti[110] had indicated that indigenous peoples should be given particular attention, and the Sub-

[107] See Zoglin, 'United Nations Action against Slavery', 337.

[108] See generally Hannum, 'New Developments in Indigenous Rights', 28 *Va. J. Int'l L.* 649 (1988); Barsh, 'Indigenous Peoples: An Emerging Object of International Law', 80 *Am. J. Int'l L.* 369 (1986).

[109] ESC Res.1982/34. Note that in the resolution, and also otherwise in UN official language, the concept used is 'indigenous populations', while in the present chapter 'indigenous peoples' is used. This is deliberate.

[110] Capotorti, *The Rights of Persons*.

Commission's response was to commission a study by Martinez Cobo.[111] The process of collecting information for the study lasted for more than ten years and made it the most comprehensive source of information available on the situation of indigenous peoples.[112]

The establishment of the Working Group resulted from a growing demand by indigenous populations for international action. Their representatives sought a forum in which to air their grievances and to seek redress. Many of the governments concerned were not enthusiastic; they argued that other bodies and procedures were available for complaints about human rights violations and saw no need for a special forum for indigenous peoples. Other governments, which were more favourably disposed, suggested that the first step should be to clarify the content of the rights of indigenous peoples. The most potentially relevant provision of the International Covenant on Civil and Political Rights, Article 27, deals with the rights of individuals rather than minority groups.[113]

The ILO has also been concerned, from its own perspective, with the prevention of discrimination against members of tribal and indigenous populations. In 1957 it had adopted its Convention No. 107 on Tribal and Indigenous Populations, which in regard to land rights was innovative and appreciated by indigenous peoples, but its traditional, assimilationist approach made them oppose other parts of the convention. Parallel to the efforts of the Sub-Commission, ILO started an effort to revise the convention in order to make it more compatible with current aspirations of indigenous peoples. This resulted in the adoption, in 1989, of ILO Convention No. 169 on Indigenous and Tribal Peoples in Independent States. While it is seen by indigenous peoples as an improvement in a number of ways, it still falls short of providing a standing international forum for the representatives of these peoples.[114]

The Working Group's mandate is:

> (a) to review developments pertaining to the promotion and protection of human rights and fundamental freedoms of indigenous peoples; and (b) to give special attention to the evolution of standards concerning the rights of indigenous peoples, taking into account both the similarities and the differences in the situations and the aspirations of indigenous peoples throughout the world.[115]

The Group has made a particular effort to obtain information directly from organizations of indigenous peoples, including those without consultative

[111] *See* n. 81, above.

[112] This was due in large part to the efforts of Secretariat member Augusto Willemsen Diez, who made the protection of indigenous populations his life-long commitment.

[113] Ramcharan, 'Peoples' Rights and Minorities Rights', 56 *Nordic J. Int'l L.* 9 (1987).

[114] For a strong critique see Berman, 'The International Labour Organisation and Indigenous Peoples: Revision of ILO Convention No. 107 at the 75th Session of the International Labour Conference, 1988', 41 *Int'l Commission of Jurists Rev.* 48 (1988).

[115] ESC Res.1982/34.

status with ECOSOC which would normally not be able to act as full participants in a UN forum. This approach has considerably strengthened the international activities of indigenous organizations. Initially, their representatives had little experience in making presentations to human rights bodies but since 1983 this has changed significantly. In 1985 a training course was organized in Geneva by, and for, indigenous persons on techniques for dealing with the international human rights system. A strategy session in Geneva has also been organized by indigenous organizations prior to each Working Group session since 1985, enabling the discussion of common platforms on some of the key issues. These efforts reveal a growing sophistication on the part of indigenous organizations in the use of international institutions to promote their interests and rights. While some governments have encouraged the Working Group and participated in a constructive dialogue with representatives of the indigenous peoples, most governments have taken, at best, a low profile. Their reluctance is an indication that the goal of adopting international standards in this field will not easily be achieved.

Indigenous representatives have told the Working Group about numerous situations in which serious violations of human rights have taken place. The Group has been cautious in response, pointing out that it is not a forum for complaints or a tribunal, and is not in a position to assess evidence of violations. The stated justification for receiving such information is to identify the most pressing issue areas, to examine the evolution of policies, laws, and practices in regard to those issues, and to draw appropriate conclusions. In practice, however, the Group has paid attention to violations and has discussed them under the following headings: (*a*) the right to life, to physical integrity and security; (*b*) the right to land and to natural resources; (*c*) the right to autonomy or self-determination and to political institutions; (*d*) the right to develop cultural traditions, language, religious practices and way of life; and (*e*) economic and social rights.

The first two categories have been the most important. Allegations of genocide and ethnocide have repeatedly been made by the representatives of indigenous peoples. From 1983 onwards, Guatemala has been singled out as the country in which the most serious violations have occurred.[116] Apart from the threats to their physical survival, the most pressing issue has been the deprivation of land and natural resources. In many parts of the world indigenous peoples have been dispossessed and resettled in places with different environmental conditions, deprived of natural resources as basic as water and natural food, and lost their sacred lands and sites. This has disrupted their lives and their social and legal orders, and has very often led to

[116] See *Report of the Working Group on Indigenous Populations in 1983*, E/CN.4/Sub.2/1983/22, para. 35.

suffering, hunger, disease, despair, and death. Some government observers have engaged in a dialogue on these and related issues, recognizing that serious harm has been done to indigenous peoples in the past, but often arguing that the present government is trying to rectify the situation. The Working Group's main task has been to develop new standards. The protection of integrity rights, collective land rights, and local autonomy or self-determination are issues on the top of the agenda for most indigenous organizations.

Governments, however, are very reluctant to accept any reference to self-determination because of its potential as a claim for secession. In the new ILO convention No. 169, the use of the word indigenous 'people' (strongly preferred by indigenous representatives) over the word 'population' which is used in the older ILO convention No. 107, gave rise to the fear among governments that it would be used to assert the right under international law of peoples to self-determination. The compromise found was to make use of the word 'people' but to include a disclaimer in Article 1(3) to the effect that its use did not give rise to rights otherwise connected with the use of the term 'people' in international law. Many indigenous representatives expressed dissatisfaction with this qualification, and have argued against the ratification of the new ILO convention partly as a result thereof. This implies that some indigenous peoples, or at least those speaking on behalf of their organizations, indeed want to obtain the legal option to secede.

The group seeks to resolve the various contradictions that have emerged through a patient process of drafting standards. In 1987, the Working Group identified fourteen draft articles to serve as a basis for discussion and comments by governments. The notion of self-determination was nowhere mentioned, but compromise provisions included the following:

> 9. The right to be secure in the enjoyment of their own traditional means of subsistence, and to engage freely in their traditional and other economic activities, without adverse discrimination.
>
> 10. The right to determine, plan and implement all health, housing and other social and economic programmes affecting them.[117]

Subsequent drafts have continued to grapple with this issue without resolving it. In the draft prepared for the Group in 1991, various proposals are included which would specifically acknowledge the right to self-determination.

The unique feature of these standard-setting efforts is that it has been carried out with the full participation of the beneficiaries, rather than being performed solely by governments and experts. Nothing comparable has happened in other standard-setting exercises. Each year since 1988 the

[117] *Report of the Working Group on Indigenous Populations in 1987*, E/CN.4/Sub.2/1987/22, Annex II, 24.

Chairman of the Group has prepared an updated text of a 'draft Universal Declaration on Indigeneous Rights' which has formed the basis for, and reflected earlier, discussions.[118]

(*d*) *The Sessional Working Group on Detention*

One of the Sub-Commission's main concerns has been the human rights of persons subjected to any form of detention or imprisonment. A sessional Working Group on Detention has been characterized by close interaction between Sub-Commission members and concerned NGOs, in particular Amnesty International and the International Commission of Jurists.[119] Another characteristic of this group has been the extensive use of expert papers written either by members or by NGOs.[120]

Matters dealt with in recent years have included the drafting of a Body of Principles for the Protection of all Persons under Detention or Imprisonment,[121] discussion of an annual review of developments concerning detainees,[122] the drafting of principles to restrain the use of force by law enforcement officials,[123] and the consideration of the repercussions of human rights violations on the families of victims.[124] The Working Group has expressed particular concern at the extent to which individuals have been detained solely as a result of attempting to exercise their rights to freedom of opinion and expression.[125]

[118] *Reports of the Working Group on Indigenous Populations* E/CN.4/Sub.2/1988/24 and Add.1 and Add.2; E/CN.4/Sub.2/1989/36; E/CN.4/Sub.2/1990/42; and E/CN.4/Sub.2/1991/40.

[119] See the following reports of the sessional Working Group on Detention: E/CN.4/Sub.2/1985/17; E/CN.4/Sub.2/1987/15; E/CN.4/Sub.2/1988/28; E/CN.4/Sub.2/1989/29; E/CN.4/Sub.2/1990/32; and E/CN.4/Sub.2/1991/27.

[120] E.g., a paper by Chernichenko and Treat on the right to a fair trial (E/CN.4/Sub.2/1991/29); another by Bautista on the violations of human rights of UN staff members (E/CN.4/Sub.2/1991/23); and reports by Joinet on the practice of administrative detention (E/CN.4/Sub.2/1990/29 and Add.1) and on ways of monitoring respect for principles concerning the independence of the judiciary (E/CN.4/Sub.2/1991/26).

[121] The first draft was finalized by the Sub-Commission in 1978 (see Sub-Commission Res.5 (XXXI) C (1978)). As of 1988, the draft was still being reviewed by the General Assembly's Sixth Committee (see A/C.6/42/L.12 (1987)). In 1987, the Sub-Commission expressly criticized some of the Sixth Committee's drafting changes (Sub-Commission Dec. 1987/108).

[122] The annual review was authorized by Sub-Commission Res.7 (XXVII) (1974). NGOs in consultative status were permitted to submit relevant information, provided that they 'acted in good faith and that their information was not politically motivated, contrary to the principles of the Charter' of the United Nations. For examples of the resulting reports, see E/CN.4/Sub.2/1988/13–15.

[123] See generally E/CN.4/Sub.2/1985/17, Annex. In Decision 1987/108, the Sub-Commission proposed the adoption of a declaration to the effect that arbitrary or abusive use of force by law enforcement personnel against persons subjected to any form of detention or imprisonment in any country should be punished as a criminal offence.

[124] CHR Res.26 (XXXVI) (1980), and E/CN.4/1985/3, paras. 235–7. See also van Boven, *Prevention of the Disappearance of Children*, E/CN.4/Sub.2/1988/19.

[125] CHR Res.1984/26, 1985/17, 1987/32, and 1988/37.

III. PLENARY DEBATES

Plenary debates have always been the core of the Sub-Commission's work, but with the growing number of studies and reports prepared by individual members prior to the session, and the increasing use of working groups before and during the sessions, much important activity now takes place outside the plenary meetings. On some issues the plenary's deliberations are becoming increasingly superficial, despite the fact that all recommendations which are submitted to the Sub-Commission's parent bodies must still be made in plenary. At present, the main substantive issues which are discussed solely in the plenary, without preparation through the working groups, are violations and racial discrimination. Together, these items took 21 of the 37 meetings of the 1987 session, leaving only 16 meetings to the remaining 15 agenda items.[126] The Sub-Commission's performance with regard to violations, which is by far the most time-consuming item on its agenda, is discussed below.[127]

Inputs that facilitate the work of the plenary come from: (*a*) studies, which often contain a set of recommendations; (*b*) working group reports, which also contain recommendations; (*c*) reports by the Secretary-General (i.e., the Centre for Human Rights) when requested; (*d*) introductory notes from the Secretariat, often referring to requests by the Commission; (*e*) submissions by NGOs, in writing or orally during the session; and, on occasion, (*f*) submissions by governments. Many Sub-Commission resolutions are 'self-sufficient' and do not require further action by other UN bodies. Those which require action by the Commission or the Council must take the form of a text containing a preamble explaining the background and the purpose of the resolution, followed by a draft resolution for adoption by the Commission, and often within it, another draft resolution for adoption by ECOSOC. This is to minimize the work required of the parent bodies by making clear what is requested from them. Authorization by the parent bodies is required whenever financial implications arise or when an entirely new activity is proposed.

Two types of activities take place during the plenary sessions: substantive interventions, and the adoption of resolutions. There are also procedural debates which, in principle, the Sub-Commission seeks to avoid. Substantive interventions by members vary considerably in depth. Some interventions are almost pro forma and contain little substance. Other interventions are carefully thought out and, on occasion, contribute significantly to elucidation of the issue. NGO interventions, which may be of great value, are normally brief, because of the time-limits imposed on them. Some NGOs also circulate very useful written material.

[126] *Report of the Sub-Commission in 1987*, E/CN.4/1988/37, paras. 10, 50, and 105.
[127] See text accompanying nn. 166–79, below.

Some interventions are carefully crafted to lay the groundwork for resolutions, providing detailed arguments and appealing for support. Much of the work on resolutions is achieved through informal interaction among the members, either during the meetings or outside. NGOs sometimes draft resolutions in collaboration with one or more of the Sub-Commission members but only the latter can introduce them. Some resolutions are generated almost spontaneously as a result of the discussions, while others are the product of long planning. They may result from activities inside the Sub-Commission itself, or in the political organs of the United Nations, or elsewhere. In some cases there is very little room for constructive work in the Sub-Commission because the majority of experts feel bound by political positions taken elsewhere. This applies in particular to resolutions dealing with the Middle East or South Africa. On some issues, resolutions are highly repetitive, and discussions closely resemble the comparable debates which have already taken place in the political organs. For some of the more independent-minded experts of the Sub-Commission, this is a frustrating experience. For those who are closely linked to their governments, it is quite normal and could not easily be otherwise.

There is also considerable interaction between the Secretariat and members of the Sub-Commission during the sessions. Each agenda item is introduced by a representative of the Secretariat, giving a summary of the background and previous discussions. The Secretariat is also at times asked to provide further information, including legal opinions on issues such as interpretation of the mandate or of the Rules of Procedure.[128] The Secretariat's attitude to involvement in the substance of the discussions has varied considerably over time. During the twenty years when John Humphrey headed the Secretariat (1946–66), initiatives desired by the Secretariat were often made by persuading individual members to take the formal responsibility.[129] In the period when Theo van Boven was head (1977–82), several initiatives were taken directly and openly by the Secretariat.[130] Since then, it has been much more reluctant to become involved, pursuing a policy of abstention and seeking to limit its role to a purely technical one.

Government observers have increasingly participated in sessions primarily, but not only, during the discussions on violations. On occasion, some of them have sought to influence decisions, and there has been a growing apprehension by the Sub-Commission with respect to the role played by some governments.[131] While interaction with governments is useful and desirable up to a

[128] Salzberg, 'The United Nations Sub-Commission on Prevention of Discrimination and Protection of Minorities', Ph.D. thesis (New York, 1973).

[129] See generally Humphrey, *Human Rights and the United Nations: A Great Adventure* (1984).

[130] See Chap. 14, below.

[131] This apprehension has been voiced on a number of occasions, usually somewhat obliquely, by various Sub-Commission members.

point, and makes the procedures more flexible, there comes a point where it tends to transform the Sub-Commission into a political, rather than an expert, body. Some government observers are aware of this danger and have sought to discourage their colleagues from overstepping the desirable limits of participation in the Sub-Commission's deliberations.

C. *Functions*

The functions of the Sub-Commission defy simple categorization. Composed of experts, many of whom actually are, and all of whom theoretically are, independent, located between the political organs of the United Nations on the one hand and the NGO community on the other, the Sub-Commission plays many different roles. As a result, it is often applauded for its flexibility while at the same time provoking confusion and frustration on the part of its parent bodies. In part, its task is to give advice on request, in part it is to organize and process information, but neither of these functions captures the essence of its role. The Sub-Commission has had to be continuously innovative in its approach. It has opened itself up to significant participation by NGOs and human rights experts and, as a result, has succeeded in harmonizing the expertise and the moral commitment of a wide constituency of concerned individuals, making possible a multi-dimensional dialogue which is otherwise rarely found in the UN system.

For analytical purposes, the functions of international human rights organs are often divided into standard-setting, promotion, and implementation.[132] It has also been argued that the work of the Commission and Sub-Commission can be divided into stages focusing consecutively on each of these functions. Although this approach tends to reflect an overly legislative conception, and to underestimate considerably the educational, consciousness-raising, and catalytic roles played by the two organs since their inception, it will nevertheless be followed for the purposes of analysis in the present context.

I. STANDARD-SETTING

As noted above, the Sub-Commission contributed to the elaboration of the anti-discrimination provisions of the Universal Declaration but failed to get a minorities provision included.[133] Its next contributions to standard-setting came as a result of the studies programme, one of the envisaged results of which was the preparation of new standards. In two instances, UN agencies took over work initiated by the Sub-Commission. The results were the

[132] Marie, *La Commission des droits de l'homme de l'ONU* (1975), 15.
[133] See text accompanying nn. 14–5 and 35–41, above.

UNESCO Convention against Discrimination in Education[134] and the ILO Convention and Recommendation on Discrimination in Employment.[135] But the Sub-Commission's most important achievements in this field were the Declaration,[136] and subsequently the Convention,[137] on the Elimination of all Forms of Racial Discrimination.

In general, however, the Sub-Commission has been more successful in drafting non-binding, rather than binding, standards. In a number of instances it has successfully laid the foundations for declarations which have eventually been adopted by the General Assembly many years after the Sub-Commission's completion of its own contribution. The following cases are illustrative of the type of process which has been followed. One early study, on Discrimination in the Matter of Religious Rights and Practices,[138] was presented in 1960. It led the Sub-Commission to recommend a set of principles[139] on that subject which the Commission did nothing about until urged to do so by the General Assembly in 1972.[140] In 1981, some twenty-five years after the study had been initiated, the Assembly adopted the Declaration on the Elimination of all Forms of Intolerance and of Discrimination Based on Religion or Belief.[141] Another example of the long and tortuous road between initial action by the Sub-Commission and the eventual adoption of a new standard began with a study of Equality in the Administration of Justice by Mr Abu Rannat.[142] He was appointed in 1963 and presented a study in 1969 which contained draft principles which were revised and endorsed by the Sub-Commission in 1970[143] and submitted to the Commission, which again delayed action until prompted by the Assembly.[144] In 1973 the latter confined itself to calling upon governments to pay attention to the draft principles, but failed formally to adopt the principles.[145] In 1979, on the initiative of the Secretariat, the Sub-Commission appointed a new rapporteur on discriminatory treatment in the administration of criminal justice.[146] The study was

[134] Adopted in 1960, by the General Conference of UNESCO. *Human Rights: A Compilation of International Instruments*, 88–95.

[135] Convention (No. 111) Concerning Discrimination in Respect of Employment and Occupation, 1958. ibid. 84–8.

[136] United Nations Declaration on the Elimination of all Forms of Racial Discrimination, adopted by GA Res.1904 (XVIII) (1963). Ibid. 52–6.

[137] International Convention on the Elimination of All Forms of Racial Discrimination, adopted by GA Res.2106 A (XX) (1965). Ibid. 56–69.

[138] Krishnaswami, *Study of Discrimination in the Matter of Religious Rights and Practices*, E/CN.4/Sub.2/200/Rev. 1 (1960).

[139] Sub-Commission Res.1 (XII) (1960).

[140] GA Res.3027 (XXVII) (1972).

[141] GA Res.36/55 (1981).

[142] Abu Rannat, *Study of Equality in the Administration of Justice*, E/CN.4/Sub.2/296 (1969).

[143] Sub-Commission Res.3 (XXIII) (1970).

[144] GA Res.2858 (XXVI) (1971).

[145] GA Res.3144 (XXVIII) (1973).

[146] Chowdhury, *Study on Discriminatory Treatment of Members of Racial, Ethnic, Religious or*

completed in 1982. Simultaneously, the Sub-Commission asked for authorization to initiate another study, on the independence and impartiality of the judiciary, jurors, assessors, and the independence of lawyers. This study, which was finalized in 1985,[147] contained a draft Universal Declaration on the Independence of Justice which the Sub-Commission began to examine in 1988.[148]

Another illustration is a study of the human rights of non-citizens, prepared by Baroness Elles, who was appointed in 1974, and reported in 1976.[149] It included a draft declaration which, after the comments of governments had been taken into account, was revised and presented to the Commission in 1978.[150] The General Assembly then established its own working group on the subject and finally adopted a declaration in 1985.[151]

In some cases the thrust of the Sub-Commission's work has been to formulate standards for the interpretation and application of existing instruments. A good example is its recent focus on the phenomenon of states of siege or emergency, which allow governments to derogate from some of their human rights obligations. The Sub-Commission, during its handling of the problem of detention, became increasingly concerned with the misuses of this technique, and in 1977 it requested a study by Ms Nicole Questiaux, which was presented in 1982.[152] The study first examined international and domestic law, in both of which there are numerous guarantees by way of limitations on State power even during emergency situations, but it pointed out that these guarantees were often deviated from in practice. It noted that states of emergency had tended to become permanent or even institutionalized and that greatly increased powers were being granted, sometimes almost clandestinely, to the executive and to military or special courts which then applied retroactive laws in a summary fashion.

The Rapporteur outlined a set of principles and measures to strengthen international monitoring of respect for human rights in such situations.[153] The Sub-Commission endorsed and submitted that study to the Commission, which in turn called on the Sub-Commission to propose measures designed

Linguistic Groups at the Various Levels in the Administration of Criminal Justice. . ., E/CN.4/Sub.2/1982/7.

[147] Singhvi, *Study on the Independence and Impartiality of the Judiciary, Jurors and Assessors and the Independence of Lawyers*, E/CN.4/Sub.2/1985/18.

[148] A revised version was presented in 1987 (E/CN.4/Sub.2/1987/18/Add.5/Rev.1).

[149] Elles, *Study on the International Provisions Protecting the Rights of Non-Citizens*, E/CN.4/Sub.2/392 and Corr. 1 (1976).

[150] Sub-Commission Res.9 (XXXI) (1978).

[151] Declaration on the Human Rights of Individuals who are not Nationals of the Country in which they Live, adopted by GA Res.40/144 (1985). *Human Rights: A Compilation of International Instruments*, 322–5.

[152] Questiaux, *Study of the Implications for Human Rights of Recent Developments Concerning Situations known as States of Siege or Emergency*, E/CN.4/Sub.2/1982/15.

[153] Ibid. Recommendation A, 44.

to ensure respect for human rights under states of siege or emergency.[154] A Sub-Commission member was entrusted with the task of preparing an annual report listing all States which have proclaimed, extended, or terminated a state of emergency, as well as the grounds given, the duration, and the measures adopted. The task was given to Leandro Despouy who presented his first report in 1987.[155] This case is thus one which began with a study deriving principles from existing human rights law and suggesting measures for better application, and was then followed up by a system of annual reporting intended to improve the capacity of the international community to monitor what States actually do when claiming that states of emergency exist.

II. PROMOTION

When international human rights standards are adopted, the next step is to see to it that they are implemented in national law and administration. An important step in this process is to have States ratify or accede to international instruments. A joint proposal by several NGOs led the Sub-Commission to establish, in 1979, a sessional Working Group on the Encouragement of Universal Acceptance of Human Rights Instruments.[156] The purpose was to request information from governments, through the Secretary-General, on the circumstances which had impeded their ratification of certain instruments, and to ask them to send representatives to provide further information to the Group. This approach was relatively audacious and gave rise to controversy over the competence of the Sub-Commission, which without authorization from its parent bodies had unilaterally decided to ask governments for information which went considerably beyond the fields of discrimination and minorities. The legal opinion of the UN Legal Office was sought and its conclusion was of major importance:

> The Sub-Commission's capacity to seek information from governments would seem to be inherent in the general mandate to undertake studies and make recommendations on matters within its competence. The capacity to collect information is a prerequisite for effective accomplishment of the Commission's tasks . . . While the action taken and envisaged by the Sub-Commission may seem to involve more than what originally seemed to be implied in the Sub-Commission's general terms of reference, it can be considered to be in line with developments in practice which have shown considerable

[154] CHR Res.1983/18, para. 2.

[155] Despouy, *Annual Report and List of States which, since 1 January 1985, have Proclaimed, Extended or Terminated a State of Emergency*, E/CN.4/Sub.2/1987/19/Rev.1; E/CN.4/Sub.2/1988/18; E/CN.4/Sub.2/1989/30 and Add.1 and Add.2/Rev.1; and E/CN.4/Sub.2/1991/28.

[156] Sub-Commission Dec. 1 B (XXXII) (1979). See generally Weissbrodt, 'A New United Nations Mechanism for Encouraging the Ratification of Human Rights Treaties', 76 *Am. J. Int'l L.* 418 (1982).

broadening of the scope of the Sub-Commission's activity (including addressing governments directly) and to which the parent bodies . . . have not objected.[157]

From the outset, more than twenty States responded in writing, even though some reserved their position as to the competence of the Working Group.[158] During its first session the Group also held oral discussions with several governments for purposes of clarification. In the process, a dialogue developed both as to the appropriate function of the Group and as to the types of factor which impeded ratification on the part of some governments. By 1985, approximately fifty governments had provided information.[159] The Group's work developed in three stages: (*a*) examination of written replies by governments; (*b*) requests for further information and clarification; and (*c*) identification of the main issues involved in non-ratification and making concrete proposals as to ways of overcoming various types of difficulties.

The competence of the Working Group came gradually to be accepted although there was some opposition to the inclusion of the Optional Protocol to the Covenant on Civil and Political Rights in the list of instruments about which information was sought, on the grounds that the term 'optional' is intended to underline that States have full freedom to become parties or not.[160] But this applies to all human rights instruments, since there is no obligation under international law to accede to any of them. Consideration of ratification is a moral obligation, however. In the process of analysing obstacles, the Working Group noted that some States had expressed difficulties due to their federal structures, but that other federal States had nevertheless found it possible (sometimes with certain reservations) to ratify. It was suggested by some members of the Group that some cases of non-ratification were due not to legal or technical, but to political, factors.[161] Most Western States, and some others, have not ratified the International Convention on the Suppression and Punishment of the Crime of Apartheid, an issue which has repeatedly been discussed in the Working Group and in the Sub-Commission itself. While the arguments are cast in legal terms, it is clear that political issues underlie the actual pattern of ratification, a point which at times has also been made in the Working Group.

[157] The text of this legal opinion is appended to the *Report of the Sub-Commission in 1980*, E/CN.4/1413, para. 296, Annex.

[158] *Report of the Sessional Working Group on the Encouragement of Universal Acceptance of Human Rights Instruments in 1980*, E/CN.4/Sub.2/453 (1980), para. 6.

[159] See the *Reports of the Working Group*: E/CN.4/Sub.2/453 (1980); E/CN.4/Sub.2/L.785 (1981); E/CN.4/Sub.2/1982/22; E/CN.4/Sub.2/1983/28; and E/CN.4/Sub.2/1984/26; in 1985, the work of the Working Group was suspended, and a member of the Sub-Commission reported on information received from governments (*Report of the Sub-Commission in 1985*, E/CN.4/1986/5, paras. 364–79).

[160] *Report of the Sessional Working Group on the Encouragement of Universal Acceptance of Human Rights Instruments in 1980*, E/CN.4/Sub.2/453 (1980).

[161] *Report of the Sessional Working Group on the Encouragement of Universal Acceptance of Human Rights Instruments in 1981*, E/CN.4/Sub.2/L.785, paras. 29–30.

For some years, the Working Group provided a useful mechanism for promoting ratifications. Whether or not it has speeded up the process is difficult to say, but the number of ratifications in regard to the main instruments has grown substantially since 1980, when it started its work. However, by 1984 it was clear, at least for the time being, that the Group had done as much as it could. Thus the Sub-Commission, while requesting that governments should continue to inform the United Nations as to any legal problems which impeded ratification, also suggested that the United Nations should offer technical assistance to help draft domestic legislation and regulations which could enable member States to ratify.[162] It also suggested that regional advisers might be designated to advise States on acceptance and implementation of human rights instruments. To follow up on these ideas the Sub-Commission decided to suspend the Working Group and to appoint one of its members to report to it annually on the information received from governments.[163]

The notion of 'promotion' also has other dimensions apart from promoting the ratification of instruments. It is obviously not enough that governments formally accept human rights; they must also be applied by ordinary human beings everywhere, otherwise their realization will never be attained. Thus, human rights education is essential. This task has been dealt with by UNESCO rather than by the human rights organs of the United Nations. But the activity of the Sub-Commission is in itself an educational activity. The presence of, and participation by, a wide range of non-governmental observers and government representatives, the reports they make to their respective constituencies, and the questionnaires which are sent out by the Sub-Commission to which they must respond, can all be seen as a wide-ranging educational process itself. The studies carried out by the Sub-Commission probably contain some of the most comprehensive educational material on human rights available. Moreover, the studies tend to reflect global rather than parochial perspectives. But this is not enough. Everybody must be made aware of their responsibility to promote and protect human rights, and they must not be hindered in their efforts to do so. Thus, in 1985 the Sub-Commission received a report by Erica-Irene Daes which included a set of 'draft principles and guidelines on the right and responsibility of individuals, groups and organs of society to promote and protect human rights'.[164] The ideas contained in the report constitute a potentially useful framework for future human rights promotional efforts. The Sub-Commission's role in that

[162] Sub-Commission Res.1984/19; see also Sub-Commission Res.1987/28.

[163] E/CN.4/Sub.2/1985/24 and Add.1–2; E/CN.4/1988/40/Add.1; and E/CN.4/Sub.2/1988/36; E/CN.4/Sub.2/1990/38; and See Sub-Commission Res.1990/24.

[164] Daes, *Draft Body of Principles and Guidelines on the Right and Responsibility of Individuals, Groups and Organs of Society to Promote and Protect Human Rights and Fundamental Freedoms*, E/CN.4/Sub.2/1985/30 and Add.1.

endeavour will be vital and could conceivably include a review of regular annual reports on the efforts made by UN agencies, governments, and NGOs in fulfilling their obligation to promote human rights.

III. MONITORING IMPLEMENTATION

By 1966 it was widely felt that the time had come for the Commission to go beyond its standard-setting and promotional activities and to attempt to ensure the effective protection of human rights in practice. Some felt that this should be the main task of the Commission, leaving the Sub-Commission to do the necessary analysis and studies. In fact, however, the Commission has given the Sub-Commission a significant role in this regard. The brief and inglorious role of the Sub-Commission (1965–7) in reviewing periodic reports by States had failed because of the inclusion of information from NGOs.[165] But this practice has long since become accepted in regard to more specific (thematic) reporting, of which several examples may be cited.

The annual report on entities engaging in business with, or in, South Africa is one illustration. Similarly the Working Group on Contemporary Forms of Slavery reviews developments in the field of slavery and slavery-like practices, which in effect amounts to a system for monitoring implementation. The same approach has been used by the Working Group on Indigenous Populations, albeit to a lesser degree. The annual report on states of emergency is another instance in which the Sub-Commission has developed an important monitoring role for itself.

These monitoring activities allow for substantial participation by NGOs in calling attention to occurrences taking place in various countries. Since the range of information available goes far beyond government reports, the procedures are thus more open and comprehensive than those of the various treaty supervisory bodies such as the Human Rights Committee.

IV. RESPONDING TO ALLEGATIONS OF VIOLATIONS

Over the years, the United Nations has gradually developed various methods for responding to alleged violations of human rights. The process has been neither smooth nor simple and in hindsight appears to have been more like a game of chess than of diplomacy. The Sub-Commission has been one of the forums in which this game of chess has been played out. But, it has not always been in the forefront; at times, it has been cautious and reluctant, and has almost had to be pushed by its parent bodies. At other times, it has plunged into activism and has been reprimanded by Commission members, though never by the Commission as a whole. There have been profound controversies

[165] See text accompanying nn. 55–61, above.

within all of the bodies involved, and alignments have proved to be as shifting as the sands. The struggle to make the United Nations respond to violations has been one in which NGOs have played a dynamic and risk-taking role. At times, they were sternly warned by the relevant UN bodies—including the Sub-Commission—that they should not overstep certain limits. If they did, they were threatened that their consultative status would be withdrawn.[166] But the limits were usually not clearly drawn, a fact which reflected the unease and controversy on the issue which characterized the attitudes of the UN bodies themselves.

In order to understand the Sub-Commission's present role it is necessary to review developments over the past twenty-five years or so. The first issue was whether the UN should in any way respond to petitions or other allegations of violations. The 'no power to act' doctrine which was sacrosanct for nearly twenty years was broken in 1965 when the Special Committee on Decolonization asked the Commission to examine petitions about human rights violations in Southern Africa.[167] In ECOSOC there was no disagreement that this request should be met[168] but it immediately raised the question as to whether the Commission should deal with allegations of violations only in regard to cases of racial discrimination and colonialism, or whether it could also do so in other cases. Opinions were divided, but the Assembly finally decided that violations anywhere in the world should be covered.[169] But this in turn raised a new issue as to the role of the Sub-Commission. Should its contribution be limited to cases involving discrimination or minorities, or should it deal with all kinds of violations? Initially the Sub-Commission was hesitant, and chose to remind the parent bodies of its limited expertise but the Commission and the Council made it clear that a wider role was envisaged for it.[170]

The question then arose as to how serious violations would have to be in order to be on a par with those taking place in Southern Africa. The Sub-Commission had been severely reprimanded by some members of the Commission in 1968 for having included the cases of Greece and Haiti

[166] ESC Res.1296 (XLIV) (1968), paras. 35–8.

[167] See Special Committee Res. 'concerning the Implementation of GA Res.1514 (XV)' (1965), para. 6; in *Report of the Special Committee on the Situation with Regard to the Implementation of the Declaration on the Granting of Independence to Colonial Countries and Peoples in 1965*, A/6000/Rev. 1 (1965), Chap. 2, para. 463.

[168] ECOSOC responded favourably by ESC Res.1102 (XL) (1966).

[169] ESC Res.1102 (XL) (1966) refers to 'all countries'. The Commission in its Res.2 (XXII) (1966) also in general terms condemned violations in 'all countries', but required more time to reflect on the means to pursue it. ESC Res.1164 (XLI) in August 1966 endorsed the Commission's concern about the means by which to deal with violations. The issue was settled in the General Assembly later that year when GA Res.2144 A (XXI), para. 12, invited the Council and the Commission 'to give urgent consideration to ways and means of improving the capacity of the UN to put a stop to violations of human rights wherever they may occur'.

[170] CHR Res.8 (XXIII) (1967) makes it clear that the Commission wanted the Sub-Commission to bring to its attention *any* situation which it has reasonable cause to believe reveals a consistent pattern of violations of human rights and fundamental freedoms in *any* country.

together with the cases of Southern Africa.[171] The Commission as a whole, however, had neither reprimanded nor praised the Sub-Commission. Over time, it gradually came to be accepted that all serious situations could be included, and comparisons with Southern Africa were not required. The next issue concerned the kind of information which could be utilized. In particular, could use be made of many thousands of petitions which were received annually by the Secretary-General and which the human rights bodies had so far dumped into 'the most elaborate waste-paper basket the world has ever seen'?[172]

If the Commission and the Sub-Commission were to deal with allegations of violations, should their deliberations be confidential or public? The procedures first proposed by the Sub-Commission were predicated on the assumption that they should be public, but the Commission and ECOSOC decided in 1970 that the handling of the communications should be confidential.[173] But the question then arose whether this arrangement meant that the Sub-Commission and the Commission were excluded from dealing with other allegations of violations in open session. For several years the position was unclear, but it was eventually settled in favour of having both types of procedures. This was probably not initially envisaged and was possibly a result of a certain degree of confusion.

The enabling resolution of the Commission[174] was vague, but included an authorization to the Sub-Commission to include on its agenda an item on violations of human rights in all countries. But the latter already had an agenda item on communications and it was under that item that it developed the procedure on communications. However, this left it, from 1968, with an agenda item on violations about which it did not know what to do. Only in 1973 did it have its first substantive debate on the issue. The alternatives were to eliminate it as being superseded by the 1503 procedure, or to have two parallel procedures. No decision was made in 1973. In 1974 the issue was clarified, primarily as a result of interventions by NGOs, whose representatives strongly argued in favour of interpreting the authorization by the Commission as allowing for two parallel procedures.[175] The debate at that time was strongly influenced by the terrible human rights violations in Chile after the military coup, and the events made it impossible for conservative actors to reject the demand for open and public debates on violations.

But, having obtained that victory, the NGOs ran into trouble the following

[171] *Report of the Commission on Human Rights in 1968*, E/4475 (1968), paras. 157–210.

[172] Humphrey, 'The United Nations Commission on Human Rights and its Parent Body', in *René Cassin: Amicorum Discipulorumque Liber* (1969) 110.

[173] ESC Res.1503 (XLVIII) (1970).

[174] CHR Res.8 (XXIII) (1967).

[175] See generally Zuijdwijk, *Petitioning the United Nations* (1982). On the role of NGOs in 1973 and 1974, see ibid. 46.

year in the Commission where the public debate on violations created friction. The Commission expressed displeasure with the NGOs and asked ECOSOC to reprimand them both in respect to the public debate and for breaking the confidentiality requirements of the 1503 procedure.[176] This brought to the fore a new question as to whether NGOs could choose between the available procedures or were restricted to the confidential one. The latter interpretation would mean that the public procedure could be initiated only by Sub-Commission and Commission members themselves.[177] For a while, the Commission and ECOSOC seemed to want a restricted role for the NGOs but it was finally acknowledged that they could use either procedure in any given case.

A more complicated issue was whether an NGO could bring the identical issue under both procedures or whether it must choose either one or the other. This issue, which is still open to debate, is connected with the question of whether the Sub-Commission can deal, under the public procedure, with a situation which is also under review by the Commission under the confidential procedure. Opinions have been divided, but the defeat of a proposal by some members of the Commission in 1985 to prohibit the Sub-Commission from presenting resolutions pertaining to situations under review under the 1503 procedure would seem to have resolved the matter.[178] The correct interpretation would now appear to be that the same *situations* can be dealt with, and the same *events* referred to, but in the open procedure there must be no mention of what happens during the confidential session, nor of the communication itself, unless the author wants to make it public. Similarly there can be no reference to responses given by the government concerned, unless that government wants it to become public, and there must be no reference to views expressed, or decisions made, by the Working Group on Communications of the Sub-Commission itself, or the Commission, in the context of the confidential procedure. As long as these limitations are respected, situations dealt with under 1503 can also be discussed publicly.

With regard to the public procedure, a difficult and enduring issue is whether it too should be regularized in terms of admissibility, time for response, and procedures for the assessment of the reliability of the evidence. Since 1983 the Sub-Commission has been unable to reach agreement on this question. In a 1986 working paper, the Yugoslav expert, Ivan Tosevski,[179] noted that Commission Resolution 8 (XXIII) called upon the Sub-Commission to perform two tasks. The first was to prepare a factual report containing

[176] CHR Res.7 (XXI) (1975).

[177] Confusion arose, owing to the language of ESC Res.1919 (LVIII) (1975), which inadvertently refers both to communications and oral presentations, and admonishes NGOs to respect the principle of confidentiality as stated in ESC Res.1503 (XLVIII) (1970).

[178] E/CN.4/1984/L.73. The defeated proposal had been presented by Brazil and Uruguay.

[179] E/CN.4/Sub.2/1984/32.

relevant information received or collected by the Sub-Commission and the second was to bring to the attention of the Commission any situation which it has reasonable cause to believe reveals a consistent pattern of violations. While the Sub-Commission has performed the second task on numerous occasions, it has only ever prepared one factual report, in 1968. Proposals in recent years to revive the practice have proved inconclusive. One of the principal problems is how to prepare the report. The Secretariat is not anxious to do it, given the sensitive nature of the issue and no single Sub-Commission member could be given such a heavy responsibility. One alternative possibility might be simply to organize and systematize the allegations presented in writing and orally by NGOs, without taking any position on them. This, however, might be of rather limited use since well-founded and baseless allegations would be treated equally, thus providing little guidance for the Commission. As it stands, the debate under the public procedure is rather unsatisfactory. Allegations of violations are presented by NGOs, by Sub-Commission members, and in some cases even by government observers who accuse other governments of violations, often in retribution for allegations made about violations in their own country. This increasingly turns the Sub-Commission into a politicized body, as is demonstrated by the rapidly growing number of government observers intervening under the item on violations. The pressure by NGOs on Sub-Commission members to raise alleged violations can also be very unfortunate, as long as the procedure exists in such a rudimentary state.

A more systematic adversarial exchange is required, in which NGOs and governments would respond to one another and Sub-Commission members would be able to play the role of impartial experts. Allegations should be made only by NGOs, orally or in writing, and government observers should be given the opportunity to respond. Sub-Commission members should be given the opportunity to ask questions of clarification and given some time to draft a proper report on the basis of the information thus collected, which would contain at least some evaluation. For political and practical reasons this is very unlikely to happen in the near future. The best that can be hoped is that some tentative steps will be taken in that direction. Perhaps the preparation of a factual report, as required by the Commission and containing no evaluation, could be a first step. It would at least serve the purpose of demonstrating to all that more stringent procedures are required.

D. *Membership and Participation*

1. MEMBERSHIP

The twenty-six Sub-Commission members are elected in their individual capacities by the Commission. Many members of the Commission share the view expressed by the delegate of Ireland on the eve of the election of Sub-Commission members in February 1988, that candidates ought to have the following qualifications:

- independence, including especially independence from their own governments,
- personal commitment to the cause of human rights; and
- expertise.[180]

Candidates must be nominated by their governments. The actual criteria for membership are vague and non-mandatory, though members are expected to be neither representatives, nor employees, of governments. The original term of office was two, and later three, years with all members being elected simultaneously. In an effort to reduce turnover and increase stability of membership the term was increased to four years in 1988 with half of the experts being elected every two years.[181]

In the initial 1947 Commission resolution it was provided: (*a*) that the Sub-Commission be composed of twelve persons selected by the Commission in consultation with the Secretary-General and subject to the consent of the government of the country of which persons are nationals; and (*b*) that not more than one person be selected from any single country.[182] This procedure was intended to give the Secretary-General an important role in the appointment procedure, but no such consultation has ever taken place.

Governments may only nominate nationals of their own country. Thus, each government can decide who among its nationals will be that State's candidate, if any. The election has thus become a regular process of nominations and competition among candidates. The members are elected on a regional basis with six from the Western European and Others group, five from Latin America, seven from Africa, five from Asia, and three from Eastern Europe.[183] In most regions, more candidates are nominated than the number of seats available.[184] In the 1988 and 1990 elections, the competition was strongest in the African and Asian groups. In both regions the number of nominations was nearly double the number of seats available. Competition has also sometimes been intense in the Western[185] and Latin American groups;

[180] E/CN.4/1988/SR.36/Add.1, para. 14.

[181] CHR Res.1986/37 and ESC Res.1986/35.

[182] Initially 12, the number of members was increased to 14 in 1959, to 18 in 1965, and to its present number of 26 in 1968. (See ESC Res.728 F (XXVII) (1959), 1974 G (XXIX) (1965), and 1334 (XLIV) (1968)).

[183] ESC Res.1334 (XLIV) (1968) and ESC Decision 1978/21.

[184] 'Election of Members of the Sub-Commission. Note by the Secretary-General', E/CN.4/1988/46.

[185] In the 'Western and Others' Group, which now holds six seats, the nominees from the United States, the United Kingdom, and France have always been elected (so far). While no country holds a permanent seat, the relative influence of the nominating country is significant. Thus, the competition in the Western group is mainly among the candidates from smaller countries.

considerable lobbying has been undertaken by some governments both for and against certain candidates—a practice which would seem to attest to the importance which Governments now attach to the Sub-Commission. Eastern Europe, on the other hand, has for a very long time not presented more candidates than the seats available, and hence there has been no genuine election.[186] That situation is sure to change in the future.

Individuals with little or no expertise in human rights, beyond diplomatic training, have on occasion been nominated and elected, and a number of experts have not sought to conceal that they see themselves essentially as governmental representatives. Salzberg found the following number of members elected in the period from 1947 to 1971 to be full-time employed in the central administration or the diplomatic service of their government: 90 per cent of those from Eastern Europe, 78 per cent of those from Latin America, 45 per cent of those from Africa, and 30 per cent of those from the West.[187]

Moreover, until 1983 the provision that an expert who was unable to attend the whole or part of a session, could designate an alternate in consultation with his government but without UN approval, enabled governments effectively to circumvent the modest safeguards that do exist. Thus, for example, in the early 1980s the elected Argentine expert was replaced by a whole succession of officials appointed by the Argentine military government, thus making nonsense of the procedures.[188] As a reaction, the Council decided, on the basis of a recommendation by the Commission, that the only alternate who may serve is one who is elected at the same time as the member and on the basis of the same requirements as to qualifications.[189]

In recent years, the Commission has increasingly underlined the importance of the independence of members. In a 1985 resolution it stressed that members and alternates should be 'independent experts not subject to government instructions in the performance of their functions as members of the Sub-Commission'.[190] But no criteria were formally laid down and no official check of qualifications takes place at any stage.[191]

While it is clearly impossible to eliminate the more subtle forms of pressure which governments can exert, it seems reasonable that the Commission should discourage the nomination of officials of the executive or diplomatic branches of government, since persons who in their daily work are directly subject to governmental instructions can hardly be expected to maintain

[186] See the list of the members of the Sub-Commission (1947 to 1971) in Salzberg, n. 128, above, 119–25.

[187] Ibid.

[188] See e.g. *Report of the Sub-Commission in 1982*, E/CN.4/1983/4, Annex I, 1.

[189] CHR Res.1983/21 and ESC Res.1983/32.

[190] CHR Res.1985/28, para. 4.

[191] The Commission has regularly called 'upon States to nominate as members and alternates person meeting the criteria of independent experts' (CHR Res.1991/56, para. 17).

complete independence in Sub-Commission matters. In the final analysis, no formula will completely suffice and vigilance will be required on the part of concerned governments with respect to both their nominees and their votes.

II. RELATIONS WITH THE COMMISSION AND THE COUNCIL

Controversies have often arisen between the Sub-Commission and its parent bodies, but their relationships have also seen some relatively tranquil periods. The first major crisis ocurred in the early 1950s, followed by a long period of gradual improvement; in the 1970s the tension started to rise again and came to a head in 1981–2, again followed by a process of increasingly positive co-operation, though some elements of friction still exist today. A number of factors explain this somewhat tense relationship. In the first place, the very activist role of NGOs *vis-à-vis* the Sub-Commission troubles many members of the Commission who, by definition, are government representatives and who thus have to take particular account of instructions designed to promote the national interest. This is particularly true of those who must seek to defend their government when it is attacked for human rights violations.

One criticism often made by the Commission is that the Sub-Commission has become too politicized. Some argue that the members have failed to apply their expertise in an objective way and have permitted NGOs to pursue political ends instead. While this contention is difficult to prove, it is not without some foundation. The application of the Commission's procedure for considering alleged violations, for example, makes it extremely difficult to avoid politically controversial, country-specific, issues being raised by NGOs, followed by responses from government observers. The outcome of all this is a politically highly charged atmosphere which makes the proper evaluation of allegations, standards, and evidence difficult.

If more formalized violations procedures were established so that the Sub-Commission, or one of its Working Groups could sit as a competent and impartial tribunal, the Sub-Commission's activities would become less political and thus less troublesome to the Commission.

Another factor making for friction is that the Sub-Commission, as a body of more or less independent experts, can more readily promote initiatives than can the Commission, whose representatives are more attuned to the political consequences of every move. Members of the Sub-Commission also take political considerations into account, but many of them do so in a less direct way than do members of the Commission. If should also be noted that tensions and disagreements exist within both the Sub-Commission and the Commission and that the alignments are not always the same in each organ.

Thus it is possible for a proposal to command strong majority support in the Sub-Commission but to be relatively unpopular in the Commission.[192]

It would be misleading, however, to depict the relationship between the Sub-Commission and its parent bodies as an entirely antagonistic one. The great majority of resolutions proposed by the Sub-Commission in recent years has been endorsed by the Commission. Where this has not been the case, the problem may well have resulted from: (*a*) the actions of a determined and relatively powerful State which sees its interests (or those of its allies) directly threatened by a particular Sub-Commission proposal; or (*b*) the fact that the issue was primarily referred to the Sub-Commission so that the Commission could avoid having to make a decision on the matter (as in the case of the proposal for a High Commissioner for Human Rights[193]).

The central problem is not *per se* the role of the two bodies *vis-à-vis* one another, and it should thus not be assumed that a fundamental antagonism must exist. On the other hand it may be argued that the absence of any such discord would be a sure sign that the Sub-Commission was no longer playing an independent or expert role. The rationale for requiring an expert sub-commission to advise and report to a governmental commission is to ensure that differing, and often conflicting, perspectives are taken into account and that the predominant concerns of one group will both complement, and to some extent offset, those of the other. Thus, the achievement of an appropriately balanced policy approach will inevitably involve some degree of tension between the two bodies, except where relatively non-controversial issues are involved.

During its first 15 years, the Sub-Commission's greatest problems were with ECOSOC, not the Commission, and the main cause of friction was the concern with protection of minorities. In 1951, the Council decided to eliminate the Sub-Commission altogether,[194] but the General Assembly forced it to reverse its decision the following year.[195] In the late 1940s and 1950s ECOSOC was essentially Western-dominated, but so was the Sub-Commission, albeit to a lesser extent. The clashes can therefore best be understood not in terms of power politics, but of the differences of approach between value-oriented independent experts and governments motivated by considerations of '*realpolitik*'.

192 e.g. Sub-Commission Res.1987/17 (adopted by 15 votes to none, with 2 abstentions), proposing a study on treaties concluded between indigenous peoples and States and their contemporary significance, became highly controversial at the Commission's 1988 session. (See *Report of the Commission on Human Rights in 1988*, E/1988/12, paras. 499–505, and CHR Res.1988/56.)

193 See *Report of the Sub-Commission in 1982*, E/CN.4/1983/4, paras. 43–61; *Report of the Commission on Human Rights in 1983*, E/1983/13, paras. 201–17; *Report of the Sub-Commission in 1983*, E/CN.4/1984/3; E/CN.4/1984/3, paras. 216–38; and *Report of the Commission on Human Rights in 1984*, E/1984/14, paras. 241–74.

194 ESC Res.414 B (XIII), Part I, para. 18(d).

195 GA Res.532 B (VI) (1952).

With the demise of ECOSOC's human rights initiating role,[196] the Sub-Commission's difficulties over the past two decades have centred entirely on its relationship with the Commission rather than the Council. Until the early 1980s the Sub-Commission often found itself frustrated, not because of rejection from the Commission, but because of a lack of guidance or response, due to competing approaches within the Commission itself. However, the Sub-Commission's increasing propensity to take initiatives forced a change of attitude on the part of the Commission. This manifested itself not only through intense debates as to the Sub-Commission's proper role, but also in improved responsiveness on the Commission's part.

Relations reached a low point in 1981–2 when the membership of both the Commission and the Sub-Commission was dominated by a majority of Third World States, many of the governments of which were accused of human rights violations. Again, the confrontation cannot be understood in terms of traditional power politics. At the 1981 session of the Commission, a large number of members criticized the Sub-Commission for going beyond its mandate.[197] In essence, the criticism was based on the view that the Sub-Commission was acting independently rather than as a preparatory body for the Commission. The main formal point of contention was that the Sub-Commission was addressing governments and other UN agencies directly rather than channelling its requests through the Commission. Many Commission members, however, came to the support of the Sub-Commission. The resolution adopted was rather bland and advised the Sub-Commission to take into account the views which had been expressed in the Commission.[198]

In response the Sub-Commission held a heated debate in 1981.[199] Some members wanted to alter fundamentally the relationship, to place the Sub-Commission on a par with the Commission, and to report directly to the Economic and Social Council. The latter would then be able to weigh up political inputs received from the Commission. Other members argued that the Commission was a much better forum for substantive discussions on human rights issues than the Council. They therefore advocated seeking a more constructive relationship with the Commission.

Recognizing the absence of consensus, the Sub-Commission abstained from adopting any resolution on the issue and, in subsequent years, a more conciliatory approach has been taken by both organs. The difficulties inherent in the relationship between the two bodies ought to be handled by closer contact between them. In 1984 and 1985 the Sub-Commission adopted a number of proposals for rationalization of its work,[200] all of which were

[196] See Chap. 4, above.
[197] E/CN.4/SR.1592–5 (1981).
[198] CHR Res.17 (XXXVII) (1981), para. 2.
[199] See E/CN.4/Sub.2/SR.896–8 and 922 (1981).
[200] Sub-Commission Res.1984/37 and 1985/34.

accepted by the Commission.[201] The Commission also underlined the need for the provision of better support services by the Secretariat to the Sub-Commission and requested the latter to bear in mind the tasks assigned to it.[202] These requests have been intended to indicate that the Sub-Commission should limit its activities to those that derive from its explicit mandate. But that mandate is vague and, in most cases in which the Sub-Commission has requested more specific guidance, the Commission has been unable or unwilling to give it. In 1991 the Commission, while reaffirming the importance of the Sub-Commission, adopted a range of measures designed to influence the Sub-Commission activities and methods of work.[203] In sum, the possibility of a completely harmonious relationship between the two bodies is small, as long as one is composed of government representatives and the other of independent experts. But the friction, at present rather modest, is probably constructive and indeed necessary if the Commission is to obtain the sort of expert input which it could not generate from within its own ranks.

From time to time it has been proposed that the Sub-Commission's title should be changed. In 1965 the new name suggested by members of the Commission, was 'Permanent Committee of Experts of the Commission on Human Rights'.[204] In 1982 several members of the Sub-Commission suggested that the Sub-Commission should enjoy a status equal to that of the Commission, should report directly to ECOSOC, and should be called 'the Committee of Experts on Human Rights'.[205] In 1984 the Sub-Commission as a whole proposed the title 'Sub-Commission of Experts of the Commission on Human Rights'.[206] On each occasion the Commission has chosen to ignore the proposal. Given the somewhat unwieldy nature of the present title and its failure to encompass many of the functions actually performed by the Sub-Commission, there are strong grounds to justify a name change. Nevertheless, the issue is of limited importance in substantive terms.

III. THE SUB-COMMISSION AS A FORUM

The Sub-Commission provides a forum in which experts, NGOs, and representatives of intergovernmental organs and of governments can meet. It thus provides a platform from which activist groups can bring the international community's attention to violations taking place in many parts of the world and facilitates the channelling of information from a wide range of sources, through the Sub-Commission and on to other UN bodies.

201 See e.g. CHR Res.1983/22, 1985/28, 1986/38, and 1988/43.
202 e.g. CHR Res.1988/43, paras. 13 and 19.
203 CHR Res.1991/56.
204 E/CN.4/L.768 (1965), para. 1.
205 E/CN.4/Sub.2/1982/L.1 and E/CN.4/Sub.2/1982/L.3.
206 Sub-Commission Res.1984/37, para. 6(b).

Its openness, however, has given rise to one problem which, as of the late 1980s, may be getting out of hand. Over the last decade, the presence and participation of observers has increased dramatically.[207] Their activity has been particularly high when the Sub-Commission deals with human rights violations, an item which grew from a minor one in 1977 (2 meetings out of a total of 39) to the central and most time-consuming one in 1990 (14 meetings out of 36).[208] As a result of this substantial shift, the Sub-Commission functions much less collegially than before, its proceedings are increasingly politicized by the observers, and the time available for in-depth discussion has been reduced substantially.[209]

IV. THE ROLE OF THE NGOS

As noted earlier, a remarkable aspect of the Sub-Commission's work is its openness to active participation by NGOs. The NGOs play a forceful and creative role. They have participated from the beginning but their numbers have increased considerably in the 1970s and 1980s. They have been most active on violations issues. Otherwise, their principal involvement has been in items dealing with the rights of detainees, indigenous peoples' rights, religious discrimination, and the new international economic order. They have been less active on issues such as racial discrimination and the organization of the work of the Sub-Commission.[210] Their representatives engage in substantial lobbying behind the scenes. Sometimes they circulate drafts of resolutions which are subsequently modified and presented by Sub-Commission experts; they provide written and oral submissions; and they present allegations of violations. They have been of particular assistance in the elaboration of principles and other forms of standard-setting. Some have developed great expertise in certain fields[211] and the larger organizations have a range of

[207] Thus, in 1977 there were probably no more than ten interventions by government observers, and even fewer by NGOs. In 1980, government observers intervened on 24 occasions, and NGOs on almost as many. In 1984, government observers took part in the discussion 64 times, and NGOs 67 times. By 1987, the figures had increased to 72 interventions from government observers, and 92 from NGOs.

[208] The role of NGOs on this item was not made clear by CHR Res.8 (XXIII) (1967); nevertheless, NGOs started very early to bring allegations of violations. In 1977, 4 government observers and 2 NGOs intervened under this item. In 1982, the figure was 12 for governments and 11 for NGOs. In 1984, government observers intervened no fewer than 20 times, and the same was true for NGOs. By 1987, government observers were up to 36 interventions, and NGOs to 23.

[209] Looking at the total number of interventions during the public, plenary meetings, and leaving aside brief statements during the adoption of resolutions, for 1987, interventions of members of the Sub-Commission (a total of 137) are outnumbered by those of the government observers and NGOs (a total of 167).

[210] In 1987, NGOs made 19, 10, 9, and 9 interventions on these respective issues.

[211] Three organizations should be particularly mentioned for their constructive role in assisting the Sub-Commission: Amnesty International, the International Commission of Jurists, and the Anti-Slavery Society.

practical experience and professional competence which may be greater than that of some of the Sub-Commission members.

NGOs have been instrumental in the creation of several working groups of the Sub-Commission. In 1979 the establishment of a Working Group on the Encouragement of Universal Acceptance of Human Rights Instruments was the outcome of an initiative by eight NGOs which joined together to propose its creation. The Working Group on Contemporary Forms of Slavery was created mainly as a result of the lobbying of the Anti-Slavery Society, and the Working Group on Indigenous Populations came about, in part, as a result of the increasingly vocal demands for such a forum by indigenous and non-indigenous organizations. In 1990, by unofficial counts, some 300 observers followed the discussions in the latter working group. Nevertheless, the relationship between the Sub-Commission and NGOs has not been entirely harmonious. Thus, for example, friction arose in the context of the study programme over the issue of how to utilize NGO information. It was also a stumbling-block in the brief venture made by the Sub-Commission into the reviewing of periodic reports. With respect to violations there is no disagreement that information can be presented by NGOs, although some Sub-Commission members continue to challenge their impartiality and objectivity. Although the majority of the Sub-Commission members are clearly appreciative of the NGO role in this respect, there are, nevertheless, great variations in the quality of submissions made by different NGOs. A few of them are highly competent, well informed, constructive, and effective. Others are not.

V. CONTACTS BETWEEN THE SUB-COMMISSION AND GOVERNMENTS

Under the studies programme, governments are often called upon to submit information in response to more or less detailed questionnaires sent out by the Secretariat on behalf of the Special Rapporteur. In compiling and completing this information, governments become sensitized to the issue under consideration in that particular study. The more publicity that surrounds the study, the more important will be this stimulation of awareness in government circles. Some studies and reports can be a source of friction if they contain information negative to some governments. A notable example is the annual 'list on banks, transnational corporations and other organizations assisting the racist regime of South Africa' which has annoyed Western governments;[212] the annual list on countries which proclaim, extend, or terminate a state of emergency[213] will undoubtedly also become a source of friction with some governments.

[212] See nn. 33 and 34, above.
[213] See n. 155, above.

Governmental representatives are increasingly prominent at Sub-Commission meetings, particularly in connection with the agenda item on violations, partly in order to report back to their governments, and partly to respond to allegations. This has turned the Sub-Commission in to something of a political body in which the experts risk becoming submerged. The participation of government experts in several of the working groups has been highly appreciated, however, since the working groups allow for more constructive dialogue and more in-depth treatment.

VI. CO-ORDINATION BETWEEN THE SUB-COMMISSION AND OTHER BODIES

Human rights activities are carried out in many bodies apart from the Sub-Commission. To a modest, but perhaps still inadequate, extent, the Sub-Commission has served as a means for promoting co-ordination. The ILO is the only specialized agency which has consistently attended the meetings. In earlier periods, UNESCO sent observers, but in recent years their presence has been token, at best. Other UN agencies and bodies have rarely attended and then only when issues of particular relevance to them have been discussed.

Somewhat regrettably there has been very little interaction between the Sub-Commission and the treaty organs. As a result, those organs tend to have little awareness of the studies and principles developed by the Sub-Commission, even when these would be directly relevant to their work. This significantly reduces the impact of the work of the Sub-Commission. Conversely, Sub-Commission members are aware of the practice and jurisprudence of the treaty organs only to a very limited extent, even when this might be of central significance to issues being discussed by them. It is probably not practical to have representatives of the treaty organs present during Sub-Commission sessions, but the Secretariat could make a greater effort to facilitate an exchange of information between those bodies, in order to improve the level of knowledge and to encourage somewhat more consistent interpretations by the different UN rights bodies.

Conclusions and Recommendations

I. CONCLUSIONS

In the final analysis, the Sub-Commission has a dual role. One is its study or 'think-tank' function, which serves several purposes; the other is its contribution to formation of UN responses to gross human rights violations. These two functions are often not kept fully separate, nor should they be; the greatest problems arise when the second role (response to violations) is sought to be singled out from its think-tank function.

The study function, we have seen, takes several forms and purposes. Two main forms have crystallized: the use of special rapporteurs, and of working groups. In both cases, sources of information include NGOs, including oral and written submissions which in effect contain allegations of violations. Based on the study of these and other sources, the Sub-Commission seeks to develop more precise and detailed standards than those contained in the general human rights provisions, which often are rather vague.

When dealing with governments which, in accordance with the Charter, are willing to co-operate with the United Nations in the realization of human rights, these efforts can have considerable impact and can be pursued without acrimonious confrontations.

Therefore, as the Sub-Commission is faced with numerous allegations of violations directed against various governments in different parts of the world, it can treat this information as indications of problems in the realization of human rights. The most constructive approach could then be to study the underlying problems and come up with its views on how these could best be solved.

An increasing number of governments co-operate in the realization of human rights. Where violations are the result of aberrations or problems which can be rectified, governments are prepared to co-operate with the United Nations to solve those problems.

Difficulties arise when violations are, indeed, systematic—i.e. where the structure of power is such that violations are inherent. When governments are non-democratic, not representing the aspirations and desires of their subjects, or when governments are unwilling to allow for a reasonable degree of autonomy to peoples living within the territory of the State, then violations can be a systematic aspect of the efforts of governments to remain in power. When this is so, it is difficult to solve the human rights problem by co-operation. Pressure may have to be brought to bear, which for the Sub-Commission and the Commission is limited to public criticism. This can, however, significantly strengthen those inside the country who struggle for democracy and openness.

It should not be overlooked, however, that governments may find themselves in extremely difficult situations due to conditions created by previous governments or as a result of irrational antagonisms between different groups in society. While the task of the government is to be equally responsive to all groups and to give equal protection, latent or open conflict makes governance very difficult at times. When social tensions are high and the different groups do not have confidence in the ability of the government to harmonize their interests and values, the government is faced with a problem which should be constructively discussed in the Sub-Commission and the Commission, seeking solutions rather than incrimination.

II. RECOMMENDATIONS

1. A basis for improving its work would be for the Sub-Commission to agree on what its main functions are. It should recognize more clearly its dual role as a study or 'think-tank' body, and as a preparatory body for the Commission in responding adequately to gross violations. While the former is the most important, the second has to be maintained as a last resort in relation to governments which do not want to co-operate. The 'think-tank' function consists not only of the studies undertaken by special rapporteurs, but also the activities of the working groups—with the exception of the working group dealing with communications under Resolution 1503. The aim of this function should be to help solve problems connected with the realization of human rights.

2. Problem-solving activities require the pursuit of at least two tasks. The first is to create awareness of the nature and dimensions of the problem. For this to happen, it is necessary to have a participatory approach to the study programme. Wherever possible, those affected should be enabled to contribute. When requesting information, particular efforts should be made to obtain information from groups affected, even if this makes it necessary to go beyond the circle of governments, intergovernmental organizations, and non-governmental organizations with consultative status.

When efforts to study selected problem areas are made by working groups, attendance by affected groups should be sought since they may have the most relevant information to bring. Simultaneously, the governments concerned should be encouraged to take part in the study efforts of the working group.

Secondly, in pursuing its study activities, the Sub-Commission should make full use of the insights gained, the recommendations proposed, and the efforts made by other UN bodies. Particular attention should be given to the treaty bodies, which have the main role in monitoring compliance with human rights standards.

3. The Sub-Commission should devote greater attention to the preferred type of recommendations it could make. They might consist of proposed new—or more precise—standards. It is recognized, however, that new human rights are often not required. New standards should therefore aim at providing more detailed and context-specific guidelines for the implementation of existing human rights, based on the insights obtained during the study of obstacles encountered in the realization of selected human rights.

In making such recommendations, the Sub-Commission should take into account that the relevant treatly bodies may in the future be in a better position to suggest such subsidiary standards, although their mode of working until now has not made that possible. A particularly important task for the Sub-Commission should be to clarify the obstacles encountered in the realization of certain human rights (e.g., economic and social rights) and indicate ways in which these obstacles might be overcome, such as by more concerted efforts by the international community.

4. Ideally, the chosen problem area should be made clear at the time of the initiation of the study (or the establishment of the working group) along with an indication of the kind of problem-solving recommendations being sought. Often, however, there will be a learning process during the course of study. Several stages may be found necessary, leading initially to partial conclusions and redefinitions of the problem area.

5. The handling of alleged violations by the Sub-Commission needs to be substantially changed and improved through a more refined use of the authorization in Commission Resolution 8 (XXIII), para. 2. Account should be taken of the work done on thematic aspects of violations, both by the Commission and the Sub-Commission, through their existing use of working groups and thematic rapporteurs. Provided additional funding for Secretariat services could be made available, the Sub-Commission should seek, preferably through the use of a new working group, to systematize the information contained in the different reports and take into account also reliable information provided by NGOs. On that basis the Sub-Commission should present to the Commission a systematic and country-specific review of the main issues involved, together with recommendations for remedial action.

These recommendations could, through decisions by the Commission, be addressed to the governments concerned. When dealing with governments which are prepared to co-operate with the United Nations in remedying the human rights problems in their country, a constructive rather than incriminating approach could then be chosen.

6. When violations are not only gross but also consistent, which they will be when the composition and the policies of the government make violations a necessary ingredient, and when the government therefore will not be genuinely prepared to co-operate in the elimination of violations, the Sub-Commission should make use of its mandate under paragraph 6 of CHR Res. 8. This calls on the Sub-Commission to bring to the attention of the Commission *situations* which it has cause to believe reveal a *consistent pattern of violations*. In such cases, only a change of government or its policies will bring violations to an end.

7

The Commission on the Status of Women

LAURA REANDA

Introduction

Concern with the elimination of sex-based discrimination is a relatively new issue on the international agenda. Certain specific problems affecting women were the object of international standard-setting by diplomatic conferences and by the International Labour Organisation in the first decades of this century.[1] However, it was only in 1935 that the question of the status of women in all its aspects was first placed on the agenda of an international organization, the League of Nations. The Assembly of the League initially referred the question to governments and women's international organizations for observations regarding possible action. In 1937, it appointed a committee of experts to carry out a comprehensive inquiry into 'the legal status enjoyed by women in the various countries of the world'. The committee's mandate was restricted to collecting and analysing information without making recommendations as to any further action, as there was no consensus over the measures to be taken at the international level, or even on whether the international community had jurisdiction in the matter. The committee, appointed in 1938, held three sessions before folding as a consequence of the war.[2]

The Charter of the United Nations and the peace treaties concluded at the end of the Second World War are therefore the first international instru-

[1] These agreements were in the following areas: (*a*) International Agreement for the Suppression of the 'White Slave Traffic' (1904) and International Convention of the same name, LNTS, i. 84–94; International Convention for the Suppression of Traffic in Women and Children, LNTS, ix. 416–33; International Convention for the Suppression of the Traffic in Women of Full Age, LNTS, cl, 431–43; (*b*) Convention Concerning the Employment of Women before and after Childbirth, Adopted by the ILO (Convention No. 3, 1919), in International Labour Organization, *International Labour Conventions and Recommendations 1919–1981* (1985), 691; Convention Concerning Employment of Women during the Night, Adopted by the ILO (Convention No. 4, 1919), ibid. 701; Convention Concerning the Employment of Women on Underground Work in Mines of All Kinds, Adopted by the ILO (Convention No. 45, 1935), ibid. 709; (*c*) nationality (Hague Convention on the Conflict of Nationality Laws, 1930; Montevideo Convention on the Nationality of Women, 1933).

[2] The papers of the committee of experts of the League were reproduced in E/HR/ST/1 (1946).

ments containing sex-equality provisions of a wide-ranging nature.[3] At San Francisco in 1945, a number of feminists working under the umbrella of the Inter-American Commission on the Status of Women were successful in having non-discrimination on the grounds of sex written into the United Nations Charter.[4] The same women were also influential in bringing about the establishment of the nuclear Sub-Commission on the Status of Women—subsequently raised to the status of a Commission of the Economic and Social Council—to promote implementation of the Charter provisions.[5]

While the mandate of the Commission on the Status of Women was not as broad as that of its sister Commission on Human Rights,[6] it is clear from the early records that the new Commission was intended to be the main policy-making body of the United Nations on all questions relating to women. Its function was to collect information, make recommendations to the Economic and Social Council, the General Assembly, and other United Nations bodies working in related fields, and to stimulate governments, private organizations, and world public opinion in favour of implementing the sex-equality provisions of the Charter.[7]

For the first quarter-century of its life the Commission did play a unique role with regard to women in the United Nations system, although not always as effectively as its supporters would have wished. Despite the many difficulties, the Commission embarked on an ambitious programme of work which in time included studies, seminars, elaboration of international standards, review of reports submitted by States, and stimulating action in favour of women by the United Nations specialized agencies and other United Nations organs, including the provision of technical assistance to benefit women in developing countries. An International Women's Year was proclaimed by the General Assembly in 1975, followed by a Women's Decade, and three world conferences were held, attended by thousands of women.[8] Today, the work of the United Nations relating to women is spread over a vast area, affecting many sectors and involving hundreds of meetings and projects.

Paradoxically, however, this great expansion in the work of the United Nations with regard to women was accompanied not by a growth in power and

[3] Sex-equality provisions are included in the UN Charter Preamble and Arts. 1, 8, 13, 55, and 76. Equal-rights clauses were inserted also in the peace treaties with Romania, Italy, Bulgaria, and Finland. (See Report of the CSOW to the ECOSOC, E/281/Rev.1, 9 (1947).)

[4] See statement by the representative of the Inter-American Commission on the Status of Women in E/CN.6/SR.29 (1948).

[5] ESC Res.1/5 (1946); 2/11 (1946); and 48 (IV) (1947).

[6] ESC Res.1/5 (1946) establishing the CHR included in its terms of reference standard-setting and the protection of minorities and prevention of discrimination, which were not included in the terms of reference of the CSOW.

[7] See statement by the Chairman of the Commission, E/CN.6/SR.20 (1948).

[8] The reports of the world conferences are contained in the following documents: *Report of the World Conference of the International Women's Year*, E/CONF.66/34 (1975); *Report of the World Conference of the UN Decade for Women: Equality, Development and Peace*, A/CONF.94/35 (1980); *Report of the World Conference to Review and Appraise the Achievements of the UN Decade for Women: Equality, Development and Peace*, A/CONF.116/28/Rev.1 (1985).

responsibility of the Commission, but by its gradual decline and loss of the focal institutional position which it occupied previously. By the late 1970s, the Commission was only marginally involved in many of the United Nations activities relating to women. The low point in the Commission's history was probably reached in 1980, when a proposal was tabled in the General Assembly for the abolition of the Commission in the context of a general restructuring of the economic and social sectors of the United Nations system.[9]

Concern by many delegations with this decline at a time when so many vital decisions affecting women are taken by the international system, led to efforts to revitalize the Commission in the past few years, particularly since the end of the Women's Decade in 1985. Problems in achieving co-ordination and consistency in the various United Nations programmes on women have pointed up the need for a centralized institutional mechanism to perform monitoring, evaluation, and co-ordination, a role for which the Commission is eminently suited. The growing concern with streamlining the United Nations system in response to its financial crisis in the late 1980s also worked in favour of a strengthened role for the Commission. The debate on the future of the Commission and on ways to strengthen it has begun and a number of changes have been initiated or proposed, as will be described later.

The historical development of the Commission on the Status of Women reflects a familiar dilemma in efforts to achieve equality for women. The creation of separate institutional mechanisms and the adoption of special measures for women are often necessary in order to rectify existing situations of discrimination. The danger of creating a 'women's ghetto' endowed with less power and resources, attracting less interest and commanding lower priority than other national policy goals is latent in this approach. On the other hand, efforts to improve the situation of women through general measures addressed to the population as a whole often result in the struggle for equality becoming submerged in global concerns.[10] The United Nations alternated between these two approaches in formulating the work of the Commission: from an initial emphasis on the definition and assertion of the rights of women as women, the creation of specialized machinery, and the formulation of special programmes, to recent efforts to integrate a women's dimension in all United Nations programmes and activities. These different

[9] Draft Res.A/C.2/35/L.20/Rev.1 (1980), submitted by Argentina and Jamaica in the Second Committee of the GA, requesting the ECOSOC to discontinue the CSOW (along with a number of other subsidiary organs) and to assume its functions directly. The proposal was later shelved.

[10] See Reanda, 'Human Rights and Women's Rights: The United Nations Approach', 3/2 *Hum Rts Q.* 12–31 (1981) for an analysis of this dilemma in relation specifically to the work of various UN human rights organs. It is perhaps a reflection of the low visibility of women in international affairs that the work of the United Nations with regard to women has received very little attention so far. In addition to the publications cited in the Bibliography, below, see: Hevener, *International Law and the Status of Women* (1983); and Bruce, 'Work of the United Nations Relating to the Status of Women', 4 *Rev. des droits de l'homme* 365 (1971).

approaches have been accompanied by a shift in emphasis from a concern with equality of rights to a concern with ensuring women's participation in all aspects of social and economic life. The latest phase in the history of the Commission, which began recently, reflects a growing understanding of the need to integrate the two approaches and to develop appropriate institutional mechanisms.

A. *Some Basic Facts about the Commission*

I. COMPOSITION AND METHODS OF WORK

The Commission on the Status of Women is one of six functional commissions established by the Economic and Social Council pursuant to Article 68 of the United Nations Charter.[11] Its members are elected by the Council from among member States of the United Nations according to a geographic distribution pattern established by the Council.[12] Originally set at fifteen, the membership of the Commission was gradually increased to reflect the growing membership of the United Nations and was set again at forty-five from 1990.[13] As with the Commission on Human Rights, the persons serving on the Commission on the Status of Women are appointed by their governments 'in consultation with the Secretary-General' and are subject to confirmation by the Council, a provision originally intended to guarantee retention of balanced expertise in the Commission membership but which has by now lost all practical meaning since neither the Secretariat nor the Council has ever challenged a nominee.

Members of the Commission accordingly sit as representatives of their countries and, like representatives in other United Nations bodies, are subject to the instructions of their governments, whose interests they promote. Members can be replaced at any time.[14] Whether the Commission should be

[11] The other functional commissions are: the Commission on Human Rights, the Commission on Social Development, the Population Commission, the Statistical Commission, and the Commission on Narcotic Drugs.

[12] ESC Res.1989/45 decided to increase the membership to 45 as of 1990 according to the following pattern: African States (13); Asian States (11); East European States (4); Latin American and Caribbean States (9); Western European and Other States (8). Members serve for a four-year term, with one-third of the membership rotating each year (no elections take place in the fourth year).

[13] The membership was increased to 18 in 1951, 21 in 1961, and 32 in 1966. The 1991 membership was the following: Austria, Bahamas, Bangladesh, Brazil, Bulgaria, Burkina Faso, Canada, China, Colombia, Costa Rica, Côte d'Ivoire, Cuba, Cyprus, Ecuador, Egypt, France, Ghana, Guatemala, India, Indonesia, Iran, Italy, Jamaica, Japan, Lesotho, Malaysia, Mexico, Morocco, Netherlands, Nigeria, Pakistan, Philippines, Poland, Rwanda, Sudan, Sweden, Thailand, Turkey, Uganda, Ukrainian SSR, USSR, United Republic of Tanzania, USA, Zaire, Zimbabwe.

[14] In order to replace its representative on the Commission a government needs simply to notify the Secretariat, which will place the new name for confirmation before ECOSOC.

composed of government representatives or experts serving in a personal capacity was a matter of some debate prior to the establishment of the Commission. Its predecessor, the nuclear Sub-Commission on the Status of Women of the Commission on Human Rights, had in fact been composed of individual experts, a number of whom were prominent activists in the women's movements of their countries. They had made wide-ranging recommendations, which will be touched upon later, and had taken the position that the future Commission dealing with women's rights should also be composed of experts serving in a personal capacity, arguing that women's rights would be better defended by persons not under the direct control of governments.[15] The Council upgraded the Sub-Commission to the status of a full Commission but decided that it should be composed of States members of the United Nations. As in the case of the sister Commission on Human Rights, this decision was to have long-lasting effects as the positions taken by the governmental representatives reflected official policies rather than the concerns of women activists. In analysing the work of the Commission on the Status of Women it should therefore be kept in mind that it is primarily an intergovernmental body, functioning within the political framework of the United Nations and following its general trends, and that the concerns and conceptualizations of the women's movement have remained somewhat marginal to its development.

Nevertheless, it must be pointed out that there is a peculiar ambiguity in the Commission, since contrary to other United Nations bodies, it is composed mostly of women.[16] An examination of the debates in the Commission shows that women members, while representing the position of their governments, have on occasion decried sex-based discrimination within their own societies, and even engaged in criticism of their own governments, as well as serving as channels for the proposals of women's groups. The other side of the coin, however, is that women serving on the Commission have often appeared to command less than full support from their governments as represented in supervisory United Nations bodies, and this resulted in a number of constraints on the work of the Commission.[17]

An examination of the working methods of the Commission shows how its activities have been circumscribed by budgetary and procedural limitations imposed by its parent bodies. Despite the fact that its growing agenda was

[15] See the summary of debates in the nuclear Sub-Commission in E/HR/ST/9 (1946).

[16] The Commission had an all-female membership until 1966, when 1 male representative was included among the 21 members. At no time has the Commission had more than a handful of male representatives. Male advisors, however, have often been attached to delegations.

[17] An early example of this was reflected in the debates at the second session of the Commission in 1948, when several members protested that representatives in the Council had 'displayed a lack of seriousness' *vis-à-vis* the Commission. A proposal to embody the protest in a resolution was withdrawn after the Chairman reported that she had already addressed a letter to the President of the Council deploring such an attitude. E/CN.6/SR.35 (1948).

causing the Commission increasing difficulties, its sessions have never been more than three weeks in length at the peak of its influence.[18] In 1969, the Council decided that the Commission should meet biennially beginning in 1971.[19] The Commission was also under pressure since the late 1960s to reduce its agenda and the volume of its documentation, as well as the number of resolutions addressed to the Council. Its entitlement to the issuance of summary records of its proceedings was discontinued in 1979. Although a majority of members opposed these decisions as having detrimental implications for the work of the Commission, no serious proposals were made to request additional resources or longer sessions in order to solve the organizational problems.[20]

Similarly, the Commission never spawned the vast array of permanent or *ad hoc* subsidiary bodies which are by now a familiar feature of the Commission on Human Rights. It has established only sessional working groups, primarily to review communications and on an informal basis to expedite consideration of certain agenda items or to draft recommendations. The device of appointing special rapporteurs to undertake studies of particularly complex or delicate issues, has also not been duplicated by the Commission. Special rapporteurs were appointed only twice in its more than forty-five-year history, both in the late 1960s, and the Commission has not reverted to this procedure since then. Budgetary constraints were mentioned repeatedly by members as militating against any proposals for the creation of subsidiary machinery.

Despite recurrent complaints in the Commission over these limitations and the frequent reliance on extra-budgetary resources in order to finance regular United Nations activities on women, its work has remained consistently underfunded, as has the work of other United Nations organs created specifically to deal with women's concerns. Recent efforts to revitalize the Commission, which have coincided with a period of financial stringency, have not appreciably changed this situation. At the 1989 session of the Commission, the Director-General of the United Nations Office at Vienna emphasized the need to look increasingly for extra-budgetary funding for the new tasks entrusted to the Commission. An appeal was also made that budgetary resources allocated to activities for the advancement of women should not suffer disproportionately from the impact of restructuring and retrenchment measures.[21]

[18] The Commission met annually for about two weeks between 1947 and 1952, and for three weeks from 1953. Only in 1976 did the Commission meet for a longer period (30 days) in order to complete its work on the Convention on the Elimination of All Forms of Discrimination against Women. In 1982, 1984, 1986, and 1988 to 1991 it met for only eight working days (Additional sessions of the Commission in its capacity as preparatory body for the 1985 world conference were held in 1983, 1984, and 1985).

[19] Decision of 8 Aug. 1969. E/4735 (1969).

[20] See the debate in the Commission. E/CN.6/SR.534 (1969).

[21] The UN budget for the biennium 1990/91 includes an appropriation of US $196,400 for the travel of Commission representatives and staff, plus US $2,587,100 for women's programmes in the Centre for Social Development and Humanitarian Affairs, which provides the substantive

This situation goes hand in hand with a relative lack of institutional weight. Compared to the Commission on Human Rights, the Commission has traditionally been subjected to much stricter control on the part of its parent body, the Economic and Social Council. Until 1986, all its decisions and resolutions, including the agenda of future sessions, were routinely submitted as drafts for adoption by the Council, while the Commission on Human Rights, for example, submits only those recommendations having financial implications, other resolutions being considered 'internal'. As the account in the following sections will show, in several instances proposals made by the Commission on the Status of Women were rejected by the Council or returned to it for further consideration.

A special session of the Commission was convened in January 1987 to review the future work of the United Nations with regard to women and its own role. Its recommendations, which resulted from new initiatives of the United States and other Western countries, were subsequently endorsed by the Council. There was general agreement that its role as the focal point in the United Nations system for all issues related to the advancement of women should be strengthened and its capacity and methods of work made more effective. It was decided that beginning in 1988 and until the year 2000, it would hold annual sessions and the officers elected to the Bureau would serve for a two-year term, and that its membership would be expanded from thirty-two to forty-five as of 1990. Its agenda for future sessions was restructured according to a long-term programme of work, and priority themes were selected for in-depth consideration at alternate sessions. A further recommendation for the regular convening of expert groups on specific themes as a supplement to the work of the Commission was also adopted. In addition, steps were taken to clarify its relationship with the United Nations organs dealing with co-ordination, on the one hand, and with the Committee on the Elimination of Discrimination against Women, on the other, and to achieve improved co-ordination of efforts.[22] These decisions, and others discussed below, did not resolve all the Commission's problems, but they constituted a welcome first step towards a more visible and influential role for it, which might be said to have reached a new stage in its long career.

secretariat for CSOW and CEDAW. The total amount corresponds to about 0.14% of the UN budget for the biennium. Some activities included in the budget are being partly financed through extra-budgetary sources, in particular the Trust Fund for the Monitoring and Review and appraisal of the Nairobi Forward-Looking Strategies for the Advancement of Women (which will pay for about half of that exercise). At the 1989 session of the CSOW, delegates also called for a continuation of the Trust Fund for the Preparatory Activities of the 1985 World Conference through the 1990–1 biennium in order to finance the convening of three expert group meetings, which could not be funded from the regular budget. (These figures do not include other activities of the UN system relating directly or indirectly to women. GAOR, Proposed Programme Budget for the Biennium 1990–1991, Supplement No. 6 (A/44/6/Rev.1), vol. i, pt. iv, sects. 4 and 8; *Report of the CSOW*, E/1989/27; ESC Res.1989/30.

[22] ESC Res.1987/21 and 1987/24; *Report of the CSOW*, E/1987/15.

II. MANDATE

The Commission's mandate was defined by the Economic and Social Council in 1947 as follows:

The functions of the Commission shall be to prepare recommendations and reports to the Economic and Social Council on promoting women's rights in political, economic, civil, social and educational fields. The Commission shall also make recommendations to the Council on urgent problems requiring immediate attention in the field of women's rights with the object of implementing the principle that men and women shall have equal rights and to develop proposals to give effect to such recommendations.[23]

This mandate was gradually modified as the Commission over the years received authority to undertake standard-setting exercises, to review communications and make general recommendations on them, and to review implementation of the documents emanating from the United Nations Decade for Women. Following recommendations made by the Commission at its special session in 1987, the Council formalized the expansion of the Commission's terms of reference since the Decade to include 'the functions of promoting the objectives of equality, development and peace, monitoring the implementation of measures for the advancement of women, and reviewing and appraising progress made at the national, subregional, regional, sectoral and global levels.'[24]

An examination of the background to the Commission's original mandate is of more than historical interest as it offers a valuable insight into the options which were open at the beginning but were not pursued, essentially for political reasons. The nuclear Sub-Commission which preceded the Commission had envisioned an activist role for the future United Nations organ dealing with women's rights and had recommended that it should have broad powers to carry out the policy goals defined by the Sub-Commission. It was recommended that the new organ should have a fourfold role involving: (*a*) an investigation function, through a study of the condition of women both in law and in fact, to be carried out world-wide on the basis of information supplied not only by governments but also by specialized agencies of the United Nations, women's organizations, academic institutions, trade unions, and others; (*b*) a mobilization function, through the convening of a women's conference and a number of activities aimed at creating a 'world-wide public opinion'; (*c*) a technical assistance function, including training of women leaders, the promotion of scholarships for women, international exchanges of women, and assistance aimed at facilitating women's participation in public affairs; and (*d*) a 'clearing house' function, meaning that all communications

[23] ESC Res.48(IV) (1947).
[24] ESC Res.1987/22.

and information received by the United Nations concerning all matters of interest to women should be referred to the new organ, and that it should be consulted on all matters pertaining to women before any decision was reached by the Council. The Sub-Commission also recommended the establishment of an Executive Committee composed of members residing near the United Nations headquarters 'in order to guard the general policy of the Sub-Commission', and of an Executive Office on Women's Affairs within the Secretariat. Some members called for the inclusion of a standard-setting role in the proposed mandate and for the drafting of an all-encompassing 'woman's charter' which, in their view, should be the primary goal of the new organ. This proposal, however, did not receive sufficient support and was not adopted.[25]

The ambitious proposals of the nuclear Sub-Commission, however, were considerably modified by the Economic and Social Council, to which the Commission on Human Rights had forwarded them unchanged, and at the first session of the new Commission on the Status of Women. In particular those recommendations which aimed at giving the Commission greater powers in monitoring implementation of equal rights for women proved controversial among the government representatives sitting in the Council and in the new Commission. Thus the recommendations that the Commission be consulted on all decisions relating to women prior to their adoption by the Council, and providing for a permanent role by an Executive Committee of the Commission, were abandoned. Its secretariat was established as a section within the Division for Human Rights (later a branch and then a division in the Centre for Social Development and Humanitarian Affairs) rather than as an office with executive powers.[26]

The proposal that all communications concerning women be referred to the Commission was also set aside in favour of a procedure which gave it no power to act in respect of such communications. The procedure was revamped in 1983 within the context of efforts to strengthen its role, but remained rather ineffective and fell far short of giving it new powers in this area, as will be described in more detail later.

Further efforts made during the early years to develop a role for the Commission in monitoring implementation of equal rights for women by individual countries largely failed. Attempts by the Eastern European countries and by certain non-governmental organizations to raise concrete situations of discrimination from the floor of the Commission were closely intertwined with the political conflicts of the cold war and were quickly defeated. An under-

[25] The recommendations of the Sub-Commission are contained in its report to the CHR, appended to the latter's report to the ESC. E/38/Rev.1 (1946). For discussion in the Sub-Commission, see E/HR/ST/2 (1946), ST/7 and ST/11 (1946).

[26] *Report of the CSOW*, E/281/Rev.1 (1947). For discussion of the issue, see E/CN.6/SR.2 and SR.16; E/AC.7/SR.18 and SR.21; E/SR.74–5 and SR.84.

standing was reached that members themselves were best qualified to speak on the situation in their own countries, thereby barring the submission of information from other sources.[27] Subsequently, the Commission became a forum for members to report on the policies and measures adopted by their governments.

However, as the role of the United Nations in requesting and reviewing reports from States in a variety of fields gradually became established, the Commission was authorized to consider reports submitted to it or to other United Nations organs under various instruments.[28] In a way, the successive reporting systems that were established did provide a form of pressure on States to examine the different aspects of the situation of women in their countries and to devise appropriate policies to deal with the problem. They therefore had a certain usefulness in encouraging a degree of accountability by governments *vis-à-vis* the international community. The Commission, however, has consistently reviewed these reports as sources of information in order to identify general trends and make recommendations for action by the international community as a whole; it has not been empowered, nor has it attempted, to review information or engage in fact-finding with a view to dealing with specific situations. The non-governmental organizations themselves have by and large refrained from commenting on, or criticizing, the situation in individual countries.[29]

It is therefore clear that the majority of States members of the United Nations did not intend to give the Commission powers to examine, let alone investigate, concrete situations of discrimination nor to take measures in order to promote compliance with UN standards. This approach appears to be rooted in a deeply held view that the condition of women, embedded as it is in cultural and social traditions, does not lend itself to fact-finding mechanisms and complaints procedures such as those developed in the human rights sphere, and should be improved primarily if not exclusively through long-term social and economic measures, responsibility for which does not lie uniquely with governments.

The Commission's function has accordingly been interpreted largely as one of general policy development, data-gathering, evaluation, promotion, inspiration, and education, and it has remained as such throughout its life. While the debate since the Women's Decade on the future of the Commission has not substantially altered this frame of reference, there appears to be a growing consensus in terms of strengthening its monitoring and evaluation functions

[27] See the CSOW debates in E/CN.6/SR.23–5, SR.31, SR.49, SR.53, SR.57, and SR.59 (1948–9).

[28] For a summary description of the various reporting systems since 1968, see E/CN.6/1986/2 and Add. 1/Corr. 1.

[29] See e.g. the statement by the representative of the International Federation of Women Lawyers in E/CN.6/SR.444 (1966).

and its co-ordinating role *vis-à-vis* other agencies and sectors of the United Nations system. The recent redefinition of the Commission's mandate may indeed result in a significant improvement in its institutional position within the United Nations system.

B. *The First Phase: The Equal Rights Orientation*

The fundamental guidelines of the work of the Commission were elaborated at its first session and remain a fundamental statement of principles guiding its work today. The principles emphasized three elements: (*a*) freedom and equality are essential to human development and therefore women as human beings are entitled to share in them with men; (*b*) the well-being and progress of society depend on the extent to which both men and women have a definite role to play in the building of their society; and (*c*) women must take an active part in the fight for peace, the prevention of aggression, and the elimination of fascist ideology.[30] The same principles were echoed, thirty years later, in the three themes of the United Nations Decade for Women: Equality, Development, and Peace.

Within this overall agenda, however, the Commission substantially shifted its priorities and approaches over time so that one can distinguish two broad historical phases in its life, with a third phase beginning since the end of the Women's Decade. In the first phase, which lasted for roughly twenty-five years, from its establishment until the early 1970s, it functioned essentially in a human rights framework. It directed its attention primarily to efforts to achieve recognition of the principle of equal rights for women through standard-setting, legal studies, and promotional activities. The second phase began in the late 1960s but was launched in full only with the International Women's Year in 1975 and lasted through the ensuing decade. The Commission's orientation shifted towards social and economic development and the stimulation of the concrete participation of women in their societies, with particular emphasis on the creation of specialized machinery at the national and international level to meet women's basic needs, while less emphasis was placed on the struggle for equality. In the third phase, which is now emerging from the conceptual work of the Women's Decade, the Commission is placing increased stress on the need to empower women and to take stronger action to integrate them into the mainstream. While there is considerable overlap between these phases of the Commission's history, they are sufficiently

[30] See *Report of the CSOW*, n. 26, above, 11–12. It may be noted that the nuclear Sub-Commission, which had elaborated these guidelines, had not included the third item, which was added by the new Commission on the proposal of the USSR.

distinct in terms of conceptual emphasis and institutional arrangements to warrant analysing each phase separately.

As elsewhere in the United Nations, the first phase in the Commission's life was dominated by Western thought and political priorities. The Western countries, with the support of a number of Latin American and Asian countries with a similar outlook, were concerned primarily with promoting equal rights and opportunities for women as individuals. For a number of years, this group argued successfully that the Commission would have greater authority if it focused on problems affecting women because of their sex, which they considered as the essence of its mandate.[31] On the opposite side, the Eastern European countries consistently argued that equal rights for women were meaningless if discussed in isolation from the global context, under which they understood problems relating to self-determination, independence, and national liberation, as well as peace, disarmament, and development. They pressed the Commission to take a position on the various political issues of the day, in particular with regard to colonial questions and the aftermath of the Second World War.[32]

The Eastern European countries were also critical of the equal rights approach for concentrating on the already better educated and professionally qualified women, and neglecting the masses of women, such as those living in rural areas, the unemployed, and those engaged in domestic service. They also took the position that the Commission should take up questions concerning social welfare rights and protective measures for women workers, issues viewed with suspicion by the Western group which considered them as having negative implications for the achievement of equal rights, as well as being within the mandate of other United Nations organs.[33]

Another line of division within the Commission during this period opposed the countries with more conservative and traditional societies and legal systems (often the Catholic and Muslim countries) against those pressing for equal rights. The former group at various times resisted recommendations aimed at altering the patriarchal order. In their view there was a need to safeguard the family and what they considered the mother's primary role in it, and they expressed fears that measures intended to promote women's rights might have a destabilizing effect on the family and on society. This group was, however, in favour of measures which it viewed as facilitating the fulfilment of

[31] See e.g. the CSOW's debate between the representative of France and that of the USSR with regard to a Soviet proposal seeking to condemn repression of women for their political activities, E/CN.6/SR.365 (1962).

[32] See debate on a proposal by the USSR to include the question of Nazism and fascism in the programme of work of the Commission in E/CN.6/SR.40, SR.41, SR.44, and SR.45 (1949). Many similar efforts were made in subsequent years.

[33] See, as one example among many, the debate on the proposal by Poland to include an item entitled 'Protection of the Mother and Child' in the agenda of the Commission. E/2727 (1955).

women's traditional role, thus providing for a measure of consensus on many of the Commission's recommendations.[34]

Despite these divisions, the countries pressing for an equal rights orientation were by and large able to keep the Commission on this course during most of this period. The Commission accordingly designed an initial programme of work geared to 'the examination of existing legal and customary disabilities of women' in the legal, political, economic, social and educational fields. In accordance with this programme, the Commission in its early years requested the Secretariat to undertake legal research on the basis of a 'Questionnaire on the Legal Status and Treatment of Women'.[35] The questionnaire was intended for use by government officials and was primarily geared to eliciting information with regard to constitutional and legal developments and to administrative and other measures taken by governments to grant equality to women. Efforts to include information on actual conditions and to draw on sources other than governments failed at an early stage, so that the information collected by the Commission remained in the nature of general surveys.[36] Despite recurrent criticisms of the questionnaire method and dissatisfaction with the scarcity of factual information reaching the Commission, surveys prepared in this manner remained its basic information-gathering tool during this period and later.

Despite these limitations, however, the documentation collected by the Commission during this period performed a valuable function in identifying the various aspects of discrimination against women in different parts of the world and in raising issues for international attention. This was a crucial element in enabling it to sensitize public opinion and to stimulate legislative and other action at both the international and the national levels. By casting its net wide, the Commission also dealt with a range of discriminatory practices which was in many respects broader than in later years. While it would be too

[34] See e.g. the statements by Spain and the United Arab Republic in the debate on day care, E/CN.6/SR.373–4; Iran, Indonesia on inheritance rights, E/CN.6/SR.377–8; the Philippines on political rights, E/CN.6/SR.415; and the debate on family planning in 1968 and subsequent years. Many other instances can be found in the records of the Commission throughout this period.

[35] The Questionnaire (E/CN.6/W.1 and Add.1–3) contained questions on the following subjects: Part I, Public Law (franchise, eligibility to hold public office, public services and functions, educational and professional opportunities, civil liberties, fiscal laws and nationality); Part II, Property Rights (full legal age, rights of action, contracts and other property transactions, business, trade, industry, or profession, property relations between husband and wife, guardianship and law of succession); Part III, Family Law (marriage, including betrothal, substantive marriage requirements, marriage formalities, polygamy, dissolution of marriage, remarriage, personal relations of spouses, relations between parents and children, relations between parents and children born out of wedlock, and adoption).

[36] A recommendation by the Commission that the emphasis in the questionnaire should be on the existence and extent of discrimination rather than on equality and that materials collected from governments be considered as only one source of information was not accepted by the Council, E/615, (1948), 27.

detailed in this context to review the substance of the areas mapped out by the Commission, it may be indicated that the research programme addressed the various fields listed in the questionnaire, priority being given to political rights.[37] Within this broad category the Commission reviewed not only questions relating to the right to vote and be elected, but also the problem of equal rights for women in the secretariats of the United Nations and other international organizations, and equal representation for women on delegations to these bodies. It also raised the issue of the status of women in colonial and trust territories, and was instrumental in ensuring the inclusion of information regarding women in the reports submitted by the colonial powers under Chapters 11 and 12 of the United Nations Charter. In connection with the information obtained in this respect, it also considered violations of women's rights under traditional customs and practices, such as female circumcision, polygamy, and bride-price. Within its examination of the status of women in family law and of the rights of married women the Commission also reviewed a range of discriminatory practices such as inequality in marriage and in the exercise of parental rights, discrimination in property relations, in inheritance rights, in the penal system, in nationality rights, and many others. In co-operation with UNESCO and the ILO it also considered questions relating to economic and cultural rights, such as equal pay for equal work and non-discrimination in employment and in educational opportunities.

This process of mapping out the various areas of discrimination against women was accompanied by the gradual development of efforts at norm-definition, which will be described in some detail in the next section. As the majority of members, however, was not in favour of developing monitoring and review mechanisms through the Commission, its recommendations remained rather shallow and general, and of limited impact. Barred from exercising a strong role, it took the path of engaging in educational and promotional activities in the hope of influencing national policies and of bringing about changes not only in public opinion but also in the attitudes and perceptions of women themselves.[38] With these ends in view, it sponsored a seminar series, a number of publications, including a newsletter on the status of women, as well as other promotional activities intended to educate women to their rights and to mobilize action by women's organizations.

Deeply conscious of the male bias of most of the United Nations system—including those organs created to promote human rights—the Commission

[37] A handy guide to the studies prepared for the Commission is contained in the survey prepared yearly by the Secretariat between 1960 and 1968, E/CN.6/372 and Add.1–6).

[38] The records of the Commission throughout this period are full of expressions of frustration at the attitudes of women, considered 'apathetic' and too attached to traditional norms of behaviour and gender stereotypes to struggle for their rights. There is very little by way of examination of the obstacles encountered by women. For the list of seminars and other information, see *United Nations Action in the Field of Human Rights*, ST/HR/2/Rev.2 (1983), 358–60.

during this period also sought actively to make them responsive to the concerns of women.[39] Because of historical and conceptual ties and a common secretariat, the Commission on Human Rights and its Sub-Commission on Prevention of Discrimination and Protection of Minorities were a natural target for its efforts. Its representatives sought actively to influence their standard-setting work, in particular the drafting of the Universal Declaration of Human Rights and of the two covenants, and were successful in inserting broad equal-rights provisions in these instruments. Later, it requested to review the periodic reports submitted by governments to the Commission on Human Rights in connection with the rights contained in the Universal Declaration and was successful in obtaining that the reports pay greater attention to equal rights for women. It also reviewed closely the drafting of a number of studies on discrimination in various fields by Special Rapporteurs of the Sub-Commission, and made efforts to ensure that the studies reflected adequately the situation of women. Representatives of the Commission regularly attended sessions of both human rights organs during this period and sought to influence a number of other activities in the field of human rights, although their reports indicate that they were not always pleased with the response received.[40]

The Commission played a similar role *vis-à-vis* UNESCO and ILO, co-operation with which had been included by the Economic and Social Council in the original mandate. The two agencies were represented at its sessions and reported on their activites, including their standard-setting efforts, on which it was asked to comment.[41] The agencies were also often requested by the

[39] For a statement on the need to put forward the views of the Commission in the Sub-Commission on Prevention of Discrimination and Protection of Minorities because of its all-male membership, see the representative of Finland in E/CN.6/SR.437 (1966). The same representative charged the following year that the CHR had reviewed all kinds of discrimination except discrimination against women. E/CN.6/SR.459 (1967).

[40] ESC Res.48(IV) (1947) authorized the Commission to be present at sessions of the CHR when sections of the International Bill of Human Rights of relevance to women were debated. It also requested the Sub-Commission to invite the Commission to be represented at its meetings when matters regarding discrimination based on sex were discussed. Participation in all relevant meetings of the CHR was extended in ESC Res.566(XIX) (1955). The Commission used its authority in particular to comment in detail on studies on discrimination in education; in religious rights and practices; in political rights; in respect of the right to leave one's country; against persons born out of wedlock; and on a report on slavery, which were prepared between 1954 and 1967. It also constantly pressed for consideration of women in the advisory services programme on human rights, which included seminars, fellowships, and expert services to governments. For a list of the human rights studies and a description of the advisory services programme, see *United Nations Action in the Field of Human Rights*, n. 38, above.

[41] The Commission played a role in particular in the elaboration of the Convention and Recommendation Concerning Equal Remuneration for Men and Women Workers for Work of Equal Value, Adopted by ILO (Convention No. 100, Recommendation No. 90, 1951), *International Labour Conventions and Recommendations*, 42; Convention Concerning Discrimination in Respect of Employment and Occupation, Adopted by ILO (Convention No. 111, 1958), ibid. 47; and Convention concerning Discrimination in Education, Adopted by UNESCO (1960), in *Human Rights: A Compilation of International Instruments* (1988), 88–95.

Commission to study aspects of the status of women falling within their frame of reference and sought guidance from the Commission in the development of their research and other programmes. The Commission was subsequently credited with having stimulated the establishment of women's programmes within the agencies and having created an awareness of the problems and needs of women.[42]

As the Commission began to shift its approach in the early 1960s, it gradually set aside the programme of surveys of the various aspects of the status of women. With regard in particular to political rights, it was felt that studies of legal and constitutional developments had largely run their course since most countries had granted equal rights to women at least on paper, and that the Commission should accordingly become involved in promoting the actual exercise of such rights.[43] The rapid achievement of independence by colonial territories resulted in much greater reluctance on its part to tackle problems rooted in cultural traditions and customs as there was a tacit consensus that these were questions for the newly sovereign governments to look into and resolve in accordance with local needs and perceptions.[44] The interest of governments in replying to the Commission's questionnaire began to wane and the questionnaire itself had to be discontinued in the mid-1960s as no replies were being received.[45] The reporting system established under the Declaration on the Elimination of Discrimination against Women, adopted in 1967, eventually replaced the system of surveys based on the questionnaire, although it quickly developed similar difficulties.

At the same time, in response to the concerns of the newly independent countries, a consensus gradually built around a new emphasis on development-related issues. A seminal study, prepared by a special rapporteur of the Commission on the interrelationships between family planning and the status of women, sought to integrate the equal-rights approach with development concepts and thus represented a bridge between the first and second phase of the Commission's life.[46]

However, it did not continue in this conceptual effort. Although the programme of studies was overhauled in the late 1960s and a long-term programme was adopted with regard particularly to the status of women in family law, subsequently reaffirmed in connection with the programme for the

[42] See e.g. the statement by the ILO representative, E/CN.6/SR.236 (1957); and by both ILO and UNESCO, E/CN.6/SR.334 and SR.338 (1961). A positive evaluation of the impact of the Commission on the work of the agencies was also made by the members. E/4175 (1966), 60.

[43] See in particular the debates on the future programme of work of the Commission in E/3606/Rev.1 (1962) and E/3749 (1963).

[44] See e.g. the statement by the USSR opposing a draft resolution proposed for adoption by the ECOSOC on the question of 'ritual operations', on the grounds that it was not for the current Commission membership to raise the issue but for the African countries themselves once they had become members. E/CN.6/SR.340 (1962). The issue was later dropped.

[45] See the report of the Secretariat, E/CN.6/425 (1965).

[46] The study is contained in E/CN.6/575 (1974). It was prepared between 1968 and 1974.

Women's Decade, none of the studies under the new programme was placed before it.[47] Documentation before the Commission did not deal again until very recently with problems specifically relating to equality of rights and discrimination.

As the Commission moved away from the equal-rights orientation of the first period, it also gradually reduced and eventually ended its participation in the work of human rights organs of the United Nations. In recent years, it has not intervened in debates or commented on studies on various human rights issues of relevance to its work, such as on traffic in persons and prostitution, slavery, and female circumcision. Similarly, the Commission has not attempted to have an input in the drafting of recent human rights instruments, such as on the right to development, the rights of children, the rights of migrant workers and non-citizens, and others. It also no longer attempted to review the standard-setting activities of the specialized agencies, although its concern with the work of the agencies expanded in other ways.

Accordingly, the work of the Commission today takes place in a conceptually and institutionally separate sphere from the human rights programme. The change in 1974 of its secretariat from the Division of Human Rights to the Centre for Social Development and Humanitarian Affairs (then part of the Department of International Economic and Social Affairs) no doubt played a role in this shift of approach, both reflecting the new orientation and further promoting it.

I. ROLE IN STANDARD-SETTING

Standard-setting was not part of the initial mandate of the Commission. As mentioned earlier, a proposal for drafting a 'woman's charter' made in the nuclear Sub-Commission was not adopted. The view prevailed that women's rights were not a separate category of rights and that the principle of equality for women should be taken into account in the global human rights instruments then to be drafted by the Commission on Human Rights and in those to be drafted by the specialized agencies in their respective fields of expertise. Hence the subsequent efforts by the Commission to influence those exercises.

Very soon thereafter, however, the need to deal at the international level with certain specific disabilities of women brought the Commission to develop a standard-setting role for itself. Its legislative activities mirror its historical development, from an exclusive concern with legal equality in specific areas, to a concern with integration and participation and efforts to achieve a global synthesis.

[47] A progress report by the Secretary-General on the legal capacity of married women to engage in independent work, the first proposed study in the new series, was submitted to the Commission in 1974. E/CN.6/584 (1974).

(*a*) *Instruments Dealing with Specific Rights of Women*

Between 1949 and 1962 the Commission drafted standards with regard to a number of specific rights enunciated in the Universal Declaration of Human Rights and which had been the object of some of its legal studies. These drafting exercises often met with a measure of disagreement within the Commission itself concerning both the appropriateness of the proposed instruments and the Commission's competence to engage in their elaboration. In a number of cases, serious obstacles were raised in the Council and it was requested to reconsider texts which it had already adopted. At least in part because of these difficulties, and the political conflicts from which they arose, these instruments have remained narrow in scope and have not been widely ratified. They also contain no implementation provisions. The follow-up activities of the Commission have accordingly remained very limited, and were dropped from its programme of work after the adoption of more comprehensive instruments.

As these instruments are of little more than historical interest at this stage, only essential details need be given here.[48]

The Convention on the Political Rights of Women, drafted by the Commission between 1949 and 1952, at the initiative of its Latin American members, grew out of dissatisfaction with the slow progress by States members of the United Nations in implementing their obligation under the Charter to grant political equality to women. The selection of this issue as the first standard-setting exercise reflects the absolute primacy with which the Commission viewed the question of political rights at the time.

The drafting, however, proved difficult, and texts already adopted were sent back to the Commission by the Council at least twice for further consideration. Eventually, the proponents of a broadly-worded instrument prevailed and the text adopted went beyond an earlier instrument which had served as a model, the 1948 Bogota Convention on the Granting of Political Rights to Women. The new Convention provided for the right of women, on equal terms with men, to vote in all elections, to be eligible for election in all publicly elected bodies, and to hold public office and exercise all public functions.[49] Although it was the most widely ratified instrument in this group, numerous reservations were made to this Convention, particularly because of the provisions of the third article which many States could not accept fully.[50]

A proposal for the establishment of a reporting system, which was not included in the Convention, was made by the Commission to the Council after its coming into force. The Council adopted the procedure, and the

[48] For an account of the background to these instruments, see Bruce, 'Work of the United Nations', and Hevener, *International Law and the Status of Women*.

[49] GA Res.640(VII) (1952).

[50] As of 31 December 1991, the Convention had been ratified or acceded to by 97 States. See E/CN.6/354 and Add.1 (1959) on the question of reservations.

Commission reviewed reports submitted by States until the early 1970s. The procedure, however, aside from being voluntary, was also used to obtain information from States that were not parties to the Convention and other sources, and was later merged with other reporting systems, thus diluting the principle of accountability of the States parties themselves.[51] The influence of the Convention has therefore been more of a moral character than that of a treaty obligation.

The Convention on the Nationality of Married Women was first proposed in 1947, in order to resolve conflicts of nationality law between countries which had resulted in hardships for many women, a situation already addressed by the League between the two World Wars.[52] The drafting of the Convention only began in 1953, as several years were spent in a debate as to whether this matter should be the object of an international treaty and, if so, whether the Commission was the most appropriate body for undertaking the exercise. The Commission eventually set aside its earlier goal of an instrument based on full equality between the sexes, for fear that it would not be widely ratified, and instead adopted a text which limited itself to protecting women against automatic loss or acquisition of nationality as a consequence of marriage, while the equality provisions were deleted.[53]

As in the case of the previous convention, the Commission submitted only the substantive articles to the Council. No reporting system was established in connection with this convention and the Commission has not specifically considered its implementation, although the question of the nationality of married women was included in the periodic surveys prepared by the Secretary-General prior to the adoption of the global instruments.

The Convention and Recommendation on Consent to Marriage, Minimum Age for Marriage, and Registration of Marriages are the last instruments dealing with specific rights adopted by the Commission. Their background lies in early efforts by the Commission to deal with the problem of traditional customs and practices which discriminate against women. The reason for drafting two instruments was that the Council rejected the Commission's initial recommendation for a legally binding instrument which would establish a universal minimum age for marriage in addition to the requirement of free consent of both parties to marriage, and compulsory registration of marriages.

[51] ESC Res.504E(XVI) (1953) requested States Parties to report to ECOSOC. The system was expanded to other States in ESC Res.961B(XXXVI) (1963) and was later merged with that under the Declaration on the Elimination of Discrimination Against Women, ESC Res.1677(LII) (1972), which was in turn merged with the reporting system under the Women's Decade, ESC Res.1978/28.

[52] For a useful statement of the problem and an account of earlier efforts in this field by the League of Nations, see E/CN.6/79 (1949); E/CN.6/82 and Add.1–4 (1949); E/CN.6/84 (1949); and E/CN.6/126 (1950).

[53] The text of the Convention was adopted by the Assembly as GA Res.1040(XI) (1957). As of 1 Jan. 1991, the Convention had been ratified or acceded to by 56 States.

As many Council members felt that deeply rooted cultural practices could be changed only through education and long-term programmes, it was decided to draft both a convention and a recommendation, with the more controversial provision to be included in the latter. Even so, the drafting was not smooth and texts adopted by the Commission were repeatedly referred back to it by the Council. The Convention was eventually adopted by the Assembly in 1962 and the recommendation in 1965. Like the earlier instruments, the Convention does not include implementation provisions but the recommendation introduced a reporting system by which States were asked to inform the Commission of the measures taken to bring the recommendation before the competent national authorities and to implement its provisions.[54] This procedure, however, was in existence for only a short time before being subsumed under the reporting system established with regard to the Declaration on the Elimination of Discrimination against Women, to which we now turn.

(*b*) *Global Instruments: Declaration and Convention on the Elimination of Discrimination against Women*

By the early 1960s, a sense of dissatisfaction with the limited scope and the difficulty of these drafting exercises, as well as with the low level of ratifications of the new instruments, led to renewed proposals for the elaboration of a global instrument covering all aspects of discrimination against women. Taking the initiative, the Eastern European members argued for a Declaration modelled after the Declaration on the Elimination of Racial Discrimination, which would in due course be followed by a convention.[55]

The Declaration on the Elimination of Discrimination against Women was accordingly drafted by the Commission between 1965 and 1967, and became an important milestone in the work of the United Nations to promote equality between the sexes. Although its provisions are not binding on States, the Declaration, like the Universal Declaration on Human Rights, was recognized as a moral force which could be invoked to urge States to take action to end discriminatory legislation and practices against women.

Although by then a consensus had developed on the need for a global statement of women's rights, the drafting process once again proved difficult because of the lack of agreement over both the form and the substance of such a statement. The draft was discussed at two sessions of the Commission before being forwarded to the Assembly; it was eventually referred back to the

[54] The text of the Convention is contained in GA Res.1763B(XVII) (1962). As of 1 Jan. 1991, the Convention had been ratified or acceded to by only 35 States. The Recommendation is in GA Res.2018(XX) (1965).

[55] See statements by the USSR, Hungary, and Poland at the Commission, E/CN.6/SR.416, SR.417 (1964). The first draft for the Declaration was tabled by Poland, E/CN.6/L.396 (1965). For a thorough analysis of the provisions of the Declaration and its background, see Bruce, 'Work of the United Nations'.

Commission for reconsideration in light of comments by governments, the Assembly, and the Council, prior to final adoption.[56] The main cleavage was between the sponsors, who argued for a text setting forth the essential obligations of States as the entities primarily responsible for implementation, and some Western countries, who viewed the future declaration as a statement of fundamental rights, similar to the Universal Declaration, without reference to obligations by governments. Eventually a compromise was reached in which each substantive article was drafted to refer to measures to be taken without spelling out who should take such measures.

Disagreement also concerned specific rights to be included in the text. While the sponsors called for a broad instrument covering all forms of discrimination against women, including some which had not been under study in the Commission, others felt the declaration should avoid setting standards which some States might be unable to accept. There was also considerable debate over the proposed inclusion of protective measures, which the sponsors saw as safeguarding acquired rights, while Western countries argued that real equality involved surrendering privileges. Eventually the sponsors were successful in including protective provisions with regard to the family and employment. The Declaration also contains broad non-discrimination provisions, including rights covered by existing instruments (political and nationality rights, freedom of choice in marriage, equal rights in education and employment, traffic in women), as well as many issues not before legislated by the Commission, in particular the abolition of discriminatory customs and practices as well as laws and regulations, equal rights in marriage, and discrimination in penal law. The Declaration, however, did not attempt to give a definition of discrimination as it was agreed that it was preferable to adopt a general formulation in an instrument of this nature.

By the late 1960s, much of the Commission's work had come to focus on the implementation of the Declaration. The earlier programme of studies and surveys, as well as the existing reporting procedures, were superseded by the reporting system established in connection with the Declaration, for which it was given responsibility.[57] This system, however, was consistently plagued with problems, in particular, a low level of responses by governments, and difficulty on the part of the Commission in establishing an effective system of review, particularly once its sessions were placed on a biennial schedule. The system was accordingly reorganized several times and was eventually

[56] Debates on the Declaration are summarized in E/4025 (1966), 16–33; E/4175 (1966), 8–40; E/4316 (1966), 9–40. Comments by States and others are contained in E/CN.6/426 and Add.1–2 (1965); E/CN.6/447 and Add.1 (1966). The Declaration was adopted by the Assembly as GA Res.2263(XXII) (1967).

[57] ESC Res.1325(XLIV) (1968) requested the Secretary-General of the UN to submit reports on a regular basis to the Commission on the information received from Member States, the specialized agencies and non-governmental organizations concerned with the implementation of the Declaration.

integrated into the reporting systems established in connection with the Women's Decade.[58]

The distinctive significance of the Declaration, in any case, was superseded with the adoption of the Convention on the Elimination of All Forms of Discrimination against Women, which the Commission began considering in 1972 and drafted subsequently as one of its most significant activities during the Women's Decade. Impetus for the new instrument was provided at least in part by unhappiness over the lukewarm response to the Declaration by governments and the fact that implementation of its provisions and the submission of reports remained voluntary. The Eastern European group again took the initiative for the new convention, arguing that the Commission should do more than collect information and pass resolutions, and should set the basis for implementation measures within the framework of a binding international instrument. As they also envisaged that implementation would be monitored by the Commission, they argued that it would thereby find a new *raison d'être* which would once and for all end proposals for its abolition.[59]

The Convention is the first international treaty dealing with the rights of women in a global manner and including provisions for a reporting system and review machinery. It is considered the crowning achievement of the Commission in the field of standard-setting. As its provisions have been analysed in detail elsewhere, only those aspects which are of relevance to the historical development of the Commission will be mentioned here.[60]

While the Convention on the Elimination of All Forms of Racial Discrimination, which the sponsors used as a precedent, was adopted within two years from the corresponding declaration, thirteen years elapsed between the adoption of the Declaration on the Elimination of Discrimination against Women and the new convention. Opposition to the new instrument came initially from the Western countries and others who feared that it might undermine existing instruments and hamper ratification of the human rights covenants, which had not yet come into force at the time. Some favoured the preparation of separate instruments limited to the fields that had not yet been covered in order to avoid possible conflicts with earlier standards. Concern was also expressed about possible conflicts with existing labour standards under the ILO.[61] Eventually, however, hesitations on the question of principle

[58] For an account of the various reorganizations of the reporting system, see E/CN.6/1986/2. Reports received from governments under the Declaration had been as low as 13 in 1972 and 31 in 1978.

[59] See debate on the draft resolution tabled by the USSR inviting the Commission to take up the drafting of the Convention in 1974. In view of the opposing arguments, however, it was decided to seek comments by governments first, and to establish a working group to make recommendations. See minutes of the Commission in E/CN.6/Min.573, 579, 588 (1972).

[60] For an article-by-article examination of the Convention, see Hevener, *International Law and the Status of Women*.

[61] See, as indicative of these various views, the statements by Finland, Norway, Egypt, Canada,

were set aside in the hope that the adoption of a convention would provide a means of giving effect to the principles of the Declaration.[62] Accordingly, the Commission proceeded to draft the Convention at its twenty-fifth and twenty-sixth sessions; the draft text was then debated by the Third Committee of the General Assembly and substantially amended prior to final adoption three years later, in 1979.[63]

The Convention, as it finally emerged from the Assembly, is a blend of the earlier equal-rights orientation with the more recent political and developmental concerns of the Commission. Its language is considerably closer to that of a political declaration than that of an international treaty. The preamble contains references to the new international economic order and to a number of political issues, such as the elimination of apartheid, colonialism, and foreign occupation, as well as the achievement of nuclear disarmament and international peace and security, as basic to the attainment of full equality between men and women. At the same time, a call is included for a change in the traditional role of men as well as the role of women in society and the family. The substantive provisions include for the first time a definition of discrimination. They incorporate most of the provisions of the earlier instruments and further spell out the rights covered in the Declaration, placing a clear responsibility on States parties to take measures for their implementation. In addition, they contain an endorsement of affirmative action as a temporary measure until equality is achieved. At the same time, a number of other issues are included which originated in the work of the Commission with regard to the integration of women in development, such as health care, financial and other economic assistance, and the role of rural women. This effort at synthesis resulted in a text which has gradually won the support of a larger number of States than any preceding instrument on women's rights. Notwithstanding this recognition, the unusually high number of reservations to the Convention and the fact that many States parties have experienced difficulties in discharging their reporting obligations have aroused concern.[64]

The drafting of the implementation provisions of the Convention is of particular interest as it generated a searching debate on the mandate and future role of the Commission. On the one hand, the Eastern European sponsors were strongly in favour of assigning the supervisory role to the

France, United Kingdom, USA, and the representative of the ILO in the minutes of the Commission, n. 59, above.

[62] See statement by Norway in E/CN.6/SR.614 (1974).

[63] Debates on the Convention are reflected in the CSOW reports E/5451 (1974) and E/5909 (1976). Comments by governments and others are contained in E/CN.6/573, 574, and 591; A/32/218 and Add.1–2 (1974). The reports of the working group of the Third Committee are in A/C.3/32/L.59, and A/34/60 (1979). The Convention was adopted by the Assembly in GA Res.34/180.

[64] On these concerns, see A/41/608 (1986). Reservations have particularly affected the provisions relating to the status of women in the family, their marital status, and their legal capacity. As of 1 Jan. 1991, the Convention had been ratified or acceded to by 105 States.

Commission, either directly or through a working group composed of States parties which were members of the Commission, on the grounds that otherwise the importance and political role of the Commission would be diminished. On the other hand, the Western countries feared that the Convention would remain a dead letter if review was left in the hands of the States parties rather than a body of experts whose mandate would flow from the Convention itself. Other delegations took the view that there was no need for a watchdog body since all countries had pledged themselves to improve the status of women, and the Commission could continue to collect information as in the past. An ancillary question was whether the new organ to be established would be empowered to review complaints and to receive information from non-governmental organizations. Proposals in this sense were made by Belgium and by a group of non-governmental organizations.[65]

Eventually, the Commission proposed the establishment of review machinery under its umbrella, but the Assembly later decided in favour of the Western proposal for a committee of experts elected by States parties and modelled after those set up under human rights instruments. The proposals for the inclusion of a procedure for reviewing complaints and for receiving information from non-governmental sources were rejected, following strong opposition by Eastern European and developing countries which could not agree that violations of women's rights should be placed on the same footing as those occurring under repressive and racist regimes.[66] The Commission, therefore, does not have a role with regard to the implementation of the Convention, and the reporting system established under the Convention in effect superseded any of its responsibilities with respect to the earlier instruments. As its mandate, however, was extended to cover implementation of the various plans of action adopted in connection with the Women's Decade, the question of defining its role *vis-à-vis* that of CEDAW has become increasingly relevant. The reports of CEDAW, which began functioning in 1983, have been made available to it for information. Recently, on its recommendation, the ECOSOC has also recognized the special relevance of the periodic reports submitted by States parties to the Convention for the Commission's monitoring efforts, and has recommended that the sessions of CEDAW be scheduled to allow for the timely transmission of the results of its work to the Commission the same year. The Commission has also been involved in efforts to promote the wider ratification and implementation of the Convention and to obtain adequate resources for the work of CEDAW.[67]

[65] See e.g. the statements by Denmark in E/CN.6/SR.661 (1976); by Pakistan, India, Iran in E/CN.6/SR.662, SR.665, and SR.666 (1976); by Belgium in E/CN.6/SR.673 and SR.674 (1976); and E/CN.6/NGO/272 (1976).

[66] See statements by Hungary, Pakistan, Togo in E/CN.6/SR.673 and SR.674 (1976).

[67] ESC Res.1989/44, adopted on the recommendation of the CSOW. See the Bibliography, below, for the document numbers of CEDAW reports.

Two additional instruments drafted by, or with the participation of, the Commission are worth mentioning here as they reflect the new concern since the early 1970s with more specifically political issues, and the Commission was subsequently entrusted with follow-up activities. Both items were proposed by the Eastern European group and gave rise to considerable controversy, as opponents charged that the issues addressed were irrelevant to the mandate of the Commission and would unduly politicize its agenda.

The Declaration on the Protection of Women and Children in Emergency and Armed Conflict, drafted by the Commission in 1974, combines the political element with the protective approach to women which until then had been eschewed by the Commission. It calls on member States of the United Nations to ensure the protection of women and children in various conflicts, with particular reference to struggles for self-determination, national liberation, and independence.[68]

The Declaration on the Participation of Women in Promoting International Peace and Co-operation was drafted by the Third Committee of the General Assembly in 1982 after an initial proposal was considered by the Commission in 1980. The text, substantially amended by the Western countries to include their concern with equal rights, calls for the full participation of women in public affairs, with particular reference to the eradication of apartheid, racism, colonialism, and foreign domination. It also calls for an equitable distribution of domestic roles between women and men to allow for such participation, and urges the adoption of appropriate measures to provide practical opportunities for women in this regard.[69]

Neither declaration provides for a reporting procedure; however, these items have been included in the Commission's agenda and have also become part of its general mandate through their incorporation in the Forward-Looking Strategies. The Commission so far has confined itself largely to reviewing reports on the situation of women in southern Africa and in the Arab territories occupied by Israel in connection with these items.

C. *The Second Phase: the 'Development' Orientation*

By the early 1960s, the Commission's hitherto almost exclusive concern with legal equality and individual rights began to give way to a concern with meeting the needs of the vast majority of the world's women, i.e., those in the developing countries. It was felt that it was moving into a crucial phase of giving effect in practice to the norms that had been established, and that it was

[68] GA Res.3318(XXIX)(1974), based on a proposal submitted by the USSR.
[69] GA Res.37/63 (1982), based on the proposal submitted by the German Democratic Republic.

necessary to seek new methods and techniques to that end. It was also increasingly argued that true equality could not be achieved in isolation from the global context and that women were the first to suffer in situations of underdevelopment, foreign occupation, and conflict.

The first formal redefinition of the Commission's programme came from the International Conference on Human Rights held in Tehran in 1968. As education was considered fundamental to achieving women's integration in society, the Conference recommended that the Commission give priority to problems concerning the education of women and their contribution to economic and social development, and that it reconsider its work with a view to meeting the needs of women in the contemporary world. The resolution also called on the United Nations system to contribute to national programmes for the advancement of women through appropriate technical assistance.[70] The resolution was adopted within a context of increased efforts by the newly independent members of the United Nations, through the Economic and Social Council and the General Assembly, to obtain expanded assistance programmes for the developing countries. It paralleled the growing recognition that development should be conceptualized not simply in economic terms but also and primarily in human terms.[71] At the same time, the Commission had begun to work out the interrelationships between the struggle for equality and that for development, and to argue that women should be viewed not only as beneficiaries but also as agents of development, calling for their contribution to be recognized and taken into account in the development strategies then under elaboration by the United Nations. An early linkage was thereby established between the goals of the first United Nations Development Decade and those of the Commission itself. Already in 1962, the General Assembly endorsed the Commission's views and requested it to develop a unified long-term programme for the advancement of women which would involve the various sectors of the United Nations system.[72]

That programme was under study in the Commission for over ten years, prior to and following the Tehran conference. The two main concerns guiding it in its debates were, on the one hand, the elaboration of concrete measures for ensuring greater participation of women in society and particularly in development programmes, and the mobilization of the agencies and bodies of the United Nations system behind this goal, and, on the other hand, the integration of the goals of equality and non-discrimination into the

[70] See *Final Act of the International Conference on Human Rights*, A/CONF.32/41 (1968), 10–11; the recommendations of the Conference were later endorsed in GA Res.2442(XXIII) (1968). It may be noted that the agenda of the Conference with regard to women and its recommendations were influenced by the Commission.

[71] See e.g. ESC Res.771H(XXX) (1960) and GA Res.1509(XV) (1960) calling for assistance by the UN system for the advancement of women in developing countries. See also statement by the representative of UNDP, E/CN.6/SR.643 (1976).

[72] GA Res.1777(XVII) (1962).

new approaches. In 1969, it recast its work programme in accordance with the priorities established by the Tehran conference, and decided to concentrate on implementation of the unified long-term programme and of the Declaration on the Elimination of Discrimination against Women. Other items on the agenda were either subsumed under those, placed on a biennial schedule, or discontinued.[73]

However, it was only with the International Women's Year in 1975 and the subsequent Women's Decade that a concrete and comprehensive action programme was set into motion. At the same time, the secretariat of the Commission was detached from the human rights programme and incorporated into the sectors dealing with social and economic matters and technical assistance, giving further impulse to the process. The proposal to call an International Women's Year devoted 'to intensified action to promote equality between men and women and to increase women's participation in national and international development' originated with a group of non-governmental organizations and was unanimously endorsed by the Commission at its twenty-fourth session. The proposal had its source in growing dissatisfaction among women's groups as well as members of the Commission about the slow pace of progress in achieving the objectives of the unified programme and of the Development Decade. On the initiative of the United States representative, the Commission subsequently recommended that a world conference be held as the focal point of the Year, with the purpose to review implementation by the United Nations system of its recommendations and to launch an action programme to achieve its goals.[74]

The Women's Year, the ensuing Decade for Women, and the three world conferences held between 1975 and 1985 (at Mexico City, Copenhagen and Nairobi) raised United Nations activities for women to a much higher level of visibility and formal commitment than they had enjoyed up to that time.[75] The conferences were attended by thousands of women both as governmental representatives and as non-governmental participants in the parallel non-governmental organization forums, and were credited with laying the foundations for an international women's movement. The political declarations and programmes of action adopted by the conferences were subsequently endorsed by the General Assembly and defined the international approach to

[73] *Report of the CSOW*, E/4619 (1969). A useful summary of the Commission's work on the unified long-term programme is contained in E/CN.6/512 (1969), 532 (1970), and 577 (1976).

[74] E/5109 (1972) and E/5451 (1974). The resolutions were subsequently adopted as ESC Res.1681(LII) (1972) and 1849(LVI) (1974). It may be noted that the proposal for the International Women's Year was supported by all regional groups in the Commission while the proposal for a conference was initially opposed by the Eastern European group on financial grounds.

[75] n. 8, above. A recent Secretariat report found that between 1975 and 1988, more than 500 legislative instruments relating to women had been adopted by the UN system, including ECOSOC, the GA, UN conferences, regional commissions, governing bodies of UN voluntary programmes and funds, other UN bodies, and specialized agencies, E/1989/19.

women's issues for the foreseeable future. These documents included the Declaration of Mexico on the Equality of Women and their Contribution to Development and Peace; the World Plan of Action for the Implementation of the Objectives of the International Women's Year; the Programme of Action for the Second Half of the United Nations Decade for Women; and the Nairobi Forward-Looking Strategies for the Advancement of Women.

Taking as their theme a simplified statement of the traditional main objectives of the Commission: Equality, Development, and Peace, those documents spelled out a new and more comprehensive analysis and awareness of the condition of women world-wide and provided a blueprint of necessary action to be taken by governments and by the intergovernmental and non-governmental community. In addition to the issues that had long been of concern to the Commission, such as political participation, education, employment, the world conferences addressed a great variety of socio-economic problems such as health, nutrition, agricultural production and marketing, access to credit, housing, industrial development, and the situation of especially vulnerable groups of women, for example refugees, the disabled, the elderly, and many others. In addition to greatly enlarging the scope of international understanding of the situation of women, the conferences also stimulated the creation of national machineries for the advancement of women and of a large number of programmes and projects involving many different bodies and agencies of the United Nations system. A recent cross-organizational programme analysis of the activities of the United Nations system benefiting women directly or indirectly, identified over 1,500 activities carried out by thirty-six organizational units and involving a total expenditure of over one billion United States dollars in the biennium 1988–9.[76]

The documents adopted during the Decade also placed the work of the Commission more firmly within the framework of the Second and then the Third United Nations Development Decade. It was entrusted with reviewing reports on implementation of the provisions of the Mexico Declaration and Plan of Action, and of the Copenhagen Programme of Action, as an input to the overall process of review and appraisal of the development decades, with particular emphasis on the integration of women in development. In 1979, that reporting system was merged with, and largely superseded, the reporting system relating to the Declaration on the Elimination of Discrimination against Women.[77] The questionnaires on the basis of which reports were prepared relied now primarily on socio-economic categories related to devel-

[76] E/1989/19. It must be noted that this figure includes all system activities relating to women, including relief activities such as those carried out by UNRWA (a total of over US $258 million for the biennium) and is therefore rather inflated. According to the same analysis, only 6% or US $72 million represents programme elements or projects entirely devoted to the advancement of women.

[77] GA Res.3490(XXX) (1975), 3520(XXX) (1975), 31/136 (1976), 33/186 (1978), and 35/136 (1980).

opment analysis, rather than on normative categories derived from existing standards.[78] The increasing programmatic emphasis on development is reflected in the medium-term plan of the United Nations for the period 1984–9, in which women are included—together with youth, the ageing, and the disabled—as a 'less advantaged population group' in the programme on social development and humanitarian affairs, whose objectives are defined by the International Development Strategy for the Third Development Decade.[79] A recent analysis showed that of the mandates concerning women adopted by the United Nations system between 1975 and 1988, more than 75 per cent related to development while 8.5 per cent related to equality and 6.4 per cent to peace, and the remainder related to issues of special concern and multiple mandates. In terms of allocation of resources, the same report indicated that in the budget period 1988–9, about 66 per cent of the system's total expenditure for women (from the regular budget and extra-budgetary sources) was earmarked for development, and less than 1 per cent for the equality objective.[80]

In many ways, the holding of the three conferences and the other activities of the Women's Decade represented the culmination of years of efforts of the Commission on the Status of Women and the realization of many of its proposals. The Commission, however, was to enter a prolonged period of crisis from which it began to emerge only towards the end of the Decade. Although its mandate was expanded in 1975 through the addition of review of the implementation of the goals of the Decade, it was not given greater powers nor additional resources to carry out this task effectively. Moreover, the reporting system established in connection with the Decade was very diffuse, involving a variety of other organs and procedures whose relationship to it was not clearly delineated. Throughout the Decade, review and appraisal have, in fact, been the primary functions of the world conferences. The conferences considered reports evaluating programmes at the national, regional, and international levels which were prepared for the conferences and were not, or not fully, reviewed by the Commission.[81] Despite its efforts, the Commission was not charged with the preparations for the first two conferences and was authorized to act as the preparatory body only for the Nairobi conference in 1985.[82]

[78] At the third session of the Commission as the preparatory body for the Nairobi conference, several delegations expressed regret that review and appraisal had not been based on existing legal instruments. A/CONF.116/PC/25 (1985).

[79] *Medium-Term Plan for the Period 1984–1989*, A/37/6 (1982), Chap. 21.

[80] E/1989/19.

[81] This state of affairs gave rise to criticism by several delegations in particular at the third session of the CSOW as the preparatory body for the Nairobi conference. A/CONF.116/PC/25 (1985).

[82] The preparatory work for the Mexico conference was carried out by a Consultative Committee of 23 member States appointed by the Chairman of the Third Committee in consultation with the regional groups, and for the Copenhagen conference by a preparatory

In addition to the conferences, review and appraisal were also increasingly carried out by both the General Assembly and the Economic and Social Council. Their direct role was strengthened by the great expansion of the range of issues addressed during the Women's Decade, and the resulting involvement of several of their subsidiary organs, particularly those concerned with development and planning, which had little co-ordination with the work of the Commission.[83] Additional machinery dealing specifically with the integration of women in development was created, in particular the International Research and Training Institute for the Advancement of Women (INSTRAW)[84] and the United Nations Development Fund for Women (UNIFEM).[85] Involvement of the Commission in this work was peripheral at best, particularly in view of its biennial schedule and the brevity of its sessions which prevented it from exercising a systematic and effective review function, or from influencing the activities of those bodies to any great extent.

Almost since the inception of the Decade, however, this gradual lessening of the central role of the Commission and the growing emphasis on development gave rise to criticism. Concern was voiced repeatedly that insufficient attention was being paid to the other two objectives of the Decade, equality and peace, and to their complex interrelationships with the development objective. It was also increasingly argued that the Commission should retain its unique position as the catalyst for all action related to women within the United Nations system and that it should play a central role with regard to co-ordinating and promoting implementation of the plans of action adopted by the world conferences.[86]

committee, also composed of 23 member States appointed by the President of ECOSOC in consultation with the regional groups.

[83] These included, in particular, the UN regional commissions, the Committee for Programme and Co-ordination, UNDP and other agencies dealing with development assistance, and the inter-agency machinery such as the Administrative Committee on Co-ordination.

[84] INSTRAW was established by ESC Res.1998(LX) (1976) following a recommendation by the Mexico City conference. It is financed by voluntary contributions and is governed by a Board of Trustees reporting to ECOSOC and the GA. According to its statute, the Institute 'is an autonomous institution within the framework of the United Nations established in accordance with the Charter . . . to serve as a vehicle on the international level for the purpose of undertaking research and establishing training programmes to contribute to the integration and mobilization of women in development, to raise awareness of women's issues world-wide and better assist women to meet new challenges and directions'. A/39/511 (1984). The 1991 report of the Board of Trustees is in E/1991/21.

[85] UNIFEM was established pursuant to GA Res.39/125 (1984). It superceded the Voluntary Fund for the UN Decade for Women, established after the 1975 conference. It functions as an autonomous technical co-operation fund in association with UNDP and under the authority of the Administrator in consultation with a Consultative Committee designated by the President of the GA. The Fund is financed from voluntary contributions. Its mandate is 'to serve as a catalyst, with the goal of ensuring the appropriate involvement of women in mainstream development activities, as often as possible at the pre-investment stage, and to support innovative and experimental activities benefiting women in line with national and regional priorities.' The 1991 report is in A/46/491 (1991).

[86] See e.g. the debate at the 1978 session of the CSOW. E/CN.6/SR.586–93 (1978). Similar

At the General Assembly in 1980, a proposal was tabled to abolish the Commission and to transfer its functions to a restructured ECOSOC. A contrary proposal, to give the Commission the central role in reviewing implementation of the World Plan of Action and of the Programme for the Second Half of the Decade for Women, was submitted to the Assembly in the report of the world conference held at Copenhagen the same year. The conference also recommended the strengthening of the Commission by reallocating budgetary resources, and improving its ability to consider communications. A parallel proposal for continuing its role in monitoring, co-ordination, and policy development was also submitted by the ECOSOC on the recommendation of the Commission itself. The Assembly eventually set aside the proposal for abolishing the Commission and adopted those for giving it an expanded role.[87] The debate over the definition of that role and the measures to be adopted, however, continued for the better part of the following decade, as will be described briefly in the next section.

D. *The Third Phase: The 'Mainstreaming' Strategy*

Efforts to revitalize the Commission have concentrated primarily on strengthening its position as the main tool of the UN system to monitor and evaluate the results of national and international policies towards women and to mobilize the resources of the system in a co-ordinated manner. Proposals were also made for expanding its terms of reference to include dealing with complaints of violations of women's rights in specific countries. The latter efforts, however, have so far been less successful than the former in modifying the role of the Commission.

Confidential communications alleging violations of women's rights were reviewed by the Commission for more than thirty years under the 'no power to take any action' doctrine, and this aspect of its mandate had soon become a routine exercise of little interest to the Commission.[88] The situation did not change following the granting of greater powers to the Commission on Human Rights and its Sub-Commission with regard to communications. However, the question came up increasingly during the debate on the draft Convention on the Elimination of All Forms of Discrimination Against Women in connection with proposals to establish a complaints procedure under the Convention. The rejection of these proposals made it clear to their proponents that no avenue of recourse for women would exist in the UN system unless the

arguments were made at subsequent sessions as well as in debates in the ECOSOC and the GA on the relevant items.

[87] ESC Res.1980/38 and GA Res.35/136 (1980).

[88] ESC Res.76(V) (1947) and 304I(XI) (1950). For a description of the operation of the procedure in practice, see E/1982/34.

Commission's role in this regard was strengthened. This concern merged with the ongoing debate on the future of the Commission and on steps to be taken for its revitalization. In 1980, the United States representative submitted a draft resolution which stressed the need for 'a United Nations body concerned with all aspects of women's rights to provide international recourse for individuals, organizations and States concerned with the status of women.'[89]

Eventually, after considerable controversy, a resolution was adopted by ECOSOC in 1983 authorizing the Commission to appoint a sessional working group to review confidential communications 'which appear to reveal a consistent pattern of reliably attested injustice and discriminatory practices against women' and to prepare a report 'which will indicate the categories in which communications are most frequently submitted to the Commission'. After reviewing the report, the Commission is 'empowered only to make recommendations to the Council, which shall then decide what action may appropriately be taken on the emerging trends and patterns of communications'.[90] The limitations of the procedure compared to that established for the Commission on Human Rights, and as a recourse mechanism, are obvious. At the same time, it could be argued that it has the potential of enabling the Commission to adopt a thematic approach to violations similar to that pioneered in recent years by the Commission on Human Rights.

In any case, it thus far has not made much use of the procedure. In the years since its coming into effect, consideration of complaints has resulted only in the adoption of resolutions on physical violence against women detainees, an issue with which it had already dealt under the old procedure. At the 1988 session, the working group did report to the Commission that many communications dealt with 'serious and extensive violations of human rights, including different forms of discrimination against women' and expressed concern at the lack of response from several governments. The group also recommended that the Commission, through ECOSOC, call on States to take appropriate measure 'to halt the current negative trends related to the status of women in their countries'. The report, however, received no follow-up in the Commission and the agenda of its 1989 session did not include an item on communications.

In 1990, however, the Commission requested the Secretary-General to prepare a report containing proposals for reform of the procedure. Having received the report,[91] the Commission devoted considerable effort at its 1991 session to the consideration of possible reforms. A reasonably sophisticated approach, with greater potential than the Commission on Human Rights' Resolution 1503 procedure, was proposed by the USA on behalf of itself and

[89] Draft Res.X. E/1980/15.
[90] ESC Res.1983/27.
[91] E/CN.6/1991/10.

eighteen other States.[92] After agreement had been reached on a number of modifications to the procedure, a proposal by China to defer further consideration until 1992 was accepted.[93] At the same session, the Commission decided, despite some opposition, to publish the report of its Working Group on Communications. The report noted the difficulty of using the communications in order to identify trends revealing 'a consistent pattern of reliably attested injustice and discriminatory practices against women' and concluded that 'the current procedure . . . should be improved to make it more efficient and useful . . .'.[94] Thus, while it remains to be seen whether meaningful reforms will prove acceptable, the need for them has been clearly recognized.

The main objective in the efforts to revitalize the Commission has been to develop ways and means of making it more effective in its historic role as a mechanism for identifying issues and making policy recommendations. Following the adoption of the recommendations of the Copenhagen conference by the General Assembly, steps were gradually taken in this direction. In 1981, the Secretary-General was directed to consult the Commission in the preparation of an important survey on the role of women in development and 'to the extent possible, regarding any survey on proposed action concerning women'.[95] Subsequently, it succeeded in obtaining designation as the preparatory body for the 1985 world conference and, even more importantly, to draft the final document of the conference, which was meant to lay the foundations for United Nations policy towards women until the year 2000.[96] Later, the Secretary-General was also instructed to report to the Commission at each session on all significant developments within the United Nations, and all parts of the system were invited to continue their co-operation and coordination with the Commission after the end of the Women's Decade.[97]

At the same time, efforts were made to adjust the Commission's agenda to achieve better integration and balance among the three objectives of the Decade—equality, development, and peace. On the initiative of the Eastern European group, it was requested to consider measures necessary to implement the Declaration on the Participation of Women in Promoting International Peace and Co-operation, and to develop assistance programmes for southern African and Palestinian women.[98] For their part, the Western countries were instrumental in adding to the agenda a number of topics of particular concern to women's groups, such as violence in the family and the need for a reordering of sexual roles in society. They also revived issues with

[92] CSOW Report, E/1991/28, para. 76.
[93] Ibid. para. 79.
[94] Ibid. para. 48.
[95] GA Res.36/127 (1981).
[96] ESC Res.1982/26.
[97] GA Res.39/128 (1984).
[98] GA Res.38/105 (1983), ESC Res.1984/17 and 1986/21.

which the Commission had been concerned in an earlier period, namely, equal rights for women working in the United Nations, and the question of the exploitation of prostitution.[99]

These efforts to revitalize the Commission were brought to a higher level following the Nairobi conference in 1985, which marked the end of the Women's Decade, and the subsequent adoption by the General Assembly of the Forward-Looking Strategies to the Year 2000. In the Strategies, the three objectives of the Decade were reaffirmed for future activities and a conscious effort was made to conceptualize their complex interrelationships and to translate them into concrete programmes for action by governments and by the United Nations system.[100] An important effect of the document was to shift emphasis from the promotion of gender-specific activities to the strategy of 'mainstreaming', i.e. taking the situation of women into account in analyses of overall economic and social trends and incorporating a women's dimension in all global planning by the United Nations system. This was accompanied by a recognition that projects designed only for women had performed a useful function in apprising policy-makers of women's needs, but had not succeeded in improving their overall position and that such activities had tended to remain marginal compared to development planning at the national level. It was also increasingly recognized that strategies for the advancement of women would remain ineffective unless they were accompanied by the empowerment of women through their participation in decision-making in all areas. In drafting the Strategies, the Commission requested, and later obtained, to be entrusted with the main responsibility for monitoring their implementation, and for carrying out review and appraisal of progress achieved. It also obtained that the mechanism of the medium-term plan be used for integrating the Strategies into planning by the entire United Nations system, and that it would review the relevant draft documents at a special session in early 1987. The session was also to be used to elaborate proposals for further strengthening of the Commission.[101]

The special session marked a new turning-point in the life of the Commission and the beginning of a third phase, in which integration among earlier approaches and better system co-ordination are being increasingly emphasized. The years following the special session of the Commission have seen the adoption of a number of measures in line with the 'mainstreaming' approach it proposed and for the strengthening of the Commission itself. The system-wide medium-term plan for women and development for the period 1990–5 recommended by the Commission gave priority to the questions of

[99] ESC Res.1984/14 and 1984/11; and GA Res.38/107 (1983) and 40/103 (1985).

[100] *Report of the World Conference to Review and Appraise the Achievements of the UN Decade for Women: Equality, Development and Peace*, n. 8, above, 2–89.

[101] ESC Res.1986/30.

discrimination, access to productive resources and services, participation in decision-making, and the need to devise comprehensive approaches to women and development and to improve means of international action. The plan was endorsed by the Economic and Social Council, which also requested all United Nations bodies, including the regional commissions, and the specialized agencies, to adopt and implement comprehensive policies for the advancement of women and to incorporate them in their own plans, programmes, and major policy statements.[102] Measures to increase the membership and to expand the schedule of meetings of the Commission and to provide it with support in the form of expert meetings and other forms of consultation were adopted. Its monitoring role was strengthened within the context of the establishment of a streamlined reporting system involving governments, intergovernmental, and non-governmental organizations, and the various sectors of the United Nations system. An expanded session of the Commission was held in 1990 to carry out the comprehensive review under the new system for the first time since the adoption of the Strategies.[103] At the same time, it restructured its agenda and adopted a systematic long-term programme of work in order to allow for in-depth consideration of priority themes drawn from each of the three main objectives of equality, development, and peace. Increased efforts were also made to address the issue of empowerment in concrete terms, by focusing on obstacles which prevent participation of women in decision-making.[104]

At this stage, it is still too early to evaluate the impact of these measures. At the 1989 session of the Commission, concern was expressed at the continued low response by governments to the new reporting system and criticisms were voiced over the insufficient emphasis given to women in the first draft of the global medium-term plan for the period 1992–7 and the continuing budgetary limitations on the work of the Commission.[105] However, the fact that the reforms that have been initiated have the support of both the Economic and Social Council and the General Assembly is a positive indica-

[102] The report of the CSOW on the special session is in E/1987/15. The proposed system-wide medium-term plan for women and development for the period 1990–5 was issued in E/1987/52. It was endorsed in ESC Res.1987/86 and 1989/105. Proposals for the strengthening of the Commission and its long-term programme for work were made in E/CN.6/1986/13 and E/CN.6/1987/3.

[103] GA Res.42/62 (1987) reaffirmed the need for the UN to develop an integrated reporting system with the CSOW at its centre in order to carry out monitoring, review, and appraisal of progress regarding the advancement of women. ESC Res.1988/22 adopted a 2-year cycle for system-wide monitoring and a 5-year cycle for review and appraisal. The system, the most comprehensive to date, was endorsed by the GA in GA Res.43/101 (1988).

[104] ESC Decision 1989/129 accepted the Commission's proposal for the convening in 1991 of a high-level inter-regional consultation on women in public life.

[105] The CSOW report is in E/1989/27. The introduction to the draft medium-term plan for 1992–7, setting out the main structure and guidelines of the plan, was submitted by the Secretary-General in A/43/329.

tion of the intention of member States to see the Commission play a stronger role in future. It will be up to the Commission and to its constituency, which by now includes large numbers of non-governmental organizations and women's groups, to take advantage of the opening that has thereby been offered.

Following a decision by the General Assembly in 1990 to hold another world conference on women in 1995 the Commission once again assumed the role of preparatory body for the conference.[106] At its 1991 session it decided to prepare a programme of action focusing on a limited number of key issues identified as representing fundamental obstacles to women's advancement and, where possible, to set quantitative goals.[107]

Concluding Observations

An evaluation of the work of the Commission on the Status of Women should begin with an assessment of its impact on the condition of women everywhere. Obviously, however, the correlation between the debates and decisions of international organs and the development of societies is extremely difficult to draw. In the case of women in particular, we are witnessing an extremely complex and varied historical process whose beginnings in many parts of the world pre-date the establishment of the United Nations, and to which the United Nations has contributed further impetus. It should be stressed in this regard that although at San Francisco a consensus was achieved on including in the Charter the principle of equality between the sexes, there was no common understanding of its meaning nor agreement on the concrete measures to be taken. Both the legal and actual condition of women varied widely from country to country, as did governmental perceptions and policies. Moreover, the vast majority of the world's women lived under the sway of traditional cultures whose development had been frozen by the colonial experience. In this context, therefore, the Commission on the Status of Women must be seen as both the product of a social reality which had begun to change and as an instrument established by governments in order to define, codify, and, as necessary, channel the new reality.

The Commission was created as an instrument of negotiation among governments, not as an agent of change. Despite its beginnings in women's activism, it was established as a body of government representatives: it was not given powers to review governmental performance, to investigate specific situations, nor to develop recourse procedures in case of violations. It was,

[106] GA Res.45/129 (1990).
[107] CSOW Res.35/4 (1991).

in fact, barred even from addressing itself directly to governments, having to couch its recommendations in general terms and to forward them through its parent bodies. Further control over its activities was exercised through budgetary constraints which have limited its field of operation throughout its life. Another consideration to be kept in mind in this respect is that the question of equality for women has never become a priority issue for governments on the same level as colonialism, racism, or economic development.

Accordingly, the role assigned to the Commission has been largely one of conceptualization, policy formulation, and promotion: articulating an international consensus over the interpretation to be given to the sex-equality provisions of the Charter, and making recommendations in an effort to influence the policies and programmes of international agencies and national governments, as well as the consciousness of the general public. The work of the Commission should therefore be evaluated with respect to this more circumscribed sphere. Its basic role so defined has not changed, although its orientation has shifted from concern with individual rights to development issues, and its strategy from an emphasis on gender-specific machinery and projects to the integration of women's concerns into all global policy-making.

The first phase of the Commission concentrated on codifying the norm of equality and influencing national legislation in this regard. Under the stimulus of the countries which had already adopted advanced legislation, it was successful in gradually widening the area of consensus. The difficulty of this endeavour and of defining norms applicable to countries with very different types of societies is shown by the fact that it took over thirty years between the time a global convention was first mooted and the adoption of the Convention on the Elimination of All Forms of Discrimination against Women in 1979. However, it is undeniable that its work during this first phase succeeded in securing the recognition in law of women's rights in many countries, as well as having an influence on the formation of public opinion in favour of equality for women. The Convention, which has attained wide support, is bound to advance this process further. The Commission should also be credited with having raised the problem of discrimination against women in various spheres of political, social, and economic life, and within the secretariats of the international organizations. Despite sporadic efforts to deal with the concrete situations identified, however, the role of the Commission in rights implementation has remained modest. Although it is no secret that the degree of implementation of women's rights has lagged far behind the enactment of legislation in most countries, and that serious violations take place in many societies, there has been no concerted attempt to expand the role of the Commission into a monitoring mechanism with powers of investigation, such as is the case with the Commission on Human Rights. The addition to the Commission's mandate of a role in monitoring, review and appraisal, and consideration of communications, has not fundamentally modified the basic approach, since the outcome has been primarily to expand the types of information reaching it, and not its powers to act on it.

Clearly, the problem of implementation of women's rights was posed differently from that of human rights. Policies were directed not at attempting to detect violations and ensure respect for basic rights, but rather at assisting governments in identifying needs and encouraging them to adopt enlightened social policies which would promote the 'advancement' of women. This approach, already evident in the first stage of the Commission's life, eventually meshed in with the growing needs for development assistance by the newly independent countries, as well as with the aid policies of the industrialized countries. The language of development and the concern with promoting development projects for women at the national and international level, have permeated the work of the Commission in its second phase.

The Commission must be credited with having contributed to the growing recognition of the importance of the human factor and of the goals of equality and justice in the development process, and with having identified the obstacles faced by women in this regard. Whether directly or indirectly through the international women's conferences, during its second phase it exercised influence on various sectors of the United Nations and on national governments to alter development policies in the direction of greater responsiveness to the needs of women, and to stimulate the creation of appropriate machinery for this purpose. The sheer number of agencies and meetings at all levels dealing with various aspects of women's contribution to development leads one to conclude that it has been largely successful in this endeavour. The concrete results in terms of improving the lives of women in the developing world, however, have been less satisfactory, as concluded in the course of the world-wide assessment carried out for the three world conferences.

At the same time, the Commission itself entered a period of crisis, appearing to have lost its basic *raison d'être* and its central institutional position amid the emphasis on development-related issues and the proliferation of programmes and bodies outside its sphere of control. Its schedule of meetings and the facilities at its disposal were reduced, and arguments for its abolition were made.

At the beginning I mentioned the dilemma between a strategy which involves creating specialized machinery to deal with women's rights, thereby running the risk of creating a 'women's ghetto' endowed with little power and resources, and the alternative strategy of 'mainstreaming', i.e., incorporating a women's dimension in programmes addressed to the population as a whole, thereby risking the subordination of women's concerns. After reviewing the experience of the Commission on the Status of Women, one is led to conclude that both strategies are necessary in order to deal with a problem as deep-rooted and complex as that of inequality between the sexes. There is a crying need both for taking women fully into account in all global policy-making, and for gender-specific programmes to redress existing situations of discrimination as well as specialized machinery with an adequate mandate to exercise effective supervision. In addition to the tasks already performed by the Commission, this mandate should ideally include powers to review specific situations, act on the basis of complaints, and address recommendations directly to the governments concerned.

In recent debates on future strategies towards women, many delegations appear to have recognized the need for just such a two-pronged approach. Since the latter part of the Women's Decade, the Commission has entered a third phase in its life, a phase in which the growing emphasis placed on the 'mainstreaming' strategy is accompanied by calls, on the one hand, for greater attention to the interlinkages between the goal of equality and those of development and peace; and on the other, for greater participation of women in all decision-making. A corollary to this have been recommendations for strengthening the role of the Commission in policy formulation and in monitoring and review of implementation. Thus far those proposals have led to an expansion of the terms of reference of the Commission and an improvement in the resources at its disposal, but have fallen quite short of granting it the full powers described above. It remains to be seen whether the process of reform that has been initiated will need to be carried further in order to bring to realization the promises contained in the new approaches.

8
The Security Council

SYDNEY D. BAILEY

Introduction

Two basic axioms of the UN Charter may sometimes be in conflict. The first, described in the Charter as a principle, is the sovereign equality of all UN Members, to which we may add another Charter concept, the territorial integrity of the State.[1] The other axiom, described in the Charter as a purpose, is to achieve international co-operation in promoting and encouraging respect for human rights and fundamental freedoms for all.[2] One particular principle or right, the claim for self-determination, is peculiarly sensitive because it can take the form of a demand for secession, thus endangering the territorial integrity of a sovereign State. It is notable that the declaration on de-colonization, approved by the UN General Assembly in 1960, gives equal weight to self-determination and to sovereignty and territorial integrity.[3]

The Security Council is one of the six 'principal organs' of the United Nations (Article 7) on which UN Members have conferred 'primary responsibility' for maintaining international peace and security, and have also agreed that the Council 'acts on their behalf' (Article 24(1)). The Council is to be 'so organized as to be able to function continuously' (Article 28(1)). It consists of five permanent members (China, France, the Soviet Union, the United Kingdom, and the United States) and ten (originally six) other members elected by the General Assembly (Article 23(1) and (2)). Decisions are now made by a vote of nine members, but in the case of substantive matters, a negative vote by one or more of the permanent members constitutes a veto (Article 27(2) and (3)). The Council may investigate potential or actual disputes or similar situations, may call on the parties to settle the matter by peaceful means, may recommend 'appropriate procedures or methods of adjustment' or 'terms of settlement', or may make other recommendations 'with a view to a pacific settlement' (Articles 33(2), 34, 36(1), 37(2), and 38). If the Council determines that there has been a threat to peace, breach of the peace, or act of aggression, it may take 'provisional measures' in order to

[1] Art. 2(1) and (4).
[2] Art. 1(3). See also Arts. 55–6.
[3] GA Res.1541 (XV) (1960), paras. 6–7.

prevent an aggravation of the situation, may decide on non-military measures so as to 'give effect to its decisions', or may impose such coercive military measures as it deems necessary to maintain or restore international peace and security (Articles 39–42). It is usually accepted that the Council's decisions are binding only if a formal determination is made under Article 39 or if words from the Article, but not synonyms, are incorporated into a decision of the Council. The procedures laid down in the Charter for military coercion (Articles 43–8) have largely remained a dead letter. UN Members have in theory agreed to accept and carry out the Council's decisions (Article 25), and when the Council decides on provisional, non-military, or military measures, UN Members are supposed to 'join in affording mutual assistance in carrying out the measures ...' (Article 49).

The General Assembly, the Economic and Social Council, and the Trusteeship Council (and their subsidiary organs), are expressly empowered to deal with human rights and fundamental freedoms,[4] but it seems not to have been envisaged at San Francisco that the Security Council might also become involved in issues of human rights. Indeed, from 1946 to the early 1960s, the Security Council's handling of such human rights issues as arose was adventitious, sporadic, and inconclusive.

An illustration of my point can be seen from the following incidents. The Council had been at work for less than a month when the Soviet ambassador raised the issue of self-determination in connection with the Ukrainian complaint about the situation in Indonesia, and the Council's lengthy resolution on terms of settlement for Indonesia dealt in considerable detail with such issues as free and democratic elections.[5] Similarly, the Council's terms of settlement for Kashmir included 'proper conditions for a free and impartial plebiscite' and 'adequate protection' of minorities.[6] In 1949, the Economic and Social Council transmitted to the Security Council a resolution and related communications concerning human rights in Palestine.[7] In 1956, the issue of human rights arose in connection with the Algerian question.[8] In 1965, in a statement of consensus, the Council 'condemned gross violations of human rights in the Dominican Republic ...'.[9] In 1969, the Republic of Ireland asked that a UN peacekeeping force should be sent to Northern Ireland following disturbances arising from the perception that human rights were being infringed.[10]

In none of these cases, however, did the Security Council pursue the human rights issues raised. The Council's resolution on Indonesia was

[4] Arts. 13(1)b, 62(2), and 76(c).
[5] SCOR 14 (1946), 200; SC Res.67 (1949), paras. 3–4.
[6] SC Res.47 (1948), sect. A and B.
[7] S/1291 (1949) (mimeo.).
[8] SCOR 729 (1956), paras. 80–1.
[9] SCOR 1233 (1965), para. 2.
[10] SCOR 1503 (1969), para. 35.

forgotten once the Netherlands and the Indonesian Republicans had agreed to hold a round-table conference. On Kashmir, India withdrew its agreement to a UN-supervised plebiscite because the necessary demilitarization was never achieved. In the Palestine case, the resolution and communications were not even discussed because the Council did not want to jeopardize the armistice negotiations. The human rights issue in the Dominican Republic was taken over by the Inter-American Commission on Human Rights. The Algerian and Northern Ireland items were not even inscribed on the Council's agenda.

Beginning in 1960, however, the Council began to concern itself with human rights in four sets of circumstances. The first was when it could be maintained that gross and persistent violations of human rights constituted a threat to international peace and security. This arose mainly in Southern Africa. The connection between infringements of human rights and threats to peace had in fact been made on one occasion in the early days (1946), when the Council was debating incidents on Greece's border. The Soviet representative introduced a draft resolution, which would have found that 'terroristic conditions' in Greece endangered peace and security;[11] but the debate on the item simply petered out without a substantive decision.

Secondly, human rights issues have arisen in connection with respect for the Geneva (Red Cross) Conventions, especially concerning those categories of persons entitled to humanitarian protection and immunity from direct attack. Thirdly, human rights issues have arisen when military forces have crossed frontiers to protect or rescue nationals or 'brothers' of the people of the intervening State. The fourth situation is in the context of UN supervision of elections and plebiscites.

A. *Human Rights Violations which Might Endanger Peace*

Allegations that violations of human rights have constituted a threat to peace have concerned Portugese colonies in Africa, Southern Rhodesia, Namibia, and South Africa, and also arose in a surprising way in connection with the US hostages in Teheran.

I. PORTUGESE TERRITORIES

The issue of Portugal's African Territories was raised in the Security Council in 1961, and six resolutions were approved between 1961 and 1972. Third World and Communist States relied heavily on the 1960 declaration of the General Assembly on de-colonization, and Portugal and her friends invariably cited Article 2(7) of the Charter, which states that the Organization is not

[11] SCOR 67 (1946), 334–5.

authorized to intervene in essentially domestic matters. Critics of Portugal's colonial policy maintained that the situation represented a threat to peace,[12] but an attempt to have the Council make a formal determination under Chapter VII of the Charter was frustrated in 1961 when the Council adopted an amendment to change a preambular reference to a 'threat to international peace and security' to 'is likely to endanger the maintenance of international peace'. Two subsequent resolutions stated that the situation was seriously disturbing international peace.[13]

There were only a few references in the debates to violations of international standards regarding human rights.[14] Four of the Council's resolutions affirmed the goals of self-determination and independence, three asked Portugal to desist from repressive measures, two asked States to refrain from helping Portugal to continue its repressive measures, three called for an amnesty, and two called for free political activity.[15] As Portugal's critics wished each resolution to be stronger than the previous one, the operative verb relating to Portugal changed from 'deprecates' in 1963, to 'deplores' in 1965, to 'condemns' in 1972.[16]

II. SOUTHERN RHODESIA

The Southern Rhodesia case in the Security Council was bedevilled from the start by a certain amount of double-thinking. From the point of view of a majority of Council members, Southern Rhodesia was a non-self-governing territory administered by the United Kingdom, and the United Kingdom was regarded as legally responsible for developments in the territory. From the United Kingdom point of view, on the other hand, Southern Rhodesia had enjoyed internal self-government since 1923, and for a time before the Unilateral Declaration of Independence (UDI) in 1965, the United Kingdom maintained that internal developments in Southern Rhodesia were essentially matters of domestic jurisdiction and therefore beyond the scope of UN intervention.[17]

The United Kingdom regarded the Unilateral Declaration of Independence as illegal and invalid, but the United Kingdom had no coercive presence in the region by which British policy could be imposed.[18] In that case, said Third

[12] SCOR 1041 (1963), paras. 11 and 37.

[13] SCOR 950 (1961), para. 37; SCOR 955 (1961), para. 66; SCOR 956 (1961), para. 157; SC Res.163 (1961); SC Res.180 (1963), para. 4; SC Res.218 (1965), para. 1.

[14] SCOR 943 (1961), para. 53; SCOR 945 (1961), para. 81.

[15] SC Res.163 (1961), para. 3; SC Res.180 (1963), para. 5(a)–(e); SC Res.183 (1963), para. 6; SC Res.218 (1965), paras. 5(a)–(e) and 6; SC Res.312 (1972), paras. 4(a) and 6; SC Res.322 (1972), paras. 1 and 3.

[16] SC Res.180 (1963), para. 3; SC Res.218 (1965), para. 2; SC Res.312 (1972), para. 2.

[17] SCOR 1064 (1963), para. 6; SCOR 1068 (1963), paras. 101–3.

[18] SCOR 1257 (1965), paras. 13, 15–16, 18–19, 21–4, and 33; SCOR 1263 (1965), paras. 10 and 23; SCOR 1479 (1969), paras. 30–3.

World countries, the United Kingdom should send an expeditionary force to repress the rebellion: 'in the recent past the United Kingdom used force, scorning right and justice, to repress what it called at the time the rebellion or insubordination of the peoples it had colonized' (Senegal).[19]

The Southern Rhodesian question first came before the Security Council in 1963, after a conference at Victoria Falls had decided to break up the Central African Federation into three separate units. African members of the Council were worried because they considered that Southern Rhodesia was to receive a disproportionate amount of the Federation's military hardware. The nature of the problem changed with the UDI by Ian Smith in 1965. The Security Council condemned this act 'by a racist minority' and called on States not to recognize or assist the illegal regime.[20]

Third World countries would have liked the Council to make an immediate formal determination under Article 39 of the Charter ('threat to the peace, breach of the peace, or act of aggression'), thus making it possible for the Council to take binding decisions, but this was resisted at this stage by the United Kingdom. US ambassador Arthur Goldberg then devised a formula which was acceptable only because its meaning was obscure: 'the situation... is extremely grave... [and] its continuance in time constitutes a threat to international peace and security'.[21] In the following year, the Council determined that the situation constituted a threat to peace, thus bringing it within the scope of Chapter VII of the Charter, and later in 1966, there were specific references in resolutions both to Chapter VII of the Charter and to Article 25, by which UN Members agreed 'to accept and carry out' decisions of the Security Council.[22]

Between 1963 and 1980, the Council held 128 meetings devoted wholly or mainly to Southern Rhodesia. The aim was variously described as 'to allow the people of Southern Rhodesia to determine their own future', 'freedom and independence', 'self-determination and independence', 'majority rule', 'genuine de-colonization', 'self-determination, freedom and independence', 'the free and fair choice of the people', and 'full independence and majority rule'.[23] There were five vetoes by the United Kingdom,[24] and two jointly by the United Kingdom and the United States.[25]

The African States were somewhat miffed that the initiative for convening

[19] SCOR 1278th (1965), paras. 36–7; SCOR 1532 (1970), para. 41.
[20] SC Res.216 (1965).
[21] SC Res.217 (1965), para. 1.
[22] SC Res.221 (1966), para. 1; SC Res.232 (1966), pream. and paras. 1, 3, and 6.
[23] SC Res.217 (1965), para. 7; SC Res.232 (1966), para. 4; SC Res.318 (1972), para. 1; SC Res.415 (1977), para 1; SC Res.423 (1978), para. 6; SC Res.460 (1979); SC Res.463 (1980), paras. 9 and 10.
[24] 13 Sept. 1963, 10 Nov. 1970, 30 Dec. 1971, 4 Feb. 1972, and 29 Sept. 1972.
[25] 17 Mar. 1970 and 22 May 1973.

the Council after UDI in 1965 had been taken by the United Kingdom.[26] At crucial junctures thereafter, there was competition as to who would be the first to put in a request for a meeting, and there was an unseemly row in 1966 when the African president of the Council (Mali) delayed calling a meeting which the United Kingdom had requested.[27] On one occasion when it was Britain's turn to preside over the Council, the UK ambassador (Lord Caradon) ceded the presidency under Rule 20 of the Council's Rules of Procedure, which allows the president to cede the presidency to the member next in alphabetical order if the question before the Council is one with which the president is 'directly connected'.[28] From time to time African members of the Council spoke on behalf of the Organization of African Unity or the group of African States.[29]

It is surprising, in retrospect, that there were not more references in the debates and resolutions on Southern Rhodesia to international human rights documents. On one occasion, Zambia cited the Universal Declaration of Human Rights,[30] and on another occasion, the Council received a statement of consensus from the Commission on Human Rights concerning 'the illegal killing [execution] of three African political prisoners and freedom fighters', leading the Council to condemn the Southern Rhodesian regime as a flagrant affront to the conscience of mankind.[31]

Because the Security Council always took the line that the United Kingdom was legally responsible for the administration of Southern Rhodesia, its appeals were addressed to Britain rather than to the Smith regime. In 1965, shortly before the UDI, the Council endorsed a request of the General Assembly, asking the United Kingdom 'to obtain' the release of political prisoners, detainees, and restrictees, the repeal of repressive and discriminatory legislation, the removal of restrictions on political activity, and the establishment of full democratic freedom and equality of political rights. Later that year, after the UDI, the United Kingdom was asked to act vigorously in quelling 'this rebellion of the racist minority' and in eliminating the authority of the usurpers. In 1968, the call to the United Kingdom to 'bring to an end the rebellion' was repeated and the United Kingdom was also asked to ensure that no settlement was reached, which failed to take account of the views of the Southern Rhodesian people; and the measures whose termination the United Kingdom had been asked 'to obtain' in 1965 were condemned. The measures were again condemned in 1970, and the United Kingdom was asked 'to rescind or withdraw' existing agreements for the presence of trade or consular

[26] S/6896 (1965), 354.
[27] SCOR 1276 (1966), para. 10; Supp. for Apr. to June 1966, 29–32, 46–8, 62–3.
[28] SCOR 1428 (1968), paras. 2–4.
[29] SCOR 1531 (1970), paras. 5–6; SCOR 2142 (1979), paras. 3–5, 7–8, 15, 37–8, 82, and 84.
[30] SCOR 1663 (1972), para. 26.
[31] S/8443 (1968), 214–15; SC Res.253 (1968), pream.

representatives in Southern Rhodesia. In 1979, the United Kingdom was asked 'to take all necessary measures' to prevent illegal executions and to ensure the departure of all external military forces, 'regular or mercenary'.[32] The request about military forces was repeated in 1980 after the Lancaster House agreement, and the United Kingdom was also asked to ensure the release of political prisoners and freedom fighters, the release of South African political prisoners and 'their safe passage to any country of their choice', the rescinding of emergency legislation, equality of treatment for all parties, and also 'to ensure that eligible Zimbabwe nationals will freely participate in the forthcoming electoral process'.[33]

In 1969 the president of the Council made a statement of consensus to the effect that a referendum in Southern Rhodesia had been illegal and that the constitution was invalid,[34] and ten years later, elections held in Southern Rhodesia were condemned and the results declared to be 'null and void'.[35]

The Security Council first called on States to apply oil sanctions, and later ordered selective economic and diplomatic sanctions, and then comprehensive sanctions.[36] In 1976, Mozambique informed the Council that it had suffered special economic problems as a result of imposing sanctions against Southern Rhodesia and was therefore consulting the Council in accordance with Article 50 of the Charter. The Council commended Mozambique and appealed to States and UN agencies to provide assistance.[37] After the conclusion of the Lancaster House agreement, mandatory sanctions were terminated, and UN Members were asked to respect 'the free and fair choice of the people of Zimbabwe'.[38]

III. NAMIBIA

Namibia, (or South West Africa, as it was known in UN documents until 1968) is the only territory which was under a League of Nations mandate which did not either become independent or was brought within the UN trusteeship system. Aspects of the Namibian question had been before the General Assembly since 1946, and subsequently before the International

[32] SC Res.202 (1965), pream.; SC Res.217 (1965), paras. 4, 5, and 9; SC Res.253 (1968), paras. 1, 2, and 17; SC Res.277 (1970), paras. 5 and 10; SC Res.445 (1979), para. 4; SC Res.460 (1979), para. 7.

[33] SC Res.463 (1980), paras. 4, 5, and 7.

[34] SCOR 1477 (1969), para. 4.

[35] SC Res.445 (1979), paras. 5–7; SC Res.448 (1979), paras. 1–2.

[36] SC Res.217 (1965), para. 8; SC Res.232 (S/7621/Rev. 1 as amended), paras. 2, 5, and 7; SC Res.253 (1968), paras. 3–10; SC Res.277 (1970), paras. 8–9, 11–5, and 17; SC Res.288 (1970), paras. 3–5; SC Res.314 (1972), paras. 1–6; SC Res.318 (1972), paras. 3–9; SC Res.320 (1972), paras. 1–5; SC Res.333 (1973), paras. 1–3; SC Res.409 (1977), paras. 1–3.

[37] SC Res.386 (1976).

[38] SC Res.460 (1979), para. 2; SC Res.463 (1980), para. 9.

Court of Justice and the Commission on Human Rights. Two resolutions of the General Assembly in 1967 asked the Security Council to concern itself with Namibia, and these were followed by a consensus resolution of the Commission on Human Rights concerning political prisoners.[39] On 24 January 1968, 52 UN Members from Asia and Africa, together with Yugoslavia, asked for an urgent meeting of the Security Council to consider the Namibian question.[40] More than one hundred and forty meetings of the Council have dealt with Namibia.

The Council made no formal determination under Chapter VII of the Charter which would have enabled the Council to take binding decisions, but one resolution included a preambular reference to Article 25 and the obligation of UN Members to comply with decisions of the Council.[41] There have been six vetoes on Namibia by the three Western permanent members, and two by the United Kingdom and the United States.[42]

The Council accepted the decision of the General Assembly in 1966 in terminating the mandate for Namibia[43] and agreed with the Advisory Opinion of the International Court of Justice to the effect that South Africa's presence in Namibia was illegal and that South Africa was under an obligation to withdraw its administration from the territory immediately.[44] The Council's aim has been to enable the Namibian people to achieve self-determination, national independence, and their territorial integrity.[45] The Council has censured, condemned, and strongly condemned South Africa.[46] States have been invited, requested, called upon, or urged to take specified forms of persuasion and pressure.[47]

South Africa abstained when the Universal Declaration of Human Rights was put to the vote in 1948, but South Africa has been asked to respect its provisions in Namibia.[48] On particular human rights issues, South Africa has been asked to discontinue illegal trials, release political prisoners, abolish

[39] GA Res.2324 (XXII) (1967), para. 4; GA Res.2325 (XXII) (1967), paras. 7–8; S/8411 (1968), 187–8.

[40] Ibid. 71–2, S/8355 and Adds.

[41] SC Res.269 (1969), pream.

[42] One on 6 June 1975, one on 19 Oct. 1976, four on 30 Apr. 1981, one on 15 Nov. 1985, and one on 9 Apr. 1987.

[43] GA Res.2145 (XXI) (1966); SC Res.264 (1969), para. 1.

[44] SC Res.284 (1970); SC Res.301 (1971), para. 6; S/10365/Rev. 1.

[45] SC Res.319 (1972), para. 2; SC Res.323 (1972), para. 4; SC Res.385 (1976), para. 7.

[46] SC Res.246 (1968), para. 1; SC Res.264 (1969), para. 6; SC Res.269 (1969), para. 2; SC Res.276 (1970), para. 1; SC Res.301 (1971), para. 3; SC Res.310 (1972), paras. 1 and 4; SC Res.385 (1976), paras. 1–3, 5, and 6; SC Res.439 (1978), para. 1; SC Res.532 (1983), para. 1; SC Res.539 (1983), paras. 1 and 2; SC Res.566 (1985), paras. 1, 3, and 6.

[47] SC Res.245 (1968), para. 2; SC Res.246 (1968), paras. 3 and 4; SC Res.269 (1969), paras. 7 and 8; SC Res.276 (1970), paras. 5 and 7; SC Res.283 (1970), paras. 1–8, 11, and 13; SC Res.301 (1971), paras. 11 and 15; SC Res.323 (1972), para. 7; SC Res.566 (1985), para. 14.

[48] SC Res.310 (1972), paras. 4 and 5; SC Res.366 (1974), para. 5(a); SC Res.385 (1976), para. 11(a).

discriminatory and repressive laws and practices, and allow the return of exiled Namibians.[49] The election held in Namibia in 1978 was declared to be null and void.[50]

IV. SOUTH AFRICA

The treatment of persons of Indian origin in South Africa came before the General Assembly in 1946, and the question of apartheid in 1952. In 1960, twenty-nine Asian and African States asked the Security Council to consider the Sharpeville killings as a danger to peace and security, and since then the Council has held more than 140 meetings on the South African race question. In 1962, the General Assembly asked the Security Council 'to take appropriate measures, including sanctions, to secure compliance with the resolutions of the General Assembly ...',[51] and at the 1965 session and since, the General Assembly has addressed similar but increasingly forceful requests to the Council.

During the debate on the item in 1963, Tunisia said that the situation in South Africa fell within the scope of Articles 55–6 of the Charter (international co-operation regarding human rights and other matters), and the Soviet Union maintained that racial discrimination was a violation of the Universal Declaration of Human Rights (which neither South Africa nor the Soviet Union had supported when it was put to the vote in 1948). The Philippines made the same points.[52] A group of experts appointed by the Secretary-General in accordance with a resolution of the Security Council recommended in 1964 that South Africa should incorporate into its constitution a bill of rights based on the Universal Declaration of Human Rights. The experts also appealed for an immediate amnesty for opponents of apartheid.[53] The communiqué issued after the 'periodic' meeting of the Security Council in 1970, held in accordance with Article 28(2) of the Charter, stated that Council members had affirmed that the peoples of Southern Africa are entitled to self-determination and 'fundamental human rights in freedom and dignity'.[54] Apartheid was later described by the Council as 'a crime against the conscience of mankind' and incompatible with the Universal Declaration of Human Rights, and the Council affirmed 'the legitimacy of the struggle of the oppressed people of South Africa ... as set forth in ... the Universal Declara-

[49] SC Res.245 (1968), para. 2; SC Res.246 (1968), para. 2; SC Res.266 (1974), para. 5(b)–(d); SC Res.385 (1976), para. 2, II(b)–(d).

[50] SC Res.435 (1978), para. 6; SC Res.439 (1978), para. 3.

[51] GA Res.1761 (XVII) (1962), para. 8.

[52] SCOR 1050 (1963), para. 42; SCOR 1054 (1963), para. 19; SCOR 1076 (1963), para. 5.

[53] S/5658 (1964), Annex, paras. 50 and 116.

[54] SCOR 1555 (1970), para. 4.

tion of Human Rights'.[55] The preamble to a resolution of the Council in 1984 reaffirmed the Universal Declaration.[56]

The Council has called upon South Africa to abandon apartheid and discrimination, cease repressive measures, to release those persons imprisoned, restricted, or sentenced to death for having opposed apartheid, abrogate the ban on parties and organizations opposed to apartheid, promote 'racial harmony based on equality', cease 'indiscriminate violence against peaceful demonstrators', abandon 'bantustanization', and release named persons.[57]

The Afro-Asian members of the Council pressed for many years for a formal determination by the Council under Chapter VII so as to make decisions mandatory,[58] but this was resisted by the main Western members.[59] The Council decided in 1960 that the situation, if continued, 'might' endanger international peace and security; in 1963, that it was then seriously disturbing international peace and security; in 1964, that it was continuing seriously to disturb peace and security; and in 1977, that violations of the arms embargo constituted a threat to peace and security.[60] The Council deplored, strongly deprecated, condemned, and strongly condemned the policy of apartheid and South Africa's refusal to comply with the Council's decisions.[61] States were called upon to take coercive measures against South Africa, including a recommended ban and later a mandatory ban on the supply of arms; and States violating the arms embargo were condemned.[62]

There have been four vetoes by the Western permanent members of the Council, and three by the United Kingdom and the United States jointly, and one by the United States alone.[63]

[55] SC Res.311 (1972), para. 3; SCOR 1806 (1974), paras. 25, 51, 77, and 80; SC Res.473 (1980), para. 3.

[56] SC Res.556 (1984).

[57] SC Res.134 (1960), para. 4; SC Res.181 (1963), para. 2; SC Res.182 (1963), paras. 2 and 4; SC Res.190 (1964), para. 1; SC Res.191 (1964), paras. 2 and 4; SC Res.311 (1972), para. 4; SC Res.392 (1976), para. 5; SC Res.417 (1977), para. 3; SCOR 2168 (1979), para. 1; 58.

[58] SCOR 1129 (1964), paras. 12–13; SCOR 1132 (1964) paras. 17–19.

[59] SCOR 1135 (1964), para. 53.

[60] SC Res.134 (1960), para. 1; SC Res.181 (1963), pream.; SC Res.182 (1963), pream.; SC Res.191 (1964), pream.; SC Res.418 (1977), pream. and para. 1.

[61] SC Res.134 (1960), paras. 2 and 3; SC Res.181 (1963), para. 1; SC Res.182 (1963), para. 3; SC Res.191 (1964), para. 1; SC Res.311 (1972), para. 1; SC Res.392 (1976), para. 1; SC Res.417 (1977), para. 1; SC Res.569 (1985), paras. 1–3.

[62] SC Res.181 (1963), para. 3; SC Res.182 (1963), para. 1; SC Res.190 (1964), para. 2; SC Res.191 (1964), paras. 12 and 13; SC Res.282 (1970), paras. 3, 4, and 6; SC Res.311 (1972), paras. 5 and 6; SC Res.417 (1977), paras. 4 and 5; SC Res.418 (1977), paras. 2–5; SC Res.473 (1980), para. 10; SC Res.503 (1982), para. 2; SC Res.525 (1982), para. 2; SC Res.533 (1983), para. 2; SC Res.569 (1985), paras. 6–7.

[63] One three-power veto on 30 Oct. 1974, and 3 on 31 Oct. 1977; the Anglo-American vetoes were on 26 July 1985 and 23 May 1986, and 20 Feb 1987; the US veto was on 8 Mar. 1988.

V. US HOSTAGES IN IRAN

From the procedural point of view, there were a number of unusual features in this case. It was not brought to the attention of the Security Council by the plaintiff but by UN Secretary-General Kurt Waldheim, on the ground that the crisis posed 'a serious threat to international peace and security'. Although the Council's president repeated the words 'serious threat to international peace and security', neither he nor the Secretary-General referred expressly to Article 99 of the Charter, on which the Secretary-General's action was presumably based.[64] While the Security Council adopted two resolutions, neither text contained a formal determination that peace was threatened, but simply referred to tension 'which could have grave consequences for international peace and security'. A third proposal, which was vetoed by the Soviet Union, would have recalled the Secretary-General's opinion that there was a serious threat to international peace and security, would have expressed the view that the continued detention of hostages constituted 'a continuing threat to international peace and security', and, acting under Articles 39 and 41 of the Charter, would have imposed non-military sanctions against Iran.[65]

Another interesting feature of the case was that part of Iran's response to the allegations of hostage-taking in contravention of the recognized rules of diplomatic immunity was to complain that US support of the Shah had represented a violation of the human rights of the Iranian people—what I have called in another context 'reversing the charges'. The consequence was that the debate revolved around two humanitarian complaints, one past and one present. The first resolution of the Security Council had asked the Secretary-General 'to lend his good offices' to secure the effective implementation of the resolution.[66] The Secretary-General commented after the adoption of this resolution that there were 'few, if any, precedents for the present situation', and he added that 'innovation may well be necessary'. After visiting Iran himself and having aired the idea of an international committee of inquiry into Iranian complaints, the Secretary-General set up a five-man commission 'to hear Iran's grievances' and thus pave the way to a resolution of the hostage crisis. This action did not, of course detract from the order of the International Court of Justice that US diplomatic premises should be vacated and the hostages released. The commission of inquiry duly visited Iran and listened to what Iranians had to say, but the hostages were not released at that stage and the commission left the country empty-handed.[67]

[64] SCOR 2172 (1979), paras. 9 and 17.

[65] SC Res.457 (1979); SC Res.461 (1979); S/13573 (1980).

[66] S/13626, S/13673 (1979), 68–9 and 103; SCOR 2175 (1979), paras. 76, 81, and 129; SCOR 2183 (1979), para. 54; S/13730 (1980), paras. 9–10; SCOR 2176 (1979), 4–5.

[67] SC Res.457 (1979), para. 4; SCOR 2178 (1979), para. 19; S/13730 (1980), 4–5; Waldheim, *In the Eye of the Storm* (1985), 1–11 and 156–9; Ramcharan, *Humanitarian Good Offices in International Law* (1987), 131–5.

The US complaint that Iran had violated diplomatic immunity was, of course, reinforced by the International Court of Justice's order to Iran to release the hostages, on which the Security Council based its second resolution, and by the Court's subsequent judgment.[68] But the US position was weakened by the attempted rescue by military action and the resignation of Secretary of State Cyrus Vance.

B. *Respect for the Geneva Conventions*

The second way in which human rights issues have come before the Security Council relates to the four Geneva Conventions of 1949, concerning wounded, sick, and shipwrecked combatants, prisoners of war, and civilians under occupation.

I. KOREA

Shortly after the outbreak of the Korean war in 1950, a memorandum was prepared in the US State Department which included the recommendation that 'the treatment of POW's . . . shall be directed toward their exploitation, training and use for psychological warfare . . .', and this policy was approved by President Truman.[69] In the event, 7,900 North Korean and 14,700 Chinese POWs and 359 POWs from the Unified Command refused repatriation. According to the Third Geneva Convention, POWs 'shall be released and repatriated . . . after the cessation of active hostilities' (Article 118), and special arrangements had to be made in the Korean case so that those POWs who refused repatriation were handed over to a Neutral Nations Repatriation Commission and an Indian Custodial Force, in accordance with an Indian formula which had been approved by the General Assembly.[70] By then, however, the Korean question had passed beyond the purview of the Security Council.[71]

II. SUEZ

At the time of the Sinai–Suez war in 1956, the United Kingdom had signed but not yet ratified the 1949 Conventions, but Prime Minister Eden assured the International Committee of the Red Cross that the United Kingdom fully intended to apply their provisions should the occasion arise.[72]

[68] S/13697 (1979); SC Res.461 (1979); S/13989 (1980).

[69] *Foreign Relations of the United States* (1980), vii. 678, 712 n. 1, and 793 n. 2.

[70] GA Res.610 (VII) (1952).

[71] SC Res.90 (1951).

[72] *Annual Report of the International Committee of the Red Cross for 1956*, 23; Forsythe, *Humanitarian Politics* (1977), 169.

III. INDIA–PAKISTAN–BANGLADESH

On 13 December 1971, shortly after the Bangladesh war, Pakistan asked the Security Council to accept a number of 'imperatives', of which the fourth was to devise means to ensure scrupulous respect for the Geneva Conventions.[73] Eight days later, the Council called on 'all those concerned' to apply the Geneva Conventions 'in full', and asked the Secretary-General to keep the Council informed on the implementation of the resolution.[74] From time to time, during the following months, Pakistan complained that India was violating the Geneva Conventions and other humanitarian norms and was ill-treating POWs and detaining them after the cessation of active hostilities.[75] India maintained that those guilty of 'grave crimes such as genocide, war crimes and crimes against humanity' were not entitled to immunity under the Geneva Conventions and that, in any case, it was India's view that the Convention 'ceases to apply' once hostilities have closed. Subject to the legal position, India said it would respect all humanitarian norms.[76]

Under the terms of the resolution of the Security Council, the UN Secretary-General appointed Vittorio Winspeare Guicciardi as his special representative for humanitarian problems. Winspeare issued two reports on his discussions with the governmental authorities in the area and with Red Cross and other relief organizations.[77] Two crucial issues for the Winspeare mission were the release of Sheikh Mujibur Rahman and the fate of the displaced Biharis. Sheikh Mujibur, who was the elected leader of the people of East Pakistan (which later became Bangladesh) was in prison in West Pakistan, but India took the view that his release was essential if Bangladesh were to become orderly and stable. Secretary-General U Thant had urged Sheikh Mujibur's release some months before the outbreak of war, and Winspeare made a new appeal to President Bhutto and other Pakistani leaders that the Sheikh should be set free. On 8 January 1972, Mujibur was released and proceeded to Bangladesh. When Winspeare visited Dhaka the following month, he was able to have a substantial talk with him.[78]

The Biharis (about 500,000 in 1971–2) are Urdu-speaking Muslims who had opted for East Pakistan at the time of partition but who found themselves unwelcome in Bengali-speaking Bangladesh. Sheikh Mujibur had appealed to his followers in Bangladesh to surrender their arms, but the Biharis had

[73] SCOR 1613 (1971), para. 291.

[74] SC Res.307 (1971), para. 3.

[75] S/10468–A/8641 (1969), 121; S/10490; S/10512; S/10560; S/10579 (1972), 2–3, 14–15, 60, 71, 73–4; S/10589 (1972), 24–5.

[76] Ibid.

[77] I am indebted to Erik Jensen who was a member of the Winspeare mission for some background information. There is a useful study of the mission in Ramcharan, *Humanitarian Good Offices*, 100–8.

[78] S/10410 (1971), 81; S/10512 (1972), 14–20; S/10512/Add.1 (1972), paras. 3, 5–7.

refused. In the ensuing clash with troops and police, many Biharis had been killed. Winspeare visited several camps for Biharis and found evidence of suffering, but he concluded that the authorities in Bangladesh were doing what they could to ameliorate the situation.[79] A permanent solution for these unfortunate stranded people has not yet been found, but Lord Ennals has been working with politicans and officials in the area for the settlement of the remaining Biharis in Pakistan.

The Winspeare mission gave a good deal of attention to providing informal links between the three capitals, as most normal diplomatic contacts had ceased. Winspeare found the Bangladesh authorities 'sympathetic in principle' to the repatriation of West Pakistani officials; as for senior officials of the former East Pakistan government, Bangladesh intended to try them as collaborators. Winspeare found great anxiety in Pakistan about the future of their POWs and about the proposed trials. He was told by the International Committee of the Red Cross that India had agreed to repatriate a number of severely wounded Pakistanis. He believed that outstanding humanitarian problems should be dealt with in direct talks between the parties.[80]

In 1973, Pakistan instituted proceedings against India in the International Court of Justice concerning 195 Pakistani POWs whom India proposed to hand over to Bangladesh to be tried for genocide and crimes against humanity. Pakistan claimed to have exclusive jurisdiction over the POWs in question and that there was no ground in international law for handing them over to Bangladesh. Later in the year, however, Pakistan informed the Court that negotiations were taking place with India and asked that proceedings should be discontinued.[81]

There were three Soviet vetoes in connection with the Bangladesh war but none of the vetoed proposals referred to the Geneva Conventions.[82]

IV. MIDDLE EAST

Following the Middle East war in June, 1967, a number of countries raised in the Council the question of respect for the principles of the Geneva Conventions, and Israel said it would fully respect the Third Convention on POWs without referring to the other three conventions. At the end of the debate, the Council called for scrupulous respect of the humanitarian principles governing the treatment of POWs and of civilians under occupation as contained in the Third and Fourth Geneva Conventions.[83] Israel, while claiming

[79] S/10512 (1972), paras. 14–15; S/10512/Add.1 (1972), paras. 2–3 and 6–9.
[80] S/10512 (1972), paras. 16, 20, and 24; S/10512/Add.1 (1972), paras. 14, 17, and 19.
[81] A/9005, paras. 44–8; A/9605, paras. 24–5.
[82] 4 Dec. 1971, 5 Dec. 1971, and 13 Dec. 1971.
[83] SCOR 1357 (1967), para. 210; SCOR 1358 (1967), paras. 113 and 225; SC Res.237 (1967), para. 2.

to respect humanitarian principles, did not regard the Fourth Convention (civilians) as applicable, on the ground that Israel had never recognized the sovereignty of Jordan over the West Bank or Egypt's right to administer the Gaza Strip.

In 1969, in a debate on the status of Jerusalem, the United States reminded the Security Council that Israel was required by the Fourth Geneva Convention 'to maintain the occupied area as intact and unaltered as possible, without interfering with the customary life of the area . . .'. Israeli actions, said the United States, had led to concern that the eventual disposition of East Jerusalem might be prejudiced.[84] This stance was quoted by Pakistan later in the year, following the fire at the Al Aqsa mosque in the Old City of Jerusalem, started by a demented Australian. The Council approved a Pakistani draft resolution which called upon Israel to observe the Geneva Conventions 'and international law governing military occupation . . .'.[85] In 1971 and 1972, the Arab States complained that Israel was violating the Conventions.[86] In 1972, Israel counter-attacked by asking for a meeting of the Council 'to consider the mutual release of all prisoners of war, in accordance with the provision of the Third Geneva Convention',[87] but no meeting was held.

In May 1976, after another Arab–Israeli war, the Islamic states again complained of Israeli violations of the Geneva Conventions,[88] but Israel counter-complained that the Arabs were the main violators of humanitarian norms.[89] The Council approved a presidential statement which deplored Israeli measures to change the status of Jerusalem,[90] from which the United States dissociated itself on the ground that the statement lacked balance. At the Camp David meeting in 1978, President Carter reaffirmed the US view that unilateral action by Israel could not change the status of Jerusalem and that East Jerusalem was occupied territory and hence subject to the international law of belligerent occupation.[91]

Islamic and Communist complaints against Israel were voiced again in November 1976, followed by another presidential statement deploring Israeli

[84] SCOR 1483 (1969), para. 97.

[85] SCOR 1507 (1969), para. 55; SCOR 1512 (1969), paras. 111–12; SC Res.271 (1969), para. 4.

[86] SCOR 1579 (1971), paras. 28 and 82; SCOR 1651 (1972), para. 192.

[87] Ibid.

[88] SCOR 1916 (1976), paras. 30–2; SCOR 1917 (1976), paras. 58 and 139; SCOR 1918 (1976), para. 30; SCOR 1919 (1976), para. 101; 1920 (1976), para. 32; SCOR 1921 (1976), para. 29; SCOR 1922 (1976), paras. 112 and 121.

[89] SCOR 1917 (1976), para. 81.

[90] SCOR 1922 (1976), para. 1.

[91] SCOR 1922 (1976), para. 9; *Search for Peace in the Middle East: Documents and Statements, 1967–79*, report prepared by the Congressional Research Service for the US House of Representatives (1979), 27.

acts,[92] which led the United States to affirm that Israel had 'acted in good faith to protect and preserve the religious rights set forth in the Fourth Geneva Convention'.[93]

After the Camp David accords, the Security Council returned to the issue of the Geneva Conventions. The Commission on Human Rights had adopted a resolution on violations of human rights in the territories occupied by Israel.[94] Third World and Communist countries, this time with cautious British and French support, again alleged that Israel was in breach of the Geneva Conventions,[95] and there were calls for mandatory sanctions against Israel under Chapter VII of the Charter.[96] Israel denied that it was violating the Geneva Conventions, accused UN organs of using double standards, and alleged that Arabs were the foremost violators of humanitarian principles.[97] The Security Council again called on Israel 'to abide scrupulously' by the Fourth Geneva Convention (civilians).[98] The debate was repeated several times the following year,[99] and the Council now determined that Israel had committed 'a flagrant violation' of the Fourth Convention, which had given rise to 'deep concern'.[100]

In 1982, following Israel's second invasion of Lebanon, the Council again based its decision on the Geneva Conventions,[101] and this was repeated in 1984.[102] The Council called upon 'all involved' to allow the International Committee of the Red Cross in Lebanon to evacuate the wounded and provide humanitarian assistance.[103] The Council has frequently condemned attacks on non-combatants and called for humanitarian assistance for them.[104]

[92] SCOR 1966 (1976), paras. 26–8, 35–8, and 89; SCOR 1968 (1976), para. 5; SCOR 1969 (1976), paras. 14, 41, and 54.

[93] SCOR 1969 (1976), para. 44.

[94] S/13419–A/34/338 (1979).

[95] SCOR 2123 (1979), paras. 148 and 172; SCOR 2124 (1979), paras. 33 and 103; SCOR 2127 (1979), paras. 7, 23, 43, 72, and 125; SCOR 2128 (1979), paras. 20, 63–4, 74, and 151; SCOR 2131 (1979), paras. 150–1; SCOR 2134 (1979), paras. 8 and 54; SCOR 2125 (1979), 66 and 71.

[96] SCOR 2123 (1979), para. 70; SCOR 2124 (1979), paras. 12 and 100; SCOR 2128 (1979), para. 49.

[97] SCOR 2124 (1979), para. 130; SCOR 2128 (1979), paras. 122–6; SCOR 2131 (1979), paras. 120–6.

[98] SCOR 2125 (1979), 21, 314, and 47–8; SC Res.446 (1979), para. 3.

[99] SCOR 2199 (1980), para. 37; SCOR 2200 (1980), para. 99; SCOR 2219 (1980), para. 37; SCOR 2221 (1980), paras. 14 and 54; SCOR 2223 (1980), paras. 24, 33, and 60; SCOR 2226 (1980), paras. 12, 86, 98, and 153; SCOR 2233 (1980), para. 28; SCOR 2234 (1980), para. 52; SCOR 2238 (1980), para. 101; SCOR 2245 (1980), paras. 15, 20, and 40; SCOR 2259 (1980), para. 15; SCOR 2260 (1980), para. 49.

[100] SC Res.465 (1980), para. 5; SC Res.468 (1980), pream.; SC Res.469 (1980), pream.; SC Res.471 (1980), paras. 2 and 4; SC Res.476 (1980), para. 3; SC Res.478 (1980), para. 2; SC Res.484 (1980), para. 1.

[101] SC Res.512 (1982), pream.; SC Res.513 (1982), pream.; SC Res.515 (1982), pream.

[102] S/16293, (1984).

[103] SC Res.436 (1978), para. 2.

[104] SC Res.332 (1973), para. 1; SC Res.347 (1974), para. 2; SC Res.450 (1979), para. 1; SC

Since the 1967 war, there has been one veto by China and the Soviet Union of an amendment on the Middle East and one of a resolution by the Soviet Union on its own,[105] and twenty-five US vetoes, of which eleven included references to the Geneva Conventions. Eight of the US vetoes were cast between the opening of the *intifadah* and the end of 1987 and the beginning of 1990.[106]

V. IRAQ–IRAN

The war between Iraq and Iran, which started in 1980, was afflicted by an unusually large number of breaches of humanitarian norms: the use of chemical weapons, direct attacks on non-combatants, and ill-treatment of POWs.

The Iranian allegation that Iraq had used chemical weapons was investigated by a group of UN experts. Under the terms of a resolution of the General Assembly in 1982, the UN Secretary-General may seek the assistance of experts in order to investigate alleged uses of chemical or biological (bacteriological) weapons, including the on-site collection and examination of evidence.[107] In the case of the Gulf war investigation, Pérez de Cuellar did not cite the resolution of the General Assembly as the authority for his action. Instead he referred to 'the humanitarian principles embodied in the Charter' and 'the moral responsibilities' vested in the office of the Secretary-General as a basis for his action, which was undertaken with the concurrence of Iraq. The allegation by Iran that chemical weapons had been used was confirmed by the UN experts and this judgment was endorsed by the Security Council in 1985; and in the following year the Council noted that chemical weapons had been used by Iraq 'on many occasions'.[108] The Council repeatedly condemned the use of chemical weapons as contrary to the obligations of the Geneva Protocol of 1925.[109]

Another group of UN experts investigated allegations about attacks on non-combatants and concluded that, while all the allegations of Iraq and Iran could not be confirmed, both countries had made attacks which had caused

Res.471 (1980), para. 3; SC Res.512 (1982), para. 1; SC Res.513 (1982), para. 1; SC Res.521 (1982), paras. 1 and 2; SC Res.542 (1983), paras. 1 and 5; S/17215 (1985); SC Res.564 (1985), para. 3.

[105] 10 Sept. 1972 and 29 Feb. 1984.

[106] 10 Sept. 1972, 26 July 1973, 8 Dec. 1975, 26 Jan. 1976, 25 Mar. 1976, 29 June 1976, 30 Apr. 1980, 20 Jan. 1982, 2 Apr. 1982*, 20 Apr. 1982*, 8 June 1982, 6 Aug. 1982, 1 Aug. 1983*, 19 Feb. 1984, 6 Sept. 1984*, 12 Mar. 1985*, 6 Feb. 1986*, 18 Jan. 1988*, 9 June 1989*, 7 Nov. 1989* (asterisked dates included references to the Geneva Conventions).

[107] GA Res.37/98D (XXXVII) (1982), paras. 4–8.

[108] S/16433–A/39/210 (1984), 108–14; S/17127 and Add.1 (1985); SCOR 2576 (1985), 2–3; SCOR 2667 (1986).

[109] SCOR 2524 (1984), 2–7; SC Res.582 (1986), para. 2; SC Res.612 (1988), para. 2; SC Res.620 (1988), para. 1.

damage to civilian targets.[110] The Council condemned all violations of the Geneva Conventions and other provisions of international humanitarian law, and called for the cessation of attacks against civilians.[111]

When the International Committee of the Red Cross (ICRC) visits POWs or political prisoners, it reports its findings in confidence to the government concerned. Occasionally part of a report has been leaked to the media in such a way as to give an incomplete picture: in such circumstances, the ICRC has little alternative but to publish its report in full. With that exception, the ICRC does not publicize the difficulties it encounters nor its findings, unless (*a*) the breaches of international humanitarian law are major and repeated, (*b*) its delegates have witnessed the violation with their own eyes or the breaches have been established by reliable and verifiable sources, (*c*) confidential representations to the governments concerned have not succeeded, and (*d*) such publicity would be in the interest of the victims.[112] The ICRC published three documents on what it learned about the treatment of POWs in Iraq and Iran.

In some respects, the two States met their obligations under the Geneva Conventions, but the first public appeal of the ICRC in 1983 drew attention to grave and repeated breaches of international humanitarian law by both sides (summary executions of captured soldiers, abandoning of the wounded on the field of battle, and indiscriminate bombing of towns and villages) as well as to the obstacles the ICRC had encountered in exercising its mandate under the Geneva Conventions.[113] In February 1984, the ICRC issued a second memorandum making similar complaints. Later in 1984, in an unusual action, the President of the ICRC made a formal public statement about official allegations in Iran that the ICRC had been spying for Iraq, and reported that Iran had first obstructed and then suspended ICRC activities.[114]

This third public statement had followed an incident in a POW camp in Gorgan in Iran, and this caused Iraq to request a UN inquiry. Another group of experts was appointed by the UN Secretary-General. After a full investigation at POW camps, the UN experts concluded that both Iraq and Iran had failed to uphold the standards and policies which they professed.[115] The Secretary-General visited the two States in 1985 and appealed for the observance of recognized international humanitarian rules, an appeal which was later repeated by the EEC members.[116]

[110] S/15834 (1983), 112–22; S/16627 (1984); S/16750 (1984), 67–8; S/16897; S/16920 (1985), 14–16 and 28–9.

[111] SC Res.540 (1983), para. 2; S/17004 and S/17036 (1985); SC Res.582 (1986), para. 2; SC Res.588 (1986), para. 1; S/18538 (1986); S/18610 (1987); S/19626 (1988).

[112] *Action by the International Committee of the Red Cross in the Event of Breaches of International Humanitarian Law*, Geneva, ICRC (reprinted from the *International Review of the Red Cross* (1981), 6.

[113] ICRC *Annual Report for 1983* (1983), 56–7.

[114] Memoranda issued by the ICRC, 10 Feb. 1984 and 23 Nov. 1984.

[115] S/16962 (1985), 48–72.

[116] S/17097, S/17161–A/39/895 (1985), 21–2, 69–70.

C. *Military Intervention to Protect or Rescue Nationals*

Military intervention across recognized borders is often justified as being to protect or rescue nationals of the intervening State—what I have called the kith and kin argument.[117] This justification is seldom used on its own: it is usually added to other reasons, sometimes almost as an afterthought.

Thus, Liaquat Ali Khan, the Prime Minister of Pakistan, justified the help which Pakistani nationals were rendering to the Azad Kashmir movement in 1947 on the ground that this was only to be expected. 'As you know,' he wrote to Pandit Nehru, 'there are large numbers of Poonchis in the Pakistan Army and if some of them, while on leave in their homes, rendered assistance to their kith and kin in defense of their hearths and homes, it is scarcely to be wondered at.'[118] When Arab armies intervened in Palestine in 1948, this was explained in the Security Council as an attempt to protect brother-Arabs and enable them to exercise self-determination: 'The majority of the people of Palestine are asking help of their neighbors to suppress the rebellion of the armed minority.'[119]

The three States which planned the Suez invasion in 1956 tried to divert attention from their own misdeeds by complaining that Egypt was mistreating Jews and British and French nationals.[120] India's seizure of Goa in 1961 was defended on the ground that 'the people of Goa are as much Indians as the people of any other part of India.'[121] Turkey explained that its actions in Cyprus in 1964 were necessary because the Turkish-speaking Cypriot community was in need of military protection and humanitarian assistance.[122] Belgium, with British and US assistance support, sent military forces to Stanleyville in the Congo (Zaire) in 1964 in order to rescue Belgian and other hostages.[123] Among the arguments used in support of US intervention in the Dominican Republic in 1965 was 'to give protection to hundreds of Americans who are still in the Dominican Republic and to escort them safely back' to the United States.[124] The Turkish invasion of Cyprus in 1974 was defended as an attempt to protect Turkish Cypriots from genocide.[125]

[117] Bailey, *How Wars End: The United Nations and the Termination of Armed Conflict, 1946–1964* (1982), 106–7.

[118] Lakhanpal, *Essential Documents on the Kashmir Dispute* (1965), 90.

[119] SCOR 292 (1948), 10 and 17–20.

[120] GAOR, 11th Session, Annexes, Agenda item 66, 22–3, 30–1, 33, A/3399, A/3400 and Add.1, A/3444, A/3457; SCOR 629 (1956), paras. 115–18.

[121] SCOR 987 (1961), para. 60; SCOR 988 (1961), para. 77.

[122] GAOR, 19th year, Supplement for July to Sept. 1964, 144, 183–5, 339, 350–1, 367–70; S/5859; S/5897; S/5950/Add.2, para. 8, S/5961.

[123] SCOR 1173 (1964), para. 9; SCOR 1174 (1964), paras. 57–8; SCOR 1175 (1964), paras. 13–14.

[124] S/6310 (1965), 65–6; SCOR 1196 (1965), paras. 68 and 76; 11 *Dep. St. Bull.* 742–8 (1965).

[125] S/11341, S/11355, and S/11365 (1974), 26–7, 51–2, 56–7; SCOR 1782 (1974), paras. 25 and 28–9; SCOR 1786 (1974), para. 87; SCOR 1792 (1974), 48–51 and 56.

Indonesia intervened in and then annexed East Timor in 1975 to protect and provide humanitarian assistance to 'its brothers in East Timor'.[126] One reason for US intervention in Grenada was to rescue US nationals.[127]

While there has been no consistent pattern in the responses of the Security Council to the kith and kin argument, Council members have in general found this justification unconvincing and not a sufficient reason for sending armed forces across recognized frontiers, even in those cases where there was an authentic invitation to intervene.

D. *Supervising Elections and Plebiscites*

The United Nations has, from the beginning, been involved in the supervision of elections or other references to the will of the people, but usually under the auspices of subsidiary organs of the General Assembly or the Trusteeship Council, or (if the parties so request) by Representatives of the Secretary-General. The role of the Security Council in this respect has hitherto been sporadic and marginal. In two cases, the plebiscite or referendum called for by the Security Council has not yet taken place (Kashmir, Western Sahara); in one case, a subsidiary organ of the Council reported on but did not itself supervise the electoral process (Indonesia); in a fourth case, the Council confirmed a report prepared by the Good Offices Mission appointed by the Secretary-General (Bahrain); only in one recent case has the Security Council sponsored a thorough monitoring of an election (Namibia).

The Security Council called for a plebiscite in Kashmir in 1948 and Fleet Admiral Chester W. Nimitz was appointed Plebiscite Administrator but, as noted above, the plebiscite never took place.[128]

The Good Offices Committee in Indonesia, appointed by the Security Council, reported on, but did not itself supervise, elections in West Java and a plebiscite in Madura in 1948.[129]

In the case of Bahrain, Iran and Britain agreed that the UN Secretary-General should appoint a Good Offices Mission to ascertain the wishes of the people about the future of the territory. The Mission was headed by Vittorio Winspeare Giucciardi, and it found that 'the overwhelming majority of the people of Bahrain' favoured 'a fully independent and sovereign state', and this conclusion was endorsed by the Security Council.[130]

The Security Council decided in 1988 in the case of Western Sahara to

[126] SCOR 1864 (1975), para. 82; SCOR 1868 (1975), paras. 8–9; S/11986 (1975).
[127] S/16076 (1983), 37–8; SCOR 2487 (1983), 93–5; SCOR 2491 (1983), 37 and 96; USIS, London, press releases, 7 Nov. 1983, 5 and 16 Nov. 1983, 5 (speeches of Kenneth Dam).
[128] SC Res.47 (1948) and SC Res.80 (1950).
[129] S/729 and S/786 (1948), 11–41.
[130] S/9772 (1970), 166–70; SC Res.278 (1970).

ask the UN Secretary-General to prepare a report 'on the holding of a referendum for self-determination'. A technical committee to work out the details of implementation met in July 1989, but Pérez de Cuellar reported two months later that a number of sensitive issues remained unresolved.[131]

In Namibia, a thorough UN supervision of elections was undertaken in November 1989. There was a very high turn-out of voters, and Marti Ahtisaari, the Special Representative of the Secretary-General, reported that the electoral process had 'at every stage, been free and fair'.[132]

E. *Improving the Procedure of the Council?*

It is difficult to review the Security Council's role regarding human rights apart from the general question of whether it is possible to improve the Council's practice and procedure. The question of increasing the size of the Council has been before the General Assembly since 1979 but has received only perfunctory attention. In any case, those who have advocated enlargement have done so in order to produce greater equity in representation rather than greater effectiveness in the Council's operations.

There have been a good many suggestions for improving effectiveness without amending the Charter. I review some of these below in the numerical order of the Articles of the Charter. While few of the suggestions for reform would require formal amendment to the Charter, most would involve a more flexible, more imaginative, or more far-sighted application of particular provisions.

I. THE VETO (ARTICLE 27(3))

While some scholars and diplomats complain that the right of the five permanent members of the Security Council to veto substantive decisions is a discriminatory provision of the Charter (which it is), I believe that it is easy to exaggerate the harm that it causes.[133] Moreover, I know of no evidence that any of the five permanent members is at present willing to give up the right of veto. The question remains, nevertheless, whether any or all of the permanent members would give up the veto on certain classes of decisions, such as substantive decisions about UN fact-finding. Personally, as a British citizen, I would be glad to see the United Kingdom give up the right to veto UN investigation or fact-finding in the United Kingdom or territories for which the United Kingdom is responsible.

131 SC Res.621 (1988).
132 S/20905 (1989), S/20906 (1989), and S/20967 (1989).
133 Bailey, *Voting in the Security Council* (1969), 18–62; and id., *How Wars End*, 205–18.

II. PERIODIC MEETINGS (ARTICLE 28(2))

The Charter provides for the holding of periodic meetings of the Council at a high ministerial level, and the Rules of Procedure provide that such meetings shall take place twice a year (Rule 4). Only one such meeting has in fact been held, in 1970, on the initiative of Finland.[134] My own conclusions about the frustrating character of the 1970 meeting were as follows:

> The lesson of the 1970 experience is not that the United Nations fails to provide a suitable framework for summit diplomacy. It is, first, that the need for summit diplomacy cannot easily be predicted; second, that the participation should be determined by the issues at stake . . . and third, that summit diplomacy cannot succeed without adequate preparation.[135]

III. SUBSIDIARY ORGANS (ARTICLE 29)

This Article simply provides that the Council may establish such subsidiary organs as it deems necessary. One idea in this connection is that the Council should ask its president, or a special rapporteur, or a select committee, to monitor each developing crisis and draw the Council's attention to the matter if action by the Council should be indicated.[136] I believe that more could be done to monitor disputes or potential disputes before they reach crisis stage, but I am not convinced that the suggested procedure would be more effective than those referred to under Article 99 below. Secretary-General Pérez de Cuellar suggested that the Council could devise 'more swift and responsive procedures' for sending missions, observers, or a UN presence to areas of conflict.[137] A similar proposal was also formulated by the Palme Commission.[138]

IV. REVISING THE PROVISIONAL RULES OF PROCEDURE (ARTICLE 30)

Yes, the Council's Rule of Procedure are still 'Provisional' after more than forty years; but it is the temporary things that last. The Charter empowers the Council to adopt its own Rules of Procedure. In my study of the procedure and practice of the Council, I drew attention to a good many instances in which the Council has never, or does not now, follow the letter of the Rules.[139] If ever the Council should decide to embark on a major review of

[134] Id., *Procedure of the UN Security Council* (1975), 34–9.
[135] Ibid. 39–40.
[136] Sohn, 'The Security Council's Role in the Settlement of International Disputes' 78 *Am. J. Int'l L.* 402 (1984).
[137] A/37/1, 3; A/42/1, 4; A/44/1, 11–12.
[138] Palme Commission, *Common Security* (1982), 163.
[139] Bailey, *Procedure of the UN Security Council*, 335–53.

procedure, these matters ought to receive attention, but I doubt whether this is a matter of great importance or urgency.

Under Rule 11, the Secretary-General is required to circulate each week a summary statement of matters of which the Security Council is seized and of the stage reached in their consideration. The Secretary-General now circulates a full list at the beginning of each year, and a weekly addendum. On 15 June 1989, the Council was seized of 150 items as follows:

inscribed 1946–55	22 items
inscribed 1956–65	32 items
inscribed 1966–75	26 items
inscribed 1976–84	52 items
inscribed 1986 to 15 June 1989	18 items

It surely would be possible to prune some of the items which have been before the Council for more than twenty-five years and which will never receive serious attention in the future (e.g. the Czechoslovak question, Hyderabad, Berlin, Egyptian assistance to Algerian nationalists, and the Congo). If these or related issues should arise again, the items could easily be re-inscribed. Some items might be combined, such as the fourteen Nicaraguan complaints against the United States since 1982.

The then Secretary-General Pérez de Cuellar noted a reluctance to bring issues to the Council's attention:

> Unfortunately there has been a tendency to avoid bringing critical problems to the Security Council, or to do so too late for the Council to have serious influence on their development. It is essential to reverse this trend if the Council is to play its role as the primary world authority for international peace and security. I do not believe that it is necessarily wise or responsible of the Council to leave such matters to the judgment of the conflicting parties to the point where the Council's irrelevance to some ongoing wars becomes a matter of comment by world public opinion.[140]

It is to meet this problem that Louis Sohn has suggested that the president for the month should report to the Council at the end of his term of office, summarizing the Council's actions during the month regarding disputes and like situations 'and appraising the threat involved in some of the disputes and situations called to his attention'; and that Rules 6 and 7 regarding the circulation of communications and the drawing up of the provisional agenda should be amended accordingly.[141] I am in no way opposed to the amendments suggested by Sohn, though I am not convinced that the changes would make a significant difference. The thrust of Sohn's suggestion could, indeed, be implemented under the existing Rules of Procedure should any presidents of the Council so wish.

[140] A/37/1, 2.
[141] Sohn, 'The Security Council's Role', 403.

The Rules provide that the Council shall meet in public unless it decides otherwise (Rule 48), when the occasion is technically known as 'a private meeting' (Rules 48, 51, 55, 56). There are no express provisions in the Rules for informal consultations: indeed, there was one famous occasion in 1973 when members of the Council knew that the meeting they were taking part in was closed to the public, but they could not agree on whether it was a private meeting, a consultative meeting, an informal discussion, or an informal consultation.[142]

During the past two decades, there has been a steady increase in the practice of holding private and informal consultations and meetings, and there have been some expressions of unease lest the practice should undermine the authority and capacity of the Council. Secretary-General Pérez de Cuellar referred to the risk 'that this process may become a substitute for action . . . or even an excuse for inaction'.[143] The risk is undoubtedly there, but it must be balanced against the contrary risk that public debate, usually involving the parties and often non-members of the Council as well, could exacerbate an already tense situation.

V. PEACEFUL SETTLEMENT OF DISPUTES (ARTICLE 33)

The Charter lists a variety of techniques for the peaceful settlement of disputes, but from time to time there are suggestions that the UN machinery for peaceful settlement is inadequate. This concern led to the setting up of a Panel for Inquiry and Conciliation in 1949 and the Panel of experts for fact-finding in 1967.[144] So far as I know, neither Panel has been used, although a person who happened to be on the first Panel was appointed mediator for the Kashmir dispute in 1951.[145] The two persons nominated by the British government to serve on the first Panel would, if they were still alive, have celebrated their 104th and 105th birthdays in 1990.[146]

A study on fact-finding was initiated by the General Assembly in 1963, leading in 1967 to the request to the Secretary-General to prepare a register of legal and other experts to engage in fact-finding at the request of parties to a dispute. The Secretary-General duly prepared the register, and subsequently issued a supplementary list, but I know of no formal resort to it.[147]

[142] Bailey, *Procedure of the UN Security Council*, 42.
[143] A/37/1, 2.
[144] GA Res.268D (III) (1949); GA Res.2329 (XII) (1967).
[145] Bailey, *How Wars End*, 166–7.
[146] S/1933, (1950); S/3398 (1955); S/3398/Add.1, 4 (1955); S/3929–A/3803, (1957); S/4199–A/4168, (1959); S/4632–A/4686, (1961).
[147] GA Res.1967(XVIII) (1963); A/5694; GA Res.2329(XXII) (1967); A/7751 (1969); A/8108 (1970).

Attention has recently been given to the possible use by the UN Secretariat of 'technical information-gathering capabilities'.[148]

In 1965–6, in response to a British initiative, the UN General Assembly gave perfunctory attention to the peaceful settlement of disputes.[149] The matter was raised again by Romania in 1979,[150] and has been before the General Assembly since then. Discussion has mainly revolved around three ideas: the approval by the General Assembly of a declaration on the peaceful settlement of disputes (the Manila Declaration); the preparation of a handbook on peaceful settlement (proposed by France); and the establishment of a permanent commission on good offices, mediation, and conciliation to prevent interstate conflict and settle disputes peacefully (proposed by Nigeria, the Philippines, and Romania).[151] The General Assembly regularly asks that work on these issues should continue, in the context of a possible review of the Charter.[152]

VI. INTERNATIONAL COURT OF JUSTICE (ARTICLES 33(1) AND 36(3))

The Charter provides that legal disputes should 'as a general rule' be referred by the parties to the International Court of Justice, and 'judicial settlement' is one of the means of peaceful settlement listed in the Charter. The reference of a dispute to the International Court of Justice was recommended by the Council once, in the Corfu Channel case in 1947,[153] but the Council usually finds it difficult to disentangle the legal from the political aspects of a dispute. In 1989, the UN Secretary-General announced the setting up of a trust fund to help countries lacking legal expertise or funds to make use of the International Court of Justice.[154]

The concept of judicial settlement of disputes has undoubtedly been damaged by the decision of the United States in 1985 that the Court was 'without jurisdiction' to entertain its dispute with Nicaragua and by subsequently vetoing two draft resolutions in the Security Council calling for full compliance with the Court's judgment of 27 June 1986.[155]

[148] S/15971 (1983), para. 13.
[149] GAOR, 20th Session, Annexes, Agenda item 99; 21st Session, Annexes, Agenda item 36.
[150] A/34/143 (1979).
[151] A/36/33, para. 87; GA Res.37/10 (1982), Annex; A/38/343 (1983).
[152] GA Res.39/79 (1984); GA Res.40/68 (1985); GA Res.41/74 (1986); GA Res.42/150 (1987); GA Res.43/163 (1988).
[153] SC Res.22 (1947).
[154] A/44/1, 13.
[155] 31 July and 28 Oct. 1988.

VII. IMPLEMENTATION OF DECISIONS (ARTICLES 33–42)

The Charter establishes procedures for the pacific settlement of disputes or similar situations, and also specifies measures that the Council may employ in situations of special danger. Pérez de Cuellar has referred to the tendency for governments 'to act as though the passage of a resolution absolved them from further responsibility . . .'. A UN resolution should, he suggests, 'serve as a springboard for governmental support and determination and should motivate their policies outside the United Nations':

> Very often the Secretary-General is allotted the function of following up on the implementation of a resolution. Without the continuing diplomatic and other support of Member States, the Secretary-General's efforts often have less chance of bearing full fruit. Concerted diplomatic action is an essential complement to the implementation of resolutions. I believe that in reviewing one of the greatest problems of the United Nations—lack of respect for its decisions by those to whom they are addressed—new ways should be considered of bringing to bear the collective influence of the membership on the problem at hand.[156]

The Secretary-General returned to the problem in following years. Resolutions were too often passed as 'the substitute for action, and indeed the antithesis of it'. Decisions should be 'the beginning, not the end, of governmental concern and action'. Efforts to secure the implementation of UN decisions should be 'an integral part of the foreign policy' of UN Members.[157]

In some cases, the Council has established a special subsidiary organ to examine reports on implementation of decisions and to study ways and means by which UN Members could carry out such decisions.[158]

VIII. INDIVIDUAL OR COLLECTIVE SELF-DEFENCE (ARTICLE 51)

Article 51 of the Charter provides that the Charter does not impair the inherent right of individual or collective self-defence 'if an armed attack occurs' and 'until the Security Council has taken measures necessary to maintain international peace and security', such measures being immediately reported to the Security Council and not affecting the Council's authority and responsibility. UN Members have often cited Article 51 in justification of military action—both Libya and the United States did so in March–April

[156] A/37/1, 3.

[157] A/38/1, 2; A/39/1, 2; see also S/16760 (1984), para. 9.

[158] This was the mandate of the committee concerned with sanctions against Southern Rhodesia: SC Res.277 (1970), para. 21.

1986—but there has been an unfortunate tendency to slide over the fact that Article 51 applies only if there has been an armed attack, and to disregard the obligation to inform the Council of action taken under this Article.[159]

IX. REGIONAL AGENCIES (ARTICLES 52–54)

These articles deal with the relationship of regional agencies to the United Nations and the obligation of such agencies to report to the Security Council on activities in contemplation or undertaken to maintain peace and security. The Security Council is to encourage the development of pacific settlement of 'local disputes' through such agencies. It has been suggested that the Council has been reluctant to entrust peacemaking activities to some regional agencies, and that regional agencies have often failed to report to the Council on activities undertaken or in contemplation.[160]

X. INITIATIVES BY THE SECRETARY-GENERAL (ARTICLE 99)

All the Secretaries-General have emphasized the great importance of Article 99, which authorizes the Secretary-General to draw the Council's attention to 'any matter which in his opinion may threaten the maintenance of international peace and security'.[161] Under the implicit responsibilities of Article 99, Secretaries-General have appointed staff, authorized research, made visits, and engaged in diplomatic consultations. In his first annual report, Secretary-General Pérez de Cuellar suggested that he might play 'a more forthright role' in bringing potentially dangerous situations to the attention of the Council, and he therefore intended to develop 'a wider and more systematic capacity for fact-finding in potential conflict areas'. Such efforts, he wrote, would be undertaken in close co-ordination with the Council. The dispatch of UN missions could inhibit the deterioration of conflict situations and might also be of real assistance to the parties in resolving incipient disputes by peaceful means.[162] The Palme Commission also proposed a more systematic use of the possibilities inherent in Article 99.[163]

I have suggested elsewhere that the United Nations could improve its early warning capability:

> If the UN is to improve its early-warning capability for dealing with threatening situations, the need is not for more staff at Headquarters in New York, but for

[159] Bailey, *Procedure of the UN Security Council*, 357–8.
[160] Ibid.
[161] Ibid. 75–8 and 358–9.
[162] A/37/1, 3.
[163] Palme Commission, *Common Security* (1982).

politically sensitive and alert men and women in the field, reporting directly to the Office of the Secretary-General on matters which might threaten international peace and security. These people should have freedom to travel within the region and to keep in touch with those developments which might justify the Secretary-General in using his power to convene the Security Council if it is his opinion that world peace is threatened.[164]

It will be apparent from the above that I do not advocate major changes in the way the Council operates. The set-backs it has suffered and the difficulties it now encounters are not primarily due to defects or gaps in the Charter or the Rules but to the fact that States assess their interests in too narrow and short-term a perspective:

It is easy to criticize the United Nations, for it has undoubted faults; and perhaps those of us who believe in the need for the organization and are close to it are more aware of the faults than the more raucous critics. The League of Nations eventually collapsed, not because of defects in the Covenant, but because the major Powers failed to meet their international obligations. If the United Nations does not prove to be an effective instrument for peace and progress over the next 40 years, the main responsibility will be on those Member States in all regions which failed to see that their long-term interests lay in a respected and effective instrument for international consultation and action.[165]

Conclusion: The Security Council's Handling of Issues of Human Rights

It is, perhaps, surprising that the Security Council has not taken human rights more seriously. Dag Hammarskjöld, a most creative Secretary-General, was so satiated by excessive diplomatic rhetoric about human rights that he banished the human rights section of the UN Secretariat to Geneva. Indeed, the index to the standard biography of Hammarskjöld contains no entry under human rights.[166] Yet an analysis of all wars between 1945 and 1964 showed that the most frequent cause of armed conflict during that period was the allegation that human rights were being denied.[167] There is no reason to think that the incidence of wars about human rights has significantly declined in the past twenty years. My own view is that any multiple strategy for the prevention of war must include work for the protection of basic rights.

The Security Council's handling of human rights issues has necessarily been haphazard because it is normally involved only when peace is endangered or armed conflict is actually taking place or has just ended. Moreover, there is

[164] Bailey, 'The Next Forty Years', 8 *Disarmament* 18 (1985).
[165] Bailey, *The United Nations — Still Humanity's Best Hope* (1986), 63.
[166] Urquhart, *Hammarskjöld* (1972).
[167] Bailey, *How Wars End*, 10; 'The United Nations and the Termination of Armed Conflict 1946–1964', 58 *Int'l Aff.* 470 (1982).

some basis in the Israeli complaint about double standards.[168] There have been appalling infractions of human rights in parts of Latin America, to cite only one region, which have not been dealt with by the Security Council, but Latin American delegates have not been inhibited in their criticism of South Africa and Israel for failing to respect international human rights standards.

The Security Council, with its primary responsibility for the maintenance of international peace and security, and being the one UN organ with the power to make decisions binding on all UN Members, has naturally been concerned with the means of enforcing its decisions. But when the Council is dealing with issues of human rights, it tends to combine appeals to do better in the future with denunciation of past failures. The Council should not, of course, depart from the high standards of the Charter and other international instruments concerned with human rights, but need it always be so censorious? One of the early Quakers wrote that

> [t]hey have a right to censure that have a heart to help. The rest is cruelty, not justice.[169]

States which find themselves on the receiving end of the Security Council's rebukes are bound to look at the domestic records of the States which voted for the Council's strictures. Jews in Israel and whites in Southern Africa have become increasingly impervious to UN advice and criticism, and even many moderates among them view the Organization with some contempt. Denunciatory debates and reproving resolutions can become counter-productive if carried to excess.

If the Council is so outraged that it imposes coercive sanctions against a State or regime, as in the case of Southern Rhodesia from 1966 to 1980, it might be useful for it to indicate what the offending State or regime must do to be relieved of the sanctions. The Council was unanimous in 1969 in describing a referendum in Southern Rhodesia as illegal and the constitutional proposals of the Smith regime as invalid, and a decade later, the Council voted that the results of so-called elections in Southern Rhodesia were null and void.[170] If the testings of public opinion by the illegal regime in Southern Rhodesia were invalid, this was because their conduct was fraudulent, not because the results happened to be displeasing to a majority of States on the Security Council.

The Council has been hampered in dealing with human rights issues because it has almost always lacked effective means to verify implementation. In four out of the five cases of subsidiary organs of the Council relating to

[168] Franck, 'Of Gnats and Camels: Is there a Double Standard at the United Nations?', 78 *Am. J. Int'l L.* 811–33 (1984); letter from Theo van Boven, 79 *Am. J. Int'l L.* 714–17 (1985).

[169] Penn, *Some Fruits of Solitude* (1963).

[170] SCOR 1477 (1969), para. 4; SC Res.445 (1979), paras. 5–7; SC Res.448 (1979), paras. 1–2.

Southern Africa, their task was not to verify whether human rights were being respected, but to encourage and supervise means of pressure against racist regimes: the one exception was the 1964 group of experts on apartheid, whose report dealt with internal and international dangers from the intensification of apartheid, the growing tide of condemnation, and the case for a multiracial national convention.[171] In the Middle East, the mandate of the special representative of the Secretary-General appointed in 1967 was to exercise good offices.[172] The main task of the other subsidiary organ on the Middle East (the commission on Arab territories occupied by Israel) was fact-finding.[173] The commission visited the Middle East for discussions with officials and for hearings, but the main emphasis of the report was on how the establishment of new Israeli settlements was affecting the Palestinians. One witness before the commission claimed that the annexation of East Jerusalem and Israeli practices in the occupied territories contravened the Geneva Conventions, a view which the commission itself shared.[174]

Even though the Council has not itself instituted procedures for verifying the appeals contained in its decisions regarding human rights in Southern Africa and the Middle East, it has at least been able to act in the knowledge that the Commission on Human Rights and other UN organs were actively involved.

What can be said of the remaining cases? Korea was unique in two senses: that an agency established by the Security Council, the Unified Command, was itself a party to the conflict; and that when it came to the disposition of POWs, there was a conflict between a humanitarian principle (no coercion against protected persons) and the actual text of the Third Geneva Convention (the right of POWs to be repatriated after the termination of hostilities). The outcome of the tortuous negotiations at Panmunjom involved the Neutral Nations Repatriation Commission and the Indian Custodial Force, but the issue was by then outside the jurisdiction of the Security Council. In the kith and kin cases, members of the Council were generally unimpressed with this justification for military intervention.

All the Secretaries-General have stressed their competence to deal with human rights, even without express authority from a policy-making organ.[175] Trygve Lie, the first Secretary-General, took up the case of missing Greek children in private discussions with East European governments, and his ten-point plan for peace included a strengthening of the work of the United

[171] SC Res.182 (1963), para. 6; SC Res.191 (1964), para. 8; SC Res.421 (1977), para. 1; SC Res.253 (1968), para. 20 (Southern Rhodesia); SC Res.276 (1970), para. 6 (Namibia).
[172] SC Res.242 (1967), para. 3.
[173] SC Res.446 (1979), para. 4.
[174] S/13450 and Add.1 (1979), 30 and 32.
[175] Ramcharan, *Humanitarian Good Offices in International Law*, 52–74.

Nations for human rights.[176] In spite of his exasperation with diplomatic oratory about human rights, Dag Hammarskjöld took up with China the question of imprisoned US fliers and with South Africa the situation after the Sharpeville massacre, in the first case at the request of the General Assembly, in the second under the authority of the Security Council.[177] In the case of the imprisoned fliers, Hammarskjöld no doubt cited the Third Geneva Convention. U Thant also took several initiatives on human rights and humanitarian issues. In an important speech just before his retirement, he maintained that the Secretary-General must always be prepared to take an initative 'whatever the consequences to his office or to him personally . . .'. But this could only be justified if the Secretary-General were truly independent, with freedom to act without fear or favour. Thant said that he had done what he could about violations of human rights within the frontiers of a State, 'knowing full well the weakness of [his] own position'. The time had come when governments should give justice a world-wide dimension.[178] Kurt Waldheim insisted that his concern for the protection of innocent civilian lives took precedence over the prohibition in the UN Charter on intervening in domestic affairs.[179]

Pérez de Cuellar wrote even more vigorously than his predecessors. In his first annual report, he stated that the human rights specified in the Charter, 'and made all the more imperative by the current state of world affairs', would in future have high priority: '[h]uman rights and peace are inextricably linked'. A year later, he reported that he had taken up a number of individual cases with governments, and was determined to persist in his efforts. In 1984, he noted that the work of the United Nations in this field had encountered constant and trenchant criticism:

> I welcome such criticism in the hope that it will spur everyone, including the critics, on to a more serious assessment of the importance—and the difficulty—of reducing injustice in an unjust world, of promoting development in a world divided between rich and poor, and of instilling the virtures of mercy and compassion into people many of whom are fighting—or believe they are fighting—for their lives.

In a vivid and much-quoted passage, Pérez de Cuellar continued:

176 Lie, *In the Cause of Peace* (1954), 235, 242–3, 245, 281, 289–90, and 304–5.

177 GA Res.906 (IX) (1954); SC Res.134 (1960). Urquhart, *Hammarskjöld*, 96–131 and 494–5.

178 'The Role of the Secretary-General', 8 *UN Chronicle* 186–7 (Oct. 1971); A/8401/Add.1, para. 147; U Thant, *View from the UN* (1978), 351–2; Ramcharan, *Humanitarian Good Offices in International Law*, 62–3; Pechota, *The Quiet Approach: A Study of the Good Offices Exercised by the United Nations Secretary-General in the Cause of Peace* (1972), 49–50.

179 A/8701/Add.1, 4; A/9001/Add.1, 5; A/9601/Add.1, 6–7; A/31/1, 9; A/32/1, 6–7; A/33/1, 7; A/34/1, 7–8; A/35/1, 7–8; 36/1/1, 8–9.

I spend much of my time, sometimes with encouraging results, on human rights and humanitarian problems, which I regard as uniquely important. Despite the existence of definitive norms developed within the United Nations, perceptions differ greatly. One person's freedom fighter is another person's terrorist; one's champion of human rights is another's subversive; one's plaintiff is another's criminal. The reality is that many are dispossessed, many confined, many tortured and many starve. This is the world we have to deal with.

Pérez de Cuellar wrote that he was concerned to help individuals whose human rights had been violated:

In particular, I seek to facilitate the release of those who may have been imprisoned or sentenced for political reasons. The criteria for judging such efforts must be whether they advance the cause of human rights and not whether they serve the political interest of one side or another.[180]

Pérez de Cuellar returned to the issue once again in 1987:

I seek, in my capacity as Secretary-General, continually to promote such respect [for human rights] and to ensure that the Secretariat carries out its important responsibilities in this area with full effectiveness.

He added a warm tribute to the 'dedicated, energetic efforts of non-governmental organizations'.[181]

What the Secretaries-General have written, said, and done accords with resolutions of the General Assembly, the Commission on Human Rights, and the Sub-Commission on the Prevention of Discrimination and Protection of Minorities.[182]

In the India–Pakistan–Bangladesh case, the Secretary-General established a UN presence to report on compliance with humanitarian norms, in accordance with an express authorization by the Security Council.[183] In the Iraq–Iran case, the investigations into alleged attacks on civilian targets were organized by the Secretary-General with the concurrence of the parties and the knowledge of the members of the Security Council. The investigation into alleged ill-treatment of POWs, which partly overlapped with the responsibilities of the International Committee of the Red Cross, was described by the Secretary-General as 'an extraordinary measure' and undertaken by Pérez de Cuellar 'in the light of his humanitarian responsibility under the Charter . . .'. In the case of alleged uses of chemical weapons, the Secretary-General followed a procedure laid down by the General Assembly in 1982, though

[180] A/37/1, 2; press release SG/SM/3353, 26 Oct. 1982; A/38/1, 3; A/39/1, 2, 4–5.
[181] A/42/1, 6.
[182] GA Res.175 (XXXIV) (1979), para. 5; CHR Res.27 (XXXVI) (1980), para. 1; Sub-Commission Res.25 (XXXIII) (1980), para. 5.
[183] SC Res.307 (1971), para. 5; S/10473 (1971), 123–4.

without citing it.[184] In no case did the Security Council expressly authorize the Secretary-General to engage in fact-finding, but the reports submitted to the Council via the Secretary-General were regarded as objective and impartial—though violations and alleged violations continued.

This reliance on the Secretary-General to act, either with the express authority of the Council or under a broad interpretation of his Charter responsibilities, may well continue to be a useful way of proceeding in the future, so long as the Council does not transfer to the Secretary-General its own primary responsibility for world peace.

In the Hammarskjöld era, the Secretary-General welcomed not only the broad interpretation of the responsibilities of the office, on which all Secretaries-General have insisted, but the practice by which UN policy-making organs defined goals but left it to the Secretary-General to secure their implementation by quiet diplomacy. For the Security Council's handling of human rights, this may in many cases continue to be a responsible course.

[184] S/15834 (1983), 113; S/16433–A/39/210 (1984), 108–14; S/16962 (1985), 48–72; S/17127 and Add.1 (1985), 48–9; S/16627; GA Res.37/98D (1982).

II
Organs Monitoring Treaty Compliance

9

The Committee on the Elimination of Racial Discrimination

KARL JOSEF PARTSCH

A. *Origins*

The Committee on the Elimination of Racial Discrimination (CERD) has the task of supervising States Parties implementation of the International Convention on the Elimination of All Forms of Racial Discrimination (the Convention).[1] The General Assembly, largely in response to Third World pressure against the South African policy of apartheid, adopted the Convention on 21 December 1965.[2] The Assembly adopted the two International Human Rights Covenants just one year later, although this proximity was not necessarily foreseen at the time of the adoption of the Convention. Of the twenty-seven States which had ratified the Convention at the time of its entry into force on 4 January 1969 (more than seven years before the Covenants became operative) nineteen were from the Third World, with five from Eastern Europe, and three from Western Europe.

B. *Composition*

Article 8 (1) of the Convention states that the Committee shall consist of

> eighteen experts of high moral standing and acknowledged impartiality elected by States Parties from among their nationals, who shall serve in their personal capacity, consideration being given to equitable geographical distribution and to the representation of the different forms of civilization as well as of the principal legal systems.

Each of the members of the Committee has to declare before his colleagues 'that I will perform my duties and exercise my powers . . . honourably, faithfully, impartially, and conscientiously'.[3] This declaration is the same as that

[1] 660 UNTS 195.

[2] A detailed account of the drafting history of the Convention is contained in Schwelb, 'The International Convention on the Elimination of all Forms of Racial Discrimination', 15 *Int'l & Comp. LQ* 996 (1966).

[3] Rule 14, Rules of Procedure, CERD/C/35/Rev.3 (1986). Between 1970 and 1984 the Committee worked on the basis of 'Provisional Rules of Procedure'. The definitive rules, which now apply, introduced headings, added a table of contents, and reordered the Rules from Rule 35 onwards.

required of the judges of the International Court of Justice (ICJ), but an examination of the two bodies' membership reveals that CERD is quite different from a court. As with the Judges of the ICJ the members of CERD are elected by a majority in a secret ballot conducted by a political body. Beyond those similarities, however, the two procedures differ significantly. In contrast to the approach used for the ICJ, in the case of CERD: (*a*) no judicial body is involved in the selection of candidates and no particular procedure is prescribed. Thus, for example, the choice may even be made by the State's Permanent Representative to the United Nations, and he may opt to nominate himself; (*b*) the candidate must be a national of the nominating State; (*c*) only one person may be nominated by a State Party; and (*d*) only one organ, the meeting of States Parties, elects the members. The preferences of States' Permanent Representatives to the United Nations, who for the most part constitute the meeting of States Parties, may be a significant factor in determining the outcome of the elections.

The rules regarding qualifications differ considerably between the two bodies. Though CERD's members are to be of 'high moral standing' and 'acknowledged impartiality', the Convention, unlike the statute of the ICJ, makes no mention of specific professional qualifications.

CERD members are to represent not only 'the different forms of civilization', but also 'the principal legal systems'; this wording indicates that legal knowledge, but not necessarily legal experience, is desirable. In fact, only about half of the Committee members to date have had a legal background; the majority have been diplomats who may have been chosen more on the basis of their rank than of their professional qualifications.

The impartiality and independence of the Judges of the ICJ is secured by the Statute's strict provision against conflicts-of-interest with other professional activities, but the Convention includes no such protections. Because a Committee member serves on a part-time, honorary basis, usually he must simultaneously maintain a separate profession. Only rarely do these dual roles create conflicts; judges, university professors, retired diplomats, or diplomats dealing only with bilateral relations are unlikely to receive directives from their authorities with respect to their work on the Committee. However, for a minority of members, primarily those belonging to the permanent missions of States Parties at New York or Geneva, such conflicts can be significant. They may find themselves in the awkward position of having to disregard their superiors' directives while at the Committee table. Clearly, it is incompatible with the Member's solemn oath of impartiality if his attitude is dictated by a member of his country's permanent mission. Nevertheless, it seems that not all States Parties attach the same importance to these proprieties.

On several occasions the Committee has had to defend its character as an independent expert body. Thus it has refused two proposals that members unable to attend Committee sessions be allowed to send alternates and it has refused to recognize a State Party's notification that a member has resigned: Committee members elected in their personal capacity must also personally submit their resignations.[4] Furthermore, each member is solely responsible for his own remarks—his committee contributions may not be attributed to his respective State.

In some cases, a Committee member may lose the confidence of his government; either because of the positions he has taken or as a result of a change of government. In either case, the next elections for the Committee permit the government involved to present a new candidate, whose election will depend both on the States Parties' attitudes and on the question of geographical distribution since the principle of 'equitable geographical distribution'[5] may at that point facilitate the election of another candidate either from within the same region or from another one. In addition, some regional groups (notably the Eastern Europeans) show great discipline in rotating the members drawn from that region.

The principle of fair geographic distribution not only applies to the election of members, but also to the composition of the Bureau (a Chairman, three Vice-Chairmen, and a Rapporteur). Concern that rotation of the Bureau's membership may have an adverse impact in terms of lack of continuity was evidently discounted when the rules of procedure were drawn up. The Chairman is selected in accordance with the following regional sequence (established at an early stage to reflect the number of ratifications from each region): Asia, Latin America, Africa, Western Europe, and Eastern Europe. The only exception was made in 1978 in order to ensure an African Chairman to coincide with the 1978 World Conference to Combat Racism. The Rapporteurship, however, has not been rotated on such a regular basis.

It is apparent therefore that the Committee's composition and structure, and the status of its members all count against its being defined as a court. For the same reasons, calling it a 'quasi-judicial body' is less accurate than referring to it simply as a 'treaty organ'.

C. *States Parties Obligations*[6]

Unlike both Covenants, the Convention emphasizes the duties of States Parties rather than the rights of individuals. The Committee's task is to ensure the implementation of these duties by seeing that the requisite internal measures are taken. Generally speaking, the Convention describes the following main duties:

[4] Ibid. Rule 13(3).

[5] Convention, Art. 8(1).

[6] See generally Meron, 'The Meaning and Reach of the International Convention on the Elimination of all Forms of Racial Discrimination', 79 *Am. J. Int'l L.* 283 (1985).

Article 1 provides a very broad definition of 'racial discrimination' which covers distinction based on colour, descent, or national or ethnic origin'. The article then goes on to detail the Convention's applicability with respect to citizenship and nationality, and to authorize 'special measures' for the 'adequate advancement of certain racial or ethnic groups or individuals' requiring them.

Article 2 specifies the Convention's goals, without always indicating how these goals are to be achieved.

Article 3 which provides that 'States Parties particularly condemn racial segregation and apartheid and undertake to prevent, prohibit, and eradicate all practices of this nature in territories under their jurisdiction', is one of the Convention's few self-executing provisions. Interpreting its reference to 'territories under their jurisdiction' has proved to be quite a controversial undertaking.

Article 4 details the States Parties' duty to penalize certain forms of racial discrimination. Committee dialogue has frequently focused on this obligation, and the Committee has performed its monitoring function most successfully in this area. Thus, for example, over half of the States Parties have adopted new, relevant legislation.

Article 5 lists the human rights to be guaranteed without discrimination. Since almost all the rights are also to be found in the the two Convenants, it is not always easy to define the respective jurisdictional competence of the three different supervisory organs.

Article 6 assures effective remedies and serves as a basis for discussion of the judicial systems of States Parties.

Article 7 requires promotional measures in the fields of teaching, education, culture, and information; areas in which UNESCO also is active.

As well as accepting the Convention's obligations, States Parties recognize the supervisory authority of the Committee. In matters within the Committee's jurisdiction, a member State may not invoke the principle of sovereignty in order to escape its obligations under the Convention. Inevitably, this principle also serves to reinforce the reluctance of many States to enlarge the Committee's jurisdiction.

D. *Relations with other Bodies*

CERD has been described as 'an autonomous body established under a Convention that is nevertheless organically linked to the UN system'.[7] It is

[7] *The Committee on the Elimination of Racial Discrimination and the Progress Made Towards the Achievement of the Objectives of the International Convention on the Elimination of all Forms of Racial Discrimination*, E.79.XIV.4 (1979), para. 67. This study, prepared by the former rapporteur F. Sayegh in 1978, will be updated by two members of the committee as a contribution to the second decade.

certainly correct to emphasize CERD's autonomy: to describe the Committee as 'linked to'—not integrated in or absorbed by—the UN system. But the word 'organically' is less accurate, since some of the relations between CERD and the UN are of a purely functional nature.

1. THE GENERAL ASSEMBLY

CERD submits annual reports to the General Assembly through the Third Committee. However, due to its heavy workload the Third Committee has not always been able to give what members of CERD would consider to be adequate attention to its reports. CERD has often complained of this neglect but has been unsuccessful in seeking the Assembly's approval to have its report introduced in the Third Committee by one of its own members. Nevertheless, in a significant number of cases the Assembly has given important guidance to the Committee by endorsing controversial proposals contained in the Committee's reports. Thus one major innovation, endorsed by the Assembly after being discussed but rejected by the Committee, led to States Parties being invited 'to be present at [the Committee's] meetings when their reports are examined'.[8]

On one occasion a direct conflict between the Assembly and the Committee arose as a result of an attempt by the former to include the Committee among bodies for which Summary Records would be either reduced or abolished. The matter was resolved in accordance with the opinion provided by the Legal Counsel to the effect that even Assembly resolutions could not override the provisions of the Convention. The same opinion was invoked when the Secretary-General sought to change the date and venue of sessions which the Committee had already approved.[9]

II. THE SECRETARIAT

The Committee's relationship with the UN Secretariat is, in general, ambiguous. Inevitably, problems have arisen, especially where money is involved. Under the terms of the Convention[10] and the Rules of Procedure[11] the Committee's Secretariat is to be provided by the Secretary-General who is also responsible for all the necessary meeting arrangements. His representative 'shall be present' at all such meetings, and may make either oral or written statements.

The Committee's own funds,[12] half of which are contributed by States

[8] GA Res. 2783 (XXIX) (1971) and Rule 64, Rules of Procedure.
[9] A/37/18 (1976), paras. 288–315.
[10] Art. 10(3).
[11] Rules 21–5, Rules of Procedure.
[12] Convention, Art. 8(6); the method of apportioning was decided by the Meeting of States Parties (originally CERD/SP/SR.3 (1969)).

Parties on an equal basis and half in proportion to their percentage contribution to the overall UN budget, cover only the travel expenses of members. This contribution imposes a heavy burden on poorer States. All other costs, including the salaries of Secretariat officials, interpreters, and précis-writers, and printing and distribution costs, are borne by the UN budget. Thus any proposed expenditure must be officially costed by the Secretariat before being approved by the Committee[13] and even then is subject to approval or rejection in accordance with the UN's standard budgetary procedures.[14]

The fact that the Committee cannot choose its own Secretary has also been the subject of criticism.[15] In practice, there has been considerable continuity in the personnel servicing the Committee and many sessions have been opened by the Director of the Centre for Human Rights who sometimes takes the opportunity to offer comments on the work of the Committee.

III. THE SPECIALIZED AGENCIES

The somewhat ambiguous relationship between the major Specialized Agencies (notably the ILO and UNESCO) and the various UN human rights organs has been examined by Samson in Chapter 16 of this volume. CERD has not been an exception in this regard. Although the Committee agreed to accept information from the two Specialized Agencies under Article 15 of the Convention (relating to non-self-governing territories) the same arrangement was not adopted with respect to Article 9 (States reports). In discussions on the issue, two Committee members, interpreting Article 9 in an extremely restrictive way, argued strongly against receipt by the Committee of written material prepared by the agencies.[16] However, a compromise solution was reached by which the material is not formally transmitted to the Committee itself but rather is distributed by the Secretariat to members of the Committee in their individual capacities.[17] As experts they can then take account of any material available to them in formulating their comments and questions on States reports.

Representatives of both UNESCO and the ILO regularly attend the Committee's sessions[18] and the reports of the ILO Committee of Experts,

[13] Rule 25, Rules of Procedure.

[14] An example of the problems raised thereby related to the proposal, made from time to time by the Committee, to hold its sessions in a developing country. However, since (almost by definition) such countries could not be expected to incur all the supplementary costs of such a session, an additional budgetary allocation by the General Assembly would be required. To date none has been forthcoming. As a result, the only meetings held away from New York or Geneva have been in Paris (hosted by UNESCO) and Vienna (hosted by Austria).

[15] Newman, 'The New International Tribunal on Racial Discrimination', 56 *Calif. L. R* 1574 (1968).

[16] A/8718 (1972), 32–5.

[17] Ibid. 39–40, Dec. 2(VI) (1972).

[18] A/8418 (1971), paras. 111–17 and A/8718 (1972), paras. 122–32.

particularly with respect to ILO Convention No. 111 dealing with discrimination in employment, provide valuable information for members of the Committee. In a number of respects the ILO Committee has also been a useful model for CERD in terms both of its techniques and its objectivity.

The problem of avoiding duplication between CERD and UNESCO, particularly in relation to the latter's activities designed to implement the 1978 Declaration on Race and Racial Prejudice, has also arisen. In 1979 the Committee appealed to UNESCO to avoid duplication as far as possible in requesting information from States reporting under both CERD and the Declaration.[19]

IV. OTHER UN HUMAN RIGHTS ORGANS

The emergence of a variety of reporting systems established under UN instruments such as the Covenants and several Conventions has considerably increased the potential for undesirable overlapping of reporting requirements. Some measures have been taken in response to this problem. Thus some States, in reporting on Article 5 of the Convention (the list of rights), have referred to reports which they may already have submitted to the Human Rights Committee but not to CERD. Other challenges still remain and it is to be hoped that the regular meetings of the chairpersons of the major human rights supervisory organs[20] will contribute to the search for constructive and innovative measures to eliminate overlapping.

E. *A Statistical Overview*

Before examining in detail the functioning of the Committee it is useful to note some basic relevant statistical data.

I. RATIFICATIONS

With 129 States Parties at 1 January 1991, the Convention is closer to achieving universal ratification than any other convention concluded under UN auspices. However, there remain some significant lacunae. China became a party to the convention on 29 December 1981; now the United States is the largest country which has still not ratified it. The United States signed the treaty in 1966, but although President Carter submitted it to the Senate in 1978 for ratification, no action on it has yet been taken. Fourteen Asian[21] and

[19] A/34/18 (1979), 111, Dec. 2(XIX).
[20] For the most recent report see A/45/636 (1990).
[21] Including Indonesia, Japan, Thailand, Myanmar, and four Gulf States, with a total of approximately 400 million inhabitants.

nine African [22] States remain non-parties, but almost all the States in Latin America,[23] as well as those in both Eastern and Western Europe,[24] and two non-UN members[25] have become parties. Some States—e.g., South Africa—have refrained from ratifying the convention for obvious political reasons. Others may be reluctant to submit to CERD's supervision, or may simply lack interest in the Convention. It is not at all surprising that several new members of the United Nations are not yet parties to the instrument.

II. INDIVIDUAL COMPLAINTS

Article 14 of the Convention, which enables the Committee to receive individual complaints, did not receive the ten declarations required to bring it into force until 1982. Eight of the fourteen States to have made the declaration are from the Council of Europe, four from the OAS, and two from Africa.

III. COMMITTEE MEMBERSHIP

CERD's membership has been relatively consistent, a factor which has proved advantageous in terms of efficiency. One member has served since the Committee's inception; ten others have served for at least two full terms. Except between 1978 and 1980, the Committee has always included a female. Seven States Parties have always had experts on the Committee.[26]

IV. COMMITTEE MEETINGS

CERD meets for two three-week sessions each year: in spring and summer. Of the committee's forty sessions to date, twenty-five have been held in New York, thirteen in Geneva, one in Vienna, and one in Paris. The sessions scheduled for August 1986, March 1988, March 1989, and March 1990 in Geneva were cancelled for financial reasons; the sessions in August 1987 and August 1988 were shortened to one and two weeks respectively; and the session in August 1989 was extended to four weeks. Each session has been open to the public with the exception of occasional private meetings.

[22] Including the Republic of South Africa, with about 24 million inhabitants, and 8 other States (among them Kenya, Malawi, Zimbabwe, and Angola), with a total of about 43 million inhabitants.

[23] With the exception of some smaller Caribbean States.

[24] With the exception of Albania, Turkey, and Ireland.

[25] Tonga and the Holy See.

[26] These states are: Egypt, the Federal Republic of Germany, Ghana, Nigeria, Yugoslavia, and the USSR. Argentina, Ecuador, France, and the Philippines also have been fairly consistently represented. Among expert members, the USSR's have changed most frequently.

The examination of States reports is usually accorded nine days during the spring session and seven in summer, when the Committee must also prepare and adopt its report to the General Assembly.

The members try to examine three reports each day, which amounts to about twenty reports per session. So far, CERD has spent more than 200 days examining States' reports, and between 1970 and 1990 it has evaluated 718 reports.[27]

One of CERD's major problems is the late receipt of States' reports. At the end of 1990, 252 reports from 103 States were overdue; some should have been submitted several years ago. States Parties have proposed that CERD lengthen the two-year period between each report required, but the Committee, at first instance, has only made the concession that States Parties combine two or more reports in one comprehensive document. In 1988 it finally agreed to follow the proposal made by the States Parties. Now a comprehensive report is due only every fourth year and in the intermediate period the States Parties are only expected to update their last report.

F. *The Functions of the Committee*

The Convention provides for four functions of the Committee: (*a*) to examine States Parties' reports (Article 9, Rules 63–68); (*b*) to consider interstate communications (Articles 11–13, Rules 69–79); (*c*) to consider individual communications (Article 14, Rules 80–97); and (*d*) to aid other UN bodies in their review of petitions from inhabitants of Trust and Non-Self-Governing Territories and of reports concerning those territories (Article 15).

To date, CERD has devoted the great majority of its work to examining States' reports received under Article 9. As of the end of 1990 the Committee has received no formal interstate and only two individual communications. Though it has acted in its Article 15 capacity, the efficacy of this action has become increasingly questionable.

The reports CERD has received from other UN bodies under Article 15 have focused mainly on promoting the independence of the territories under examination, and significant information on the territories' racial situations has been lacking. Moreover, CERD has received most of these reports too late to take effective action on them. Where action has been taken it has not gone beyond either a request for futher information[28] or the formal endorsement of decisions already taken by other UN bodies. It is doubtful if such responses

[27] This number includes some supplementary reports, and some covering more than one reporting period. During the last five years, 10–20% of all reports submitted have been of the latter type.

[28] Convention, Art. 15(4).

adequately satisfy the requirements of Article 15(3) which provides for 'expressions of opinion and recommendations . . . relating to the said petitions and reports'.

Since the former Portuguese and many other dependent territories achieved their independence, and since Namibia ratified the Convention (in 1982), the number of territories to which Article 15 applies has decreased considerably. Given the procedure's reduced applicability, coupled with its lack of practical results, the need for its continuation should be re-evaluated. In 1989 the Committee refused to comment on the material presented, and in 1990 it deferred consideration due to lack of time.

G. *The Reporting Systems*

Under Article 9(1) of the Convention

> States Parties undertake to submit . . . for consideration by the Committee, a report on the legislative, judicial, administrative or other measures which they have adopted and which give effect to the provisions of this Convention: (*a*) within one year after the entry into force of the Convention for the State concerned; and (*b*) thereafter every two years and whenever the Committee so requests. The Committee may request further information from the States Parties.

The States Parties have almost complete control over the preparation of their reports. Each State itself decides who is to write its report, and may even entrust this task to its Permanent Mission to the United Nations. In most States the job is done by a central ministry—either the Ministry of Foreign Affairs or one of the Ministries for Internal Affairs (e.g., the Home Office or the Ministry of Justice). Certain States have established special reporting committees which include all authorities concerned and even some academic experts;[29] by so broadening their preparing group, however, States are likely to prolong the time of preparation of the report.

Federal States frequently have difficulties collecting and co-ordinating reporting data from their various regions. In those States where regional authorities are responsible for specific concerns (e.g., education), central authorities must try to interconnect all regional data into one overall report.

Sometimes, however, diverse regional data are included in a State report without further explanation and it falls to the Committee itself to interpret and evaluate the heterogeneous body of information.[30]

[29] e.g. Italy. CERD/C/46/Add.1 (1979), 3.
[30] e.g. Reports of Canada. CERD/C/50/Add.6 (1980), paras. 45–84; C/107/Add.8; C/132/Add.3 and comments thereto in A/42/18 (1987), para. 389.

H. *The Periodicity of Reports*

CERD can work effectively only if it receives States' reports on time. Article 9's periodicity requirement is not discretionary on the Committee's part, and CERD has always recognized its duty to enforce this obligation. When reports are late, the Committee sends reminders to governments through the Secretary General, and a list of those reminders appears in its annual report to the General Assembly. Where such reminders have been ignored, letters have been written to Heads of government, direct contacts undertaken with the States' delegations at UN Headquarters, and Secretariat advice has been offered to the State concerned.

As other human rights Conventions involving reporting obligations have come into force, CERD's reporting situation has begun to deteriorate. As noted above, the Committee has agreed to permit States to submit several overdue reports in one comprehensive document, and where a government has explained the reasons for the delay in its report, the Committee has abstained from sending reminders. Nevertheless, between 1977 and 1982, the percentage of delayed reports increased from 32.6 to 41.75.[31] In 1982 CERD appealed to the General Assembly to 'use its authority in order to ensure that the Committee could more effectively fulfill its obligations under the Convention'.[32] The Committee suggested that the reporting systems under the different human rights Conventions be better co-ordinated, and that States be offered technical assistance to facilitate the preparation of their reports. At the Assembly's request[33] the Secretariat prepared an analysis of the reporting system based on observations made by States Parties. The report proposed an extension of the periodicity from two to four years; the convening of periodic meetings of the Chairman of the major human rights supervisory bodies; and intensification of the technical assistance provided to States in the form of seminars, training programmes, and expert advice.[34]

In March 1984, the Committee gave its full support to the latter two suggestions but firmly opposed the first. The Committee noted that whether the reporting difficulties of certain States Parties were due to a lack of personnel, a lack of political will, or excessive international reporting obligations, the extension of the required periodicity would only 'have a negative effect . . . since it will weaken the obligations assumed by States . . .'. It also noted that its own Rules of Procedure provided for a degree of flexibility which could readily be used to ease the burden on States

[31] A/38/393 (1983), Table 2; since then it has risen further, probably due to the cancellation or curtailment of different sessions.

[32] A/37/18 (1982), General Recommendation VI (1982).

[33] GA Res.37/44 (1982).

[34] A/38/393 (1983); see also A/37/18 (1982), Annex IV and A/38/18 (1983), Annex VI.

experiencing temporary difficulties with their reporting.[35] The new decision taken in 1988 is mentioned above.

I. *The Content of Reports*

The Committee has always recognized that States Parties need to know as precisely as possible which information their reports should include. Unfortunately, the 'Convention' does not authorize it to issue a questionnaire as a basis on which States could prepare their reports,[36] so it has instead produced guidelines describing the desired content of the reports. While the original guidelines did not follow the system of the Convention,[37] they have since been rewritten so as to refer systematically to the various articles.[38] In addition, the revised guidelines request or invite information on, *inter alia*: the demographic composition of the population (in connection with the general scope of the Convention); the existence of diplomatic, economic, or other relations with racist regimes (Article 3); implementation of the provision prohibiting activities that incite racial hatred (Article 4); and the documentation requested by the Committee (such as the texts of relevant laws and judicial decisions).

Of those provisions dealing with States' obligations, Article 7 presents particular reporting difficulties. It requires States Parties to:

> undertake to adopt immediate and effective measures, particularly in the fields of teaching, education, culture and information, with a view to combating prejudices which lead to racial discrimination and to promoting understanding, tolerance and friendship among nations and racial or ethnical groups, as well as to propagating the purposes and principles of the Charter of the United Nations, the Universal Declaration of Human Rights, and the United Nations Declaration on the Elimination of All Forms of Racial Discrimination, and this Convention.

CERD has complained that reporting on these obligations has been scant, general, and perfunctory[39] although neither the Committee's first nor its second set of reporting guidelines did more than repeat the provisions of the Article. Eventually the Committee asked UNESCO to help draft reporting guidelines. The response consisted of an extensive list of more than ninety questions. On the basis of UNESCO's draft and of other proposals by its

[35] A/39/18 (1984), 127–8, Dec. 1 (XXIX) (1984).

[36] Art. 88 of the UN Charter authorizes the Trusteeship Council to use such an approach.

[37] CERD/C/R/12; and A/8027 (1970), Annex IIIA. These guidelines were issued as a 'Communication to States Parties' on the basis of the Committee's authority to request further information.

[38] For the revised general guidelines adopted on 9 Apr. 1980, see A/35/18 (1980), Annex IV.

[39] A/32/18 (1977), Annex; General Recommendation V (1977). Prior to the adoption of the Recommendation some reports contained little concrete information beyond assertions that ethnic groups were permitted to engage in folklore, that UN Human Rights Day had been celebrated, etc.

members, the Committee issued a short text which defines (with examples) the States' reporting duties with respect to each of Article 7's distinct topics: education and teaching, culture, and information.[40] The guidelines also refer to *General Recommendation IV* in requesting 'States Parties to endeavour to include in their reports . . . information on the demographic composition of the population . . .'.[41] However, the Committee has not always succeeded in obtaining this information. Not all States recognize the concept of 'national' or 'ethnic' groups. Others consider an investigation into ethnicity to be inherently discriminatory and thus do not request such details in national censuses. Even where such information has been provided, based on census results, it may be untrustworthy since minority group members may tend to conceal their ethnic background in order to avoid social or civic disadvantages.

In recent discussions on the issue the Committee has, despite vehement objections by one member, confirmed the practical importance of receiving such information and reiterated its 'invitation' to States Parties.[42]

CERD's current guidelines were adopted in 1980. Though some of the reports submitted since their adoption have been praised, others have still lacked sufficient information. Nevertheless the new guidelines enable the Committee to ask more specific questions, and hopefully this will lead to the receipt of increasingly adequate answers.

J. *The Committee's Source of Information*

Article 9(2) provides that CERD:

> shall report annually, through the Secretary-General, to the General Assembly of the United Nations on its activities and may make suggestions and general recommendations based on the examination of the reports and information received from the States Parties. Such suggestions and general recommendations shall be reported to the General Assembly together with comments, if any, from States Parties.

The interpretation of this provision has caused significant Committee debate. Some members have sought to construe the article narrowly and have argued that CERD could make suggestions to a State Party *solely* on the basis of information submitted by that State.[43] The limitations of this interpretation,

[40] A/37/18 (1982), chap. 9; Dec. 2 (XXV) (1982); incorporated into the Revised General Guidelines (CERD/C/70/Rev.1 (1983)). The committee also requested one of its members, Mr Tenekides, to prepare a report on Art. 7 to be submitted to the Second World Conference to Combat Racism and Racial Discrimination. See A/CONF.119/11 (1983). Cf. criticism of the report by The Netherlands, A/C.3/38/SR.9 (1983), para. 5.

[41] A/9018 (1973).

[42] For recent discussions on this issue, see CERD/C/SR.653 (1984); CERD/C/SR.714 (1985) (report of Greece); and CERD/C/SR.719 (1985) (report of Afghanistan).

[43] At one point several Committee members even opposed taking account of the provisions of a State's Constitution on the grounds that the text had not been provided in the States' report.

however, led to its early rejection.[44] Eventually, the Committee decided that Article 9(2) permits it to consider any official documents of the reporting State, including legislation, government declarations, and parliamentary papers (which might include speeches by the Government's opponents)—whether or not these are quoted in the State's report.[45] In addition, Committee members may take account of materials from intergovernmental organizations.

CERD's decision to accept this range of sources constitutes considerable progress towards the establishment of an effective reporting system. Unfortunately, the Committee cannot tap comparable information sources in every reporting State: data availability differs between countries with one-party governments and those with pluralistic systems, and also depends on the extent to which each government controls the media. Thus the Committee inevitably obtains unequal amounts of information and of varying reliability with respect to the actual situation in the various States.

The Committee will not examine information obtained from the mass media or from non-governmental organizations.[46] However, if significant news in the press bears on a reporting State's conditions, a member may request the State's official version of that news. Similarly, if a non-governmental organization publishes an analysis of a State's laws or provides information collected on the spot, such material may influence the questions posed by Committee members when evaluating States' reports. The material would then constitute information which the Committee members 'might have as experts'.[47] Nevertheless, the Committee does not solicit NGO inputs. Its

See CERD/C/SR.30 (1970), 19–23; SR. 31, 27–33; and SR. 32, 47. No decision was reached, but the chairman drew a distinction between CERD's use of material not mentioned in the report in order to request further information, and its use of such material as a basis for making suggestions. CERD/C/SR.31 (1970), 27. An attempt to insert a provision into the Rules of Procedure that members during the examination of reports 'may raise any matter relevant to the situation described in the documents before the Committee or related to the implementation of the Convention' was not approved. Some members objected on the grounds that it would introduce an element of rigidity into the Committee's procedures. The proposal was finally withdrawn, but the Chairman stated that the practice of the Committee allowed 'members to use any information they might have as experts'. A/8718 (1972), paras. 27–33.

[44] Ibid., para. 66.

[45] Confirmed by the Chairman, CERD/C/SR.296 (1976), para. 57; but still challenged by Starushenko (USSR). CERD/C/SR.719 (1985) (concerning the report of Afghanistan).

[46] In the view of Lamptey (Ghana), this rule should also be observed by States Parties when presenting their reports, on the grounds that it would otherwise be impossible to exclude political controversies in the media from the Committee's discussions (CERD/C/SR.661 (1984), 6). Recently CERD decided its members should have access even to non-governmental material.

[47] A/8718 (1972), 11. A degree of flexibility was hinted at in a 1972 opinion of the UN Office of Legal Affairs which noted that the Convention does not specify 'that the Committee is limited to these sources (i.e., States Parties' reports) in its preliminary consideration of the reports of States and in particular in formulating requests for further information'. Legal Opinion of the UN Office of Legal Affairs to the Assistant Secretary-General for Inter-Agency Affairs, *1972 UN Jud. YB* 164 (1974).

reluctance to use such information reflects the fear that such organizations may be politically motivated even though they may have been accorded consultative status with ECOSOC.

When States reports are submitted late, Committee members are often left without enough time to collect the information required to review it adequately. Even with respect to 'acceptable' sources of information practical difficulties may arise. Thus even though the Secretariat automatically provides the Committee with copies of certain documents from intergovernmental organizations[48] other such documents must be identified and obtained by the members themselves.

The task would be simpler if the Secretariat could provide a list of intergovernmental documents of potential relevance to the examination of a State's report. However, even such an apparently innocuous proposal might well be resisted by members of the Committee because it could refer to controversial documents such as reports prepared by UN forces operating in an occupied territory. It is not always possible to predict what materials the Committee might be prepared to take into account.[49]

It remains to be seen whether the same rules governing sources of information to be used in the evaluation of States reports will also be applied by the Committee in dealing with interstate and individual complaints.

K. *Examination of Reports*

I. ACCEPTANCE OF REPORTS

The decision to examine a State's report is CERD's alone; even if a report appears totally unsatisfactory the Secretariat is not authorized to reject it. The Committee's decision to accept certain reports has been quite controversial, for example, in the cases of reports submitted by Chile[50] and Israel.[51] Some Committee members felt that those reports should not be examined in view of large-scale human rights violations in the countries concerned. However, in each case the Committee opted to review the report on the assumption that criticism is most appropriately expressed in the context of the evaluation process.

[48] These documents include those mentioned in Art. 15 as well as the relevant records of the General Assembly concerning the annual reports of CERD, the annual reports of the Human Rights Committee, and the ILO Committee of Experts.

[49] When the situation in the Panama Canal Zone was discussed the majority of the Committee refused to consult the relevant treaties between Panama and the USA. A/8418 (1971), para. 64(ii).

[50] Second report by Chile. For discussion see A/10018 (1975), para. 159.

[51] First report by Israel. For discussion, see A/35/18 (1980), paras. 330–4.

II. STATES' REPRESENTATIVES PARTICIPATION AT COMMITTEE MEETINGS

Once CERD decides to examine a State's report, its Chairman invites the representatives of the reporting State to attend the relevant meetings of the Committee. This system, which is not specifically authorized by the Convention, was only instituted after great deliberation. CERD first discussed the issue at its third session, when one member expressed his discomfort at having to act, during the Committee's examination of his own country's report, both as an impartial member and in defence of his State. He pointed out that when experts on the Committee engaged in such a defence of their respective States, their reports were examined more leniently than those of other States Parties. He proposed that CERD adopt a procedure like that of the Trusteeship Council, which invites representatives from the administering powers to participate in its meetings.[52]

The initial proposal was rejected and when, one week later, the Pakistani delegation requested permission to comment on CERD's examination of its report, that request was refused.[53] However, later in the same year the matter was taken up by the General Assembly which recommended that CERD invite representatives of States Parties to be present for the discussions of their reports.[54] Although some Committee members still objected to the proposal on the grounds that an expert committee should not operate like a court,[55] the practice was adopted in 1972.[56] Since its adoption, the majority of States Parties have sent representatives—often senior government officials—to introduce their reports and to respond directly to questions. The dialogue established as a result of this very significant innovation has proved to be a valuable element in the relationship between CERD and the States Parties.[57] Recently, doubts were expressed by some members on whether the Committee should examine a State report in the absence of a representative. These doubts have no legal basis.

[52] CERD/C/SR.46 (1970).

[53] CERD/C/SR.58 (1971) and A/8418 (1971), paras. 84–8.

[54] GA Res. 2783 (XXVI) (1971).

[55] A/8718 (1972), para. 23.

[56] Ibid. para. 37, Dec. 1(V), Rule 64A. As Rule 64 it now reads: 'The Committee shall, through the Secretary General, notify the States Parties (as early as possible) of the opening date, duration, and place of the session at which their respective reports will be examined. Representatives of the States Parties may be present at the meetings of the Committee when their reports are examined. The Committee may also inform a State Party from which it decides to seek further information that it may authorize its representative to be present at a specified meeting. Such a representative should be able to answer questions which may be put to him by the Committee and make statements on reports already submitted by his State, and may also submit additional information from his State.'

[57] In drafting its Rules of Procedure the Human Rights Committee unhesitatingly included similar provisions for having States' Representatives attend its meetings. CCPR/C/L.1/Add.1, Rule 69.

III. COMMITTEE DISCUSSIONS

The examination of reports usually begins with an introductory statement by the representative of the reporting State. This statement need only consist of general remarks, although in practice new, substantive information is often provided. In some instances, the introductory remarks have contained even more information than the State's written report.[58]

Following the introductory statement, the Committee is free to discuss the report at will. Frequently, a member will initiate the discussion by providing a systematic survey of the report. This does not necessarily prevent other members from presenting their own analyses, or even from repeating what has already been said. Considerable time can also be taken up by lengthy compliments which some members seem to feel should be addressed to the reporting government's representatives.

CERD has made many attempts to avoid wasting valuable time and to discipline its discussions. One such proposal was to assign one or more reports to a rapporteur (or group of rapporteurs) and to limit the other members' reviews to additional questions.[59] Though some members feared that such a practice would curtail the non-rapporteur-members' rights, practice has shown that short and pertinent questions often evoke the most thorough and complete answers. Only in 1988 did the Committee decide to introduce on an experimental basis a rapporteur-system according to the model used by ILO for decades.

At that session the reports already available for the next session were distributed to some members who declared themselves ready to act as rapporteurs and to prepare analyses for a certain number of reports. After this first experience the Committee came to the conclusion that this working method 'has contributed to the reduction of time for the consideration of each State report and strengthens the dialogue with State Parties representatives.'[60] Accordingly this system has been adopted.

After the Committee members have completed their observations and questioning, the State's Representative is once again invited to take the floor. Some representatives simply thank the Committee for its attention, and promise that all of its questions and remarks will be transmitted to the government. However, most representatives use the opportunity to clarify issues, correct misunderstandings, or provide information which may have been either unintentionally or deliberately omitted from the report.[61]

[58] Introductory remarks of the representative of China. See CERD/C/101/Add.3 (1983), supplementary to the initial Report contained in CERD/C/101/Add.2 (1983).

[59] Dec. 1(XXIX), para. 3(h), in A/39/18 (1984), where the need to reconsider the Committees' method of work is emphasized.

[60] A/44/18 (1989).

[61] Usually, such additional information will be confirmed in the State's next periodic report.

IV. REQUESTS FOR FURTHER INFORMATION

Article 9(2) authorizes CERD to 'request further information from the States Parties'. The Committee has indicated how it shall implement this provision in Rule 67 of its Rules of Procedure which states (in part) that:

(1) When considering a report submitted by a State Party under Article 9, the Committee shall first determine whether the report provides the information referred to in the relevant communications of the Committee.
(2) If a report of the State Party to the Convention, in the opinion of the Committee, does not contain sufficient information, the Committee may request that State to furnish additional information.

In applying this Rule the Committee evaluates each State's report with respect to the formal reporting guidelines, taking account of that State's previous reports. The members seek to determine:

(*a*) what information requested has been delivered in earlier reports;
(*b*) whether information missing in previous reports is included in the report under consideration;
(*c*) whether questions initially incompletely answered have now been responded to fully; and
(*d*) whether new developments in the reporting country give rise to a need for additional information.

Usually, this phase of the review results in a request for further information —a request which the Committee almost always makes without a formal decision.[62] Recently, States have responded to these requests by including the desired data in their next periodic reports, sometimes in the context of a special chapter.

In their early reports States frequently declared, with little or no analysis to support the assertion, that no racial discrimination existed in their country—an assertion the Committee never accepted. Many of the recent reports include substantial details of the situation prevailing in the State concerned. Such detail signifies an increasing compliance with CERD's formal reporting guidelines. In addition, the Committee's information gathering efforts have in themselves had an impact in so far as they have encouraged reforms which otherwise might not have been made. For example, about half the States Parties have adopted new penal provisions against acts of racial discrimination.[63]

[62] CERD's Rule of Procedure 64 provides for a 'specified meeting' with States' representatives to discuss requests for further information. However, CERD has not used this procedure, and only rarely has the Committee concluded a session by taking a formal decision to make a request for further information.

[63] Ingles, *Study on the Implementation of Article 4 of the International Convention on the Elimination of all Forms of Racial Discrimination*, A/CONF. 119/10 (1983).

Therefore, though CERD's fact-finding capabilities are still far from adequate, even the technique of simply requesting further information may prove to be a valuable means of encouraging anti-discrimination measures.

L. *Evaluation of States' Reports*

Article 9(1) declares the States Parties' reporting duties to CERD; Article 9(2) states CERD's subsequent reporting duties to the General Assembly. By separating these sets of obligations into two paragraphs, the Convention indicates that the Committee's work is to proceed through two stages: first, fact-finding; and secondly, making suggestions or general recommendations.

During its early years, CERD made little distinction between these two stages. The Committee would conclude its examination of reports by qualifying them as 'satisfactory' or 'unsatisfactory' without indicating whether 'unsatisfactory' reports lacked sufficient information, or whether the reporting State had failed to comply with its substantive obligations under the Convention.[64] In 1972 the Committee amended its Rules of Procedure (now Rule 67) in order to distinguish more clearly the two phases of its evaluation. In addition to paragraphs 1 and 2 of Rule 67 (quoted above) it introduced Rule 67(3) which provides that

> If, on the basis of its examination of the reports and information supplied by the State Party, the Committee determines that some of the obligations of that State under the Convention have not been discharged, it may make suggestions and general recommendations in accordance with Article 9, Paragraph 2, of the Convention.

Almost simultaneously with the adoption of this Rule, however, the Committee introduced the practice of inviting States' representatives to be present during the review of their report. This important innovation inadvertently blurred the newly emphasized distinction between the two supervisory phases since, when States' representatives are present, it is almost impossible to avoid discussing the States' fulfilment both of its technical reporting duties and of its substantial Conventional obligations.[65]

The resulting merger of CERD duties has been criticized,[66] but the dialogue does have significant advantages. For instance, if at a reviewing session the Committee determines that a State has failed to conform to the Convention's standards, it can discuss remedial measures with the State's Representative

[64] This practice was abandoned by the Committee in 1974. A/9618 (1974), para. 23.

[65] In addition, CERD has begun to combine its first- and second-stage functions by including in its reports to the General Assembly details on the results of its requests for further information from States. This new practice was first introduced in 1973. Beginning in 1979, CERD also reported on the States' representatives responses at Committee sessions to its request for further information.

[66] Buergenthal, 'Implementing the UN Racial Convention', 12 *Tex. Int'l LJ*, 202 (1977).

immediately. Then, if the Representative assures the Committee that his country will undertake the required measures, his State may avoid the ramifications of a formal Committee evaluation. Thus, in effect, the dialogue is transformed into a process of conciliation which may have much greater practical effect than more formal supervisory measures which are not supported by possible sanctions. Though Rule 67(3) enables the Committee to declare that a State Party is in default of its obligations, the Committee has, as established by its recent practice, confined itself to formulating 'concluding observations'.

By contrast, specific suggestions have been adopted in cases where accusations have been made against States which were *not* parties to the Convention.[67] In such cases the Committee has adopted a specific procedure. If, having established the relevant facts, it decides to begin discussing a proposed suggestion or recommendation the States representative is asked 'to withdraw from the Committee table' although he may 'be present when the Committee's decision is announced'.[68] The same procedure would be used to formulate a suggestion directed to a State Party.

M. *Problems of Interpretation Related to the Reporting Process*

In seeking the most effective means by which to exercise its supervisory function the Committee must take account of various constraints. Thus, for example, in its fact-finding endeavours the Committee has to rely very heavily on information provided by the reporting State itself. It is not empowered to summon witnesses or undertake on-the-spot investigations, and it can make only indirect use of materials from non-governmental organizations. Compliance with the Committee's suggestions and general recommendations therefore depends on the voluntary co-operation of the State concerned, since by publicizing any findings of discriminatory practices, the Committee must hope to provoke the adoption of appropriate remedial measures. The Committee has chosen to seek such co-operation through a working dialogue with States in the knowledge that the acceptability of new initiatives designed to strengthen its procedures will inevitably be limited by States' conceptions of their own national sovereignty.

Nevertheless, the Committee has often sought to promote an expansive interpretation of the substantive obligations contained in the Convention. By way of illustration several cases may briefly be mentioned.[69]

[67] See e.g. the Committee's discussions of the situation in the Panama Canal Zone, the Golan Heights, the West Bank, Sinai, and Cyprus, reviewed in Lerner, *The UN Convention on the Elimination of all Forms of Racial Discrimination* (1980), 131–43.

[68] A/34/18 (1979); Dec. 1(XIX) (1979).

[69] For other examples, see Meron, 'The Meaning and Reach of the International Convention', 310–12.

Article 3 of the Convention provides that: 'States Parties particularly condemn racial segregation and apartheid and undertake to prevent, prohibit and eradicate all practices of this nature in territories under their jurisdiction.' While this Article limits the States Parties' anti-discrimination duties to their own territories, Committee members have argued that the Convention's preamble, which declares that the States Parties are 'resolved ... to build an international community free from all forms of racial segregation and discrimination', authorizes them to request from States information on their relations with the racist regime in South Africa.[70] Initially, this matter was pursued cautiously. The Committee noted that it would welcome the submission of information from the States 'which choose to do so';[71] later, it 'Invite[d] all States Parties to include, in their reports ... information on the status of their relations with the racist regimes of southern Africa.'[72] Although the General Assembly has supported this interpretation,[73] a significant number of States Parties have rejected it.[74] Several States have refused to include the relevant information in their reports, but have offered it orally after explaining their legal reservations.[75]

The Committee has also sought to interpret Article 4 broadly. In that Article:

> States Parties condemn all propaganda and all organizations ... which attempt to justify or promote racial hatred and discrimination in any form, and undertake to adopt immediate and positive measures designed to eradicate ... discrimination ... with due regard to the principles embodied in the Universal Declaration of Human Rights and the rights expressly set forth in Article 5 of this Convention ...

Several States have held that the obligations deriving from Article 4 must be interpreted so as not to jeopardize the employment of other human rights.[76] However, CERD's Special Rapporteur José D. Ingles[77] and other Committee members have argued that Article 29 of the Universal Declaration authorizes the specific limitations embodied in the Convention. The Declaration's Article 29(2) permits limitations 'for the purpose of securing

[70] A/8718 (1972), Dec. 1(VI) (1972). In seeking to justify this approval, Committee members have argued that the decision to export goods or to send diplomatic or consular representatives are matters determined by States within their own jurisdictions. This argument rests on a debatable assumption: that a State's maintenance of commercial or diplomatic relations constitutes support for the governmental practices of the receiving country.

[71] A/8718 (1972), General Recommendation 6 (III) (1972).

[72] A/10018 (1975), Dec. 2(XI) (1975).

[73] GA Res. 31/81 (1976), and GA Res. 39/21 (1984), para. 12 which was adopted by a separate vote with 20 abstentions.

[74] e.g. the UK. A/38/18 (1983), para. 173.

[75] See e.g. sections of the Committee's 1983 report (A/38/18 (1983)) dealing with the reports of: Venezuela (para. 216), Federal Republic of Germany (para. 309), France (para. 323), and Canada (para. 403).

[76] e.g. CERD/C/60 (1980) (Italy).

[77] Ingles, *Study of the Implementation of Article 4*, paras. 209 and 227–8.

due recognition and respect for the rights and freedoms of others and of meeting the just requirements of morality, public order, and the general welfare in a democratic society', while Article 29(3) declares that 'rights and freedoms may in no case be exercised contrary to the purposes and principles of the United Nations'. On this basis it has been argued that Article 4 of the Convention requires the penalization of acts of racial hatred or hostility regardless of the intention or motivation underlying such acts.

This argument, however, seems to overlook Article 30 of the Universal Declaration, which denies 'any State, group or person any right to engage in any activity or to perform any act aimed at the destruction of any of the rights and freedoms set forth herein'. This express provision against limitations supports the interpretation that in no case should Article 4's obligations be interpreted so as to 'jeopardize' basic human rights.[78]

CERD's application of Article 5 has been more cautious. The Committee has asked reporting States whether the rights listed in the article are guaranteed by their national legal systems, but it has not indicated that the absence of such guarantees constitutes a failure to comply with the Convention. Specifically, CERD's inquiries have aimed at ensuring that where the rights in question are in fact safeguarded by a State's legal order, they are also enjoyed without discrimination, and that any suspension of those rights—such as might occur during an emergency or state of siege—has been justified.[79]

N. *Interstate Complaints*

Articles 11–13 of the Convention authorize the Committee to deal with complaints submitted by States alleging discriminatory practices on the part of other States Parties. Article 11(1) provides that:

> If a State Party considers that another State Party is not giving effect to the provisions of this Convention, it may bring the matter to the attention of the Committee. The Committee shall then transmit the communication to the State Party concerned. Within three months, the receiving State shall submit to the Committee written explanations or statements clarifying the matter and the remedy, if any, that may have been taken by that State.

Although the Covenant on Civil and Political Rights also provides for interstate complaints, those procedures apply only between States which

[78] The importance of this provision is illustrated by Art. 19(2) of the Basic Law of the Federal Republic of Germany which provides that in no case may the essential content of a basic right be infringed upon. An express reservation to this effect is not necessary. See, however, Meron, 'The Meaning and Reach of the International Convention', 315.

[79] See Partsch, 'Elimination of Racial Discrimination in the Enjoyment of Civil and Political Rights', 14 *Tex. Int'l LJ* 225–6 (1979). On the relationship between Art. 5 and Art. 1(2), with respect to discrimination against aliens, see Meron, 'The Meaning and Reach of the International Convention', 311–13.

have specifically recognized the relevant competence of the Human Rights Committee.[80] By contrast, CERD's procedures apply automatically to all States Parties.

The Committee has received several Article 9 reports claiming that the reporting State has been prevented by a non-party State from fulfilling its Conventional obligations. Jordan, Syria, and Egypt submitted such claims when Israel occupied their territories, as did Cyprus when Turkey intervened in the northern part of Cyprus. Since Article 11 provides for interstate procedures only between States Parties, the Committee had to determine if and when complaints about non-parties could be considered under Article 9 reports. In the case of territorial occupation by a non-party State, CERD has decided that information on the situation may appropriately be included by States Parties in their Article 9 reports.[81] However, when transmitting such information to the General Assembly, the Committee has tried to avoid making any political or legal value judgments, although it has not always succeeded in abiding by this restriction.[82] One commentator has pointed out that as more States ratify the Convention, the Committee should more readily be able to avoid 'getting embroiled in political disputes that it is not equipped to resolve'.[83]

In light of recent European history, given the successful use of interstate complaint procedures in the context of the European Human Rights Convention, it seems remarkable that no State Party to CERD has yet initiated an Article 11 proceeding. However, some States' Article 9 reports have raised what have been called 'disguised inter-state disputes'.[84] CERD must determine if and when such 'disguised disputes' between States Parties demand Article 11 treatment, which requires that the Committee interpret what the Convention means by the term 'inter-state communication'.

The original draft of Article 11 referred to interstate 'complaints' but in the Third Committee of the General Assembly Mexico proposed substituting 'complaints' with 'communications', and the draft's sponsors readily adopted this less juridical, more inclusive term.[85]

[80] International Covenant on Civil and Political Rights, Art. 41(1).

[81] See the study of the *Committee* quoted *supra* note 7, paras. 15–16; and analysis by Buergenthal, 'Implementing the UN Racial Convention', 211–18.

[82] e.g. in 1983 when the Committee adopted a decision in which, *inter alia*, it reiterated 'its hope that the Government of Cyprus will, without further delay, be enabled to exercise its full responsibility for the implementation of all its obligations under the Convention in its whole national territory, and that the unacceptable state of affairs in Cyprus, due to the foreign occupation of part of its territory, will finally be brought to an end' (A/38/18 (1983); Decision 1(XXCII) (1983)). Two Committee members dissociated themselves from the consensus on the grounds that the decision 'dealt with matters which fell outside the scope of the Committee's competence' (ibid. para. 96).

[83] Buergenthal, 'Implementing the UN Racial Convention', 218.

[84] Ibid. 211.

[85] *Report of the Third Committee*, A/6181 (1965), paras. 118–20.

As it reads now, Article 11 permits informal procedures: it does not even require, as does Article 41(1) (a) of the Convenant, that interstate communications be 'written'. Some Committee members have argued that such informality leads to the conclusion that when States include interstate information in their Article 9 reports, they automatically initiate Article 11 proceedings. In such a case, the Committee is required to 'transmit the communication to the State Party concerned'.[86]

Past Article 9 reports have contained various forms of 'disguised inter-state disputes'. Several States have reported that part of their territory has been occupied by another State Party, and that the latter 'is not giving effect to the provisions of the Convention'.[87] A series of reports by the Syrian Arab Republic have made such claims with respect to Israel's occupation of the Golan Heights. When Israel became a party to the Convention, some Committee members refused to accept Syria's claim under Article 9;[88] however, Syria clearly was unwilling to initiate an Article 11 proceeding.[89] Though several of CERD's members considered Syria's information regarding Israeli racial discrimination acceptable under Article 9 on the basis of political, moral, or ethical concerns,[90] the Committee in this case did not table a draft decision to condemn Israel for its practices in the occupied territory.

In another case, the Netherlands reported that 'some countries' (which remained unspecified) were requesting official proof of 'non-Jewish faith' before permitting foreigners to enter their territories. It had refused to issue its citizens certificates of 'non-jewish faith' for purposes of trade or travel, claiming that this would 'conflict with the spirit and tenor of the Convention'.[91] When asked why the Netherlands government had not submitted this information under Article 11, its representative explained that 'the countries concerned had not, at the time in question, all been parties to the Convention'.[92] He admitted that his State had taken no further steps to ascertain if these countries had in the mean time ratified the Convention. Apparently, the Netherlands was not inclined to invoke Article 11 procedures, and by choosing to include interstate information in its Article 9 report, it was able to avoid accusing any particular State of violating the Convention.

[86] Cf. Lamptey's argument that a formal complaint under Art. 11 is required in order to activate the relevant procedures. In his view the Committee might otherwise be led 'to resolve a conflict that might not exist' (CERD/C/SR.662 (1984)). However, the use of Art. 9 to raise disguised interstate disputes, without providing the accused State with an opportunity to defend itself, would seem even more problematic.

[87] In accordance with Art. 11(1) of the Convention.

[88] See Syria's sixth periodic report (CERD/C/66/Add. 22) and discussion in A/36/18 (1981), paras. 169–73 and CERD/C/SR.507 and 508 (1981). As regards the seventh periodic report (CERD/C/91/Add. 39), see CERD/C/SR.661 and 662 (1984).

[89] CERD/C/SR.507 (1981), para. 37, and CERD/C/SR.661 (1984), para. 3.

[90] CERD/C/SR.661 and 662 (1984).

[91] Netherlands third periodic report. CERD/C/9 (1977), para. 2.

[92] A/32/18 (1977), paras. 227–8.

O. *Individual Complaints*

Both Article 14 of the Convention and the Optional Protocol to the Convenant authorize procedures whereby individuals may submit petitions directly to the respective supervisory Committees. Each procedure requires ten States' specific acceptance to become effective, but receiving these acceptances took much longer for Article 14 than for the Protocol. Once Article 14 became operative in 1982, CERD drafted applicable Rules of Procedure based on the approach adopted by the Human Rights Committee.

Article 14 differs from the Protocol in that it provides that:

(*a*) 'Groups of individuals' as well as 'individuals' may present communications to the Committee;[93]

(*b*) The identity of the petitioner(s) shall not be revealed to the State Party criticized without his or their express consent;[94]

(*c*) A State Party may establish or indicate a national body competent to receive and consider individuals' petitions. This body must keep a register of the submitted petitions, and file copies annually with the Secretary-General;[95]

(*d*) CERD is not barred from considering communications which are being examined under another procedure of international investigation or settlement;[96]

(*e*) CERD may forward its 'suggestions and recommendations'[97] rather than just its 'views'[98] to the State Party concerned and to the petitioner(s).

To date the Committee has only received two individual communications. A decision on the merits of the first was taken in 1988.[99] In 1989 one other communication was received which was decided in 1991.

P. *Other Functions*

The Committee functions are defined in Part II (Articles 9–16) of the Convention and it is clear that it could not justify the usurpation of entirely

[93] Art. 14(1).

[94] Art. 14(6)(a).

[95] Art. 14(2) and (4). According to Rule 91(e) the establishment of such a body is optional. A contrary view has, however, been expressed by one member of the committee. CERD/C/SR. 325, para. 21.

[96] The Human Rights Committee is not permitted to do this (see Art. 5(2)(a) of the Optional Protocol to the International Covenant on Civil and Political Rights). Denmark, Iceland, Italy, Norway, and Sweden have made reservations underlying their interpretation of this provision (ST/HR/4/Rev.4 (1982)).

[97] Art. 14(7)(b).

[98] As provided for in the Optional Protocol, Art. 5(4).

[99] *Yilmaz-Dogan v. The Netherlands*: Procedure on admissibility. See A/42/18 (1987), para. 849. For the opinion of the Committee, see Annex IV to A/43/18 (1988).

new powers for itself by, for example, using the argument that these are necessary in order to enable it to carry out its general mandate. By the same token, however, there are inevitably instances in which the Committee must consider undertaking tasks which, although not specifically enumerated in the Convention, are consistent with the authority vested in it. Indeed the Committee has often done so although it is submitted that the legitimacy or appropriateness of the activities undertaken has sometimes been questionable.

The Committee produced studies for each of the two World Conferences to Combat Racism and Racial Discrimination, and CERD's Chairman and one other member participated in the Conferences. Because these activities aimed at a systematic analysis of CERD's accomplishments within the framework of the goals of the Conference, and because they were consistent with the Committee's official functions, they were clearly within the Convention's authorized scope.

However, the participation of some of the Committee's members in seminars organized in relation to the Decade for Action to Combat Racism and Racial Discrimination[100] is of more dubious legitimacy. Though they are well qualified to contribute to such gatherings, it is submitted that the expression of individual viewpoints cannot be reconciled with the status of official representatives of the Committee. Since the seminars in question involved scholarly discussions and the expression of personal opinions it would seem more appropriate for the Committee's representatives to have limited their participation to the status of observers.

Also in connection with the Decade, the Committee expressed its readiness in 1974 to 'take an active part in a world-wide information campaign' and to 'speak on United Nations radio broadcasts'.[101] In the same decision, CERD endorsed the recommendation 'that the General Assembly continue to decline to accept the credentials of the representatives of the Republic of South Africa'. These actions involve CERD directly in the media and put it squarely in the political arena. As a committee of experts—unlike many other UN bodies—CERD is not authorized to assume such involvements.

Q. *Future Perspectives*

During its first twenty-two years the Committee has certainly not been able to eliminate all forms of racial discrimination in the world. Though the Convention is binding for 129 States with about 85 per cent of the world population, there remain important lacunae. Thus, the Committee does not dispose of any means to interfere directly in the Republic of South Africa and

[100] e.g. A/38/18 (1983), para. 15.
[101] A/9618 (1974); Dec. 2(X) (1974).

to eliminate its policy of apartheid. Whether its indirect attempts to contribute to this goal have had a decisive effect is difficult to decide.

By its monitoring work the Committee has generally made the governments of the member States better aware of relevant problems. This results from the progressively improving quality of State reports, the increasing number of States which penalize discriminatory acts, and the establishment of special new authorities for treating the relevant problems in some States.

Numerous special measures could be suggested in order to improve the legal and political situation of ethnic and linguistic minorities, including indigenous groups, and their better integration into society. There is no doubt, however, that much has to be done even in those member States which have accepted a policy of non-discrimination and shown sincere intention of its realization.

The future enhancement of CERD's effectiveness is essentially dependent on the implementation of appropriate procedural innovations. Any realistic effort to identify such possible reforms must be taken with full regard to the political environment in which the Committee functions. The Committee itself may implement certain changes, particularly with respect to matters dealt with in its Rules of Procedure which it may expand or amend of its own accord. Other changes, however, can only be brought about by action by the State Parties, either informally though the endorsement of innovative approaches, or formally through amendment of the Convention. The latter possibility should be considered only with the utmost caution.

I. THE COMMITTEE'S PROCEDURES

There is inevitably a degree of tension in the operation of any large committee of this type and the challenge is to strike a balance between, on the one hand, the need not to cramp the style and initiative of individual members and, on the other hand, to achieve a level of discipline and organization which is conducive to the smooth functioning of the Committee as a whole. In the past a number of measures designed to encourage more disciplined discussion of States' reports have been proposed but rejected. Some members have been concerned that such measures would prejudice the opportunity of all members to contribute equally to the work of the Committee.

Nevertheless, measures designed to reduce unnecessary repetition of questions could involve considerable savings of time and need not necessarily impinge unduly on the rights of members. Such measures could include: (*a*) the adoption of a rule that the Chairman alone, on behalf of the Committee, would be entitled to congratulate the States representatives for their participation in the supervisory process; (*b*) insisting that Committee meetings begin on time; and (*c*) allocating responsibility (on a rotating basis) for the preparation of a summary of the contents and shortcomings of a particular report to one or two members and urging other members to limit themselves to pertinent questions on matters not already raised.

While such measures might at first appear trivial to an outside observer the increasing number of States Parties to the Convention and the growing demands placed on the Committee make it essential to adopt such measures, which could significantly enhance the Committee's efficiency. It remains to be seen whether the system of introducing a rapporteur system will prove to be effective in the long run.

II. SOURCES OF INFORMATION

The range of sources of information to which the Committee may refer in its review of States' reports has been broadened significantly over the years but the limits attainable under the terms of the Convention may still not have been reached. In particular, it is to be hoped that in the future the Committee might be able to take greater account of NGO reports provided that: the organization concerned has consultative status with ECOSOC, the information provided is based on an analysis of the laws of the country concerned, and that the reports are distributed to all Committee members without exception. While acknowledging the sensitivity of this issue, the importance of ensuring access to a diversity of sources of information must not be underestimated.

III. THE MAKING OF FORMAL RECOMMENDATIONS AND SUGGESTIONS

In the field of international human rights law there is sometimes a tendency to equate effectiveness with the development of a relatively formalized system of reaching conclusions and making recommendations with respect to the human rights situation in the State under review. However, given the positive results which CERD has achieved to date by means of an evolving dialogue with States Parties and appeals for voluntary co-operation it would seem to be potentially counter-productive at this stage for the Committee to make greater use of its powers to issue either formal suggestions or general recommendations.

IV. IMPARTIALITY OF MEMBERS

The nomination and election of Committee members is the exclusive prerogative of the States Parties and the Committee itself may not interfere. Thus it is up to the States to ensure that the Committee members are 'of acknowledged impartiality'[102] by seeking to minimize any potential conflicts of interest. While no universally applicable criteria for determining impartiality can be identified, it is clear that States Parties should never seek to instruct their nationals on matters within the Committee's jurisdiction and that they should not nominate individuals for whom an automatic conflict of interest would exist (such as diplomatic members of their permanent missions to the United Nations).

V. PERIODICITY OF REPORTING

This question was for years controversial between the Committee and the States Parties.[103] As a matter of fact, human rights reporting systems introduced after the drafting of the Convention provide for longer periods than does Article 9 of the Convention. The Committee, however, expressed concern that a reform would mean a weakening of the commitments made by the States Parties and would therefore need a formal amendment of the Convention.[104] As the relevant provision does not define the exact nature of these reports it seemed appropriate to request from States Parties only every four years a comprehensive report which has to be updated two years later. When necessary, the Committee is entitled to require an additional report in any case.

VI. THE COMMITTEE'S ROLE IN DE-COLONIZATION

The Committee's efforts to implement Article 15 of the Convention which authorizes it to contribute to the work of UN bodies dealing with Trust and Non-Self-Governing Territories, have to date produced few substantive results. Moreover the bureaucratic approach adopted has been particularly time-consuming. While it is certainly not desirable to deprive the relevant bodies of CERD's support in their efforts to combat racial discrimination, a far better alternative to the present formalistic approach would be for the Committee to become involved only when specifically requested to do so.

VII. FACT-FINDING CAPACITY

The Committee's lack of an independent fact-finding capacity has been identified by one commentator as the major obstacle to its effectiveness.[105] In the case of both the European and the Inter-American Human Rights

[102] Art. 8(1).
[103] A/38/393 (1983), para. 30.
[104] A/39/18 (1984), Dec. 1 (XXIX) (1984), para. 3(b).
[105] Buergenthal, 'Implementing the UN Racial Convention', 202.

Commissions comparable organs have been authorized to undertake a broad range of fact-finding activities including the examination of relevant documentation, the hearing of witnesses and experts, and the making of on-the-spot visits to any locality.[106] In the case of CERD no such general mandate is specifically provided for in the Convention and some of the Committee's members would be reluctant to undertake such quasi-judicial activities. Financial constraints raise a further obstacle to the development of such a role. Nevertheless, given the critical importance of an independent fact-finding capacity, it may not be unrealistic to envisage steps, at least in the longer term, towards the achievement of such a goal.

[106] Art. 28 of the European Convention (1950) reads: 'The Commission . . . shall . . . undertake . . . if need be, an investigation, for the effective conduct of which the States concerned shall furnish all necessary facilities, after an exchange of views with the Commission.'

10
The Human Rights Committee

TORKEL OPSAHL

Introduction

The Human Rights Committee was established in 1976 under the International Covenant on Civil and Political Rights. It was soon described as 'the most important of the UN's human rights bodies'[1] and its work has frequently been favourably commented upon in General Assembly debates and resolutions. Nevertheless, even six years after its creation one commentator suggested that it was 'still struggling to define its role and refine its procedures'.[2] Each of these assessments may still be warranted.

The purpose of this chapter is to analyse the structure, functions, and achievements of the Committee. First comes a general overview of its status, activities, relations and functions in the light of experience. Further parts deal more in detail with its functions in terms of both law and practice. The principal thrust of the analysis is to emphasize the independence of both the Covenant as a legal system in itself, and of the Committee as an institution for its implementation. It is also assumed that its functions, which are only loosely defined by the Covenant, can, over time, evolve significantly beyond its present practice. In the final part of the chapter a critical appraisal of the Committee's work to date is undertaken, and consideration is given to its possible future evolution.

A. *General Features*

I. A BRIEF DESCRIPTION

Technically speaking, the Human Rights Committee is a body of 'experts' working part-time, and assisted by the UN Secretariat. Its functions are

[1] See e.g. Nowak, 'The Effectiveness of the International Covenant on Civil and Political Rights: Stocktaking after the First Eleven Sessions of the UN Human Rights Committee', 1 *Hum. Rts. LJ* 163 (1980). For the most recent and comprehensive study of the Committee see McGoldrick, *The Human Rights Committee: Its Role in the Development of the International Covenant on Civil and Political Rights* (1991).

[2] Avery, 'The Human Rights Committee after Six Years: Thirty Operational Issues' unpub. MS (Columbia University School of Law, 1982), 1.

defined and limited by the International Covenant on Civil and Political Rights of 16 December 1966, which entered into force for thirty-five States Parties on 23 March 1976, as well as by the Optional Protocol to that Covenant.[3] Despite the Committee's more pretentious name, it would more accurately be described as the 'Civil and Political Rights Committee'. This fact became clear when the Committee on Economic, Social and Cultural Rights was set up in 1987, if not before.

Part IV of the Covenant sets out the Committee's composition, status, functions, and procedures. These provisions, together with the relevant parts of the Optional Protocol, provide the legal basis for all its activities. In brief, it may be described as the guardian of the Covenant, with responsibility for monitoring its implementation.[4] Indeed, all of its work is directly or indirectly devoted to this task.

Its two main functions, which we shall discuss in detail below, are to consider *reports* from, and *complaints* against, the States Parties. The former is obligatory for all States Parties, while the latter is optional and exists in two forms: interstate 'communications' under the Covenant, as well as individual 'communications' under the Optional Protocol.

The basic obligation of States Parties is to implement the rights provided for in Parts I and III of the Covenant.[5] Part IV, in addition to dealing with the Committee, contains provisions concerning the relationship of this system to the United Nations, the procedure for ratification, and so forth.

This chapter does not deal with the substantive rights contained in the Covenant except in so far as is necessary to illustrate trends and issues in the work of the Committee. However, the purpose of the Covenant is to promote and protect exactly these human rights, and the Committee's role in this respect is a central one in so far as one accepts the assumption that effective national implementation requires a degree of international accountability.[6] By the same token, the Committee is not the only factor in the overall equation.

[3] International Covenant on Civil and Political Rights, and Optional Protocol to the International Covenant on Civil and Political Rights, adopted by GA Res.2200 A (XXI) (1966), in United Nations, *Human Rights: A Compilation of International Instruments* (1988), 18–42.

[4] No description of the Committee's functions is entirely neutral. 'Monitoring' is preferred here over more controversial terms such as 'supervising', 'enforcing', or 'protecting' rights.

[5] They are laid down in Arts. 6–27 (Part III), International Covenant, and concern mainly the rights to life, integrity, personal freedom, humane treatment, movement, fair trial, legal personality, privacy, freedom of conscience and religion, expression, assembly, association, family, children, political rights, non-discrimination, and certain rights of persons belonging to minorities, all of which must be read together with Art. 1 (Part I) on the right of all peoples to self-determination and Arts. 2–5 (Part II) which contain a number of general provisions affecting the substance of the rights and freedoms enshrined in the Covenant.

[6] Even those who reject 'interventionist' approaches, or 'supervision' or 'condemnation' of States by international institutions may find value in co-operation through such organs, as do, for example, Graefrath, 'New Version of the Interventionist Proposal for a UN High Commissioner

Indeed, the first requirement of the Covenant is national implementation, which is the alpha and omega of human rights even when the latter are internationally recognized and the obligations accepted as binding.[7] In some countries the Covenant is regarded as self-executing, but for many reasons such a doctrine does not ensure perfect implementation. Furthermore, like any other treaty, the Covenant also lays down mutual obligations between States, and may therefore be invoked in bilateral relations.[8] Such use of the Covenant may happen from time to time, but it is difficult to obtain systematic knowledge about it. In addition the Covenant provisions are of major relevance to the work of many other international bodies, including the political organs of the United Nations, from the General Assembly and the Councils to the Commission on Human Rights. Nevertheless, the more States Parties engage in active co-operation with the Human Rights Committee, the more clearly the Committee becomes the central world forum for matters concerning the Covenant, even if we acknowledge that the role of international machinery is essentially of a subsidiary nature.

II. BACKGROUND

The Committee's historical origins reflect the struggle to reach agreement on measures of implementation for the International Bill of Human Rights.[9] On that question the *travaux préparatoires* reveal considerable differences among the various State groupings. The draft Covenant prepared in 1954 by the Commission envisioned a quasi-judicial Human Rights Committee quite different in its powers and functions from that which actually came into existence. It was another twelve years before the General Assembly's Third Committee debated the proposed implementation provisions, at which time they were drastically altered. The majority was opposed to making obligatory

for Human Rights', 2 *GDR Committee Hum. Rts. Bull.* 43 (1983); and Mohr, 'Questions of Procedure under International Law in the Implementation of Human Rights Instruments', ibid. 61.

[7] Art. 2(1), International Covenant. See e.g. Opsahl, 'Human Rights Today: International Obligations and National Implementation', 23 *Scandinavian St. L.* 153 (1979). Cf. ibid. 158–62 for a discussion of 'the double duty of implementation', contained in that provision's expression 'to respect and to ensure'.

[8] Henkin, 'Introduction', in id. (ed.), *The International Bill of Rights: The Covenant on Civil and Political Rights* (1981), 14 and 17.

[9] See e.g. Das, 'United Nations Institutions and Procedures Founded on Conventions on Human Rights and Fundamental Freedom', in K. Vasak and P. Alston (eds.), *The International Dimensions of Human Rights* (1980), 303; Robertson, 'The Implementation System: International Measures', in Henkin (ed.) (n. 8 above), 332; Jhabvala, 'The Practice of the Covenant's Human Rights Committee, 1976–82: Review of State Party Reports', 6 *Hum. Rts. Q.* 81 (1984). Study of the process is facilitated by Bossuyt, *Guide to the 'Travaux Préparatoires' of the International Covenant on Civil and Political Rights* (1987).

the procedure for interstate communications. The Soviet-led group was originally opposed to the establishment of any Committee at all, while the Afro-Asian group preferred that similar, but not identical, measures should be adopted for the two Covenants and that the proposed Committee should not be linked to the International Court of Justice.

All of the various positions, except that of dispensing with the Committee altogether, were taken into account by a formula worked out by the Afro-Asian group.[10] According to this version, the Committee's only compulsory role would be to study and comment generally upon the reports of States Parties, a function originally intended for the Commission on Human Rights. Many of the details of this proposal were amended, which later caused doubts and disagreements about the proper role of the Committee in the reporting system.[11] The functions relating to communications were made entirely optional, and arrangements providing for the consideration of individual complaints of violations were separated from the Covenant and put in the Optional Protocol.[12] In other words, the result was a compromise between those States which favoured strong international measures and those which emphasized the primacy of national sovereignty and responsibility. As is inevitably the case with such compromises, many specific issues were left unresolved, perhaps intentionally. As a result the subsequent evolution of the arrangements has had to be shaped by a continuing give-and-take within the Committee over many years.

III. ELECTION, COMPOSITION, AND ORGANIZATION

The eighteen members of the Committee are elected by the States Parties.[13] They must be nationals of those States[14] and be nominated by their own States.[15] With respect to individual candidates, the Covenant provides only that they shall be 'persons of high moral character and recognized competence in the field of human rights'.[16] Other requirements relate to the election process rather than to the candidates themselves. Thus the Covenant says that 'consideration' shall be given to 'the usefulness of the participation of some persons having legal experience',[17] and to the achievement of 'equitable

[10] Jhabvala, 'The Practice of the Covenant's Human Rights Committee', 86.

[11] For example, the insertion in Art. 40(4) of 'general' before 'comments', retained after a vote split 44–29–12 in the Third Committee. See Bossuyt, *Guide to the 'Travaux Préparatoires'*, 629–30. On its implications, see text accompanying nn. 169–202, below.

[12] The history of the Protocol is summarized by Møse and Opsahl, 'The Optional Protocol to the International Covenant on Civil and Political Rights', 21 *Santa Clara L. Rev.* 274–6 (1981).

[13] Arts. 28(1) and 30(4), International Covenant.

[14] Ibid. Art. 28(2).

[15] Ibid. Art. 29(2).

[16] Ibid. Art. 28(2).

[17] Ibid.

geographical distribution of membership and to the representation of the different forms of civilization and of the principal legal systems'.[18]

Members serve for terms of four years, with half of the positions being subject to election every two years.[19] The possibility of re-election, however, has been important in practice. The Committee was originally elected in 1976 by the then thirty-seven States Parties to the Covenant. Since that time the membership has changed, but only gradually.

Thus, in 1986, after ten years, five regular elections and three elections to fill single vacancies caused by death (twice) or resignation (once), seven of the original eighteen members still remained. The seven were from Cyprus, Ecuador, East and West Germany, Mauritius, Norway, and the Soviet Union. Meanwhile the number of States Parties had increased to eighty-five. There had thus been a significant continuity of membership. However, three of these seven did not stand for re-election in 1986. Thus, only four of the veterans (from Cyprus, Ecuador, Mauritius, and the Soviet Union) still went on into the second decade.[20] Elections in 1988 resulted in the three former continuing to serve in the Committee.[21]

Most members have come to the Committee with considerable legal experience or with other relevant professional backgrounds. Given the rather limited power and emoluments accompanying the task, the prestige factor must have been central in attracting a high calibre of nominees. Many members have been professors of law, most of whom have also had practical legal and international experience, and a number of others have been diplomats with legal training. In addition to these two dominant categories, the membership has also included judges, cabinet ministers, and individuals who serve or have served on other international human rights bodies.[22]

[18] Ibid. Art. 31(2). This formula has been applied more or less consistently during election consultations among States Parties, but the regional approach based on the five groupings of UN members seems open to various objections in this case; moreover, no authority can enforce the requirements of the Covenant.

[19] Art. 32, International Covenant.

[20] The membership after each election is listed, *inter alia*, in the annual reports of the Committee: A/32/44 (1977); A/33/40 (1978); A/34/40 (1979); A/35/40 (1980); A/36/40 (1981); A/37/40 (1982); A/38/40 (1983); A/39/40 (1984); A/40/40 (1985); A/41/40 (1986); A/42/40 (1987); A/43/40 (1988); A/44/40 (1989); A/45/40 (1990); A/46/40 (1991). A total of 45 individuals from 36 States Parties served on the Committee during the first 15 years. The 1986 election brought in 5 of them (for the years 1987–90), the 1988 election 3 (for the years 1989–92). Of these 8, 5 came from States Parties which had not had members elected before (Egypt, Hungary, Japan, Netherlands, and Sweden). In 1990, one new member (from Austria) and one (from Jordan) who had served an earlier term (1979–82) were elected.

[21] CCPR/SP/SR.13–14 (1988). The election brought in three new members, from Costa Rica, Hungary, and the USSR.

[22] In alphabetical order: Mr Aguilar (Venezuela, elected 1980 and 1984) was a former president of the Inter-American Commission of Human Rights; Mr Ermacora (Austria, elected 1980) was a member of the European Commission of Human Rights since 1958; Mr Evans (United Kingdon, elected 1976 and 1980) was a judge in the European Court of Human Rights

At any one time, only about one-fifth of the States Parties (98 as at 5 October 1991) can have members elected to the Committee. But they can all nominate candidates, and there have always been more candidates than seats to be filled. An exception is the filling of vacancies, where so far another national of the same State Party has been returned every time without contest. Astonishingly few of the many and important States which have ratified the Covenant since its entry into force have nominated candidates, despite the opportunity to do so. Most of the States Parties which have nominated candidates for the seven regular elections 1976–88, either did so at the first elections, or were among those thirty-seven States Parties which could have done so. Of the majority of States which have become parties later, only a minority have availed themselves of this right. The 1984 elections attracted fewer nominations then the 1976 election (21 as against 26), the 1986 elections even fewer (19), and likewise in 1988 (15), despite the fact that the number of States Parties had more than doubled.[23] Of course, later ordinary elections concerned only 9 seats and not 18 as the first time; still, increasing competition for the available seats might have been expected. It is difficult to say whether the existing composition has been found satisfactory; or whether a bias in favour of existing members has been tacitly accepted for the sake of continuity. Obviously some groups of States Parties consult among themselves before nominations are made.

At the election itself, several factors seem to affect the outcome. The most important appear to be geographical distribution and the lobbying effectiveness of the nominee's country's representatives at the United Nations.[24] Bloc voting and general diplomatic bargaining may also play their roles. As a result, a high premium is not always placed on those individual qualities which are most important from the Committee's viewpoint, such as competence, energy, ability to co-operate, negotiating skill, and propensity to attend meetings.

The geographical distribution of elected members has only roughly corresponded to the 'electorate', so that, for example, Africa was under-represented until 1984.[25] Moreover, the global distribution of the States Parties has had a different profile from that of the UN membership as a whole. Thus, for example, Asia 'proper', with eleven States Parties including

since 1980; and Mr Opsahl (Norway, elected 1976, 1978, and 1982) was a member of the European Commission of Human Rights in 1970–84. When the Committee started its work, the last was the only member who was at the same time sitting at one of the other bodies.

[23] 'Election of Members of the Human Rights Committee . . .', CCPR/SP/3 and 6 (1976); CCPR/SP/9, 10, and Add.2 (1978); CCPR/SP/13 and Add.1 (1980); CCPR/SP/16 (1982); CCPR/SP/26 (1984); CCPR/SP/29 and Add.1 and 4 (1986); CCPR/SP/32 and Add.1–2 (1988).

[24] Tarnopolsky, 'General Course on the International Protection of Human Rights', in *International Institute of Human Rights Collection of Lectures* (1984), 22.

[25] Bojji, 'Le Comité des droits de l'homme institué par le pacte international relatif aux droits civils et politiques', 17, Diploma thesis (Univ. of Geneva, 1985), presents tables and discusses the sources of under-representation.

populous nations like India and Japan, until 1986 had only one (from Sri Lanka) of the eighteen Committee members. The internal distribution of Committee positions has been made in accordance with the five regional groupings recognized in the United Nations. This concerns, in particular, the composition of the Bureau and Working Groups (below), as well as informal discussions, for example, about rotation in the election of officers of the Committee. However, these groupings have had different numbers of members in the Committee. Prior to 1985 there were six members counted as 'Western and others', three Latin Americans, two Africans, four Eastern Europeans, and three members from the Middle East and Asia. As a result of the 1984 elections both the Western and Asian nations lost a seat, while the African group gained two.[26] The geographical balance was thus improved. In 1986 Eastern Europe's turn to lose a seat came, Asia again gaining one;[27] both of these regions since then have had three members, which corresponds better to their number of States Parties. Among sub-regions the five Nordic countries will probably continue to co-operate in order to keep one seat.

The geographical groupings in UN terms are, however, of limited relevance in the human rights context. One obvious illustration is the fact that the Committee's Chairman for the first ten years, Andreas Mavrommatis (Cyprus), comes from a country which in the United Nations is counted as Asian (Middle East) but at the same time is a member State in the Council of Europe and a party to the European Convention.

For the first seven years of the Committee, no women were elected or even nominated. The first woman member, a Canadian elected in 1983 to fill a vacancy,[28] was not re-elected at the ordinary election the following year despite her strong qualifications. However, another woman, from the United Kingdom, was then nominated and elected.[29] In 1986 only France followed this good example,[30] and in 1988 no country did. That is, of course, quite unsatisfactory. Blame for the male domination must be borne by those (ninety odd) States Parties which so far have not nominated any women at all.

Members are elected and serve in their personal capacity and are, in UN terminology, described as 'experts'.[31] This requires, ideally, independence

[26] Mr Lallah (Mauritius) returned after an absence of two years and Mr Wako (Kenya) was elected for the first time. Mr Pocar (Italy) came in instead of outgoing members from Austria and Canada; the other seat that can be said to have gone to Africa was that of an outgoing member from Iraq.

[27] No new East European was elected in 1986, when Mr Graefrath (German Democratic Republic) left the Committee. A member from Japan was elected for the first time.

[28] Ms Cote-Harper replaced Mr Tarnopolsky, who resigned upon his appointment to the Ontario Court of Appeal.

[29] Ms Higgins, elected after the expiry of the second term of Mr Evans.

[30] Ms Chanet, elected after the expiry of the term of Mr Errera (France).

[31] Art. 28(3), International Covenant, about 'personal capacity' and Art. 43 (ibid.) about entitlements of 'experts on mission' for the United Nations. The term 'expert from (country)' is also consistently used by the UN administration regarding Committee members, *inter alia*, for financial and information purposes.

from the governments which have nominated them, a point underlined by the solemn declaration required of each member to 'perform his functions impartially and conscientiously'.[32] Inevitably, however, independence is relative and varies with the backgrounds of the members and the practices of their governments. It is not unique to this body that some experts seem to have been in closer contact with the authorities of their own countries than other members, if they have not acted directly under instructions; others have at the same time as their Committee membership been serving their governments in an official capacity. Some have even combined posts by being cabinet ministers, UN ambassadors, advisers to the Foreign Ministry, and so on in a way which could easily prejudice the independence of their contribution to the work of the Committee.[33] However, the personality factor is equally important, and members' links with governments may mean that influence is exerted in both directions.

The ideological and political background of members is another important factor affecting the dynamics of the Committee. Members' attitudes are usually quite representative of their national backgrounds, although they explicitly, and often rightly, refuse to be identified with the official positions of their governments. At any rate, traditional political and ideological differences are reflected in the Committee's work. As we shall see, however, for several reasons such differences have never paralyzed the Committee, although they may have dominated certain issues. Members arriving with different attitudes and experiences soon share common experiences and begin to form common views modifying their differences. The formal and informal interaction among members has created friendships across ideological divisions, and has promoted a degree of mutual confidence and rapport. Superficially, there is a common human desire to succeed in the task at hand, and, at a somewhat deeper level, there is also a certain meeting of minds on points of substance and values.

The fact that only one superpower so far was a State Party has made the Committee much less of an arena for confrontation and struggle than if the others had also been present. The USSR member has had an interesting role to play in the Committee, and has often played it well.[34] Although Europe as a

[32] Art. 38, International Covenant.

[33] There have been cabinet ministers from Iran and Colombia (during the 1977–80 term), UN ambassadors from several countries (Cyprus, Jordan, Tunisia, and Venezuela), and various holders of other government posts.

[34] Elected in 1976, 1980, and 1984, Anatoly P. Movchan made many important contributions to the Committee's work. With his experience from the UN Secretariat (Legal Division), he always stressed the need for correct procedures and consistent application of the Covenant, the Rules of Procedure, and Committee decisions; he proposed at the outset that the Committee's work should be based on consensus (see below). He often found solutions to drafting and other problems; he also took very firm positions opposing other members whose views were different from his. Mr Movchan resisted some initiatives and efforts to develop the work of the Committee. But despite his often strong and sometimes even rude language, he also showed commendable

whole—East and West—has recruited a number of very active members, politically speaking divisions among them for many years tended to neutralize them and give decisive influence to others. From 1989, new developments in Europe have removed old sources of friction and because the patterns of work are now established without the domination of any superpower, the risk of paralysis would be less if members from the United States or China were eventually to join.

The Committee elects its Officers for terms of two years.[35] It has a Chairman, three Vice-Chairmen, and a Rapporteur who in practice have virtually always been elected by consensus. This 'Bureau' has helped the Committee to plan its work and sometimes to negotiate the necessary consensus in private meetings. The Chairman for the first ten years, Andreas Mavrommatis, is a man of wide experience and great skill as a lawyer and a diplomat. When he was again elected Chairman in 1985, one member, exceptionally, expressed reservations.[36] When Mr Mavrommatis was not a candidate for re-election as Chairman, he was succeeded in 1987 by Mr Prado Vallejo (Ecuador), in 1989, by Mr Lallah (Mauritius), and in 1991 by Mr Pocar (Italy). The Chairman has always played a key role in presiding over the Committee's work, guiding its deliberations, and, when necessary, conducting informal consultations to achieve a consensus. In recent years such consultations have been conducted more frequently outside, rather than within, the Bureau. The position of Committee Rapporteur was seen as a key post at the first election. However, he has not in practice been given any special functions other than those connected with the drafting of the Committee's annual report, which in itself is important. Nevertheless, there has been frequent rotation in this post.[37]

Subsidiary bodies of the Committee are foreseen in the Rules of Procedure[38] and are regularly used in practice, usually in the form of Working Groups

realism and ability to compromise. Together with other Eastern European members, his participation clearly facilitated the Committee's dialogue with socialist countries. His successor, elected in 1988, Mr Rein A. Myullerson, represented the 'new thinking' in the USSR, and since 1991 has been an Estonian expert.

[35] Art. 39(1), International Covenant.

[36] Mr Bouziri (Tunisia) observed that consultations had failed to achieve consensus. CCPR/C/SR.574 (1985), paras. 6–8. He also requested that certain matters, such as the role of the Secretariat, be taken up separately. CCPR/C/SR.575 (1985), para. 2.

[37] The first Rapporteur (Mr Uribe Vargas, Colombia, 1977–8) was twice temporarily replaced in his absence by acting Rapporteurs from the same region, while the second (Mr Lallah, Mauritius) served for four years, 1979–82. In the following four-year period, three different Rapporteurs were elected and served (Mr Tarnopolsky from Canada, Mr Opsahl from Norway, and Mr Graefrath from the German Democratic Republic). They were succeeded by Mr Dimitrijevic (Yugoslavia) in 1987, Mr Pocar (Italy) in 1989, and Mr Ando (Japan) in 1991.

[38] Rule 89 of the 'Provisional Rules of Procedure as Adopted at the First and Second Sessions of the Human Rights Committee', *Report of the Human Rights Committee*, A/32/44 (1977), Annex II. When amending the Rules in 1989, the term 'provisional' was dropped from the title. A/44/40 (1989), para. 23 and Annex IX.

(three to five members) to make recommendations to the Committee on communications under the Optional Protocol. Since 1980, other Working Groups have made important recommendations relating to States reports under Article 40 of the Covenant, and the drafting of 'general comments' under that Article.[39] From time to time, Special Rapporteurs have been appointed to make recommendations on cases and other matters.

IV. ACTIVITIES

The Covenant, and thus the 'jurisdiction' of the Committee, extends as at the beginning of 1992 to almost one hundred States Parties[40] with a combined population of nearly 3 billion people. This includes most of the important UN member States, with the notable exceptions of the United States and China. Former socialist States were among the first to ratify the Covenant, while developing countries make up about two-thirds of the current membership.

In order to monitor the implementation of civil and political rights on this vast scale it might be assumed that the Committee would need to work year-round, and have considerable staff and resources at its disposal. The reality, however, is very different from what the magnitude of the task and the terms of the Covenant suggest.[41] Although the Committee's functions demand a certain permanence or at least continuous effort, the Committee only operates during its sessions, usually nine weeks in a year. The permanence of the Secretariat can do little—far too little—to outweigh this handicap.

(a) *Sessions*

The Covenant states that the Committee shall meet at such times as shall be provided in its rules of procedure, normally at UN Headquarters or at the UN Office at Geneva.[42] The rules adopted at its first session provide for future sessions 'as may be required for the satisfactory performance of its functions',[43] and prescribe 'normally . . . two regular sessions each year'.[44]

[39] The issues discussed in text accompanying nn. 169–202 have usually been examined first by such a Working Group.

[40] Information on ratifications as of Jul. 1991 is given in *Report of the Human Rights Committee*, A/46/40 (1991), Annex I.

[41] Art. 36, International Covenant, requires that the Secretary-General provide 'the necessary staff and facilities' for 'the effective performance of the functions' of the Committee. Art. 35 (ibid.) mentions that members shall receive emoluments 'having regard to the importance of the Committee's responsibilities'. These provisions are, however, subject to what the UN General Assembly decides.

[42] Art. 37(2) and (3), International Covenant.

[43] Rule 1, Rules of Procedure.

[44] Ibid. Rule 2.

But after extensive debate at the second session in 1977 the Committee decided that necessary measures should be taken to include a third regular session the following year.[45] Without any amendment of the rules this became the normal pattern, with sessions in the spring in New York, and in summer and autumn in Geneva, each of three weeks. The Committee may meet elsewhere, but has only done so once, in Bonn, in 1981, and after being invited by the Federal Republic of Germany.[46] The Committee had hoped to receive more such invitations in order to become more visible in different regions.

Working groups usually meet one week prior to the sessions. The autumn session of 1986 had to be cancelled because of the UN's financial crisis. While the Committee maintained that the decision in this regard came within its purview, it was forced to concede that it had no choice in the matter. Also, the venue of the first session in 1987 was changed from New York to Geneva.[47] With these exceptions, the customary schedule of meetings and venues has been resumed.

Fulfilment of the Committee's main functions under the Covenant naturally takes up most of its meeting time, and also requires much preparation and follow-up work on the part of the members and the Secretariat. Other activities include determination of the methods and programmes of work and of the rules of procedure, the holding of elections, the drafting of annual reports, and the adoption of measures to promote publicity. Most activities take place in public plenary meetings, which are interrupted occasionally for informal consultations. About one-third of the meetings are held in private, as is required for the handling of complaints (communications). Most members attend regularly, but the quorum of twelve[48] has on a few occasions not been achieved.

Only State representatives attending for reporting purposes are regularly invited to participate and address the Committee. In a few instances others have been given the floor, such as representatives of UN specialized agencies

[45] *Report of the Human Rights Committee*, A/32/44 (1977), paras. 165–7 reflects this discussion and the decision. For further details, see CCPR/C/SR.37 (1977); CCPR/C/SR.42 (1977), paras. 1–7; and CCPR/C/SR.44 (1977), paras. 20–68.

[46] *Report of the Human Rights Committee*, A/37/40 (1982), para. 4 put on record the Committee's appreciation of this valuable experience.

[47] Ibid. A/41/40 (1986), paras. 425–34. The General Assembly had already decided that one of the 1986 sessions should be cancelled (GA Dec. 40/472 (1986), ibid. para. 427); however, the Committee stated the case for the existing pattern (ibid. para. 428) and said, *inter alia*, that '[t]he decision to cancel that session could be taken by the Committee only with the utmost reluctance as an exceptional and drastic measure' (ibid. para. 429). Cf. ibid. para. 434 (restating the importance attached by the Committee to the maintenance of its schedule). See, further, text accompanying n. 94, below. In 1989, the Committee stressed the necessity of annual sessions at the UN Headquarters. A/44/40 (1989), para. 27.

[48] Art. 39(2)(a), International Covenant; cf. Rule 37, Rules of Procedure.

who have explained their position in matters relevant to the Covenant,[49] but this has not developed into any regular form of participation.[50]

The UN Secretariat also participates in the meetings and is represented by a Committee secretary, and a higher ranking official of the Centre for Human Rights, sitting as the representative of the Secretary-General.

Finally, a number of non-governmental organizations regularly have observers present in the public meetings, although they do not sit with name-shields at the Committee table and cannot formally address the Committee.[51] In principle the public has access to the meetings except when they are closed for such purposes as the handling of communications.[52] Apart from NGO observers, meetings are poorly attended by visitors since neither the press nor the public at large have paid much attention to the work of the Committee. The actual extent of personal interaction depends not only on the shape and size of the meeting room but also on the venue. In Geneva informal contacts are not difficult whereas in New York the room is big and impersonal and access to the building is rather restricted.

In addition to the participants and observers, a comprehensive apparatus of technical services surrounds the meetings for the purposes of simultaneous interpretation into all working languages of the Committee (English, French, Spanish, Russian, and since 1984, Arabic); documentation, in principle, in the same languages; the writing of summary records;[53] and, the preparation of press releases. In this way considerable resources are invested in the Committee's work.

However, as regards the substance of the Committee's activities, the organized input is less impressive. Thus, members of the Committee are left completely to their own devices, studying the documentation and preparing their interventions as best they can in their hotel rooms. They have no

[49] The question of the Committee's co-operation with the specialized agencies occupied it for some time.

[50] See e.g. the discussion between Mr Vasak (UNESCO) and members of the Committee, CCPR/C/SR.78 (1978), paras. 18–49.

[51] The most faithful observers have been representatives of Amnesty International, International Commission of Jurists, International League for Human Rights, International Confederation of Free Trade Unions, and the Quakers. A few scholars have joined them.

[52] Rule 33, Rules of Procedure, provides for meetings to be held in public unless the Committee decides otherwise or it appears from the relevant provisions of the Covenant or the Protocol that the meeting should be held in private. Art. 5(4) of the Optional Protocol requires 'closed meetings when examining communications'.

[53] Rule 35, Rules of Procedure, requires the Secretariat to prepare summary records of all meetings. For years, the United Nations has sought to dispense with summary records in a number of bodies, because of the high cost involved; the financial crisis in 1986 brought the matter to an acute stage. Before the Committee had responded to the request from the General Assembly, the Conference Services Division announced that they would not be provided during the third week of the session (CCPR/SR.691 (1986), para. 1). See the discussion during that meeting (CCPR/C/SR.691 (1986)), as well as its summary and the Committee's decision, *Report of the Human Rights Committee*, A/41/40 (1986), paras. 430 and 432.

secretarial assistance, nor office space, much less any advisers, researchers, or speech writers, as is otherwise usual in public life. The provision that members are to 'serve in a personal capacity',[54] or as 'independent experts', is thus applied perhaps all too literally. As a result, 'all members have had to fall back on their own missions for support facilities'.[55] Also absent are any country or regional files to which members can refer for general information. The general UN library facilities are of limited practical use during sessions, so that information provided by non-governmental organizations consequently assumes critical importance. Compared to many other UN bodies, strain and time pressures on members are considerable. They must follow all proceedings while at the same time preparing their interventions, which, in the case of comments and questions on State reports, may amount to hour-long statements, covering many complex issues of law and fact. The burden of work on members during sessions is heavy, and most of them then do more than can reasonably be expected. By contrast, little or no work by members is foreseen between sessions.

Despite these constraints, the output achieved by the Committee has been considerable. In the course of its first fifteen reporting periods the Committee held 1091 meetings during forty-two sessions. It examined eighty-five initial State reports in public meetings with representatives of the States concerned, thirteen 'supplementary reports', and second periodic reports from forty-eight States Parties, as well as third periodic reports from eleven of them. It also dealt with 468 private complaints.[56]

The documents of the Committee run into tens of thousands of pages. They are, in accordance with UN practice, divided into those of general and restricted distribution, respectively.[57] Documents are, however, never issued in large numbers[58] and some complain that they are difficult to obtain.

The most important sources for study of the Committee's activities are the summary records of its meetings[59] and the annual reports.[60] After considerable delay, the publication of a Yearbook was also begun in 1986[61] but it will take several years to catch up with the existing backlog. Volume I of each

[54] Art. 28(3), International Covenant.

[55] Tarnopolsky, 'General Course', 22.

[56] The figures are based on the *Report of the Human Rights Committee*, A/46/40 (1991).

[57] See Rules 36, 64(1) and (3), and 64(2) for the definition of documents of general and restricted distribution Rules of Procedure.

[58] For example, 3,600–4,300 copies of the Report seem to be issued each year. (See back covers of the annual reports, n. 20, above.)

[59] Identified by the symbol CCPR/C/SR.

[60] Issued each year as *Report of the Human Rights Committee*, General Assembly Official Records: Session, Supplement No. 40 (A/ /40). Cited here by title, UN document number, and year, and listed in n. 20 above.

[61] *Yearbook of the Human Rights Committee 1977–1978*, i (CCPR/1) and ii (CCPR/1/Add.1) appeared in 1986; *Yearbook of the Human Rights Committee 1979–1980*, i (CCPR/2) in 1988; ii (CCPR/2/Add.1) and the volumes for 1981–1982 in 1989; CCPR/4 for 1983–1984 in 1991.

Yearbook contains the summary records of public meetings while Volume II contains, *inter alia*, all of the States reports.

The UN press releases issued regularly during the Committee sessions can provide a superficial introduction to the work, but they cannot be relied on for accuracy. In the author's experience, even the summary records are often far from perfect because most speakers do not avail themselves of the opportunity to correct them. In any event, the Corrigendum which contains the corrections has only a very limited readership.

(*b*) *Rules of Procedure and Methods of Work: Voting v. Consensus*

The Covenant provides that the Committee shall establish its own rules of procedure.[62] At its first session the Committee considered and, after detailed deliberations and negotiations on certain issues,[63] adopted much of a draft prepared by the Secretariat, which was based mainly on the rules of the Committee on the Elimination of Racial Discrimination (CERD). The second session had the benefit of a working group's recommendations, and a revised draft on the rules concerning the admissibility and consideration of communications was adopted.[64] A chapter on interstate communications was left open until the relevant article came into force in 1979 and the lacuna was filled after some considerable discussion,[65] although the chapter has yet to be put to use.

Because the original Secretariat draft was taken from other texts, particularly the rules adopted by CERD, and because the Committee had no experience of its own when it adopted the rules, many of them have later shown themselves not to be particularly well suited to the Committee's evolving practices. The general part has to some extent remained a dead letter, in particular the chapter on voting. Even the parts dealing with the specific functions of the Committee have been overtaken by later developments on some points, and have not often been invoked in the deliberations even when they might have provided answers to controversial questions. Instead, supplementary decisions have been taken by the Committee on its programme and methods of work, guidelines for States Parties reporting, periodicity of reporting, and other matters. Since they embody and codify the Committee's practices, the importance of these decisions is far greater than that of the Rules of Procedure. No published collection exists, but most of the relevant decisions are annexed to the annual reports of the years in which they have

[62] Art. 39(2), International Covenant.

[63] See for the preliminary draft CCPR/C/L.2 and Add.1–2 (1977); for the discussions, see CCPR/C/SR.3–17 (1977) or their summary in the *Report of the Human Rights Committee*, A/32/44 (1977), paras. 16–57.

[64] The debates are summarized in *Report of the Human Rights Committee*, A/32/44 (1977), paras. 58–94.

[65] The debates in CCPR/C/SR. 125–6, 139, 150–1, 156, and 169 (1979) are summarized in *Report of the Human Rights Committee*, A/34/40 (1979), paras. 28–53.

been adopted. These reports also describe other practices, whether arising out of, or codified in, Committee decisions or not. The growth of the Committee's procedures and practices therefore warrants special attention, although it cannot be fully accounted for here.

Practices of questionable formal status, such as tacit understandings on the status of unofficial information, rotation of the membership of the Bureau, and the need to obtain States Parties' consent to certain procedures, are particularly precarious. On a number of occasions views have differed sharply as to whether or not an alleged 'gentlemen's agreement' existed, and, if so, on what it said. Moreover, new members have sometimes objected to being bound by earlier informal practices.

The central issue in this regard concerned the basis on which the Committee's decisions were to be taken. The problem arose at a very early stage of deliberations when, at the first session, the member from the USSR, supported by other Eastern European members, proposed a procedural rule providing for the use of 'consensus' in making decisions.[66] This proposal initially met with considerable scepticism, particularly off the record. Members noted that the Covenant itself provided for decisions to be taken by majority vote.[67] But, at the same time, all members acknowledged the value of seeking consensus whenever possible. An intense discussion ensued.[68] Eventually a deadlock was averted through the adoption of a principle of seeking consensus *as a method of work*. The discussions had in themselves amounted to a successful search for consensus, and had brought valuable experience with this method of work. The solution was, however, to be without prejudice to the Covenant rule, or to the right of any member to ask for a vote at any time.[69] At the time, it was felt by some members that while this approach might be workable with respect to procedural matters, it would be less feasible

[66] A first proposal was made in the third meeting, when, dealing with Rule 9 (agenda), Mr Movchan suggested using consensus (CCPR/C/SR.3 (1977), para. 80), after several speakers (Mr Evans, Mr Tarnopolsky, the Chairman, and Mr Lallah) had referred to majority vote (ibid. paras. 75–8). Other members (Mr Opsahl, Mr Evans, and Mr Espersen) agreed that consensus was a good principle of work, but given Art. 39(2) of the Covenant, it could not easily be adopted as a rule of procedure (ibid. paras. 83–4 and 86). The debate continued at length at the next meeting, when the proposal for Rule 9 was reworded by another Eastern European member (Mr Hanga) (CCPR/C/SR.4 (1977), Paras. 2–34).

[67] Art. 39(2), International Covenant states that the 'rules shall provide that: . . . (b) Decisions of the Committee shall be made by a majority vote of the members present.'

[68] The consideration of draft Rule 9 (n. 66, above) led into Rules 49 and 51. The summary records (CCPR/C/SR.6–7, 12–14 (1977)) and the summary of the discussion (*Report of the Human Rights Committee*, A/32/44 (1977), paras. 27–34) do not reflect its intensity, since most of the discussion took place in informal consultations which extended over a number of days.

[69] *Report of the Human Rights Committee*, A/32/44 (1977), paras. 32–34, reflects the Committee agreement to seek consensus before voting, but subject to the Covenant and Rules of Procedure, and without such attempts unduly delaying the Committee's work. It was also decided to include a footnote to this effect in Rule 50, restating Art. 39(2) of the Covenant on decisions by majority vote (see n. 67, above).

on matters of substance. Nevertheless, for better or worse, and sometimes at the price of vague compromise formulas, decisions by consensus have since become the general rule. No formal vote has ever been taken by the Committee; the detailed chapter on voting in the Rules of Procedure as well as the exact interpretation of the Article on voting in the Covenant[70] have thus never been tested. The original decision refers to the seeking of consensus '*before* voting', but it has always been applied as if it read '*instead of* voting'. Thus, the decisions reached are never confirmed by a vote. However, the recording of disagreements does occur, as illustrated by the separate and individual opinions filed in cases under the Optional Protocol.[71]

V. RELATIONS WITH UN BODIES

(*a*) *Point of Departure: Independence*

In legal terms the Covenant establishes an independent regime, of which the Committee is an integral part. More precisely, the Covenant is a treaty creating a separate and independent set of obligations for States Parties, as well as providing the basis for the Committee which it establishes. Moreover, when the Covenant states that members shall act 'in their personal capacity', it means in this context that they act as members of a treaty organ and not as subordinates in any hierarchy, whether national or international. Thus, they are not to take instructions from any body including the United Nations. Nevertheless, the Covenant is a creation of the world organization and neither its substantive rights nor its measures of implementation are conceivable in a vacuum. In formal legal terms it may be insisted that the basis of the Committee is not the UN Charter, nor any UN organ, such as the Commission on Human Rights or the General Assembly under whose auspices the Covenant was adopted. Rather it is a separate treaty and could not under the Charter have become binding in any way other than ratification. Over one-third of the member States of the United Nations are not as yet States Parties to the Covenant and have neither obligations nor functions under it. Still, the United Nations itself has both, and the impact of its obligations and functions under the Covenant is felt in every meeting of the Committee and in every aspect of its work. In times of crisis, the Committee's independence may seem unreal.

(*b*) *Absence of an 'International Organization for Civil and Political Rights'*

The meeting of States Parties provided for under the Covenant could have been conceived of as the highest organ within this separate system of law. The

70 See on this subject Das, 'United Nations Institutions and Procedures Founded on Conventions on Human Rights and Fundamental Freedom', *The International Dimensions of Human Rights*, 303.

71 See text accompanying nn. 239–67, below.

Covenant might thus have created a kind of 'International Organization for Civil and Political Rights' with the meeting of States Parties as a general assembly and an executive body in the form of a committee elected by it. But the present structure is far from such a vision. It has no separate budget, for example, and the meeting of States Parties consists of representatives of permanent missions in New York. The meeting of States Parties nevertheless does have a role in the procedure for amending the Covenant.[72] It has been proposed that its functions could be be enlarged in practice, so that, for instance, the meeting could consider matters relating to reporting by States, or to the Committee's needs. Such hints have so far yielded few, if any, results. The USSR reserved its position on the agenda item 'Other matters' in 1982 when the Netherlands took up the matter of derogation in times of emergency, which was thought to be of concern to all States Parties. This attempt to engage the meeting in debate found little or no response, at least officially.[73] However, at the meeting in 1986 to elect Committee members Tunisia raised the matter of the effect of the financial crisis on the work of the Committee, and several delegations took up the issue.[74]

Still, the Covenant provides an independent legal basis for the Committee's work. In this way it is not a 'United Nations Committee'. Moreover, the task of the Committee is to monitor the implementation of human rights, not to propose others. Further, it has to be recalled that its mandate is limited to the States Parties, and that its members are not serving as representatives of governments. On all these points the Committee differs clearly from the UN Commission on Human Rights, with which it is often confused.

(*c*) *Role of UN Organs*

Despite this formal independence, the Covenant links the Committee and its work to various UN Charter organs: the General Assembly provides for members' emoluments and receives the annual report;[75] ECOSOC transmits the report and may receive the Committee's general comments along with copies of State reports;[76] and the Secretary-General provides staff and facilities and convenes sessions.[77] In practice a range of UN bodies on lower levels are concerned with the Committee's work. They include the Assembly's Third Committee, and to a lesser extent, the Commission and its various offspring, and, above all, the Centre for Human Rights.

This interaction with the UN organs, which is both essential and difficult,

[72] Art. 51, International Covenant, provides for a special conference of the States Parties to be called for that event. Election meetings are governed by Art. 30(4), ibid.

[73] CCPR/SP/SR.5 (1982), paras. 19–24.

[74] CCPR/SP/SR.11 (1986), paras. 30–40.

[75] Arts. 35 and 45, International Covenant.

[76] Ibid. Arts. 40(4) and 45.

[77] Ibid. Arts. 36 and 37.

poses a number of characteristic problems for 'treaty organs' like the Committee, CERD,[78] CEDAW,[79] and the Committee against Torture.[80] On a different formal basis they also arise for the Committee on Economic, Cultural and Social Rights.[81]

During one of its sessions in New York the Committee was described as 'a prisoner in the basement of the UN'. Not only was it physically confined to an underground meeting room to which only people with a security clearance could obtain access, despite the principle of public meetings, but some members also felt figuratively imprisoned in the structure of the organization. The higher UN organs have so far not concerned themselves with the Committee to any large extent beyond the minimum required by the Covenant. If anything, the Committee has felt somewhat neglected, particularly by the General Assembly and the Secretary-General. The former, despite a suggestion by the Committee that its Chairman be invited to introduce its first annual report in 1977, has never agreed to such a practice.[82] And the latter has never personally attended any meeting of the Committee. Interviewed in 1983, Mr Pérez de Cuellar expressed, in a non-committal manner, his interest in attending a meeting of the Committee,[83] but this idea apparently has never been taken up seriously. ECOSOC on the other hand, later suggested a rescheduling of the Committee's annual report in order to be able to deal with it in substance. This time, however, it was the Committee which did not want to accommodate the request.[84]

Nevertheless, the General Assembly, through its Third Committee, has shown a natural interest in the Committee's work when dealing with its annual report. Gradually, more and more delegations have made observations of substance concerning its opinions, practices, and problems as reflected in the

[78] Committee on the Elimination of Racial Discrimination, established under Art. 8 of the International Convention on the Elimination of all Forms of Racial Discrimination, adopted by GA Res.2106 A (XX) (1965), *International Instruments*, 56–69. See Chap. 9, above.

[79] Committee on the Elimination of Discrimination against Women, established under Art. 17 of the Convention on the Elimination of all Forms of Discrimination against Women, adopted by GA Res.34/180 (1979), *International Instruments*, 112–25. See Chap. 11, below.

[80] Established under Art. 17 of the Convention against Torture and other Cruel, Inhuman or Degrading Treatment or Punishment, adopted by GA Res.39/46 (1984), *International Instruments*, 212–26. See Chap. 13, below.

[81] Created by ESC Res.1985/17, to assist the Economic and Social Council in monitoring States Parties' compliance with their obligations under the International Covenant on Economic, Social and Cultural Rights, adopted by GA Res.2200 A (XXI) (1966), *International Instruments*, 7–18. See Chap. 12, below.

[82] Members of the Third Committee of the General Assembly were of the opinion that 'there did not seem to be sufficient precedent to justify the sending of an invitation to the Chairman', CCPR/C/L.8 (1978), para. 4, and further references therein.

[83] 'Bedre midler til a lose problemene (Better Means to Solve the Problems)', 3 *Mennesker og Rettigheter* 90 (1983).

[84] *Report of the Human Rights Committee*, A/39/40 (1984), para. 25 refers to ECOSOC's decisions and the consultations which took place; *Report of the Human Rights Committee*, A/40/40 (1985), para. 13 refers to the Committee's negative conclusion.

report. The Assembly has regularly adopted resolutions about the need for universal ratification and observance of the Covenant and it has expressed appreciation and support for the work of the Committee.[85] But the sponsors of these resolutions have avoided any suggestion of reviewing the decisions or views of the Committee, even though such suggestions have occasionally been made in the debate in the Third Committee. Uruguay, in 1979, raised objections to the Committee's views under the Optional Protocol, but no action was taken by the Assembly; the same response occurred when a suggestion was made by Italy in 1982 that the Assembly should express its views on the Covenant.[86] It seems to have been the policy of the Assembly to de-emphasize the links between the Committee and the United Nations; at least it has clearly not sought to influence the substance of its work by direct intervention. Any such attempt would almost certainly be resisted by the Committee, which in law must maintain that it takes no instructions from any other body inside or outside the United Nations in matters of substance. The Committee, for its part, has dealt with the Assembly's debate on its annual report as a separate item on its agenda. In this way a slow dialogue between the two organs has been conducted.[87] The substance discussed between them has occasionally touched on the Committee's competence,[88] but more often on the organization and progress of its work.

The dilemma of preserving the Committee's substantive independence from the United Nations, while at the same time securing from the United Nations the necessary support and resources, cannot be solved by a simple formula. This is realized by all Committee members although they might differ as to how the dilemma should be resolved; in particular, some would obviously be more activist than others. This has to do with whether or not they want a Committee with 'teeth'; an independent body exercising real supervision. In the past some members seemed to prefer, instead, a Committee acting mainly as a forum for interstate co-operation and a clearing-house for ideas, and not much more. Until recently, realism, and the principle of

[85] See e.g. GA Res. 41/119, 41/120, and 41/121 (1986) referred to in *Report of the Human Rights Committee*, A/42/40 (1987), paras. 26–31, and GA Res. 43/114 and 43/115 (1989), in *Report of the Human Rights Committee*, A/44/40, paras. 29–34 (1989).

[86] Uruguay's letter was distributed as an official document in the Third Committee, 'Letter dated 12 October 1979 from the Permanent Representative of Uruguay to the United Nations addressed to the Secretary-General', A/C.3/34/3 (1979), and a reply came in 'Letter dated 1 November 1979 from the Permanent Representative of Panama to the United Nations addressed to the Secretary-General', A/C.3/34/6 (1979); cf. Mose and Opsahl, 'The Optional Protocol', 327 n. 253. For Italy's intervention in the Third Committee, see A/C.3/SR.51 (1982), paras. 29–34.

[87] See e.g. *Report of the Human Rights Committee*, A/39/40 (1984), paras. 18–23; A/40/40 (1985), paras. 23–30; A/41/40 (1986), paras. 21–8; A/42/40 (1987), paras. 26–32; A/43/40 (1988), paras. 26–9; A/44/40 (1989), paras. 29–34; A/45/40 (1990), paras. 20–6.

[88] This concerned its general comment 14(23) on the right to life and the threat of war, especially of arms of mass destruction. *Report of the Human Rights Committee*, A/40/40 (1985), para. 27.

consensus, have perhaps weighed in their favour. Since 1989 a new approach has been evident and new iniatives are expected.

UN rules and principles are important constraints on the Committee's actions. For example, from the very beginning the Committee experienced difficulties in the exercise of its authority to schedule its own meetings. In its first annual report it expressed 'its strong reservations' about the manner of setting the next year's calendar,[89] and more recently the venue in Spring 1990 caused controversy. In practice, not only the number and duration of the sessions, but also their timing, are matters beyond its control. This is but one of the organizational and financial implications of the Covenant's approach in making the Committee dependent on the Secretariat for staff and facilities.[90]

Such outside constraints also affect the way the Committee understands its mandate and its ability to carry out its functions. The complex factors, mainly of a political nature, which frustrate so many UN activities also contribute to the 'prisoner in the basement' syndrome. There is, of course, no permanent conspiracy of hostile forces. When members occasionally criticize the Secretariat, they are protesting against the political reality that prevents the development of the Committee in the way they would like to see it. Each Committee member must decide whether to accept the status quo or to struggle to break down the external constraints. The financial crisis of 1986 made this major problem acute. The ways in which the UN's crisis management affected the human rights programme were much debated both inside the Committee and within the human rights movement.[91]

(*d*) *The Secretariat*

A particularly ambiguous role is played by the Secretariat. In principle, the Charter-based activity of the Secretariat in human rights matters can and must be separated from its treaty-based functions, such as serving the Committee. But in practice it is difficult to serve two masters. Beginning from the top of the hierarchy, it is obvious that the Secretary-General in person normally must respond to the political atmosphere in the organization rather than to the wishes of a Committee of experts. Imagine, for instance, that the Committee were to ask him to offer his 'good offices' in the human rights situation in a State Party during an emergency which had been notified in accordance with the relevant provisions of the Covenant.[92] His political

[89] Ibid. A/32/44 (1977), para. 163; see also CCPR/C/SR.923 (1989), paras. 14–40.

[90] Rule 27, Rules of Procedure, prescribes a special procedure before any proposal which involves expenditure is approved by the Committee.

[91] In particular at an NGO seminar in Geneva, 8–10 Sept. 1986. See its recommendations and conclusions, as well as a number of background papers, in 4 *Mennesker og Rettigheter* 30–43 (1986).

[92] Art. 4(3), International Covenant deals with notification of emergencies. See the discussion of reporting obligations in such situations in CCPR/C/SR.334, 349, and 351 (1982), summarized in *Report of the Human Rights Committee*, A/37/40 (1982), paras. 340–4.

advisers would certainly point out the risk of disapproval from influential UN member States, whether they had ratified the Covenant or not, no matter how irrelevant their views would be in terms of the treaty. In an interview in 1983 the Secretary-General, while confirming the importance of his good offices in human rights matters, stated only that in such a situation the legal aspects would have to be carefully examined.[93] Even more obviously, when the UN financial situation is in crisis, recourse to the terms of the treaty cannot make the Committee immune to proposed budget cuts. It has enjoyed neither autonomy nor influence in budget matters, and until 1986 was not even consulted. The question whether the General Assembly can insist on cuts despite the objections of the Committee can never be authoritatively answered in legal terms. The decisions taken by the Assembly in May 1986 were in substance accepted by the Committee in July, although many members said it would have been preferable if the Committee had been better informed and had been allowed to decide for itself among alternative solutions, provided that the necessary savings were made.[94]

The Secretariat consists, in principle, of a single hierarchical structure. This, however, gives rise to potentially troublesome issues of loyalty since those Secretariat members who serve the Committee must do so in accordance with the Committee's wishes, while at the same time upholding the policies of the Secretariat. Thus, officials serving the Committee may not act against the Committee's wishes. But if they are aware that conflicts may arise with the interests and policies of the Secretariat they may have to inform their superiors or risk being sanctioned by them. More than once, Secretariat members have been caught in the cross-fire between the Committee or its members and the Secretariat hierarchy. Minor examples include difficulties regarding the timing and venue of meetings and public access to them, and criticism of the information services. A controversy concerning the editing of the annual report for 1983 revealed the structural dilemma and led to a decision by the Assistant Secretary-General to appoint a new Committee Secretary.[95]

The dilemma is visibly demonstrated by the seating arrangement in the Committee: to the Chairman's left sits the (Committee) Secretary, to his right the Representative of the Secretary-General. The former takes his or her instructions from the Committee itself, but also acts as a permanent channel of communication between the Committee and the Secretariat. It seems to be

[93] 'Bedre midler til a lose problemene', 90, (n. 83, above).

[94] See in particular CCPR/C/SR. 690–1, 694, and 696 (1986), but also earlier, CCPR/C/SR. 677 (1986), para. 12. In the Chairman's opinion, the Assembly was not entitled under the Covenant to cancel the autumn session; a question of principle was involved. The Committee itself could cancel it; he added later, however, that the Committee should be realistic rather than legalistic (ibid., para. 21).

[95] Referred to in *Report of the Human Rights Committee*, A/39/40 (1984), para. 17, in neutral terms.

the latter who, in principle, has to answer for the Secretariat whenever its institutional authority is involved. In practice, the division of functions may be less clear-cut. The Under-Secretary-General for Human Rights, or his deputy, normally represents the Secretary-General at the opening of the Committee's sessions. But neither is able to follow the work by being personally present all the time thereafter. Most days, another senior official takes this place. Thus, in practice, no particular individual is totally in charge of the Secretariat functions. This, of course, is a weakness which could be remedied. The selection of personnel to service the Committee, including its Secretary, is a matter for the Secretariat itself to handle. Nevertheless, it would seem appropriate, if only to enhance the prospect of smooth relations, for the Committee to be consulted.

At present, the Secretariat's work is divided between two separate units: general matters, including reporting, come under the International Instruments Unit, while communications come under the Communications Unit. Both have numerous other responsibilities. In order to cope with the expanding work of the Committee, the Centre has only been allowed to redeploy existing staff members, and once or twice to add an officer. With two exceptions—the Committee Secretary and her secretary—the persons now serving it do not do so on a full-time basis. The Communications Unit serves several groups and procedures and conducts an immense correspondence with individuals who address themselves to the United Nations at large; the International Instruments Unit serves several other Committees besides the Human Rights Committee.

The concept of the neutral and permanent Committee Secretariat, linked nevertheless to the UN Secretariat, has certain advantages, but also considerable drawbacks. As presently applied, it does not seem to ensure efficient and satisfactory working conditions for the staff and divided responsibilities and even personal rivalries may result. The Committee, or individual members, have more than once complained about the overall functioning of the Secretariat. Sometimes these matters appear on record; more often they are dealt with informally. Little of this goes into its reports, however, and, when it does, it is only in a diluted form.[96]

The Secretariat itself always faces many problems. Budgetary cuts, and cumbersome administrative procedures may explain why the Committee's needs enjoy no particular priority. But the 1986 budget crisis only accentuated problems which had already existed for some time. In hindsight it could be said that the Committee was vulnerable because so little had been built up earlier; there was thus little room for cuts. Pious exhortations to improve services, contained in General Assembly resolutions, are of little help when

[96] Ibid. As Rapporteur, the present writer had in mind more specific points which caused concern at different Secretariat levels; the draft report limited itself to certain generalities.

the available resources are simply insufficient. Take, for example, the immense task of providing all the voluminous documentation in five working languages. It is understandable that at times the Conference-servicing machinery cannot cope with the demands. But, as a result, valuable momentum is lost when, for example, summary records only appear weeks or months after the end of the relevant sessions. The issuance of the Committee's decisions and views are for the same reasons delayed beyond the comprehension of those concerned. Other problems include the lack of qualified staff. Thirdly, the Secretariat cannot give absolute priority to any one committee or other activity; its role generally requires caution and impartiality.

These factors also help to explain the striking difference of treatment accorded by the Secretariat to the two main functions of the Committee. Thus, State reports, no matter how long or convoluted, receive very little professional input from the Secretariat: initial reports are merely translated into the working languages. No official is expected to read or analyse them or to check them against any relevant guidelines. By contrast, an individual communication, no matter how trivial it may be, is read, analysed, and summarized, and clarification is sought from the author where required. This discrepancy is explained in part by the Committee's limited mandate and powers as well as by the political constraints on its actions under the reporting system. The communications system applies only to States Parties which have accepted it, and experience has shown it to be less sensitive politically. Although some differences in treatment between the two categories of work are inevitable, the differences are exacerbated by the structure and composition of the Secretariat. More Secretariat input, in the form of initiative, imagination, and effort could probably have produced results without causing disagreement within the Committee. The Secretariat's failure to provide more substantive assistance in analysing State reports may be due in part to a lack of trained staff and to a reluctance to risk accusations of partiality. The ILO has, however, successfully overcome these problems and the UN situation might seem also to result in part from inertia or lack of interest.

Committee relations with the United Nations, and in particular with the Secretariat, are, in other words, multi-dimensional, and this discussion cannot be exhaustive. The Committee's rules state that it has to co-operate with the United Nations on everything which has financial implications.[97] But in addition to the problems outlined above, there is also in the UN system an unwritten law saying that anything that has 'political implications' will involve problems and frustrations, not least at the Secretariat level. Human rights initiatives are no exception, as many new Committee members have had to learn the hard way.

[97] Cf. n. 90, above.

VI. RELATIONS WITH THE OUTSIDE

The Committee's contacts with the world outside the United Nations vary greatly. Its primary interaction is, of course, with the States Parties, and, under the Optional Protocol, with the authors of communications. From this perspective, all other relations are secondary but sometimes no less essential. They range from the official role of the UN Specialized Agencies (foreseen in the Covenant[98]), via other human rights bodies (as also envisaged there[99]), to the NGOs which lack formal standing, but in practice constitute a most important part of the environment for the Committee's activities. Both the Covenant and its Optional Protocol are silent about them, although their freedom of association is, of course, to be protected.[100] Their role in the implementation system can only be determined by reference to other sources and practice. They help where the Committee's present weaknesses are most obvious, especially by providing independent sources of information and by giving valuable and much-needed publicity to the Committee's work.

(*a*) *Specialized Agencies*[101]

Several Specialized Agencies work on matters falling under the Covenant. They include the ILO as regards forced labour and freedom of association; UNESCO as regards freedom of expression, research, and education; WHO in matters affecting the rights to life and integrity; and possibly other agencies in less obvious ways. They also contributed to drafting the two Covenants and some kind of co-operation between them and the Committee was clearly foreseen.[102] Inter-agency consultations on collaboration in the implementation of the Covenants took place before the Committee began its work.[103] Their experience is relevant to the Committee, and co-ordination of activities might seem useful, and indeed necessary.

Initially, the Committee adopted Rules of Procedure to enable the specialized agencies both to receive and, after being invited, to comment upon, relevant parts of State reports.[104] This original consensus disappeared,

[98] Art. 40(3), International Covenant. Cf. ibid. Arts. 44 and 46.

[99] Ibid. Art. 44: 'other procedures' which may be in force between States Parties.

[100] Ibid. Art. 22.

[101] The relationships of the Committee with the specialized agencies was primarily discussed during its first years, as reflected in *Report of the Human Rights Committee*, A/32/44 (1977), paras. 156–9; A/33/40 (1978), paras. 592–606; and A/35/40 (1980), paras. 410–14.

[102] Their intended role was, however, not clear from its provisions, notably in Art. 40(3), International Covenant, on parts of State reports.

[103] These are referred to in letters from ILO to the Secretary-General, 'Letter dated 29 November 1976 from the Director-General of the International Labour Office to the Secretary-General', CCPR/C/L.3 (1977), A; and 'Letter dated 16 February 1977 from the Assistant Director-General of the International Labour Office to the Secretary-General', CCPR/C/L.3 (1977), B.

[104] Rule 67(2), Rules of Procedure.

however, when the Eastern European members declared that the latter aspect went beyond the Covenant.[105] The Committee then decided that the specialized agencies should not be so invited 'since the Covenant contained no provisions to that effect'.[106] The role they might instead be granted was the subject of protracted consultations within the Committee, leading to a decision in 1979 according them a very limited role. The Committee decided that information from the agencies on their 'interpretation of and practice in relation to the corresponding provisions of their instruments should be made available to members of the Committee on a regular basis, and that information can be made available to them on request during meetings of the Committee'.[107] No such requests have yet been made.

The attention shown by some of the specialized agencies, notably the ILO and UNESCO, to the Committee and their declared readiness to co-operate clearly waned because of the Committee's initial period of unresponsiveness. They have since rarely, if ever, sent representatives to Committee meetings. Only the ILO has sent regular notes concerning States Parties whose reports were being considered, as envisaged in the decision, which has been applied very literally. The notes are only for Committee members individually, are only made available during sessions, not beforehand, and have not been treated as official documents of the Committee. Committee members have sometimes used this information in their questions and comments, but without any official acknowledgement. Thus, the much debated co-operation has dwindled to almost nothing.

The cool attitude of the Committee to the specialized agencies, and its change of approach, was mainly caused by the emerging polarization of views within the Committee as regards its own functions. The controversy over whether it could and should adopt reports or comments on individual State reports, a concept which was strongly resisted by members from Socialist countries, caused these members also to oppose the idea of such comments from the specialized agencies.[108] Struggles within the ILO as well as developments in UNESCO also caused some members certain worries. Finally, the thorough and professional work of the ILO Secretariat, which enables its supervising bodies to make detailed comments within their field of competence, may not have been an attractive model to some members, in view of their different conception of the proper role of the Human Rights Committee.

The whole struggle about co-operation with the specialized agencies now

[105] Ibid. Rule 67(2) could only relate to information about the practice and experience of the specialized agencies: *Report of the Committee*, A/33/40 (1978), para. 595; requests for comments would be exceeding the Committee's powers. Several members stated in 1979 that the rule went beyond the Covenant; see Mr Graefrath, CCPR/C/SR.181 (1979), para. 6; Mr Lallah, ibid. para. 8; Mr Movchan, ibid. para. 12; and Mr Hanga, ibid. para. 13.

[106] *Report of the Human Rights Committee*, A/33/40 (1978), para. 605.

[107] CCPR/C/SR.181 (1979), para. 14.

[108] See e.g. Mr Graefrath, ibid. para. 2.

seems distant. In retrospect some opportunities for developing certain aspects of the Committee's work may have been lost, while the strong opposition may have been due to exaggerated fears. The East–West battle pursued within some of the agencies was carried over into the Committee, and similar battles were apparently fought in other organs. The same issue was later raised in the Committee for the Elimination of Discrimination against Women (CEDAW).[109] The formalism and dogmatism of this struggle is somewhat artificial. The meagre result achieved by the Committee in 1979 has not proven to be a serious handicap in practice;[110] other constraints are far more serious.

(*b*) *Other International Organs*

The Covenant makes it clear that the Committee cannot ignore the existence and activities of bodies applying other procedures in the field of human rights.[111] This may require co-operation for special purposes whether or not any express mandate exists. Thus, at the Secretariat level the Committee has had contact with the European and Inter-American Commissions on Human Rights in its handling of communications. Such contact is needed because of the rule in the Optional Protocol which precludes the Committee's competence if the same matter is being handled elsewhere.[112] It has also had visits from other international bodies (such as Council of Europe Parliamentarians) and has from time to time delegated officers or members to attend conferences. More often members are invited in their personal capacities to participate in conferences where their Committee work is of interest.

(*c*) *Relations with the Public at Large*

After fifteen years of activity the Committee is still virtually unknown to the public at large, at least in Western Europe and North America. To speak about its 'public relations' therefore sounds almost like a joke. The mass media report very little about its work. The Committee's activities may be 'news' in a very real sense, but not in the view of the press, which finds its procedures slow, its examinations of the human rights situation even in the most controversial countries low-key, and its documents and records of

[109] See *Report of CEDAW*, A/39/45 (1984), i, paras. 23–5; ibid. ii, para. 368; and *Report of CEDAW*, A/42/38 (1987), para. 580. See also Chap. 11, below.

[110] Brar, 'International Law and the Protection of Civil and Political Rights: A Critique of the United Nations Human Rights Committee's Nature, Legal Status, Practices, Procedures and Prospects', MA thesis (The Fletcher School of Law and Diplomacy, 1985), sees this differently, especially at 46.

[111] Art. 44, International Covenant, reserves recourse to 'other procedures' in disputes between States Parties; it would apply to inter-State communications under Art. 41, ibid. See text accompanying nn. 209–14.

[112] Already *Report of the Human Rights Committee*, A/33/40 (1978), para. 585, refers to such co-operation.

general distribution voluminous and difficult to find or use. Even the regular press releases issued by the UN Information Service, which are drafted in a form more convenient for the mass media, are rarely reflected there. Feature articles seem to have a better chance than news reports. Some interested journalists, however, have complained about the inefficiency, unreliability and lack of professionalism of the UN Information Service in this regard.[113]

Against this background, the Committee's own ambitions must be modest. It cannot expect to obtain much publicity for its work and even less for itself. It has, however, consistently asked governments to publicize the Covenant, the measures of its implementation on the national level, and to some extent its examination of State reports and the views it adopts. Besides the official documents, of which the annual report is the most important, some further publications are slowly forthcoming, including selected decisions and bound annual volumes of its documents and records.

The masses cannot be the Committee's main audience. When their attention is drawn to human rights issues, as is daily the case, it is because of the reporting of violations and suffering; sometimes a case dealt with by an international organ gets publicity, but not the organ itself. This is really neither surprising nor troublesome. What is crucial for the work of the Committee is not to catch the attention of the masses or the media, but that of the human rights movement and the emerging human rights profession including non-governmental organizations, educators, scholars, government officials, and, of course, certain specialized media people. This now seems to be the realistic aim of the measures taken on behalf of the Committee. To this end, it is more necessary to have a successful publications programme than a large public gallery during meetings.

The Committee's relations with the world outside the United Nations are more important the less formalized they are. Apart from its main dealings with governments and the authors of communications, institutionalized relations are insignificant for its work. But the flow of information and ideas to and from the Committee is as necessary as the air the Committee members have to breathe.

VI. THE COMMITTEE'S FUNCTIONS: GENERAL REMARKS

In law, the Committee's functions may be described in terms of its competence and duties under the Covenant and the Optional Protocol.[114] In

[113] On these matters, see e.g. Guest, Sandvig, Gastaut, and van Boven, 4 *Mennesker og Rettigheter* (1986), papers from a seminar for the press held in Geneva in September 1986.

[114] Arts. 40–2, International Covenant, and Arts. 1–5 of the Protocol, ibid. Whether or how far the Committee has any legal duty to exercise its competence is a theoretical question of limited interest, since it cannot be forced to do so.

practice, its role is to act as the guardian of the Covenant. Disagreements on the scope and limits of its competence as well as constraints of a practical nature have caused the Committee to refrain from exercising its competence to the fullest conceivable extent.

The competence and duties of the Committee have three main components: to request and consider State reports, to receive and consider State complaints, as well as receiving and considering private complaints. They are partly general, that is, accepted as obligatory by all States Parties,[115] and partly optional, that is dependent upon special recognition by a State Party.[116]

Apart from this, the best way to describe the functions and role of the Committee has been a matter of controversy. Is it an organ for promotion and co-operation, or for protection and supervision? Is it quasi-judicial or conciliatory? The Covenant, avoiding any such description of the Committee, states laconically that it 'shall carry out the functions hereinafter provided'.[117] The Committee is careful in its manner of presenting itself so as not to provoke underlying disagreements.[118] The field is, in other words, open for analysis and opinion, and above all for development through practice.

The Committee has no functions under the International Covenant on Economic, Social and Cultural Rights. Its functions are exhaustively enumerated in the Covenant on Civil and Political Rights and the Optional Protocol. It follows that the Committee cannot and does not act *ex officio* in any way, and does not take initiatives outside those functions. It does not intervene in 'situations', however acute or frustrating, unless its functions under the Covenant and Protocol justify the action. What kinds of action are possible within these limits remains a somewhat controversial question.

It is sometimes argued that the Committee cannot do anything which is not explicitly stated in the Covenant and Optional Protocol. But this is misleading. There is an obvious need, confirmed by practice, to fill in many gaps created by the wording of the Covenant and the Optional Protocol. First, the question arises as to the Committee's 'implied' or 'inherent' powers. At the very least, the functions explicitly given to it may imply certain steps which are not expressly mentioned. On this basis, the Committee has often taken such action as has seemed useful for its work. Examples will be mentioned elsewhere in this chapter.[119] Above all, while its functions are defined in the

[115] See n. 40, above.

[116] Ibid. As of 26 Jul. 1991, 55 States Parties were bound by the Protocol and 31 by Arts. 41–2 of the Covenant.

[117] Art. 28, International Covenant.

[118] The three roles have been termed respectively 'advisory and supervisory' (Art. 40), 'conciliatory' (Arts. 41–2), and 'investigatory' (Optional Protocol), Brar, 'International Law', 3. This description seems inexact, but must be taken from terms once used by the Committee without any recorded discussion: *Report of the Human Rights Committee*, A/35/40 (1980), para. 374. It is unlikely that the Committee would commit itself to such a description.

[119] The problem of the Committee's 'inherent powers', deserves further study. Cf. Møse and Opsahl, 'The Optional Protocol', 279 n. 33.

Covenant and the Protocol, its procedures and methods of work in carrying out those functions are neither fully prescribed nor limited by these instruments. To some extent the text leaves matters open, or empowers the Committee to decide them. Other steps may be inherent even if they are not clearly implied in any provision. The scope for experimentation and practical initiative is probably less limited by legal barriers than by the Committee's resources and other practical constraints.[120]

It is also possible to extend its functions by amendments to the Covenant or by adopting new instruments. Such action depends not on the Committee itself, but on States concluding new agreements such as additional Optional Protocols. The situation could become complex because different sets of States Parties might be involved.[121]

B. *The Reporting System*

The Committee's primary function to date concerns the reporting system. This accords with the drafting history and the obligatory character of the reports, and is confirmed by its predominant share in the Committee's work. The system affects all States Parties, and when fully activated is able to provide a more comprehensive picture, generate more useful public documentation, and attract more publicity than its other main function of considering communications.

I. THE SUBMISSION OF REPORTS: DUTIES OF STATES PARTIES

All States Parties have undertaken to submit reports for consideration by the Committee on the measures they have taken to implement the Covenant. The first two paragraphs of Article 40 concerning the duties of States Parties mainly deal with the timing and content of reports, and are silent about the dialogue arising from them.

(*a*) *Timing*

Reports are due according to Article 40 as follows: '(*a*) Within one year of the entry into force of the present Covenant for the States Parties concerned; (*b*) thereafter whenever the Committee so requests.'

[120] For example, when a suggestion is made under the reporting procedure to send observers to a country in agreement with the government, CCPR/C/SR.608 (1985), para. 52.

[121] This point was discussed during the drafting of the International Convention on Protection against Torture. The idea was abandoned, but it is hardly 'principally impossible', as stated by Mohr, 'Questions of Procedure under International Law', (n. 6, above) 68, with references. Thus,

(i) *Initial Reports* Reports under sub-paragraph (*a*) are in practice known as *initial reports* and in most cases have become the first test of the State Party's commitment.[122] The large majority of States Parties have discharged their duty to submit initial reports[123] but only a minority of them have done so on time. Delays have caused the Committee to send reminders, as foreseen in its Rules of Procedure.[124] In a number of cases more than one reminder has had to be sent. The Committee has never gone straight from the first reminder to noting the non-submission in its annual report, as provided for in its Rules.[125] Such special mention has, however, been made in cases involving delays of several years. A few such reports have arrived only after four or five reminders.[126] One report, that of Zaire, came more than nine years after it was due, after ten reminders as well as a number of informal contacts and meetings with State representatives.[127]

The Committee has often discussed how, in the absence of any enforcement power, to underline the importance of, and how to induce compliance with, the crucial obligation to submit the initial report; publicity, direct contacts, offers of encouragment and even assistance, seem to be the best options. These matters are not controversial within the Committee: it has exercised, and sometimes in vain exhausted, its limited influence with varying energy

a Second Optional Protocol to the Covenant, relating to the abolition of the death penalty, was adopted by GA Res. 44/138 (1989). The Committee has welcomed this and noted that the reporting obligations of a State Party under Article 40 will extend to this Protocol, *Report of the Human Rights Committee*, A/45/40 (1990) para. 21.

[122] Some, like Canada, Uruguay, and Zaire, however, had communications brought against them even before their initial reports were submitted. *Report of the Human Rights Committee*, A/33/40 (1978), para. 574 and Annex III.

[123] 82 of 87 due until July 1989, *Report of the Human Rights Committee*, A/44/40 (1989), Annexes I, IV, and V.

[124] Rule 69(1), Rules of Procedure, which deals equally with 'reports or additional information requested'. See below.

[125] Ibid. Rule 69(2), which again applies both to reports and to additional information. The Committee decided that a second reminder and a warning to this effect should precede such a statement in the annual report. *Report of the Human Rights Committee*, A/35/40 (1980), para. 36.

[126] Bojji, 'Le Comité des drôits de l'homme', 59–61, tabled all 36 cases of more than a year's delay of initial reports until July 1984, and described in detail the measures taken by the Committee, including a letter to the election meeting of States Parties in 1980, and their results. After the tenth session (1980), no formal decision to State delays in the annual report was taken until 1985, but the facts have always appeared from the annexes. A decision under Rule 69 to make a specific statement of the non-submission was once more taken for six States Parties in 1985. *Report of the Human Rights Committee*, A/40/40 (1985), para. 43. Despite the increasing seriousness of the situation (discussed ibid. A/41/40 (1986), paras. 29–42; A/42/40 (1987), paras. 33–51; and A/43/40 (1988), paras. 30–41), this formula was not repeated in the following years. Ibid. A/44/40 (1989), para. 44, mentions the 7 States whose reports were overdue as of 7 Apr. 1989, as well as the 29 and 6 States whose second and third reports respectively were overdue. See also A/45/40 (1990) paras. 27–36 and Annex IV.

[127] The steps taken are described, for example, ibid. A/38/40 (1983), paras. 49–50; A/39/40 (1984), para. 49; and A/41/40 (1986), paras. 35–42.

over the years.[128] The long delays mainly concern developing countries which are admittedly lacking in resources and qualified staff. Thus, for example, Lebanon met with particular understanding because of its exceptional difficulties.[129] The Secretariat has always given some informal assistance if asked by a State Party, and since 1985 its programme of Advisory Services has included regional training seminars for national civil servants responsible for the preparation of reports.[130] This is one of the most promising developments in the reporting system, and would have been inconceivable only a few years earlier.

(ii) *Subsequent Reports: Periodic and Others* The duty under Article 40(1)(b) to report 'whenever the Committee so requests' remained hypothetical until the Committee's fourth year of work because of the difficulty of achieving consensus on any action such as a formal request to a particular State Party. Certain cases, such as those of Chile and Iran, in 1979, might have offered the opportunity, but events took different directions.[131]

In 1981, the Committee adopted a general decision on periodicity which required new reports every five years. It was slightly amended in 1982.[132] Under it, a number of 'second periodic reports' were due in 1983 although the Committee could still request subsequent reports at any time. The possibility of making such requests was raised early in 1982, when Poland and Nicaragua had notified derogations under Article 4 of the Covenant. Although various proposals were made, no decision was taken.[133]

[128] Until 1986, the Committee paid less attention to the growing delays, since 1983, in the submission of 'second periodic reports' (below); see, however, *Report of the Human Rights Committee*, A/41/40, para. 35.

[129] Ibid. A/35/40 (1980), para. 37, and, again, A/37/40 (1982), paras. 48–51, where, in a departure from the ordinary style of other reports the controversial situation in the country was also commented upon. Nevertheless a report from Lebanon was submitted and examined in 1983 A/38/40 (1983), paras. 336–73), causing long and in part political debate within the Committee.

[130] Such seminars were organized in co-operation with the UN Institute for Training and Research (UNITAR) and supported financially by the Ford Foundation. The first ones were held in Barbados, Bolivia, Senegal, and Philippines and seem to have been very successful (ibid. A/40/40 (1985), para. 19; A/41/40 (1986), para. 14; A/42/40 (1987), para. 17; and A/43/40 (1988), para. 17).

[131] On the request to Chile, n. 135 below, a suggestion that the Committee ought to consider whether to apply Art. 40(1)(b) to Iran, in view of the events, CCPR/C/SR.123 (1979), para. 23, prompted a representative of Iran to appear and promise a report 'in due course . . . in conformity with Article 40'. *Report of the Human Rights Committee*, A/34/40 (1979), para. 60. No Committee decision was then taken.

[132] See 'Decision on Periodicity', in *Report of the Human Rights Committee*, A/36/40 (1981), Annex V, as modified in 1982; A/37/40 (1982), Annex IV. A paragraph was added to provide for the possibility of deferring the date for a subsequent periodic report if the Committee has held a new hearing (a 'second round') on 'additional information'. Cf. below.

[133] CCPR/C/SR.334, 340, and 342 (1982). An alternative to a decision of principle as suggested would be to request reports *ad hoc*, but in practice this too remains only a possibility.

In addition to initial and subsequent reports under Article 40, the Rules of Procedure also provide for the possibility of requesting additional written information.[134] In practice, this rule has not been applied. Instead the Committee has in many cases received supplementary information without having made any formal request. It seems to have taken the position that receiving, or even suggesting, the provision of such supplements is not an exercise of its powers under Article 40(1)(b). It should follow that there is no duty to furnish them, although the Rule does not make this clear. The Committee has, however, encouraged such submissions, which in practice are often termed 'supplementary reports', implying that the first report was found incomplete. Although the legal position is thus unclear they have proved useful, and in several cases were clearly needed. During the early years of the Committee, separate hearings were held on 13 such reports. Many others were promised but never submitted.[135] If the Committee wished to make a State Party legally obliged to submit more information than volunteered in its report and oral answers,[136] it would have to rely on the power granted to it by the Covenant to request a report at any time, or, as foreseen in the relevant Rule, to request 'additional information' which might be seen as a type of specified request for a report. In practice, it has hesitated to do either.

(*b*) *Contents: Requirements and Guidelines*

The content of the reporting obligation is described by the Covenant in qualitative rather than quantitative terms. States Parties are required to submit reports 'on measures they have adopted' which give effect to the rights recognized in the Covenant, and 'on the progress made in the enjoyment of those rights'.[137] To these terms is added: 'Reports shall indicate the factors and difficulties, if any, affecting the implementation of the present Covenant.'[138] No distinction is made between initial and other reports. Obviously the former must cover the whole Covenant while it seems clearly to be implied that a subsequent request may be limited and specific.[139]

[134] Rule 70(2), Rules of Procedure.

[135] Special decisions were taken in a few cases. For example, having examined the reports and answers from Chile, the Committee stated that the information was 'still insufficient' and, with calculated ambiguity, invited the government 'to submit a report in accordance with Article 40'. *Report of the Human Rights Committee*, A/34/40 (1979), para. 108. A controversy with Chile over its reporting obligations ensued. See ibid. Annex V, as well as, *inter alia*, *Report of the Human Rights Committee*, A/36/40 (1981), para. 36, and A/37/40 (1982), paras. 32, 39, and 42. Another case concerned the inadequate report and absence of Guinea, which was reflected ibid. para. 47, ibid. A/38/40 (1983), paras. 57–8, and A/39/40 (1984), para. 136 (decision to consider even in the absence of a representative), and para. 156 (request for 'a new report' after contacts with representatives). Relations with these countries were later gradually normalized without clarification of the legal position.

[136] See text accompanying nn. 150–68, below.

[137] Art. 40(1), International Covenant.

[138] Ibid. Art. 40(2).

[139] Ibid. Art. 40(1)(b). Cf. Rule 70(2), Rules of Procedure.

The manner in which States have understood their duties has varied considerably. Reports have ranged from one or two pages of generalities to hundreds of pages of detailed accounts of national laws and practices. There is no fixed format, but the Committee has sought to assist by issuing guidelines. The guidelines for initial reports were drawn up as early as 1977, after the first reports had reached the Committee. These reports differed greatly in quality, and some were clearly incomplete by any standards. The guidelines informed States Parties of the Committee's 'wishes regarding the form and contents of reports'.[140]

The guidelines indicated that information should be given about each right and article separately, as well as information of a more general character on the constitutional and legal background, the status of the Covenant in national law and the remedies available. Limitations or restrictions on the rights should be specifically explained. It was decided not to refer in the guidelines to reservations or derogations.[141] General guidelines for subsequent reports were adopted in 1981, after the introduction of the system of periodicity.[142]

The terms used in the Covenant—'measures', 'progress', 'factors', and 'difficulties'—indicate that it is not enough to report solely on constitutions, laws, or regulations relevant to the implementation of civil and political rights. The purpose of reporting also suggests that facts are as important as law. The consistent attitude of the Committee[143] has confirmed what its guidelines might have perhaps made more clear that no matter how adequately the relevant rights are reflected on paper, the reports must also refer to actual practice. In this regard, statistical data is often useful and sometimes even necessary.[144] Other monitoring bodies have adopted a similar position.[145]

Measured by these criteria few, if any, initial reports have been perfect even when an obvious attempt has been made to observe the guidelines. Additional information is often submitted by reporting governments as a result of requests by Committee members eager to supplement the 'file', which is, figuratively speaking, never closed. With periodicity or follow-up reports the need for also maintaining files in the literal sense for each country, is

[140] *Report of the Human Rights Committee*, A/32/44 (1977), Annex IV; the debate is summarized ibid. paras. 136–41.

[141] Ibid. para. 138; the reasons given seem insufficient in light of later experience.

[142] 'Guidelines Regarding the Form and Content of Reports from States Parties under Article 40, paragraph 1 (b) of the Covenant', *Report of the Human Rights Committee*, A/36/40 (1981), Annex VI.

[143] See, *inter alia*, its general comment 2(13), ibid. Annex VII, paras. 2–3.

[144] They have often been asked for, and provided, on such matters as sexual equality (Art. 3, International Covenant); the right to life; use of capital punishment, infant mortality (ibid. Art. 6); participation in political life (ibid. Art. 25); or minorities (ibid. Art. 27).

[145] Reporting to CERD and CEDAW (see Chap 9, above, and Chap. 11, below seems to involve the use of statistics to an even larger extent.

obvious.[146] The main rationale for periodic reports is precisely to maintain a 'constructive dialogue' between the Committee and the reporting States. The experience so far with periodicity is that it deepens the knowledge and brings the Committee's probing much closer to the realities of each country.

Reports and additional information are normally printed in documents of 'general distribution',[147] which are available in mimeographed form, but they are not given wide circulation by the United Nations. Only a few States Parties seem to have publicized them domestically. As a result, the public is generally unaware that such reports are prepared, let alone that they might be available for scrutiny. Some countries have attempted to secure broader participation in the preparation of reports, either instead of, or in addition to, the inputs by government ministries.[148] Knowledge of the report and freedom to discuss its content are essential if the exchange between the Committee and the State Party is to become a dialogue with 'the people of a particular country through their Government'.[149]

Whether States Parties have further obligations under Article 40 of the Covenant, beyond the submission of appropriate reports, is unclear. In practice, however, their co-operation with the Committee goes much further.

II. THE PROCESS OF EXAMINING STATE REPORTS

(a) *Stages, Procedures, and Methods*

The main importance of State reports is to provide a basis for an active examination of the situation by the Committee through a process of direct co-operation with representatives of the reporting States. Such a process may have been envisaged by the drafters, but the Covenant is surprisingly laconic about it. The procedures and methods of work are left almost entirely to the Committee's discretion. The competence and duties of the Committee follow from Article 40(4), which states only that the Committee '*shall* study' States' reports, and '*shall* transmit its reports, and such general comments as it *may* consider appropriate, to the States Parties' (emphasis added). For many years the proper role of the Committee in the light of this provision 'proved to be the most controversial issue of all'.[150] However, when the process started in 1977, consensus had already been reached on some essential points through

[146] In practice it is, however, left to individual members to establish such files and add to them from other sources, such as NGO materials. See text accompanying nn. 167–8, below.

[147] Rule 64(3), Rules of Procedure. Cf. the discussion at the first session, summarized in the *Report of the Human Rights Committee*, A/32/44 (1977), paras. 41–6.

[148] e.g. Norway. See Egeland and Eide, 'The Systems of Reports by States Parties as a Human Rights Implementation Mechanism: The Norwegian Experience', SS-82/CONF.002/2(a), 11–19. The practical effects in this case, however, appear to have been very limited.

[149] A diplomatic formula used by the Assistant Secretary-General (Dr Herndl), CCPR/C/SR.676 (1986), para. 22.

[150] Avery, 'The Human Rights Committee after Six Years', 15.

the adoption at the first session of Provisional Rules of Procedure.[151] These Rules followed the philosophy and embodied the central formulations of those adopted earlier by the Committee on the Elimination of Racial Discrimination.

According to this model, States Parties are notified that they may send representatives to the meetings for the purpose of introducing their report and to answer questions from Committee members or refer them to their governments for additional information.[152] Before any reports had been examined, agreement was reached in 1977 'at least' for 'the present (second) session'.[153] Despite some shortcomings experienced over the years, it has been followed ever since.

In practice, the ideal of a collective study, with prepared questions and comments by the Committee as a whole, had to be abandoned as impracticable. There was very little public discussion of the decision, but it was clear that members would not have been able to agree on formulations because of their different backgrounds and outlook on many issues. Moreover, there were no precedents which could have assisted the Committee in overcoming such difficulties. Thus for initial reports, 'study' by the Committee became an examination by its members in public meetings, commenting one by one—favourably or critically—and questioning. They often went into the details and employed legalistic terms, usually in light of what they knew about the specific human rights situation in a particular country. That information did not necessarily come from the government.

It was expedient for such a diverse group to keep the controversy over the Committee's mandate in the background. Although the Covenant speaks of the competence and duties of the Committee as such, its performance has been dominated by members speaking individually. The result was uncertainty and disagreement, sometimes open and sometimes concealed, regarding the legal scope and limits of the Committee's action. In these circumstances, the Committee developed a pattern and methods of work in which legalism generally yielded to pragmatism. The practical aspects of the process deserve attention.

The most important achievement of this process is to make the examination in most cases more rewarding than the initial report itself. As a rule, and especially when the written basis is clearly insufficient, the questioning and answering has brought forward much more information from the State Party, orally or in additional written submissions.

The examination of each State report extends over several meetings and sometimes includes hundreds of questions. If members work under certain

[151] *Report of the Human Rights Committee*, A/32/44 (1977), paras. 16–94; the (then Provisional) Rules of Procedure can be found ibid. Annex II.

[152] Rule 68, Rules of Procedure. The model was described as a 'groundbreaker' by Roemer, 'Human Rights—UN Monitors Progress', *Free Lab. World* 24 (Dec. 1984).

[153] *Report of the Human Rights Committee*, A/32/44 (1977), para.111.

handicaps the representatives of States Parties certainly do so as well. An observer once wrote that it was 'unlikely' that the delegates drafting the Covenant 'knew what they were letting their governments in for' when they provided for the Committee and its role in the reporting system; 'in fact, it is hard to imagine where else top government officials would find themselves being so closely questioned about their country's law and policies, and needing to justify them.'[154]

Representatives have to take notes during long and intense sessions of questioning; they are normally listening to a foreign language, often through simultaneous interpretation. Thus, they do not get easily the exact wording, or even the main point, of a question. The questioning can be repetitive, since members often wish to underline some points or raise related points in different ways.

There is a regrettable, although perhaps inevitable, lack of co-ordination in this procedure, inasmuch as the Summary Records reflecting the questions and comments are never available when answers are due a day or two later. The possibility of members submitting their questions in writing, in order to save meeting time and achieve more precision, although aired,[155] has never been considered to be a practicable alternative probably because it would require even more work by members and reduce the immediacy and publicity of the examination process.

Not unexpectedly, oral replies from States Parties are often considered by the questioners to be far from satisfactory, and many questions receive no reply. After a while members realized that this could be pointed out, once the answers had been given.[156] This has been frequently done. In some cases it leads to new answers, but there may be a difference of opinion as to what constitutes an answer. The representatives of the States Parties often respond by promising supplementary information in writing. While such information was often forthcoming in the Committee's early years, it has been less reliable since the decision on periodicity. Including further answers in the second periodic report is less satisfactory from the point of view of establishing a dialogue.

Apart from situations considered exceptional by all members—Chile in 1979 and Guinea in 1983—the Committee has not resorted to the request for a new report which it is clearly authorized to make at any time. Moreover, it has hardly ever made explicit requests for additional information as foreseen

[154] Ms Rachel Malcomson (Quaker observer), quoted by Opsahl, 'The Protection of Human Rights in the Council of Europe and in the United Nations', 26 *European YB*. 106 (1978).

[155] See e.g. a suggestion made by Opsahl in 1979, during the examination of the initial report of the Ukrainian SSR, CCPR/C/SR. 155 (1979), para. 37.

[156] The innovator was Mr Bouziri, whose well-founded insistence on a question to the Ukrainian SSR concerning the Crimean Tartars also caused a controversy within the Committee concerning sources. CCPR/C/SR. 160 (1979), paras. 18–32.

under its Rules of Procedure,[157] relying instead on vague promises by representatives of States Parties. Deeper disagreements as to the Committee's proper role caused its failure to act as a unified body which could exercise its full powers during the consideration of reports.[158]

The first attempts to organize the debate in a different manner were made in 1978–80 during the 'second rounds' of initial reporting, which took place with a number of States Parties which had kept their promise to submit additional information after an initial round of questioning, in some cases, on clearly inadequate reports. Their 'supplementary reports' formed the basis for a more direct dialogue when members agreed to group their questions and invited immediate answers during the same meetings. Most members and State representatives found this method more useful, but its use declined after the introduction of periodicity, despite an amendment which should provide an incentive in the possibility of deferring the next periodic report.[159]

In 1980, the Committee adopted a statement[160] which reflected the agreement on instituting periodicity in reporting. A more organized approach to the examination process was foreseen. The new method required preparatory work by the Secretariat as well as a Working Group that would define and organize the issues for the Committee's consideration of second periodic reports.[161] The details were further considered in the autumn session of 1983, before being first put into practice with the second report from Yugoslavia.

Since the summer session of 1984, the Committee has regularly examined second periodic reports although many have been late. Seven years later about half of the States Parties had gone through the procedure.[162] According to the last published annual report (1991) four second periodic reports were pending before the Committee, twenty-seven more were due but not received (although some had had the due date extended) and two more had an extension still running[163] and many reminders had been sent to most of the States in this category.[164] Meanwhile, many third periodic reports have become due.[165]

[157] Rule 70(2), Rules of Procedure.

[158] See text accompanying nn. 169–88, below.

[159] The only such case was that of Canada in 1984. CCPR/C/SR. 569 (1984), paras. 77–80. See also *Report of the Human Rights Committee*, A/40/40 (1985), para. 40. Cf. ibid. para. 250.

[160] 'Statement on the Duties of the Human Rights Committee under Article 40 of the Covenant', adopted on 30 Oct. 1980, in *Report of the Human Rights Committee*, A/36/40 (1981), Annex IV.

[161] The Working Group and the Secretariat analyses were foreseen in the statement, ibid. paras. (i) and (j).

[162] Compiled from the annual reports, most recently, *Report of the Human Rights Committee*, A/46/40 (1991).

[163] Ibid. Annexes IV and V.

[164] Ibid. Annex IV.

[165] Ibid. Twenty-nine periodic reports were already overdue.

The method for second and third periodic reports is to invite the State representatives to address each issue on a list approved by the Committee and communicated to the State Party in advance. Thus, they have to answer what may be seen as questions posed by the Committee as such, while members have the right to ask additional questions and make any comments they wish. These have tended to be numerous, unless the representative of the State Party has already answered convincingly and exhaustively. Opinions on this new method were already divided after its first application. On the one hand, it takes at least as much time as the examination of the initial report. On the other hand, it provides a better organized, and usually much more penetrating examination. But self-discipline is required of members and of State representatives for the dialogue to become interesting and useful. Unfortunately, the more or less prepared answers heading by heading have in some cases taken up too much time, making the dialogue difficult.[166]

(*b*) *Other Information: Role of Non-Governmental Organizations*

Even when States Parties submit elaborate reports, additional information is crucial for the examination process. Members of the Committee have been particularly concerned about obtaining more facts and examining existing limitations on rights and their justifications. Quite often they raise particular events, not referred to by the State, or indicate problems and situations which require further study and answers. Members have sometimes openly disagreed concerning the degree to which such material, from academic studies to newspaper articles, could be brought into their comments and questions and how to refer to it.[167]

The restrictive attitude advocated by some, in particular the Eastern European members, was partly based on considerations of principle. It was argued, notably, that under Article 40 the Committee is not an investigatory body for allegations made against a State Party of violations of the Covenant. It is true that an accusatory or condemning approach by the Committee would be contrary to the purpose of the reporting system, but an inquisitive role of individual members in matters of implementation is different and legitimate under Article 40. In practice, it is obvious that experts, as admitted and sometimes underlined by Eastern European members, are not limited to State reports in their search for knowledge and ideas. However, part-time members cannot do all the work required for the study of the reports together with other material between sessions. In the absence of Secretariat support, the

[166] A case in point was that of Czechoslovakia in July 1986. CCPR/C/SR. 679–83 (1986). The summary in *Report of the Human Rights Committee*, A/41/40 (1986), paras, 315–70, does not reveal this aspect.

[167] See, *inter alia*, Fischer, 'Reporting under the Covenant on Civil and Political Rights: The First Five Years of the Human Rights Committee', 76 *Am. J. Int'l L.* 146 (1982).

role of the non-governmental organizations has become of paramount importance, but at the same time controversial.

From the beginning, non-governmental organizations sent documents to members on an individual basis and their representatives met informally with members during sessions. Gradually a few of them have approached the work of the Committee more systematically, providing information, comments, and 'critiques' of State reports. Some members have actively solicited such help, and others have gratefully accepted it, while still others have considered the information tainted. It is generally accepted by the non-governmental organizations that they have to be tactful and not seek visibility during Committee sessions. Amnesty International, the International Commission of Jurists, and the International League for Human Rights in particular have provided useful information without which many members would have felt rather helpless.

Members do not, of course, lightly accept or present such material as evidence of violations of the Covenant, although this is usually the thrust of it and members may individually point this out. Most of them use the material as a basis for their own comments or questions; they thus avoid limiting the examination process to an inquiry into a State report which in many cases bears little resemblance to reality.[168]

III. 'FOLLOW-UP' PROBLEMS UNDER THE REPORTING PROCEDURE

The consideration of reports engages the Committee in a continuing dialogue with the States Parties about implementation of the Covenant. According to a minimalist view, the proper role of the Committee under Article 40 is to contribute to the promotion of the Covenant in this manner. This view has been articulated by some members, especially from Eastern Europe, and in the literature.[169] Its proponents stress the consideration of reports as a form of co-operation between States through the Committee and strongly oppose the idea that the Committee should criticize individual States

[168] Tomuschat refers to the reports of North Korea (CCPR/C/22/Add. 3 and 5 (1984)), and their examination (CCPR/C/SR. 509, 510, and 516 (1984)), to show 'how difficult it is to come to grips with facts and not to remain in a mollifying nirvana of sheer verbalism'. Tomuschat, 'Human Rights in a World-Wide Framework: Some Current Issues', 45 *Zeitschrift für Ausländisches Öffentliches Recht und Völkerrecht* 577 (1985), with ref.

[169] A leading spokesman of this view—in both capacities—was Professor Bernhard Graefrath from the then German Democratic Republic, member of the Committee from 1977 to 1986. See, for instance, his intervention in CCPR/C/SR. 231 (1980), paras. 9–17, or his article, 'Trends Emerging in the Practice of the Human Rights Committee', 1 *GDR Committee for Hum. Rts. Bull.* 3 (1980).

Parties or determine that they do not fulfil their obligations to implement the Covenant.[170]

Other members did not share this view. They wanted the Committee's study to lead to some conclusion in each case. But the practice of consensus has so far frustrated their ambitions on the Committee's behalf. This disagreement as to the proper role of the Committee arose early[171] and has since taken on many aspects. The differing views were described in the Committee's annual report for 1980, published shortly after a major debate on the topic.[172] The report pointed out that many members were of the view that individual questioning was not sufficient, and that 'the Committee had not yet, collectively as a Committee, "studied" the reports.' The problem was defined in terms of Article 40 as follows:

> Since States Parties, by the submission of their reports under article 40(1) and (2) of the Covenant, and the Secretary-General, by the transmission of those reports under article 40(3) of the Covenant, had fulfilled their obligations, it was incumbent on the Committee to fulfill its obligations under article 40(4) of the Covenant which requires the Committee as such to 'study the reports' and 'transmit its reports, and such general comments as it may consider appropriate, to the States Parties.' The Committee should, therefore, as a Committee and as distinct from its individual members, now continue and complete its work in relation to the reports of States Parties which it had examined.[173]

However, opinions differed as to what the end result should be, and as to whether reports and comments by the Committee should be made to States Parties individually or to all the States Parties as a whole:

> Two main trends of opinion evolved in the course of the discussions. One trend of opinion, which was supported by most members, favoured the approach that the functions of the Committee . . . ought to be viewed in the context of the very objects of the Covenant as a whole . . . to promote and ensure the observance of the civil and political rights . . . [S]ince . . . the Covenant imposed a duty on the Committee to study those reports, there must inevitably be some purpose to that study. It was in the light of this very purpose, that rule 70(3) of the provisional rules of procedure was adopted.[174]

[170] Rule 70(3) of the Committee's Rules of Procedure, assumes that its general comments could state that a State Party has not discharged its obligations under the Covenant. It has been argued that this provision is *ultra vires* and must have been adopted by mistake. See e.g. CCPR/C/SR. 231 (1980), para. 12 (Mr Graefrath). Be this as it may, it does not determine what the Committee may say in its reports under Art. 40(4), International Covenant.

[171] CCPR/C/SR. 48–50 (1978); CCPR/C/SR. 219/Add. 1 (1979); and *Report of the Human Rights Committee*, A/34/40 (1979), paras. 15–20.

[172] *Report of the Human Rights Committee*, A/35/40 (1980), paras. 370–83.

[173] Ibid. para. 373. These views had introduced the discussion, CCPR/C/SR.231 (1980), paras. 2–8 (Mr Opsahl), and were opposed by the next speaker, Mr Graefrath (ibid. paras. 9–17), but supported by other members Mr Prado Vallejo, Mr Sadi, Mr Bouziri, Mr Dieye, and Mr Lallah (ibid. paras. 18–39).

[174] *Report of the Human Rights Committee*, A/35/40 (1980), para. 375.

This majority opinion would divide the functions of the Committee under Article 40 into three specific parts, each explicitly mentioned in paragraph (4): the Committee's 'study', 'its reports', and 'general comments', the last function being optional whereas the first two were obligatory, as the wording indicated. This opinion went on to explain *how* the Committee's study could be completed (e.g., via Working Groups) 'for the purpose of enabling the Committee to adopt its own reports, which might include general comments'. The study

> should lead to the adoption of separate reports by the Committee on each State Party's report. The exercise would, however, be conducted in such a way as not to turn the reporting procedure into contentious or inquisitory proceedings, but rather to provide valuable assistance to the State Party concerned in the better implementation of the provisions of the Covenant.[175]

General comments would highlight matters of common interest to the States Parties.

Despite these concessions, the minority clearly feared that the reporting procedure might be abused,[176] and no agreement could be reached on the main points. The minority held that the Committee's role was limited to the exchange of information and promotion of co-operation among States and to the maintenance of a dialogue with them; 'the study did not have in it any element of assessment or evaluation' which would go 'far beyond the wording of the Covenant'.[177] The term 'its reports' in Article 40(4) was seen as a reference to the annual reports of the Committee to the General Assembly under Article 45. Although the Covenant did not empower the Committee to interfere in internal affairs, there was a wide range of constructive opportunities for influence with the present method.

Facing this disagreement, the Committee reported in July 1980 that there was 'a convergence of opinion on the need for the Committee, at the very least, to make general comments' and that it wished to proceed to that task 'pending a decision on further work, if any, under Article 40 of the Covenant'.[178] A working Group representing the main trends was established to make appropriate recommendations on these two points.[179] After difficult negotiations, the next session was able to reach consensus on a 'Statement on

[175] Ibid. para. 378.

[176] The Committee 'should not allow itself to be converted into an instrument for interference in the internal affairs of States'. CCPR/C/SR.231 (1980), para. 10 (Mr Graefrath).

[177] *Report of the Human Rights Committee*, A/35/40 (1980), para. 380.

[178] Ibid. paras. 382–3.

[179] The members were Mr Graefrath, Mr Lallah (the Committee Rapporteur), and Mr Opsahl. In the absence of Mr Lallah, Mr Mavrommatis (the Committee Chairman) formed part of the group. It made its recommendations to the next (eleventh) Session in Oct. 1980, *Report of the Human Rights Committee*, A/36/40 (1981), para. 14.

the Duties of the Human Rights Committee under Article 40 of the Covenant',[180] which has since governed the Committee's role in the reporting system.

Of the ten points in that statement, the three first concerned the Committee's intention to begin drafting general comments according to agreed principles and relating to certain kinds of subjects. The Committee tacitly adjourned the idea of concluding its study of each state report, aiming instead at a more permanent dialogue with each State Party. The statement announced that this 'constructive dialogue' would be conducted on the basis of periodical reports, that guidelines had proved useful, and that a second periodic report would be due four years after the first examination. It also envisaged considering supplementary reports already examined (the 'second round' of some initial reports) to be second periodic reports. Guidelines would be developed for new reports, outlining their essential elements. A list of questions most frequently asked would be circulated to States Parties; a working group would review the information received and identify those matters which it would seem most helpful to discuss with the representatives presenting second periodic reports; finally, the Secretariat would prepare an analysis of the examination of each report, setting out systematically both questions and responses.

This statement represented a considerable achievement in so far as it demonstrated a common will to get on with meaningful work. A compromise close to the minimalist line had been necessary, but the majority made sure that it was expressly 'without prejudice to the further consideration of the Committee's duties under Article 40, paragraph 4 of the Covenant'.[181] A number of questions regarding 'follow-up' to State reports were thus solved, while others were postponed. The consensus reached enabled the Committee to adopt (in 1981) and put into operation its decision on periodicity, and also to adopt the envisaged guidelines regarding form and content of reports under Article 40(1)(b).[182]

Putting the rest of the statement into effect proved more problematic. The list of 'questions most frequently asked' existed only in an unofficial Secretariat draft and was never approved or even considered by the Committee. It was nevertheless given some unofficial circulation. The more organized preparation for the study of subsequent reports has been only partly successful. The Committee has approved lists of headings and issues recommended by Working Groups subject, as foreseen, to the right of every member to take up other matters. The concept of 'questions of the Committee' as such, despite some reluctance in the beginning, has become a

[180] 'Statement on the Duties of the Human Rights Committee', n. 160, above.
[181] Ibid. pream. para. 2.
[182] See nn. 132 and 142, above.

reality, especially since the examination in 1984–5 of the reports of the United Kingdom, Spain, and the Ukrainian SSR.[183]

One of the weak points in the follow-up procedure is the Secretariat analysis of the initial report and its examination by the Committee. This work has relied solely on summary records. Without any comment or deeper analysis, these documents have become less useful than was hoped. It was soon made clear that the decision to ask for this service from the Secretariat could not be given retroactive effect.[184] The studies have been carried out only immediately before the next report is to be considered.[185] Thus, the Committee has so far been unable to use that analysis to decide whether or not to request a supplementary report, instead of waiting five years to see whether the previous report would be adequately completed.

The method for examining reports has thus been changed from initial to subsequent reports. Instead of only individual questioning by members, awaiting combined replies in a later meeting, the Committee prepared a more systematic list of issues to be addressed by government representatives. There was controversy, until 1986, over whether the 'new' procedure of seeking immediate answers to groups of issues could be imposed on States Parties. The first Working Group, in order to reach agreement, suggested the new method only as an alternative, after first stating that the method need not differ essentially from that adopted for initial reports.[186] This was a concession to the view which preferred the least possible development beyond the 'anarchy' still prevailing for initial reports. In 1985, however, the idea of a more rational and organized approach, even to initial reports, was taken up again.[187] Together with other weaknesses of the reporting system, such as co-ordination problems and the need for revised guidelines, these matters have again in the last few years had the attention of the Committee.

The difficulties and uncertainties of the reporting system have not prevented the development of routines of which the Committee has become rather

[183] When preparing the lists of issues in the first cases, Yugoslavia (1983), Chile, German Democratic Republic, and Byelorussian SSR (1984), care was taken to define subjects rather than asking questions, but this was later given up. *Report of the Human Rights Committee*, A/39/40 (1984), paras. 60–6.

[184] Ibid. A/36/40 (1981), para. 383. It was pointed out that the Secretariat did not have the capacity to go back and do this for all States Parties whose reports had been examined in the past. And the analysis was only intended for internal use. It would not be distributed to the States Parties (ibid. para. 382).

[185] Since this has become the practice, it has in fact meant going back to examinations dating from the period preceding the decision, despite the point made in n. 184, above.

[186] The recommendation made by the Working Group is set out in *Report of the Human Rights Committee*, A/39/40 (1984), para. 59. The Committee's attitude, experience, and debate are summarized ibid. paras. 60–5.

[187] A suggestion to reconsider some of these issues was also made at the 25th Session by Mr Aguilar, chairman of the Working Group under Art. 40, CCPR/C/SR.601 (1985). Years have passed, however, without substantial changes. In 1986 the financial crisis overshadowed the reporting crisis. On developments in 1990, see A/46/40 (1991) para. 14.

proud, and which have even received some praise from States Parties as well as certain criticisms. But the pragmatism and caution required has left several fundamental follow-up questions unresolved,[188] such as whether States Parties have an obligation to attend the Committee meetings and answer questions, and whether or how the Committee as such can formally express criticisms of individual States for the contents of their reports or for non-implementation of the Covenant.

IV. THE GENERAL COMMENTS OF THE COMMITTEE UNDER ARTICLE 40 (4)

Since 1981, the Committee has devoted some attention and applied its experience to the drafting of general comments.[189] In the first four years, it issued fourteen texts. Five were adopted at the Thirteenth Session in July 1981, with an introduction setting out their purpose (general comments 1–5(13)); then four followed in July 1982 (6–9(16)), two in 1983 (10–11(19)), another two early in 1984 (12–13(21)) and yet another later in the same year (14(23)).

From 1985, however, the rate has decreased. No general comment was adopted that year, while only one was adopted in 1986 (15(27)).[190] Work on another went on throughout 1987 and was only concluded with its adoption in the spring session of 1988 as general comment 16(32).[191] Since 1989 four more were added (17(35), 18(37), 19(39), and 20(43)).

The framework for general comments adopted in 1980 was the result of a compromise, required by the deadlock on other follow-up issues. As a record of the Committee's experience, the adoption of general comments offers interesting possibilities which have not yet been fully utilized.

The agreed framework implies that comments shall be 'addressed to the States Parties' which so far has been applied to them collectively, not individually. Comments should summarize the Committee's experience with reports and promote certain obvious goals such as co-operation between States Parties, improvement of reporting, and Covenant implementation.[192] Subjects

[188] Even when its competence is clear, it has remained mostly passive to such challenges as declarations of a state of emergency; see n. 195, below.

[189] See, generally, Opsahl, 'The General Comments of the Human Rights Committee', in *Des Menschen Recht zwischen Freiheit und Verantwortung, Festschrift für Karl Josef Partsch zum 75. Geburtstag*, 273 (1989). The texts adopted during the first four years are in *Report of the Human Rights Committee*, A/36/40 (1981), Annex VII; A/37/40 (1982), Annex V; A/38/40 (1983), Annex VI; A/39/40 (1984), Annex VI; and A/40/40 (1985), Annex VI.

[190] *Report of the Human Rights Committee*, A/41/40 (1986), Annex VI.

[191] Ibid. A/43/40 (1988), Annex VI; A/44/40 (1989), Annex VI; and A/45/40 (1990), Annex VI.

[192] The detailed formulations are found as five principles in the 'Statement on the Duties of the Human Rights Committee', n. 160, above, para. (b).

treated could be (*a*) the implementation of the reporting obligations, (*b*) the implementation of the obligation to guarantee the rights set forth in the Covenant, (*c*) the application and content of its individual articles, and (*d*) suggestions for State co-operation in Covenant matters.[193]

The first set of comments belonged to several of these categories: two related to the Committee's experience with reporting under Article 40 (No. 1 and 2), and one sought to clarify some points concerning the implementation obligation in Article 2 (No. 3). There were also two which dealt with category (*c*), commenting on Covenant Articles 3 (sexual equality), and 4 (states of public emergency). Category (*d*) has so far remained a dead letter.

During the following years, the Committee's general comments, always explaining its understanding of important articles and substantive rights, have covered: particularly, Article 6, on the right to life (1982, and later with particular reference to nuclear arms in 1984); Article 7, on the prohibition of torture and other ill-treatment (1982); Article 10, on treatment of detainees (1982); Article 19, on freedom of expression (1983); Article 20, on prohibition of war propaganda and incitement to racial hatred (1983); Article 1, on the right of self-determination of peoples (1984); Article 14, on the right to equality before the courts and fair administration of justice (1984); Article 17, on the right to privacy (1988); Article 23, on the family (1990); Article 24, on the rights of children (1989); and on Article 7, updated (1991).

The Committee's deliberations have thus usually been directed towards comments on the substantive articles one by one. This seems to have been regarded as the normal, and even the natural, approach.[194] But in 1986 the Committee once more adopted a general comment which in fact confirmed that the article-by-article approach should not be the only one feasible within category (*c*). In taking up the general question of the application of the Covenant to aliens, many provisions had to be taken into account, including, of course, Article 13 (concerning expulsion). But the subject-matter was certainly not limited to that particular provision, which in practice affects only a very small number of the millions of aliens who are protected by the Covenant in relation to States Parties.

The introduction to the first set of comments in 1981 restated the purposes of general comments in more specific terms, making it clear that they did not purport to be exhaustive or limitative, nor did they attribute any priority as between different aspects of the implementation of the Covenant. Very often, comments express regret for the absence of relevant information in many

[193] For the wording of these subject descriptions, see ibid. para. (c).

[194] It was, however, from time to time pointed out that problem- or issue-oriented comments on substance were also desirable, and, *inter alia*, *Report of the Human Rights Committee*, A/39/40 (1984), para. 556 refers to 'articles . . . or other subjects' to take up. The suggestion which later became general comment 15(27), n. 190, above, was introduced as an illustration of this approach.

reports, without naming countries as examples. They also make interesting points of interpretation, sometimes clearly inspired by, but not referring to, cases under the Optional Protocol. Thus, the Committee has clarified the nature of many of the substantive obligations of the State Parties, by pointing out aspects often ignored in reports. It has mentioned, for example, the need for specific activities to enable individuals to enjoy their rights, linking the point to the duty not only to 'respect' but also to 'ensure' these rights. It has explained that States which take measures of derogation under Article 4 must also fulfil their reporting obligations under Article 40.[195]

The Committee has explored the scope of the right to life in neglected areas such as killings by security forces, disappearances, and other threats to individuals, including certain health risks, and has also related this right firmly to matters of war and weapons of mass destruction. In this way, its progressive comments relating to capital punishment are made against a wider background (comments no. 6(16) and 14(23)). The Committee has declared that prohibiting or punishing torture or ill-treatment is not sufficient, and that States must also ensure an effective protection through some machinery of control, and has listed alternative measures to prevent treatment contrary to Article 7 (comments no. 7(16)). These comments have also sought to clarify the meaning of Article 7 in other important respects, such as other forms of prohibited treatment, and its application to institutions other than prison, or to experimentation.

When entering the politically sensitive areas of the right of self-determination (12(21)), freedom of expression, and prohibition of certain kinds of progaganda (10(19)) and (11(19)), the Committee's results were perhaps somewhat less helpful in providing guidance for practice. Then again, its complex and detailed comment on the right to a fair administration of justice and guarantees for the defendant (13(21)) offered many useful suggestions, and was soon taken up in various contexts.[196]

From the perspective of the Committee's functions as the guardian of the Covenant the most important benefit derived from this work is perhaps procedural. Years after the Committee's establishment, and after many struggles, the draft general comments offered the Committee its first opportunity to deliberate matters of substance, the very contents of the Covenant, in

[195] Comment no. 13(13), para. (1), and comment no. 5(13), para. (3), *Report of the Human Rights Committee*, A/36/40 (1981), Annex VII; emergency derogations under Art. 4 International Covenant would seem to be among the occasions where the power of the Committee to request a report at any time under Art. 41(1)(b)(ibid.) might be resorted to. Otherwise the Committee would abdicate from its monitoring role when it might be most needed. As noted above (n. 137), however, no such decision has been taken.

[196] Points made by this comment (*Report of the Human Rights Committee*, A/39/40 (1984), Annex VI) were often raised by members with reporting States. The lists of issues to be taken up in connection with second periodic reports (see text accompanying n. 186, above) have also included a general request to respond to this comment.

public session.[197] It is thus applying the Covenant, discussing interpretations, and drawing conclusions, in the manner of a quasi-legislative body.

The preparation of draft general comments was entrusted to the Working Group which had originally been created to seek a basis for consensus on the so-called 'follow-up' issue under Article 40. A single member's draft has usually been the basis for work in this group. From his own experience in the area, the present author became aware of certain weaknesses in the process. The Committee was unwilling or unable to lay down a programme of work, apart from the general framework adopted in 1980 and only partially adhered to. Too much depended on the initiatives of a few members and their willingness to produce drafts. Secretariat assistance was very limited. The time and resources available for preparatory work did not allow systematic study even of the Committee's own materials, let alone the *travaux préparatoires* of the Covenant, or relevant literature and related materials from other organs or organizations.

The plenary Committee feels entirely free to reopen any discussion in the Working Group and to change nearly every point. Its debates are recorded and offer interesting insights on the comments. Since the Working Group is normally 'politically balanced', the basic orientation of the comment is usually taken from its recommendation. As regards drafting and reasoning, however, the experts in the plenary do not easily abdicate their responsibility, so that much hair-splitting is repeated.[198] Another role of the Working Group has been that of stopping topics and drafts on which there was no consensus.

It is true that the general comments are neither scholarly studies nor secondary legislative acts. And since they are couched in general terms their interpretation may easily create problems of application to specific cases, while their possible implications may indeed be insufficiently considered. But they carry some practical authority because they represent an important body of experience in considering matters from the angle of the Covenant. The ideas expressed, even if emanating from a single member, are tested and modified in detailed and exhaustive debates, on and off record.

The elaboration of general comments has opened several new processes.[199] Under the Covenant they go to the General Assembly as part of the annual report, but also to ECOSOC (Article 40(5)), and to States Parties. The guidelines for subsequent reports ask States Parties to refer to general comments in those reports. However, under Article 40(5) of the Covenant, the States Parties may also submit separate observations. Responses to general

[197] The quasi-judicial function under the Optional Protocol requires much debate on substantial issues, but it is exercised in closed meetings (Art. 5(3) of the Optional Protocol).

[198] The *Report of the Human Rights Committee*, A/39/40 (1984), paras. 546–7 briefly describes the process. In 1990 the Committee decided to begin work on updating some existing comments. See ibid. A/45/40 (1990), para. 586.

[199] Ibid. paras. 550–5. A/39/40 (1984)

comments have come both from speakers in the Third Committee and from some subsequent State reports. The Committee and its members have also brought them up and provoked answers during the examination of State reports. In 1985, the first separate observations under Article 40(5) arrived from two States Parties (Congo and Madagascar).[200] ECOSOC has also offered an opportunity to debate the general comments treated as a separate point on its agenda, as part of an effort to revitalize the role of this organ in human rights matters.[201]

The impact of these general comments outside the formal UN system is probably more interesting and promising, particularly in the work of non-governmental organizations and the scholarly community. Amnesty International has relied on them in its work on such issues as deprivation of life, disappearances, and ill-treatment.[202]

V. DECLINE OR DEVELOPMENT?

Because reporting is the only obligatory procedure to review implementation of the Covenant, the purpose of the Committee's function in this regard should be seen as twofold. The first concern must be to establish whether the particular State Party has reported as it should (i.e., fulfilled Article 40). This question is less controversial than the second, whether it may also be held to have implemented the Covenant as it should (i.e., fulfilled Article 2). However, during the many years when the system has been able to develop only along the minimalist line, the Committee as a rule has not formalized country-specific conclusions on any of these points.

This fact may seem regrettable, but it has not paralyzed the Committee. In particular, many observations and findings made by members have been expressed individually and reflected in the summary records.[203] They have found their way to some extent into the annual report, in the very brief and cautious summaries of the examinations ('Many members said . . . it was

[200] 'Observations regarding general comments 12(21) (Art. 1) and 13(21) (Art. 14) submitted by the Congo and Madagascar', CCPR/C/40 (1985). These documents were, however, rather partial reports on the articles in question, which did not address the substance of the general comments.

[201] The effect of this new departure was rather thin. In 1986 ECOSOC had before it general comment 15(26) on the position of aliens, E/1986/16, but it was referred to only in vague terms and by a few delegations e.g. Norway, E/1986/SR.9, 22.

[202] On reports on countries and issues, Amnesty International has invoked the general comments as authoritative explanations of the duties of states. See e.g. Amnesty International, *Torture in the Eighties* (1984), 16. A newer organization, draws on them as well. Article 19, *Information Freedom and Censorship: World Report 1991*, 441.

[203] However, the summary records are, of course, only summaries, covering about 25% of what has actually been said. Although often well done, they have a tendency to give priority to questions put by members during the consideration of reports, rather than their comments on the interpretation of the Covenant or the situation in a given country.

commonly felt that . . .'). Since the text of the annual report is approved by the Committee as such, this process has become significant and sometimes delicate. Depending on the terms used, the annual report may be said to reflect a position taken by the Committee. Only a subtle content analysis can reveal whether deliberations on and adoption of its different paragraphs amount to such a position, or merely reproduce what is already on record.[204] The practice by members of making general observations at the end of the consideration of a State report began in 1983–4 with the second periodic reports. Their reflection in the annual report could serve as a substitute for Committee reports on each State report, as could a summing-up by the Chairman if endorsed or accepted by the Committee. A development in this direction may gain momentum as older members of the Committee are replaced. For new members, the idea that the Committee as such should hold views even on State reports and country situations need not be anathema. In particular, the departure of the original GDR and USSR members in 1986 and 1988, and the presence from 1989 of a Hungarian and a new USSR member seems to have opened a new era in this respect.

The question that must be faced, however, is whether the reporting system is capable of meaningful development or whether it will degenerate into a routine of lessening interest.

Of course, any conclusions drawn by the Committee or its members are in any event only valid at the time. New facts and laws always require, in principle, that the situation be kept under constant review. For this reason alone periodicity need not mean stagnation. The absence at one stage of conclusions, which would anyway soon be outdated, is not fatal for the vitality of the system as a whole. Indeed, a case can be made for the view that establishing a continuing dialogue, a choice imposed on the Committee so far by its consensus practice, is more important than researching a conclusion after each stage of study of a report.

In principle, therefore, the system need not decline even if it does not develop beyond the present practice. Some improvements in the dialogue have also been achieved, and more can be done. Individual members have obtained

[204] The comments on Lebanon and Israel in the *Report of the Human Right Committee*, A/37/40 (1982), para. 48–51, referred to above (n. 129), illustrate a balanced taking of positions during the adoption of the annual report. The custom is not to take summary records of the deliberations on this point of the agenda, which is being dealt with in the last few days of the summer sessions. Exceptionally, however, records were requested in 1984. CCPR/C/SR.542–4 (1984). The debates on how to reflect members' general observations almost caused the resignation of the Rapporteur in the end (see, in particular, CCPR/C/SR.544 (1984), paras. 51–62). The episode no doubt contributed to his being replaced at the next election in 1985 (*Report of the Human Rights Committee*, A/40/40 (1985), para. 8). Nevertheless, similar points, about whether to say 'some' or 'a few' members as regards certain comments made, arose off-record later that year. In the atmosphere of 1989–90, the Committee has reverted to the problem under discussion with clear indications that progress is now possible. See, in particular, Pocar and Myullerson in CCPR/C/SR.950 (1989); and A/45/40 (1990), paras. 9–13.

a closer understanding of the countries and their legal systems during the second round of reporting. This is likely to benefit the Committee as an institution during the third round.[205]

Drastic changes should perhaps neither be predicted nor advocated. However, even if one is willing to settle for the present practices, concern must be felt on several points. Critical comments from persons who have represented governments before the Committee, should receive particularly careful attention.[206] In practice, even present standards are threatened, because States Parties do not fulfil their reporting obligations.[207] In the last years, the number of pending State reports has been low and diminishing, rather than increasing. Moreover, the rate of new ratifications has slowed down and in fact came to a standstill from spring 1984 to autumn 1985. During the previous seventeen years since 1966 the average annual rate had been nearly five ratifications, increasing in the first years after the Covenant entered into force (1976). Even if it were to be assumed that the UN members which have ratified the Covenant are more interested in human rights than the rest, it is not easy to say why the number of ratifications should not grow at the same rate as before, at least for some time. It may be that the world community is losing interest, since the 1970s. Increased awareness that the obligations are to be taken seriously—at least the reporting—may also be a factor, in which case the Committee may claim some credit. But it would be disappointing to find the reporting obligation becoming a deterrent, especially in view of the consideration shown for States' interests in the procedure. Better publicity might be of help, if this is the case. Advisory services to assist governments in reporting are also useful. Another factor which may explain both delays in reporting and reluctance to ratify is the proliferation of instruments with similar procedures. Some States parties have for some time complained about overlapping and lack of co-ordination between the different bodies.[208]

[205] But the membership is changing and the Committee's collective memory is weak. New members may find it almost impossible to take advantage of past experience via back reading, unless new ways are found to make it more readily accessible.

[206] A crisis in the reporting systems under different instruments has been building up, overshadowed for a while by the UN financial crisis (cf. text accompanying n. 91, above). Both the methods of work and the lack of co-ordination between the different treaty monitoring bodies have put government representatives into difficulties. See e.g. the criticism by Nordenfelt (Sweden) in 'Konventioner i kris (Conventions in Crisis)', 1 *Mennesker og Rettigheter* 45 (1987) (see n. 83, above). Recent reports and debates have increased the awareness of the system. See, *inter alia*, GA Res. 42/105 (1987). A meeting of chairpersons of the supervisory bodies was held in October 1988 to discuss the problems and remedial actions as well as co-ordination of future activities. E/CN.4/1989/62, Annex. See also Alston and Rodriguez-Bustelo, *Taking Stock of United Nations Human Rights Procedures: Report of a January 1988 Workshop* (1988), 30–7.

[207] See text accompanying nn. 128 and 162–5, above.

[208] See text accompanying n. 206, above. Also the coexistence with regional systems entails some problems. See e.g. Opsahl, 'Ten Years of Co-existence Strasbourg–Geneva', in *Protecting Human Rights: The European Dimension (Essays in Honour of G. J. Wiarda)* (1988), 431.

So far, the reporting system has mainly served to promote the Covenant, not to protect victims. When asking how reporting can develop, it should be admitted, however, that reporting was not intended as, and cannot become, a procedure to determine individual violations of the Covenant. Its direct purpose is to help in ensuring the implementation of the Covenant, and this can perhaps indirectly assist actual or potential victims. To prevent decline and promote a useful development in this respect, the Committee must combine its efforts to preserve the confidence of States Parties and to maintain its seriousness. It should search for innovations in its method of work, adjusting its guidelines and requests, making them more specific, and using persuasion and firmness to induce compliance with reporting obligations. But it should also be able to indicate somehow to States and others that the study of reports raises in many cases serious concerns as to the human rights situation, generally or in specific ways. Its strategy can be based for some years on the continued use of the consensus principle. But it is for the majority to reconsider this strategy at any time, and to face the costs and the benefits of adopting a new line.

C. *The Complaints System*

In addition to the reporting procedure, the Committee carries out two other procedures, which may be described together as the complaints system. They are set in motion by what is euphemistically called 'communications' from States or individuals claiming that the Covenant is being violated. All three procedures are designed to ensure compliance with the Covenant, but from different angles. This is important for the strategic choices facing States, the Committee, and the public (non-governmental organizations and individuals). They have to ask whether to seek to develop the optional complaints procedures, hoping that they will become more widely accepted and used, or whether to focus on the obligatory reporting system. Any attempt to reach an answer must be based on past experience with the respective systems.

I. INTERSTATE COMPLAINTS: IN FORCE BUT UNUSED

Interstate complaints were originally intended to become the main method for implementation of the Covenant, as proposed by the Commission on Human Rights in the early years (draft Covenant of 1954, Articles 41–3). In 1966, the Third Committee of the General Assembly changed the system and made the possibility of interstate complaints optional. It is only applicable between States Parties that have made a declaration recognizing the competence of the Committee to consider such 'communications'.[209] As adopted, Article 41

[209] Robertson, 'The Implementation System', (n. 9, above) 334–6, with refs.

basically provides that the Committee 'shall make available its good offices to the States Parties concerned with a view to a friendly solution of the matter . . .'. If a solution is not reached under Article 41, States Parties may consent to the Committee's appointment of an *ad hoc* Conciliation Commission, as provided for by Article 42.

To date, the procedure has not been used, although it has been formally in force since 1979 and thirty-one States Parties had, by the summer of 1991, made the necessary declarations.[210] In 1979, the Committee adopted detailed Rules of Procedure for such a case.[211] However, this is likely to remain a theoretical possibility for quite some time. Of the States which have accepted it, many are members of the Council of Europe and have as such given priority to their regional procedures in case of concurrent jurisdiction. Among remaining States are Argentina, Canada, Congo, Ecuador, Gambia, New Zealand, Peru, the Philippines, Poland, Senegal, and Sri Lanka. They do not seem likely to raise human rights problems between themselves or with any of the others, although events in some of these countries could perhaps change this prediction. Some observers have suggested that State complaints systems are simply impractical: '[t]here is something almost naïve about a system that assumes that a government will gratuitously come to the help of foreigners at the risk of compromising its relations with other governments.'[212] Although this scepticism may be exaggerated, other interstate complaints systems seem to confirm that this measure will be resorted to only very sparingly.[213] As one commentator has stated, '[t]he issue is not the nature of the Committee's role under the inter-state procedure, but whether the Committee will have a role at all.'[214] Therefore, it would not be useful to discuss this hypothetical function in further detail.

II. THE INDIVIDUAL COMPLAINTS SYSTEM IN OUTLINE

Under the Optional Protocol to the Covenant, States Parties undertake further duties and grant the Human Rights Committee a certain competence which has become the basis for its second main activity. It allows the Committee to consider complaints, or 'communications', from individuals.

[210] See n. 116, above.

[211] Rules 72–7 of the Rules of Procedure, n. 38, above. For refs. to the debate, see n. 65, above.

[212] Avery, 'The Human Rights Committee after Six Years', 92, with further references.

[213] Art. 24 of the [European] Convention for the Protection of Human Rights and Fundamental Freedoms, signed at Rome on 4 Nov. 1950, 213 UNTS 221 makes the interstate application system binding on all parties. Since 1953, only 11 applications have been dealt with, relating to no more than 6 conflicts (Cyprus before independence, South Tirol, Greece, Northern Ireland, Cyprus, and Turkey), while 17568 optional individual applications were registered by 1990. Council of Europe, *Survey of Activities and Statistics 1990*, 19.

[214] Avery, 'The Human Rights Committee after Six Years', 93.

More ambitious proposals for the handling of such complaints were discarded at an early stage. No private complaints system, to a Court or otherwise, could be made obligatory. Not even in an optional form was any such procedure allowed to become part of the Covenant itself. But a majority of the General Assembly decided at the eleventh hour to create a separate document, the Optional Protocol, allowing for 'communications from individuals claiming to be victims of violations of any of the rights set forth in the Covenant'. They would be dealt with by the Committee as soon as ten of the States Parties to the Covenant had ratified this Protocol.[215]

This separate treaty had in fact already obtained twelve ratifications when the Covenant entered into force for the first thirty-five States Parties. Thus, the Committee has been competent from the outset to receive and consider such communications. In 1991, fifty-five of the ninety-six States which had ratified or acceded to the Covenant had accepted the obligations following from the Optional Protocol.[216] If communications are admissible, the Committee examines their substance and forwards 'its views' to the State Party and to the individual concerned.[217]

On some points, this system resembles those of the Council of Europe and the Organization of American States, but it is much simpler. The Committee is the only competent organ and its procedure is not very elaborate. Its 'views' are not to be understood as strictly binding in law and cannot be enforced. The Protocol itself seems to consider a case closed as soon as the views have been forwarded to the parties. There is no follow-up procedure leading, as in the European system, from the report of a Commission to binding decisions by other competent organs (such as the European Committee of Ministers or Court of Human Rights).

The consideration of communications takes place in closed meetings.[218] The files and summary records of the Committee's deliberations remain confidential, but the texts of its final decisions, called 'views', [219] have been made public from the beginning. The decision to publish the views was taken without any express authority from the Optional Protocol[220] and did not correspond to any explicit rule in the then Provisional Rules of Procedure. Thus it was a bold and important precedent, which later became an

[215] Møse and Opsahl, 'The Optional Protocol', 274–6. cf. the text of the Preamble to the Optional Protocol, n. 3, above.

[216] *Report of the Human Rights Committee*, A/46/40 (1991) para. 659.

[217] For the status of 468 cases 1977–1991 see ibid., para. 661.

[218] Art. 5(3) of the Optional Protocol, n. 3, above.

[219] Ibid. Art. 5(4).

[220] Decision at the Seventh Session, summarized in 'Selected Decisions under the Optional Protocol', CCPR/C/OP/1 (1985), Introduction, para. 6, with refs. The first views were published in *Report of the Human Rights Committee*, A/34/40 (1979), Annex VII; see comments in Møse and Opsahl, 'The Optional Protocol', 332, with further refs. Art. 5(4) of the Protocol (n. 3, above) says that the '[c]ommittee shall forward its views to the State Party concerned and to the individual', and Art. 6 (ibid.) that its annual report shall include 'a summary of its activities under

established practice. It enables, but does not oblige, the Committee to give publicity to its views. If it did not, a risk of less objective, or selective, publicity from the parties would have existed. Nevertheless, it is noteworthy that the Committee could agree on this practice in the absence of express authority, in contrast for instance to the practice of the European Commission on Human Rights.[221]

The Committee's annual report summarizes its activities under the Protocol, with the already published decisions joined as annexes. These summaries describe the procedure and practice in general terms and include relevant statistics. In 1984, an expanded version of such a 'summary' gave a survey of the practice and case law since the beginning. A separate volume of selected decisions, whose publication the Committee had decided in 1982, appeared in 1985.[222] The volume also contains procedural decisions and decisions declaring communications inadmissible, which were not published separately until 1981. Thus, despite the confidentiality of the proceedings under the Optional Protocol, ample material is now available. However, as a source of case law, the material is less developed than in, for instance, the European system, because the Committee does not go to the same lengths in its published reasoning.

Lack of more widespread publicity may be one of the reasons why individual communications have not arrived in greater numbers, compared to the European system, and which hardly amount to a representative selection of problems in the countries concerned. In the first fifteen years only 468 complaints had arisen from thirty-six States Parties, and their distribution was very uneven.[223] The absence of cases against, for instance, the Central African Republic and the Congo might simply reflect lack of knowledge about the procedure. In other cases, such as the States Parties that are also bound by the European Convention on Human Rights, the more effective regional procedure may be preferred by most people who wish to complain.[224]

the present Protocol'. These provisions, together with the rule on closed meetings in Art. 5(3) (ibid.) impose duties ('shall'), but do not, of course, say what else the Committee 'may' do; thus, the practice of publishing views could not be said to be contrary to the Optional Protocol.

[221] The European Commission has always considered itself bound to preserve the confidentiality of its reports as a necessary implication of Arts. 31 and 32 of the European Convention, n. 213, above. However, the issue is different, because the European Court of Human Rights or the Committee of Ministers are authorized and in some measure duty-bound to publish the Commission's reports as well as their own decisions in the same cases.

[222] *Report of the Human Rights Committee*, A/39/40 (1984), paras. 558–625. 'Selected Decisions under the Optional Protocol', n. 220, above, covers only cases up to July 1982; another volume, covering the seventeenth to the thirty-second Sessions, was published in 1990 (CCPR/C/OP/2). De Zayas, Möller, and Opsahl, 'Application of the International Covenant on Civil and Political Rights under the Optional Protocol by the Human Rights Committee', 28 *German YB Int'l L.* 9 (1985), gives an analytical survey of the case law until the end of 1986.

[223] *Report of the Human Rights Committee*, A/46/40 (1991), para. 660.

[224] The treaty provisions give them a choice. However, once the choice has been made, the treaties, as well as reservations made by a number of European states to the Optional Protocol

The number of cases per year has not increased as noticeably in the 1980s as might have been expected, and for a while was in fact lower than in the first few years. This was related to the situation in Uruguay, which was the main source of complaints from 1977 to 1984. The Committee found many instances of serious violations of the Covenant in Uruguay. Important measures were taken after the change of government there, such as the release of all political prisoners. The Committee was thanked by the new Uruguayan government for its attention to the relevant communications.[225] The Committee has also found violations of very different kinds by other States, such as Bolivia, Canada, Colombia, Dominican Republic, Finland, France, Madagascar, Jamaica, Mauritius, The Netherlands, Peru, Suriname, Venezuela, and Zaire. Cases have been declared admissible and examined on their merits without the finding of any breach of the Covenant; in the cases of yet other States Parties, admitted cases are still pending. In 1989 the Committee also reported a recent 'exponential growth' in the number of pending cases submitted to it.[226]

One of the noticeable differences from the restrictive practice of the European regional system is the high percentage of cases declared admissible (almost 50 per cent as against less than 3 per cent). This is due, typically, to the serious facts of many of the cases, in particular those from Uruguay in the early years, but also to certain differences in legal conditions and procedures.

III. ADMISSIBILITY: CONDITIONS AND PROCEDURE

A communication is only admissible if it is compatible with the Covenant, i.e., concerns one of the rights and freedoms recognized in the Covenant, does not represent an abuse, and is not anonymous. Moreover, it must be submitted by or on behalf of the alleged victim. All domestic remedies must have been exhausted, and the same matter must not at the same time be under examination by another international procedure. These conditions follow from the Optional Protocol itself, and are comparable to those under the European Convention, with certain notable exceptions.[227]

(except The Netherlands), seek to prevent a second reference of the same matter to the other organ; see, for further discussion of the provisions and the emerging practice, Opsahl, 'Ten Years of Co-existence Strasbourg-Geneva', 435–7.

[225] CCPR/C/SR.599 (1985), paras. 14–16 summarizes Uruguay's message of 12 Apr. 1985, about steps taken in implementation of the Committee's views. See also *Report of the Human Rights Committee*, A/40/40 (1985), para. 703.

[226] See e.g. *Report of the Human Rights Committee*, A/44/40 (1989), para. 618, and A/46/40 (1991), para. 667, asking for a substantial staff increase.

[227] The conditions of admissibility summarized in the text follow from Arts. 1, 2, 3, and 5 of the Optional Protocol and are restated in Rule 90, Rules of Procedure. Comparable conditions under the European Convention (n. 213, above) are set out in its Arts. 24–7 which include, in addition, a time-limit: 'within a period of six months from the date on which the final decision was taken' by which all remedies were exhausted (ibid. Art. 26). Art. 27(1)(b) says that 'manifestly ill-founded' petitions shall be inadmissible.

The Protocol, however, says little about the procedure to be followed. The Committee adopted its rules of procedure on the assumption that the stages of admissibility and merits are normally separate. No case can be declared *admissible* without prior reference to the State Party for its observations.[228] In practice, only clear cases are declared *inadmissible* without such referral.

For the preparation of cases, a Working Group, or, since 1989, a Special Rapporteur is appointed to make recommendations as to the procedure and the decisions on admissibility, assisted by the Secretariat. The rules and practice of the Committee require, in particular, that the Secretariat (the 'Secretary-General') seek the necessary clarification 'from the author of a communication' concerning the applicability of the Protocol.[229] The actual author of the communication need not personally be the alleged victim. The author may be a duly appointed representative, normally a lawyer, or any person with whom there exists a sufficient link when it appears that the alleged victim is unable to act for himself or herself. The Working Group and Special Rapporteurs are authorized to determine whether the State Party concerned should be requested to submit 'additional written information *or observations relevant to the question of admissibility*'.[230] In other words, the important first screening, which is of a procedural order, has been delegated to the Working Group or Special Rapporteurs.

Both the State Party and the author of the communication must be allowed sufficient time to prepare their submissions. The time-limit for a State's observations on admissibility is from six weeks to two months. Since the Working Group only meets for a week before each of the three annual sessions of the Committee and recommendations or decisions are not always reached at the earliest opportunity, a decision on admissibility can only be taken between six months and a year after the initial submission. Since 1989, a unanimous Working Group may declare a case admissible.

The procedure may seem somewhat cumbersome, particularly since all the documentation of the Committee and Working Groups must be prepared in the several working languages. Some States Parties have been slow or unwilling to co-operate, while others have submitted voluminous pleadings even at the stage of admissibility. It has also become apparent that the confidential oral deliberations of the Working Group and the plenary Committee (whose summary records for these closed meetings are, of course, restricted in distribution), require considerable time and effort. The Committee has allowed dissenting or separate opinions to be expressed in its published

[228] Rule 91(2), Rules of Procedure.

[229] Ibid. Rule 80. In 1989, Rules 89, 91, and 94 were amended to allow a Special Rapporteur to carry out some preparatory functions. *Report of the Human Rights Committee*, A/44/40 (1989), para. 620 and Annex IX.

[230] Ibid. Rule 91(1) (emphasis added).

decisions, even on admissibility, but the search for consensus without voting necessarily takes time at both stages.

In the decisions on admissibility, interesting indications have been given on the requirements of exhaustion of domestic remedies, on preclusion when the 'same matter' is being examined under another international procedure or the standing of the authors and alleged victims, and on the extent of the responsibility of States Parties towards 'individuals subject to its jurisdiction'.[231] The Committee has also concluded a number of cases by discontinuing or suspending their consideration without declaring them inadmissible, or because they have been withdrawn by the author.[232]

The protocol does not say whether the Committee can consider communications inadmissible because they are submitted after a certain time-limit or are unsubstantiated.[233] The Committee has not wished to introduce any time-limit, without prejudging the legal issue of whether this is possible.[234] But it has repeatedly and on various grounds, declared inadmissible cases which do not seem to raise any real issues. If the communication is clearly outside the provisions of the Covenant, the claim is, of course, held 'incompatible'[235] *ratione materiae*. National law and decisions are often questioned in communications and where they raise issues or interfere with rights under the Covenant the cases may be admissible. However, the Committee is not competent to deal with the application of national law as such. To use the unofficial term coined in Strasburg for a similar purpose, it is not a 'fourth instance'. In that light, the Committee may declare a communication asking the Committee to review the application of national law inadmissible as incompatible *ratione materiae*.[236]

On the factual basis, the Committee has had to admit that at the stage of admissibility the author 'need not prove his case', but it has required that he

[231] Art. 1 of the Optional Protocol. For an analytical survey with case references, see *Report of the Human Rights Committee*, A/39/40 (1984), paras. 570–89; and, including more material, de Zayas, Möller, and Opsahl, 'Application of the International Covenant', 17–30. For a detailed discussion of the conditions of admissibility in terms of what the Optional Protocol decides or allows, see Møse and Opsahl, 'The Optional Protocol', 291–311.

[232] The statistics, given most recently in *Report of the Human Rights Committee*, A/46/40 (1991), para. 661, do not separate these categories. For their discussion at the stage of admissibility, see Møse and Opsahl, 'The Optional Protocol', 311–17.

[233] In contrast to much-used provisions in the European Convention.

[234] The matter was debated in 1977 on the basis of a Secretariat draft with a time-limit of twenty-four months. *Report of the Human Rights Committee*, A/32/44 (1977), paras. 60–2, but left open in the Rules of Procedure. See also Bossuyt, *Guide to the 'Travaux Préparatoires'*, 147–8, with refs., and Møse and Opsahl, 'The Optional Protocol', 310.

[235] The concept of incompatibility 'with the provisions of the Covenant', Art. 3 of the Optional Protocol, is discussed *ratione temporis*, *materiae*, *loci*, and *personae* (including the notion of 'victim'), in Møse and Opsahl, 'The Optional Protocol', 295–302.

[236] e.g. communication no. 174/1984, *J.K.* v. *Canada*, *Report of the Human Rights Committee*, A/40/40 (1985), Annex XIV, para. 7.2, and further cases discussed in de Zayas, Möller, and Opsahl, 'Application of the International Covenant', 27–30.

'submit sufficient evidence in substantiation of his allegations as will constitute a prima facie case'.[237] Thus non-substantiation of allegations became a ground for inadmissibility. Later, the Committee disposed of such cases by declaring that the author 'has no claim under Article 2 of the Optional Protocol', [238] a stand formalized in 1989 by adding words to that effect in the Rules of Procedure—a somewhat surprising but useful innovation, disposing of the merits in a way similar to the missing category of 'manifestly ill-founded' cases.

IV. MERITS—AND THEREAFTER

The haste in which the Optional Protocol was drafted may explain its ambiguity and brevity on essential points. It does not distinguish so clearly between admissibility and merits as the Rules of Procedure do. Articles 4 and 5 envisage the consideration of the merits of admissible cases without laying down stages or procedures.[239] Article 4(1) makes it a duty to bring such cases to the attention of the State Party concerned. Under the rules and practice set out above, this has already been done at the stage of admissibility. At the merits stage, the decision declaring the case admissible and containing procedural requests is also communicated to the State Party. Article 4(2) then requires the State Party to react within six months; it has to submit 'written explanations or statements clarifying the matter and the remedy, if any, that may have been taken by that State'. Further, the Protocol says that the Committee shall 'consider' the communication 'in the light of all written information made available to it' by the parties (Article 5(1)). Lastly, the Protocol prescribes that the Committee shall forward 'its views' to the parties (Article 5(4)), without explaining how these views shall be reached, for which purpose, and to which effect.

However, the Committee never doubted that it should state its opinion on whether or not it considered that there had been a breach of the Covenant. It has also applied basic principles of a judicial, or quasi-judicial nature

[237] *Report of the Human Rights Committee*, A/39/40 (1984), para. 588, and, similarly, A/40/40 (1985), para. 696.

[238] Ibid. A/40/40 (1985), para. 692, and Annexes XIII and XIV. In one case, a decision of admissibility was reviewed and set aside. Ibid. para. 695 and Annex XV. See also the amendments to the Rules of Procedure in 1989. Rule 90(b) now requires that a claim has to be 'sufficiently substantiated'. A/44/40 (1) (1989), para. 633 and Annex IX.

[239] Delays could be avoided and effectiveness increased by a more integrated approach. However, joining objections against admissibility to the merits has not been practised, and a proposal to amend the Rules of Procedure to allow provisional decisions when a case at once appears to be admissible was never acted upon (Mr Evans, 1981). But the Committee developed a new practice to expedite a case in 1987, ibid. A/42/40 (1987), para. 399; when the admitted case had already been sufficiently argued and the State party agreed, an earlier decision on the merits could be taken.

concerning, for instance, contradictory proceedings, assessment of evidence, and reasoning in support of its results.

At the same time, the Committee has not, or not yet, displayed much initiative or allowed for much development of its procedures at the merits stage. Besides recalling the time-limit of six months for the State Party, and transmitting any replies to the author for possible further information or observations, the Committee's decisions reveal that it has remained largely passive.[240] The paucity of the relevant rules on the subject[241] is evidence that the Committee has not taken such an active role as an investigative body might be expected to do. Some members have expressed the opinion that the Optional Protocol does not permit the Committee to take such steps as carrying out a more independent inquiry by specifying its requests, resorting to active fact-finding by sending delegates, arranging for oral hearings of the parties and witnesses, or taking steps towards mediation or settlement of the matter. It is true that the Protocol only refers to the duty of the Committee to consider 'all *written* material made available to it' by the *parties*. But this clause only says what the Committee shall consider, not what, in addition, it *may* consider or do. In the absence of consensus on the Committee's powers and policy as regards a more active role, a minimalist line has again prevailed in its practice.

In its handling of complaints, however, the Committee has been able to reach substantive conclusions on a large number of issues, often unfavourable to States Parties. And a flexible approach may, once the practical need for it is demonstrated, outweigh the cautious interpretation which holds that the Committee cannot do anything not expressly foreseen under the Protocol.

The Committee has in many cases not only expressed its 'view' that there have been violations of specific rights, but also added what in its opinion should follow, stating as a separate conclusion a duty to provide individual reparation and take preventive measures for the future. This is now a settled interpretation of its role. The Committee could go further in seeking solutions in co-operation with the parties. Certainly it might, with their consent, develop its fact-finding role and allow oral pleadings.

The numerous cases where 'views' have been expressed[242] represent a considerable amount of case law, and many instances have already occurred where an earlier case may be seen as a precedent. The views are not reasoned in great detail, but sufficiently to explain the Committee's understanding and

[240] The 1987 precedent for shortening the merits stage (n. 239, above) is, however, a welcome initiative.

[241] Rules 93 and 94, Rules of Procedure, add little to the minimum provisions of the Optional Protocol; see also Bossuyt, *Guide to the 'Travaux Préparatoires'*, 149–52, and Møse and Opsahl, 'The Optional Protocol', 317–26, about the many issues left unanswered.

[242] Until the forty-second Session, July 1991, they were 119 in all, and violations had been found in 93 of them. *Report of the Human Rights Committee*, A/46/40 (1991), para. 701.

application of the Covenant. Separate or dissenting opinions of individual members have been expressed in appendices to these views.

Some trends of this case law can be summarized as follows. Once the Committee has established the facts on which it should formulate its views, the result is often obvious, as in cases of arbitrary deprivations of life contrary to Article 6, or torture and other ill-treatment prohibited under Article 7.[243] The recurring question in such cases has instead been the burden of proof. The Committee has held that such burden cannot rest alone on the author, especially because the parties' access to evidence is not always equal; frequently the State alone has such access. In the absence of contrary evidence from the State Party, corroborated allegations have been deemed substantiated, and a refutation of the allegations in general terms has not been found sufficient (Uruguay).[244]

The Committee has emphasized the duty of States under Article 6 to protect the right to life, for instance when justifying legislation facing certain police action resulting in deaths (Colombia),[245] or when deliberate action by military police causes numerous prominent persons to lose their lives (Suriname).[246] 'Disappearances' and unexplained death in prison have also been considered under Article 6 (Uruguay).[247] Under Article 7 (torture and other ill-treatment) the content has been at times difficult to circumscribe,[248] but violations of this Article in conjunction with 10(1) prescribing humane treatment of detainees, have been found in the context of bad conditions in detention (Madagascar).[249] Mental anguish suffered by a mother because of the disappearance of her daughter also constituted a violation of Article 7 (Uruguay).[250]

Deprivation of liberty is often carried out according to the law of the State Party. It has therefore been more difficult for communications, in the absence of an independent fact-finding machinery, to succeed in the claim that deprivation of liberty has been 'arbitrary' in a specific case and thus contrary to

[243] e.g. communication no. R.7/30, *Bleier* v. *Uruguay*, ibid. A/37/40 (1982), Annex X, para. 13.3.

[244] Communication no. R.2/11, *Grille Motta* v. *Uruguay*, ibid. A/35/40 (1980), Annex X, para. 14 and a number of other cases.

[245] Communication no. R.11/45, *Camargo* v. *Colombia*, ibid. A/37/40 (1982), Annex XI, paras. 13.1–13.3 and 15.

[246] Communications no. 146/1983 and 148–154/1983, *Baboeram-Adhin et al.* v. *Suriname*, ibid. A/40/40 (1985), Annex X, paras. 14.3–16.

[247] Communication no. 30/1978, n. 243, above, paras. 13.4 et sqq. and communication no. 85/1981, *Barbato* v. *Uruguay*, ibid. A/38/40 (1983), Annex IX, para. 9.2.

[248] De Zayas, Möller, and Opsahl, 'Application of the International Covenant', 35–36.

[249] Communication no. 49/1979, *Marais* v. *Madagascar*, *Report of the Human Rights Committee*, A/38/40 (1983), Annex XI, para. 17.4, and communication no. 115/1982, *Wight* v. *Madagascar*, ibid. A/40/40 (1985), Annex VIII, para. 17.

[250] Communication no. 107/1981, *Quinteros* v. *Uruguay*, ibid. A/38/40 (1983), Annex XXII, para. 14.

Article 9(1), but in particular circumstances, it has been found so.[251] In any event, further guarantees in cases of deprivation of liberty can be of considerable importance, even if the arrest or detention as such is not held contrary to the Covenant. In particular, those who are arrested or detained on a criminal charge have the right to be brought 'promptly' before a judicial officer (*habeas corpus*), and to 'trial within a reasonable time', or to be released. The case law shows many violations of these provisions.[252] The more general right to challenge one's arrest and detention under Article 9(4) before a court (*habeas corpus* outside of criminal cases, such as administrative detention for reasons of health, state security, etc.) has also been applied, especially in cases of political detention; for example, as a result of 'prompt security measures' in Uruguay.[253] Likewise, the right to compensation for unlawful arrest or detention has been applied to cases where these provisions had been violated.[254]

Besides such violations of the right to life, limb, and liberty, the Committee has also considered and applied the Covenant to many cases where other rights and freedoms were affected. Typically, such cases are less simple in fact and law, and they require more subtle legal reasoning than can be properly explained in the space available here. By way of illustration, the Committee has held that the right of freedom of movement and to leave any country (Article 12), may be violated by the refusal to issue a passport;[255] while it has yet to clarify how far Article 14 and the right to a fair hearing extend to disputes about 'rights and obligations in a suit at law', in particular whether it covers only private disputes or also 'public law disputes'[256] (other Articlc 14

[251] e.g. communication no. R.6/25, *Amendola and Baritussio* v. *Uruguay*, ibid. A/37/40 (1982), Annex XVIII, para. 13, and other cases, see de Zayas, Möller, and Opsahl, 'Application of the International Covenant', 36–8.

[252] De Zayas, Möller, and Opsahl, 'Application of the International Covenant', 38–9. The meaning of the key terms is also addressed in the Committee's general comment on Art. 9, International Covenant, which states that 'promptly' means that 'delays must not exceed a few days', for judicial review of arrest or detention as such. General comment 8(16) (Art. 9), *Report of the Human Rights Committee*, A/37/40 (1982), Annex V, para. 2. 'Another matter' is the length of pre-trial detention which should be 'as short as possible'. Ibid. para. 3.

[253] Numerous cases from communication no. 4/1977 are listed in de Zayas, Möller, and Opsahl, 'Application of the International Covenant', 39–40. In communication no. 265/1987, *Vaolanne* v. *Finland*, a breach of Art. 9(4) was found in a case concerning military disciplinary procedure. *Report of the Human Rights Committee*, A/44/40 (1989), para. 633 and Annex IX.

[254] Art. 9(5), International Covenant, has been applied as an aspect of the duty to provide remedies, including such compensation; see de Zayas, Möller, and Opsahl, 'Application of the International Covenant', 40.

[255] See, *inter alia*, communication no. 106/1981, *Pereira Montero* v. *Uruguay*, *Report of the Human Rights Committee*, A/38/40 (1983), Annex VII, para. 9.4; and de Zayas, Möller, and Opsahl, 'Application of the International Covenant', 42–3. Art. 12, International Covenant, was also violated by administrative banishment within the State territory. Communication no. 138/1983 *Ngalula et al.* v. *Zaire*, *Report of the Human Rights Committee*, A/41/40 (1986), Annex VIII, A, and communication no. 157/1983, *Mpaka-Nsusu* v. *Zaire*, ibid. D.

[256] Communication no. 112/1981, *YL* v. *Canada*, concerning decisions by a pensions review board, was found inadmissible; the guarantees of Art. 14(1) did not apply because a 'suit at law' was not involved. But there was disagreement about the reasoning: the majority did not conclude

aspects, in particular the minimum guarantees in criminal cases, have been frequently explained and applied);[257] issues concerning privacy, freedom of thought, and of expression (Articles 17 to 19) have been considered in a series of cases but standards here are far from having crystallized;[258] the right to family life (Articles 17 and 23) and those of persons belonging to a minority (Article 27) have been highlighted in several significant cases where violations of these rights were found, combined with discrimination on grounds of sex (Mauritius and Canada).[259] A good part of the communications considered on their merits have also included elements affecting the enjoyment of political rights (Article 25) and related issues of freedom of expression, assembly, and organization (Articles 21 and 22). In many of the cases of this kind (relating mostly to Uruguay but with some from Zaire, Madagascar, and Suriname),[260] such issues have often been secondary to the main complaints concerning the right to life, limb, liberty and fair trial. With the end of the heavy oppression in Uruguay, subtler legal aspects may dominate the future case law under the Optional Protocol.

A main point concerning the scope of the provision that all are 'equal before the law', etc. (Article 26) was decided in 1987.[261] Discrimination against married women in social security legislation (unemployment benefits) —a field which as such belongs under the other Covenant—was held to be contrary to the clause requiring 'equal protection of the law'. The outcome and reasoning shows that the Committee considers the provision to contain a separate and general right to equality as soon as any law is made in any field, whether inside or outside the substantive provisions of the Covenant, of the other Covenant or of any other international instrument. The Committee has

'incompatible' *ratione materiae*, but that the 'author has no claim under Article 2 of the Optional Protocol', *Report of the Human Rights Committee*, A/41/40 (1986), Annex IX, A and Appendix; cf. text accompanying n. 238, above. The individual opinion of three members is also less than clear. The corresponding problem under Art. 6(1) of the European Convention (relating to 'determination of civil rights and obligations') has caused much discussion in numerous important cases, as cited by de Zayas, Möller, and Opsahl, 'Application of the International Covenant', n. 102.

[257] A rich case law is grouped by de Zayas, Möller, and Opsahl, 'Application of the International Covenant', 46–51. On *nulla poena sine lege* (Art. 15), see ibid. 51–2 and a further discussion by Opsahl and de Zayas, 'The Uncertain Scope of Article 15(1) of the International Covenant on Civil and Political Rights', 1 *Canadian YB Hum. Rts.* 237 (1983).

[258] See de Zayas, Möller, and Opsahl, 'Application of the International Covenant', 52–6.

[259] In particular, communication no. R.9/35 *Aumeeruddy-Cziffra et al.* v. *Mauritius*, *Report of the Human Rights Committee*, A/36/40 (1981), Annex XIII; amending legislation reported in the *Report of the Human Rights Committee*, A/38/40 (1983), Annex XXXII, and communication no. 24/1977, *Lovelace* v. *Canada*, ibid. Annex XXXI, which had similar effect.

[260] Examples are found in de Zayas, Möller, and Opsahl, 'Application of the International Covenant'.

[261] Communication no. 172/1984, *S. W. M. Broeks* v. *The Netherlands*, *Report of the Human Rights Committee*, A/42/40 (1987), Annex VIII, B; and communication no. 182/1984, *F. H. Zwaan-de Vries* v. *The Netherlands*, ibid. D.

thus apparently vastly extended its competence, but at the same time, it seems to have reserved for itself full control of this development.[262]

The views of the Committee have not been concerned merely with the finding of possible violations of the Covenant. Their impact depends on whether the views presented are acceptable to the parties, in particular to the States concerned. There are no means of enforcement, apart from the Committee's moral authority and the potential pressure of public opinion. Normally, it may be expected that States ratifying the Protocol will show themselves inclined to follow the opinion of the Committee, even when it goes against them.[263] This has been confirmed in practice, especially when a long-term impact, such as that of the Uruguayan cases, is taken into account. The Committee cannot *ex officio* supervise the impact of its views, but it 'takes an interest in any action taken' and invites States Parties to inform it accordingly. It has been able to report such action in a number of cases. From this perspective, the question of 'follow-up' after views might seem less vital, but the Committee, finding the original approach insufficient, has recently decided on further measures in a strategy for monitoring compliance, *inter alia*, appointment of a Special Rapporteur.[264]

Discussion of the Committee's views in the General Assembly are without legal effect and could be unfortunate, in view of the Committee's independence. A suitable balance of publicity and confidentiality concerning its activities under the Protocol is equally important.[265] The Committee has received a number of requests from parties for reconsideration and has had to decide whether it could take further action in cases concluded by views or inadmissibility. In 1984, the Committee expressed the opinion that its decisions are final, and that it might agree to reconsider them only in exceptional circumstances. 'Basically, this would only occur when the Committee is satisfied that new facts are placed before it by a party claiming that these facts were not available to it at the time of the consideration of the case and that these facts would have altered the final decision of the Committee.'[266] In other words, normally no further action will be taken.

There remains another possibility for increasing the impact of the Com-

[262] In particular because discrimination does not include 'differentiation based on reasonable and objective criteria', n. 261, above, para. 13 in both cases. For details of these and related cases and comparison with European practice, see Opsahl, 'Equality in Human Rights Law', in Nowak, Steurer, and Tretter (eds.), *Festschrift für Felix Ermacora* (1988), 51. Following these cases, an increasing number of similar allegations were received, although several were declared inadmissible. *Report of the Human Rights Committee*, A/44/40 (1989), paras. 647–56.

[263] Møse and Opsahl, 'The Optional Protocol', 323. This assessment, made in 1981, is difficult to verify, but later events have at least not weakened it.

[264] *Report of the Human Rights Committee*, A/45/40 (1990), paras. 632–8, A/46/40 (1991), paras. 703–9.

[265] Møse and Opsahl, 'The Optional Protocol', 327, with refs.

[266] *Report of the Human Rights Committee*, A/39/40 (1984), para. 621.

mittee. Any State Party to the Optional Protocol may propose to amend it, and one-third of them may cause a Conference to be convened for that purpose. If a majority there adopts the amendment, and the latter is approved by the General Assembly, it will come into force when two-thirds of the States Parties have accepted it.[267] Therefore, the amendment procedure seems to offer a realistic opportunity for States Parties which wish to clarify and improve the Committee's powers and procedures under the Optional Protocol.

D. *Discussion, Conclusions, and Recommendations*

I. PURPOSE

In 1984, a survey of the Committee's work concluded by recalling how recently this 'kind of supervision' has been accepted, stating that it is 'unfair to gauge progress in this field from one hundred percent. Rather, one has to measure from zero. And from that point of view there has been progress'.[268]

Undoubtedly. But what does 'progress' mean when studying reports on implementation, or considering communications about alleged violations? This basic question cannot be ignored, although it is too difficult to be fully discussed here. The ultimate test must be progress in the enjoyment of rights in the States Parties, and in as many other States as possible. In other words, better implementation, fewer violations, and more ratifications.

However, when the Committee is assessing its role, or others do so, additional indicators come to mind.[269] For practical purposes, it is often tempting to measure the progress of the Committee in simpler terms, such as

[267] Art. 11 of the Optional Protocol. Both the initiative and the majority requirement relate to the States Parties to the Optional Protocol, not to the States Parties to the Covenant as such (the latter were, as of Dec. 1989, 89, the former only 48. See nn. 115 and 116, above). However, the latter as well as non-States Parties can, of course, block any such reform via the General Assembly.

[268] Tarnopolsky, 'General Course on the International Protection of Human Rights', 33. For a more recent assessment, see McGoldrick, *The Human Rights Committee*, 498–504.

[269] The Committee declared early that the study of reports should assist State Parties in promoting the Covenant, *inter alia*, 'taking fully into account the need to maintain and develop friendly relations among Member States of the United Nations'. *Report of the Human Rights Committee*, A/32/44 (1977), para. 105. The goals might to some extent seem conflicting. At least in a short- and middle-term perspective, experience shows that concern for the human rights situation in a country may threaten friendly relations to its regime. Fischer, 'Reporting under the Covenant', 142–53, assessed the practical effectiveness of the reporting procedure of the Committee by reference to five criteria (four taken from Robertson, 'The Implementation System'): quality and independence of members, co-operation of governments, information from other sources, the power to make recommendations, and, fifthly, 'the key test', whether changes in the law and the practice of the States Parties are effected. All of these important elements will be reflected below, together with other matters.

its efficiency in carrying out its business (e.g. in avoiding backlogs), or even the amount of criticism it allows itself in the study of reports, or the frequency of findings of violations in its views on communications.[270]

It seems useful to distinguish short-, middle- and long-term perspectives in the defence of human rights. Lasting progress is achieved only when defence mechanisms have become superfluous. From a long-term perspective, a focus on the Committee would be too narrow; factors beyond its control—from Covenant amendment to a better world—are more important. Middle-term progress also depends less on what the Committee can do, or can do better, than, for instance, on the States Parties or the Secretary-General. But from a short-term perspective, any critical appraisal should mainly consider the Committee's own performance and situation, bearing in mind what other actors can and ought to do in that respect.

An internationalist approach with Western-inspired priorities cannot be taken for granted. Thoughtful and competent spokesmen of socialist States and of some developing countries have in the past held the view that the Committee should not be an organ of supervision. They saw it instead as a forum for the exchange of information and for co-operation among sovereign States, helping to achieve consensus between different approaches. This view should not be lightly dismissed. The present trend, like this analysis, is nevertheless based on the idea that the Committee should identify with the interests of individuals rather than with those of governments; that the Covenant and the Committee are instruments of protection, however weak, and not intended to be window-dressing; that States Parties are internationally accountable to the Committee for their obligations; and that its task in considering reports and communications is to make that responsibility as real as possible. The Committee should not try to arrogate to itself powers not granted by its basic texts. But those powers which are granted should be understood and applied so as to enable the Committee to achieve results along these lines.

II. GENERAL ASPECTS, INCLUDING COMPOSITION, QUALITY, AND INDEPENDENCE

Many important developments have taken place during the years 1977–91:

(*a*) Parallel to the increase from thirty-five to over ninety-six parties, the Committee has asserted itself and become recognized as the proper forum to address most Covenant matters.

(*b*) The Committee has also gained a reputation for serious work and ability to overcome the difficulties inherent in its task.

[270] The apparent paradox is avoided provided that the findings have practical effects.

(*c*) Its composition has ensured sufficient expertise and independence, but it should be better balanced geographically, ethnically, and as regards sex in particular.

(*d*) The Committee has had the co-operation of most States Parties but not all.

(*e*) The adoption of the principle of consensus as a method of work has meant that progress has been slower, but perhaps surer, than it would have been using majority vote.

Above all, the changed international situation in 1989–90 resulting from the revolutionary changes occurring within many States Parties has removed many of the obstacles to progress in the field of international human rights supervision.

Among the positive results the continuity of the Committee's efforts, despite its infrequent sessions and little inter-sessional activity, should also be counted. Public support from various non-governmental organizations, as well as their informal assistance to Committee members, has also been a positive development.

The Committee's main output is its continuous application of the Covenant, expressed through general comments and views, which contain a significant contribution to doctrine and case law. The Committee's independence and authority give this contribution a particular weight.

Apart from the last point, these favourable observations could be considered rather bureaucratic. They do not answer the more substantial question: *has the Committee become an effective guardian of the Covenant?*

Giving a brief answer to this many-sided question is more difficult. The Committee's role is changing, as is the effectiveness of the UN itself as a guardian of the Charter.[271] Factors contributing to this situation include the Committee's mandate and other outside constraints as well as the opportunities emerging through the changes in world order together with its own performance of its functions.

III. MANDATE AND OTHER OUTSIDE CONSTRAINTS

As shown above, the Committee has never fully exercised its mandate. The main reasons have been political, administrative, and financial constraints as well as internal disagreements combined with the consequences of the

[271] 'Despite all polite official comments about its importance, which reflects the overwhelmingly persuasive strength of the ideas of the Covenant rather than the realities which the Committee is facing, the Committee lacks support, publicity and resources.' Møse and Opsahl, 'The Optional Protocol', 330.

consensus principle. From the Committee's point of view a change of mandate is not foreseeable. The Committee's mandate follows from the Covenant and Optional Protocol, which are not likely to be amended during this century. Extending the Committee's functions through new instruments is a possibility, as shown in practice by the Second Optional Protocol.[272]

The only development which could affect the Committee's general mandate, and which is not wholly unlikely, would be some modification in its present functions, including necessary co-ordination with other bodies. Since these functions are described in terms open to interpretation, the limits of the mandate could be determined in a broad and dynamic manner through the adoption of liberal positions by the Committee itself.[273] This has happened, for example, with the adoption of a rule that the Committee could determine under Article 40 that a State Party had not discharged its obligations, and with the Committee's decision to publish its views and other decisions under the Optional Protocol.[274] The practical implementation of its mandate can be much developed through the active and innovative use of guidelines and specific requests to States Parties. Resistance to the Committee's own interpretation of its mandate is more likely if this interpretation assumes additional or implied duties for States Parties than if it only concerns action that the Committee may take on its own or with their co-operation and consent. The Committeee was for a long time quite cautious as regards the limits of its mandate on points in dispute, because resistance would not only come from at least some States Parties, but also from within the Committee. Such points were well-known but usually not touched on, without prejudice to their ultimate solution one day. New trends and moods since 1988 may have changed this approach.

Most of the outside constraints have to be accepted by the Committee, like its own composition and mandate. But is the Committee doomed, as once warned by Fischer, to 'degenerate into an empty political forum, a familiar fate indeed of United Nations bodies'.[275] or will it be able to liberate itself to some extent from the United Nations?

The answer depends to a large degree on the members themselves. They risk not being renominated or re-elected if they antagonize their environment, especially the States Parties. The Committee as such has no way to confront or break away from the United Nations. But this does not mean that it must be silent about its needs and how it wishes to develop.

[272] n. 121, above, and accompanying text.

[273] States Parties wishing to strengthen the individual communications system could, however, propose amendments under Art. 11 of the Optional Protocol. See text accompanying n. 267, above.

[274] Rule 70(3), Rules of Procedure. See text accompanying nn. 170 and 220, above.

[275] Fischer, 'Reporting under the Covenant', (n. 167, above) 153.

IV. THE COMMITTEE'S OWN PERFORMANCE

The favourable comments often heard in the past about the Committee should not mislead anyone. While the flattering remarks are often of a very general nature, criticisms can be quite specific, regarding, for instance, the Committee's procedures, planning, methods of work, and discipline.[276] The tasks of the Committee are many and there is much room for improvement.

The major focus, however, should be on how the Committee has discharged its main functions:

(a) *Has the Committee Promoted Implementation through its Operation of the Reporting System?*

In view of the controversies about the proper role of the Committee and the aim of the system, all of its methods have been only tentatively adopted, so that any assessment becomes subjective and provisional. The main factor that should be considered is the degree of active co-operation between the States Parties and the Committee. Limited co-operation is not exceptional. Judging from the Committee's past experience, the Covenant has only a marginal impact in perhaps one-third of the ninety-six States Parties.[277] Some of the reports it has received have been nearly worthless, and the representatives of States have been of such low rank or so lacking in knowledge that the examination has been an empty exercise. It may be feared in these cases that the Covenant and the Committee are being ignored or neglected. This is not to say that the situation in any such country is otherwise necessarily bad, since very different States have sent poor reports or representatives to the Committee.

The picture is brighter when one turns to the many States Parties—a majority—whose co-operation with the Committee must be described as satisfactory. Although the Committee has refrained as a rule from drawing specific conclusions for each State, the expression of its concerns may have an impact. Not only better reporting but, more importantly, better implementation, has been in evidence through different stages in the Committee's work. Whether ratification and reporting are the causes, or rather symptoms, of such improvement is much more difficult to tell. Awareness of international obligations cannot but increase with reporting and examination of the kind described when it becomes institutionalized and is taken seriously by the authorities concerned.

[276] These are factors depending mostly on the Committee itself. Without going into detail here, experience has revealed weaknesses on such points as punctuality in attendance and discipline in debate, preparing for interventions and deliberations, etc.

[277] Some facts and figures on reports due, received, and considered are given above, text accompanying nn. 122–9 and 162–5, above. But the poor quality of a number of reports and oral answers is well known off record, and suggests that the estimate of one-third is not too pessimistic.

(*b*) *Has the Committee Protected Individual Victims of Violations through its Operation of the Optional Protocol System?*

Again, a general assessment is not possible due to the differences between States Parties and between cases. The impact of individual decisions—particularly views on the merits of communications—is, however, controllable. In a number of cases concerning Uruguay, eventual recognition by the State Party vindicated the Committee's efforts, which at times had seemed futile. In other cases, concerning other countries, the efforts were immediately rewarded. Given the present limits on the exercise of its mandate, not much more could be expected. The basic weakness in the system is the absence of direct and effective fact-finding. The possibility of recourse to the Optional Protocol also seems to be very little known.

(*c*) *Relations between the Main Functions*

The respective impacts of the reporting and communications procedures have been differently assessed. Some think that reporting is a very successful method, and consider the outcome under the Optional Protocol to be negligible. This is too one-sided. It seems true that reporting brings up more issues and sometimes more important matters, and that its public nature enables public opinion, non-governmental organizations, and other governments to support the Committee's work and contribute to any influence it may have. But the evidence of its effect on national laws and policies, apart from benevolent statements during Committee meetings or before other UN bodies, is scarce. Being unrelated to actual facts, vague answers and comments may not reflect or affect the real situation.

As a contribution to the development of case law, the communications procedure has proved its value. And there is already ample evidence that the reporting and communications procedures may benefit each other. The Committee cannot apply two standards of understanding as regards the Covenant, one for reports and another for communications. Therefore, the findings made under the Optional Protocol will influence the thinking of the Committee when dealing with State reports. Several of the general comments adopted under Article 40 are clearly influenced by decisions under the Protocol, and the opposite influence of general comments on later individual cases is also becoming a matter of course.

One may be struck, however, by an imbalance between the ways in which these two main functions of the Committee are performed in practice. The Committee and the Secretariat invest much less preparatory and follow-up work in State reporting than in the handling of communications. Yet, the former takes up more meeting time, concerns all States Parties, and always covers many more subjects. Thus, some change of approach and priorities seems necessary.

V. THE FUTURE OF THE HUMAN RIGHTS COMMITTEE

(a) *Predictions*

Past results and present trends make it possible to sketch a short-term, a middle-term, and a long-term prognosis, varying, of course, from the obvious to the very uncertain.

By 1994 the Covenant will have perhaps 120 States Parties. After the election in the autumn of 1992 few if any of the original members of the Committee will remain, and more members will be women. The balance between regions is not likely to change very much; a majority of the members will be from the Third World.

Third periodic reports are being considered, while the Committee's Article 40 practice will develop without any major breakthrough. A gradual focusing on findings, or conclusions, for each country may be expected to occur, in one way or another. This will be the most important new development in the Committee's functioning. In addition, general comments are likely to be adopted before 1994 on most of the substantive articles and probably also on a number of other subjects. They will be increasingly invoked during Article 40 proceedings and also in other contexts.

One or more interstate communications may have occurred, which would offer an opportunity to test this machinery. It is most likely to happen by tacit advance agreement between the parties involved, in the context of efforts to solve local or regional problems (e.g., of minorities). This experience will not, however, lead to any spectacular or speedy results.

The Optional Protocol system will not undergo any revolutionary development, although communications will have come in greater numbers. But since many new States will have accepted the system, the pattern of decisions on admissibility is likely to change. The proportion of cases where violations are found will be decreasing rather than increasing, apart from special crisis situations. The system will find a more 'normal' level, with a representative selection of cases where violations will be more exceptional than in the past.

By the year 2000 when the Covenant becomes almost universally—if not always genuinely—accepted, the Committee will be dominated by Third World members not only in numbers but also in outlook. Newly industrialized countries, including China, will take the lead. Industrialized Western and Eastern States Parties, including at last the United States, will have about one-third of the members. Smaller countries like the Scandinavian ones will exert pressure to have the Committee membership increased in order to regain seats.

The workload will increase because the reporting system will develop into more regular supervision, including country visits by rapporteurs and working groups, requiring more staff assistance than before. The development of standards, and political struggles, will occupy the Committee less than the question of how to cope with its regular business. Interstate cases will remain, however, exceptional, occurring mostly in Article 4 situations or *de facto* emergencies in regions where political unrest continues. Work on communications under the Optional Protocol will stagnate as regards numbers, but selected test cases will lead to investigations on the spot and oral hearings before the Committee, with the consent of the States Parties concerned. A certain pressure will develop to make the Committee permanent and its membership salaried. The creation of a separate Secretariat unit will have removed some of the present problems. States Parties' meetings, which will have become more and more comparable to a special session of the General Assembly (Third Committee), will develop into a superior forum where the Covenant and the Committee's work will be debated. Annual reports will be rescheduled to be considered in substance there, and the discussion of the report in the General Assembly will become more formal. The States Parties' meeting will last several days and will open with a general debate on the human rights situation in the world.

Present trends cannot continue forever, but all states will learn to keep the peace despite their earlier attitude to international supervision, and they will realize that they all need the United Nations. Thus, the Human Rights Committee will at last have that superpower co-operation which until 1991, and in a very limited way, was only offered by the USSR. In this hopeful alternative, it would seem that this body is likely to continue in existence for decades along the lines already suggested. However, structural reform of the system will be both possible and desirable, so that it may be replaced, after about fifty years, by a more subtle machinery. To supervise implementation of the Covenant, which will also be ripe for substantial amendments, at least a High Commissioner and a Court will take over and share all the controlling, mediating, and dispute-settling functions of the Committee. These functions will be redefined and more effectively carried out, and, when necessary, sanctioned by the executive organs of the United Nations. However, regional protection systems will gradually take over much of the supervision, in the tradition of the European, American, and African institutions created in the second half of the twentieth century.

(*b*) *Recommendations*

Any suggestion for a desirable development of the Human Rights Committee in the short, middle, and long term must bear in mind that the 'withering away' of all such institutions as they become superfluous, is Utopian. The question is, therefore, whether, in the long term, the Human Rights Committee should be strengthened or whether it should be replaced by more adequate machinery.

The main long-term aim should be for the Committee to develop into the world guardian of the *implementation* of civil and political rights, through various forms of general supervision. Such supervision could take the form of the studying of State reports, the development of rights through their application in case law and through general comments, as well as the drafting of proposals for amendments to the Covenant. The principles guiding the elaboration of general comments and the subjects which these could address are already listed in the Committee's statement of its duties under Article 40. The Committee should also strive to assert its role as the proper world forum in all matters concerning the Covenant, being a body of experts with continuity and a global outlook in its supervising and quasi-lawmaking functions. This body will remain necessary for the promotion of universal standards until more adequate machinery is created, probably decades into the next century.

The other side of this approach concerns monitoring *violations* of these rights through complaints procedures. This should not be more than a secondary aim. Universality in such procedures is less necessary and more difficult to apply. It is true that complaints procedures, more than abstract inquiries, may throw specific light even over matters of general interest. Case law can also be more specific than general comments on how provisions ought to be understood. Nevertheless, the Committee will never be able to control violations in all parts of the world through complaints procedures. It would not be practical to develop its machinery to the extent which this control would require, since this would include hearings, fact-finding, visits, investigations, use of many languages, etc. Theoretically the procedures could become permanent and deal annually with thousands of cases rather than dozens. But there is a better alternative; building and strengthening regional complaints systems, like the European, American, and African ones, offers several advantages in the areas of logistics, local trust, and homogeneity. States Parties from the regions which have such systems in place have already shown their preference for them through reservations.

For the Committee to fulfil these functions satisfactorily in the future, attitudes must change, and resources must be made available. The Committee cannot 'lift itself by its bootstraps', but it can describe its own situation more clearly. The support it gets from States Parties and the United Nations is not adequate, and the Committee should say so. The result of this lack of support is that the Committee's effectiveness is reduced. The Committee should insist on its independence in substantial matters; in others, it must be diplomatic but firm. A task force of the Committee and Secretariat should draw up a list of demands in light of the real needs and challenges facing the Committee, assuming that the words of the Covenant are seriously intended. Those demands should be presented to the States Parties' meeting, and to the ESC and the General Assembly, where they might receive the support of the press and the NGOs. The Committee has nothing to lose by 'going public'.

These demands should include the staff and facilities needed to prepare and carry out a programme of work giving effect to the Committee's duties under Article 40. In particular, the Committee needs resources to enable it to use rapporteurs and working groups for each reporting country; they would make inquiries, hear witnesses, and make visits to the territories concerned in connection with the study of State reports.

An improved information and documentation system, relating to the various dimensions of the Committee's activities under Article 40 is also required. It should include:

- material necessary to decide when to request reports;
- material for the study of reports;
- material relating to the Committee's study of reports, and follow-up to the reporting; and
- material relating to measures taken by the States Parties as a result of the reporting procedure.

This system has to be structured and indexed so that it can be used not only on a country-by-country basis, but also by subject. Some Secretariat staff members should be trained to deal with particular States Parties or groups of States. The Committee should draw up a programme to diversify the reporting system according to need. Needs would be different for cases of large-scale reforms of legislation and constitutions, for particular problem areas, such as minorities, migration, or those accompanying macro-social phenomena (unemployment, illiteracy, poverty, political upheavals, etc.), and for emergencies. The Committee could develop blueprints for reporting for federal States, for multi-racial societies, for countries emerging from dependence or civil warfare, or for countries returning to democracy after periods of unrepresentative government. While the two present sets of guidelines for reporting adopted by the Committee—initial and subsequent reports—only foresee general reports on all matters covered by the Covenant, the future programme should be much more diversified.

It should be possible to limit reports to special matters, such as recent events like public emergencies affecting implementation, or to limit them to certain rights selected for deeper study, with a view to preparing general comments on such rights. The Committee might also adopt particular questionnaires.

Further assistance to States Parties should be offered. In this process, the need for co-ordination between reporting systems under different instruments should be met, and the special needs of less developed States must be taken into account.

Reporting cannot assume that progress in implementation is taking place everywhere. It should aim at deepening the process and the dialogue. So far, the Committee itself has never sent a delegate, rapporteur, or working group to a country. Going into the individual countries must now be a priority concern; and should be co-ordinated with similar measures, such as the provision of 'advisory services', developed elsewhere in the UN system.

To prevent the reporting cycle from becoming an empty circle, the gap between input to, and output of, the Committee should be bridged. The Committee should report on its study of a State Party report in order to maintain the dialogue with every State Party, within the system of periodicity now established. This means that any report from the Committee would be just one stage in the dialogue, and never a final one. It would seem convenient for the Committee to make such a report, under whatever name, after its consideration of third periodic reports.

In most cases, certain aspects of the procedure which have become crystallized could form the basis of the Committee's report. Although majority voting is likely to remain a hypothetical possibility in the short term, members should insist on having proposals to this effect elaborated. The Committee should take stock of the outcome of the study of prior State reports, draw provisional conclusions, point out problem areas, express appreciation at progress, and comment favourably or unfavourably on matters of reporting and implementation. The practice of having members make general observations at the conclusion of the examination of second and third periodic reports could be the basis on which such reports would be drafted. They might well be described as surveys of the implementation of the Covenant by the State party concerned.

The Committee should also lay down a clear programme for its drafting of general comments, giving due attention to the usefulness of taking up other matters besides pure article commentaries. In this way, general comments can be useful for a long time ahead. They are capable of development in many directions which have not yet been explored.

The need for improvement is also obvious for the handling of communications. The procedure should be developed to include fact-finding, pleadings, and conciliation. There are inherent weaknesses in the present procedure, although most of them could be overcome by a liberal interpretation of the Protocol, especially with the consent of the parties. Amendment of the Protocol should also be considered.

The interaction between the two procedures, reporting and communications, should go further. The submission of communications is an indicator of the situation in a country whose reliability depends on how well known this remedy is. The Committee, as the guardian of the Covenant monitoring its implementation, might consider that a need for requesting subsequent reports could be revealed by an upsurge in the number of communications. Conversely, subsequent and even periodic reports may be less necessary if the absence of communications confirms that the Covenant is being observed. A more radical stand would be to distinguish within the system of periodicity between States Parties to the Optional Protocol and other States Parties. The argument would be that for the former, periodic reports are in any event less necessary and could thus be less frequent. This distinction would also provide an incentive for ratification of the Optional Protocol.

As a first step, the Committee should request the Secretary-General to establish for it a Secretariat unit of its own. Next, it should ask the United Nations to grant it the resources and the freedom of action required to carry out programmes along the lines suggested above, and it should appeal to public opinion to support its demands. The non-governmental organizations which have proved their loyalty to the Covenant and the Committee may be counted upon to speak up for these demands.[278]

[278] These and other proposals are considered in *Making the Reporting Procedure under the International Covenant on Civil and Political Rights More Effective*, Publication No. 8 (1991), Norwegian Institute of Human Rights.

11

The Committee on the Elimination of Discrimination against Women

ROBERTA JACOBSON

Introduction

From the outset, international bodies concerned with women's rights and gender-based discrimination have faced a dilemma: should women's rights be considered to be a part of human rights in general or as a separate issue? The UN, recognizing the enormity of the problem of discrimination and the need for a broader range of approaches than was employed in the human rights field, separated the two issues and set up the Commission on the Status of Women in 1947. It is now generally agreed that women's rights are a specialized subset of human rights and are appropriately dealt with by distinct bodies. In addition, the sheer magnitude of the issues arising under the two rubrics warrants the establishment of separate organs. By the same token, however, there is no question that women's rights bodies must be considered to be an integral part of the overall international institutional framework in the field of human rights.[1]

The Committee on the Elimination of Discrimination against Women, or CEDAW, is in many ways testimony to what the UN can do when there exists the elusive quality of political will. Many countries that had focused little if any attention on women's rights in the past do so today in large part because of the treaty under which the Committee was established—the Convention on the Elimination of all Forms of Discrimination against Women.[2] Thus, although the principal purpose of this chapter is to be constructively critical of CEDAW's work and to provide recommendations for improvement, such a focus should not be permitted to obscure the considerable achievements of the Committee in the course of its brief existence, dating only from 1981.

[1] This study was researched through extensive interviews conducted with Committee and UN Secretariat members concerned with CEDAW. For obvious reasons the opinions they expressed cannot be attributed to specific individuals. The author wishes to thank Ms Maria Rodriguez-Bustelo for assistance in the preparation of this article.

[2] Convention on the Elimination of all Forms of Discrimination against Women, adopted by GA Res.34/180 (1979), in United Nations, *Human Rights: A Compilation of International Instruments* (1988), 112–25.

The UN Decade for Women culminated in 1985 in a major conference in Nairobi to discuss its accomplishments and failures as well as future strategies for national and international action. With the end of the Decade has come a plethora of writing on women's issues at the UN, regional, and national levels but much of it has scrupulously avoided analysis of the institutions created to promote the aims of the Decade. CEDAW is potentially the most enduring, and from the perspective of international human rights law, the most important of those institutions. While its history is far shorter than that of most of the bodies dealt with in this volume, this very fact should make it more amenable to constructive criticism than its more deeply entrenched counterparts.

A. *Background to the Convention*

The Convention was opened for signature on 1 March 1980 and entered into force on 3 September 1981. Its impetus came from the 1967 Declaration on the Elimination of Discrimination against Women,[3] but almost seven years elapsed from the initial proposal by the Commission on the Status of Women (CSW) to draft a Convention until its final adoption by the General Assembly. Along the way, working groups of both the Commission and the Assembly's Third Committee agonized over each article.[4]

The Commission's 1976 session was expected to discuss a draft convention. What thc Commission got, however, in the form of the Working Group's report, were four draft conventions.[5] The first was the text based on replies from governments and the report of the original Working Group. Three other draft texts texts came from Benin, Indonesia, and the All African Women's Conference. During the 1976 session an additional draft was presented by Belgium.[6] Some portions of the Belgian text were taken into account in the context of the discussion of individual articles but the original Working Group text constituted the basis for most of the discussion, while the other texts were hardly mentioned. By the end of the Commission's session, its role in drafting the Convention was basically completed. From 1977 to 1979 a 'Working Group of the Whole' of the General Assembly's Third Committee discussed the draft articles and amendments.

[3] GA Res.2263 (XXII) (1967).

[4] In 1974 the Commission decided to produce a single comprehensive legal document without prejudice to recommendations for other documents in specific fields. See *Report of the Commission on the Status of Women in 1974*, E/5451 (1974).

[5] 'Working Paper prepared by the Secretary-General on the Draft Convention on the Elimination of all Forms of Discrimination against Women', E/CN.6/591 (1976).

[6] 'Addendum to the Working Paper prepared by the Secretary-General on the Draft Convention on the Elimination of all Forms of Discrimination against Women', E/CN.6/591/Add.1 (1976).

Although the Working Group began with what amounted to a finished draft its deliberations were nevertheless long and painful. Part of the difficulty stemmed from the structure of the Convention and particularly its 15 preambular paragraphs. In some respects the preamble 'diverges further from the central issues ... than does the preamble to any other human rights treaty'.[7] In contrast, the Convention on the Elimination of all Forms of Racial Discrimination, with 12 preambular paragraphs, is a good deal more circumscribed in its scope. It touches upon issues which many delegations considered to be outside the scope of the Convention and to be politically controversial. For example, the statement in the sixth preambular paragraph that discrimination against women still exists despite the existence of various human rights instruments provoked the Socialist country representatives to disagree with such a 'broad formulation since discrimination against women had been eliminated in their countries'.[8] A longer and more intractable debate ensued over preambular paragraphs 10 and 11 which deal with issues as diverse as: equality between men and women in the context of apartheid and racism, international peace and security, general and complete disarmament, and self-determination of all peoples.[9]

After its tortuous discussions on the preamble, the first meeting of the Third Committee's Working Group ended by only getting up to Article 10 of the Convention, and the next session, in March of 1979, covered only Articles 10–16.[10]

Although the drafting of the Convention took several years, the Third Committee as a whole discussed the draft for only two days (6–7 December 1979)[11] before recommending its adoption by the General Assembly.[12] Such uncharacteristic speed can be explained either by the comprehensiveness of the preparatory work or by the Third Committee's relative lack of interest in the issue, or both.

B. *Structure and Substance of the Convention*

The convention opens with a definition of discrimination intentionally designed only to cover discrimination against women rather than all discrimination based on sex. Article 2, which is the heart of the Convention, embodies

[7] Burrows, 'The 1979 Convention on the Elimination of all Forms of Discrimination against Women', 32 *Netherlands Int'l L. Rev.* 420 (1985).

[8] *Report of the Working Group of the Whole on the Drafting of the Convention on the Elimination of all Forms of Discrimination against Women in 1977*, A/C.3/32/L.59 (1977), para. 34.

[9] Ibid. paras. 44–9.

[10] *Report of the Working Group of the Whole on the Drafting of the Convention on the Elimination of all Forms of Discrimination against Women in 1978*, A/34/60 (1979).

[11] A/C.3/34/SR.70–3 (1979).

[12] The Third Committee had 43 meetings to discuss the Convention on Racial Discrimination. See Burrows, 'The 1979 Convention', 420 n. 7.

the obligation of States Parties to eliminate discrimination. As such it was the subject of intense debate during the various Working Group meetings and is often still the focus of CEDAW's discussions.[13] Many of the subsequent articles in the Convention require States Parties to take measures, 'including legislation', to overcome discrimination in areas such as employment (Article 11), education (Article 10), health care (Articles 12 and 14), and rights relating to marriage (Article 16). Some articles are relatively specific as to the measures that should be taken, including action going beyond legislation, such as efforts to overcome discriminatory social and cultural patterns and stereotyping in educational patterns. Notwithstanding such provisions, most States tend to report only on legislative measures they have taken.

Article 4 of the Convention permits the temporary use of discriminatory measures 'aimed at accelerating de facto equality' and provides that measures to protect maternity will not be considered discriminatory. Thus measures such as temporary affirmative action programmes to increase women's access in fields like education and employment are permitted although they must be discontinued once the inequality is remedied. At the drafting stage this article was surprisingly uncontroversial although some governments have subsequently expressed difficulties with it either in the context of ratification or implementation.[14] The provision dealing with maternity appears quite straightforward, but has also been the subject of debate. One State Party, for example, reported that measures used to protect maternity included the transfer of a pregnant woman from her job if that job put her in contact with the public (a role considered unsafe by government officials).[15]

An important decision as to the structure of the Convention was the adoption of separate articles dealing with areas such as education, employment, health care, nationality and marriage issues, and prostitution. Implementation and supervision of the treaty have thereby been substantially facilitated. This is because in reporting on progress made, even the most cursory of States Parties' reports must refer to each article of the Convention and the relevant aspects of national legislation and practice. The more specific the Convention is in both substance and structure, the more issues a government must address in its report.[16]

[13] Much of the recent discussion has centred on whether reservations to Art. 2 are 'incompatible with the object and purpose of the Convention and thus prohibited under Article 28'. (See n. 2, above.)

[14] The United States, for example, has had numerous court cases on affirmative action and the issue has been highly controversial. Interestingly, the working of Art. 4 was suggested by the representative of the United States. See Burrows 'The 1979 Convention', 427–8.

[15] The issue was discussed during questioning of the representative of El Salvador at the Committee's fifth session. See the report of El Salvador, CEDAW/C/5/Add.19 (1983).

[16] The specificity of the Convention also means that its provisions overlap with other UN treaties such as the Convention on Nationality of Married Women (1957), the UNESCO Convention against Discrimination in Education (1960), various ILO Conventions, and the two UN Human Rights Covenants (1966).

C. *Comparison with other Bodies: CERD and CSW*

An assessment of the effectiveness of CEDAW's approach and procedures is facilitated by a comparison with the experience of similar supervisory bodies. While such comparisons are inevitably invoked by commentators to justify reforms of, and innovations in, CEDAW's approach, it must nevertheless be borne in mind that there are significant differences between it and a body such as the Committee on the Elimination of Racial Discrimination (CERD). For example, whereas the latter generally meets for three weeks twice a year (its Convention being silent on that point), CEDAW is specifically limited by its Convention to a single two week annual meeting. The constraints this places on CEDAW will be discussed in detail below. CERD requires initial reports from States Parties within one year of the Convention's coming into force and thereafter every two years, whereas CEDAW only requires reports every four years. This has led to suggestions by some commentators that the two-year period is preferable. The four-year decision, however, was designed to give countries enough time to implement and monitor *de facto* as well as *de jure* changes, since tasks such as changing attitudes and stereotypes can hardly be completed within two years. Moreover, since the late 1980s, it is CERD that has actually emulated CEDAW by adopting, for all practical intents, a four-year reporting periodicity.

Other comparisons with CERD might also appear to make the Women's Convention potentially less effective. The Convention on Racial Discrimination includes a process for rejecting reservations by States Parties if they are deemed incompatible with the purposes of the Convention provided that at least two-thirds of the States Parties object.[17] While CEDAW could conceivably provide in its rules of procedure for some sort of system it has not yet done so, and in any event its inclusion in the Convention would have given it more weight. Indeed the absence of any applicable procedure for assessing the compatibility of reservations with the Convention has given rise to serious problems for the Committee. As one commentator has noted: 'Discrimination [against women] is particularly subversive of the Convention when states parties justify it by reference to reservations made under the regime of the Convention itself'.[18]

Some commentators have criticized the Convention for not providing for the submission of complaints either by States or individuals.[19] CERD has

[17] International Convention on the Elimination of all Forms of Racial Discrimination, adopted by GA Res. 2106 A (XX) (1965), *International Instruments*, 56–69, Art. 20(2).

[18] Cook, 'Reservations to the Convention on the Elimination of all Forms of Discrimination against Women', 30 *Va. J. Int'l L.* 707–8 (1990). Cf. Oeser, 'Legal Questions in the Committee on the Elimination of Discrimination against Women', 14 *GDR Committee Hum. Rts. Bull.* 86 (1988). On this issue generally, see text accompanying nn. 90–7, below.

[19] Meron, 'Enhancing the Effectiveness of the Prohibition of Discrimination against Women', 84 *Am. J. Int'l L.* 213 (1990).

both interstate and individual complaint mechanisms. While they have to date been used only rarely, their existence gives CERD the possibility of expanding the scope of its action beyond the constraints of the reporting system.

Some critics believe that such procedures would be inappropriate or unnecessarily cumbersome for CEDAW, and in any event there already exists a recourse procedure for individuals established by the Commission on the Status of Women. The Commission began the individual communications procedure in 1982 partly in response to the wide range of sex discrimination allegations being referred to it from various other parts of the United Nations system. FAO, for example, would refer complaints charging such things as confiscation of land or discrimination in agricultural employment or rural lending programs. The Commission thus began to refer these confidential and non-confidential communications to a working group. Under the 1982 procedure, when the Commission receives a complaint, the Secretariat informs the relevant government of the allegations and gives it an opportunity to respond before a certain date. Both the complaint and the response are then examined by the working group. The Commission's report reflects trends observed in the communications, rather than details of individual complaints.[20] The first trend noted by the Commission was the proliferation of acts of violence against women under detention in many countries. It therefore requested the Secretary-General to obtain information from States on the treatment of women detainees.[21]

The absence of a complaints procedure in the CEDAW Convention is thus partly explained by the existence of the Commission's procedure. Given CEDAW's existing time constraints and backlog of States reports, the omission of a time-consuming complaints procedures is probably for the best. The absence of a complaints procedure diminishes the potential for confrontation between the Committee and governments and facilitates the evolution of a constructive dialogue. On the other hand, the experience of the Human Rights Committee in this respect is that the detailed examination of individual complaints provides an invaluable context in which to develop a body of jurisprudence elaborating upon the scope and content of the various treaty provisions. While Meron has characterized the absence of such a

[20] At its 1986 session, for example, the Commission's 'Working Group on Communications on the Status of Women' produced a six-sentence report on the basis of its review of all communications received. It concluded that many of the communications were not relevant, and on the basis of the remainder, observed only 'the exposure of women, while officially detained, to physical violence, still continued'. *Report of the Commission on the Status of Women in 1986*, E/1986/24, chap. 5, para. 94. At its 1991 session the Commission considered a comprehensive review paper proposing major changes in the manner of dealing with communications.

[21] 'Report of the Secretary-General on Physical Violence against Detained Women that is Specific to their Sex', E/CN.6/1986/11. In 1986 the Commission called for a follow-up report on the same issue to be submitted to it by the Secretary-General in 1987 (ESC Res. 1986/29, paras. 3–4).

procedure in the CEDAW context as a 'major inadequacy', he has also noted that considerable additional resources would need to be allocated to the Committee to enable it to carry out such a function.[22]

D. *The Committee (CEDAW)*

Part V of the Convention (Articles 17–22) outlines the form and functions of CEDAW. The Committee consists of twenty-three members who serve in their individual capacities. They are elected by the States Parties for four-year terms and their travel and expenses are paid for by the UN rather than by the States Parties, as in the case of CERD. The Convention also stipulates that the Secretary-General will provide the necessary facilities and staff to service the meetings of the Committee. Unlike all of the other treaty-based supervisory bodies the Committee's secretariat is provided not by the Centre for Human Rights, in Geneva, but by the Branch for the Advancement of Women, based in Vienna.

The provisions of the Convention are relatively specific as to both the format and content of CEDAW's work by outlining the qualifications required for Committee membership, duration of sessions, what issues are appropriate for the agenda, and other matters. There has been much debate over the qualifications and independence of members of the Committee. The Convention says only that experts should be 'of high moral standing and competence in the field covered by the Convention'.[23] Although the distinction between governmental representatives and independent experts is an important one in the UN setting, throughout the 1980s experts from Socialist countries regularly consulted with diplomats from their missions during CEDAW meetings. For this reason the Chairperson usually found it necessary at the relevant sessions to remind the members that they were serving in their individual capacities. At the fifth session of the Committee, one member slipped during a discussion and referred to the views of 'my delegation'. No one seemed to notice, but the Chairperson did make the obligatory statement on independence later in that session.

Some experts have expressed a desire that members be professionals, not employed directly by their governments, in order to ensure their independence. For example, the member from the Soviet Union (through the fifth session) Ms Aleksandra Biryukova, was elected in 1986 a member of the Supreme Soviet, the highest official post ever attained by a Soviet woman.[24]

[22] Meron, 'Enhancing the Effectiveness of the Prohibition of Discrimination against Women', 216–17.

[23] Art. 17(1) of the Convention. (See n. 2, above.)

[24] Ms Biryukova was nominated for re-election at the States Parties meeting after the fifth session, but her nomination was withdrawn by the Soviet Union after her election to the

While this clear sign of Ms Biryukova's close governmental links raises doubts as to her independence, such a status may have some advantages even from the Committee's viewpoint. In the first place, it is inevitably difficult to find qualified professional women from Socialist countries who have no connection to their governments. Secondly, in the case of Ms Biryukova, there is every likelihood that she would be a force for change in her country and would be well placed to promote positive action on women's issues reflecting the approach of CEDAW. Ms Biryukova was a member of CEDAW from its inception and showed great dedication to the cause; it is thus likely that her promotion will further enhance the Committee's prestige and impact in the Soviet Union. Notwithstanding the theoretical desirability of complete independence, one cannot automatically conclude that an expert's proximity to her government is inversely correlated to her effectiveness on the Committee.

It has also been suggested that the country of origin may explain a member's attitude better than any governmental links. In fact, the feminist background common to most CEDAW members seems to have been more important than government employment, and has ensured a collective critical attitude.[25]

The Convention's provisions concerning staffing and facilities available to CEDAW have also given rise to some controversy. Some members of the Secretariat claim problems with inadequate staffing are indicative of the Organization's low priority for women's issues, especially since the Convention states that the Secretary-General 'shall provide the *necessary* staff and facilities for the *effective* performance' of CEDAW.[26] For example, the Convention provides that meetings should take place 'normally' at UN Headquarters (a phrase which in itself has been contentious, as some argue that the Organization has headquarters in Vienna and Geneva as well as New York),[27] or at any other convenient place determined by the Committee. This provision has typically been inserted into conventions to reflect a preference for New York rather than other UN offices. However, in this case meetings held in New York are severely hampered by administrative inadequacies. The Branch for the Advancement of Women (part of the Centre for Social Development and Humanitarian Affairs), which provides the support staff for CEDAW, is located in Vienna. Partly to discourage the holding of meetings in New York and partly due to severe financial constraints, the Secretary-General has provided so few staff members to service CEDAW in New York

government body. See 'Amendment to the Note by the Secretary-General on the Election of Twelve Members of the Committee on the Elimination of Discrimination against Women', CEDAW/SP/9/Amend.3 (1986).

[25] Byrnes, 'The "Other" Human Rights Treaty Body: The Work of the Committee on the Elimination of Discrimination against Women', 14 *Yale J. Int'l L.* 10–12 (1989).

[26] Art. 17(9) of the Convention, emphasis added. (See n. 2, above.)

[27] For example, the Legal Officer in 1982. See *Report of CEDAW in 1982*, A/38/45 (1983), para. 39.

as to render almost impossible the 'effective performance' of the Committee. The Committee's sessions are now held in Vienna except when there is a States Parties' meeting for elections, which occurs every two years.

As a result of pressure exerted by various States through the debates in the General Assembly and by the 1988 and 1990 Meetings of the Chairpersons of the Human Rights Treaty Bodies,[28] the 1991 session of the Committee saw various proposals by the Secretariat to improve its performance in this regard. As, in effect, a *quid pro quo*, the Committee decided to defer consideration of a proposal made by the Chairpersons in 1990 that CEDAW should instead be serviced by the Centre for Human Rights in Geneva, until the benefits of the proposed improvements could be evaluated.

Article 18 of the Convention requires States Parties to submit reports to the Secretary-General within one year after the entry into force of the Convention, on 'legislative, judicial, administrative or other measures which they have adopted to give effect' to the Convention, and to submit subsequent reports every four years thereafter. Most States Parties have concentrated on legislative developments and have included all too few other details in their reports. Moreover, many States have been tardy in their submission of reports. As of January 1991, twenty-nine initial reports, forty-nine second reports, and twenty-six third reports were overdue out of a total of 103 States Parties.[29] While other committees, such as CERD and the Human Rights Committee, as well as the General Assembly, have expressed serious concern at the proportion of overdue reports,[30] in recent years the problem has assumed increasing significance for CEDAW as well. The only positive dimension of the problem is that because of the grossly inadequate length of its annual sessions, CEDAW could not possibly cope with submissions by all States that have ratified the Convention. Even giving each report only superficial consideration and working at breakneck speed, it is estimated that the Committee could not discuss more than eight initial reports per session (ten working days). At their 1986 session, Committee members all agreed that this represented the maximum speed at which they could process reports.[31] In 1991, the Committee was able to examine two initial reports and eight second reports.

[28] The Meeting of Chairpersons, in 1990, concluded that 'strong and active consideration should be given to relocating the functions relating to the Convention' from Vienna to Geneva. It noted that existing arrangements 'were not at all conducive to facilitating the type and level of interaction [among the different treaty bodies] that was necessary', and that 'the benefits that the Committee had derived from proximity to the secretariat of the Commission on the Status of Women had been minimal . . .'. A/45/636 (1990) para. 19.

[29] *Report of CEDAW in 1991*, A/46/38 (1991), Annexes I and II.

[30] GA Res. 45/85 (1990). For the report of the Third Meeting of the Chairpersons, see A/45/636 (1990).

[31] *Report of CEDAW in 1986*, A/41/45 (1986), para. 26. The Committee has noted that this is an unusually heavy load and that the Human Rights Committee, for example, treats no more than four reports per session; see CEDAW/C/SR.40 (1984), para. 58.

CEDAW's final reports are submitted to the Economic and Social Council and then to the General Assembly. The consideration given to the report by those bodies has been cursory at best, the reasons for which will be discusssed below.

I. WORKING METHODS

In many respects CEDAW is still relatively young in terms of an evaluation of its working methods. The Committee held its tenth session in 1991, but has only been carrying out its major task of reviewing States Parties' reports since 1983, because its first session was occupied with organization matters.

It is useful to consider briefly certain of CEDAW's Rules of Procedure as they, like the Convention, help to set the tenor of the Committee's work. Controversy began in drafting the rules of procedure with Article 1 on 'annual sessions'. Although the rule on the length and number of meetings comes directly from Article 20 of the Convention, pressure for longer or more frequent sessions has been a continual theme of debate.[32] Discussions focused on the meaning of the word 'normally' and whether exceptional (additional) meetings could be held. It was immediately clear to members that the scheduled sessions would not be sufficient to accomplish even the most modest of proposed agendas. The Committee's fifth session was scheduled to propose to the General Assembly that a third week be added to the annual session. Instead, the Committee merely 'considered the implications of requesting longer sessions in the light of the present financial crisis'[33] and agreed that 'States Parties and the Economic and Social Council should be informed about the constraints faced by the Committee'.[34] At its sixth session, the Committee decided to request the General Assembly to approve 'on an exceptional basis, eight additional meetings of the Committee in 1988'.[35] Thus in 1988, the Committee had four extra working days, an arrangement which was again requested for its 1989 session, without success.[36] A request for additional time at future sessions, albeit on an exceptional basis, was also foreshadowed at the Committee's 1991 session.

As if to underscore the inadequacy of CEDAW's allotted time, during the Committee's first session there was insufficient time (one week) for discussion of the draft guidelines on the content of States Parties' reports. The

[32] See, *inter alia*, *Report of CEDAW in 1982*, paras. 26–31; CEDAW/C/SR.34 (1984), paras. 46–8; and CEDAW/C/SR.40 (1984), paras. 47–70.

[33] *Report of CEDAW in 1986*, para. 20.

[34] Ibid. para. 21.

[35] Draft resolution for the General Assembly, para. 1, in *Report of CEDAW in 1987*, A/42/38 (1987), para. 580, Dec. 1.

[36] Committee Suggestion 1, *Report of CEDAW in 1988*, A/43/38 (1988), para. 772. The General Assembly decided to keep the request 'under review', GA Res. 43/100 (1988), para. 10.

Committee was therefore authorized to meet for three weeks in 1983 to consider the guidelines.

On many of the contentious issues involved in drafting the Rules of Procedure the Committee looked to both the Human Rights Committee and CERD for precedents.[37] Although in many ways its situation resembles that of CERD, CEDAW has sometimes opted for the Human Rights Committee's approach, and, in recent years, has adopted a significant number of the innovations introduced by the Committee on Economic, Social and Cultural Rights.

The Committee simply reiterated in its Rules of Procedure (Rule 48) the provisions for suggestions and recommendations contained in Article 21 of the Convention. The issue has been discussed at almost every session[38] because of the existence of strongly divergent views on the part of Committee members as to the nature and focus of the recommendations which the Committee is entitled to make. In 1986, the Committee adopted its first general recommendations[39] and, the following year, it decided that it could also make suggestions.[40] The principal issue remaining unresolved[41] was whether either of these two categories of comments could deal directly with the situation in a particular State.[42] By 1991, general recommendations had been adopted on a range of issues including the implementation of the Convention, reporting approaches, procedures and resource problems, as well as substantive issues, such as violence against women, equal remuneration for unpaid women workers in family enterprises, and disabled women.[43]

The major task of the Committee is consideration of the reports of States Parties. When the Convention was opened for signature on 1 March 1980, the first countries to ratify it were Cuba, Guyana, Portugal, Sweden, and the German Democratic Republic. As of January 1991, there were 103 States Parties to the Convention.[44] Although some observers had speculated that it would be difficult to get countries to sign, ratify, or accede to the treaty, this has not been the case.[45] In part as a result of the enthusiasm generated by the

[37] *Report of CEDAW in 1982*, paras. 25–77, esp. paras. 27, 29, 45, and 77.

[38] See e.g. CEDAW/C/SR.34, 46, 68, 78, 97, and 131 (1984, 1985, 1986, 1987, and 1988).

[39] *Report of CEDAW in 1986*, paras. 357–65.

[40] *Report of CEDAW in 1987*, paras. 56–60.

[41] *Report of CEDAW in 1988*, para. 58 and CEDAW/C/SR.131 (1988), paras. 38–51.

[42] For a more detailed examination of the issue, see Byrnes, 'The "Other" Human Rights Treaty Body', 42–5.

[43] The Committee adopted three general recommendations in 1987, four in 1988, five in 1989, three in 1990, and three in 1991. See *Report of CEDAW in 1987*, paras. 577–9; *Report of CEDAW in 1988*, para. 770; *Report of CEDAW in 1989*, A/44/38 (1989), para. 392; *Report of CEDAW in 1990*, A/45/38 (1990), para 438; and the *Report of CEDAW in 1991*, A/46/38 (1991), para. 1.

[44] *Report of CEDAW in 1991*, Annex I.

[45] See Tinker, 'Human Rights for Women: The UN Convention on the Elimination of all Forms of Discrimination against Women', 3 *Hum. Rts. Q.* 42–3 (1981).

end of the UN Decade for Women and the Nairobi conference, the number of States Parties increased greatly during 1985. The high number of ratifications has significant implications for the Committee's work. First, it attests to the importance of the Convention and generates a large number of reports to be examined, thereby ensuring CEDAW's survival at a time of drastic budget-cutting in the Organization. In addition, the requirement that a State report to the Committee within one year after the Convention's coming into force places pressure on the country to begin looking closely at its domestic laws and practices. This frequently results in the first detailed, official examination of the situation of women in the ratifying State. Although the reports are usually delayed and are frequently poor in quality, 'the process of preparing a Report could bring to light aspects of discrimination in the State concerned which may not have been given official recognition previously'.[46]

II. STATES PARTIES' REPORTS

(*a*) *General Characteristics*

When the 'General Guidelines Regarding the Form and Contents of Reports Received from States Parties under Article 18 of the Convention' (hereafter referred to as the Guidelines), were adopted, members hoped that these would be sufficient to ensure reasonable detail and uniformity of data.[47] However, a sampling of States Parties' reports reveals the great diversity in content and style which results from the vagueness of the Guidelines. They run the gamut from 200-plus page documents with statistical appendices to two-page reports.[48] Although additional information may be contained in a representative's oral introduction or during the Committee's question and answer period, the written reports should provide the most complete picture of the situation of women in the country concerned. The fact that countries may submit reports of such uneven quality and quantity, all of which are in conformity with the Committee's rules and are accepted by it, reflects not only differing levels of commitment to the principles of the Convention but also the shortcomings of the Guidelines.

In order to ascertain whether a State Party report conforms to the Committee's requirements, one must look carefully at the Guidelines. They suggest that a State divide its report into two parts. The first is to cover

[46] Evatt, 'The United Nations Convention on the Elimination of Discrimination against Women and CEDAW' (mimeo., Canberra, Dec. 1985), 14.

[47] The guidelines are contained in 'General Guidelines Regarding the Form and Contents of Reports Received from States Parties under Article 18 of the Convention', CEDAW/C/7 (1983); See discussion of them in *Report of CEDAW in 1983*, A/39/45 (1984), i. paras. 26–34; and CEDAW/C/SR.10, 11, 23, and 24 (1983).

[48] See the reports for Australia (CEDAW/C/5/Add. 40 (1986) and Amend. 1 (1988)) and Mali (CEDAW/C/5/Add.43 (1987)).

measures taken to eliminate discrimination against women, legislation, or other measures taken to implement the Convention and those institutions or organizations charged with implementing the Convention. The second is to list 'specific information in relation to each provision of the Convention' and to elaborate upon difficulties encountered in their implementation.[49] The guidelines were discussed in great detail, both in an informal working group and within the Committee itself.[50] The apparent reason for dividing the reports into two sections was that it was recognized that a difference existed between what was provided in the legislation in different countries and how that legislation was applied in practice.[51] Most States Parties feel justified in devoting the majority of their reports to national legislation that embodies the spirit and letter of the Convention, the implication being that such provisions ensure implementation. Such information, however, provides at best a very partial view of the situation of women.

Although a number of issues are omitted from many States Parties' reports, including difficulties or obstacles to full implementation and information about courts or tribunals available to women, none has been as repeatedly ignored as that contained in item 5 of the Guidelines: statistics. That guideline advises States not to present 'mere lists of legal instruments' but to include 'data concerning [the reality in their country] and conditions . . . with a breakdown of the statistics on the category of sex'.[52] Countries frequently include general demographic figures and occasionally indicate the number of women at certain educational levels, but only very few have provided more detailed statistics. During the Committee's fifth session, the Working Group drew up a list of statistical categories to be included in each State Party report.[53]

State compliance with more detailed and specific Guidelines would greatly improve the consistency and comparability of reports.[54] It would also create the kind of database which CEDAW could profitably use in formulating suggestions and recommendations to States Parties, as well as in shaping its agenda. However, the collection of such data is a monumental task in countries that do not have the requisite institutions or staff. Two proposals have been made which would reduce the burden. During the Committee's fourth session, a suggestion was made that the UN Institute for Research and

[49] 'General Guidelines', para. 7.

[50] For the Committee discussion, see e.g. CEDAW/C/SR.23–4 (1983).

[51] *Report of CEDAW in 1983*, para. 27.

[52] 'General Guidelines', para. 5.

[53] The Annex to CEDAW/C/11/CRP.4 (1986), contains eight general categories related to articles in the Convention and then breaks down specific items for inclusion, e.g.: level of female participation in trade unions, in elections as voters, women as a percentage of the work force, etc.

[54] Indeed, Byrnes sugests that part of the problem of non-compliance lies precisely in the fact that the guidelines are too general. For his examination of the problem, see Byrnes, 'The "Other" Human Rights Treaty Body', 15–17.

Training for the Advancement of Women (INSTRAW) could be utilized to 'assist developing countries that lacked suitable data'.[55] The suggestion has not yet been explored in any detail but is very valuable. Its implementation would strengthen the supervision and co-ordination functions of the UN organs concerned with women's issues and greatly improve the quality of States parties reports. In order not to overburden countries, States Parties are requested to provide comprehensive data only in their initial report, in subsequent reports they may simply update statistics in which *substantial* changes had occurred.

States Parties' reports are usually produced by the foreign ministry. On some occasions, however, reports have been drawn up by, or in collaboration with, national non-governmental or quasi-governmental bodies concerned with women's issues. The report of the Philippines, discussed during CEDAW's third session, was prepared by the National Commission on the Role of Filipino Women, a quasi-governmental body created in 1975.[56] The National Commission had been created to monitor the implementation of laws concerning the integration of women in national development. It included at least one important NGO leader, the President of the Civil Assembly of Women, an umbrella organization under which 75 women's organizations operated.[57]

The report of Portugal presented at CEDAW's fifth session was based upon a unique mixture of governmental and non-governmental sources.[58] The first portion of the report covers governmental and legislative actions undertaken in accordance with the Convention. The second part of the document, issued as a corrigendum, contains a report prepared by the Portuguese Commission on the Status of Women, a governmental body located within the office of the President of the Council of Ministers. The Commission's report, which is over three times the length of the initial governmental submission, is a comprehensive document, containing basic statistical data, a historical time-line of events of significance to women's rights in Portugal, details of governmental bodies charged with implementing policy on women, a bibliography of publications concerning Portuguese women, a list of non-governmental organizations participating in the Commission, and a more detailed legislative analysis than that contained in the initial submission.[59] Although its statistics are still not comprehensive, the

[55] Report of CEDAW in 1985, A/40/45 (1985), para. 26. INSTRAW, located in the Dominican Republic, was set up during the UN Decade for Women (1975–85).

[56] Report of the Philippines, CEDAW/C/5/Add.6 (1984). The report was also prepared with the assistance of other governmental and non-governmental bodies.

[57] See the *Report of CEDAW in 1984*, A/39/45 (1984), ii, para. 107.

[58] Report of Portugal, CEDAW/C/5/Add.21 (1984) and Corr.1 (1985).

[59] The Commission's report is in the Corrigendum to the report of Portugal, CEDAW/C/5/Add.21/Corr.1 (1985), Annex II.

Portuguese report should be considered a valuable model to be followed by other States.

(*b*) *The Oral Presentation*

To open the Committee's discussion of a State Party report, a representative of the government is invited to introduce it.[60] Such introductions are as diverse as the reports they precede, and range from mere presentations of the documentation to the provision of information that may be far more comprehensive than the report itself.[61] Whatever the intention of the representative, the introduction often provides the most insight into the State's real intentions with respect to compliance with the convention and co-operation with CEDAW. On some occasions these insights have come in the form of errors made by representatives who are quite unfamiliar with the issues under discussion.

The representative may be a diplomat in the country's UN mission, or on some occasions, the ambassador. During the Committee's early sessions there was occasionally tension between the Committee member serving in her individual capacity, and the representative of her country who was presenting the State's work. In part this was the result of asymmetrical knowledge on the subject, the member having been nominated in recognition of her detailed knowledge of women's issues whereas the ambassador's expertise might lie in very different fields. This tension was exacerbated in the early years by the extent to which the nationals of reporting States were members of the Committee since the few countries who were States Parties were presenting both candidates for membership, and reports. Thus at CEDAW's second session, seven reports were presented and five of these countries had nationals on the Committee.[62] In a notorious incident during the introduction of the report of the Philippines to the third session of CEDAW, the Filipina member of the Committee was eventually unable to contain herself in the face of inaccurate statements by the State representative. When a Committee member asked a question of the representative, the Summary Records indicate that she took it upon herself to reply before the State representative had a chance to do so.[63]

It would be incorrect to leave the impression that such difficulties have arisen only in the context of the Philippine case; they have not. Many (if not all) countries' representatives have been less knowledgeable than the

[60] See Rule 49 of the Rules of Procedure, in *Report of CEDAW in 1982*, Annex III.

[61] An example of the latter can be found in the introduction of Rwanda's report during CEDAW's third session; see CEDAW/C/SR.37 (1984), paras, 13–24.

[62] The five were Cuba, the German Democratic Republic, Mexico, Sweden, and the Soviet Union. The other two countries presenting reports were the Byelorussian SSR and the Ukranian SSR. (CEDAW/C/S/Add.4,1,2,8,12,5,11 (1983)).

[63] CEDAW/C/SR.33 (1984), para. 8: 'Ms Cortes said that, while she had not intended to participate in the debate, she wished to refer . . .'.

Committee member of the same nationality and the tension between these groups is unlikely to disappear. It is simply that the Philippine case presents the most dramatic example because in the words of one Committee member it 'plunged the Committee into confusion and perplexity'.[64] It is therefore worth recounting in some detail.

During his oral presentation to the Committee, the representative of the Philippines, stated, *inter alia*, that, 'Filipinos wanted women to remain as they had been in the past; they did not want them to lose their femininity and wanted to protect them', and concluded that 'because Filipinas understood their complementarity to men, there was no women's liberation movement in the Philippines'.[65] The representative continued his remarks to a stunned and silent chamber, and the Committee rapidly moved on to introduce the report of China. Many members of the Committee subsequently voiced strong criticism of and demanded apologies from the Philippine mission. A few days later, when another representative of the country faced a hostile CEDAW,[66] she took the extraordinary step of emphasizing that the Ambassador's views were personal and did not reflect government policy and formally apologized for offense caused by his comments.[67]

The incident brings up another important issue that often arises in the context of the oral presentation of States Parties' reports. This is the issue of tension between an all-female Committee dealing with women's issues and the States representatives who, more often than not, are male. CEDAW has only had one male member, Mr Johan Nordenfelt of Sweden, whose credentials on women's issues were above question. He had been his country's representative to the Third Committee when the Decade for Women was initiated and had participated in both the UN Women's Conferences in Mexico and Copenhangen. Mr Nordenfelt is no longer on the Committee, and since 1984 CEDAW has been all female, a situation unlikely to change in the near future.[68] The resulting division between representatives and experts along gender lines has often resulted in the questions and questioners becoming adversarial in nature, as a result of which the representative often feels victimized and responds defensively.[69]

[64] CEDAW/C/SR.37 (1984), para. 5.

[65] CEDAW/C/SR.33 (1984), para. 13.

[66] Often while a country's ambassador will be given the honour of introducing a report, questions on substantive matters are turned over to other officials from the mission who are more knowledgeable on the issues.

[67] CEDAW/C/SR.37 (1984), paras. 9–10.

[68] Members elected in 1990 ensure that the Committee will be all female at least until 1992. *Report of CEDAW in 1991*, Annex III.

[69] This situation could be seen during questions and answers to the Salvadoran representative during the fifth session. When the representative began to feel more defensive and unable to reply to questions, he chastised Committee members for their lack of understanding of his country's political situation. Committee members responded by charging the representative with bringing up irrelevant matters. See CEDAW/C/SR.80 (1986), paras. 1–20.

The existence of such tensions in the work of the Committee greatly detracts from the achievement of its goals. Having more male members on the Committee is not the answer. In the first place, it is questionable whether the presence of one or two male members would greatly ease the representatives' discomfort. In addition, finding men with the requisite experience and interest in women's issues is not an easy task. An alternative would be to encourage the practice that representatives who introduce reports and take questions be women. Such formal encouragement would seem unwise and should be unnecessary. It is simply incumbent upon members of the Committee, despite their occasional frustration with incomplete information and the ignorance of some representatives, to work harder to prevent the development of an adversarial atmosphere which conflicts with the goal of achieving constructive dialogue.

A final issue of concern regarding the oral presentations is that of recording such presentations, especially when they contain useful information not found in the written reports. Proposals to transcribe the representatives' statements were discussed informally during the second session. Under the present system the representative's remarks are not part of the State Party report, and will appear only in an abbreviated form in the Committee's summary records. In addition, those records are available only after an often considerable delay. For this reason, it was proposed that the Secretariat create a 'reference file' containing any and all material on a specific country, to be made available to Committee members when that country's report was to be considered.[70] During the third session, a number of proposals were made, including annexing the introductory remarks to the country's report for circulation among the members and requesting that representatives summarize their remarks and replies in written form.[71] At the fifth session, the working group which was created to work informally on other issues discussed the topic yet again. They decried the lack of institutional memory for CEDAW, and noted the problems this will raise when second reports begin to come in to a Committee most of whose members will not have participated in consideration of the initial reports.[72]

The problem is indeed serious but the solutions proposed are all flawed in the same manner: they require the State Party representative to prepare his or her introductory remarks and replies in a more formal manner for submission and future use. Many representatives read from note cards or base their comments on statistics. Many of them would apparently prefer not to be obligated to formalize their comments any further. Moreover, the proposals all require the Secretariat office servicing CEDAW to serve a greater in-

[70] *Report of CEDAW in 1983*, para. 20.
[71] *Report of CEDAW in 1984*, para. 346.
[72] See CEDAW/C/11/CRP.4 (1986).

formation-processing or database function despite the fact that it is already labouring under budgetary constraints. Nevertheless, a greater capacity to record and store the data presented by representatives during CEDAW meetings must be found if the value of the information presented therein is not to be lost.

A related problem is that the written questions submitted to each State Party by the pre-sessional Working Group are also not recorded in either the summary records or the annual report.

(c) The Question and Answer Procedure

After a State has presented its written report to the Committee, members may ask questions, request additional information, or seek clarification on a range of subjects. Often the representative will not have such information at his fingertips but will note all of the questions and return with as much information as possible on the second day of discussion of the report.[73] All States Parties reports are given two scheduled days of discussion, the first for introduction and initial questions, the second for information and follow-up. The actual period of time devoted to discussion varies in length, but rarely exceeds the two days allotted. Moreover, it never occupies the entirety of either day's work. The major problem with the procedure is the repetitive and therefore time-consuming nature of questions.[74] Each member seems to feel compelled to repeat congratulatory remarks and to reiterate questions already posed by a colleague. An even worse tendency is to associate one's self with the questions of another, often at greater length than the initial question. The most frequently asked question concerns the lack of good statistical data in the reports. Members also occasionally feel compelled to demonstrate that they have read the report by quoting whole sections before finally arriving at their question. Soemtimes questions are so esoteric in nature that an answer would not be likely to contribute to the dialogue on the report. Similarly, as in any UN body, political, ideological, and other differences find their way into the questioning procedure. At the fifth session, for example, issues of political pressures on women, foreign domination, and general and widespread human rights violations did not arise except in the questioning of the representative of El Salvador, and then only from certain members.

There is obviously a need, especially in light of CEDAW's already packed agenda, to cut down on all unnecessary or repetitive comments or questions. A 1986 Working Group proposal contemplated dividing questions into major substantive areas most commonly asked such as education, legislation, legal

[73] Elizabeth Evatt describes this process as days of 'feverish activity' on the part of the delegation; Evatt, 'The United Nations Convention against Women and CEDAW', 6.

[74] See e.g. a series of comments saying in essence nothing more than thank you, CEDAW/C/SR.17 (1983), paras. 27–36.

systems, family practices, health care, etc. Members could ask as many questions as they liked and all members would be free to ask questions, but only on the area under discussion. These discussion areas would be open only for periods of time determined by the Committee. This proposal ran into stiff opposition from those who felt that members would be constrained in their questioning and thus not elicit as much information, and also because some members saw it as a first step to restricting certain questions to certain members in a sort of division of labor.[75]

In 1987 and 1988 Working Group I suggested assigning individual members to co-ordinate questions on specific articles. Although the Committee agreed to try this method it did not seek to reflect it in its formal rules.[76] It did decide, in 1988, to adopt on a trial basis a new procedure based on the transmission to States Parties' representatives of lists of questions before the discussion of second or subsequent periodic reports. In 1989 the Committee decided that the lists should be prepared by a pre-sessional working group, subject to authorization by the General Assembly.[77]

E. *Relations to other UN Bodies*

I. HUMAN RIGHTS BODIES

While CEDAW is the only specialist body in the UN system with responsibility for supervising State's compliance with their treaty obligations with respect to women's rights (a task not performed by the Commission on the Status of Women, for example), it nevertheless remains almost entirely isolated from the UN's other human rights organs. This is in part because while the latter are almost all serviced by the Centre for Human Rights in Geneva, CEDAW, as noted earlier, is separately serviced from Vienna. Moreover, its Secretariat is located within the Centre for Social Development and Humanitarian Affairs, an umbrella unit which is also responsible for matters relating to youth, the ageing, the handicapped, and crime prevention. While these issues are of undoubted relevance to human rights, they are not dealt with substantively or institutionally in the same manner as human rights issues *per se*.

[75] In fact the working group's report was published with a dissenting opinion from Ms Peytcheva (Bulgaria). See CEDAW/C/11/CRP.4 (1986), 2. It was finally decided to leave it to each expert to decide whether to repeat a question, and experts would only 'endeavour to ask questions in the same order as the articles of the Convention' (*Report of CEDAW in 1986*, para. 22).

[76] *Report of CEDAW in 1987*, para. 33; *Report of CEDAW in 1988*, para. 32; and CEDAW/C/SR.128 (1988), paras. 3–12.

[77] Byrnes, 'CEDAW's 10th Session: Building on a Decade of Achievement' (mimeo. International Women's Rights Action Watch, 1991), 11.

Most observers accept the appropriateness of establishing separate organs and secretariats to deal with human rights and women's rights. It has, nevertheless, been suggested that this separation has enabled the UN to downgrade the latter in a number of respects (shorter meetings, truncated summary records, etc.) while at the same time professing the equal importance of the two sets of issues.

The problem cannot be resolved by the abolition of CEDAW or the absorption of its functions into human rights bodies, nor by moving its Secretariat to Geneva (although this proposal was explicitly endorsed by the 1990 Meeting of the Chairpersons of the Human Rights treaty bodies). What is required is an effort to achieve improved co-operation and co-ordination. A major step in this direction was taken in 1985 by the General Assembly when it decided to include the Chairperson of CEDAW in any future meetings of the Chairpersons of the various principal human rights bodies. When that group met for the first time in August 1985 CEDAW was not included. The decision to remedy this omission for the 1988, 1990, and subsequent meetings was a welcome one and could provide the basis for serious partnership among the various bodies.[78]

II. OTHER BODIES DEALING WITH WOMEN'S ISSUES

Another body with which CEDAW has little formal or institutional contact is the Commission on the Status of Women. The Convention contains a provision that the Secretary-General will transmit CEDAW's reports to the CSW for its information (Article 21) but there is little evidence that the Commission has utilized them in any real way, and there is no provision for the Commission to send information to CEDAW. While the nature of the Commission's work differs from CEDAW's, there is little doubt that increased communication would benefit both bodies.

CEDAW had very little to do with the preparations for, or the proceedings of the UN Decade for Women Conference in Nairobi in 1985, but it clearly benefited from the activities of the Decade and the Conference through the receipt of additional ratifications. At its second session the Committee decided to transmit the reports of its second and third sessions to the Nairobi Conference in order to give an indication of the progress made in implementing the Convention.[79]

[78] GA Res. 40/116 (1985), para. 12. The reports of the Meetings of Chairpersons are contained in: A/39/484 (1984); A/44/98 (1989); and A/45/636 (1990).

[79] The document they submitted was 'Achievements and Obstacles Experienced by States Parties in the Implementation of the Convention on the Elimination of all Forms of Discrimination against Women', CEDAW/C/1985/CRP.1/Rev. 1 (also circulated at the Nairobi 1985 Conference as A/CONF.116/13). See also the discussion of this contribution in CEDAW/C/SR.22 (1983), paras. 47–57 and CEDAW/C/SR.41 (1984), paras. 59–74.

Now that a second decade of activities to promote the status of women has begun, efforts should be made to link CEDAW to such activities. A recent comparison of the Convention with the major document adopted by the Conference, the 'Nairobi Forward-Looking Strategies for the Advancement of Women',[80] reveals the complementarity of concerns dealt with in the two instruments. The comparative analysis concluded that certain areas of the Strategies are more specific and far-reaching than the comparable provisions of the Convention but that in other areas the Convention is actually more advanced. Such comparisons demonstrate that there are important lessons to be learned from the Committee's work and that these can be applied to other areas of the UN's work on women, and vice versa.

Since the Commission on the Status of Women was the preparatory body for the Nairobi Conference and will play an important role in implementing its recommendations, co-ordination between it and CEDAW are even more important. To date there has been little study within or outside the Organization of the relationship between the two bodies and of the ways in which their activities could be better co-ordinated so as to ensure coverage of the entire spectrum of issues. One body which grew out of the Decade but which has had little or no contact with CEDAW is the Voluntary Fund for the UN Decade for Women, recently renamed the UN Development Fund for Women or UNIFEM. UNIFEM has projects in many States, whose governments have been or will be reporting to CEDAW. Its efforts concentrate on grassroots activities to provide women with greater economic resources in developing countries. While it is true that CEDAW and the Convention deal with government activities and not those of the 'micro' level development projects of UNIFEM, the latter's activities could have important consequences and lessons for countries wishing to comply with provisions of the Convention. Article 14 of the Convention is particularly relevant since it deals with issues concerning rural women such as the teaching of technical skills, establishment of co-operatives, access to credit and participation in community activities, all of which have been among the chief concerns of UNIFEM projects. These projects have not been government administered and therefore do not fall within the scope of the States Parties' reports, but information about successful projects in countries reporting to CEDAW would prove useful to Committee members in gaining an understanding of the difficulties and obstacles to implementation.[81]

Both UNIFEM and INSTRAW, the two bodies created during the Decade, should also be utilized to a greater extent to provide States Parties

[80] Stumpf, 'Re-examining the UN Convention on the Elimination of all Forms of Discrimination against Women: The UN Decade for Women Conference in Nairobi', 10 *Yale J. Int'l. L.* 384 (1985).

[81] The guidelines in fact suggest that the States Parties should report on any obstacles or difficulties encountered in implementing the rights contained in the Convention; see 'General Guidelines', para. 7.

with data they could use in the preparation of their reports. Data is provided to UNIFEM when project proposals are submitted and this also could be tapped by both Committee members and the reporting State. In general, the more information provided to the Committee through increased co-ordination among the relevant UN bodies, the more accurate the picture Committee members will have, and the more informed and appropriate will be their questions and recommendations on implementation of the Convention.

III. REPORTING TO ECOSOC AND THE GENERAL ASSEMBLY

There is very little to say about the treatment which CEDAW's report receives from ECOSOC and the General Assembly. This is principally because of the paucity of attention which it receives. It would be unfair to suggest that this is entirely due to the chauvinism or lack of interest of those bodies. As the Committee's reports are now structured, they are essentially a summary of activities during the session. As such, there is usually little controversial to be discussed. When the Committee decided to request the promotion of UN studies on the status of women under Islamic law, it was strongly criticized in ECOSOC and was asked by the General Assembly to reconsider its request.[82] In general, the Committee will only get serious attention if its suggestions and recommendations prove more interesting, albeit more controversial, than its summary of examination of reports. Whilc there are some within the Secretariat who argue that increased scrutiny will hamper even CEDAW's modest achievements thus far, it is also true that recommendations and suggestions endorsed by the Council and the General Assembly would carry greatly increased weight. Such recommendations, even if watered down by those bodies through political debate, would be infinitely more powerful than those made solely by CEDAW.

F. *Relations with Specialized Agencies and NGOs*

I. SPECIALIZED AGENCIES

Both the Convention and the Rules of Procedure[83] contain provisions for representation of UN specialized agencies at CEDAW meetings and for

[82] The studies were requested by Dec. 4 (*Report of CEDAW in 1987*, para. 580). GA Res.42/60 (1987), para. 9, requested 'the Committee to review that decision, taking into account the views expressed by delegations at the first regular session of 1987 of the Economic and Social Council and in the Third Committee of the General Assembly . . .'. The Committee did not withdraw its request, although it clarified that no criticism of any religion had been intended (*Report of CEDAW in 1988*, paras 64–71). For further discussion of this incident, see Byrnes, 'The "Other" Human Rights Treaty Body', 54–5, and Evatt, 'Towards a Common Standard of Achievement' (mimeo., Sydney, May 1989), 6–7.

[83] Ibid. Art. 22 and rule 52(1).

CEDAW to request reports from those agencies on relevant activities. It was assumed that such input could help the Committee in its major task of evaluating States Parties' reports. The Committee therefore discussed the role of the specialized agencies and their reports at both its second and third sessions.[84] At the former session the Committee decided to invite the specialized agencies to submit information, but did not determine the status or attention such documents would receive during Committee sessions.[85] There was debate on whether the Committee should be concerned with such reports when its primary task was the examination of States Parties' reports. During its third session, having received reports from FAO, ILO, and UNESCO, the Committee debated their status. It decided that they would be circulated as background papers (bearing symbols such as 'CEDAW/ background paper/L . . .') provided this entailed no financial implications.[86] During its seventh session, the Committee again called on the specialized agencies to submit reports on their activities and on information provided to them by States Parties to the Convention.[87]

Although the background papers have been distributed to members and thereby hopefully influence debate, they could be used more productively. It is difficult to recommend any action that requires more time, since it is the Committee's scarcest commodity. It would be better however, if the Committee (perhaps in a working group), discussed strategies and programmes contained in these reports and how they might be utilized in CEDAW's work. Not only would this aid Committee members, it would also assist States Parties because discussion of such agencies' programmes would be entered into the Committee's report, and presumably be read by governmental offices charged with implementing the Convention.

An encouraging development which occurred at the 1991 session was the active involvement of a representative of the ILO in the meetings of the Working Group responsible for drafting the Committee's general recommendations. This precedent could usefully be followed by the representatives of other agencies in the years ahead.

II. RELATIONS WITH NGOS

The most glaring omission in the work of the Committee is the lack of information from non-governmental organizations. NGOs have no formal role

[84] See e.g. CEDAW/C/SR.22 (1983), paras. 2–30; CEDAW/C/SR.31 (1984), paras. 12–65; and CEDAW/C/SR.41 (1984), paras. 75–7.

[85] *Report of CEDAW in 1983*, paras. 23–5.

[86] *Report of CEDAW in 1984*, para. 368.

[87] *Report of CEDAW in 1987*, para. 580, Dec. 2. For a general discussion on the present and possible role of the specialized agencies, see Byrnes, 'The "Other" Human Rights Treaty Body', 38–42.

in the provision of information to CEDAW, although NGO members often attend the public meetings to observe. Their absence is an acute problem because many women's rights NGOs have been working far longer than governments in this area, and many therefore have more information and experience than the reporting States.

NGO inputs may come to the Committee's attention through several, albeit circuitous, paths. Their impact, however, can generally be described as minimal. First, they may be requested by governments to provide information for the drafting of the State Party report. This mechanism was used in the case of Portugal, discussed earlier, in which NGOs participated in the national Commission on the Status of Women, whose report was annexed to the governmental one. NGOs may also, on their own initiative, submit information to individual Committee members for their use during the question and answer sessions. As one Committee member noted, this would provide members with the kind of 'ammunition' needed to delve beneath the surface of reports and get a more accurate overall picture of the situation of women. This means of achieving access to the Committee is difficult for NGOs to exploit effectively for at least three reasons: (1) they may not know how to reach Committee members; (2) they may not know in advance which States Parties reports are to be discussed; and (3) they may not have the resources to send information to all Committee members.

At every session of the Committee, in working and informal groups, members have informally discussed ways to enlarge the access of NGOs to the Committee's debates. There has always been strong resistance to such proposals from Committee members who feel it is inapppropriate to expand the provisions of the Convention. States Parties might also resist increased NGO input, especially when they submit reports or reply to questions. Some States may fear that if, as was noted above, an asymmetry of knowledge exists now, it would be even more pronounced if members had additional information. While it would be unfortunate if increased NGO participation fuelled antagonism between States Parties' representatives and CEDAW members, it is equally regrettable that members must rely on often skimpy reports and haphazard additional information, especially once CEDAW begins making specific recommendations.

Given the Committee's reluctance to act, a recent initiative promises to provide enhanced access for NGOs to the Committee. The International Women's Rights Action Watch has begun to serve as a kind of clearing-house and channel for NGOs to get information to Committee members.[88] The

[88] This group was formed by the Women, Public Policy, and Development Project at the University of Minnesota and the Development Law and Policy Program at Columbia University to 'facilitate and monitor law and policy reform using the UN Convention . . . [as] a model and symbol'. From IWRAW Information Sheet, mimeo., 1986. See also Byrnes, 'The "Other" Human Rights Treaty Body'.

organization notifies major NGOs in countries scheduled to report to CEDAW, requests data or reports from those bodies on the condition of women in their country, and endeavours to receive the information before CEDAW meets. It then compiles all NGO information on countries whose reports are on the agenda at CEDAW's next meeting and sends it to Committee members. It is an ambitious scheme and has drawn a few mixed reviews. Some feel that increased NGO participation and input potentially disrupts and hinders some of CEDAW's more activist achievements that are aided by its relative obscurity among international bodies. Others fear increased hostility in the event that a Committee member feels compelled to debate an issue with a State Party representative on the basis of conflicting information.

While such potentially negative consequences cannot be dismissed altogether, it has been the general theme of this study that increased information can only contribute to CEDAW's overall effectiveness. A spin-off effect of NGO participation could be government reports which are prepared more carefully and comprehensively since detailed information from other sources may be available to Committee members. CEDAW has been an extremely cautious body. Perhaps because women's issues are so inherently volatile it seems to fear any but the most tentative of innovations. In the area of NGO participation, however, the Committee must take some risks because it is in this area that there is the greatest opportunity for improvement in the quality of its work.

G. *Problems and Recommendations*

Many of CEDAW's problems, and recommendations for responses to them, have been outlined in the preceding sections. It is appropriate in concluding to recall the most important of them and to add several that have not been mentioned earlier.

(i) One of the most serious problems, but also among the most difficult to remedy, is the lack of input from NGOs. There are no standardized procedures for NGO access which is currently achieved only through haphazard contacts with Committee members or at the pleasure of national governments. Since NGOs do important work on relevant issues, increased access can only enhance the Committee's work. Until such time as the Committee itself is prepared to take the initiative (which it should do, sooner rather than later) the best option would seem to be to rely upon the inputs of groups such as the Women's Rights Action Watch.[89] The group's role of eliciting information from appropriate NGOs in countries due to report,

[89] Ibid.

synthesizing the information, and sending it to all Committee members (or those who express a desire to receive it) has the potential greatly to improve the quality of questions from members.

(ii) The Committee continues to discuss but has not reached a conclusion as to whether reservations from States which are deemed incompatible with the Convention should be determined, upon a vote of the Committee, to nullify ratification.[90] CERD has such a procedure, though it is yet to be tested. Whether the adoption of a specific procedure for resolving disputes over reservations would improve the Committee's work is difficult to say. While it might encourage ratifying States to work harder to make national legislation conform to the Convention, it also might dissuade other States from ratifying at all. In addition, there appears to be no consensus on which reservations should be deemed incompatible, although there is some agreement on the necessity to adhere to Article 2. In 1987, Working Group II (on ways and means of implementing Article 21 of the Convention), suggested that the question of reservations might be addressed in general recommendations,[91] and general recommendation 4 (sixth session, 1987) suggested that 'all States Parties concerned reconsider such reservations with a view to withdrawing them'.[92] However, the issue of reservations has mainly been addressed, although so far inconclusively, at the meetings of the States Parties.[93] The third meeting, in 1986, did go as far as to express concern over the possible incompatibility of some of the reservations and sought the views of States Parties on the issue.[94] However, the next two meetings, in 1988 and 1990, took no substantive action on the issue.[95] It is hoped that, in the not too distant future, the General Assembly will be able to muster the political will needed to enable it to make a formal request to the Internatinal Court of Justice for an advisory opinion on the compatibility of specific reservations with the Convention.[96] The Inter-American Court of Human Rights might also address itself to the issue in accordance with article 64(1) of the American Convention on Human Rights.[97]

(iii) An issue not discussed earlier in this study, and rarely addressed explicitly within CEDAW, is the tension that arises from the Committee being

[90] Some examples of reservations include, *inter alia*, Egypt as concerns nationality of children and equality of men and women in marriage due to Islamic law; Austria's reservation *vis-à-vis* women in the armed forces, and Mauritius, reservations to equal remuneration and equality of husband and wife. See 'Achievements and Obstacles'; see also n. 18, above.

[91] *Report of CEDAW in 1987*, para. 56, recommendation 15.

[92] Ibid. para. 579 (General recommendation 4, para. 4).

[93] For a more detailed discussion of reservations, see Byrnes, 'The "Other" Human Rights Treaty Body', 51–6.

[94] CEDAW/SP/10 (1986).

[95] CEDAW/SP/14 (1988) and CEDAW/SP/17 (1990).

[96] A clean precedent exists in this regard by virtue of the Advisory Opinion on Reservations to the Genocide Convention, 1951 *ICJ*, 15 (Advisory Opinion of 28 May).

[97] See generally on the point Cook, 'Reservations', 711.

treaty-based but none the less subject to decisions by the Secretary General or the General Assembly to curtail its activities during budgetary crises. Because of its treaty basis, certain aspects of the Committee's work are beyond the control of either the Secretary-General or the Assembly. These include the minimum length of meetings, the number of experts, the venue of meetings, and other provisions explicitly defined by the Convention. Simultaneously, however, budgetary and most administrative provisions are within the purview of the Assembly. During the UN's 1980s budgetary crisis the natural tendency of the main political organs was to cut back on expenditures for functional bodies. The contractionary impulse was compounded by a feeling that the Organization had done more than enough for women's issues by setting up the Decade, CEDAW, and the two institutions that grew directly out of Decade conferences, UNIFEM and INSTRAW.

As a result of this paradox, many observers fear that since the Assembly cannot completely abolish CEDAW, it will 'nickel and dime' it to death. In other words, it could so underfund and understaff the Committee as to completely undermine its work and effectiveness. These financial constraints are felt even more sharply as CEDAW's agenda has expanded due to the increase in ratifications. As one Committee member points out, although various resolutions have urged States which have not submitted their reports to do so, and 'requested the Committee . . . to ensure that the reports of States are adequately reviewed within the quadrennial cycle envisaged', the Committee has not been given the additional resources which it would require in order to complete this task.[98]

There is no real solution to this dilemma except one that is likely to appear radical to many UN observers: CEDAW should seek alternative financing arrangements. It would be difficult for the Organization to object to the use of outside funds which might enable the Committee to expand its work. Outside financing arrangements are presently utilized when meetings are held other than at UN Headquarters, with countries paying the difference between holding them at Headquarters and at other venues. There is always the danger, however, that funds coming from governmental sources bring with them influence over the Committee's work. In addition, economic hardship world-wide makes the availability of such funds scarce. Nevertheless, more imaginative and innovative approaches to the financing of functional bodies of the UN will have to be sought as the severity of the budgetary crisis increases.

(iv) The inadequate length of meetings is clearly a problem for the Committee. When one compares CEDAW with other UN human rights organs the inadequacy of CEDAW's two weeks a year is striking. CERD normally meets for six weeks and the Human Rights Committee for nine. Although the financial climate may not be right, CEDAW must increase the length of its

[98] From ESC Res.85/18, para. 4, as quoted in Evatt, 'The United Nations Convention', 8.

sessions. An extension from two weeks to three would be the minimum necessary to speed up review of initial reports by States Parties.[99] At the present rate of eight reports per two-week session it will take over ten years to discuss the initial reports, during which time many States Parties will be submitting their second and third reports.[100] While this optimistic prediction ignores delinquency, it is absurd for the Committee to operate on the assumption that many States will not submit reports on time and thereby encourage tardiness.

(v) Proposals for restructuring the question and answer procedure have been outlined above. Informal co-ordination arrangements seem to work reasonably well and repetition of questions has been somewhat curtailed. Although Committee members have expressed concern that proposals to divide the process into subject areas would be too restrictive, it need not reduce their ability to elicit information. If each area is left open long enough for all members to exhaust their questions, there should not be an overall reduction in the ability of any one member to ask questions. Formalizing the co-ordinating procedure would cut down on repetition and might impose some discipline on members by requiring them to be present at meetings designated for discussion of themes on which they have questions.

(vi) The decisions, suggestions, and recommendations adopted by the Committee have tended to deal with procedural matters or general exhortations. It only started to develop jurisprudence on the Convention, based on its consideration of country reports, in 1989.[101] Since the other treaty-supervisory bodies have emphasized such a practice, it is to be hoped that CEDAW will also develop in this direction. In particular, there are strong grounds for encouraging the Committee to begin the systematic adoption of General Comments dealing with the interpretation of each of the articles contained in the Convention. The Committee took the first step in this direction in 1991 when it decided to establish a programme for examining specific articles or themes at each of its sessions between 1992 and 1994. The themes chosen are: violence against women (in 1992), the family (in 1993), and equality in political participation and public life (in 1994). In terms of the procedures for examining these themes the Committee decided to follow the precedents set by the Committee on Economic, Social and Cultural Rights and invite inputs into its deliberations on these themes from the Secretariat, Specialized Agencies, and other UN bodies as well as relevant NGOs.

(vii) A major complaint by many Committee members is that CEDAW has

[99] See CEDAW/C/11/CRP.4 (1986).

[100] The 'exceptionally' extended sessions held in 1988 and requested for 1989 are no solution, since Art. 20 of the Convention refers explicitly to two weeks as the normal meeting period (n. 2, above).

[101] See e.g. general recommendation no. 13, on 'Equal remuneration for work of equal value', *Report of CEDAW in 1989*, para. 392. For a more detailed discussion of this issue, see Byrnes, 'The "Other" Human Rights Treaty Body', 42–5.

no institutional memory and that certain important information is therefore being lost. This problem relates to a number of issues discussed earlier, including the problem of 'truncated' summary records, the failure to record written questions and oral presentations in detail and inadequate servicing. All of those problems could be solved by General Assembly action, but CEDAW will have to make a convincing case, which it has so far not done.

(viii) The independence of members of the Committee has been a contentious issue since the Committee was set up.[102] Real independence is not taken as seriously as it might be. Twelve of the 1986 nominees were either members of government ministries or in their countries' diplomatic service.[103] This number represents more than half of the total nominees. As noted earlier, governmental connections do not necessarily diminish a member's effectiveness. The Committee should decide however, whether direct government is appropriate for so many of its members now that its pool of nominees has been widened by increased ratifications. More specific guidelines about independence from governments might result in a more professional and independent Committee.

(ix) A final problem to be addressed is the lack, as noted early in the work of the Committee, of provision for any 'exchange of views or dialogue between the members of the committee about the content of particular Reports... [which] means that the efforts...are largely undirected'.[104] Although Committee members may have informal discussions on such matters these often end inconclusively and rarely include more than two or three like-minded members. During its fifth session the Committee set up a working group to deal with the more controversial issues, the 'working group on ways and means of improving the efficiency of the work of the Committee'.[105] In 1987, the working group was set up again (Working Group I), and another met to discuss the implementation of Article 21 of the Convention (Working Group II).[106] They have now become standing working groups, with flexible membership, and should go a long way towards solving the problem. It is to be hoped that the Committee's decision in 1991 to examine, at its 1992 session, the most effective means by which to reach some conclusions following the examination of each State Party's report will lead it to follow the precedents set by the Committee on Economic, Social and Cultural Rights which adopts a set of concluding observations after the examination of each report.

[102] See Tinker, 'Human Rights for Women', 38 n. 22.

[103] 'Note by the Secretary-General on the Twelve Members of CEDAW', CEDAW/SP/9 (1986).

[104] Evatt, 'The United Nations Convention', 8.

[105] *Report of CEDAW in 1986*, para. 12.

[106] *Report of CEDAW in 1987*, paras. 26, 28. The two groups were set up on the basis of rule 50 of the Rules of Procedure (n. 60, above) and GA Res. 41/108 (1986).

12

The Committee on Economic, Social and Cultural Rights

PHILIP ALSTON

Introduction[1]

Although both of the Covenants came into force in early 1976, and the Human Rights Committee was established to monitor the Covenant on Civil and Political Rights the following year, it was not until 1979 that the Economic and Social Council's arrangements to monitor States' compliance with the International Covenant on Economic, Social and Cultural Rights[2] got under way. Thereafter followed eight years of thoroughly ineffectual monitoring by a succession of Working Groups set up, nominally at least, as a part of the Council's own machinery. In 1986, almost in desperation as a result of the Working Group's inadequacies, the Council decided to 'subcontract' its responsibilities under the Covenant to an independent cxpert committee which was expected to emulate, as far as practicable, the approach followed by the Human Rights Committee.

The body that was thereby created, the Committee on Economic, Social and Cultural Rights,[3] held its first session in 1987 and, as of February 1991 had held five sessions.[4] During that period it has succeeded in evolving a set of procedures which goes significantly beyond the simple mimicking or replication of those followed by the other UN treaty bodies. It has devoted, and seems likely to continue to devote, much of its energies to streamlining and refining procedures and to laying the foundations upon which a serious

[1] The first part of this chapter draws in part on an analysis previously published in Alston, 'Out of the Abyss?: The Challenges Confronting the New UN Committee on Economic, Social and Cultural Rights', 9 *Hum. Rts. Q.* 332 (1987).

[2] GA Res.2200 A (XXI) (1966).

[3] The Committee was established pursuant to ESC Res.1985/17.

[4] The Committee's reports are contained in the following documents: 1st Session, E/1987/28; 2nd Session, E/1988/14; 3rd Session, E/1989/22; 4th Session, E/1990/23; 5th Session, E/1991/23. For some commentary on specific sessions, see Alston and Simma, 'First Session of the UN Committee on Economic, Social and Cultural Rights', 81 *Am. J. Int'l L.* 747 (1987); eid., 'Second Session of the UN Committee on Economic, Social and Cultural Rights', 82 *Am. J. Int'l L.* 603 (1988); and Craven, 'Analytical Report of the Fourth Session of the Committee on Economic, Social and Cultural Rights, February 1990' (1990).

effort can be made to promote respect for economic, social, and cultural rights.

In many respects the Committee has confronted problems which are common to all of the treaty bodies. In other respects, however, the challenges that confront it and the context in which it must work are significantly different from those of the other committees. Among the many factors that tend to distinguish its task are: the lack of conceptual clarity of many of the norms reflected in the Covenant; the ambivalence of most governments towards economic, social, and cultural rights; the strong ideological undertones of the debate, not only in the 1980s but also, albeit in a different form, in the 1990s; the absence of national institutions specifically committed to the promotion of economic rights *qua* rights; the complexity and scope of the information required in order to supervise compliance effectively; the largely programmatic nature of some of the rights; the more limited relevance of formal legal texts and judicial decisions; and the paucity of non-governmental organizations with a developed and sophisticated interest in economic rights as such.

But despite these different factors, it remains as true for this Committee as it does for the others that its ultimate success or failure will largely reflect the commitment and strength of its own expert members. In this regard, experience with the Covenant's European regional counterpart, the European Social Charter, is particularly pertinent. According to Harris, the Charter's 'success in establishing itself during the first years of its life has been the result not of loving nurture by the states that conceived it, who have instead tended to neglect their offspring, but of the care and attention of the foster mother charged with the Charter's implementation, the Committee of Independent Experts.'[5]

A. *An Overview of the Covenant's Implementation Provisions*

Before analysing the procedures actually followed by the Committee it is necessary to begin with a quick glance at the implementation provisions contained in Part IV of the Covenant. Articles 16–22 may be summarized, in formalistic language that approximates that used in the Covenant, as follows.

The States Parties are required to report, in accordance with a programme to be determined by the Economic and Social Council, after consultation with the specialized agencies concerned and the States Parties, on the measures they have adopted and the progress they have made in achieving the observance of the rights recognized in the Covenant. The reports may indicate 'factors and difficulties' affecting the degree of fulfilment of the obligations. They are to be submitted to the Secretary-General, who is required to

[5] Harris, *The European Social Charter* (1984), p. xiv.

transmit copies to the Council and copies of all of the relevant parts to the agencies. Where information has already been furnished to an agency, it is sufficient for the report to refer thereto.

Provision is made for arrangements between the Council and the agencies whereby the latter will report on progress achieved in the observance of the Covenant. The Commission on Human Rights may receive from the Council copies of both the State and agency reports and may make 'general' recommendations thereon. The agencies and States parties are entitled to submit their comments on any such recommendations to the Council. The Council, in turn, may submit reports to the General Assembly with recommendations of a general nature and a summary of the information received. It may also bring to the attention of the agencies matters that might warrant the provision of technical assistance or the taking of other international measures.

By far the most striking feature of these provisions is the very limited extent to which they reflect the actual practice that has evolved in the implementation of the Covenant. As we shall see below, the creation of the Committee and the entrusting to it of virtually all of the Council's substantive functions is the most significant departure from the actual text of the Covenant. In addition, however, the resulting institutional and procedural arrangements have evolved to an extent that they would barely be recognizable by an observer informed only by the formal provisions of the Covenant. Thus, for example, the respective roles played by the Commission, the specialized agencies, and the Council have all been radically different from that foreseen for each of them in the Covenant. Moreover, the constructive dialogue that has taken place between the Committee and States parties bears only a remote resemblance to the rather constipated form of paper warfare apparently envisaged by the drafters of the Covenant. By the same token, one must also be struck by the extent to which the arrangements that have emerged, albeit in a very piecemeal fashion, resemble some of the proposals that were made, but firmly rejected, during the drafting process. We turn now to examine briefly some of those proposals.

B. *Background to the Committee's Establishment*

The context in which the decision to establish the Committee was taken is, in several respects, without precedent in the UN system. In the first place, the creation of such a committee had been debated at length when the Covenant was being drafted but two specific proposals, championed by the United States and Italy respectively, conspicuously failed to win support. As a result, the Covenant makes no provision for the establishment of any specialist supervisory body.

Secondly, the decision to establish an expert committee was taken after relatively limited and somewhat inconclusive consultations with States Parties and with surprisingly few objections being raised in advance. Thirdly, and perhaps most significantly, the decision can be seen, in a sense, as a last-ditch effort to establish a meaningful international implementation system for the Covenant in the wake of the failure of earlier approaches.

I. EARLIER PROPOSALS FOR AN EXPERT COMMITTEE

The drafting of the Covenant's implementation provisions was effectively completed by 1954.[6] The debates were complex and drawn out, and the final proposals reflected major concessions on the part of almost all of the concerned parties. As the Polish delegate correctly observed at the time, the drafting of these procedures had proven to be 'the most difficult and controversial aspect of the covenant'.[7] Among the issues that had delayed agreement were: the nature of the relationship between the two sets of rights (and therefore between the two Covenants); the extent to which States Parties should be held 'accountable' to an international body; the desirability of supplementing a reporting system with individual or interstate complaints procedures; the extent to which the Covenant's provisions could be applicable to non parties; the respective roles to be played by the General Assembly, the Economic and Social Council, and the Commission on Human Rights; and the appropriate division of competence, in technical and formal jurisdictional terms, between the UN and the specialized agencies.

The first formal suggestion that economic, social, and cultural rights should be dealt with by a specialist committee was made by the representative of Lebanon in April, 1951.[8] According to the original version of the Lebanese proposal, a 'Committee on Economic, Social and Cultural Rights' would be established and would comprise fifteen members with 'recognized experience' in the field. Members would be nominated by States Parties to the Covenant, be elected by the Economic and Social Council for a five-year term, and be eligible for re-election. The proposed provisions were extremely detailed and ran to nine pages.[9]

Ironically the proposal which is remarkably similar to the arrangements now in existence received little support in the Commission. The Chinese representative, for example, opposed it on the grounds that the creation of a separate body would lend support to the contention that economic, social, and cultural rights were of a very different nature from civil and political rights.[10] Another objection was based on the argument that the specialized agencies

[6] See *Report of the Commission on Human Rights, Tenth Session*, E/2573 (1954).
[7] E/CN.4/SR.424 (1954), 12.
[8] E/CN.4/570 (1951).
[9] Ibid.
[10] E/CN.4/SR.242 (1951), 15.

should bear the principal responsibility for supervision, given that they alone possessed the necessary technical expertise.[11] Finally it was argued, in terms of the need for co-ordination and economy, that 'the time had come to call a halt to the process of setting up new committees'.[12]

A revised version of the Lebanese proposal, submitted less than two weeks after the initial version, provided that the Committee would be established on an annual basis by the ECOSOC, with members serving in their individual capacities.[13] Under that version, a considerably more prominent role was foreseen for the specialized agencies, including even a potential (but unspecified) role in the election of the members of the Committee.[14] By the time a third version[15] was submited, a week later, the Commission had before it four separate proposals.[16] Of those, only one—that of Lebanon, as revised—provided for the creation of a committee. In the event, the Commission established a Working Group to assist it in elaborating a compromise approach. The result of the Working Group's deliberations was a set of proposals very similar to those embodied in the Covenant as finally adopted.[17]

Although the notion of establishing a separate committee had thus been rejected, the debate was briefly reopened in 1954 when France proposed that the Human Rights Committee (to be established under the Civil and Political Rights Covenant) might also be given responsibility for examining reports under the Economic, Social and Cultural Rights Covenant.[18] The French representative, Mr Juvigny, argued in favour of the proposal on the grounds that economic and social rights would, over time, 'tend to become semi-enforceable or even fully enforceable by judicial action'.[19] However, in the face of opposition by various States,[20] he withdrew the proposal before it was put to a vote.[21]

A final attempt to create a committee came in 1966 when the General Assembly's Third Committee was putting the finishing touches to the draft Covenant. An Italian proposal suggested the establishment of an '*ad hoc* Committee of Experts' on the basis of whose proposals the Council would carry out its functions under the Covenant.[22] The Italian representative emphasized that, in undertaking an initial study of States Parties' reports, the 'committee of experts would not work alone but in collaboration with the

[11] E/CN.4/SR.241 (1951), 28 (UK).
[12] Ibid. 33 (Pakistan).
[13] E.CN.4/570/Rev.1, Art. 1 (1951).
[14] Ibid.
[15] E/CN.4/570/Rev.2 (1951).
[16] The various proposals are reproduced in E/CN.4/AC.14/2/Add.5 (1951).
[17] E/CN.4/629 (1951).
[18] E/CN.4/L.388 (1954).
[19] E/CN.4/SR.432 (1954), 10.
[20] e.g. China, ibid. 6–7; Australia, ibid. 7–9; UK, ibid. 9–10; Greece, ibid. 10.
[21] Ibid. 11.
[22] A/C.3/L.1358 (1966).

Economic and Social Council and its establishment would in no way change the character of the draft Covenant'.[23]

The Italian proposal was overshadowed, however, by a much more radical United States proposal that called for the establishment of an independent committee in terms similar to those provided for in the Convention on the Elimination of all Forms of Racial Discrimination which the General Assembly had adopted one year earlier.[24] Under the US proposal, committee members would need to have 'recognized competence' in the field and would be elected by States Parties. The committee would examine all reports, be responsible for establishing the reporting cycle, report annually to the Council and to States Parties, and make suggestions and recommendations based on its examination of reports.[25] The US proposed committee would thus have much of the autonomy of the Human Rights Committee and would take responsibility for many of the activities that the Council had been expected to perform.

Arguments adduced in favour of the creation of a Committee included: the superiority of 'a technical body unhampered by political or other considerations';[26] the advantage that non-States parties would thus not be involved in the supervisory process as would be the case if the Council performed the task;[27] the fact that the existing system of considering periodic reports, for which the Commission was primarily responsible, had been a failure;[28] and the fact that the Council was already overburdened even without the additional responsibilities the Covenant would place under it.[29] Proponents of the two proposals also sought to assure other States' representatives that a committee would be no more likely than the Council to interfere in States' domestic affairs.[30] While a number of States expressed support for the establishment of a new committee, almost all of those opted for the Italian rather than the stronger US version.[31]

Opposition to the proposal was widespread, however. The USSR argued that it 'would complicate the reporting procedure, create confusion and inevitably give rise to constitutional conflicts with the Council'.[32] African States in particular were opposed on the grounds that an undue proliferation of

23 A/C.3/SR.1398 (1966), 3.
24 A/C.3/L.1360 (1966).
25 Ibid.
26 A/C.3/SR.1398, 3 (Italy).
27 Ibid.
28 A/C.3/SR.1400 (1966), 51.
29 Ibid. 14 (The Netherlands).
30 Ibid.
31 e.g. Canada A/C.3/SR.1399 (1966), para. 28; Finland, ibid. para. 30; Ireland A/C.3/SR.1400, para. 2; Madagascar, ibid. paras. 10–11; Netherlands ibid. paras. 13–16; Ceylon, ibid. paras. 19–23; Norway, ibid. paras. 24–6; Panama, ibid. para. 33; Israel, ibid. paras. 50–2.
32 A/C.3/SR.1399, para. 23.

new bodies should be avoided,[33] that the UN bureaucracy should not be increased,[34] that developing countries would have difficulty finding candidates with the required qualifications,[35] and that the committee would, in any event, not be free of political influences.[36] Specifically, several States made it clear that the International Court of Justice's recent decision on South-West Africa had cast considerable doubt on the desirability of entrusting authority to 'expert' bodies.[37]

In the face of strong opposition both proposals were withdrawn by their respective sponsors.[38] Nevertheless, several speakers left open the possibility that the Council might some day wish to establish an expert committee to assist it to fulfil its responsibilities under the Covenant. Jamaica, for example, noted that it 'did not interpret the decision . . . as precluding the establishment by the Council of a committee of experts to examine the reports in the first instance'.[39] Similarly the representative of Dahomey (now Benin) indicated that he would not object to such an action provided that the committee of experts was 'an advisory organ reporting to the' Council.[40] Thus while the time was clearly not ripe in 1966 for the establishment of an expert committee the door was not irretrievably closed.

II. THE CHANGE FROM A WORKING GROUP TO A COMMITTEE OF INDEPENDENT EXPERTS

(*a*) *The Working Group and its Shortcomings*

Shortly after the Covenant entered into force on 3 January 1976, the Economic and Social Council met to consider the best means of operationalizing the implementation procedures laid down in Part IV (Articles 16–23). It decided from the outset to establish a 'Sessional Working Group' of the Council to assist it in the consideration of reports due under the Covenant,[41] thereby exercising the discretion it retained to determine for itself the most appropriate arrangements for ensuring effective supervision. Members of the Group were appointed by the President of the Council after

[33] Ibid. para. 25.
[34] Ibid. para. 12.
[35] A/C.3/SR.1401 (1966), para. 11.
[36] Ibid. para. 7.
[37] Ibid. para. 11 ('The peoples of Africa had recently seen an example of what experts were capable of, and they would never forget what the judges of the International Court of Justice had done to the people of South West Africa'). The speaker was referring to the South West Africa Cases (*Ethiopia* v. S. *Africa*, *Liberia* v. *S. Africa*), 1966 *ICJ* 6 (Judgment of July 18).
[38] A/C.3/SR.1401, para. 19; ibid. para. 21.
[39] Ibid. para. 26.
[40] A/C.3/SR.1399, para. 20.
[41] ESC Res.1988 (LX) (1976).

due consultation with the regional groups.[42] After a review of the experience of that Group's first four sessions (1979–82),[43] the Council concluded that specialist expertise was required in the Group's membership. It therefore renamed the Group the Sessional Working Group of Governmental Experts and decided that its members were to be elected by the Council for three-year terms from among nominees put forward by the States Parties to the Covenant.[44]

A detailed review of the performance of the Working Group in each of its two incarnations would not serve to shed very much light on the work of the Committee which eventually succeeded it and will thus not be undertaken here. Nevertheless, it seems clear that the vast majority of observers would have no difficulty endorsing the typically understated comment by the British representative to the Commission on Human Rights in 1986 that his delegation was 'somewhat dissatisfied over the way in which the implementation of the . . . Covenant . . . had been supervised by the Economic and Social Council'.[45] A survey by the International Commission of Jurists of the work of the Sessional Working Group at its first three sessions identified a large number of shortcomings,[46] many of which continued to characterize the work of the expert group between 1983 and 1986. Among the criticisms most commonly cited,[47] mention may be made of the following:

(*a*) [t]he examination of reports [was] cursory, superficial, and politicized;[48]
(*b*) the Group failed to establish standards for the evaluation of reports;
(*c*) the Group's reports to the Council contained very few substantive conclusions, were largely procedural, and failed to indicate whether reporting States were complying with their obligations under the Covenant;
(*d*) the participation of the specialized agencies, and notably the International Labour Organisation (ILO), in the work of the Group was consistently blocked or impeded;
(*e*) attendance by members of the Group was irregular and alternates used too frequently;[49]

[42] Ibid. para. 9(a).
[43] E/1981/6 (1981).
[44] ESC Res.1982/33, para. b.
[45] E/CN.4/1986/SR.26, para. 65 (1986).
[46] Commentary, 'Implementation of the International Covenant on Economic, Social and Cultrual Rights: ESOSOC Working Group', 27 *ICJ Review* (Dec. 1981), 26.
[47] Sources of criticism include ibid; Westerveen, 'Towards a System for Supervising States' Compliance with the Right to Food', in Alston and Tomasevski (eds.) *The Right to Food* (1984) 119; comments by governments reproduced in E/1981/6 and Add.1–2; comments by members of the Sessional Working Group, E/1985/WG.1/SR.19–20 and 22.
[48] Commentary, 'Implementation of the International Covenant', 28; and Westerveen, 'Towards a System for Supervising States' Compliance', 125.
[49] One of the members of the Group noted during its 1985 session that 'while in theory there were 15 members, in fact there were only 13 [since two seats remained vacant] and there were never more than 10 present, in contrast to other human rights bodies'. E/1985/WG.1/SR.22, para. 13.

(*f*) membership of the Group manifested a lack of continuity, to the detriment of efforts to build up expertise and a sense of group solidarity;
(*g*) States' reports had to be considered too quickly because of the inadequate time allotted to the Group;
(*h*) the Group's examination of reports was often ritualistic and repetitive because 'all members felt the need to ask questions on all reports'[50] and because the Group 'generally avoided attempting to assess the reality behind a State's legal provisions';[51] and
(*i*) the Group's discussion often ignored the broader context in which States Parties pursued their policies relating to economic, social and cultural rights.[52]

However, the most significant shortcomings of the Group's work related to its output. The Group failed to include any summary of States' reports, or its deliberations thereon, in its own reports to the Council and, for the most part, abstained from making recommendations on other than procedural matters. As a result, it did not provide the Council with anything of substance on the basis of which the latter could, if it wished, have exercised its right under Article 21 of the Covenant to 'submit from time to time to the General Assembly reports with recommendations of a general nature and a summary of the information received from the States Parties . . . and the specialized agencies . . .". Accordingly, over a period of eight years the Council was never once able to make any such report to the Assembly.

(*b*) *Rejecting the Option of Involving the Commission*

Prior to the creation of the Committee the majority of the Covenant's Articles dealing with implementation remained inoperative. In other words, the Council failed to exercise any of the options available to it under Articles 19–22. Two of those provisions (Articles 19 and 20) concern the role the Commission on Human Rights might play if the Council chose to transmit the various reports to it 'for study and general recommendation or, as appropriate, for information'.

The role the Commission should play in implementation became surprisingly contentious during the drafting of the Covenant. When the Commission established a Working Group on implementation in 1951 this issue was characterized as 'the most controversial' with which it had to deal.[53] This was so despite the fact that an earlier Working Group on the same subject,

[50] E/1985/WG.1/SR.19, para. 17.
[51] Commentary, 'Implementation of the International Covenants', 35; see also ibid. 38.
[52] In 1985 one member of the group indicated that he 'found it odd that discussion could take place without any reference to the critical situation in the [world] in general and in the developing countries in particular, specifically in such reporting States as Portugal, Iraq and Nicaragua'. 1985/WG.1/SR.19, para. 13.
[53] E/CN.4/AC.15/SR.3 (1951), 8.

established in 1947, was unanimously of the opinion that the Economic and Social Council, whilst still retaining the whole of its prerogatives, and therefore its rights to make recommendations with respect to human rights, should also delegate this latter right to the Commission on Human Rights.[54] The arguments in favour of involving the Commission in the process included the fact that the Council was already (even in 1947) overburdened with work,[55] the need to reaffirm the role of the Commission as the central body dealing with all human rights issues,[56] the fact that the Commission was the principal repository of expertise in the field, and the prospect that the Commission's general understanding would be enhanced by its study of this issue.

Despite the force of these arguments a role for the Commission was opposed by a significant coalition of States. It included the Soviet Union and its allies which, in line with their initial general opposition to the implementation provisions, objected on the grounds that the proposed approach 'would confer new powers on the Commission . . . which would in some respects exceed those of the . . . Council and even those of the General Assembly'.[57] The United States was equally opposed to giving the Commission such a role, ostensibly on the grounds that it would make 'the implementation machinery . . . unnecessarily cumbersome'.[58] Its real motivation seems more likely to have been a desire to minimize the effectiveness of whatever implementation procedure was devised in order to deal with economic, social, and cultural rights, a category of rights it recognized only grudgingly on the basis of a pragmatic calculation that overt opposition to the concept itself would either scuttle the entire endeavour or would lead to a far less acceptable treatment of civil and political rights. The third source of opposition to giving the Commission a role came from a diverse group of States which sought to give the substantive responsibility for implementation to the relevant specialized agencies and to vest formal responsibility in the Council alone.[59] In support of this position they argued that the Commission already had more than enough on its plate and that, in any event, it lacked the technical expertise necessary to undertake such a task.[60]

Notwithstanding this opposition, the Commission adopted a text in 1951 according to which the 'Council *shall* transmit to the Commission . . . for study and recommendation' the various reports submitted by States and specialized agencies.[61] When the matter was again considered by the Commission in

[54] E/CN.4/53 (1947), 11.
[55] Ibid. 12.
[56] E/CN.4/SR.238 (1951), 19; E/CN.4/SR.248 (1951), 4.
[57] E/CN.4/SR.421 (1954), 8.
[58] E/CN.4/SR.247 (1951), 11.
[59] Ibid. 11 (UK); ibid. 12 (Pakistan).
[60] Ibid. 12 (Pakistan).
[61] *Report of the Commission on Human Rights, Seventh Session*, E/1992 (1951) (emphasis added). The vote was 10–6–2. Ibid.

1954, three amendments, which were adopted on the proposal of the United Kingdom,[62] succeeded in very significantly altering the import of the earlier agreed formulation. On this basis, the word 'shall' was replaced by 'may', the word 'general' was inserted before 'recommendation', and the phrase 'or, as appropriate, for information' was added after the word 'recommendation'.[63] The effect was to make it entirely optional for the Council to involve the Commission and to give it the additional option of involving the Commission only in a formal sense by transmitting the reports solely 'for information'. The argument was that the Covenant could not, and should not, purport to tie the hands of the Council on a matter over which the Charter gave the Council general authority.[64] Since the justification offered by the sponsor was thus procedural rather than substantive the Secretary-General was justified in concluding that '[t]he text adopted reflects a predominance of support for the view that the interest of the Commission on Human Rights in the matter should be expressly recognized'.[65]

Immediately after the entry into force of the Covenant in January 1976, the Commission debated the role it should play in the Covenant's implementation process. Most speakers assumed that its role would be an important one and expressed a strong willingness to assist the Council in accordance with Article 19.[66] This approach was reflected in a proposal put to the Council in 1976 by the Secretary-General to the effect that full use should be made of the Commission's assistance in evaluating reports.[67] These suggestions were not, however, taken up by the Council in its 1976 resolution laying down the implementation procedures to be followed.[68]

The Council's failure to accord the Commission any role has not subsequently given rise to any expression of regret on either side. Moreover, in 1981 when States were requested to comment on the future arrangements for implementation, none of the responding States made any mention whatsoever of the desirability of giving a role to the Commission.[69] The issue would thus appear to be closed. The Commission's already overcrowded agenda, its reluctance to take economic, social, and cultural rights very seriously, and the undoubted need for specialist expertise in monitoring such rights would all seem to confirm the wisdom of that approach now that a committee of independent experts has been given the principal responsibility.

[62] E/CN.4/SR.424, 10.
[63] See *Report of the Commission on Human Rights, Tenth Session*, E/2573 (1954), paras. 122–32.
[64] E/CN.4/SR.424,7.
[65] *Annotations on the Text of the Draft International Covenants on Human Rights* (Prepared by the Secretary-General), A/2929 (1955), 120.
[66] *Report of the Commission on Human Rights, Thirty-Second Session*, E/5768 (1976), paras. 11–14.
[67] E/5764 (1976), 14.
[68] ESC Res.1988 (LX) (1976).
[69] E/1981/6, 11–30.

(c) *Re-Emergence of Proposals for a Committee of Independent Experts*

In 1980, at the Council's request,[70] the Secretary-General consulted all States Parties to the Covenant as well as members of the Council as to the type of arrangements under which the Working Group should operate in the future. Only eighteen States replied but those that bothered to do so clearly took the matter seriously.[71] Almost half of them indicated a lack of satisfaction with existing arrangements and suggested the desirability of establishing a new committee along the lines of the Human Rights Committee.[72] By contrast the other half were more or less satisfied with the existing arrangements.[73] In the event, the Council opted in 1982 for a compromise, but one that had very little impact in terms of making the Group resemble more closely the Human Rights Committee.[74] At the same time it resolved to review the arrangements again in 1985.[75]

Between 1982 and 1985 nothing of any import was said in any UN setting about the possibility of transforming the Working Group into a committee of independent experts. It thus came as a surprise when the Working Group, at its 1985 session, proposed such a transformation to the Council,[76] which in turn promptly endorsed it on the basis of very little discussion.[77] The question that arises is how and why such an apparently major change of attitude came about in such a short period of time. There appear to be three explanatory factors.

The first lies in the increasing dissatisfaction with the performance of the Working Group. This is clearly reflected in the various criticisms cited above,[78] and came through strongly in the Group's own discussion of possible reforms.[79] In that context, only the Japanese member seemed to be opposed to the adoption of major changes.[80] In the Council itself one of the principal sponsors of reform, the Netherlands, concluded that the 'Council had clearly fallen short in the exercise of its duties with regard to the Covenant',[81] a state of affairs for which the representative of Denmark blamed the Working Group which 'had not been able to elaborate a sufficiently satisfactory basis

[70] ESC Res.1980/24, para. 2.

[71] The replies are reproduced in E/1981/6 and Add.1–2.

[72] See E/1981/6: replies of Canada, the Federal Republic of Germany, Italy, Senegal, and the UK. See E/1981/6 Add.1: replies of Australia and The Netherlands.

[73] See E/1981/6: replies of Byelorussian SSR, Hungary (the 'Working Group completes its task well and lends effective support to the Council', 19), Ukrainian SSR, and USSR. See E/1981/6/Add.1: reply of Thailand. See E/1981/6/Add.2: reply of Bulgaria.

[74] ESC Res.1982/33.

[75] Ibid. para. f.

[76] E/1985/18, para. 39.

[77] ESC Res.1985/17.

[78] See text accompanying n. 47–52, above.

[79] E/1985/WG.1/SR.19–22.

[80] E/1985/WG.1/SR.22, paras. 2–3.

[81] E/1985/SR.18, 2.

for the Council's deliberations'.[82] It was thus apparent to the Council that major reforms were necessary if the Covenant's implementation procedures were to amount to anything significant.[83]

The second factor is the increasing emphasis placed on economic, social, and cultural rights by various other UN bodies, such as the Sub-Commission on Prevention of Discrimination and Protection of Minorities, which had undertaken a study on the relationship between 'the New International Economic Order and the promotion of human rights'[84] and a separate study on the concept of the right to adequate food as a human right.[85] Similarly, the Commission on Human Rights had begun to take economic and social rights more seriously, first in the late 1970s in the context of the right to development,[86] and then in the early 1980s in the context of a concern to spell out more clearly the implications of various specific rights such as the rights to work, housing, education, health care, and food.[87] During the same period the General Assembly was engaged in a continuing ideological struggle over the relative importance of the two sets of rights.[88] In such a setting it became increasingly difficult to defend the view that the UN was taking economic, social, and cultural rights just as seriously as civil and political rights when the treaty-related, institutional arrangements for implementing the former were clearly inferior to those relating to the latter.

The third and final factor relates to the attitude of the Eastern European States in particular. Initially, when the Commission on Human Rights was debating implementation procedures for the Covenant in 1951, the Soviet representative had strongly opposed the establishment of a reporting system on the basis that it would infringe State sovereignty and thus be contrary to Article 2(7) of the UN Charter.[89] By 1963, however, when the matter was before the General Assembly's Third Committee, the Eastern European representatives had reversed their earlier stand. Thus, for example, the USSR was not only favourably disposed to the proposed reporting system but went so far as to suggest that implementation measures with respect to economic,

[82] Ibid. 4.

[83] Compelling evidence of the perceived unimportance of the Working Group was provided by the fact that several regional groups consistently failed to nominate a sufficient number of candidates to fill the vacancies in the Group's membership. E/1985/17, paras. 17–18.

[84] Ferrero, *The New International Economic Order and Promotion of Human Rights*, E/CN.4/Sub.2/1983/24/Rev.1 (1986).

[85] Eide, *Study on the Right to Adequate Food as a Human Right: Progress Report*, E/CN.4/Sub.2/1984/22 and Add.1–2.

[86] See *The International Dimensions of the Right to Development as a Human Right*, E/CN.4/1334 (1979); Declaration on the Right to Development, GA Res.41/128 (1986) Annex.

[87] See E/CN.4/1986/38 and Add.1–3.

[88] See Donnelly, 'Recent Trends in the U.N. Human Rights Activity: Description and Polemic', 35 *Int'l Org.* 633 (1981); cf. Alston, 'The Alleged Demise of Political Human Rights at the U.N.: A Reply to Donnelly', 37 *Int'l Org.* 537 (1983).

[89] E/CN.4/SR.246 (1951), 14.

social, and cultural rights 'might well have to be stricter [than those relating to civil and political rights] lest some governments should use the principle of progressive implementation as an excuse for doing nothing'.[90] While some Western representatives suggested at the time that the Soviet position was motivated more by a desire to weaken the reporting procedure under the Covenant on Civil and Political Rights than by any wish to strengthen the procedures under the other Covenant[91] the fact remains that the representatives of various Socialist States went on record in the early 1960s as supporting strong implementation procedures with respect to economic, social, and cultural rights.[92]

While the Council's 1976 decision to establish the Working Group was supported by the Eastern European countries,[93] those States made it clear in 1981 that they were not yet willing to contemplate any substantial reforms.[94] Whey then were they prepared to join the consensus in 1985 to upgrade the Working Group into a Committee? The answer, particularly in the case of the Soviet Union, is to be found in the assumptions on which its agreement was predicated. The first assumption was that acceptance of the proposed upgrading would facilitate an implicit enhancement of the overall status of economic, social, and cultural rights.[95] The second assumption was that the proposed change could be brought about without entailing any significant procedural or substantive changes in the way in which the Group had operated since its inception in 1979. Thus the Soviet member of the Working Group, who also represented the USSR in the relevant discussions in the Council, insisted that 'the Group's method of work was effective and that its organizational structure should remain intact'.[96] In the same vein he rejected proposals that greater account be taken of reports by the specialized agencies (particularly, the ILO),[97] suggested that the Working Group's arrangements for a rotating bureau chosen on the basis of regional groupings be maintained,[98] and termed 'unacceptable' proposals to include in the Committee's report a summary of the reports submitted and of the Committee's consideration thereof.[99] In his view these points were part of the 'package' of points to which the Working Group had agreed in formulating its proposals for the new Committee.[100] In effect, therefore, he was seeking to endorse the principle of

[90] A/C.3/SR.1264 (1963), para. 12.
[91] A/C.3/SR.1396 (1966), para. 38.
[92] e.g. ibid. para. 24; A/C.3/SR.1397 (1966), para. 14.
[93] ESC Res.1988 (LX) (1976), para. 9.
[94] See n. 73, above.
[95] E/1985/WG.1/SR.19, para. 21.
[96] E/1985/SR.18, para. 10.
[97] E/1985/WG.1/SR.22, para. 58.
[98] Ibid. para. 32.
[99] Ibid.
[100] Ibid. paras. 26–7.

change while at the same time insisting that it be accompanied by no substantial changes.

It is noteworthy, however, that while the USSR was not among the twenty-four co-sponsors of the resolution to establish the new Committee, Bulgaria, the German Democratic Republic, and Mongolia were.[101] The position of the GDR was of particular significance given its strong support for the Human Rights Committee (and the important and constructive contribution which its nominee made to that Committee) and its suggestion in 1981 that the Working Group should adopt the organizational approach and procedures of the Human Rights Committee.[102]

When the Council voted to establish the new Committee in 1985 only one State opposed the move.[103] In explaining that vote the representative of the United States opined that 'at a time of extreme budgetary austerity, the proposals . . . did not justify the related expense'.[104] Curiously, he made no mention of the position of his government in opposing the very concept of economic, social, and cultural rights, a position that would seem to be a more likely explanation of the US opposition to the new Committee than the budgetary concern cited. The only other representative to explain his vote was that of the United Kingdom who suggested that it was 'important for the Covenant to be treated with due respect, seriousness and diligence'. In his view, 'the proposed changes would enhance the application of the Covenant and the attitude of the States toward it'.[105]

C. *The Composition and Terms of Reference of the Committee*

The Committee resembles in several respects the Human Rights Committee. Thus, for example, its members are designated as 'experts with recognized competence in the field of human rights, serving in their personal capacity'.[106] In contrast to the members of the old Working Group, they therefore do not act as representatives of governments. Also like its counterpart, the Committee has eighteen members with 'due consideration' being given in their election to 'equitable geographical distribution and to the representation of different forms of social and legal systems'.[107] However, this general principle has been translated into a relatively inflexible formula whereby each of the five

[101] *Report of the Economic and Social Council*, A/40/3/Rev.1 (1985), 176, para. 10.
[102] E/1981/6, 17.
[103] The vote was 43 to 1, with 4 abstentions (Bangladesh, Brazil, Japan, and Malaysia). *Report of the Economic and Social Council*, 176–7, para. 13.
[104] E/1985/SR.22, para. 11.
[105] Ibid. para. 12.
[106] ESC Res.1985/17, para. b.
[107] Ibid.

geopolitical regional groupings has three members and an additional three seats are allocated 'in accordance with the increase in the total number of States Parties per regional group'.[108] At the first elections in 1986 and subsequently, this formula resulted in one extra seat each going to the Latin American, African, and Western European and Other groups.[109]

Only States Parties to the Covenant can nominate persons for election to the Committee.[110] Although there appears to be nothing to prevent the nomination of an individual who is not a national of a State Party, there have been no precedents and the chances of election would probably be slight. Unlike elections for the Human Rights Committee in which only States Parties can vote, all members of the Economic and Social Council, whether or not they are parties to the Covenant, are entitled to take part in the secret ballot by which the members of the Committee are elected.[111]

Members of the Committee are elected for four years with elections for half the membership being held every two years. Members are eligible for re-election.[112] These provisions are of particular importance in view of the detrimental consequences flowing from the unduly high rate of turnover in membership of the old Working Group. This has helped to ensure a significant degree of continuity in the three elections that have been held, as of February 1991.

The Committee meets annually in Geneva for sessions of three weeks each. Its first four sessions were held at the beginning of the respective years but its fifth session was held at the end of 1990, thus initiating what is intended to be a continuing practice. In order to facilitate this scheduling transition it held two sessions in 1990. While one annual session will probably suffice for the next few years, more frequent sessions may well be required within a few years time. The travel and subsistence expenses of its members are paid by the United Nations,[113] thus underlining their independence from the governments that nominated them.

The principal differences between the Committee and the Human Rights Committee relate to their status and independence as committees. Whereas the latter is a treaty-based organ whose mandate is laid down in the Covenant on Civil and Political Rights and which is responsible directly only to the States Parties to that Covenant, the former exists entirely at the pleasure of ECOSOC. Its terms of reference, its composition, and its working arrangements can thus be altered at any stage by the Council. Moreover, its mandate is in a sense only an indirect one in that its task is 'to assist the Council' in

[108] Ibid.
[109] ESC Decision 1986/150.
[110] ESC Res.1985/17, para. c.
[111] Ibid.
[112] Ibid. para. c(i), (ii).
[113] ESC Res.1985/17, para. e.

fulfilling the Council's role under the Covenant[114] rather than to be directly responsible, in its own right, for supervisory activities.

But while this remains a potentially significant difference, the Council has, in practice, permitted the Committee to act in all important respects as an independent Committee. The latter is dependent upon the former in all matters involving financial implication, but so too in reality is the Human Rights Committee dependent upon the Assembly in such matters. Otherwise, the Committee has tended to adopt all of its working methods without reference to the Council. The only significant exception relates to its Rules of Procedure, for which it sought the Council's endorsement after its third session.[115] However, even that arrangement seems in retrospect to have been ill-advised because it inhibits the Committee's ability to adjust its procedures promptly to changing circumstances and places it at the mercy of the Council's efficiency or inefficiency in considering and approving proposed changes. It would thus be desirable for the Committee to be given full control over its own Rules of Procedure as soon as practicable. The only other matters of significance to have been referred to the Council for decision have concerned the role of NGOs in submitting information to the Committee[116] and the creation of a 'blacklist' of States whose reports are dramatically overdue.[117]

D. *The Principal Activities of the Committee*

A detailed micro-analysis of the methods and procedures followed by the Committee in the course of its first five sessions is of rather limited utility for those whose objective is to develop an appreciation of the principal challenges confronting the Committee, and the progress it has made in meeting them. Thus, rather than adopting a more traditional, and inevitably tedious, analytical breakdown of the Committee's activities,[118] the analysis that follows concentrates primarily upon the Committee's efforts to: (1) clarify the norms contained in the Covenant; (2) expand the information base relevant to its work; and (3) design an effective system for monitoring States' performance in the field of economic, social, and cultural rights. Taken together, these issues

[114] Ibid. para. f.
[115] *Report on the Third Session*, E/1989/22, paras. 333–4.
[116] *Report on the First Session*, E/1987/28, paras. 312–13.
[117] *Report on the Fifth Session*, E/1991/23, chap. 1, draft decision I.
[118] It should be noted that, from its fourth Session onwards, the Committee had included in each of its sessional reports a separate chapter entitled 'Overview of the Present Working Methods of the Committee'. The stated purpose of this overview is 'to make the Committee's current practice more transparent and readily accessible so as to assist States Parties and others interested in the implementation of the [Covenant]'. *Report on the Fourth Session*, E/1990/23, para. 19.

constitute the most important of the tasks that the Committee has set for itself.

I. CLARIFICATION OF THE COVENANT'S NORMS

One of the most striking features of the Covenant is the vagueness of the normative implications of the various rights it recognizes. While some of the formulations are no more vague or ill-defined than some of those in the other Covenant, the difference in the extent of elaboration of their normative content undertaken both before and after the adoption of the Covenant is immense. Several factors account for this discrepancy. In the first place, the content of the Covenant on Economic, Social and Cultural Rights was not based upon any significant bodies of domestic jurisprudence as was the case with civil and political rights. Thus, phrases like 'cruel, inhuman or degrading treatment or punishment' had been the subject of in-depth judicial and academic analysis long before their inclusion in the Covenant on Civil and Political Rights. By contrast, the range of rights recognized in the other Covenant was, with the exception of labour-related rights, considerably in advance of most national legislation. Indeed, this is still the case today so that international lawyers seeking enlightenment as to the meaning of rights such as those pertaining to food, education, health care, clothing, and shelter will find little direct guidance in national law.[119]

The second reason for the discrepancy lies in the failure of the international community to develop jurisprudence of any significance on many of the principal economic rights since the Covenant's adoption in 1966. By contrast, the meaning and precise policy implications of specific civil and political rights have been the subject of detailed legal analysis and of carefully honed judicial and quasi-judicial interpretation, as well as being spelled out in much greater detail in specialized instruments such as the Standard Minimum Rules for the Treatment of Prisoners[120] and the Convention Against Torture.[121] Economic, social, and cultural rights have been the beneficiaries of remarkably few such endeavours and those that have been undertaken have not been very revealing. Indeed, some of the relevant United Nations reports have served principally to demonstrate that in the field of economic rights it is easy to generate a large amount of heat (by detailing the statistics of infant mortality, death by starvation, adult illiteracy, and general homelessness) but infinitely more difficult to generate even a small amount of light (by identifying the core requirements stemming from recognition of particular rights).[122]

[119] See e.g. Alston 'International Law and the Human Right to Food', in *The Right to Food*, 9.
[120] ESC Res.663 C (XXIV) (1957).
[121] GA Res.39/46 (1984) Annex.
[122] e.g. Ganji, *The Realization of Economic, Social and Cultural Rights: Problems, Policies, Progress*, UN Sales No. E.75.XIV.2 (1975).

Clarification of the normative content of the rights recognized in the Covenant has thus been a priority concern for the Committee. In theory this function, in so far as it is to be performed at all, should be achieved through the examination of States Parties' reports. In other words, the approaches adopted by States themselves in their internal arrangements (and explained in their reports to the Committee) will shed some light upon the norms, while the dialogue between the State and the Committee will contribute further to deepening the understanding of the central issues in that regard.

In practice, however, States' reports have not proven especially enlightening in this respect and States' representatives have manifested a distinct reluctance to engage in any exchange of views with the Committee on these issues. As a result, the Committee has sought to devise other, additional, means by which to develop an improved understanding of the applicable norms. In particular, it has done so through the scheduling of a day of 'general discussion' at each session and through the adoption of detailed 'general comments'. While the latter technique is a well-proven one that is already used effectively by other committees, the former constitutes an innovative and potentially much more flexible approach. We turn now to an examination of each of these three activities.

(*a*) *The Examination of States Parties' Reports*

A rapid review of the relevant provisions of the Covenant, as well as of the procedures followed by the Committee, could well lead a casual observer to the conclusion that the examination of a State Party's report by the Committee (albeit in the name of the Council) is the ultimate objective of the entire exercise. If, however, that exercise is seen in its proper perspective it should be considered to be a relatively routine and modest part of a far grander enterprise: the taking of measures designed to promote realization of the economic, social, and cultural rights of every individual living within the jurisdiction of the State concerned. Viewed in this light, reporting is only one part of a continuing process, the domestic rather than the international ramifications of which should be far more significant.

Perhaps the principal reason why States' reports have failed to shed any significant light on the normative content of the rights is that their function has not been viewed in this way by the responsible national authorities. Rather, the task of compiling and presenting the reports has tended to be seen almost exclusively as a diplomatic chore. Accordingly, the accepted 'wisdom' has been that it should be carried out with the least possible expenditure of diplomatic staff resources, with little involvement on the part of those in government who are actually concerned with the rights in question, and with no involvement at all of the broader range of social partners in the community. In fact, the great majority of States have adopted an attitude to reporting which is entirely consistent with this vision. The result is an all too often sterile reporting system that yields few, if any, genuine insights into the social system in the country concerned and provides the Committee with very little to go on in its quest to inject some meaning into the process.

The procedural measures adopted by the Committee in an effort to improve the mechanics of the reporting process are evaluated in section D. III below. The point to be made in the present context, however, is that the Committee has not simply acquiesced in the view that the reporting process consists solely of an isolated and occasional diplomatic exchange between a State and the Committee. To the contrary, it has indicated through its questions to representatives as well as through its General Comments that it views that process as a far more demanding and continuous one than many States might have wished it to be. This is borne out in particular by the fact that its first General Comment was devoted to the question of 'reporting by States Parties'.[123] In its analysis the Committee specifically rejected the view that 'reporting is essentially only a procedural matter designed solely to satisfy each State Party's formal obligation to report to the appropriate international monitoring body'. To underscore its point it identified seven different objectives which reporting should promote. In brief, they are: (1) to ensure that a comprehensive initial review of national legislation, administrative rules and procedures, and practices is undertaken either before or very soon after ratification; (2) 'to ensure that the State Party monitors the actual situation with respect to each of the rights on a regular basis and is thus aware of the extent to which the various rights are, or are not, being enjoyed . . .'; (3) 'to provide the basis for the elaboration of clearly stated and carefully targeted policies, including the establishment of priorities which reflect the provisions of the Covenant . . .'; (4) to facilitate public scrutiny of relevant government policies and to encourage the involvement of the various sectors of society in the formulation, implementation, and review of the policies in question; (5) 'to provide a basis on which the State Party itself, as well as the Committee, can effectively evaluate the extent to which progress has been made towards the realization of the obligations contained in the Covenant . . .'; (6) 'to enable the State Party itself to develop a better understanding of the problems and shortcomings encountered in efforts to realize progressively the full range of economic, social and cultural rights'; and (7) 'to facilitate the exchange of information among States and to develop a better understanding of the common problems faced . . .'.

The principal significance of this conception of the reporting process lies in the emphasis it places upon the vital importance of a range of activities taking place at the national level, quite apart from the actual examination of the report by the Committee. It also serves to emphasize that reporting is much more than a gesture requiring a flurry of diplomatic activity for a short time every five years.

[123] *Report on the Third Session*, E/1989/22, Annex III.

Nevertheless, despite the potentially far-reaching implications of the General Comment, it has made little, if any, impact to date upon the parties to the Covenant. In responding to it they have used a potent weapon; it has simply been ignored. This will presumably continue to be the case: until the Committee itself can convey its message more effectively; until Governments are prepared to take their obligations more seriously; and, perhaps most importantly, until domestic pressure groups are prepared to invest time and effort into pushing governments to take the reporting process seriously.

In the mean time, the Committee's task will be to develop the procedures surrounding the reporting process in such a way that States are more or less compelled to take it seriously.

(*b*) *The Day of General Discussion*

The Committee realized at an early stage of its work that the task of fleshing out the normative framework of the Covenant could not be left to Governments alone. Instead the need was to mobilize other forces with the necessary expertise and interest and to ensure that the Committee itself was closely involved in that work. For that purpose the Committee has designated one day to be set aside at each of its sessions as a 'day of general discussion'. The stated purpose is to focus upon 'one specific right or a particular aspect of the Covenant in order to develop in greater depth [the Committee's] understanding of the relevant issues'.[124] In practice, this day has been used as a vehicle for ensuring that the Committee is able to detach itself, temporarily, from the grind of its day-to-day examination of reports and is able to invite a wide range of experts to talk with it on relevant issues.

This 'agenda item' was begun at the third session when the focus was on the right to food. At the next session the issue discussed was the right to housing while at the sixth session the focus will be on the place of economic and social indicators in the work of the Committee. Lack of time prevented a discussion at the fifth session. Within the framework provided by these general discussions the Committee has engaged in active discussions with several rapporteurs of the Sub-Commission, heard from the representatives of specialized agencies who would not otherwise have contributed to its work, and invited individual experts (often closely associated with NGOs) to discuss specific issues with it. The general thrust of these discussions has been summarized in a separate chapter of the Committee's annual report.[125] The discussions have provided an invaluable means by which the Committee has been able to open up its dialogue and has given it the opportunity to invite a

[124] *Report on the Fifth Session*, E/1991/23, paras. 37–41.

[125] *Report on the Third Session*, E/1989/22, paras. 310–26; *Report on the Fourth Session*, E/1990/23, paras. 255–85.

much wider range of inputs from individuals or groups that feel they have something to offer to the Committee.

The general discussions also enable the Committee to discuss broader, sometimes more theoretical, issues which are directly relevant to its role of examining States' reports and especially to the task of elaborating General Comments.

(c) *General Comments*

The Committee was not originally given any specific authorization to adopt General Comments, although it was generally expected to apply many of the approaches developed by the Human Rights Committee to its own work. It therefore sought the Council's authorization and has subsequently received active encouragement from both the Committee and the Council 'to continue using that mechanism to develop a fuller appreciation of the obligations of States Parties under the Covenant'.[126] This accords fully with the Committee's own understanding of the purposes of its General Comments which it has expressed in the following terms:

> The Committee endeavours, through its General Comments, to make the experience gained so far through the examination of [States'] reports available for the benefit of all States Parties in order to assist and promote their further implementation of the Covenant; to draw the attention of the States Parties to insufficiencies disclosed by a large number of reports; to suggest improvements in the reporting procedures and to stimulate the activities of the States Parties, the international organizations and the specialized agencies concerned in achieving progressively and effectively the full realization of the rights recognized in the Covenant.[127]

The role played by General Comments in the work of the UN treaty bodies as a whole should not be underestimated. During the 1970s and 80s, the Human Rights Committee was able, in a period when ideological disputes blocked many other avenues, to develop its collection of General Comments into a strong body of jurisprudential insights into the various provisions of the Covenant. While the Committee on Economic, Social and Cultural Rights has given clear indications that it intends to follow suit in this regard, it has also made use of the technique of elaborating General Comments as a means of laying down some solid foundations for the future development of its jurisprudence.

By the end of its fifth session (December 1990), it had adopted three General Comments. The first, which is analysed above, deals with the nature of the reporting system.[128] The second deals with international technical assistance measures, particularly in connection with Article 22 of the

[126] ESC Res.1990/45, para. 10.
[127] *Report on its Fourth Session*, E/1990/23, para. 39.
[128] See text accompanying n. 123, above.

Covenant.[129] It was warmly welcomed by the Council and has also received considerable attention in the Commission and the Assembly.[130] Its principal concern is with the means by which the various UN agencies working in the development field could integrate measures designed to promote full respect for economic, social, and cultural rights.

However, it is the third General Comment[131] that is of the greatest significance in the present context. It constitutes an explicit statement by the Committee on 'the nature of States Parties' obligations' with particular reference to Article 2(1) of the Covenant. As such it provides the intellectual and legal framework within which the Committee can begin to interpret the normative implications of each of the specific rights recognized in the Covenant. In brief, the Committee notes that the Covenant *does* impose 'various obligations which are of immediate effect', contrary to the assertions of those who argue that the Covenant is wholly aspirational. It singles out two such obligations in particular: the non-discrimination provisions and the undertaking 'to take steps'. With respect to the latter it says that appropriate steps 'must be taken within a reasonably short time after the Covenant's entry into force for the States concerned' and that they should be 'deliberate, concrete and targeted as clearly as possible towards meeting the obligations recognized in the Covenant'.

The Committee also notes that legislation may sometimes be an indispensable requirement, but that it will rarely be sufficient *per se*. It notes that judicial or other effective remedies should be provided wherever possible and that suggestions that the provisions of the Covenant 'are inherently non-self-executing would seem to be difficult to sustain', at least in respect to certain rights.

Most importantly of all, the Committee observes that 'a minimum core obligation to ensure the satisfaction of, at the very least, minimum essential levels of each of the rights is incumbent upon every State Party'. This leads it to the conclusion that 'a State Party in which any significant number of individuals is deprived of essential foodstuffs, of essential primary health care, of basic shelter and housing, or of the most basic forms of education is, *prima facie*, failing to discharge its obligations under the Covenant'. The only qualification it adds is that a State may be able to demonstrate that resource constraints make it impossible for anything positive to be done in this regard. The burden of proving that this is the case would, however, be a difficult one to discharge and falls upon the State itself.

In normative terms, this is a very significant development. The Committee would appear to be well justified in suggesting, as it has, that without such an

[129] *Report on the Fourth Session*, E/1990/23, Annex III.
[130] e.g. ESC Res.1990/45, para. 8; and E/C.12/1990/SR.36, paras. 6–7 (Mr Martenson).
[131] *Report on the Fifth Session*, E/1991/23, Annex VI.

approach the very *raison d'être* of the Covenant would be undermined. It thus follows the reasoning reflected in the Limburg Principles, an important statement by an international expert group convened prior to the Committee's creation to examine the nature of the Covenant's obligations.[132]

II. EXPANDING THE INFORMATION BASE

One of the most enduring myths of the UN's work in the human rights field was that governments alone hold a monopoly of reliable information on the situation in their own countries and that other sources of information, by contrast, are inherently unreliable. It took the dramatic growth of international NGOs such as Amnesty International and others to prove conclusively that the opposite is more likely to be the case. The point was also emphasized by the highly frustrating experiences of both the treaty and the political organs whenever they were deprived of access to non-governmental sources of information. But despite the fact that effective monitoring is simply impossible in the absence of such information, members of several of the treaty supervisory bodies have persisted in their efforts to ensure a restrictive information policy.[133]

It was clear from the first session of the Committee on Economic, Social and Cultural Rights, however, that the expansion of the Committee's information base, to enable it to reach out far beyond governmental sources alone, was a matter of the highest priority. Indeed, the first session witnessed a major confrontation between the three Eastern European experts, led by Mr Eduard Sviridov from the USSR, and their colleagues over the questions of: whether NGOs would be permitted to submit written statements to the Committee; whether the representatives of the specialized agencies could participate in the proceedings; and whether outside sources of information (such as World Bank reports) could be cited. Although the Summary Records of the relevant debates inevitably tend to eliminate all of the urgency and drama that characterized the proceedings, the Committee came very close to abandoning the consensus approach[134] which is widely assumed to be essential to the smooth functioning of the various committees. In the event, a crisis was averted by the

[132] 'The Limburg Principles on the Implementation of the International Covenant on Economic, Social and Cultural Rights', E/CN.4/1987/17, Annex. See also 9 *Hum. Rts. Q.* 122 (1987). Principle 25 states that: 'States Parties are obligated, regardless of the level of economic development, to ensure respect for minimum subsistence rights for all'.

[133] For a recent example, see positions adopted in the Committee on the Elimination of Racial Discrimination detailed in International League for Human Rights, 'Sources of Information used by Treaty Committees' (New York, Sept. 1990).

[134] Indeed, at one stage during the Committee's first session, two of the Eastern European experts took particular exception to the phrase 'procedural innovation' and indicated that there was absolutely no need for any such reforms. See generally Alston and Simma, 'First Session of the UN Committee on Economic, Social and Cultural Rights'.

Perestroika-related withdrawal of the Soviet expert prior to the second session and his replacement at the third session by Professor Valeri Kouznetsov. The latter was a genuine expert who manifested a clear determination to ensure the success of the Committee's work (and who succeeded to such an extent in winning the confidence of his colleagues that they elected him Chairman at the fifth session).

Since the settling of the *brouhaha* caused by this incident, the Committee has been able to move towards a much more systematic expansion of its general information base. We turn now to examine the different ways in which this has been achieved.

(*a*) *Reporting Guidelines*

Each of the treaty bodies has adopted a set of reporting guidelines designed to indicate to reporting States the type of information that is required under each of the relevant treaty provisions. However, the Committee on Economic, Social and Cultural Rights 'inherited' a set of guidelines that had been put together in 1976–7 by the Secretariat, on the basis of technical proposals drafted by the key specialized agencies (ILO, FAO, WHO, and UNESCO).[135] During the eight years of the Working Group the guidelines were never changed to reflect the Group's experience, despite the fact that the reports received from States Parties were rarely satisfactory.

The principal shortcoming of the original guidelines was that they combined inordinate length with generality and vagueness. On issues such as 'safe and healthy working conditions' (Article 7(b)) the guidelines requested each State to submit, *inter alia*, all of its 'principal laws, administrative regulations, collective agreements and court decisions', along with details of the 'principal arrangements and procedures (including inspection services and various bodies at the national, industry, local, or undertaking level entrusted with the promotion or supervision of health and safety at work) to ensure that these provisions are effectively respected in individual work-places'. Only the arrival of semi-trailer loads of documents at the Palais des Nations in Geneva could have signified that a medium-sized industrialized State was taking such a reporting requirement seriously.

The Committee thus decided at its first session to revise those guidelines and it spent considerable time between then and its fifth session in doing so. The task proved to be difficult and to necessitate a choice between two alternative approaches. The first was to ask only a very limited number of specific questions, each of which would be capable of being answered concisely. The principal advantage of this alternative was that it would greatly reduce the burden upon States and would leave them with no justification for not providing all of the requested information. The Committee's task would

[135] The guidelines were reproduced in E/C.12/1987/2.

also be greatly simplified. The disadvantage was that large numbers of rights dealt with by the Covenant would be ignored or glossed over and the examination of the resulting report would give the Committee only the most superficial indication of both the *de facto* and the *de jure* positions within the reporting State.

The second alternative was to compile a lengthy but none the less quite precise list of key questions designed to cover systematically each of the issues raised in the Covenant. The disadvantage of this approach is that it entails a significant reporting burden and requires the compilation of a large amount of information. The advantage, however, is that the resulting report should constitute a detailed, informative, and focused evaluation of the present situation and enable the reporting process to fulfil several, if not all, of the objectives of reporting identified by the Committee in its General Comment No. 1.[136]

Not surprisingly, the Committee opted for the second alternative, on the understanding that it would continue to refine and revise its guidelines in the light of experience. Thus the reporting guidelines adopted by the Committee at its fifth session are quite extensive[137] and represent a major departure from the previous guidelines. One major innovation is that States that have already submitted detailed information, of direct relevance, to a specialized agency or other international organization need not reproduce that information but can simply refer to it. The objective is to reduce the burden imposed upon States that are already reporting to ILO, WHO, UNESCO, etc. on economic, social and cultural rights-related issues. In order to maximize the utility of the new guidelines from the Committee's point of view, the Committee has instructed its Secretariat to undertake a comparison of States reports with the guidelines in order to identify any issues which the report fails to address.[138] This in turn should facilitate the Committee's task and provide a more consistent and systematic basis for the examination of reports.

(b) The Role of the Specialized Agencies

The 'big four' agencies (ILO, WHO, UNESCO, and FAO) each played a significant role in the drafting of the Covenant. In addition, it was always envisaged that they would have an important role to play in relation to its implementation.[139] Thus it is noteworthy, although unsurprising, that every article but two in Part IV of the Covenant (dealing with implementation) makes a specific reference to the role of the agencies.

136 See text accompanying n. 123, above.
137 *Report on the Fifth Session*, E/1991/23, Annex IV.
138 Ibid. para. 282.
139 See generally Alston, 'The United Nations Specialized Agencies and Implementation of the International Covenant on Economic, Social and Cultural Rights', 19 *Colum. J. Transnat'l L.* 79 (1979).

Nevertheless, the relationship between the agencies (and particularly ILO and UNESCO) and the UN Centre for Human Rights has always been uneasy and an unproductive element of competitiveness has often crept into their relationships.[140] This was enormously exacerbated once the Working Group was established in 1979 mainly as a result of the deep-seated antipathy of the Soviet Union and its allies to the agencies and to the ILO in particular. The problem was made even more acute by the fact that the ILO was prepared to take its role seriously and to furnish detailed and specific information about the situation in reporting States. The result was a relentless battle against the ILO, waged with obessive intensity, which succeeded in taking up an inordinate amount of the Working Group's limited time. It was especially unproductive. The ILO was only permitted to present its information after all other aspects of the examination of the State Party's report had been completed; in other words, only when it no longer mattered. In response, the ILO eventually decided, ostensibly on budgetary grounds, to cease preparing special reports under the Covenant and instead to provide the Working Group only with excerpts from reports prepared by the ILO's Committee of Experts for other purposes.[141] Nevertheless, it has continued to send an observer to each session of the Committee who has made a very valuable contribution both formally and informally.

The contribution of the other agencies has been very mixed. WHO has provided only one very formalistic and brief written report under the Covenant,[142] but at recent sessions it has been represented by individuals who have provided the Committee with valuable advice on appropriate issues. UNESCO has submitted two written reports, each considerably different from the other, and has expressed a desire to contribute more actively.[143] In practice, however, its contribution has been rather token to date. FAO has submitted one report[144] and has been represented at one session but has not manifested any intention of contributing to the Committee's work.

Overall then the situation is not encouraging. In part, the Working Group is to blame for its earlier bloody-mindedness. In part, also, the problem is the almost compulsive inability of the UN and 'its' agencies to collaborate effectively on almost anything in the human rights field. Another problem is the tendency of some of the agencies to continue to assume that human rights is a deeply politicized field and that they should avoid it at all costs. Nevertheless,

[140] See Chap. 16 below.

[141] For a detailed analysis of the entire episode from the ILO viewpoint, see *Impact of ILO Policies on the United Nations*, ILO Doc. GB.225/10/3/3, paras. 92–5 (1984). The ILO's reports under the Covenant have been reproduced in the following documents: E/1978/27; E/1979/33; E/1980/35; E/1981/41; E/1982/41; E/1983/40; E/1985/63; E/1986/60; E/1987/59; E/1988/6; E.1989/6; E/1990/9; E/1991/4.

[142] E/1980/24.

[143] E/1982/10 and E/1988/7.

[144] E/1981/22.

the possibilities for future collaboration remain enormous and it is to be hoped that the past will not be an accurate guide to the future. If nothing else, at least the attitude of the Committee has changed radically and it remains anxious to explore new forms of co-operation.

(c) *Other United Nations Bodies*

The Committee has consistently sought to make use of information available from other UN sources. In particular, it has requested its Secretariat to ensure that it has available to it the World Bank's annual *World Development Report* and UNICEF's annual *State of the World's Children Report*. In addition, it has begun to make use of the statistical publications of UNESCO, the International Monetary Fund, FAO, and the UN Development Programme. However, much work needs to be done in order to ensure that the Committee is able to make effective use of these statistical indicators. The fact that it is an area fraught with difficulty has recently been demonstrated in an excellent report on the subject to the Sub-Commission by Danilo Turk.[145]

The Committee has not, however, come close to making the most important breakthrough in using relevant information generated by the agencies. That is to say, it has never had access to the detailed reports prepared by some of those agencies on the economic and social situation in many of the countries that report under the Covenant. For example, the position with respect to the right to food or the right to education in a given country would be described in infinitely more detail and in a far more informative way in internal reports regularly prepared by the World Bank, the FAO, UNICEF, and other agencies than in the reports submitted to the Committee by the States themselves. So far, the insistence that such agency reports are confidential has always deterred the Committee from even requesting access to them. But at some stage this reticence will need to be overcome and both the Committee and the agencies will need to attach to the human rights monitoring process the importance that it clearly warrants.

(d) *United Nations Human Rights Organs*

One source of information which was long neglected by the Committee is the reports prepared by either Special Rapporteurs or Working Groups of the Commission on Human Rights and the Sub-Commission dealing with the situation in specific countries. Sometimes these reports contain information specifically on economic, social, and cultural rights which could readily be used by the Committee. In other instances, the reports deal only with civil and political rights issues, but these should also be of relevance to the Committee given the reality of the interdependence of the two sets of rights and the consequent impossibility of understanding the situation in a country on the

145 E/CN.4/Sub.2/1990/19, especially paras. 96–105.

basis of only half the overall picture. The same applies to the reports of the other treaty monitoring body. If the Committee is considering the situation in, say, Australia it should at least have some idea of any conclusions recently reached on the situation in that country by CEDAW, CERD, or the Human Rights Committee.

There are several reasons why these types of information have not consistently been taken into account by the Committee. The first is a sense that the work of different bodies should be kept entirely separate. This is difficult to justify, however, and, if accepted, would ensure that efforts to co-ordinate the work of the different bodies, albeit only in some very general sense, are doomed to failure. The second is the sheer volume of work that would be entailed by efforts to take all relevant reports into account. This is a very real problem but it is to be hoped that recent initiatives to promote the creation and use of a computerized database within the UN human rights programme[146] as well as a greater emphasis on the servicing responsibilities of the Committee's Secretariat will help to mitigate it.

(*e*) *Non-Governmental Organizations*

As noted above, one of the most important features of the way in which the international human rights regime has evolved over the last two decades is the extent to which NGOs have come to be accepted not merely as partners in the overall enterprise but as indispensable ones. Within the framework of the political organs this is already a well-established fact and it is coming to achieve that status within the treaty body system. Nevertheless, many of the committees continue to have their holdouts and the result has been the evolution of an informal rather than a formal set of arrangements to facilitate NGO inputs. The Committee on Economic, Social and Cultural Rights broke the mould in 1988, however, when it became the first of the committees to permit the formal submission of written statements by NGOs. It has subsequently also adopted the practice of permitting NGO representatives to participate in their capacity as experts in the day of general discussion. In addition, virtually all members of the Committee have evinced a clear willingness to ask State representatives to respond specifically to information emanating from NGO sources.

It is noteworthy that the Committee has not yet sought to involve NGOs directly in the oral dialogue with States Parties and indeed there would not seem to be any particular sentiment in favour of such a move. If anything, the Committee has been disappointed by the very low level of interest in its work demonstrated by NGOs. Only Rights and Humanity and the Habitat International Coalition has shown any consistent interest and made constructive

[146] See 'Study on Computerizing the Work of the Human Rights Treaty Monitoring Bodies', E/CN.4/1990/39, Annex.

contributions. Written submissions from other NGOs, let alone any form of active attendance at sessions, have been few and far between. Similarly, national NGOs have not mobilized themselves around the Committee's work to any significant extent. There is no doubt that the NGO community should consider itself culpable on this score. Its neglect of the only body seeking to do serious and sustained work in the field of economic, social, and cultural rights tends to undermine the purported attachment by so many of its members to those rights.

At the same time, however, the Committee itself must also share a large part of the blame. The application of free market principles, which have been much in vogue in the 1980s and early 90s, provides a compelling indication of consumer dissatisfaction with the way in which the Committee functions and, in particular, with the results that it is perceived to be capable of achieving. Ultimately, it is for the Committee to demonstrate that the investment of time and effort in its work on the part of NGOs is capable of yielding satisfactory returns. While it has not yet been able to do this, it is to be hoped that it has succeeded in laying the procedural foundations for a process that might one day achieve the desired results.

(*f*) *The Future*

In the information area the Committee finds itself in something of a bind. It usually meets once a year for three weeks, with a Working Group also meeting for one week. Its members all have full-time jobs and have little opportunity to devote themselves to Committee work during the year. It might be added, in this connection, that it is almost alone among the treaty bodies in not providing its members with an honorarium. Thus, while access to an extensive information base is indispensable for the carrying out of its principal functions, the effective use of that information requires time and facilities which are not currently available. The only means by which these competing demands might be reconciled is through the development of an active servicing role on the part of the Secretariat. Up until the end of its fifth session the Secretariat had provided virtually no substantive assistance of any kind to the Committee. Its role was confined to that of providing secretarial services and drafting the routine parts of the report. Once the annual session was finished, members received no more than one or two perfunctory administrative communications until the following session began. It must be acknowledged that the overall level of human resources made available by the General Assembly for the purpose of assisting the treaty bodies as a whole has been entirely unsatisfactory. Nevertheless, this has been no more than part of the problem as far as the Committee is concerned.

As a result of increasing dissatisfaction with this situation the Committee has sought to explore other approaches. Since its third session it has called for the establishment of a 'Committee Resource Room' to be available for use by the members of all of the treaty bodies. Although this proposal was also endorsed by the Meeting of Chairpersons of the Human Rights Treaty Bodies, the Committee was forced at its fifth session to note 'with regret that at both its fourth and fifth sessions only vague and non-committal information had been provided [by the Secretariat] in response to this request'.[147] Having asked that a room be set aside for a purpose that it considered to be of the highest importance, the Committee was apparently not overly impressed by assurances that the construction of a new building at the UN might eventually resolve the problem.[148]

An equally important, and perhaps more productive initiative (at least in the sense that the Secretariat cannot, in effect, just ignore it) taken by the Committee at the same session was to 'invite all concerned bodies and individuals to submit relevant and appropriate documentation to it'[149] To ensure that all such information is taken advantage of, the Committee requested the Secretariat to establish a separate file for each State which is reporting to it and it specified that the file should contain at least the following information: (1) all relevant country-specific Commission and Sub-Commission reports; (2) information pertaining to the State concerned taken from the two most recent Annual Reports of the other major human rights treaty bodies (except for CAT); (3) relevant country-specific information from recent ILO reports; (4) relevant country-specific information available from the WHO; (5) relevant statistical indicators from World Bank and UNICEF sources; (6) the text of any report submitted to an international agency and to which specific reference is made by the State Party in its report; and, perhaps most importantly, (7) 'any other relevant documentation submitted to the Secretariat for inclusion in the file'.[150]

In adopting this decision, the Committee noted that 'an information base of this type is indispensable to enable it to carry out its monitoring functions effectively'. Its significance is that it formalizes arrangements which in the past had been initiated only on an *ad hoc* and very uneven basis. It thus ensures that the range of information formally before the Committee when it is examining any given report will be far greater than it has ever previously been. While this will make the Committee considerably better informed than any of its treaty monitoring counterparts, it may be expected that the precedent will soon be followed by those committees.

III. DEVELOPING AN EFFECTIVE MONITORING SYSTEM

Clarification of the normative content of the rights and expansion of the information base are essential if the Committee is to be effective, but they

[147] *Report on the Fifth Session*, E/1991/23, para. 262. [148] E/C.12/1990/SR.36, para. 18 (Mr Martenson). [149] *Report of the Fifth Session*, E/1991/23, para. 280. [150] Ibid.

constitute means more than the end. The objective is to facilitate the development of an effective monitoring system which not only gives the overall process a strong degree of credibility but also contributes significantly towards the promotion of respect for economic, social, and cultural rights. Such a system requires a number of additional components, to which we now turn.

(a) Reporting Periodicity

The first step taken by the Committee to make the pre-existing reporting system manageable for States and to make the reports self-contained and comprehensible was to change the reporting cycle, or periodicity. Under the system established by the Council in 1976 States Parties presented initial reports at three-yearly intervals, each dealing with one-third of the rights recognized in Part III of the Covenant (i.e., Articles 6–9, 10–12, and 13–15). An entire cycle thus took nine years to complete and neither the State itself nor the Committee ever got an up-to-date and comprehensive picture of the situation. Subsequent periodic reports did not take quite so long: two-yearly intervals added up to a six-year cycle. Combined with delays in submitting and often in considering reports, the result was a most unsatisfactory basis for monitoring. The principal explanation for the system was to facilitate the involvement of the specialized agencies, since each of the clusters of rights corresponded to the concerns of specific agencies. But this convenience was hardly sufficient to justify the continuation of a system that, in almost every other respect, was inefficient.

Thus at its second session the Committee decided to introduce a system of single 'global' reports to be presented by each State party at five-yearly intervals.[151] The objectives of the change were to: reduce the total number of reports submitted; ease the workload of the national officials responsible for preparing reports; facilitate the Committee's appreciation of the overall situation in the relevant State; make the reports more comprehensible to concerned NGOs and the public at large; and synchronize the reporting schedule with that applying under most other human rights treaties. In terms of evaluation, the transition period from the 'old' to the 'new' system has inevitably been slow and it is yet too soon to say with any certainty how much the change will contibute to increasing the Committee's effectiveness.

(b) Responding to Non-Submission of Reports

The problem of a failure by States Parties to report pursuant to the obligations they have assumed under the various human rights treaties has reached chronic proportions in recent years. The International Covenant on Economic, Social and Cultural Rights has been far from exempt from this trend. As of 1 August 1990, there were ninety-seven States Parties to the

[151] *Report on the Second Session*, E/1988/14, para. 351.

Covenant which, between them, had accumulated a total of 147 overdue reports.[152] But as unsatisfactory as this statistic is, it tells only a small part of the story. Delays of several months, or even a year, are not unusual and give rise to very little concern. What is disturbing is the number of States that, after many years as parties to the Covenant, have still not submitted even one initial report.[153] As of January 1991, twenty-eight States Parties to the Covenant had never reported. The response of the treaty bodies to this situation has been to submit repeated reminders and requests to the States concerned and sometimes to seek meetings with the relevant Foreign Minister of Permanent Representative to the UN.[154] These measures have met with only very limited success. The political organs have, as a matter of course, long expressed grave concern at the situation[155] but have consistently stopped short of any measures that would put significant pressure on individual States, no matter how grave their delinquency.

In an effort to break through this impasse the Committee, at its fifth session, requested the Council to adopt a Decision in which it would appeal 'to the following States which have been parties to the [Covenant] for more than 10 years but which have yet to submit even the initial report required by the Covenant, to do so as soon as possible . . .'.[156] The draft Decision then lists the countries by name. If adopted by the Council, it will come close to being a 'blacklist' of States which have failed, dismally, to take the Covenant seriously. It would be the first of its kind and would constitute an important precedent for other committees. If the draft is watered down, or rejected, by the Council it will be a sad demonstration of the unwillingness of the political organs to support the treaty bodies on issues in which there are some perceived political costs involved.

(c) *Responding to Non-Appearance before the Committee*

Even when a report has been submitted, it may not always be easy to persuade the reporting State to schedule a session at which to present it. The Committee was confronted with this problem on a significant scale at its fifth

[152] Statistics contained in HRI/MC/1990/L. 2, 10 (prepared for the Meeting of Chairpersons of the Human Rights Treaty Bodies).

[153] Thus, as of 1 Dec. 1990, there were five States which were original parties (i.e. since 3 Jan. 1976, when the Covenant first entered into force) and which had still not reported almost fifteen years later (Kenya, Lebanon, Mali, Mauritius, and Uruguay). There were seven which had been parties for over ten years (El Salvador, The Gambia, Guinea, Iceland, Morocco, Sri Lanka, and Suriname) and nine which had been parties for over seven years (Belgium, Bolivia, Central African Republic, Egypt, Gabon, Honduras, St Vincent and the Grenadines, Solomon Islands, and Vietnam). *Report on the Fifth Session*, E/1991/23, Annex I.

[154] See e.g. the approaches pursued by the Human Rights Committee, A/44/98, para. 12.

[155] e.g. GA Res.44/135 (1989) pream. para. 7 ('Expressing concern about the continuing and increasing backlog of reports . . .') and para. 5 ('Again urges States Parties to make every effort to meet their reporting obligations . . .').

[156] *Report on the Fifth Session*, E/1991/23, chap. 1, Draft Dec. I.

session. Iran, which had on three previous occasions deferred consideration of its report, informed the Committee that it wished to do so again. Afghanistan and Panama also indicated that they wished to defer consideration of pending reports for a third time. Before determining its response, the Committee engaged in a protracted debate. On one side the view was expressed that there was a need to be very diplomatic with States and to be especially solicitous of States facing particular difficulties. On the other side, it was felt that such States were in greater need of scrutiny by the Committee than others and that to permit them to sidestep their treaty obligations would call the seriousness of the entire procedure into question.[157]

In the event, the Committee decided 'that on the third occasion that a State Party's report is scheduled for consideration, it will, except in truly exceptional circumstances, proceed with the consideration of the report whether or not a representative of the State Party concerned is able to be present'.[158] This policy of insistence immediately paid dividends. Iran announced that it would, after all, be sending a delegation from Teheran to present its report, which it indeed did. Panama sent an official letter undertaking to present an updated report at the very next session and Afghanistan sent its Permanent Representative to appear before the Committee and assure it that an up-to-date, global report would be submitted within six months. The lesson to be learned was that a body that takes itself seriously is far more likely to be taken seriously by States than one that does not.

(*d*) *A Truly Constructive Dialogue*

Each of the treaty bodies is committed to maintaining a 'constructive dialogue' with the States parties by means of putting questions to representatives when they submit the report of their State. For this process to work, a number of ingredients, in addition to those discussed earlier, are necessary. The first is for the State to be represented by individuals who have the stature and expertise required to be able to answer the questions put in relation to relatively technical matters. The Committee has long stressed the importance of this factor and the political organs have endorsed the position.[159] In an effort to encourage such representation the Committee has, unlike any of its counterparts, listed in its reports the name and position of each of the representatives to appear before it.[160] This has not, however, deterred a number of States from sending only diplomatic personnel from their Missions

[157] For details of the debate, see E/C.12/1990/SR.27, paras. 16–43 and E/C.12/1990/SR.28, paras. 1–7.

[158] *Report on the Fifth Session*, E/1991/23, para. 35.

[159] e.g. GA Res.44/129 (1989), para. 8 (expressing the hope 'that all States Parties to both Covenants will arrange [expert] representation in the future').

[160] e.g. *Report on the Third Session*, E/1989/22, Annex V.

in Geneva, whose ability to deal with the issues in sufficient depth has often proven quite limited.

Another essential ingredient is for the State's representatives to be given reasonable notice of at least the principal questions that they will be expected to answer. In order to ensure this the Committee has developed the practice of entrusting to a pre-sessional Working Group, which should meet for one week a minimum of one month before the relevant session, the task of drawing up a detailed list of the major questions to which answers appear to be required.[161] This procedure is still relatively new and is not yet working as well as it might. Time and experience will be required to enable it to be perfected.

But the biggest challenge confronting the Committee is to marshal a sufficient knowledge of the *de facto* situation in a country, to pose precise and carefully targeted questions, and to oblige the representative to respond honestly and unequivocally. All of this is, of course, much easier said than done. The Committee has been prepared to be very tough on occasion with States when it has felt that the situation was either being misrepresented or was clearly unsatisfactory. To date, however, it has been very much of a hostage to the continuing shortcomings of the procedures that it has inherited and under which other committees have also had to labour. The result, all too frequently, has been a most unsatisfactory dialogue when seen from the viewpoint of those whose rights are patently being violated in the country concerned. There is no shortage of examples that might be invoked in this regard but the 'safest' are those of governments that have fallen and where subsequent exposés have revealed terrible suffering or persecution that was barely, if at all, touched upon during the Committee's dialogue with the offending government. The cases of Romania and the German Democratic Republic[162] fall most easily into that category but many others would also warrant a mention.

As noted earlier, the Committee has taken many steps designed to lay the groundwork for a more effective dialogue and these will inexorably begin to bear fruit over time. The principal issue that remains to be resolved, however, is how to achieve a meaningful and frank evaluation of the performance of a reporting State. In the early years of the UN treaty-monitoring system it was argued by some States, and invariably supported by the experts from those States, that the objective of the exercise was to avoid evaluation at all costs. In other words, the constructive dialogue should have no conclusion. But, in the longer term, such an approach is patently unacceptable. The whole exercise

[161] The Working Group's methods of work are described in detail in *Report on the Fifth Session*, E/1991/23 chap. III.

[162] For the Committee's discussions on the GDR, see *Report on the First Session*, E/1987/28, paras. 115–49, and on Romania, see *Report on the Second Session*, E/1988/14, paras. 90–116.

risks becoming a charade if a monitoring committee is not prepared to put itself on the line and draw some conclusions from all the paper and talk that is generated. Those conclusions have to be considered, nuanced, precise, and thoroughly justified but that, surely, is the whole purpose of having an expert committee.

None of the committees has yet dealt satisfactorily with this crucial issue, although several have begun to grapple seriously with it. The Committee on Economic, Social and Cultural Rights has (as of its fifth session) been able to develop a procedure whereby an individual member is given the principal resonsibility for evaluating the dialogue with a given State. He or she then presents a set of 'concluding observations' which other members are free to supplement, or if they wish, to contradict. In practice, a consensus evaluation is emerging more and more frequently and the observations are becoming gradually more precise and more pertinent. Nevertheless, the system has a long way to go before it is perfected.

Conclusion

Most of this Article has been devoted to identifying the measures that will be required in the future to make the Committee on Economic, Social and Cultural Rights effective. It is not particularly useful to recall or restate those measures yet again at this point. Before concluding, however, it is essential to note that the procedural developments which assume such exaggerated importance in an analysis such as this are no more than some of the means by which a single overriding objective might be promoted. That objective is the realization of basic economic, social, and cultural rights throughout the world, and in particular in those States that are parties to the Covenant.

This point warrants emphasis not only so that the significance of the various procedural issues is not overstated but also so that the role of the Committee itself is kept in perspective. Ultimately, as in all international endeavours on behalf of human rights, those efforts will succeed or fail primarily in response to domestic achievements or shortcomings. In other words, a body such as the Committee can make some contribution and might be a useful catalyst, but what ultimately matters is what is done, perhaps in conjunction with those measures, at the national level.

13
The Committee against Torture

ANDREW BYRNES*

Introduction

The Committee against Torture (CAT) is one of the newest of the expert supervisory bodies established pursuant to human rights treaties adopted within the UN system. CAT was set up in accordance with Article 17 of the Convention against Torture and other Cruel, Inhuman or Degrading Treatment or Punishment (the 'Torture Convention'),[1] which entered into force on 26 June 1987. By the end of 1991 the Committee had held seven sessions.[2]

The purpose of this chapter is to examine the structure and functions of the Committee and to analyse its work to date, as well as to identify the challenges and difficulties which the Committee is likely to face in its future work and to suggest some responses to those. The chapter deals in some detail with a number of substantive issues to which the Convention gives rise. In view of the relatively recent commencement of work by the Committee, the manner in which it addresses these issues will determine the scope of its work and the nature of its contribution to the elaboration and implementation of international standards relating to torture and other forms of ill-treatment.

The function of the Committee against Torture is to monitor the implementation by State Parties of the obligations they have assumed under the Torture Convention. With a couple of important exceptions, the Committee's

* I would like to thank Lisa Stearns and the UN Centre for Human Rights, Geneva, in particular Alessio Bruni, for their assistance in helping me obtain UN and other materials for this Chapter. I would also like to thank Philip Alston, Peter Burns, Felice Gaer, and David Stuart for similar assistance, as well as for helpful comments on earlier drafts and in response to my queries.

[1] GA Res.39/46, Annex, A/39/51, 197 (1984), 6 *Eur. Hum. Rts. Rep.* 259, reprinted in United Nations, *Human Rights: A Compilation of International Instruments* (1988), 212, Sales No. E.88.XIV.1 ('Human Rights'), draft reprinted in 23 *Int'l Legal Materials* 1027 (1984), substantive changes noted in 24 *Int'l Legal Materials* 535 (1985), opened for signature 4 Feb. 1985, entered into force 26 June 1987. As of 10 Dec. 1991, there were 64 States Parties to the Convention. E/CN.4/1992/15.

[2] For the reports of the Committee to the General Assembly, see A/43/46 (1988) (first session), A/44/46 (1989) (second session), A/45/44 (1990) (third and fourth sessions), and A/46/44 (1991) (fifth and sixth sessions). For a good overview of the work of the Committee up to the end of its third session, see Dormenval, 'UN Committee against Torture: Practice and Perspectives', 8 *Netherlands Q. Hum. Rts.* 26 (1990).

functions, powers, and procedures are modelled on those of the other treaty bodies, in particular those of the Human Rights Committee.[3]

The Committee has commenced its work at a problematic time. The system of reporting under UN human rights treaties is in difficulties and the resources available within the UN system to support the work of the treaty bodies are inadequate. CAT is likely to fare no better than the other committees in terms of the resources provided to support its work. It will be serviced by the same secretariat, while the financing of the Committee's operations will be largely dependent on the State Parties' continued willingness to fund them, an unsatisfactory and precarious way of ensuring the Committee's effectiveness.

Apart from these systemic and financial problems, the Committee will face other challenges. It will need to minimize unnecessary duplication of the work of existing international and regional bodies and procedures dealing with torture. The Committee will also need to address important substantive issues in interpreting the Convention; the need here will be to ensure a creative approach derived from the Convention that is consistent so far as possible with the jurisprudence and pactice of other bodies involved in the struggle against torture and other ill-treatment. The Committee will also be faced with the challenge not just of dealing with individual communications in an efficient and effective way, but also with the task of developing its *sua sponte* procedure into an effective tool for achieving the goals of the Convention.

A. *Origin and Composition of the Committee*

During the drafting of the Convention, various proposals were put forward for an appropriate monitoring mechanism for the Convention. These included the suggestion that there be no special supervisory procedure at all, supervision by a body appointed by the Chairperson of the Commission on Human Rights, and establishment of a supervisory committee of independent experts.[4] The solution finally adopted evolved from the original Swedish draft which proposed that the Human Rights Committee established under the International Covenant on Civil and Political Rights (the ICCPR) act as the supervisory body for the purposes of the Convention.[5]

This proposal was motivated by a desire to ensure consistency in the interpretation of the overlapping guarantees of freedom from torture or

[3] Established under the *International Covenant on Civil and Political Rights*, GA Res.2200 A (XXI) (1966), 999 UNTS, 171 ('ICCPR').

[4] See generally Rodley, *The Treatment of Prisoners under International Law* (1987), 126–7; Burgers and Danelius, *The United Nations Convention against Torture* (1988), 74–7, 80–9, 96–8.

[5] E/CN.4/1285 (1978), reprinted in Burgers and Danelius, *The United Nations Convention against Torture*, Appendix 6, 203–7, Art. 16–21. Ibid. 74–7, 80–4, 85–9.

cruel, inhuman, or degrading treatment and punishment contained in the Convention and in Article 7 of the ICCPR, as well as to draw on existing expertise in the field and to avoid unnecessary procedural duplication and complexity. Expense was also a factor in the original proposal to have substantial overlap of personnel.[6]

Various objections were raised to this arrangement, mainly on the ground that the Human Rights Committee, as the creation of the ICCPR, could perform only the functions conferred on it by that treaty and could not assume to carry out functions conferred on it by other treaties without an appropriate amendment to the Covenant.[7] While these problems may have ultimately been surmountable, the outcome was the decision to establish the Committee against Torture as a separate body of independent experts to monitor the implementation of the Convention.

The Committee comprises ten experts elected by the States Parties to serve in their personal capacity.[8] CAT is thus, together with the Committee on the Rights of the Child, the smallest of the independent treaty bodies, the size of its membership justified no doubt by the relatively limited scope of the Convention and considerations of expense.

The original aim of ensuring an overlap of personnel with the Human Rights Committee is realized only in so far as Article 17(2) provides that States Parties 'shall bear in mind the usefulness of nominating persons who are also members of the Human Rights Committee ... and who are willing to serve on the Committee against Torture'. The impact of this provision has been limited to date: only one of the ten members of the Committee elected in 1987 was at the time a member of the Human Rights Committee.[9]

The Convention mentions two other factors which are to be taken into consideration by States parties in the election of members of the Committee. The first factor is equitable geographical distribution; this is based on similar provisions in a number of other treaties.[10] As in the case of some of the other

[6] *Report of the Open-Ended Working Group of a Draft Convention against Torture and other Cruel, Inhuman, and Degrading Treatment or Punishment*, E/1982/12/Add.1, 12, para. 57.

[7] This was the view of the Legal Counsel of the United Nations: Burgers and Danelius, *The United Nations Convention against Torture*, 76.

[8] The first meeting of the States Parties to the Convention, at which the first ten members of the Committee were elected, was held in Nov. 1987. The second meeting was held in Nov. 1989. See CAT/SP/SR.1 (1987) and CAT/SP/SR.2 (1989).

[9] Christine Chanet of France. See CAT/SP/3 and Add.1–3 (1987) and CAT/SP/SR.1 (1987). One other nominee who was not elected (Felix Ermacora) had previously served as a member of the Human Rights Committee.

[10] *International Convention on the Elimination of all Forms of Racial Discrimination*, GA Res.2106 A (XX) (1966), 660 UNTS, 195, Art. 8(1); ICCPR, Art. 31(1); and *Convention on the Elimination of all Forms of Discrimination against Women*, GA Res.34/180, Annex (1979), reprinted in *International Instruments*, 112, Art. 17(1). The additional requirement in these treaties that consideration be given 'to the representation of the different forms of civilization as well as of the principal legal systems' does not appear in the Torture Convention. While the difference in wording and likely effect is minimal, in view of the possible divergence of views as to whether

treaty bodies, however, the Committee has a slight over-representation of Western Europeans and a slight under-representation of Africans.[11]

The second factor to be taken into account is the usefulness of the participation of some persons having legal experience.[12] This provision seems curious in view of the domination of the other treaty bodies by persons with a legal background; one might have thought that ensuring the participation of persons with expertise in medicine, health administration, and, law enforcement would have been just as important.[13] The members of the committee who served from 1988 to 1991 were predominantly lawyers: seven of the ten members of the Committee had legal backgrounds, while the other three had backgrounds which included medicine, public health, and communications.[14]

B. *The Scope of the Convention*

I. THE TASK OF SUBSTANTIVE INTERPRETATION

An important part of the work of CAT will be giving substantive content to the concepts of torture and other cruel, inhuman, or degrading treatment or punishment ('other ill-treatment') in the context of the Convention. The prohibition of torture and other ill-treatment appears in many international

various punishments ordained or lawful under Islamic law which would otherwise amount to torture or other ill treatment constitute 'lawful sanctions' within the meaning of Art. 1, the presence of a member with some expertise in relation to Islamic laws and culture would seem highly desirable.

[11] At the first meeting of States Parties in 1987 which elected the members of the Committee, a number of African delegations expressed unhappiness with the fact that only 1 African member was elected to the Committee, while 4 Western members were elected, despite a consensus reached in preliminary consultations that there would be 3 Western European members and 2 African members. CAT/SP/SR.1, para. 49 (1987). The Committee decided to elect a Bureau of 5, so that the principle of geographical distribution could be observed. Nowak, 'First Session of the UN-Committee against Torture', 6 *Netherlands Q. Hum. Rts.* 111 (1988). However, at the second meeting of States Parties in 1989, the meeting agreed that continuity in the composition of the Committee was important in its early stages and should be given primacy over strict geographical distribution. As a result, the 5 retiring members of the Committee were re-elected unopposed. The African and Latin American groups supported this result on the clear understanding that the geographical imbalance would be corrected at future elections. CAT/SP/SR.2, paras. 28–41 (1989). It was to some extent in 1991: CAT/SP/SR.3, paras. 20–40.

[12] Art. 17(1) and (2).

[13] Art. 4(1) of the European Torture Convention, for example, provides that members of the European Committee for the Prevention of Torture are to be chosen 'from among persons of high moral character, known for their competence in the field of human rights or having professional experience in the areas covered by [the] Convention'. *European Convention for the Prevention of Torture and Inhuman or Degrading Treatment or Punishment*, opened for signature 26 Nov. 1987, entered into force 1 Feb. 1989, Council of Europe Doc. H (87) 4, reprinted in 27 *Int'l Legal Materials* 1152 (1988).

[14] See CAT/SP/3 and Add.1–4 (1987), CAT/SP/7 and Add.1 (1989), and CAT/SP/SR.1 (1987) and SR.2 (1989).

treaties and other instruments and the nature and existence of these concepts has been explored in considerable depth.

Although this experience provides a valuable resource for CAT, ultimately the Committee must ground its interpretation of those concepts in the text and history of the Convention. While it is obviously desirable that international bodies concerned with the prevention and punishment of torture not work at cross purposes, it is also important to keep in mind that there is no one, standard definition of torture or other ill-treatment that applies in every context. What 'torture' means for the work of one body will depend on the text, purpose, and history of its enabling instrument, as well as on its own practice and the relevant practice of States.

Thus, while there may be a large measure of substantive overlap, the term 'torture' in the mandate of the Special Rapporteur on Torture does not necessarily have an identical meaning to 'torture' as defined in the Convention. Furthermore, the steps which a State is obliged to take to prevent or punish 'torture' may well vary depending on the source and wording of the obligation. Accordingly, a State may have different obligations under the ICCPR than it does under the Convention. None the less, it is obviously desirable that the Committee should keep its interpretation of these terms as consistent with those adopted by other bodies as is possible.

There are a number of important issues relating to the definition of torture and cruel, inhuman, or degrading treatment that CAT will need to address. They include the difference between torture and cruel, inhuman, or degrading treatment, and the extent to which the acts of private individuals can amount to torture or other ill-treatment, as well as other issues.[15]

(a) *The Distinction between Torture and Cruel, Inhuman, or Degrading Punishment*

While there has been much discussion in academic commentary and a number of important international cases of the distinction between 'torture' and 'cruel, inhuman, or degrading treatment or punishment', where it appears in various international instruments, the juridical consequences of classifying actions as one or the other have been relatively unimportant.[16] In the case of the Torture Convention, the distinction does have important legal con-

[15] For example, the issue of lawful sanctions and the limits the Convention places on the types of sanctions that can be inflicted under national law, and whether particular forms of human rights violations such as 'disappearances', extra-judicial executions, incommunicado detention, and other abuses necessarily or ever amount to torture or other ill-treatment within the meaning of the Convention. See generally Lerner, 'The UN Convention on Torture', 16 *Israel Y B Hum. Rts.* 130–4 (1986); Tardu, 'The United Nations Convention against Torture and other Cruel, Inhuman or Degrading Treatment or Punishment', 56 *Nordic J. Int'l L.* 307–8 (1987), and Boulesbaa, 'The Nature of the Obligations Incurred by States under Article 2 of the UN Convention Against Torture', 12 *Hum. Rts. Q.* 53 (1990).

[16] Tardu, 'The United Nations Convention against Torture', 309–11; Villán Durán, 'La Convención contra la tortura y su contribución a la definición del derecho a la integridad física y moral en el derecho internacional', 37 *Rev. Española de Derecho Int'l* 392–3 (1985).

sequences, affecting both the extent of the obligations undertaken by States Parties and the availability of the various procedures. Thus, it will be necessary for the Committee to distinguish in particular cases between conduct which amounts to torture and that which does not fall within that concept but which none the less amounts to 'cruel, inhuman, or degrading treatment or punishment'.

The difference affects in the first place the extent of obligations assumed by States Parties. States Parties assume a general obligation to take steps to prevent both torture and cruel, inhuman, or degrading treatment or punishment in territory under their jurisdiction and a number of the specific obligations contained in the Convention apply to both categories of behaviour.[17] However, a number of important obligations relate only to torture, at least as far as their express language is concerned.[18]

In addition to differences in substantive obligations, the distinction is also important in the context of the initiation of the various investigative procedures upon which the Committee is empowered to embark. The investigative procedure established by Article 20 can only be invoked in a case where there are indications that *torture* is being systematically practised. Similarly, the distinction may have to be drawn when examining individual communications.[19] The Committee may also need to distinguish between the two categories under the interstate procedure (if it is ever used), though any 'determination' by the Committee might well be purely informal.

In view of the difficulty that other bodies have experienced in formulating a meaningful distinction between torture and other ill-treatment[20] and the need to apply the terms in the context of individual cases, it is likely and desirable that CAT will deal with the issue on a case-by-case basis, until it has accumulated enough experience to be in a position to make a more general pronouncement about the sorts of actions that fall into one category or another.

[17] Art. 10 (education and training of law enforcement and prison personnel), Art. 11 (review of interrogation procedures and custody arrangements), Art. 12 (duty to investigate where there are grounds to believe torture or other ill treatment may have occurred), Art. 13 (duty to investigate individual complaints and protection against retaliation).

[18] Art. 3 (obligation not to return or expel person to country where s/he faces the risk of torture), Art. 4 (to criminalize acts of torture with appropriately severe punishments), Art. 5 (establishment of 'universal jurisdiction' over torturers), Art. 6 (obligation to take into custody alleged torturers), Art. 7 (obligation to extradite or try alleged torturers), Art. 8 (obligation to ensure that extradition is available for torture), Art. 9 (provision of assistance in proceedings relating to torture), and Art. 14 (obligation to provide legal remedies including compensation).

[19] For example, an individual may complain that s/he had been subjected to torture, but has received no compensation as required by Art. 14. It would be open to the State Party concerned to argue that the actions complained of amounted only to cruel, inhuman, and degrading treatment or punishment and that Art. 16 did not require compensation to be paid in the circumstances of the case.

[20] See Rodley, *The Treatment of Prisoners*, 71–95; Villán Durán, 'La Convención', 386–95.

II. THE SCOPE OF THE DEFINITION OF TORTURE AND OTHER ILL-TREATMENT

Apart from the difficulty of distinguishing between torture and other ill-treatment, the definitions of torture and other ill-treatment contained in the Convention[21] give rise to a number of problems. Two issues of particular importance will need to be dealt with by the Committee. The first is whether the Convention definition is confined to the protection of 'detainees', narrowly or broadly defined, from maltreatment, or whether the prospective victims of such maltreatment can be more broadly defined. The second is determining under what circumstances the acts of private individuals can amount to torture or other ill-treatment. These issues overlap to some extent.

(*a*) *Protection of Detainees*

It is clear from the text and history of the Convention that it is primarily intended to protect 'detainees', that is, persons who are serving prison sentences in State institutions or who are in the lawful or unlawful custody of law enforcement or security forces pending trial or for some other purpose.[22] Maltreatment[23] of such persons by a State official is plainly conduct covered by Articles 1 and 16.

The prohibition of maltreatment presumably also applies to persons who, while not prisoners or in detention for some law enforcement purpose, are confined in State institutions. Persons who are compulsorily confined in State mental institutions would thus seem to come within the scope of the protection afforded by the Convention.[24]

A more difficult question is whether the protection afforded by the Convention extends beyond detention in State institutions to include maltreatment which occurs in other contexts of State control or supervision. Does the Convention apply, for example, to the treatment of students by teachers in public schools?[25]

A number of commentators, while conceding that the definitions are not

[21] Art. 1 provides that torture means 'any act by which severe pain or suffering, whether physical or mental, is intentionally inflicted on a person [for specified purposes, not exhaustive] . . . when such pain or suffering is inflicted *by or at the instigation of or with the consent or acquiescence of a public official or other person acting in an official capacity*' (emphasis added).

[22] Burgers and Danelius, *The United Nations Convention against Torture*, 120–1.

[23] The term 'maltreatment' is used here to encompass conduct of such severity that it would qualify as either torture or other ill-treatment had it been directly carried out by State officials.

[24] The Human Rights Committee has interpreted the prohibition of torture, and other ill-treatment contained in Art. 7, ICCPR as protecting 'not only persons arrested or imprisoned, but also pupils in educational and medical institutions'. *Report of the Human Rigths Committee in 1982*, A/37/40 (1982), Annex V (General comment 7 (16), para. 2). See also CAT/C/SR.26, para. 25 (1989) (France).

[25] *Campbell & Cousans* v. *United Kingdom*, Ser. A, No. 48, 4 *Eur. Hum. Rts. Rep.* 293, 67 *Int'l L. Rep.* 480 (Eur. Ct. Hum. Rts. 1982).

restricted to maltreatment of individuals in State custody of one form or another, have expressed the view that the phrase should be read relatively narrowly. They point out that the primary motivation of the Convention was the elimination and punishment of 'the systematic use of torture by governments as a means of crushing political opposition';[26] an approach which suggests that the Convention was not intended to cover categories of conduct that do not fall within the traditional categories of torture.

None the less, the text of the Convention does not expressly limit its protection against State maltreatment only to those in custody and the Committee should consider whether there are other forms of public maltreatment that it must examine. Examples of actions which might not have been traditionally brought within the rubric of torture or other ill treatment would include genital mutilation carried out in State-run or State-licensed hospitals, sexual harassment by public officials of public employees or others, and the mistreatment of children by social workers. Although most States parties have so far taken a more traditional approach in selecting the topics covered in their reports to the Committee, a number of States Parties have indicated that a broader view might be appropriate by incorporating in their reports descriptions of laws and measures which prevent or punish acts of this sort.[27]

The experience of other treaty bodies has shown that the Committee does not have to be forever shackled by a narrow interpretation of its mandate, even if that was how it was conceived by the drafters of the Convention. By adopting a creative approach to the interpretation of the Convention and its powers, the Committee will be able to ensure that its mandate evolves to take account of changing circumstances and perceptions of the nature and extent of torture and other ill-treatment. It is to be hoped that the Committee will see its role in these terms.

(b) The Application to a State's Response to the Acts of Private Persons

An even more difficult issue is the extent to which the Convention's definition covers maltreatment of private individuals by other private individuals. The text of the Convention does not require that a State official directly inflict the ill-treatment for it to be characterized as torture or other ill-treatment; it is sufficient if the maltreatment is carried out 'at the instigation of' or 'with the consent or acquiescence of' a public official. This definition, requiring some sort of official complicity, was the compromise reached between those who proposed that the definition of torture apply to all acts of torture whether carried out by government officials or private individuals and those who

[26] Tardu, 'The United Nations Convention against Torture', 306.

[27] See e.g. Canada's initial report, CAT/C/5/Add.15, paras. 53, 64–8 (1989) (listing measures to prevent sexual harassment in public employment, abuse of children by teachers, social workers, and other public officials in positions of trust, treatment of victims of crime and individuals confined in mental institutions). Cf. CAT/C/SR.31, para. 42 (GDR).

considered that the national criminal justice system was the appropriate procedure for dealing with the acts of private individuals.[28]

Recognizing conduct which is performed 'at the instigation of' a public official does not cause major conceptual problems, though it may give rise to problems of proof. It would certainly cover acts such as the beating of one prisoner by other prisoners at the urging of a prison official. However, the words are also capable of applying to actions directed against persons who are not under the custody or control of State officials. A private individual, employed or used by a State official to inflict maltreatment on other private individuals who are not detainees or patients, would seem to be capable of committing 'torture' within the meaning of Article 1 (assuming the extent of his involvement does not render him 'a person acting in an official capacity').

A fairly direct relationship between the request or desire of the State official and the infliction of torture by the private individual would seem to be required by the use of the word 'instigation'. However, the acts of private individuals may also amount to torture or other ill-treatment if they are of sufficient severity and are carried out 'with the consent or acquiescence' of a public official. The definition adopted is broader than the one contained in the 1975 UN Declaration against Torture[29] which limits torture to acts carried out by State officials or at the instigation of a public official.[30] How far does this definition extend? It would certainly seem to push the Convention beyond being restricted primarily to protecting detainees or patients in State institutions, but what sort of acts are covered and what level of State knowledge and ability to prevent their occurrence is necessary before it can be said that the acts have been done with the consent or acquiescence of the State?

In this context commentators have argued that the purpose of the Convention was limited and have pointed out that acts inflicted by one private individual on another would normally be expected to be dealt with through the national criminal justice system.[31] However, where private individuals or groups have the explicit or tacit support or encouragement of a government in any actions taken to suppress governmental opponents, it is not likely that the criminal justice system will provide an adequate remedy. As a result, it seems to be accepted that the definition of torture includes cases in which 'public officials . . . turn a blind eye to atrocities committed against opponents of the

[28] See E/1979/36, paras. 17–18.

[29] *Declaration on the Protection of All Persons from Being Subjected to Torture, and Other Cruel, Inhuman or Degrading Treatment or Punishment*, Art. 1, GA Res.3452 (XXX) (1975), reprinted in *International Instruments*, 209.

[30] The Inter-American Convention to Prevent and Punish Torture contains a similar definition to that of the Declaration, but it also applies to the case of a public official who, 'being able to prevent [the use of torture], fails to do so', which may be broader than the definition of the Declaration. OAS Treaty Series, No. 67, OEA/Ser.A/42 (1986), Art. 3(a), 25 *Int'l Legal Materials* 519.

[31] See E/1979/36, paras. 17–18; Burgers and Danelius, *The United Nations Convention against Torture*, 119–20.

government in power by unofficial groups',[32] the so-called 'death squads' and paramilitary or vigilante groups.[33] While there may be difficulties in demonstrating the requisite level of knowledge of such conduct, of the ability to prevent it, or of unwillingness to punish such conduct necessary to show State 'acquiescence', it would seem that these types of activity fall within the scope of the Convention's definition. It is, however, far from clear which other acts of private individuals involve the acquiescence of the State to a degree sufficient to bring them within the Convention's definition. It can be argued that many, if not most, acts committed by one individual against another take place with the acquiescence of the State, if the State has failed to prevent an act knowing of the likelihood of its occurrence, has no law penalizing a particular action, or does not enforce its law.

The failure of a State to prevent or to respond to acts of torture or other ill-treatment inflicted by one private individual on another may constitute a breach of the ICCPR.[34] However, it is by no means clear that the obligations imposed by the Convention extend to the prevention, punishment, and remedying of as broad a range of private actions as do the obligations imposed by the ICCPR. Ultimately, it is a question of interpreting two different but overlapping treaties, each of which has to be construed in the light of its own text, purpose, and history.

It seems improbable that a very broad interpretation of the definition was intended by the drafters of the Convention and unlikely that the Committee will take a radically expansive approach in interpreting it.[35] None the less, the Committee should eschew an unduly narrow approach and should not be reluctant to bring within its purview instances of private torture or ill treatment in which State failure to take preventive, punitive, or remedial action is particularly egregious.

In this regard the Committee should address itself not just to the traditional paradigms of torture and other ill-treatment by State law enforcement or security forces, or by paramilitary groups of uncertain status. It should also explore instances in which private organizations with some form of State licence or approval (such as private medical institutions) engage in activities in circumstances in which torture or other ill-treatment is likely to occur.[36]

[32] Rodley, *The Treatment of Prisoners*, 91.

[33] Tardu, 'The United Nations Convention against Torture', 306.

[34] The definition contained in the Convention does not seem to go as far as do the corresponding obligations under Arts. 1 and 7, ICCPR to 'ensure' the enjoyment of the right not to be subjected to torture or other ill treatment, as that obligation has been interpreted by the Human Rights Committee. See in particular General comment 7 (16), n. 24, above.

[35] For example, the presence of the obligations to exercise universal jurisdiction for torture may lead the Committee to interpret the scope of the definitions narrowly.

[36] See e.g. Argentina's initial report, CAT/C/5/Add.12 (1989), paras. 15 and 19 (accepting that acts of private individuals can constitute torture or other ill-treatment).

(c) *Awareness of and Concern with the Position of Women*

One important criticism that has been levelled at a number of the treaty bodies is their alleged neglect of women's experiences and of types of violations which may have a specific impact on women. Critics have claimed that some of the treaty bodies have not been sufficiently sensitive to sex and gender in defining and identifying human rights violations. They have also argued that the conceptual framework within which much of the examination takes place renders invisible many of the objective violations that women suffer, because it focuses mainly on direct violations by the State or State agents and leaves out of account the many violations that women suffer at the hands of men in the private sphere.

To date the Committee has not demonstrated any great interest in identifying the role that sex and gender may play in the infliction of torture and other ill-treatment.[37] CAT must be responsive to these criticisms of the treaty bodies in so far as it is possible within the framework laid down by the Convention. Unfortunately, the conceptual framework of the Convention is based on a public/private distinction which excludes from consideration many of the violations suffered by women at the hands of private individuals which, if inflicted by public officials, would come within the scope of the Convention.

None the less, even within the more traditional framework, there are a number of steps the Committee needs to take. It must seek sex-specific information, for example, information about the numbers of male and female prisoners and detainees, the reasons for their detention, and the conditions under which they are being held. CAT must show that it realizes that conditions of interrogation may pose quite different threats to women than to men or that there are some types of violation that may asymmetrically affect women. The Committee must also seek to ascertain whether there are particular forms of torture or other ill-treatment which are directed mainly against women or which have a more severe impact on women than on men.[38]

To the extent that it will be relying on NGOs to provide this sort of information, CAT must make an effort to involve not only the well-established mainstream NGOs in its work, but also women's groups which may have considerably more detailed information of this sort.

Secondly, the Committee must adopt a liberal approach when interpreting the provisions of the Convention to ensure that experiences of torture or of other ill-treatment which affect women more than men are not neglected.

[37] For example, in its consideration of the report of Senegal, CAT/C/SR.44–5 (1990), the Committee did not raise the issue of genital mutilation, although it is well known that such practices are widespread in that country (WIN News Autumn 1989), 15/4, 29–30).

[38] See *Cyprus* v. *Turkey*, 4 *Eur. Hum. Rts. Rep.* 482, 62 *Int'l. L. Rep.* 4, paras. 358–74 (Eur. Commission Hum. Rts. 1976) (rape by Turkish soldiers constituted inhuman treatment under Art. 3 of the European Convention).

This would involve interpreting the Convention as applying not only to those who are held in some form of detention but to anyone subjected to maltreatment at the hands of government officials. Examples of the types of issues that could be raised have been mentioned above.[39]

Finally, to the extent that the Committee is prepared to adopt a broader view of what actions take place 'with the consent or acquiescence of a public official', it may be able to address various private violations against women to which the State has not responded adequately in a preventive or punitive manner.

(*d*) *The Relevance of other International Standards to the Work of the Committee*

The Convention is one of many international instruments that seek to eradicate torture, punish its perpetrators, and provide remedies for victims of torture. A number of instruments lay down detailed standards in relation to matters covered relatively briefly in the Articles of the Convention. Of particular importance are the Standard Minimum Rules for the Treatment of Prisoners,[40] the Code of Conduct for Law-Enforcement Officials,[41] the Principles of Medical Ethics,[42] and the Body of Principles for the Protection of all Persons under any Form of Detention or Imprisonment.[43] Each of these provides detailed guidance on particular issues dealt with by the Convention and none of them appears to conflict with the norms laid down by it.

There are a number of ways the Committee may wish to use these instruments. The first is to use these standards as the basis for questions and recommendations when examining the reports of individual States Parties. Indeed, a number of governments have already referred to some of these instruments in their reports to the Committee.[44] The Committee should also take full account of these standards in its consideration of complaints and in its investigations under Article 20. Finally, if the Committee decides to formulate general comments relating to individual articles of the Convention, it should reflect the relevant standards in those comments.

[39] For example, genital mutilation carried out in State-run or State-sponsored hospitals or clinics, sexual harassment of women by public officials, and the treatment of women victims or survivors of crimes by law enforcement officials and the justice system.

[40] *First United Nations Congress on the Prevention of Crime and the Treatment of Offenders: Report by the Secretariat*, UN Sales No. 1956.IV.4, Annex I.A, approved by ESC Res.663 C (XXIV), E/3048 (1957), and amended by ESC Res.2076 (LXII), E/5988 (1977), reprinted in *International Instruments*, 190.

[41] GA Res.34/169, Annex (1980), reprinted in *International Instruments*, 226.

[42] Principles of Medical Ethics Relevant to the Role of Health Personnel, particularly Physicians, in the Protection of Prisoners and Detainees against Torture and other Cruel, Inhuman, or Degrading Treatment or Punishment, adopted by GA Res.37/194 (1982), reprinted ibid. 233.

[43] GA Res.43/173 (1988), Annex.

[44] See e.g. the initial reports of Mexico, CAT/C/5/Add.7, para. 67 (1989) and Canada, CAT/C/5/Add.15, para. 12 (1989).

C. *Institutional Difficulties*

I. FINANCES

The Convention adopts a system for financing the operations of the Committee which is unsatisfactory and which has the potential to undermine the Committee's performance of its functions. Articles 17(7) and 18(5) provide that the States Parties are responsible for both the expenses of Committee members in the performance of their Committee duties and for expenses connected with the meetings of the Committee, including the cost of staff and facilities provided by the United Nations in servicing the Committee. This arrangement represents a departure in important respects from the financial arrangements made for most of the other committees.[45] With one exception of little practical importance,[46] the expenses of the Human Rights Committee (including its work under the Optional Protocol), CEDAW, and the ESCRC are paid out of the UN budget: members receive emoluments from the United Nations, which also provides the necessary servicing with no requirement that States Parties reimburse the Organization.

The model for the Torture Convention was the Racial Discrimination Convention, Article 8(6) of which provides that States Parties are responsible for the expenses of Committee members while in performance of their duties. Even in the case of CERD, however, the costs of secretariat servicing are covered out of the regular UN budget; the Torture Convention moves beyond that model. The provision, which did not appear in the original Swedish draft, was introduced at the insistence of the United States,[47] presumably as part of efforts to reduce overall UN spending.

Although the recent UN financial crisis has shown that financing the activities of the treaty bodies out of the regular UN budget has its drawbacks, the method adopted in the Convention is an even less secure and satisfactory arrangement from the Committee's point of view. Apart from possibly deterring some States from becoming parties to the Convention because of the financial implications,[48] the recent experience of CERD has shown the dis-

[45] 'Methods Applied under Different Human Rights Instruments as Regards their Financial Implications, Note by the Secretary-General', E/1988/85.

[46] Under the interstate complaints procedure under Art. 41, ICCPR, the expenses of any conciliation commission appointed are to be borne by the States Parties concerned (ICCPR, Art. 42). A similar provision is made by Art. 12 of the Race Convention in relation to any conciliation commission appointed under that Article. Neither of these procedures has yet been invoked.

[47] See E/CN.4/1983/63, para. 45; E/CN.4/1984/72, paras. 46–8; Nowak, 'The Implementation Functions of the Committee against Torture', in Nowak *et al.* (eds.), *Fortschritt im Bewußtsein der Grund und Menschenrechte: Festschrift für Felix Ermacora* (1988), 495.

[48] The fear related mainly to less affluent States (E/CN.4/1983/63, para. 47), but there have been suggestions that even some developed countries have been slow to ratify for this reason. Zoller, 'Second Session of the Committee against Torture', 7 *Netherlands Q. Hum. Rts.* 253 (1989).

ruptive effect that the failure by States Parties to pay their assessed contributions can have on a committee's activities.[49] To exist in a state of uncertainty as to whether sufficient funds will be received in time to permit the holding of its next scheduled session does little to assist the Committee in carrying out the functions it has been assigned under the Convention.[50]

To date adequate funds have been received from States Parties sufficiently in advance for the Committee to hold its scheduled sessions.[51] However, this apparently healthy financial situation is less secure than it seems: by the third States Parties' meeting in 1991, twenty-two of the assessed States Parties were in arrears with their contributions.[52] Solvency is due in large measure to the fact that a number of States had contributed more than their finally assessed amounts for the period. As the Committee moves to a regular cycle of two sessions a year (with perhaps a working group as well) and its workload under the complaint procedures increases, so will its operating costs. The experience of CERD is a distressing one and it would seem that the Committee would be much better served if its operations were to be funded out of the regular UN budget,[53] which now looks increasingly likely.

The financial security of the Committee (and thereby its efficacy) also came under attack from another direction early in the Committee's existence. When the German Democratic Republic ratified the Convention in 1987, it made a declaration to the effect that it would bear its share only of those expenses 'arising from activities under the competence of the Committee as recognized by the [GDR]'[54] As the GDR had not made a declaration under either Article 21 or 22 and had opted out of the Article 20 procedure, when it ratified the Convention, it was declaring its intention to pay its share only of the expenses incurred by the Committee in its work of reviewing reports.[55]

The declaration seemed inconsistent with the express terms of the Convention, certainly violated its spirit, and was probably incompatible with the object and purpose of the Convention.[56] If other States had followed the GDR's

[49] 'Chaos Threatens UN Treaties', 12 (2) *Hum. Rts. Internet Reporter* 106–7 (1988).

[50] At the first meeting of States Parties, it was decided that States Parties would be liable to contribute on the basis of the UN scale of assessment with a maximum contribution by any one State of 25% in any given year, CAT/SP/SR.1, paras. 54–5 (1987) and CAT/SP/4 (1987), and that meetings would not take place until sufficient funds had been collected from States Parties. Burgers and Danelius, *The United Nations Convention against Torture*, 112–13.

[51] See Dormenval, 'UN Committee against Torture', 28–9.

[52] See CAT/SP/11 (1991), and CAT/SP/SR.2, para. 47 (1989).

[53] See generally A/44/668 (1989).

[54] CAT/C/2, 7 (1988).

[55] See Nowak, 'The Implementation Functions', 495; Burgers and Danelius, *The United Nations Convention against Torture*, 110; Gaer, 'Human Rights at the United Nations: Treaties to Enforce Human Rights', 4 *In Brief* 2–3 (1988).

[56] For a detailed discussion of the reservation of the GDR concluding that it is incompatible with the object and purpose of the Convention, see Gornig and Ney, 'Die Erklärungen der DDR zur UN-Anti-Folterkonvention aus völkerrechtlicher Sicht', 43 *Juristenzeitung* 1048 (1988).

lead, the Committee's ability to function effectively may have been severely undermined.

Seventeen States Parties objected to this declaration[57] and the GDR withdrew it in September 1990 (shortly before its accession to the Federal Republic of Germany) at the same time as it accepted the competence of the Committee under Articles 20, 21, and 22.[58] In view of the strong reaction to the GDR's declaration, it seems unlikely that any other State will make a similar declaration.[59]

II. MONITORING PROCEDURES

(*a*) *The Procedures*

The Convention establishes four procedures[60] for the monitoring of the implementation of the Convention by States Parties to it.[61] As under the other treaties, States are obliged to report to the Committee on the measures they have adopted to implement the Convention. This reporting procedure is the only compulsory form of monitoring to which States Parties are subject. The Convention also establishes procedures for the consideration by the Committee of complaints by individuals against States Parties alleging violations of the Convention and of complaints by one State Party against another.

[57] See CAT/SP/SR.1, paras. 56–9 (1987) and the objections in CAT/C/2/Rev.1 (1991).

[58] CAT/C/2/Rev.1 (1991), para. 13. The GDR itself appeared to accept the obligation to pay its full contribution as assessed by the meetings of States Parties see CAT/SP/8 (1989) and CAT/SP/SR.2 (1989), paras. 42–53. For its earlier stance, see CAT/SP/SR.1 (1987), para. 59.

[59] Reservations to substantive provisions have also drawn objections from other States Parties. For example, the reservation entered by Chile to article 2(3) (obedience to orders no defence in case of torture) and article 3 (CAT/C/2/Rev.1, pp. 6–7) drew objections from 20 States Parties and was subsequently withdrawn (CAT/C/2/Rev.1 (1991), para. 13). The Federal Republic of Germany entered a reservation to Article 3 which stated that the article 'prohibits the transfer of a person directly to a State where this person is exposed to a concrete danger of being subjected to torture' and that German domestic law was consistent with the Convention in this regard: ibid. para. 9. Although the declaration does not refer to the similar obligation under Article 16, it appears to have been a response to the decision of the European Court of Human Rights in *Soering* v. *U.K.*, Judgment of 7 July 1989, Series A, No. 161, (1989) 11 *Eur. Hum. Rts. Rep*. 439, 28 *Int'l Leg. Mat.* 1063. See generally, and in relation to the impact on the US proposals to ratify the Convention: Lillich, 'The Soering Case', (1991) 85 *Am. J. Int'l L.* 128, in particular at pp. 145–9.

[60] Article 30 of the Convention also provides for reference to arbitration of disputes between two States Parties over the interpretation or application of the Convention, which cannot be resolved by negotiation. If the arbitration cannot be organized within 6 months, any one of the States Parties concerned may refer the dispute to the International Court of Justice. However, the Convention provides that reservations to this article may be made. As of 1 Jan. 1991, 8 States Parties maintained reservations (Afghanistan, Bulgaria, Chile, China, Czechoslovakia, France, Panama, and Turkey), while 6 other States Parties had withdrawn reservations they had earlier entered (Byelorussain SSR, GDR, Guatemala, Hungary, Ukrainian SSR, USSR): CAT/C/2/Rev.1 (1991).

[61] For a good discussion of the procedures, see Donnelly, 'The Emerging International Regime against Torture', 33 *Netherlands. Int'l. L. Rev.* 1 (1986).

Both of these communication procedures are optional.[62] All these procedures are based on similar procedures of the other human rights treaty bodies.

The fourth procedure represents an innovation in the context of supervision by the treaty bodies, although it does have other international analogues. The Convention confers on the Committee the power to investigate, on its own initiative, cases in which it receives 'reliable information which appears to it to contain well-founded indications that torture is being systematically practised in the territory of a State Party'.[63] It, too, is optional, but the Convention provides that a State Party must 'opt out' of the provision if it does not wish to be bound by it.[64]

(*b*) *The role of NGOs*

The Convention and the rules of procedure of the Committee provide for a greater degree of formal involvement by NGOs in the work of the Committee than in the case of any other committee, although much NGO input into other committees occurs on an informal basis. Provision is made for the Committee to invite NGOs to furnish it with relevant information under all its procedures;[65] it can be expected that NGO information will have particular prominence in the Article 20 procedure as well as in the reporting procedure. So far, NGOs have shown relatively limited interest in the Committee's sessions.[66] However, it is early days yet and, in view of the fact that many NGOs have been prominent in the struggle against torture, it can be expected that they will eventually provide considerable input into the work of the Committee.[67]

(*c*) *Reporting Procedure (Article 19)*

The reporting procedure is the only mandatory part of the Convention's monitoring procedure. Under Article 19 each State Party undertakes to submit to the Committee within one year after the entry into force of the Convention for that State a report on the measures it has taken to carry out its

[62] The obligation accepted under Art. 21 is also subject to a condition of reciprocity. Only those States which have themselves accepted the Art. 21 procedure can lodge communications against other States Parties which have done so: Art. 21(1).

[63] Art. 20(1).

[64] Art. 28.

[65] See CAT *Rules of Procedure*, CAT/C/3/Rev.1 (1989), Rule 62 (a consolidated and renumbered version of the rules adopted at the first and second sessions, which appear in *Report of the Committee against Torture in 1988*, A/43/46 (1988), Annex III, and in *Report of the Committee against Torture in 1988*, A/44/46 (1989), Annex IV). However, the Committee did not adopt a proposal which would have permitted NGOs to address the Committee in public session subject to its approval. See CAT/C/SR.2 (1988), paras. 82–8; CAT/C/SR.5 (1988), paras. 45–59; and CAT/C/SR.6 (1988), paras. 2–4.

[66] Dormenval, 'UN Committee against Torture', 44.

[67] At the Committee's fourth session, a large amount of material was supplied to the Comittee on individual countries, in particular on China. Amnesty International and other organizations also supply background country material to the Committee on a regular basis.

obligations under the Convention. Each State Party is then required to submit a supplementary report every four years on any new measures it has taken, as well as to provide any other reports the Committee requests.[68]

The Committee has adopted guidelines which indicate to States Parties the information it wishes to see included in the report.[69] *Mutatis mutandis*, the guidelines for initial reports are much the same as those of the Human Rights Committee.[70] They request that reports be divided into two parts, the first a general section outlining the constitutional and legal structure within which the Convention is to be implemented, the second providing detailed information about the steps taken to implement individual Articles of the Convention, including the difficulties the State has experienced in implementing the Convention and providing details of specific cases and situations where the guarantees have been enforced. The guidelines for periodic reports ask for information to be provided on new developments since the last report, in particular legislative, institutional or administrative changes, relevant case law and details of complaints of torture and other ill treatment and their outcome, as well as information requested by the Committee at the consideration of the previous report.

The Committee will doubtless be faced with many of the problems that have confronted the other bodies: late submission of reports, inadequate reports, and refusal to provide promised additional information. Some of these are systemic problems and will have to be dealt with in conjunction with the efforts of the other treaty bodies; others may be specific to the Convention. Forewarned is forearmed, however, and if the Committee draws on the experience of the other committees, it may be able to avoid at least some of the problems they have encountered.

Already a number of States are overdue with their reports. By 16 November 1991, of the fifty-four reports due for submission since 1988, sixteen were overdue with about half being more than a year overdue.[71] While one may partly attribute this lack of punctuality to a lack of familiarity with the Committee's work and its requirements, the experience of other committees would not justify a prediction that the situation will improve dramatically in the future.

[68] Although the term used is 'supplementary reports' rather than 'periodic reports', in practice it is unlikely that the difference will have any great practical impact. Nowak, 'The Implementation Functions', 497.

[69] The guidelines for initial reports have been revised twice. The latest version appears at A/46/44 (1991), Annex VII (which replaced earlier versions in CAT/C/4/Rev.1 (1989) and A/43/46 (1988), Annex IV. The Committee has also adopted the consolidated guidelines proposed by the meeting of Chairpersons for the initial parts of reports (A/46/44 (1991), Annex VI). These two sets of guidelines together set out the information which should be made available to the Committee in initial reports. The guidelines for second and subsequent reports appear at A/46/44 (1991), Annex VIII.

[70] See *Report of the Human Rights Committee*, A/32/44 (1977), Annex IV (initial reports) and A/36/40 (1981), Annex VI.

[71] A/46/44 (1991), Annex III and CAT/C/SR.88 (1991), paras. 23–31.

One of the major organizational challenges the Committee will face will be getting through its work in the time available. Currently, the Committee plans to hold two regular sessions of two weeks each annually,[72] assuming that sufficient funds are available for these sessions. The work of the Committee under Article 19 will continue to increase, and it is likely that the Article 20 and Article 22 procedures will add considerably to the Committee's workload. It is difficult to predict whether the four weeks annually will be sufficient for the Committee's work; it certainly should be if the Committee makes judicious use of working groups and rapporteurs to get through its work,[73] and if members are willing to deal with a certain amount of work between sessions. To date the Committee has worked very efficiently[74] and has no backlog of reports after its first seven sessions. Indeed, it could almost be said to have had time to spare compared with the time limitations faced by the Committee on the Elimination of Discrimination against Women[75]—it has even been able to consider the additional reports it has requested from States Parties. It is difficult to predict the likely increase in the Committee's workload, but other committees have generally faced a fairly steady increase the longer they have been in existence. While CAT is not at present faced with any significant time constraints, that may change in the future as more States become parties to the Convention and greater use is made of the communications procedures.

(i) *Reports Submitted to Date*[76] It would be excessively optimistic to expect that the standard of reports submitted to CAT would necessarily be higher than those submitted to the other treaty bodies. On the other hand, the scope of the Convention is more limited than that of the other human rights treaties, a fact which presumably would make it easier to prepare a detailed and thorough report. In particular, a number of articles of the Convention call primarily for detailed information about legal provisions (e.g. extradition).

On the whole, the reports submitted to CAT follow the pattern of those submitted to other treaty bodies, varying considerably in quality and length, although there are a number of extremely good reports among them. Reports submitted to date have consisted largely of descriptions of legal provisions

[72] CAT *Rules of Procedure*, n. 65, above, Rule 2(1).

[73] At its fourth Session the Committee decided to appoint a rapporteur for each report received to review the report and prepare questions for the State Party. A/45/44 (1990), para. 14.

[74] See Dormenval, 'UN Committee against Torture', 35–6.

[75] See Byrnes, 'The "Other" Human Rights Treaty Body: The Work of the Committee on the Elimination of Discrimination against Women', 14 *Yale J. Int'l L.* 58–9 (1989).

[76] This description is based on the following reports to CAT: CAT/C/5/Add.1–16. These were the reports of Sweden (Add.1), France (Add.2), Norway (Add.3), Denmark (Add.4), Egypt (Add.5), Philippines (Add.6 and Add.18), Mexico (Add.7), Senegal (Add.8), Hungary (Add.9), Austria (Add.10), USSR (Add.11), Argentina (Add.12), German Democratic Republic (Add.13), Byelorussian SSR (Add.14), Canada (Add.15), Cameroon (Add.16), Switzerland (Add.17), Ukrainian SSR (Add.20); and CAT/C/7/Add.1–5, Colombia (Add.1), Chile (Add.2), Tunisia (Add.3), Czechoslovakia (Add.4), and China (Add.5).

which make acts of torture unlawful[77] and of the steps taken to provide preventive education or to ensure remedies for those who are the victims of torture. These descriptions have varied from the perfunctory[78] to the detailed and informative.[79]

What has been lacking is information about the number of persons detained in individual countries, the categories of detainees, and the conditions under which they are held. There has also been relatively little information provided about the extent of torture and other ill-treatment in the territory of the States nor about the frequency of allegations that persons have been subjected to it. In some cases, the existence of torture or allegations of it are denied or ignored in cases where a country has been accused by an organization such as Amnesty International of engaging in acts which would constitute torture or cruel, inhuman, or degrading treatment within the meaning of the Convention.[80]

Such reticence on the part of governments is, of course, not unusual, but it underlines the important role that NGOs will have in the context of the work of the Committee. The Committee has recognized this, too, by making formal provision for the involvement of NGOs in its work. No doubt NGO information will be provided to CAT in abundance, as there is already a well-established network of organizations with considerable experience in the fight against torture.

(ii) *CAT's Consideration of Reports* The Committee has followed the practice of the other treaty bodies in its consideration of States Parties' reports. It has embraced the notion of a constructive dialogue with the representatives of States.[81] The Committee invites a representative of each State to give a brief introduction to its report, followed by questions from members of the Committee. The representative returns at a subsequent meeting to provide information in response to those questions, followed in some cases by further comments by individual members of the Committee.[82] The Committee may then or subsequently formulate any general comments it considers appropriate on the report of each State Party.

The questioning of the Committee has so far been reasonably incisive and

[77] One common feature has been States claiming that they have criminalized acts of torture by pointing to a large number of criminal statutes which would apply to many acts of torture. However, in cases in which the Convention's definition has not been incorporated in national law, the coverage of existing criminal laws may not be adequate.

[78] See e.g. the initial report of Egypt, CAT/C/5/Add.5 (1988).

[79] See e.g. the initial report of Canada, CAT/C/5/Add.15 (1989).

[80] Among the countries which made no mention in their reports of allegations made by Amnesty were Senegal, Mexico, France, and the USSR: see *Amnesty Int'l Rep. 1988*, 65–7, 123–5, 199–201, and 218–21 (1989). A number of countries did refer to allegations of torture made against State officials. See CAT/C/5/Add.5 (1988), para. 10 (Egypt).

[81] CAT *Rules of Procedure, supra* n. 65, above, Rule 66.

[82] See the summary records of the second Session, CAT/C/SR.8–24 (1989), and the report of the Committee on its second session, A/44/46 (1989).

efficient, with an informal division of responsibility for certain areas.[83] While credit has been given to States where it is due, members have also asked a number of questions which reveal the limitations of the measures taken by States Parties so far and of the inadequate coverage of particular subjects in reports. In a positive step, the Chairperson of the Committee, in conjunction with the Rapporteur, has taken it upon himself to summarize his understanding of the Committee members' response to individual State reports, making a number of general observations in the process.[84] With the appointment of country rapporteurs, primary responsibility for formulating such conclusions has now been assigned to them.

The vigour and seriousness with which the Committee is taking its task is also manifest in the steps it has taken to ensure that States Parties which submit inadequate reports do not simply escape scrutiny by promising to provide additional information in their next report, thus delaying further scrutiny for another four years.

For example, the Committee has adopted a practice of sending reminders not just to States whose reports are overdue, but also to States which have promised to submit additional information but which have failed to do so—an important procedural step.[85]

More importantly, the Committee has been prepared to request additional reports from States whose reports are in its view inadequate.[86] The Committee has requested additional reports from a number of countries, including Cameroon, Senegal, Chile, Colombia, and China.[87] So far most of the States requested to provide additional reports have done so.[88]

(iii) *The role of NGOs* In the context of reviewing States Parties' reports, the Committee has adopted a rule of procedure whereby it may formally invite NGOs in consultative status to submit information to it. As yet, CAT has not dealt with the issue of whom it should invite and how information should be made available to members. Perhaps the best way for the Committee to proceed would be to invite a number of organizations with a reputation and

[83] Zoller, 'Second Session of the Committee', 250.

[84] See Dormenval, 'UN Committee against Torture', 42–3; CAT/C/SR.38 (1989), paras. 75–84; A/45/44 (1990), para. 11.

[85] CAT/C/SR.3 (1989), paras. 1–18. Such requests have been made of Denmark, Egypt, and Spain, among others. It would also be a useful procedural innovation if the Committee were to ensure that the replies received from governments became part of the public record, by being issued as official UN documents (see e.g. the additional information supplied by Egypt, CAT/C/5/Add.23 (1990)). If such information is not included in subsequent reports, it remains unavailable to the public.

[86] The Committee has the power under Art. 19 of the Convention to require States Parties to submit 'such other reports as the Committee may request'. Rule 67 of the CAT *Rules of Procedure*, n. 65, above, makes similar provision.

[87] CAT/C/SR.73, para. 27 (1991).

[88] Ibid. Of the States mentioned, only China has so far failed to submit an additional report.

expertise in the fields covered by the Convention to assist it and to invite them to seek information from national organizations in the countries whose reports are being considered. Or a request for thematic information could be made. To date CAT has not made any formal decision to invite NGOs to participate in its work; the limited NGO interest shown to date could well be increased in this way.

The Committee should seriously consider using its power under the rules (or amending them if necessary) to allow some NGO material to be received and circulated formally as Committee documents. The fact that NGOs may supply material informally in a language with which a significant number of members may not be comfortable means that the Committee does not benefit fully from the information supplied to it. Translation and circulation of some of this material as official documents would alleviate this problem somewhat.

(iv) *The Power of the Committee to make 'General Comments'* The Committee is empowered to make 'such general comments' on each report as it may consider appropriate.[89] It must forward these to the State Party concerned and may decide to include them in its annual report, together with any observations received from the State Party concerned.[90]

The Convention thus makes clear what has been in dispute in the case of a number of the other treaties,[91] namely that the Committee may formally comment on a report submitted by an individual State Party.[92] The phrase indicates that the Committee should not address itself to individual cases of alleged violations, but to more general issues relating to the implementation of the Convention in that State.

The original draft provision, amended late in the drafting process, provided that the Committee could make 'comments and suggestions' on a State Party's report. However, the Committee has been left without an explicit power to make 'general comments' or 'general recommendations' addressed to all States Parties,[93] a power which is possessed by all the other treaty bodies.[94] In

[89] Art. 19(3).

[90] Art. 19(4). It is not clear whether the Committee can publish its comments when made or whether that is only possible once the State Party has responded or been given a reasonable time to respond. Burgers and Danelius, *The United Nations Convention against Torture*, 158–9.

[91] In relation to the power of CERD and CEDAW to make comments on the report of an individual State Party, see Byrnes, 'The "Other" Human Rights Treaty Body', 42–4, and sources cited there. In relation to the Human Rights Committee, see Empell, *Die Kompetenzen des UN-Menschenrechtsausschusses im Staatenberichtsverfahren* (1987), 141–94.

[92] Burgers and Danelius, *The United Nations Convention against Torture*, 158–9; Nowak, 'The Implementation Functions', 499–502.

[93] Nowak, 'The Implementation Functions', 501. Burgers and Danelius, *The United Nations Convention against Torture*, 159, comment that lack of power to make general comments addressed to all States Parties 'is certainly not something the authors of the Convention intended'.

[94] On the powers possessed by the other committees, see Byrnes, 'The "Other" Human Rights Treaty Body', 42–51.

the case of the Human Rights Committee, that power has been an important vehicle for developing a jurisprudence of the Convention. None the less, it could be argued that the Committee possesses an implied power to make general comments of this sort in its reports as part of its function of monitoring and encouraging the better implementation of the Convention. It is to be hoped that the Committee itself will adopt this view and that it will develop its own detailed understanding of the Convention in this format.

(*d*) *Investigation on its own Initiative (Article 20)*

While Article 20 represents a procedural innovation so far as the treaty bodies are concerned, the procedure has international parallels and was inspired by the ECOSOC Resolution 1503 procedure and supervisory procedures of the International Labour Organisation.[95]

The Article 20 procedure is not a compulsory procedure for States Parties, but a State Party is bound by it unless it expressly declares at the time of its ratification or accession that it does not accept the competence of the Committee under Article 20.[96] This contrasts with the procedures under Articles 21 and 22, which require the making of a declaration of acceptance of the competence of the Committee under those articles. Despite some early predictions that the Article 20 procedure would be blunted by States Parties opting out of it,[97] the fact that States have to opt out expressly has apparently inhibited their doing so. As of 31 December 1991, only seven of the sixty-four States Parties had not accepted the procedure;[98] fifty-seven States Parties had thus accepted the competence of the Committee. This can be compared with the acceptance by States Parties of the Article 21 and 22 procedures: only twenty-nine and twenty-eight States Parties respectively had made declarations under those Articles.

The procedure consists of four stages.[99] While the Committee is required to seek co-operation and input from the State Party concerned at every stage of the procedure, the failure of a State Party to co-operate does not prevent the Committee from proceeding with its inquiry. Apart from limiting the

[95] Tardu, 'The United Nations Convention against Torture', 318; Burgers and Danelius, *The United Nations Convention against Torture*, 160; Nowak, 'The Implementation Functions', 503.

[96] Art. 28(1).

[97] Marx, 'Die Konvention der Vereinten Nationen gegen Folter und andere grausame, unmenschliche oder erniedrigende Behandlung oder Strafe', 19 *Zeitschrift für Rechtspolitik*, 84 (1986).

[98] Those states were Afghanistan, Belarus, Bulgaria, Chile, China, Czech and Slovak Federal Republic, Israel, and the Ukraine. Chile, Guatemala, the GDR, Hungary, and the USSR (Russian Federation), while opting out of the procedure at the time they ratified the Convention, subsequently accepted the procedure: CAT/C/2 Rev.2 (1992).

[99] For the rules adopted by the Committee to regulate the conduct of inquiries under Art. 20, see CAT *Rules of Procedure*, n. 65, above, Rules 69–84 (consolidated version of rules adopted at the second session which appeared in Report of the Committee against Torture in 1989, A/44/46 (1989), Annex IV).

material before the Committee, the only consequence of non-co-operation is that the members of the Committee delegated to conduct an inquiry will not be able to pay a visit to the country concerned.

All stages of the procedure are confidential until the inquiry has been completed and the Committee has sent its findings to the State concerned, together with any comments or suggestions it feels appropriate to make. At this stage the Committee may decide to publish a summary of the proceedings. While it must consult with the State concerned before doing so, publication by the Committee is not contingent on the State's agreement.

The procedure is triggered by the receipt by the Committee of 'reliable information which appears to it to contain well-founded indications that torture is being systematically practised in the territory of a State Party'.[100] It does not appear that local remedies must be exhausted before the procedure can be invoked.[101] The provision requires that the Committee be satisfied that the source of the information and/or the information itself can be relied on;[102] it must then determine that this information contains well-founded indications that torture is being practised systematically on the territory of a State Party. The procedure applies only in cases in which *torture* appears to be involved; it does not apply to cruel, inhuman, or degrading treatment or punishment. It is to be hoped that the Committee takes a relatively liberal approach at the initial screening stage.

There are a number of sources from which the Committee could receive information that might be sufficient to cause it to initiate the inquiries procedure. The most obvious and likely source is NGOs which submit information about individual countries, whether in conjunction with the Committee's review of reports under Article 19 or independently of that review. Other sources include material coming to the Committee's attention under the individual complaints procedure. If a large number of complaints are made against a particular country (as was the case with Uruguay under the ICCPR), the Committee may consider it appropriate to initiate an investigation. However, it will also need to give consideration to the issue of how best to go about an Article 20 investigation when there are individual complaints against a country being examined simultaneously.

[100] Art. 20(1).

[101] Exhaustion of domestic remedies is required under the Resolution 1503 procedure. Trindade, 'Co-existence and Co-ordination of Mechanisms of International Protection of Human Rights' 202 *Rec. des cours* (1987) 219, but CAT has not adopted any rule of procedure imposing a similar requirement under Art. 20. Nor does the similar procedure under Art. 26 of the ILO Constitution appear to be subject to the requirement of exhaustion of local remedies. See International Labour Office, *Manual of Procedures Relating to International Labour Conventions, and Recommendations* (1984), 25–6; United Nations, *United Nations Action in the Field of Human Rights*, ST/HR/2/Rev.3, (1988), paras. 168–73.

[102] In so doing, it may obtain information about the nature of the source or may obtain information from elsewhere to determine the reliability of the information. CAT *Rules of Procedure*, n. 65, above, Rule 75.

States Parties' reports themselves may even provide information sufficient to justify the invocation of the procedure, though in the case of a State that has been sufficiently honest to describe torture of a systematic nature, there may be little point in launching an inquiry when the same advice and assistance could be given through the report review process itself. The reports of other UN bodies, in particular those of the Special Rapporteur on Torture, might also provide information sufficient to lead to the initiation of an inquiry.

After the Committee has determined that the information satisfies the threshold test, it must then refer the matter to the State Party concerned, seeking its co-operation and input.[103] At this stage the Committee may also seek other information, from UN sources, NGOs, and individuals. Once it has received this information, the Committee must then decide whether an inquiry is appropriate. If it does so decide, one or more members of the Committee are to be appointed to carry out the inquiry and to report to the Committee urgently. If the State Party agrees, the inquiry may include a visit to the territory of the State. Those conducting the inquiry may also enlist the aid of medical experts or persons with experience in relation to the detention of prisoners.[104]

Once the inquiry is concluded, the Committee is to consider the result and to forward its findings and any comments or suggestions it considers appropriate to the State Party, after which it may decide to publish a summary of findings in its annual report. One can expect that fairly extensive 'summaries' of investigations will be published, following in the steps of the Human Rights Committee which publishes detailed 'summaries' of its proceedings under the Optional Protocol.[105]

At its fourth session, the Committee embarked on its first investigation under Article 20.[106] However, by November 1991 the work of the Committee under Article 20 had not yet reached the stage when information about its progress can be made public, so it is still too early to tell whether the procedure will be effective. If it does turn out to be an effective procedure, then it is likely to be used increasingly.

However, inquiries of this sort take considerable time and money, both of which are likely to be in short supply so far as the Committee is concerned. Delegation of much of the preparatory work to individual members of the Committee is clearly going to be necessary, but even that may not be sufficient to cope with the workload of the Committee which is likely to increase. There is a further danger the Committee must avoid: if the confidential procedure is

[103] Ibid. Rule 76.

[104] Ibid. Rule 82.

[105] Nowak, 'The Implementation Functions', 510.

[106] UN Press Release HR/3466. Apparently the country involved has also been the recipient of a visit from the Special Rapporteur on Torture, thus necessitating co-ordination between the two mechanisms. See text accompanying n. 161, below.

drawn out and there is inadequate public disclosure of what has gone on, the procedure may attract the criticism that some human rights organizations have levelled at the Resolution 1503 procedure, of being a way States can escape from international accountability rather than being held responsible for their failure to fulfil their obligations.

(*e*) *Interstate Complaints (Article 21)*

Article 21 of the Convention establishes a procedure for processing complaints by one State Party that another State Party is not giving effect to the provisions of the Convention.[107] The procedure is optional and binds only those States which have made a declaration accepting the competence of the Committee under Article 21 on the basis of reciprocity. Five declarations were necessary for the procedure to enter into force; that occurred prior to the entry into force of the Convention and the Article 21 procedure which itself entered into force on 26 June 1987 as between the States which had made such declarations. As of 31 December 1991, twenty-nine States had made declarations accepting the competence of the Committee under Article 21.[108]

The procedure is essentially the same as that laid down by Article 41 of the ICCPR.[109] It is initiated by one State communicating to another State Party its view that the other State is not fulfilling its obligations under the Convention. The other State is required to respond within three months. If the matter is not settled within six months of the original communication, then either State may refer the matter to the Committee. The Committee, after satisfying itself that the communication is admissible, is then to offer its good offices in an attempt to settle the matter, essentially a function of conciliation. In order to do this, it may appoint an *ad hoc* conciliation commission.[110] The Committee is required to submit a report within twelve months of having the matter referred to it. In the case of a matter that has been settled, the report is to consist simply of a statement of the facts and of the solution reached; if the matter has not been settled, the report is to include a statement of the facts and the written and oral submissions made to it by the States Parties concerned. While the report must be given to the States Parties concerned, the Convention does not indicate whether it can also be made public, though it

[107] See generally Nowak, 'The Implementation Functions', 510–17.

[108] E/CN.4/1992/15, para. 5. The GDR had made such a declaration, but presumably this lapsed with its accession to the FRG.

[109] As supplemented by Rules 72–7 of the Provisional Rules of Procedure of the Human Rights Committee, contained in *Report of the Human Rights Committee in 1979*, A/34/40 (1979), Annex III.

[110] Unlike Art. 42, ICCPR, which makes detailed provision for the composition of an *ad hoc* conciliation commission, the Convention makes no such provision. Nor do the CAT *Rules of Procedure* make detailed provision in this regard. CAT *Rules of Procedure*, n. 65, above, Rule 92, para. 2.

would be reasonable to assume that the Committee has the power to do so.[111]

Despite the description of the procedure by one commentator as a 'very modest and badly drafted means of implementation',[112] it still remains to be seen what, if anything, the Committee can make of it. While the procedure is quite different from the procedures for interstate complaints established under the European and American Conventions, the Committee may be able to use the procedure effectively if it deals with any case it receives in a principled but sensitive manner. The problem is likely to be that the procedure will probably be little utilized.

While interstate complaints procedures appear in a number of human rights treaties, for a variety of reasons little or no use has been made of them.[113] It seems likely that the factors that inhibit recourse to these procedures will also apply in the case of the Torture Convention. However, it is worth nothing that allegations of systematic torture or other ill-treatment have been an important element in a number of the interstate complaint cases which have been brought under the European Convention on Human Rights.[114] It may be that in particularly egregious cases some States Parties may be prepared to bring complaints against others. However, the procedure is optional and, unlike Article 24 of the European Convention, does not result in a binding decision by a judicial or quasi-judicial body. Furthermore, as a similarly effective investigation can be initiated under Article 20 without the adverse political consequences that might flow from an interstate complaint, it does not seem likely that the interstate procedure will be much utilized, despite the number of States that have accepted the Committee's competence under the Article 21 procedure.

(*f*) *Individual Complaints (Article 22)*

(i) *The Procedure* Article 22 establishes an individual complaints procedure, permitting the Committee to consider communications from individuals 'who claim to be victims of a violation by a State Party of the provisions of the Convention'.[115] The procedure is an optional one and only those States making a declaration recognizing the competence of the Committee to con-

[111] Nowak, 'The Implementation Functions', 517, and CAT *Rules of Procedure*, n. 65, above, Rule 6/21, which provides that the Committee may after consultation with the States parties issue communiqués for the use of the information media and the general public regarding the Committee's activities under Art. 21.

[112] Nowak, 'The Implementation Functions', 511.

[113] See generally Leckie, 'The Inter-State Complaint Procedure in International Human Rights Law: Hopeful Prospects or Wishful Thinking?' 10 *Hum. Rts. Q.* 249 (1988).

[114] 213 UNTS 211. See Leckie, 'The Inter-State Complaint Procedure', 271–6; and, among other cases, *Ireland* v. *United Kingdom*, Ser. A, No. 25, 2 *Eur. Hum. Rts. Rep.* 25; 58 *Int'l. L. Rep.* 188 (Eur. Ct. Hum. Rts. 1978); and *Cyprus* v. *Turkey*, 4 *Eur. Hum. Rts. Rep.* 482; 62 *Int'l. L. Rep.* 4 (Eur. Commission Hum. Rts. 1976).

[115] Art. 22(1). See generally Nowak, 'The Implementation Functions', 517–24; Burgers and Danelius, *The United Nations Convention against Torture*, 166–7.

sider such communications are bound by the procedure. Five ratifications were necessary before the individual communications procedure could enter into force. At the time of entry into force of the Convention itself, there were already more than the required number of ratifications, so the procedure entered into force together with the Convention. As of 31 December 1991, twenty-eight States had made declarations accepting the competence of the Committee to examine individual complaints.[116]

The procedure is modelled on the individual communications procedure contained in the First Optional Protocol[117] to the ICCPR, those governing the Human Rights Committee's consideration of individual communications.[118] The rules of procedure adopted by the Committee[119] largely reproduce those of the Human Rights Committee and the Committee will obviously look to the practice and jurisprudence of the latter[120] in developing its own practice under Article 22 of the Convention.

Generally speaking, any communication must first be declared admissible before it can be considered on its merits. The conditions of admissibility are laid down in Article 22 of the Convention and amplified somewhat in the rules.[121] Once a communication has been declared admissible,[122] the Committee considers the merits of the complaint, having invited both the individual and the State Party concerned to submit material to it and to comment on each other's submissions. The final outcome is the 'adoption of views' by the

[116] E/CN.4/1992/15, para. 5. The only State Party which has accepted the Article 21 procedure but not the Article 22 procedure is the UK.

[117] 999 UNTS 302.

[118] See *YB Hum. Rts. Committee 1977–78*, CCPR/1/Add. 1 (1986), ii, Annex II.

[119] See CAT *Rules of Procedure*, n. 65, above, Rules 1/22–17/22, A/43/46 (1988), Annex III.

[120] See Opsahl, chap. 10, above; McGoldrick, *The Human Rights Committee: Its Role in the Development of the International Covenant on Civil and Political Rigths* (1991), 120–202; Nowak, *UNO-Pakt über bürgerliche und politische Rechte und Fakultativprotokoll: CCPR Kommentar* (1989), 693–771; de Zayas, Möller, and Opsahl, 'Application by the Human Rights Committee of the International Covenant on Civil and Political Rights under the Optional Protocol' 3 *Canadian YB Hum. Rts.* 101 (1986); ibid. 'Application of the International Covenant on Civil and Political Rigths under the Optional Protocol by the Human Rights Committee', 28 *German YB Int'l L.* 9 (1985); Meron (ed.), *Human Rights Law-Making in the United Nations: A Critique of Instruments and Processes* (1985), 217–19. See also *Human Rights Committee, Selected Decisions under the Optional Protocol (Second to Sixteenth Sessions)*, CCPR/C/OP/1 (1985), Sales No. E. 84. XIV. 2; and *Selected Decisions of the Human Rights Committee Under the Optional Protocol*, Vol. 2 (1990), UN Sales No. E. 89. XIV. 1.

[121] The communication must not be anonymous, it must emanate from an individual subject to the jurisdiction of a State Party which has accepted the competence of the Committee, it must be submitted by the individual, a relative, or designated representative, or by others who can justify their submission of a complaint on behalf of the victim, must not be an abuse of the right to submit a communication nor incompatible with the provisions of the Convention, the same matter must not have been examined under another procedure of international investigation or settlement, and local remedies must have been exhausted where to do so is reasonable and likely to be effective. Art. 22(5); CAT *Rules of Procedure*, n. 65, above, Rule 107.

[122] Much of the preliminary work on questions of admissibility and also on substance is likely to be carried out by a working group of the Committee, as is the case with the Human Rights Committee. See CAT *Rules of Procedure*, n. 65, above, Rule 106.

Committee. While these are not formally binding on the State Party, no doubt they will have a similar status to the views adopted by the Human Rights Committee, which are formulated by that Committee as if they were a court decision and which have generally been given effect to by the State Party concerned.[123]

There are a number of differences between the procedure laid down in the Optional Protocol and the Human Rights Committee's provisional rules, and those of the Torture Convention. However, these differences are not likely to lead to any major divergences in practice between the approaches of the two bodies.

Two differences are likely to have little practical impact. While Article 22(1) of the Convention provides that communications made be submitted not only 'by' but also 'on behalf of' an individual, the Covenant only provides for the consideration of communications submitted 'by' an alleged victim.[124] However, as the Human Rights Committee has permitted close relatives and others who can show that they have been authorized by the victim to lodge complaints on behalf of the victim,[125] there appears to be little difference between the provisions. The only suggestion that has been made is that Article 22 may permit non-governmental organizations to play a greater role in lodging communications than under the Optional Protocol, as the Human Rights Committee insists in such cases that there be some form of authorization by the victim. However, it seems likely that CAT will also impose a requirement of this sort rather than allowing the provision to develop into a form of *actio popularis*, though there may be exceptional cases in which it may entertain such communications.[126]

A second difference between the Convention and the Optional Protocol relates to the requirement of exhaustion of domestic remedies. The Covenant states simply that domestic remedies must have been exhausted for a communication to be considered by the Committee, with an exception where the 'application of the remedies is unreasonably prolonged'.[127] The Convention contains a similar requirement but qualifies it by not requiring exhaustion of domestic remedies if the process is unlikely to bring the person alleging the violation effective relief. It is doubtful that this difference in wording has any

[123] See Opsahl, chap. 10, above.

[124] Optional Protocol, Art. 1.

[125] Rule 90(1)(b) of the Provisional Rules of Procedure, n. 118, above, 246, provides that normally an individual or his representative should submit an application but allows the Committee to consider a communication submitted on behalf of an alleged victim 'when it appears that he is unable to submit the communication himself'.

[126] CAT *Rules of Procedure*, n. 65, above, Rule 107, para. 1(b) provides that a communication 'should be submitted by the individual himself or by his relatives or designated representatives or by others on behalf of an alleged victim when it appears that the victim is unable to submit the communication himself, and the author of the communication justifies his acting on the victim's behalf'.

[127] Optional Protocol, Art. 5(2).

practical effect.[128] The general international law requirement of exhaustion of local remedies is subject to exceptions in cases of unreasonable delay or futility[129] and the Human Rights Committee has taken the approach that the Optional Protocol only requires domestic remedies to be exhausted to the extent that these remedies are effective and available.[130]

A third difference between the Optional Protocol and the Convention is that the Convention provides that communications that have been or are presently being examined under another procedure of international investigation or settlement are not admissible; the Optional Protocol mentions only those matters that are simultaneously being so examined. Overall, however, in determining whether the Committee is precluded from considering a particular communication, the Committee is likely to follow the fairly strict approach that the Human Rights Committee has taken in defining what is the 'same matter' and what amounts to 'another procedure of international investigation and settlement'.[131]

Thus, an individual will not be able to seek redress under the Covenant or a regional human rights convention and then come to the Committee (at least not if the complaint has been given more than formal consideration). However, CAT is also likely to take the view that an individual case that has been the subject of representations by the Special Rapporteur on Torture of the Commission on Human Rights as a result of a complaint by the victim will not be thereby rendered inadmissible.[132]

One further difference may be of some importance in relation to CAT's procedures. The Convention provides that the Committee shall take into account all information made available to it by or on behalf of the individual and State Party concerned,[133] while the Optional Protocol provides that the Human Rights Committee shall take into account 'written' information made

[128] Tardu, 'The United Nations Convention against Torture', 316.

[129] See generally Cançado-Trindade, *The Application of the Rules of Exhaustion of Local Remedies in International Law* (1983), 57–8.

[130] *Report of the Human Rights Committee in 1984*, A/39/40 (1984), para. 584; de Zayas, Möller, and Opsahl, 'Application by the Human Rights Committee', 116–117. Both the Human Rights Committee and CAT have adopted a similar approach to the question of proving the exhaustion of local remedies. While an individual is generally required to give some details of the steps taken to exhaust local remedies, a State Party cannot have a communication declared inadmissible by stating generally that the individual has failed to exhaust local remedies. Rather the State will be required to give 'details of the effective remedies available to the alleged victim in the particular circumstances of the case'. CAT *Rules of Procedure*, n. 65, above, Rule 13/22, para. 7. See also de Zayas, Möller, and Opsahl, op. cit., 116.

[131] De Zayas, Möller, and Opsahl, 'Application by the Human Rights Committee', 113–15.

[132] *Baboeram et el.* v. *Suriname* in which the Human Rights Committee expressed the view that the consideration of an individual's case in the context of a broader study such as that of the Special Rapporteur on Summary and Arbitrary Executions would not bar consideration of the case under the Optional Protocol. Communications No. 146/1983, and 148 to 154/1983, *Report of the Human Rights Committee in 1985*, A/40/40 (1985), Annex X, para. 9.1.

[133] Art. 22(4).

available to it.[134] In practice the Human Rights Committee has restricted itself to an exclusively written procedure, although it has been suggested that it could hold oral hearings and conduct fact-finding visits if it wished.[135] The word 'written' was dropped in the course of the drafting of the Convention and it seems that it is open to the CAT to hold oral hearings and examine witnesses if it considers this to be appropriate in a particular case.[136] Whether the Committee will have at its disposal the necessary time and resources to hold oral hearings as a routine matter may be open to doubt.

One question with which the Committee will also have to deal is the relationship between the individual communication procedure and the Article 20 procedure. The Committee may very well receive a number of individual complaints about a particular country which, taken together, might suggest that there is a systematic practice of torture in the country concerned. In such a case, there would seem to be no reason why the Article 20 procedure should not be invoked while simultaneously dealing with the individual communications; information supplied in support of individual complaints would also presumably be available for use in the Article 20 procedure assuming it satisfies the criteria laid down by the Convention and the Rules relating to Article 20.

Another issue that is likely to arise is the power of the Committee to request interim relief for an alleged victim pending the adoption of final views by the Committee if the victim is likely to suffer irreparable harm were interim relief not granted. Such cases are easy enough to imagine: a person who is to be extradited or deported to a country where there is a likelihood that he or she will be subject to torture; or a person who has been sentenced to a particular form of punishment which may amount to torture within the meaning of the Convention; or a person who has been convicted of an offence in proceedings as the result of a confession extracted by torture. The Human Rights Committee has dealt with similar situations, particularly in the context of persons sentenced to death and persons who are to be extradited or deported, and has on a number of occasions requested States Parties to delay taking such actions until after the Committee has dealt with the merits of a communication.[137] CAT has adopted rules of procedure enabling it to take

[134] Optional Protocol, Art. 5(1).

[135] Opsahl, chap. 10, above.

[136] Tardu, 'The United Nations Convention against Torture', 317; Nowak, 'The Implementation Functions', 532, Burgers and Danelius, *The United Nations Convention against Torture*, 167.

[137] Rule 86 of the Provisional Rules of Procedure, n. 118, above, empowers the Committee to make such a request of a State Party. It has done so on a number of occasions. See e.g. Communication No. 22/1977, *Selected Decisions*, 5, 6–7 (request to a State Party that a person not be expelled to a country from which he had sought refuge). The Committee has authorized one of its members to take Rule 86 decisions on behalf of the Committee. *Report of the Human Rights Committee in 1988*, A/43/40 (1988), para. 656.

similar action[138] and will no doubt follow the practice of the Human Rights Committee in appropriate cases.

(ii) *Cases to Date* By the end of its seventh session, the Committee had adopted decisions in only seven cases under Article 22. Three of these communications, lodged by relatives of persons who had been allegedly tortured by Argentine military authorities in 1976, alleged that the adoption of the Due Obedience Act in 1986 (which exempted lower-ranked military officials from liability for criminal acts on the assumption that they were acting under orders) and the Finality Law of 1987 (limiting the period within which new criminal proceeedings in relation to events of the 'dirty war' of 1976–83 could be brought) violated the Convention. The two statutes were adopted (or proclaimed) after Argentina signed and ratified the Convention, but before it entered into force for Argentina.

The Committee declared the communications inadmissible, *ratione temporis*, holding that all the acts complained of took place before Argentina was bound by the Convention. None the less, it made its position on the substantive issues clear; it stated that the adoption of these statutes was, in its view, 'incompatible with the spirit and purpose of the Convention' and declared that Argentina was 'morally bound to provide a remedy to victims of torture and their dependants, notwithstanding the fact that the acts of torture occurred before the entry into force of the Convention, under the responsibility of a de facto government which is not the present Government of Argentina'.[139]

Four other communications have also been rejected on admissibility grounds.[140]

III. OVERLAP WITH THE WORK OF OTHER HUMAN RIGHTS BODIES

(*a*) *General*

In addition to CAT, there are already a number of international and regional intergovernmental bodies which have some form of monitoring responsibility in the areas covered by the Convention and at least some of these overlap

[138] CAT *Rules of Procedure*, n. 65, above, Rule 108, para. 9 and Rule 110, para. 3.

[139] A/45/44 (1990), Annex V, para. 9. The Committee thus implicitly accepted the argument that Argentina had violated its obligation under Art. 18 of the Vienna Convention on the Law of Treaties 1969, 1155 UNTS 331, not to defeat the object and purpose of the Convention between signature and ratification. The Committee also called on the Argentine Government to give details of the remedial steps that had been taken to compensate the victims of the 'dirty war' or their dependants. For the reply of Argentina, see A/45/44 (1990), Annex VI. For a similar decision on admissibility under the Optional Protocol, see *S.E.* v. *Argentina*, Communication No. 275/1988, A/45/40 (1990) Annex X.J.

[140] The first, *W.J. v. Austria*, Communication No. 5/1990, was rejected as inadmissible because the same matter was already under consideration by the European Commission of Human Rights ((1991) 12 *Hum. Rts. LJ* 26), although that application has recently been rejected

areas of responsibility assigned to CAT.[141] While it is impossible and probably undesirable to eliminate some substantive and procedural overlap among the various procedures at the international and regional level designed to attack the problem of torture,[142] avoidance of excessive duplication of procedures is obviously desirable, as is consistency in the formulation and interpretation of standards.

The existence of other supervisory institutions with overlapping jurisdiction presents the Committee with two main challenges. The first is how to ensure that its work harmonizes with and draws on the substantive work that has been already done by other bodies; the second is how to avoid unproductive duplication of work.

Although there is jurisdictional and substantive overlap between the Committee and a number of bodies, the most important are the overlaps with the Human Rights Committee and the Special Rapporteur on Torture.

So far as individual communications are concerned, there is overlap with the jurisdiction of the Human Rights Committee, as well as with bodies empowered under the regional human rights conventions to receive individual communications.[143] Because of the requirements governing admissibility of communications under Article 22 mentioned above, it is unlikely that the work of the Committee will significantly duplicate the work of any of these bodies.

As far as the Article 20 investigation procedure is concerned, there are other similar procedures, both within the UN system and at the regional level.[144] If the Committee receives information about a country which it knows is being examined by another body, the Committee does have a discretion under Article 20 to decide against initiating an investigation. This discretion will need to be exercised carefully in a case where there is evidence of systematic torture, taking into account factors such as whether the torture is the focus of the other investigation and whether the State concerned is seeking to play one procedure and body off against another in an attempt to escape scrutiny.[145]

as indamissible by the Commission ((1991) 12 *Hum. Rts. LJ* 173). The other three rejected on admissibility grounds were: *R.E.G. v. Turkey*, Communication No. 4/1990, *H.V.P. v. Spain*, Communication No. 6/1990, and *L.B. v. Spain*, Communication No. 9/1990.

141 See generally on the problem of overlap and duplication, Meron, *Human Rights Law-Making*.

142 Ibid. 241–3.

143 The European Commission and Court of Human Rights under the European Convention, 213 UNTS 221, Art. 25, and the Inter-American Commission and Court of Human Rights under the American Convention on Human Rights, OAS Treaty Series No. 36, reprinted in 9 *Int'l Legal Materials* 673 (1970), Art. 44.

144 For example, the Resolution 1503 procedure, and the procedure permitted under Art. 18(g) of the Statute of the Inter-American Commission, in *Basic Documents Pertaining to Human Rights in the Inter-American System (updated to 1 March 1988)*, OEA/Ser.L.V/II.71 Doc.6 Rev.1 (1988), 65. See Cançado-Trindade, 'Co-existence and Co-ordination', 366–70.

145 See Zoller, 'Second Session of the Committee against Torture', 253–4.

An additional international mechanism proposed to further the campaign to eradicate torture has been a system of periodic visits by independent experts to places of detention, a procedure designed to serve a preventive and educative function. Costa Rica proposed such a system for the Convention, but the matter was not taken up at the time the Convention was adopted and has only recently been reactivated.[146] However, the idea has been taken up in the Council of Europe in the form of the European Torture Convention,[147] which establishes a committee to conduct such visits. There are also efforts within the Inter-American system to develop a similar procedure.[148] However, in view of the largely preventive and educative nature of the supervisory body under such a procedure, such an arrangement is unlikely to interfere with or duplicate the work of the Committee.[149]

In the area of reporting, there is a major overlap with the Human Rights Committee, at least for States which are parties to both the ICCPR and the Convention.[150] States Parties to both treaties are required to report on the measures they have taken to prevent and punish torture and other ill-treatment. While the obligations under the two treaties are somewhat different in scope, nearly all the material provided to CAT will be of relevance to a State Party's obligations under the Covenant, in particular under Article 7.

Reports to CAT will generally contain more detailed information than the sections of reports dealing with corresponding rights under the ICCPR. It would be preferable for the Human Rights Committee simply to request that copies or summaries of States Parties' reports to CAT be provided to it, together with updates or more extensive material in other areas.[151]

There is also potential for duplication and inconsistency in the case of suggestions made by the two bodies to individual States Parties about steps they might take to fulfil their obligations, as well as in the case of substantive interpretation of the corresponding provisions of the two treaties. In these

[146] Draft Optional Protocol, E/CN.4/1409 (1980), reprinted in Burgers and Danelius, *The United Nations Convention against Torture*, Appendix 8, 213. The issue has been taken up by the Commission on Human Rights, which by its decision 1991/107 decided to consider a draft Optional Protocol submitted by Costa Rica (E/CN.4/1991/66) at its 1992 session.

[147] n. 13, above. See generally Cassese, 'A New Approach to Human Rights—the 1987 Convention for the Prevention of Torture', 83 *Am. J. Int'l L.* 128 (1989); Vigny, 'La Convention européene de 1987 pour la prévention de la torture et des peines ou traitements inhumains ou dégradants', 43 *Schweizerisches Jahrbuch für Internationales Recht* 62 (1987). See also A/45/44 (1990), 6.

[148] Cassese, 'A New Approach to Human Rights', 133 n. 29.

[149] Ibid. 136–7.

[150] See also the reporting procedures provided for under the American Convention on Human Rights, n. 125, above, Art. 43, and the Inter-American Convention to Prevent and Punish Torture, n. 30, above, Art. 17 (both provisions requiring reports only when the Inter-American Commission requests them).

[151] On the problem of duplication of reporting requirements and suggestions as to how the problem might be alleviated, see generally 'Reporting Obligations of States Parties to the United Nations Instruments on Human Rights, Note by the Secretary-General', A/44/98 (1989).

areas each Committee will need to keep itself apprised of developments in the other Committee so that unnecessary divergences can be avoided. In this respect overlapping membership can facilitate the exchange of information and needs to be maintained.

(b) The Special Rapporteur on Torture

The major area of potential overlap is between the work of CAT and that of the Special Rapporteur on Torture.[152] The Special Rapporteur was appointed in 1985 pursuant to a resolution of the Commission on Human Rigths;[153] he is one of the 'theme' rapporteurs of the Commission on Human Rights.[154] Originally appointed for one year, his mandate has been renewed on a number of occasions;[155] as of 1991 he had submitted six annual reports to the Commission.[156]

The Special Rapporteur has so far undertaken four types of activities in carrying out his mandate. First, he has requested information from governments as to the steps that they have taken to prevent or combat torture and to establish safeguards designed to protect the individual against torture. Secondly, he has received allegations of the practice of torture from various sources and forwarded them to governments seeking a response; these have included a number of requests for urgent action. Thirdly, he has visited a number of countries to consult with governmental and non-governmental representatives on methods that can be adopted to prevent torture; he has also compiled reports on these visits which contain specific recommendations to individual governments. Finally, he has analysed the phenomenon of torture generally and the conditions under which it occurs, and has made general recommendations as to the steps that States should take to prevent its occurrence.

While the Committee and Special Rapporteur are pursuing similar goals, they go about the task in somewhat different ways and, with one exception, there does not appear to be any great likelihood of significant duplication of

[152] Both the Committee and the Special Rapporteur have expressed concern about the desire to avoid unnecessary overlap between their work, as well as to ensure that their work is complementary both substantively and procedurally. See E/CN.4/1988/17, paras. 4–13, in which the Special Rapporteur argues that there is little overlap in function or jurisdiction between the mandate of the Committee and his own mandate; see also CAT/C/SR.11 (1989), paras. 39–67 (discussion between the Special Rapporteur and the Committee). The Chairman of the Committee and the Special Rapporteur have consulted informally on a number of occasions.

[153] CHR Res. 1985/33.

[154] See Weissbrodt, 'The Three "Theme" Rapporteurs of the UN Commission on Human Rights', 80 *Am. J. Int'l L.* 693–5 (1986); Rodley, *The Treatment of Prisoners under International Law*, 120–5.

[155] In 1986 for one year (CHR Res. 1986/50), in 1987 for another year (CHR Res. 1987/29), in 1988 for two years (CHR Res. 1988/32), and in 1990 for a further two years (CHR Res. 1990/34).

[156] E/CN.4/1986/15; E/CN.4/1987/13; E/CN.4/1988/17 and Add. 1; E/CN.4/1989/15; E/CN.4/1990/17; and E/CN.4/1991/17.

work. The exception is the requests the Special Rapporteur has made to States to inform him about the steps they have taken to prevent and punish torture; this is essentially the same information that States Parties to the Convention are required to provide to the Committee in their reports under Article 19. This area of overlap can easily be eliminated by the Special Rapporteur's obtaining copies of the reports of States Parties to the Committee, a measure he has already suggested.[157] However, as regards States which are not yet parties to the Convention, there is no overlap in this respect.

So far as the allegations of torture received by the Special Rapporteur are concerned there does not seem to be unnecessary duplication. The Special Rapporteur can respond to complaints against any State, whereas the Committee's ability to take cognizance of allegations of torture is restricted to States Parties to the Convention and, in the case of its investigative powers, to those States Parties which have accepted one of the optional procedures.

Secondly, the Special Rapporteur can respond immediately to allegations of torture, something which the Committee, meeting only twice a year, may not be in a good position to do, even if it develops inter-sessional procedures to respond to violations (which would in any event apply only to those States that have submitted to the relevant procedure). Additionally, domestic remedies will ordinarily be required to be exhausted before the Committee can consider individual complaints; no such procedural limitation applies to the Special Rapporteur's actions. The Committee's role in adopting views on individual communications is also quite different from that of the Special Rapporteur who comes to no conclusion on whether the allegations are well-founded in a particular case.

In the case of the Committee's power to investigate systematic violations under Article 20, there is a higher threshold for the initiation of that procedure than for a decision by the Special Rapporteur to raise allegations of torture with governments;[158] and, in any event, the Article 20 procedure binds only those States Parties to the Convention which have accepted the Article 20 competence of the Committee.[159]

There are a couple of areas in which the jurisdiction of the Committee and

[157] CAT/C/SR.11 (1989), para. 42.

[158] The Special Rapporteur has cautioned the Committee against assuming that it can commence an Art. 20 investigation into every country mentioned in his reports against which a number of allegations of torture have been made; in his view the Committee will need to test that information against the threshold criteria laid down in Art. 20: CAT/C/SR.11 (1989), paras. 54 and 64.

[159] Some countries have suggested that States Parties to the Convention should not be subject to the jurisdiction of the Special Rapporteur because they are already subject to the supervision of the Committee. In the case of States which have not submitted to any of the optional procedures, removing them from the jurisdiction of the Special Rapporteur would have the result of subjecting them to less scrutiny than if they had not ratified the Convention. Gaer, 'Human Rights at the United Nations: Preventing Torture', 8 *In Brief* 3 (1988).

the Special Rapporteur do overlap and in which some care will need to be taken to ensure consistency of approach. In the case of general recommendations about the steps necessary to the eradication of torture, it would be undesirable if the analysis and approach taken by the Special Rapporteur were to diverge significantly from or conflict with that taken by the Committee in any general guidance it wishes to give to States Parties to the Convention. This outcome seems unlikely, in view of the fact that the Special Rapporteur has taken the Convention as the central framework for much of his work, as well as endorsing the various non-binding international instruments relating to torture on which the Committee is also likely to draw.

Similarly, significant conflicts seem unlikely in regard to recommendations directed to individual countries, provided that the Committee and the Special Rapporteur keep each other informed of any relevant actions they have taken in relation to a given country. The Special Rapporteur has already completed a number of individual country reports and has made specific recommendations about steps that should be taken by those States. Some of these countries are also parties to the Convention[160] and presumably the Committee could make similarly detailed suggestions when reviewing their periodic reports or when exercising one of its investigative functions.[161] Provided that each body is aware of what the other has done, it seems unlikely that there will be major conflicts.

However, one important issue on which the Committee and the Special Rapporteur might adopt different approaches has already emerged: the definition of torture. While the Special Rapporteur may be in a position to interpret 'torture' in his mandate broadly by drawing on various international norms defining that concept, the Committee may have less freedom in that regard. It must ground its understanding of 'torture' in the text and drafting history of the Convention. While that may permit or require that other international developments be incorporated in the substantive definition of torture adopted by the Committee, ultimately the Committee is constrained by the Convention. The distinction the Convention draws between torture and other ill-treatment also limits the extent to which the Committee can adopt an expansive view of what constitutes torture, while the Special Rapporteur, his mandate relating explicitly only to 'torture', has an incentive to adopt a more expansive definition.

The Special Rapporteur's mandate confines itself to 'torture' and it does

[160] Turkey, for example, which was visited by the Special Rapporteur and which was the subject of a report and recommendations (E/CN.4/1989/15, paras. 209–33), ratified the Convention in Sept. 1988. One member of the Committee suggested that the information contained in the Special Rapporteur's report might be sufficient to initiate the Art. 20 procedure in respect of Turkey; in such a case consistency of approach in recommendations would obviously be highly desirable.

[161] See n. 106 above.

not explicitly authorize him to take actions with respect to other ill-treatment; indeed, references to cruel, inhuman, or degrading treatment or punishment were deleted from the substantive parts of the mandate. None the less, the Special Rapporteur has concerned himself with other ill-treatment in a number of contexts, as well as violations of other human rights. He has, for example, addressed such practices as corporal punishment, inhuman detention, and prolonged stays on death row. He has justified this approach on the grounds that the distinction between torture and other ill-treatment is often difficult to draw and that various forms of ill-treatment and violations of other rights are conducive to the occurrence of torture so that therefore any attempt to ensure that torture does not occur must necessarily prevent the common preconditions under which it occurs.[162]

To the extent that his concern with these matters extends beyond a commonly accepted international definition of torture, it can be justified by invoking some doctrine of implied powers in construing his mandate. In so far as he attempts to bring these particular practices generally within a definition of 'torture', the Committee is under no obligation to follow his approach and, indeed, may not be able to do so because of the limitations imposed by the Convention. While it might be desirable that both the Committee and the Special Rapporteur are operating with substantially similar definitions of torture,[163] that may not be possible or even desirable if the Convention definition is interpreted in an unduly narrow fashion by the Committee.

Overall, however, it seems that there will be relatively little unproductive duplication of work by the Committee and the Special Rapporteur, nor does it seem very likely that there will be major disagreements between them over what constitutes torture. It is to be hoped that the Committee will involve the Special Rapporteur in its work, by inviting him to provide it with information on specific countries under the reporting and investigation procedures, by seeking his assistance in those investigations, and by recommending to States Parties that they invite him to visit their countries in order to provide them with expert assistance.

Thus, apart from the problem of duplication in reporting, it does not seem likely that there will be wasteful duplication between the work of the Committee and that of the Special Rapporteur. Close co-operation between the two bodies will be necessary to ensure that their general approaches and recommendations in specific cases do not diverge markedly.

The Committee has considered whether it might assume some of the functions of the Special Rapporteur in relation to States Parties to the Convention.[164] In particular, members have suggested that the Committee

[162] See E/CN.4/1986/15, paras. 122–40; E/CN.4/1988/17, paras. 40–9.
[163] See CAT/C/SR.11, para. 61 (1989).
[164] CAT/C/SR.37 (1989), paras. 43–7 and CAT/C/SR.42 (1989), paras. 1–22.

could carry out visits of the type carried out by the Special Rapporteur, as well as adopting an urgent action mechanism.[165] It has also been suggested that the Special Rapporteur devote himself primarily to dealing with States which are not parties to the Convention.

While these suggestions are designed to avoid unproductive overlap and to increase the efficiency of both the Committee and the Special Rapporteur, they give rise to some concern. Not only is the formal power and actual capability of the Committee to take urgent action far from clear at this stage, but the possibility that States Parties might be subject to only periodic scrutiny if excluded from the Special Rapporteur's mandate is a disturbing one. Further, suggestions that the mandate of the Special Rapporteur be limited are politically dangerous at a time when many members of the Commission on Human Rights are inclined to undermine mechanisms such as this which have proved to be effective in practice. The best solution for the forseeable future would be for the Committee and the Rapporteur to continue to liaise closely, ensuring that they are not duplicating but complementing each other's work.

Conclusion

The Committee has commenced its work at a difficult time. Its work is likely to be affected by the general malaise of the treaty-reporting system and the Committee can hardly remain untouched by the generally inadequate resources available to support the work of the treaty bodies, exacerbated in its own case by the insecure financing arrangements laid down in the Convention.

None the less, there are reasons to feel reasonably optimistic about the future work of the Committee. It is in an excellent position to benefit from the experience of the other treaty bodies and to avoid the pitfalls they have encountered. The Committee can draw on the enormous amount of work that has already been done in relation to torture. Finally, the work of the Committee is likely to be given significant support by NGOs, many of whom played a major role in the genesis and adoption of the Convention. The real organizational challenge will come as the Committee's workload increases and its credibility as an enforcement mechanism will depend on how effectively it deals with complaints against States. Its activities will certainly not eliminate torture and other forms of ill-treatment but they may give the struggle additional momentum.

[165] See A/45/44 (1990), paras. 21–22. Initially, the Committee apparently considered that there was unlikely to be a major overlap of functions, but as members of the Committee have begun to envisage a more ambitious role for it, the proposed new activities may well lead to unproductive duplication. However, the relationship is an evolving one and much will depend on how heavy the workload of the Committee under its existing responsibilities becomes.

III

Other Issues

14

The Role of the United Nations Secretariat

THEO C. VAN BOVEN

Introduction

The United Nations Charter lists[1] the Secretariat among the principal organs of the Organization and lays down a number of important rules and principles with regard to its status and responsibilities. While a great deal has been written on the role of the Secretary-General, on the perception of that role by the successive holders of the office, and on the ways in which they carried out their functions, the literature on the sector of the Secretariat responsible for the human rights programme is scarce.[2] This chapter will discuss the role of the main actors in that domain. They are, first of all, the Secretary-General who is 'the chief administrative officer of the Organization', and secondly, what is now the Centre for Human Rights and its Executive Head, who currently holds the rank of Under-Secretary-General. Rather than giving a detailed description of all the functions and tasks of these actors the emphasis will be on issues of policy and responsibility.

The analysis is premised on several assumptions. First, the Secretariat's role in promoting respect for, and observance of, human rights should always be guided by: the provisions of the Charter governing the activities of the Organization as a whole and its Secretariat in particular; the principles contained in the UN human rights instruments; and the policies established by the United Nations' policy organs. Secondly, in accordance with the Charter, the promotion and encouragement of respect for human rights is directly related to other major objectives of the Organization, in particular the maintenance of international peace and security and the creation of conditions for economic and social progress and development. Thirdly, the human rights policies of governments as well as the human rights aspirations and expectations of peoples and individuals are bound to have a bearing upon the role

[1] Arts. 7 and 97–101.

[2] A principal exception is the autobiographical work by John P. Humphrey, the first Director of the Human Rights Division from 1946 to 1966. This book gives interesting historical insights into the early years of the United Nations human rights programme and the role played by the Secretariat. Humphrey, *Human Rights and the United Nations: A Great Adventure* (1984).

and responsibilities of the Secretariat. Fourthly, while the Secretariat has its own distinct status and its own exclusively international character, it functions in close association with the policy-making organs of the Organization. These assumptions are elaborated upon in the analysis that follows. The author should first note, however, that his views and the choice of issues for discussion are marked by his own experiences during a period of five years (1977–82) as Director of what was then the UN Division of Human Rights (subsequently renamed the Centre for Human Rights).

The purposes and principles of the Organization not only provide a framework for international co-operation; they also represent intrinsic values which are basic to the dignity and welfare of peoples and individual human beings. The preamble of the UN Charter is an eloquent statement of the great values which 'the peoples of the United Nations' are determined to pursue. They include the reaffirmation of faith in fundamental human rights, in the dignity and worth of the human person, in the equal rights of men and women and of nations large and small, and the promotion of social progress and better standards of life in larger freedom.[3] These basic values are further spelled out in other Charter provisions, in particular in Articles 55 and 56, and of course in numerous international human rights instruments such as the Universal Declaration of Human Rights and the International Covenants.

When the Universal Declaration addresses itself to 'every individual and every organ of society' to secure the universal recognition and observance of human rights, it is obvious that such a statement is not only important to the world at large but that it affects in a very special manner the Secretary-General and all other UN staff members who carry responsibilities in the field of human rights. In that respect the Secretariat's actions should be constantly guided by human rights concerns and by the United Nations' policy responses to these concerns. If the Secretariat pursues narrow self-interest instead of being guided and inspired by the human rights principles proclaimed by the Organization itself, it would be failing in its responsibilities towards both the Organization and the peoples in whose name the Charter has been drawn up. If the Secretariat were to be an institution in which the common interests of mankind and the rights of human beings were not to be the determining factor and inspiration, it would betray the values underlying the Organization. Consequently there can be no neutrality on the part of the Secretariat where human rights are at stake, either in its internal structure or in its external relations. Such an approach may certainly bring the Secretariat into conflict with member States. This in turn poses major problems in terms of its partiality or impartiality, its loyalty towards the principles of the Organization or towards the governmental interests of member States, and the nature of the international civil service as an instrument of internationalism or as an

[3] UN Charter, pream. paras. 2 and 4.

extension of intergovernmental interests. These complex issues are of such a fundamental nature as to require analysis in much greater depth.

In international policy terms there is an increasing awareness of the interdependence among human rights, international peace and security, and economic and social progress and development. UN reports and resolutions have underlined this interdependence and it is now widely recognized that human rights considerations should be taken into account in the United Nations' efforts to maintain peace and promote development. This recognition should have practical implications for the totality of the Organization's activities, including those of the Secretariat. In reality, however, such an integrated approach has not yet materialized. On the Secretariat level, the human rights programme is largely carried out in isolation from other programmes with little interaction, co-ordination, or co-operation between the two spheres. This state of affairs warrants critical and continuing attention, particularly by the Office of the Secretary-General and by the Under-Secretary-General for Human Rights, who heads the Centre for Human Rights.[4] Efforts should be pursued to integrate human rights interests into the work of the other major departments of the UN Secretariat.

In the last ten to fifteen years a veritable explosion of international interest in human rights has taken place. During his Presidency from 1977 to 1981, Jimmy Carter officially proclaimed human rights as one of the central objectives of US foreign policy. Earlier in the 1970s a bloody military *coup d'état* had struck the people of Chile and the resulting massive violations of human rights caused widespread international concern. The Helsinki Accords (Final Act of the Conference on Security and Co-operation in Europe, 1975) and their focus on human rights also mobilized large sectors of public opinion. Thus, by the end of the seventies human rights had become a fashionable topic at diplomatic conferences and a great deal of human rights rhetoric was indulged in by distinguished speakers in UN General Assembly policy debates. At the same time non-governmental organizations stepped up their human rights activities as new non-governmental organizations emerged and grass roots groups and movements became more vocal. Although the United Nations is in some respects far removed from the realities of the world, the Organization does not function in isolation and tends to reflect developments in the world at large.

Increasing awareness of human rights issues among large sectors of public opinion, rising expectations and aspirations, and more urgent demands by many people that their appeals be heeded, inevitably had an impact on the orientation of the United Nations' human rights programme. A substantial

[4] See generally 'Situation and developments regarding the logistical and human rights resources support for the activities of the centre for Human Rights in the field of human rights', E/1990/50.

number of member States were increasingly prompted to utilize the platform of human rights organs to raise matters of concern. They were more prepared to take initiatives, collectively or individually, some of a rhetorical, but others of a substantive nature, some prompted by political motives and others mainly by humanitarian concerns.

Similarly, non-governmental organizations became increasingly interested in the potential of the Organization and raised numerous issues in the framework of their consultative relationship.[5] Complaints, petitions, and communications from victims of violations of human rights or other concerned individuals and groups began to reach the United Nations in rapidly growing numbers. This broadening political and public concern with human rights created a climate favourable to the establishment of new sub-organs and the development of new fact-finding techniques. It prompted demands for research and studies in new areas, particularly those dealing with the deeper 'structural' causes of human rights violations. The same climate led to a broader stream of complaints and other expressions of concern, and increasing demands from representatives of governments, non-governmental organizations, and individuals for advice, guidance, and information. In quantitative and qualitative terms the result was a 'broadening and deepening of the human rights programme'.[6] Such developments inevitably have a considerable impact on the nature of the role and responsibilities of the Secretariat and require, in terms of both policy and management, constant readjustment in determining priorities, and utilizing staff and other resources. It is obvious under such circumstances that a Secretariat that perceives itself as a trustee of human rights interests may run into serious difficulties with repressive governments that seek to protect their own interests. Yet a Secretariat genuinely committed to human rights principles both in its internal and external relations will hardly be able to avoid such difficulties.

An important function of the Human Rights Secretariat is the rendering of services to UN organs. Some of those organs are policy-making bodies, such as the Third Committee of the General Assembly, the Economic and Social Council and its Social Committee, and the Commission on Human Rights and its Sub-Commission. Other bodies monitor the observance of international instruments; they include, for instance, the Committee on the

[5] Although the focus of the present analysis is on the formal human rights actors in the Secretariat it should be noted that various other units of the Secretariat are also concerned with specific human rights problems. They include the Centre against Apartheid which forms part of the Department of Political and Security Council Affairs, the Centre for Social Development and Humanitarian Affairs with responsibilities for social development, the advancement of women, the advancement of youth, the ageing and disabled persons, crime prevention and criminal justice, and of course the Office of the United Nations High Commissioner for Refugees dealing with international protection of refugees, the provision of material assistance, and the execution of special humanitarian operations.

[6] See my statement on this theme before the Third Committee of the UN General Assembly on 23 Sept. 1981, reprinted in van Boven, *People Matter: Views on International Human Rights Policy* (1982), 28–39.

Elimination of Racial Discrimination, the Human Rights Committee, the Committee against Torture, the Committee on Economic, Social and Cultural Rights, and the Committee on the Rights of the Child. Others still are subsidiary bodies that carry out studies and investigations regarding specific countries and territories or with respect to particular issues of great concern to the international community. The formal function of the Secretariat *vis-à-vis* all these organs is largely to provide administrative servicing in accordance with their respective rules of procedure (preparation of the provisional agenda, securing conference facilities, handling documentation, assisting chairmen and rapporteurs with respect to such questions as lists of speakers, the preparation of the draft report, etc.). It is also the duty of the Secretariat to function as the institutional memory and to remind the policy organs of decisions and guidelines adopted by themselves or by higher organs of the UN hierarchy, with a view to maintaining consistency and coherence in substantive and administrative matters.

Other duties include representing the Secretary-General and making oral or written statements on his behalf and detailing the budgetary implications of proposals which entail financial consequences. The Secretary-General and the Secretariat also receive numerous requests from the organs to collect information or to carry out research and studies. An important issue is the extent to which the Secretariat, in particular its Executive Head, can exercise discretion in implementing policies in the light of practical needs and actions which appear to him to be necessary and appropriate with due regard to political feasibility. Since the pursuit of virtually all human rights objectives has political implications, the Secretariat has to act, whether publicly or privately, in close consultation and co-operation with the competent organs. It is clear that suggestions and advice on the part of the Secretariat as to possible courses of action will only lead to results if it and its leadership enjoy the respect and confidence of a substantial number of delegates. In this chapter examples will be given of concrete policy suggestions put forward by the Secretariat in the Commission and the Sub-Commission which were followed-up on and translated into important elements of the human rights programme. The publicly verifiable examples can be matched by many other instances of discreet action by the Secretariat which are not reflected in the public records. It should be emphasized that the relationship between the Secretariat and the human rights organs should be one of active partnership, without prejudice to the distinct status and the truly international character of the Secretariat.

A. *Neutrality versus Advocacy*

The successive holders of the office of Secretary-General have repeatedly emphasized the need for an independent international civil service. To that effect they have all highlighted the importance of Article 100 of the Charter.

Hammarskjöld, in a noteworthy lecture delivered at Oxford in May 1961 on 'The International Civil Servant in Law and Fact',[7] discussed the meaning and implications of that Article[8] at length. It is on the concept of 'neutrality' that Hammarkjöld's comments are of particular interest:

> If a demand for neutrality is made, by present critics of the international civil service, with the intent that the international civil servant should not be permitted to take a stand on political issues, in response to requests of the General Assembly or the Security Council, then the demand is in conflict with the Charter itself. If, however, 'neutrality' means that the international civil servant, also in executive tasks with political implications, must remain wholly uninfluenced by national or group interests or ideologies, then the obligation to observe such neutrality is just as basic to the Charter concept of the international civil service as it was to the concept in the Covenant of the League.[9]

In the same lecture Hammarskjöld also observed:

> It is obvious from what I have said that the international civil servant cannot be accused of lack of neutrality simply for taking a stand on a controversial issue when this is his duty and cannot be avoided. But there remains a serious intellectual and moral problem as we move within an area inside which personal judgment must come into play. Finally, we have to deal here with a question of integrity or with, if you please, a question of conscience.[10]

It is clearly no coincidence that 'integrity' along with 'efficiency' and 'competence' are mentioned in Article 101 of the Charter as requirements for the employment of the staff and the determination of the conditions of service. On the first of these requisite qualities Hammarskjöld commented that 'if integrity in the sense of respect for law and respect for truth were to drive him (the international civil servant) into positions of conflict with this or that interest, then that conflict is a sign of his neutrality—and not of his failure to observe neutrality—then it is in line, not in conflict with, his duties as an international civil servant'.[11]

It is clear from the above quotations that Hammarskjöld did not equate neutrality with a failure to take positions. He did, however, consider identification with national or group interests to conflict with neutrality. It should

[7] Reprinted in Kay (ed.), *The United Nations Political System* (1967), 142–60.

[8] Art. 100 reads: '1. In the performance of their duties the Secretary-General and the staff shall not seek or receive instructions from any government or from any authority external to the Organization. They shall refrain from any action which might reflect upon their position as international officials responsible only to the Organization. 2. Each member of the United Nations undertakes to respect the exclusively international character of the responsibilities of the Secretary-General and the staff and not to seek to influence them in their discharge of their responsibilities.'

[9] Hammarskjöld, in Kay, *The United Nations Political System*, 150.

[10] Ibid. 159.

[11] Ibid. 160.

also be noted, as Hammarskjöld states, that respect for law and for truth are matters of integrity and conscience and a demonstration of neutrality. While fully agreeing with both the substance and lines of Hammarskjöld's arguments I consider the word 'neutrality' (which was apparently used in response to his critics) to be ill chosen. I believe that being in the service of, and solely responsible to, the United Nations (in accordance with Article 100) is not a neutral affair since a servant of the United Nations must be guided by the Organization's principles, purposes, and policies which are *per se* not neutral but represent basic values concerning the dignity and welfare of peoples and individual human beings. This applies to the staff of the United Nations as a whole and, *a fortiori*, to the international civil servants carrying special responsibility for the human rights programme. In this respect the various elements of international human rights law, referred to earlier, set out a framework, demanding respect for law and morality and observance of truth and integrity.

While the staff of the United Nations and in particular its human rights officers can therefore not remain neutral in the performance of their duties, they are of course bound to base themselves on the law and on a fair and objective interpretation of the facts. They should not be partisan towards group or national interest but should rather be partners in the advancement of human welfare and the promotion of human rights. As I stated at the opening of the session of the Commission on Human Rights in February 1978:

> If one tries to work for the cause of human rights, as we do on a daily basis in the Division of Human Rights, it is impossible to remain indifferent when confronted with the many appeals which are directed to the United Nations. Peoples, groups of persons, and individuals are vesting their hopes in the United Nations, which has proclaimed ideals of freedom, justice, and peace and which has reaffirmed faith in fundamental human rights, in the dignity and worth of the human person. Large masses, many of them children and young people, see no meaningful future because they lack the most basic needs of existence. Large groups of people live in desperate situations because of their race, their sex, their religion, their ethnic origin, or their convictions. It would appear that in particular those who are underprivileged, who are victims of discrimination and oppression should be of primary concern, in a joint effort of the United Nations and its Commission on Human Rights together with all organs of society, national and international.[12]

These words were meant to indicate partisanship in favour of human rights, in particular the rights of the oppressed and the underprivileged. In the face of flagrant violations of human rights, responsibility to the Organization is incompatible with an attitude of strict neutrality, despite the risk of conflicts with governmental interests.

The major issue at stake is the fact that the ideals and principles which

[12] van Boven, *People Matter*, 48–9.

underlie a 'peoples-oriented' approach, are at variance with the prevailing realities of the United Nations, which are geared toward harmonizing the interests of governments. The Human Rights Secretariat forms part and parcel of the overall administration of the Organization and as such is subject to the policies, rules, instructions, and guidelines which govern the UN Secretariat as a whole, under the leadership of the Secretary-General. The question arises whether the Secretary-General, given the broad range of interests he has to serve, can afford to take a principled stand on human rights matters if he is not to lose the support of the major powers. Commentators who have studied and analysed the role played by successive Secretaries-General have rightly observed that each has perceived his role to be primarily in the area of solving political conflicts.[13] Inasmuch as an outspoken and principled stand on human rights tends to cause conflicts with governments rather than to solve them, an activist human rights policy does not fit well into the concepts and strategies of the average Secretary-General. From his perspective, channels of communication with governments should remain open if he wishes to play a role in conflict resolution and in promoting political settlements, even when the governments concerned might be among the worst violators of human rights and deserve no moral credit whatsoever. Consequently, the UN Secretariat is caught in a conflict between political or diplomatic pragmatism and convenience on the one hand, and the principles of morality and human rights on the other. The Secretary-General and his immediate associates are naturally inclined to favour 'quiet diplomacy' and confidential procedures. On the other hand, some staff members who are further removed from the political centre of the Secretariat and more directly in touch with human rights problems, may wish to see more visible action. As long as a Secretary-General insists on a uniform, centralized approach by the entire UN administration, neutrality and caution will inevitably be the watchwords at all levels.

B. *The Secretary-General*

In his enlightening study on the Secretary-General's humanitarian good offices role, Ramcharan[14] analysed the extent to which Secretaries-General Lie, Hammarskjöld, U Thant, and Waldheim sought to make human rights an integral part of their overall strategies in leading the Organization. Largely on the basis of the Annual Reports of these Secretaries-General on the Work of the Organization, he concluded that the answer to the question whether these officials perceived the need to include human rights within their core strategies appeared to be in the negative, with the exception of U Thant:

[13] Weiss, *International Bureaucracy* (1975), 89.
[14] Ramcharan, *Humanitarian Good Offices in International Law* (1983).

Lie and Hammarskjöld served during the formative years of the Organization and it would be unrealistic to have expected them to go further... U Thant continued Hammarskjöld's work in handling political crises, sought to utilize his good offices in dealing with humanitarian crises and left office openly pointing out the need for the Organization to face up to humanitarian crises, including violations of human rights. U Thant came nearest to including human rights questions within his core strategy. Secretary-General Waldheim was certainly mindful of the need to deal with humanitarian crises and also used innovative methods for dealing with them, but the evidence suggests that he approached human rights more in a compartmentalized than an integrated manner.[15]

Ramcharan cites many cases where the Secretary-General, through a variety of means, sought to exercise good offices in response to urgent humanitarian cases or situations. It is striking, however, that in none of the major situations in which the Secretary-General got substantially involved when exercising his good offices role (for instance, East Pakistan (Bangladesh); refugees and displaced persons in South-east Asia; Cyprus; American hostages in Iran), was his involvement related to actions by the UN's human rights organs. Notably, Waldheim considered his good offices role to be a matter within his own discretion and competence, and sought to avoid interference by the human rights organs.[16] In recent years the Commission on Human Rights, acting confidentially under the 1503 procedure or publicly, has on many occasions requested the Secretary-General to use his good offices or to contact governments in relation to alleged serious violations of human rights and to report to the Commission.[17] In these instances, the Secretary-General was bound to respond, given that Article 98 of the Charter requires him 'to perform such other functions as are entrusted to him'. Nevertheless, for the most part, his attitude was characterized by reluctance and caution, and little reliance was placed on the expert services of the Human Rights Secretariat. Requests from the Commission were usually not carried out expeditiously but were acted upon at a very late stage when the duty to report to the next session of the Commission or the General Assembly was imminent. A case in point is that relating to Guatemala. In 1980 and 1981 the Commission requested the Secretary-General to establish direct contacts with that government and to report to the Commission.[18] The government succeeded, however, in frustrating virtually all 'velvet glove' efforts by the Secretary-General.

Another enlightening case is that of Poland. In March 1982 the Commission requested the Secretary-General to arrange for the preparation of a report on the situation in that country. Although the Commission's request

[15] Ibid. 32.
[16] Ibid. 83.
[17] Ibid. 75.
[18] CHR Res. 32 (XXXVI) (1980) and 33 (XXXVII) (1981).

was confirmed by ECOSOC in early May,[19] it was not until 21 December 1982 that Secretary-General Pérez de Cuellar designated as his representative Under-Secretary-General Hugo Gobbi. The latter's report was noted principally for its diplomatic caution.[20] In March 1983 the Commission renewed the mandate and requested 'the Secretary-General or a person designated by him to update and complete the thorough study of the human rights situation in Poland requested in its Resolution 1982/26, based on such information as he may deem relevant, including comments and materials the Government of Poland may wish to provide, and to present a comprehensive report to the Commission at its fortieth session'.

The report subsequently presented by Under-Secretary-General Patricio Ruedas in March 1984, amazed many observers because of its brevity, incompleteness, and restraint.[21] It indicated that the Secretary-General did not find it possible to give full effect to the mandate entrusted to him, because his representative Mr Gobbi had left the United Nations and had had to be replaced for present purposes by Patricio Ruedas. Because of those staff changes the report did not purport to be 'comprehensive' nor was it the result of a 'thorough study'. But such a justification cannot be considered to be either valid or convincing.

The Secretary-General has the responsibility of ensuring that tasks entrusted to him are carried out effectively. He cannot be blamed if governments fail to co-operate, but changes within his own staff cannot legitimately be adduced as a reason for inadequate fulfilment of his duties. The real explanation in this case is revealed in correspondence between the Helsinki Committee on Poland and the Secretary-General in which Mr Ruedas, writing on behalf of the Secretary-General, emphasized 'that the Secretary-General remains committed to promote human rights throughout the world, including in Poland. In this respect, he continues to believe that he can pursue this objective most effectively through the exercise of quiet diplomacy.'[22] By noting that the Secretary-General was at that time engaged in efforts to obtain the release of political prisoners in Poland, including a UN staff member, the letter's reference to 'quiet diplomacy' implies that the presentation on his behalf of a comprehensive factual report would not be conducive to the specific human rights interests he was pursuing. In effect, the Commission's mandate was thus unilaterally reinterpreted by the Secretary-General.

The Polish case clearly demonstrates that the Secretary-General should as a general rule not be entrusted with public fact-finding and reporting duties in the area of violations of human rights. Such duties complicate his other

[19] CHR Res. 26/1982, confirmed by ESC Dec. 1982/133.

[20] E/CN.4/1983/18. The newspaper *Le Monde* wrote on 2 Mar. 1983: 'The report on Poland shines by its insignificance.'

[21] E/CN.4/1984/26.

[22] Helsinki Watch, *No Mention of Solidarity: UN Report on Human Rights in Poland* (Sept. 1984).

functions and he is unlikely to be the most appropriate authority to carry them out effectively. It would therefore appear that in the light of experience and given the fact that the Secretary-General's actions are characterized by political restraint and diplomatic caution, it would seem that the task of investigating and reporting on violations of human rights should be entrusted to independent experts rather than to the Secretary-General or members of his staff. Such experts can of course make full use of the experience of the staff of the Secretariat.

This approach need not, however, diminish the humanitarian role the Secretary-General can play within the domain of his own competence and on the basis of his own authority. Ramcharan refers to the dual competence of the Secretary-General, stemming on the one hand from his general powers under the Charter to use his good offices at his own discretion, and on the other hand from the requirement 'to perform such other functions as are entrusted to him' by UN organs.[23] It is submitted that in general, human rights fact-finding should be entrusted to Working Groups or Special Rapporteurs serving in their individual and expert capacities, rather than to the Secretary-General. However, in cases which call for discreet intercession, in particular when the lives or the physical integrity of individual human beings are at stake, the Secretary-General's diplomatic role may be beneficial. Although it is true that such requests to governments to grant favours on humanitarian grounds in cases where such action should in any event be taken as of right amount to legitimating injustice, the Secretary-General is not only a servant of justice: he also has to be mindful of the fate of individual human beings.

Successive Secretaries-General have publicly acknowledged their good offices role, but details are not publicly available on this score and it is difficult to assess the effectiveness of their actions.[24] What seems to be needed, however, is a more systematic effort to bring individual cases to the attention of the Secretary-General; a process which would be facilitated if more effective procedures of communication were to be created with the competent services of the Human Rights Secretariat.

C. *The Human Rights Sector of the Secretariat*

The human rights sector of the Secretariat was established in the early days of the United Nations as a Division. Although the Division had long satisfied the

[23] Ramcharan, *Humanitarian Good Offices*, 82–3.

[24] U Thant was apparently quite successful in obtaining the exit of many Jews from the USSR. See ibid. 63. Pérez de Cuellar stated in his Report on the Work of the Organization in 1983: 'I have been in contact with a number of governments regarding particular human rights situations or individual cases. I am heartened by the instances in which co-operation has been extended to me in these contacts, and I am determined to persist in my efforts'. A/38/1 (1983).

criteria[25] necessary for upgrading within the Secretariat to the status of a Centre, it was not until 28 July 1982 that the Secretary-General redesignated it accordingly as the Centre for Human Rights. In fact, both the General Assembly and the Commission had on a number of occasions requested such a change of status[26] but Secretary-General Waldheim had deferred the decision on the grounds that 'further consideration of the matter was required'.[27] Waldheim was obviously anxious to avoid any controversy in the matter since some States, notably those of Eastern Europe, were opposed to such a change. It was also suggested that Waldheim did not wish to jeopardize his bid for a third term of office and thus preferred to act on the matter, which was after all not of great urgency, only after his re-election.

Waldheim's successor, Javier Pérez de Cuellar, who took office on 1 January 1982, and whose first action affecting the Human Rights Secretariat was the non-renewal of my own contract as Director of the Division of Human Rights, had a special interest in demonstrating his good will towards the human rights programme. He thus gave the redesignation his early blessing. Subsequently, he sought and obtained the Assembly's approval to upgrade the directorship of the Centre to the Assistant-Secretary-General level as from 1 January 1983 because 'the official in charge of the Centre bears an extra heavy responsibility in representing the Secretary-General in the meetings of human rights bodies in Geneva and in dealing with ranking dignitaries in that diplomatic community' and because this official 'with substantive day-to-day responsibility for carrying out these important and sometimes sensitive contacts, as well as supervising and managing the Organization's human rights programme as a whole on behalf of the Secretary-General, should have a rank commensurate with such important responsibilities'.[28]

The post of head of the Human Rights Secretariat was subsequently upgraded again, although it was in another sense downgraded at the same time. In 1986, at the height of the United Nations' financial crisis, the Secretary-General undertook to reduce the total number of senior executive level positions in the Organization. In the process, he abolished the post of Assistant-Secretary-General for Human Rights (occupied at the time by an Austrian, Kurt Herndl) and transferred that responsibility to an Under-Secretary-General who, since that time, has also served as Director-General of the UN Office in Geneva. Two very senior posts were thus, in effect, amalgamated and the appointee (a Swede, Jan Martenson) has been required

[25] The criteria are set forth in A/C.5/32/17 (1977).

[26] See GA Res. 34/47 (1979), CHR Res. 22 (XXXVI) (1980), and ESC Dec. 1980/132.

[27] 'Report of the Secretary-General on the Service of the Secretariat Concerned with Human Rights'. A/35/607 (1980).

[28] A/C.5/37/82 (1982), paras. 34–5.

to perform both sets of functions simultaneously, thus clearly reducing the amount of time available to be devoted to the human rights portfolio.

As of 1 July 1990 the internal administrative arrangements of the Centre were changed significantly. It now consists of three major branches, in addition to the Office of the Under-Secretary-General for Human Rights, an Administrative Unit, and a Liaison Office based in New York. Within the Legislation and Prevention of Discrimination Branch are the Research and Standards Section and the Prevention of Discrimination Section. The Implementation Branch consists of the International Instruments Section, the Special Procedures Section, and the Communications Section. The Advisory Services, Technical Assistance and Information Branch consists of the Advisory Services and Technical Assistance Section and the External Relations Section. A formal description of the organization and duties of the Centre is published regularly in the Secretary-General's Bulletin. In 1990 the authorized staffing table consisted of a total of 45 professional officers.

Without seeking to trace the history of more than forty years of work of the Human Rights Secretariat, one particular event deserves to be singled out for special attention. In 1974 the Division of Human Rights was transferred from Headquarters in New York to the European Office at Geneva. The official rationale for this move was strictly administrative and financial, but, as usual, political considerations were prevalent. It was suggested that East European and Arab nations in particular wanted the Human Rights Secretariat moved away from the active American Jewish lobby. It was also believed that the Secretary-General had an interest in relocating this sensitive part of the Secretariat, which for all political purposes was considered more of a liability than an asset, at a suitable distance from the political centre. Leaving aside the real motivations for the transfer, it is my view that in the final analysis the move to Geneva was a blessing in disguise. It is true that location in New York has certain advantages inasmuch as political and administrative co-ordination can be better secured at Headquarters, given the presence of the political and administrative leadership of the Organization. It is also true that location in New York might ideally be conducive to integrating human rights into other major UN programmes in the areas of development and disarmament. There would thus seem to be weighty arguments for a return of the Human Rights Secretariat to Headquarters.

On the other hand, if one favours a functioning of the human rights programme in a manner which is somewhat removed from the political control and pressures at Headquarters, if one favours closer co-ordination and co-operation with other humanitarian organizations and with a broad gamut of non-governmental organizations, if one favours a 'people-oriented' approach to human rights with open communication to the outside world and easier access of concerned groups and individuals to the Secretariat, the Centre for Human Rights should remain in Geneva.

However, inasmuch as in recent years the political organs of the United Nations in New York and the Office of the Secretary-General are getting increasingly involved in intra-state conflicts requiring solutions with direct human rights implications, the physical separation between Geneva and New York may well become more of a liability than an asset. No senior official at UN Headquarters in the vicinity of the Secretary-General presently carries special responsibility for human rights. This situation should be remedied, either by moving the Centre back to New York or by substantially strengthening the role and the status of the Centre's New York Liaison Office.

The Secretariat's principal role is to support and implement the human rights programme developed by the relevant policy organs. It has been rightly observed that the main thrust of the human rights programme has evolved through various stages focusing on promotional activities, implementation, and a structural approach.[29] While in the first decade of its existence the Secretariat provided a considerable intellectual input in the drafting of the International Bill of Human Rights,[30] it embarked in the fifties and in later years upon the preparation of a number of important studies which were officially brought out in the name of Special Rapporteurs but in reality were largely and sometimes entirely the product of research and study by the Secretariat.[31] Through this means the Secretariat was able to carry out a large amount of creative research and to provide useful insights and approaches for tackling human rights questions. While many of the early studies were concerned with aspects of discrimination, in later years the Secretariat has been asked to study some of the causes and conditions that lead to violations of human rights, such as denial of the right to self-determination, the causes of racism and other manifestations of discrimination, and the effects of the present unjust international economic order and of the unbridled continuation and escalation of the arms race. This 'structural' approach to human rights found clear political expression in General Assembly Resolution 32/130 of 1977 and in many subsequent pronouncements of the General Assembly and the Commission. The same approach also led to requests by the Commission for studies on the international, regional, and national dimensions on the right to development which in their scope and content proved to be pioneering products of creative thinking and research.[32] These in turn have provided a basis for further standard-setting and, hopefully, for the framing of international and national policies aimed at bringing about improved conditions for the realization and enjoyment of human rights. Such studies prove that the

[29] See in particular Marie, *La Commission des droits de l'homme de l'ONU* (1975) and Alston, *Development and the Rule of Law: Prevention Versus Cure as a Human Rights Strategy* (1981).

[30] See Humphrey, in his autobiographical work, *The Great Adventure*.

[31] For information on studies which the Secretariat prepared or contributed to, see *United Nations Action in the Field of Human Rights* (1988), 337–40.

[32] E/CN.4/1334 (1978); E/CN.4/1421 (1981); and E/CN.4/1488 (1981).

Secretariat can play a leadership role in study and research, provided it does not content itself with mere compilation and a lowest common denominator approach and provided also that the studies are action-oriented and not undertaken on abstract, academic, or marginal topics.[33]

Since 1969 various conventions as well as the two Human Rights Covenants and the Optional Protocol have entered into force. The demands on the services of the Secretariat have expanded accordingly. Thus, for example, the preliminary draft Rules of Procedure for the Committee on the Elimination of Racial Discrimination and for the Human Rights Committee were drafted by the Secretariat. The Racial Discrimination Convention states that that Committee's Secretariat shall be provided by the Secretary-General (Article 10, para. 3). Similarly, the Covenant on Civil and Political Rights stipulates that the Secretary-General shall provide the necessary staff and facilities for the effective performance of the functions of the Committee (Article 36). Similar provisions are included in the Convention Against Torture (Art. 18(3)) and the Convention on the Rights of the Child (Art. 43(11)).

It is somewhat anomalous that although these Committees are not technically UN bodies but rather function within the treaty framework of States Parties, matters of staffing, administration, and finance for those bodies nevertheless fall within the decision-making competence of organs of the United Nations, notably the General Assembly and the Secretariat. This state of affairs has occasionally led to some friction between these independent expert bodies and the Organization, inasmuch as the former, or at least a part of their membership, felt that their activities were subject to unduly restrictive UN rules, practices, and facilities regarding such matters as the timing of meetings, publicity and information, staff resources, travel arrangements, emoluments, etc. Some East European members also felt at the time that the non-United Nations, *sui generis*, status of the Human Rights Committee required the representative of the Secretary-General to adopt a position of utmost restraint when discussing general policy matters affecting that body.[34] But although, from the strictly legal point of view, there may be a difference

[33] Many UN reports and studies suffer from lack of imagination and creativity and avoid raising the relevant issues. In this regard the critical notes and recommendations in a 1984 report prepared by Maurice Bertrand of the Joint Inspection Unit entitled 'Reporting to the Economic and Social Council' (JIU/REP/84/7) deserve full attention. Bertrand wrote very aptly: 'Interpretations of the political situation lead staff members in many cases to apply a form of self-censorship which is not favourable to the dissemination of information, the development of initiatives, or the formulation of constructive proposals' (para. 4). One of the main recommendations put forward by Bertrand is to have more recourse to outside expertise. This should assist the Secretariat in constantly improving its effectiveness, breathing new 'life into its dialogue with Member States and devising a new style in many fields' (para. 67).

[34] At the opening of the seventh session of the Human Rights Committee on 30 July 1979 I raised a number of policy issues regarding, *inter alia*, the supervisory role of the Committee, its consideration of communications, and its relationship with Specialized Agencies (cf. van Boven,

between UN human rights organs and human rights treaty bodies in their respective relationships to the Secretary-General and his staff, in practice this difference is more artificial than real. Some members of the treaty-based bodies have expressed the wish that the Secretariat should provide more substantive services than merely handling matters of a largely administrative nature. It is indeed true that the Secretariat could do more to assist the members of these organs in the preparation of their work, in particular by furnishing them with technical analyses of the reports of States Parties on the basis of criteria and guidelines established by the treaty organs. In this connection proposals made in a report to the Commission by its Task Force on Computerization go in the right direction.

Complaints by private groups and individuals alleging violations of human rights run annually into some tens of thousands, and impose a considerable workload on the Human Rights Secretariat. It is not intended to discuss here in detail the duties of the Secretariat which flow from the relevant ECOSOC Resolutions 728 F (XXVIII) and 1503 (XLVIII) and from subsequent decisions of the Commission relating to the procedures. Suffice it to say that the many thousands of communications which reach the Secretariat are of a highly diverse nature, ranging from a few words to hundreds of pages per communication, sometimes written in languages which are not the working languages of the Organization. Regularly complainants present themselves in person and it is the policy of the Secretariat to receive them, to listen, and to give advice as to the functioning of UN procedures. While the procedures are rudimentary and provide neither legal standing to the authors of communications nor real possibilities for redress, the workload of the Secretariat is a very heavy one and entails not only administrative duties but also policy issues because of the co-existence of a variety of procedures. Time and again this requires decisions as to the procedure under which a given communication should be handled, in particular when authors have given no specific indication of the body or procedure to which they wish to address themselves. The Provisional Rules of Procedure of the Human Rights Committee give some guidance in this matter by requiring the Secretary-General to bring to the attention of the Committee communications which are, or appear to be, submitted for its consideration under Article 1 of the Protocol (Rule 78) and by providing that the Secretary-General may also request clarification from the author concerning the applicability of the Protocol to his communication (Rule 80).[35] But in many other cases where additional procedural avenues are available (such as Working Groups or Special Rapporteurs having a mandate regarding a special country or a specific human rights concern), no guidelines

People Matter, 125–31). Some Committee members from East European countries felt strongly that the representative of the Secretary-General should abstain from dealing publicly with such policy issues while other members expressed support for my position.

[35] See E/CN.4/1317 (1979), paras. 6–13.

or instructions from policy organs exist and the Secretariat finds itself in the position of having to devise its own policies, keeping in mind the interest of the authors of communications, and the efficacy of the respective procedures.

In a number of instances, governments involved in special procedures have criticized the Secretariat for bringing to the attention of special investigatory bodies communications relating to the mandate of such bodies. Those governments, feeling more at ease with the confidential and rather ineffective procedures under ECOSOC Resolutions 728F and 1503, argued that for the handling of communications the Rules of Procedure had to be applied without exception and that the Secretariat had thus violated the prescribed procedure. Such was, for instance, the position of Argentina in connection with individual communications on disappeared persons that were brought to the attention of the Working Group on Enforced or Involuntary Disappearances. The Director of the Division of Human Rights replied in writing, with the authority of the Working Group, that the contentions of Argentina could not be sustained. In his letter he reviewed the relationships between different UN procedures for dealing with human rights problems or with allegations of violations of human rights and concluded that a specialized procedure for dealing with the problem of disappeared persons should be complementary to other existing procedures and not be subordinated to any pre-existing procedure.[36]

The practice pursued by the Secretariat is that, whenever specialized procedures exist, relevant communications or copies thereof are brought to their attention.

One of the most dynamic responsibilities of the Human Rights Secretariat is the servicing of fact-finding exercises.[37] The policy organs have increasingly resorted to the creation of working groups and special rapporteurs as mechanisms of investigation, dialogue, and advice. In addition to a wide variety of specific country situations, special phenomena of major human rights concern, such as disappeared or missing persons, slavery and slavery-like practices, and summary or arbitrary executions, religious discrimination, and torture have become subjects of investigative mandates. The role of the Secretariat with regard to these special fact-finding bodies is very substantive. It extends to such matters as: advising groups and rapporteurs on their methods of work; the collection of information; analysing facts, practices, and legislation; preparing field trips and contacts with relevant authorities; organizing the hearing of witnesses; contacting a diversity of sources of information; servicing Working Groups and Rapporteurs while in session or on mission; and preparing drafts for the reports to be submitted to policy organs. Many

[36] 'First Report of the Working Group to the Commission on Human Rights', E/CN.4/1435 (1981), paras. 75–6. For more details see Annexes IX and X of this Report.

[37] See generally Ramcharan (ed.), *International Law and Fact-Finding in the Field of Human Rights* (1982).

of these activities require the highest professional standards in terms of expertise, dedication, and diplomatic skills. In this respect the experience gained in other international organizations with respect to the qualifications of the staff also applies to UN fact-finding exercises. As a senior ILO official has noted:

> Any serious inquiry calls for thorough preliminary research by technically qualified and experienced officials who are used to working with the utmost objectivity, possess sound judgment, and are able to adopt a balanced approach to controversial situations. This technical staff needs to be co-ordinated by a senior official, whose duty is to give guidance in the light of his wider experience and particular knowledge of the background and political context of the case under examination.[38]

It would go beyond the scope of this chapter to spell out in detail the functions of the Secretariat in fact-finding exercises. However, it is worth stressing that the quality and effectiveness of these operations are significantly enhanced by the skills of the Secretariat. The latter should not hesitate to make use of the advice, the insights, and the assistance of knowledgeable and reliable partners in other sectors of the UN Secretariat or in other intergovernmental or non-governmental organizations. Two examples may serve as an illustration. The first pertains to an on-site fact-finding mission in Latin America. Prior to the mission and during the stay in the country the Secretariat of the investigatory group not only benefited from the existing UN facilities in the country, but also and very importantly, from the insights and advice voluntarily offered by UN officials serving in that country and who were able to establish contacts with persons and groups providing invaluable information to the investigatory group. Such assistance, often provided by local officials without the explicit and formal authority of their superiors at headquarters proves that effective co-operation and co-ordination which may be difficult to achieve at the top bureaucratic levels may with a sense of goodwill be effectuated in the field.

The other example, from 1980, relates to the challenge of devising methods of work to be followed by the newly established Working Group on Enforced or Involuntary Disappearances. At the outset of this operation, the Human Rights Secretariat convened an informal meeting with representatives of some six or seven non-governmental organizations that had already acquired a great deal of experience in dealing with questions of disappearances. The discussion touched upon such issues as channelling of information, verification of reports, procedures for urgent actions relating to information on recent disappearances, etc. Such an informal consultation with experienced and knowledgeable NGO representatives and in which due regard was paid to the position and responsibilities of each of the partners contributed significantly to

38 Von Potobsky, 'On-the-spot Visits: An Important Cog in the ILO's Supervisory Machinery', 120 *Int'l Lab. Rev.* 593 (1981).

the type and degree of assistance that the Secretariat could render to the Working Group. Particularly when dealing with concrete situations and the individuals involved, a major requirement for the effectiveness of the Secretariat is that of partnership, in the first place *vis-à-vis* the expert body the Secretariat is called upon to serve, but also in co-operation with other intergovernmental organizations and with reliable non-governmental organizations and groups. It is indeed essential, not only in fact-finding activities but with respect to the entire human rights programme, that the Secretariat maintains effective and close contacts with the non-governmental sector. As regards relationships with non-governmental organizations in consultative status, Article 71 of the UN Charter and ECOSOC Resolution 1296 (XLIV) provide for detailed arrangements for consultation, including consultation with the Secretariat. Open channels of communication and easy access to the Secretariat by the non-governmental sector can only enhance the effect and the impact of the human rights programme.

The effectiveness of special fact-finding procedures tends to be jeopardized by rules and regulations of an administrative and budgetary nature. Although it is anticipated that in the years to come there will be 'an accentuated trend towards more fact-finding and direct contacts, in the field of human rights as well as efforts of the Secretary-General in situations of mass and flagrant violations of human rights' and that 'ways and means will be considered by the Commission on Human Rights and other relevant bodies to provide urgent United Nations responses to situations of gross violations of human rights',[39] the regular biennial budgets for the human rights programme present serious obstacles for the Human Rights Secretariat in its efforts to respond expeditiously in the servicing of fact-finding exercises. It is assumed in the regular budget that special procedures in the area of fact-finding, irrespective of whether they relate to specific country situations or to general phenomena of serious concern, are of a non-recurring nature and that the funds needed for servicing and carrying out these activities should therefore not form part of the regular budget. This assumption is based on the expectation that special situations or phenomena under investigation are of a temporary nature and that funds can only be allocated for activities and needs relating to those situations and phenomena after policy organs have issued or renewed the mandates pertaining to the investigations. As a consequence, sufficient staff and resources are not available under the regular budget, in spite of the fact that special procedures have become a permanent feature of the human rights programme and that 'an accentuated trend towards more fact-finding and direct contacts' is expected. By upholding the fiction that these special procedures are non-recurrent in nature, and thus require additional allocations from the budgetary authorities, in particular the Advisory Committee

[39] 'Medium-Term Plan for the Period 1984–1989', A/37/6 (1982), para. 6.23.

for Administrative and Budgetary Questions (ACABQ) and the General Assembly, these authorities are able to exercise, often in a less visible manner, not only administrative but also political control over the proposed implementation of human rights mandates. One of the ensuing complications is a delaying effect on the implementation of mandates that usually concern urgent situations. The fiction of the non-recurrent nature of the activities also ensures that the number of established posts earmarked for this type of work are far below what is required. Moreover, even when additional allocations are eventually authorized, most of them must be used to employ temporary assistance staff.

The utilization of temporary staff in the sensitive and politically controversial area of fact-finding poses considerable problems from the point of view of management and efficiency. Since temporary staff are only recruited on a short-term basis and the Organization is most reluctant for reasons of personnel policy to renew their contracts, the benefit of training is naturally lost when the staff member leaves and little expertise can be built up on a continuing basis, although expertise is of the essence in the servicing of investigations. Another problem which deserves emphasis is governmental interference and pressures with respect to certain aspects of internal staff management and utilization. Two examples, each of which is a matter of public record, serve to illustrate this point.

During the 1978 session of the Commission the representative of the USSR insisted repeatedly that, in view of relevant General Assembly resolutions, the Division of Human Rights had to comply with the principle of equitable geographical distribution of posts, and that this principle should apply not only with respect to the Secretariat as a whole but to each division or administrative unit. As the Director of the Division, I replied in essence that, in the light of the various criteria for the employment of staff laid down in Article 101 of the Charter and the wording of the relevant Assembly Resolution,[40] the principle was applicable to the Secretariat as a whole but not automatically to each and every individual unit of the Secretariat.[41] I also insisted that the distribution and utilization of staff in the various units of the Secretariat is a question of internal administration and efficiency and that the work of the Division had to be organized in the most efficient and rational manner. The real motivation of the USSR's complaint was their wish to see an East European staff member assigned to the Communications Unit which handles complaints from individuals and private groups, including, naturally, complaints pertaining to East European countries. The management of the Division never yielded to this desire of the USSR. At the following session of the Commission the Soviet delegate repeated the same criticism and also

[40] GA Res. 31/26 (1976).

[41] See *Report of the Commission on Human Rights*, E/1978/34, paras. 204–5.

made other remarks critical of the leadership of the Division. These related to matters such as the views expressed in opening statements and at press briefings, the circulation of NGO documents critical of General Assembly Resolutions (in particular the one equating Zionism with racism), etc.

Another example of governmental interference relates to the problem discussed above of the utilization of temporary staff for fact-finding purposes, in particular in connection with the Working Group on Enforced or Involuntary Disappearances. Since the practice of disappearances was particularly widespread and alarming in Latin American countries, notably Argentina, some temporary staff members were recruited because of their knowledge of the Spanish language and their familiarity with the prevailing legal systems in Latin America. These staff members, supervised on a daily basis by experienced staff on permanent posts, soon developed the necessary competence and efficiency and performed their functions with dedication. The Argentine government felt significantly threatened by the activities of the Working Group and made every effort to challenge its methods of work, to discredit its sources of information and to attack and intimidate the Secretariat. The government representative went so far as to allege that 'terrorists'[42] were on the staff of the Working Group.

It was against this background that Argentina, supported by some other Latin American countries, consistently criticized the leadership of the Human Rights Secretariat, ostensibly for its use of temporary staff. Attacks were mounted not only in the Commission[43] but also in ECOSOC, the Assembly, and even in the ACABQ. It was probably not by coincidence that, in the wake of this campaign of harassment by Argentina, the personnel services of the United Nations did not see fit to approve renewal of temporary contracts of the persons who had been the special target of Argentina's allegations. This decision was taken despite the judgment of their immediate supervisors that the temporary staff members had carried out their work with the highest standards of efficiency, competence, and integrity. This example illustrates how political pressure and interference by a major human rights violator, partly applied overtly but perhaps more effectively through invisible and unverifiable means, can threaten to undermine the effectiveness of the Secretariat. In order to protect the independence of the staff and to ensure that performance and merit are the criteria for professional advancement, as

[42] It should be noted that former president Jorge Rafael Videla of Argentina once defined a 'terrorist' as 'not just someone with a gun or a bomb but also someone who spreads ideas that are contrary to western civilization' (quoted by Kinzer, 'Argentina in Agony', *New Republic*, 23 and 30 Dec. (1978), 18). Reference may also be made to Sydney Bailey's comment that '[n]o Secretary-General would knowingly appoint a person who had engaged in acts of subversion against any State; but the commission of subversive acts is a very different thing from mere disagreement with the policy of a particular government'. Bailey, *The Secretariat of the UN* (1964), 26.

[43] See e.g. *Report of the Commission on Human Rights*, E/1981/25, para. 209.

successive Secretaries-General have stressed so aptly time and again,[44] the leadership of the Secretariat should make every effort to ensure that the practice of yielding to undue government pressures is put to an end. Otherwise Article 100 of the UN Charter will become a dead letter and the erosion of the independence of the international civil service will continue. It is evident that this applies *a fortiori* to that sector of the Secretariat that has a special responsibility for advancing human rights.

A major challenge facing the human rights sector of the Secretariat—and this applies *mutatis mutandis* to the entire UN Secretariat—is the need for more rational planning and more efficient organization and use of available resources. It cannot be said that the Secretariat has been very successful in these areas in the field of human rights. In theory, planning should find concrete expression in the Medium-Term Plan which should highlight the policy orientations of the UN system and indicate the medium-term objectives and strategy and the trends deduced from the mandates which reflect the priorities set by the intergovernmental organs.[45]

The Medium-Term Plan should indicate trends and developments established by policy organs. It should also, however, identify activities that have been completed, are obsolete, of marginal usefulness, or ineffective. The question arises to what extent a rational planning of human rights activities is at all possible in view of the great variety of interests and views on the part of member States regarding the orientation and contents of the human rights programme. Ideally, the Commission as the main policy organ should be in a position to take the necessary measures in order to secure efficient and adequate planning, but it has proved unable to play this role. The reason is that the same conflicting interests which complicate human rights policy-making and prevent rational organization and harmonization in general are as much at work in the Commission as in any other human rights body. Thus, when the Commission had to examine the proposed Medium-Term Plan for 1984–9, it was informed by the Deputy Director of the Division, Mr Nyamekye, that:

> The Division had in recent years been faced with a situation in which the level of repetition, duplication and lack of planning and co-ordination had resulted in great difficulties and wastage of scarce resources. It had sometimes received requests for studies on similar topics by different bodies or for reports which had little practical value and often remained on the shelves . . . [T]he decision to initiate standard-setting was much too haphazard, unplanned, and unco-ordinated, and it was far from certain that the priorities decided upon were the optimum ones.

In preparing the draft Medium-Term Plan, the Secretariat could only provide

[44] See Pérez de Cuellar, Annual Report of the *Secretary-General on the Work of the Organization 1982*, A/37/1 (1982).
[45] GA Res. 34/224 (1979), para. 2(g).

guidance on objectives and strategies with regard to the prevention of discrimination, standard-setting, research, and studies. The specific areas of activities were to be decided upon by the human rights organs.[46]

Commenting on the conflict arising out of great pressures to contain expenditures and continuous requests by the human rights organs to undertake new activities, he stressed that 'the Commission on Human Rights would have to indicate priorities and specify which tasks should be postponed, if necessary'. He informed the Commission that 'if necessary, the Secretariat might be forced to determine such priorities and to postpone activities which did not appear to be very urgent or important'.[47] It would indeed seem necessary, insofar as the Commission is unwilling or unable to agree upon coherent and effective policy planning, that the Secretariat with the support of the Secretary-General should act in accordance with the general policy spelled out in the Medium-Term Plan which may be invoked as a suitable framework for guidance. On the other hand, it should not serve as a bureaucratic strait-jacket which would impede imaginative responses to urgent human rights needs and stand in the way of dynamic programme development. If maximum planning and management efficiency were to be the ultimate goal of the human rights programme, its essence, which should be measured by its human rights impact, would surely suffer.

D. *The Executive Head*

The formal role of the Executive Head of the Human Rights Secretariat does not differ significantly from that played by the Executive Heads of other major UN programmes, the key tasks being representation and management. It is obvious that the Head cannot successfully perform his functions without the close collaboration and support of his colleagues in the Human Rights Secretariat, in particular his Deputy, his special assistant(s), the chiefs of sections and units, and the staff in charge of personnel, finance, and administration. It is also obvious that the Head, and in fact the entire staff of the Human Rights Secretariat, cannot function properly in isolation from the UN administration as a whole. Constructive relationships with the Secretary-General together with his immediate associates are essential as also are good working relations with the administrative, personnel, and financial services of the Organization and with the Department of Public Information. Similarly, because of the human rights implications of the activities of many other sectors of the Organization, frequent consultation and co-ordination is needed with all of the relevant departments and offices. This is particularly important

[46] E/CN.4/SR.1640 (1981), paras. 54–5.
[47] Ibid. para. 57.

in light of the desirability of integrating human rights into the other major activities of the Organization. In fact, some of the programmes conducted by other departments call for particularly frequent co-ordination between the Centre for Human Rights and the relevant officials dealing with, for example, apartheid, Palestinian rights, Cyprus, refugees, status of women and other special groups (youth, ageing, disabled persons), crime prevention, population, etc.

It is submitted, nevertheless, that the Executive Head of the Human Rights Secretariat and his staff, while forming part and parcel of the entire UN Secretariat, find themselves in a somewhat special position in view of the nature of the human rights programme. Many governments that are politically very active in UN organs, including the Commission on Human Rights, are serious human rights violators and seek through various means to protect their interests. Views on the content and implications of international human rights norms differ and this is inevitably also reflected in the opinion of individual staff members, who come from different regions of the world with different political systems. Moreover, there is hardly any UN programme in which non-governmental organizations and groups take such an active interest. Representatives of those groups, many of whom are strongly opposed to certain governmental policies and practices, seek access to the Human Rights Secretariat and wish in particular to have access to its Executive Head. He may thus find himself in the middle of controversies between governments and human rights proponents who represent and defend victims of oppression and discrimination. His attitude will be largely influenced by the way in which he perceives his role. He may be guided principally by intergovernmental interests and by formal bureaucratic rules, or he may see his function as the promotion of human rights ideals proclaimed by the Organization. His choice in this regard will often make a considerable difference in terms of the Secretariat's impact.

The Director's responsibilities for representation and management are of course inter-related. It is clear that his managerial duties relate to such matters as staffing, finance, organization of work, and programme planning on the basis of the mandates received from policy organs and other human rights bodies. There can be no doubt that, as an official of the Organization, the Director is subordinated to the Secretary-General. Nevertheless, it would appear that a distinction can be made between the formal role of the Director as 'Representative of the Secretary-General' and his role as an authoritative adviser and expert or a trustee of the human rights programme. The representational role of the Director flows from the duty of the Secretary-General to act in that capacity in meetings of the main organs of the Organization as prescribed in Article 98 of the Charter and from the fact that under the Rules of Procedure of the human rights organs the Secretary-General may designate a member of the Secretariat to act as his representative. He may also request the Director to represent him at meetings or on occasions other than sessions of UN organs.

But the role of the Director should not be perceived only in relation to the authority of the Secretary-General. The Director also works in close collaboration with human rights policy organs, particularly the Commission. It is therefore fair to say that the policies of these organs do and should provide the basis and framework for the Director's actions and pronouncements. In that sense, his role is based on dual authority, on the one hand deriving from the Secretary-General; and on the other hand, from the human rights policy organs. He carries out many outside activities in which he expresses views, gives advice and information, or consults. Such may be the case in contacts with delegations, non-governmental organizations, journalists, or other interested persons. It cannot be said that he acts in those instances as the 'Representative of the Secretary-General' but rather that he then acts under the authority of the Secretary-General and of the human rights policy organs. When carrying out the latter type of activities the Director has certainly more latitude than when he acts, *in stricto sensu*, as the representative of the Secretary-General.

While it is useful to keep in mind the variety of functions carried out by the Director, the extent to which he may develop a personal role by making statements on matters of policy that identify programme gaps and needs and include suggestions for specific action depends very much on the policy of the Secretary-General, his personal interest in the human rights programme, and his wish to exercise control. In a centralized bureaucratic system with full policy control exercised by the leadership there exists, of course, less scope for such an approach than under a system of delegated authority. In this connection it would seem that Secretary-General Pérez de Cuellar was in favour of a system of centralized control.[48] Another major factor is whether the Director, who is in constant touch with human rights policy organs and who can be considered to be a trustee of the human rights programme, seeks to respond not only to bureaucratic interests but also to human rights needs and interests.

In practice, as noted earlier, successive Secretaries-General have not taken a keen interest in the human rights programme and as a result a great deal of room has been left to the Director, perhaps not so much by way of express delegation of authority but rather by the inclination of the Secretary-General not to get too involved in human rights matters. Thus it proved possible for

[48] See the *Report of the Secretary-General on the Work of the Organization 1983*: 'One trend, however, deserves mention here, namely the tendency to establish more or less autonomous units to carry out certain functions—organs over which the Secretary-General does not have clear control. This trend raises serious questions of organizational responsibility and authority and may sometimes not be altogether consistent with the Charter concept of a unified Secretariat working as a team under a single leadership'. A/38/1 (1983), 13.

the Director to develop a policy of expounding publicly his own views and suggestions, based on insights gained in his daily work and on frequent contacts with delegations, non-governmental organizations, and groups, and members of the human rights staff. There are, however, limits of a political nature to the latitude and independence of the Director, since at a certain point the Secretary-General might encounter what he may consider adverse political consequences flowing from misgivings on the part of some governments. This is illustrated by the anomalous situation that resulted when I was instructed to include in my opening statement of 1 February 1982 to the thirty-eighth session of the Commission on Human Rights, the main focus of which was the protection of human life and the incidence of political assassinations in a number of named countries, the following phrase: 'I have to state that certain parts of my statement reflect my personal views.'[49] The insertion of this sentence, the significance of which did not escape the attention of certain delegations, was an indication that the Secretary-General did not wish to accept political responsibility for certain parts of my statement, despite the fact that its essence was a reflection of reports which were formally before the Commission. It is, however, a matter of record that an Executive Head, given conditions which leave room for a certain degree of independence and latitude, can play a public role in relation to the human rights policy organs, in addition to his important 'behind-the-scenes' role. The manner in which this public role is exercised is a matter of careful judgement which should take account of the overall content and orientation of the human rights programme, the prevailing views of policy organs, the probability of a meaningful follow-up, and objective needs and requirements in the light of the Organization's responsibility to promote and protect human rights. Public proposals for action should not amount to a voice 'crying in the wilderness' but rather reflect a process of weighing the views and sentiments of the main governmental and non-governmental actors in the human rights area, together with an assessment of objective needs and requirements by the Executive Head and his staff. Examples of such an approach in practice are given below.

The opening meetings of organs such as the Commission and the Sub-Commission always provide a good occasion on which to influence delegates and interested public opinion and provide an appropriate opportunity for the Executive Head to emphasize certain principles, to review developments, to formulate objectives, and to put forward concrete suggestions. During the years 1977–82, as Director of the Division of Human Rights, I repeatedly drew the attention of the Commission and the Sub-Commission to possible means by which to tackle gross and massive violations of human rights, building upon the experience already gained in investigations in particular

[49] The background to the addition of this sentence is outlined by Hans Thoolen, 'Introduction', van Boven, *People Matter*, 7–8.

situations, such as South Africa and Chile.[50] I pleaded that the United Nations should undertake appropriate fact-finding exercises by appointing rapporteurs, establishing panels of experts, or sending emissaries on behalf of human rights organs or the Secretary-General with respect to various situations allegedly involving serious human rights violations. I also suggested that UN organs should respond more expeditiously to human rights emergencies and come to the assistance of victims of violations. I brought before the Commission and the Sub-Commission the plight of vulnerable groups whose very existence and survival was at stake and recommended in particular more effective action in favour of disappeared persons and indigenous peoples. I stressed the need for the protection of human rights advocates who in many countries run great risks and drew attention to the desirability of providing humanitarian assistance to overcome the effects of serious violations of human rights that certain countries had experienced under regimes of repression. I also impressed upon the Commission that, in view of many situations of deliberate killings and the taking of human lives by organized power, the protection of human life should rank highest on the human rights agenda and required urgent and meaningful action.

Several of these and other suggestions for concrete policy action were taken up by the human rights organs. Rapporteurs were appointed to investigate and to report on human rights situations in Equatorial Guinea, El Salvador, Bolivia, and Guatemala. The Secretary-General was asked to report on Nicaragua, Iran, and Poland. The Commission established, after a long political and procedural struggle, a Working Group on Disappearances. It also endorsed a proposal to set up a Working Group on Indigenous Populations, decided to appoint a Special Rapporteur on Summary or Arbitrary Executions, and recommended that under the advisory services programmes expert services be rendered to Nicaragua, Equatorial Guinea, the Central African Republic, and Uganda. A common feature to all these actions was the objective of making the United Nations more operational in concrete human rights situations and of creating instruments for dialogue, recourse, relief, and pressures rather than keeping the Organization's activities at the level of verbal exercises, abstractions, and generalities.

It would, however, be an error to over-emphasize the role of the Executive Head by attributing these developments to him alone. He occupies an important position in terms of advice, encouragement, and stimulation, but, at the end of the day, government delegates are the political decision-makers. Part of the membership of the policy organs may be receptive to his ideas and may ask him or his immediate associates for advice and assistance to reflect

[50] The texts of my statements at the opening of sessions of the Commission and the Sub-Commission and at meetings of other human rights organs can be found, ibid. 40–84 and 85–124.

the ideas in a draft resolution. Delegations may also consult the Director and his staff on the resolution of controversies arising out of draft proposals which are circulating. They may consult the Director on the legal and financial aspects of such proposals. He may in his regular contacts with them discreetly point out the merits and weaknesses of certain courses of action. He may advise non-governmental organizations and groups as to how best to pursue their aims in lobbying members of UN organs.

The Director is in a position to function as a sort of focal point for information, advice, and consultation, provided he is generally considered to be a reliable resource person and has the effective and constructive assistance of his staff. Whatever policy objectives he would like to achieve, he can succeed only in close consultation with the political decision-makers. Since most human rights policy issues are controversial, in particular in so far as these issues are related to violations of human rights and affect the interests of UN member States, he may run the risk of antagonizing certain governments. How far he can actually go in public statements and in private advice depends, as stated above, on the room for action and the latitude left to him by his superiors, on the confidence policy organs invest in him as a reliable and objective human rights actor, and on his own sense of responsibility and judgment.

E. *Final Remarks*

This chapter does not purport to provide a comprehensive description of the duties and activities of the UN Secretariat in human rights matters. Much more could have been said on the complicated procedures, the political intricacies, and the bureaucratic pressures in matters of staff recruitment. Mention could also have been made of the insufficient financial resources allocated to the human rights programme so that basic facilities such as a reference service and a data bank on human rights issues are not available to staff members and experts who have to collect information and carry out research. More room, politically, financially, and physically, should also be provided for the training of interns and for the provision of technical assistance in the field of human rights. Public information activities and the quality and volume of human rights publications should also be improved. The main focus of this chapter, however, is on the potentials and limitations of the Human Rights Secretariat, on the responsibility of the international civil service in human rights matters, and on questions of integration versus separation or of centralization versus decentralization of the human rights programme in relation to the totality of work of the United Nations.

The author of this chapter is under no illusion that his views and ideals on these issues will be shared by everyone. He wishes, however, to insist on the fundamental importance of Article 100 of the UN Charter. As long as the exclusively international character of the responsibilities of the Secretary-General and the staff are not fully respected, the role of the Secretariat and, *a fortiori*, of the sector of the Secretariat that carries special responsibility for human rights, is in constant jeopardy. The ultimate rationale of the Secretariat and of the Organization as a whole can be found in the opening phrase of the United Nations Charter, as the then Secretary-General rightly pointed out in his address to Headquarters Staff in January 1982, shortly after taking office. He stated:

> The Charter begins with the words, 'We, the peoples of the United Nations . . .'. In serving the Organization, members of the Secretariat here at Headquarters and at some 160 other duty stations are working together to serve these peoples, north and south, east and west. They are our constituents and, ultimately, it is to them we are held to be accountable. They have a right to expect the best of our services in promoting peace, progress, and justice on their behalf.[51]

Summary of Conclusions

The following conclusions and recommendations are distilled from the foregoing analysis.

I. NEUTRALITY AND ADVOCACY

(*a*) The observance of Article 100 of the UN Charter is of capital importance in order to uphold the exclusively international character of the responsibilities of the Secretary-General and the staff.

(*b*) Servicing the United Nations in light of its overall responsibilities precludes an attitude of neutrality inasmuch as the purposes and principles of the Organization are not neutral but affirm basic values. This applies to the entire staff of the Organization and, *a fortiori*, to members of the Human Rights Secretariat, who should always be mindful of the dignity and welfare of peoples and of individual human beings.

(*c*) While the staff of the United Nations and in particular the human rights officers should not remain neutral in the performance of their duties, they are bound to act on the basis of a fair and objective application of the law in light of the facts. They should not pursue national or group interests but seek to serve the common interest in good faith and with integrity.

II. THE ROLE OF THE SECRETARY-GENERAL

(*a*) Since the Secretaries-General have seen their major role to be in conflict resolution and the maintenance of good relations with member States, human rights issues usually have not fitted well in their overall strategies.

[51] ST/IC/82/13, Annex.

(*b*) The good offices role of the Secretary-General should in general be exercised independent of actions by human rights policy organs.

(*c*) In view of the Secretary-General's attitude of political restraint and diplomatic caution, mandates for public investigation and reporting should be entrusted to independent experts rather than to the Secretary-General or members of his staff.

III. THE HUMAN RIGHTS SECTOR OF THE SECRETARIAT

(*a*) The decision which led to the transfer of the Human Rights Secretariat from New York to Geneva raises the issue of integration versus separation of the human rights programme in relation to other United Nations' programmes. On balance the move was not an unfavourable one because in Geneva the Secretariat is in a better position to respond to humanitarian concerns and needs than it would be at Headquarters in New York.

However, in view of the present trend that the political leadership of the UN gets increasingly involved in intra-state conflicts requiring solutions with direct human rights implications, the physical separation between Geneva and New York may be reconsidered. Consequently, either the Centre for Human Rights should be moved back to New York or the role and the status of the Centre's New York Liaison Office should be substantially strengthened.

(*b*) The entry into force of major human rights instruments and the creation of a variety of fact–finding mechanisms not only greatly increased the workload of the Human Rights Secretariat but also involved it more in policy issues affecting member States and large numbers of peoples whose basic human rights are at stake. These new tasks have to be carried out by the Secretariat in close co-operation with the expert bodies concerned and require the highest standards of expertise, dedication, and objectivity.

(*c*) It is in the interest of the human rights programme as a whole and in particular of fact-finding operations that the Secretariat should benefit from the experience and information available in other intergovernmental and non-governmental organizations and maintain open channels of communication with interested groups and individual persons.

(*d*) Since the human rights programme is increasingly touching upon issues of immediate concern to Member States, there is a stronger tendency on their part to exert political pressures and to interfere overtly and covertly in the management and administration of the Human Rights Secretariat. In order to prevent further erosion of the political independence and morale of the Secretariat it is essential that its leadership vigorously resists such pressures and interferences.

(*e*) The Medium-Term Plan should serve as a framework for guidance towards a more efficient and coherent approach to planning by human rights policy bodies and the Secretariat. On the other hand, planning and co-ordination should not become ends in themselves such that they hamper imaginative responses to urgent human rights concerns or obstruct dynamic developments and processes.

IV. THE ROLE OF THE DIRECTOR OF THE HUMAN RIGHTS SECRETARIAT

(*a*) The role of the Executive Head (Director) of the Human Rights Secretariat is based on a dual authority, deriving on the one hand from the Secretary-General and on the other from the human rights policy organs, in particular the Commission. To carry out his tasks effectively he needs a fair degree of latitude and independence.

(*b*) As a trustee of the human rights programme and as someone who is in constant touch with policy organs, with representatives of governments, and of intergovernmental and non-governmental organizations, the Executive Head is in an ideal position to be an authoritative focal point for information, advice, and consultation.

(*c*) He should also play a meaningful public role and indicate to the policy organs the objectives which he deems important and attainable on the basis of an objective assessment of needs and requirements, taking into account the responsibility of the Organization to promote and protect human rights, as well as the prevailing views of the relevant policy organs. Such public statements may well include suggestions for concrete action by the policy organs.

15

Lessons from the Experience of the International Labour Organisation

VIRGINIA A. LEARY

Introduction

The International Labour Organisation (ILO) has the most highly developed intergovernmental system for the protection of human rights, but scholars and activists conversant with the human rights activities of the UN remain surprisingly ill-informed concerning its work. This lack of knowledge has meant that lessons drawn from the ILO experience have rarely been utilized in debates on improving UN human rights policies and procedures. The ILO experience is especially relevant to the incipient UN system for the implementation of economic and social rights; promotion of these rights is the particular area of concern of the ILO.

The ILO is well known among specialists in international organizations and labour matters who give it high praise for its implementation of international labour conventions.[1] Lack of knowledge of the ILO among human rights experts may be due to the perception that the Organisation is concerned only with labour standards and not with human rights. This perception reflects a narrow conception of human rights as encompassing civil and political rights but not economic and social rights. Non-governmental human rights organizations (NGOs) have largely directed their efforts to participation in UN activities, since the ILO provides only limited scope for participation by NGOs other than employer and workers' organizations. Whatever the reasons for the lack of general awareness and knowledge concerning ILO activities, it is a lacuna in the human rights area.

A critical examination of UN human rights work would be incomplete if it failed to include an analysis of the long experience of the ILO. The purpose of the present chapter is to highlight the salient features of ILO human rights activities, not for their own sake, but to suggest that lessons from the ILO experience may prove useful for other UN organs.

[1] 'Its [ILO's] history is often regarded as a success story of the international protection of human rights. In recognition of its achievements, the ILO was awarded the Nobel Peace Prize in 1969 . . .'. Vincent-Daviss, 'Human Rights Law: A Research Guide to the Literature. Part III', 15 *NYUJ Int'l L. & Pol.* 213 (1982).

The following aspects of the ILO which are particularly relevant to UN human rights activities will be examined in this chapter:

(a) The ILO's Integrated Approach to Human Rights

A dichotomy has arisen within the UN between economic rights on the one hand, and civil and political rights on the other hand. The result has been an unfortunate ideological dispute and a less developed UN system for implementing economic and social rights. The ILO has avoided the dichotomy by adopting a broad conception of human rights and establishing essentially the same supervisory system for all rights within its area of concern, including economic and social rights.

(b) The Systematic ILO Procedure for the Adoption of Conventions

Human rights standard-setting within the UN has been haphazard and has often been an inordinately long process. Initiatives for human rights conventions come from a number of UN bodies and the standard-setting procedure is uncoordinated. In contrast, the ILO system for adoption of conventions is systematic, regular, and relatively expeditious.

(c) The Highly-Developed ILO System for Supervising Conventions

This is the most widely praised aspect of ILO human rights activities. The Organisation uses numerous methods to encourage compliance by governments with ratified conventions, including reporting systems, complaints procedures, Commissions of Inquiry, and direct contacts of ILO officials with government representatives. The UN employs many of the same procedures but less efficiently and effectively.

(d) The Role Played by Non-Governmental Occupational Organisation Representatives within the ILO

Worker and employer representatives participate fully in ILO activities, including the drafting and supervision of conventions. This feature of the ILO structure cannot be duplicated within the UN, but the ILO experience illustrates the efficacy of human rights systems which grant major roles to non-governmental actors.

(e) The Co-ordination of ILO Human Rights Work with other Activities of the Organisation

The ILO has endeavoured—not always successfully—to relate technical assistance to human rights concerns, particularly the implementation of conventions. Such an effort has not yet been made within the UN.

(f) The Activist ILO Secretariat (the 'Office')

ILO officials have traditionally played a more active role within the Organisation than have UN officials. They have regarded themselves as dynamic partners of governments, workers, and employers within the Organisation, and much of the credit for ILO human rights activities has been attributed to the competence of the staff.

Part A of this chapter provides a general overview of the human rights activities of the UN and ILO, including sections on the similarities and differences between the organizations, on standard-setting, technical assistance, and the integrated approach of the ILO to human rights. Part B describes extensively the ILO systems, techniques, and procedures for implementing conventions and promoting trade union rights and compares them with similar methods employed by the UN. The role of the secretariat of the two organizations is discussed in Part C.

A. *An Overview of ILO and UN Human Rights Activities*

I. SIMILARITIES AND DIFFERENCES IN AIMS AND ACTIVITIES

Comparing the work of the UN and the ILO may seem to be comparing apples with oranges. The ILO has a mandate, history, and institutional development which differs from that of the United Nations Organization and from that of other UN specialized agencies. In the area of human rights, however, substantial similarities exist between the two organizations. Human rights are a concern of both organizations and human rights conventions have been adopted by both, but the ILO has had the advantage of a long period of trial and error not yet equalled by the UN. The ILO has been adopting conventions and supervising their implementation for more than sixty years; UN human rights activities date only from 1945 and the two major UN human rights conventions came into force only in 1976.

The ILO is a specialized agency of the UN, but it antedates the UN by 26 years. Established by the Treaty of Versailles in 1919 to abolish the 'injustice, hardship, and privation' which workers suffered and to guarantee 'fair and humane conditions of labour', it was conceived as the response of Western countries to the ideologies of Bolshevism and Socialism arising out of the Russian Revolution. The ILO was the only major intergovernmental organization to survive the Second World War and the demise of the League of Nations. In 1945, it became a specialized agency within the UN system.

The substantial similarities between the UN and the ILO in the area of human rights should not obscure their differences. Collective security is the primary goal of the United Nations, while the mandate of the ILO lies in the field of labour and social policy. Economic development, trade, and human rights are also UN concerns but they are not as central as the concern for collective security. The UN has, nevertheless, accomplished remarkable work in the field of human rights, particularly the adoption of the Universal Declaration of Human Rights, the International Covenant on Civil and Political Rights, and the International Covenant on Economic, Social and Cultural Rights.

UN human rights activities have attracted widespread interest; less attention has been given to the ILO and questions relating to labour and human rights. Yet, the extent to which the rights of workers are protected provides a touchstone for evaluating a nation's respect for human rights. The rights of an individual to join a trade union and to work under decent conditions are among the most important human rights. Trade unions can function effectively only in a climate of civil and political liberties and the suppression of freedom of association for workers is a warning sign of the overall deterioration of the human rights situation. Independent trade unions often provide the only organized opposition to repressive governments. The importance of workers' rights places the ILO in the forefront of international efforts to promote and protect human rights.

ILO human rights work has a long history dating from the founding of the Organization in 1919, but the terminology 'human rights' was not used by the ILO in relation to its own work until after the Second World War. The term 'human rights' does not appear anywhere in the ILO Constitution. The phrase 'social justice' was used rather than 'human rights' in early ILO history. Nevertheless, just as Monsieur Jourdain in Molière's *Le Bourgeois Gentilhomme* discovered that he had been speaking prose all his life, so the ILO seems to have discovered after thirty years of existence that it had been 'doing human rights' since its inception.

The adoption of international labour conventions and recommendations is the primary means chosen to carry out the aims of the ILO. Since its founding, the ILO has given central importance to the adoption of international conventions (which become binding through ratifications) and the supervision of government compliance with such standards. In recent years the ILO has increasingly emphasized technical co-operation, research, and diplomatic contacts as means of promoting and protecting human rights, but the normative approach to human rights remains the heart and core of ILO human rights work.

Only ten of the 171 conventions adopted by International Labour Conferences[2] (as at Jan. 1991) have been officially classified by the ILO as 'basic human rights conventions', although a broader conception of human rights might consider all ILO conventions as human rights treaties. The conventions which are included under the human rights rubric concern freedom of

[2] The International Labour Conference can be likened to the General Assembly of the United Nations. All member States participate in annual conferences. However, delegations also include representatives of employers and workers. One of the Conference's major functions is the adoption of conventions and recommendations establishing labour standards.

association and the right to organize trade unions, freedom from forced labour, freedom from discrimination in employment, and equal remuneration.[3] Following the Second World War, the relationship of civil liberties to social policy was made explicit by the ILO in the 1944 Declaration of Philadelphia. This post Second World War restatement of ILO aims refers to the importance of freedom of expression and association as well as to non-discrimination in the pursuit of social justice.

All but two of the 'basic human rights conventions' were adopted after the Second World War, and, in recent years, the ILO has increasingly emphasized the importance of civil and political rights in the protection of labour rights. The emphasis on human rights aspects of ILO activities owes much to the late C. Wilfred Jenks, an international lawyer who served as ILO Legal Advisor for many years and ultimately as Director-General. He wrote:

> Virtually all of the ILO Conventions and Recommendations are in some measure a contribution to the promotion and protection of human rights in the broad sense... for even the most technical of them may be regarded as measures for the implementation of the right to just and favourable conditions of work affirmed by the Universal Declaration [of Human Rights] and recognized by the Covenant on Economic, Social and Cultural Rights.[4]

One of the most significant organizational features of the ILO has no counterpart within the UN, i.e., 'tripartism', the participation of representatives of non-governmental occupational organizations as full members in the ILO. Representatives of employers' and workers' organizations participate in all ILO deliberative bodies and activities, including the drafting of conventions and recommendations and supervision of their implementation. To most observers, this full participation of workers' and employers' representatives in

[3] The official titles of these conventions are: Convention Concerning Freedom of Association and Protection of the Right to Organise, adopted by the ILO (Convention No. 87, 1948), in *International Labour Organisation: International Labour Conventions and Recommendations 1919–1981* (1985), 4; Convention Concerning the Application of Principles of the Right to Organise and Bargain Collectively, adopted by ILO (Convention No. 98, 1949), ibid. 7; Convention Concerning the Rights of Association and Combination of Agricultural Workers, adopted by ILO (Convention No. 11, 1921), ibid. 3; Convention Concerning Protection and Facilities to be Afforded to Workers' Representatives in the Undertaking, adopted by ILO (Convention No. 135, 1971), ibid. 9; Convention Concerning Organisations of Rural Workers and their Role in Economic and Social Development, adopted by ILO (Convention No. 141, 1975), ibid. 15; Convention Concerning Protection of the Right to Organise and Procedures for Determining Conditions of Employment in Public Service, adopted by ILO (Convention No. 151, 1978), ibid. 25; Convention Concerning Forced or Compulsory Labour, adopted by ILO (Convention No. 29, 1930), ibid. 29; Convention Concerning the Abolition of Forced Labour, adopted by ILO (Convention No. 105, 1957), ibid. 39; Convention Concerning Discrimination in Respect of Employment and Occupation, adopted by ILO (Convention No. 111, 1958), ibid. 47; Convention Concerning Equal Remuneration for Men and Women Workers for Work of Equal Value, adopted by ILO (Convention No. 100, 1951), ibid. 42.

[4] Jenks, 'Human Rights, Social Justice and Peace: The Broader Significance of the I.L.O. Experience', in Eide and Schou, *International Protection of Human Rights* (1968), 235–6.

the ILO is responsible for much of its success in adopting and implementing Conventions. They supplement information provided by governments and, when truly independent, are less politically motivated than governments. The same type of non-governmental representation does not exist within the UN. It is unfortunate that an aspect of ILO human rights work which has proved to be particularly helpful is structurally incapable of duplication within the UN.

As regards non-occupational NGOs, however, the UN has been more advanced than the ILO in opening the door to non-governmental participation. There has been considerable progress within the UN in recent years in utilizing the contribution of non-governmental organizations. Latitude has been given to organizations with consultative status with the ECOSOC to speak before various organs, to contribute information informally to committees monitoring human rights reports and to participate in Working Groups of the Sub-Commission on Prevention of Discrimination and Protection of Minorities. Especially striking has been the participation of representatives of indigenous peoples within the Working Groups of the Sub-Commission. Extensive lobbying for human rights is carried on in the corridors of the Palais des Nations in Geneva and at the General Assembly in New York by the most active human rights organizations such as Amnesty International, the International Commission of Jurists, and the Anti-Slavery Society. As a result, human rights NGOs have made substantial contributions to human rights at the UN and have publicized UN human rights activities.

The well-known human rights NGOs are conspicuously absent from participation in ILO human rights activities. Within the ILO, full non-governmental participation is restricted to representatives of organizations of employers or workers. Trade union organizations play a very active role but their preoccupations are not always the same as those of human rights NGOs. Individuals and human rights organizations may not bring complaints under ILO procedures. Human rights organizations do not lobby in the corridors at ILO meetings and the ILO has not found the means of sufficiently encouraging information, consultation, and participation by such groups. Human rights organizations have generally failed to study ILO procedures in order to see how they might influence them.[5] Since they lack the possibility of an active role within the rather highly formalized procedures of the ILO, the human rights NGOs have evidenced little interest in the Organisation. This is unfortunate for the ILO, the NGOs, and the cause of human rights. When the ILO is attacked for its human rights work, the constituencies of the

[5] The International Commission of Jurists has attempted to increase knowledge of ILO procedures among NGOs by organizing seminars in Geneva on ILO conventions and procedures for human rights NGOs. See 21 *Int'l Commission of Jurists Newsletter* Appendix A (1984), and 25 *Int'l Commission of Jurists Newsletter* 20–1 (1985).

NGOs are not alerted to its defence and NGOs have not found direct means of influencing ILO activities in a positive manner. It would be a gain for human rights if the ILO could find the means to make it possible for human rights non-governmental organizations, in addition to workers and employers organizations, to participate more strongly in its activities if only in an informal manner.[6]

ILO human rights activities play a central role in the total work of the Organisation, particularly evidenced by the commitment of substantial institutional resources to the ILO departments concerned with international labour standards and by the emphasis at the annual Conference on the adoption and supervision of labour standards. The same emphasis on human rights activities is not evident within the overall work of the UN: substantial resources are not committed to the Centre for Human Rights nor to the Committees set up under various human rights treaties. The relationship between human rights activities and other major concerns such as technical assistance have not been developed within the UN. There is little co-ordination among the units of the Secretariat dealing with human rights. With the exception of apartheid, little attention is given to human rights by the political organs. Yet the relationship between human rights and the other major goals of the UN, in particular, the maintenance of peace and economic development, has become increasingly evident. The broader mandate of the UN and the relegation of human rights to a compartmentalized role within the overall organization may be the cause.

II. STANDARD-SETTING

Human rights standard-setting plays a more major role within the ILO than within the UN. Standard-setting has been an aspect of UN human rights work, particularly between 1948 and 1968, but it can scarcely be said to occupy as important a position within the totality of the work of the UN as it does within the ILO. By January 1991, 171 conventions and 178 recommendations on freedom of association, discrimination in employment, hours of work, occupational safety and health, maritime employment, labour inspection, and social security and other labour matters had been adopted by annual International Labour Conferences. The UN has adopted some major human rights conventions.

Economic and social rights, which are usually stated in general terms, have

[6] Non-governmental human rights organizations may, of course, maintain close contacts with international workers organizations which have consultative status with the ILO and thus indirectly contribute to ILO activities. They may also maintain informal links with the International Labour Office and submit any information they wish to the Office. They may apply to the ILO Director-General to be placed on a list of organizations whose objectives are in harmony with the ILO. This entitles them to receive notice of meetings, documentation, and, with special permission, to distribute documents and make oral interventions in some meetings.

been given a more precise and concrete definition by the ILO. Thus, the 'right of everyone to just and favourable conditions of work' (Article 7 of the International Covenant on Economic, Social and Cultural Rights) has been given specificity by the adoption of detailed norms in conventions and recommendations on employment security, wage fixing machinery, protection of wages, hours of work, weekly rest, and paid leave. These specific norms have given content to the general right and made it possible to determine a State's conformity with the rights.

There are fundamental differences in methods of standard-setting within the UN and the ILO. Human rights standard-setting in the UN context tends to be haphazard, since suggestions for the adoption of human rights conventions may originate with States (which provide initial drafts), or with the Human Rights Commission, the Sub-Commission on Prevention of Discrimination and Protection of Minorities, or the General Assembly. Drafting may take place by working groups in any one of these bodies and often requires many years before completion of a Convention. There is no single body engaged in overall planning or setting of priorities for the adoption of human rights treaties or declarations by the UN. The result is a burgeoning multiplicity of human rights standards adopted by various bodies, the creation of a number of separate supervisory systems, and general lack of co-ordination, and a duplication of efforts.

In contrast, a unified and standardized system for the adoption of conventions has been developed within the ILO. The Governing Body[7] provides overall planning and co-ordination. It determines the agenda of annual ILO Conferences which adopt new conventions and recommendations, thus setting priorities in standard-setting. Conventions are adopted relatively expeditiously by ILO Conferences after consideration at two consecutive annual Conferences. The Governing Body and the International Labour Office (the Organisation's secretariat) engage in periodic reviews of the standard-setting work of the Organisation.[8]

From 1948 to 1966 the UN was engaged in the drafting of the two major international human rights covenants. The specialized agencies were associated with this drafting process and the ILO was particularly active in the process because of its extensive experience. John Humphrey, then Director of the UN Human Rights Division, has written that the ILO was uncooperative and parochial in its approach to these UN efforts and guilty of 'agency

[7] The Governing Body is the executive organ of the ILO. It meets frequently between annual sessions of the Conference and consists of government, employer, and worker representatives

[8] Theodore Meron has commented on the effectiveness of ILO lawmaking procedures: 'Outside the United Nations, the ILO procedure for the adoption of conventions and recommendations by the International Labour Conferences deserves interest because of its proven effectiveness and highly structured character . . . [T]here is no reason why some of its features could not inspire appropriate reforms in UN human rights law-making'. Meron, 'Reform of Lawmaking in the United Nations: The Human Rights Instance', 79 *Am. J. Int'l L.* 664 (1985).

imperialism'.[9] He reports jurisdictional conflicts between the ILO and the UN concerning human rights, claiming that the attitude of the ILO may have been due to 'its thwarted ambition to become, after the effective demise of the League of Nations, the principal organ of the international community responsible for the promotion of respect for all economic and social rights'.[10] In 1949, Humphrey had favoured a joint UN-ILO Commission for the protection of trade union rights but the Fact-Finding and Conciliation Commission on Freedom of Association—eventually set up by agreement between the ILO and the ECOSOC—was solely an ILO institution due to the influence of the 'ILO lobby', according to Humphrey. Humphrey held that the safeguarding of trade union rights was intimately related to other human rights which were the 'direct concern of the United Nations'. He pointed out that the conflict concerning freedom of association was only the first of the jurisdictional conflicts with the ILO over human rights responsibilities.[11]

From the point of view of the UN and many observers, the ILO must have appeared intransigent and unduly protective of its turf. One can appreciate, however, the reluctance of the ILO, in view of its experience, to relinquish the protection of trade union rights to the untried, newly created UN human rights programme. Since 1949 when the ILO succeeded in obtaining primary responsibility for protecting trade union rights, it has developed a remarkable system for protecting freedom of association for trade union purposes—a system which is explained later in this chapter. In retrospect, it is difficult to regret that the ILO won the jurisdictional battle. Given the political and institutional developments in the UN since 1949, it is unlikely that such extensive supervisory machinery would have been developed had the UN been an equal partner with the ILO. The ILO procedures for freedom of association developed since 1949 stand in marked contrast to the slow development of UN procedures for protecting other human rights since that date.

Humphrey also accused the ILO of using its influence to water down articles of the draft UN covenants on civil and political rights and on economic, social, and cultural rights relating to labour—again in order to protect its own jurisdiction—and lauded the co-operative attitude of the World Health Organization and the Food and Agriculture Organization. The articles on labour eventually included in the Covenant on Economic, Social and Cultural Rights, however, are more detailed and precise than the articles dealing with food and health.[12]

[9] See Humphrey, *Human Rights and the United Nations: A Great Adventure* (1984), 12 and 103.

[10] Ibid. 12.

[11] Ibid.

[12] The role of the ILO Committee of Experts in contributing to the implementation of the Covenant on Economic, Social and Cultural Rights is an important aspect of ILO human rights work and is discussed in Chap. 12, above.

III. TECHNICAL ASSISTANCE

The importance of standard-setting within the ILO has been underscored by its efforts to integrate standard-setting and technical assistance. No comparable efforts are yet apparent within the UN. The ILO provides technical assistance to developing countries in the area of its competence, particularly assistance in vocational training, labour legislation, and employment promotion, and, especially in developing countries, assistance in overcoming difficulties in implementing labour standards. ILO experts sent on technical co-operation missions are provided with a memorandum explaining ILO's standard-setting activities,[13] and, in theory, briefed before departure concerning the State's ratification of and compliance with ILO conventions. In reality, many of them are only slightly conversant with ILO human rights standards and have had only superficial briefings. The workings of this system is currently undergoing review within the Office in order to improve the integration of these two major activities.

Since States generally wish to receive ILO technical co-operation, the effort to emphasize standards in connection with technical assistance could act as a 'carrot' or an inducement for States to be more receptive to the norm-setting work of the Organisation. The withdrawal of technical assistance has not, however, been used by the ILO as a sanction for failure to implement human rights or labour standards.

At the annual Conference, ILO officials are available to consult with and encourage government representatives to promote ratification of ILO conventions. The ILO provides technical assistance to member States to assist them in drafting legislation which will ensure conformity with conventions they have ratified, maintains a system of regional advisers on labour standards, organizes regional seminars on standards, and, through direct contacts, assists States in overcoming difficulties in implementing conventions. These activities are aimed at assisting States to maintain labour standards rather than judging them for delinquencies, although they are not always so perceived by member States.

Utilizing the ILO example, the UN might well institute technical assistance programmes relating to ratification and implementation of human rights conventions. Recommendations to this effect are now being made in UN circles. In 1984, the Sub-Commission on Prevention of Discrimination and Protection of Minorities adopted a resolution calling for the Secretary-General to:

> examine the idea [of technical services in the field of human rights] and to report on the possibility of offering technical assistance in the form of legal training of the local

[13] Memorandum for the Use of ILO Experts, *International Labour Standards and Technical Cooperation*, D. 18. 1971 (Rev. 1978).

staff or by providing human rights experts to assist in the drafting of the necessary legislation and regulations, with a view to enabling the member states to ratify or accede to international human rights instruments and requested the Secretary-General to consider the possibility of designating regional advisers on international human rights standards whose function would include advising the States concerned on acceptance and implementation of human rights standards.[14]

The resolution resulted from a study by a Working Group of the Commission in which NGOs participated. The inspiration from the experience of the ILO is apparent. The International Commission of Jurists was particularly active and proposed a number of points which should be given special attention in designing the programme.[15]

At each of their three sessions to date (from 1984 to 1990) the chairpersons of the UN's human rights treaty bodies have strongly recommended that UN advisory services and assistance be expanded in the field of human rights, particularly in relation to implementation of human rights conventions.[16]

The ILO experience demonstrates that an advisory service programme can contribute to implementation of human rights standards. In developing a UN programme in this regard a detailed study should be made of the methods employed by the ILO and the successes and difficulties involved in carrying out the programme.

IV. INTEGRATED APPROACH TO HUMAN RIGHTS

The ILO has made a major contribution to theory and practice by its 'holistic'[17] or integrated approach to human rights. In contrast, the promotion and protection of human rights within the UN has been marred by controversy over the relative importance of, and priority to be accorded to, economic and social rights as compared with civil and political rights. The perceived dichotomy between these two sets of rights, created—or exacerbated—by the adoption within the UN of two separate human rights covenants, one on civil and political rights and one on economic, social, and cultural rights, has been largely avoided within the ILO.

The original ILO emphasis on the concept of 'social justice', as well as its consistent emphasis on the intrinsic links between the material advancement of peoples and their civil and political rights have provided a broader philosophical approach to human rights than is often evident in UN circles. The 1944 Declaration of Philadelphia stated: 'all human beings, irrespective of

[14] Quoted in *The Need for Technical Services in the Field of Human Rights*, 22 *Int'l Commission of Jurists Newsletter* Appendix C, 57 and 60 (1984).

[15] Ibid.

[16] A/45/636 (1990), paras. 34–37.

[17] 'Holistic: emphasizing the importance of the whole and the inter-dependence of the parts', *American Heritage Dictionary* (1982).

race, creed, or sex have the right to pursue both their material well-being and their spiritual development in conditions of freedom and dignity, of economic security and equal opportunity . . .'.[18] In brevity and scope, this sentence ranks as one of the finest succinct statements of the rights of the individual. It avoids problems of distinctions and priorities among different types of rights, and gives equal value to material well-being, economic security, freedom, and non-discrimination. The ILO approach to human rights has been to place them within the broader concept of social justice.

ILO conventions on hours of work, minimum working age, social security, occupational safety and health, employment policy, and labour inspection relate to economic and social rights but conventions have also been adopted on freedom from forced labour, discrimination (in relation to employment), and equal remuneration, which are generally classified as civil and political rights. Freedom of association for trade union purposes is considered both a civil right and an economic right. It is referred to in Article 8 of the Economic Covenant and in Article 22 of the Civil and Political Rights Covenant. The ILO itself has not classified the rights with which it is concerned into the UN categories. ILO conventions relating to all the above subjects have established standards and been subject to measures of implementation.

'Freedom of association' provides a useful example of the integrated approach of the ILO. Protecting basic economic rights such as fair working conditions requires giving an effective voice and influence to those most directly concerned. From its earliest beginnings, the ILO recognized that freedom of association for both employers and workers was an important principle of social justice. Freedom of association is mentioned in the 1919 Constitution, reaffirmed in the 1944 Declaration of Philadelphia, and translated into binding standards for ratifying States by the adoption in 1948 of the Freedom of Association and Protection of the Right to Organise Convention, and in 1949 of the Right to Organise and Collective Bargaining Convention. Today, all member States of the ILO are obligated, by virtue of their membership in the Organisation, to protect freedom of association whether they have ratified these Conventions or not.

The ILO has spelled out the close relationship between trade union rights and civil liberties. In 1970, the International Labour Conference adopted a resolution stating that 'there exist firmly established, universally recognized principles defining the basic guarantees of civil liberties which should constitute a common standard of achievement for all peoples and all nations' and that 'the rights conferred upon workers' and employers' organizations must be based on respect for those civil liberties which have been enunciated, in

[18] *Declaration of the Aims and Purposes of the International Labour Organisation*, known as the 'Declaration of Philadelphia', attached as an annex to the text of the Constitution as revised, UST No. 874, 26 *ILO Off. Bull.* 1–3 (1944).

particular, in the Universal Declaration of Human Rights and in the International Covenant on Civil and Political Rights and that the absence of these civil liberties removes all meaning from the concept of trade union rights.'[19]

In a 1983 case alleging violations of freedom of association by Sri Lanka, the ILO Governing Body Committee on Freedom of Association[20] drew the government's attention to the importance of civil liberties.[21] The Ceylon Federation of Labour, the World Federation of Trade Unions, and eleven Sri Lankan national federations of unions complained to the Committee concerning alleged infringements of trade union rights. One complaint concerned Sri Lanka's Prevention of Terrorism Act which permits a suspect to be detained by administrative order for up to eighteen months without charges. The Act had been widely criticized both within Sri Lanka and by international human rights organizations as violative of fundamental human rights.[22] The government denied that the Act was concerned with trade union rights or activities: the Committee did not comment specifically on the Act but implicitly invoked its relationship to trade union rights by drawing the government's attention to the principle that every government should ensure observance of human rights and more especially the right of all accused persons 'to receive a fair trial at the earliest possible moment'.[23]

Different measures of implementation have been adopted for various ILO conventions, but the distinction is not based on a classification of the rights concerned as economic and social or civil and political. Some conventions contain simple negative prohibitions such as 'women . . . shall not be employed during the night in any public or private industrial undertaking'; others such as the Maternity Protection Convention require that public funds be provided or a system of insurance be set up to guarantee maternity benefits; some conventions such as the Employment Policy Convention are 'promotional conventions' which state objectives and programmes of action which can only be achieved by gradual measures. Some conventions require the adoption of penal sanctions. The Freedom of Association and Protection of the Right to Organise Convention uses traditional rights language, 'Workers and employers . . . shall have the right to establish and . . . to join organizations of their own choosing without prior authorization.'

The same ILO supervisory system is used for monitoring the implementation of all conventions: those that deal more directly with civil rights, such as

[19] ILO, Record of Proceedings, ILC, 54th Session, 1970, 733. See also ILO, *Freedom of Association and Collective Bargaining*, General Survey, ILC, 69th Session, 1983, para. 49–75.

[20] See the next section for explanation of the work of this Committee.

[21] 230th Report, ILO Governing Body Committee on Freedom of Association, 15–17 Nov. 1983, Cases Nos. 988 and 1003, paras. 351–75.

[22] See Leary, *Ethnic Conflict and Violence in Sri Lanka*, International Commission of Jurists (1983).

[23] n. 21, above, paras. 372 and 375.

discrimination in employment, as well as those which deal with more clearly economic matters such as conditions of work or social security.

Within the UN, the belief that economic, social, and cultural rights are fundamentally different from civil and political rights and that they require totally different means of implementation resulted in the adoption of two separate human rights covenants with different implementation systems. It was argued that economic and social rights required positive action of the State rather than abstention from State action and therefore could not be implemented in the same manner as civil and political rights.[24] Since a weaker implementation system was provided in the Economic, Social and Cultural Rights Covenant than in the Civil and Political Rights Covenant, the impression was conveyed that civil and political rights were more important than economic and social rights.

Some States found it difficult to accept the concept of economic and social 'rights'. The controversy over one covenant or two accentuated ideological differences concerning human rights from which the UN has not yet recovered. Eastern European Socialist countries, and developing nations have most frequently emphasized economic and social rights; civil and political rights are the favoured rights of the Western market-economy countries. Categorization of the rights has worsened ideological conflicts and impeded the promotion of human rights.

In 1977, the United Nations General Assembly adopted Resolution 32/130 which emphasized the importance of economic and social rights and stressed the relation between those rights and civil and political rights. But the Resolution stirred more controversy. Although it stated that 'all human rights and fundamental freedoms are interrelated and indivisible', the Resolution as a whole, by its emphasis on 'economic, social, and cultural realities', seemed to suggest that a failure to protect civil and political rights might be justified by economic difficulties. A laudable effort to adopt a resolution conveying the importance of economic and social rights thus stumbled over what it left unexpressed. The key questions of the relative importance of the two categories of rights and the manner in which they interrelate were left unresolved.

The most serious impact of the ideological controversy is its practical impact on the UN system for implementing the two types of rights. The Civil and Political Rights Covenant provides for the setting up of a Human Rights Committee composed of independent persons elected by the ratifying States. The Committee receives and studies reports of States concerning imple-

[24] Henry Shue has pointed out that differentiating economic rights from civil and political rights by contending that the former require positive State action and the latter only State abstention is simplistic. Some civil and political rights such as the development of an adequate judicial system require positive State action. See Shue, *Basic Rights* (1980), 35–64. See also comments of the Human Rights Committee, n. 26, below.

mentation and, under the Optional Protocol to the Covenant, considers allegations from individuals of violation of the Covenant. Although the Committee's history is short it has earned the respect of observers for its serious and committed approach to its work. It currently meets for several weeks three times a year.

In contrast, the Economic, Social and Cultural Rights Covenant does not set up a separate committee to analyse State's reports but simply provides that they should be submitted to the ECOSOC. In 1978 the Economic and Social Council set up a Sessional Working Group of Governmental Experts who met for three weeks before one of the the ECOSOC sessions to assess the implementation of the Covenant by States Parties. These experts often had other major responsibilities and it had often been difficult to obtain a quorum. Some States Parties failed to designate experts for the Working Group.[25] The experts have been unwilling to accept input from the specialized agencies.

In May 1985, the ECOSOC made a major advance in implementation of the Covenant by transforming the Working Group into the Committee on Economic, Social and Cultural Rights. A more effective implementation body for the Economic Covenant has resulted, but the initial creation of two Covenants and continued ideological controversy have slowed effective development and implementation of economic rights within the UN.

The Human Rights Committee has referred to economic factors in relation to civil rights in its general comments on articles of the Civil and Political Covenant.[26] The institutionalized separation of the implementing bodies of the two Covenants will result in the future either in duplication, as both bodies move towards a realization of the interrelation of rights, or a continued inability to present a coherent approach to human rights.

The UN conceptualization of rights into distinct categories is not part of the ILO experience. The ILO is not, of course, exempt from the economic and political forces in the world—on both the left and the right—which emphasize certain rights and ignore others. Criticisms of ILO practice in the mid-1980s by both blocs, as well as differences over reforming the ILO's structures are examples. But as an institution, it has refused the division among types of rights, social justice, and development, and has shown that 'economic rights' as well as 'civil and political rights' may be subject to precise definition and enforcement.

[25] A/39/484 (1984), para. 14.

[26] In its general comments concerning Art. 6 of the Civil and Political Rights Covenant on the right to life the Committee notes: 'the right to life has been too often narrowly interpreted. The expression "inherent right to life" cannot properly be understood in a restrictive manner, and the protection of this right requires that States adopt positive measures. In this connection, the Committee considers that it would be desirable for States parties to take all possible measures to reduce infant mortality and to increase life expectancy, especially in adopting measures to eliminate malnutrition and epidemics'. *Report of the Human Rights Committee*, A/37/40 (1982), Annex V, para. 5.

B. *Implementing Human Rights: The ILO and UN Experience*

The ILO system for the supervision of conventions and consideration of complaints is often cited as a model for other systems for implementing human rights. But it is not easy to assess the effectiveness of such systems. The relationship of cause and effect in this area is difficult to measure: too many factors influence progress in human rights to make it possible to document precisely the role of international supervisory systems. The ILO itself has undertaken studies of the impact of ILO supervision and others have carried out similar examinations.[27] While these studies may be lacking in precise mathematical proof they have nevertheless led to the general view that ILO supervision of the implementation of conventions has been relatively successful.

The ILO systems are highly structured and have been periodically re-examined—including very recently—by the ILO constituency after initial study by the Office. The result is a cohesive system which employs a wide array of measures all designed to exercise persistent tactful pressure on States to comply with conventions and trade union rights. The various measures are interrelated and are integrated into the work of the Organisation as a whole.[28]

The ILO system has been perfected over a period of more than seventy years while the UN system of implementation of human rights conventions is of much more recent origin. But aspects of the ILO system provide examples which may be useful for the development of procedures within the UN. The UN systems for implementation and promotion of human rights evidence duplication of functions by many UN organs, a lack of co-ordination, and a failure to integrate human rights implementation within the wider work of the Organisation. Specific examples of both the ILO and the UN systems are provided later in this section.

I. REPORTING SYSTEMS

The main method used in international organizations to implement human rights standards is a system of reporting by States on their compliance with norms they have accepted, and examination of these reports by committees.

The ILO system of reporting, which is referred to as the 'regular system of supervision', consists of a two-tier examination of reports on ILO conventions: first by a small (twenty-member) Committee of Experts, and, secondly,

[27] ILO, *The Impact of International Labour Conventions and Recommendations* (1976). This report contains an extensive bibliography on studies concerning the impact of ILO standards. See also Haas, *Human Rights and International Action: The Case of Freedom of Association* (1970); Landy, *The Effectiveness of International Supervision: Thirty Years of ILO Experience* (1966).

[28] For an extensive bibliography relating to the ILO implementation of conventions and other supervisory procedures, see Vincent-Daviss, 'Human Rights Law', 212.

by a much larger Committee at the annual Conference, composed of representatives of governments, employers, and workers. Reports on all 171 ILO conventions are examined by the same two Committees. In contrast, within the UN, separate reporting systems have been set up under the Covenant on Civil and Political Rights, the Covenant on Economic, Social and Cultural Rights, the Convention on the Elimination of Racial Discrimination, the Convention against Torture, the Convention on the Elimination of Discrimination against Women, the International Convention on the Suppression and Punishment of the Crime of Apartheid and the Convention on the Rights of the Child. There is no structural relationship among these systems.

The UN systems of reporting seem to have been modelled on the relatively successful ILO reporting system which had many years of experience before the UN systems began functioning. Yet, the UN systems lack many of the ingredients which have been responsible for the success of the ILO system, in particular extensive assistance provided to Committees by a large number of highly trained secretariat officials (discussed in the next section), the technical examination of reports by experts selected in a manner which minimizes political influence, a subsequent examination by a body more sensitive to political issues and also more capable of bringing political pressure to bear in a public manner, and by making the examination an integral part of the annual political meeting of the Organisation.

The initial examination of reports by the ILO is carried out by the twenty-member Committee of Experts on the Application of Conventions and Recommendations. Members are prominent judges, professors, and labour law experts from selected geographic areas. The work of the Committee of Experts resembles the supervisory work of the Committees set up under conventions adopted by the UN, which also examine reports of States on compliance with conventions. Like the ILO Committee of Experts, the UN Committees are small bodies of persons serving in their individual capacities. The method of naming members of the ILO and UN committees[29] differ, however. Members of the Committee of Experts are appointed by the tripartite ILO Governing Body on the nomination of the ILO Director General. States members of the ILO are not directly involved in the process. The members of the UN Committees are elected by the States which have ratified the conventions. While all Committees have, in general, consisted of individuals of high reputation and experience, the ILO method of appointment ensures the protection of the process from government pressures to a greater degree than the UN election method.

[29] The term 'UN Committees' will be used in the remainder of the chapter to refer to Committees set up under various human rights conventions. Strictly speaking most are not 'UN Committees' but the conventions were adopted under UN auspices and the UN provides secretariat assistance for them.

The perception that the members of the ILO Committee of Experts are objectively selected rather than politically appointed has contributed to its reputation for objectivity and competence. The reputation of the Committee has become an issue as the Committee has become more explicit in pointing out discrepancies between the law and practice of States and the norms in ratified conventions. The Committee of Experts has, by the early 1990s, acquired a reputation for objectivity, competence, and integrity among virtually all ILO member States, although during the 1980s some few States, particularly in the Eastern European Socialist group, had contested its objectivity.[30] The respect accorded a supervisory organ is a crucial element in the continued acceptance by States of the supervision of human rights.

The ILO Committee of Experts undertakes a technical examination of reports submitted on ratified conventions in a closed session, without the presence of representatives of States. The meetings of the UN Committees, including the questioning of government representatives, are carried out in public (with the exception of the examination of individual complaints and the preparation of general comments). This is often conducive to political stands by government representatives but it also guarantees publicity for the Committee's work. There is no media publicity covering the work of the ILO Committee of Experts. Closed meetings, lack of publicity, and the lack of presence of government representatives have depoliticized the ILO procedure at this stage and enhanced the reputation of the Committee of Experts, but it has also meant little media attention to the work of the Committee.

The Committee of Experts examines reports on the basis of Office (secretariat) analysis and addresses 'direct requests' or 'observations' to governments, requesting further information, or pointing out discrepancies between a State's law and practice and the relevant convention. The 'observations' are published in annual Committee reports and concern more serious matters.

[30] At the 1983 ILO Conference nine Socialist countries presented a memorandum critical of the ILO supervisory system. It stated in part: 'the ILO supervisory machinery . . . refuses to take into account the objective realities of the contemporary world, makes tendentious and one-sided assessments of the legislation and practice of Socialist and developing countries, and arbitrarily expands its functions in an effort to become a kind of supranational tribunal.' 1983 Record of Proceedings, International Labour Conference, 7/18. The memorandum was submitted by the government representatives of Byelorussia, Bulgaria, the GDR, Cuba, Mongolia, Czechoslovakia, Hungary, the Ukraine, and the USSR. It is noteworthy, however, that since the dramatic political changes of the late 1980s most of these States have gone out of their way to express their satisfaction with, and even their admiration for, the ILO.

More recently, some Employer Representatives and a few governments have been critical of the role of the Committee of Experts. Their criticism brought a careful response from the Committee in its 1991 Report. The Committee observed that 'it is essential for the ILO system that the views that the Committee is called upon to express in carrying out its functions . . . should be considered as valid and generally recognized, subject to any decisions of the International Court of Justice which is the only body empowered to give definitive interpretations of Conventions', *Report of the Committee of Experts on the Application of Conventions and Recommendations*, International Labour Conference, 78th Session, 1991, para. 12.

The 'direct requests' are sent to the governments but are not published, although mention is made of them in the published report. The Committee of Experts does not 'condemn' States for 'violations' of human rights. Rather, it directs questions or comments to a government in the most polite terms when it finds that a convention is not being fully implemented. The Committee may state in its report that it 'hopes' or 'trusts' that 'measures will be taken to ensure application of the Convention'. Or it may state that it would be 'glad' or 'grateful' if the government 'would supply further information'. While the Committee's communications with governments are always polite, they are also persistent if the Committee believes a continued discrepancy exists. Comments may continue for years if the Committee is not satisfied with the government's response. Failure to bring law and practice into line with the convention may lead the Committee to express 'concern' or note 'with regret'. Improvements in implementation are noted 'with interest' or 'with satisfaction'.

The Committee has developed a highly stylized, understated language to express its views. When it notes 'with concern' or 'with regret', those phrases are meant to be understood as a serious criticism of a government's failure to implement a convention. But the Committee's circumspect language in referring to government delinquencies is sometimes criticized. Thus at one ILO Conference, a worker representative from Uruguay referred to the 'excessively diplomatic language used in conclusions and recommendations' of the ILO Committee.[31]

In the overwhelming majority of cases, the Committee's comments represent a consensus, but in rare cases, especially concerning comments during the 1980s on the legislation of Eastern European countries, members from Poland and the USSR dissented from the Committee's findings.

The Committees set up under various UN conventions publish their reports, which include questions asked by individual members and requests for further information but, unlike the reports of the ILO Committee of Experts, do not contain any common agreed consensus regarding the conformity of the State with the particular convention. Even the polite and circumspect language of the ILO Committee—which nevertheless conveys the Committee's judgment—is not employed. Thus, there is no agreed technical analysis of a State's legislation which may serve as a basis for criticism of a State.

The next stage of the ILO regular supervisory procedure is public. At each annual Conference, the Conference Committee on Standards chooses some of the more serious cases raised by the Committee of Experts for discussion. States' representatives appear before the Conference Committee to reply to

[31] Baldassari, Workers' Member of Uruguay, at the meeting of the Conference Committee on the Application of Standards, 71st Session of the International Labour Conference, 8 June 1985.

questions. The Committee consists of government delegates and employees' and workers' representatives. The sessions are open to the public.

The ILO Conference Committee is a political body, not an expert committee. It differs substantially in composition from the Committee of Experts, consisting usually of some 200 members, of whom one-third are government delegates, one-third representatives of workers' organizations, and one-third representatives of employer organizations. Cases selected for discussion by the Conference Committee frequently concern application of the basic human rights conventions.

There are some similarities between the ILO Conference Committee and the UN Committees, but also many differences. Government representatives appear before the UN Committee and the ILO Committee to respond to questions. But the questions asked by the ILO Committee are based on the previous technical examination and report by the Committee of Experts. The questions asked by the UN experts are based on their own individual analyses not on a previous technical analysis by an expert body. The ILO Conference Committee is also a large body and not a small group as are the UN Committees.

Two aspects of the ILO Conference Committee procedure are particularly worthy of note: (*a*) the active, and critically important, participation of employer and worker representatives in addition to the government delegates, and (*b*) the reference in the Committee's report to certain governments who have failed to implement ratified conventions. An observer of Conference Committee proceedings quickly notes that worker and employer representatives are more active in the Committee than government members. Worker representatives call attention to aspects of the trade union situation not mentioned in government reports and take the lead in questioning government representatives.

It has been possible for the Conference Committee, because of the two-thirds non-governmental participation, to cite governments in its reports—including even major countries—for failure to implement conventions. It is unlikely that the Committee would have done so had it been composed of government representatives only. In the past the Committee report contained a 'special list' of States which had not adequately implemented ratified conventions. The list soon came to be considered a 'blacklist'. Its purpose was to draw the attention of the Conference to cases where governments apparently encountered serious difficulties in discharging their obligations under the ILO Constitution or under ratified Conventions. States cited in the list increasingly objected to it, considering it a serious form of censure. On occasion, they raised objections to acceptance of the Committee report in plenary sessions of the Conference, evidencing how seriously governments react to any reference to their failure to live up to international obligations.

UN Committees which consider States' reports on human rights do not make specific findings concerning a particular State's conformity with the relevant convention with the exceptions of complaints raised under the Optional Protocol to the Civil and Political Rights Covenant. As a result, the 'mobilization of shame' sanction, which to date remains the most substantial international sanction for human rights violations, does not function in UN reporting systems. The Human Rights Committee *qua* committee has confined itself thus far to general comments on various provisions of the Covenant. A difference of opinion presently exists within the Committee as to whether it should make specific comments on a State's implementation of the Covenant. There is no intrinsic reason why this could not be done: the controversy is primarily a political one. So far, only the comments of individual members have been recorded.

In the face of persistent criticism, Working Parties of the ILO Conference Committee were established in 1979 and 1980 to examine the question of the special list. It was argued, by those opposed to it, that the list amounted to a sanction which had no basis in the ILO Constitution, that the list consisted almost exclusively of developing and Socialist countries, and that technical assistance and regional study courses could have a greater effect on implementation than pointing a finger to countries in a special list. It was mentioned that the membership of the Committee included States, such as the United States, which had not ratified major ILO conventions and that the Committee should not act as a tribunal. Defenders of the special list argued that moral sanctions of some kind were necessary and its abolition would weaken supervision, that States had full opportunities to explain their position, and that the Committee had an obligation to arrive at conclusions. They pointed out that the ILO Constitution did not prohibit such a moral sanction.

As a result, 'special paragraphs' replaced the 'special list' in the Committee's report. In place of the list, the report now states that in some countries there has been continued failure fully to implement conventions, that the Committee notes this with grave concern, and that such cases will be discussed in subsequent paragraphs of the report. The change is more of form than substance and governments appear to be no less sensitive to mention in a special paragraph than they were previously to have been included in the special list. The impact of the supervisory procedure has apparently not been lessened. Governments may still be singled out for particular mention if there has been a serious failure to implement a convention.

The reaction of governments to special mention in the report is evidence that such publication as a means of 'mobilizing shame' is a sensitive matter and one which governments do not lightly ignore. Ministry of labour officials have stated that public citation of their government for failure to implement conventions has had positive results, on occasion, by drawing the attention of other ministries and the legislative branch to the need for changes previously urged without effect by labour officials.

The effectiveness of the work of the Conference Committee owes much to the participation of representatives of non-governmental occupational organizations which have a two-thirds majority in the Committee. In the plenary sessions of the Conference each national delegation has four votes, only two of which are allocated to employers and workers. Thus, government delegates have a greater role in the plenary session and they are often reluctant to criticize other governments unless there is a political conflict at issue.

In 1974, 1977, and 1982 the report of the Conference Committee failed adoption in the plenary because of a deliberately engineered lack of quorum. The report was controversial in 1974 because it cited the failure of the USSR to implement the Forced Labour Convention of 1930 (No. 29). In 1977, a controversy concerning the application of conventions in the territories occupied by Israel was the major factor in the non-adoption of the report. In 1982 an issue involving the Conference's Resolutions Committee spilled over into the plenary and caused the lack of a quorum. In the plenary, where governments have fifty per cent of the votes (and considerably more since many trade unions and employers organizations are not independent of governments), it becomes difficult to adopt a report which treads on the sensibilities of important governments. Many observers interpreted the failure to adopt the Committee's reports in 1974, 1977, and 1982 as a serious attack on the supervisory organs of the ILO.

The ILO experience establishes that criticisms of States, however diplomatically couched, elicit strong opposition from the criticized State and its allies and may in the end threaten the very existence of a reporting system. Probably only a well-established and prestigious Committee which has a firm reputation for objectivity and competence and is backed by an international organization as a whole can withstand the resulting political opposition. A 'go-slow' approach to specific findings of non-compliance may be a wise precaution for the relatively new UN supervisory organs, unfortunate as this may seem.

The supervisory work of the ILO Conference Committee is enhanced because the Committee forms an integral part of the annual ILO Conference. The Conference is a major annual international event attracting 2,000–3,000 government, worker, and employer representatives. Since all Member States (with a few minor exceptions) send delegations to the Conference, it is difficult for them to refuse to provide a representative to respond to questions in the Committee. The report of the Committee is one of the major events of the plenary session. The supervisory work is thus clearly demonstrated to be an important aspect of ILO institutional activities. To the extent that governments wish to participate in the general activities of the ILO, they are motivated to participate in the supervisory activities.

The UN Committees lack the second-tier of the ILO regular supervisory procedure, since there is no serious discussion of the reports of the UN human rights committees within UN political bodies such as ECOSOC or the General Assembly. This depreciates the importance of the work of the UN supervisory committees in the work of the UN as a whole and is a serious deficiency of UN human rights activities.

II. FREEDOM OF ASSOCIATION SUPERVISORY PROCEDURES

In addition to the regular system of ILO supervision based on reports by States, the ILO has developed a special procedure for complaints concerning violations of freedom of association for trade union purposes. All member States of the ILO are subject to the supervisory procedures for freedom of association whether or not they have ratified the freedom of association conventions. Complaints of violation of freedom of association are examined by the Freedom of Association (FAS) Committee of the Governing Body.[32]

The most comparable procedure within the UN system is the '1503' procedure established in 1970.[33] Like the ILO freedom of association procedures the 1503 procedure may be invoked regardless of whether the State concerned has acceded to a human rights convention. It may even be invoked against a non-member of the UN, as it has been against the Republic of Korea. Under the 1503 procedure, persons with knowledge that a State is engaged in a 'consistent pattern of gross violations of human rights' may file a 1503 communication. The communication is first considered by a Working Group of the Sub-Commission on Prevention of Discrimination and Protection of Minorities, then by the full Sub-Commission, and then by the Human Rights Commission. The procedure is secret until the Human Rights Commission announces its conclusions and it often requires four to five years from the time a communication is filed until a resolution is reached by the Human Rights Commission.

Although the ILO system for the supervision of freedom association is a separate system from the regular supervisory system the two systems interact when the country concerned has ratified the main ILO conventions on freedom of association (the Freedom of Association and Protection of the Right to Organise Convention, No. 87, adopted in 1948, and the Right to

[32] Information concerning the FAS Committee procedure is contained in *Outline of the Existing Procedure for the Examination of Complaints Alleging Violations of Trade Union Rights*. GB/LS/May 1982. Organizations which may present complaints are national occupational organizations with a direct interest in the matter, an international organization of employers or workers having consultative status with ILO, or another international organization of employers or workers where the allegations relate to matters directly affecting its affiliated organizations.

[33] ESC Res.1503 (1970). For an extensive discussion of the 1503 procedure, see Chap. 5, above.

Organise and Collective Bargaining Convention, No. 98, adopted in 1949). There is limited interaction between the 1503 procedure and the procedures for supervision set up under human rights covenants, even if the State referred to in a 1503 procedure has ratified the relevant human rights covenant.

The ILO freedom of association system developed at a much later date than the regular supervisory systems. Following negotiations with the Economic and Social Council of the United Nations in 1950, the ILO set up a Fact-Finding and Conciliation Commission on Freedom of Association. The Economic and Social Council decided that allegations of violations of trade union rights by UN members who were also members of the ILO should be referred to the ILO. Allegations of violations of trade union rights by non-members of the ILO may also be referred to the Fact-Finding and Conciliation Commission. The Commission functions only with the consent of the government concerned and has therefore been used sparingly. As a result, the Committee on Freedom of Association (the 'FAS Committee'), composed of nine members of the Governing Body appointed by the ILO Governing Body and representing government, workers, and employers has gradually become the major ILO organ for examining allegations of infringements of freedom of association. It was originally established, however, only to make a preliminary examination with a view to presentation of the case to the Fact-Finding and Conciliation Commission. The FAS Committee may examine cases without the specific agreement of the country concerned. The responsibility of the Committee is to determine whether cases are worthy of examination by the Governing Body. As of July 1991, the Committee had presented findings and recommendations to the Governing Body for decision in almost 1,600 cases of allegations of infringements of freedom of association. The Governing Body normally rubber-stamps the Committee decisions. At each of its meetings in 1990–1 the Committee had before it an average of 70 cases concerning more than 40 countries.

Complaints may be submitted to the FAS Committee by workers' or employers' organizations or by governments, but not by individuals. Nearly all of the complaints are received from workers' organizations. Under the UN 1503 procedure, individuals or others with reliable knowledge of violations may file communications. The FAS Committee functions in a quasi-judicial manner, although its members are not independent experts but members of a political organ, the ILO Governing Body. The Committee's hearings are conducted in private and no representative or national of the State against which a complaint has been lodged or person occupying an official position in the national association of employers or workers which has lodged the complaint may participate in the Committee's deliberations or be present in the room during the hearing. Following each session of the Committee at which a complaint has been considered the complainant is notified of the action taken by the Committee. Under the UN 1503 procedure, complainants are not kept informed officially of any action taken concerning their complaint and may hear nothing of its disposition unless it reaches fruition before the Human Rights Commission four or five years later.

The FAS Committee meets three times a year, before each session of the ILO Governing Body. 1503 complaints are considered only once a year by the Working Group of the Sub-Commission on Prevention of Discrimination and Protection of Minorities.

A wide variety of factual and legal situations have been presented to the Committee over the years. The majority of ILO member States have ratified one or both of the major freedom of association conventions and the Committee is guided in reaching its conclusions by the terms of the Conventions, but has added greater precision to them by its decisions in the many cases it has considered. The FAS Committee does not itself make on-the-spot investigations, but conducts an examination of the allegations, normally on the basis of written statements by the complainants and the government. In some cases, representatives of the government or the complainants may be invited to make oral presentations.

The Committee has a special procedure for dealing with what it considers urgent cases. These are cases 'involving human life or personal freedom, or new or changing conditions affecting the freedom of action of a trade union movement as a whole, and cases arising out of a continuing state of emergency and cases involving the dissolution of an organization'.[34] The Committee gives priority to such cases and specially requests the government to give a particularly speedy reply to the allegations. Nevertheless, even many urgent cases seem to require an inordinately lengthy period of consideration by the FAS Committee. The 1503 procedure makes no provision for the disposition of urgent cases, although many situations involving gross violations are clearly urgent. The Commission on Human Rights may, of course, at its annual meetings, discuss and adopt resolutions on what it considers to be urgent matters. But the consideration of the matter will not have been handled through a systematic procedure and the result has been that consideration of human rights matters by the Commission have too frequently been politically motivated.

The FAS Committee, following its consideration of a case, submits recommendations to the Governing Body concerning action the government might take with regard to what are referred to as 'anomalies' that have been uncovered in hearing the case. The Governing Body may then transmit the recommendations to the government. Care is taken to avoid direct accusations or the use of the term 'violation'.

[34] See generally *Freedom of Association: Digest of Decisions and Principles of the Freedom of Association Committee of the Governing Body of the ILO*, 3rd end. (1985).

Although the Governing Body Committee does not itself make on-the-spot investigations, procedures have been developed for visits to the country concerned where a continuing problem exists with regard to trade union rights. A representative of the Director-General may visit the country at the invitation of the government, or at least with its consent, to discuss matters relating to trade union rights. This procedure is discussed more fully below in the section on 'Direct Contacts'. A panel of the Fact-Finding and Conciliation Commission may also be appointed by the Governing Body on nomination of the Director-General to investigate the situation on-the-spot if the allegations are sufficiently serious and the country consents to establishment of the Commission. Only a small number of cases have been submitted to the Commission including matters concerning Lesotho, the United States (Puerto Rico), Chile, Japan, and Greece. In February 1991 the Government of South Africa consented for the first time to a complaint being referred to the Commission.

The case of Chile provides an example of the interplay between the FAS Committee and the Fact-Finding and Conciliation Commission. Immediately after the overthrow of the Allende regime in Chile in 1973, the ILO received a series of complaints from trade unions and trade union federations concerning infringements of trade union rights in that country. The most serious allegations related to arrests, killings, and disappearances of labour leaders. The FAS Committee submitted two reports to the Governing Body dated November 1973 and February 1974[35] noting the seriousness of the situation in Chile. In May 1974, the Governing Body decided, with the agreement of the Chilean government, to submit the matter to a panel of the Fact-Finding and Conciliation Commission. Thus, within a period of eight months following the coup in Chile, plans were well under way for an ILO on-the-spot investigation.

Chile had not ratified the two main freedom of association Conventions but accepted on-site investigations by the Commission by virtue of its membership in the ILO. The final report of the Commission in 1975[36] and some of its recommendations were accepted by the Chilean government, but problems continued to exist.

Following the report of the Commission in 1975, the Governing Body requested the Chilean government to continue to transmit to the ILO regular information on the development of the situation and actions taken on the recommendations made by the Commission. For almost fifteen years there-

[35] See 139th Report of the Freedom of Association Committee, paras. 553–68 and the 142nd Report, paras. 22–271. These reports were respectively approved by the Governing Body at its 191st and 192nd sessions.

[36] See ILO, *The Trade Union Situation in Chile: Report on the Fact-Finding and Conciliation Commission on Freedom of Association* (1975). The report was examined by the Governing Body during the 196th Session in May 1975.

after the Committee continued to urge the Chilean government to adopt amendments bringing the trade union legislation into conformity with the principles of freedom of association and asked that the Committee be kept informed of developments. It also requested the Chilean government to keep it informed of the development of inquiries into the disappearance of trade unionists.

The Chile case illustrates one of the most notable aspects of the ILO supervisory procedures: polite but long-term, persistent pressure on governments to improve human rights. The FAS Committee appears never to let go of a case until it has been satisfactorily resolved. Steady ILO pressure will be maintained on Chile until the trade union situation becomes satisfactory.

The ILO has published the principles on freedom of association enunciated by the FAS Committee in the Digest of Decisions of the FAS Committee on Freedom of Association (1985). It is claimed that these principles, which make the right of freedom of association more concrete, have become principles of customary international law.[37]

In 1978 and 1979 the FAS Committee, at the suggestion of the Governing Body, reviewed its procedures to determine what improvements might be made and measures adopted to speed up the Committee's work and increase its efficiency. The Committee concluded that its influence was primarily a moral one deriving from: 'conclusions unanimously reached on the basis of established principles and to some extent from the publicity which the conclusions of an international body entail.'[38] It considered that one of its main achievements was to have gained wider recognition for principles of freedom of association and emphasized the importance of public opinion as one of the most important elements in its work.

In the 1979 review, the FAS Committee analysed the result of its efforts:

> [A]mong the numerous cases examined by the Committee, a substantial proportion have raised issues relating to fundamental human rights, particularly in connection with the arrest, detention or exile of trade unionists ... In many of these cases—including, in particular, cases where such measures had not been taken within the context of judicial proceedings—the government concerned finally released the persons in question or allowed their return from exile. While there is no doubt that, in a large number of cases, the positive results achieved can be directly linked to the action of the Committee, it can also be said that in other cases of achievement, the Committee's efforts, coupled with other factors, have contributed to a large extent in obtaining the desired results from governments ... Thus, since the beginning of 1976 the Committee, in the course of its examination of certain cases involving the arrest, detention, or exile of trade unionists, has been informed of the release of over 250 trade unionists, and in one case the Committee was informed of the granting of a

[37] Caire, *Freedom of Association and Economic Development* (1977).

[38] 193rd Report of the Committee on Freedom of Association, 9B.209/6/9, 209th Session, Geneva, 27 Feb.–2 Mar. 1979, para. 8.

general amnesty which enabled large numbers of trade unionists to be released from detention or to return from exile.[39]

Despite the cautiously optimistic statement of the results of the Committee's work, the 1979 review suggested a number of measures to improve its efficiency, in particular: wider publicity for the Committee's findings when governments are unwilling to co-operate with the Committee, approaches to government delegates at the annual ILO Conference in order to obtain government co-operation, increasing use of the direct contacts procedures (see below, under 'Direct Contacts'), added approaches by ILO regional offices to elicit government co-operation.[40] The Governing Body adopted these suggestions for improving the work of the FAS Committee.[41] When governments fail to supply information concerning a complaint within a reasonable time they may be mentioned in a special introductory paragraph of the Committee's report. If there is a continued failure the governments concerned are informed that the Chairman of the Committee will make contact with their representatives attending the session of the International Labour Conference to draw attention to the particular case and to discuss the reasons for delay and then report to the Committee. If there is still continued failure to reply, the governments are warned in a special introductory paragraph to the Committee's report—and by an express communication from the ILO Director-General—that the Committee may submit a report on the case even if the government has failed to supply information. In certain cases where replies are not sent, ILO external offices may approach governments to elicit information. Finally, the outline of procedure states: 'In cases where the governments implicated are obviously unwilling to co-operate, the Committee may recommend, as an exceptional measure, that wider publicity be given to the allegations, to the recommendations of the Governing Body and to the obstructive attitude of the governments concerned'.[42]

More radical proposals by the Workers' members, of the Governing Body were rejected by the FAS Committee. The Workers members suggested that severe measures should be adopted for governments which persistently refused to carry out Committee recommendations. Such measures could include the withholding of technical co-operation, refusal to hold meetings, and the closure of ILO field offices in countries where there were serious violations of freedom of association.

The Committee as a whole did not support the suggestions of the Workers' members and expressed 'certain doubts' about the proposals. It rejected the

[39] Ibid. paras. 9 and 10.
[40] 193rd Report of FAS Committee, GB.209/6/9, 209th Session, Geneva, 27 Feb.–2 Mar. 1979, para. 33.
[41] n. 30, above.
[42] n. 34, above, para. 34.

idea of a 'special list' of uncooperative countries which was suggested by Workers' members on the grounds, in part, that it would be drawn up only on the basis of countries against which a complaint had been lodged; other countries with serious trade union problems would not be included and the list would therefore not be objective. In rejecting the special list it emphasized the need for co-operation from governments. The report noted that in order to carry out its activities:

> the Committee needs the co-operation of governments and it is only by a strong measure of government support that the persuasive and moral influence of the Committee can lead to practical results being obtained . . . [I]f it protected governments against unreasonable accusations, governments on their side should recognize the importance for the protection of their good name of formulating for objective examination detailed factual replies to such factual charges as might be put forward.[43]

The Committee did, however, as referred to above, adopt the suggestion of mentioning governments in a special paragraph of its report. The Committee felt that decisions regarding withholding of technical assistance, refusal to hold meetings, and closure of ILO offices were matters for the Governing Body to decide in particular cases.

As the FAS Committee has pointed out, its influence is primarily a moral one. 'Objectivity, perseverance and the weight of public opinion are the most valuable means at its disposal.'[44] That this influence is not negligible is evidenced by the fact that trade unions and trade union federations continue to file an average of eighty to ninety new cases each year with the Freedom of Association Committee.

The confidence which trade union members and others place in the FAS procedures appear to be based on the following aspects of the procedures:

(*a*) expeditious handling of complaints of violations by means of frequent meetings (three times a year) and procedures for handling urgent cases;
(*b*) participation of representatives of workers' organizations who maintain constant pressure to improve procedures;
(*c*) maintaining the confidence of complainants (normally trade unions) through information regarding the status of complaints and published information concerning cases;
(*d*) methods for applying progressively mounting pressure on uncooperative governments or governments guilty of egregious violations of trade union rights by publicizing violations; and
(*e*) integration of the FAS procedures with other aspects of ILO activities: reference to the Fact-Finding and Conciliation Commission, or to the

[43] 193rd Report of the FAS Committee, GB.209/619, 209th Session, Geneva, 27 Feb.–2 Mar. 1979, paras. 33–7.
[44] n. 37, above, para. 35.

Committee of Experts for continued follow-up, approaches to government delegates at the annual Conference, reference of cases to regional offices, and ultimately possible intervention of the Director-General.

In contrast, the UN 1503 procedure is not expeditious, and does not permit non-governmental participation other than the initial filing of the communication. The filing of a communication is a secret procedure and the procedure is not linked with other UN activities and thus lacks the support of the Organisation as a whole. However, the Human Rights Commission under the 1503 procedure may eventually publish the names of particular governments considered engaged in a 'consistent pattern of gross violations of human rights' and, thus, unlike UN reports systems, utilizes the 'mobilization of shame'. The 1503 procedure also makes it possible for individuals or persons with reliable knowledge of violations to file communications, a possibility which does not exist under ILO procedures.

III. CONSTITUTIONAL COMPLAINTS PROCEDURES AND COMMISSIONS OF INQUIRY

Articles 24–6 of the ILO Constitution provide procedures for the filing of complaints against States for failing to implement ratified conventions and for the establishment of Commissions of Inquiry in particular cases. Until recently, these procedures had been rarely used. They have been increasingly used recently but the regular supervisory system and the freedom of association procedures remain the most commonly employed ILO procedures.

The UN Charter makes no specific provision for the filing of human rights complaints or the setting up of Commissions of Inquiry. The *Ad Hoc* Working Group set up by the Human Rights Commission of the UN in 1974 to investigate the human rights situation in Chile, deriving its mandate implicitly from the Charter, undertook a fact-finding mission in 1975 analogous to the missions of ILO Commissions. But the work of such working groups and Special Rapporteurs remains something of an anomaly in UN practice. Fact-finding procedures are less formally developed in the UN than within the ILO.[45]

Article 26 of the ILO Constitution provides that a State which has ratified a particular convention may file a complaint that another ratifying State is not effectively observing the provisions of the convention. The same Article provides that the Governing Body may appoint a Commission of Inquiry to investigate the complaint if it sees fit. The Governing Body may also appoint Commissions of Inquiry on its own motion or on receipt of a complaint from a delegate of the Conference. States have rarely filed complaints under this

[45] See generally Chap. 5. above.

Article, although in recent years several complaints have been filed by conference delegates.

Article 24 of the Constitution provides that industrial associations of employers or workers may make 'representations' that a member State has failed to observe a convention. Between 1924 and 1970 only eight such representations were made but there has been an increasing number recently. Thus, for example, in its 1991 report the Committee of Experts noted Article 24 representations relating to Turkey, Argentina, Mauritania, Iraq, and Libya. Representations are examined by a tripartite committee appointed by the Governing Body from among its members and the representation and the government's reply may be published if the Governing Body so decides.

Relatively few Commissions of Inquiry have been appointed, although in recent years the number has increased. Thus Commissions have examined situations in the Dominican Republic, the Federal Republic of Germany, Nicaragua, and Romania. A particularly important Commission was named in 1982. In that year, two workers' delegates to the International Labour Conference from France and Norway filed a complaint under Article 26 of the ILO Constitution against the government of Poland for failure to observe the freedom of association conventions which it had ratified. The Governing Body established a three-person Commission of Inquiry to investigate the allegations. The Commission was informed, however, that the government of Poland would not co-operate in the proceedings. It was thus unable to carry out its investigations within Poland. The Governing Body informed Poland that the 'competence of the Commission is . . . beyond doubt in international law, under Article 26 of the Constitution of the ILO, which has been accepted by Poland. The non-co-operation of your Government in this connection would constitute a breach of an international obligation on the part of your Government'.[46] The Commission was able to obtain sufficient information outside Poland to support its conclusion that Poland was not in conformity with the freedom of association conventions in a number of regards. When the Governing Body took note of the Report, Poland announced its intention to withdraw from the ILO. This threat was never carried out and the ILO's role was overwhelmingly vindicated by developments in Poland in the late 1980s.

Commissions of Inquiry remain an exceptional but important ILO measure. They are quasi-judicial inquiries carried out by respected independent persons under formal procedures which normally include on-the-spot investigations and hearings of witnesses. Other ILO implementation systems, the

[46] In 1983 Poland became the first country to refuse to co-operate with an ILO Commission of Inquiry: 'Report of the Commission Instituted under Article 26 of the Constitution of the International Labour Organisation to Examine the Complaint of the Observance by Poland of the Freedom of Association and Protection of the Right to Organise Convention, 1948 (No. 87) and the Right to Organise and Collective Bargaining Convention 1949 (No. 98) presented by delegates at the 68th session of the International Labour Conference', GB 227/3/6, (1984).

regular supervisory system, and the Committee on Freedom of Association, both include a political aspect, i.e., the participation of government representatives during stages of the procedures. The Commissions of Inquiry are the best guarantee of impartiality and objectivity among the various ILO implementation procedures. Surprisingly, they have been accepted by some governments with reputations for serious violations of human rights. The care in which the Commissions have undertaken their work has inspired the confidence of governments and, with the recent exception of Poland, led them to accept on-site investigation.

The importance of independent fact-finding Commissions is illustrated by a comparison of the ILO treatment of the case of Poland with that of the UN. The ILO appointed a Commission composed of three highly respected independent persons, conducted many hearings, and published a lengthy substantive and well-documented report on the labour situation in Poland. In contrast, the Secretary-General of the UN designated his representative, Under-Secretary-General Hugo Gobbi, in December 1982 to prepare a report on human rights in Poland to be presented to the Human Rights Commission several months later. The report has been referred to as 'noted for its diplomatic caution' and 'insignificance'.[47] This incident reminded observers of the political nature of much of UN human rights activity reinforcing the cynicism so often prevailing regarding the UN and human rights.

IV. 'DIRECT CONTACTS'

Although it might appear from the variety of ILO supervisory mechanisms previously described that no additional measures were needed to implement labour rights, the ILO in recent years has found 'direct contacts' to be particularly useful. 'Direct contacts' are personal visits by ILO officials or an independent person (named by the ILO Director-General), to ILO member States in order to assist them in overcoming difficulties in application of ratified conventions or to fulfil other responsibilities of an ILO member.[48] Such contacts have been used, *inter alia*: to follow up recommendations of the Commission of Inquiry which examined the implementation by Portugal of the Forced Labour Convention in Angola and Mozambique, to examine complaints concerning trade union situations in Uruguay, Bolivia, and Argentina, and to examine a complaint filed by France against Panama relating to maritime conventions, in regard to freedom of association in Argentina (April 1990), and to consider the situation of Haitian workers on sugar plantations in the Dominican Republic (January 1991).

[47] See Chap. 14, above. See also Franck, 'Of Gnats and Camels: Is there a Double Standard at the United Nations?', 78 *Am. J. Int'l L.* 830 (1984). See also n. 50, below.

[48] The information in this section is based largely on Valticos, 'Une nouvelle forme d'action internationale: Les "contacts directs"', 27 *Ann. français de droit int'l* 481–2 (1981).

The visits are carried out with considerable discretion and are generally of a short duration—usually a few days. They are often requested by governments but in some cases are proposed by the Office. The ILO representative meets with high officials of the government, generally the Minister of Labour, and with employers' and workers' organizations. Direct contacts relating to freedom of association are particularly sensitive since they may concern the evaluation of facts relating to complaints lodged against the government.

The procedure of direct contacts was established because of limitations in other ILO procedures:

> The examination of reports on ratified conventions by the Committee of Experts takes place entirely through written documents. The discussion of a case before the Conference Committee on Application of Conventions, where government representatives may be heard, is often too heated and too brief to lead to positive results. In addition, the size of the Conference Committee (over 120 members) makes it difficult to arrive at a solution.[49]

Direct contacts have proved to be a particularly efficacious means of reaching solutions or establishing the existence of contested facts. The success of such contacts is due to the rapidity with which they can be arranged and to the low-key discreet manner in which they are carried out. They are primarily informal means of entering into negotiations with government representatives. They have been widely used in recent years and have become an important complement to the other more formal ILO procedures.

Direct contacts have been further supplemented by the appointment of Regional Advisors on international labour standards in Africa, America, and Asia. Their role is primarily providing continuing advice and assistance rather than investigating facts.

The UN has, with increasing frequency, named Special Rapporteurs to look at abuses of human rights in particular countries. This procedure is roughly comparable to the ILO 'direct contacts' procedure but has clearly been far less effective. One 1984 assessment reported that:

> on four of the six recent occasions when the United Nations has resorted to this mechanism, the Special Rapporteurs have pursued ends other than the documentation of human rights abuses. In so doing, these four Rapporteurs—those assigned to report on Chile, Guatemala, Iran and Poland—have done a disservice to the human rights cause. In addition, they have injured the United Nations as an institution, further inspiring cynicism about its capacity to conduct itself fairly in assembling and evaluating information about human rights abuses.[50]

[49] Ibid. 478.

[50] *Four Failures: A Report on the U.N. Special Rapporteurs on Human Rights in Chile. Guatemala, Iran and Poland*, prepared by Americas Watch, Asia Watch, Helsinki Watch (1984).

C. *The International Labour Office—An Activist International Secretariat*

The Office of the ILO corresponds to the secretariat of the various UN bodies and organs and consists of the permanent employees of the Organisation at the Geneva headquarters and in regional and field offices. The Office is one of the main organs of the ILO together with the Governing Body and the annual Conference. The activist role which the Office has claimed for itself since the founding of the ILO has given it more importance within the Organisation than secretariats within most UN bodies.

The term 'secretariat' to describe the work of the Office is not one with which ILO officials are comfortable, since it seems to connote a role secondary to that of other organs. The Office plays a leadership role in promoting the objectives of the ILO and keeping it 'on course' as well as embodying the institutional memory of the Organisation. ILO officials have been initiators in the work of the Organisation, considering themselves not as simple executors of the desires of member States, but rather as collaborators in the pursuit of social justice.

This attitude by ILO officials is due in large part to the dynamism and commitment of Albert Thomas, a Frenchman who was the first Director-General of the ILO. Thomas was a man of strong personality, exceptional ability, and political 'sagesse'. He established the principle that the Director-General of the ILO had a role of leadership within the Organisation. The precedent set by Thomas has been followed by his successors, not all of whom, however, have had the political skills of Thomas. Because of the role played by the Director-General, the ILO has been referred to as a 'limited monarchy'.[51] The first Secretary-General of the League of Nations, Eric Drummond, had a more humble conception of his role than Thomas did. Drummond considered that his role, and that of the Secretariat of the League of Nations, was one of service to member States and not one of initiating and leading. To a certain extent, this concept may be said to prevail still in the UN. Thomas established a dynamic conception of the role of an ILO official and an *esprit de corps* which has influenced the ILO throughout its subsequent history.[52]

Albert Thomas was the first of the active and influential members of the Office but many others have followed. No study of the International Labour Office would be complete without emphasizing the importance of the individ-

[51] Cox, 'ILO: Limited Monarchy', in Cox and Jacobson (eds.), *The Anatomy of Influence* (1974), 102.

[52] It has been suggested that some of the differences between the Drummond and the Thomas approach may have been due to the different conceptions of the civil service prevailing in the British and French governments.

ual personalities who have served as ILO Directors-General or as heads of major ILO departments.[53]

The ILO Committee of Experts and the Governing Body Committee on Freedom of Association must necessarily depend to a great extent on the Office because of the large volume of work. At its 1991 session, the Committee of Experts examined 1,409 reports from member States on ratified conventions, 322 reports on Conventions declared applicable to non-metropolitan territories, 281 reports on paid educational leave and human resources development, concerning which it issued a general survey, and 10 reports on the International Covenant on Economic, Social and Cultural Rights. All of this was accomplished by the Committee during its three-week session in March 1991. The 1991 session was in no way atypical. It is obvious that only substantial preparatory work and efficient working methods could enable to Committee to accomplish such a large volume of work. It has called upon ILO officials to undertake preparatory work.

The preparatory work of the Committee is carried out by officials of the International Labour Standards (ILS) Department. In 1991 this Department employed thirty-five officials at the professional level, all of whom were trained lawyers and most of whom were hired through competitive examinations. Each official specializes in the examination of reports on a particular group of conventions: social security, employment policy, forced labour, maritime conventions, etc. Reports are due in October, and between October and March (when the Committee of Experts meets) the officials examine each report from a country concerning conventions for which he or she is responsible. The examination may involve independent research into the laws of the country, study of judicial decisions of the country, and examination of comments by workers' and employers' organizations. The Office maintains an extensive library of the laws and decrees of member States and further information is often available at the UN library in Geneva.[54]

The official may also consult reports of regional advisors, reports of the Committee on Freedom of Association, and Commissions of Inquiry. Account is taken of any previous comments of the Committee of Experts or the Conference Committee on the Application of Conventions. If the report is the first one received from a country after ratification, a very extensive 'comparative analysis' is made of the provisions of the convention and national law and practice.

Finally, if the official believes the examination shows a discrepancy between the convention and national law and practice, draft comments will be prepared

[53] David Morse, C. Wilfred Jenks, and Nicolas Valticos are names which come immediately to mind.

[54] Nevertheless, one of the problems uncovered by the ILO is difficulty in obtaining in Geneva all the relevant legislation and judicial decisions. For this reason recourse is sometimes had to ILO regional offices to obtain information which may be delayed in receipt from governments.

for submission to the member of the Committee of Experts charged with responsibility for the convention. The Expert may accept the comment as drafted or make whatever changes are felt desirable. The draft comments as approved or changed by the Expert are then presented to the entire Committee for approval. Frequent changes are made where important human rights aspects are involved, but in the great majority of cases the comments to governments finally presented are substantially as prepared by the officials. Thus, the exceptional amount of work accomplished by the Committee of Experts is understandable. The Committee of Experts has expressed its appreciation for the 'invaluable assistance . . . rendered to it by the officials of the ILO whose competence and devotion to duty make it possible to accomplish its increasingly complex tasks in a limited period of time'.

Other ILO supervisory bodies are also serviced by the Office. The Governing Body Freedom of Association Committee is serviced by officials of the FAS Branch of the ILS Department. Commissions of Inquiry are provided with officials from the ILS Department who undertake a substantial amount of the necessary research, accompany the members of the Commission at on-site investigations, and draft major parts of the report of the Commission.

The ILS Department is one of the major departments of the ILO and has been provided with the necessary staffing and funding for the responsibilities assigned to it. The head of the Department holds a high rank within the Organisation and has traditionally been one of the most important Office officials. The ILS Department has been given high priority within the Office. The constituency of the ILO—the member States and, particularly, workers' organizations—have also placed a high priority on the work of the Department. This institutional support is clearly one reason for the high quality work produced. The support of workers' organizations has made it possible for ILO officials to undertake important initiatives.

The ILO has the usual complement of bureaucratic employees who are not committed individuals, but there has traditionally been a relatively high degree of commitment to ILO goals within the Office. Cox has written:

> The International Labour Office emerged from World War II as a small staff with a high sense of commitment to building a new world order. The staff members were united by their efforts to survive the debacle of the League of Nations, by the tradition of strong executive leadership, and by their conviction that they had a right to express collectively an independent international viewpoint on the postwar issues of social policy.[55]

Many of the officials who were with the ILO immediately following the Second World War are now retired and the *esprit de corps* of this small group no longer permeates the entire organization in the same manner. Neverthe-

[55] n. 46, above.

less, the tradition of quality work and a sense of responsibility to ILO ideals among officials in the Standards Department is evident to close observers.

It has already been observed that the UN Secretariat has not taken as dynamic a leadership role within the UN as the Office has taken within the ILO. In addition, the branch of the UN responsible for human rights activities—the Centre for Human Rights—has not been granted the importance within the UN which the ILS Department has been given within the ILO. Its upgrading from a Division to a Centre was a positive step, but it occurred simultaneously with the failure to renew the contract of a dynamic and committed Director. Mixed messages were therefore conveyed regarding the importance of the overall UN committment to human rights.

Other chapters of this book contain extensive information on the work of the UN secretariat and human rights and it is not necessary to enter into detail here, but some points warrant emphasis in this context. The Committees set up under human rights conventions have an anomalous role within the UN. For the most part they are not strictly speaking 'UN Committees' but rather structures created under specific conventions. Nevertheless, they are dependent on the UN secretariat for assistance and support in their activities. Their lack of a clear structural role within the UN has repercussions in their relations with the secretariat, particularly with regard to the allotment of resources. This is to be contrasted with the importance the ILO places on the work of the Committee of Experts and the Conference Committee as evidenced by adequate secretariat resources.

The extent of support provided by the UN secretariat for the work of the various human rights committees appears deficient to an observer familiar with the ILO system although the Communications Unit of the Centre is reputed to provide excellent and extensive assistance with respect to the consideration of petitions. The ILO experience demonstrates that effective work by human rights organs is heavily dependent on secretariat assistance. None of the UN committees has been provided a secretariat unit of its own. They do not have the benefit of substantive assistance from the secretariat in either the study of reports or the drafting of comments. A member of the Human Rights Committee has written:

> The Secretariat has not been expected to do any such advance study and might have felt unable to do so as it would require not only specially trained staff but perhaps also the exercise of judgment in framing comments and questions; which the Secretariat seems slow to undertake.[56]

Thus far such assistance to the various committees appears to have been provided in an unstructured manner by non-governmental human rights organizations.

[56] See Chap. 10, above.

Conclusion

What lessons can be learned from the ILO experience? And can the lessons be usefully applied to the human rights work of the United Nations?

The ILO and the UN differ in aims, structure, and historical development; practices and procedures cannot easily be transposed from one to another. Keeping in mind this precautionary note, however, there are elements of the ILO experience, outlined in the preceding pages, which are particularly relevant to the development of UN human rights work. The ILO experience provides evidence of the positive role played by non-governmental actors in international human rights monitoring. Observers of the UN are discouraged by the political nature of much of its human rights activity. Governments criticize or do not criticize other governments largely for political reasons. The participation of non-governmental representatives in the ILO tends to de-politicize its human rights monitoring. The full participation of workers' and employers' organizations in the ILO Conference Committee on the Application of Standards and the Governing Body Committee on Freedom of Association has made an important contribution to the effective work of these Committees. They provide information not contained in government reports and insist that steady pressure be applied on governments to comply with labour standards.

Given the nature of the UN, it is not possible to duplicate the 'tripartite' structure of the ILO. But there is no intrinsic reason, given the necessary political will, why NGOs should not be offered a more expansive role within the UN. It has been suggested, for example, that the role of NGOs in supplying briefs to UN monitoring committees or other organs should be officially recognized and the documents distributed to members and governments.[57] This is a modest but useful suggestion—many more could be made. UN human rights activities will elicit increased respect to the extent that they are de-politicized and greater participation of non-governmental human rights organizations is essential if this is to be accomplished.

The ILO experience may prove most useful to the UN in illustrating that economic and social rights may be precisely defined and their implementation monitored by international organs. In particular, the Committee on Economic, Social and Cultural Rights could use ILO analyses of legislation and practice more extensively in its examination of Articles 6–9 of the Covenant.

The ILO Committees which supervise the implementation of conventions and investigate the application of labour standards have acknowledged their considerable reliance on the technical expertise of the ILO staff. The Organisation has provided the necessary resources to develop a large and competent

[57] Niall MacDermot, 'Human Rights Implementation Procedures in the UN and Council of Europe', 25 *Int'l Commission of Jurists Newsletter* Appendix B (1985).

staff within the International Labour Department which supports the work of the supervisory organs. As a result, it has been possible for the Committees, meeting only for brief periods during the year, to carry out their functions. The supervisory bodies set up under UN conventions have an anomalous relationship with the UN, and it has not always been clear to what extent they may draw on UN secretariat resources. Members have commented on lack of secretariat assistance. It is essential that the Centre for Human Rights be provided with sufficient resources to assist the committees set up under UN conventions. The political bodies of the UN carry the ultimate responsibility for the human rights work of the Organisation, but this work will depend to a large extent on the resources provided to the Centre. An adequately funded and supported Centre might lead to a more active UN Secretariat which could provide needed impetus to improvement of UN human right activities.

ILO techniques for the supervision of conventions and the implementation of labour rights are highly developed and regarded as relatively effective but the use of such techniques is not unique to the ILO. Reporting systems, complaint procedures, Commissions of Inquiry, and Special Rapporteurs are all used by the UN to monitor and promote human rights. They have not been as effective as the ILO procedures. The participation of non-governmental representatives and the active support of the ILO staff have been mentioned, but other factors are also important. In appointing members of Commissions of Inquiry and individuals to undertake direct contacts, the ILO Governing Body and Director General have been careful to appoint independent and experienced persons who can be relied on to report accurately on the situation of human rights in the country concerned. Unfortunately, members of UN Commissions and Special Rapporteurs have not always been perceived as politically independent or as reporting fully and accurately. As a result, UN human rights work has too often been depreciated and criticized. The ILO experience demonstrates that intergovernmental organizations are capable of fair and dispassionate inquiries into human rights situations if attention is paid to the selection of individuals assigned to investigate human rights. The UN Human Rights Commission should give particular attention in the future to the naming of Special Rapporteurs who will carry out their functions in an independent and competent manner.

The ILO has profited from long experience in supervising trade union rights and the civil liberties necessary to ensure those rights. It has developed its effective techniques over many years. A number of the techniques discussed in the section of this chapter on supervisory procedures are presently being emulated within the UN, to a limited extent. However, the UN supervisory committees are not yet sufficiently experienced or sufficiently supported by the political organs of the UN to adopt certain of the more effective ILO practices. The ILO procedures were originally established for the supervision of technical labour standards. There was little opposition to the procedures because they related to technical matters and not human rights. When ILO human rights conventions were adopted after the Second World War, the supervisory procedures were already well established and it was considered normal to extend them to the human rights conventions. Such was not the case with the development of supervisory procedures for UN human rights treaties. New supervisory procedures had to be established and political opposition arose to the intrusion of international organization activity into such a sensitive area as domestic human rights practices. UN human rights supervision has necessarily proceeded gingerly, lacking the long experience of the ILO. But the primary obstacle to development of highly effective rights monitoring within the UN has been the lack of political will.

The ILO could also profit from the experience of the UN. The UN has developed procedures for receiving petitions from individuals and from human rights organizations. The ILO has no procedure for receiving individual complaints (other than by a delegate to its annual Conference) and human rights NGOs have not found an easy means of participating in ILO activities. The ILO has not done a good job in conveying to the international human rights constituency the importance of labour rights within the human rights picture. Very little writing on labour rights appears in national and international journals on human rights. As a result, the work of the ILO has not been strongly supported by the human rights constituency.

ILO human rights work is not without its critics. The United States withdrew from the ILO from 1977 to 1980 on the grounds, *inter alia*, that ILO human rights activities were lacking in due process, evidenced a double standard, and were increasingly politicized. On the opposite side of the political spectrum, Eastern European Socialist countries have been waging a systematic attack on the ILO human rights supervisory organs in recent years. Despite such criticisms, the ILO constituency, particularly trade union representatives, have strongly defended the Organisation. During the withdrawal of the United States a number of countries made voluntary contributions to the Organisation. The criticisms by both political blocs have had some influence on the human rights work of the ILO.

While it may be a tribute to the impartiality of the ILO that it has been criticized by opposing political blocs, the attacks illustrate the precariousness of even long-established and respected mechanisms for the protection and promotion of human rights. All international efforts to protect human rights are fragile. If the ILO has achieved some success, it has been by cautious and slow steps. The UN may be able to advance more rapidly by profiting from the ILO experience.

16

Human Rights Co-ordination within the UN System

KLAUS T. SAMSON

Introduction

Organigrams showing the relationships between the various parts of the UN system give the impression of an orderly system with a rational division of responsibilities. The actual picture is far less clear. This is particularly so in the human rights field in which the proliferation of organs, expert committees, standard-setting instruments, procedures, and general activities, while underlining the importance of co-ordination, has at the same time rendered it ever more difficult to achieve. Constant reaffirmation of the need for greater co-ordination has been matched in practice by frequent disregard for such concerns.

One must bear in mind that the UN system does not provide for the subordination of its component parts to a supreme authority, but instead is based on the principle of functional decentralization and autonomy. Moreover, in the vast range of activities with which the system is concerned, encompassing practically every aspect of human endeavour and mobilizing the thought and energies of innumerable individuals from every part of the globe, it would be unrealistic to expect a complete measure of consistency. What the system should seek is a co-ordinated approach to the identification of priorities, policies, programmes, and the use of limited resources, in order to arrive at an appropriate allocation of functions and responsibilities among the various agencies concerned. This supposes a series of institutional arrangements and rules. The initial parts of this chapter will therefore examine the formal framework for co-ordination of human rights activities in the UN system, as well as the purposes and limits of such co-ordination.

The main part of the chapter will be devoted to an examination of the way in which attempts to secure co-ordination of human rights activities have fared in practice in respect of a representative sample of issues. A number of these have arisen in relation to the work of the ILO. Their inclusion is due not only to the author's special familiarity with them, but also to two factors which have made co-ordination of the work of the ILO and of other international agencies particularly sensitive. One arises from the major role played in the work of the ILO by standard-setting and supervisory procedures, where lack of adequate co-ordination is especially liable to cause conflict. The other arises from its tripartite composition: the direct institutional participation of non-governmental representatives in the work of the ILO gives its deliberations a perspective different from that of purely intergovernmental organizations.

In my conclusion, I express concern about what I consider negative trends in human rights co-ordination in practice. I place the main responsibility for those trends on the UN, since it is there that I perceive the principal constraining elements in structures, methods, and attitudes. Established habits are not easy to change. My suggestions for improving co-ordination in the human rights field are therefore of an essentially practical nature, aimed particularly at ensuring greater awareness of relevant considerations by all those who participate in international efforts to promote and protect human rights.

A. *The Formal Framework*

The framework for co-ordination of human rights activities within the UN system is provided by the UN Charter and the relationship agreements between the United Nations and the specialized agencies. Article 55 (c) of the Charter requires the United Nations to promote 'universal respect for, and observance of, human rights and fundamental freedoms for all without distinction as to race, sex, language or religion'. Articles 57 and 63 provide for other intergovernmental organizations to be brought by agreement into relationship with the UN as specialized agencies. Under Article 58, the UN is to make recommendations for co-ordination of the policies and activities of the specialized agencies. According to Article 60, these functions are vested in the General Assembly and, under its authority, in the Economic and Social Council. By virtue of Article 63, the Council may co-ordinate the activities of the specialized agencies through consultation with and recommendations to them and through recommendations to the Assembly and to member States. Under Article 62, the Council may make or initiate studies and reports with respect to international economic, social, cultural, educational, health, or related matters and may make recommendations with respect to them, *inter alia*, to the specialized agencies; it may also make recommendations for the purpose of promoting respect for, and observance of, human rights and fundamental freedoms for all.[1] These provisions are reflected in the relationship agreements between the UN and the specialized agencies. Other features of these agreements concern arrangements for reciprocal representation at meetings and for exchange of information.

[1] Similar powers are vested in the General Assembly itself by Art. 13 of the Charter.

A network of agreements has also been concluded among the specialized agencies with a view to ensuring, on similar lines, continuing consultation and collaboration on matters of common interest.

In the field of human rights, the discharge of its responsibilities by the Economic and Social Council is largely dependent on the work, proposals, and recommendations of the Human Rights Commission. In 1979, the Commission's terms of reference were amplified to include the function of assisting the Council in the co-ordination of activities concerning human rights in the UN system.[2] Parallel to these provisions, the Committee for Programme and Co-ordination has a general responsibility to assist the Council in the performance of its co-ordination functions.[3]

Concern for co-ordinated use of the UN system finds expression also in the Rules of the Economic and Social Council. Thus, under Rule 77, when proposals are made in the Council for new activities to be undertaken by the UN relating to matters which are the direct concern of the specialized agencies, the Secretary-General is to enter into consultations with the agencies concerned and to report to the Council on the means of achieving co-ordinated use of the respective agencies. More generally, the Administrative Committee on Co-ordination (consisting of the UN Secretary-General, the executive heads of the specialized agencies, and the heads of various other UN agencies or programmes) is required to keep under constant review measures to be suggested to the Council, in order to ensure the most effective implementation of the agreements between the UN and the specialized agencies.[4]

Since 1977, it has been the practice to organize, normally once a year, informal consultation meetings of services responsible for human rights matters in organizations of the UN system and in regional organizations. They have provided an opportunity for review of current activities, exchange of information, and timely identification of questions on which more formal measures of co-ordination might be required.

Inter-agency co-ordination should not be seen merely in terms of initiatives and deliberations in the UN. It is very much a continuing preoccupation of the specialized agencies themselves. For example, already in 1948 the Governing Body of the International Labour Office established an International Organizations Committee, which is kept informed of developments in other organizations of concern to the ILO and is called upon to consider issues of inter-agency relations.

A further dimension of co-ordination concerns relations between the UN

[2] ESC Res.1979/36.

[3] ESC Res.2008(LX) (1976).

[4] ESC Res.13(III) (1946) and 1643(LI) (1971). See also GA Res.32/197 (1977) concerning the restructuring of the economic and social sectors of the UN system.

system and regional organizations, which have developed important human rights programmes. The UN Charter (in Chapter VIII) envisages regional arrangements only in relation to the settlement of disputes. However, in 1966 the Economic and Social Council laid the basis for attendance of representatives of regional bodies concerned with human rights at sessions of the Commission on Human Rights and of the Sub-Commission on Prevention of Discrimination and Protection of Minorities and for exchange of information between them and the Commission.[5] Various specialized agencies have concluded relationship agreements with the regional organizations.

B. *Purposes and Limits of Co-ordination*

Co-ordination may be aimed at various objectives: the avoidance of duplication and waste by allocating responsibility and resources for given activities to a specified organization or group of organizations; consistency in the standards and policies enunciated, advocated, and pursued by the organizations concerned (including individual organs and programmes within an organization); the development of programmes which, taken together, will represent an effective response to a recognized set of needs; or the establishment of a common set of programme priorities.

The extent to which such objectives can realistically be pursued within the UN system is dependent, amongst other things, on the structure of that system. It will also vary according to the nature of the activity concerned, and is liable to be significantly influenced by personal attitudes and relationships among the actors and the pursuit of particular policy objectives.

The UN system has been described as one of functional decentralization.[6] This finds expression in the very provisions of the Charter concerning the specialized agencies, which defines them as organizations 'having wide international responsibilities, as defined in their basic instruments, in economic, social, educational, health, and related fields'. The system is characterized by the existence of a series of distinct organizations, each governed by its own constitution, with its distinctive competence, its own organs of government, its own programme, and its own budget.

In the case of the ILO, there is a major additional factor to be taken into account: its tripartite structure, by virtue of which the representatives of employers and workers, together with those of governments, determine the Organisation's policies and programmes. Already at the San Francisco

[5] ESC Res.1159(XLI) (1966).

[6] See Jenks, 'Co-ordination: A New Problem of International Organisation', 77 *Rec. des cours* 172 (1950); Hill, *The UN System: Co-ordinating its Economic and Social Work* (1978), 11–12; Luard, *International Agencies: The Emerging Framework of Interdependence* (1977), 265 and 324–48.

Conference in 1945 at which the UN Charter was formulated, the ILO delegation insisted that that tripartite form of organization must be respected, as well as the Organisation's direct relations with governments.[7]

As early as its second session, the UN General Assembly called upon member States to ensure on the national level a co-ordinated policy of their delegations to the UN and the specialized agencies,[8] but that advice has been honoured more in the breach than in the observance. Various factors explain this situation.[9] Frequently arrangements for communication and consultation among the government departments which ensure representation in various agencies are lacking or tenuous. These departments are liable, in any case, to have divergent views, interests, and priorities, and to be influenced by the climate of discussion within each agency.

Looking at the efforts at co-ordination in the UN system as a whole, it appears that there are two areas where a considerable measure of systemization and harmonization has been achieved. One involves matters of an administrative nature, such as conditions of employment, information systems, budgetary procedures, etc. The other concerns operational activities, where it has been necessary to determine which organizations should have responsibility for projects in given fields and how to ensure the collaboration of other interested agencies. A series of specific agreements and arrangements have been concluded on such matters. Examples are the agreements between the ILO, FAO, and UNESCO concerning agricultural education and training, or the arrangements between the World Food Programme and the ILO concerning the vetting of WFP project requests.[10] Results of this kind have been achieved on questions of a relatively concrete nature, primarily as a result of discussions and negotiations at secretariat level, not always without difficulty, but on a basis of reciprocal good will and mutual interest.

In considering co-ordination of human rights activities, it must be borne in mind that the extent of involvement in such activities of the various specialized agencies differs greatly, having regard to their mandate. Furthermore, the concern for co-ordination has manifested itself most strongly in regard to certain forms of action, such as standard-setting, supervisory mechanisms, and studies (particularly studies aimed at preparing the ground for possible standards). Prominence has been given to problems which have arisen on such questions because they had to be discussed and settled in policy-making bodies rather than at secretariat level. These factors explain why issues of

[7] See International Labour Conference, *Report IV(1)* (1945), 54.

[8] GA Res.125(II). See also *Report on Co-ordination at the National Level*, E/3107 (1958) and 694B(XXVI) (1958).

[9] See Luard, *International Agencies*, 266 and 284; Nicol and Renninger, 'The Restructuring of the UN Economic and Social System: Background and Analysis', 4 *Third World* 89–90 (1982).

[10] See the application of international labour standards to WFP activities, WFP Intergovernmental Committee, Fourth Session (Nov. 1963), WM/IGC, 4/10.

human rights co-ordination have come to the fore especially in relations among certain agencies, such as the UN, ILO, and UNESCO.

In the late 1950s the Economic and Social Council undertook a comprehensive appraisal of the activities of the UN and specialized agencies in the economic, social, and human rights fields with a view to the development of closer co-ordination.[11] The appraisal was aimed at ascertaining the general direction and trend of programmes rather than at defining individual programmes and projects. It was not meant to imply that the programmes and budgets of the UN or the specialized agencies should, or could, be determined outside the constitutional framework of each organization.[12] A consolidated report was drawn up by a Committee of the Council in 1960.[13] It was little more than a balance sheet, rather than a basis for programme decisions.[14] The exercise has not been repeated. Subsequent discussions on the co-ordination of the economic and social work of the UN system have focused essentially on development activities, without examination of their human rights dimension.[15]

The Commission on Human Rights has been the principal forum in which the general issue of co-ordination of human rights activities within the UN system has been considered in recent years, within the context of its discussions on the further promotion and encouragement of human rights and on alternative approaches and ways and means within the UN system for improving the effective enjoyment of human rights. Arising out of resolutions adopted by the Commission itself,[16] as well as by the General Assembly[17] and the Council,[18] secretariat reports on the human rights activities of the various agencies and bodies concerned and on arrangements and procedures for co-operation and co-ordination were presented to the Commission in 1976 and 1980.[19] The latter report set out and analysed information and comments received from UNICEF, ILO, FAO, UNESCO, WHO, and the Council of Europe. These replies stressed both the desire of the various agencies to collaborate and the extent to which, in a series of activities, arrangements for co-operation had already been made. Significantly, the replies did not address

[11] ESC Res.664A(XXIV), and 665A(XXIV) (1957).

[12] ESC Res.694D (xxvi) (1958).

[13] *Five-Year Perspective 1960–64: Consolidated Report on the Scope, Trend and Costs of the Programmes of the UN, ILO, FAO, UNESCO, WHO, WMO and IAEA in the Economic, Social and Human Rights Fields*, E3347/Rev.1 (1960).

[14] See ESC Res.791(XXX) (1960), stating that the consolidated report 'provides a picture of what is being achieved and attempted through international action and brings into sharper focus the inter-relationship between the work of different organisations'.

[15] See the study by Hill, former UN Assistant-Secretary for Inter-Agency Affairs, *The UN System*.

[16] CHR Res.10(XXXI) (1975).

[17] GA Res.33/54 (1978).

[18] ESC Res.1979/36.

[19] E/CN.4/1193 and E/CN.4/1433.

themselves to difficulties encountered in ensuring co-ordination or suggest any new initiatives. The discussions in the Commission and its working groups have not touched further on this question, although it has been identified as among the relevant issues.[20]

In the past twenty years or so, items specifically referring to human rights have only rarely appeared on the agenda of the Administrative Committee on Co-ordination. One such item concerned arrangements for the contribution by the specialized agencies to the implementation of the Human Rights Covenants. The matter was brought before the ACC by the ILO in 1974, following the failure by the then Director of the Division of Human Rights to respond to repeated requests for discussions, and led to the holding of two *ad hoc* meetings at secretariat level, in September 1974 and January 1976. Another item, also considered at the initiative of the ILO, concerned the co-ordination of legislative work in the UN system. Although this question appeared to go beyond human rights issues, it was brought up because of concern at problems liable to arise from overlap between comprehensive UN human rights instruments and more specific standards adopted within specialized agencies.

This discussion resulted in the adoption of conclusions which represent one of the rare guidelines for co-ordination of UN human rights activities.[21] By reference to the overriding purpose of developing an integrated system of international treaty law, these conclusions identified the following fundamental concerns of co-ordination of the legislative work of international organizations:

(*a*) to prevent unnecessary duplication;
(*b*) to prevent conflict between the obligations undertaken by States under different instruments, as well as in the interpretation of instruments adopted by various organisations; and
(*c*) to ensure that statutory provisions on complex technical subjects are established and supervised by those most competent to do so.

ACC considered that, with a view to achieving uniform interpretation of standards, analysis of compliance should be carried out by those with the greatest competence in the field, and that, where more than one organization was concerned, provision for co-operation should be made in the instrument itself and should bear both on mutual representation and on full exchange of information and observations, as appropriate.

These ACC conclusions recognized that ultimate responsibility for taking relevant decisions would rest with the competent legislative organs, but

[20] See the informal listing of relevant issues by the Chairman of the Working Group established by the Human Rights Commission at its 39th Session in 1983, E/CN.4/1983/64.

[21] See *Annual Report of the Administrative Committee on Co-ordination 1973–74*, E/5488, paras. 200–8.

stressed the importance of the provision by secretariats of information which would ensure full knowledge and understanding of the needs for co-ordination, precedents, and possible solutions.

A similar concern had been expressed by the Economic and Social Council twenty years earlier as regards the carrying out of studies. Arising out of proposals by the Sub-Commission to undertake a series of studies on discrimination in various fields, the Council stated that studies which fall within the scope of specialized agencies or other bodies should normally be carried out by the specialized agencies or other bodies directly concerned.[22]

C. *Co-ordination in Practice*

The effectiveness of co-ordination depends not only on formal guidelines and procedures, but also on the continuing awareness by those participating in deliberations in the various organs of the UN system of the importance of an orderly development of human rights activities within the system. It is therefore necessary to see how far this concern has found expression in specific instances. A sample of cases is reviewed below.

I. EARLY ISSUES BROUGHT BEFORE THE ECONOMIC AND SOCIAL COUNCIL BY TRADE UNION ORGANIZATIONS

At early sessions of the Council, a series of issues was submitted by trade union organizations which raised the question of the relationship between the Council and the ILO. They concerned action in the field of trade union rights, forced labour, and equal pay for men and women.

Proposals for international action to protect trade union rights were presented to the Council in 1947 both by the World Federation of Trade Unions and by the American Federation of Labor. Discussion in the Council centred on whether these proposals should be examined by it or should be referred to the ILO, in accordance with the UN–ILO relationship agreement. The Council decided to transmit them to the ILO with the request that the question be placed on the agenda of the next session of the International Labour Conference. It also transmitted the documents to the Commission on Human Rights.[23] Immediate action by the ILO Governing Body led to the addition of the item 'freedom of association and industrial relations' to the agenda of the Conference, meeting in June 1947, and to the adoption the following year of the Convention concerning Freedom of

[22] ESC Res.502(H(XVI) (1953).
[23] ESC Res.52(IV) (1947).

Association and Protection of the Right to Organise (No. 87, 1948) and, subsequently, of the Convention concerning the Right to Organise and Collective Bargaining (No. 98, 1949).

Acting upon another part of the proposals originally made in the Economic and Social Council, and following discussions at secretariat level, the Governing Body decided in January 1950 to establish a Fact-finding and Conciliation Commission for examination of allegations of infringement of trade union rights, whose services would also be available to the UN. The Council, which had previously requested the ILO to proceed with the establishment of such machinery, decided to accept the services of the ILO and the Commission on behalf of the United Nations.[24] Subsequently, it also decided that all allegations of violation of trade union rights received by the UN relating to States Members of the ILO should be forwarded to the ILO Governing Body.[25]

Another issue on which effective inter-agency co-ordination was achieved was the question of forced labour which was brought before the Economic and Social Council in 1947 by the American Federation of Labour. It proposed that the ILO be asked to undertake a comprehensive survey on the extent of forced labour in all UN member States and to suggest measures for its elimination.[26] Following consultations, the Council decided in 1951, in agreement with the ILO Governing Body, to establish an *Ad Hoc* Committee on forced labour, to be appointed jointly by the UN Secretary-General and the Director-General of the ILO, to survey systems of forced labour and to report to the two bodies.[27] The *Ad Hoc* Committee's 1953 report was considered by the UN General Assembly and the Economic and Social Council and by the ILO Governing Body. One outcome was a decision by the latter to bring the matter before the International Labour Conference for the adoption of new international standards. Both the Council and the Assembly encouraged these efforts,[28] which led to the adoption of the Convention concerning Abolition of Forced Labour (No. 105, 1957).

The question of equal pay was raised in January 1948 by the World Federation of Trade Unions. It submitted to the Council a declaration of

[24] ESC Res.277(X) (1950). See generally, *ILO Official Bulletin*. (1950), xxxiii. 74–90, and United Nations, *United Nations Action in the Field of Human Rights* (1980), 188–9. In several instances, States which at the time were members of the UN but not of the ILO gave consent to the reference to the ILO commission of cases concerning them—Lesotho (1972), United States (1978), and South Africa (1983).

[25] ESC Res.474(XV) (1953).

[26] It is not without interest to recall that the adoption by the ILO of the Forced Labour Convention, 1930 (No. 29) resulted from an initiative taken by the Assembly of the League of Nations when it approved the text of the 1926 Slavery Convention.

[27] ESC Res.350(XII) (1951).

[28] See, in particular, ESC Res.524(XVII) (1954) and 602(XXI) (1956), and GA Res.842(IX) (1954).

principles and a survey on the remuneration of women workers and asked it to consider the question of equal pay for equal work for male and female labour. The Council decided to transmit the WFTU memorandum to the ILO and invited it to proceed as rapidly as possible with the consideration of the subject. The Council also invited the Commission on the Status of Women to submit to it suggestions on the matter.[29] Informed of these developments, the International Labour Conference in 1948 called for further studies on the issue by the International Labour Office with a view to the early adoption of appropriate standards. This led to the adoption in 1951 of the Convention and Recommendation concerning Equal Remuneration (No. 100 and No. 90 respectively).

In all the above instances, matters of concern to the ILO which were raised in the Council were referred to the ILO for action and found a ready and rapid response, thus ensuring effective co-operation between the ILO and the Council.

II. THE DRAFTING OF THE HUMAN RIGHTS COVENANTS

The specialized agencies participated directly in UN discussions on the Covenants, and, in particular, had considerable influence in shaping the contents of the Covenant on Economic, Social and Cultural Rights, which was recognized to deal with matters which fell primarily within their field of action.[30] This participation was actively sought by the UN. Thus, when the General Assembly decided in 1950 that provisions concerning economic, social, and cultural rights should be included in the draft Covenant, it called upon the Economic and Social Council to obtain the co-operation of the specialized agencies in that connection.[31] The Council invited the specialized agencies to send representatives to the 1951 Session of the Commission on Human Rights to participate in its work on the subject.[32] High-level delegations from the ILO, WHO, and UNESCO participated in that session. In subsequent years, the specialized agencies continued to follow the issue in both the Commission and the Assembly and frequently presented observations, covering both the substantive provisions of the Covenants and the measures of implementation.[33]

[29] ESC Res.121(VI) (1948). Certain principles recommended by the Commission on the Status of Women were subsequently transmitted to the ILO by the Council. ESC Res.242(D) (1949).

[30] See, generally, Alston, 'The UN Specialized Agencies and Implementation of the International Covenant on Economic, Social and Cultural Rights', 18 *Colum. J Transnat'l L.* 79 (1979).

[31] GA Res.421(V) (1950).

[32] ESC Res.349(XII) (1951).

[33] See e.g. GA Res.543(VI), 544(VI) and 833(IX), and ESC Res.501(XVI).

During the discussions in the Commission and in the Third Committee of the Assembly, reference was frequently made to the standard-setting work of the specialized agencies, particularly of the ILO, as a factor to be borne in mind in formulating the Covenant provisions.[34] There was a clear concern not to duplicate or enter into conflict with the agencies' instruments, and to leave to the agencies the task of detailed definition of concepts within their specialized fields of action. It was this view which led to the drafting of the Covenant in terms of broadly defined rights. It was pointed out that the Covenants were not the only or final human rights instruments, and that the rights in question could be elaborated in more detailed conventions adopted under the auspices of the UN and the specialized agencies.[35] This possibility is expressly envisaged in Article 23 of the Covenant.

The competence of the specialized agencies also found recognition in the implementation provisions of the Covenant. They require communication to the agencies of copies of States Parties' reports relating to matters within their responsibilities (Article 16, paragraph 2(b)). They allow States Parties to refer to information previously furnished to specialized agencies instead of repeating that information in their reports on the Covenant (Article 17, para. 3); in that case, the UN in effect becomes dependent on the agency for knowledge of the situation in the country concerned. Article 18 provides for reporting by the agencies to the Economic and Social Council on 'progress made in achieving the observance of the provisions of the present Covenant falling within the scope of their activities; these reports may include particulars of decisions on such implementation adopted by their competent organs'. Provision is also made for specialized agencies to comment on proposed general recommendations concerning the implementation of the Covenant, and for reference to the specialized agencies, for their consideration, of matters arising out of States Parties' reports which may call for technical assistance (Articles 20 and 22).

Subsequent developments concerning the involvement of the specialized agencies in the actual operation of the supervisory systems under the Covenants, following their entry into force in 1976, will be reviewed later in the present chapter.

[34] Already in 1948, following the adoption by the ILO of the Convention on the Freedom of Association and Protection of the Right to Organise and of a resolution aimed at the creation of additional international machinery for safeguarding freedom of association, the Economic and Social Council, in ESC. 193(VIII) (1948), had invited the Human Rights Commission to consider these texts when drawing up the Covenant provisions and the implementation articles.

[35] See, A/2929, Chap. 2, paras. 13–23, and Chap. 5, para. 25, and Alston, 'The UN Specialized Agencies', 85. The most striking example of broad formulation is the one-sentence Art. 9 of the Covenant on Economic, Social and Cultural Rights, recognizing the right of everyone to social security including social insurance. It was decided not to spell out the content of this right in the Covenant, having regard to ILO standards. A/3525, para. 80.

III. STUDIES AND STANDARD-SETTING IN THE FIELD OF DISCRIMINATION

Important questions of principle as to the division of responsibility within the UN system for action against discrimination arose when in 1952 the Sub-Commission drew up a programme of work which provided for studies of discrimination in specific fields, including education, employment and occupation.[36] The Sub-Commission's mandate requires it to undertake studies and to make recommendations to the Commission on Human Rights concerning the prevention of discrimination of any kind relating to human rights and fundamental freedoms. At the same time, questions concerning education, employment and occupation fall within the field of activity of UNESCO and of the ILO. It was therefore a matter of how to deal with a situation of overlapping competence.

Although the Sub-Commission's work programme was in the form of proposals for approval by the Commission, the Sub-Commission decided at the same time to initiate the study of discrimination in education and to appoint a special rapporteur for this purpose. When the question came before the Economic and Social Council, the latter, in order not to delay the study, decided to approve the appointment of a rapporteur and invited UNESCO to co-operate with him, but it also indicated that future studies within the scope of specialized agencies should normally be carried out by them.[37]

The special rapporteur experienced considerable difficulty in obtaining support from UNESCO. It declined to undertake any research specifically for the study, limiting itself to providing information already in its possession. It declined to comment on the available factual information, emphasizing that the rapporteur would bear sole responsibility for his work.[38] It also declined the special rapporteur's request for appointment of consultants to conduct field investigations. The Director-General of UNESCO expressed the view that, by focusing attention on instances of discrimination, the UN 'had embarked on a somewhat dubious path', in contrast to the positive aim pursued by UNESCO of promoting the achievement of equality.[39]

The special rapporteur's study was presented to the Sub-Commission and the Commission in 1957. Before the Commission considered the report, UNESCO initiated action with a view to the preparation of international instruments on discrimination in education. In 1958, the UNESCO General Conference decided that UNESCO should take responsibility for drafting

[36] See *Report on the Ninth Session of the Commission on Human Rights* (1953), 31–2 and 77–80.

[37] ESC Res.502H(XVI) (1953).

[38] E/CN.4/Sub.2/163, paras. 115–17.

[39] UNESCO, 49 Ex/SR.18, 28 Nov. 1957, 162.

these instruments and a Convention and Recommendation were adopted two years later. This action was noted with appreciation by the Council.[40]

As regards discrimination in employment and occupation, the Sub-Commission envisaged a preparatory study by the ILO, on the basis of which it would itself examine the question. However, in the Commission and the Council the view prevailed that, since the question fell within the scope of the ILO, the entire study should be left to the ILO, including the formulation of conclusions and any further action which might be considered appropriate.[41]

The ILO likewise felt that responsibility for adopting international instruments on this question should 'rest squarely with the ILO'.[42] The Governing Body decided in 1955 to place the matter on the ILO Conference agenda, leading to the adoption of a Convention and Recommendation in 1958. The Economic and Social Council noted the adoption of these instruments with great satisfaction.[43]

It will thus be seen that the course of events in relation to discrimination in education and in employment and occupation was determined less by a process of consultation than by a series of unilateral decisions taken by the various actors. Effective co-ordination was achieved in part because of the relevant agency's perceptions that its purposes would best be served by determined action on its part and because of the Sub-Commission's lack of resources to undertake the required studies itself.

IV. INDIGENOUS POPULATIONS

In contrast to the strains which manifested themselves in determining spheres of action on questions of discrimination, measures taken during the same period within the UN system in favour of indigenous populations were marked by a genuine sense of collaboration in a common endeavour.

In 1949 a Conference of American Member States of the ILO adopted a programme of action for indigenous peoples in Latin America, and called for ILO activities in this field to be co-ordinated with those of the UN, other specialized agencies and the Organization of American States. The question of assistance to raise the living standards of aboriginal populations in the American continent was also taken up in the General Assembly and the Economic and Social Council.[44] Following discussions initiated by the ILO with the UN, UNESCO, FAO and WHO, the UN Technical Assistance Board in 1952 approved an exploratory mission by experts from these organ-

[40] ESC Res.821VB(XXXII) (1961).

[41] See Commission on Human Rights, *Report of the Tenth Session* (1954), paras. 54–7, and ESC Res.545C(XVIII) (1954).

[42] ILO, *Minutes of the 127th Session of the Governing Body of the ILO* (1954), 24–5 and 71–82.

[43] ESC Res.728D(XXVIII) (1959).

[44] See, in particular, GA Res.275(III) (1949) and ESC Res.313(XI) (1950).

izations and a representative of the Organization of American States, to visit Bolivia, Ecuador, and Peru to determine the type of assistance to be provided for improvement of conditions of their indigenous populations. A regional technical assistance programme for the three countries was approved by the Board in 1953, involving the collaboration of the various agencies concerned. The Board entrusted the co-ordination of this programme to the ILO. In 1960 it was extended to Colombia.[45]

In 1954 the ILO Governing Body decided to place the question of the living and working conditions of indigenous workers in independent countries on the agenda of the ILO Conference in 1956. The report on this item was drafted in close collaboration with the UN (as regards general questions), FAO (land), UNESCO (education, communication, and socio-anthropological aspects of integration), and WHO (health).[46] At the Conference in 1956, several Governments noted that the proposed conclusions submitted for discussion covered a wide range of subjects, many of which fell outside the constitutional or traditional competence of the ILO. In the ensuing discussion it was stressed that the living and working conditions of the populations concerned should be considered as an integral problem, calling for a broad and comprehensive approach. The representatives of the UN, UNESCO, WHO, and FAO intervened to stress that they had collaborated in the preparation of the reports and of the proposed conclusions and to indicate their organizations' satisfaction with the results. An amendment to limit the conclusions to labour and social security matters was rejected.[47] The following year the Conference adopted the Convention and Recommendation concerning Indigenous and Tribal Populations (Nos. 107 and 104 respectively), which embody the comprehensive approach initially envisaged.

Fruitful inter-agency collaboration in this instance was facilitated by the fact that the interest on the part of the UN came from the technical assistance side of the organization, thus minimizing potential jurisdictional conflicts.

V. INTER-AGENCY COLLABORATION IN SUPERVISING THE IMPLEMENTATION OF INTERNATIONAL INSTRUMENTS

By the early 1970s, the increasing volume of standard-setting within the UN system and the entry into force of several major Conventions and supervisory

[45] For a fuller description of the programmes developed by the various agencies and their subsequent collaboration, see International Labour Conference, *Report VIII(1): Living and Working Conditions of Indigenous Populations in Independent Countries* (1956), 5–46. An appraisal of the Andean Indian Programme was presented to an ILO panel of consultants on indigenous and tribal populations in 1962. PCITP/1962/I/2.

[46] See International Labour Conference, *Report VIII(1)* (1956), 2.

[47] See International Labour Conference, *Record of Proceedings* (1956), 533–4 and 737–8.

procedures made it necessary to consider more specific means of collaboration and co-ordination.

This question arose, for example, in the field of discrimination, where Conventions had been adopted by the UN, ILO and UNESCO. Following the entry into force of the UN Convention on the Elimination of all Forms of Racial Discrimination and the establishment of the Committee on the Elimination of Racial Discrimination (CERD) in 1969, the ILO and UNESCO offered their co-operation to that Committee. The matter was the subject of considerable discussion at the Committee's fourth and sixth Sessions, in which differing views were expressed as to what arrangements would be compatible with the terms of the Convention. Finally, the Committee decided that representatives of the ILO and UNESCO be invited to attend its meetings and that its reports and other official documents be made available to the supervisory bodies of the two organizations. It agreed that written information might be submitted to the Committee by these agencies concerning the application in dependent territories of their Conventions and Recommendations concerning discrimination in employment and occupation and in education. Any written information concerning the application of these instruments in countries other than dependent territories would be distributed not to the Committee as such, but directly to the members for their personal information.[48] It was understood that the agencies would not be entitled to submit oral information to the Committee. Subsequently, following the entry into force of the provisions of Article 14 of the Convention relating to the examination of communications alleging violation of its provisions, the Committee decided to include in its rules of procedure on this question a provision making it possible to request from UN bodies and specialized agencies any documentation which might assist in disposing of a case.[49]

The above-mentioned arrangements have made possible exchange of information regarding the work of supervisory bodies in the various organizations in regard to problems of discrimination. Reciprocal arrangements have been made for UN representation at the meetings of the ILO and UNESCO supervisory bodies. Similar collaboration arrangements have also been made between the ILO and UNESCO.

As already noted, the original ILO Convention on indigenous and tribal populations was drawn up in collaboration with the UN and other agencies concerned. The preamble to that Convention, in recalling this fact, indicated the intention to seek the continuing co-operation of the organizations in question in promoting and securing the application of the Convention. Similar statements are made in the preambles to various other ILO Conventions dealing with such matters as safety of seafarers, vocational training, rural

[48] See *Report of the Committee on the Elimination of Racial Discrimination*, A/8718, paras. 122–32.

[49] *Report of the Committee on the Elimination of Racial Discrimination*, A/38/18, para. 56.

workers' organizations, nursing personnel, and migrant workers. In all these cases, the ILO has made arrangements to transmit copies of the reports received from ratifying States and comments made by ILO supervisory bodies to the other organizations concerned, inviting them to provide information or comments for consideration by the Committee of Experts on the Application of Conventions and Recommendations and to be represented at that Committee's meetings when it deals with those Conventions.[50]

An example of joint action by two organizations in the drawing up and implementation of international standards is provided by the Recommendation concerning the Status of Teachers of 1966. UNESCO and the ILO had been active for many years in considering questions of training, status, career, employment conditions, civil liberties, and trade union rights of teachers. In 1963 the two organizations decided to combine their efforts which culminated in the calling of a special intergovernmental conference in 1966, at which the Recommendation was adopted. The UNESCO Executive Board and the ILO Governing Body invited States Members of their organizations to report periodically on the action taken on the Recommendation. They also decided to establish a joint expert committee, half of whose members would be appointed by each of these two bodies, to examine the reports.[51] Up to 1983, that committee had examined three sets of reports, with the technical support of the secretariats of the two organizations. The committee's reports are presented to the deliberative bodies (governing body and conference) of each organization.

The entry into force of the Human Rights Covenants made it necessary to consider the manner in which the specialized agencies might collaborate in their implementation.

In May 1976, the Council adopted Resolution 1988 (LX) concerning procedures for implementation of the Covenant on Economic, Social and Cultural Rights. The Council 'called upon' the specialized agencies to report to it in terms of Article 18 of the Covenant[52] and requested the Secretary-General, in co-operation with the agencies concerned, to draw up guidelines for the reports to be submitted by States Parties. It decided to establish a sessional working group to assist the Council in the consideration of reports; representatives of specialized agencies might take part in the proceedings of the working group when matters within their field of competence were considered.

The ILO Governing Body agreed to reporting by the ILO to the Council in

[50] See International Labour Conference, *Report of the Committee of Experts on the Application of Conventions and Recommendations, Report III(Part 4A)*, paras. 25–6 (1983).

[51] See Report of the Joint ILO/UNESCO Committee of Experts on the Association of the Recommendation Concerning the Status of Teachers, Second Session, Apr.–May 1970, introduction.

[52] One may question whether this an appropriate manner of 'making arrangements' with the agencies, as envisaged by Art. 18.

accordance with Article 18 of the Covenant and decided, for that purpose, to entrust the Committee of Experts on the Application of Conventions and Recommendations with the task of examining the reports and other available information on the implementation of the Covenant.[53]

The Executive Board of UNESCO decided to entrust its Committee on Conventions and Recommendations with the preparation of its reports.[54] In the absence of comparable bodies, the reports of WHO and FAO were prepared by the secretariats.

The ECOSOC Sessional Working Group provided for in Resolution 1988 (LX) was established in 1978. At its first session, in 1979, devoted to consideration of its methods of work, one of the most controversial issues was the significance to be attributed to the reports from the specialized agencies. One view was that such reports would make a valuable contribution, and should be examined by the Working Group concurrently with individual State Party reports.[55] The opposing view—pressed particularly by the USSR member—was that the Working Group should consider *only* reports from States Parties, that the agencies' reports could not be put on the same footing as reports from States Parties, and that it was improper for an outside opinion to be imposed on the Working Group before it considered the reports from States Parties.[56] Following informal consultations, it was proposed to provide merely that the Working Group be entrusted also with the task of considering the reports of the specialized agencies submitted to the Council under Article 18 of the Covenant. Even this formulation ran into opposition, mainly from Eastern European representatives, but was ultimately maintained.[57] The methods of work as proposed by the Working Group were approved by the Council.[58]

When the sessional Working Group embarked on the examination of reports in 1980, a renewed attempt was made by Eastern European members to limit consideration to State reports.[59] Other members argued that any member of the Working Group was entitled to refer to any document before it and to seek a reply from the representative of the country concerned, and that it would be unfair to discuss agency reports separately, without the presence of a representative of a State Party to which those reports might refer.[60]

[53] *Minutes of the 201st Session of the ILO Governing Body* (1976), pp. VIII/18–21. The Committee of Experts, from 1978 to 1987, presented nine reports on progress in regard to provisions dealing with matters within the scope of ILO activities.

[54] UNESCO 107 EX/Decision 4.4.1 and 109 EX/Decision 5.4.3. The first UNESCO report was presented in 1982, after approval by the Executive Board (113 EX/Decision 5.4.1).

[55] See E/1979/WG.1/SR.4, para. 5.

[56] See E/1979/WG.1/SR.3, para. 21, SR.4, paras. 4, 14, 16, and 17.

[57] See E/1979/WG.1/SR.7, paras. 19, 33, 43, and 44.

[58] ESC Res.1979/43.

[59] See E/1980/WG.1/SR.2, paras. 12, 19, 26–8, 34.

[60] See, in particular, ibid. para. 31.

Following informal consultations, the objections were not maintained, and in practice the reports of the ILO Committee of Experts were referred to by members of the Working Group, and by the ILO representative, in the course of examination of individual State Party reports. This became so much part of the Working Group's procedure that, when other agencies (WHO, FAO, and UNESCO) subsequently presented reports which—in contrast to the ILO reports—did not contain country-specific indications, the Working Group nevertheless expected them to be considered within the framework of the State-by-State examination. The Working Group in fact failed to examine those reports.

An attempt was also made in 1980, again by Eastern European members, to prevent the representatives of the specialized agencies from speaking.[61] Such a denial would have been contrary not only to the terms of the Council Resolution establishing the Working Group and to the Rules of Procedure of the Council, which were expressly applicable, but to the relationship agreements between the UN and the specialized agencies. After informal consultations, the Working Group announced a compromise decision that, at the end of the discussion by the working group of a State Party report, representatives of specialized agencies might be allowed to make a general statement on matters relating to their field of competence.[62]

It is generally recognized that the Working Group originally established by the Council did not achieve any significant results. It made no recommendations to the Council for action in pursuance of its responsibilities under the Covenant, and concerned itself almost exclusively with questions of a procedural nature.[63]

The situation changed significantly, however, once the Committee on Economic, Social and Cultural Rights was set up in 1987. The Committee moved rapidly to accord the specialized agencies every opportunity to contribute to all aspects of its work and the reporting guidelines it adopted in 1990 make very extensive reference to the role of the agencies.[64]

The Covenant on Civil and Political Rights, although it covers several matters of concern to certain specialized agencies,[65] does not deal with their contribution to its implementation. It merely contains a provision (Article 40, para. 3) authorizing the UN Secretary-General, after consultation with the Human Rights Committee, to transmit to specialized agencies copies of such

[61] See E/1980/WG.1/SR.4, paras. 43–7, 54–66, paras. 10–17, 51–8.

[62] E/1980/WG.1/SR.5, paras. 1–3.

[63] See e.g. the Working Group's *Report on the 1983 Session*, E/1983/41, para. 24. An evaluation of ILO experience in the implementation of the Human Rights Covenants may be found in a paper entitled 'Impact of ILO policies on the UN', GB.225/IO/3/3 (1984), 16–22.

[64] E/C.12/1991/1. On the role of the agencies see Chap. 12, section II(*b*), above.

[65] For example, the provisions on forced labour, the right to form and join trade unions, freedom of opinion and expression, parental rights regarding the religious and moral education of children, and the rights of ethnic, religious, and linguistic minorities.

parts of reports from States Parties as may fall within their field of competence. Any arrangements for collaboration between the Committee and the agencies were therefore a matter for agreement. Following the establishment of the Committee in 1976, both the ILO and UNESCO sent communications offering their assistance. The matter was discussed by the Committee in 1978 and 1980.

Some members of the Committee felt that the purpose of communicating extracts from States' reports to the agencies, as provided for in Article 40(3), was to elicit comments from them. Others argued that the purpose was merely to bring the information to the knowledge of the agencies. The Committee decided in favour of transmission to the agencies concerned of relevant parts of the reports, but agreed that the agencies should not be invited to comment on the reports, since the Covenant contained no provision to that effect. The Committee also decided to inform the agencies concerned that it would welcome attendance by their representatives at its public meetings (an invitation which, in the absence of any opportunity to intervene, is essentially of symbolic value).[66]

When the question was further discussed in 1980, the Committee concluded that there was a need for all possible information from the specialized agencies relevant to its work. It accordingly agreed that information, mainly on the specialized agencies' interpretation of, and practice in relation to, the corresponding provisions of their instruments should be made available to members of the Committee on a regular basis.[67] At the same time, the Committee confirmed its earlier decision not to invite comments from the agencies on State Party reports.[68]

Since then, the ILO has, prior to each session of the Committee, sent notes on the position in the States whose reports were due to be examined as regards ratification of relevant Conventions and comments made by ILO supervisory bodies. Members of the Committee can use these notes as a basis for comments and questions, and have indeed done so. Other agencies have not submitted information to the Committee.

In contrast to the recent decision of the Committee on the Elimination of Racial Discrimination providing for the possibility of seeking information from other UN organs and specialized agencies in connection with communications submitted by individuals or groups, the Rules of Procedure of the Human Rights Committee do not envisage any similar action in the examination of communications received under the Optional Protocol to the Covenant. However, in one case raising issues of trade union rights, the Committee

[66] *Report of the Human Rights Committee*, A/33/40 (1978), Chap. 5.

[67] This decision was no doubt influenced by the knowledge that some members were already obtaining such information, which in general is publicly available.

[68] *Report of the Human Rights Committee*, A/33/40 (1978), Chap. 5.

carefully considered the relevant ILO standards and decisions of ILO supervisory bodies.[69]

The Convention on the Elimination of all Forms of Discrimination against Women provides for supervision on the basis of the examination of government reports by a committee elected by the States Parties (the Committee on the Elimination of Discrimination against Women). The Convention contains provisions on various matters within the competence of specialized agencies, such as education and training, employment, social security, health care and participation in cultural life.[70] According to Article 22, the specialized agencies are entitled to be represented at the consideration by the Committee of the implementation of the provisions of concern to them. The Committee may also invite the agencies to submit 'reports on the implementation of the Convention in areas falling within the scope of their activities'. At its 1983 Session, when the Committee discussed the question of participation of specialized agencies, several members expressed reservations about the usefulness of requesting such reports, and also about interventions by representatives of the agencies. The Committee decided to invite the agencies 'to prepare reports on such programmes as might promote the implementation of the Convention and to provide the Committee with additional information'—language which appeared to be at variance with the terms of the Convention.[71]

Since that time, however, the Committee has shown itself to be very open to the receipt of information from the agencies. At its 1991 session it decided that the preliminary analysis of each State Party's report, to be prepared by its secretariat, should make use of all information available from UN agency sources. It also decided to encourage the full participation of experts from the specialized agencies in its work of elaborating upon the normative content of the provisions of the Convention and noted that 'when appropriate, such persons should be invited to participate as resource persons in the work of the Working Groups'.[72]

In summary, it will be seen that a series of arrangements have been

[69] *Report of the Human Rights Committee*, A/41/40 (1986), 151–63.

[70] It was concern about the degree of detail with which the draft Convention sought to deal with matters of employment, with the consequent danger of conflicting provisions in different organizations, that led the ILO to initiate the discussion of co-ordination of legislative work of international organizations in the Administrative Committee on Co-ordination in 1974 (see n. 21, above). Art. 23 of the Convention contains a saving clause, according to which nothing in the Convention shall affect provisions in the legislation of a State Party or in an international convention in force for a State Party which are more conducive to the achievement of equality between men and women. In so far as this clause seeks to regulate the relationship between different international instruments, it is open to criticism, since it implies that the ratification of a Convention adopted by one international organization may affect obligations accepted under Conventions adopted by other Organizations.

[71] See CEDAW/C/SR.16, paras. 32–9, SR.22, paras. 2–30, and SR.23, paras. 30–6, and A/39/45, paras. 23–5.

[72] A/46/38 (1991), paras. 368 and 373.

established within the UN system whereby supervisory bodies responsible for examining the implementation of international instruments can be informed of activities undertaken and conclusions reached in other organizations which may be relevant to their work. Specialized agencies such as the ILO and UNESCO have been relatively flexible in providing for the consideration of such information, whereas the supervisory bodies in the UN tended for many years to adopt a more restrictive approach.

Among the reasons for the reluctance shown by UN supervisory bodies are: a restrictive interpretation of the instruments pursuant to which they have been created, an apparent fear that closer collaboration might limit their autonomy or prejudge their deliberations, and a conscious desire by at least some members to forestall the strengthening of human rights supervisory mechanisms which would result from greater co-operation and cross-fertilization. The practice of UN supervisory bodies of seeking to operate on the basis of consensus has given disproportionate influence to those members who have desired to limit any input from specialized agencies, even when they have represented a minority view.

The inhibitions shown by UN bodies also reflect a fundamental difference in approach to international supervision. The idea of specific conclusions indicating the extent of compliance by individual States with their obligations under conventions, which has been regarded as normal in the ILO for the past sixty years, did not find acceptance in the terms of UN instruments and is only very gradually being accepted in the practice of the supervisory bodies. The members of UN supervisory bodies representing or coming from the USSR and other Socialist countries consistently opposed any such development throughout the 1970s and for most of the 1980s. More recently, however, their attitudes have changed dramatically and new opportunities for sustained, substantive co-operation are emerging.

VI. SOME RECENT DEVELOPMENTS: POTENTIALS FOR AND IMPEDIMENTS TO CO-ORDINATION

It is evident from developments in the fields already discussed that, whatever arrangements may be made to facilitate inter-agency co-ordination, a variety of factors of a political, jurisdictional, budgetary, personal, or other nature may intervene to frustrate them. Because of this diversity of elements, any one of which may at a given time be decisive, an empirical review of specific experiences tends to be more revealing than any abstract or academic analysis. In the present section it is proposed to examine some recent developments which bring out the potential for collaboration and problems encountered. To begin with, one may contrast two different cases of standard-setting, relating respectively to the protection of prisoners and detainees and to the rights of migrant workers. Reference will also be made to action concerning slavery and slavery-like practices, child labour, the right to education, and indigenous populations.

(*a*) *Protection of Prisoners and Detainees*

For a decade after 1975, the General Assembly initiated a series of measures for drawing up additional standards for the protection of prisoners and detainees. In this, it consistently relied upon the advice of the competent specialized bodies within the UN system. Thus, proposals for the 1975 declaration on the protection of all persons from being subjected to torture and other forms of cruel, inhuman or degrading treatment or punishment were drawn up by the Fifth UN Congress on the Prevention of Crime and the Treatment of Offenders, following a request addressed to it by the Assembly the previous year.[73] At the same time as it adopted this declaration, the Assembly called for further action by the Commission on Human Rights, the Committee on Crime Prevention and Control, and the World Health Organization.[74] The Commission was asked to consider the formulation of a body of principles for the protection of all persons under any form of detention or imprisonment. Two years later, it was asked to draw up a Convention on torture and other cruel, inhuman, and degrading treatment or punishment.[75] This work led to the adoption of a Convention by the Assembly in 1984.[76] The Committee on Crime Prevention and Control was asked to draw up a code of conduct for law enforcement officials. On the basis of proposals made by the Committee, such a code of conduct was adopted by the Assembly in 1979.[77] WHO was asked to consider the elaboration of principles of medical ethics relevant to the protection of persons subjected to any form of detention or imprisonment against torture and other cruel, inhuman, and degrading treatment or punishment. On the basis of proposals drawn up by the Council for International Organizations of Medical Sciences and endorsed by the WHO Executive Board in 1979, the General Assembly adopted such principles in 1982.[78]

It will be seen that, in these instances, effective collaboration between the General Assembly and the relevant expert body or agency was achieved.

(*b*) *The Rights of Migrant Workers*

Questions concerning migrant workers are of interest to various organizations within the UN system. The UN itself is concerned with demographic,

[73] See GA Res.3218(XXIX) (1974) and A/10260. The declaration was adopted by GA Res.3452(XXX) (1975).

[74] GA Res.3453(XXX) (1975).

[75] GA Res.34/62 (1977).

[76] GA Res.39/46 (1984).

[77] GA Res.34/169 (1979) and A/34/431.

[78] GA Res.37/194 (1982).

economic, political, and legal aspects of migration. The constitutional mandate of the ILO includes both the manpower aspects of migration for employment and the protection of the interests of workers when employed in countries other than their own. Educational and cultural questions affecting migrants call for consideration by UNESCO, and health problems by WHO.

To place recent decisions in this field in perspective, it is necessary to refer to co-ordinating measures initiated by the Economic and Social Council soon after the establishment of the UN. In March 1947 the Council called for a practical plan for the allocation of functions, without duplication of work, among the various organs concerned in the field of migration, and asked the Secretary-General to make the necessary preliminary studies.[79] Discussions between officials of the UN and the ILO led to an exchange of letters approving arrangements for a working division of responsibilities. The competence of the ILO was to include the rights and situation of migrants in their capacity as workers (recruitment, training, employment, working conditions, social insurance, etc.), whereas the UN, in addition to the population, economic, and financial aspects of migration, should deal with the rights and situation of migrants in their capacity as aliens (conditions of residence, expulsion, naturalization, relief in case of indigency, etc.). These arrangements were noted with satisfaction by the Council.[80]

In 1947 the American Federation of Labor had requested the Council to consider the question of the protection of migrant labour and submitted a memorandum on the subject. The Council, noting that the ILO was then considering the revision of its existing Conventions and Recommendations on migration, decided to transmit the memorandum to the ILO as the competent specialized agency, and invited it actively to pursue its consideration of the problem.[81] The ILO adopted revised standards on migration for employment (Convention and Recommendation) in 1949.

In 1971 and 1972 the International Labour Conference adopted resolutions concerning the conditions and equality of treatment of migrant workers, in response to which it was proposed that additional standards be framed to supplement the instruments of 1949, to deal with such matters as non-discrimination against migrant workers, social services, and housing for migrant workers, protection against arbitrary expulsion, family reunion, etc.[82]

In July 1972, while ECOSOC was meeting, press reports appeared concerning a particularly flagrant case of illegal trafficking in workers from Africa for employment in a European country. This led the Council to adopt a resolution condemning such practices, instructing the Human Rights Commission to consider the question, and inviting the ILO to pursue energetically

79 ESC Res.42(IV) (1947).
80 ESC Res.156(VII) (1948).
81 ESC Res.85(V) (1947).
82 *Minutes of the 186th Session of the Governing Body of the ILO* (1972), 54–5.

its examination of the matter.[83] The resolution of the Council was brought to the attention of the ILO Governing Body in November 1972, when it decided to place the question of migrant workers on the agenda of the Conference in 1974, with a view to the adoption of supplementary standards. In addition to the questions previously envisaged, it was decided, in response to the resolution of the Council, to deal with international trafficking in labour.[84] Consideration of the item by the ILO Conference led to the adoption in 1975 of a supplementary Convention (No. 143) and of a Recommendation (No. 151) dealing with migrations in abusive conditions, equality of opportunity and treatment for migrant workers and their families, social policy and services, and the protection of residence rights of migrant workers. These instruments were drawn up in consultation with the UN, UNESCO, and WHO.

In 1973 the Council welcomed the action taken by the ILO in initiating the adoption of further standards for the protection of migrant workers, but at the same time asked the Sub-Commission to consider the question of illicit trafficking in migrant workers.[85] The Sub-Commission entrusted one of its members, Mrs Warzazi, with the preparation of a study on the question, which was completed in 1975.[86] In her draft recommendations, the rapporteur called for ratification of the new Convention adopted by the ILO in 1975, and also suggested that a review be made of relevant standards set by the UN, in order to consider the desirability of preparing new instruments to render more explicit certain human rights relevant to the protection of migrant workers.[87] Following further discussions in the Commission, the Council, and the Assembly, the latter decided in 1979 to draw up a convention on the protection of the rights of all migrant workers and their families.[88]

In the discussions leading up to this decision, the question had been raised how far the adoption of such standards by the UN would be appropriate, having regard to the constitutional competence of the ILO and the international instruments already adopted by it. In the General Assembly, an amendment was proposed providing in the first instance for the preparation of a report on the need for additional standards, but this was rejected. The majority view was that the competence of the ILO and other specialized agencies was sectoral in character, and that a global instrument covering all aspects of the protection of migrant workers and their families should therefore be adopted by the UN.[89] Accordingly, between 1980 and 1989 a Working Group of the General Assembly embarked on the drawing up of

[83] ESC Res.1706(LIII) (1972). The UN General Assembly adopted a similar resolution in GA Res.2920(XXVII) (1972).

[84] *Minutes of the 188th Session of the Governing Body* (1972), 116.

[85] ESC Res.1789(LIV) (1973).

[86] E/CN.4/Sub.2/L.629.

[87] E/CN.4/Sub.2/L.636.

[88] GA Res.34/172 (1979).

[89] See, in particular, A/34/535, Add. 1 and A/34/535, 22 and A/C.3/34/SR.63.

such a global UN Convention. The work was completed and the Convention adopted by the Assembly in 1990.[90]

The foregoing developments call for a number of comments.

The UN action arose from consideration of illicit trafficking in migrant workers. As an aspect of recruitment of labour, this was clearly within the competence of the ILO, as confirmed by the 1947 understanding between the UN and the ILO, and had indeed already been dealt with in the ILO's instruments of 1949. In 1972, the Economic and Social Council invited the ILO to act on the question. Why then, should the Sub-Commission have been called upon, in 1973, to study it? This decision appears to have ignored both the 1947 UN–ILO arrangements and the Council's decision of 1953 that studies within the scope of specialized agencies should be carried out by them.[91]

In essence, the Convention deals with two types of questions. There are a series of provisions, based mainly on the Covenant on Civil and Political Rights, which seek to guarantee protection against arbitrary interference with individual liberty and security of the person and the enjoyment of various freedoms. These are matters which affect migrant workers in their capacity as aliens, irrespective of the exercise of economic activity. They are proper subjects for UN action, according to the 1947 agreement. Other provisions, however, concern the interests of migrants as workers, such as recruitment procedures, access to employment, equality of treatment in employment, exercise of trade union rights, and social security. These questions are all within the competence of the ILO, and were already the subject of ILO standards. Inevitably there are overlaps in the detailed standards framed within the two organizations, and also variations between them. Once the UN Convention enters into force, there will be two distinct sets of standards on this important question, with separate supervision procedures.[92] Employers and workers, who are directly interested in the regulation of the matter and who participate in ILO standard-setting, had no direct part in drawing up the UN Convention although an ILO official did participate actively. Nor will employers and workers have the same possibilities to participate in supervising the implementation of the Convention as they enjoy in regard to ILO standards. The governments which pressed for a UN convention appear to

[90] GA Res.45/158 (1990), Annex.

[91] n. 22, above.

[92] According to one assessment, the principal issue in the drafting process was whether or not the Convention 'would detract from the work of the ILO and to what extent the final Articles would be stronger or weaker than existing ILO standards. The results are mixed. Some articles go beyond ILO instruments and some fall short'. Hune and Niessen, 'The First UN Convention on Migrant Workers', 9 *Neths Q. of Hum. Rts* (1991) 133. For a detailed discussion of the relevant standards see Hasenau, 'Setting Norms in the United Nations System: The Draft Convention on the Protection of the Rights of All Migrant Workers and Their Families in Relation to ILO Standards on Migrant Workers', 28 *Int'l Migration* (1990) 133.

have sought deliberately to remove the question from a tripartite forum in order to enjoy greater influence over the outcome of the discussions. Although Article 74 of the Convention allows for the ILO to provide the UN Committee with technical analysis and advice, the relevant arrangements would seem to fall well short of those which apply to ILO supervision of its own standards. From the point of view of technical as well as legal competence, one may thus doubt whether the action taken by the General Assembly is the most suitable way of dealing with these complex matters. In this instance, neither the interests of migrant workers nor the interests of inter-agency co-ordination were of paramount concern. Rather, political considerations succeeded in setting aside the previously aggreed co-ordination arrangements.

(*c*) *Slavery and Slavery-like Practices*

In 1974 the Sub-Commission established a Working Group on Slavery, with a view to reviewing developments in this field.[93] The Working Group has considered a variety of situations and problems, including—in addition to actual instances of slavery—questions of debt bondage, forced labour, traffic in persons, sale of children, and child labour. The main input for its work has come from submissions by non-governmental organizations. The Working Group has also been anxious to have the collaboration of the specialized agencies, through the provision of information and representation at its meetings. It has frequently recommended to the Sub-Commission that matters brought to its attention which fell within the area of activity of a specialized agency should be referred to that agency. In this way, a number of communications alleging the existence of forced labour, exploitation of children, or debt bondage have been brought to the notice of ILO supervisory bodies. A particularly interesting illustration of this interaction is provided by the manner in which allegations of exploitation of Haitian cane-cutters on the sugar plantations of the Dominican Republic were examined. Originally international attention was drawn to this problem by documents submitted to the UN Working Group on Slavery by the Anti-Slavery Society.[94] This led subsequently to the filing of complaints by worker delegates to the International Labour Conference and a thorough investigation by an ILO Commission of Inquiry.[95]

(*d*) *Child Labour*

The protection of children and young persons in regard to work is among the responsibilities of the ILO. It has adopted many international instruments

[93] Sub-Commission Res.11(XXVII) (1974).
[94] See E/CN.4/Sub.2/434, para. 22.
[95] See the Report of the Commission of Inquiry in ILO, *Official Bulletin*, 66 (1983), ser. B, Special Supplement (1983).

dealing with the minimum age for admission to work and the protection of young workers. Wider questions concerning the status and protection of children are of concern to the UN. The General Assembly adopted a Declaration and a Convention on the Rights of the Child in 1959 and 1989 respectively. The Supplementary Convention on the Abolition of Slavery, adopted by the UN in 1956, includes among slavery-like practices the delivery of a person under 18 years to another person with a view to exploitation of his labour.

Instances of exploitation of child labour have frequently been brought to the attention of the Working Group on Slavery, which has generally recommended that such information, in addition to being communicated to the States concerned, should be transmitted to the ILO.[96] It has been taken into account by ILO supervisory bodies in examining compliance with ILO Conventions.

In 1979, the Sub-Commission decided to review the question of child labour annually, and also recommended that a report on the question be prepared by one of its members, Mr Bouhdiba.[97] Following approval of this proposal by the Economic and Social Council, Mr Bouhdiba presented his report in 1981.[98] It referred to ILO standards and activities, and drew extensively on ILO sources of information. It formulated a series of conclusions, including an appeal for the implementation and ratification of ILO instruments on minimum age for employment and continuing examination of the question of child labour by the Working Group on Slavery. The Sub-Commission and the Commission subsequently envisaged the adoption of a programme of action to combat violations of human rights through the exploitation of child labour.[99]

What implications do these developments have for principles of co-ordination? That non-governmental organizations should bring situations of child labour before the Working Group on Slavery is normal and useful, as a means of bringing the force of international public opinion to bear on those issues. Through reference of this information to the ILO, it receives cognizance by the supervisory bodies of the competent specialized agency, to which the organizations concerned would ordinarily not have access. It may also be regarded as normal for the Working Group on Slavery and the Sub-Commission to review the question of exploitation of child labour, in view of its possible ramifications in areas in which action would be the primary responsibility of the UN, such as false adoptions, prostitution, and debt bondage. However, while recognizing the excellence of the comprehensive and penetrating report by Mr Bouhdiba, one may wonder whether that study

96 See e.g. Sub-Commission Res.8(XXXIII) (1980), para. V.3.
97 Sub-Commission Res.7(XXXII) (1979).
98 E/CN.4/Sub.2/479.
99 Sub-Commission Res.18(XXXIV) (1981) and CHR Res.1982/21.

should not have been requested from the competent specialized agency and whether further action to combat child labour should not be regarded as the primary responsibility of that agency, from the point of view of technical expertise as well as the concentration of resources. The proper conclusion to draw from the Bouhdiba report would be to call on the ILO to intensify its action on the problem, in collaboration with other organizations active in related fields,[100] and to explore the possibilities of providing increased resources for that purpose.

(*e*) *The Right to Education*

In the early 1980s, resolutions of the General Assembly on the right to education raised important issues concerning the relationship between the UN and the specialized agencies. In 1979 the Assembly adopted a resolution in which it invited the Director-General of UNESCO to present reports containing information on UNESCO activities in relation to support for education and training of national personnel of developing countries, as well as views and suggestions on reinforcing UNESCO action for adequate education in developing countries, and information on problems encountered in the full implementation of the right to education, particularly in developing countries, and action to be taken in that regard.[101]

The Director-General of UNESCO brought this request to the attention of the UNESCO Executive Board. While inviting the Director-General to draw up a brief report in response to the Assembly's resolution, the Board expressed concern at UN interference in UNESCO affairs. It reaffirmed UNESCO's competence in education within the UN system and expressed the wish that the deliberative organs of other organizations of the system should consult the competent organs of UNESCO before adopting decisions concerning education. The Board also invited member States to ensure respect for the distribution of technical competence and responsibilities within the UN system, since this was essential for effectiveness of action.[102]

The Director-General of UNESCO, in his draft programme and budget for 1981–3, also criticized the tendency of the UN General Assembly and the Economic and Social Council 'to step up to an exaggerated degree' requests for contributions and reports and for the Assembly to take measures plainly within the province of the specialized agencies. In addition to the resolution on the right to education, he referred to decisions relating to information and to science and technology.[103]

[100] The wider social problems which lie at the root of child labour are indicated in the Boubdiba report, n. 94, above. See, similarly, International Labour Conference, *Report of the Director-General*, Part I (1983).

[101] GA Res.34/170 (1979).

[102] 109 EX/Decision 7.1.1, reproduced in A/35/148.

[103] UNESCO General Conference, *Draft Programme and Budget for 1981–83*, paras. 295–302 (1980).

In 1980, the General Assembly had before it a brief report by UNESCO concerning its activities in support of education and training in developing countries, and referring also to the UNESCO Medium-Term Plan for 1977–82, the draft Programme and Budget for 1981–3, and the report of the Director-General on UNESCO activities for 1977–8.[104] The report ended by stressing that the objectives of the Assembly's resolution on the right to education had been central to UNESCO action since its foundation.

Further resolutions were adopted by the General Assembly in 1980, 1981, and 1982, in which, in addition to calling on States to adopt measures for the implementation of the right to universal education, it requested the Director-General of UNESCO to report on the action taken by his Organization with a view to fostering the full implementation of the right to education.[105] In response to these resolutions, the UNESCO Executive Board initially instructed the Director-General to submit to the Assembly a report setting out the relevant parts of the Draft Medium-Term Plan for 1984–9 and to recall that various reports on the activities of UNESCO were regularly transmitted to the UN Secretary-General in accordance with the agreement between the UN and UNESCO.[106] In 1983, the Board decided that no further special reports on the subject were required, and that the Director-General's Report on the activities of UNESCO and its approved programme and budget, which were regularly transmitted to the UN, would constitute the appropriate forms of keeping the General Assembly informed.[107]

Given the general terms of the UN resolutions and their implicit assumption that UNESCO's action to promote the realization of the right to education was insufficient and needed to be given further impetus by pressure from the General Assembly, one can understand the irritation displayed by the UNESCO authorities. The position would have been different if the resolutions had asked UNESCO to consider specific action, such as additional standard-setting to define the measures to be adopted for the realization of the right to education. Such a request could have been based on the provisions of Article 23 of the Covenant on Economic, Social and Cultural Rights, which envisage the conclusion of conventions and the adoption of recommendations among measures for the realization of the rights recognized in the Covenant. However, that is not what the UN resolutions asked for, nor does it appear from the discussions at the General Assembly that action of this kind was what the sponsors of the resolutions had in mind. The incident suggests that, if the General Assembly—and UN organs generally—wish to exercise their co-ordinating functions in a credible and effective manner, they

[104] See A/35/148.
[105] GA Res.35/191 (1980), 36/152 (1981), and 37/178 (1982).
[106] 114 EX/Decision 7.1.3, reproduced in A/37/521.
[107] 116 EX/Decision 7.1.3.

should seek to be precise in their analysis of problems and in their recommendations.

(f) Indigenous Populations

Reference has already been made to the collaboration among organizations in the UN system in the preparation of the ILO Convention and Recommendation of 1957 relating to indigenous and tribal populations. But, in so far as those instruments envisaged a process of integration of indigenous populations in their national communities, their incompatibility both with current thinking and with the wishes of the populations themselves, soon became apparent. As a result, the International Labour Conference adopted a revised Convention on Indigenous and Tribal Peoples (No. 169) in 1989. The work on the revised instrument began in 1985 and involved extensive efforts to consult with and involve all those interested in the issues. These developments did not, however, seem to make much difference to parallel work being undertaken during this period, and still continuing in 1991, on related issues within the UN.

In 1971 the Sub-Commission appointed a special rapporteur to make a comprehensive study of the problem of discrimination against indigenous populations.[108] Various parts of the study were prepared over a period of years, and the special rapporteur's conclusions and recommendations were presented to the Sub-Commission in 1984.[109]

Pending completion of the study, the Sub-Commission decided in 1981 to recommend the establishment of a Working Group on Indigenous Populations to review developments pertaining to the promotion and protection of human rights and fundamental freedoms of such populations and to give special attention to the evolution of standards concerning the rights of indigenous populations.[110] Following ECOSOC authorization,[111] such a Working Group has met since 1982. Among the questions being considered by the Working Group are the content of possible new standards, the kind of implementation machinery to be envisaged, and the relation of new standards to the relevant ILO instruments.[112]

Although no final version of a UN declaration on the rights of indigenous peoples has yet emerged, the likelihood of the eventual adoption of such standards raises the question of their relationship to the ILO's standards.[113] Even if the UN standards are adopted in the form of a declaration or other

108 Sub-Commission Res.8(XXIV) (1971).
109 See E/CN.4/Sub.2/1983/21/Add.8.
110 Sub-Commission Res.2(XXXIV) (1981).
111 ESC Res.1982/334.
112 See *Report of the Working Group on Indigenous Populations at its Second Session*, E/CN.4/Sub.2/1983/22, paras. 101–8.
113 On the current status of the drafting see Chap. 6, above.

non-mandatory instrument, problems will arise as to which of the existing standards should be considered by governments and by international organizations as an authoritative source of guidance in subsequent policy formulation and action on questions concerning indigenous populations.

It is thus difficult not to conclude that important opportunities have been missed for consultation and collaboration among the organizations concerned in order to arrive at properly co-ordinated solutions. Such efforts should have sought to avoid conflicting international guidelines and to provide a basis for an effective division of responsibilities for a range of measures covering standards, review of problems and developments, promotional action, and technical co-operation.

VII. SPECIAL PROCEDURES AND INVESTIGATIONS TO EXAMINE ALLEGATIONS OF HUMAN RIGHTS VIOLATIONS

A considerable number of procedures have been established under which international organizations may examine either individual complaints of non-observance of human rights or the general human rights situation in a given country.[114] Some function within the UN system, others in the framework of regional organizations. Some are based on international instruments and acceptance by States through an act of ratification or adhesion, and are aimed at determining whether obligations under the instrument in question are being respected and at securing compliance. Others are available even in the absence of specific obligations, and may have wide-ranging terms of reference.

Within the UN itself, reference may be made to the possibility of considering interstate disputes concerning the observance of the Covenant on Civil and Political Rights provided for in Article 41 of the Covenant, to the procedure under the Optional Protocol to that Covenant permitting consideration by the Human Rights Committee of communications from individuals claiming to be victims of violations of rights set forth in the Covenant, and to the similar optional procedure under the Convention on the Elimination of all Forms of Racial Discrimination. There is the procedure for examination of communications alleging consistent patterns of gross violations of human rights under ECOSOC Resolution 1503 (XLVIII) as well as a variety of procedures for reviewing human rights in particular regions or countries.

In the ILO, there are the constitutional procedures for examining complaints and representations alleging non-observance of ratified Conventions, as well as special machinery (applicable irrespective of ratifications) for com-

[114] See generally Hannum (ed.), *Guide to International Human Rights Practice*, 2nd edn. (forth coming).

plaints of violation of trade union rights. *Ad hoc* methods of fact-finding have also been used; for example, on-the-spot missions have taken place annually since 1978 to examine the situation of workers of the Arab territories occupied by Israel.

In UNESCO, apart from the possibility of interstate proceedings under the Protocol to the Convention on Discrimination in Education, there is the procedure for consideration of communications alleging violation of human rights within the fields of competence of UNESCO, established by the Executive Board in 1978.

At the regional level, there are the procedures established under the European and American Conventions on Human Rights, opening avenues for examination both of interstate complaints and individual petitions. In addition, the Inter-American Commission on Human Rights has competence to examine communications alleging violation of human rights by States which are not parties to the American Convention. Reference may also be made to the procedures currently being developed by the African Commission on Human Rights.

The question thus arises to what extent this multiplicity of procedures may lead to duplication of investigations or, what may be more serious, conflicting conclusions on facts or law. It has been sought, to some extent, to guard against multiple recourse to procedures, for instance by providing against consideration of cases which are substantially the same as matters already submitted to another procedure of international investigation or settlement (in the case of individual petitions under the European Convention on Human Rights)[115] or which are currently being examined under another procedure (in the case of communications under the Optional Protocol to the Covenant on Civil and Political Rights[116] and under the American Convention on Human Rights).[117] The latter limitation would not prevent successive recourse to different procedures. For this reason, a number of European States, acting on a recomendation made by the Committee of Ministers of the Council of Europe, have made reservations upon ratifying the Optional Protocol to the Covenant on Civil and Political Rights, so as to exclude recourse to its provisions also in respect of matters which have been examined under another international procedure. Under ECOSOC Resolution 1503, the appointment of an *ad hoc* committee to examine allegations of gross violation of human rights is excluded if the situation is being examined under other procedures established by the constitutions or conventions of the UN or the specialized agencies or in regional conventions or if the State concerned wishes to submit it for examination under an international agreement to which it is a party; the

[115] Art.27(1)(b).
[116] Art.5(2)(a).
[117] Art.46(c).

decision to appoint an *ad hoc* committee is, moreover, subject to the consent of the State concerned.[118] The UNESCO communications procedure excludes cases only when they have already been settled by the State concerned in accordance with human rights principles.[119]

In considering the question of duplication of procedures, it seems appropriate to distinguish between those aimed at throwing light upon the general human rights situation in a given country or region and those concerned with individual cases.

Where investigations of a general nature have been undertaken by several organizations, they have related to situations involving major human rights problems—for example, South Africa, the Israeli occupied territories, Chile, Poland, Portuguese territories prior to independence, or Greece at the time of the military regime. The fact that in such cases inquiries or studies are pursued by various bodies within the UN system and at the regional level (and frequently also by non-governmental organizations) is not in itself objectionable. The terms of reference and the perspectives within which the different agencies operate are generally not the same, even if there is a certain amount of overlap. Some inquiries may be aimed at ascertaining whether specific human rights standards have been violated, while others are directed at a more general assessment of the human rights situation. The means and powers of investigation available to the organs involved may also vary. The initiation of several procedures in such circumstances reflects a widespread concern to secure international intervention when serious human rights violations occur, as a means of informing and mobilizing international public opinion and thus exerting a moderating influence when internal safeguards have been removed or have proved ineffective.

Where such parallel investigations take place, there is generally no formal requirement for consultation among the organizations concerned. In practice, consultations and exchange of relevant documentation frequently occur, but this depends on the awareness and initiative of those involved in carrying out the study or inquiry, particularly at secretariat level. ILO Commissions of Inquiry have regularly invited information from non-governmental organizations, and have, on occasion, also invited information from the UN and relevant regional organizations.[120] The fact that documentation available from other organizations has been taken into account is often reflected in the reports issued as a result of a study or inquiry.[121]

[118] ESC Res.1503(XLVIII), para. 6(b).

[119] 104 EX/Decision 3.3, para. 14(a)(x).

[120] Case of the Dominican Republic and Haiti. See ILO, *Official Bulletin*, 66 (1983), ser. B, Special Supplement, para. 18.

[121] See e.g. the references in the reports of the UN Special Rapporteur on the human rights situation in Chile to the conclusions of the ILO bodies with respect to trade union rights, E/CN.4/1983/9, paras. 145–148.

The above measures of course cannot guarantee that in all cases there is consistency in findings or conclusions. For example, while it was concluded in the ILO in 1971, following on-the-spot investigations in Angola and Mozambique, that there was no evidence that forced labour was any longer in use,[122] in 1973 the UN *Ad Hoc* Group of Experts, after hearing witnesses, came to a contrary conclusion.[123] Similarly, a UN report on the human rights situation in Poland,[124] placing considerable emphasis on encouraging developments, stands in contrast to the report of an ILO Commission of Inquiry which examined the trade union situation there.[125] Significant differences are also to be found in early assessments of the human rights situation in Guatemala made by the special rapporteur appointed by the UN Commission on Human Rights[126] and by the Inter-American Commission on Human Rights.[127]

Where such divergent conclusions are reached, they are liable to affect the credibility and thrust of the procedures. They raise the question how thorough and objective the investigation has been, both in seeking to obtain information from a sufficient range of reliable sources and in weighing up the evidentiary value of whatever information has been gathered. This in turn underlines the need to carry out such inquiries in accordance with principles and procedures which respect the concept of due process of law.[128]

In the case of individual complaints of human rights violations, it seems undesirable, in principle, for applicants to seek redress from more than one international organ. As already noted, some restrictions are imposed by the procedural rules laid down for such cases, although most of them appear to exclude only concurrent proceedings. In any case, multiple proceedings should be regarded as undesirable only where the issues are in fact identical. Often this is not the case. The parties may not be the same. There can also be differences in the wording of the relevant international instruments. For example, in several cases involving labour matters, the divergent positions taken by the organs of the European Convention on Human Rights and by ILO supervisory bodies have reflected such textual differences.

In dealing with individual complaints, as in the case of general human rights investigations, it is important that account should be taken of relevant

[122] See International Labour Conference, *Report of the Comittee of Experts on the Application of Conventions and Recommendations* (1971), 160–3 and the appended report on the on-the-spot mission.

[123] E/5245, 56.

[124] E/CN.4/1984/26.

[125] See ILO, *Official Bulletin*, 67 (1984), ser. B, Special Supplement.

[126] E/CN.4/1984/30.

[127] OEA/Ser.L/V/II.61, Doc. 47, Rev.1. (5 Oct. 1983).

[128] See, in this connection, Franck and Fairley, 'Procedural Due Process in Human Rights Fact-Finding by International Agencies', 74 *Am. J. Int'l L.* 308–45 (1980) and Ramcharan (ed.), *International Law and Fact-Finding in the Field of Human Rights* (1982).

standards and documentation in other agencies, even in the absence of formal requirements. In practice this tends to be done.[129]

An important aspect in efforts to secure some measure of co-ordination and consistency in human rights investigations is that information on the issues examined and the conclusions reached should be publicly available. The confidential nature of certain procedures—such as the UN procedure under ECOSOC Resolution 1503 and the UNESCO communications procedure—represents an obstacle. Information which would be relevant to investigations undertaken elsewhere is not available. There is no means to become aware of inconsistent findings or conclusions under confidential and non-confidential procedures. Nor is it possible to ascertain to what extent the competence of other agencies or organs is respected in the operation of the confidential procedures. It may be recalled that concern was expressed by members of the Human Rights Committee, when informed of the establishment of the UNESCO communications procedures, that this might involve overlapping with their own functions under the Optional Protocol to the Covenant on Civil and Political Rights, particularly in view of the absence of any clear definition of what human rights questions would be regarded as falling within the competence of UNESCO.[130] Given the confidentiality of the UNESCO procedure, there is no means of knowing how far those fears were justified.

VIII. CO-ORDINATION WITHIN THE UNITED NATIONS

The question of ensuring an appropriate measure of co-ordination of human rights activities at the international level requires consideration not only in terms of inter-agency relations, but also as regards action within individual organizations. This aspect calls for examination particularly for the UN, in view of its wide-ranging responsibilities and complex structure.

A considerable number of UN organs concern themselves with human rights questions, either pursuant to their specific mandate or because they deal with closely related matters. Among the former are the General Assembly, the ECOSOC, the Commission on Human Rights, the Sub-Commission, working groups set up to draft standards upon or to examine particular subjects, and bodies established to follow the human rights situation in particular regions or countries. Other bodies include the Commission for Social Development and the Commission on the Status of Women, as well as a variety of *ad hoc* bodies.

The primary responsibility for co-ordinating these activities rests upon

[129] See e.g. case of van der Mussele, 7/1982/53/82, Judgment of 23 Nov. 1983 of the European Court of Human Rights, the Advisory Opinion of the Inter-American Court of Human Rights of 13 Nov. 1985 regarding compulsory membership in an association prescribed by law for the practice of journalism, and n. 69, above.

[130] CCPR/C/SR.78.

ECOSOC, with the assistance of the Commission on Human Rights. Many decisions, both on substance or on proposals for action, are indeed referred to these two bodies. A number of problems have arisen, however.

One of them concerns the duplication of discussion on questions such as apartheid, the Israeli occupied territories, and the human rights situation in Chile, as well as on certain general subjects, such as human rights and development. Serious issues are involved which are rightly of concern to the UN system. One may nevertheless question whether repetitive discussions and repetitive resolutions by a series of UN organs represent a rational use of resources, in terms of the likely impact on the situations or problems concerned, and in the light of the resulting limitations upon the ability of bodies such as the Commission and the Sub-Commission to devote adequate time and attention to other problems within their field of responsibility. To give one illustration, for many years the Sub-Commission's Working Group on Slavery ritually discussed as an item on its agenda 'the slavery-like practice of apartheid'. Whatever the merit of that characterization, discussions in that limited context could make no contribution to further action on the question, which was in any case discussed every year by the Sub-Commission, as well as by the Commission. The time would have been better spent considering action on other issues specific to the Working Group's mandate. The Commission's discussions on this and other perennial topics tend often not to go beyond a series of prepared speeches for the purpose of maintaining and defending established positions.

At the end of the 1983 Session of the General Assembly, its President expressed doubt as to whether it had directed its energies in the best and most practical ways. He wondered whether the 63 resolutions adopted on disarmament and the 20 resolutions on the Arab–Israeli conflict would achieve practical results. He urged the Assembly to reverse the trend towards an ever-increasing agenda and to concentrate on essential issues with fewer resolutions on each, with the aim of seeing the resolutions it adopted implemented in fact and not relegated to the realms of hope.[131] These reminders are of general relevance in the context of the present study.

There is the tendency for the Commission and the Sub-Commission, once a question has been considered, to maintain it on their agenda indefinitely, with the result that their agendas become overloaded. Both bodies are aware of this problem and have been discussing means of rationalizing their methods and programme of work.[132]

The Sub-Commission's basic mandate requires it to consider questions concerning the prevention of discrimination of any kind relating to human rights and the protection of racial, national, religious, and linguistic

[131] A/38/PV.104, 52–3.
[132] See generally Chaps. 5 and 6 above.

minorities.[133] Over the years, in large measure on account of additional tasks assigned to it but also as a result of initiatives taken within the Sub-Commission itself, its work has come to embrace a far wider range of questions. This evolution led to suggestions in the Sub-Commission that its title be changed to that of 'Committee of Experts on Human Rights' and also that it might report directly to the Economic and Social Council.[134] On the other hand, it has also led to criticisms in the Commission on Human Rights, on the ground that the Sub-Commission was exceeding its terms of reference and ignoring its subordinate status by taking decisions on matters which should rather be referred to the Commission or the Economic and Social Council for decision. The Commission has, from time to time, called on the Sub-Commission to consider and make recommendations to it on how, within the existing terms of reference of the Sub-Commission, its work might best be harmonized with that of the Commission, so as to ensure complementarity and co-ordination.

The continuing examination by the main UN human rights organs of their programmes and methods and of their relationship appears to be a potentially useful exercise, with the prospect of rationalization and better co-ordination. One must recognize, however, that the trend towards expansion of the field of action of the Sub-Commission and also the debate which has gone on in recent years concerning its role reflect political differences on the thrust of UN human rights activities. Frustration over prospects of securing effective action by the Commission appears to lie at the root of initiatives to shift issues to the Sub-Commission. The widening range of questions dealt with by the Sub-Commission increases its involvement in politically controversial matters, and is thus liable to affect its character as a supposedly independent, expert body. The discussions which have taken place so far in the Commission and the Sub-Commission have led to some organizational changes and to a measure of stock-taking, but not to any major developments or shift of emphasis.

Beyond the relative functions of the Commission and the Sub-Commission, there is the more general question of co-ordination with their work of the activities of other bodies within the UN. For example, the Ad Hoc Working Group on the social aspects of the development activities of the UN, established by the ECOSOC in 1979, dealt with matters closely related to human rights and considered co-ordination within the UN system. The Working Group, however, made only a passing reference in its report to the importance of social development for enjoyment of human rights, without examining the organizational implications of that relationship.[135] The

[133] E/1371 (1949), para. 13.

[134] *Report of the Sub-Commission on Prevention of Discrimination and Protection of Minorities on its 35th Session*, E/CN.4/1983/4 (1982), Chap. 3.

[135] E/1981/3, para. 54.

Advisory Committee for the International Youth Year discussed proposals for a draft declaration on the rights and responsibilities of youth which covered important aspects of the rights provided for in the Universal Declaration of Human Rights and the Human Rights Covenants and were seemingly in conflict with those texts.[136] No suggestion was made that the proper place for examining proposals of this nature would be the Commission on Human Rights.

The last-mentioned case exemplifies a factor which works against co-ordination, namely, the absence of any standardized procedure for proclaiming human rights and for drawing up standards in this field.[137] There would be obvious advantages in the development by the UN of a standard procedure which, in addition to determining the body responsible for drawing up instruments on human rights questions, would ensure proper technical preparation by preliminary secretariat studies and a process of consultation of governments and relevant international, regional, and non-governmental organizations.[138] Such a standard procedure exists for the adoption of Conventions and Recommendations in the ILO. There is no technical reason—as distinct from possible political obstacles—why a similar practice should not be adopted in the UN. Initiatives by the General Assembly in 1986[139] and the Commission in 1991[140] in this direction are thus to be welcomed but much more remains to be done.

With an increasing number of human rights instruments, problems also arise with respect to their mutual compatibility. For example, Article 1 of the Declaration on the Elimination of all Forms of Intolerance and of Discrimination Based on Religion or Belief[141] recognizes only the right to have a religion or belief of one's choice, whereas Article 18 of the Universal Declaration of Human Rights expressly recognized also the right to change a religion or belief and Article 18 of the Covenant on Civil and Political Rights guarantees the right to have *or to adopt* a religion or belief of one's choice. Since the later declaration otherwise follows closely the terms of the Covenant, the variation of wording on this point cannot be devoid of significance. On the other hand, Article 8 of the Declaration contains a saving clause to ensure that it may not be construed as restricting or derogating from the Universal Declaration or the Covenant. If that was the intention, why should there have

[136] A/37/348, Appendix I. See also the comments on the draft declaration in A/AC.209/8.

[137] See Alston, 'Conjuring up New Human Rights: A Proposal for Quality Control', 78 *Am. J. Int'l L.* 607 (1984).

[138] Ibid. The suggestions made by the author with regard to the proclamation of new human rights appear valid for the preparation of instruments in the field of human rights generally. See also Meron, 'Reform of Law Making in the United Nations: The Human Rights Instance', 79 *Am. J. Int'l L.* 664 (1985).

[139] GA Res.41/120 (1986).

[140] CHR Res.1991/20.

[141] GA Res.36/55 (1981).

been the derogation in wording noted above?[142] Similar questions may arise in regard to the rights of aliens as flowing respectively from the UN Declaration on the human rights of individuals who are not nationals of the country in which they live[143] and from the Universal Declaration and Human Rights Covenants.[144]

Problems arise not only from the proliferation of standards, but also from the proliferation of supervisory procedures. In contrast to ILO practice, where a single supervisory system operates in respect of all Conventions adopted by the General Conference, UN practice is to provide in obligation-creating instruments for the establishment of distinct supervisory bodies. One thus finds in operation some seven different committees and an eighth (dealing with migrant workers) to be set up in due course. There is a considerable amount of overlap in the provisions of the various instruments, for example, in regard to questions of discrimination or on substantive rights guaranteed by the Human Rights Covenants and by more limited instruments (e.g., as regards rights of women, children, and migrants, and protection against torture).[145] Organic links between the different procedures are lacking and, while first efforts have been made at co-ordination by the exchange of documentation and the convening of meetings of the chairpersons of UN supervisory bodies,[146] the diffuse nature of the arrangements and the distinct composition, methods, and traditions of the organs concerned will make it difficult to secure a sufficient degree of consistency in evaluations and views.

The proliferation of procedures also gives rise to material problems for governments which are required (in addition to obligations which they have in respect of instruments adopted by other organizations of the UN system and at the regional level) to participate in the work of the numerous UN organs concerned, through reporting, attendance of their meetings, and study of their proceedings and reports. As a result a substantial backlog has developed in reporting on UN human rights instruments.

Considerable efforts thus appear to be needed to rationalize the supervisory processes and methods used in the UN, with the aim of limiting the burden on governments, and avoiding duplication and inconsistency. It would in particular be desirable to refrain from adopting further wide-ranging instru-

[142] Similar questions also arise in relation to Art.14(1) on the Convention on the Rights of the Child (GA Res.44/25 (1989) Annex) which provides only that 'States Parties shall respect the right of the child to freedom of thought, conscience and religion'.

[143] GA Res.40/144 (1985).

[144] Reference may be made, in this connection, to the general comments of the Human Rights Committee on the position of aliens under the Covenant on Civil and Political Rights in A/41/40, 117–19.

[145] For an important analysis in this regard see List of Articles Showing the Nature and Extent of Overlapping under Six International Human Rights Instruments: Report of the Secretary-General, EIC.12/1989/3.

[146] A/39/484 (1984); A/44/98 (1989); and A/45/636 (1990).

ments which seek to restate existing rights for particular categories, and instead to concentrate attention on questions where there is a lack of international standards. One should also examine the feasibility of bringing together in a single body responsibility for supervising the implementation of a number of conventions.[147] Whatever the obstacles to such fusion for existing instruments, that possibility should be explored for future standards.

IX. REGIONAL STANDARDS AND MACHINERY FOR THE PROTECTION OF HUMAN RIGHTS

Reference has already been made to the coexistence of universal and regional mechanisms of investigation of human rights violations. It is proposed here to consider more generally the questions of co-ordination which arise as a result of the adoption of instruments for the protection of human rights by regional organizations. Such action has been grounded in the belief that the more homogenous membership and shared traditions in a regional organization as well as the degree of mutual confidence among its members would facilitate agreement upon substantive guarantees and the acceptance of more incisive systems of supervision.[148] In the case of the European Convention, there was also the fact that action remained to be taken by the UN to embody the rights proclaimed in the Universal Declaration of Human Rights in obligation-creating instruments and to provide for 'measures of implementation'.

In the preparation of the European and American Conventions, great care was exercised to take into consideration the corresponding standard-setting already completed or in progress in the UN. The rights selected for inclusion in the European Convention were drawn from the Universal Declaration of Human Rights, and in defining them account was taken both of the text of the Universal Declaration and of the early drafts of the Human Rights Covenants already worked out in the Commission on Human Rights.[149] In preparing the American Convention, both the European Convention and the Covenants were drawn upon. A comparative study was made of the preliminary draft and

[147] For a comprehensive examination of these questions, see Meron, 'Norm-Making and Supervision in International Human Rights: Reflections on Institutional Order', 76 *Am. J. Int'l L.* 754 (1982); and A/44/668 (1989). See also Morgenstern, 'International Legislation at the Crossroads', *Brit. YB Int'l L.* 101 (1978).

[148] See, as regards the European Convention on Human Rights, *UN YB Hum. Rts.* 418 (1950), and Robertson, 'The Relations between the Council of Europe and the UN', UNITAR Regional Study No. 1 (1972), 48–9. As regards the American Convention on Human Rights, see Gros Espiell, 'The Organisation of American States', in *The International Dimensions of Human Rights*, UNESCO (Paris, 1982), ii, 556–7, and the *Inter-American YB Hum. Rts.* 383–7 (1968).

[149] Robertson, *Human Rights in Europe* (1977), 6–11. See, in particular, *Consultative Assembly of the Council of Europe, First Session*, Doc. 77, para. 6 (1949), where reference is made to the desire to co-ordinate the activities of the Council of Europe and of the UN as well as to the moral authority of the Universal Declaration of Human Rights.

the Covenant on Civil and Political Rights and its Optional Protocol. When the OAS Council called upon the Inter-American Commission on Human Rights to complete work on the draft, it directed that the text should be in harmony with the UN Covenants.[150] The Commission's report prepared in response to this request shows its systematic efforts to bear that directive in mind.[151] The Conference in San Jose at which the Convention was adopted was attended by representatives of the UN and of various specialized agencies, who were able to contribute to the final shaping of the text.

Following adoption of the Human Rights Covenants, the Council of Europe initiated studies of the problems arising from the coexistence of the Covenants and of the European Convention. The identification of differences in the rights guaranteed led to the preparation of the seventh Protocol to the European Convention.[152]

As a counterpart to the protection of civil and political rights by the European Convention on Human Rights, the Council of Europe adopted the European Social Charter in 1961. The drafting of this Charter was largely guided by ILO standards. At the request of the Council of Europe, the ILO convened a tripartite conference in Strasburg in 1958 to examine the draft. The conference had before it a comparative study of the draft Charter and corresponding ILO standards. Its deliberations led to substantial modifications in the draft.[153] In recent years, consideration has been given in the Council of Europe to the updating of the European Social Charter, as well as to the possibility of including certain social rights in the system of protection of the European Convention on Human Rights. In the study of these questions, regard has again been had to relevant ILO standards, and representatives of the ILO have participated in the discussions.[154]

The preceding indications show the concern of regional organizations, in their work of standard-setting in the field of human rights, to co-ordinate their efforts with those undertaken within the UN system. There have, however, been signs in recent times that the requirements of co-ordination are not always given sufficient weight. Examples can be cited from three regions: Africa, the Americas, and Europe.

Although the preparation of an African human rights instrument received its impetus from a UN seminar held in Monrovia in 1979, the actual drafting was undertaken without any participation or consultation of organizations of the UN system. The African Charter of Human and People's Rights, adopted

[150] See *Inter-American YB Hum. Rts.* 65–93 and 169–213 (1968).

[151] Ibid. 93–155.

[152] See Council of Europe: *Text of Protocol No. 7 to the Convention for the Protection of Human Rights and the Fundamental Freedoms and Explanatory Memorandum*, H(84)5.

[153] See 'The European Social Charter and International Labour Standards', *Int'l Lab. Rev.*, lxxiv. 354–75 and 478–98.

[154] See generally Council of Europe, *Charte sociale européenne* (1989); and Betten (ed.), *The Future of European Social Policy* (1989).

in 1981, while containing some innovative features, at the same time departs in important respects from the guarantees laid down in the Human Rights Covenants and other international conventions, notwithstanding that many African States are parties to those instruments. The Charter generally defines rights more succinctly, and restrictions more amply, than the earlier texts. The scope of the protection afforded by it is further reduced by the long list of widely defined duties imposed on individuals by Articles 27–9. To take but one example, although Africa was *par excellence* the continent which had experienced forced labour, the Charter—in contrast both to the Covenant on Civil and Political Rights and to the European and American Conventions on Human Rights—contains no prohibition of this practice; on the contrary, several of the duties of individuals set out in Article 29 appear to provide a basis for its imposition. It is also to be noted that—again in contrast to the Human Rights Covenants and to the European and American Conventions—the Charter contains no saving clause for rights enjoyed by virtue of other international conventions.

As already mentioned, the Council of Europe has been considering the strengthening of its protection of social rights, both by updating the European Social Charter and by examining the possibility of including certain social rights within the European Convention system. One of the rights looked at in both contexts has been the guarantee of equality of men and women in employment and occupation. Attention was drawn to the fact that the guarantees of equality in this field already laid down in the Convenant on Economic, Social and Cultural Rights and in ILO Conventions were not limited to sex, but aimed at elimination of discrimination on a series of grounds, such as race, colour, sex, religion, political opinion, national extraction, and social origin. The European Convention itself contains, in respect of the rights recognized in it, a similarly general non-discrimination clause. Notwithstanding this situation and the fact that most member States of the Council of Europe are already parties to the relevant Covenant and ILO Conventions, the non-discrimination clause in respect of employment and occupation contained in the Additional Protocol of 5 May 1988 to the European Social Charter remains limited to sex.[155] The adoption of such limited provisions, far from representing advance, would appear to be a step backwards as compared with existing standards and obligations.

The American Convention on Human Rights contains, in Article 26, a general undertaking by States Parties for the progressive realization of economic, social, educational, scientific and cultural rights. A preliminary draft protocol to the Convention, dealing with economic, social, and cultural rights, was presented to the OAS General Assembly in November 1983. The General Assembly decided to seek comments from the governments of

[155] See *European Treaty Series*, No. 128 (1988), Article 1.

member States, as well as from the Inter-American Commission and Court of Human Rights.[156] The original draft text was prepared by the OAS secretariat without consultation with interested UN agencies. Although the explanatory report by the secretariat mentioned the Universal Declaration of Human Rights and the Covenant on Economic, Social and Cultural Rights as among the sources used, the annotations to individual articles of the draft showed that this was rarely the case. However, this disregard of earlier international standards appears to have been corrected in the final version of the Additional Protocol, adopted in 1988.[157]

The above-mentioned developments show that, while regional measures to safeguard human rights may constitute a valuable supplement to action on the universal level, they will achieve that aim only if they add to or strengthen protection available under universal instruments. Care must be taken to ensure that regional action does not result in confusion or in the erosion of existing standards. These observations underline a conclusion which also emerges from the study of problems of co-ordination within the UN system, namely, that an unchecked proliferation of standards may be counter-productive in calling into question, rather than reinforcing, guarantees which have already been established.

X. HUMAN RIGHTS AND DEVELOPMENT ASSISTANCE

There has been much discussion in the past decade on the desirability and feasibility of linking the promotion and protection of human rights to measures in the field of aid and trade. The present context is not appropriate for a general review of these issues. It is, however, necessary to consider to what extent the human rights objectives proclaimed in the UN Charter and the rights stated in the Universal Declaration and Covenants on Human Rights influence the contents of the large-scale assistance programmes of the UN system, positively or negatively. This question raises issues both of consistency of policy in the different forms of action pursued by international organizations and of inter-agency co-ordination.

Suggestions have been made at various times that assistance under UN programmes should be denied to States guilty of human rights violations, but no general policies to that effect have been adopted within the UN system.[158]

[156] See OEA/Ser.P/AG/doc.1656/83 and AG/RES. 657 (1983).

[157] For the text see 28 *Int'l Legal Materials* (1989) 156.

[158] For a discussion of this question in regard to violations of trade union rights, see *193rd Report of the Committee on Freedom of Association of the ILO Governing Body*, ILO, *Official Bulletin*, 62 (1979), ser. B, No. 1, 163–5. See also the criticism of UN agencies for providing assistance to Equatorial Guinea under oppresive regime of Francisco Mancias in Cronje, *Equatorial Guinea—The Forgotten Dictatorship* (1976), 39–43. The author overlooked the fact that the projects mentioned were initiated in the period immediately following the country's independence and subsequently were either not continued or substantially reduced.

In a specific instance, in a series of resolutions adopted from 1965 onwards, the General Assembly called upon all international institutions, including the specialized agencies, to withhold financial, economic, technical, and other assistance from the governments of Portugal (prior to the change of regime in 1974) and of South Africa until they renounced their policies of colonial domination and racial discrimination.[159] The Secretary-General has regularly reported to the General Assembly on the action taken by organizations of the UN system in response to these resolutions. For most agencies, for reasons ranging from non-membership to absence of assistance in practice, no major problems have been encountered.[160]

In the case of the World Bank, however, a serious dispute of principle arose. The Bank took the view that it could not accede to the request made by the General Assembly, because its Articles of Agreement prohibited it from interfering in the political affairs of its member States and from being influenced in its decisions by the political character of the State concerned and because they also required the Bank to take decisions only by reference to economic considerations.[161] This restrictive interpretation of the Bank's powers and of its ability to take account of requests of the kind addressed to it by the Assembly has been questioned, both by the UN[162] and by outside commentators.[163] The Bank has stated that it has made no loans to South Africa since 1966 and that since 1972 South Africa has not participated in elections for executive directors of the Bank Group. Notwithstanding these indications, the General Assembly has expressed regret at the maintenance of links with South Africa by the Bank, and also by the International Monetary Fund, as exemplified by South Africa's continued membership in both agencies. It has also condemned the persistent collaboration between the IMF and South Africa, particularly the granting of a loan of $1.1 billion in 1982.[164]

In questioning the legal position adopted by the World Bank on the issue of its relations with South Africa, attention was drawn to the fact that, under its Articles of Agreement, the Bank's objectives include the encouragement of 'international investment for development of productive resources of members, thereby assisting in raising productivity, the standard of living and

[159] See e.g. GA Res.2105(XX) (1965) and 2704(XXV) (1970). Resolutions maintaining this position have continued to be adopted in respect of South Africa. See e.g. GA Res.38/51 (1983).

[160] See, however, the policy statement adopted by the ILO Governing Body in Nov. 1968 concerning the conditions for granting assistance under technical co-operation programmes, which reserved the Organisation's freedom of decision in such matters, with due regard to its obligations to its members under the ILO Constitution and towards the UN in relation to decisions of the General Assembly: A/8314 (1971), 7–9.

[161] Art. IV, Sect. 10 of the Articles of Agreement.

[162] See, in particular, the *Report of the Secretary-General*, A/6825 (1967).

[163] Bleicher, 'UN v IRBD, a Dilemma of Functionalism', 24 *Int'l Org.* 31 (1970); Marmorstein, 'World Bank Power to Consider Human Rights Factors in Loan Decisions', 13 *J. of Int'l L. & Econ.* 113 (1974).

[164] GA Res.38/51 (1983).

conditions of labour in their territories'.[165] It is accordingly significant that, since the dispute concerning the South African issue first arose, the Bank has taken an increasingly comprehensive view of the development process, involving greater attention to the social aspects of economic growth, including population, employment, income distribution, health, nutrition, and the impact on the environment, and emphasis on investments that can directly affect the well-being of the masses of poor people as partners in development.[166]

This raises the question how far UN development programmes in general are used to promote the enjoyment of human rights. The need to direct them to that end has certainly been recognized[167] and found reflection, for example, in the international development strategy for the Fourth UN Development Decade. The latter called for 'an environment that supports the evolution everywhere of political systems based on consent and respect for human rights, as well as social and economic rights, and of systems of justice that protect all citizens'.[168]

As can be seen from the specific example of the World Bank already referred to, such policy statements undoubtedly have an influence on the overall conception and thrust of development programmes in the UN system. On the other hand, human rights standards, such as those contained in the Universal Declaration of Human Rights and other instruments, are generally not referred to in any specific manner to determine the choice or content of projects.

The idea has been put forward of requiring the preparation of human rights impact statements as part of the formulation of project requests.[169] While this is an attractive suggestion, it is not certain that it would prove effective. In many instances—such as loans for carrying out development projects or assistance in improving food supply, health care, education and training, or opportunities for gainful employment—the human rights benefits would be easy to establish. On the other hand, one may wonder whether the existing normative basis would prove adequate. It is only in the area covered by ILO Conventions and Recommendations that there is available a comprehensive

[165] Art.I(iii).

[166] See the letter by Robert McNamara, President of the Bank, reproduced in E/5476/Add.5 (1974), 5; E/CN.4/1334 (1979), Annex, 4–7; and *World Bank Annual Report 1983*, 3.

[167] See e.g. the reports of the Secretary-General on the right to development in E/CN.4/1334 (1979), 152–6, and E/CN.4/1488 (1981), 81–5. Also, in 1990 the Director-General of the ILO endorsed the approach taken by the UN Under-Secretary-General for Human Rights and the UNDP Administrator in writing to all UNDP Resident Representatives to encourage them to consider technical cooperation projects aimed at promoting respect for human rights. *Report of the Committee of Experts on the Application of Conventions and Recommendations*, International Labour Conference, 78th Session, 1991, para. 44.

[168] GA Res.45/199 (1990), Annex, para. 13.

[169] E/CN.4/1488 (1981), 83.

and relatively detailed corpus of standards for guidance. In the many other areas to which UN development programmes relate there exist as yet no comparable sources of reference, and the generally worded provisions of the Human Rights Covenants may not provide a sufficient substitute.

Having regard to the above observations, it may be useful to give a brief summary of ILO experience. As a general policy, its standards should be taken into account in the formulation and implementation of technical co-operation projects, and there exist instructions to experts on their duties in this respect. Attempts are also made to identify cases in which technical co-operation could be useful in overcoming difficulties in the observance of ILO Conventions. Having regard to the manner in which the choice of country programmes is ultimately determined, it remains exceptional for projects to be chosen with the specific aim of ensuring the application of particular Conventions. It is rather at the stage of execution of projects that these instruments may serve as tools. Even here, many projects are of a nuts-and-bolts nature in which practical considerations predominate over policy. There are, however, others in which Conventions provide models or guidelines (for instance, in establishing or improving systems of labour administration or social security) or inject important policy principles, such as the participation of employers and workers in the determination and implementation of programmes or the exclusion of compulsory measures of labour mobilization.[170] Apart from formal assistance projects and as part of its current work, the ILO provides advice to member States on implementation of its standards, and for several years now regional advisers have been functioning for this purpose.[171] Suggestions have been made for similar action in the UN.[172]

As has already been observed, the relevance of positive aid to the promotion of human rights can be readily perceived. The position is different when international agencies are called upon not merely to provide aid, but to advise on general economic policies, particularly to countries in economic difficulties where stabilization measures, generally involving austerity, have to be put into operation. In such circumstances, how effectively is the principle of balanced economic and social development observed? A complaint repeatedly voiced at ILO meetings, not only by trade union representatives but also by governments, is that the measures which the international financial institutions have required governments to take have imposed a disproportionate burden on the poorer sections of the population, have caused severe hardship and social

[170] See *Report of the Director-General, International Labour Conference, 70th Session* (1984), 55–6.

[171] See generally *Human Rights: A Common Responsibility*, Report of the Director-General, International Labour Conference, 75th Session, 1988.

[172] See General Comment No. 2 (1990) adopted by the Committee on Economic, Social and Cultural Rights on the subject of international technical assistance measures. *Committee on Economic, Social and Cultural Rights, Report on the Fourth Session*, E/1990/23, Annex III.

disturbance, and have been at variance with ILO standards.[173] In 1984, a group of trade union confederations of Costa Rica lodged a formal complaint with the ILO against the government of Costa Rica and the International Monetary Fund alleging that measures required by the IMF had led to the violation of ratified ILO Conventions.[174] Involved here are both issues of the compatibility of the economic policies advocated by individual UN agencies with UN human rights objectives and with the principles of the International Development Strategy and issues of co-ordination between the policies pursued by the various agencies. Discussions have been undertaken by the ILO with the World Bank and the IMF to collaborate in finding solutions to these problems.

Apart from the role which may be played by general aid programmes in promoting the enjoyment of human rights, the question has arisen of how UN services may be used to eliminate human rights violations. The Human Rights Commission has been giving increasing attention to this matter, as a result of recommendations made by various special rapporteurs in respect of countries where oppressive regimes have been replaced by governments desirous of repairing the damage inflicted by their predecessors.[175] Such remedial measures can, however, be applied only in relatively limited cases. Greater opportunities for the UN to provide assistance specifically to improve the protection of human rights at the national level may arise in the framework of implementation of the Human Rights Covenants and other human rights instruments.[176] It remains to be seen to what extent governments will wish to avail themselves of such assistance and how imaginatively any requests of this nature will be dealt with.

Conclusions—A Forty-five Year Perspective

Looking at the experience of the past forty-five years, what conclusions emerge? The formal framework of the UN system provides for a rational distribution of tasks and for means of keeping the co-ordination of the activities of the various components of the system under review. The concern to ensure an orderly development of the system, including its work in the social field and more specifically in regard to human rights, has been repeatedly stressed, and a series of rules and guidelines have been established.

[173] n. 70, above, p. vii, and *Record of Proceedings, International Labour Conference, 70th Session*, 44/14, and ILO doc. GB.228/3/5 (1984).

[174] ILO doc. GB.227/8/13 (1984).

[175] See e.g. the resolutions adopted by the Commission in 1984 concerning assistance to Bolivia (CHR 1984/45), to Uganda (CHR 1984/45), and to Equatorial Guinea (CHR 1984/51).

[176] See generally Samson, 'Human Rights Assistance: The Experience of ILO', in Radda Barnen *et al.*, *UN Assistance for Human Rights* (1988), 53.

These include the ECOSOC rules providing for consultation of the specialized agencies concerning proposals on matters within their field of action, the principles enunciated by the Administrative Committee on Co-ordination concerning the legislative activities of the UN system, the ECOSOC decision concerning the carrying out of studies on questions within the competence of specialized agencies by the agency concerned, and individual arrangements on division of work or collaboration in specific fields such as migrant workers or machinery for dealing with complaints of violation of trade union rights.

In the earlier part of the period under consideration, considerable results were achieved in co-ordinating the human rights work of the UN system. A number of issues first brought up in UN organs, especially the Economic and Social Council, were referred to specialized agencies for action because it was recognized that they fell wholly or primarily within the agencies' competence. This resulted in the adoption of a series of important human rights instruments, including those on trade union rights, abolition of forced labour, equal pay, and discrimination in employment and in education. The active involvement of the specialized agencies was sought in the framing of the Human Rights Covenants, leading to the recognition of the place of the standard-setting work of the agencies in their respective fields as a means of spelling out and supplementing the generally worded provisions of the Covenants and to the assignment to the agencies of a significant role in the implementation of the Covenant on Economic, Social and Cultural Rights. Machinery for the protection of trade union rights was set up by agreement between the UN and the ILO, and certain activities were undertaken jointly, such as the inquiry into forced labour or the system-wide collaboration on questions concerning indigenous populations.

Over the years, the picture has changed. While much day-to-day consultation and collaboration still occurs, UN organs have increasingly taken up subjects, for study, standard-setting, or other action, which—had earlier decisions and guidelines been followed—ought rather to have been referred to specialized agencies, and which in any case should have been the subject of prior consultations with the agency concerned. Such decisions have not been taken in ignorance of the responsibilities and activities of the specialized agencies, but rather because of the political advantages which a majority in the organs concerned saw in dealing with the matter in the UN context. The clearest example is provided by the decision to draw up a UN Convention on migrant workers, when a proposal to study in the first instance the need for additional measures, which would have permitted an analysis of existing ILO standards and of gaps or deficiencies in those standards, was rejected out of hand. There was, for a considerable period, a persistent campaign waged with determination and a measure of success by certain governments within the UN to limit specialized agency contributions to supervision of the implementation of human rights instruments. There is also the increasing lack of order within the UN itself, resulting from the proliferation of instruments each having its distinct supervisory mechanism, the absence of any consistent and technically solid method for drawing up international standards, and the self-effacing role imposed on the main potential agent for promoting co-ordination (the secretariat). These are ingrained habits and attitudes, and will take a long time to be reversed.

These difficulties appear to be due to a number of factors.

There has been a substantial change in the size and composition of the main UN organs concerned with human rights activities and co-ordination. For instance, ECOSOC originally had a membership of only eighteen. Having recently been involved in the negotiation of the relationship agreements with various specialized agencies, the members were conscious of the need to give practical effect to the arrangements for collaboration provided for in them. Several States were represented by persons of major stature who at times had themselves participated in the work of certain specialized agencies and who were sensitive to the concern for system-wide co-ordination. Today, the Council has fifty-four members and is much more varied in composition.

The change in size and composition of the UN Organization itself is another important factor, including the development of various groupings of countries. Delegations at the General Assembly are often more concerned to promote action on topics of particular interest to their country than to secure co-ordination in the activities of the UN system as a whole. Representing foreign affairs ministries, they may have only limited knowledge and no experience of the work of specialized agencies, and will tend to consider questions in terms of their implications for foreign relations rather than on the basis of technical considerations. Group loyalties are liable to prove more important than the orderly development of international law and institutions, particularly when there are trade-offs in mutual support among groups on different, frequently unrelated issues. These tendencies are reinforced by the notorious lack of co-ordination in the policies pursued by governments in the UN and in other agencies.

All States tend to proclaim their attachment to human rights. Far too often actual conduct or conditions fall sadly short of these professions or aspirations. It is thus not surprising that international measures to safeguard human rights are not regarded everywhere with equal enthusiasm. This finds reflection in human rights discussions in the UN system. There are the centrifugal tendencies, which seek to direct attention to general questions, away from specifics, and centripetal forces, which seek to give greater emphasis to action on concrete problems and situations. The issue of co-ordination—which ultimately is one of effectiveness—is part of the tug-of-war between these tendencies.

Discussions on human rights questions in the UN take place in a large number of bodies, from the General Assembly to the Economic and Social

Council, various commissions subordinate to the Council and their own subordinate bodies. Human rights issues often arise in *ad hoc* bodies, such as those concerned with preparations for international years or particular conferences, and also in the consideration of technical co-operation programmes. It is a large, sprawling edifice where it is difficult to keep track of, and a hold on, all that is going on.[177] These problems are compounded by the physical separation of competent secretariat services in at least three distinct centres (New York, Geneva, and Vienna). This is very different from the situation in the specialized agencies, where there is generally much closer control of activities by a single governing body and greater cohesion in a centrally located headquarters secretariat. In principle, ECOSOC should provide the unifying force, but it is doubtful whether it is doing so effectively. Be it remembered that the Council took many years to reach conclusions on its own 'revitalization'.

Despite the continuing difficulties, it should be noted that several encouraging developments have emerged recently. Firstly, the Commission on Human Rights has acknowledged, at least formally, the need for improved co-ordination. In two separate resolutions in 1991 the Commission expressed its support for efforts to enhance the role of the Centre for Human Rights 'as a coordinating unit in the system of bodies dealing with the promotion and protection of human rights'.[178] Secondly, the Third Committee of the General Assembly, in the context of 'rationalizing' its own work, has placed particular emphasis on the need to achieve improved overall co-ordination.[179] And thirdly, ECOSOC has, in the context of its own 'restructuring' efforts, recognized the need to improve its co-ordinating role.[180] While it remains to be seen what practical results will emerge from these initiatives, the mere fact of their adoption signals an encouraging awareness of the extent of the problems outlined in this chapter.

Why do the specialized agencies themselves not exert a bigger influence on the human rights discussions in the UN, particularly when co-ordination issues are at stake? In this regard, there has been a great change in the situation from the early days of the UN. Then the specialized agencies tended to be represented by high-level delegations. The ILO, for instance, sent tripartite Governing Body delegations (generally headed by the Chairman of the Governing Body and comprising also influencial employer and worker members) to the early sessions of the General Assembly and ECOSOC. The Director-General or one of his deputies might also attend. These representatives were sometimes closely acquainted with several of the dominant per-

[177] See Jenks, n. 6, above, 160–3.
[178] CHR Res.1991/22, para. 1 and CHR Res.1991/26, para. 2.
[179] GA Res.45/175 (1990), Annex.
[180] GA Res.45/264 (1991), Annex, para. 4(a).

sonalities in UN bodies, and in any case were listened to. Today it is not feasible, in terms of time and resources, for the specialized agencies to be similarly represented. Nor is there the same propensity to listen to the agencies, in the different membership structure referred to above. Many delegates appear to conceive of the UN family as similar to a Victorian family, where the children (in this instance, the specialized agencies) should be seen, not heard. This is not unrelated to the non-active, essentially secretarial role which UN bodies expect from their secretariat. Given that tradition, why should officials of other agencies presume to influence their deliberations? In this setting, the agency representatives tend to place greater reliance on indirect influence through discussions with delegations inclined to listen to their views. This discreet manner of seeking to contribute to the course of debate may, however, be insufficient to overcome the structural problems within the UN noted above.

Another obstacle to the airing of specialized agency views is the practice in UN bodies of conducting important discussions outside formal meetings, either through negotiations between groups of delegations or in informal consultations which, in all but name, are meetings of the bodies concerned. The specialized agencies have no recognized standing in such discussions. Even where matters of direct concern to them are under consideration, they may find themselves altogether excluded (obliged to find out from well-disposed delegates what is transpiring) or merely tolerated to be present. These practices result in the negation of the rights of representation provided for in the agreements between the UN and the agencies.[181]

Given these various difficulties, it is perhaps not surprising that the agencies' representatives in UN human rights bodies tend not to entertain great expectations as to their ability to inject an original contribution, and are concerned primarily to explain that given problems are receiving attention in their organization and to prevent decisions which would conflict with or inhibit their agency's policies or activities. It is revealing that in the information on human rights activities and co-ordination which the agencies sent to the UN Secretary-General, they sought to bring out their awareness of the need for co-ordination and the considerable efforts made to that end, but did not refer to the difficulties which they had encountered or to improvements which would be desirable in their relations with the UN.[182] In informal secretariat consultations on the matter, difficulties have been recognized to exist, but the general assumption has been that they were the inevitable consequence of the attitudes and prerogatives of the deliberative organs concerned.

One should, however, not look solely at the UN in discussing the current

[181] See Hill, n. 6, above, 70.
[182] E/CN.4/1433 (1981).

difficulties in human rights co-ordination. One of the reasons why in the earlier years questions of concern to the specialized agencies, when raised in UN bodies, were referred to the agencies was that the latter were prepared to act, and to act rapidly. This was the essence of the ILO response on such issues as trade union rights, forced labour, and discrimination in employment. The best manner of asserting competence is to exercise it in fact. A more recent example is provided by the proposal to cover matters of employment, training, conditions of work and life and industrial relations in the UN Code of Conduct on Transnational Corporations by a reference to the ILO Tripartite Declaration of Principles—adopted as long ago as 1977. In other areas, the record of specialized agency action has at times been less impressive. For example, the problems of migrant workers were relatively neglected by the ILO in the sixties and only received closer attention again from the early seventies. This may have contributed to the UN decisions first to study the problem of illicit trafficking in migrant workers and then to adopt a convention on the rights of migrant workers. Similarly, ILO action in regard to child labour—apart from adoption of more up-to-date standards in 1973—had become very limited, and was only intensified as a result of the general interest aroused by the International Year of the Child and the attention given to the problem by certain non-governmental organizations. Would it have been relevant to propose, as was done by a UN special rapporteur in 1981, a UN programme for the abolition of child labour if a solid programme of this kind had already existed in the ILO, the competent specialized agency? One can understand the irritation of UNESCO at UN General Assembly resolutions on the right to education, which led its Executive Board to recall UNESCO's competence in education, the division of responsibilities within the UN system as an essential condition for the effectiveness of that system, and the need for organs of other organizations to consult UNESCO before adopting decisions concerning education. But might there not be room for further standard setting by UNESCO to spell out the contents of the right to education? Similarly, would it not have been advisable for UNESCO to consult other agencies, and especially the UN, before establishing its own human rights communications machinery, in view of the need for avoiding overlap and conflict with already existing machinery?

Questions are frequently taken up in UN human rights bodies because of documents and proposals submitted by non-governmental organizations or suggested to individual delegations or members by the representatives of such organizations. One reason why issues of primary concern to the ILO (such as child labour and the treatment of Haitian cane-cutters on sugar plantations in the Dominican Republic) have been brought before UN organs is that they were raised by non-governmental organizations which—not being employers' or workers' organizations—had no direct access to ILO procedures. Even if it may be difficult to change the rules governing those procedures, the

ILO might be well advised to maintain closer links with non-occupational organizations.

More generally, what action might realistically be envisaged to improve human rights co-ordination in the UN system?

To begin with, it is necessary to consider the aims which arrangements for co-ordination should seek to meet. Action by the UN General Assembly in adopting the Universal Declaration of Human Rights and the Human Rights Covenants was of vital importance in establishing a general conceptual framework for the human rights activities of the international community. The various UN agencies have unquestionably accepted these instruments as an authoritative basis of reference in developing their own action to promote and protect human rights. One may question whether today there is further need and scope for general programme orientation of a similar nature by the UN for the system as a whole. Through deliberations on their programmes and policies, the agencies identify the main tasks with which they are faced and try to work out considered responses. Both as a matter of autonomy of decision-making within the organizations belonging to the UN system and as a matter of understanding and expertise in the specialized fields covered by the various agencies, there appears to be no reason to look to the organs of the UN itself for a shrewder, more profound appreciation of the needs of the times.

One may refer, in this connection, to some cases in which the UN General Assembly has sought to provide overall guidance. In 1977, in Resolution 32/130, the Assembly enunciated a series of concepts to be taken into account in approaching the future work in the UN system with respect to human rights. Leaving aside the procedural question whether a decision of this kind, purporting to apply to the entire UN system, should have been taken without detailed prior consultation with the other agencies concerned, one may wonder whether the Resolution was in fact capable of influencing the direction of human rights work in those agencies, in view of the generality of the terms in which the concepts were defined and the divergent interpretations to which the Resolution lent itself. The fact that in 1982 the Assembly adopted two Resolutions concerning further human rights work,[183] both of which invoked the 1977 resolution but which were regarded by their main proponents as conflicting with one another, bears out these doubts. In retrospect, Resolution 32/130 appears more as a barometer to gauge the relative strength of different schools of thought in the UN about the thrust of its human rights work than as the seminal text which many at first believed it to be.

Another illustration is provided by General Assembly resolutions[184] requesting the specialized agencies to take full account in their programmes

[183] GA Res.37/199 and 37/200 (1982).
[184] GA Res.35/130A (1980) and 36/56A (1981).

and activities of the Declaration adopted by it in 1975 on the use of scientific and technological progress in the interests of peace and for the benefit of mankind.[185] This Declaration seeks to ensure that scientific and technological developments are used to promote economic and social progress and the enjoyment of human rights and not misused to infringe those rights. Scientific progress and technological change are such major determinants of contemporary economic and social conditions and problems that it would be naïve to think that they would not receive the closest attention in the studies, policy discussions, and operational activities of the various agencies within the UN system. In the ILO, for example, this has been true in such fields as employment, training, conditions of work, and occupational health and safety.

UN human rights co-ordination should thus be directed to more specific objectives: to ensure that problems which arise are dealt with by the best qualified agencies and bodies and, where they involve several organizations, are the subject of the necessary collaboration, and to avoid duplication and conflict.

It would be useful to prepare a compilation of the various rules, decisions, guidelines, and agreements previously adopted or concluded within the UN system which have a bearing on human rights co-ordination, as a reminder both to secretariats and to deliberative bodies of the rules and practices which should be followed. Such a compilation might be prepared jointly by the secretariats of the UN and the specialized agencies and presented, for example, to the Commission on Human Rights to take into account in its consideration of future work in the field of human rights. It would provide a basis of reference for attempts to secure more consistent attention to the needs of co-ordination.

In its conclusions concerning co-ordination of legislative work in the UN system, the Administrative Committee on Co-ordination recognized the important role of secretariats in providing information on co-ordination needs, precedents, and possible solutions to the deliberative organs concerned. There are many statements of principle by the main UN organs stressing the importance of co-ordination. Building on those statements, might one not suggest that practices be developed to ensure that any relevant elements concerning co-ordination were brought systematically to the attention of deliberative organs before decisions were taken? This might be done by instructions to the UN secretariat to include the necessary indications in the annotated agendas of these organs and, whenever appropriate, to submit data on the co-ordination implications of proposals, as is already done regarding financial implications. Indications of this kind should relate not only to co-ordination as between the UN and other agencies, but also to co-ordination within the UN. For instance, in relation to standard-setting work, they should

[185] GA Res.3384(XXX) (1975).

examine the relationship of the proposed texts to earlier standards or other current standard-setting, both within and outside the UN. In future this will be assisted by the inventory of all international human rights standard-setting activities which the commission requested the secretariat to prepare in 1991.[186]

A question for consideration by the specialized agencies is whether they should seek to play a more active role in the proceedings of UN organs, not only out of concern for considerations of co-ordination but also with a view to enhancing the work of the UN through a distinctive contribution. This would require a much larger allocation of resources than is at present the case. Is that an appropriate priority, in an era of financial stringency and consequent difficulty for the agencies in responding to all the needs of their own constituents, and having regard to the fact, noted earlier, that action by agencies to meet their technical responsibilities is an important element in securing respect for their competence? Beyond this material factor, how effective would such a strategy be? Would there be prospects of significantly influencing decisions or conclusions, or might the results be limited to secondary points of detail? To what extent are the decisions on major human rights issues in UN organs dependent on an alignment of political forces which it would be difficult for any input from the specialized agencies to modify? Might their efforts, which would inevitably have to include a considerable element of lobbying, be resented and thus prove counter-productive? Clearly this is a question to be handled with care. In all the circumstances, although increased participation by the specialized agencies in the work of UN organs dealing with human rights might over the years produce some results, it would probably not bring about any major modification in the policies pursued by those organs or in the relationship between the UN and the specialized agencies in this field.

As regards human rights standard-setting, attention should be given to the problems arising from the proliferation of instruments and supervisory mechanisms. Before embarking on the drawing up of new instruments, one should carefully consider whether there is a real need for such action, and whether it might not be preferable to concentrate on improving or filling gaps in existing standards. It would also be useful to analyse the consequences of the approaches to standard-setting adopted hitherto, with a view to proposing improved methods. In particular, the UN should establish a regular procedure for the drawing up of human rights standards, covering such matters as the bodies to which this work should be assigned, the technical analyses and other preparatory material to be provided by the secretariat, and the manner of ensuring consultation of member States, specialized agencies, and other

[186] CHR Res.1991/20, para. 17.

interested organizations.[187] As regards supervision, all possibilities of rationalization should be explored. The suggestion has been made that reporting procedures should be consolidated by legislating for the establishment of one or two bodies to replace the present multitude of organs.[188] Such a move would have obvious advantages and may not be beyond the wit of lawyers, but major political resistance as well as legal complexities would have to be overcome before it could secure acceptance and take effect. At best, this could only be a long-term development. In the mean time, two more limited ideas merit consideration. One should examine how far new standards might be made subject to an existing supervisory mechanism. In the Council of Europe, the practice of establishing new rights through protocols to the European Convention on Human Rights has precisely that effect. The possibility of proceeding in a like manner in the UN context—for example, by means of protocols to the Covenant on Civil and Political Rights—would be worth exploring. Beyond this, one might study the possibility of establishing a supervisory system of general scope to be given responsibility for the implementation of instruments which may be adopted in the future.

In the case of human rights standard-setting at the regional level, care is required to ensure that it retains its distinctive mission of action going beyond what is possible, in substance or procedurally, in the UN system, and does not result in a regional retreat from universally accepted standards.

A major responsibility rests upon the secretariats of the various organizations to identify at the earliest possible date issues on which co-ordination questions are likely to arise, with a view to entering into consultations and placing relevant suggestions before the competent organs. It has been suggested that an inter-organization committee of legal advisers and other experts be established for co-ordination of human rights standard-setting.[189] Dealing with such questions in a formal body, comprising representatives of agencies which might not be affected by particular issues which arose, would prove unduly cumbersome and slow. Moreover, early consultation should cover human rights activities generally and not be confined to legislative work. What matters is that the need for such consultation should be accepted as a general principle and actively pursued by all the agencies concerned.

[187] See the suggestions regarding these matters made by Alston, n. 140, above, and Meron, n. 141, above.

[188] See Meron, n. 147, above, 775.

[189] Ibid. 774.

SELECT BIBLIOGRAPHY*

* This bibliography does not purport to be comprehensive. Only those references which deal directly or indirectly with some aspect of the United Nations role (or that of the ILO in the case of section 13) have been included.

Where available, references to the relevant literature in French, German and Spanish have been included.

Since each reference has been included only once in the bibliography, the placement of references dealing with issues of relevance to two or more of the subject headings has inevitably been somewhat arbitrary. However, when the reader knows an author's name the Author Index may be used to trace the reference.

In the case of official (UN and ILO) documents, an attempt has been made to select those reports or studies which seem to be of some enduring interest. The listing is, however, by no means exhaustive.

1. *The United Nations and Human Rights: General Issues*

DOCUMENTS

(1968)

Final Act of the International Conference on Human Rights, E.68.XIV.2.

(1975)

Report on Protection of Broad Sectors of the Population against Social and Material Inequalities, as well as other Harmful Effects which may Arrive from the Use of Scientific and Technological Developments, by the Secretary-General, A/10/146.

(1977)

Report on Respect for Human Rights in Armed Conflicts, by the Secretary-General, A/32/144 & Add.1.

(1979)

Report of the World Conference to Combat Racism and Racial Discrimination, E.79.XIV.2.

(1981)

Study on Ways and Means of Ensuring the Implementation of International Instruments such as the International Convention on the Suppression and Punishment of the Crime of Apartheid, including the Establishment of the International Jurisdiction Envisaged by the Convention, E/CN.4/1426.

(1988)

Human Rights: A Compilation of International Instruments, E.88.XIV.1, ST/HR/1/Rev.3.

United Nations Action in the Field of Human Rights, E.88.XIV.2.

BOOKS AND ARTICLES

Abellán Honrubia, V., 'La protección internacional de los derechos humanos: Métodos internacionales y garantías internas', *Pensamiento Jurídico y Sociedad Internacional: Libro-homenaje al Profesor D. Antonio Truyol Serra*, 29–58 (1986).

Abram, J., 'The United Nations and Human Rights', 47 *Foreign Aff.* 361–74 (1969).

Allen, F., 'Human Rights and the International Court: The Need for a Juridical World Order', 35 *ABAJ* 713–16, 788–9 (1949).

Allen, P. D., 'The Baha'is of Iran: A Proposal for Enforcement of International Human Rights Standards', 20 *Cornell Int'l LJ* 337–61 (1987).

Alston, P., 'Human Rights and the New International Development Strategy', 10 *Bull. of Peace Proposals* 281–90 (1979).

—— 'The Universal Declaration at 35: Western and Passé or Alive and Universal', 31 *Int'l Commission of Jurists Rev.* 60–70 (1983).

—— 'Conjuring Up New Human Rights: A Proposal for Quality Control', 78 *Am. J. Int'l L.* 607–21 (1984).

—— 'The United Nations and the Elliptical Notion of the Universality of Human Rights', in United Nations, *Is Universality in Jeopardy?* INF/86/9, 51–64 (1987).

—— and RODRIGUEZ-BUSTELO, M., *Taking Stock of United Nations Human Rights Procedures, Workshop Report* (Fletcher School of Law and Diplomacy, Boston, 1988).

ARMSTRONG, J. D., 'Non-Governmental Organizations', in R. J. Vincent (ed.), *Foreign Policy and Human Rights: Issues and Responses*, 243–60 (Cambridge UP, Cambridge, 1986).

ASBECK, F. VAN (ed.), *The Universal Declaration of Human Rights and its Predecessors (1679–1948)* (Brill, Leiden, 1949).

BADAWI, I., 'U.N. and Violations of Human Rights', 36 *Rev. égypt. de droit int'l* 133–60 (1980).

BAILEY, S., 'U.N. Fact Finding and Human Rights Complaints', 48 *Int'l Aff.* 250–66 (1972).

BALLALOUD, J., *Droits de l'homme et organisations internationales* (Montchrestien, Paris, 1986).

BALLINGER, R. B., 'U.N. Action on Human Rights in South Africa', in E. Luard (ed.), *The International Protection of Human Rights*, 248–85 (Praeger, New York, 1967).

BARSH, R. L., 'Making the United Nations Human Rights Machinery Cost-Effective', 56 *Nordic J. Int'l L.* 183–97 (1987).

—— 'The Ethnic Factor in Security and Development: Perceptions of United Nations Human-Rights Bodies', 31 *Acta Sociologica: J. of the Scandinavian Soc. A.* 333–41 (1988).

—— 'The Right to Development as a Human Right: Results of the Global Consultation', 13 *Hum. Rts Q.* 322–38 (1991).

BASSIOUNI, C., 'The U.N. Procedures for the Effective Implementation of the Standard Minimum Rules for the Treatment of Prisoners', in *Festschrift für Dietrich Oehler zum 70. Geburtstag* 525–39 (Berlin, 1985).

BASSIOUNI, C., *et al.*, 'Final Report on The Establishment of an International Criminal Court for the Implementation of the Apartheid Convention and other Relevant International Instruments', 9 *Hofstra L. Rev.* 523–92 (1981).

BAYEFSKY, A., 'Human Rights: The 1966 Covenants Twenty Years Later: A Panel', 80 *Am. Soc. Int'l L. Proc.* 408–28 (1986).

BECKETT, W. E., 'Human Rights', 2 *Int'l LQ* 228–30 (1948).

BEITZ, W. (ed.), *Begrenzte Menschrenrechte für Fluchtlinge?* (Nomos, Baden Baden, 1979).

BENNET, W. H., 'A Critique of the Emerging Convention on the Rights of the Child', 20 *Cornell Int'l LJ* 1–64 (1987).

BERNHARDT, R., 'Domestic Jurisdiction of States and International Human Rights Organs', 7 *Hum. Rts. LJ* 205–16 (1986).

—— 'General Report', in R. Bernhardt, and J. A. Jolowitz (eds.), *International Enforcement of Human Rights*, 143–58 (Springer-Verlag, Berlin, 1987).

BERNHEIM, J. C., 'Le Rôle des organisations non-gouvernementales dans la mise en œuvre du droit international des droits de la personne au Canada et au Québec', 2 *Rev. québécoise de droit int'l* 231–55 (1985).

BILDER, R. B., 'International Promotion of Human Rights: A Current Assessment', 58 *Am. J. Int'l L.* 728–34 (1964).

—— 'Rethinking International Human Rights: Some Basic Questions', 2 *Rev. des droits de l'homme* 557–608 (1969).

—— 'Integrating International Human Rights Law into Domestic Law—U.S. Experience', 4 *Houston J. Int'l L.* 1–12 (1981).

BISSELL, J., 'Negotiations by International Bodies and the Protection of Human Rights', 7 *Colum. J. Transnat'l L.* 90–134 (1968).

BITKER, B., 'Application of the United Nations Universal Declaration of Human Rights within the United States', 21 *De Paul L. Rev.* 337–95 (1971).

BLAUSTEIN, J., 'Human Rights: A Challenge to the United Nations and to Our Generation', in A. W. Cordier, and W. Foote (eds.), *The Quest For Peace: The Dag Hammarskjöld Memorial Lectures*, 315–30 (Columbia, New York, 1965).

—— *Human Rights Sourcebook* (Paragon House, Washington, DC, 1987).

BOLINTINEANU, A., 'The Significance of International Covenants on Human Rights', 21 *Rev. roum. d'ét. int'l* 175–7 (1987).

BOSSUYT, M., 'United Nations and Civil and Political Rights in Chile', 27 *Int'l & Comp. LQ* 462–71 (1978).

BOVEN, T. C. VAN, 'Partners in the Promotion and Protection of Human Rights', 24 *Netherlands Int'l L. Rev.* 55–71 (1977).

—— 'The United Nations and Human Rights: A Critical Appraisal', 8 *Bull. of Peace Proposals* 198–208 (1977).

—— 'Human Rights Fora at the United Nations. How to Select and Approach the Most Appropriate Forum: What Procedural Rules Govern?', in J. C. Tuttle (ed.), *International Human Rights Law and Practice: The Roles of the United Nations, the Private Sector, the Government, and their Lawyers*, 83–92 (American Bar Association, Chicago, 1978).

—— 'Menschenrechte: Moglichkeiten und Grenzen der Vereinten Nationen', 27 *Vereinte Nationen* 95–9 (1979).

—— 'United Nations Policies and Strategies: Global Perspectives?', in B. Ramcharan (ed.), *Human Rights: Thirty Years after the Universal Declaration* (Martinus Nijhoff, The Hague, 1979).

—— 'Les Nations Unies et les droits de l'homme', 43 *Ann. de droit de Louvain* 165–75 (1983).

BROWNLIE, I., *Basic Documents on Human Rights* (Oxford UP, Oxford, 1981).

BRUDNER, A., 'The Domestic Enforcement of International Covenants on Human Rights: A Theoretical Framework', 35 *U. Toronto LJ* 219–54 (1985).

BRUNET, R., *La Garantie internationale des droits de l'homme: D'après la charte de San Francisco* (Grasset, Geneva, 1947).

BUERGENTHAL, T., 'The United Nations and the Development of Rules Relating to Human Rights', 59 *Am. Soc. Int'l L. Proc.* (1965).

—— 'International and Regional Human Rights Law and Institutions: Some Examples of their Interaction', 12 *Tex. Int'l LJ* 321–30 (1977).

—— 'International Human Rights Law and Institutions: Accomplishments and Prospects', 63 *Wash. L. Rev.* 1–19 (1988).

—— *International Human Rights in a Nutshell* (West Publishing Company, St Paul, Minn., 1988).

BURKE, K., 'New United Nations Procedure to Protect Prisoners and other Detainees', 64 *Calif. L. Rev.* 201–28 (1976).

BURROWS, N., 'Monitoring Compliance of International Standards Relating to Human Rights in the World', 31 *Netherlands Int'l L. Rev.* 332–54 (1984).

CANHAM, E., 'International Freedom of Information', 14 *Law & Contemp. Prob.* 584–98 (1949).

CAREY, J., 'UN and Human Rights: Who Should Do What?', 10 *ABA Soc. Int'l & Comp. L.* 9–29 (1966).

—— 'Procedures for International Protection of Human Rights', 53 *Iowa L. Rev.* 291–324 (1967).

—— *International Protection of Human Rights* (Oceana Publications, New York, 1968).

—— 'United Nations Response to Government Oppression', 3 *Int'l L.* 102–8 (1968).

—— UN Protection of Civil and Political Rights (Syracuse University Press, Syracuse, NY, 1970).

—— 'Progress on Human Rights at the U.N.', 66 *Am. J. Int'l L.* 107–9 (1972).

CARRILLO SALCEDO, J. A., 'Human Rights: Universal Declaration', 8 *Encyclopedia of Public International Law* 303 (Heidelberg, Max Planck Institute, 1985).

CASSESE, A., 'The Admissibility of Communications to the UN on Human Rights Violations', 5 *Rev. des droits de l'homme* 375–97 (1972).

—— (ed.), *UN Law/Fundamental Rights: Two Topics in International Law* (Alphen aan den Rijn, Sijthoff and Noordhoff, 1979).

CASSIN, R., 'La Déclaration universelle et la mise en œuvre des droits de l'homme', 79 *Rec. des cours* 241–367 (1951).

—— 'Twenty Years after the Universal Declaration', 8 *Int'l Commission of Jurists Rev.* 1–16 (1967).

—— 'De la place faite aux devoirs de l'individu dans la Déclaration universelle des droits de l'homme', in *Mélanges offerts à Polys Modinos: Problèmes des droits de l'homme et de l'unification européenne* 479–88 (Pedone, Paris, 1968).

—— 'Looking Back on the Universal Declaration of 1948', 15 *Rev. of Contemp. L.* 13–26 (1968).

CHANDRA, S., *Individual's Petition in International Law* (Deep & Deep Publications, New Delhi, 1985).

CHAKRAVARTI, R., *Human Rights and the United Nations* (Progressive Publishers, Calcutta, 1958).

CHATTERJIE, R., 'The United Nations', in R. J. Vincent (ed.), *Foreign Policy and Human Rights: Issues and Responses*, 227–42 (Cambridge UP, Cambridge, 1986).

CLARK, R. S., *A United Nations High Commissioner for Human Rights* (Martinus Nijhoff, The Hague, 1972).

—— 'The United Nations and Religious Freedom', 10 *NYUJ Int'l L. & Pol.* 197–220 (1978).

—— 'Human Rights and the United Nations High Commissioner for Refugees', 10 *Int'l J. Legal Info.* 287–307 (1982).

—— and NEVAS, L., 'U.N. and Human Rights: Some Modest Proposals', 59 *ABAJ* 1393–7 (1973).

—— —— 'First Twenty-Five Years of the Universal Declaration of Human Rights—and the Next', 48 *Conn. Bus. J.* 111–60 (1974).

CLAYDON, J., 'The Treaty Protection of Religious Rights: UN Draft Convention on the Elimination of all Forms of Intolerance and of Discrimination Based on Religion or Belief', 12 *Santa Clara L. Rev.* 403–23 (1972).

COHEN, B., 'Human Rights under the United Nations Charter', 14 *Law & Contemp. Prob.* 430–7 (1949).

COHEN, C. P., 'Elasticity of Obligation and the Drafting of the Convention on the Rights of the Child', 3 *Conn. J. of Int'l L.* 71–109 (1987).

COHEN, R., 'International Covenant on Civil and Political Rights', *Int'l Probs.* 38–49 (1968).

COLARD, D., 'Les Droits de l'homme trente ans après la Déclaration universelle', 31 *Stud. Diplomatica* 555–74 (1978).

COLLIARD, L., 'L'Adoption par l'Assemblée Générale des Nations Unies de la Déclaration sur le droit au développement', 33 *Ann. français de droit int'l* 614–28 (1987).

Comment, 'The International Human Rights Treaties: Some Problems of Policy and Interpretation', 126 *U. Pa. L. Rev.* 886–929 (1978).

Commission to Study the Organization of Peace, *The United Nations and Human Rights* (Oceana Publications, New York, 1968).

CONFORTI, B., 'Prolifération organique, prolifération normative et crise des Nations Unies: Réflexions d'un juriste', in D. Bardonnet (ed.), *The Adaptation of Structures and Methods at the United Nations* 153–70 (Martinus Nijhoff, Boston, 1986).

Consultative Council of Jewish Organizations, *A United Nations Attorney-General or High Commissioner for Human Rights: A Memorandum Submitted to the Commission on Human Rights* (Consultative Council Of Jewish Organizations, New York, 1950).

CRAWFORD, J. (ed.), *The Rights of Peoples* (Clarendon Press, Oxford, 1988).

DANELIUS, H., 'The United Nations Fund for Torture Victims: The First Years of Activity', 8 *Hum. Rts.* 294–305 (1986).

DAVIES, P. (ed.), *Human Rights* (Routledge, London, 1988).

DESCHÊNES, J., 'Variations sur le thème des droits humains à L'ONU', *Canadian Hum. Rts. YB* 159–84 (1987).

DETZNER, J. A., 'Utilización de mecanismos internacionales en la protección de los derechos Humanos: El caso chileno', 6 *Rev. Inst. Interam. de derechos hum.* 3–21 (1987).

DÍAZ MULLER, L., *América latina: Relaciones internacionales y derechos humanos* (Fondo de Cultura Económica, Mexico, 1986).

—— 'El derecho al desarrollo y los derechos humanos', 4 *Rev. Inst. Interam. de derechos hum.* 5–13 (1986).

DIMITRIJEVIC, V., 'International Supervision over Respect for Human Rights', 38 *Rev. of Int'l Aff.* 29–31 (1987).

DINU, M., 'The Role of the United Nations Organization in the Efforts for Finding a Solution to the Problem of the Palestinian People: Romanian Positions and Proposals', 17 *Rev. roum. d'ét. int'l* 271–87 (1983).

DONNELLY, J., 'International Human Rights: A Regime Analysis', 40 *Int'l Org.* 599–642 (1986).

—— 'Human Rights: The Impact of International Action', 43 *Int'l J.* 241–63 (1988).

—— 'Human Rights at the United Nations, 1955–85: The Question of Bias', 32 *Int'l Stud. Q.* 275–303 (1988).

—— and HOWARD, R. E. (eds.), *International Handbook of Human Rights* (Greenwood Press, New York, 1987).

—— and HOWARD, R. E., 'Assessing National Human Rights Performance', 10 *Hum.*

Rts. Q. 214–48 (1988).

DORE, I. I., 'United Nations Measures to Combat Racial Discrimination: Progress and Problems in Retrospect', 10 *Den. J. Int'l L. & Pol.* 299–330 (1981).

DUPUY, R., 'La France devant les droits de l'homme à l'Organisation des Nations Unies', 5 *Rev. des droits de l'homme* 52–78 (1972).

EGGERS, W., *Die Staatenbeschwerde* (Duncker & Humblot, Berlin, 1978).

EL-SHEIK, I. A. B., 'International Implementation of the International Covenants on Human Rights', Ph.D. thesis (Cairo Univ., 1984).

ELLES, D. L., 'Aliens and Activities of the United Nations in the Field of Human Rights', 7 *Rev. des droits de l'homme* 291–320 (1974).

EMPELL, M., *Die Kompetenzen des UN-Menschenrechtsausschusses im Staatenberichtsverfahren: Art. 40 des Internationales Paktes über bürgerliche und politische Rechte* (Peter Lang, New York, 1987).

ERMACORA, F., 'Human Rights and Domestic Jurisdiction: Art. 2, Sec. 7 of the United Nations Charter', 124 *Rec. des cours* 371–481 (1968).

—— 'Zu den Menschenrechtspakten der Vereinten Nationen', 16 *Vereinte Nationen* 133–9 (1968).

—— 'Partiality and Impartiality of Human Rights Inquiry Commissions of International Organizations', in *René Cassin: Amicorum Discipulorumque Liber*, i. 64 (Pedone, Paris, 1969).

—— *Menschenrechte in der sich wandelnden Welt: Historische Entwicklung der Menschenrechte und Grundfreiheiten* (Vienna, Der Osterreichischen Akademie der Wissenschaften, 1974).

—— 'UN and Human Rights in Chile', 1 *Hum. Rts. Rev.* 145–55 (1976).

—— 'Uber das Kumulationsverbot in Menschenrechtsverfahren', in P. Fisher, P. Kock, and A. Verdross (eds.), *Volkerrecht und Rechtsphilosophie Internationale Festschrift für Stephen Verosa* (1980).

—— *Theory und Praxis: Die Verwirklichung der Menschenrechte in Afrika und im Nahen Osten* (Vienna, Der Osterreichischen Akademie der Wissenschaften, 1983).

—— 'The Protection of Minorities before the United Nations', 182 *Rec. des cours* 247–370 (1983).

—— 'Die Menschenrechte im Rahmen der Vereinten Nationen', 19 *Aus. Pol. & Zeitgeschichte* 3–20 (1986).

ETRA, A., 'International Protection of Human Rights: The Proposal for a UN High Commissioner', 5 *Colum. J. Transnat'l L.* 150–8 (1966).

FALK, R. A., 'Responding to Severe Violations', in J. Dominguez, N. Rodley, B. Wood, and R. Falk (eds.), *Enhancing Global Human Rights* 207–57 (McGraw-Hill, New York, 1979).

FARER, T. J., 'The United Nations and Human Rights: More than a Whimper, Less than a Roar', 9 *Hum. Rts. Q.* 550–86 (1987).

—— 'Human Rights in Law's Empire: The Jurisprudence War', 85 *Am. J. Int'l L.* 117–27 (1991).

FAWCETT, J. E. S., 'Role of the United Nations in the Protection of Human Rights—Is it Misconceived?', in A. Eide, and A. Schou (eds.), *International Protection of Human Rights* 95–102 (Almquist and Wiksell, Stockholm, 1969).

FERGUSON, J. A., 'The Third World', in R. J. Vincent (ed.), *Foreign Policy and Human Rights: Issues and Responses* 203–26 (Cambridge UP, Cambridge, 1986).

FISEK, H., 'Les Droits de l'homme et l'Organisation des Nations Unies', in I. Kufuradi (ed.), *The Philosophical Foundations of Human Rights* (Hecettepe University, Ankara, 1982).

FIX ZAMUDIO, H., 'A Global Survey of Governmental Institutions to Protect Civil and Political Rights', 13 *Den. J. Int'l L. & Pol.* 17–52 (1983).

FLORETTA, H., and OHLINGER, T., *Die Menschenrechtspakte der Vereinten Nationen* (Braumuller, Vienna, 1978).

FONSAR BELLOCH, E., 'El derecho internacional de protección del menor: El Consejo de Europa y la Organización de las Naciones Unidas', 11 *documentación jurídica* 109–45 (1984).

FORSYTHE, D., 'The United Nations and Human Rights, 1945–1985', 100 *Pol. Sci. Q.* 249–69 (1985).

—— 'The Politics of Efficacy: The United Nations and Human Rights', in L. S. Finkelstein (ed.), *Politics in the United Nations System*, 246–73 (Duke Univ. Press, Durham, 1988).

—— 'The United States, the United Nations, and Human Rights', in M. P. Karns, and K. A. Mingst (eds.), *The United States and Multilateral Institutions: Patterns of Changing Instrumentality and Influence*, 261–88 (Unwin Hyman, Boston, 1990).

—— *The Internationalization of Human Rights* (Lexington Books, Lexington, Mass., 1991).

FRAMBACH, R., 'Menschenrechtsfragen in der UNO 1985/86', 40 *Neue Justiz* 310–12 (1986).

—— 'Menschenrechtsfragen in der UNO 1986/87', 41 *Neue Justiz* 356–8 (1987).

FRANCK, T., 'Of Gnats and Camels: Is there a Double Standard at the United Nations?', 78 *Am. J. Int'l L.* 811–33 (1984).

FRANKEL, M. E., 'International Human Rights: Who Cares?', 57 *NY St. BJ* 12–15 (1985).

GANJI, M., *International Protection of Human Rights* (Droz, Geneva, 1962).

GANSHOF VAN DER MEERSCH, W., 'Quarantième anniversaire de la Déclaration universelle des droits de l'homme', 107 *J. des tribunaux* 697–9 (1988).

GARMENT, L., 'Majoritarianism at the United Nations and Human Rights', in D. Sidorsky (ed.), *Essays on Human Rights: Contemporary Issues and Jewish Perspectives* (Jewish Publication Society of America, Philadelphia, 1979).

GIBNEY, M. (ed.), *World Justice: U.S. Courts and International Human Rights* (Westview Press, Boulder, Colo., 1991).

GOLSONG, M., 'Implementation of International Protection of Human Rights', 110 *Rec. des cours* 1–151 (1963).

GÓMEZ DEL PRADO, J. L., 'Órganos y mecanismos internacionales de supervisión establecidos por las convenciones de las Naciones Unidas sobre derechos humanos', 6 *Rev. Inst. Interam. de derechos hum.* 21–46 (1987).

GONZALES, T. D., 'Political Sources of Procedural Debates in the United Nations: Structural Impediment to Implementation of Human Rights', 13 *NYUJ Int'l L. & Pol.* 427–72 (1981).

GONZÁLEZ CAMPOS, J. D., 'The Protection of Human Rights in the United Nations', in *Twenty Years of the United Nations 1946–1966* (Tecnos, Madrid, 1966) (in Spanish).

GOOLSBY, R. H., 'Progress Report on United Nation Human Rights Activities to

Protect Prisoners', 7 *Ga. J. Int'l & Comp. L.* 467–76 (1977).

GORMLEY, W. P., 'The Relevance of the Universal Declaration to Emerging Human Rights Protection at the International and Regional Levels: The Common Standard of Mankind', 76 *Am. Soc. Int'l L. Proc.* 299 (1982).

GOSSMER, R., 'The United Nations and Human Rights', 23 *Blatter für deutsche & int'l Pol.* 33–47 (1978) (in German).

GRAEFRATH, B., 'The Promotion of Human Rights: A Universal Task of the United Nations', 9 *German Foreign Pol.* 372–84 (1970).

—— 'Détente and Human Rights: On Some Results of the 30th UN General Assembly', 2 *GDR Committee Hum. Rts. Bull.* 3–17 (1976).

—— 'On The Sixth Version of the Proposal for A High Commissioner for Human Rights', 4 *GDR Committee Hum. Rts. Bull.* 26–42 (1978).

—— 'The Application of International Human Rights Standards to States with Different Economic, Social and Cultural Systems', *UN Bull. Hum. Rts.* 7–16 (Special Issue, Human Rights Day 1985).

GRAF, N., 'Unteilbarkeit der Menschenrechte—ein Neuer Anlauf in der UNO', 40 *Neue Justiz* 181–3 (1986).

GREEN, J. F., *The United Nations and Human Rights* (Brookings Institution, Washington, DC, 1956).

—— 'Changing Approaches to Human Rights: The United Nations, 1954 and 1974', 12 *Tex. Int'l LJ* 223–38 (1977).

GREEN, L. C., 'Institutional Protection of Human Rights', 2 *Cahiers de droit* (Quebec) 547–74 (1987).

GREENBERG, J., 'Race, Sex and Religious Discrimination in International Law', in T. Meron (ed.), *Human Rights in International Law: Legal and Policy Issues* 307–43 (Clarendon Press, Oxford, 1984).

GRIEF, N. J., 'The International Protection of Human Rights: Standard-Setting and Enforcement by the United Nations and the Council of Europe', 16 *Bracton LJ* 41–65 (1983).

GROS ESPIELL, H., 'En torno al derecho a la libre determinación de los pueblos', 3 *An. de derecho int'l* 49–74 (1979).

—— 'El derecho a la libre determinación de los pueblos y los derechos humanos', in 1 *An. de derecho int'l* 129–46 (1981).

—— 'Las Naciones Unidas y los derechos humanos' 40 *Rev. de la Facultad de Derecho de la Universidad Complutense* 75–106 (1987).

GUYOMAR, G., 'Nations Unies et organisations régionales dans la protection des droits de l'homme', 68 *Rev. gen. du droit int'l pub.* 687–707 (1964).

HAEDRICH, M., 'Die Einheit der Menschenrechte—ein zentrales Thema der Vereinten Nationen', 41 *Neue Justiz* 15–18 (1987).

HAEGENDOREN, G. VAN., 'International Election Monitoring', 20 *Belgian Rev. of Int'l L.* 86–123 (1987).

HALDERMAN, J., 'Advancing Human Rights through the United Nations', 43 *Law & Contemp. Prob.* 275–88 (1979).

HALPERN, P., 'Activities of the UN in the Field of Human Rights', 79 *NY St. BA Bull.* 156–70 (1954).

HANNUM, H. (ed.), *Guide to International Human Rights Practice* (Univ. of Pennsylvania Press, Philadelphia, 1984).

—— 'International Law and Cambodian Genocide: The Sounds of Silence', 11 *Hum. Rts. Q.* 82–138 (1989).

HASSAN, K., 'Human Rights and the UN', 27 *Pakistan Horizon* 66–77 (1974).

HASSAN, P., 'The International Bill of Human Rights', 26 *Pakistan Horizon* 28–42 (1973).

—— 'The Word "Arbitrary" as used in the Universal Declaration of Human Rights: "Illegal" or "Unjust"?', 10 *Harv. Int'l LJ* 225–62 (1969).

HASSAN, T., 'Human Rights in the Implementation Phase: A Comparative Study of International Instruments', 30 *Pakistan Horizon* 3–26 (1977).

HAUSER, R. E., 'Foreword: Universal Declaration of Human Rights', 11 *Colum. J. Transnat'l L.* 1–13 (1972).

—— 'UN and Human Rights: A Long and Winding Road', 8 *Vista* 81–3 (1972).

HAZARD, J. N., 'The Soviet Union and a World Bill of Rights', 47 *Colum. L. Rev.* 1095–117 (1947).

HAZZARD, S., 'How the UN Betrays its Own Staff', 9 *Hum. Rts.* 20–3 (1980).

HENDERSON, C., 'Human Rights and Regimes: A Bibliographical Essay', 10 *Hum. Rts. Q.* 525–43 (1988).

HENKIN, L., 'The United Nations and Human Rights', 2 *Int'l Org.* 504–17 (1965).

—— 'The Constitution, Treaties, and International Human Rights', 116 *U. Pa. L. Rev.* 1095–132 (1968).

—— 'The International Bill of Rights: The Universal Declaration and the Covenants', in R. Bernhardt, and J. A. Jolowitz (eds.), *International Enforcement of Human Rights* 1–20 (Springer-Verlag, Berlin, 1987).

—— *The Age of Rights* (Columbia University Press, New York, 1990).

HERNDL, K., 'Die Vereinten Nationen und die Verwirklichung der Menschenrechte', 35 *Die Vereinten Nationen & Oesterreich* 21–32 (1986).

—— 'The Role of the United Nations in the Development of Human Rights', 2 *UN Bull. Hum. Rts.* 1–6 (1986).

—— 'Recent Developments Concerning United Nations Fact-Finding in the Field of Human Rights', in N. P. Engel (ed.), *Fortschritt im Bewusstsein der Grundund Menschenrechte*, 1–36 (Springer-Verlag, Strasburg, 1988).

HEVENER, N. K., 'Drafting the Human Rights Covenants: An Exploration of the Relationship Between U.S. Participation and Non-Ratification', 148 *World Aff.* 233–44 (1986).

HIGGINS, R., *The Development of International Law through the Political Organs of the United Nations* (Oxford UP, Oxford, 1963).

—— 'Technical Assistance for Human Rights: A New Approach to an Old Problem', 19 *World Today (London)* 174–80 (1963).

—— 'Compliance with the United Nations Decisions on Peace and Security and Human Rights', in S. M. Schwebel (ed.), *The Effectiveness of International Decisions* (Oceana Publications, New York, 1971).

—— 'Derogations under Human Rights Treaties', 48 *Brit. YB Int'l L.* 281–320 (1979).

—— 'The United Nations: Still a Force for Peace', 52 *Mod. L. Rev.* 1–21 (1989).

HOARE, S., 'Recent Developments in the United Nations Concerning the Protection of Human Rights', in *Rene Cassin: Amicorum Discipulorumque Liber*, i. 101 (Pedone, Paris, 1969).

Humphrey, J. P., 'Draft International Declaration of Human Rights', 26 *Canadian. B. Rev.* 1106–12 (1948).

—— 'United Nations and Human Rights', 11 *How. LJ* 373–8 (1965).

—— 'The UN Charter and the Universal Declaration of Human Rights', in E. Luard (ed.), *The International Protection of Human Rights*, 39–58 (Praeger, New York, 1967).

—— 'Human Rights and the United Nations', 9 *Int'l Commission of Jurists Rev.* 1–13 (1968).

—— 'United Nations High Commissioner for Human Rights: The Birth of an Initiative', 11 *Canadian YB Int'l L.* 220–5 (1973).

—— 'International Bill of Rights: Scope and Implementation', 17 *Wm. & M. L Rev.* 527–41 (1976).

—— 'Implementation of International Human Rights', 24 *NYL Sch. L. Rev.* 31–61 (1978).

—— 'The Just Requirements of Morality, Public Order and the General Welfare in a Democratic Society', in R. S. J. MacDonald, and J. P. Humphrey (eds.), *The Practice of Freedom* (Butterworths, Toronto, 1979).

—— 'The Universal Declaration of Human Rights: Its History, Impact and Judicial Character', in B. G. Ramcharan (ed.), *Human Rights: Thirty Years after the Universal Declaration* 21–37 (Martinus Nijhoff, The Hague, 1979).

—— *Human Rights and the United Nations: A Great Adventure* (Transnational Publishers, Dobbs Ferry, NY, 1984).

—— 'Political and Related Rights', in T. Meron (ed.), *Human Rights in International Law: Legal and Policy Issues* 171–203 (Clarendon Press, Oxford, 1984).

—— 'The United Nations Human Rights Advisory Programme', 1 *UN Bull. Hum. Rts.* 38–41 (1986).

Huston, J., 'Human Rights Enforcement Issues of the United Nations Conference on International Organization', 53 *Iowa L. Rev.* 272–90 (1967).

Imai, T., 'Guarantee of Human Rights under the Charter of the United Nations', 39 *Osaka L. Rev.* 25 (1961).

International Commission of Jurists, *Gross Violations of Human Rights: A Practical Guide for Nongovernmental Organizations Wishing to File Communications with the United Nations* (International Commission of Jurists, Geneva, 1973).

—— 'The Convention on the Rights of the Child: Time for a New Look at Implementation', 36 *Int'l Commission of Jurists Rev.* 30–4 (1986).

—— and Rädda Barnen, *UN Assistance for Human Rights: An Analysis of Present Programs and Proposals for Future Development of the UN Advisory Services, Technical Assistance, and Information Activities in the Field of Human Rights* (International Commission of Jurists, Stockholm, 1988).

Irigoin, B. J., *La protección de los derechos del hombre en las organizaciones internacionales* (Instituto de Estudios Internacionales, Univ. de Chile, Santiago, 1988).

Janca, D., 'U.N. Legal Activity in the Field of Human Rights', *Int'l Probs.* 41–57 (1969).

Jessup, P. C., 'The Conquering March of an Idea', 21 *Dep. St. Bull.* 432–5 (1949).

Jha, S. K., 'The United Nations and Human Rights', 29 *India Q.* 239–49 (1973).

Jhabvala, F. 'The Soviet-Bloc's View of the Implementation of Human Rights Accords', 7 *Hum. Rts. Q.* 461–91 (1985).

JIMÉNEZ DE ARECHAGA, E., 'The Background to Article 17 of the Universal Declaration', 8 *Int'l Commission of Jurists Rev.* 34–9 (1967).

JOHNSON, L., 'The United Nations System for the Protection of Human Rights', 20 *Ga. J. Int'l & Comp. L.* 363–76 (1990).

JOHNSON, M. G., 'The Contributions of Eleanor and Franklin Roosevelt to the Development of International Protection for Human Rights", 9 *Hum. Rts. Q.* 19–48 (1987).

KARTASHKIN, V. A., 'Human Rights and the Modern World: Thirty Years of the Universal Declaration of Human Rights', 1 *Int'l Aff.* (Moscow) 48–56 (1979).

KAUFMAN, N. H., and WHITEMAN, D., 'Opposition to Human Rights Treaties in the United States Senate: The Legacy of the Bricker Amendment', 10 *Hum. Rts. Q.* 309–37 (1988).

KEITH, K. J. (ed.), *Essays on Human Rights* (Sweet and Maxwell, New Zealand, 1968).

KHARE, S., *Human Rights and United Nations* (Metropolitan Book Co., New Delhi, 1977).

KHOL, A., *Der Menschenrechtskatalog der Volkerrechtsgemeinschaft—Die Menschenrechtskonventionen der Vereinten Nationen* (Braumuller, Vienna, 1968).

KIMMINICH, O., *Der Internationale Rechtsstatus des Fluchtlings* (Heymanns, Cologne, 1962).

KIZILBASH, M. H., 'United Nations and Human Rights: A Failure Report', 27 *Pakistan Horizon* 50–60 (1974).

KNITEL, H. G., 'La Protection du détenu et notamment du détenu politique, en droit international des droits de l'homme', 10 *Rev. des droits de l'homme* 39–96 (1977).

KOREY, W., 'The Key to Human Rights: Implementation', 570 *Int'l Conciliation* 1–70 (1968).

—— 'UN Human Rights: Illusion and Reality', 42 *Freedom at Issue* (New York) 27–34 (1977).

KUBOTA, Y., 'Consideration of the Relationship between Scientific and Technological Developments and Human Rights Fora', 56 *Nordic J. Int'l L.* 334–56 (1987).

KUNZ, P., 'United Nations Declaration of Human Rights', 43 *Am. J. Int'l L.* 316–23 (1949).

LABRADOR, A., 'Universal Declaration of Human Rights', 28 *Philippines LJ* 830–6 (1953).

LA CHAPELLE, P. DE., *La Declaration universelle des droits de l'homme et le catholicisme* (Librairie Générale de Droit et de Jurisprudence, Paris, 1967).

LALIGANT, M., 'Le Projet de Convention des Nations Unies sur l'élimination de toutes les formes d'intolerance religieuse', 5 *Rev. belge de droit int'l* 175–206 (1969).

LAMBERT, P., 'Quarante ans après . . .', 107 *J. des tribunaux* 706–8 (1988).

LAMBORN, L. L., 'The United Nations Declaration on Victims: Incorporating "Abuse of Power"', 19 *Rutgers LJ* 59–85 (1987).

LATTANZI, F. *Garanzie dei diritti dell'uomo nel diritto internazionale generale* (Giuffre, Milan, 1983).

LAUREN, P. G., 'First Principles of Racial Equality: History and the Politics and Diplomacy of Human Rights Provisions in the United Nations Charter', 5 *Hum. Rts. Q.* 1–26 (1983).

LAUTERPACHT, E., 'Some Concepts of Human Rights', 11 *Harv. Int'l LJ* 264–74 (1965).

LAUTERPACHT, H., *An International Bill of the Rights of Man* (Columbia UP, New York, 1945).

—— 'Universal Declaration of Human Rights', 25 *Brit. YB Int'l L.* 354–81 (1948).

—— *International Law and Human Rights* (Stevens, London, 1950).

LEACH, R. A., 'The Domestic Enforcement of the Law of Nations: A Proposed International Human Rights Organization', 15 *Calif. W. Int'l LJ* 705–33 (1985).

LEARY, V., 'When does the Implementation of International Human Rights Constitute Interference into the Essentially Domestic Affairs of a State?—The Interactions of Articles 2(7), 55 and 56 of the Charter', in J. Tuttle (ed.), *International Human Rights Law and Practice: The Roles of the United Nations, the Private Sector, the Government, and their Lawyers* 15–21 American Bar Association, Chicago, 1978).

LEBLANC, L. J., 'The United Nations Genocide Convention and Political Groups: Should the United States Propose an Amendment?', 13 *Yale J. Int'l L.* 268–95 (1988).

—— *The United States and the Genocide Convention* (Duke University Press, Durham, NC, 1991).

LELOUP, P., 'L'ONU au service des droits de l'homme', *Rev. de l'action populaire* 118–22 (1964).

LERNER, N., 'Toward a Draft Declaration against Religious Intolerance and Discrimination', 11 *Israel YB Hum. Rts.* 82–105 (1981).

LILLICH, R. B., and NEFF, S. C., 'The Treatment of Aliens and International Human Rights Norms: Overlooked Developments at the U.N.', 21 *German YB Int'l L.* 97–118 (1978).

—— 'The Paris Minimum Standards of Human Rights Norms in a State of Emergency', 79 *Am. J. Int'l L.* 1072–81 (1985).

—— 'Civil Rights', in T. Meron (ed.), *Human Rights in International Law: Legal and Policy Issues* 115–70 (Clarendon Press, Oxford, 1986).

LINIGER-GOUMAZ, M., *ONU et dictatures: De la démocratie et des droits de l'homme* (L'Harmattan, Paris, 1984).

LISKOFSKY, S., 'The United Nations and Human Rights: Alternative Approaches', in D. Sidorsky (ed.), *Essays on Human Rights: Contemporary Issues and Jewish Perspectives* (Jewish Publishing Society of America, Philadelphia, 1979).

LORD, S., 'Individual Enforcement of Obligations Arising under the United Nations Charter', 19 *Santa Clara L. Rev.* 195–216 (1979).

LOWENSTEIN, A., 'The United Nations and the Human Rights Issue', 43 *Law & Contemp. Prob.* 268–74 (1979).

LUARD, E., 'Promotion of Human Rights by U.N. Political Bodies', in E. Luard (ed.), *The International Protection of Human Rights* 132–59 (Praeger, New York, 1967).

MACBRIDE, S., 'The Meaning of Human Rights Year', 8 *Int'l Commission of Jurists Rev.* pp. iii–xi (1967).

—— 'Strengthening of International Machinery for the Protection of Human Rights', in A. Eide and A. Schou (eds.), *International Protection of Human Rights. Proceedings of the Seventh Nobel Symposium, Oslo, September 25–27, 1967*, 149–65 (Almquist & Wiksell, Stockholm, 1968).

MCCARTHY, T., 'Human Rights and Internal Conflicts: Some Aspects of The United Nations Approach', 13 *Ga. J. Int'l & Comp. L.* 335–9 (1983).

MACCHESNEY, B., 'International Protection of Human Rights in the United Nations',

47 *Nw. U. L Rev.* 198–222 (1952).
—— 'United Nations Machinery for Implementing Human Rights', 62 *Am. J. Int'l L.* 901–12 (1968).
MacDonald, R., 'United Nations High Commissioner for Human Rights', 5 *Canadian YB Int'l L.* 84–117 (1967).
—— 'United Nations High Commissioner for Human Rights: The Decline and Fall of an Initiative', 10 *Canadian YB Int'l L.* 40–64 (1972).
—— 'The United Nations and the Promotion of Human Rights', in R. MacDonald, D. M. Johnson, and G. L. Morris (eds.), *The International Law and Policy of Human Welfare* (Sijthoff and Noordhoff, Alphen aan den Rijn, 1978).
McDougal, M. S., and Bebr, G., 'Human Rights in the United Nations', 58 *Am. J. Int'l L.* 603–41 (1964).
—— Lasswell, H. D., and Chen, L. C., 'Human Rights and World Public Order: A Framework for Policy-Oriented Inquiry', 63 *Am. J. Int'l L.* 237–69 (1969).
Malik, C., 'The Drafting of the Universal Declaration of Human Rights', 1 *UN Bull. Hum. Rts.* 18–26 (1986).
Mansuy, G., 'Un médiateur des Nations Unies pour les droits de l'homme', 6 *Rev. des droits de l'homme* 235–59 (1973).
Mantzoulinou, A. D., 'Protection of Human Rights within the Framework of the United Nations', 20 *Ncon Dekaion* 461 (1964).
Marie, J. B., 'Les Pactes internationaux relatifs aux droits de l'homme confirment-ils l'inspiration de la Déclaration universelle?', 3 *Rev. des droits de l'homme* 397–425 (1970).
—— 'Relations between Peoples' Rights and Human Rights: Semantic and Methodological Distinctions', 7 *Hum. Rts. LJ* 195–204 (1986).
Marinic, D., 'The United Nations and the Protection and Advancement of Human Rights', 31 *Rev. of Int'l Aff.* 9–12 (1980).
Marks, S., 'UNESCO and Human Rights: The Implementation of Rights Relating to Education, Science, Culture and Communication', 13 *Tex. Int'l LJ* 35–67 (1977).
Matas, D., 'Domestic Implementation of International Human Rights Agreements', *Canadian YB Hum. Rts.* 91–117 (1987).
Mbaye, K., 'L'Organisation des Nations Unies et les droits de l'homme', in D. Bardonnet (ed.), *The Adaptation of Structures and Methods at the United Nations* 289–318 (Martinus Nijhoff, Boston, 1986).
Meibner, F., *Die Menschenrechtsbeschwerde vor den Vereinten Nationen* (Nomos, Baden Baden, 1976).
Meissner, E., *Human Rights Grievances before the United Nations* (Nomos, Baden Baden, 1976) (in German).
Meléndez, F., *La suspensión de los derechos fundamentales en el derecho internacional convencional: Aspectos comparativos* (IDHUCA, Univ. Centroamericana José Simeón Canas, San Salvador, 1987).
Meron, T., 'Norm Making and Supervision in International Human Rights: Reflections on Institutional Order', 76 *Am. J. Int'l L.* 754–78 (1982).
—— 'Reform of Lawmaking in the United Nations: The Human Rights Instance', 79 *Am. J. Int'l L.* 664–81 (1985).
—— *Human Rights in Internal Strife: Their International Protection* (Grotius, Cambridge, 1987).

—— *Human Rights Law-Making in the United Nations: A Critique Of Instruments and Processes* (Oxford UP, New York, 1987).

—— *Human Rights and Humanitarian Norms as Customary Law* (Clarendon Press, Oxford, 1989).

MICHALSKA, A., 'Universalisme et régionalisme dans la protection internationale des droits de l'homme', 7 *Pol. YB Int'l L.* 169–208 (1975).

—— 'Control Competences of U.N. Organs in Connection with Communications about Violations of Human Rights', *Stud. Prawnicze* 3–39 (1984).

MILLER, R., 'United Nations Fact-Finding Missions in the Field of Human Rights', *Australian YB Int'l L. 1970–1973* 40–50 (1975).

MIRKINE-GUETZEVITCH, B., 'Quelques problèmes de la mise en œuvre de la Déclaration universelle des droits de l'homme", 86/3 *Rec. des cours* 255–375 (1954).

MOJSOV, I., 'The Human Rights Struggle: Thirty Years of the Universal Declaration of Human Rights', 29 *Rev. of Int'l Aff.* 1–4 (1978).

MORSINK, J., 'The Philosophy of the Universal Declaration', 6 *Hum. Rts. J.* 309–34 (1984).

MOSKOWITZ, M., *Human Rights and World Order: The Struggle for Human Rights in the United Nations* (Oceana Publications, 1958).

—— *The Politics and Dynamics of Human Rights* (Oceana Publications, New York, 1968).

—— 'The Meaning of International Concern with Human Rights', in *René Cassin: Amicorum Discipulorumque Liber*, (Pedone, Paris, 1969).

—— *International Concern with Human Rights* (Oceana Publications, New York, 1974).

—— 'Whither the United Nations Human Rights Program?', 6 *Israel YB Hum. Rts.* 81–90 (1976).

MOSLER, H., 'Protection of Human Rights by International Legal Procedure', 52 *Ga. LJ* 800–23 (1964).

MOURGEON, J., 'Les Pactes internationaux relatifs aux droits de l'homme', *Ann. français de droit int'l* 326–63 (1967).

MUELLER, G. O. W., 'Crime Prevention as a Human Right: The Task of the United Nations', in *Festschrift für Dietrich Oehler zum 70. Geburtstag* 517–24 (Berlin, 1985).

NANDA, V. P., 'Implementation of Human Rights by the United Nations and Regional Organizations', 21 *De Paul L. Rev.* 307–36 (1971).

NARTOWSKI, A. S., 'Human Rights in the United Nations System: Development Trends', in W. Morawiecki (ed.), 5 *Ann. polonais de droit int'l 1972–1973* (Polish Academy of Sciences, Warsaw, 1974).

NATH MUKHERJEE, S., 'Human Rights in India and in the U.N.', 11 *Law QJ of the Indian L. Inst.* 266–72 (1974).

NATH NAG, M., 'Universal Declaration of Human Rights', 12 *Law QJ of the Indian L. Inst.* 155–64 (1975).

NAYAR, M. G. K., 'Human Rights: The United Nations and United States Foreign Policy', 19 *Harv. Int'l LJ* 813–43 (1978).

NDIAYE, B., 'De l'individu et de sa collaboration avec les organismes internationaux de protection des droits de l'homme", *Ann. Afr.* 25–42 (1974).

NEAL, M., 'The United Nations and Human Rights', 489 *Int'l Conciliation* 113–76 (1953).

NEFF, S., 'An Evolving International Norm of Religious Freedom: Problems and Prospects', 7 *Calif. W. Int'l LJ* 543–90 (1977).

NEWMAN, F. C., 'Ombudsmen and Human Rights: The New UN Treaty Proposals', 34 *Univ. Chi. L. Rev.* 951–62 (1967).

—— 'Interpreting the Human Rights Clauses of the UN Charter', 5 *Rev. des droits de l'homme* 283–91 (1972).

NICKEL, J., *Making Sense of Human Rights: Philosophical Reflections on the Universal Declaration of Human Rights* (Univ. of California Press, Berkeley, Calif., 1987).

NIKKEN, P., 'Los derechos del niño, de los ancianos y de la mujer: Su protección internacional', 4 *Rev. Inst. Interam. de derechos hum.* 15–42 (1986).

—— *La protección internacional de los derechos humanos: Su desarrollo progresivo* (Instituto Interamericano de Derechos Humanos, Madrid, 1987).

NISET, J., 'Droits de l'homme, 25 ans après la Déclaration universelle', 89 *J. des tribunaux* 53–8 (1974).

NOLDE, O. F., 'Human Rights and the United Nations: Appraisal and Next Steps', 25 *Proc. Acad. Pol. Sci.* 171–8 (1953).

NOLL-WAGENFELD, M., 'Feasibility of Action of the United Nations for Human Rights Violations', 25 *Vereinte Nationen* 180–6 (1977) (in German).

NOTE, 'The International Declaration of Human Rights—The Proposed Treaty and Current Discussions about it and its Effects on American Government, State and Federal', 34 *Mass. LQ* 45–84 (1949).

—— 'The Universal Declaration of Human Rights', 8 *Int'l Commission of Jurists Rev.* 17–26 (1967).

—— 'The United Nations Human Rights Covenants, Problem of Ratification and Implementation', 62 *Am. Soc. Int'l L. Proc.* 83–123 (1968).

—— 'The Universal Declaration of Human Rights 1948–1968', 15 *Rev. of Contemp. L.* 9–162 (1968).

—— 'U.N. "Human Rights" Conventions', 1 *Int'l L.* 589–666 (1967).

—— 'UN High Commissioner for Human Rights: A Call for Support', 30 *Int'l Commission of Jurists Bull.* 1–7 (1967).

—— 'Preliminary Survey of Action to Further Human Rights in the Asian Region specifically by the United Nations through its Programme of Advisory Services in the Field of Human Rights', *Australian YB Int'l L. 1970–1973* (Oceana Publications, New York, 1975).

—— 'United Nations Standard Minimum Rules on the Treatment of Prisoners', 11 *Crim. L. Bull.* 637–46 (1975).

—— 'Report of Workshop on the Role of International Organizations', 7 *Colum. Hum. Rts. L. Rev.* 261–2 (1975).

—— 'Human Rights in the United Nations', 12 *Tex. Int'l LJ* 129–250 (1977).

NOWAK, M., 'UN-Ausschuss fur Menschenrechte—Rechtsprechungsbericht Juli 1984 bis Juli 1986', 13 *Europäische Grundrechte-Zeitschrift* 641–8 (1986).

OLIVER, C. T., 'The Treaty Power and National Foreign Policy as Vehicles for the Enforcement of Human Rights in the United Nations', 9 *Hofstra L. Rev.* 411–32 (1980).

OPSAHL, T., 'The Protection of Human Rights in the Council of Europe and in the United Nations', 26 *European YB* 94–118 (1978).

ORTIZ MARTÍN, G., 'Algunos aspectos del orden público y la soberanía relacionados con los tratados multilaterales sobre derechos humanos', 13 *Curso de derecho int'l* 151–8 (1987).

PADILLA, A., 'Universal Declaration of Human Rights: Expression of Past

Achievements and Future Aspirations', 37 *Philippines LJ* 739–47 (1962).

PAHLAVI, A., 'The International Conference on Human Rights', in R. N. Swift (ed.), *Annual Review of United Nations Affairs 1967–1968* (Oceana Publications, New York, 1969).

PARK, A. I., 'Human Rights and Basic Needs: Using International Human Rights Norms to Inform Constitutional Interpretation', 34 *UCLA L. Rev.* 1195–264 (1987).

PARTSCH, K. J., 'Religions—und Weltanschauungsfreiheit als Menschenrecht', 30 *Vereinte Nationen* 82–6 (1982).

—— 'Recent Developments in the Field of Peoples' Rights', 7 *Hum. Rts. LJ* 177–82 (1986).

PEDRONCINI, A. P., 'Droits de l'homme: Sur la thèse de l'indivisibilité', 1 *Rev. int'l de droit contemporain* 13–21 (1988).

PETRENKO, A., 'The Human Rights Provisions of the United Nations Charter', 9 *Manitoba L. J.* 53–92 (1978).

PIERSON-MATHY, P., 'Actions des Nations Unies contre l'apartheid', 7 *Rev. belge de droit int'l* 148–98 (1971).

POPESCU, T. R., 'The Significance of the Universal Declaration of Human Rights, Two Decades after its Adoption', 33 *Rev. roum. d'et. int'l* 11–124 (1968).

POSSER, D., 'How the United Nations Would Like to Protect Human Dignity', 22 *Vereinte Nationen* 1–27 (1974) (in German).

PREMONT, D., 'United Nations Procedures for the Protection of all Persons Subjected to any Form of Detention or Imprisonment', 20 *Santa Clara L. Rev.* 603–32 (1980).

QUINTANO RIPOLLES, A., 'La protección de los derechos humanos en lo universal y en lo regional O. N. U. y Consejo de Europa', XIV *Rev. española de derecho int'l* 537–51 (1961).

RABOSI, E. A., *La Carta Internacional de Derechos Humanos* (EUDEBA, Buenos Aires, 1987).

RAJAN, M. S., *United Nations and Domestic Jursdiction* (Asia Publishing House, Calcutta, 1961).

RAMCHARAN, B. G. (ed.), *Human Rights: Thirty Years after the Universal Declaration* (Martinus Nijhoff, The Hague, 1979).

—— 'Evaluating Human Rights Performance: Some Relevant Criteria', in *Human Rights: From Theory to Practice* (Centre for Applied Study in International Negotiations, Geneva, 1981).

—— (ed.), *International Law and Fact-Finding in the Field of Human Rights* (Martinus Nijhoff, The Hague, 1982).

—— (ed.), *The Right to Life* (Nijhoff, The Hague, 1985).

—— 'The Legal Status of the International Bill of Human Rights', 55 *Nordic J. Int'l L.* 366–83 (1986).

—— 'The Concept of Protection in the International Law of Human Rights', in *International Law at a Time of Perplexity: Essays in Honour of Shabtai Rosenne* (Martinus Nijhoff, Boston, 1989).

—— *The Concept and Present Status of International Protection of Human Rights: Forty Years after the Universal Declaration* (Martinus Nijhoff, Boston, 1989).

—— 'Strategies for the International Protection of Human Rights in the 1990s', 13 *Hum. Rts Q.* 155–69 (1991).

RANDALL, K. C., *Federal Courts and the International Human Rights Paradigm* (Duke University Press, Durham, NC, 1990).

RAUBE-WILSON, S., 'The New World Information and Communication Order and International Human Rights Law', 9 *BC Int'l & Comp. L. Rev.* 107–30 (1986).

REISMAN, M., 'Sovereignty and Human Rights in Contemporary, International Law', 84 *Am. J. Int'l L.* 866–76 (1990).

RITTERBAND, C., *Universeller Menschenrechtsschutz und volkerrechtliches Interventionsverbot* (Paul Haupt, Bern, 1982).

ROBERTSON, A. H., and MERRILLS, J., *Human Rights in the World: An Introduction to the Study of the International Protection of Human Rights* (St Martin's Press, New York, 3rd. edn., 1989).

ROBIN, M. A., 'Soviet Emigration Law and International Obligations under United Nations Instruments' 13 *J. Int'l L. & Econ.* 403–31 (1979).

ROBINSON, J., *Human Rights and Fundamental Freedoms in the Charter of the United Nations: A Commentary* (Institute of Jewish Affairs, New York, 1946).

RODLEY, N. S., 'United Nations and Human Rights in the Middle East", 38 *Social Research* 217–40 (1971).

—— 'Monitoring Human Rights by the UN System and Non-Governmental Organizations', in D. Kommers, and G. Loescher (eds.), *Human Rights and American Foreign Policy* (University of Notre Dame Press, Notre Dame, Ind., 1979).

—— *The Treatment of Prisoners Under International Law.* (Oxford UP, Oxford, 1986).

—— 'UN Action Procedures against 'Disappearances', Summary or Arbitrary Executions, and Torture', 8 *Rev. des droits de l'homme* 700–30 (1986).

—— 'Human Rights and Humanitarian Intervention: The Case Law of the World Court', 38 *Int'l & Comp. LO* 321–33 (1989).

ROOSEVELT, E., 'The Promise of Human Rights', 26 *For. Aff.* 470–7 (1948).

ROUSSEAU, C., 'Place de la Déclaration universelle des droits de l'homme dans la hiérarchie des actes juridiques', *Rev. gén. du droit int'l pub.* 661–3 (1987).

RYCROFT, R., 'United Nations High Commissioner for Human Rights: A Proposed International Government Control Agency', 4 *Rutgers Camden LJ* 237–59 (1973).

SAARIO, V. V., 'Nordic Initiatives in the Field of Human Rights in the United Nations and other International Organizations', 8 *Rev. des droits de l'homme* 95–111 (1975).

—— and HIGGINS, C. R., 'The United Nations and the International Protection of Human Rights: A Legal Analysis and Interpretation', 3 *Calif. W. Int'l LJ* 591–614 (1977).

SAKSENA, K. P., 'International Covenants on Human Rights', 15–16 *Indian YB. Int'l Aff.* 596–613 (1970).

SALZBERG, J. P., 'The Struggle for Human Rights in the UN and Regional Groups', 12 *War/Peace Report*, 16–21 (1973).

—— 'UN Prevention of Human Rights Violations: The Bangladesh Case', 27 *Int'l Org.* 115–27 (1973).

SANDIFER, D. V., 'New International Frontiers in Human Rights', 20 *Dep. St. Bull.* 258–63 (1949).

SANTOS, V. A., 'Study on Proposed International Court of Human Rights', 24 *Philadelphia LJ* 372 (1949)

SCALI, J., HOFFMAN, P., MOYNIHAN, D., and GARMENT, L., 'The United Nations and

Human Rights: The American Viewpoint', in W. S. Veenhoven (ed.), *Case Studies on Human Rights and Fundamental Freedoms: A World Survey*, v. 563–83 (Martinus Nijhoff, The Hague, 1976).

SCHACHTER, O., 'Charter and the Constitution: The Human Rights Provisions in American Law', 4 *Vand. L. Rev.* 643–59 (1951).

SCHECHTER, L. F., 'The Views of "Charterists" and 'Skeptics' on Human Rights in the World Legal Order: Two Wrongs Don't Make a Right', 9 *Hofstra L. Rev.* 357–98 (1981).

SCHAUMANN, W., 'International Legal Protection of Human Rights and Freedom: Their Realization through the United Nations', in E. Menzel (ed.), 10 *German YB Int'l L. 1967* (Vandenhoeck und Ruprecht, Göttingen, 1967).

SCHLUTER, B., 'The Domestic Status of the Human Rights Clauses of the United Nations Charter', 61 *Calif. L. Rev.* 110–64 (1973).

SCHOENBERG, H. O., 'The Implementation of Human Rights by the United Nations', 7 *Israel YB Hum. Rts.* 22–52 (1977).

SCHREIBER, M., 'Les Nations Unies et les droits de l'homme', 2 *Rev. des droits de l'homme* 95–112 (1969).

—— 'Les Tendances nouvelles de l'action des Nations Unies dans le domaine des droits de l'homme', in *René Cassin: Amicorum discipulorumque Liber*, i. 300 (Pedone, Paris, 1969).

—— 'Les Organisations non-gouvernementales et l'œuvre des Nations Unies dans le domaine de la protection des droits de l'homme', 25 *Synthèses* (Dordrecht) 58–63 (1970).

—— 'Réflexions à l'occasion de la commémoration du vingt-cinquième anniversaire de l'adoption de la Déclaration universelle des droits de l'homme', 34 *Ann. de droit* 189–200 (1974).

—— 'La Pratique récente des Nations Unies dans le domaine de la protection des droits de l'homme', 145 *Rec. des cours* 297–392 (1975).

SCHREUER, C., 'The Impact of International Institutions on the Protection of Human Rights in Domestic Courts', 4 *Israel YB Hum. Rts.* 60–88 (1974).

SCHWELB, E., 'The Influence of the Universal Declaration of Human Rights on International and National Law', 53 *Am. Soc. Int'l L. Proc.* 217–29 (1959).

—— *Human Rights and the International Community: The Roots and Growth of the Universal Declaration of Human Rights 1948–1963* (Quadrangle Books, Chicago, 1964).

—— 'United Nations and Human Rights', 11 *How. LJ* 356–72 (1965).

—— 'New Steps for the Enforcment of International Law through the United Nations', 13 *Archives des Volderrechts* (Tubingen) 14–36 (1966) (in German).

—— 'International Court of Justice and the Human Rights Clauses of the Charter', 66 *Am. J. Int'l L.* 337–51 (1972).

—— 'Interpretation of Human Rights Clauses by the International Court of Justice', in *Report of the Fifty-fifth Conference held at New York, August 21 to August 26, 1972* (Int'l Law Assoc., London, 1974).

—— and ALSTON, P., 'The Principal Institutions and other Bodies Founded under the Charter', in K. Vasak, and P. Alston (eds.), *International Dimensions of Human Rights*, 231–302 (Greenwood, Westport, Conn., 1982).

SCHWEBEL, S. M., 'Wars of Liberation as Fought in UN Organs', in J. N. Moore (ed.),

Law and Civil War in the Modern World (Johns Hopkins UP, Baltimore, 1974).

SCOBLE, K. M., and WISEBERG, L. S., 'Human Rights NGO's: Notes Towards Comparative Analysis', 9 *Rev. des droits de l'homme* 611–44 (1976).

SHITLOV, A. P., 'Rights and Their Guarantees: 30th Anniversary of the Universal Declaration of Human Rights', 12 *Socialism: Theory and Prac.* 60–7 (1978).

SIMSARIAN, J., 'United Nations Action on Human Rights in 1948', 20 *Rep. St. Bull.* 18–23 (1949).

SINGH, B., 'The Human Rights Covenant and Indian Social Policy', 26 *Indian J. of Soc. Work* 57–68 (1965).

SINGH, N., 'The Declaration of Human Rights and Customary International Law', in L. Singvi (ed.), *Horizons of Freedoms* (National Pub., Delhi, 1969).

—— *Enforcement of Human Rights in Peace and War and the Future of Humanity* (Martinus Nijhoff, Boston, 1986).

SKOLER, D. L., 'World Implementation of the United Nations Standard Minimum Rules for Treatment for Prisoners', 103 *Int'l L. & Econ.* 453–82 (1975).

SLUSNY, M., 'Quelques observations sur les systèmes de protection internationale des droits de l'homme', in *Mélanges offerts à Rolin, problèmes de droit des gens* (Pedone, Paris, 1964).

SOHN, L. B., 'Universal Declaration of Human Rights: A Common Standard of Achievement? The Status of the Universal Declaration in International Law', 8 *Int'l Commission of Jurists Rev.* 17–26 (1967).

—— 'A Short History of United Nations Documents on Human Rights', in C. M. Eichberger (ed.), *The United Nations and Human Rights: 18th Report of the Commission to Study the Organization of Peace* (Oceana Publications, New York, 1968).

—— 'Protection of Human Rights through International Legislation', in *René Cassin: Amicorum Discipulorumque Liber*, i. 440 (Pedone, Paris, 1969).

—— *The United Nations: The Next Twenty-Five Years* (Commission to Study the Organization of Peace, New York, 1969).

—— 'The Human Rights Law of the Charter', 12 *Tex. Int'l LJ* 129–40 (1977)

—— 'The Improvement of the UN Machinery on Human Rights', 23 *Int'l Stud. Q.* 186–215 (1979).

—— 'The International Law of Human Rights: A Reply to Recent Criticism', 9 *Hofstra L. Rev.* 347–56 (1981).

—— and BUERGENTHAL, T., *International Protection of Human Rights* (Bobbs-Merrill, Indianapolis, 1973).

SPIEGEL, W. E., 'Prior Consent and the United Nations Human Rights Instruments', in *Regulation of Transnational Communications* (Clark Boardman Co., New York, 1984).

SRNSKA, M., 'Comparisons between Universal and Regional Human Rights Conventions', *GDR Committee Hum. Rts. Bull.* 40–9 (1980).

STEPHEN, M., 'Natual Justice at the United Nations: The Rhodesia Case', 67 *Am. J. Int'l L.* 479–90 (1973).

STOTTER, C. W., 'Self-Executing Treaties and the Human Rights Provisions of the United Nations Charter: A Separation of Powers Problem', 25 *Buffalo L. Rev.* 773–86 (1976).

SUDRE, F., *Droit international et européen des droits de l'homme* (Presses universitaires de France, Paris, 1989).

SULLIVAN, D. J., 'Advancing the Freedom of Religion or Belief through the UN Declaration on the Elimination of Religious Intolerance and Discrimination', 82 *Am. J. Int'l L.* 487–520 (1988).

SZABO, I., 'The Legal Importance of the Declaration', 15 *Rev. Contemp. L.* 41–54 (1968).

—— 'La Portée juridique de la déclaration universelle', *Rev. de droit contemporain* 39–51 (1968).

TANBANDAHI, S., *A Muslim Commentary on the Universal Declaration of Human Rights* (Goulding, Guildford, 1970).

TAMM, H., 'Observance of Human Rights and Fundamental Freedoms in Bulgaria, Romania, and Hungary in Relation to the Peace Treaties and the UN Charter', 1 *Jus Gentium* 359–83 (1949).

TARDU, M. E., *Human Rights: The International Petition System* (Oceana Publications, New York, 1979–85).

TARNOPOLSKY, W. S., 'Human Rights, International Law and the International Bill of Rights', 50 *Saskatchewan L. Rev.* 21–37 (1985).

TAUBENFELD, H. J., and TAUBENFELD, R. F., 'Human Rights and the Emerging International Constitution', 9 *Hofstra L. Rev.* 475–514 (1981).

TCHIRKOVITCH, S., 'La Déclaration universelle des droits de l'homme et sa portée internationale', 53 *Rev. gen. du droit int'l pub.* 359–86 (1949).

TEDIN, K. L., 'Developing of the Soviet Attitude toward Implementing Human Rights under the UN Charter', 5 *Rev. des droits de l'homme* 399–418 (1972).

THOOLEN, H., and VERSTAPPEN, B., *Human Rights Missions: A Study of the Fact-Finding Practice of Non-Governmental Organizations* (Martinus Nijhoff, The Hague, 1986).

THORNBERRY, P., 'Self-Determination, Minorities, Human Rights: A Review of International Instruments', 38 *Int'l & Comp. LQ* 867–89 (1989).

TOMUSCHAT, C., 'Menschenrechtsschutz durch die Vereinten Nationen' 24 *Vereinte Nationen* 133–74 (1976).

—— 'Die Bundesrepublik Deutschland und die Menschenrechtspakte der Vereinten Nationen', 26 *Vereinte Nationen* 1–10 (1978).

—— 'The Protection of Human Rights through the United Nations at the Present Day', 20 *Universitas* (Stuttgart) 1–10 (1978).

—— 'Der Ausschub für Menschenrechte—Recht und Praxis', 29 *Vereinte Nationen* 141–8 (1981).

—— 'Menschenrechtpolitik der Vereinten Nationen', 36 *Europa-Archiv* 587–96 (1981).

—— 'Das Recht auf Etwicklung', 25 *German YB Int'l L.* 85–112 (1982).

—— 'International Standards and Cultural Diversity', *UN Bull. Hum. Rts.* 24–35 (Special Issue, Human Rights Day 1985).

—— 'Human Rights in a World-Wide Framework—Some Current Issues', in 45 *Zeitschrift fur auslandisches offentliches Recht und Volkerrecht* 566–84 (1986).

—— 'Zehn Jahre Menschenrechtsausschub—Versuch einer Bilanz', 35 *Vereinte Nationen* 157–63 (1987).

—— 'Die Vereinten Nationen und die Menschenrechte', 49 *Aus Pol. und Zeitgeschichte* 14–24 (1988).

TUMANOV, V. A., 'International Protection of Human Rights: Soviet Report', in R. Bernhardt, and J. A. Jolowitz (eds.), *International Enforcement of Human Rights*,

21–4 (Springer-Verlag, Berlin, 1987).

TÜRK, D., 'Promotion of Human Rights within the UN System', 25 *Socialist Thought and Prac.* 89–106 (1985).

—— 'La Préparation et la présentation des rapports périodiques du Canada en application des traités relatifs aux droits et libertés', 24 *Canadian YB Int'l L.* 161–212 (1986).

VAN DIJK, P., 'International Law and the Promotion and Protection of Human Rights', 244 *Wayne L. Rev.* 1529–53 (1978).

VASAK, K., 'A 30 Year Struggle: The Sustained Efforts to Give Force of Law to the Universal Declaration of Human Rights', *Unesco Courier* (Paris), 29–32 (1977).

VERDOODT, A., *Naissance et signification de la Déclaration universelle des droits de l'homme* (Naulwaerts, Louvain, 1964).

—— 'Signification de la Déclaration universelle des droits de l'homme: Bilan et perspectives d'avenir', *Rev. int'l de la Croix-Rouge* 257–66 (1966).

—— 'Influence des structures ethniques et linguistiques des pays membres des Nations Unies sur la rédaction de la Déclaration universelle des droits de l'homme', in *René Cassin: Amicorum discipulorumque liber*, i. 404 (Pedone, Paris, 1969).

VIJAPUR, A. P., 'The UN Mechanisms and Procedures for the Promotion and Implementation of Human Rights', 25 *Indian J. Int'l L.* 576–611 (1985).

VOITTO SAARIO, V., and CASS, R. H., 'United Nations and the International Protection of Human Rights: A Legal Analysis and Interpretation', 7 *Calif. W. Int'l LJ* 591–614 (1977).

VUKAS, B., 'La Protection internationale des droits de l'homme dans le système des Nations Unies', 28 *Rev. de pol. int'l* 43–8 (1977).

WEISSBRODT, D., 'The Role of International Non-Governmental Organizations in the Implementation of Human Rights', 12 *Tex. Int'l LJ* 292–320 (1977).

—— 'New United Nations Mechanism for Encouraging Ratification of Human Rights Treaties', 76 *Am. J. Int'l L.* 418–29 (1982).

WILLIAMS, P., *International Bill of Human Rights* (Entwhistle, Glen Ellen, Calif. 1981).

YIU, M. K., 'Legal Character of the Charter Provisions Concerning Human Rights', 28 *India Q.* 52–60 (1972).

—— 'The Competence of the United Nations Organs Concerning Human Rights', 30 *India Q.* 133–41 (1974).

ZUIJDWIJK, T., *Petitioning the United Nations: A Study in Human Rights* (St Martin's Press, New York, 1982).

2. *The General Assembly*

DOCUMENT

(1989)

Study on 'Possible Long-term Approaches to Enhancing the Effective Operation of Existing and Prospective Bodies Established under United Nations Human Rights Instruments', Prepared by an Independent Expert, Mr. Philip Alston, for the General Assembly, A/44/668.

BOOKS AND ARTICLES

ALSTON, P., 'The Alleged Demise of Political Human Rights at the UN: A Reply to Donnelly', 37 *Int'l Org.* 537–46 (1983).

Anon., 'The Domestic Jurisdiction Limitation in the UN Charter', 47 *Colum. L. Rev.* 268–79 (1947).

BAILEY, S., *The General Assembly of the United Nations: A Study of Procedure and Practice* (Praeger, New York, 1964).

COLLIARD, C.-A., 'L'Adoption par l'Assemblée Générale de la déclaration sur le droit au développement (4 December 1986)', 33 *Ann. francais de droit int'l* 614–28 (1987).

DONNELLY, J., 'Recent Trends in Human Rights Activity: Description and Polemic', 35 *Int'l Org.* 633–55 (1981).

—— 'The Human Rights Priorities of the UN: A Rejoinder to Alston', 37 *Int'l Org.* 547–50 (1983).

GURADZE, H., 'Are Human Rights Resolutions of the United Nations General Assembly Law-Making?', 4 *Rev. des droits de l'homme* 453–62 (1971).

HASENAU, M., 'Setting Norms in the United Nations System: The Draft Convention on the Protection of the Rights of All Migrant Workers and Their Families in Relation to ILO in Standards on Migrant Workers', 28 *Int'l Migration* 133–57 (1990).

HUNE, S., and NIESSEN, J., 'The First UN Convention on Migrant Workers', 9 *Neths O. of Hum. Rts.* 130–41 (1991).

MARINIC, D., 'Human Rights at the 34th General Assembly Session', 31 *Rev. of Int'l Aff.* 8–10 (1980).

OT, J., and PELLET, A., *La Charte des Nations Unies* (Economica, Paris, 1985).

OZGUR, O., *Apartheid: The United Nations and Peaceful Change in South Africa* (Transnational, Dobbs Ferry, NY, 1984).

PETERSON, M. J., *The General Assembly in World Politics* (Allen & Unwin, Boston, 1986).

ROOSEVELT, E., 'General Assembly Adopts Declaration of Human Rights', 19 *Dep. St. Bull.* 751–4 (1948).

ROWE, T., 'Human Rights Issues in the UN General Assembly 1946–1966', 14 *J. of Conflict Resolution* 425–37 (1970).

RUSSELL, R., 'The General Assembly: Patterns, Problems, Prospects Carnegie Endowment for International Peace, New York 1970', 42 *Int'l Conciliation* 5–141 (1970).

SCHACHTER, O., 'Interpretation of the Charter in the Political Organs of the United Nations', in *Law State and International Legal Order: Essays in Honor of Hans Kelsen* (Univ. of Tennessee Press, Knoxville, Tenn., 1964).

SCHAPIRO, L. B., 'Domestic Jurisdiction in the Covenant and the Charter', 2 *Int'l & Comp. LO* 64–7 (1948).

STULTZ, N., 'Evolution of the United Nations Anti-Apartheid Regime', 13 *Hum. Rts. Q.* 1–23 (1991).

WEISSBRODT, D., 'The Role of International Organizations in the Implementation of Human Rights and Humanitarian Law in Situations of Armed Conflict', 21 *Vand. J. of Transnat'l L.* 313–65 (1988).

XIDES, S. G., 'The General Assembly', in J. Barros (ed.), *The United Nations: Past, Present and Future* (Free Press, New York, 1972).

3. *The Economic and Social Council*

DOCUMENTS

(1954)

Freedom of Information 1953, Report by S. P. López, E/2426 & Add.1–5.

(1955)

Concise Summary on Information on Slavery, Report by H. Engen, E/2673 & Add.1–4.

The Problem of Protecting Sources of Information from News Personnel, Study by the Secretary-General, E/2693 & Add.1–3.

Legal Aspects of the Rights and Responsibilities of Media of Information, Study by the Secretary-General, E/2698 & Add.1.

(1961)

Report on Developments in the Field of Freedom of Information since 1954, Report by H. Eek (Sweden), E/3443.

Study on Capital Punishment, Study by M. Ancel, ST/SOA/SD9.

(1966)

Report on Slavery, Report by M. Awad, E/4168/Rev. 1.

(1983)

Suppression of the Traffic in Persons and the Exploitation of the Prostitution of Others, Report by J. Fernand-Laurent, E/1983/7 (1983).

(1984)

Reporting to the Economic and Social Council, Report by M. Bertrand, Geneva Joint Inspection Unit Report, 84/7 (1984).

(1989)

In-Depth Evaluation of the Human Rights Programme, Report of the Secretary-General, E/AC.51/1989/2.

BOOKS AND ARTICLES

CHIANG, P., *Non-Governmental Organizations at the United Nations* (Praeger, New York, 1981).

GOODSPEED, S., 'Political Considerations in the United Nations Economic and Social Council', *YB of World Aff. 1961* (Stevens, London, 1961).

HUMPHREY, J., 'The United Nations Commission on Human Rights and its Parent Body', in *René Cassin: Amicorum Discipulorumque Liber*, i. 108 (Pedone, Paris, 1969).

KAUFMANN, J., 'The Elusive Quest for World Economic Policies: The Economic and Social Council and Related Bodies', in *United Nations Decision Making*, 53–70 (Sijthoff and Noordhoff, Alphen aan den Rijn, 1980).

LOVEDAY, A., 'Suggestions for the Reform of the United Nations Economic and Social Machinery', 7 *Int'l Org.* 325–41 (1953).

MALINOWSKI, W. R., 'Centralization and Decentralization in the United Nations Economic and Social Activities', 16 *Int'l Org.* 521–41 (1962).

RUCZ, C., *Le Conseil économique et social de l'ONU et la coopération pour le développement* (Economica, Paris, 1983).

United Nations, '*Review and Reappraisal of the Role and Functions of the Economic and Social Council: Report of the Secretary-General*, A/3109 (1965).

—— '*A New United Nations Structure for Global Economic Co-operation: Report of the Group of Experts on the Structure of the United Nations System*, E/AC.62/9 (1975).

WILCOX, F., and MARCY, C., *Proposals for Changes in the United Nations*, 223–66 (Brookings, Washington, DC, 1955).

4. *The Commission on Human Rights*

DOCUMENTS

(*Note*: Studies focusing on a single State or groups of States are not included in this selection.)

(1947–)

Commission on Human Rights, Reports on the Sessions. Supplements to the Official Records of the Economic and Social Council Sessions, years and UN doc. nos. as follows: 1, 1947, E/259; 2, 1947, E/600; 3, 1948, E/800; 4, 1949, E/1315; 5, 1949, E/1371; 6, 1950, E/1681; 7, 1951, E/1992; 8, 1951, E/2256; 9, 1952, E/2447; 10, 1954, E/2573; 11, 1955, E/2731; 12, 1956, E/2844; 13, 1957, E/2970/Rev.1; 14, 1958, E/3088; 15, 1959, E/3229; 16, 1960, E/3335; 17, 1961, E/3456; 18, 1962, E/3616/Rev.1; 19, 1963, E/3742; 20, 1964, E/3873; 21, 1965, E/4024; 22, 1966, E/4184; 23, 1967, E/4322; 24, 1968, E/4475; 25, 1969, E/4621; 26, 1970, E/4816; 27, 1971, E/4949; 28, 1972, E/5113; 29, 1973, E/5625; 30, 1974, E/5664; 31, 1975, E/5635; 32, 1976, E/5768; 33, 1977, E/5927; 34, 1978, E/1978/34; 35, 1979, E/1979/36; 36, 1980, E/1980/13; 37, 1981, E/1981/25; 38, 1982, E/1982/12; 39, 1983, E/1983/13; 40, 1984, E/1984/14; 41, 1985 E/1985/22; 42, 1986, E/1986/22; 43, 1987, E/1987/18; 44, 1988, E/1988/12; 45, 1989, E/1989/20; 46, 1990, E/1990/22 & Add.1; 47, 1991, E/1991/22 & Add.1.

(1950)

Study of the Legal Validity of the Undertakings Concerning Minorities, Study by the Secretary-General, E/CN.4/367 & Add.1 & Corr.1.

(1952)

Activities of the United Nations and of the Specialized Agencies in the Field of Economic, Social and Cultural Rights, Report by the Secretary-General, E/CN.4/364/Rev.1.

(1957)

Right of Asylum, Memorandum by the Secretary-General, E/CN.4/738 & Corr.1 and 2.

Freedom of Information, Special Report of the Ad Hoc Committee on Freedom of Information Established by Commission on Human Rights Resolution IX (XIII), E/CN.4/762 & Corr.1.

(1964)

Economic and Social Consequences of Racial Discrimination, Report of the Executive-Secretary of the Economic Commission for Africa (1962).

Study on the Right of Everyone to be Free from Arbitrary Arrest, Detention and Exile, 65.XIV.2.

(1966)

Question of the Applicability of Statutory Limitation to War Crimes and Crimes against Humanity, Study by the Secretary-General, E/CN.4/906.

(1968)

Study of Apartheid and Racial Discrimination in Southern Africa, Study by M. Ganji, E/CN.4/979 & Add.1–8.

Capital Punishment: Developments 1961–1965, Study by N. Morris.

(1969)

Study of the Right of Arrested Persons to Communicate with Those whom it is Necessary for Them to Consult in Order to Ensure their Defence or to Protect their Essential Interests, Study Prepared by the Committee on the Right of Everyone to be Free from Arbitrary Arrest, Detention, and Exile, E/CN.4/996.

(1970)

Report on Certain Aspects of Human Rights and Technological Developments, Report by the Secretary-General, E/CN.4/1028 & Add.1–3 (1970).

(1972–)

The Impact of Scientific and Technological Developments on Economic, Social and Cultural Rights, Reports of the Secretary-General, E/CN.4/1084; E/CN.4/1115; E/CN.4/1141; E/CN.4/1198 (1972, 1973, 1974, and 1976).

Study Concerning the Question of Apartheid from the Point of View of International Penal Law, Study by the Ad Hoc Working Group of Experts on Southern Africa, E/CN.4/1075.

(1974)

Respect for the Privacy of Individuals and the Integrity and Sovereignity of Nations in Light of Advances in Recording and other Techniques, Report by the Secretary-General, E/CN.4/1116 & Add.1–3.

(1975)

Protection of the Human Personality and its Physical and Intellectual Integrity, in Light of Advances in Biology, Medicine and Biochemistry, Report by the Secretary-General, E/CN.4/1172 & Add.1–3.

The Realization of Economic, Social and Cultural Rights: Problems, Policies, Progress, Study by M. Ganji, E.75.xiv.2.

Use of Electronics which may Affect the Rights of the Person and the Limits which Should be Placed on Such Use in a Democratic Society, Report by the Secretary-General, E/CN.4/1142 & Add.1–2.

(1976)

The Balance which Should be Established between Scientific and Technological Progress and the Intellectual, Spiritual, Cultural and Moral Advancement of Humanity, Report by the Secretary-General, E/CN.4/1199 & Add.1.

(1977)

The Human Rights Implications of the Genetic Manipulation of Microbes, Report by the Secretary-General, E/CN.4/1236.

(1979–)

Right to Development, Studies by the Secretary-General E/CN.4/1334 (1979); E/CN.4/1421 (1980); E/CN.4/1488 (1982).

Study on Ways and Means of Insuring the Implementation of International Instruments such as the International Convention on the Suppression and Punishment of the Crime of Apartheid, including the Establishment of the International Jurisdiction Envisaged by the Convention, E/CN.4/1426 (1981).

Human Rights and Mass Exoduses, Study by Sadruddin Aga Khan, E/CN.4/1503 (1982).

Working Group of Governmental Experts on the Right to Development: E/CN.4/1489 (1982); E/CN.4/1983/11; E/CN.4/1984/13; E/CN.4/1985/11; E/CN.4/1987/10; E/CN.4/1988/10; E/CN.4/1989/10.

Working Group on Enforced or Involuntary Disappearances: Reports E/CN.4/1435 (1981); E/CN.4/1492 (1982); E/CN.4/1983/14; E/CN.4/1984/21 & Add.1–2; E/CN.4/1985/15 & Add.1; E/CN.4/1986/18 & Add.1; E/CN.4/1987/15 & Add.1; E/CN.4/1988/19 & Add.1; E/CN.4/1989/18 & Add.1; E/CN.4/1990/13; E/CN.4/1991/20 & Add.1.

Summary of Arbitrary Executions, Reports by A. Wako, E/CN.4/1983/16; E/CN.4/1984/29; E/CN.4/1985/17; E/CN.4/1985/21; E/CN.4/1986/21; E/CN.4/1987; E/CN.4/1988/22 and Add.1–2; E/CN.4/1989/25; E/CN.4/1990/22 & Add.1; E/CN.4/1991/36.

Study on the Effects of the Policy of Apartheid on Black Women and Children, Study by the Ad Hoc Working Group of Experts on Southern Africa, E/CN.4/1497; E/CN.4/1983/38 (1982; 1983).

Implementation of the Declaration on the Elimination of all Forms of Intolerance and of Discrimination Based on Religion or Belief, Reports by A. Vidal d'Almeida Ribeiro, E/CN.4/1987/35; E/CN.4/1988/45 & Add.1; E/CN.4/1989/44; E/CN.4/1990/46.

Study on the Criminal Effects of Apartheid, Study by the Ad Hoc Working Group of Experts on Southern Africa, E/CN.4/1985/14 (1987).

The International Dimensions of the Right to Development as a Human Right in Relation with other Human Rights based on International Co-operation Including the Right to Peace,

Taking into Account the Requirements of the New International Economic Order and the Fundamental Human Needs, Report by the Secretary-General, E/CN.4/1334.

Torture and other Cruel, Inhuman, or Degrading Treatment or Punishment, Reports by P. Kooijmans, E/CN.4/1986/15; E/CN.4/1987/13; E/CN.4/1988/17 and Add.1; E/CN.4/1989/15; E/CN.4/1990/17 & Add.1; E/CN.4/1991/17.

Traditional Practices Affecting the Health of Women and Children, Study by a Working Group of Experts, E/CN.4/1986/42.

Global Consultation on the Right to Development as a Human Right, E/CN.4/1990/9.

BOOKS AND ARTICLES

Anon., 'A Preliminary Survey of Action to Further Human Rights in the Asian Region Specifically by the United Nations through its Programme of Advisory Services in the Field of Human Rights', *Australian YB Int'l L.* 51–67 (1970–3).

Bettati, M., 'De Pénélope à Antigone; Fonctionnement politique de la Commission de L'ONU', *Projet 151*, 31–42 (1982).

Bossuyt, M. J., 'United Nations and Civil and Political Rights in Chile', 27 *Int'l & Comp. LQ* 462–71 (1978).

—— 'The Development of Special Procedures of the United Nations Commission on Human Rights', 6 *Hum. Rts. LJ* 179–210 (1985).

Boven, T. C. van, 'The United Nations Commission on Human Rights and Violations of Human Rights and Fundamental Freedoms', 15 *Netherlands Int'l L. Rev.* 374–93 (1968).

—— 'The United Nations and Human Rights: A Critical Appraisal', 8 *Bull. of Peace Proposals*, 198–208 (1977).

—— 'The International Protection of Human Rights, Appraisal and Perspectives: The United Nations Commission on Human Rights', unpublished lectures (1980).

—— 'La Comisión de Derechos Humanos', in *La protección internacional de los derechos humanos: Balance y perspectivas* (Mexico, 1983).

Brody, R., Parker, P., and Weissbrodt, W., 'Major Developments in 1990 at the UN Commission on Human Rights', 12 *Hum. Rts. Q.* 559–90 (1990).

—— and Weissbrodt, D., 'Major Developments at the 1989 Session of the UN Commission on Human Rights', 11 *Hum. Rts. Q.* 586–611 (1989).

Brunet, R., *La Garantie international des droits de l'homme d'après la Charte de San Francisco* (Geneva, 1947).

Carey, J., '"United Nations" Double Standard on Human Rights Complaints', 60 *Am. J. Int'l L.* 792–803 (1966).

—— 'United Nations Scrutiny of South African Prisons', 1 *Rev. des droits de l'homme* 531–43 (1968).

—— *UN Protection of Civil and Political Rights* (Syracuse UP, New York, 1970).

Cassese, A., 'Admissibility of Communications to the United Nations on Human Rights Violations', 5 *Rev. des droits de l'homme* 375–93 (1972).

—— 'The New United Nations Procedure for Handling Gross Violations of Human Rights', 30 *Communita int'l* 49–61 (1975).

Cassin, R., 'La Commission des droits de l'homme de l'ONU, 1947–1971', in *Miscellanea W. J. Ganshof van der Meersch* 397–433 (Établissements Émile Brulant, Brussels, 1972).

CONTRERAS MAZARIO, J., 'La libertad religiosa y la no discriminación por motivos religiosos en la Comisión de Derechos Humanos de las Naciones Unidas', 6 *An. de derecho eclesiástico* (1989).

DJORDJEVIC, M., 'The United Nations Commission on Human Rights and Yugoslavia', 12 *Socialist Thought and Prac.* 154–63 (1984).

ERMACORA, F., 'International Enquiry Commissions in the Field of Human Rights', 1 *Rev. des droits de l'homme* 80–218 (1968).

—— 'Procedure to Deal with Human Rights Violations: A Hopeful Start in the United Nations', 7 *Rev. des droits de l'homme* 670–89 (1974).

ESCOBAR HERNÁNDEZ, C., *La Comisión de Derechos Humanos de las Naciones Unidas y la violación de derechos humanos y libertades fundamentales: Estudio de los procedimientos públicos especiales* (Editorial de la Universidad Complutense, Madrid, 1988).

FEGLEY, R., 'The UN Human Rights Commission: The Equatorial Guinea Case', 3 *Hum. Rts. Q.* 34–47 (1981).

FEYLER, K. DE., 'The International Protection of Political Prisoners: The Practice of the United Nations Commission on Human Rights, the International Committee of the Red Cross and Amnesty International', 20 *Rev. belge de droit int'l* 290–312 (1987).

GONZALES, T. D., 'The Political Sources of Procedural Debates in the United Nations', Structural Impediments to Implementation of Human Rights', 13 *NYUJ Int'l L. & Pol.* 427–72 (1981).

GREEN, J. F., 'Changing Approaches to Human Rights: The United Nations, 1954 and 1974', 12 *Tex. Int'l LJ* 223–38 (1977).

GUGGENHEIM, M. H., 'Key Provisions of the New United Nations Rules Dealing with Human Rights Petitions', 6 *NYUJ Int'l L. & Pol.* 427–54 (1973).

HOARE, S., 'The UN Commission on Human Rights', in E. Luard (ed.), *The International Protection of Human Rights*, 59–98 (Praeger, New York, 1967).

—— 'The United Nations and Human Rights: A Brief Survey of the Commission on Human Rights', 1 *Israel YB Hum. Rts.* 29–34 (1971).

HUMPHREY, J. P., 'Human Rights: New Directions in the U.N. Program', 4 *NYLF* 391 (1958).

—— 'The Right of Petition in the United Nations', 4 *Rev. des droits de l'homme* 463–75 (1971).

International Commission of Jurists, *The Review*, Commentaries on the UN Commission of Human Rights, published regularly from 1973 to date.

KAMMINGA, M. T., 'The Thematic Procedures of the UN Commission on Human Rights', 34 *Netherlands Int'l L. Rev.* 299–323 (1987).

KRAMER, D., and WEISSBRODT, D., 'The 1980 UN Commission on Human Rights and the Disappeared', 3 *Hum. Rts. Q.* 18–33 (1981).

LEBLANC, P., 'Canada at the UN Human Rights Commission', *Int'l Persp.* 20–2 (1985).

LILLICH, R. B., 'The United Nations and Human Rights Complaints: U Thant as Strict Constructionist', 64 *Am. J. Int'l L.* 610–14 (1970).

LISKOFSKY, S., 'Coping With the Question of the Violation of Human Rights and Fundamental Freedoms', 8 *Rev. des droits de l'homme* 883–914 (1975).

LOWENSTEIN, A. K., 'The United Nations and the Human Rights Issue', 43 *Law &*

Contemp. Prob. 268–74 (1979).

MacChesney, B., 'Development in Recent Years of Human Rights in the United Nations with Particular Reference to the Draft Covenants', in *Human Rights: Protection of the Individual under International Law* (Rothman, NJ, 1970).

Malik, C., 'How the Commission on Human Rights Forged its Draft of a First Covenant', 8 *UN Bull. Hum. Rts.* 471–3, 501 (1950).

Marie, J. B., 'La Commission des droits de l'homme des Nations Unies à sa vingt-neuvième session', 6 *Rev. des droits de l'homme* 369–433 (1973).

—— *La Commission des droits de l'homme de l'ONU* (Pedone, Paris, 1975).

—— 'Situation des droits de l'homme au Chili: Enquête de la Commission des droits de l'homme des Nations Unies', 22 *Ann. français de droit int'l* 305–35 (1976).

—— 'La Pratique de la Commission des droits de l'homme de l'ONU en matière de violation des droits de l'homme', 15 *Rev. belge de droit int'l* 355–80 (1980).

Michalska, A., 'Petition as a Means of International Control over the Implementation of Human Rights', 38 *Panstwo i Prawo* 50 (1983).

Möller, J., 'Petitioning the United Nations', 1 *Universal Hum. Rts.* 57–72 (1979).

Murphy J. F., 'The United Nations and Human Rights: The Human Rights Commission in 1973–1974', 4 *Israel YB Hum. Rts.* 48–59 (1974).

Newman, F. C., 'New United Nations Procedures for Human Rights Complaints: Reform, Status Quo or Chamber of Horrors', 34 *Ann. de droit* 129–46 (1974).

Pastor Ridruejo, J. A., 'La acción de la Comisión de derechos humanos de las Naciones Unidas ante las violaciones de los derechos del hombre', 2 *An. de Derechos Hum.* 319–30 (1983).

Pastor Ridruejo, J. A., 'La Función del relator espceial de la Comisión de Derechos Humanos de la ONU en el caso de El Salvador', 2 *Rev. Inst. Interam. de derechos hum.* 5–16 (1985).

Prasad, N., 'The Role of Non-Governmental Organizations in the New United Nations Procedures for Human Rights Complaints', 5 *Den. J. Int'l L. & Pol.* 441–62 (1975).

Questiaux, N., 'Procédure des rapports triennaux devant la Commission des droits de l'homme des Nations Unies', 1 *Rev. des droits de l'homme* 544–8.

Rachlin, R. D., 'Report of the 26th Session of the United Nations Commission on Human Rights', 3 *Rev. des droits de l'homme* 487–97 (1970).

Ramcharan, B. G., 'Good Offices of the United Nations Secretary-General in the Field of Human Rights', 26 *Am. J. Int. L.* 130–41 (1982).

Resich, Z., 'La Commission des droits de l'homme des Nations Unies', 15 *Rev. de droit contemporain* 25–37 (1968).

Rodley, N., *The Treatment of Prisoners under International Law* (Oxford UP, Oxford, 1986).

—— 'UN Action Procedures against "Disappearances" Summary or Arbitrary Executions and Torture', 8 *Hum. Rts. Q.* 700–31 (1986).

Ruzie, D., 'Le Droit de petition individuelle en matière de droits de l'homme à propos de la Résolution 1503 (XLVIII) du Conseil économique et social des Nations Unies', 4 *Rev. des droits de l'homme* 89–101 (1971).

Schreiber, M., 'Les Nations Unies et les droits de l'homme', 2 *Rev. des droits de l'homme* 95–112 (1969).

—— 'Les Organisations non-gouvernmentales et l'ôeuvre des Nations Unies dans le domaine de la protection des droits de l'homme', *Synthesis*, 58–63 (1970).

SCHWELB, E., 'Complaints by Individuals to the Commission on Human Rights: 25 Years of an Uphill Struggle (1947–1971)', in C. Bonsson (ed.), *The Changing International Community* 119–40 (The Hague, 1973).

SHESTACK, J. J., 'The Commission on Human Rights: Pitfalls, Progress and a New Maturity', in S. M. Finger, and J. R. Herbert (eds.), *U.S. Policy in International Institutions* 71–82 (Westview Press, Boulder, Colo., 1982).

SIMSARIAN, J., 'Third Session of United Nations Commission on Human Rights', 42 *Am. J. Int'l L.* 879–83 (1948).

—— 'Human Rights: Draft Covenant Revised at Fifth Session of Commission on Human Rights', 21 *Dep. St. Bull.* 3–12 (1949).

—— 'Draft International Covenant on Human Rights at 1950 session of United Nations Commission on Human Rights', 45 *Am. J. Int'l L.* 170–7 (1951).

SMOGER, G., 'Whither the Commission on Human Rights: A Report after the 35th Session', 12 *Vand. J. Transnat'l L.* 943–68 (1979).

SUTER, K. D., 'The U.N. Commission on Human Rights', *Australian Outlook* 289–309 (1979).

TARDU, M. E., 'United Nations Response to Gross Violations of Human Rights: The 1503 Procedure', *Santa Clara L. Rev.* 559–602 (1980).

TOLLEY, H., *The U.N. Commission on Human Rights* (Westview Press, Boulder, Colo., 1967).

—— 'Decision-Making at the United Nations Commission on Human Rights', 5 *Hum. Rts. Q.* 27–57 (1983).

—— 'The Concealed Crack in the Citadel: The United Nations Commission on Human Rights Response to Confidential Communications', 6 *Hum. Rts. Q.* 420–62 (1984).

TURLINGTON, E., 'Human Rights Commission at the Crossroads', 45 *Am. J. Int'l L.* 531–8 (1951).

US House Committee on Foreign Affairs, Subcommission on Human Rights and International Organizations, *Review of the UN Commission on Human Rights: Hearings* (99th Cong, 2d Sess., 1986).

VUKAS, B., 'Projet de déclaration sur les droits des personnes appartenant à des minorités nationables, ethniques, religieuses et linguistiques', 25 *Ann. français de droit int'l* 281–94 (1979).

WEISSBRODT, D., 'The Three "Theme" Special Rapporteurs of the UN Commission on Human Rights', 80 *Am. J. Int'l L.* 685–99. (1986).

—— 'Country-Related and Thematic Developments at the 1988 Session of the UN Commission on Human Rights', 10 *Hum. Rts. Q.* 544–58 (1988).

—— 'The United Nations Commission on Human Rights Confirms Conscientious Objection to Military Service as a Human Right', 35 *Netherlands Int'l L. Rev.* 53–72 (1988).

WHITEMAN, MARJORIE, 'Mrs. Franklin D. Roosevelt and the Human Rights Commission', 62 *Am. J. Int'l L.* 918–21 (1969).

ZUIJDWIJK, T. J. M. 'Right to Petition the United Nations because of Alleged Violations of Human Rights', 59 *Canadian B. Rev.* 103–23 (1981).

5. *The Sub-Commission on Prevention of Discrimination and Protection of Minorities*

DOCUMENTS

(1947–)

Sub-Commission on Prevention of Discrimination and Protection of Minorities, Reports on the Sessions, year and UN doc. nos. as follows: 1, 1947, E/CN.4/52; 2, 1949, E/CN.4/351; 3, 1950, E/CN.4/358; 4, 1951, E/CN.4/641; 5, 1952, E/CN.4/670; 6, 1954, E/CN.4/703; 7, 1955, E/CN.4/711; 8, 1956, E/CN.4/721; 9, 1957, E/CN.4/740; 10, 1958, E/CN.4/764; 11, 1959, E/CN.4/778; 12, 1960, E/CN.4/800; 13, 1961, E/CN.4/815; 14, 1962, E/CN.41830; 15, 1963, E/CN.4/846; 16, 1964, E/CN.4/873; 17, 1965, E/CN.4/882; 18, 1966, E/CN.4/903; 19, 1967, E/CN.4/930; 20, 1967, E/CN.4/947; 21, 1968, E/CN.4/976; 22, 1969, E/CN.4/1008; 23, 1970, E/CN.411040; 24, 1971, E/CN.4/1970; 25, 1972, F./CN.4/1101; 26, 1973, E/CN.4/1128; 27, 1974, E/CN.4/1160; 28, 1975, E/CN.4/1180; 29, 1976, E/CN.4/1218; 30, 1977, E/CN.4/1261; 31, 1978, E/CN.4/1296; 32, 1979, E/CN.4/1350; 33, 1980, E/CN.4/1413; 34, 1981, E/CN.4/1512; 35, 1982, E/CN.4/1983/4; 36, 1983, E/CN.4/1984/3; 37, 1984, E/CN.4/1985/3; 38, 1985, E/CN.4/1986/5; 1986 session cancelled; 39, 1987, E/CN.4/1988/37; 40, 1988, E/CN.4/1989/3; 41, 1989, E/CN.4/1990/2; 42, 1990, E/CN.4/1991/2; 43, 1991, E/CN.4/1992/2.

Working Groups

Working Group on Detention: 1, 1981, E/CN.4/L.774; 2, 1982, E/CN.4/Sub.2/1982/34; 3, 1983, E/CN.4/Sub.2/1983/14; 4, 1984, E/CN.4/Sub.2/1984/16; 5, 1985, E/CN.4/Sub.2/1985/17; 6, 1987, E/CN.4/Sub.2/1987/15; 7, 1988, E/CN.4/Sub.2/1988/28; 8, 1989, E/CN.4/Sub.2/1989/29; 9, 1990, E/CN.4/Sub.2/1990/32; 10, 1991, E/CN.4/Sub.2/1991/27.

Working Group on Indigenous Population: 1, 1982, E/CN.4/Sub.2/1982/33; 2, 1983, E/CN.4/Sub.2/1983/22; 3, 1984, E/CN.4/Sub.2/1984/20; 4, 1985, E/CN.4/Sub.2/1985/22 and Add. 1; 5, 1987, E/CN.4/Sub.2/1987/22 and Add. 1; 6, 1988, E/CN.4/Sub.2/1988/24 and Add. 1; 7, 1989, E/CN.4/Sub.2/1989/36; 1990, E/CN.4/Sub.2/1990/42; 1991, E/CN.4/Sub.2/1991/40.

Working Groups on Slavery: 1, 1976, E/CN.4/Sub.2/373; 2, 1977, E/CN.4/Sub.2/389; 3, 1978, E/CN.4/Sub.2/410; 4, 1979, E/CN.4/Sub.2/434; 5, 1980, E/CN.4/Sub.2/447; 6, 1981, E/CN.4/Sub.2/486; 7, 1982, E/CN.4/Sub.2/1982/21; 8, 1983, E/CN.4/Sub.2/1983/27; 9, 1984, E/CN.4/Sub.2/1984/25; 10, 1985, E/CN.4/Sub.2/1985/25; 11, 1987, E/CN.4/Sub.2/1987/25; 12, 1988, E/CN.4/Sub.2/1988/32; 13, 1989, E/CN.4/Sub.2/1989/39; 14, 1990, E/CN.4/Sub.2/1990/44; 15, 1991, E/CN.4/Sub.2/1991/41.

Studies, Reports, etc.

(1949)

The Main Types and Causes of Discrimination, Memorandum of the Secretary-General, E/CN.4/Sub.2/40/Rev.1.

Report on the Prevention of Discrimination, Report by the Secretary-General, E/CN.4/Sub.2/40.

(1950)

Definition and Classification of Minorities, Memorandum by the Secretary-General, 1950.xiv.3.

Memorandum on the Population of the Aaland Islands, by E. E. Ekstrand, E/CN.4/Sub.2/101.

Memorandum on the German Minority in Denmark, by E. E. Ekstrand, E/CN.4/Sub.2/102.

(1951)

Prevention of Discrimination and Denial of Fundamental Freedoms in Respect of Political Groups, Memorandum of the Secretary-General, E/CN.4/Sub.2/129.

The Suppression of Slavery, Memorandum by the Secretary-General, 1951.XIV.2.

(1954)

Preliminary Report on the Proposed Study on Discrimination in the Matter of Religious Rights and Practices, by P. Halpern, E/CN.4/Sub.2/162.

(1955)

Preliminary Study of Discrimination in the Matter of Emigration, Immigration and Travel, by J. D. Ingles, E/CN.4/Sub.2/167.

(1956)

Measures for the Cessation of National, Racial or Religious Hostility, Report by the Secretary-General, E/CN.4/Sub.2/172.

(1957)

Discrimination in Education, Study by C. Ammoun, 1957.XIV.3 (1957).

(1960)

Discrimination in the Matter of Religious Rights and Practices, Study by A. Krishnaswami, 60.XIV.2.

(1963)

Discrimination in the Matter of Political Rights, Study by H. Santa Cruz, 63.XIV.2.

Discrimination in Respect of the Right of Everyone to Leave Any Country, Including His Own, and to Return to His Country, Study by J. Inglés, 64.XIV.2.

(1966)

Report on Slavery, Study by M. Awad, 67.XIV.2.

(1967)

Discrimination against Persons Born out of Wedlock, Study by V. Saario, E.68.XIV.3.

(1971)

Equality in the Administration of Justice, Study by M. A. Abu Rannat, E.71.XIV.3.

Racial Discrimination in the Political, Economic, Social and Cultural Spheres, Study by H. Santa Cruz, E.71.XIV.2.

(1975)

Study of the Exploitation of Labour through Illicit and Clandestine Trafficking, Study by H. E. Warzazi, E/CN.4/Sub.2/L.640.

(1977)

Racial Discrimination, Study by H. Santa Cruz, E.76.XIV.2.

(1978)

Impact of Foreign Economic Aid and Assistance on Respect for Human Rights in Chile, Report by A. Cassese, E/CN.4/Sub.2/412, i–iv.

Question of the Prevention and Punishment of the Crime of Genocide, Study by N. Ruhashyankiko, E/CN.4/Sub.2/416.

(1979)

The Rights of Persons Belonging to Ethnic, Religious and Linguistic Minorities, Study by F. Capotorti, E.78.XIV.1.

(1980)

International Provisions Protecting the Rights of Non-Citizens, Study by Baroness Elles, E.80.XIV.2.

The Right to Self-Determination: Implementation of United Nations Resolutions, Study by H. Gros Espiell, E.1979.XIV.5.

(1981)

The Right to Self-Determination: Historical and Current Development on the Basis of United Nations Instruments, Study by A. Cristescu, E.80.XIV.3.

(1982)

Exploitation of Child Labour, Study by A. Bouhdiba, E.82.XIV.2.

Study on Discriminatory Treatment against Members of Racial, Ethnic, Religious or Linguistic Groups at the Various Levels in the Administration of Criminal Justice Proceedings, Study by A. S. Chowdhury, E/CN.4/Sub.2/1982/7.

The Implications for Human Rights of Recent Developments concerning Situations known as States of Siege or Emergency, Study by N. Questiaux, E/CN.4/Sub.2/1982/15.

(1983)

The Individual's Duties to the Community and the Limitations of Human Rights and Freedoms under Article 29 of the Universal Declaration of Human Rights, Study by E.-I. A. Daes, E.82.XIV.1.

(1984)

Reports on the Mission to Mauritania, Reports by M. J. Bossuyt, E/CN.4/Sub.2/1984/23; E/CN.4/Sub.2/1985/26; E/CN.4/Sub.2/1987/27 (1984, 1985, 1987).

(1985)

Slavery, Study by B. Whitaker, E.84.XIV.1 (1984). Updated version, E/CN.4/Sub.2/1985/6 & Corr. 1.

Conscientious Objection to Military Service, Study by A. Eide, and C. Mubanga-Chipoya, E.85.XIV.1.

Revised and Updated Report on the Question of the Prevention and Punishment of the Crime of Genocide, Report by B. Whitaker, E/CN.4/Sub.2/1985/6 & Corr. 1.

Draft Body of Principles and Guidelines on the Right and Responsibility of Individuals, Groups and Organs of Society to Promote and Protect Human Rights and Fundamental Freedoms, by E.-I. A. Daes, E/CN.4/Sub.2/1985/30 & Add.1.

The New International Economic Order and the Promotion of Human Rights, Study by R. Ferrero, E.85.XIV.6.

Principles, Guidelines and Guarantees for the Protection of Persons Detained on Grounds of Mental Ill-Health or Suffering from Mental Disorder, Report by E.-I. A. Daes, E.85.XIV.9.

Amnesty Laws and their Role in the Safeguard and Promotion of Human Rights, Study by L. Joinet, E/CN.4/Sub.2/1985/16.

The Independence and Impartiality of the Judiciary, Jurors and Assessors and the Independence of Lawyers, Study by L. Singhvi, E/CN.4/Sub.2/1985/18 & Add. 1–6; E/CN.4/Sub.2/1988/20 & Add. 1.

Proposal Concerning a Definition of the Term 'Minority', by J. Deschênes, E/CN.4/Sub.2/1985/31.

(1986)

Exploitation of Labour through Illicit and Clandestine Trafficking, Study by H. Warzazi, E.86.XIV.1.

The Problem of Discrimination against Indigenous Populations, Study by J. Martínez Cobo, E/CN.4/Sub.2/1986/7 & Add. 1–3.

(1987)

Analysis Concerning the Proposition to Elaborate a Second Optional Protocol to the International Covenant on Civil and Political Rights Aiming at the Abolition of the Death Penalty, Study by M. J. Bossuyt, E/CN.4/Sub.2/1987/20.

The Current Dimensions of the Problem of Intolerance and of Discrimination on Grounds of Religion or Belief, Study by E. Odio Benito, E.CN.4/Sub.2/1987/26.

The Right to Adequate Food, Study by A. Eide, E/CN.4/Sub.2/1987/23.

(1988)

Analysis of the Current Trends and Developments Regarding the Right to Leave any Country including One's Own, and to Return to One's Own Country, and Some other Rights or Considerations Arising Therefrom, Report by C. Mubanga-Chipoya, E/CN.4/Sub.2/1988/35 & Add. 1.

Human Rights and Disability, Report by L. Despouy, E/CN.4/Sub.2/1991/31.

International Peace and Security as an Essential Condition for the Enjoyment of Human Rights, Above All the Right to Life, Report by the Secretary-General, E/CN.4/Sub.2/1988/2.

Guidelines for the Regulation of Computerized Personal Data Files, Report by L. Joinet, E/CN.4/1988/22.

Prevention of the Disappearances of Children in Argentina, Report by T. C. van Boven, E/CN.4/Sub.2/1988/19.

Study on the Legal and Social Problems of Sexual Minorities, Study by J. Fernand-Laurent, E/CN.4/Sub.2/1988/31.

(1989)

Annual Report and List of States which, since 1 Jan 1985, have Proclaimed, Extended or Terminated a State of Emergency, by L. Despouy, E/CN.4/Sub.2/1989/30 & Add. 1.

Assistance to Racist Regimes in Southern Africa: Impact on the Enjoyment of Human Rights, Study by A. Khalifa, E.79.XIV.3 (1979). See also updated lists issued annually including E/CN.4/Sub.2/1991/13 & Add. 1.

Discrimination against Persons with the HIV Virus or Suffering from AIDS, Progress Report by L. Varela Quiros, E/CN.4/Sub.2/1991/10.

Hopi-Navajo Relocation, summary of information submitted by E.-I. A. Daes, J. Carey, E/CN.4/Sub.2/1989/35, parts I & 2, & Add.1.

Possible ways and Means to Facilitate the Peaceful and Constructive Resolution of Situations involving Racial, National, Religious and Linguistic Minorities, Working Paper by C. Palley, E/CN.4/Sub.2/1989/43.

Respect for the Right to Life: Elimination of Chemical Weapons, Report by the Secretary-General, E/CN.4/Sub.2/1989/4.

Status of the Individual and Contemporary International Law, Report by E.-I. A. Daes, E/CN.4/Sub.2/1989/40.

The Achievements Made and Obstacles Encountered during the First Decade to Combat Racism and Racial Discrimination, Study by A. Eide, E/CN.4/Sub.2/1989/8 & Add. 1.

The Right to Freedom of Opinion and Expression, Report by L. Joinet and D. Türk, E/CN.4/Sub.2/1991/9.

The Sale of Children, Report by the Secretary-General, E/CN.4/Sub.2/1989/38.

The Status of the Individual and Contemporary International Law, Study by E.-I. A. Daes, E/CN.4/Sub.2/1989/40.

Treaties Concluded between Indigenous Peoples and States, Preliminary Report by A. Martinez, E/CN.4/Sub.2/1991/33.

Ways and Means for Establishing an Effective Mechanism for the Implementation of the Slavery Convention, Study by the Secretary-General, E/CN.4/Sub.2/1989/37.

Realization of Economic, Social and Cultural Rights, Progress Reports by D. Turk, E/CN.4/Sub.2/1989/19 (1989); E/CN.4/Sub.2/1990/19 and E/CN.4/Sub.2/1991/17.

(1990)

The Right to Restitution, Compensation and Rehabilitation for Victims of Gross Violations of Human Rights and Fundamental Freedoms, Preliminary Report by T. van Boven, E/CN.4/Sub.2/1990/10.

The Practice of Administrative Detention, Report by L. Joinet, E/CN.4/Sub.2/1990/29.

The Adoption of Children for Commercial Purposes and the Recruitment of Children into Government and Non-Governmental Armed Forces, Report of the Secretary-General, E/CN.4/Sub.2/1990/43.

Possible Ways and Means of Facilitating the Peaceful and Constructive Solution of Problems involving Minorities, Progress Report by A. Eide, E/CN.4/Sub.2/1990/46.

Human Rights and Youth, Study by D. Mazilu, E/CN.4/Sub.2/1991/12.

Violations of Human Rights of Staff Members of the United Nations System, Report by M. Bautista, E/CN.4/Sub.2/1991/23.

The Right to a Fair Trial, Preliminary Report by S. Chernichenko and W. Treat, E/CN.4/Sub.2/1991/29.

Human Rights of Detained Juveniles, Report by M. Bautista, E/CN.4/Sub.2/1991/24.

Administrative Detention without Trial or Charge, Report by L. Joinet, E/CN.4/Sub.2/1990/29 & Add. 1.

Recent Developments with Regard to Traditional Practices Affecting the Health of Women and Children, Study by H. E. Warzazi, E/CN.4/Sub.2/1991/6.

Study on Treaties, Agreements and other Constructive Agreements Concluded between States and Indigenous Peoples, Preliminary Report by M. Alfonso Martínez, E/CN.4/Sub.2/1991/33.

Compensation for Victims of Gross Violations of Human Rights, Progress Report by T. van Boven, E/CN.4/Sub.2/1991/7.

Human Rights in Times of Armed Conflict, Report of the Secretary-General, E/CN.4/Sub.2/1991/5.

Human Rights and Extreme Poverty, Report by E. Svescún Monroy, E/CN.4/Sub.2/1991/18.

Study on Possible Ways and Means of Facilitating the Peaceful and Constructive Solution of Problems involving Minorities, Preliminary Report by A. Eide, E/CN.4/Sub.2/1991/43.

Human Rights and the Environment, Preliminary Report by F. Ksentini, E/CN.4/Sub.2/1991/8.

BOOKS AND ARTICLES

ALFREDSSON, G., 'Fourth Session of the Working Group on Indigenous Populations', 55 *Nordic J. Int'l L.* 22–31 (1986).

Anon. 'The Rights of Indigenous Populations: The Emerging International Norm', 16 *Yale J. Int'l L.* 127–75 (1991).

BARSH R. L., 'Indigenous Peoples: An Emerging Object of International Law', 80 *Am. J. Int'l L.* 369–85 (1986).

BRENNAN, K., BRODY, R., and WEISSBRODT, D., 'The 40th Session of the UN Sub-Commission on Prevention of Discrimination and Protection of Minorities', 11 *Hum. Rts. Q.* 295–324 (1989).

BRODY, R., 'Commentary on the Draft UN "Declaration on the Protection of All Persons from Enforced or Involuntary Disappearances"', 8 *Neths. Q. of Hum. Rts.* 381–401 (1990).

—— CONVERY, M., and WEISSBRODT, D., 'The 42nd Session of the Sub-Commission on Prevention of Discrimination and Protection of Minorities', 13 *Hum. Rts. Q.* 260–90 (1991).

BRUEGEL, J. W. 'A Neglected Field: The Protection of Minorities', 4 *Rev. des droits de l'homme* 413–42 (1971).

CAPORTORTI, F., 'The Protection of Minorities under Multilateral Agreements on Human Rights', 2 *Italian YB Int'l L.* 3–32 (1976).

—— 'Les Développements possibles de la protection internationale des minorités', 27 *Cahiers de droit* (Quebec) 239–54 (1986).

CLAYDON, J., 'The Transnational Protection of Ethnic Minorities: A Tentative Framework for Enquiry', 13 *Canadian YB Int'l L.* 25–60 (1975).

DAES, E.-I. A., 'Native People's Rights', 27 *Cahiers de droit* (Quebec) 123–33 (1986).

DELBRÜCK, J., *Die Rassenfrage als Problem des Volkerrechts und nationaler Rechsordnungen* (Athenaum, Frankfurt, 1971).

DESCHÊNES, J., 'Le Rôle de la sous-commission sur la lutte contre la discrimination et la protection des minorités', 2 *Rev. québécoise de droit int'l* 215–29 (1985).

DINU, M., 'The Role of the United Nations Organization in the Efforts for Finding a Solution to the Problem of the Palestinian People: Romanian Positions and Proposals', 17 *Rev. roum. d'ét. int'l* 271–87 (1983).

EGGLESTON, E. M., 'Prospects for United Nations Protection of the Human Rights of Indigenous Minorities', 5 *Australian YB Int'l L. 1970–3* 68–74 (1975).

ENGRAM, J. M., 'Conscientious Objection to Military Service: A Report on the United Nations Division of Human Rights', 11 *Ga. J. Int'l & Comp. L.* 359–99 (1982).

ERMACORA, F., *Protection of Minorities in the Work of the United Nations* (Braumueller, Vienna, 1965) (in German).

—— 'The Protection of Minorities before the United Nations', 82 *Rec. des cours* 247–370 ((1983)

FAWCETT, J. E. S., *The International Protection of Minorities* (Minority Rights Groups Report, No. 41, London, 1979).

FONSECA, J. C., and QUINTERO, M., 'Las Naciones Unidas y los derechos humanos. La Subcomisión sobre prevención de discriminación y protección de las minorías', 1 *Cuadernos de Derechos Hum.* (1985).

GALEY, M. E., 'Indigenous Peoples, International Consciousness-Raising and the Development of International Law on Human Rights', 8 *Rev. des droits de l'homme* 21–39 (1975).

GARDENIERS, T., 'The UN Sub-Commission on Prevention of Discrimination and Protection of Minorities: Recent Developments', 4 *Hum. Rts. Q.* 353–70 (1982).

—— *et al.*, 'Current Developments: The 1981 Session of the UN Sub-Commission on the Prevention of Discrimination and Protection of Minorities', 76 *Am. J. Int'l L.* 405–12 (1982).

HADJICONSTANTINOU, C., 'The United Nations Sub-Commission on the Prevention of Discrimination and the Protection of Minorities', 2 *Thesaurus Acroasium* 395–404 (1976).

HASRAR, U., *Minority Protection and International Bill of Human Rights* (Allied Publishers, Bombay, 1974).

HANNUM, H., 'Current Developments: The Thirty-Third Session of the UN Sub-Commission on Prevention of Discrimination and Protection of Minorities', 75 *Am. J. Int'l L.* 172–9 (1981).

—— 'Human Rights and the UN: Progress at the 1980 Session of the UN Sub-Commission on Prevention of Discrimination and Protection of Minorities', 3 *Hum. Rts. Q.* 1–17 (1981).

—— 'New Developments in Indigenous Rights', 28 *Va. J. Int'l L.* 649–78 (1988).

HANTKE, H., 'The 1982 Session of the UN Sub-Commission on Prevention of Discrimination and Protection of Minorities', 77 *Am. J. Int'l L.* 651–62 (1983).

HAVER, P., 'The Mandate of the UN Sub-Commission on the Prevention of Discrimination and Protection of Minorities', 21 *Colum. J. Transnat'l L.* 103–34 (1982).

HEINZ, W. S., *Indigenous Populations, Ethnic Minorities and Human Rights* (Springer-Verlag, Berlin, 1988).

HISCOCKS, R., 'The Work of the UN for the Prevention of Discrimination', in G. Liebholz and K. D. Bracher (eds.), *Die moderne Demokratie und ihr Recht: Festschrift für Gerhard Leibholz* (Mohr, Tubingen, 1966).

HUMPHERY, J. P., 'The United Nations Sub-Commission on the Prevention of Discrimination and the Protection of Minorities', 62 *Am. J. Int'l L.* 869–88 (1968)

International Commission of Jurists, *The Review*: Commentaries on the Work of the Sub-Commission, published from 1973 to date.

JONES, M., 'National Minorities: A Case Study in International Protection', 14 *Law & Contemp. Prob.* 599–626 (1949).

KIM, C. K., 'Some Minority Problems in International Law', 27 *Pophak* (Seoul Law Journal, Korea) 30–3 (1986).

KULIKOW, I. P. 'Sub-Commission on Prevention of Discrimination and Protection of Minorities: Tasks and Results', *GDR Committee Hum. Rts. Bull.* 33–9 (1980).

KUSSBACH, E., 'Die Vereinten Nationen und der Schutz des religiösen Bekenntnisses', 24 *Österreichische Zeitschrift für öffentliches Recht* 267–338 (1973).

LASSEN, N., 'Slavery and Slavery-like Practices: United Nations Standards and Implementation', 57 *Nordic J. Int'l L.* 197–227 (1988).

MCKEAN, W., *Equality and Discrimination under International Law* (Clarendon Press, Oxford, 1983).

MAHER, R. M., and WEISSBRODT, D., 'The 41st Session of the UN Sub-Commission on the Prevention of Discrimination and Protection of Minorities', 12 *Hum. Rts. Q.* 290–327 (1990).

MANKE, I., 'Exhaustion of Domestic Remedies in the United Nations Sub-Commission on Prevention of Discrimination and Protection of Minorities', 24 *Buffalo L. Rev.* 643–81 (1975).

MODEEN, T., *The International Protection of National Minorities in Europe* (Åbo Akademi, Åbo, 1969).

MONTIGNY, Y., 'L'ONU et la protection internationale des minorités depuis 1945', *Rev. juridique Thémis* 389–447 (1978).

NISET, J., 'La Sous-commission de la lutte contre les mesures discriminatoires et de la protection des minorités des Nations Unies à la vingt-sixième session', 5 *Rev. des droits de l'homme* 565–602 (1973).

NOVA, R. DE, 'The International Protection of National Minorities and Human Rights', 11 *Howard LJ* 275–90 (1965).

O'CONNOR, C. M., and GARBER, L., 'The 1984 UN Sub-Commission on Prevention of Discrimination and Protection of Minorities', 79 *Am. J. Int'l L.* 168–80 (1985).

PIRCHER, E., *Der vertragliche Schutz ethnischer, sprachlicher und religiöser Minderheiten im Völkerrecht* (Stampfli, Bern, 1979).

ROBINSON, J., *et al.*, *Were the Minorities Treaties a Failure?* (Institute of Jewish Affairs, New York, 1943).

ROSEN, S., and WEISSBRODT, D., 'The 39th Session of the UN Sub-Commission on Prevention of Discrimination and Protection of Minorities', 10 *Hum. Rts. Q.* 487–508 (1988).

ROY, B., and ALFREDSSON, G., 'Indigenous Rights: The Literature Explosion', 13 *Transnat'l Persp.* 19 (1987).

SALZBERG, J. P., 'A Report on the Twenty-Second Session of the Sub-Commission on the Prevention of Discrimination and Protection of Minorities', 3 *Rev. des droits de l'homme* 129–40 (1970).

SANDERS, D., 'The UN Working Group on Indigenous Populations', 11 *Hum. Rts. Q.* 406–33 (1989).

SAXENA, J. N., 'International Protection of Minorities and Individual Human Rights', 23 *Indian J. Int'l L.* 38–55 (1983).

SCHACHTER, O., 'How Effective Are Measures against Racial Discrimination?', 4 *Rev. des droits de l'homme*, 293–310 (1971).

SOHN, L., 'The Rights of Minorities', in L. Henkin (ed.), *The International Bill of Rights* 270–89 (Columbia UP, New York, 1981).

STAVENHAGEN, R., 'Derechos Humanos y derechos de los pueblos: La cuestión de las minorías', 4 *Rev. Inst. Interam. de derechos hum.* 43–62 (1986).

TRETTER, H., 'Entwicklung und gegenwärtige Bedeutung der Internationalen Sklavereiverbote', in M. Nowak, D. Steurer, and H. Tretter (eds.) *Fortschritt im Bewußtsein der Grund- und Menschenrechte* (Engel, Kehl, 1988).

TREVES, T., 'The UN Body of Principles for the Protection of Detained or Imprisoned Persons', 84 *Am. J. Int'l L.* 578–85 (1990).

VUKAS, B., 'Project de déclaration sur les droits des personnes appartenant à des minorités nationales, ethniques, religieuses et linguistiques', *25 Ann. français de droit int'l* 281–94 (1979).

WEISSBRODT, D., 'A New United Nations Mechanism for Encouraging the Ratification of Human Rights Treaties', 76 *Am. J. Int'l L.* 418–29 (1982).

WILLIAMS, R. A., 'Encounters on the Frontiers of International Human Rights Law: Redefining the Terms of Indigenous Peoples' Survival in the World', 1990 *Duke LJ* 660–704.

ZOGLIN, K., 'United Nations Action against Slavery: A Critical Evaluation', 8 *Hum. Rts. Q.* 306–39 (1986).

6. *The Commission on the Status of Women*

DOCUMENTS

Commission on the Status of Women, Reports on the Sessions. Supplements to the Official Records of the Economic and Social Council. Sessions, years and UN doc. nos. as follows: 1, 1947, E/281/Rev.1; 2, 1948, E/615; 3, 1949, E/1316; 4, 1950, E/1712; 5, 1951, E/1997/Rev.1; 6, 1952, E/2208; 7, 1953, E/2401; 8, 1954, E/2571; 9, 1955, E/2727; 10, 1956, E/2850; 11, 1957, E/2968; 12, 1958, E/3096; 13, 1959, E/3228; 14, 1960, E/3360; 15, 1961, E/3464; 16, 1962, E/3606/Rev.1; 17, 1963, E/3749; 18, 1964, E/4025; 19, 1966, E/4175; 20, 1967 E/4316; 21, 1968, E/4472; 22, 1969, E/4619; 23, 1970, E/4831; 24, 1972, E/5109; 25, 1974, E/5451; 26, 1976, E/5909; 27, 1978, E/1978/32/Rev.1; 28, 1980, E/1980/15; 29,

1982, E/1982/14; 30, 1984, E/1984/25; 31, 1986, E/1986/24; 31A, 1987, E/1987/15; 32, 1988, E/1986/15/Rev.1; 33, 1989, E/1989/24; 34, 1990, E/1990/25; 35, 1991, E/1991/28. The Commission also acted as the preparatory body for the World Conference to Review and Appraise the Achievements of the United Nations Decade for Women. See: A/CONF.116/PC/9 (1983) (Report on First Session) and A/CONF.116/PC/19 (1984) (Report on Second Session).

(1969)

Constitutions, Electoral Laws and other Legal Instruments Relating to Political Rights of Women, Report of the Secretary-General, E.69.IV.2.

(1970)

Participation of Women in the Economic and Social Development of their Countries, Report of the Secretary-General, E.70.IV.4.

(1971)

The Status of the Unmarried Mother: Law and Practice, Report of the Secretary-General, E.71.IV.4.

(1972)

International Instruments and National Standards Relating to the Status of Women: Study of Provisions in Existing Conventions Related to the Status of Women, Report of the Secretary-General, E/CN.6/552.

(1975)

Human Rights Questions: Relevant Resolutions and Procedures Dealing with Communications Concerning Human Rights and Status of Women, Explanatory Report of the Secretary-General, E/5628.

Report of the World Conference of the International Women's Year, E.76.XIV.1.

(1980)

Report of the World Conference of the United Nations Decade for Women: Equality, Development and Peace, E.80.XIV.3.

(1985)

Report of the World Conference to Review and Appraise the Achievements of the United Nations Decade for Women: Equality, Development and Peace, A/CONF.116/28.

Equality in Political Participation and Decision-Making, Report of the Secretary-General, E/CN.6/1990/2.

Negative Effects of the International Economic Situation in the Improvement of the Status of Women, Report of the Secretary-General, E/CN.6/1990/3.

BOOKS AND ARTICLES

Anon., 'The United Nations Commission on the Status of Women', 2 *Int'l LQ* 60–2 (1948).

BARRY, K., 'Female Sexual Slavery: Understanding the International Dimensions of Women's Oppression', 3 *Hum. Rts. Q.* 44–52 (1981).

BOKOR-SZEGO, H., 'Influence of Social Development on Treaties Relating to the Rights of Women', 18 *Acta Juridica Academica Scientiarium Hungaricae* 315–34 (1976).

BOALS, K., 'Women's Transnational Privileges and Disabilities', 69 *Am. Soc. Int'l L. Proc.* 107–13 (1975).

BRUCE, K., 'Work of the United Nations Relating to the Status of Women', 4 *Rev.des droits de l'homme* 365–412 (1971).

BRUCE, M. K., 'Work of the United Nations Relating to the Status of Women', 4 *Rev. des droits de l'homme* 365–412 (1971).

BUNCH, C., 'Women's Rights as Human Rights: Towards a Re-Vision of Human Rights', 12 *Hum. Rts. Q.* 486–98 (1990).

BURROWS, N., 'Monitoring Compliance of International Standards Relating to Human Rights; The Experience of the United Nations Commission on the Status of Women', 31 *Netherlands Int'l L. Rev.* 332–54 (1984).

—— 'International Law and Human Rights—the Case of Women's Rights', in T. Campbell, *et al.* (eds.), *Human Rights: From Rhetoric to Reality* (Blackwell, London, 1986).

CHAION, J. H., 'The Unesco Long-Range Program for the Advancement of Women', *Annals of the American Academy of Political and Social Science* 145–53 (1968).

COLIVER, S., 'United Nations Commission on the Status of Women: Suggestions for Enhancing its Effectiveness', 9 *Whittier L. Rev.* 435–44 (1987).

—— 'United Nations Machineries on Women's Rights: How they could Better Help Women whose Rights are being Violated?', in E. L. Lutz, H. Hannum, and K. J. Burke (eds.), *New Directions in Human Rights* 25–49 (Univ. of Pennsylvania Press, Philadelphia, 1989).

Commission to Study the Organization of Peace, *International Protection of Women's Rights: Preliminary Report* (New York, 1975).

COOK, R. J., 'U.S. Population Policy, Sex Discrimination, and Principles of Equality under International Law', 20 *J. Int'l L. & Pol.* 93–142 (1988).

DAW, R., 'Political Rights of Women: A Study of the International Protection of Human Rights', 12 *Malaya L. Rev.* 308–36 (1970).

EVATT, E., 'Discrimination against Women: The United Nations and CEDAW', in L. Spender (ed.), *Human Rights: The Australian Debate*, 27–38 (Redfern Legal Centre Publishing, Sydney, 1987).

FEARN, C. R., 'Status of Women: United Nations and Mexico', 8 *Calif. W. Int'l LJ* 93–129 (1978).

GALEY, M. E., 'Promoting Nondiscrimination against Women: The UN Commission on the Status of Women', 23 *Int'l Stud. Q.* 273–302 (1979).

—— 'International Enforcement of Women's Rights', 6 *Hum. Rts. Q.* 463–90 (1984).

—— 'The Nairobi Conference: The Powerless Majority', 19 *Pol. Sci.* 255–65 (1986).

GINSBURG, R. B., *et al.*, 'International Women's Year: Focus on Transnational Needs and Initiatives for Women', 69 *Am. Soc. Int'l L. Proc.* 1–39 (1975).

GUGGENHEIM, M. H., 'The Implementation of Human Rights by the UN Commission on the Status of Women: A Brief Comment', 12 *Tex. Int'l LJ* 239–49 (1977).

—— and DE FEIS, E. F., 'United States Participation in International Agreements

Providing Rights for Women', 10 *Loy. of LA L Rev.* 1–71 (1976).

HALLER-ZIMMERMAN, M., 'The UN Human Rights Covenants and the Legal Status of Women in Switzerland' (Schulthess, Zurich, 1973) (in German).

HEVENER, N. K., 'International Law and the Status of Women: An Analysis of International Legal Instruments Related to the Treatment of Women', 1 *Harv. Women's LJ* 131–56 (1978).

—— *International Law and the Status of Women* (Westview Press, Boulder, Colo., 1983).

HOSKEN, F. P., 'Toward a Definition of Women's Rights', 3 *Hum. Rts. Q.* 1–10 (1981).

HUGHES, M. M., 'Women's Rights: A Selected Biblography', 4 *Int'l J. Legal Info.* 216–48 (1976).

IRELAND, P. 'International Advancement and Protection of Human Rights for Women', 10 *Law. of the Am.* 87–98 (1978).

KASCHITZ, H., 'The Commission on the Status of Women with Particular Reference to its Work on Communications', 6 *Netherlands Q. Hum. Rts.* 22–8 (1988).

KHUSHALANI, Y., *Dignity and Honour of Women as Basic and Fundamental Human Rights* (Martinus Nijhoff, The Hague, 1982).

KRAEMER-BACH, M., 'The United Nations Commission on the Status of Women', *Rev. of Contemp. L.* 227–35 (1960).

Lebanese Women's Organization, *Women in the Arabic World under the International Agreements of the United Nations* (Beirut, 1975).

MCDOUGAL, M., LASSWELL, H., and CHEN, L.-C., 'Human Rights for Women and World Public Order: The Outlawing of Sex-Based Discrimination', 69 *Am. J. Int'l L.* 497–533 (1975).

—— —— —— 'The Outlawing of Sex-Based Discrimination', in *Human Rights and World Public Order* 612–52 (Yale UP, New Haven, Conn., 1980).

MORSINK, J., 'Women's Rights in the Universal Declaration', 13 *Hum. Rts. Q.* 229–56 (1991).

PARPORT, J., 'Women's Rights and the Lagos Plan of Action', 8 *Hum. Rts. Q.* 180–96 (1986).

PICADO SOTELA, S., 'La mujer y los derechos humanos: Decenio de Naciones Unidas: Igualdad, desarrollo y paz', 2 *Rev. Inst. Interam. de derechos hum.* 17–40 (1985).

POLSON, T. E., 'Rights of Working Women: An International Perspective', 14 *Va. J. Int'l L.* 729–46 (1974).

REANDA, L., 'Human Rights and Women's Rights: The United Nations Approach', 3 *Hum. Rts. Q.* 11–31 (1981).

—— 'Prostitution as a Human Rights Question: Problems and Prospects of United Nations Action', 13 *Hum. Rts. Q.* 202–28 (1991).

RICAFRENTE, C. L. S., 'International Labor Standards for Working Women', 50 *Philoppine LJ* 55–79 (1975).

SEIFERT, K. H., 'The United Nations Commission on the Status of Women', 16 *Vereinte Nationen* 188–90 (1969) (in German).

SHAPIRO-LIBAI, N., 'The Concept of Sex Equality: The UN Decade for Women', 11 *Israel YB Hum. Rts.* 106–32 (1981).

SWEENEY, J. P., 'Promoting Human Rights through Regional Organizations: Women's Rights in Western Europe', 6 *Hum. Rts. Q.* 491–506 (1984).

TAUBENFELD, R. F., and TAUBENFELD, H. J., 'Achieving the Human Rights of

Women: The Baseline, the Challenge, the Search for a Strategy', 4 *Hum. Rts. Q.* 125–69 (1975).

—— —— *Sex-Based Discrimination: International Law and Organization* (Oceana Publications, New York, 1978).

TINKER, I., and JAQUETTE, J., 'UN Decade for Women: Its Impact and Legacy', 15 *World Dev.* 419–22 (1987).

WOODRICK, R. L., 'Women 1982: Has the United Nations Decade for Women Significantly Advanced the Goal of Equality between the Sexes?' 13 *Calif. W. Int'l LJ* 413–57 (1983).

7. *The Security Council*

BAILEY, S, *Voting in the Security Council* (Indiana UP, Bloomington, Ind., 1969).

—— *How Wars End: The United Nations and the Termination of Armed Conflict, 1946–1964* (Clarendon Press, Oxford, 1982).

—— *The Procedure of the UN Security Council* (Clarendon Press, Oxford, 1975, 1988).

BETTATI, M., and KOUCHNER, B., *Le Devoir d'ingérence: Peut-on les laisser mourir?* (Denoël, Paris, 1987).

BRAND, R. A., 'Security Council Resolutions: When do they Give Rise to Enforceable Legal Rights? The United Nations Charter, the Byrd Amendment and a Self Executing Treaty Analysis', 9 *Cornell Int'l LJ* 298–316 (1976).

CLAUDE, I., Jr., 'The Security Council', in E. Luard (ed.), *The Evolution of International Organizations* (Praeger, New York, 1966).

COT, J. P., and PELLET, A., *La Charte des Nations Unies* (Economica, Paris, 1985).

FRANCK, T., 'Unfulfilled by UNIFIL: The Security Council in Search of a Role', in T. Franck (ed.), *Nation against Nation*, 161–83 (Oxford UP, New York, 1985).

HIGGINS, R., 'The Place of International Law in the Settlement of Disputes by the Security Council', 64 *Am. J. Int'l L.* 1–18 (1970).

—— 'Compliance with United Nations Decisions on Peace and Security and Human Rights Questions', in S. M. Schwebel (ed.), *The Effectiveness of International Decisions*, 32–50 (Sijthoff, Leyden, 1971).

HISCOCKS, R., *The Security Council: A Study in Adolescence* (Free Press, New York, 1974).

KAHNG, T. J., *Law Politics and the Security Council: An Inquiry into the Handling of Legal Questions Involved in International Disputes and Situations* (Martinus Nijhoff, The Hague, 1969).

KERLEY, E., 'The Power of Investigation of the United Nations Security Council', 55 *Am. J. Int'l L.* 892–918 (1961).

KUYPER, P. S., 'Limits of Supervision: The Security Council Watchdog Committee on Rhodesian Sanctions', 25 *Netherlands Int'l L. Rev.* 159–94 (1978).

MCDOUGAL, M., and REISMAN, M., 'Rhodesia and the United Nations: The Lawfulness of International Concern', 62 *Am. J. Int'l L.* 1–19 (1968).

MASON, P., and MARSTELLER, T., 'U.N. Mediation: More Effective Options', 5 *Sch. Adv. Int'l Stud. Rev.* 271–84 (1985).

NEWCOMBE, H., 'Reform of the U.N. Security Council', 8 *Peace Res. Rev.* 419–42 (1979).

NICOL, D., *et al.*, *The United Nations Security Council: Towards Greater Effectiveness* (UNITAR, New York, 1982).

NKALA, P., *The United Nations, International Law, and the Rhodesian Independence Crisis* (Clarendon Press, Oxford, 1985).

NOTE, 'Proposed Resolution Providing for the Authorization of Intervention by the United Nations, A Regional Organization, or a Group of States in a State Committing Gross Violations of Human Rights', 13 *Va. J. Int'l L.* 340–74 (1973).

POGANY, I., *The Security Council and the Arab–Israeli Conflict* (St Martin's Press, New York, 1984).

RAMCHARAN, B. G., '*Humanitarian Good Offices in International Law* (Martinus Nijhoff, The Hague, 1983).

—— 'The Security Council and Humanitarian Emergencies', 9 *Neths. Q. of Hum. Rts.* 19–35 (1991).

ROBEN, V., 'A Report on Effective Protection of Minorities', 31 *German YB Int'l L.* 621–38 (1988).

ROESSER, T., 'The Arms Embargo of the UN Security Council against South Africa: Legal and Practical Aspects', 31 *German YB Int'l L.* 574–94 (1988).

SCHWELB, E. 'An Instance of Enforcing the Universal Declaration of Human Rights-Action By the Security Council', 22 *Int'l & Comp. LQ* 161–3 (1973).

SOHN, L., 'The Security Council's Role in the Settlement of International Disputes', 78 *Am. J. Int'l l.* 402–4 (1984).

SUY, E., 'Some Legal Questions Concerning the Security Council', in I. von Munch (ed.), *Festschrift für Han-Jurgen Schlochauer*, 677–89 (Walter de Gruyter, Berlin, 1981).

TIEWUL, S. A., 'Binding Decisions of the Security Council within the Meaning of Article 25 of the United Nations Charter', 15 *Indian J. Int'l L.* 195–215 (1977).

WHITE, N. D., *The United Nations and the Maintenance of International Peace and Security* (Manchester Univ. Press, Manchester, 1990).

8. *The Committee on the Elimination of Racial Discrimination*

DOCUMENTS

Committee on the Elimination of Racial Discrimination, Reports on the Sessions. Supplement to the Official Records of the UN General Assembly. Sessions, years and UN doc. nos. as follows: 1 and 2, 1970, A/8027; 3 and 4, 1971, A/8418; 5 and 6, 1972, A/8718; 7 and 8, 1973, A/9018; 9 and 10, 1974, A/9618; 11 and 12, 1975, A/10018; 13 and 14, 1976, A/31/18; 15 and 16, 1977, A/32/18; 17 and 18, 1978, A/33/18; 19 and 20, 1979, A/34/18; 21 and 22, 1980, A/35/18; 23 and 24, 1981, A/36/18; 25 and 26, 1982, A/37/18; 27 and 28, 1983, A/38/18; 29 and 30, 1984, A/39/18; 31 and 32, 1985, A/40/18; 33, 34, and 35, 1986–7, A/42/18 (see also A/41/561); 36, 1988, A/43/18; 37, 1989, A/44/18; 38, 1990, A/45/18.

(1979)

Committee on the Elimination of Racial Discrimination and the Progress Made Towards the Achievement of the Objectives of the International Convention on the Elimination of all

Forms of Racial Discrimination, (E.79.XIV.4).

The Committee on the Elimination of Racial Discrimination and the Progress Made Towards the Achievement of the Objectives of the International Convention on the Elimination of all Forms of Racial Discrimination, E.79.XIV.4.

(1983)

Experience in Developing Public Awareness of the Provisions of International Standards on Human Rights, Study by S. Sadiq Ali, HR/GENEVA/1983/BP.1.*Study on the Implementation of Article 4 of the International Convention of the Elimination of all Forms of Racial Discrimination*, Study by J. Ingles, A/CONF.119/10.

Study on the Implementation of Article 7 of the International Convention on the Elimimation of all Forms of Racial Discrimination, Study by G. Tenekides, A/CONF.119/11.

(1986)

Rules of Procedure of the Committee on the Elimination of Racial Discrimination (Embodying Amendments and Additions Adopted by the Committee up to 31 July 1984), CERD/C/35/Rev. 3.

BOOKS AND ARTICLES

Badawi el Sheikh, I. A., 'The Implementation by Egypt of the International Convention on the Elimination of all Form of Racial Discrimination', 38 *Rev. egyptienne de droit int'l* 103–18 (1982).

Bernard-Maugiron, N., '20 Years after: 38th Session of the Committee on the Elimination of Racial Discrimination', 8 *Neths. Q. of Hum. Rts.* 395–415 (1990).

Bitker, B., 'The International Treaty against Racial Discrimination', *53 Marq. LR* 68–81 (1970).

Buergenthal, T., 'Implementing the UN Racial Convention', 12 *Tex. Int'l LJ* 187–221 (1977).

Burrowes, M. R., 'Implementing the UN Racial Convention: Some Procedural Aspects', 7 *Australian YB Int'l L.* 236–78 (1981).

Cassese, A., 'A New Reservations Clause: Article 20 of the United Nations Convention on the Elimination of all Forms of Racial Discrimination', in *Recueil d'études de droit international: En Hommage à Paul Guggenheim* 266 (University of Geneva, Geneva, 1968).

Coleman, H. D., 'Rules of Procedure for the New Tribunal (on Racial Discrimination): A Proposed Draft', 56 *Calif. LR* 1569–600 (1968).

—— 'The Problem of Anti-Semitism under the International Convention on the Elimination of all Forms of Racial Discrimination', 4 *Rev. des droits de l'homme* 609–31 (1969).

Corriente Cordoba, J. A., 'El proyecto de Convención de las Naciones Unidas sobre la eliminación de todas las formas de intolerancia y discriminación fundadas en la religión o la creencia', XIV *Ius Canonicum* 121–48 (1972).

Das, K., 'Measures of Implementation of the International Convention on the Elimination of all Forms of Racial Discrimination with Special Reference to the Provisions Converning Reports from States Parties to the Convention', 4 *Rev. des droits de l'homme*, 313–62 (1971).

—— 'The International Convention on the Elimination of all Forms of Racial Discrimination', in K. Vasak, and P. Alston (eds.), *The International Dimensions of Human Rights*, 307–30 (Greenwood Press and UNESCO, Westport and Paris, 1982).

DORE, I., 'United Nations Measures to Combat Racial Discrimination: Progress and Problems in Retrospect', 10 *Den. J. Int'l L. & Pol.* 299–330 (1981).

ELKIND, J., 'Discrimination: A Guide for the Fact Finder (International Convention for the Elimination of all Forms of Racial Discrimination)', 32 *Pittsburgh LR* 307–46 (1971).

ERMACORA, F., *Diskiminierungsschutz und Diskriminierungsverbot in der Arbeit der Vereinten Nationen* (Bräumüller, Vienna, 1971).

FERGUSON, C. C., 'United Nations Convention on Racial Discrimination: Human Rights by Treaty', 1 *Law Transition Q.* 61–75 (1964).

GÓMEZ DEL PRADO, J., 'United Nations Conventions on Human Rights: The Practice of the Human Rights Committee and the Committee on the Elimination of Racial Discrimination in Dealing with Reporting Obligations of States Parties', 7 *Hum. Rts. Q.* 492–513 (1986).

HAUSER, R., 'United Nations Law on Racial Discrimination', 64 *Am. Soc. Int'l L. Proc.* 114–19 (1970).

HEINTZE, H. J., 'The Ban on Propaganda Advocating Racism and War: On Some Topics Debated in CERD', 14 *GDR Committee Hum. Rts. Bull.* 129–41 (1988).

KELSEY, R., 'A Radical Approach to the Elimination of Racial Discrimination', 1 *U. New South Wales LJ* 56–96 (1975).

KOH, T., 'United Nations Law on Racial Discrimination', 64 *Am. Soc. Int'l L. Proc.* 119–21 (1970).

KUBOTA, Y. (ed.), *Peoples for Human Rights: IMADR Yearbook 1988: Special Issue on International Efforts to Eliminate Discrimination* (International Movement against all Forms of Discrimination and Racism, Tokyo, 1989).

LAUREN, P. G., 'First Principles of Racial Equality: History and the Politics and Diplomacy of Human Rights Provisions in the United Nations Charter', 5 *Hum. Rts. Q.* 1–26 (1983).

LERNER, N., 'Anti-Semitism as Racial and Religious Discrimination under United Nations Conventions', 1 *Israel YB Hum. Rts.* 103–15 (1971).

—— 'The Golan Heights Case and the UN Committee on Racial Discrimination', 3 *Israel YB Hum. Rts.* 118–35 (1973).

—— *The UN Convention on the Elimination of all Forms of Racial Discrimination* (Sijthoff & Noordhoff, Alphen aan den Rijn, 1980).

—— 'Curbing Racial Discrimination: Fifteen Years CERD', 13 *Israel YB Hum. Rts.* 170–82 (1983).

MCKEAN, W. A., *Equality and Discrimination under International Law* (Clarendon Press, Oxford, 1983).

MAHALIC, D., 'The Limitation Provisions of the International Convention on the Elimination of all Forms of Racial Discrimination', 9 *Hum. Rts. Q.* 74–101 (1987).

MERON, T., 'The International Convention on the Elimination of all Forms of Racial Discrimination and the Golan Heights', 8 *Israel YB Hum. Rts.* 222–39 (1978).

—— 'The Meaning and Reach of the International Convention on the Elimination of all Forms of Racial Discrimination', 79 *Am. J. Int'l L.* 283–318 (1985).

NATHANSON, J., and SCHWELB, E., *The United States and the United Nations Treaty on Racial Discrimination* (American Society of International Law, Studies in Transnational Legal Policy, Washington, DC, 1975).

NEWMAN, F., 'The New International Tribunal on Racial Discrimination', 56 *Calif. LR* 1559–68 (1968).

NJENGA, F. X., 'Role of the United Nations in the Matter of Racial Discrimination', 1 *E. Afr. L. Rev.* 136–57 (1968).

PARTSCH, K. J., 'Die Konvention zur Beseitgung der Rassendiskriminierung', 19 *Vereinte Nationen* 1–5 and 46–53 (1971).

—— 'Elimination of Racial Discrimination in the Enjoyment of Civil and Political Rights', 14 *Tex. Int'l LJ* 191–250 (1979).

PIERSON-MATHY, P., 'Droit international et élimination du racism', 35 *Civilisations* (Brussels) 85–111 (1985).

REISMAN, M., 'Responses to Crimes of Discrimination and Genocide: An Appraisal of the Convention on the Elimination of Racial Discrimination', 1 *Den. J. Int'l L. & Pol.* 29–64 (1971).

RICHARDSON, E. R., 'Will the Rapidly Accumulating Body of U.N. Law on Racial Discrimination Truly be Effective?', 64 *Am. Soc. Int'l L. Proc.* 110–14 (1970).

SCHACHTER, O., 'How Effective Are Measures against Racial Discrimination?', 4 *Rev. des droits de l'homme* 293–310 (1971).

SCHAFFER, T., and WEISSBRODT, D., 'Exhaustion of Remedies in the Context of the Racial Discriminations Convention', 2 *Rev. des droits de l'homme* 632–52 (1969).

SCHROTH, R., and MUELLER, G., 'Racial Discrimination: The United States and the International Convention', 4 *Hum. Rts.* 171–203 (1975).

SCHWELB, E., 'The International Convention on the Elimination of all Forms of Racial Discrimination', 15 *Int'l & Comp. LQ* 996–1068 (1966).

TENEKIDES, G., 'L'Action des Nations Unies contre la discrimination raciale', 168 *Rec. des cours* 269–487 (1980).

TRINDADE, A. A., C., 'Exhaustion of Local Remedies under the United Nations International Convention on the Elimination of all Forms of Racial Discrimination', 22 *German YB Int'l L.* 374–83 (1979).

WHITEHEAD, M., 'The Elimination of Racial Discrimination: The U.N. Proposed Solution', 11 *How. LJ* 583–93 (1965).

9. *The Human Rights Committee*

DOCUMENTS

Human Rights Committee, Reports on the Sessions, Supplements to the Official Records of the General Assembly. Sessions, years, and UN doc. nos. as follows: 1 and 2, 1977, A/32/44; 3, 4, and 5, 1978, A/33/40; 6 and 7, 1979, A/34/40; 8, 9, and 10, 1980, A/35/40; 11, 12, and 13, 1981, A/36/40; 14, 15, and 16, 1982, A/37/40; 17, 18, and 19, 1983, A/38/40; 20, 21, and 22, 1984, A/39/40; 23, 24, and 25, 1985, A/40/40; 26, 27, and 28, 1986, A/41/40; 29 and 30, 1987, A/42/40; 31, 32, and 33, 1988, A/43/40; 34, 35, and 36, 1989, A/44/40; 37, 38, and 39, 1990, A/45/40.

Yearbook of the Human Rights Committee 1977–8 E.85.XIV.5 & 10 (1986); 1979–80, E.85.XIV.12 and E.86.XIV.2; 1981–2, E.87.XIV.1 and E.87.XIV.3; 1983–4, E.88.XIV.8.

Human Rights Committee, Selected Documents under the Optional Protocol (2–16th Sessions), E.84.XIV.2.

Selected Documents of the Human Rights Committee under the Optional Protocol, ii (17th–32nd Sessions), E.89.XIV.1.

BOOKS AND ARTICLES

BAAB, C., 'The Process for United States Ratification of Human Rights Instruments', 20 *Ga. J. Int'l & Comp. L.* 265–78 (1990).

BAYEFSKY, A., 'The Human Rights Committee and the Case of Sandra Lovelace [Human Rights Communication R.6/24]', 20 *Canadian YB Int'l L.* 244–66 (1982).

BERGESEN, H. O., 'Human Rights: The Property of the Nation State or a Concern for the International Community? A Study of the Soviet Positions Concerning UN Protection of Civil and Political Rights Since 1975', 14 *Co-operation & Conflict* 239–54 (1979).

BHALLA, S. L., *Human Rights: An Institutional Framework for Implementation* (Docta Shelf Publications, New Delhi, 1991).

BLAY, S. K. N., 'The International Covenant on Civil and Political Rights and the Recognition of Customary Law Practices of Indigenous Tribes: The Case of Australian Aborigines', 19 *Comp. & Int'l LJ of S. Afr.* 199–219 (1986).

BOKOR-SZEGO, H., 'Après l'entrée en vigueur des pactes relatifs à la protection des droits de l'homme', 19 *Acta Juridica Acad. Sci. Hungaricae* 423–39 (1977).

BOSSUYT, M., 'Le Règlement intérieur du Comité des droits de l'homme', 14 *Rev. belge de droit int'l* 104–56 (1978–9).

—— *Guide to the 'Travaux Préparatoires' of the International Covenant on Civil and Political Rights* (Martinus Nijhoff, The Hague, 1987).

BOYD, S., 'The United Nations Human Rights Covenants: Problems of Ratification and Implementation', 62 *Am. Soc. Int'l L. Proc.* 83–123 (1968).

BRAR, P., 'The Practice and Procedures of the Human Rights Committee under the Optional Protocol of the International Covenant on Civil and Political Rights', 25 *Indian J. Int'l L.* 506–43 (1985).

BUERGENTHAL, T., *et al.*, 'UN Human Rights Covenants Become Law: So What?' 70 *Am. Soc. Int'l L. Proc.* 97–105 (1976).

—— 'Codification and Implementation of International Human Rights', in A. H. Henkin (ed.), *Human Dignity: The Internationalization of Human Rights* 15–22 (Oceana Publications, New York, 1979).

—— 'To Respect and to Ensure: State Obligations and Permissible Derogations', in L. Henkin (ed.), *The International Bill of Rights* 72–91 (Columbia UP, New York, 1981).

CAPOTORTI, F., 'The International Measures of Implementation included in the Covenant on Human Rights', in A. Eide and A. Schou (eds.), *International Protection of Human Rights*, 131–48 (Almquist & Wiksell, Stockholm, 1969).

CAREY, J., 'Implementing Human Rights Conventions: The Soviet View', 53 *Ky. LJ* 115–34 (1964).

CASSESE, A., 'The Self-Determination of Peoples', in L. Henkin (ed.), *The International Bill of Rights*, 92–113 (Columbia UP, New York, 1981).

CHEE, C. I., 'Alien Registration Law of Japan and the International Covenant for Civil and Political Rights', 10 *Korea & World Aff.* 649–86 (1986).

COHEN, R., 'International Covenant on Civil and Political Rights', 6 *Int'l Prob.* (Tel Aviv) 38–49 (1968).

COHN, C., 'The Early Harvest: Domestic Legal Changes Related to the Human Rights Committee and the Covenant on Civil and Political Rights', 13 *Hum. Rts Q.* 295–321 (1991).

'Comment, The Remedies of Law of the International Covenant on Civil and Political Rights: Current Trends and a Conceptual Framework for the Future', 20 *NYUJ Int'l L. & Pol.* 525–55 (1988).

Committee of Experts on Human Rights, *Human Rights: Problems Arising from the Co-Existence of the United Nations Conventions on Human Rights and the European Commission on Human Rights Differences as Regards the Rights Guaranteed* (Council of Europe, Strasburg, 1970).

COPITHORNE, M. D., 'Notes sur l'élaboration des pactes de 1966 sur les droits de l'homme', 9 *Etudes internationales* 531–7 (1978).

COTE, M.-J., 'Le Recours au Comité des droits de l'homme de l'O.N.U.: Une illusion', 26 *Cahiers de droit* (Quebec) 531–47 (1985).

COTE-HARPER, G., 'Le Comité des droits de l'homme des Nations Unies', 28 *Cahiers de droit* (Quebec) 533–46 (1987).

COÚSSIRAT-COUSTERE, V., 'L'Adhésion de la France au protocole facultatif se rapportant au pacte relatif aux droits civils et politiques', 29 *Ann. français de droit int'l* 510–32 (1983).

CRAIG, M., 'The International Covenant on Civil and Political Rights and United States Law: Department of State Proposals for Preserving the Status Quo', 19 *Harv. Int'l LJ* 845–86 (1978).

DAS, K., 'United Nations Institutions and Procedures Founded on Conventions on Human Rights and Fundamental Freedom', in K. Vasak and P. Alston (eds.), *The International Dimensions of Human Rights*, 303–62 (Greenwood, Westport, Conn., 1982).

DECAUX, E., 'La Mise en vigueur de pacte international relatif aux droits civils et politiques', 84 *Rev. gén. du droit int'l pub.* 487–534 (1980).

DEUTSCH, E. P., 'The International Covenants on Human Rights and our Constitutional Policy', 54 *ABAJ* 238–45 (1968).

DHOMMEAUX, J., 'Le Comité des droits de l'homme: 10 ans de jurisprudence (25 août 1977–9 juillet 1987)', 33 *Ann. français de droit int'l* 447–77 (1987).

—— 'Méthodes du comité des droits de l'homme dans l'examen des rapports soumis par les états partes au pacte sur les droits civils et politiques', 34 *Ann francais du droit int'l* 331–64 (1988).

DIMITRIJEVIC, V., 'Activity of the Human Rights Committee', 34 *Rev. Int'l Aff.* 24–7 (1983).

DINSTEIN, Y., 'The Rights to Life, Physical Integrity and Liberty', in L. Henkin (ed.), *The International Bill of Rights* 114–37 (Columbia UP, New York, 1981).

EISSEN, M., 'The European Convention on Human Rights and the United Nations Covenant on Civil and Political Rights: Problems of Co-Existence', 22 *Buffalo L. Rev.* 181–216 (1972–3).

ELKIND, J. B., 'The International Covenant on Civil and Political Rights: A Breakthrough', 75 *Am. J. Int'l L.* 169–72 (1981).

ERMACORA, F., 'Human Rights Covenants of the United Nations', 16 *Vereinte Nationen* 133–9 (1968) (in German).

—— 'Die Probleme der Durchsetzung der UN-Konvention über zivile und politische Rechte in westlichen Ländern', in G. Zieger, H. Brunner, O. Mampel, and F. Ermacora (eds.), *Die Ausübung staatlicher Gewalt in Ost und West nach Inkrafttreten der UN-Konvention über zivile und politische Recht* (1978).

—— 'Are the UN Human Rights Covenants an Integral Part of the Austrian Legal Order?', 101 *Juristische Blatter* (Vienna) 191–6 (1979) (in German).

FAUNDEZ LEDESMA, H., 'The Reporting System on the Civil and Political Rights Covenant', Ph.D. thesis (Harvard, 1979).

FAWCETT, S., 'A British View of the Covenant', 14 *Law & Contemp. Prob.* 438–50 (1949).

FERGUSON, C., 'The United Nations Human Rights Covenants: Problems of Ratification and Implementation', 62 *Am. Soc. Int'l L. Proc.* 83–96 (1968).

FISCHER, D. D., 'Reporting under the Covenant on Civil and Political Rights: The First Five Years of the Human Rights Committee', 76 *Am. J. Int'l L.* 142–53 (1982).

FISHER, H., 'Human Rights Covenants and Canadian Law', 15 *Canadian YB. Int'l L.* 42–83 (1977).

GARIBALDI, O. M., 'On the Ideological Content of Human Rights Instruments: The Clause "in a Democratic Society"', in T. Buergenthal (ed.), *Contemporary Issues in International Law: Essays in Honor of Louis B. Sohn* 23–68 (Engel, Kehl, 1984).

GHANDI, P. R., 'The Human Rights Committee and the Right of Individual Communication', 57 *British YB Int'l L.* 201–51 (1986).

—— 'The Human Rights Committee and Derogation in Public Emergencies', 32 *German YB Int'l L.* 321–64 (1989).

GÓMEZ DEL PRADO, J., 'United Nations Coventions on Human Rights: The Practice of the Human Rights Committee and the Committee on the Elimination of Racial Discrimination in Dealing with Reporting Obligations of States Parties', 7 *Hum. Rts. Q.* 492–513 (1985).

GRAEFRATH, B., 'Trends Emerging in the Practice of the Human Rights Committee', *GDR Committee Hum. Rts. Bull.* 3–23 (1980).

—— 'Background Paper Prepared for United Nations Seminar on the Experience of Different Countries in the Implementation of International Standards on Human Rights, Geneva, 1983', HR/Geneva/1983/BP.2 (1983).

—— *Menschenrechte und internationale Kooperation. 10 Jahre Praxis des internationalen Menschenrechtskomitees* (Akademie-Verlag, Berlin, 1988).

GURADZE, H., 'Die Menschenrechtskonventionen der Vereinte Nationen vom 16. Dezember 1966', 15 *Jahrbuch für internationales Recht* 242–73 (1971).

HAIGHT, G. W., 'International Covenants on Human Rights', 1 *Int'l Law.* 475–88 (1967).

—— 'Human Rights Covenants', 62 *Am. Soc. Int'l L. Proc.* 96–116 (1968).

HARTMAN, J. F., 'Derogation from Human Rights Treaties in Public Emergencies: A Critique of Implementation by the European Commission and Court of Human Rights and the Human Rights Committee of the United Nations', 22 *Harv. Int'l LJ* 1–52 (1981).

HASSAN, P., 'International Covenants on Human Rights: An Approach to Interpretation', 19 *Buffalo L. Rev.* 35–50 (1969).

—— 'The International Covenant on Civil and Political Rights: Background and Perspective on Article 9 (I)', 3 *Den. J. Int'l L. & Pol.* 153–83 (1973).

HENKIN, L. (ed.), *The International Bill of Rights: The Covenant on Civil and Political Rights* (Columbia UP, New York, 1981).

HEVENER, N. K., and MOSHER, S. A., 'General Principles of Law and the UN Covenant on Civil and Political Rights', 27 *Int'l & Comp. LQ* 596–613 (1978).

HIGGINS, R., 'Liberty of Movement within the Territory of a State: The Contribution of the Committee on Human Rights', in *International Law at a Time of Perplexity: Essays in Honour of Shabtai Rosenne* (Martinus Nijhoff, Boston, 1989).

HYMN, J., 'Constitutional Aspects of the Covenant', 14 *Law & Contemp. Prob.* 415–78 (1949).

ILO, 'Comparative Analysis of the International Covenants on Human Rights and International Labour Conventions and Recommendations', 52 *ILO Official Bull.* 181–216 (1969).

International Commission of Jurists, *The Review*: Commentaries on the Work of the Human Rights Committee, published regularly from 1977 to date.

JAGERSKIOLD, S., 'The Freedom of Movement', in L. Henkin (ed.), *The International Bill of Rights*, 166–84 (Columbia UP, New York, 1981).

JAKUBOWSKI, J., 'Pactes des droits de l'homme de l'O.N.U. et le droit international privé', 4 *Polish YB Int'l L.* 207 (1977–8).

JENKS, C. W., 'The United Nations Covenants on Human Rights Come to Life', in *Recueil d 'études de droit international en hommage à Paul Guggenheim* 805 (Univ. of Geneva, Geneva, 1968).

JHABVALA, F., 'The Practice of the Covenant's Human Rights Committee, 1976–82: Review of State Party Reports', 6 *Hum. Rts. Q.* 81–106 (1984).

—— 'Domestic Implementation of the Covenant on Civil and Political Rights', 32 *Netherlands Int'l L. Rev.* 461–86 (1985).

—— 'The International Covenant on Civil and Political Rights as a Vehicle for the Global Promotion and Protection of Human Rights', 15 *Israel YB Hum. Rts.* 184–203 (1985).

—— 'The Soviet-Bloc's View of the Implementation of Human Rights Accords', 6 *Hum. Rts. Q.* 461–91 (1985).

JONES, C., 'Toward Equal Rights and Amendment of Section 12(1)(b) of the Indian Act: A Postcript to Lovelace v. Canada', 8 *Harv. Women's LJ* 195–214 (1985).

KARTASHKIN, V. A., 'Legislation, Decisions and Practice: Covenants on Human Rights and Soviet Legislation', 10 *Rev. des droits de l'homme* 97–115 (1977).

KAUFMAN, E., HEVENER, N., and MOSHER, S. A., 'General Principles of Law and the UN Covenant on Civil and Political Rights', 27 *Int'l & Comp. LQ.* 597–613 (1978).

KAWASHIMA, Y., 'The International Covenants on Human Rights and the Japanese Legal System', in S. Yamamoto (ed.) *The Japanese Annual of International Law 1978* (Int'l Assoc., Tokyo, 1979).

KISS, A., 'Permissible Limitations on Rights', in L. Henkin (ed.), *The International Bill of Rights*, 290–310 (Columbia UP, New York, 1981).

KOULICHEV, L., 'Garanties juridiques concernant l'application des pactes relatifs aux droits de l'homme', in E. Kamenov (ed.), *La République Populaire de Bulgarie et les droits de l'homme: Recueil d'études et de documents* (Sofia-Press, Sofia, 1970).

LANGER, R., 'Der Kampf um die Menschenrechtskonventionen in den Vereinten Nationen', 9 *Osterreichische Zeitschrift für offenliches Recht* 1–65 (1958).

LECKIE, S., 'The Inter-State Complaint Procedure in International Human Rights Law: Hopeful Prospects or Wishful Thinking?', 10 *Hum. Rts. Q.* 249–303 (1988).

LEMMENS, P., 'Contestation sur des droits et obligations de caractère civil', 11 *Admin. Pub.* 90–3 (1987).

LILLICH, R. B., 'United States Ratification of the United Nations Covenants', 20 *Ga. J. Int'l & Comp. L.* 279–92 (1990).

LIPPMAN, M., 'Human Rights Revisited: The Protection of Human Rights under the International Covenant on Civil and Political Rights', 10 *Calif. W. Int'l LJ* 450–513 (1980).

LOCKWOOD, J. E., 'Drafts of International Covenants and Declaration on Human Rights', 42 *Am. J. Int'l L.* 401–5 (1948).

LUCHTERHANDT, O., *Human Rights: UN Covenants and Soviet Law* (Bundesinstitut fur Ostwissenschaftliche and Internationale Studien, Cologne, 1980) (in German).

MACCHESNEY, B., 'Should the United States Ratify the Covenants? A Question of Merits, Not of Constitutional Law', 62 *Am. J. Int'l L.* 912–17 (1968).

MCGOLDRICK, D., 'Canadian Indians, Cultural Rights and the Human Rights Committee', 40 *ICLQ* 658–69 (1991).

—— *The Human Rights Committee: Its Role in the Development of the International Covenant on Civil and Political Rights* (Clarendon Press, Oxford, 1991).

MAMPEL, S., 'Observations on the Report of the GDR to the Human Rights Committee of the United Nations', 22 *Recht in Ost und West* 149–57 (1978) (in German).

MARIE, J. B., 'Les Pactes internationaux relatifs aux droits de l'homme: Confirment-ils l'inspiration de la Déclaration Universelle?', 3 *Rev. des droits de l'homme* 397–425 (1970).

MICHALSKA, A., 'L'Application des pactes internationaux relatifs aux droits de l'homme, 8 *Polish YB Int'l L.* 183–200 (1976).

—— 'Interpretation of the International Covenant on Civil and Political Rights in the Light of Reports of the Human Rights Committee', 15 *Polish YB Int'l L.* 45–70 (1986).

MØSE, E., and OPSAHL, T., 'The Optional Protocol to the International Covenant on Civil and Political Rights', 21 *Santa Clara L. Rev.* 271–331 (1981).

MOHR, M., 'Questions of Procedure under International Law in the Implementation of Human Rights Instruments', 2 *GDR Committee Hum. Rts. Bull.* 61–71 (1983).

—— 'Experience Gained in the Human Rights Committee: Reflections on Professor Graefrath's Book, "Human Rights and International Co-operation"', 14 *GDR Committee Hum. Rts. Bull.* 100–12 (1988).

MOURGEON, J., 'L'Entrée en vigueur des pactes internationaux relatifs aux droits de l'homme', 22 *Ann. français de droit int'l* 290–304 (1976).

MOWER, A. G., Jr., 'Implementation of the UN Covenant on Civil and Political Rights', 1 *Rev. des droits de l'homme* 271–95 (1977).

—— 'Organizing to Implement the UN Civil/Political Rights Covenant: First Steps by the Committee', 3 *Hum. Rts. Rev.* 122–31 (1978).

MUNGER, K., *Burgerliche und politische Rechte im Weltpakt der Vereinten Nationen und im schweizerischen Recht* (Schulthess Polygraphischer, Zurich, 1973).

NAWAZ, M. K., 'Ratification of or Accession to Human Rights Convention', 13 *Indian J. Int'l L.* 576–88 (1973).

NEWMAN, F., 'Natural Justice, Due Process and the New International Covenants on Human Rights', *Pub. L.* 274–313 (1967).

NOBLE, A. A., 'The Covenant on Civil and Political Rights as the Law of the Land', 25 *Vill. L. Rev.* 119–40 (1979).

NOOR MUHAMMED, H. N. A., 'Guarantees for Accused Persons Under the UN Human Rights Covenants', 20 *Indian J. Int'l L.* 179–215 (1980).

—— 'Due Process of Law for Persons Accused of Crime', in L. Henkin (ed.) *The International Bill of Rights*, 138–65 (Columbia UP, New York, 1981).

Note, 'The Draft International Declaration and Covenant on Human Rights', 26 *Can. B. Rev.* 548–63 (1948).

—— 'Ratification and Implementation of International Conventions on Human Rights', 32 *ILJ Bull.* 1–12 (1967).

—— 'The UN Human Rights Covenants: Soon to be in Force', 15 *Int'l Commission of Jurists Rev.* 33–6 (1975).

—— 'Rights of Relatives of Victims: Views of the Human Rights Committee in the Quinteros Communication', 25 *Harv. Int'l LJ* 470–7 (1984).

NOWAK, M., 'Die Durchsetzung des Internationalen Paktes über burgerliche und politische Rechte. Bestandsaufnahme der ersten 10 Tagungen des UN-Ausschusses für Menschrenrechte', 25 *Europäische Grundrechte Zeitschrift* 532–44 (1980).

—— 'The Effectiveness of the International Covenant on Civil and Political Rights: Stocktaking after the First Eleven Sessions of the UN Human Rights Committee', 1 *Hum. Rts. LJ* 136–70 (1980).

—— 'UN Human Rights Committee: Survey of Decisions Given up till July 1984', 5 *Hum. Rts. LJ* 199–219 (1984).

—— 'UN Human Rights Committee: Survey of Decisions Given up till July 1986', 7 *Hum. Rts. LJ* 287–307 (1986).

—— *UNO-Pakt über bürgerliche und politische Rechte und Fakultativprotokoll: CCPR-Kommentar* (Springer-Verlag, Kehl, 1989).

OPSAHL, T., 'Equality in Human Rights Law with Particular Reference to Article 26 of the International Covenant on Civil and Political Rights', in N. P. Engel (ed.), *Fortschritt im Bewußtsein der Grund-und Menschenrechte*, 51–67 (Springer-Verlag, Strasburg, 1988).

—— and DE ZAYAS, A., 'The Uncertain Scope of Article 15 (1) of the International Covenant on Civil and Political Rights', 1 *Canadian YB Hum. Rts.* 237–54 (1983).

OUTRATA, V., 'Some Notes on the Implementation of the Covenants on Human Rights and its Control', 25 *Bull. of Czechoslovak L.* (Prague) 293–309 (1967).

OXENKNECHT, R., *Der Schutz ethnischer, religiöser und sprachlicher Minderheiten im Art. 27 des Internationalen Paktes über bürgerliche und politische Rechte vom 16. Dezember 1966* (Lang, Frankfurt, 1988).

'Panel, The UN Human Rights Covenants: Problems of Ratification and Implementation', 62 *Am. Soc. Int'l L. Proc.* 83–116 (1968).

—— 'UN Human Rights Covenants become Law: So What?', 70 *Am. Soc. Int'l L. Proc.* 97–105 (1976).

PARTSCH, K. J., 'Freedom of Conscience and Expression and Political Freedoms', in

L. Henkin (ed.), *The International Bill of Rights* 209–45 (Columbia UP, New York, 1981).

PECHOTA, V., 'The Development of the Covenant on Civil and Political Rights', in L. Henkin (ed.), *The International Bill of Rights* 32–71 (Columbia UP, New York, 1981).

PLAINE, H. H. E., 'The Covenant on Human Rights', 73 *New Jersey LJ* 367–9 (1950).

PREMONT, D., 'État d'acceptation du Pacte international relatif aux droits civils et politiques et du Protocole facultatif s'y rapportant', 32 *Ann. français de droit int'l* 570–90 (1986).

PROUNIS, O., 'The Human Rights Committee: Towards Resolving the Paradox of Human Rights Law', 17 *Colum. Hum. Rts. L. Rev.* 103–19 (1986).

RAMCHARAN, B. G., 'Implementing the International Covenants on Human Rights', in B. G. Ramcharan (ed.), *Human Rights: Thirty Years after the Universal Declaration* (Martinus Nijhoff, The Hague, 1979).

—— 'The Emerging Jurisprudence of the Human Rights Committee', 6 *Dalhousie LJ* 7–40 (1980).

—— 'Equality and Nondiscrimination', in L. Henkin (ed.), *The International Bill of Rights* 246–69 (Columbia UP, New York, 1981).

RAMELLA, P. A., 'Human Rights Covenants', 143 *Rev. jurídica Argentina: La ley* 1042–51 (1971) (in Spanish).

RESICH, Z., 'Covenants on Human Rights', 20 *Pol. Persp.* 27–35 (1977).

ROBERTSON, A., 'United Nations Covenant on Civil and Political Rights and the European Convention on Human Rights', 43 *Brit. YB Int'l L.* 21–48 (1968–9).

ROBERTSON, A. H., 'The Implementation System: International Measures', in B. G. Ramcharan (ed.), *Human Rights: Thirty Years after the Universal Declaration*, 332–70 (Martinus Nijhoff, The Hague, 1979).

RUSK, D., 'A Personal Reflection on International Covenants on Human Rights', 9 *Hofstra L. Rev.* 515–22 (1981).

RYAN, H. R. S., 'Seeking Relief under the United Nations International Covenant on Civil and Political Rights', 6 *Queen's LJ* 389–407 (1981).

SAITO, Y., 'The Adoption of the Two Treaties on Human Rights at the General Assembly of the United Nations Organization', 10 *World Just.* (Louvain) 188–201 (1968).

SAKSENA, K. P., 'International Covenants on Human Rights', in T. S. Rama Rao (ed.), *Indian YB Int'l Aff. 1966–1967* (Univ. of Madras, 1970).

SCHACHTER, O., 'The Obligation of the Parties to Give Effect to the Covenant on Civil and Political Rights', 73 *Am. J. Int'l L.* 462–5 (1979).

—— 'The Obligation to Implement the Covenant in Domestic Law', in L. Henkin (ed.), *The International Bill of Rights* 311–31 (Columbia UP, NY, 1981).

SCHWELB, E., 'The Work of Codification of the United Nations in the Sphere of Human Rights', 8 *Archiv des Volkerrechts* (Tubingen) 16–49 (1959) (in German).

—— 'International Conventions on Human Rights', 9 *Int'l & Comp. LQ.* 654–75 (1960).

—— 'Civil and Political Rights: The International Measures of Implementation', 62 *Am. J. Int'l L.* 827–68 (1968).

—— 'Notes on the Early Legislative History of the Measures of Implementation of the Human Rights Covenants', in *Mélanges offerts à Polys Modinos: Problèmes des droits de*

l'homme et de l'unification européene 270–89 (Pedone, Paris, 1968).
—— 'Some Aspects of the International Covenants on Human Rights of December 1966', in A. Eide and A. Schou (eds.), *International Protection of Human Rights*, 103–30 (Almquist & Wiksell, Stockholm, 1969).
—— 'The Nature of the Obligations of the States Parties to the International Covenant on Civil and Political Rights', in *René Cassin: Amicorum Disciopulorumque Liber*, i. 301 (Pedone, Paris, 1969).
—— 'The United Kingdom Signs the Covenants on Human Rights', 18 *Int'l & Comp. LQ* 457–67 (1969).
—— 'Entry into Force of the International Covenants on Human Rights and the Optional Protocol to the International Covenant on Civil and Political Rights', 70 *Am. J. Int'l L.* 511–19 (1976).
—— 'The International Measures of Implementation of the International Covenant on Civil and Political Rights and of the Optional Protocol', 12 *Tex. Int'l L. Rev.* 141–86 (1977).
SCOTT, C., 'The Interdependence and Permeability of Human Rights Norms: Towards a Partial Fusion of the International Covenants on Human Rights', 27 *Osgoode Hall LJ* 770–859 (1989).
SEELEY, J. J., 'Article Twenty of the International Covenant on Civil and Political Rights: First Amendment Comments and Questions', 10 *Va. J. Int'l L.* 328–47 (1970).
SHELTON, D. L., 'Supervising Implementation of the Covenants: The First Ten Years of the Human Rights Committee', 80 *Am. Soc. Int'l L. Proc.* 413–19 (1986).
SIMSARIAN, J., 'Progress in Drafting Two Covenants on Human Rights in the United Nations', 46 *Am. J. Int'l L.* 710–18 (1952).
SKELTON, J. W., 'The United States Approach to Ratification of the International Covenants on Human Rights', 2 *Hous. J. Int'l L.* 103–25 (1979).
SOHN, L. B., 'The Rights of Minorities', in L. Henkin (ed.), *The International Bill of Rights* 270–89 (Columbia UP, New York, 1981).
—— 'United States Attitudes Towards Ratification of Human Rights Instruments', 20 *Ga J. Int'l & Comp. L.* 255–64 (1990).
STARR, R., 'International Protection of Human Rights and the United Nations Covenants', 4 *Wis. L. Rev.* 863–90 (1967).
SUTER, K. D., 'Australia and the Covenant on Civil and Political Rights', 4 *Dyson House Papers: Australia, Asia, and the World* 1–16 (1978).
SYMPOSIUM, 'Limitation and Derogation Provisions in the International Covenant on Civil and Political Rights', 7 *Hum. Rts. Q.* 1–157 (1985).
TARDU, M., 'The Protocol to the UN Covenant on Civil and Political Rights and the Inter-American System: A Study of Co-Existing Petition Procedures', 70 *Am. J. Int'l L.* 778–800 (1976).
TIMMERMANS, W. A., 'Eastern Europe and the UN Human Rights Covenants', 4 *Rev. of Socialist L.* (Leiden) 85–90 (1978).
TOMUSCHAT, C., 'Der Schutz der Familie durch die Vereinten Nationen', 100 *Archiv des offentlichen Rechts* 402–15 (1975).
—— 'Protection of Minorities under Article 27 of the International Covenant on Civil and Political Rights', in R. Bernhardt, W. Geck, G. Jaenicke, and H. Steinberger (eds.), *Völkerrecht als Rechtsordnung: International Gerichtsbarkeit-Menschenrechte*,

Festschrift für Hermann Mosler 949–79 (Berlin, Springer, 1983).
—— 'Evolving Procedural Rules: The UN Human Rights Committee's First Two Years of Dealing with Individual Communications', 1 *Hum. Rts. LJ* 249–57 (1980).
—— 'Equality and Non-Discrimination under the International Covenant on Civil and Political Rights', in I. von Munch (ed.), *Festschrift für Hans-Jurgen Schlochauer*, 691–716 (Walter de Gruyter, Berlin, 1981).
—— 'National Implementation of International Standards on Human Rights', R/Geneva/1983/B.P.3 & Add. 1 (1983).
TRIGGS, G., 'Australia's Ratification of the International Covenant on Civil and Political Rights: Ratificaiton or Repudiation?', 31 *Int'l & Comp. LQ* 278–306 (1982).
TRINDADE, A. A. C., 'Exhaustion of Local Remedies under the UN Covenant on Civil and Political Rights and its Optional Protocol', 28 *Int'l & Comp. LQ* 734–65 (1979).
TUTTLE, C., 'Are the Human Rights Coventions Really Objectionable?' 3 *Int'l Law.* 385–96 (1969).
TYAGI, K., 'Cooperation between the Human Rights Committee and Nongovernmental Organizations: Permissibility and Propositions', 18 *Tex. Int'l LJ* 273–90 (1983).
VOLIO, F., 'Legal Personality, Privacy and the Family', in L. Henkin (ed.), *The International Bill of Rights*, 185–208 (Columbia UP, New York, 1981).
WAGNER, W., *Die Verwirklichung der Menschenrechte im Pakt der Vereinten Nationen über bürgerliche und politische Rechte vom 16. Dezember 1966, im Grundvertrag und den ihn begleitenden Nebeninstrumenten* (Peter Lang, Frankfurt, 1977).
WALKATE, J. A., *The Human Rights Committee: Monitoring the Implementation of the International Covenant on Civil and Political Rights* (Oegstgeest, The Netherlands, 1980).
—— 'The Human Rights Committee and Public Emergencies', 9 *Yale J. World Pub. Ord.* 133–46 (1982).
WEISSBRODT, D., 'United States Ratification of the Human Rights Covenants', 63 *Minn. L. Rev.* 35–78 (1978).
WILLIAMS, P., *Treatment of Detainees: Examination of Issues Relevant to Detention by the United Nations Human Rights Committee* (Henry Dunant Institute, Geneva, 1990).
ZAYAS, A. DE, 'The Potential for the United States Joining the Covenant Family', 20 *Ga. J. Int'l & Comp. L.* 299–310 (1990).
—— and MOLLER, J., 'Optional Protocol Cases Concerning the Nordic States before the United Nations Human Rights Committee', 55 *Nordic J. Int'l L.* 384–402 (1986).
—— —— and OPSAHL, T., 'The Case Law of the Human Rights Committee, 1977–1982', 1 *Canadian YB Hum. Rts.* 237–54 (1983).
—— —— —— 'Application of the International Covenant on Civil and Political Rights under the Optional Protocol by the Human Rights Committee', 28 *German YB Int'l L.* 9–64 (1985).
—— —— —— 'Application by the Human Rights Committee of the International Covenant on Civil and Political Rights under the Optional Protocol', 3 *Canadian YB Hum. Rts.* 101–53 (1986).
ZIEGER, G., 'Die Konvention der UN über die zivilen und politischen Rechte', in G. Zieger, H. Brunner, O. Maupel, and F. Ermacora (eds.), *Die Ausübung staatlicher Gewalt in Ost and West nach Inkrafttreten der UN-Konvention über zivile und politische Rechte* (Muller, Heidelberg, 1978).

10. *The Committee on the Elimination of Discrimination against Women*

DOCUMENTS

Committee on the Elimination of Discrimination against Women, Reports on the Sessions. Supplement to the Official Records of the UN General Assembly. Session years and UN doc. nos. as follows: 1, 1983, A/38/45; 2, 1984, A/39/45/, vol. i; 3, 1984, A/39/45, vol. ii; 4, 1985, A/40/45; 5, 1986, A/41/45; 6, 1987, A/42/38; 7, 1988/A/43/38; 8, 1989/A/44/38; 9, 1990, A/45/38; 10, 1991, A/46/38.

Commonwealth Secretariat, *The Convention on the Elimination of all Forms of Discrimination against Women: Explanatory Documentation Prepared for Commonwealth Jurisdictions* (Commonwealth Secretariat, London, 1985).

Report of the Committee on the Elimination of Discrimination against Women on the Achievements of, and Obstacles Encountered by, States Parties in the Implementation of the Convention on the Elimination of all Forms of Discrimination against Women; Submitted to the World Conference to Review and Appraise the Achievements of the United Nations Decade for Women: Equality, Development and Peace, A/CONF.116/13 (1985).

BOOKS AND ARTICLES

BURROWS, N., 'The 1979 Convention on the Elimination of all Forms of Discrimination against Women', 32 *Netherlands Int'l L. Rev.* 419–60 (1985).

BYRNES, A., 'Australia and the Convention on Discrimination against Women', 62 *Australian LJ* 478–9 (1988).

—— 'The "Other" Human Rights Treaty Body: The Work of the Committee on the Elimination of Discrimination against Women', 14 *Yale J. Int'l L.* 1–67 (1989).

CARON, M., 'Les Travaux du Comité pur l'élimination de la discrimination à l'égard des femmes', 2 *Rev. québécoise de droit int'l* 295–303 (1985).

CLARK, B., 'The Vienna Convention Reservations Regime and the Convention on Discrimination against Women', 85 *Am. J. Int'l L.* 281–321 (1991).

COOK, R. J., 'Bibliography: The International Right to Nondiscrimination on the Basis of Sex', 14 *Yale J. Int'l L.* 161–81 (1989).

—— 'Reservations to the Convention on the Elimination of all Forms of Discrimination against Women', 30 *Va. J. Int'l L.* 643–716 (1990).

—— 'The Women's Convention: Opportunities for the Commonwealth', *Commonwealth Law Bulletin* (Apr. 1990), 610–19.

CORTES, I. R., 'The Philippine Commitments under the United Nations Convention on the limitation of Discrimination against Women', 11 *Philippine YB Int'l L.* 53–60 (1985).

DELBRÜCK, J., 'Konvention des Vereinten Nationen zur Beseitigung jeder Form der Diskriminierung der Frau von 1979 im Kontext der Bemühungen um einen völkerrechtlichen Schutz der Menschenrechte', in I. von Munch (ed.), *Festschrift für Hans-Jurgen Schlochauer*, 691–716 (Walter de Gruyter, Berlin, 1981).

EISLER, R., 'Human Rights: Toward an Integrated Theory for Action', 9 *Hum. Rts. Q.* 287–308 (1987).

ERNST-HENRION, M., 'Le Rôle normatif de l'ONU dans l'élimination de la discrimination à l'égard des femmes', 107 *J. des Tribuneaux* 708–11 (1988).

GALEY, M., 'International Enforcement of Women's Rights', 6 *Hum. Rts.* Q. 463–90 (1984).

HALBERSTAM, M., and DEFEIS, E., *US Women's Legal Rights: International Covenants an Alternative to ERA?* (Transnational, Dobbs Ferry, NY, 1987).

HEVENER, N. K., 'An Analysis of Gender Based Treaty Law: Contemporary Developments in Historical Perspective', 8 *Hum. Rts. Q.* 70–88 (1986).

International Women's Rights Action Watch, *Assessing the Status of Women: A Guide to Reporting using the Convention on the Elimination of all Forms of Discrimination against Women* (International Women's Rights Action Watch, New York, 1988).

JAYME, R., 'Economic Implications of the Philippine Accession to the United Nations Convention on the Elimination of All Forms of Discrimination against Women', 7 *Philippines YB Int'l L.* 150–79 (1981).

LORANGER, B., 'Convention on the Elimination of All Forms of Discrimination against Women', 20 *Canadian YB Int'l L.* 349–50 (1982).

MCKEAN, W., 'The Convention and Declarations (4): Equality of the Sexes', in *Equality and Discrimination under International Law*, 166–93 (Clarendon Press, Oxford, 1983).

MERON, T., 'The Convention on the Elimination of All Forms of Discrimination against Women', in T. Meron (ed.), *Human Rights Law-Making in the United Nations: A Critique of Instruments and Processes*, 53–82 (Clarendon Press, Oxford, 1986).

—— 'Enhancing the Effectiveness of the Prohibition of Discrimination against Women', 84 *Am. J. Int'l L.* 213–17 (1990).

OESER, E., 'Legal Questions in the Committee on the Elimination of Discrimination against Women', 14 *GDR Committee Hum. Rts. Bull.* 86–100 (1988).

OSCHINSKY, S., 'Un nouvel instrument international destiné à promouvoir l'égalité entre femmes et hommes: La Convention sur la discrimination à l'égard des femmes des Nations Unies', 95 *J. des tribunaux* 385–6 (1980).

REANDA, L., 'Human Rights and Women's Rights: The United Nations Approach', 3 *Hum. Rts. Q.* 11–31 (1981).

RICHTER, R., 'Frauenkonvention—bedeutendes Ergebnis in der UN-Dekade der Frau', 6 *Deutsche Außenpolitik* 105–12 (1980).

STUMPF, A., 'Re-Examining the UN Convention on the Elimination of All Forms of Discrimination against Women: The UN Decade for Women Conference in Nairobi', 10 *Yale J. Int'l L.* 384–405 (1985).

TINKER, C., 'Human Rights for Women: The UN Convention on the Elimination of All Forms of Discrimination against Women', 3 *Hum. Rts. Q.* 32–43 (1981).

WADSTEIN, M., 'Implementation of the UN Convention on the Elimination of All Forms of Discrimination against Women', 6 *Netherlands Q. Hum. Rts.* 5–21 (1988).

11. *The Committee on Economic, Social and Cultural Rights*

DOCUMENTS

Annual Reports of the Committee and its Predecessor Working Groups: E/1979/64; E/1980/60; E/1981/64; E/1982/56; E/1983/41; E/1984/83; E/1985/18; E/1986/49; E/1987/28; E/1988/14; E/1989/22; E/1990/23; E/1991/23.

(1967)

Seminar on the Realization of Economic and Social Rights Contained in the Universal Declaration of Human Rights. ST/TAO/HR/31.

(1969)

Preliminary Study of Issues Relating to the Realization of Economic and Social Rights Contained in the Universal Declaration of Human Rights and in the International Covenant on Economic, Social, and Cultural Rights: Prepared by the Secretary-General. E/CN.4/988 and Add. 1.

(1975)

The Realization of Economic, Social, and Cultural Rights: Problems, Policies, Progress, Study by M. Ganji, E.75.XIV.2.

(1989)

Bibliography of Published Materials Relating to the International Covenant on Economic, Social, and Cultural Rights and the Work of the Committee, E/C.12/1989/L.3.

List of Articles Showing the Nature and Extent of Overlapping under Six International Human Rights Instruments, E/C.12/1989/3.

Selected Resolutions and Decisions of the Economic and Social Council Relating to the Implementation of the International Covenant on Economic, Social, and Cultural Rights, E/C.12/1989/4.

BOOKS AND ARTICLES

ALSTON, P., 'Human Rights and Basic Needs: A Critical Assessment', 12 *Rev. des droits de l'homme* 19–67 (1979).

—— 'United Nations Specialized Agencies and Implementation of the International Covenant on Economic, Social and Cultural Rights', 18 *Colum. J. Transnat'l L.* 79–118 (1979).

—— 'International Law and the Human Right to Food', in P. Alston and K. Tomasevski (eds.), *The Right to Food*, 9–68 (Martinus Nijhoff, The Hague, 1984).

—— 'Out of the Abyss?: The Challenges Confronting the New UN Committee on Economic, Social and Cultural Rights', 9 *Hum. Rts. Q.* 332–81 (1987).

—— 'US Ratification of the Covenant on Economic, Social and Cultural Rights: The Need for an Entirely New Stategy', 84 *Am. J. Int'l L.* 365–93 (1990).

—— and QUINN, J., 'The Nature and Scope of States Parties Obligations under the International Covenant on Economic, Social and Cultural Rights', 9 *Hum. Rts. Q.* 156–229 (1987).

—— and SIMMA, B., 'First Session of the UN Committee on Economic, Social and Cultural Rights', 81 *Am. J. Int'l L.* 747–56 (1987).

—— and SIMMA, B., 'Second Session of the UN Committee on Economic, Social and Cultural Rights', 82 *Am. J. Int'l L.* 603–15 (1988).

BARD, R., 'The Right to Food', 70 *Iowa L. Rev.* 1279–92 (1985).

BEITZKE, G., 'Verwirklichung sozialer Menschenrechte durch internationale

Kontrolle', 29 *Vereinte Nationen* 149–53 (1981).

BERENSTEIN, A., 'Economic and Social Rights: Their Inclusion in the European Convention on Human Rights: Problems of Formulation and Interpretation', 2 *Hum. Rts. LJ* 257–80 (1981).

BOSSUYT, M., 'La Distinction juridique entre les droits civils et politiques et les droits économiques, sociaux et culturels', 8 *Rev. des drotis de l'homme* 783–820 (1975).

BROWNLIE, I., *The Human Right to Food* (Commonwealth Secretariat, London, 1987).

Commentary, Implementation of the International Covenant on Economic, Social and Cultural Rights: ECOSOC Working Group', International Commission of Jurists, 27 *The Rev.* 26–39 (1981).

CRAVEN, M., and DOMMEN, C., 'Making Room for Substance: Fifth Session of the Committee on Economic, Social and Cultural Rights', 9 *Neths Q. of Hum. Rts.* 83–95 (1991).

DANKWA, E. V. O., 'Working Paper on Article 2(3) of the International Covenant on Economic, Social and Cultural Rights', 9 *Hum. Rts. Q.* 230–49 (1987).

DE LA PRADELLE, P., 'Le Droit fondamental de l'homme à la protection de la santé', 31 *Ann. de droit int'l médical* 75–9 (1983).

DJORDJEVIC, M., 'Implementation of the International Pact on Economic, Social and Cultural Rights', 785 *Rev. of Int'l Aff.* 15–17 (1982).

ECHTERHOLTER, R., 'United Nations Covenant on Economic, Social and Cultural Rights', 22 *Vereinte Nationen* 9–13 (1974) (in German).

EIDE, A., *et al.*, (eds.), *Food as a Human Right* (United Nations University, Tokyo, 1984).

FERNÁNDEZ LÓPEZ, A., (ed.), *Garantía internacional de los derechos sociales: Contribución de Naciones Unidas al progreso y desarrollo social, los derechos del niño, la eliminación de la discriminación de la mujer y desarrollo del voluntariado* (Ministerio de Asuntos Sociales, Madrid, 1990).

GINSBERG, M., and LESSER, L., 'Current Developments in Economic and Social Rights: A United States Perspective', 2 *Hum. Rts. LJ* 237–56 (1981).

GONZAGA, M. P., and VILLATUYA, E. O., 'Social and Economic Rights in the Universal Declaration of Human Rights', 27 *Philippines LJ* 92 (1952).

GOODWIN-GILL, G., 'Obligations of Conduct and Result', in P. Alston and K. Tomasevski (eds.), *The Right to Food*, 111–18 (Martinus Nijhoff, The Hague, 1984).

HALVOREN, K., 'Notes on the Realization of the Human Right to Education', 12 *Hum. Rts. Q.* 341–64 (1990).

HARRIS, D., *The European Social Charter* (UP of Virginia, Charlottesville, Va., 1984).

HARVEY, P., 'Monitoring Mechanisms for International Agreements Respecting Economic and Social Human Rights', 12 *Yale J. Int'l L.* 396–420 (1987).

HENKIN, L., 'Economic-Social Rights as "Rights": A United States Perspective', 2 *Hum. Rts. LJ* 223–36 (1981).

HOOF, G. J. H. VAN, 'The Legal Nature of Economic, Social and Cultural Rights: A Rebuttal of Some Traditional Views', in P. Alston and K. Tomasevski (eds.), *The Right to Food*, 97–110 (Martinus Nijhoff, The Hague, 1984).

KARTASHKIN, V., 'Economic, Social and Cultural Rights', in K. Vasak and P. Alston (eds.), *The International Dimensions of Human Rights*, 111–33 (Greenwood Press and UNESCO, Westport, Conn., and Paris, 1982).

KLERK, Y., 'Working Paper on Article 2(2) and Article 3 of the International Covenant on Economic, Social and Cultural Rights', 9 *Hum. Rts. Q.* 250–73 (1987).

KOHLER, P., *Sozialpolitische und sozialrechtliche Aktivitaten der Vereinten Nationen* (Nomos, Baden Baden, 1987).

KOTSCHNIG, F., 'The UN as an Instrument of Economic and Social Development', in R. Gardner, and M. Millikan (eds.), *The Global Partnership: International Agencies and Economic Development*, 16–43 (Praeger, New York, 1968).

LEBLANC, L., 'Economic, Social, and Cultural Rights and the Inter-American System', 19 *J. of Inter-Am. Stud. & World Aff.* 61–82 (1977).

LECKIE, S., 'The UN Committee on Economic, Social and Cultural Rights and the Right to Adequate Housing: Towards an Appropriate Approach', 11 *Hum. Rts. Q.* 522–60 (1989).

LOTILLA, R. P. M., 'State Implementation of the International Covenant on and Cultural Rights', 61 *Philippines LJ* 259–301 (1986).

PECES-BARBA, G., 'Reflections on Economic, Social and Cultural Rights' 2 *Hum. Rts. LJ* 281–94 (1981).

MACDERMOT, N., 'How to Enforce the Torture Convention: A Draft Optional Protocol', *Int'l Commission of Jurists Rev.* 31–6 (1979).

MACDONALD, R. S. J., 'The United Nations and the Promotion of Human Rights', in R. S. J. MacDonald, D. M. Johnston, and G. L. Morris (eds.), *The International Law and Policy of Welfare* (Martinus Nijhoff, Alphen aan den Rijn, 1978).

MARKS, S., 'UNESCO and Human Rights: The Implementation of Rights Relating to Education, Science, Culture and Communication', 13 *Tex Int'l LJ* 35–67 (1977).

MARTÍ DE VESES PUIG, C., 'El proceso de positivación de los derechos económicos, sociales y culturales en el derecho internacional', 3 *An. de derechos hum.* 175–220 (1984).

MOHR, M., 'Procedural Problems Pertaining to the Work of the Committee on Economic, Social and Cultural Rights', 14 *GDR Committee Hum. Rts. Bull.* 112–29 (1988).

PREMONT, D., TOM, M., and MAYENZET, P., *Essais sur le concept de 'droit de vivre': En mémoire de Yougindra Khishalani* (Bruylant, Brussels, 1988).

RAMCHARAN, B. G., 'Implementation of Economic, Social and Cultural Rights after the Entry into Force of the International Covenant on Economic, Social and Cultural Rights', 9 *E. Afr. L. Rev.* 27–49 (1976).

—— 'Implementation of the International Covenant on Economic, Social and Cultural Rights', 23 *Netherlands Int'l L. Rev.* 151–61 (1976).

SCHWELB, E., 'Some Aspects of the International Covenant on Economic, Social and Cultural Rights', 1 *Rev. des droits de l'homme* 363–77 (1968).

SHELTON, D., 'The Duty to Assist Famine Victims', 70 *Iowa L. Rev.* 1309–20 (1985).

SIEGEL, R., 'Socioeconomic Human Rights: Past and Future', 7 *Hum. Rts. Q.* 255–63 (1985).

SIMMA, B., 'Der Ausschuß fur wirtschaftliche, soziale und kulturelle Rechte (CESCR)—Ein neues Menschenrechtsgremium der Vereinten Nationen', 37 *Vereinte Nationen* 191–96 (1989).

—— and BENNIGSEN, S., 'Wirtschaftliche, soziale und kulturelle Rechte im Völkerrecht—Der Internationale Pakt von 1966 und sein Kontrollverfahren', in J. F. Baur, K. S. Hopt, and K. P. Mailänder (eds.), *Festschrift für Steindorff* 1477–502 (de Gruyter, Berlin, 1990).

STEWART, F., 'Basic Needs Strategies, Human Rights, and the Right to Development', 11 *Hum. Rts. Q.* 347–74 (1989).

SYMPOSIUM, 'The Implementation of the International Covenant on Economic, Social and Cultural Rights', 9 *Hum. Rts. Q.* 121–287 (1987).

TAMAMES, R., 'Economic Rights in the Declaration of Human Rights', in J. Aranguren *et al.* (eds.), *Los derechos humanos* (Editorial Ciencia Nueva, Madrid, 1967) (in Spanish).

TOMASEVSKI, K., 'Human Rights Indicators: The Right to Food as a Test Case', in P. Alston and K. Tomasevski (eds.), *The Right to Food*, (Martinus Nijhoff, The Hague, 1984).

—— 'Human Rights: The Right to Food', 70 *Iowa L. Rev.* 1321–8 (1985).

—— (ed.), *The Right to Food: Guide through Applicable International Law* (Martinus Nijhoff, Dordrecht, 1987).

TRUBEK, D., 'Economic, Social and Cultural Rights in the Third World: Human Rights Law and Human Needs Programs', in T. Meron (ed.), *Human Rights in International Law: Legal and Policy Issues* 205–71 (Clarendon Press, Oxford, 1984).

UMOZURIKE, U., 'Freedom From Hunger: A Third World View', 70 *Iowa L. Rev.* 1329–38 (1985).

VALTICOS, N., 'The International Protection of Economic and Social Rights', in *Rechten van de Mens in Mundial en Europees Perspectif* (Ars Acqui Libri, Maarsen, The Netherlands, 1978).

VIERDAG, E., 'The Legal Nature of the Rights Granted By the International Covenant on Economic, Social and Cultural Rights', 9 *Netherlands YB Int'l L.* 69–105 (1978).

WESTERVEEN, G., 'Towards a System for Supervising States' Compliance with the Right to Food', in P. Alston and K. Tomasevski (eds.), *The Right To Food*, 119–34 (Martinus Nijhoff, The Hague, 1984).

ZWADZKI, S., 'Le Pacte international des droits économiques, sociaux et culturels et les constitutions des pays européens', *Pologne et les affaires occidentales* 217–28 (Warsaw, 1967).

12. *The Committee against Torture*

DOCUMENTS

Committee against Torture, Report on the Sessions, Supplement to the Official Records of the UN General Assembly. Sessions, years, and UN doc. nos. as follows: 1, 1988, A/43/46; 2, 1989, A/44/46; 3 and 4, 1990, A/45/44.

BOOKS AND ARTICLES

ACKERMAN, S., 'Torture and other Forms of Cruel and Unusual Punishment in International Law', 11 *Vand. J. Transnat'l L.* 653–70 (1978).

Amnesty International, *Torture in the Eighties* (Amnesty International Publications, London, 1984).

BASSIOUNI, C., and DERBY, D., 'Appraisal of Torture in International Law and Practice: The Need for an International Convention for the Prevention and

Suppression of Torture', 48 *Rev. int'l de droit penal* 23–310 (1977).

BONIN, J.-F., 'La Protection contre la torture et les traitements cruels, inhumains et dégradants: L'Affirmation d'une norme et l'évolution d'une définition en droit international', 3 *Rev. québécoise de droit int'l* 169–229 (1986).

BOULESBAA, A., 'An Analysis of the 1984 Draft Convention against Torture and other Cruel, Inhuman or Degrading Treatment or Punishment', 4 *Dick. J. Int'l L.* 185–211 (1986).

BURGERS, J. H., and DANELIUS, H., *The United Nations Convention against Torture: A Handbook on the Convention against Torture and other Cruel, Inhuman or Degrading Treatment or Punishment* (Martinus Nijhoff, Boston, 1988).

CASSESE, A., 'A New Approach to Human Rights—the 1987 Convention for the Prevention of Torture', 83 *Am. J. Int'l L.* 128–53 (1989).

CHANET, C., 'La Convention des Nations Unies contre la torture et autres peines ou traitements cruels, inhumains ou dégradants', 30 *Ann. français de droit int'l* 625–36 (1984).

DANELIUS, H., 'The United Nations Fund for Torture Victims: The First Years of Activity', 37 *Int'l & Comp. LQ* 35–42 (1986).

DOSWALD-BECK, L., 'What does the Prohibition "Torture or Inhuman or Degrading Treatment or Punishment" Mean? The Interpretation of the European Commission and Court of Human Rights', 25 *Netherlands Int'l L. Rev.* 24–50 (1978).

DRAPER, G. I. A. D., 'Juridical Aspects of Torture', 10 *Acta Juridica* 221–32 (1976).

DOMINICE, C., 'Convention contre la torture de l'ONU au Conseil de l'Europe', in *Volkerrecht im Dienste des Menschen: Festschrift für Hans Haug*, 57–68 (Verlag Paul Haupt, Bern, 1986).

DONNELLY, J., 'The Emerging International Regime against Torture', 33 *Netherlands Int'l L. Rev.* 1–23 (1986).

DORMENVAL, A., 'UN Committee against Torture: Practice and Perspectives', 8 *Netherlands Q. Hum. Rts.* 26–44 (1990).

GORNIG, G., and NEY, M., 'Die Erklärung der DDR zur UN-Anti-Folterkonvention aus Völkerrechtlicher Sicht: Ein Beitrag zur Zulassigkeit von Vorbehalten und ihren Rechtsfolgen', 43 *Juristenzeitung* (Tubingen) 1048–53 (1988).

HAILBRONNER, K., and RANDELZHOFER, A., 'Zur Zeichnung der UN-Folter-konvention durch die Bundesrepublik Deutschland', 13 *Europäische Grundrechte-Zeitschrift* 641–8 (1986).

HAQUANI, Z., 'La Convention des Nations Unies contre la torture', 90 *Rev. gen. du droit int'l pub.* 127–70 (1986).

HAUG, H., 'Internationale Konventionen gegen die Folter', 'in C. Swinarski (ed.), *Studies and Essays on International Humanitarian Law and Red Cross Principles* 713–23 (Martinus Nijhoff, Dordrecht, 1984).

—— 'Efforts to Eliminate Torture through International Law', 77 *Int'l Rev. of the Red Cross* 9–27 (1989).

HOFFMAN, P. L., and BRACKINS, L. W., 'The Elimination of Torture: International and Domestic Developments', 19 *Int'l Law.* 1351–64 (1985).

'International Protection of Fundamental Freedoms and Human Rights: The Convention against Torture and other Cruel, Inhuman or Degrading Treatment or Punishment', 8 *ASILS Int'l LJ* 67–101 (1984).

KLAYMAN, B. M., 'The Definition of Torture in International Law', 51 *Temp. LQ* 449–517 (1978).

KRIEKEN, P. J. VAN, 'Torture or Asylum', 16 *Israel YB Hum. Rts.* 143–61 (1986).

LANGBEIN, J.-H., *Torture and the Law of Proof* (Univ. of Chicago Press, Chicago, 1977).

LERNER, N., 'The UN Convention on Torture', 16 *Israel YB Hum. Rts.* 126–42 (1986).

LEWIS, A., 'Torture dans le monde', 10 *Diritto int'l* 1–10 (1977).

LIPPMAN, 'The Protection of Universal Human Rights: The Problem of Torture', 1 *Universal Hum. Rts.* 25–55 (1979).

MACDONALD, R. S. J., 'International Prohibitions against Torture and other Forms of Similar Treatment or Punishment', in Y. Dinstein (ed.), *International Law at a Time of Perplexity: Essays in Honour of Sahbtai Rosenne* 385–406 (Martinus Nijhoff, Dordrecht, 1987).

MAIER, I., 'Wirksamere Ächtung der Folter erstrebt: Menschenrechtskommission legt Entwurf einer UN-Konvention vor', 32 *Vereinte Nationen* 77–82 (1984).

—— 'Wichtiger Schritt zur Abschaffung der Folter: Generalversammlung verabschiedet UN-Konvention', 33 *Vereinte Nationen* 1–6 (1985).

MARIE, J.-B., 'La Convention européenne pour la prévention de la torture—un instrument pragmatique et audacieux', 19 *Rev. gén. du droit* 109–25 (1988).

MARX, R., 'Die Konvention der Vereinten Nationen gegen Folter und andere grausame, unmenschliche oder erniedrigende Behandlung oder Strafe', 19 *Zeitschrift für Rechtspolitik* 81–5 (1986).

MOHR, M., and KAMPA, R., 'On the UN Anti-Torture Convention: Committee against Torture (CAT) Started its Work', 15 *GDR Committee Hum. Rts. Bull.* 208–22 (1989).

NAGAN, W., 'The Politics of Ratification: The Potential for United States Adoption of the Convention against Torture, the Covenants on Civil and Political Rights and Economic, Social and Cultural Rights', 20 *Ga. J. Int'l & Comp. L.* 311–42 (1990).

NOWAK, M., 'Die UNO-Konvention gegen die Folter vom 10 Dezember 1984', 12 *Europäische Grundrecht Zeitschrift* 109–16 (1985).

—— 'Die Europäische Konvention zur Verhntung von Folter', 15 *Europäische Grundrechte-Zeitschrift* 537–42 (1988).

—— 'The Implementation Functions of the UN Committee against Torture', in N. P. Engel (ed.), *Fortschritt im Bewusstsein der Grundund Menschenrechte: Festschrift für Felix Ermacora* 493–526 (Springer-Verlag, Strasburg, 1988).

RAESS, M., *Der Shutz vor Folter im Volkerrecht* (Springer Verlag, Zurich, 1989).

RAMELLA, P. A., 'Convención internacional sobre la tortura', *Rev. jurídica argentina la ley* 1051–4 (1986).

RIKLIN, A. (ed.), *Internationale Konventionen gegen die Folter* (Paul Haupt, Berne, 1979).

SKUPINSKI, J., 'Prohibition of Torture and other Inhuman Treatment (the Development of International Legal Regulation within the United Nations)', 15 *Pol. YB Int'l L.* 136–92 (1986).

SOHN, L., 'Torture as a Violation of the Law of Nations', 11 *Ga. J. Int'l & Comp. L.* 307–9 (1981).

STEWART, D., 'The Potential for United States Adoption of the Genocide Convention and the Convention against Torture', 20 *Ga. J. Int'l & Comp. L.* 343–52 (1990).

TARDU, M. E., 'The United Nations Convention against Torture and other Cruel, Inhuman or Degrading Treatment or Punishment', 56 *Nordic J. Int'l L.* 303–21 (1987).

TRECHSEL, S., 'Zum Verhaltnis zwischen der Folterschutzkonvention (FSK) und der Europäischen Menschenrechtskonvention (EMRK)', in P. Haupt (ed.), *Völkerrecht im Dienste des Menschen: Festschrift für Hans Haug* 355–62 (Springer-Verlag, Bern, 1986).

VIEIRA, M. A., 'La tortura en las convenciones internacionales', 12 *Curso de derecho int'l* 53–68 (1986).

VILLÁN DURÁN, C., 'La Convención contra la tortura y su contribución a la definición del derecho a la integridad física y moral en el derecho internacional', 37 *Rev. española de derecho int'l* 377–402 (1985).

VOORHIS, R. A., 'Enforcing the Proposed International Convention against Torture', 5 *ASILS Int'l LJ* 17–38 (1981).

YAHIA-BACHA, M., 'La Convention des Nations Unies contre la torture', 24 *Rev. algérienne des sc. jur. écon. et pol.* 529–38 (1986).

13. *The International Labour Organisation*

DOCUMENTS

Abolition of Forced Labour: General Survey of the Reports Relating to the Forced Labour Convention, 1930 (No. 29) and the Abolition of Forced Labour Convention, 1957 (No. 105), International Labour Conference, Report III (Part 4B).

Comparative Analysis of the International Covenants on Human Rights and International Labour Conventions and Recommendations, 51 *Official Bull.* 181–216.

Conventions and Recommendations Adopted by the International Labour Conference (1981). Conventions and Recommendations adopted since 1981 are printed in the *ILO Official Bull.*

Employment of Women with Family Responsibilities: General Survey of the Reports Relating to the Employment (Women with Family Responsibilities) Recommendation, No. 123. International Labour Conference, Report III (Part 4B).

Equality of Opportunity and Treatment for Women Workers, International Labour Conference, Report VIII.

Human Rights—A Common Responsibility, Report of the Director-General, Part I, International Labour Conference, 75th Session, Geneva, 1988.

International Law Organization, *Fighting Discrimination in Employment and Occupation. A Worker's Educational Manual* (1975).

—— *Freedom of Association: Digest of Decisions and Principles of the Freedom of Association Committee of the Governing Body of the ILO* (1985).

The ILO and Human Rights, Report of the Director-General, Part I, International Labour Conference, 52nd Session, Geneva, 1968.

International Labour Standards: A Worker's Education Manual (1978).

The Impact of International Labour Conventions and Recommendations (1976).

Minimum Age: General Survey by the Committee of Experts on the Application of Conventions and Recommendations. International Labour Conference, Report II (Part 4B) (1981).

Reports by the Committee of Experts on the Application of Conventions and Recommendations of the International Labour Organisation on Progress in Achieving Observance of the Provisions of Articles 6 to 9 of the International Covenant on Economic, Social, and Cultural Rights. UN docs. E/1978/27; E/

1979/33; E/1980/35; E/1981/41; E/1982/41; E/1983/40; E/1985/63; E/1986/60; E/1987/59; E/1988/66; E/1989/6; E/1990/9; and E/1991/4.

Reports of the Committee of Experts on the Application of Conventions and Recommendations, General Report and Observation Concerning Particular Countries. Submitted each year to the International Labour Conferences as Report II (Part 4A).

BOOKS AND ARTICLES

ABOUGHANEM, A., *Étude sur les relations entre les normes internationales du travail et la coopération technique* (ILO, Geneva, 1985).

ALCOCK, A., *History of the International Labour Organisation* (Macmillan, London, 1971).

ALFORD, W. P., 'The Prospective Withdrawal of the United States from the International Labor Organization: Rationales and Implications', 17 *Harv. Int'l LJ* 623–38 (1976).

BAJWA, D. K., 'Human Rights Standards of ILO: Their Impact in India', 24 *Civ. & Mil. LJ* (New Delhi) 39–47 (1988).

BARNES, G. N., *History of the International Labour Office* (Williams and Norgate Ltd., London, 1926).

BARTOLOMEI DE LA CRUZ, H. G., *Protection against Anti-Union Discrimination* (ILO, Geneva, 1976).

BEIGBEDER, Y., 'The United States Withdrawal from the International Labour Organization', 34 *Industrial Relations (Quebec)* 223–40 (1979).

BENNETT, G. I., 'The ILO Convention on Indigenous and Tribal Populations—The Resolution of a Problem of "Vires"', 46 *Brit. YB Int'l L.* 382–97 (1972–3).

BETHGE, H., and DAMMANN, K., 'Der ILO-Bericht zu den Berufsverboten', 32 *Blätter fur Deutsche und Int'l e Pol.* 582–7 (1987).

BEUTLER, L. A., 'The ILO and IMF: Permissibility and Desirability of a Proposal to Meet the Contemporary Realities of the International Protection of Labor Rights', 14 *Syracuse J. Int'l L. & Com.* 455–77 (1988).

CAIRE, G., *Freedom of Association and Economic Development* (ILO, Geneva, 1977).

DAHL, K. N., 'The Role of ILO Standards in Global Integration Process', 5 *J. of Peace Research* 309–51 (1968).

FOLLOWS, J. W., *Antecedents of the International Labour Organisation* (Clarendon Press, Oxford, 1951).

GALENSON, W., *The ILO: An American View* (Univ. of Wisconsin Press, Madison, Wis., 1981).

GHEBALI, V. Y., 'Vers la réforme de l'Organisation Internationale du Travail', 30 *Ann. français de droit int'l* 649–71 (1984).

—— *The International Labour Organisation: A Case Study on the Evolution of UN Specialised Agencies* (Martinus Nijhoff, Dordrecht, 1989).

GORMLEY, W. P., 'Emerging Protection of Human Rights by the International Labour Organization', 30 *Alb. L. Rev.* 13–51 (1966).

GOULD, W. B., 'The Rights of Wage Earners: Of Human Rights and International Labor Standards', 3 *Indus. Rel. LJ* 489–516 (1979).

GROS ESPIELL, H., *La Organización Internacional del Trabajo y los derechos humanos en América Latina* (EUDEBA, Buenos Aires, 1986).

HODGES-AEBERHARD, J., and ODERO DE DIOS, A., 'Principles of the Committee on Freedom of Association concerning Strikes', 126 *Int'l Lab. Rev.* 543–63 (1987).

HOEFER-VAN DONGEN, P., 'The Right to Strike within the Framework of the ILO', *Netherlands Int'l L. Rev.* (Special Issue) 109–19 (1977).

JENKS, C. W., 'The Protection of Freedom of Association by the International Labour Organization', 28 *British YB Int'l L.* 348–59 (1951).

—— 'The International Protection of Freedom of Association for Trade Union Purposes', 87 *Recueil des cours* 6–115 (1955).

—— *The International Protection of Trade Union Freedom* (Stevens, London, 1957).

—— *Human Rights and the International Labour Standards* (Praeger, New York, 1960).

—— 'Human Rights: Social Justice and Peace: The Broader Significance of the ILO Experience', in A. Eide, and A. Shou (eds.), *International Protection of Human Rights* (Almquist & Wiskell, Stockholm, 1968).

—— *Social Justice in The Law of Nations: The ILO Impact after Fifty Years* (Oxford UP, London, 1970).

JOHNSTON, G. A., *The International Labour Organisation: Its Work for Social and Economic Progress* (Europa Publications, London, 1970).

JOYCE, J., *World Labour Rights and their Protection* (Croom Helm, London, 1980).

JOYNER, C. C., 'United States' Withdrawal from the ILO: International Politics in the Labor Arena', 12 *Int'l Law.* 721–39 (1978).

JUVIGNY, P., 'Organisation Internationale du Travail et les droits de l'homme', in *Rene Cassin: Amicorum Discipulorumque Liber*, i. 121 (Pedone, Paris, 1969).

HAAS, E. B., *Human Rights and International Action: The Case of Freedom of Association* (Stanford University Press, Stanford, Calif., 1970).

LANDY, E. A., 'The Influence of International Labour Standards: Possibilities and Performance', 101 *Int'l Lab. Rev.* 555–604 (1970).

—— *The Effectiveness of International Supervision: Three Decades of ILO Experience* (Oceana Publications, New York, 1966).

—— 'The Implementation Procedures of the International Labour Organization', 20 *Santa Clara L. Rev.* 633–63 (1980).

LEARY, V., *International Labour Conventions and National Law* (Martinus Nijhoff, The Hague, 1981).

LUBIN, C. R., and WINSLOW, A., *Social Justice for Women: The International Labor Organization and Women*, (Duke University Press, Durham, NC, 1990).

MAINWARING, J., *The International Labour Organization: A Canadian View* (Labour Canada, Ottawa, 1986).

MANIN, A., 'Quelques réflexions sur la fonction de controle de l'OIT—à propos du rapport sur la liberté syndicale en Pologne', 30 *Ann. français de droit int'l* 672–91 (1984).

—— 'La Commission d'enquête de l'OIT institué pour examiner l'observation de la Convention 11 par la république fédérale d'Allemagne: De nouveaux renseignements', 34 *Ann. français de droit int'l* 365–81 (1988).

MAUPAIN, P., 'La Réforme de l'Organisation Internationale du Travail', 33 *Ann. français de droit int'l* 478–97 (1987).

MCMAHON, J. F., 'The Legislative Techniques of the International Labour

Organization', 41 *British YB Int'l L.* 1–102 (1965–6).

MELANSON, R. A., 'Human Rights and the American Withdrawal from the ILO', 1 *Universal Hum. Rts.* 43–61 (1979).

MERON, T., 'Violations of ILO Conventions by the USSR and Czechoslovakia', 74 *Am. J. Int'l L.* 206–11 (1980).

MOYNIHAN, D. P., 'The United States and the ILO, 1889–1934', Ph.D. thesis (Fletcher School of Law and Diplomacy, 1960).

OSIEKE, E., *Constitutional Law and Practice in ILO* (Kluwer, Dordrecht, 1985).

POTOBSKY, G. VON., 'Protection of Trade Union Rights: Twenty Years' Work by the Committee on Freedom of Association', 105 *Int'l Lab. Rev.* 69–83 (1972).

POTTER, E. E., *Freedom of Association, the Right to Organize, and Collective Bargaining: The Impact on US Law and Practice of Ratification of ILO Conventions No. 87 & No. 98* (Labor Policy Association, Washington DC, 1984).

POULANTZAS, N. M., 'International Protection of Human Implemention Procedures within the Framework of the International Labour Organisation', 25 *Rev. hellénique de droit int'l* 110–41 (1972).

POUYAT, A. J., 'The ILO's Freedom of Association Standards and Machinery: A Summing Up', 121 *Int'l Lab. Rev.* 287–302 (1982).

ROCKWOOD, B. L., 'Human Rights and Wrongs: The United States and the ILO—A Modern Morality Play', 10 *Case W. Res. J. Int'l L.* 359–413 (1978).

ROOD, M. G., 'ILO en Mensenrechten', 12 *Nederlands Juristen Comite voor de Mensenrechten-Bull.* 429–36 (1987).

ROSSILLON, C., 'ILO Examination of Human Rights Situations', 12 *Int'l Commission of Jurists Rev.* 40–9 (1974).

SAMSON, K. T., 'International Labour Organisation and Human Rights in 1970', 5 *Rev. des droits de l'homme* 103–17 (1971).

—— 'The Changing Pattern of ILO Supervision', 118 *Int'l Lab. Rev.* 569–7 (1979).

—— 'International Labour Organisation', 9 *Hum. Rts.* 32–5 (1980).

SERVAIS, J. M., 'ILO Standards on Freedom of Association and their Implementation', 123 *Int'l Lab. Rev.* 765–81 (1984).

—— 'Flexibility and Rigidity in International Labour Standards', 125 *Int'l Lab. Rev.* 193–209 (1986).

SWEPSTON, L., 'Indigenous and Tribal Populations: A Return to Centre Stage', 126 *Int'l Lab. Rev.* 447–57 (1987).

—— and PLANT, R., 'International Standards and the Protection of the Land Rights of Indigenous and Tribal Polpulations', 124 *Int'l Lab. Rev.* 91–106 (1985).

VALTICOS, N., 'International Labour Organisation: Its Contribution to the Rule of Law and the International Protection of Human Rights', 9 *Int'l Commission of Jurists Rev.* 3–34 (1968).

—— 'Fifty Years of Standard-Setting Activities by the International Labour Organisation', 100 *Int'l Lab. Rev.* 201–37 (1969).

—— 'Organisation Internationale du Travail et les droits de l'homme en 1968', 2 *Rev. des droits de l'homme* 113–38 (1969).

—— 'Organisation Internationale du Travail et les droits de l'homme en 1969', 3 *Rev. des droits de l'homme* 109–28 (1970).

—— 'Les Normes de l'Organisation Internationale du Travail en matière de protection des droits de l'homme', 4 *Rev. des droits de l'homme* 691–771 (1971).

—— 'The Future Prospects for International Labour Standards', 118 *Int'l Lab. Rev.* 679–97 (1979).

—— 'The Role of the ILO: Future Perspectives', in B. G. Ramcharan (ed.), *Human Rights: Thirty Years After the Universal Declaration* (Martinus Nijhoff, The Hague, 1979).

—— *Le Droit international du travail* (Dalloz, Paris, 1980).

—— 'L'Evolution du système de controle de l'Organisation International du Travail', in Giuffre (ed.), *International Law at the Time of its Codification: Essays in Honour of Roberto Ago* 505–21 (Milan, 1987).

—— 'The Sources of International Labour Law: Recent Trends', in W. Heere (ed.), *International Law and its Sources: Liber Amicorum Maarten Bos* 179–96 (Kluwer, Deventer, 1989).

WERNERS, S. E., 'New Dimensions to Tripartism in the International Labour Organisation', *Netherlands Int'l L. Rev.* (Special Issue) 323–34 (1977).

WIRTH, D., 'Trade Union Rights in the Workers' State: Poland and the ILO', 13 *Den. J. Int'l L. & Pol.* 269–82 (1984).

WOLF, F., 'Aspects judiciaires de la protection internationale des droits de l'homme par l'OIT', 4 *Rev. des droits de l'homme* 773–838 (1971).

—— 'ILO Experience in the Implemention of Human Rights', 10 *J. Int'l Law & Econ.* 599–625 (1975).

—— 'Human Rights and the International Labour Organization', in T. Meron (ed.), *Human Rights in International Law: Legal and Policy Issues* 273–305 (Clarendon Press, Oxford, 1984).

WOOD, J., 'International Labour Organisation Conventions: Labour Code or Treaties?', 40 *ICLQ* 649–57 (1991).

ZENGER, A., 'Les Droits de l'homme et le contrôle de leur application au sein de l'Organisation Internationale du Travail', in *Volkerrecht im Dienste des Menschen: Festschrift für Hans Haug* 401–16 (Berne, 1986).

14. *Human Rights Co-ordination*

ASBECK, F. M. VAN, 'The Universal Declaration of Human Rights and its Implementation in International Organizations', in H. F. van Panhuys and M. Leeuwen Boomkamp (eds.), *International Society in Search of a Transnational Legal Order*, 554–65 (Sijthoff Noordholf, Leyden, 1976).

BASTID, S., 'Sur quelques problèmes juridiques de coordination dans la famille des Nations Unies', in *Mélanges offerts à Paul Reuter: Le Droit international: Unité et diversité*, 75–101 (Pedone, Paris, 1981).

BERTELING, J., 'Inter-Secretariat Co-ordination in the United Nations System', 24 *Netherlands Int'l L. Rev.* 21–42 (1977).

DAGORY, J., 'Rapports entre les institutions spécialisées et l'Organisation des Nations Unies', 73 *Rev. gén. de droit int'l pub.* 285–377 (1969).

HANSEN, P., and MATHIASON, J., 'Coordination in the United Nations System', in M. S. Rajan, V. S. Mani, and C. S. R. Murthy (eds.), *The Nonaligned and the United Nations*, 223–44 (Oceana Publications, New York, 1987).

HILL, M., *The UN System: Co-ordinating its Economic and Social Work* (Cambridge UP, Cambridge, 1978).

JENKS, C. W., 'Co-ordination: A New Problem of International Organization', 77 *Rec. des cours* 157–301 (1950).

JIMENEZ de ARECHAGA, E., 'Cooperative Relations between the United Nations and its Specialized Agencies', 8 *Acad. interam. de derecho comp. e int'l* 101 (1960) (in Spanish).

LEWIN, A., 'La Coordination au sein des Nations Unies—mission impossible?', 29 *Ann. français de droit int'l* 9–22 (1983).

NICOL, D., and RENNINGER, J., 'The Restructuring of the UN Economic and Social System: Background and Analysis', 4 *Third World Q.* 74–90 (1982).

PARTAN, D. G., 'Population in the UN System: Developing the Legal Capacity and Programs of UN Agencies', 7 *Colum. Hum. Rts. L. Rev.* 207–29 (1975).

QUADRI, P., 'The Question of Coordination of International Human Rights Instruments', 19 *Rev. de derecho int'l y ciencias diplomaticas* (Rosario) 90–9 (1970) (in Spanish).

SCHMIDT, M., 'Achieving Much with Little: The Work of the United Nations Centre for Human Rights', 8 *Neths. Q. of Hum. Rts.* 371–94 (1990).

TRINDADE, A. A. C., 'Co-existence and Co-ordination of Mechanisms of International Protection of Human Rights (at Global and Regional Levels)', 202 *Rec. des cours* 9–435 (1987).

WILLIAMS, D., *The Specialised Agencies and the United Nations: The System in Crisis* (St Martins Press, New York, 1987).

ZARB, A., *Les Institutions spécialisées du système des Nations Unies et leurs membres* (Pedone, Paris, 1980).

INDEX OF SUBJECTS

INDEX OF AUTHORS

The following index is based on textual as well as bibliographical references.